30106021537161

CW01522787

# LENIN REDISCOVERED

# Historical Materialism Book Series

Haymarket Books is proud to be working with Brill Academic Publishers (http://www.brill.nl) and the journal *Historical Materialism* on the new Historical Materialism Book Series. This is Haymarket's second paperback edition of a title initiated in hardcover by Brill.

Other titles in the series from Haymarket Books include:

**The Theory of Revolution in the Young Marx**
Michael Löwy

**Between Equal Rights: A Marxist Theory of International Law**
China Miéville

**The German Revolution 1917–1923**
Pierre Broué

**About the series**

More than ten years after the collapse of the Berlin Wall and the disappearance of Marxism as a (supposed) state ideology, a need for a serious and long-term Marxist book publishing program has risen. Subjected to the whims of fashion, most contemporary publishers have abandoned any of the systematic production of Marxist theoretical work that they may have indulged in during the 1970s and early 1980s. The Historical Materialism book series addresses this great gap with original monographs, translated texts and reprints of "classics." At least three titles will be published every year. For more details, see http://www.brill.nl/download/HiMaBookseries.pdf.

Editorial board: Paul Blackledge, Leeds; Sebastian Budgen, London; Jim Kincaid, Leeds; Stathis Kouvelakis, Paris; Marcel van der Linden, Amsterdam; China Miéville, London; Paul Reynolds, Lancashire.

# LENIN REDISCOVERED
## *WHAT IS TO BE DONE?* IN CONTEXT

## LARS T. LIH

**Haymarket**
Books
Chicago, Illinois

First published in 2005 by Brill Academic Publishers, The Netherlands
© 2006 Koninklijke Brill NV, Leiden, The Netherlands

Published in paperback in 2008 by Haymarket Books
P.O. Box 180165
Chicago, IL 60618
773-583-7884
www.haymarketbooks.org

Trade distribution:
In the U.S. through Consortium Book Sales, www.cbsd.com
In the UK, Turnaround Publisher Services, www.turnaround-psl.com
In Australia, Palgrave MacMillan, www.palgravemacmillan.com.au

Cover art: Detail from *Composition IV* by Wassily Kandinsky, 1911 © 2008 Artists
Rights Society (ARS), New York / ADAGP, Paris, –Roethel T. I n°383 p.366.

This book was published with the generous support of the Wallace Global Fund.

Printed in Canada

10 9 8 7 6 5 4 3 2 1

Library of Congress Cataloging-in-Publication Data
Lih, Lars T.
  Lenin rediscovered : what is to be done? In context / by Lars T. Lih.
     p. cm. -- (Historical materialism)
  Includes bibliographical references and index.
  ISBN 978-1-931859-58-5 (pbk.)
  1. Socialism--Russia. 2. Rossiiskaia sotsial-demokraticheskaia rabochaia partiia. 3.
Lenin, Vladimir Il?ich, 1870-1924. Chto delat??  I. Lenin, Vladimir Il?ich, 1870-1924.
Chto delat?? English. 2005. II. Title.
  HX314.L57 2008
  335.430947--dc22
                                        2008010318

to
Robert Tucker

*The basic mistake made by people who polemicise with* What Is to Be Done? *at the present time is that they tear this production completely out of a specific historical context, out of a specific and by now long-past period in the development of our party.*

Lenin, 1907

# Contents

## TRANSLATION

# List of Illustrations

# Note on the Text

All Lenin quotations are taken from the *Polnoe sobranie sochineniia* (Complete Collection of Works), 5th edition, published in Moscow from 1958 to 1965. References are in the following form: Lenin 1958–65, 6, p. 101 (= volume 6, p. 101).

In the 1920s and 1930s, the 2nd and 3rd editions of Lenin's *Sochineniia* (Works) were published in the Soviet Union. The relation between these two editions is difficult to pin down, since they were issued to a large extent concurrently and the 3rd edition describes itself as only a reprint of the 2nd edition. Political changes seem to account for this odd procedure. The chief editor of the 2nd edition was Lev Kamenev (a Stalin foe) and the chief editors of the 3rd edition are listed as V.V. Adoratski, V.M. Molotov (!), and M.A. Savelev. Although the 3rd edition is more easily available, I believe it is more proper to cite the 2nd edition (1926–35, Moscow: Gosizdat) as the original source. This edition is used here for its invaluable notes and appended documents and is cited in the following form: Lenin 1926–35, 6, p. 101 (= Volume 6, p. 101).

When I refer to a chapter in WITBD itself, I use a Roman numeral (for example, Chapter I). When I refer to a chapter in my commentary, I write the number out (for example, Chapter One).

I drop the soft sign in the transliteration of Russian words when I find it interferes with readability, which is most of the time.

For a number of key terms, I have chosen translations different from the usual ones. The following Glossary lists these terms and provides references where appropriate to more extended discussions of the rationale for my choices.

# Glossary

Artisanal limitations [*kustarnichestvo*]. Translated by others as 'amateurism', 'primitivism'. See Chapter Eight.

Awareness [*soznanie*]. Normally translated as 'consciousness'. See Chapter Six.

Bourgeois democracy [*burzhuaznaia demokratiia*]. At the time when WITBD was written, *burzhuaznaia demokratiia* did not mean primarily a particular system of government but the non-worker social/political groups that were willing to fight for democratic transformation. In tsarist Russia, these groups were revolutionary. Thus Lenin can accuse Martynov of overlooking the existence of *burzhuaznaia demokratiia* in tsarist Russia. We need to be careful not to see Lenin's comments on 'bourgeois democracy' in anachronistic fashion as the kind of critique of bourgeois democracy as a system that is associated with the communist movement after the Bolshevik Revolution.

Cause to stray [*sovlech'*]. Normally translated as 'divert'. See Annotations Part Two.

*Intelligenty* [adjective form *intelligentnyi*]. Usually translated as 'intellectuals'. The Russian *intelligent* at the turn of the century was a social type not much like intellectuals today. I use the Russian term when I feel that 'intellectual' would be seriously misleading.

Indictment [*oblichenie*]. Translated by others as 'exposure' or 'arraignment'. The term refers to leaflets and articles that point to abuses at either the factory level or the political level in order to indict the system as a whole.

*Konspiratsiia.* Often translated as 'secrecy'. See Chapter Eight.

Kow-towing [*preklonenie*]. Found in the phrase 'kow-towing to *stikhiinost*' that Lenin uses as a catch-all for the sins of his opponents. Translated by others as 'bowing' or 'worshipping' *stikhiinost*. I chose 'kow-towing' to bring out the idea of abject devotion. The origin of the phrase is described in Annotations Part Two.

Leader/guide [*rukovoditel'*]. Usually translated 'leader'. The Russian word *rukovodstvo* is often translated as 'guidance'. I have adopted this translation and used 'leader/guide' to translate *rukovoditel'*, first to preserve the vital textual link with *rukovodstvo* and second to distinguish *rukovoditel'* from other, more emotive words for leaders (such as *vozhd'*).

Legally-permitted. A *legal'nyi* publication is not one that deals with legal issues but rather one that has been passed by the censor. It is the opposite of an underground publication. 'Legally-permitted Marxism' was Marxism that was inoffensive enough to be passed by the tsarist censor. More specifically, it referred to a group of writers in the 1890s of whom Petr Struve was the most prominent.

*Narod.* Usually translated 'people' or (in words such as *narodnik*) 'populist'. I have kept the Russian word when I thought it was important to keep the resonance of the common people, the *Volk*, as opposed to the élite.

*Proval.* Underground slang for the break-up of a local committee by police arrests. See Chapter Eight.

Purposive [*soznatel'nyi*] and purposiveness [*soznatel'nost'*]. Usually translated 'conscious' and 'consciousness'. See Chapter Six.

Revolutionary by trade [*revoliutsioner po professii* or *professial'nyi revoliutsioner*]. Usually translated 'professional revolutionary'. See Chapter Eight.

*Stikhiinost* [adjective form *stikhiinyi*]. Usually translated 'spontaneity' and sometimes (when in adjective form) 'elemental'. For full discussion, see Annotations Part Two.

*Tred-iunionizm.* Usually translated 'trade-unionism'. *Tred-iunionizm* does not primarily mean 'activities associated with trade unions' but rather 'the ideology that urges the workers to limit themselves to trade unions'. By definition, *tred-iunionizm* is the enemy of Social Democracy.

Worker class [*Arbeiterklasse, rabochii klass*]. For an explanation of my unidiomatically literal translation of this and similar key terms, see Chapter One.

# Acknowledgements

This study was undertaken and completed without any institutional support. I mention this to bring out how much I relied on the support of family and friends. For this reason, contrary to custom, I begin rather than end with an expression of gratitude toward my family. My extended family – parents, siblings, in-laws – gave support in all possible ways. My daughters Emelyn and Ariadne treated the project that sometimes threatened to drown their father under a mountain of manila folders with unfailing sympathy, interest and respect. My wife Julie Cumming gave the manuscript a much-needed critical reading and copy-editing that added immeasurably to the clarity of presentation. I can do no better than to quote my words from an earlier book: 'She has been as merciless to the defects of any one sentence as she has been generous to the overall spirit of the book. She has made the usual hectic completion of a manuscript seem almost peaceful. It is heartening indeed to think that everything I write in the future will profit in the same way.'

Encouragement from friends provided much-needed psychological support. In particular, Lewis Siegelbaum and Sebastian Budgen understood the importance of what I was doing long before I did. Without Sebastian Budgen's determined prodding, this study would not have been undertaken, much less completed.

After I completed a full draft of this book I learned of Reginald Zelnik's death in an accident in Berkeley, California. Only then did I realise how much of this book was written in intellectual dialogue with Zelnik – a dialogue now brutally cut off. I repeat the words from the first draft of my acknowledgements: I owe a special intellectual debt to the late Allan Wildman as well as to Gerald Surh and especially Reginald Zelnik. These scholars ask the interesting questions about Russian Social Democracy and the Russian workers – indeed, I learned from them what these questions were. After being inspired by them to ask the same questions, I came up with different answers.

In this book, I feel a duty to explain why our answers differ. All the more reason to emphasise here the far deeper solidarity that comes from asking the same questions and from insisting on a historical approach to *What Is to Be Done?*. Like Lenin, I polemicise at greatest length with the people closest to my own position.

Earlier versions of some of the arguments presented in this study were presented at the conference held in Essen, Germany in February 2001 on the centennial of *What Is to Be Done?* as well as at the round table devoted to the WITBD centennial held at the convention of the American Association for the Advancement of Slavic Studies in autumn 2001. The participants on both occasions listened to my views, gave me forthright criticism and helped me with references and texts. Besides those already mentioned, I would like to thank Kevin Anderson, Michael Melancon, Henry Reichman, and Alan Shandro.

Conversations with Anna Krylova and David Mandel stimulated me to ask further questions about Lenin's text. Sally Boniece and Kevin Murphy provided helpful comments on earlier drafts. The commentary as a whole benefitted greatly from the detailed reaction of an anonymous reader.

Christoph Neidhöfer provided me with invaluable help on the German passages, both on translation matters and correct spelling. (Since I was unable to show him all the German-language quotations and titles, the usual disclaimer doubly applies.)

Material from my article 'How a Founding Document was Found' that appeared in *Kritika* in 2003 has been incorporated into this study. I asked the editors for permission and I was told that their policy was not to require permission. Therefore I will just thank them for running such an excellent journal.

The Interlibrary Loan service at McGill played a fundamental role in my research. They never failed me in finding the most out-of-the-way Russian-language pamphlets and I greatly appreciated their friendly and professional demeanour. Regine Reincke at Brill managed to prod me in so friendly and engaging a way that I truly regretted the many times I had to come up with excuses for missed deadlines.

The ideal person to write a study of Lenin's *What Is to Be Done?* would have to be someone equally at home in European Marxism and Russian Bolshevism, someone who has written on Marx's outlook as well as on Soviet politics, someone who is engaged by the philosophical issues at stake as well as the political ramifications not only for Russia but for revolutionary movements world-wide, someone who can balance a sense of the importance of personality and of the importance of political context. Unfortunately, Robert Tucker is engaged in his own monumental study of Stalin. Therefore, I undertook this commentary, following as I did so the path pointed out by Tucker's insightful description of *What Is to Be Done?* quoted several times in the course of this study. I remember, way back when, how Bob congratulated me as I drove back to Princeton loaded down with the fifty-odd volumes of Lenin's complete works. I also listened when just recently he did not just encourage me in this study – he told me I *had* to write it. I therefore cannot imagine dedicating this book to anyone but Robert Tucker.

Montreal, May 2005

# Commentary

# Introduction

*And a sower went forth sowing seeds . . .*

This image from the Gospels unexpectedly turns up in *Chto delat?*, a political pamphlet published just over a century ago as part of an internecine struggle over policy and leadership within the ranks of the fledgling Social-Democratic Party of Russia. The parable of the sower points directly to the disputed issues in this struggle. All sides agreed on the task of sowing the seeds of the Social-Democratic message among the workers. All sides were confident that the seeds would ultimately bear fruit in revolutionary action by the workers. But many difficult choices remained. What is the best way to spread the seeds in autocratic Russia? What parts of the message will strike root immediately and what parts will fall on barren ground? What kind of conditions are propitious for sowing the seed and how can they be attained?

The author kept his identity hidden by using a recently coined pseudonym. Yet his political profile was clear to any perceptive reader. Here was a Russian revolutionary activist inspired by the mighty Social-Democratic Party of Germany and determined to import as much of the model as was possible under the very different conditions of autocratic Russia. He resolutely opposed the sceptical voices in Russia who expressed doubts about the applicability of this model.

He was confident that the Russian workers were rapidly acquiring a revolutionary outlook, so much so that he promised the young and inexperienced Social-Democratic activists in Russia that they could accomplish miracles by preaching the revolutionary message. At the centre of his political programme was a passionate insistence on the overriding necessity of bringing political freedom to Russia.

*Chto delat?* had a solid success among the narrow audience to whom it was addressed. Nevertheless, the responses to the questions posed in the pamphlet were strongly tied to the concrete conditions of Russia's Social-Democratic movement in 1901–2. So, the book was read widely only for a brief period. In 1903, the Russian Social Democrats created a national party organisation of sorts. In 1905, a revolution transformed the political landscape in Russia. *Chto delat?* was remembered, if at all, as a salvo in the pamphlet wars of yesteryear. Even the author of the pamphlet never referred to it after 1907.

In 1917, this author – one Vladimir Ulianov, who wrote under the pseudonym 'N. Lenin' – became the founder of the new political system of Soviet Russia. Since this political system lasted for most of the rest of the century – and since both the achievements and crimes of this system shocked and awed the world during its existence – much attention was directed towards the beliefs and outlook of the system's founder. Eventually, the spotlight was turned on the long-forgotten pamphlet *Chto delat?*, especially after the late 1920s, when the Soviet government made Lenin's major works available in the major European languages. The title chosen for the English translation of *Chto delat?* was *What Is to Be Done?*.

Here, it was felt by many in the West, was the key to it all, the source of the beliefs that led to so grandiose a political experiment. *What Is to Be Done?* became enshrined in the textbooks as the founding document of Bolshevism. In the words of one of the most prominent American experts on Soviet Russia, 'the argument and the flavour of *What Is to Be Done?* have remained imbedded in the values and beliefs of the Soviet system. They are evident in the pronouncements of Khrushchev as they were in those of Stalin and Lenin.'[1]

Thus *What Is to Be Done?* (WITBD) became everybody's introduction to Lenin's beliefs and a basic teaching tool for understanding the essence of Bolshevism.

---

[1] Ulam 1962, p. 615.

There could hardly have been a worse choice. *WITBD* was written to score off some very specific opponents and to advocate some very specific policies that were relevant only for a fleeting moment. It certainly was not written with the intention of making Lenin's basic beliefs clear to readers decades later. If we want to pry out these beliefs, we must go the circuitous route of deducing them from his policy choices and his arguments in the context of the assumptions he shared with his intended readership. And yet this information is nowhere available in English or indeed in any language, so that even learned specialists wrestle with the text and fail to pin it down. How paedagogically perverse to confront the beginner with a text that should frighten the expert!

The experts regarded *WITBD* as the founding document of Bolshevism, the book where Lenin first revealed the essence of his outlook. But even the experts worked without a proper knowledge of context – particularly the large context of international Social Democracy and the small context of the polemical in-fighting among Russian Social Democrats in late 1901. To speak plainly, they misread *WITBD* and therefore misunderstood Lenin, and then successfully raised up this image of Lenin to textbook status.

As a result, the textbook status of *WITBD* is the main barrier to a serious rethinking of Lenin, since everybody thinks they have a basic idea of what Lenin stood for. But this barrier can turn into a bridge if we make the effort to put the book into context. The aim of this commentary and new translation is to provide the basic background information needed to do this. We will then literally *rediscover* a Lenin who is close to the complete opposite of the Lenin of the textbooks.

## Lenin: A Russian Social Democrat

Although *WITBD* is focused on certain specific issues, the basic beliefs that animate it are the same ones reflected in all of Lenin's writing, at least prior to World War I. These beliefs can be summed up by using the label Lenin certainly would have used for himself: a Russian Social Democrat. He must be thought of as a Social Democrat because his fundamental inspiration was the Social-Democratic workers' movement in Western Europe. He must be thought of as a Russian Social Democrat because his fundamental project was to help build a party in Russia that was as much like Western Social-Democratic parties as conditions allowed – and, where conditions did not allow, to change them by revolutionary overthrow of the tsar.

I have coined the term 'Erfurtian' to describe the bundle of beliefs, institutional models and political strategies that constituted orthodox Marx-based Social Democracy. Erfurt was the German town where the Sozialdemokratisches Partei Deutschland (SPD) held a congress in 1891 at which they celebrated their victory over Bismarck's repressive anti-socialist law and also adopted a new programme. An Erfurtian is someone who accepts the SPD as a model party, accepts the Erfurt Programme as an authoritative statement of the Social-Democratic mission, and accepts Karl Kautsky's tremendously influential commentary the *Erfurt Programme* as an authoritative definition of Social Democracy. On all counts, Lenin was a passionate Erfurtian.

The self-defined mission of Social Democracy was to make the workers aware of their own world-historical mission, namely, to conquer state power as a class and use it to introduce socialism. To borrow an image from Kautsky, the Social Democrats were bringing good news to the proletariat and they confidently expected the proletariat to respond (if not immediately, then in the near future) with acceptance and enthusiasm. In order to carry out their mission, the Social Democrats created a party of a new type, dedicated to bringing enlightenment and organisation to the proletariat. As embodied in the SPD, this new type of party possessed a clear commitment to the final goal of socialism, it was centralised and disciplined, it was as democratic as possible, and it was organised on a nation-wide scale, allowing effective use of specialisation and division of labour.

Lenin observed all this from Russia and wanted to be part of it. But there was a big and obvious obstacle to applying the Social-Democratic model to Russia. This obstacle was not Russia's backward industrial development and the relatively small size of its urban proletariat. There was plenty of work for Social Democrats to do even with this relatively small proletariat. No, the obstacle was the absence of political freedom. Political freedom was light and air to Social Democracy. Without political freedom, the vigorous political participation, the organisation on a national scale, the flourishing press – in fact, all the ways by which Social Democracy sought to enlighten and organise the proletariat for its world-historical mission – were impossible.

Lenin is often pictured as impatiently telling naïve Russian activists that a democratic mass movement in the Western style was impossible under tsarist repression. But nobody was that naïve. Everyone was aware of the obvious fact that a full application of the Social-Democratic model was only possible after the overthrow of tsarism. The real debate was over whether the model could be applied at all to tsarist Russia, and if so, to what extent? Was something resembling a mass movement even possible under these circumstances? An affirmative answer required some very confident assumptions about workers' receptivity to the Social-Democratic message and about the ability of underground activists to build and sustain a nation-wide political organisation, one that could both put down roots in the worker milieu and escape destruction at the hands of the police.

The debate over these questions was essentially an empirical one, a political judgement about what was and was not feasible in Russia. The terms of the debate changed over the years as a real-life Social-Democratic underground organisation was built up in the mid-1890s and as the opportunities and limitations of underground organisation became more clear. In each of the various clashes over these issues within Russian Social Democracy, Lenin can be easily located. He is always on the side making the most confident assumptions about the empirical possibility of a mass underground Social-Democratic movement. Among the Russian revolutionaries, Marxists were more confident than populists in the mid-1890s. Among the Marxists, the orthodox were more confident than the 'economists'. Among the orthodox, the *Iskra* group was more confident than their main leadership rival, the *Rabochee delo* group. Among the *Iskra*-ites, the Bolsheviks were more confident than the Mensheviks. Among the Bolsheviks, Lenin was more confident that many of the faction's underground *praktiki*.

Much of the following commentary is devoted to describing these clashes and prying out the empirical assumptions underlying the various positions taken. On what might Russian Social Democrats base their confidence about the viability of a mass movement under police-state conditions? One source was a particular reading of 'the history of all countries', to employ a phrase often used by Lenin in this context – in other words, the inspiring example of Western Social Democracy. The working class in Western Europe was also scattered and disorganised at the beginning, it also suffered under repressive conditions – and yet Social Democracy was able to win it over and build it into a mighty political force.

Confidence could also be based on optimistic assumptions about the receptivity of Russian workers to the Social-Democratic message. Lenin generally argued that the 'advanced workers' were already committed Social

Democrats and that these advanced workers were in an ideal position to spread the message further, since they would be accepted by other workers as their natural leaders.

A relatively confident judgement could also be grounded in optimism about the survival ability of underground organisations. Underground committees were continually destroyed by the police (three or four months was a typical life span), open communication between local organisations was impossible, while strikes, demonstrations and petition campaigns were all illegal. In order to have any confidence at all about the stability of underground organisations, you had to make some fairly heroic assumptions about a continual supply of activists, about their dedication, about their ability to outwit the police, about the possibility of setting down protective roots in the worker milieu. Lenin made all these assumptions. The very fact that he campaigned to raise the professionalism of the underground activists showed that he thought that they were capable of honing their skills and that this would have a payoff in survival value – opinions by no means universally shared.

Finally, confidence could be based on the possible impact that a mass underground movement guided by Social Democracy could make on the rest of Russian society. If Russia was entering into a period of revolutionary crisis, if almost all of Russian society was turning in anger against the tsar, if everyone was waiting for some sort of mass action against the tsar before revealing their own radical dissatisfaction, if an underground organisation would receive support not only from the workers but from all groups – then, indeed, even a pathetically small and weak Social-Democratic organisation could make a major impact and genuinely lead a revolutionary transformation of Russia. For Lenin, all of these 'ifs' were facts.

As is often observed, Lenin devoted all his energy to 'the revolution'. But, in itself, this observation is so abstract that it is quite misleading. Lenin was working for the upcoming anti-tsarist revolution that would destroy absolutism and introduce political freedom to Russia. One way of putting it is to say he was working for a 'bourgeois revolution'. This phrase, accurate enough as far as it goes, misleadingly puts the emphasis on what were, for Lenin, the negative and limited aspects of the upcoming revolution. At this point in his career, Lenin was a passionate advocate of political freedom – in particular, of what might be called the 'five S's', *svoboda slova, soiuzov, sobraniia, stachek* (freedom of speech, association, assembly, strikes). If you were willing to fight for political freedom, you were Lenin's ally, even if you were hostile to socialism. If you downgraded the goal of political freedom in any way, you were Lenin's foe, even if you were a committed socialist.

Attachment to political freedom confirms his Erfurtian loyalties and his confident assumptions about Russia. Marx, Engels and Kautsky – Lenin's three central authorities – all insisted that political freedom was light and air to the proletariat and its struggle. Political freedom was not an end in itself, but it was an absolutely necessary means to accomplishing the socialist goal. Bourgeois political freedom was thus much too important to be left to the bourgeoisie, and so Kautsky's authoritative writings sketched out a role for Social Democracy as leader of the whole people in the fight for expanded political freedom.

The rise of Marx-based Social Democracy among the revolutionaries in Russia depended crucially on the growing conviction that a political revolution had to precede a social revolution. The populist revolutionaries of the 1870s had by and large been very pessimistic about the effects of political freedom. Would not political freedom simply give the bourgeoisie greater access to the masses, thus allowing them to corrupt and mislead them? And, indeed, anyone who was sceptical about the revolutionary inclinations of the workers would be ill-advised to fight for a political freedom that would benefit conservatives and liberals at least as much as socialists and probably more. But this certainty evidently did not bother Lenin as he single-mindedly worked for a revolution to destroy absolutism.

Lenin's Erfurtian loyalties and confident assumptions about Russia can be found in everything he produced, before, during and after the writing of WITBD. And they structure the whole argument of WITBD as well. In order to see this clearly, we must look at the micro-context, the situation Lenin faced in late 1901 when he sat down to write WITBD. Lenin's urgency and polemical zeal have led most readers to suppose Lenin was reacting to a *crisis*. His argument is put in a strikingly different light when we realise he was reacting to an *opportunity*.

The fundamental cause of this sense of opportunity was the approaching revolutionary storm in Russia. The young Social Democrat Boris Gorev had the Rip Van Winkle experience of returning to European Russia in August 1902 after several years in Siberian exile. When he had left Russia in 1897, a single strike in Petersburg was cause for Social-Democratic joy. When he returned, the entire country seemed on the brink of the long-awaited overthrow of the tsar. When Gorev met his younger brother Mikhail – now known as Liber and one of the leaders of the Jewish Bund – he was struck by his brother's assurance that the time of revolution had finally arrived.[2]

This sense of excitement was widely shared. One émigré newspaper was entitled *On the Eve* [*Nakanune*]. L. Nadezhdin, a Social-Democratic critic of *Iskra*, entitled his group's journal *Eve of Revolution* [*Kanun revoliutsii*]. In the lectures that he gave in America in 1903–4, Paul Miliukov told his audience that Russia was in a state of revolutionary ferment. The book based on these lectures – aptly titled *Russia and its Crisis* – particularly stressed the role of worker militancy in creating the atmosphere of revolutionary storm.[3]

Social Democrats such as Lenin were even more encouraged by the rise of worker militancy and its galvanising effect on the rest of Russian society. Always in the background of *WITBD* is the sense of excitement vividly expressed by Vera Zasulich, one of Lenin's fellow editors on the underground newspaper *Iskra*, when she described workers' demonstrations to German readers:

> The new revolutionary Russia is the growth of revolutionary courage and the refusal to submit to the powers that be, it is the wide dissemination of illegal literature and the constant demand for it, it is the speed and the ease with which the ranks of organised Social Democracy pulls together and grows, despite the countless arrests, it is the street demonstrations themselves, carried out by crowds of people many thousands strong who support the protests of the students, it is the huge masses during the present year [1902] who made the watchword 'Down with the autocracy!' heard all over Russia – and this watchword was not rejected by the rest of the population. All of this compels those loyal to the government and the government itself to understand just how stormily and uncontrollably the number of their enemies is growing, just how irreconcilable are the contradictions between its hired defenders and the mass of the people.[4]

All this activity strengthened the position of Lenin's *Iskra* group vis-à-vis its Social-Democratic rivals. As Miliukov put it in *Russia and its Crisis*, the success

---

[2] Gorev 1924, pp. 44, 49.
[3] Miliukov 1962.
[4] Zasulich 1983b, p. 378 (originally in *Neue Zeit* 1902).

of the 'orthodox' Marxists grouped around *Iskra* 'is easily explained by the fact that their tendency coincided with the ascending line of the whole movement and was powerfully supported by the whole trend of the increasing revolutionism of the Russian socialists'.[5]

Lenin was delighted by these developments. In late 1901, the very time that he was writing *WITBD*, he wrote:

> We should draw new faith in the universal power of the worker movement guided by us when we see how the excitement in the advanced revolutionary class is transmitted to the other classes and strata of society – how this excitement leads not only to an unbelievable upsurge of revolutionary spirit among the students but also to the awakening in the village that is now beginning.[6]

But, if 'economism' – the downgrading of political freedom as an urgent goal for Russian Social Democracy – was on the rocks by 1901, why did Lenin devote *WITBD* to conducting a polemic against it? The answer to this question is simple: he did not. The polemic in *WITBD* is not against economism – rather, it is a polemic which uses economism as a stick to beat the main leadership rivals of *Iskra* (the *Rabochee delo* group). Lenin correctly assumed that, if he could pin the 'economist' label on his rivals, they would be discredited. The *Rabochee delo* group loudly – and, as I think, justifiably – denied they had anything to do with economism. In the close to fifty articles Lenin wrote for *Iskra* during the years 1900–3, polemics directed against economism are very hard to find, whereas polemics against terrorism or nationalism within the Party are prominent.

The polemics directed against *Rabochee delo* are, for the most part, confined to two short chapters tacked on to the original plan for the book (due to circumstances described in Chapter Five). The business part of *WITBD* consists the three long chapters in which Lenin makes the case for his positive policy proposals. These proposals include the urgency of a particular agitation technique ('political indictments'), the urgency of transcending the prevailing 'artisanal limitations' in party organisations, and the urgency of using a party

---

[5] Miliukov 1962, p. 355. See also Miliukov's mostly positive review of *WITBD* that I have translated as an appendix to Chapter Three.

[6] Lenin 1958–65, 5, p. 334 (from an article in *Iskra*'s sister journal *Zaria*, No. 2/3, published December 1901).

newspaper as a tool in tying together the existing local organisations into an effective national organisation. But, again, all this urgency sprang out of a sense of opportunity, not of crisis. From Lenin's point of view, the groundwork of a national party organisation had been laid, the viability of a truly mass underground movement had been demonstrated. All that remained was to take the logical next step toward unification on a Russia-wide scale.

In his first, although unpublished, presentation of his policy package in 1899, Lenin describes the past achievements and vast future potential of underground Social Democracy:

> The Russian worker movement finds itself at the present time in a transitional period. A brilliant beginning that saw Social-Democratic organisations of the workers in the Western regions, Petersburg, Moscow, Kiev and other towns was crowned by the formation of the 'Russian Social-Democratic Worker Party' (spring 1898). After taking this giant step forward, Social Democracy seemed to have exhausted all its forces and fell back to its previous fragmented work of separate local organisations. The Party did not go out of existence – it only turned inward to gather up its forces and put the work of uniting all Russian Social Democrats on a secure basis . . .
>
> Local Social-Democratic work in Russia achieved a rather high level. The seeds of Social-Democratic ideas were sown everywhere in Russia; worker leaflets – that primary form of Social-Democratic literature – are now familiar to all Russian workers, from Petersburg to Krasnoyarsk, from the Caucasus to the Urals. All that is lacking is precisely bringing together all this local work into the work of one *party*.[7]

Because of this underlying sense of urgency, opportunity and excitement, WITBD had inspiring qualities that communicated itself to many of its first readers above and beyond its angry polemics. One of these first readers, N. Valentinov, has left the following account (all the more valuable because Valentinov broke with Lenin very early):

> In his pamphlet on the Kiev revolutionary movement of 1901–3, published in 1926 by the Kiev section of the Institute of Party History, Vakar wrote the following:

---

[7] Lenin 1958–65, 4, pp. 187–8.

'Volsky [= Valentinov], a student of the Polytechnic, took an extremely active part in the work of the Social-Democratic Committee at that time. He was an athletically built, healthy, and cheerful youth. His energetic and expansive nature always drove him to the most dangerous and different enterprises which demanded daring and determination, and sometimes skill and physical strength. Struggle, risk and danger attracted comrade Volsky'.

Apart from the word 'youth' (I looked younger than my age), the description is broadly correct. I only quote it here because it applied equally well to *all of us* in those years. 'Daring and determination' were common to us all. For this reason *What Is to Be Done?* struck just the right chord with us and we were only too eager to put its message into practice. In this sense, one may say, we were one hundred per cent Leninists at that time.[8]

## Worry about workers

The [Russian] Marxists faced a problem that had plagued radicals in the 1870's and would be a perennial obstacle for them: the political inertia of the masses. If the *narod* (the people), revered by many Russian radicals, refused to be budged toward activism, how could the revolution ever be made? . . . Lenin turned to the issue of the masses' political inertia and analysed it most comprehensively in 1902 in the pamphlet *What Is to Be Done?*'.[9]

This statement by the distinguished American historian Abraham Ascher brings us up short. Could Ascher be talking about the same Lenin I have just described? Could he be talking about the same WITBD? I described a confident and excited Lenin who wrote WITBD in the midst of a revolutionary upsurge. Ascher describes a gloomy, anxious Lenin trying to figure out what went wrong.

We are indeed talking about the same Lenin and the same WITBD, and furthermore, Ascher here expresses the outlook of a strong consensus of informed experts. I call this consensus 'the textbook interpretation' because, at least from the mid-1950s, this reading of WITBD has found its way into

[8] Valentinov 1968, p. 27. Valentinov's whole discussion of WITBD is valuable.
[9] Ascher 1988, p. 37.

textbooks of political science and of Russian history, and, from there, into almost any secondary account that has reason to touch on Lenin. The two or three famous passages that form the textual basis of this reading are endlessly recycled from textbook to popular history to specialised monograph and back again.

In my description of the textbook interpretation, I will restrict myself to those writers who backed up their reading with factual historical research. These writers can be divided into two groups, the academics and the activists. The academic historians who laid the basis of the textbook interpretation constituted the first generation in postwar Soviet studies: Leopold Haimson, Alfred G. Meyer, Adam Ulam, Leonard Schapiro, John Keep, Samuel Baron, Allan Wildman, Israel Getzler, Abraham Ascher, Richard Pipes, Jonathan Frankel. Although not full-time Soviet specialists, Barrington Moore and Herbert Marcuse also belong on this list.[10]

The monographs written by these specialists, starting in the early 1950s and petering out in the early 1970s, are dedicated to various aspects of the revolutionary and labour movement in the period when Lenin wrote WITBD. WITBD itself plays a somewhat strange role in these books. On the one hand, there is no extensive examination of WITBD as a text. On the other hand, WITBD invariably provides what can be called the narrative hinge of these books. It is in and through WITBD that Lenin first reveals himself and creates Bolshevism almost as a demiurge.

In the 1970s, activists in the Trotskyist tradition began to issue their own historically based readings of WITBD. Writers such as Tony Cliff, John Molyneux and more recently Paul Le Blanc wrote partly in reaction to the academic specialists but mainly out of a desire to bring Leninist lessons to the movement of their own day.[11] Their attitude to Lenin is very favourable but not completely

---

[10] Wolfe 1948, Meyer 1957, Geyer 1962, Baron 1963, Keep 1963, Ulam 1965, Wildman 1967, Getzler 1967, Frankel 1969, Schapiro 1987 [1969], Ascher 1972, Moore 1956, Marcuse 1958, Haimson 1955. Leopold Haimson has recently published essays on Lenin in which he modifies some conclusions of his highly influential study of 1955 (Haimson 2004, pp. 61–2) but does not break fundamentally with the textbook interpretation. Further references in my commentary are only to Haimson's recent essays: Haimson 1999, Haimson 2004, Haimson 2005. Also somewhat difficult to categorise is Harding 1977. Harding mounts a critique of the academic tradition, but ultimately does not break away from the 'worry about workers' interpretation (for further discussion, see Lih 2003).

[11] Cliff 1975; Molyneux 1978; Le Blanc 1990; Liebman 1975; Mandel 1971.

uncritical. Despite the political differences between them and the academics, there is enough overlap in their interpretation of WITBD to justify including the activists among the advocates of the textbook interpretation. The activist take on the academic interpretation can be summed up as 'Yes, but . . .'. Yes, WITBD does show a mistrust of workers, emphasis on the role of intellectuals and so on – but, first of all, Lenin had a point, even if a one-sided point, and, second, he radically changed his emphasis later. I shall first describe the academic reading of WITBD and then the activist reaction.

The fundamental tenet of the textbook interpretation is that WITBD expresses Lenin's 'worry about workers'.[12] In this book, Lenin reveals a 'distrust of the mass, a conviction that socialist consciousness was given to few'.[13] Lenin's pessimistic assumption about the workers' natural reformist inclinations is what drove him to make his other theoretical and organisational innovations.

The textual basis for this description of Lenin's outlook are his pronouncements on the subject of 'spontaneity' and 'consciousness'. Lenin was preoccupied with this question.[14] He feared the 'spontaneous' development of the workers' movement, he demanded that the workers' movement be 'diverted' from its natural course and be directed 'from without' by non-workers, in fact, by bourgeois revolutionary intellectuals. It is hardly an exaggeration to say that the textual basis for this portrait of Lenin is not just one book, not just one chapter in this book, not just two famous paragraphs from this chapter that are inevitably quoted, but three words found in these paragraphs: 'spontaneity', 'divert', and 'from without' (one word in Russian).

Lenin's worry about workers was caused by a crisis, a development that threatened his view of the world and poisoned his previous optimism. Disputes over the exact nature of this crisis have led to a major division within the textbook interpretation. The majority view locates Lenin's conversion to the rise of 'revisionism'.[15] Deep down inside, Lenin agreed with the revisionists

---

[12] This felicitous phrase is taken from the title of Zelnik 2003b.

[13] Baron 1963, p. 239.

[14] Haimson 2004, pp. 57–9. I tend to put 'spontaneity' in quotation marks because I believe 'spontaneity' to be an inaccurate and misleading translation of the Russian word *stikhiinost* (see Annotations Part Two).

[15] For accounts that locate the radical transformation in Lenin's views to the year 1899, see Schapiro 1987 [1969] and Pipes 1968.

that the workers were becoming more and more reformist, less and less socialist. A very common trope is that Lenin was a secret revisionist himself. Adam Ulam – the Harvard political science professor who was instrumental in making WITBD a standard textbook item – put it this way:

> Although the argument is directed at German revisionism and its alleged Russian followers, there is this basic agreement between Lenin and Eduard Bernstein: the forces of history are not making of the workers a *revolutionary* class; the spontaneous organization of the workers leads them not to revolution but to the struggle for economic and professional improvement. Why, then, is Bernstein a 'revisionist' and Lenin an 'orthodox' Marxist? Because Bernstein believes in the workers' party following the inclinations of the workers and bowing to the inherent labourism of the industrialized worker, whereas Lenin believes in forcible conversion of the worker to revolutionary Marxism.[16]

The other explanation for Lenin's turn to pessimism might be called the 'uppity worker' explanation, or, more gravely, the 'anti-worker-phile' explanation. According to Reginald Zelnik, at the end of the 1890s, Lenin

> had learned from afar that some of Russia's most militant, dedicated workers were now engaged in the dramatic (though in some ways ambivalent) rejection of intelligentsia tutelage, a 'worker-phile' trend that echoed trends in other parts of Europe, and one that Lenin fought with all his heart.[17]

The scholars who pioneered this explanation of Lenin's crisis – Allan Wildman, Zelnik and Gerald Surh – do not actually call Lenin a 'worker-phobe', but they do see him as driven by a profound unease, even outrage, at the sight of workers taking their fate into their own hands. A desire to exclude workers from leadership positions is the natural result.[18]

Lenin's new-found pessimism (whatever motivated it) caused him to reject the more optimistic Marxism of Western Social Democracy, with its deterministic faith in the 'spontaneous' revolutionary inclinations of the workers. 'Lenin

---

[16] Ulam 1960, p. 170.
[17] Zelnik 2003a, p. 28.
[18] Wildman 1967; Surh 1999 and Surh 2000. Of the two explanations of Lenin's alleged crisis, the 'anti-worker-phile' scholars have much the better case. For my response to their interpretation, see Chapter Four.

is quite ready to reinterpret Marx, while, claiming, of course, that he is merely following the letter of the doctrine'.[19] Others, more charitably, allow that Lenin may have sincerely believed he was orthodox and that therefore he was only an unconscious heretic.

Lenin's rejection of Marxism as understood by Western Social Democracy led logically to his rejection of 'the popular, open, and more or less democratically organised parties of Western Europe and the huge, trade-union-affiliated German party in particular' and therefore his reversion to 'populist conspiratorial ideas of revolution-mongering'.[20] This reversion to populist models constituted a profound innovation within the Marxist tradition. As Bertram Wolfe put it in 1961,

> In two pamphlets, and a number of articles published between 1902 and 1904, Lenin had been hammering away at his new organization plan for a 'party of a new type,' that is, one differing fundamentally from all previous Marxian parties, whether those founded while Marx and Engels were alive, or since.[21]

The 'party of a new type' was to be hyper-centralised, confined to a few 'professional revolutionaries' recruited from among the intelligentsia, and dedicated to conspiracy.

Naturally, these innovations caused a huge split within Russian Social Democracy, dividing those who remained true to the Social Democracy of civilised Europe and those who updated the traditions of barbarous Russia. Part of the attraction of the textbook interpretation is the compelling narrative of this fateful split between Bolshevik and Menshevik – a split whose huge stakes were only vaguely sensed by the participants themselves. The first major and in many ways still most compelling statement of the textbook interpretation was Bertram Wolfe's *Three Who Made a Revolution*, published in 1948, in which he says:

> the real issue [was] between 'Economists' and Marxists, then between Mensheviks and Bolsheviks, then between Workers Opposition and Lenin,

---

[19] Ulam 1962, p. 615.
[20] Wesson 1978, pp. 22–3.
[21] Wolfe 1961, p. 11. This is the earliest use of 'party of a new type' in English that I have found; Wolfe took it over from Soviet historians and implied, incorrectly, that Lenin himself used the term.

between Tomsky and Stalin, changing forms of the protean battle between Westernizer and Slavophile. One path led closer to the parties and trade unions of the West, which were democratically organized, comfortably adapted to the sizeable legality permitted them, and long since devoid of insurrectionary spirit except as a banner for festal occasions. The other led to concentration on conspiracy and insurrection under the leadership of a self-selected, rigidly centralized, secret and conspirative band of revolutionary intellectuals under a self-appointed leader, formed on the pattern of the early 'professional revolutionaries' of the *Narodnaya Volya*.[22]

Putting all the assertions of the textbook interpretation together, we realise that *WITBD* is a profound theoretical and organisational innovation, the charter document of Bolshevism, and the ultimate source of Stalinism. Given the strong link thus forged between *WITBD* and Stalinism, the textbook interpretation has little motivation to bring out the centrality of political freedom in Lenin's platform. The specialists who wrote about the political history of Russian Social Democracy in this period were surely aware that Lenin and the *Iskra* group strongly insisted on the urgency of political freedom for Russia, but they somehow managed to talk about it in such a way that nobody else knew it (I certainly did not). They put as little emphasis on political freedom as possible while putting as much emphasis on any hint (often very tenuous indeed) that Lenin was 'impatient', wanted to skip stages, leap to socialism, and so forth. One sometimes gets the impression that Lenin's 'revolution-mongering' in favour of political freedom was not quite seemly. His insistence on political freedom begins to look captious and sectarian. Richard Pipes tells us that Lenin demanded revolution despite the fact that by 1900 Russia was moving toward a 'mature trade-unionism' – and this at a time when trade unions and even strikes were illegal in Russia, and one of the main motives for *Iskra*'s insistence on revolution was precisely to make them legal![23]

The activist interpretation advanced by Cliff, Molyneux, Le Blanc and others vehemently rejects the link between *WITBD* and Stalinism. Their overall portrait of Lenin contrasts strongly with the one presented by the academic tradition. Yet, on the specific issue of *WITBD*, the contrast with the academic tradition

---

[22] Wolfe 1964 [1948], pp. 160–1.
[23] Pipes 1968, pp. 45–6. On the absence of political freedom in Russia at this time (including freedom of association and strikes), see Chapter Three.

is less striking than the overlap. With minor differences of emphasis, the activist writers tell the following story.

Marx-based Social Democracy in Western Europe had a fatalistic and deterministic view of political organisation. This view had roots in Marx's own 'optimistic evolutionism'.[24] The great breakthrough to a vanguard conception of the party came with Lenin in WITBD, although Lenin himself was unaware of his originality and thought he was applying standard Marxist conceptions. In making this breakthrough, Lenin was led to make formulations about spontaneity and the role of intellectuals that were one-sided and therefore false. But this was just Lenin's way of doing things – he was always 'bending the stick' too far in the particular direction he needed to emphasise at a particular point. In 1902, the stick needed bending toward the importance of centralism, and so Lenin emphasised centralism at every turn.

Lenin's formulation led to the split within Russian Social Democracy, because the Mensheviks remained loyal to the standard Social-Democratic position of a passive, fatalistic, deterministic, 'economist' confusion between party and class. But Lenin's own views continued to develop, particularly in response to the revolution of 1905.

> In the face of the enormous and spontaneous revolutionary achievements of the Russian working class, the tone of Lenin's writings changes completely. . . . The break with economistic fatalism that was achieved in *What Is to Be Done?* and *One Step Forward* is maintained and developed, but freed of the elitist foundation that Lenin had at first given it.[25]

Lenin moved so far ahead of other Bolsheviks that when he tried to get more workers on party committees in 1905, his own followers rejected him, imbued as they were with the spirit of WITBD.

Thus the activists. When we compare this account given by the activists to the standard academic account, we see that the two sides agree that Lenin made an unwittingly original breakthrough in the area of party organisation. The new 'vanguard' type of party constitutes a dramatic break with Western traditions. The difference here is only one of evaluation: the academic writers

---

[24] Molyneux 1978, p. 34.

[25] Molyneux 1978, pp. 59–60. In his recent essays, Haimson also argues that Lenin was 'intoxicated' with the spontaneous revolutionary activism of the workers in 1905, leading to 'radical changes' in his views on party organisation (Haimson 2004, p. 64).

prefer the 'mass democratic' parties of the West while the activist rejects these parties as over-representative and insufficiently revolutionary.[26] The two sides also agree that Lenin's formulations on the question of spontaneity and consciousness are the heart of WITBD. In this case, the activists to a large extent subscribe to the evaluation of these formulations as unfortunately élitist. The difference here is that the activists claim that Lenin himself later realised these formulations were one-sided, so they cannot be said to constitute the heart of Lenin's outlook. Finally, both sides agree that the message sent out by WITBD was 'worry about workers'. So intense was this message that only the mighty events of 1905 caused Lenin to change his mind – and, even then, his followers were determined to keep workers off the committees.

As should already be clear, I reject all the central propositions of the textbook interpretation. The keynote of Lenin's outlook was not worry about workers but exhilaration about workers. The formulations about spontaneity are not the heart of WITBD but a tacked-on polemical sally (if Lenin's opponent Boris Krichevskii had not used the word in his critique of Iskra published in September 1901, it would not have appeared in WITBD published a few months later). These formulations are confusing, unedifying and should be bracketed until all other evidence about Lenin's outlook is considered. WITBD was not a gloomy response to a crisis (however defined) but an exuberant response to an opportunity. WITBD did not reject the Western model of a Social-Democratic party but invoked this model at every turn. Lenin certainly advocated a 'vanguard party', for this was the common understanding of what Social Democracy was all about. Lenin thus did not revert to the populist tradition in any way. WITBD not advocate hyper-centralism or an élite, conspiratorial party restricted to professional revolutionaries from the intelligentsia. The positions advanced in WITBD were not the cause of the party split in 1904. The centrality of political freedom in Lenin's platform makes it impossible to draw a direct link between WITBD and Stalinism.

How is it that such a wide and long-standing consensus has (in my view) gone so wrong? The political outlook of the various writers can hardly be

---

[26] The activists have a more accurate sense than the academics of Lenin's vision of the party (see Le Blanc 1990, p. 67). What is misleading is their stress on the originality of this vision and its stark contrast with Western Social Democracy. (Cliff, in particular, also agrees with the academic tradition in tracing the origins of Lenin's thinking to populism.)

decisive, given the strange coalition just observed between pro-Lenin and anti-Lenin authors. One explanation for this coalition is that it goes back to a similar coalition in 1904. At that time, two heroes of the activist tradition – Lev Trotsky and Rosa Luxemburg – were Mensheviks or, at any rate, were prepared to work with the Mensheviks in combatting Lenin. Even today, a few oft-quoted sentences from Trotsky and Luxemburg are among the main props of the textbook interpretation.[27]

Another reason is the common fascination with the question of Lenin's attitude toward 'spontaneity'. For a variety of reasons to be set out later, this is a profitless exercise. One ill effect of the exclusive focus on this issue is the exiguous textual base used to ascertain Lenin's views, since Lenin simply did not talk about this topic very much. Two passages to the exclusion of much else in Chapter II of *WITBD*, one chapter to the exclusion of much else in *WITBD* as a whole, one book to the exclusion of almost everything else Lenin wrote in the *Iskra* period (1900–3) – no wonder there are some surprises when a more extensive range of writings is taken into account.[28]

Lenin cannot be understood just by reading Lenin. Three other vital contexts have been largely overlooked by the textbook interpretation. The first is the context of international Social Democracy – what I call the Erfurtian outlook. The two wings of the textbook interpretation have different motives for neglect of this context. Specialists on Russia enjoy tracing the Russian roots of Lenin's thinking and tend not to have a detailed knowledge of, say, German Social Democracy. Trotskyist activists have inherited a disdain for the Second International, and for Kautsky in particular, that is so total as to preclude any serious inquiry into their actual views.

A second context is the growing revolutionary storm in Russia at the turn of the century. Of course, any informed specialist is aware of the crisis in Russia that was gathering momentum in 1901–2, but this never seems to have any impact on their presentation of Lenin as a worried man singing a worried song. At the time Lenin wrote his book, the entire spectrum of revolutionary opinion was encouraged and energised by the willingness of workers to

---

[27] I owe Alan Shandro thanks for pointing out this explanation for the activist/academic overlap.

[28] The surprisingly total neglect of Lenin's other *Iskra*-period writings is a feature of the activist writers as well as the academic ones. For a survey of some of these writings, see the section 'The unknown Lenin' in Chapter Three.

demonstrate their political dissatisfaction in the streets. This growing excitement has been leached out of the standard picture of Social Democrats wringing their hands over (in Ascher's words) 'the political inertia of the masses'.

A third context is the shared assumptions among the participants in the polemical infighting within Russian Social Democracy. If we do not realise that everybody took for granted that the SPD model could only be applied to Russia in a severely distorted underground version, we will miss the import of Lenin's proposals. If we do not realise that Lenin fully expected all his readers and even his opponents to regard 'economism' as a very bad thing indeed, we will miss the import of his polemics. And so forth.

Although I cannot help being worried by the impressive array of experts who support the textbook interpretation, there are two circumstances that encourage me. The first is that when the more knowledgeable and conscientious advocates of the textbook interpretation try to bring in a wider range of evidence in support of Lenin's worry about workers, they regularly end up with a thoroughly incoherent picture. The second is that there exists a solid counter-tradition on WITBD – so much so that I can safely say I am rediscovering Lenin rather than presenting an original new picture. Let us look at these two sources of encouragement in turn.

## Flip-flops and stick-bending

Every interpretation of a complicated and messy reality faces anomalies, that is, data that at least on the surface gives rise to serious problems for their proposed interpretation. My approach to WITBD can be labelled the 'good news' interpretation.[29] Lenin believed that Social Democracy had a mission to carry to the workers the good news of their own world-historical mission and that, furthermore, this message would be on the whole enthusiastically received and acted upon.[30] Social Democracy was *needed* and would be *heeded*.

---

[29] This term is taken from a comment by Kautsky in the *Erfurt Programme*: 'Socialism is no message of woe for the proletariat but rather good news, a new gospel [*ein neues Evangelium*]' (Kautsky 1965, pp. 230–1). For further discussion of this passage, see Chapter One.

[30] I have added the qualifier 'on the whole' because, obviously, Social Democrats were aware that there would be periods of depression and retreat (see Chapter One). Lenin too was aware of this possibility, but, more characteristically, he insisted on a rapid spread of awareness, particularly in the period studied in this commentary.

The anomaly for this interpretation consist of the famous formulations about combatting spontaneity and so on. I deal with this anomaly, first, by laying out the massive evidence for my interpretation and, second, by giving reasons why the famous formulations do not in fact pose a serious threat.

The 'worry about workers' interpretation also faces a long and grave list of anomalies. To start with, the views attributed to Lenin by the textbook interpretation are 'ridiculous' and 'remarkably illogical'. This is demonstrated quite insightfully and convincingly by Adam Ulam, a scholar who was instrumental in turning the 'worry about workers' interpretation into a textbook staple:

> 'To combat spontaneity . . .' The literal statement sounds almost ridiculous, doubly so in the circumstances of its first formulation. Who is to divert the growing working movement in Russia from its natural course? A handful of revolutionaries – some of them in Tsarist jails – operating through a newspaper published abroad. But the statement contains the essence of Leninism, the perception that the *natural* development of material forces and the *natural* response of people to them will, in time, lead far away from Marx's expectations about the effects of industrialization on the worker. You do not jettison Marxism because it failed to predict the psychology of the worker in an advanced industrialized country. You 'improve' and advance this psychology in the revolutionary direction by means of a party. A remarkably illogical performance. You reject the major premise of your ideology, yet you claim strict orthodoxy. Your argument is rationalistic and materialistic, and yet you set out, almost in Sorel-like fashion, to propagate the myth of revolution, the necessity of which, you have just asserted, the workers will feel less and less![31]

Advocates of the textbook interpretation will sometimes admit that Lenin did not explicitly advance the views attributed to him, although this fact does not seem to worry them much, For example, Richard Pipes summarises a Lenin article of 1899 by telling us that Lenin's '*unspoken* assumption is that the majority of the population is actually or potentially reactionary; his *unspoken* conclusion, that democracy leads to reaction'.[32] Pipes is absolutely right: these

---

[31] Ulam 1960, pp. 170–1. Note the emphasis on 'natural', a word not used by Lenin in this context. (Despite the quotation marks, Lenin did not use the word 'improve'.)
[32] Pipes 1968, p. 49 (emphasis added).

particular assumptions and conclusions are definitely unspoken. Lenin's *spoken* assumptions and conclusions – a subject in which Pipes shows less interest – are all about the majority of the population charging the citadel of the autocracy in order to achieve democratic political freedom as the necessary next step toward socialism.

Direct evidence that Lenin held quite other views than the ones assigned to him are dealt with by making Lenin incoherent. In an important book in the academic tradition, Alfred Meyer's *Leninism*, we read that 'Lenin tended to assume that the workingman was forever doomed to insufficient consciousness, no matter how miserable his conditions'. Yet – again, precisely because Meyer is more informed and conscientious than most – he promptly starts to make Lenin incoherent. He immediately adds: 'as an "orthodox" Marxist, Lenin denied the revisionist thesis that the workers had lost their class consciousness (or had never possessed it in the first place). But as a Leninist he accepted it, at least as a short-run proposition'. A little later we read:

> While it is true that in the main he denied rationality to the workingman, he did not maintain this attitude unhesitatingly. On the contrary, he more than once allowed himself to be led astray [!] by an unusually optimistic appraisal of proletarian consciousness.[33]

Turning to the most recent and up-to-date scholarship in the 'worry about workers' tradition, we find that it also insists – is forced to insist – on Lenin's incoherence. Earlier scholarship had often posited some sort of sudden conversion on Lenin's part prior to WITBD.[34] But, lately, the number of conversions and flip-flops in Lenin's outlook has dramatically increased. In independent studies, Robert Mayer and Anna Krylova both advance what I call a double flip-flop hypothesis: Lenin had a crisis of faith immediately before WITBD and then had a radical change of mind very soon thereafter, thus leaving WITBD disconnected both to Lenin's past and his future.[35] Krylova,

---

[33] Meyer 1957, pp. 31, 44.

[34] For example, Leonard Schapiro writes that between summer 1899 and the end of the year there occurred 'a complete transformation in Lenin's outlook' (Schapiro 1987, pp. 234–5).

[35] Mayer 1996, pp. 307–20. In an earlier article, I wrote the following about Robert Mayer's study: 'This double flip-flop hypothesis may not find many adherents, but it represents a serious attempt to deal with genuine difficulties that need to be confronted'

for example, states that *WITBD*'s view of the workers is 'in striking contrast' to Lenin's previous writings, that *WITBD* itself is an 'encyclopedia' of modernist doubt, and that soon after the publication of *WITBD* Lenin put an end to his doubts with a brand-new view of the workers as motivated entirely by class instinct.[36]

Another way to dismiss anomalous evidence about Lenin's views is simply to claim that Lenin was consciously or unconsciously hypocritical. According to Reginald Zelnik, Lenin could not be fully explicit about his worry about workers because of 'the dangerous political implications' of clarifying his real views, even to himself.[37] The activist writers also talk as if they knew Lenin's beliefs better than he did himself. John Molyneux writes, for example, that 'Lenin at this stage [1904] was not aware that he diverged in any fundamental way from social democratic orthodoxy' and therefore incorrectly identified himself with the mainstream of SPD luminaries such as Karl Kautsky and August Bebel.[38] We are left with the following picture. There was probably no one in Russia who had read in Kautsky's voluminous writings so attentively, extensively and admiringly as Lenin, yet he remained completely unaware that he diverged in fundamental ways from Kautsky. I am not sure whether we are supposed to explain this by Kautsky's deceitfulness, Lenin's inability to understand what he read, or Lenin's unawareness of his own beliefs.

'Bending the stick' is the activist tradition's favourite device for explaining away anomalies. Of course, Lenin did tend to put exclusive emphasis at any one time on one or a few points. Certainly, we need to keep this in mind when we are trying to make sense of his pronouncements. Nevertheless, over-frequent recourse to this explanation ends up making Lenin look like a rather incompetent and incoherent leader. Tony Cliff is a great admirer of Lenin and yet his picture of Lenin from 1895 to 1905 is not an attractive one. In 1895, Lenin thought 'class consciousness, including political consciousness, develops automatically from the economic struggle'. A few years later he veered away from that extreme belief:

---

(Lih 2003). While the compliment in the second clause still applies, I find I must retract the somewhat sarcastic comment in the first clause. The double flip-flop hypothesis *is* finding adherents.

[36] Krylova 2003.

[37] Zelnik 2003a, pp. 24–33; Zelnik 2003b, p. 216.

[38] Molyneux 1978, pp. 52, 56.

> It was fear of the danger to the movement occasioned by the rise of Russian 'economism' and German revisionism in the second half of 1899 that motivated Lenin to bend the stick right over again, away from the spontaneous, day-to-day fragmented economic struggle and towards the organisation of a national political party.[39]

'Lenin's "bending of the stick" right over to mechanical over-emphasis on organisation in *What Is to Be Done?*' was 'quite useful operationally', since 'the step now necessary was to arouse, at least in the politically conscious section of the masses, a passion for political action'. But, as Cliff himself makes clear, by the time Lenin sat down to write WITBD in late 1901, economism was on the rocks and the workers were becoming 'the main active political opponents of Tsarism'. Evidently, Lenin was so out of touch that he bent the stick exactly where it was not needed.[40]

Lenin's stick-bending in WITBD had unfortunate consequences, since he managed to convince the Bolshevik *praktiki* that it was unwise to allow workers on party committees. No doubt, these Bolsheviks did yet not realise their leader's habit of always exaggerating and so took him seriously. When Lenin himself began to bend the stick in yet another direction, he could not convince his followers to relent.[41]

Lenin himself used the 'bend the stick' image in some remarks he made about WITBD. Given the importance of this image in commentary on WITBD (especially in the activist tradition), we should be clear in our minds about exactly what it is that we take Lenin to be saying. There are two ways of understanding the 'bend the stick' image. If a stick is bent in one direction, then you bend it in the other direction in order to get it back to centre. In this case, you are explaining why you bent the stick in a certain direction and no other – or, less figuratively, why you chose to make some points and not others. Or, alternatively, the stick is so firmly bent in one direction that in order to correct it, you must bend it *too far* in the other direction, in the expectation that, upon release, it will revert to an upright position. Less figuratively, you exaggerate and overstate your case in order to get people's attention.

---

[39] Cliff 1975, p. 69.
[40] Cliff 1975, pp. 52, 69, 82, 95–8.
[41] For a more accurate account of this supposed clash between Lenin and the *praktiki*, see Chapter Nine.

Turning to Lenin's actual words, we find he never said he bent the stick too far. On the contrary, he said at the Second Congress in 1903:

> We all know now that the 'economists' bent the stick in one direction. In order to make the stick straight it was necessary to bend the stick in the other direction, and that is what I did. I am sure that Russian Social Democracy will always straighten [*vypriamliat'*] the stick that is bent by any kind of opportunism, and that our stick will therefore always be straight as possible and as ready as possible for action.[42]

It is not inconceivable that Lenin's outlook was indeed as incoherent as it is portrayed by many advocates of the textbook interpretation. Yet, as a matter of basic methodology when trying to interpret a person's world-view, the assumption of incoherence should be our *last* resort, not our first.[43] We wish to understand the outlook of people operating in a long-ago historical environment, who rely on all sorts of unfamiliar assumptions, who use language for intensely polemical purposes. On first or even second reading, their views seem ridiculous, remarkably illogical, shot through with contradictions, completely at odds with their earlier and later outlook, and such that even they are not conscious of their own views. If this is the result of our first and second reading, I urge a third or fourth one, coupled with a more concerted effort to uncover the unfamiliar assumptions governing their views and the situation they faced when making any particular expression of them.

In any event, I find it a rather attractive feature of my own interpretation that it allows Lenin to know his own beliefs and to maintain a fundamental consistency in his outlook. These two points go together, since Lenin himself often asserted the fundamental continuity of his views, even in writings put

---

[42] Lenin 1958–65, 7, p. 272. In 1907, he responded to the Menshevik use of this comment: 'The sense of these words is clear: WITBD was a polemical correction of "economism" and to consider its content outside this task of the book is incorrect' (Lenin 1958–65, 16, p. 107). Lenin's actual words thus provide no justification for Trotsky's later statement that 'the author of *What Is to Be Done?* himself subsequently acknowledged the biased nature, and therewith the erroneousness, of his theory' (cited by Le Blanc 1990, p. 62). Note also that Lenin made his 'bend the stick' comment in 1903, at a time when all his fellow *Iskra* editors still defended WITBD. If the 'bend the stick' comment meant a renunciation of WITBD, then Lenin had renounced it *before* the party split of 1904. Authors who cite the 'bend the stick' comment usually mean it to support the claim that Lenin veered to the other extreme only in 1905.

[43] I found Bevir 1999 useful on these questions of basic method.

forward as evidence of his flip-flops. They also make it possible to explain how WITBD's first readers could see it as an inspiring expression of 'passionate and insistent' revolutionary will (in the words of Boris Gorev, a member of WITBD's original audience).[44] One is inclined to doubt that Gorev and his fellows could have been inspired in this way by an encyclopædia of modernist doubt written in obfuscatory language by an anxious pessimist.

## Lenin rediscovered

So far, I have talked as if it were myself against the field. Fortunately, this is not the case. The present study is part of a tradition of WITBD interpretation that stretches back to the time of its publication. Indeed, when we look at the *longue durée* of WITBD studies, the textbook interpretation appears to be in a minority position.[45]

We saw earlier how the textbook interpretation traces its lineage back to the 1904 pamphlets of Rosa Luxemburg and Lev Trotsky. There are some ironies associated with their iconic status as the prophets who immediately realised the evil consequences of WITBD. Luxemburg's article does not mention WITBD at all and Trotsky's pamphlet confines its critique of WITBD to a few passing pot-shots at some of Lenin's *obiter dicta*. Both works aim their fire at Lenin's factional sins during and after the Second Congress in August 1903 and make no serious effort to trace these sins back to WITBD.[46] More importantly, if we listen to what Trotsky and Luxemburg actually say, we find that their anti-Lenin critique does fatal damage to the textbook interpretation. The most glaring example is the role of intellectuals, since both Luxemburg and Trotsky

---

[44] Gorev 1924, p. 46.

[45] For a detailed study of a century of WITBD interpretation, see Lih 2003.

[46] Something similar holds true for other critics of Lenin in 1904 who are sometimes described as reacting with horror to WITBD (Service 1988). As far as I know, Pavel Akselrod, the ideological leader of the Mensheviks, never criticised WITBD or even suggested that Lenin had made theoretical mistakes. Plekhanov wrote a critique of WITBD in summer 1904, but aimed his principal fire at a passage more or less forgotten by the textbook interpretation (see Annotations Part Two). A few months later, he wrote an article criticising Lenin for abandoning the correct tactical position of WITBD (Plekhanov 1905). As documented by J. Kautsky 1994, Kautsky never criticised WITBD in 1904 or later, nor did he ever protest against Lenin's use of his term 'from without'. Kautsky criticised Lenin's factional behaviour in 1904, but on many substantive issues he was considerably closer to the Bolsheviks.

vigorously attack Lenin for his hostility to intellectuals. In fact, as we shall see later, Trotsky and Luxemburg share many of the assumptions that the textbook interpretation sees as unique to Lenin's 'élitism'.[47]

Meanwhile, one opponent of Lenin did produce an extensive reading of WITBD that has been totally forgotten. In a series of articles in 1904–5, Aleksandr Potresov, one of Lenin's fellow editors on *Iskra* and now a determined foe, analysed WITBD as the classic expression of the grandiose romanticism and self-deceiving optimism of the underground *praktik*. These *praktiki* had a totally unrealistic idea of what they could accomplish and the mass support they could expect. True, Lenin severely chastised the *praktiki*, but (to use an anachronistic image to express Potresov's thought) this was the pep-talk of a coach at half-time, aimed at conveying the invigorating conviction to the team that it could do much, much better. As such, Lenin's sermons made him the hero precisely of these *praktiki*.[48]

Potresov's hostile but perceptive critique brings out an important point. The thrust of the textbook interpretation is that Lenin's pessimism and distrust of the masses is a bad thing (although there are occasional compliments to his 'pragmatic realism'). As a result, an interpretation stressing Lenin's confidence will *ipso facto* be considered 'pro-Lenin'. The present study is neither pro-Lenin nor anti-Lenin. Its aim is to give an accurate account of Lenin's outlook and his empirical judgements. Potresov opens the possibility that Lenin's confidence was a mistaken view of reality that was capable of doing much damage. This possibility can only be assessed in the course of a full-length consideration of Lenin's entire career.

Another extended analysis of WITBD in 1905 came from the pen of a then obscure Georgian *praktik* named Iosif Dzugashvili (Stalin). Stalin mounted an energetic defence of WITBD against Menshevik critics who described it as anti-worker. Although Stalin was a fierce Bolshevik, his defence of WITBD coincides with Potresov's analysis on an essential point: Lenin was confident that the workers would heed the Social-Democratic message.[49] Stalin's essay was his

---

[47] Something similar holds true of WITBD's critics from the right wing of Social Democracy, Aleksandr Martynov and Vladimir Akimov. See Chapter Nine for further discussion.

[48] These articles, entitled *Nashi zlokliucheniia* or 'Our Misadventures', are reprinted in Potresov 2002, pp. 67–120.

[49] Stalin 1946–52, Vol. 1.

contribution to the Bolshevik polemics of 1904–5 that was conducted by Lenin partisans such as Aleksandr Bogdanov, Mikhail Olminskii, M. Liadov, Vatslav Vorovskii. The writings of these Bolsheviks do not defend anything remotely similar to what the textbook interpretation would predict their views to be.[50]

After 1905, Russian Social Democracy moved on to other issues and other crises, and WITBD was never discussed, even by its author, outside the context of party history. Looking back, Lenin's closest lieutenants and first biographers – Grigorii Zinoviev, Lev Kamenev, Nadezhda Krupskaya – saw WITBD as an outstanding and characteristic product but certainly not as a break-though or a charter document of Bolshevism. Zinoviev's recollection serves as a good introduction to our account of the dispute between the orthodox and the 'economists':

> The economist critics would say: 'So what, in your opinion, is the working class, a Messiah?' To this we answered and answer now: Messiah and messianism are not our language and we do not like such words; but we accept the concept that is contained in them: yes, the working class is in a certain sense a Messiah and its role is a messianic one, for this is the class which will liberate the whole world. . . . We avoid semi-mystical terms like Messiah and messianism and prefer the scientific one: the *hegemonic proletariat*.[51]

The role of WITBD in later Bolshevism is perhaps best illustrated by a representative of a younger generation than Zinoviev's, namely, Nikolai Bukharin, who joined the Party after 1905, that is, after the WITBD episode had come and gone. If there is a single reference to WITBD in all of Bukharin's writings, I have not yet found it. WITBD, for example, is missing from the extensive reading lists provided for the up-and-coming Bolshevik in the party textbook *ABC of Communism* that Bukharin co-authored in 1919. Bukharin twice wrote specifically about Lenin's status as a original theorist and his contributions to Marxism. WITBD is not mentioned either time – in fact, the whole topic of party organisation is not taken up.[52]

---

[50] These Bolshevik writings are discussed in more detail in Chapters Eight and Nine.

[51] Zinoviev 1924, p. 74 (for an English translation of Zinoviev's party history, see Zinoviev 1973).

[52] Bukharin and Preobrazhensky 1919; Bukharin 1989 [1920], pp. 177–80; Bukharin 1990 [1924], pp. 50–85.

After the Bolshevik Revolution, informed outsider observers described Lenin in terms that are incompatible with the textbook interpretation. The American journalist W.H. Chamberlin, author of the classic study *The Russian Revolution*, wrote in 1930 that 'boundless hatred for the capitalist system and its upholders, boundless faith in the right and the ability of the working class to dominate a new social order – these were certainly the two dominant passions of Lenin's strong and simple character'.[53]

In the late 1930s, the Soviet government issued a fundamental textbook of party history usually referred to as the *Short Course*. The sections on the *Iskra* period are by Stalin personally. Stalin's interpretation of WITBD differ from the Western textbook interpretation in two fundamental respects. First, he did not see WITBD as the charter document of a 'party of a new type'. To be sure, this term is used, but applied only to later developments.[54] As for WITBD, it 'brilliantly substantiated the fundamental Marxist thesis that a Marxist party is a merger of the worker movement with socialism'.[55] Stalin knew perfectly well that Karl Kautsky was the one who formulated this fundamental Marxist thesis, since he cited Kautsky's formula as the epigraph for his 1905 article. He knew perfectly well that this formula was an authoritative commonplace within international Social Democracy, since the whole brunt of his 1905 defence of WITBD rests on this fact. And, because he knew these things, it did not occur to him to see WITBD as the origin of a party of a new type.

Stalin also challenges the 'worry about workers' interpretation because he presents WITBD as *more* confident about the workers than were foes of Lenin such as the 'economists'. Why is it bad to bow down to spontaneity and to disparage consciousness? Answer: because to do so was 'to insult the workers, who strive toward consciousness as to light'. Furthermore, 'Lenin showed that to draw the working class away from the general political struggle against tsardom' was a crime because 'the workers wanted to fight not only for better terms . . . but also for the abolition of the capitalist system itself'.[56]

---

[53] Chamberlin 1930, p. 88.
[54] According to the *Short Course*, the Prague conference of 1912 'inaugurated a party of a new type' because it eliminated the Mensheviks and thus created a party 'free of opportunist elements' (*Kratkii kurs* 1938, pp. 134–9). Only after Stalin's death did Soviet historians attach the 'party of a new type' label to WITBD – although, unlike many Western scholars, Soviet historians did not put these words in Lenin's mouth.
[55] *Kratkii kurs* 1938, pp. 37–8.
[56] *Kratkii kurs* 1938, pp. 35–6 (order of passages reversed).

Thus I stand with Stalin against the academic and activist consensus. This is no doubt rather embarrassing – but for whom? For me, because I find myself on the same side with a man not known for scrupulous history-writing? Or for advocates of the textbook interpretation, who are wrong when even Stalin (because of his roots in prewar Russian Social Democracy) was right?

The textbook interpretation is thus, on the whole, a postwar creation. One reason for its rise is a great forgetting of what prewar international Social Democracy was all about.[57] The principal reason for this loss of context is the watershed of the 1917 revolution, which split prewar Social Democracy in two and gave the name 'Social Democracy' only to the more moderate side. On the Left, a number of writers with no or very shallow roots in the Second International – Georg Lukács, Antonio Gramsci, Karl Korsch – created a theory (*not* shared by Lenin) that Leninism was the principled rejection of the fatalistic Marxism of the Second International and of Kautsky in particular. In my view, the insistence on seeing a great gulf between Kautsky on the one hand and Lenin, Luxemburg and Trotsky on the other has condemned those in the postwar Trotskyist tradition to a deep misunderstanding of their own heroes. A similar forgetting occurred in the academic tradition, due in large part to the exclusive focus on Russia, resulting in a similar misunderstanding of the heroes of many in the academic tradition, namely the 'economists' and the Mensheviks.[58]

Even in postwar scholarship, the textbook interpretation has not gone unchallenged. Two teachers of mine from the generation that created the textbook interpretation, John Plamenatz and Robert Tucker, saw the excitement and urgency underlying *WITBD*.[59] In recent years, persistent challenges to the

---

[57] A full discussion of this question would include consideration of English-speaking scholarship on German socialism. All I can do here is record my debt, particularly to Gary Steenson and Vernon Lidtke.

[58] The main statement of the Menshevik case available in English is by Fyodor Dan (Dan 1964). Dan was a prominent Menshevik in 1904 and his view of *WITBD* reflects the partisan struggle of that year. Nevertheless, his overlap with the textbook interpretation is not very extensive.

[59] Plamenatz 1947, Plamenatz 1954, Tucker 1987. I will have occasion to quote these authors later. Although he does not have much to say directly about *WITBD*, Stephen Cohen's challenge to the reigning 'continuity thesis' (what I call the 'Soviet politics, made easy' approach) remains an inspiration to the critique mounted here. See Cohen 1977.

textbook interpretation have continued to appear in the scholarly literature. I am indebted in particular to Moira Donald's study of Kautsky's overwhelming impact on Russian Social Democracy and to Henry Reichman's groundbreaking article that asks how WITBD might have looked in the eyes of a militant worker of Lenin's time.[60]

Given the existence of two strongly contrasting views on such an important document, we would expect some sort of debate or some attempts to convince one other. But not so. There was, neither then or later, any sort of extended academic debate about the meaning of WITBD. Advocates of the textbook interpretation simply took no cognisance of any respectable challenge to their interpretation. As stated earlier, it is difficult to find *any* argued analysis of WITBD in the *Iskra*-period monograph cycle or in the historical literature generally.[61] None of the challengers took on the job of putting WITBD into historical context or explaining the striking passages that give prima facie plausibility to the textbook interpretation (combatting spontaneity, consciousness from without, diverting the worker movement, and the like). This is where the present study comes in.

## Commentary and translation

The present commentary is divided into three parts. Part I examines the outlook of Marx-based Social Democracy. After introducing the term 'Erfurtianism' as a label for that outlook, I argue that Lenin was a Russian Erfurtian who saw Russian Social Democracy as one episode in a larger overarching narrative. Within Russian Social Democracy, Lenin was a member from 1900 to 1903 of the editorial board of the underground newspaper *Iskra*. Since both friends and foes of WITBD saw it as a classic expression of *Iskra*-ism, I devote a chapter to explaining the outlook of *Iskra* and its reaction to the growing revolutionary crisis in Russia.

Part II examines the immediate polemical context of WITBD by looking at Lenin's 'significant others', that is, the Russian Social Democrats against whom

---

[60] Donald 1993 and Reichman 1996. For other accounts that step outside the consensus on one point or another, see Daniels 1957; Treadgold 1955; Himmer 2001.

[61] The only exception I know is Reginald Zelnik's recent articles (Zelnik 2003a and 2003b), written partially in response to the challenge to the textbook interpretation mounted by Henry Reichman and myself.

he defined his own position in WITBD. The key question in all these disputes is the usefulness of the SPD model under Russian conditions and, in particular, the chances for a successful spread of Social-Democratic awareness. In every dispute, Lenin is found insisting on a rapid spread of awareness that would become even more rapid if the Social Democrats shaped up.

Part III examines the world of WITBD: the view of the world implicit in its arguments and the source of its organisational proposals. The Social-Democratic underground, as it evolved in various localities in the 1890s, had set itself the task of combining the secrecy needed to survive police prosecution with the presence of genuine roots in the worker milieu. Lenin's contribution was to make explicit the norms of this newly-created institution and then to promise the *praktiki* that they could accomplish miracles if they observed these norms. In a final chapter, I survey the Bolshevik/Menshevik dispute of 1904. WITBD played a much smaller role in this episode than is generally realised and I had not originally planned to discuss it at length. I eventually came to see that clarity about the real issues underlying the Bolshevik/Menshevik split in 1904 was a necessity, given the iconic status of Trotsky and Luxemburg as critics of WITBD.

A new translation of the entire 1902 text of WITBD is appended to the commentary. One may well ask, why is a new translation needed? There now exist four different English translations of WITBD. The first one was done in 1929 when Lenin's works were issued by the Soviet government in English, German and French. The English version was done by Joe Fineberg, a Russian-born British leftist who returned to Russia soon after the Revolution (he gave a report on the British situation at the founding congress of the Communist International in 1919). Fineberg made the basic translation choices that have governed how English speakers have read WITBD ever since.

In 1962, the Soviet government issued Lenin's *Complete Works* in English. For this edition, Fineberg's translation was revised by George Hanna, whose changes are usually but not always for the better. Finally, a Penguin translation edited by Robert Service was published in 1988. Service tinkered further with the Fineberg/Hanna translation and his changes are also sometimes an improvement.[62]

---

[62] For Fineberg, see Lenin 1929; for Hanna, see Lenin 1962; for Service, see Lenin 1988.

Meanwhile, the only translation of *WITBD* independent of the Fineberg tradition was published by Oxford University Press in 1962. Sentence by sentence, this translation by S.V. and Patricia Utechin is superior to the other translations. Unfortunately, as a scholarly edition, the Utechin translation is a failure. Not only is it abridged, but the passages left out are precisely those that might have caused trouble for Utechin's own interpretation.[63]

So we now have the three synoptic translations (Fineberg, Fineberg/Hanna and Fineberg/Hanna/Service) plus the translation according to Utechin. All four are aimed at making Lenin's texts readable and understandable without extensive commentary. As such, there is much to recommend them. They are accurate for the most part and they often succeed admirably in rendering Lenin's passionately convoluted sentences into usable English. The version provided here is a new one translated directly from the Russian text and yet I am glad to acknowledge my debt to earlier translations.

The fact remains that *WITBD* simply is not understandable without an extensive commentary. The present translation therefore pursues a different goal: *consistency and clarity in the rendition of key terms*. This goal requires, first, motivated translation choices for key terms. Second, it requires that a Russian term always be rendered by the same English word and that no English word be used to render more than one Russian word. Third, insofar as possible, closely related Russian words should be translated in such a way that the link between them is clear. These requirements could not always be fully met. But the closer the translation comes to the goal of consistency and clarity in the rendition of key terms, the more 'commentary friendly' it is.

A central example of my translation goals is the contrast between 'consciousness' and 'spontaneity'. This contrast is crucial for the textbook interpretation and yet no one restricted to the English text can have an adequate grasp of it. On the one hand, the English word 'consciousness' translates two related but quite distinct Russian terms, *soznanie* and *soznatel'nost'*. After much consideration of Lenin's usage of these terms, I have decided on 'awareness' for *soznanie* and 'purposiveness' for *soznatel'nost*.

On the other hand, the Russian word rendered by 'spontaneity' – *stikhiinost* – is also sometimes rendered in its adjectival form as 'elemental'. I have thrown

---

[63] Lenin 1963. Utechin was convinced of Lenin's ties to earlier Russian populism and removed most of the passages that invoke the German model (see the section in Chapter Seven entitled 'Look at the Germans').

up my hands on this one and simply retained the Russian word *stikhiinost*, since the term is simply too contentious and idiosyncratic for me to impose an interpretation via translation.

In the existing translations, then, one English word, 'consciousness', represents two distinct Russian words, while one Russian word, *stikhiinyi*, is represented in English by two distinct terms (spontaneous and elemental). The English-language contrast 'consciousness vs. spontaneity' thus seriously distorts what is going on in Lenin's text.

Sometimes the existing translations muffle even the existence of a key term. Take the Russian word *konspiratsiia*. It does *not* mean 'conspiracy'. It refers to all the rules and procedures needed to enable an underground organisation to survive: the fine art of not getting arrested. The earlier translators were certainly aware of this general meaning and usually render *konspiratsiia* as 'secrecy' or some such term. Given that there is no term in English remotely similar to *konspiratsiia*, 'secrecy' is in many ways a defensible translation choice.

Nevertheless the result is unacceptable for anyone interested in a genuine engagement with Lenin's text via the English translation. According to the textbook interpretation, Lenin in WITBD advocates a 'conspiratorial' form of party organisation. How can we seriously assess this claim when the very term *konspiratsiia* is hidden from view? What is more, *konspiratsiia* was a key term in the vocabulary of Russian revolutionaries. It had an emotional and even romantic aura. Much of Lenin's argument revolves around the need for inculcating a culture of *konspiratsiia*. The term must be restored to view. Since it is a foreign word transliterated into Russian, I have found it simplest just to transliterate it back and keep it as *konspiratsiia*.

In other cases, a translation choice that is too obvious can be severely misleading. *Professiia* is such a *faux ami*. This word often means 'trade', as in *professional'nyi soiuz*, the standard term for 'trade union'. As such, *professiia* plays an important role in the rhetoric of WITBD, since Lenin takes over Kautsky's argument that economic struggle tends to focus on particular *trades* while political struggle unites the entire *class*. But *professiia* also turns up in Lenin's most celebrated coinage *revoliutsioner po professii*. This is always translated 'revolutionary by profession' or 'professional revolutionary', but I believe we should respect the verbal link in Lenin's text and translate as 'revolutionary by trade'. In Chapter Eight, I will show why this more prosaic rendering is closer to Lenin's intention. Other *faux amis* are *tred-unionizm* and *burzhuaznaia demokratiia*.

A Glossary contains all the renderings that differ significantly from earlier translations and points the reader to relevant discussions in the commentary.

The translation is provided with two sets of annotations of approximately equal size. One set is devoted to two paragraphs, the other set is devoted to the rest of the book. The two paragraphs are what I call the 'scandalous passages' – the endlessly recycled sentences about 'from without' and 'combatting spontaneity'. These are the heart of the textbook interpretation. For reasons given at the beginning of Chapter Seven, I bracket the scandalous passages during the course of my commentary and build my interpretation without using them one way or the other. In Annotations Part Two, I open up the brackets and give these two paragraphs the close reading they need in order to be understood.

*WITBD* has five chapters and each chapter is broken up into several sections that are the real building blocks of the book. In Annotations Part One, I proceed section by section, explaining the key assertions and how they fit into the larger argument. I also provide such background information as is necessary for understanding Lenin's text. Some readers may find it useful to get a sense of what Lenin's book is all about by perusing the section-by-section annotation before plunging into the commentary, since the commentary does not get to *WITBD* itself until Part III.

LEEDS UNIVERSITY LIBRARY

# Part One

## **Erfurtianism**

# Chapter One

# The Merger of Socialism and the Worker Movement

Anyone reading Lenin's early writings will often run across the formula 'Social Democracy is the merger of socialism and the worker movement.' At one point he describes this formula as 'Karl Kautsky's expression that reproduces the basic ideas of the *Communist Manifesto*'.[1] In this way, Lenin draws a link between what for him were two foundational books: the *Communist Manifesto* of Marx and Engels (1848) and the *Erfurt Programme* by Karl Kautsky (1891). So important were these books to the young Lenin that he translated both of them into Russian (unfortunately, neither translation survives).[2]

We shall follow Lenin's lead and describe developments from the 1840s to the 1890s with the merger formula as unifying theme. The aim is not so much to advance a particular interpretation of the history of nineteenth-century Marxist socialism as to bring out how Lenin and others of his generation saw this history. The merger formula is a condensation of a *narrative*. Key to the considerable emotional charge of this narrative is the idea of a *mission* – both the world historical mission of the *workers* to take power and introduce socialism and the mission of

---

[1] Lenin 1958–65, 4, p. 189, an unpublished newspaper article from late 1899.
[2] The *Manifesto* in 1889 and the *Erfurt Programme* in 1894.

the *Social Democrats* to merge socialism and the worker movement. To bring out this emotional aspect out, I shall be quoting some flowery rhetoric of a type that does not often make its way into secondary accounts. Anyone who pictures Social Democracy as based on dry and deterministic 'scientific socialism' and overlooks the fervent rhetoric of good news and saving missions has missed the point.

The merger formula also implied a concrete political strategy that is as often overlooked as the formula's emotional fervour. In order to further the desired merger, certain kinds of organisations need to be set up, certain kinds of political conditions need to be established, and certain social forces need to be assessed as either friends or foes. When the Russian Social Democrats put forth this strategy, observers found it innovative and even heretical. But although the Russians may have come up with the new name of 'hegemony', the basic logic had been fairly thoroughly worked out by the Germans.

My label 'good news interpretation' underscores these two vital but under-appreciated aspects of nineteenth-century Social Democracy: the proselytising fervour of the Social Democrats plus some hard-headed thinking about how best to spread the word.

## Marx and Engels

> One element of success the workers possess – numbers; but numbers weigh only in the balance, if united by combination and led by knowledge. (Karl Marx, Inaugural Address, 1864.)

At its highest level, the merger narrative is a world-historical epic about the coming of socialism. In its full scope, the epic surveys both 'the history of all hitherto existing societies' and the future.[3] In a biographical sketch of Marx written during his lifetime, Engels summarises the crucial final episodes of this epic in one monster sentence:

> [Marx's 'new conception of history' teaches that] the ruling big bourgeoisie has fulfilled its historic calling [*Beruf*], that it is no longer capable of the leadership of society and has even become a hindrance to the development of production . . . that historical leadership [*Leitung*] has passed to the

---

[3] Marx and Engels 1959, p. 462.

proletariat, a class which, owing to its whole position in society, can only free itself by abolishing altogether all class rule, all servitude and all exploitation, and that the productive forces of society, which have outgrown the control of the bourgeoisie, are only waiting for the associated proletariat to take possession of them in order to bring about a state of things in which every member of society will be enabled to participate not only in production but also in the distribution and administration of social wealth, and which so increases the productive forces of society and their yield by planned operation of the whole of production that the satisfaction of all reasonable needs will be assured to everyone in ever-increasing measure.[4]

While this particular formulation brings out the key feature of Marx's narrative – classes having a 'calling' for 'historical leadership' – it does not bring out the central task of proletarian class leadership, namely, the conquest of political power. The *Communist Manifesto* states this task as follows: 'The immediate aim of the communists is the same as that of all the other proletarian parties: formation of the proletariat into a class, overthrow of bourgeois rule, conquest of political power by the proletariat'.[5] Marx's Inaugural Address in 1864 for the Working Men's International Association puts it more succinctly: 'To conquer political power has therefore become the great duty of the working classes.'[6]

Scientific socialism is a reasoned recounting of this world-historical epic. We are here primarily interested in the political strategy that differentiates Marx-based Social Democracy from other nineteenth-century socialists and revolutionaries. Thus we now focus on one particular episode from the overall story, namely, the episode in which the worker class realises its great duty and carries it out.

As long as we remain on the level of the world-historical epic as a whole, we can content ourselves with saying 'the worker class realises its great duty', as if this process occurs more or less automatically. But, once we start to examine this episode in detail, we immediately see that the episode has a dramatic plot of its own, since it describes the outcome of interaction of

[4] Engels 1962c, pp. 103–4.
[5] Marx 1996, p. 13 (Carver translation).
[6] Marx and Engels 1978, p. 518 (Marx 1984a, p. 12).

historical actors who strive to overcome obstacles to their chosen goals. The plot of this episode is summarised by the merger formula: 'Social Democracy is the merger of socialism and the worker movement.' 'Socialism' here means socialist *doctrine*, and Social Democracy is the historical actor that prepares the worker class for its great deed.

According to both Kautsky and Lenin, the first person to set forth the logic of the merger narrative was Engels in *Condition of the Working Class in England*, published in 1845. In a tribute to Engels written after his death in 1895, Kautsky summarised the argument of this book in these words: 'the worker movement must be the power to bring socialism into birth; socialism must be the goal the worker movement sets before itself'.[7] In his own tribute to the recently deceased Engels, Lenin closely followed Kautsky in giving a high evaluation to *Condition of the Working Class*. This book shows that Engels was 'the *first* to say that the proletariat is *not only* a suffering class'. Lenin also summarised Engels's argument:

> All that the socialists had to understand was which social force, owing to its position in contemporary society, has a deep interest in the realisation of socialism – and then communicate to that force an awareness of its interests and historical task. The proletariat is such a social force. . . . The political movement of the worker class inevitably leads the workers to the awareness that there is no escape outside of socialism. On the other hand, socialism only becomes a force when it becomes the aim of the *political* struggle of the worker *class*.[8]

Engels's argument is set forth in the chapter of *Condition of the Working Class* entitled 'Worker Movements'. In it Engels delineates two separate forces. The first is the worker movement that achieved its highest expression in Chartism, a radical political movement on a national scale. The second is the 'socialist agitation' inspired by Robert Owen. The socialists are 'thoroughly tame and peaceable . . . They understand, it is true, why the working man is resentful against the bourgeois, but regard as unfruitful this class hatred, which is, after all, the only moral incentive by which the worker can be brought nearer the goal'. And so, 'in its present form, Socialism can never become the common

---

[7] Kautsky 1899, pp. 5–6.
[8] Lenin 1958–65, 2, p. 8. Lenin's emphasis.

creed of the working class; it must condescend to return for a moment to the Chartist standpoint'.

Engels confidently outlines the next episode in the story in what is evidently the first explicit statement of the merger narrative:

> It is evident that the worker movement is divided into two sections, the Chartists and the Socialists. The Chartists are the more backward, the less developed, but they are genuine proletarians all over, the representatives of their class. The Socialists are more far-seeing, propose practical remedies against distress, but, proceeding originally from the bourgeoisie, are for this reason unable to amalgamate completely with the working class. The merger [*Verschmelzung*] of Socialism with Chartism, the reproduction of French Communism in the English style, will be the next step, and has already begun. Then only, when this has been achieved, will the worker class be the true leader of England. Meanwhile, political and social development will proceed, and will foster this new party, this new departure of Chartism.[9]

I have quoted Kautsky's and Lenin's summary of Engels in order to bring out the crucial importance of this chapter for both men. They saw it as the first statement of the essence of their political creed. And yet it is well-nigh impossible to find any mention of this chapter in the secondary literature. Thus the view from WITBD implies a revised Marxist canon.

The logic of the merger narrative is deeply embedded in the *Communist Manifesto* – or, in any event, Lenin strongly believed this to be the case. The *Communist Manifesto* states that the Communists 'fight [*kämpfen*] for the attainment of those aims and interests of the working class that lie immediately to hand, but they are also the voice in the present movement of the future of the movement'.[10] This sentence expresses the specifically Marxist road-map to socialism: merging the day-to-day interests that gave rise to the worker movement with the final aim of socialism. It was precisely this road-map, and perhaps even this very sentence, that finally persuaded Georgii Plekhanov,

---

[9] Engels 1959, p. 453. The nineteenth-century English translation supervised by Engels and published in the 1880s adds two noteworthy glosses: the Chartists are '*theoretically* the more backward', etc., and the post-merger worker class will be 'the true *intellectual* leader of England' (Engels 1993, pp. 244–5, emphasis given to added words).

[10] Marx and Engels 1959, p. 492.

the most important founder of Russian Social Democracy, to become a Marxist in the early 1880s.[11]

It is not too fanciful to see the merger formula reflected in the overall structure of the *Manifesto*. The *Manifesto* is divided into three large sections: 'Bourgeois and Proletarians', 'Proletarians and Communists', 'Socialist and Communist Literature'. The first section, 'Bourgeois and Proletarian', tells the story of the worker movement up to the point of revolution. The basic theme in this section is the resistance of the workers and their growing organisation, that is, the replacement of mutual isolation through competition by the merger [*Vereinigung*] of the workers into revolutionary associations.[12]

The next section, 'Proletarians and Communists,' describes the aims of the revolution, that is, 'the future of the movement'. The communist is said to reflect only the beliefs of the most decisive part of the worker movement, the one that ever drives forward [*der entschiedenste, immer weiter treibende Teil*].[13] Thus the worker movement as a whole still needs to be persuaded of its great duty.

So we see that the first section describes the worker movement and the second section describes socialism. The third section turns to the question of *how* to merge these two. This section – 'Socialist and Communist Literature' – is where the political strategy inherent in the merger formula first begins to be worked out. Marx invites us to observe the self-destruction of all forms of socialism *except* the kind that reaches out to the worker movement. The aggressively polemical tone is in its way a compliment to the socialists. Marx wants to persuade other socialists that *their* great duty is to further this process. *They* are the aware element, they are the ones who can be directly convinced by abstract reasoning and literary polemics. When the socialists have been swung round, they themselves will start spreading awareness in the worker milieu.

---

[11] I have read somewhere that this sentence was indeed crucial for Plekhanov, but I have been unable to track down the reference. In his memoirs, another founder of Russian Social Democracy, Pavel Akselrod, quotes this sentence from Plekhanov's introduction to his 1882 translation of the *Manifesto*: 'The *Manifesto* can prevent Russian socialists from two equally sorry extremes: a negative attitude toward political activity [= working to overthrow tsarism] on the other hand, and forgetting the future interests of the party, on the other'. Akselrod 1975, p. 423.

[12] Marx and Engels 1959, p. 474.

[13] Ibid.

The five targets subjected to critique in the final section of the *Manifesto* are not just a random assortment but represent most of the logical possibilities of opposition to the merger strategy. As such, they foreshadow the bulk of the polemics unleashed later by Social Democracy against its competitors. The first target is feudal or reactionary socialists. The merger strategy will not work here because these are the wrong socialists. Their demagogic flirting with the workers covers up a will to dominate the worker movement. Various forms of 'state socialism' continued to challenge Social Democracy throughout the nineteenth century.

In his next target – 'petty-bourgeois socialism' – Marx argues that the merger strategy will fail because it is based on the wrong workers. The interests of the petty bourgeoisie – peasants and shopkeepers – do not lead them toward a viable socialist society but toward a 'reactionary utopia' in which economic independence is based on small individual property.

The third target ('True Socialists') will be examined later when we look at the *Manifesto*'s tactical implications. In the fourth and fifth targets, we see the right workers and the right socialists – but *outside* the merger, outside the great synthesis. If the worker movement refuses to adopt the revolutionary-socialist point of view, it becomes mere bourgeois reformism that vainly seeks to emancipate workers *inside* the framework of bourgeois society. If the socialists continue to regard the workers as incapable of emancipating themselves, they will dwindle into a set of cranks. The *Manifesto* does not blame the early worker movement and the early socialists for not immediately seeking the merger – indeed, they are praised for their embattled resistance on the one hand and for their critical insight on the other. It is the *continued* refusal of the great synthesis that is reprehensible.

Having established the foundational impact of the merger narrative, we now turn to an outline of the political strategy therein implied, as set forth in various remarks by the masters. The key idea is 'the emancipation of the working classes must be conquered by the working classes themselves'. The famous motto of the First International can be understood in two ways. On one reading, the motto tells revolutionaries from other classes that they are not wanted: the emancipation of the worker class is the business of the workers and no one else. The motto was understood in this way by the French Proudhonists who were perhaps the most important constituency within the First International.

On another reading, the motto not only refuses to close the door to non-proletarian revolutionaries but actually invites them in. If only the workers themselves can bring about their liberation, then it is imperative that they come to understand what it is they need to do and that they obtain the requisite organisational tools. This mission of preparing the worker class for its mission was incumbent upon *any* socialist who accepted the Marxist class narrative, no matter what his or her social origin. As the programme of the Austrian Social-Democratic Party put it in 1890, the aim of Social Democracy is 'to organise the proletariat politically, to fill it with the awareness of its position and its task, and to make and keep it spiritually and physically fit for struggle'.

It follows that the job of the socialists is to ensure that the workers are 'united by combination and led by knowledge'. 'Combination' – disciplined organisation – is necessary on both the national and international level if the workers are not be 'chastised by the common discomfiture of their incoherent effort', as Marx elegantly put it in the Inaugural Address.[14] When Marx and Engels speak of the knowledge that must lead the workers, they mean, of course, scientific socialism. A crucial couple of sentences by Engels defines the role of scientific socialism in the Social-Democratic political strategy. These sentences conclude Engels's immensely influential *Socialism, Utopian and Scientific*. I despair of reproducing the rhetorical force made possible by German syntax and therefore present this passage in both languages.

> Diese weltbefreiende Tat durchzuführen, ist der geschichtliche Beruf des modernen Proletariats. Ihre geschichtlichen Bedingungen, und damit ihre Natur selbst, zu ergründen und so der zur Aktion berufnen, heute unterdrückten Klasse die Bedingungen und die Natur ihrer eignen Aktion zum Bewusstsein zu bringen, ist die Aufgabe des theoretischen Ausdrucks der proletarischen Bewegung, des wissenschaftlichen Sozialismus.
>
> To carry out this world-freeing deed – this is the historical calling of the modern proletariat. The task of the theoretical expression of the proletarian movement – scientific socialism – is to solidly explicate the deed's historical conditions and therefore its very nature. By so doing, scientific socialism

---

[14] Marx 1984a [1864].

will bring the conditions and the nature of the proletariat's own act into the awareness of a class that, although oppressed today, is called to this [great] action.[15]

*Beruf*, 'calling', is an expressively intense word that summons up echoes of a high religious calling. The proletariat is almost defined as 'die zur Aktion berufnen Klasse', 'the called-to-a-great-deed class.' Scientific socialism's own task [*Aufgabe*, another key word] is not only to explicate the proletariat's calling but also to make the class aware of it – that is, to get involved in the nuts and bolts of propaganda and agitation. Thus, scientific socialism tells the proletariat a story about itself: its past ('historical conditions'), its present ('oppressed') and its future ('world-freeing deed'). Since this story will itself inspire the proletariat to carry out the great deed, telling the story is a precondition for freeing the world.

The great duty of taking political power implies that the aim of all this insight and organisation will be a nation-wide, class-based and therefore independent, political party.[16] Marx sketches the development of such a party in Part I of the *Manifesto*. One theme in this sketch is of particular importance for understanding Lenin's rhetoric in WITBD: the parallel Marx draws between the nationalisation of the *economy* and the nationalisation of *political organisations*. The bourgeoisie nationalises the economy by dislodging it from its original starting point of local, parochial, scattered and low-technology production and progressively moving it toward the endpoint of national, urban, centralised and industrial production. The bourgeois transformation of society is mirrored by the transformation of society's own political organisations. Thus 'the confrontations between individual workers and individual bourgeois increasingly take on the character of confrontations between two classes'. The drive toward nation-wide combination is furthered by 'the growing means of communication generated by large-scale industry that put the workers of different localities in contact with one another. But this contact is all that is

---

[15] Engels 1962b, p. 228.
[16] The necessity of some sort of organisation aimed at political power is inherent in the new world view. Marx's views on the role of 'the party' are less basic, especially since the appropriate institutions and terminology were still inchoate at this period. With this proviso, the discussions by Molyneux 1978 and Johnstone 1967 of Marx's view of the party provide valuable insights.

needed to centralise the many local struggles of a generally similar kind into a national – a class – struggle'.[17]

Thus, the merger formula sets the socialists the task of organising and propagandising on a national level. From this definition of the task flows an enormous tactical implication: the necessity of freedom of assembly, freedom of the press and other political freedoms. This implication is already drawn without any ambiguity in the *Communist Manifesto*. As discussed earlier, the third section of the *Manifesto* outlines the nature of the merger between socialism and the worker movement in the negative form of showing how *not* to do it. In the third of the five targets attacked in the third section, Marx draws a contrast between the German 'True Socialists' and the German communists. As described by Marx, the True Socialists were a set of intellectuals who 'hurled traditional anathemas against liberalism, against representative government, against bourgeois competition, bourgeois freedom of the press, bourgeois right, bourgeois freedom and equality'. They were so eager to use socialist demands as a way of discrediting any striving for political freedom that they became tools of the nobility and the German absolutist governments. Far different are the German communists, who fight *alongside* the bourgeoisie 'as soon as it shows itself revolutionary – against the absolutist monarchy, the feudal landowners, the petty bourgeoisie'.[18]

Exactly these passages are cited by Plekhanov in *Socialism and the Political Struggle*, the book he issued in 1883 to announce his conversion to Social Democracy. As Plekhanov's title implies, the aim of the book is to convince Russian socialists that the struggle for political freedom must be their most urgent priority.[19] But the insistence on political freedom was basic not only to Russian but to all Social Democrats: it was what distinguished the political strategy of Marx-based Social Democracy from all other nineteenth-century socialists, revolutionaries and worker-movement activists.

---

[17] Marx and Engels 1959, pp. 470–1. This section of the *Manifesto* forms the background to Lenin's metaphor of 'artisanal limitations' as a stage in the development of party organisation (see Chapter Eight).

[18] Marx and Engels 1959, pp. 485–8. According to Gareth Stedman Jones, Marx is unfair here to the actual 'True Socialists' (Stedman Jones 2002). Jones's assertion does not detract from the centrality of the tactical point Marx is making.

[19] In his biography of Plekhanov, Samuel Baron brings out the importance of this section of the *Manifesto* for Plekhanov. Unfortunately, he also argues that this section and its tactical implications were 'little more than an aside' for Marx and Engels (Baron 1963, p. 112).

The central importance of political freedoms for Social Democracy is brought out in another revealing but overlooked text by Engels, 'The Workingmen of Europe in 1877'.[20] In this survey of the progress of worker parties all over the continent, the state of political freedom is a touchstone of the aims and successes of the various national parties. Engels's description of the French worker class is particularly revealing. By 1877, the French worker class had suffered two recent traumas. The first was

> the eighteen years of the Bonapartist Empire, during which the press was fettered, the right of meeting and of association suppressed and the working class consequently deprived of every means of inter-communication and organisation.

This repressive régime was followed by the crushing of the Paris Commune in 1871. The ones who held power in France now were the very middle-class radicals who (as Engels angrily put it) had betrayed the workers and the country.

Nevertheless, Engels's political advice is to support these hateful bourgeois democrats against monarchist attacks. The worker class has

> but one immediate interest: to avoid the recurrence of such another protracted reign of repression [as it had experienced under Bonapartism], and with it the necessity of again fighting, not for their own direct emancipation but for a state of things permitting them to prepare for the final emancipatory struggle.

Only the republic, despicable as it was, gave them a chance to 'obtain such a degree of personal and public liberty as would allow them to establish a working-class press, an agitation by meetings and an organisation as an independent political party, and moreover, the conservation of the republic would save them the necessity of delivering a separate battle for its future re-conquest'.

Political freedoms are so fundamental that even political independence should be temporarily sacrificed for them if need be. In 1877, the worker class supported the republicans from an attack by the monarchists. Engels comments:

---

[20] Engels 1989, pp. 209–29 (written in 1878 for a New York socialist newspaper). Hal Draper first pointed out the importance of this article (Draper 1977–90, Vol. 2).

No doubt in this they acted as the tail of the middle-class Republicans and Radicals, but a working class which has no press, no meetings, no clubs, no political societies, what else can it be but the tail of the Radical middle-class party? What can it do, in order to gain its political independence, but support the only party which is bound to secure to the people generally, and therefore, to the workmen too, such liberties as will admit of independent organisation?[21]

Thus the new view of history set out in the *Communist Manifesto* came attached with a political strategy, one that is firmly outlined in the *Manifesto* itself and one to which its authors remained loyal over the years. Some writers see a contrast between the revolutionism of the Address to the Communist League in 1850 and the reformism of the Inaugural Address of the Working Men's International Association in 1864. Yet both are based on the same fundamental political strategy: strive to obtain political liberties and use them once attained to bring combination and knowledge to a nation-wide, independent, worker political party whose goal is to conquer political power in order to introduce socialism. Despite the fierceness of the cry *Die Revolution im Permanenz!*, the 1850 address is engaged in giving electoral advice ('even where there is no prospect whatsoever of their being elected, the workers must put up their own candidates in order to preserve their independence, to count their forces and to bring before the public their revolutionary attitude and party standpoint') under the assumption of a 'lengthy revolutionary development'.[22] Despite the mildness of the Inaugural Address's salute to legislation such as the English Ten Hours Bill, Marx still insists that the great duty of the worker class is to conquer political power in order to abolish hired labour.

The Marx presented here is not the Marx of Leszek Kolakowski, who opens his trilogy with what he considers the most important fact about Marx, namely, 'Marx was a German philosopher'.[23] Nor is it the Marx of Geoff Eley, who writes that 'Marx's most important legacy for the pre-1914 social democratic

---

[21] Engels 1989, pp. 222–3.
[22] Marx and Engels 1960, p. 251. As we shall see, the German SPD followed this electoral advice to the letter.
[23] Kolakowski 1978, 1, p. 1. It is hard to find in Kolakowski's account even a mention of the conquest of state power by the proletariat, much less a recognition of its central role.

tradition' was an economic theory that emphasised 'the determining effects of material forces on human achievement, and the linking of political opportunities to movements of the economy'.[24] Nor yet is it the Marx of Eric Hobsbawm, who says that Marx's greatest impact came from the assertion of socialism's inevitability.[25] On the other hand, the Marx presented here is akin to the Marx of Hal Draper. Draper's great achievement was to put Marx in the company not so much of Hegel and his followers, not so much of Ricardo and his followers, but of the nineteenth century's other radical, socialist, revolutionary and worker leaders – the likes of August Blanqui, Ferdinand Lassalle, and Mikhail Bakunin.[26]

Of course, Marx was indeed a major philosopher and economist. But the Marx who was central for Lenin and his generation was the one whose new view of the *path* to socialism gave rise to a new view of the *tasks* of the socialists – a new political strategy that, in turn, inspired some of the most impressive and innovative political institution-building of the nineteenth century. In 1917, in his notebook on Marxism and the state, Lenin commented on 'the basic idea of Marx: the conquest of *political power* by the proletariat'.[27] Marx the philosopher and Marx the economist tried to give these few words the most solid foundation possible. But the Marx who had the greatest impact on the nineteenth century was the activist who tried to draw out all the implications for political strategy that lay hidden in these few words.

## Ferdinand Lassalle

In Italy at the turn of the century, so we are told, Italian socialists named their sons Lassalo and their daughters Marxina.[28] Some informed observers

---

[24] Eley 2002, p. 38. Eley has an excellent description of the new 'independent mass party of labour': 'independent, because it organised separately from liberal coalitions; mass, because it required broadly based public agitation; labour, because it stressed the need for class-based organisation; and a party, by proposing permanent, centrally organised, programmatically co-ordinated, and nationally directed activity' (pp. 39–40). Unfortunately, he contrasts this to 'vanguardism', although this strategy is precisely what Social Democrats (including Lenin) meant by a vanguard party.

[25] Hobsbawm 1962, p. 289.

[26] Draper 1977–90.

[27] Lenin 1958–65, 33, p. 226.

[28] Michels 1962 [1911], p. 95.

were ready to give Ferdinand Lassalle top billing: 'To Lassalle, even more than to Marx, modern Socialists are deeply indebted; Marx set the world of culture thinking and arguing, Lassalle set the people organising'.[29] In the German Social-Democratic Party, Lassalle remained the hero-founder, and meetings were opened by an anthem that affirmed:

> Der Bahn, der kühnen, folgen wir,
> Die uns geführt Lassalle.
> (We follow that bold path on which Lassalle has led us.)[30]

These days, in contrast, Lassalle has more or less dropped off the historical radar screen. A recent 600–page book on the history of the European Left in the last 150 years does not even mention him.[31] A direct motive for bringing out his contribution here is that Lassalle makes an appearance in a crucial passage in WITBD. A wider motive is the conviction that one cannot understand the emotional world of Social Democracy nor the logic of its institutions without looking at its forgotten founding father.

Lassalle's career as a leader of nascent German Social Democracy was incredibly short, given its impact on the rest of the century. In 1863, he was asked by a German worker group to give his opinion on the best political course for the workers. In his *Open Letter* (also known as his *Manifesto*), Lassalle advised them to organise an independent political party aimed at achieving universal suffrage. He then plunged into a whirlwind round of setting up just such an organised party. Only a year and a half after the start of his campaign, he was killed in a duel that arose out of his love affair with a German countess. His death was probably a good career move, since his organising efforts had achieved little in concrete results and his flirtation with conservatives such as Bismarck might soon have sorely discredited him. As it was, he remained a martyr and an icon of the cause.

Lassalle's impact on his contemporaries was in large part due to his larger-than-life flamboyance. The English critic George Brandes, writing in 1881,

---

[29] Villiers 1908, p. 86.

[30] Russell 1965 [1896], 130. On the importance of this song in SPD culture, see Lidtke 1985, pp. 112–14. Lidtke observes that 'throughout the nineties numerous localities still held Lassalle Festivals, but no one seems ever to have thought of holding a Marx Festival' (Lidtke 1985, p. 195).

[31] Eley 2002.

declared that the fundamental feature of his temperament was 'apparent in the quality best expressed by the Jewish word "Chutspo", which connotes presence of mind, impudence, temerity, resolution, and effrontery'.[32] Lassalle's legacy to German Social Democracy was a very mixed bag indeed and the movement spent many years shedding many of his policy nostrums as well as his proclivities toward dictatorial party organisation. In our discussion, however – with one important exception – we are going to focus on the permanent contribution that even otherwise suspicious Marxists were prepared to grant. There were two sides to Lassalle's permanent contribution. He brought out the emotional underpinning of the merger narrative more vividly and effectively than either Marx or Engels. He also brought the political strategy inherent in the merger formula out on the national stage for all to see.

The emotional fervour latent in the merger formula arises most profoundly from the idea of a *mission*: a noble task that one has an obligation to accept. In the texts by Marx and Engels we have looked at, we have seen references to a *Beruf*, to a 'world-freeing deed', to the workers' 'great duty' and their 'historic mission'. But Marx and Engels were perhaps too sardonic to wax eloquent on this theme. Lassalle was just the opposite. While his melodramatic rhetoric has no doubt dated more than Marx's, it was extremely effective at the time. Thirty years later, propagandising among the workers of Petersburg, K.M. Takhtarev found that Lassalle's 'idea of the worker estate' made a very strong impression on the workers in his study circle.[33]

Lassalle explained the 'idea of the worker estate' by telling the following story. Originally, the workers had been united with the bourgeoisie as part of the revolutionary Third Estate, but then the bourgeoisie separated itself off due to its egoism and desire for privilege. For the workers, in contrast, self-interest and group solidarity coincided.

> The more earnestly and deeply the lower classes of society strive after the improvement of their condition as a class, the improvement of the *lot of their class*, the more does this *personal* interest, instead of opposing the movement of history and being thereby condemned to that immorality [that is exemplified by the bourgeoisie], assume a *direction* which thoroughly accords

---

[32] Brandes 1911, p. 16 (preface dated 1881).
[33] Takhtarev 1924, p. 24

with the development of the whole *people*, with the victory of the *idea*, with the advance of *culture*, with the living principle of history itself, which is no other than the development of *freedom*. Or in other words . . . *its* interest is the interest of the entire human race.[34]

The workers now constituted a Fourth Estate that possessed a historical *mission* to transform society.

You are able therefore to devote yourselves with *personal passion* to this historical development, and to be certain that the more strongly this *passion* grows and burns within you . . . the higher is the moral position you have attained. . . . We may congratulate ourselves, gentlemen, that we have been born at a time which is destined to witness this the most glorious work of history, and that we are permitted to take a part in accomplishing it.[35]

But this destiny imposes the obligation of a quasi-religious earnestness, as revealed by the following widely-quoted passage from one of Lassalle's most influential writings, *The Worker Programme*:

Nothing is more calculated to impress upon a class a worthy and moral character, than the awareness that it is destined to become a ruling class, that it called upon to raise the principle of its class to the principle of the entire age, to convert *its idea* into the leading idea of the whole of society and thus to form this society by impressing upon it its own character.

The high and world-wide honour of this destiny must occupy all your thoughts. Neither the burden of the oppressed, nor the idle dissipation of the thoughtless, nor even the harmless frivolity of the insignificant, are henceforth becoming to you. You are the rock on which the Church of the present is to be built.

It is the lofty moral earnestness of *this* thought which must with devouring exclusiveness possess your spirits, fill your minds, and shape your whole lives, so as to make them worthy of it, conformable to it, and always related to it. It is the moral earnestness of this thought which must never leave you,

---

[34] Lassalle 1899, p. 53 (*Worker Programme*). When possible, I have used translations made in the nineteenth century as less academic and closer to Lassalle's agitational spirit. Quoted passages have been checked against the original German text (Lassalle 1919a, pp. 193–4).

[35] Lassalle 1899, pp. 53–9; Lassalle 1919a, pp. 194, 199 (*Worker Programme*).

but must be present to your heart in your workshops during the hours of labour, in your leisure hours, during your walks, at your meetings, and even when you stretch your limbs to rest upon your hard couches, it is *this* thought which must fill and occupy your minds till they lose themselves in dreams.

The more exclusively you immerse yourselves in the moral earnestness of this thought, the more undividedly you give yourselves up to its glowing fervour, by so much the more, be assured, will you *hasten the time* within which our present period of history will have to fulfil its task, so much the sooner will you bring about the accomplishment of this task.[36]

Lassalle was also remembered because he 'showed the path', that is, he set out the fundamentals of the party's political strategy. This strategy was first announced in the *Open Letter*: 'The working class must constitute itself an independent political party and make universal, equal and direct suffrage the primary watchword and banner of this party.'[37] Thus Lassalle called for an *independent political organisation*: all three terms have equal emphasis. At the time that Lassalle put forth his strategy, all of its facets were innovative, not to say outrageous.[38] By insisting on a *political* organisation, Lassalle was flying in the face of an opinion widespread even among the workers themselves that (as Lassalle put it in his *Open Letter*) 'you have *no* business to trouble yourselves about a *political* movement, for this is something in which you have no interest'.[39]

The content of worker politics comes from the uplifting *mission* of the workers and their loyalty to 'the idea of the Fourth Estate'. Lenin in WITBD makes a distinction between '*tred-iunionist* politics' and 'Social-Democratic politics'. The essence of this distinction is already in Lassalle:

---

[36] Lassalle 1899, pp. 59–60; Lassalle 1919a, pp. 200–1 (*Worker Programme*). Note how this passage combines determinism (you are *destined* to be a ruling class) with a call to passionate activity to bring about this inevitable denouement.

[37] Lassalle 1919c, p. 47 (*Open Letter*). The nineteenth-century English translation of the *Open Letter* freely adds considerable glosses to Lassalle's text. For example, it says in this passage that universal suffrage is for the worker party 'a sentiment to be inscribed on its banners, and forming the central principle of its action' (Lassalle 1898, p. 8).

[38] For background on the emergence of the SPD, see Barclay and Weitz 1998.

[39] Lassalle 1919c, p. 42 (*Open Letter*); compare Lassalle 1898, pp. 4–5.

You want to found Savings-banks, Invalid and Sick-help Societies; institutions whose relative but subordinate importance I readily recognise. [But] is it your aim to ameliorate the condition of the worker – guarding him against the results of recklessness, sickness, age and accidents, the unguarded effects of which press individual workers below the ordinary condition of their class?

If so, the establishment of such institutions will be fully equal to meet your aims. But for such an aim, it would hardly be worthwhile to instigate a movement throughout all Germany and commence a universal agitation of the entire worker estate.

A movement of such magnitude as the universal agitation of the workingmen of the nation, however, would be far from finding its reward in accomplishing so little when so much could be done.[40]

Lassalle also insisted on political *independence*, a goal which in 1861 had a very concrete meaning: to break away from the liberal Progressive Party that to a large extent had summoned up the worker societies in the first place in order to recruit followers in its struggle for a liberal constitution. Lassalle violently attacked the Progressives because their bourgeois interests were in conflict with those of the workers. He also attacked them because of their lack of energy, weakness and pusillanimity in fighting for their own goal of political freedom. This sort of accusation against the liberals became a standard feature of Social Democracy both in Germany and in Russia.

Finally, Lassalle insisted on effective *organisation*. One aspect of this theme was a rather dictatorial and 'cult of personality' mode of inner-party organisation. What I want to stress here is rather how Lassalle's ideal of organisation followed from the fundamental aim of spreading the good news of the 'idea of the Fourth Estate'.

But how to effect the introduction of universal direct suffrage? Look at England. The great agitation of the English people against the Corn Laws lasted for over five years. And then the laws had to go: a Tory Ministry itself had to abolish them.

---

[40] Lassalle 1898, pp. 9–10; Lassalle 1919c, pp. 48–9 (*Open Letter*). Later Social-Democratic opinion concluded that Lassalle overdid his hostility to reforms as such.

> Organise yourselves as a Universal Union of German Workers for the purpose of a legal and peaceful but unwearying, unceasing agitation for the introduction of universal direct suffrage in every German state.[41]

Lassalle wanted a party of agitation that openly inscribed its sentiments on its banners. In order to succeed in this aim, the new party had to set up treasuries based on membership dues. These treasuries will support a powerful agitation force:

> Found and publish newspapers, to make this demand daily and to prove the reasons for it from the state of society. With the same funds circulate pamphlets for the same purpose. Pay agents out of the Union's funds to carry this insight into every corner of the country, to thrill the heart of every worker, every house-servant, every farm-labourer, with this cry. Indemnify out of the Union's funds all workers who have been injured or prosecuted for their activity. Repeat daily, unwearyingly, the same thing, again the same thing, always the same thing.[42]

In this way, Lassalle evoked the image of the spreading circle of awareness that was later central to Lenin's idea of class leadership:

> Propagate this cry in every workshop, every village, every hut. May the workers of the towns let their higher insight and education [Bildung] overflow on to the workers of the country. Debate, discuss, everywhere, every day, without pausing, without ending as in the great English agitation against the Corn Laws, now in peaceful public assemblies, now in private conferences, the necessity of universal direct suffrage. The more the millions who echo your voice, the more irresistible will be its influence.[43]

The key to effective agitation, Lassalle believed, was to keep it simple by focusing on one basic message. In the case of his own agitation, the message was to be 'universal suffrage in order to obtain state aid to worker co-operatives'. This programme was a very distorted first approximation of the programme of conquering political power in order to introduce socialism.

---

[41] Ensor 1910, pp. 45–6; Lassalle 1919c, pp. 89–90. Note Lassalle's inspiration by the middle-class anti-Corn Laws agitation campaign in England.

[42] Ensor 1910, p. 46; Lassalle 1919c, pp. 90–1 (Open Letter).

[43] Ensor 1910, p. 46; Lassalle 1919c, p. 90 (Open Letter).

Thus Lassalle had his own version of the merger formula: 'The great destiny of our age is precisely this – which the dark ages had been unable to conceive, much less to achieve – the dissemination of scientific knowledge among the body of the people'.[44] What Lassalle means by 'science' here is essentially his popularised version of Marx's historical materialism. And what he meant by 'disseminate' was not adult education lectures, but the excited agitation machine described in the *Open Letter*.

Many features of Lassalle's programme, tactics and organisation were rejected by German Social Democracy as the years went by. One of the most important Marxist criticisms of Lassalle could have been predicted on the basis of the *Manifesto* passages cited previously. According to the Marxist wing of the early Social-Democratic movement, Lassalle's hostility toward the bourgeoisie led him to dangerously underestimate the importance of political freedom. Wilhelm Liebknecht, one of these early Marxist leaders, used the opportunity of his trial for high treason in 1872 to make this point:

> I showed that a one-sided procedure against the bourgeoisie could only be of service to the aristocracy, that the contemplated universal suffrage, without freedom of the press, of meeting, and of combination, was nothing but an instrument of the reaction, and that 'State-help' from a government of lordlings could only be granted to corrupt the workmen and make them useful for the purposes of the reaction.[45]

It is easy to pick holes in Lassalle's programme and tactics and certainly his rhetoric has badly dated. Put next to Marx, he is, as Jeeves would say, intellectually negligible. Yet his current absence from historical memory must distort our view of Social-Democratic activists such as Lenin, for whom Lassalle was a hero even after all the criticisms were accepted. Lassalle put the political strategy adumbrated in the *Communist Manifesto* on the map. He caught two essential features of that strategy: the emotional appeal of the call to a historical mission and the organisational implications of preparing the workers to carry out that mission. He can indeed be called the first Social Democrat.

---

[44] Lassalle 1900, p. 44 (*Science and the Workingman*, translated by Thorstein Veblen); Lassalle 1919b, p. 247. Compare Lassalle's dictum 'die Wissenschaft an das Volk zu bringen' with Lenin's notorious formula about bringing socialist awareness to the workers from without.

[45] As cited by Russell 1965 [1896], pp. 77–9.

We may conclude with an appreciation of Lassalle penned by Eduard Bernstein in his orthodox, pre-revisionist days. His book *Ferdinand Lassalle as a Social Reformer* (1893) was heavily influenced by Engels and translated into English by Marx's daughter Eleanor. Engels's role in the book was so great that Hal Draper practically treats him rather than Bernstein as the author.[46] The book as a whole is hostile to Lassalle and insists on his weaknesses at great length. All the more valuable, then, is the book's summary of Lassalle's enduring achievements. The value of organisation was one such contribution: 'If the German Social Democracy has always recognised the value of a strong organisation, if it has been so convinced of the necessity of the concentration of forces, that even without the outer bond of organisation it has yet known how to perform all the functions of one, this is largely a heritage of the agitation of Lassalle.' But Lassalle's central contribution was to turn the idea of historical mission into practical politics:

> Where at most there was only a vague desire, he gave conscious effort; he trained the German workers to understand their historical mission, he taught them to organise as an independent political party, and in this way at least accelerated by many years the process of development of the movement. . . . The time for victory was not yet, but in order to conquer, the workers must first learn to fight. And to have trained them for the fight, to have, as the song says, given them swords, this remains the great, the undying merit of Ferdinand Lassalle.[47]

## Party of a new type: the SPD model

> It is rather startling to one whose observation of socialist movements has been confined almost entirely to the United States, to enter one of the largest and most beautiful halls in the world, – a hall seating 10,000 persons – and find it packed to the point of suffocation with delegates, members, and friends of the Social-Democratic Party of Germany . . . It was an impressive sight.[48]

---

[46] Draper 1977–90, 4, pp. 266–9. According to Draper, 'this book was one of the most acute Marxist analyses ever published'.

[47] Bernstein 1970, pp. 190–2 (translated by Eleanor Marx Aveling). The song is the anthem quoted at the beginning of this section.

[48] Hunter 1908, p. 1.

The American socialist Robert Hunter was not the only one impressed by the Sozialdemokratische Partei Deutschlands (SPD). The strength and prestige of the SPD was a source of confidence – no, *the* source of confidence – for socialists the world around. Hunter reels out the facts on which this confidence rested:

> The German party is the oldest and largest socialist organisation in Europe. It represents the thought of a very large proportion of the working men of the entire nation. There are more socialists in Germany than there are people in Spain, or Mexico, or in Belgium, Holland, Denmark, and Norway put together. Its present vote would have elected the President of the United States up till the time of Grant's second term. It polls a million more votes than any other party in Germany.[49]

Hunter stresses some other features that made contemporaneous observers regard the SPD as something unseen before, as a party of a new type in European politics. 'The German socialist movement is a democratically controlled organisation of a character unknown in American politics'. Furthermore, 'the party carries on a propaganda of incredible dimensions'. Finally, it was truly a working man's party – and

> they were of that type of working men one too rarely sees outside of Germany. . . . They were serious minded, ruddy-faced, muscular; one could see that they had saved from the exploitation of the factory enough physical and mental strength to live like men during their leisure hours; and my belief is that physically and mentally they can hold their own in the essentials with any other class in Germany.[50]

Most discussion of the SPD today, whether from the Left or the Right, is heavily tinged with irony. The party was not as revolutionary as it thought, it was not as Marxist as it thought, it was not as democratic as it thought, and (more recently) it was not as committed to gender equality as it thought. The textbook interpretation of *WITBD* in particular operates with a contrast between Lenin's fierce revolutionary party and the SPD's mild-mannered party of reform. In Bertram Wolfe's words, the parties and trade

---

[49] Hunter 1908, pp. 4–5.
[50] Hunter 1908, pp. 1–2, 5.

unions of the West were 'democratically organised, comfortably adapted to the sizeable legality permitted them, and long since devoid of insurrectionary spirit except as a banner for festal occasions'.[51]

No doubt there is much that gives support to all this irony. But perhaps we can understand the more dramatic view taken by contemporaneous observers when they heard August Bebel, the leader of the Party, exclaim 'I shall remain the mortal enemy of this society and social system, in order to sap its very life and, if I can, to eliminate it altogether'. Or when they heard Prussian officials say that the SPD was not 'a reformist party . . . but a revolutionary party, whose aim is the destruction of the existing state and social system'.[52] In any event, if we want to understand the impact of the SPD model on *WITBD*, we must, for a time, bracket the irony of hindsight. For this reason, I will document my discussion with comment from contemporaneous observers.

Every institution has an idealised model of itself – 'idealised' in the sense that it is abstracted from everyday concrete practices, in the further sense that it reflects the ideals and goals of the institution, and in the final sense that it pictures the institution and its members as more heroic and pure-hearted than reality warrants. Such a model is not just a self-flattering pat on the back but plays a crucial role in the working of the organisation. It determines what is seen as normal and what abnormal. Debates within the organisation and proposals for innovation are steeped in a rhetoric imposed by the model. Such a model is in fact the unwritten constitution of the organisation.[53]

This idealised model can sometimes have a greater impact on foreigners than on the institution itself. The ideal model of the English Parliament is a

[51] Wolfe 1964 [1948], pp. 160–1.

[52] Hall 1977, pp. 17, 58 (Bebel in 1903, Prussian official in 1897). The cited comment by Prussian Minister of the Interior von der Recke was in defence of a bill that would have prohibited the SPD from holding public meetings. This bill almost passed. Hall's excellent study is an effective response to Wolfe's rosy view cited above.

[53] A comparison can be made to what John Kay calls the American Business Model: an idealised model of the American economy that is not a reliable empirical guide to the actual workings of this economy but that nevertheless is fervently believed in by many of the practitioners within the economy and that has acquired prestige throughout the world as an explanation of the perceived successes of the American economy (Kay 2003).

case in point. In a similar way, the SPD model was normative for all of European Social Democracy, as described by Gary Steenson:

> When Jean Dormoy wrote his first-hand account of the founding congress of the first French workers' party, he referred to the congress's decision 'to organise itself into a party similar to that which existed in Germany'; seven years later in a letter to Engels, Paul Lafargue referred to his group as 'we who hold up the German party as a model'. An anarchist opponent of the first united workers' political party in Austria objected strongly to the repeated, almost exclusive reference at its founding congress to the German model. And one prominent historian of the Italian worker-socialist movement has argued that the German organisational example was at least as influential with the founders of the first national socialist party as was the northerners' presumed marxian theory, and, in fact, that the former fostered widespread acceptance of the latter.[54]

Although Steenson might be surprised to hear it, he could and should have added the Russian Social-Democratic Worker Party to this list. As we sketch out the features of the SPD model that are particularly relevant to *WITBD*, we shall see that the model was fundamentally narrative in form: it told a story about the SPD's past, present and future. We shall start with the ways in which the Party in the 1890s saw its own past. When the Party looked back, it saw its origin in a double act of independence from liberals and bourgeois democrats. We have already seen how Lassalle urged the workers to reject the tutelage of the liberal Progressive Party. The other wing of the movement – the more Marx-oriented groups led by August Bebel and Wilhelm Liebknecht – had a more gradual but no less determined break with its radical-democratic middle-class sponsors. In the case of Bebel and Liebknecht, it was an internal evolution in their views as well as an external organisational evolution that led them by 1869 to embrace the programme of Marx's International and the accompanying ideal of an independent, class-based political party.[55] In contrast to Lassalle, however, Bebel and Liebknecht retained from their days as radical democrats a firm conviction of the primordial importance of political freedom.

---

[54] Steenson 1991, p. 80.
[55] Steenson 1981; Barclay and Weitz 1998.

The next great episode in the Party's story of itself was the heroic outlaw period. In 1878, at Bismarck's instigation, very harsh anti-socialist laws were put into effect that essentially outlawed the Party with the bizarre but crucial exception of its ability to elect parliamentary representatives.[56] The period of persecution ended in 1890 with a resounding victory for the SPD and a resounding defeat for the Iron Chancellor. Despite the persecution, the SPD votes swelled during this period until it became the largest single party in the German Empire. In 1890 the laws were allowed to lapse. By the end of 1890, Bismarck was gone but the SPD was still there.

The tactics used by the German socialists during this period were, of course, of consuming interest to Russian Social Democrats, for whom absolutist repression was an ongoing reality and not just a matter of 'exceptional laws'. At the centre of these tactics was the role of exile organisations in giving the movement a continuing voice and sense of direction. The most important role here was played by Eduard Bernstein as editor of the newspaper weekly *Sozialdemokrat*, published in Switzerland. One of the sagas of the outlaw period told how this paper continued to be distributed by the 'red postal service' right under the noses of the Imperial gendarmerie. As Bertrand Russell remarked in the 1890s, 'this paper, which was secretly distributed with the greatest energy, and soon began to make a large profit for the party funds, restored, in some measure, the connection between the central authority and the individual members'.[57]

*Sozialdemokrat*'s role in keeping the Party together was due just as much to its editorial line as to its succesful distribution. In his influential party history first published in 1898 (just when the *Iskra* plan was taking shape in Lenin's mind), Franz Mehring commented that 'Bernstein well understood how to maintain the newspaper as an organ of the whole party and to give it, at the same time, a definite, firm, clear direction that took into account all tactical demands without violating principle'.[58] Thus the Russians had a ready-made model for the party-building role of a newspaper published abroad.

---

[56] 'Not only were party organisations proper outlawed, but also trade unions with even the faintest socialist connections, cultural and exercise clubs, workers' lending libraries, consumer co-operatives, and on occasion even taverns and cafes popular with workers were shut down by overzealous police officials' (Steenson 1981, p. 35).

[57] Russell 1965, p. 106. The man who ran the red postal service was Julius Motteler; for detailed discussion, see Lidtke 1966, pp. 89–97.

[58] Mehring 1898, 2, p. 463; see also Gay 1962, pp. 60–1.

Above and beyond the tactical and organisational successes of the outlaw period, it demonstrated what a sympathetic but not uncritical British observer called 'the extraordinary vitality of the movement' – so vital that absolutist repression could not destroy it (an encouraging thought for Russian Social Democrats). This British observer, Thomas Kirkup, goes on to explain:

> The Social Democrats had shown a patience, resolution, discipline, and, in the absence of any formal organisation, a real and effective organisation of mind and purpose which are unexampled in the annals of the labour movement since the beginning of human society. They had made a steady and unflinching resistance to the most powerful statesman since the first Napoleon, who wielded all the resources of a great modern State, and who was supported by a press that used every available means to discredit the movement; and as a party, they had never been provoked to acts of violence. In fact, they had given proof of all the high qualities which fit men and parties to play a great *rôle* in history. The Social-Democratic movement in Germany is one of the most notable phenomena of our time.[59]

The triumphal outcome of the outlaw period did more to confirm a sense of the coming revolution's 'natural necessity' than all the learned proofs of scientific socialism.

We turn now the SPD's view of the present, that is, the 1890s. The SPD model interpreted the innovative institutions of the Party as the embodiment of the Marxist political strategy, namely, to bring to the workers the *insight* and *organisation* that they needed to enable them to carry out their great mission. The emphasis on insight led to the Party's educational thrust. The Party's job was to teach the workers not only *how* to carry out their mission but, more fundamentally, the very fact that they *had* a mission. As Gary Steenson states, a key assumption of the SPD model was that 'while the conditions of their experience might predispose workers to adhere to social democracy, specifically socialist consciousness had to be taught and learned'.[60]

This essential point is stated in more detail by H.-J. Schulz:

---

[59] Kirkup 1906, p. 222. I suspect that this passage comes from the first edition of 1892, that is, fresh after the triumph of the SPD.

[60] Steenson 1981, p. 130.

In a movement which began in the 1860s with the establishment of liberal education clubs for craftsmen and workers, the original and paradigmatic act of proletarian emancipation was not the strike or street protest but the reading of authorised texts, the acquisition of approved knowledge for the intellectual, moral and aesthetic improvement of the individual. The equation 'knowledge is power' attended the birth of the socialist movement and remained, despite all criticism, a central metaphor of its discourse. . . . The progressive worker who entered the movement was obliged to become, first of all, a reader of canonised texts. He was taught to approach each of these texts as containing coherent, self-evident and class-transcending *scientific* truth.[61]

This educational thrust was supported by an agitation machine of unprecedented elaborateness. Already in the 1870s, prior to the anti-socialist laws, this machine amazed observers:

A staff of skilful, intelligent, and energetic agitators advocated the new creed in every town of Germany, and they were supported by an effective machinery of newspapers, pamphlets, treatises, social gatherings, and even almanacs, in which the doctrines of socialism were suggested, inculcated, and enforced in every available way.[62]

In 1911, the German sociologist Robert Michels made a similar observation.

The tenacious, persistent, and indefatigable agitation characteristic of the socialist party, particularly in Germany, never relaxed in consequence of casual failures, nor ever abandoned because of casual successes, and which no other party has yet succeeded in imitating, has justly aroused the admiration even of critics and of bourgeois opponents.

Michels goes on to note that the emphasis on agitation means that 'in democratic organisations the activity of the professional leader is extremely fatiguing, often destructive to health, and in general (despite the division of labour) highly complex'.[63]

---

[61] Schulz 1993, p. 2.
[62] Kirkup 1906, p. 214. (Kirkup is describing the causes of the Party's excellent showing in the Reichstag election of 1877.)
[63] Michels 1962, p. 91.

The single most impressive feature of this agitation machine was the party press. In 1895 there were 75 socialist newspapers, of which 39 were issued six times a week. These newspapers catered to a broad variety of workers. There were newspapers for worker cyclists and worker gymnasts, for teetotaling workers and even for innkeepers. By 1909 the total circulation was over one million, a figure that implies a great many more actual readers.[64] But the printed word was embedded in an even wider context of the face-to-face spoken word. Social-Democratic agitation was carried on by public meetings, smaller conferences for the party militants and agitation by individual members.[65]

Nor did the SPD confine itself to political propaganda and agitation. The Social-Democratic movement in Germany consisted of a wide range of institutions that attempted to cover every facet of life. Party or Party-associated institutions included trade unions, clubs dedicated to activities ranging from cycling to hiking to choral singing, theatres and celebratory festivals. The broad scope of the movement's ambitions justifies the title of Vernon Lidtke's classic study *The Alternative Culture*. Looking just at Lidtke's index under the letter 'W', we find the following: workers' athletic clubs, workers' chess societies, workers' consumer societies, workers' cycling clubs, workers' educational societies, workers' gymnastic clubs, workers' libraries, workers' rowing clubs, workers' samaritan associations, workers' singing societies, workers' swimming clubs, workers' temperance associations, workers' theatrical clubs, workers' youth clubs.[66]

The reader will have noticed the repetition of the word 'worker'. This observation leads us to the central importance of the word *Arbeiter*, worker, as the symbolic core of the SPD model. The centrality of *Arbeiter* is also reflected in the high ideological discourse of the SPD. The key terms in this discourse are *Arbeiter*, *Arbeiterklasse* [worker class], *Arbeiterbewegung* [worker movement], *Arbeiterpartei* [worker party]. This close verbal and symbolic link is also present in the vocabulary of Russian Social Democracy. An individual worker is *rabochii*, *rabochii klass* is 'worker class', and so on.

---

[64] Steenson 1981, pp. 132–3.
[65] Russell 1965 [1896], pp. 124–31, based on Paul Göhre's first-hand reporting toward the end of the time of the anti-socialist laws.
[66] Lidtke 1985, pp. 298–9. The full title of Lidtke's book is *The Alternative Culture: Socialist Labor in Imperial Germany*.

In English, these verbal links are broken. One German-English dictionary translates the terms given above as 'working class', 'labour movement' and 'workers' party'.[67] The English language cannot jam nouns together as easily as German. (The Russians could match German usage in this instance because the noun *rabochii* happens to be adjectival in form.) At the cost of subverting the genius of the English language, I translate the key Social-Democratic terms as 'worker class', 'worker movement', 'worker party'. A few words in justification of this decision will not be amiss.

One motive is to preserve the centrality of the complex of associations attached to the word *Arbeiter* in the German Social-Democratic movement. Lidtke calls it 'the central code word' of the movement. On the one hand, the symbolic and ideological use of *Arbeiter* marked the separateness of the workers, their sense of exclusion, their hostility to German society. On the other hand, the word emphasised the unity of *all* participants in the movement, and this usage had paradoxical implications.

> This broad ideological usage [of *Arbeiter*], in conjunction with the ubiquitous *comrade* (*Genosse*), sanctioned the presence of a substantial number of middle-class people, found especially among the movement's intellectuals, in a party that proclaimed both its confidence in the necessity and ability of workers to emancipate themselves and its unrelenting hostility to everything bourgeois and capitalist.[68]

Preserving 'worker' as a link between the key terms of Social-Democratic discourse also helps us see the underlying *narrative* in which the worker class is a subject, an actor, a protagonist, in a world-historical epic. The English term 'working class' defines the class in terms of a *function*, one function among many needed for society. Engels once wrote:

> The moment the workers resolve to be bought and sold no longer, when, in the determination of the value of labour, they take the part of *human beings* [*Menschen*], possessed of a will as well as of working power [*Arbeitskraft*], at that moment the law of wages and the whole political economy of today is finished.[69]

---

[67] See the *Collins German-English English-German Dictionary* 1981, s.v. Arbeiter.
[68] Lidtke 1985, p. 200.
[69] Engels 1959, p. 436; Engels 1993, p. 227.

We might put this as follows: bourgeois political economy ends when the workers stop seeing themselves as 'the working class' with the function of providing labour power, and begin seeing themselves as 'the worker class', possessed of a will that allows them to play an active role in world history.

'Worker class' also defines the class in terms of the concrete and active individuals making it up. Nineteenth-century English usage allowed another way to bring this out. For example, the first German editions of Engels's book on the English working class had a dedication in English which began: 'Working Men! To you I dedicate this book'.[70] For obvious reasons, this usage is no longer acceptable. At least when translating and paraphrasing the historical documents of Social Democracy, I compensate by using 'worker class' to preserve the sense that the class is made up of living, breathing individuals.

The Social-Democratic narrative relied heavily on preserving the links between the various key terms. Take the following crucial sentence from Kautsky's *Erfurt Programme*:

> So bildet sich allmählich aus qualifizierten und unqualifizierten Proletariern die Schicht der in Bewegung befindlichen Arbeiterklasse – die Arbeiterbewegung.[71]

My translation tries to preserve this narrative thrust: 'From skilled and unskilled proletarians there gradually forms the stratum of the worker class that finds itself in movement – the worker movement.'

One final motivation for using 'worker class' is that German Social Democrats also used the term 'working class', *die arbeitende Klasse*. Engels, for instance, uses this in the title of his book that is appropriately translated *The Condition of the Working Class in England*. Often, the term 'working classes' means everybody in the class *except* the urban proletariat. In the same passage as the quotation just given, Kautsky talks about the growing influence of the militant proletariat on 'die anderen arbeitenden Klassen'.[72]

---

[70] Engels 1959, p. 235; Engels 1993, p. 9. See also the title of the International under Marx: The International Working Men's Association.

[71] Kautsky 1965, p. 216.

[72] Kautsky 1965, pp. 216–17. In Russian Social Democracy, the term *trudiashchiesia* has the same technical meaning of workers in a very broad sense, as opposed to the industrial proletariat by itself.

Returning now to the SPD model, we note that the job of the Party itself was to ensure that all these institutions worked together to carry out the movement's central mission of raising proletarian awareness. Thus observers were impressed not only by the scope of the SPD agitation but also by its superb organisation. 'So efficient is the organisation that the Socialists boast of being able to flood all Berlin with agitation leaflets in two hours.'[73] Particularly striking was the extent of what might be called the SPD's *apparat*: the salaried bureaucracy both in the Party itself and its offshoots. The party *apparat* was the outward and visible sign of the inward and invisible grace of discipline and organisation. For the SPD model, these were highly positive qualities. As Karl Kautsky put it in a comment cited by Lenin:

> The proletarian is never an isolated individual. He feels great and strong as part of a strong organisation. . . . His individuality counts little beside it. He struggles with full devotion as a part of an anonymous mass, without prospect of personal gain or personal fame, fulfils his duty in the post in which he is placed, in voluntary discipline which fills his whole feeling and thought.[74]

Another innovative feature of the SPD model that arose out of the *Manifesto* strategy was the fact that it was a truly *nation-wide* party – indeed, in many ways, it was the only truly nation-wide party in the German Empire. The SPD attempted to run candidates in as many electoral districts as possible, including many in which it had no chance of victory. Its aim, here as everywhere, was 'to spread the word to the masses, even to the reluctant, unhearing, and scornful masses'.[75]

A final aspect of the SPD that was extremely important for Lenin can be described using Lenin's own image: it acted as the *people's tribune*. As an English journalist put it in 1912, the German Social Democrats were

> the only unterrified, tooth-and-nail foes of reaction, insensate militarism and class rule, the one voice which cries out insistently, fearlessly, implacably, against the injustices which, in the opinion of many patriotic men, are

---

[73] Russell 1965 [1896], p. 124.
[74] Pierson 1993, p. 170; written by Kautsky in 1903–4 and cited in Lenin in *Two Steps Forward* (1904), Lenin 1958–65, 8, pp. 309–10.
[75] Steenson 1981, p. 45.

retarding the moral progress and sapping the vital resources of the German nation.[76]

Thus, the Party stood not just for worker-class interests and not even just for socialist transformation, but for the principles of democratic decency in society as a whole. One central forum for this activity was parliament. We sometimes tend to equate 'parliamentary activity' with mild-mannered reformism. But, at the end of the nineteenth century, when oratory in general and parliamentary oratory in particular was much more popular and prestigious than today, the SPD's use of the parliamentary forum was an essential means of taking its stand and spreading its message. Since later we will hear Lenin talk of 'Russian Bebels', we should remember that the basis of Bebel's vast influence was his activity as a parliamentary orator whose enormous talent was all the more striking because he personified 'the entrance to power of the men of toil . . . No other member [of the Reichstag] exercises a personal influence equal to his and one can actually feel a thrill of excitement pass through the chamber when he rises to speak'.[77] At a time when parliamentary debates could attract excited crowds, Bebel was a figure of Europe-wide import. Bebel's prestige should be kept in mind when we consider Lenin's dream of 'hegemony' – leadership in the revolutionary movement as a whole – for Russian Social Democracy.

The existence of parliament and especially the right of interpellation (the right of an ordinary member to demand an answer of a cabinet minister on any topic) allowed small parliamentary minorities to obtain a nation-wide hearing for their criticism of the government. An observer such as the American Robert Hunter felt that the right of interpellation as employed by the Social Democrats in their role as tribune was one of the main bulwarks of political liberty in Europe.

> Except in Russia, and a few of the more backward countries, it is inconceivable that in Europe men should be shot, deported from their homes, denied every constitutional protection, and put at the mercy of martial law, – as happened for a period of many months a year or so ago in Colorado, – without the entire country knowing both sides of the case.[78]

---

[76] Hall 1977, p. 20, citing Frederick William Wile.
[77] Hunter 1908, pp. 225–7.
[78] Hunter 1908, pp. 213–14.

Another weapon used by the SPD in its role as people's tribune – one of central importance to Lenin and *Iskra* – was what Lenin called political indictments: the exposure of corruption and scandal. Uncovering abuses, often with the help of sympathetic whistle-blowers who passed on incriminating documents, was a major activity of the socialist press. Observers attributed an 'incredible influence' to the embattled Party due to the 'unfriendly and relentless eye' it cast on events affecting all classes of society.[79]

Besides its heroic past as defier of Bismarck and besides its energetic present as educator and organiser of the worker class and as people's tribune, the SPD also included the future in its narrative of identity – that is, it defined itself as a party inspired by a final goal of social transformation and, as such, unique. The inspiration provided by the final goal had two sources: the idea of the mission, the task, the calling, the great duty, plus the idea that the final outcome was guaranteed by the forces of history. Much commentary on Marxism and Social Democracy is fascinated by a supposed contradiction between these two sources. If the outcome is inevitable, why devote your life to ensuring that it will come about? Such commentary misses the point that in practice the two sources complemented and strengthened each other. I will close with two contemporaneous observers who made exactly this point, so we can better understand some of the reasons why the would-be founders of the Russian Social-Democratic Party thought that 'theoretical clarity' was a life-and-death matter.

Bertrand Russell, writing in a book published in 1896 – that is, prior to the furore caused by Bernstein's revisionism – tells us:

> Those who have seen the daily support, in the midst of the most wretched conditions, which the more intelligent working men and women derive from their fervent and religious belief in the advent of the Socialist State, and from their conviction that historical development is controlled by irresistible forces, in whose hands men are only puppets, and by whose action the diminution and final extinction of the capitalist class is an inevitable decree of fate – those who have seen the strength, compactness and fervour which this religion gives to those who hold it, will hardly regard its decay as likely to help the progress of the party.[80]

---

[79] Hunter 1908, p. 30. For a full-length study of SPD indictments, see Hall 1977.
[80] Russell 1965, p. 161.

Russell was a sympathetic outsider. The Austrian Social-Democratic leader Victor Adler may be considered an insider. Writing after the Stuttgart Congress of 1898 – that is, after the German Party had semi-officially repudiated Bernstein's position, but before his famous book *Presuppositions of Socialism* had appeared, Adler exclaimed:

> How unpractical these practical people so often are! The strength of our party, the efficiency of every single one of our comrades depends on his knowledge that the extraordinary amount of labour, sacrifice, courage, and endurance which he must daily exact from himself and from others is not just devoted to the welfare of the individual groups around him, but that he is the vehicle for a bit of history, that he is working not only for the present but also for the future.[81]

## Kautsky and class leadership

In support of his argument in WITBD, Lenin quoted a rather long passage by Karl Kautsky. Much ink has been spilled on the relationship between Lenin's views and Kautsky's views as presented in this passage.[82] But most of this discussion is beside the point, since Lenin's real debt to Kautsky is much earlier and much more basic. One might say that Kautsky's influence is hidden in plain view, since the crucial text is the final chapter of Kautsky's *Erfurt Programme* – probably the most fundamental statement of what Social Democracy is all about.

Kautsky is remembered as the most influential theoretician of international Social Democracy, but in certain key respects – particularly in the case of the fledgling Russian Social Democracy – Kautsky's role went beyond influence. In 1892, Kautsky wrote the *Erfurt Programme*, a semi-official commentary on the recently adopted programme of the Social-Democratic Party of Germany. This book *defined* Social Democracy for Russian activists – it was the book one read to find out what it meant to be a Social Democrat. In 1894, a young provincial revolutionary named Vladimir Ulianov translated the *Erfurt Programme* into Russian just at the time he was acquiring his life-long identity

---

[81] Tudor and Tudor 1988, pp. 316–17.
[82] This Kautsky passage is discussed in detail in the Annotations Part Two.

as a revolutionary Social Democrat. Despite the canonical status of the *Erfurt Programme* for Lenin's generation, it is ignored today, at least by English-speaking scholars. Few are even aware that the existing English translation – first issued in 1912 – is a bowdlerised abridgement that serves only to obscure what someone like Lenin might have taken out of the book.

Besides the *Erfurt Programme*, the principal text for my reconstruction of Kautsky's outlook is *Parliamentarism* (1893), cited directly by Lenin in WITBD as an authority for some of his key arguments. This book really has been totally forgotten (the copy I read was one of the hardest to obtain and most decrepit of the texts I consulted for this commentary).[83] *Parliamentarism* is unjustly forgotten, since it is one of the very few works in the Marxist tradition dealing entirely with political theory and, in my view, compares favourably with Lenin's *State and Revolution*. And, since I have mentioned *State and Revolution*, let me say that we should not anachronistically see Kautsky defending parliamentary democracy as opposed to, say, soviet democracy. What Kautsky means by 'parliamentarism' in the 1890s is essentially representative democracy. As such, it cannot really be opposed to soviet-style democracy, itself a form of representative democracy. For our purposes, *Parliamentarism* is important not only because of the arguments that Lenin uses explicitly but also because the book brings together better than anywhere else the logic behind what the Russians labelled the strategy of proletarian hegemony in the democratic revolution.

I occasionally use revealing passages from other works by Kautsky, including one or two that were written after the publication of WITBD. But since both the *Erfurt Programme* and *Parliamentarism* are, in different ways, forgotten works and since their influence on Lenin is indisputable, I rely mainly on them for my exposition.[84]

*Circles of awareness*

Kautsky conceived of Social Democracy as the inner ring in a series of concentric circles. A key passage in the *Erfurt Programme* describes these circles and their

---

[83] Kautsky 1893. The French translation is more easily located (Kautsky 1900).
[84] Among the useful secondary literature on Kautsky is Steenson 1978, Geary 1987, Hünlich 1981, Gilcher-Holtey 1986, Salvadori 1979, J. Kautsky 1994, Donald 1993.

mutual relationship. (NB: the term usually translated 'conscious', *bewusst*, is here translated 'aware.')

> From skilled and unskilled proletarians there gradually forms the stratum of the worker class that finds itself in movement – the worker movement. This is the part of the proletariat that fights for the common interests of its class, its *ecclesia militans* (fighting church).[85] This stratum grows at the expense of the arrogant worker 'aristocrats' sunk in their egoism as well as the dull 'rabble', the lower strata of the wage proletariat that vegetates in hopelessness and powerlessness.
>
> We have seen that the worker proletariat is constantly increasing; we know further that it becomes ever more decisive for the other working classes, whose living conditions and whose way of feeling and thinking is ever more influenced by it. Now we see that in this ever-growing mass the fighting section grows not only absolutely but proportionately. No matter how fast the proletariat grows, the *fighting section* grows even faster.
>
> *But the fighting proletariat is by far the most important and productive recruiting ground for Social Democracy.* Social Democracy is nothing other than the part of the fighting proletariat that is aware of its goal. [In turn,] the fighting proletariat has a tendency to become more and more synonymous with Social Democracy; in Germany and Austria the two have in actuality become one.[86]

Using this passage, I have created a diagram called 'Kautsky's Circles of Awareness' (see Figure 1.1). The remainder of this discussion of Kautsky will be devoted to teasing out the implications hidden in this chart.

The first point – a very important one for understanding WITBD – is that the term 'worker movement' used in the merger formula is a technical one with a fairly precise meaning within Social-Democratic discourse. The worker movement is neither the proletariat as a whole, nor is it Social Democracy. It is the militant or fighting proletariat – the section of the proletariat animated by a spirit of organised resistance.

---

[85] The usual translation of *ecclesia militans* in English is 'church militant'. Note the strong verbal link in German between 'fighting church', *kämpfende Kirche*, and class struggle, *Klassenkampf*.

[86] Kautsky 1965, pp. 216–17.

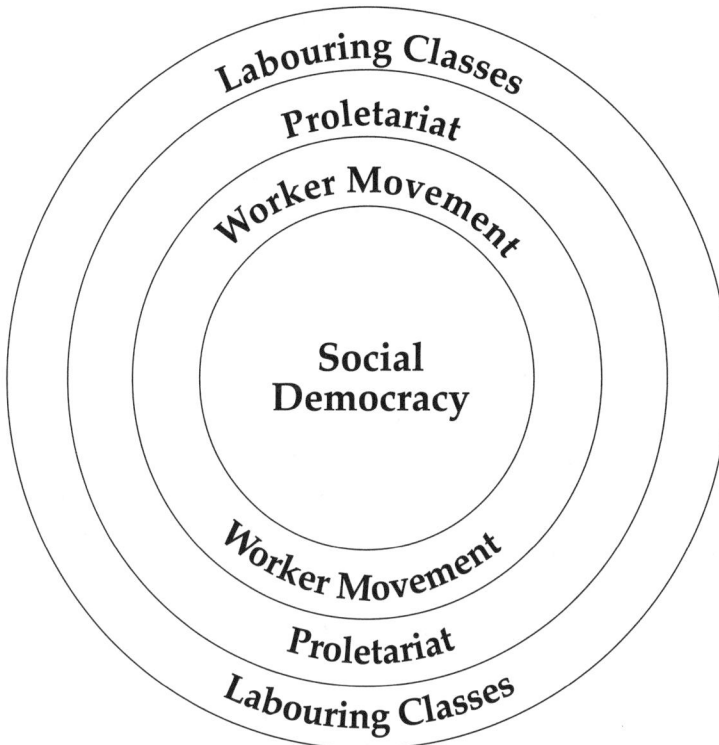

Figure 1.1: Kautsky's Circles of Awareness

At any one point in time, members of the outside circles will always have less awareness – that is, less insight into their own class position, basic interests, and therefore historic mission. Yet, viewed over time, there is a tendency for the inner, more aware, circles to expand. Social Democracy becomes a greater and greater portion of the worker movement, while the worker movement becomes a greater and greater portion of the whole proletariat. At the limit, all the circles collapse into one circle of complete awareness.

What we still do not know is the nature of the forces that are working to bring the circles together. Kautsky's brief description of the process might leave the impression that the whole thing is automatic. This impression is strengthened by the frequent occurrence of one of Kautsky's favourite words, *Naturnotwendigkeit*, natural necessity. We therefore need to ask, what are the amalgamating forces in Kautsky's model and in what direction do they operate? Does the worker movement give rise to the highly aware inner circle through forces internal to itself? Or does Social Democracy move out to transform the worker movement in its own image?

The answer is somewhat complicated by the fact that Kautsky has two aims in this section of the *Erfurt Programme*. One is to provide an ideal model of the past and future of Social Democracy: its origin and its destiny. The other aim is to set out an explicitly counterfactual and highly unlikely scenario in order to make a theoretical point about the 'natural necessity' of socialism. We will first examine Kautsky's thought experiment, which is all the more important to us because it was cited at length in disputes within Russian Social Democracy about the orthodoxy of *WITBD*.[87]

For various rhetorical and theoretical purposes, Kautsky wants to show that socialism is an inevitable natural necessity even if there were no Social Democracy – in fact, even if the workers did not accept socialist ideas. He therefore invites us to consider the outcome *even if* Social Democracy were absent from the picture. The chain of inferences proceeds as follows:

- It is inevitable that the workers will resist capitalist exploitation, that is, it is inevitable that there *be* a worker movement.
- It is inevitable that this resistance lead to a nation-wide worker political party.
- It is inevitable that this party will take over control of the state.
- It is inevitable that the workers will use this power to introduce socialism, because – as they will discover after much trial and error – socialism is the only way to protect their essential interests.[88]

Thus, only at the very last minute, just as the curtain goes down, the workers discover and accept the merits of socialism (NB: this last-minute conversion could also be called Social Democracy). The point of this thought experiment is to show that even in a worst-case scenario, socialism is still inevitable. Nevertheless (Kautsky immediately adds), this is indeed a *worst* case scenario because socialism arrives only after 'a great many misconceptions, errors and unnecessary sacrifices and useless expenditure of strength and time'.[89]

I call this the 'sooner or later' argument. It turns up rather frequently in Social-Democratic writings as a way of combining the core Social-Democratic

---

[87] For example, by Plekhanov in his 1904 article attacking *WITBD* (*Iskra*, No. 70 and 71 [25 July and 1 August 1904], reprinted in Plekhanov 1923–7, 13, pp. 116–40).

[88] Kautsky 1965, pp. 225–31.

[89] Kautsky 1965, p. 229.

claim of inevitability with the core Social-Democratic urgency about proselytising the workers. As the young Stalin put it when he recycled Kautsky's argument in 1905 in order to defend the orthodoxy of WITBD:

> Of course, at some point, after long wanderings and sufferings, the *stikhiinyi* [elemental] movement, even without the help of Social Democracy, will come into its own and arrive at the gates of socialist revolution.[90]

Having made his worst case scenario, Kautsky returns from his thought experiment to the real world. He hastens to assure us that the chances that events will play out in this manner are vanishingly small. The following extensive but crucial passage explains the forces that actually are at work to expand the circles of awareness.

> Nevertheless there is absolutely no reason to expect that the proletariat of any country will adopt such a negative attitude [toward socialism] after it comes to power. This would mean that in relation to awareness and knowledge it remains at the level of a child, while economically, politically and morally it has become an adult, one with the power and the capability of overcoming its powerful opponent and imposing its will. Such a misshapen development of the proletariat is highly unlikely. We have already noted more than once that thanks to [mechanised industry], there is in the proletariat (once its original degradation has been overcome) a theoretical sense, a capacity for great problems and goals that lie outside the realm of immediate interests, that one searches for in vain in the other working and labouring classes under it and over it.
>
> At the same time, furthermore, the economic development of present-day society proceeds so rapidly and manifests itself in such a mass of conspicuous phenomena that it is recognised even by an uneducated person, once his attention is called to it. And there won't be any lack of attention-calling, since simultaneously, thanks to the continuation by Karl Marx of the work begun by bourgeois classical economy, insight into the course of economic development and the whole economic mechanism becomes exceptionally deep and comprehensive.

---

[90] Stalin, 1946–52, 1, p. 98, see also 1, p. 105. For other instances of the same kind of argument, see Gorin, a speaker at the Second Congress cited by Stalin (Stalin 1946–52, 1, p. 104) and Kanatchikov 1986, p. 267.

This all comes together to make the fighting proletariat extremely receptive to the socialist teaching. Socialism is no message of woe for the proletariat but rather good news, a new gospel [*ein neues Evangelium*]. The ruling classes cannot recognise socialism without committing moral suicide. The proletariat finds in socialism new life, new power, inspiration and the joy of hope. Will the proletariat remain indifferent or even hostile to such a teaching for any length of time?

Once an independent worker party has been formed, it will with natural necessity sooner or later adopt a socialist outlook – if it has not been filled with such an outlook from the very beginning – and finally it must become a *socialist* worker party, that is, Social Democracy.

We now see the chief recruiting ground [of Social Democracy] set out clearly before us. In brief, the conclusion of our discussion is as follows: the bearer of the socialist movement is the fighting strata of the industrial proletariat that has attained political self-awareness. The more the influence of the proletariat on the social strata nearest to it grows and the more the thinking and emotions of these strata are influenced, all the more will they also be drawn into the socialist movement.

The class struggle of the proletariat has socialist production as its natural goal; it cannot end before this goal is reached. Just as the proletariat will with certainty come to be the ruling class in the state, so equally is the victory of socialism certain.[91]

We can now describe more concretely the forces at work in Kautsky's model. First, there is a force that comes about automatically from *within* the worker movement: the spirit of resistance. As we have seen, this resistance is capable of eventually getting us to socialism all by itself, but this point is almost irrelevant in real life. What is more important is that the spirit of resistance (along with other features of the industrial proletariat) makes the worker movement *receptive* to the good news brought by Social Democracy. And, since Social Democracy and its message *do* exist, we have a new natural necessity: any worker party will 'sooner or later' adopt a socialist programme.

This natural necessity does not detract from the fact that, in real life, Social Democracy is the *active* force that transforms the worker movement by

---

[91] Kautsky 1965, pp. 230–1.

expanding awareness. Social Democracy realises that the militant proletariat is the ideal 'recruiting ground' and so it directs its efforts there. Social Democracy definitely does *not* emanate automatically from the worker movement in order to serve the movement's own ends more efficiently. It is, rather, the force of a particular *insight* that comes originally from Marx and Engels.

We can now see the relevant meaning of 'confidence' in the Social-Democratic context. In terms of the worst case scenario, the Social Democrat is confident that the workers will *eventually* introduce socialism. In terms of the *real-life* scenario, the Social Democrat is confident that the worker movement will hear, mark and inwardly digest the Social-Democratic message as soon as it is in a position to receive it. Even the unlearned, the *Ungelehrter*, will achieve this insight.

Since this new natural necessity – 'a worker party will sooner or later adopt the socialist programme' – is dependent on *insight*, the actual timing is not closely tied to the course of capitalist development.[92] The most advanced Social Democracy need not be found in the most advanced capitalist country. It could conceivably be found, say, in Germany rather than England. Indeed (says Kautsky at one point), even the workers in economically backward Russia are more politically advanced in their thinking than the English workers.[93] The driving force in this respect is the quality of class leadership rather than the level of productive forces.

Thus, we see that the circles of awareness are constantly shifting in their relation to one another. The basic formula defines Social Democracy as the merger of socialism and the worker movement. But only context can inform us, when Social-Democratic writers use the term 'worker movement', whether they mean the worker movement *prior* to Social Democracy (defined by its militant resistance alone) or after its transformation by Social-Democratic insight and organisation.

Much of the misunderstanding about the orthodoxy of this or that formulation is caused by the resulting ambiguities. The best way to avoid such misunderstanding is to keep in mind the underlying narrative. On one side, we have a worker movement animated by the spirit of resistance, and, on the other, we have Social Democracy animated by the insight that a merger

---

[92] Kautsky 1901b (this article is cited by Lenin in *WITBD*).
[93] Kautsky 1902, pp. 55–6.

is necessary. (Note that when an individual worker becomes convinced of the truth of scientific socialism, he becomes by virtue of that very fact a part of Social Democracy rather than simply the worker movement – thus making it almost a matter of definition to assert that awareness comes from Social Democracy.) The inner forces of the two protagonists drive them in each other's direction and eventually lead to their melding.

We may sum up the moral of the circles of awareness in the following way: Social Democracy is *needed* and will be *heeded*. It is not needed to achieve socialism, since this will come about regardless. It is needed to avoid the human tragedy that would be caused by socialism coming 'later' rather than 'sooner'. It will be heeded because its good news brings the proletariat new life, new power, inspiration and the joy of hope.

### Merger vs. continued isolation

In order to bring out the crucial importance of the Social-Democratic merger, Kautsky stresses that the two partners – socialism and the worker movement – were originally *separate*. What might be called the foundation myth of Social Democracy describes how these two separate forces come together. Kautsky's rendition of this story served as a template for many other more detailed accounts of Social-Democratic origins, including the one given by Lenin in *WITBD*.

In the *Erfurt Programme*, Kautsky traces the growth of the worker movement from its early beginnings in the Middle Ages. The driving force of the movement was always resistance to capitalist exploitation. This resistance grew more and more organised and effective, but resistance in and of itself does not generate the realisation that capitalist private property had to be abolished. To make this point, Kautsky sets out the thought experiment described earlier and describes a worker movement that remains separate from socialism until long after it takes political power.

Just as worker resistance in and of itself does not generate insight into the need for socialism, possession of the insight about socialism does not in and of itself generate the realisation that only a militant worker movement can bring it about. Kautsky's narrative tells how 'socialism' (= all those who advocated social control of the economy as the only answer to the problems of society and the problems of the poor in particular) comes to the worker movement from without – in other words, how socialism was originally separate from the worker movement. But the intention of the narrative is not to laud the socialists. On the contrary, their haughty condescension towards the militant worker movement and indeed their overt fear of it meant that worker rejection of socialism as a bourgeois whim was entirely understandable.

From the early socialists' point of view, the proletariat was much too crude and raw to be credited with the capacity for independent political initiative. And, when a militant worker movement did come into existence in the 1830s, the socialists were hostile because worker militancy threatened to scare off the bourgeois philanthropists and the élite politicians whom the socialists wanted to win over. The 'utopian' rejection of the worker movement can be illustrated with a North-American example. Edward Bellamy's *Looking Backward* is a classic of utopian socialism: published in 1888, it contrasts the world of its time with the enlightened world of 2000.[94] Bellamy made no distinction between 'the labor parties', 'followers of the red flag', and bomb-throwing anarchists. In the following exchange, the narrator who grew up in the world of the nineteenth century learns the point of view of the enlightened twentieth century from the lips of his host, Doctor Leete:

> As we sat at table, Doctor Leete amused himself with looking over the paper I had brought in. There was in it, as in all the newspapers of that date [1887], a great deal about the labor troubles, strikes, lockouts, boycotts, the programs of labor parties, and wild threats of the anarchists.
>
> 'By the way', said I, as the doctor read aloud to us some of these items, 'what part did the followers of the red flag take in the establishment of the new order of things? They were making considerable noise the last thing that I knew.'
>
> 'They had nothing to do with it except to hinder it, of course', replied Doctor Leete.

Doctor Leete then announces as historical fact that the followers of the red flag were subsidised by the capitalists in order to delay reform. (The narrator adds in a footnote that this assertion is undoubtedly incorrect even though it is the only theory that makes intelligible their actions.) Doctor Leete then explains that the 'national party' that ushered in the utopian system of 2000 had nothing to do with the labour parties:

---

[94] [Editorial note: for more on Bellamy and other late-Victorian utopias, see another book in the *HM* Book Series, Beaumont 2005.]

The labor parties as such never could have accomplished anything on a large or permanent scale. For purposes of national scope, their basis as merely class organisations was too narrow. It was not till a rearrangement of the industrial and social system on a higher ethical basis, and for the more efficient production of wealth, was recognised as the interest, not of one class, but equally of all classes, of rich and poor, cultured and ignorant, old and young, weak and strong, men and women, that there was any prospect that it could be achieved.[95]

Kautsky lays great stress on this kind of hostility toward militant labour on the part of the early socialists. Even worker socialists shared this hostility. The point of Kautsky's narrative is not that socialism was originally separate from the *workers* as such but that it was originally separate from the *worker movement*. Individual workers such as Wilhelm Weitling could and did become socialists – but that very fact alienated them from the worker movement and kept them apart from the militant day-to-day struggle. An 'elemental' [*urwüchsig*] class instinct of hatred for the bourgeoisie made early worker socialists reject any doctrine coming from it. As a result, their own rough-hewn theories were crude and violent [*gewalttätig*]. Furthermore, despite their hostility to bourgeois intellectuals, they themselves had no real faith in the worker movement.

This early form of proletarian socialism lacked the patience and the confident sense of strength needed to contemplate a long, drawn-out class struggle. It remained a form of utopian socialism, only instead of hoping like earlier utopians for a bourgeois millionaire to bankroll the new Jerusalem, it placed its hopes on 'the Revolution' with a capital R that would give power to a small dictatorial group of visionaries. Any form of class struggle besides an immediate call to the barricades was perceived as a betrayal of 'mankind's cause'.

Usually such worker revolutionaries end up as anarchists, or, if they do join in the day-to-day class struggle, they forget about socialism altogether. This kind of 'elemental' revolutionary militancy is one of the growing pains [*Kinderkrankheit*] of a genuinely socialist worker movement, since it tends to

---

[95] Bellamy 1968, pp. 263–5 (this particular example of utopian socialism, originally published 1888, is not used by Kautsky).

crop up whenever recent backward recruits to the proletariat still lack 'clear insight' into social relations. The paradoxical conclusion of this discussion is that even a socialism that grew directly out of proletarian soil failed to overcome the gap between socialism and the worker movement.

How then to overcome the gap – indeed, conflict – between socialism and the worker movement? Kautsky provides the answer in a basic passage that brings together the *Communist Manifesto*, Social Democracy, and the logic of the merger formula. The following paragraph begins the climactic section entitled 'Social Democracy as the Merger of the Worker Movement and Socialism'.

> In order for the socialist and the worker movements to become reconciled and to become fused into a single movement, socialism had to break out of the utopian way of thinking. This was the world-historical deed of *Marx* and *Engels*. In the *Communist Manifesto* of 1847 they laid the scientific foundations of a new modern socialism, or, as we say today, of Social Democracy. By so doing, they gave socialism solidity and turned what had hitherto been a beautiful dream of well-meaning enthusiasts into a earnest object of struggle and [also] showed this to be the necessary consequence of economic development.[96] To the fighting proletariat they gave a clear awareness of its historical task and they placed it in a condition to speed to its great goal as quickly and with as few sacrifices as possible.
>
> The socialists no longer have the task of freely *inventing* a new society but rather of *uncovering* its elements in existing society. No more do they have to bring salvation from its misery to the proletariat from above, but rather they have to support its class struggle through increasing its insight and promoting its economic and political organisations and in so doing bring about as quickly and as painlessly as possible the day when the proletariat will be able to save itself. *The task of Social Democracy is to make the class struggle of the proletariat aware of its aim and capable of choosing the best means to attain this aim* [*zielbewusst und zweckmässig*].[97]

---

[96] 'Necessary' = *naturnotwendig*. Note the combination of will and determinism in this sentence that many commentators find so paradoxical but which Kautsky evidently saw as mutually supporting.

[97] Kautsky 1965, pp. 238–9.

The heroic contribution of Marx and Engels could only have come from people who had mastered all of modern 'scientific' political economy and extended it further – in other words, bourgeois intellectuals (albeit very exceptional ones). This is one reason for the failure of the early self-taught proletarian socialists. The *necessary* role of bourgeois intellectuals, however, begins and ends with Marx and Engels. Once the great insight is achieved, anybody can understand, accept and pass on the good news.

Furthermore, the great contribution of Marx and Engels should not be seen as a *rejection* but as a *synthesis* of what went before. As Kautsky put it later, each of the warring socialist sects contained a little bit of the truth, 'ein Stückchen des Richtigen'.[98] In what we can now see as a version of the 'sooner or later' argument, the contribution of Marx and Engels is to bring clarity and insight to what was previously instinctive groping.

> A glance at these beginnings [of early socialist organisations always reveals] a chaotic germ, an uncertain, instinctive seeking and groping of numerous proletarians, none perceptibly more prominent than the others, all moved forward on the whole by the same tendencies, but often displaying the most striking individual deviations. Such a picture is, for instance, presented by the beginnings of the proletarian socialistic movement in the thirties and forties of the nineteenth century. . . . Had it not been for Marx and Engels, the teachings [of the League of Communists] would have continued to remain in the stage of ferment for a long time. The two authors of the *Communist Manifesto* were only enabled to secure their dominant and determining position by virtue of their mastery of the science of their times.[99]

Kautsky's narrative stresses the original *separation* of socialism and the worker movement in order to bring out the absolute necessity of their *merger*. And this is not just an inspiring story of the past – it also defines the tasks of Social-Democratic polemics in the present. Even at the present time, some participants of both the worker movement and the socialist movement still refuse the great synthesis, with the result that even their little bit of truth becomes debased. What was pardonable one-sidedness in the past becomes dangerously harmful in the present.

---

[98] Kautsky 1908.
[99] Kautsky 1925 [1908], p. 442.

Thus, the merger narrative laid the foundation for a two-front polemical war aimed against all who defend the continued isolation of either socialism or the worker movement. The technical term within Social-Democratic discourse for the effort to keep the worker-class struggle free from socialism was *Nur-Gewerkschaftlerei*, 'trade-unions-only-ism'. A similar *'Nur'* term could have been coined for bomb-throwing revolutionaries who continued to think that it was a waste of time to try to propagandise and educate the worker class as a whole prior to the revolution.

These two enemies of Social Democracy are often invoked by means of national stereotypes. Over here, we see the frantic French anarchist or syndicalist who scorns parliamentary politics. Over there, we see the stolid British trade unionist who is a brilliant organiser but who openly rejects socialism. And, somewhere in the middle, the German Social Democrat who is both solidly organised *and* inspired by a high ideal.

If we only look at one front in this polemical war, we will come away with a equally one-sided view of the Social-Democratic outlook. This is the conclusion reached by Robert Stuart in his very useful study of the French Marxists led by Jules Guesde and Paul Lafargue. The standard comment on the French Marxists is that they flip-flopped back and forth between a sectarian hard-line and an opportunist soft line. After reading party literature throughout the period, Stuart stresses rather the *continuity* in outlook, once we take into account the Party's multiple targets.[100] One aim of my commentary is to bring out in a similar way the continuing two-front polemical war in Lenin's *Iskra*-era writings, very much including WITBD.

*Insight and organisation*

Now that we have witnessed the origins of the great synthesis, we can look closer at Social Democracy as the active force that works to bring about the merger. The key goals are summarised by the eloquent German words Kautsky used in the passage just cited, *zielbewusst* and *zweckmässig*, 'aware of one's aim' and 'capable of choosing the best means to attain it'. Or, as Kautsky elaborated in 1899,

---

[100] Stuart 1992. Unfortunately, Stuart's book does not take up the question of the influence of the SPD model or of Kautsky on French Marxists during this period.

> Social Democracy is the party of the militant proletariat; it seeks to enlighten
> it, to educate it, to organise it, to expand its political and economic power
> by every available means, to conquer every position that can possibly be
> conquered, and thus to provide it with the strength and maturity that will
> finally enable it to conquer political power and to overthrow the rule of the
> bourgeoisie.[101]

Out of Kautsky's extensive discussion of this topic, we will concentrate on
the themes with the most impact on Russian Social Democracy. These include
the primordial importance of political freedom; the strength that a clear final
goal gives to the struggle here and now; the high value given to party
organisation and discipline; the Social Democrats' own exalted sense of
mission.

The Social-Democratic mission of educating and organising on a national
level is crippled at the outset if political freedom is absent. Secret organisations
are a highly ineffectual substitute for 'open' [öffentlich, public] ones for purposes
of a nation-wide class struggle. The crucial weapon of the socialist press is
particularly dependent on political freedom.

> To bring these masses into contact with one another, to awaken their awareness
> of their broad community of interests and to win them over for organisations
> capable of protecting their interests – this implies the possibility of speaking
> freely to the great masses, this implies freedom of assembly and the press. . . .
> Without the help of the press, it is absolutely impossible to unite the huge
> masses of today's wage-labour into organisations and to get them to the
> level of unified action.[102]

For all these reasons and more, there is no worse sin from a Social-Democratic
point of view than to disparage the crucial role of political freedom:

> Where the working class bestirs itself, where it makes the first attempts to
> elevate its economic position, it puts political demands next to purely
> economic ones – namely, demands for freedom of association, of assembly,
> of the press. These freedoms have the greatest significance for the working
> class: they are among the conditions that makes its life possible and to which

---

[101] Cited by J. Kautsky 1994, p. 86.
[102] Kautsky 1965, p. 218.

it unconditionally owes its development. They are light and air for the proletariat; he who lets them wither or withholds them – he who keeps the proletariat from the struggle to win these freedoms and to extend them – that person is one of the proletariat's worst enemies. It doesn't matter how great a love for the proletariat he feels or fakes, it doesn't matter whether he calls himself an anarchist or a Christian-Socialist or whatever. He harms the proletariat just as much as a declared foe; it is all the same whether he does this from evil will or simply from ignorance – he must be fought against in the same way as acknowledged opponents of the proletariat.[103]

The history of the 'light and air' metaphor is a revealing one. It can be traced back at least to 1865, when Engels wrote 'The Prussian Military Question and the German Worker Party'. On the subject of proper relations to liberal bourgeois opposition to absolutism (a subject with obvious relevance to Russia), Engels gave this advice:

Even if the worst came to the worst and the bourgeoisie was to scurry under the skirts of reaction for fear of the workers and to appeal to the power of those elements hostile to itself for protection against the workers – even then the worker party would have no choice but, notwithstanding the bourgeoisie, to continue its agitation for bourgeois freedom, freedom of the press and rights of assembly and association which the bourgeoisie had betrayed. Without these freedoms it will be unable to move freely itself; in this fight it is fighting to establish its own life-element, to obtain the air it needs to breathe.[104]

In 1882, Engels wrote a letter to Kautsky in which he remarked

Polish socialists who fail to put the liberation of the country at the forefront of their programme remind me of those German socialists who were reluctant to demand the immediate repeal of the Anti-Socialist Law and freedom of association, assembly and the press. To be able to fight, you must first have a terrain, light, air and elbow-room. Otherwise you never get further than chit-chat.[105]

---

[103] Kautsky 1965, p. 219.
[104] Engels 1962a, p. 77.
[105] Letter of 7 February 1882 in *Marx Engels Werke*, Band 35, p. 270; *Marx Engels Collected Works*, vol. 20, p. 192.

Whether he got the phrase from 'The Prussian Military Question' or from Engels's letter, Kautsky used it when he wrote the *Erfurt Programme* in 1892. The Russian Social Democrats immediately understood its application to their own situation. In 1897, the underground Social-Democratic paper *Rabochaia gazeta* [*Worker Newspaper*] wrote:

> The Russian worker movement is still tightly held in the iron grip of governmental oppression. As a living being needs air, so we need *political freedom*. Without achieving freedom of strikes, assembly, unions, speech and press, without achieving the right to take part in the administration of the country or in making its laws, we will never cast off the chains of economic slavery that oppress us. That is why the struggle with the autocratic government for political freedom is the most urgent task of the Russian worker movement.[106]

In 1898, the abortive First Congress of the Russian Social-Democratic Worker Party (RSDWP) declared *Rabochaia gazeta* the official organ of the new party – although the paper was never able to publish another issue. The First Congress also issued an influential manifesto drafted by Petr Struve. In this document – the first official programmatic document of the RSDWP – we read that 'political freedom is as necessary for the Russian proletariat as fresh air is for healthy breathing. It is the fundamental condition for its free development and for its successful struggle both for partial improvements and final liberation'.[107] In the first issue of *Iskra* that came out in late 1900, the same point is hammered home using the same metaphor.[108] To complete the circle, Kautsky repeated the metaphor in his *Social Revolution* – published in 1902 and promptly translated into Russian with Lenin as editor.

We can now understand why it was fatal for a Russian Social Democrat to be labelled as an 'economist'. An individual or group who really did argue that political rights were unimportant, or that it was no part of Social Democracy's job to fight for them, or that political goals should be restricted to economic legislation – such a person, if the charge held, was not a 'moderate'

[106] Lead article from *Rabochaia gazeta* No. 2, November 1897, from a reprint of the article in Lenin 1958–65, 2nd edition, 2, pp. 612–15.

[107] Lenin 1926–35, 2, p. 616 (an English translation of the Manifesto of the First Congress can be found in Harding 1983).

[108] 'Achievements of International Social Democracy', *Iskra*, No. 1 (December 1900).

Social Democrat and certainly not (as some scholars seem to think) a more orthodox Marxist than his 'political' opponents. No, such a person had read himself out of Social Democracy altogether. 'He who lets political freedoms wither or withholds them – he who keeps the proletariat from the struggle to win these freedoms and to extend them – that person is one of the proletariat's worst enemies.'

Thus, a nation-wide political party – *not* nation-wide economic organisations – was the highest form of the class struggle. As Kautsky rather extravagantly defends the crucial role of a worker political party:

> The adherents of trades-union-only-ism are conservative even when they put on radical airs, while [in contrast] all worker parties are revolutionary by their very nature even when their attitude or indeed the awareness of their members is moderate.[109]

The creation of a nation-wide and effective organisation – whether political or economic – has implications that were rejected by anarchists and the old-style liberals of Kautsky's time but accepted by Social Democrats. The Social-Democratic movement requires 'permanent organs in the course of its growth, a sort of professional bureaucracy in the party, as well as in the unions, without which it cannot function, which are a necessity for it, which must continue to grow and to obtain duties that grow in importance'.[110] This bureaucracy consists not only of salaried officials but parliamentary representatives and party journalists.[111] Coupled with this functional division of labour is a spirit of discipline unique to a worker-class organisation.

These organisational imperatives were partly the result of the capitalist transformation of society and partly a necessary condition of *any* effective fighting organisation. 'One finds [these features] present any time that the large-scale masses are fighting for a weighty battle-prize and where victory can be won only with the strictest co-ordination and the most decisive unity of action all tending toward the same end'.[112] Thus Kautsky laughs at liberals who excoriate trade-union tyranny but who always vote at their party's call

---

[109] Kautsky 1900, p. 188.
[110] Kautsky 1925 [1908], p. 463.
[111] Kautsky 1925 [1908], pp. 464–6.
[112] Kautsky 1893, p. 42. In German, Kautsky calls for a combination of *Zusammenhalten* and *Zusammenwirken*.

and never think of thinking for themselves at all. Equally ridiculous are anarchists who sneer at the discipline of parliamentary parties while praising trade unions – proletarian trade unions! – as the home of unconstraint.

In order to combat the dangers inherent in this situation, representative democracy *within* the party is required. But representative democracy is in its way just another manifestation of a modern division of labour and the spirit of voluntary discipline. Any effective nation-wide political organisation will follow this imperative: 'our century is not only the century of parliamentarism but also the century of [party] congresses'.[113] Leave to the anarchists the absurdity of assembling in party congresses in order to denounce the inevitable corruption of representative democracy![114]

But worker-class parties have a better chance than others of keeping organisational bureaucracy under control precisely because of the proletarian sense of discipline. This sense of discipline does not only mean the workers are good at following orders – it also means that the workers will stand for no nonsense from party officials, parliamentarians and journalists. The class origin of party spokesmen is no predictor of their behaviour: middle-class activists have been among the workers' best defenders while worker activists have sometimes betrayed their class. What is crucial is the workers' ability to 'constantly oversee and influence' those who speak in their name.[115] Neither the middle classes nor the non-proletarian classes of the people (peasants and urban petty bourgeoisie) are capable of such organisational discipline.

Social-Democratic political organisations are powerful not only because they are modern large-scale organisations and not only because they are proletarian organisations that understand the value of discipline but also because they are *Social-Democratic* Parties and therefore inspired by a grand historical mission. Only a few years after the Erfurt Congress, Eduard Bernstein became notorious for his epigram 'The movement is everything, the final goal is nothing'. We can understand the horror occasioned by the epigram when

---

[113] Kautsky 1893, p. 79; Kautsky 1900, pp. 110–12.

[114] As Lenin observes in *WITBD* (1958–65, 6, pp. 142–3 [802–3]), there is a substantial overlap between Kautsky's defence of representative democracy within organisations and the similar defence mounted by Sidney and Beatrice Webb a few years later in *Industrial Democracy* (Webb, Sidney and Beatrice 1965 [1897]). I note that Kautsky's *Erfurt Programme* is listed in the Webbs' bibliography.

[115] Kautsky 1893, p. 109.

we look at the *Erfurt Programme* and *Parliamentarism* – both written prior to any revisionist controversy – and observe Kautsky's insistence that an inspiring final goal was a unique source of strength for the Party in its ongoing day-to-day struggle.

Any worker movement – especially when operating under the oppressive environment of semi-absolutist countries like Germany and Austria – is going to face heartbreaking defeats as well as victories. The only thing that can prevent these failures from wreaking devastating demoralisation is a firm sense of the big story in which all failures are no more than passing episodes. After the class struggle is transformed by 'the fusion of the socialist and the worker movement',

> the worker movement now has an aim to which it visibly comes closer, now all sides of the struggle are significant, including those that do not bring any immediate practical consequences, if only they further the self-awareness and prestige of the proletariat, its comradely unity and discipline. Now many battle that seems to end in defeat is equivalent to a victory, now every strike and every rejected legislative proposal that would have served the interests of the proletariat is a step forward toward the aim of achieving an existence worthy of mankind.[116]

Kautsky's mention of prestige and human dignity point to larger themes. Faced with the formidable self-righteousness of Victorian bourgeois civilisation, a worker political party faced a life-and-death problem of protecting what we might now call worker self-esteem. Kautsky argued that scientific socialism provided a goal that was superior in its sweep and generosity of vision to bourgeois parties. Not only that, it also provided the necessary confidence that this goal could and would be achieved. Thus only a firm sense of the final goal could give the workers self-respect and the respect of other classes.[117]

The final goal was also the only thing that made a unified nation-wide class party even feasible.

> What gives a political party cohesion – especially if, like the socialist party, it has a great historical task to fulfil – is the final goal. . . . There will always be differences of opinion within the party and sometimes these differences

---

[116] Kautsky 1965, pp. 241–2.
[117] Kautsky 1965, Section 12, pp. 238–42.

reach a disquieting intensity. But the more the great common goals really live in the awareness of party members, the less easily will these internal disputes cause party splits.[118]

The final goal is not just words inscribed on a banner. It imposes the obligation of learning to grasp the big picture. As Kautsky wrote in 1908:

> Today, in a society whose market embraces the entire world, a society which is in a process of constant transformation, of industrial and social revolution, in which the workers are organising themselves into an army of millions, and the capitalists are accumulating billions in money, it is impossible for a rising class – a class that cannot content itself with the retention of the *status quo* and that is obliged to aim at a complete reconstruction of society – to conduct its class struggle intelligently and successfully by a mere resort to 'plain common sense' and to the detail work of practical men.
>
> It becomes a necessity for every combatant to broaden his horizon through scientific understanding, to grasp the operation of great social forces in time and space, not in order to abolish the work in detail, or even relegate it to the background, but in order to align it in a definite relation with the social process as a whole.[119]

The dire consequences of the absence of a final goal are exemplified by the fate of the English workers. The power of individual trade unions was hardly compensation for the resulting narrowness of spirit that caused the 'worker aristocrats' who should have been the champions of the masses to act instead as their oppressors. Even more striking was the political helplessness of even these economically powerful workers. Writing in 1902 and citing the research of Beatrice and Sidney Webb, Kautsky stated that the impact of the English workers on British politics was in fact steadily decreasing.

> Even the latest scourgings by their opponents have not served to rouse the proletariat of England. They remain dumb, even when their unions are rendered powerless, dumb when their bread is made more costly. The English workers today stand lower as a political factor than the workers of the most economically backward and the least politically free country in Europe –

---

[118] Kautsky 1900, p. 183 (written before Bernstein's 'revisionism').
[119] Kautsky 1925, pp. 16–17.

Russia. It is their thriving revolutionary awareness that give the Russian workers their great practical strength. It is the renunciation of revolution, the narrowing of interest to the interests of the moment, their so-called *Realpolitik*, that have made the English workers a nullity in actual politics.[120]

If the inspiring final goal was so vital for effective worker-class influence, then the mandate for Social Democrats was clear: it is

> the duty of every man who has made the advancement of the proletariat his life work, to oppose this tendency toward spiritual stagnation and stupidity, and to direct the attention of proletarians to great points of view, to large prospects, to worthy goals.[121]

This comment leads us to one final aspect of Kautsky's outlook: the insistence not only on the proletariat's but also on Social Democracy's own high and inspiring mission. Just as the Social-Democratic narrative gave strength to the workers to fight against seemingly hopeless odds, it also gave strength to the Social-Democratic activists who devoted themselves to their *Kleinarbeit*, the seemingly insignificant detail work needed to run the impressive party machinery.

> To lead the economic and political class struggle – to carry out enthusiastically one's small duties but also to fill them with thoughts of a wide-encompassing socialism – to bring together by these means the organisations and activities of the proletariat, in a unified and harmonious way, into a massive whole that rises up ever more irresistible – this is what Marx and Engels taught was the task of anyone, whether proletarian or not, who adopts the viewpoint of the proletariat and wishes to liberate it.[122]

We end this section with the final words of Kautsky's *Path to Power*, written in 1909 and much admired by Lenin. This kind of exalted rhetoric rarely makes it into secondary accounts, yet it is a vital part of the context for a book like WITBD.

> Already today the élite [of the proletariat] forms the strongest, the most far-sighted, most selfless and boldest stratum – the one united in the largest

---

[120] Kautsky 1902, p. 55.
[121] Kautsky 1925, pp. 16–17.
[122] Kautsky 1908, p. 37.

free organisations – of the nations of European culture. And in the same way the proletariat will, in and through struggle, take up into itself the most selfless and farsighted elements of all classes; it will organise and educate in its own bosom even its own most backward elements and fill them with the joy of hope and with insight. Its élite will be raised up to the height of culture, making it capable of leading the immense economic transformation that will finally, throughout the whole world, put an end to the misery that arises out of slavery, exploitation and ignorance.

Happy are they who are called to take part in this high struggle and this glorious victory![123]

### Leadership of the people (the hegemony scenario)

Social Democracy, Kautsky tells us, has a tendency

to become more and more a *national* party – that is, a *Volkspartei*, in the sense that it is the representative not only of the industrial wage-labourers but of all the labouring and exploited strata – and therefore the great majority of the population, what is commonly known as 'the *Volk*'.[124]

This feature of the Social-Democratic narrative was overwhelmingly important for Russian Social Democracy.

Social Democracy will ultimately be able to lead the non-industrial labouring classes because socialism is in the interest of *all* labouring classes. But this long-term perspective does not exhaust the potential for leadership of the *Volk* in the here and now. Precisely because Social Democracy is the merger of socialism and the worker movement, it is not restricted to preaching socialism and defending worker interests.

Social Democracy cannot defend exclusively the interests of the proletariat. Its historical mission is to precipitate social evolution in every domain in which it can act, and to take in its hands the cause of all the exploited and all the oppressed.[125]

---

[123] Kautsky 1909, p. 104.
[124] Kautsky 1965, p. 250.
[125] Kautsky 1900, p. 165.

Thus Social Democracy encourages the proletariat to see itself as 'the sworn enemy of any exploitation or oppression, in whatever form they might take – it is the champion [*Vorkämpfer*] of all exploited and oppressed'.[126]

What this means in concrete terms is that Social Democracy can defend the *present-day, acknowledged* interests of all labouring classes better than any other party. These interests are enshrined in the so-called 'minimum programme'. The logic of the minimum programme would be easier to grasp if it were called the *maximum* programme – that is, the maximum that can be achieved prior to proletarian rule. (Conversely, the logic of the so-called 'maximum programme' is that it contains the *minimum* that has to be realistically achievable before the worker class is justified in taking power.) 'Minimum' indeed seems a misleading epithet for a set of measures that would have entailed a vast political and social transformation of Imperial Germany: full representative democracy, full political liberties, religious tolerance, 'socialised' medicine, progressive tax, labour protection laws. This list also shows how justified the SPD was in regarding itself as the principal voice of the ethical decency of modernism in Imperial Germany. According to Kautsky, some of these demands can only be championed by an anticapitalist party. Others are officially part of the programme of 'bourgeois democracy', that is, those sections of the middle classes that are actively (or at least publicly) interested in democratic transformation. But – and this is a crucial observation – 'even the bourgeois-democratic demands will not be championed by any party with as much energy as by Social Democracy'.[127]

Along with Social Democracy's role as the champion of the interests of all labouring classes as a whole is the influence that results as the proletarian way of life becomes more of a model for other classes. I have already cited Kautsky on this point, so I will document this aspect of the Social-Democratic narrative with some words written in 1898 by Parvus, a Russian-born Social-Democratic activist who was at this time an influential spokesman for the SPD Left:

> The overwhelming majority of the population are in industry, trade, etc.
> These are therefore the people who determine the *economic character* of the

---

[126] Kautsky 1965, p. 251.
[127] Kautsky 1965, pp. 254–6.

country. This is not merely a matter of numerical superiority; it means that this industrial urban population with its interests, conflicts, views, and demands dominates the historical character of Germany, brings all other things under its sway, shapes them in its own likeness, makes them dependent upon itself, and, inevitably, establishes its moral hegemony over them by the vast tide of public opinion it generates.[128]

The reader will notice that Parvus used the word 'hegemony' in the passage just quoted. This allows us to segue nicely into the political strategy labelled 'hegemony' by the Russian Social Democrats. Our interest is much more in the logic of this political strategy than in the word used to label it (for a word-history of 'hegemony', see the appendix to this chapter). 'Hegemony' was used to describe Social-Democratic hopes for inter-class leadership in the Russian context. The core idea of the hegemony strategy is that the Russian *proletariat* is the only force capable of leading the *bourgeois*-democratic revolution that would overthrow the tsar. As Plekhanov put it in 1889, 'The Russian revolution [Plekhanov means the anti-tsarist revolution] will either triumph as a revolution of the worker class or it will not triumph at all'.[129]

This strategy has struck many as a surprising, even paradoxical, one for Marxists to adopt. According to the Marxist schema, it is said, the bourgeois revolution is carried out by the bourgeoisie – otherwise, why label it a 'bourgeois revolution'? – while the proletariat carries out the socialist revolution at a later date. What I want to show here is that the hegemony strategy follows – perhaps even with natural necessity – from the accepted premises of Social-Democratic thinking that I have already described. In fact, the appropriate conclusions from these premises were already drawn by Kautsky in his book on parliamentarism in 1893.[130]

Premise Number One is that political freedom is an absolute necessity for Social Democracy. From this premise, it follows that 'in countries where there

---

[128] Tudor and Tudor 1988, p. 182, originally published in *Sächsische Arbeiter-Zeitung*, 6 February 1898, as part of a series directed against Bernstein. I have consulted only the English translation provided by the Tudors and therefore I am not absolutely certain that 'hegemony' appears in the German text.

[129] Zinoviev 1924, p. 54. On the basis of this statement, Zinoviev labels Plekhanov the father of the idea of the hegemony of the proletariat.

[130] Kautsky 1893 and Kautsky 1900 (French translation). All further Kautsky citations in this section are from this book.

is only a pretend parliamentary régime [*Scheinkonstitutionalismus*], another weighty task falls to the proletariat: the conquest of a genuinely parliamentary régime'.[131] Perhaps, before the rise of Social Democracy, a revolutionary could really believe that a parliamentary régime would only benefit the élite and not the people, but 'today it becomes clearer every day that [the struggle for proletarian political power] takes the form, at least in the east of Europe, of a struggle for a parliamentary régime, against militarism and absolutism'.[132]

Premise Number Two is that the people as a whole also have an interest in the political freedom that will protect them from abuse of power. Of course, Social Democracy is the force that will most effectively use political freedom to fight abuses. A parliamentary system – even such a 'servile and weak' one as Austria – ensures that a single 'inflexible and brave' individual can throw the glare of publicity on abuses and set a certain limit to arbitrary action. Parliament provides 'a tribune from whose height the accusers of present-day society can speak to the entire people'.[133]

Premise Number Three is that the bourgeoisie's interest in political freedom goes down as the proletariat's interest in it goes up. The bourgeoisie certainly would not mind having political freedom for themselves, and they have no qualms about enlisting proletarian help in getting these freedoms – *as long as* the bourgeoisie can be sure that the proletariat will not use them in a dangerous way. Perhaps the proletariat can simply be banned from political participation, as in France after 1830, or perhaps the bourgeoisie feels unthreatened by a docile proletariat, as in England.

But the bourgeoisie has begun to notice, correctly, that it can no longer exploit the revolutionary services of the proletariat in this way. In fact, the evident success of Social Democracy makes political freedom itself rather less attractive. For German Social Democrats, it was axiomatic that the cowardly bourgeoisie had betrayed their own cause after 1848. As Kirkup recounts:

> It is a standing charge brought against German liberalism by the Social
> Democrats, that it has never led the progressive forces against the reaction
> with any degree of courage or resolution. They maintain that in the

---

[131] Kautsky 1900, p. 166.
[132] Kautsky 1893, p. 138; Kautsky 1900, pp. 193–4.
[133] Kautsky 1900, p. 105. Lenin explicitly wanted the newspaper *Iskra* to be a temporary substitute for parliament as a tribune that could address the whole people.

revolutionary struggles of 1848 the German Liberals never trusted the working class, that when the choice came to be made between the reaction and a strenuous democratic policy supported by the proletariat, they preferred to transact with the reaction, and so committed treason on the sacred cause of progress . . . 'The treason of the bourgeoisie', 'the abdication by the bourgeoisie' of its historic place at the head of the democratic movement: these phrases sum up the worst accusations brought by the Social Democrats against the German middle class.[134]

Kautsky generalised the failure of the German bourgeoisie with the following epigram:

> In fact, the European bourgeoisie east of the Rhine has become so weak and so cowardly that in all likelihood the regime of the sabre and of the bureaucracy cannot be broken until the proletariat is in a position to conquer political power, so that the fall of absolutist militarism will lead directly to the seizure of political power by the proletariat.[135]

Put all these premises together, and we see that 'Social Democracy, the party of the class-aware proletariat, is by that very fact the most solid support of democratic aspirations, a much more reliable support than – the [bourgeois] democrats themselves'.[136] The Social-Democratic proletariat was the most reliable supporter of democracy *because* it saw democracy not as an end in itself but as a means – an absolutely vital means. Social Democracy would love democracy less, loved it not socialism more.

The Russians may have been the first to use the word 'hegemony' to describe proletarian leadership in the bourgeois revolution, but the strategy itself was impeccably Social-Democratic. The basic idea was simply this: bourgeois

---

[134] Kirkup 1906, pp. 200–2. Compare the comment by Michels on German liberalism's 'partisan struggle against socialism and its simultaneous and voluntary renunciation of all attempts to complete the political emancipation of the German bourgeoisie' (Michels 1962, pp. 49–50).

[135] Kautsky 1900, p. 194. Compare this statement from the Manifesto issued by the Russian Social-Democratic Worker Party at its first congress in 1898: 'The further east we go in Europe, the more weak, cowardly and base becomes the bourgeoisie in regard to politics and the greater are the cultural and political tasks that fall to the lot of the proletariat.' *Kommunisticheskaia partiia . . . v rezoliutsiiakh* 1983, pp. 15–18. If he had been so minded, Lenin could have cited this statement in justification of the Bolshevik revolution in 1917.

[136] Kautsky 1900, p. 194.

political freedoms are much too important to be left to the bourgeoisie. The bourgeoisie would try to exploit the revolutionary services of the proletariat to get as much for themselves and as little for the labouring classes as possible. A proletariat led by Social Democracy would instead lead the whole people to ensure the most extensive democratic constitution available. Political freedom made Social Democracy possible and it was therefore the duty of Social Democracy to make political freedom possible.

According to the hegemony scenario, Social Democracy assumes leadership not just of the worker movement and of the proletariat, but the people [das Volk, the narod] as a whole. Thus we find ourselves now in the outer circles of the spread of awareness. The battle for leadership is more difficult in these outer circles. There is more incomprehension, vacillation and even hostility. The resulting complex set of expectations is brought out in a passage written by Kautsky in the 1920s:

> As the mass, the economic importance, and the intelligence of the industrial population grow, so too does the attraction exerted by the proletariat on strata of the people that do not entirely belong to it but are close to it with respect to their standard of living and their economic relations. This attraction becomes the stronger, the greater the intellectual and organisational independence and unity of the proletariat are. . . .
>
> The classes in society are in reality not so rigorously distinct as they have to be in theory. . . . Thus, there are numerous intermediate grades between the class of wage-labourers and the other working classes, peasants, artisans, and petty trades, just as there are between them and the intellectuals. Vacillating between the proletariat and capital, individual members and even whole groups of these classes and strata decide more in favour of or against the proletariat, depending on particular personal influences, historical situations, and economic constellations. Thus, a part of the peasants, petty bourgeois, and intellectuals can become ever more bitterly antagonistic to the proletariat. A constantly growing part, especially of the poorer strata, will be drawn to the proletariat and make the proletarian cause its own. . . . In this way, too, the mass army grows that marches under the proletariat banner.[137]

---

[137] Kautsky 1988, p. 409. If this commentary aimed at providing a full account of

## Social Democracy as good news

We have canvassed Karl Kautsky's pronouncements on a number of topics and we shall see echoes of all of them in Lenin's writings. The power of these pronouncements does not stem merely from Kautsky's authoritative status. His various opinions are unified and anchored in three ways: by the narrative logic of the merger formula, by the authority of the *Communist Manifesto*, and by the prestige of actually existing Social Democracy in Germany. We might even say that, for a reader such as Lenin, the *Communist Manifesto* and the *Erfurt Programme* stand in a Old Testament/New Testament relation to each other. The New Testament tells us a story that is supposed to govern our lives and then backs up this claim by arguing that the events of the story have unfolded *secundum scripturas*, as predicted by earlier authoritative writings. The *Erfurt Programme* tells an idealised version of the story of the SPD – past, present and future – as a confirmation of the predictions of the *Communist Manifesto*. In this way, it strengthens the authoritative status both of the *Manifesto* and the SPD model.

The merger formula – 'Social Democracy is the merger of socialism and the worker movement' – pulls all Kautsky's various arguments together. The expanding circle of awareness, the original and nearly fatal separation of socialism and the worker movement, the two-front polemical war against those who refuse the great Marxian synthesis, political freedom as light and air for the proletariat, the strength that comes from an inspiring final goal, the need for disciplined modern parties of nation-wide scope, the aspiration to become a *Volkspartei*, the need to carry out the democratic tasks that the bourgeois is too scared to undertake, and finally, Social Democracy's own exalted sense of mission – all these flow from the merger narrative. In order for the worker class to accomplish its socialist mission, it must understand this mission and make itself capable of overcoming all resistance to its completion. Social Democracy can provide the requisite insight and organisation only if it builds up an efficient nation-wide organisation. It can only do this if it has obtained political freedom. Political freedom, along with the many

---

Bolshevism, we would have to go into the subject of inter-class leadership in much greater detail. In particular, the figure of the vacillating peasant or urban petty bourgeois is central to the Bolshevik view of the world. I have examined various aspects of inter-class leadership in Bolshevik doctrine in Lih 1999, Lih 2000 and Lih 2002.

other demands of the 'minimum programme', allows and indeed compels Social Democracy to become a tribune of the people.

The merger formula was not confined to Kautsky. In fact, if there was one thing that united both orthodox and 'opportunist', it was loyalty to the merger formula as a definition of Social Democracy. A brief survey will bring out the foundational nature of the merger formula.

Conrad Schmidt was a member of the German Social-Democratic Party who leaned toward revisionism. In an article devoted to showing the many ways in which the *Communist Manifesto* had become dated, he started off with an appreciation of its fundamental contribution (NB: 'modern socialism' is a synonym for 'Social Democracy'):

> The essence of modern socialism lies in the *connection* between the working class movement and a final goal *beyond* bourgeois-capitalist society. Modern socialism found itself faced, firstly, with a spontaneous working class movement which had arisen as a reaction to unrestricted capitalist exploitation and, secondly, with the conception of collectively organised production and distribution of goods, which had arisen outside the mainstream of practical life, from criticism of the irrationality of bourgeois property. What socialism achieved was the combination and mutual interaction of both these moments, an interaction which stripped the actual working class movement of its native limitations and the socialist idea of its utopian character. The materialist conception of history . . . provided the conceptual means of achieving this reconstructive combination.[138]

In 1908, our American socialist Robert Hunter published an informative and useful survey of the European socialist movement. In this book, he looks into the conflict within Social Democracy between 'Marxists' and 'reformists', but he insisted that there was still a fundamental difference between committed

---

[138] Tudor and Tudor 1988, pp. 205–10 (originally published in *Vorwärts*, 20 February 1899). I do not know what German word is here translated as 'spontaneous'. Note this statement by Bernstein himself in 1898: 'We talk of "proletarian" ideas. And the way this is sometimes presented in our literature suggests that these ideas are not merely accepted by a large section of the workers of all civilised countries but were actually first *produced* by the intelligence of the modern working class. But this is at best a metaphor, an ideological inversion of the actual process. . . . Just think how much ideology is required for workers to see themselves as proletarians!' (Tudor and Tudor 1988, pp. 233–9).

Social Democrats of either camp and socialists such as the Fabians who thought they could dispense with an independent political organisation of the proletariat. To bring out the fundamental difference, he cited with approval the words of the 'reformist' Jean Jaurès, one of the leaders of the French Socialist party. The reader will find little that is new in Jaurès's words, but some repetition is inevitable when one wants to document the existence of a commonplace:

> To Marx belongs the merit, perhaps the only one of all attributed to him that has fully withstood the trying tests of criticism and of time, of having drawn together and unified the labour movement and the socialist idea. In the first third of the nineteenth century, labour struggled and fought against the crushing power of capital, but it was not conscious itself toward what end it was straining; it did not know that the true objective of its efforts was the common ownership of property. And, on the other hand, socialism did not know that the labour movement was the living form in which its spirit was embodied, the concrete practical force of which it stood in need. . . . [Marx] enriched the practical movement by the idea, and to the theory he added practice; he brought the socialist thought into proletarian life, and proletarian life into socialist thought.[139]

I have just given the words of a Frenchman as cited by a contemporaneous American, and now I will give the words of a Belgian, Emile Vandervelde, as cited by a contemporaneous Russian: 'The theory of socialism, born of compassion, remained divided from day-to-day socialism, born of suffering. It required long years, full of heavy ordeals, for the thinkers and proletarians to join forces and extend a hand to each other.' The Russian Social Democrat who cited these words, Vladimir Akimov, did not himself like the emphasis on separation, but nevertheless acknowledged that 'this image has been used repeatedly as a figurative description of the development of the social labour movement'.[140]

The merger narrative was used as a template for developments in Russia by Iulii Martov when he published a pioneering historical sketch of the struggle of the Russian proletariat in 1900. The work begins with the words

---

[139] Hunter 1908, pp. 206–7.
[140] Akimov 1969, p. 118. The Vandervelde citation is from 1898.

'The contemporary international socialist worker movement consists of two streams that for a long time developed independently of each other'. There follows a very familiar account of Western developments lifted from Kautsky's *Erfurt Programme*, ending with the consummation devoutly to be wished:

> Socialism came to the economic movement of the worker class, it took on itself the task of becoming the expression of the common interests of this class movement. And meanwhile the worker movement came to socialism: the worker masses started to see in socialism the final aim of their own historical movement. Thus took place the fusion of the practical worker movement with theoretical thought – thus was realised what Lassalle called the union of science with the workers. The idea of socialism became the idea of the worker class, the socialist party became its advance detachment [or 'vanguard'].
>
> This is how things turned out in all countries. Speaking of the history of the Russian revolutionary movement, we also must trace both the development of the economic struggle of the worker masses and the development of socialist thought up to the moment when it became the patrimony of the proletariat.[141]

In the rest of the pamphlet, Martov traces the intermingling of socialism and the worker movement in a way that brings out both the canonical essence and the local peculiarities of the Russian story. Thus, in absolutist Russia the Social Democrats themselves had to take over much of the job that trade unions and the like had done in the West, namely, 'to give an organised and sensible character to the *stikhiinyi* [elemental] worker movement'. The trust earned by the Social Democrats in this line of activity helped them in their more basic task of

> sowing in the masses an awareness of the class interests of the proletariat, of the necessity of uniting in the struggle for socialism, and of the necessity of conquest of political freedom as the first stage on the path to the full liberation from exploitation.[142]

We have seen the merger narrative's canonical status endorsed in various ways by a Czech, a German, a Belgian, an American, a Frenchman and a

---

[141] Martov 1900, pp. 27, 30.
[142] Martov 1900, pp. 92–3.

Russian. I believe we may consider as established its role as a central part of international Social Democracy's doctrinal identity.

The aim of this chapter has been to provide the Social-Democratic context for *WITBD*. Today, when scholars can affirm that the *Communist Manifesto* was neglected by Kautsky and by Social Democrats in general or that Marx was nihilistic about political freedom, the view of Social Democracy presented here may be surprising. A hundred years ago, it was a commonplace to any informed observer. To bring this out, I will conclude this chapter by looking at the spirit of Social Democracy through the eyes of two observers, one from the beginning and the other towards the end of the era of pre-World-War Social Democracy.

These two passages will anchor my 'good news' interpretation of Social Democracy. According to this interpretation, the self-appointed mission of Social Democracy was to bring the good news of their world-historical mission to the workers in the confident expectation that they would receive the message and carry out the mission. The first passage by John Rae reveals the Marxian roots of the political strategy implied by Social Democracy's mission and the second passage by Robert Hunter reveals the emotional exaltation that surrounded the mission.

John Rae was a learned economic historian who wrote one of the first scholarly biographies of Adam Smith, from which we may accurately deduce his hostility to socialism. Nevertheless, his 1884 publication *Contemporary Socialism* contains a chapter on Karl Marx that must be one of the very first academic discussions of Marx in any language – and, in my opinion, an excellent one (in particular due to his recognition of the importance of Marx's Young-Hegelian background). In the first edition of 1884, Rae noted that it was remarkable that the works of Marx were so little known in England even as they stirred up a commotion as far away as Russia, especially since *Das Kapital* is so imbued with things English. But an English translation of *Das Kapital* had appeared in 1887, leading Rae to remark in the second edition of 1891 that 'we have therefore grown more familiar of late with the name and importance of Karl Marx'.[143] In his chapter on Marx he quotes Marx's criticism of the original outlook of the Communist League (the organisation for which he drafted the *Communist Manifesto*):

---

[143] Rae 1891, pp. 128–9.

its work could have no tenable theoretical basis except that of a scientific insight into the economic structure of society, and this ought to be put into a popular form, not with the view of carrying out any utopian system, but of promoting among the working classes and other classes a self-conscious participation in the process of historical transformation of society that was taking place under their eyes.[144]

Rae comments that 'this is always with Marx the distinctive and ruling feature of his system'. After noting Marx's belief in inevitable economic evolution, he describes at length the practical political strategy implied in Marx's system. I cite this passage *in extenso*, not only because I think it one of the best things ever written by an academic scholar about Marx but because it proves that even in 1884, the year after Marx's death, when German Social Democracy was still struggling to come into existence, the political strategy that inspired Lenin was clearly apparent to an attentive reader of Marx.

Marx thought the League should also change its method and tactics. Its work, being that of social revolution, was different from the work of the old political conspirators and secret societies, and therefore needed different weapons; the times, too were changed, and offered new instruments. Street insurrections, surprises, intrigues, *pronunciamentos* might overturn a dynasty, or oust a government, or bring them to reason, but were of no avail in the world for introducing collective property or abolishing wage labour. People would just begin the day after to work for hire and rent their farms as they did before.

A social revolution needed other and larger preparation; it needed to have the whole population first thoroughly leavened with its principles; nay, it needed to possess an international character, depending not on detached local outbreaks, but on steady concert in revolutionary action on the part of the labouring classes everywhere. The cause was not political, or even national, but social; and society – which was indeed already pregnant with the change – must be aroused to a conscious consent to the delivery.

What was first to be done, therefore, was to educate and move public opinion, and in this work the ordinary secret society went but a little way.

---

[144] Rae 1884, p. 127. The passage comes from Marx's *Herr Vogt* (Marx 1984, p. 107). Rae's translation is rather free but (I believe) does not betray the spirit of Marx's point.

A secret propaganda might still be carried on, but a public and open propaganda was more effectual and more suitable to the times. There never existed greater facilities for such a movement, and they ought to make use of all the abundant means of popular agitation and intercommunication which modern society allowed. No more secret societies in holes and corners, no more small risings and petty plots, but a great broad organisation working in open day, and working restlessly by tongue and pen to stir the masses of all European countries to a common international revolution. Marx sought, in short, to introduce the large system of production into the art of conspiracy.[145]

I present the next passage by Robert Hunter with some hesitation. I read it out in 2001 at a conference on *WITBD* in Essen, Germany, and was told later that I was perceived as making a hysterical attack on Lenin. I was also told that any comparison between Marxism and religion was nothing but a typical bourgeois ploy. But, speaking as a historian, I say that the emotional fervour and dedication evoked by this passage was an essential part of Social Democracy, very much including the Russian Social Democrat Lenin. Anyone who is embarrassed by Hunter's rhetoric will also be embarrassed by the Marxist Left at the turn of the nineteenth and twentieth centuries. But my motive in bringing the passage forth here is not to make the should-be-banal point that the socialism of this era can be compared to religious belief in its intensity and its demands (a point that the revolutionaries themselves often made). I rather want to demonstrate how this socialist fervour expressed itself in the story of the inspired and inspiring activist who is spreading the word of Social Democracy and by this means is building up a world-wide army of fighters for the cause.

Almost unknown to the world outside of Labour a movement wide as the universe grows and prospers. Its vitality is incredible, and its humanitarian ideals come to those who labour as drink to parched throats. Its creed and programme call forth a passionate adherence, its converts serve it with a daily devotion that knows no limit of sacrifice, and in the face of persecution, misrepresentation, and even martyrdom, they remain loyal and true.... From Russia, across Europe and America to Japan, from Canada to Argentina,

---

[145] Rae 1884, pp. 127–9.

it crosses frontiers, breaking through the barriers of language, nationality, and religion as it spreads from factory to factory, from mill to mill, and from mine to mine, touching as it goes with the religion of life the millions of the underworld.

Its converts work in every city, town and hamlet in the industrial nations, spreading the new gospel among the poor and lowly, who listen to their words with religious intensity. Tired workmen pore over the literature which these missionaries leave behind them, and fall to sleep over open pages; and the youth, inspired by its lofty ideals and elevated thought, leave the factory with joyous anticipation to read through the night.[146]

## Appendix on 'hegemony'

Given the notoriety of the term today, the following history – although, I stress, highly speculative – might be of interest to readers. According to the *Oxford English Dictionary*'s account of late nineteenth-century usage, 'hegemony' meant most particularly the leadership deriving from a predominant position of one state in a confederacy or union of states. Applied originally to ancient Greece, it was transferred thence to the multi-state system of pre-imperial Germany. In 1860, the *Times* wrote 'it is no doubt a glorious ambition which drives Prussia to assert her claim to the leadership, or as that land of professors phrases it, the "hegemony" of the Germanic confederation'.[147] Of course, Social Democrats were greatly interested in the Prussian question – indeed, it was a principal bone of contention between the Lassalleans who favoured German unification under Prussian auspices and the Bebel-Liebknecht group who opposed it. So, the word was a natural one to use when evoking the influence of the worker class beyond the borders of the urban industrial workers, as in the Parvus citation above. In 1900, the French translation of Kautsky's *Parliamentarism* used it to translate Kautsky's description of the confident class domination of the English bourgeoisie.[148]

The first Russian to apply the word to Social-Democratic political strategy seems to have been Pavel Akselrod in the late 1890s. Akselrod's use of the

---

[146] Hunter 1908, pp. v–vi. Compare to Lassalle's rhetoric half a century earlier.
[147] Oxford English Dictionary, s.v. 'hegemony'.
[148] Kautsky 1900, pp. 56, 146.

*term* should not, of course, suggest that he originated the *strategy*. The credit here belongs to Plekhanov. Lenin later defined Bolshevism as the faction most loyal to the original strategy of hegemony, and his close lieutenants Kamenev and Zinoviev imbibed this respectful use of the term. After the 1917 revolution, Zinoviev made hegemony the centrepiece of his own exposition of Leninism and even described the dictatorship of the proletariat as the hegemony strategy applied *after* taking power. As head of the Communist International, Zinoviev no doubt expounded the conception to Comintern activists such as Antonio Gramsci. Gramsci's use of the word – when rediscovered decades later – started it off on its way to its present eminence (although, in my own opinion of Gramsci's usage, the originality of his concept and its alleged anti-Leninist thrust have been greatly overestimated). As we look over the history of the term, we are struck by the movement over time from a confident and even daring set of connotations ('we can use proletarian influence over other classes to achieve great aims') to a fearful and pessimistic set ('the influence of the bourgeoisie over even the proletariat keeps us from achieving very much').

# Chapter Two

# A Russian Erfurtian

*Our outlook is this: we share all the fundamental
ideas of Marxism (as they are expressed in the*
Communist Manifesto *and in the programmes
of the West European Social Democrats).*

(Lenin, 1900)

One episode in the overarching narrative of the
proletariat's world-historical mission was the story
of Social Democracy, the merger of socialism and the
worker movement. The basic plot content of this
episode was Social Democracy's efforts to bring
insight and organisation to the proletariat. It is time
now to go down one narrative level and examine
Russian Social Democracy as one episode in the story
of international Social Democracy.

Russian Social Democracy traced its roots back to
the early 1880s and the programmes and polemics
of the émigré Emancipation of Labour group led
by Georgii Plekhanov. But Social Democracy as a
practical movement within Russia itself only got
going in the 1890s. Throughout the 1890s, one
member of the small band of committed Social
Democrats within Russia had a special interest in
coming up with programmatic statements that tried
to set forth the aims and outlook of the Party as a
whole. Since these statements focused on Social-
Democratic consensus, they provide the best starting
place for our search for Russian Social Democracy's
narrative self-definition.

Conveniently for our purposes, this avid programme writer was Lenin himself. The bulk of the first four volumes of his collected works are devoted to polemics with populists and studies of Russian agriculture, including his magnum opus *The Development of Capitalism in Russia* (1899). Scattered among these weighty studies is a group of smaller writings whose aim was to define Social Democracy.[1] Twice Lenin actually drafted party programmes along with commentary. Other writings responded to attacks on Russian Social Democracy by affirming basic principles. A third group of writings in 1899 was aimed at fellow Social Democrats, but the brunt of Lenin's case was that his opponents had stepped outside the fundamental Social-Democratic consensus. (See Table 2.1 for a list of writings discussed in this chapter.)

### Table 2.1
### List of Lenin's Programmatic Writings in the 1890s

1. *Who are These 'Friends of the People' and How Do They Fight Against the Social Democrats?* (1894)
2. 'Friedrich Engels' (1895)
3. 'Draft and Explanation of a Programme for the Social-Democratic Party' (Prison Programme Draft) (1895–6)
4. *Tasks of the Russian Social Democrats* (1897)
5. Protest Writings (1899)
   a. 'A Protest by Russian Social Democrats' (against Kuskova's *Credo*)
   b. 'A Retrograde Trend in Russian Social Democracy' (against *Rabochaia mysl*)
   c. 'Apropos of the *Profession de foi*' (against a statement issued by the Kiev Social Democratic Committee)
6. Articles for *Rabochaia gazeta* (1899)
   a. 'Our Programme'
   b. 'Our Immediate Task'
   c. 'An Urgent Question'
7. 'A Draft Programme for our Party' (1899)

What should we expect to find in these writings? To sharpen this question, I introduce the label 'Erfurtian'. I want to avoid the usual diffuse discussions

---

[1] One of the few writers to take Lenin's programmatic efforts seriously is Paul Le Blanc (Le Blanc 1990).

about whether Lenin was an orthodox Marxist or Social Democrat. Let us consider the case of a young Russian revolutionary trying to find a secure political orientation around the time (1891) that the SPD was holding its Erfurt Congress in an atmosphere of triumph for having emerged from Bismarck's anti-socialist persecution even stronger than before. Such a Russian revolutionary might well be inspired by this massive and imposing Marxist party. He might well have become an Erfurtian, which we define as someone who (a) accepts the SPD party that met at Erfurt as a model in both organisation and activity; (b) accepts the programme adopted by the Erfurt Congress as a model Social-Democratic programme; (c) accepts Kautsky's commentary on the Erfurt Programme as authoritative.

The material presented in the previous chapter leads us to expect to find the following in the programmatic writings of a Russian Erfurtian in the 1890s:

(i) *Erfurt allegiance.* An explicit acknowledgement of the three sources of authority: the party, the programme, Kautsky's writings.

(ii) *Merger formula.* A commitment to the merger formula ('Social Democracy is the merger of socialism and the worker movement'). This commitment shows itself in (a) the merger account of the origins of Social Democracy and (b) the two-front polemical war against those who refuse the merger.

(iii) *Good news.* A definition of Social Democracy's mission as spreading the good news of the workers' world-historical mission. This definition further implies (a) a political strategy aimed at bringing insight and organisation to the worker class; (b) a commitment to the 'circles of awareness' model of the labouring classes; (c) confidence that the workers will respond to the message.

(iv) *Party ideal.* An aspiration to establish an independent class-based political party. Such a party will have a clear commitment to the final goal of socialism, it will be centralised and disciplined, it will be as democratic as possible, and it will be organised on a nation-wide scale, making effective use of specialisation and division of labour, including full-time officials.

(v) *Political freedom.* An insistence on the urgent priority of achieving political freedom, which in Russia means overthrowing the autocracy.

(vi) *Popular leadership.* An expectation that the Social-Democratic Party will be able to become a party of the whole people.

(vii) *Hegemony*. A commitment to the hegemony strategy. Precisely because the first priority of the workers is to achieve socialism, they are the natural leaders in the national struggle for political freedom.

(viii) *Internationalism*. An aspiration to join and be worthy members of the international Social-Democratic movement.

Using this checklist, we shall show that Lenin was a completely committed Erfurtian. Of course, Lenin's outlook was not a pale photocopy of Western models. This could not be, since the fierce absolutism of tsarist Russia and the entire absence of political freedom posed a challenge to the mere existence of anything resembling Social Democracy in Russia. Populist revolutionaries were quick to point this out to the fledgling Social Democrats. The clash between populists and Social Democrats in the mid-1890s was the first of many disputes over the applicability of the SPD model in tsarist Russia. Later in the decade, Social-Democratic voices sounded the same note of scepticism – but, while the populists counselled terrorism to replace the impossible Social-Democratic underground, the Social-Democratic 'economists' counselled economic struggle as the only one possible until political freedom was achieved.

Lenin had to show the sceptics that Russian Erfurtianism was a coherent political stance. It is here, in this extraordinary stubbornness about the possibility of a genuine underground Social Democracy, that a passionately individual profile emerges. Lenin's stubbornness springs from a commitment more intense and emotional than usual to certain aspects of the standard Social-Democratic narrative. The joke of the time had it that Karl Kautsky was the pope of Social-Democratic ideology. If so, then Lenin comes across as more Social-Democratic than the pope.

One way of proceeding would be to take these programmatic writings as a whole and illustrate each theme in the checklist with appropriate passages from any of the writings. In my view, this procedure would be justifiable, since I believe that Lenin retained the same Erfurtian outlook throughout the 1890s – indeed, at least up to 1917. But it would be imprudent to adopt a procedure that assumes what many dispute, namely, the continuity of Lenin's views. We will therefore proceed chronologically and go through each writing with checklist in hand.

In one sense, the material in this chapter does not provide a direct threat to the 'worry about workers' interpretation of WITBD. The writers in this tradition usually grant that Lenin was 'orthodox' throughout much of the

1890s. They even use these earlier writings to show just how much Lenin changed when he had his crisis of faith and became a secret revisionist.

Nevertheless, Lenin's Erfurtianism in the 1890s ultimately poses some severe difficulties for the textbook interpretation. It is one thing to say 'yes, prior to WITBD Lenin seemed more confident about the spread of awareness' and it is another thing to observe the strength and intensity of that commitment in writing after writing. We shall also find Lenin making arguments that upon examination are very hard to distinguish from his allegedly heretical assertions in WITBD – and, yet, they are embedded in writings whose orthodoxy remains unchallenged. We shall also obtain a rounded view of Lenin's two-front polemical war that will help us put his WITBD focus on 'economism' into context.

### Friends of the People (1894)

In 1894, the 24-year-old Lenin wrote a book-length polemical manifesto entitled *Who are These 'Friends of the People' and How Do They Fight Against the Social Democrats?*.[2] The work was circulated in samizdat-type fashion; it takes up 220 pages of the first volume of Lenin's *Collected Works* – and one-third of it is missing. This is the work of one who has fully assimilated an existing doctrine, who is thrilled by its power and scope, and who is itching to demonstrate its power by taking on all comers.

For a long time, all copies of *Friends of the People* were presumed missing. When two-thirds of it showed up in 1923, shortly before Lenin's death, Lenin's companions and first biographers – Grigorii Zinoviev, Lev Kamenev and Nadezhda Krupskaya – were thrilled. They saw *Friends of the People* as proof that right at the start of his career Lenin had acquired the essentials of the world-view that guided him for the rest of his life, up to and including the NEP of the 1920s. In her memoirs, Krupskaya made this work sound more fundamental than WITBD: 'Whereas *Friends of the People* had immense significance in setting out the path to be followed by the revolutionary

---

[2] Lenin's polemic was directed against the moderate populists [*narodniki*] N. Mikhailovsky and S. Krivenko. 'While in general claiming to present the ideas and tactics of true "friends of the *narod*" in their journal, these gentlemen are arch-enemies of Social Democracy' (Lenin 1958–65, 1, p. 129).

movement, *What Is to Be Done?* defined a plan for wide revolutionary work and pointed to a definite task'.[3]

I agree with Lenin's lieutenants about the significance of *Friends of the People*. Amidst all the violent polemical abuse are passages that set forth in relatively straight-forward fashion a Social-Democratic political strategy. These programmatic passages do indeed reveal Lenin as a rare example of a person who makes his entrance on the political scene with his world-view fully formed.

Zinoviev was particularly taken with the last sentence of the main text: 'These words, written almost thirty years ago, sound as if they had been written today'.[4] This final sentence was clearly crafted by Lenin with some care to provide a fitting climax. It is, in fact, the most succinct statement of what Lenin meant by 'Social Democracy' and what he thought Social Democracy's role in Russia should be. In *Friends of the People*, 'worker' [*rabochii*] means specifically urban factory workers as one section of the much wider Russian proletariat that included all labourers suffering under capitalist exploitation. After stating that 'the Russian Social Democrats concentrate all their attention and all their activity on the class of [urban industrial] workers', Lenin proceeds to sketch out the aim of this activity (I have retained the emphatic capitalisation of the original):

> When the advanced representatives of this class assimilate the ideas of scientific socialism, the idea of the historical role of the Russian worker – when these ideas receive a broad dissemination – when durable organisations are created among the workers that transform the present unco-ordinated economic war of the workers into a purposive class struggle, – then the Russian WORKER, elevated to the head of all democratic elements, will overthrow absolutism and lead the RUSSIAN PROLETARIAT (side by side with the proletariat of ALL COUNTRIES) by the *direct road of open political struggle to* THE VICTORIOUS COMMUNIST REVOLUTION.[5]

We note first of all that this climactic programmatic sentence presents the Social-Democratic political strategy in narrative form, as a scenario of future developments. When we turn to the checklist, we discover that every single

---

[3] Krupskaya 1969, 1, p. 250 (see also 1, p. 217).
[4] Zinoviev 1973, p. 220 (writing in the 1920s).
[5] Lenin 1958–65, 1, pp. 311–12.

element on the list – with the exception of an explicit statement of Erfurtian allegiance, an element found elsewhere in *Friends of the People* – is at least foreshadowed in this remarkable sentence. Let us go down the list.

*Merger formula.* This is foreshadowed by the eloquent word 'assimilate' [*usvoiat'*]. The ideas of scientific socialism already exist. They do not emanate from the Russian working class itself, they are assimilated. Although these ideas originate from outside the working class, Social Democracy only really starts its work when they have become part of the very identity of at least some of the workers.

*Good news.* Social Democracy's job is to ensure that the inspiring insight about the historic role of the workers receives a broad dissemination and that economic war is turned into a genuine class struggle by purposive organisation. The circles of awareness are clearly delineated in Lenin's sentence: starting from advanced representatives of the factory workers, Social-Democratic awareness moves out, in turn, to factory workers, the proletariat as a whole, and finally 'democratic elements' (that is, urban and rural 'petty bourgeoisie' who are not ripe for socialist propaganda but are potential supporters of a thorough democratic transformation of Russia). Lenin's confidence in the successful spread of the Social-Democratic good news is conveyed simply by the narrative form of the sentence.

*Party ideal.* The ideal of an independent class-based political party is strongly implied by the assertion that organisations based on the class struggle will undertake the political task of overthrowing absolutism.

*National leadership.* The Russian worker is called upon to lead *all* democratic elements to accomplish a task of the most pressing urgency for Russia as a whole, namely, the overthrow of the autocracy that dooms Russia to barbarism.

*Political freedom.* Overthrowing the autocracy – in other words, achieving political freedom – is vital not only for Russia but for the workers who can then set out on the *direct* road of *open* political struggle. 'Open' should be understood as meaning 'without the censorship and repression that keeps us from bringing insight and organisation to the workers in the most effective way possible'.

*Hegemony.* The anti-tsarist revolution will only occur when the workers organised by Social Democracy take their place at the head of all democratic elements.

*Internationalism.* One reason for overthrowing autocracy is to be able to work openly with the proletariat of all countries.

If I were asked to present my interpretation of Lenin as concisely as possible, I would quote Lenin's sentence from 1894 and then merely add: this was his story – and he stuck to it.

*Friends of the People* contains many other revealing programmatic passages. One of the most famous of the 'heretical' passages in WITBD starts with the words 'The history of all countries bears witness . . .'. This was no new procedure for Lenin. As we shall see again and again, the most natural way for him to set forth his political ideal was to point to West-European and particularly German experience. The historical material in *Friends of the People* is the best source for putting flesh on the narrative skeleton evoked in the final sentence.

Lenin starts with the failure of the pre-Marx utopian socialists to merge with the worker movement:

> Despite a whole phalanx of extremely talented people who set out these ideas and of [many] completely committed socialists, their theories remained apart from life, their programme remained apart from the political movements of the people, until large-scale machine industry drew the masses of the worker proletariat into the whirlpool of political life and until the true watchword of their struggle was found.[6]

The people Lenin was polemicising against in the 1890s were also 'utopian' in outlook, but they did not have the excuse of living *before* Marx found the true watchword of the struggle. According to the merger story, the curse that afflicts utopian socialists who refuse the great synthesis even *after* Marx found the correct watchword of the struggle is to degenerate into harmless reformists. The brunt of Lenin's polemic against the Russian populists of the 1890s uses this narrative template. The revolutionary populists of the 1870s did not really understand the nature of the class struggle, but at least they were fighters. The present-day populists who claim to be their heirs still refuse to understand the necessity of the class struggle and thus are reduced to begging for reforms from élite society and the tsarist state.[7]

Where the utopian socialists failed, the SPD succeeded. They had the two things needed for success: a receptive worker movement and the proper

---

[6] Lenin 1958–65, 1, p. 187.
[7] Lenin 1958–65, 1, pp. 284–95, 303.

Marxist watchwords. But was this SPD success relevant to Russia? This was the crucial question. Lenin had to respond to the argument made by Russian populists that Marx and Social Democracy were all right for the West but not for Russia. In Western Europe, the argument runs, Marx was dealing with a worker movement that capitalism had already created. In Russia, in contrast, capitalism was obviously unable to create a worker movement. At the time of these polemics, there were hardly any signs of organised worker resistance in Russia, although the situation was shortly to change. The question thus became: is Marx correct in predicting that capitalism would 'socialise' the Russian workers, that is, make of them a historical agent on a society-wide scale that would be capable of carrying out their assigned historical mission? Lenin's answer to this question is one of the best presentations of the narrative core of his outlook.

> Only the most superficial acquaintance with the facts could inspire the idea that Marx operated with a ready-made proletariat. Marx's communist programme was worked out by him even before 1848. What kind of worker movement was there in Germany at that time? At that time there weren't even any political freedoms, and the work of the communists was limited to secret circles (as with us today). It was the Social-Democratic worker movement that brought home to everybody the revolutionary and uniting role of capitalism – and this movement began two decades later, when the doctrine of scientific socialism had been thoroughly worked out, when large-scale industry had spread wider and when a series of talented and energetic disseminators of that doctrine in the worker milieu were found.
>
> Putting historical facts into an incorrect light, forgetting about the mass of labour put by socialists into bringing purposiveness and organisation to the worker movement, our philosophers on top of that also attribute to Marx an utterly senseless viewpoint of historical fatalism. According to Marx – we are told – the organisation and socialisation of the workers occurs all by itself and therefore, it seems, if we look at capitalism and don't see a worker movement, then that's because capitalism has not fulfilled its mission – and not because we are still working feebly at the job of organisation and propaganda among the workers. This philistine and cowardly trick of our home-grown philosophers is not worth refuting: it is refuted by the entire activity of Social Democrats in all lands, it is refuted by every public speech of whatever Marxist you wish.

Social Democracy – as Kautsky says with complete justice – is the merger of the worker movement with socialism. And for the progressive work of capitalism to 'appear' among us as well as elsewhere, our socialists must get down to their own work with all energy: they must work out a detailed Marxist understanding of Russian history and actuality while investigating more concretely all forms of class struggle as well as the exploitation that is especially obscure and hidden in Russia. Further, they must popularise that theory, bring it [*prinesti*] to the worker, help the worker assimilate it and work out *a form of organisation,* **appropriate** to our conditions, for the purpose of spreading Social Democratism and for the cohesion of the workers into a political force. Russian Social Democrats have never claimed that they have already finished or completed the work of ideologues of the working class (there is no end to this work in sight) – on the contrary, they have always emphasised that they have only begun it, that a lot of effort from a lot of people will be required before anything durable is created.[8]

Just as in *WITBD*, Lenin here says that the Social Democrats must 'bring' [*prinesti*, the word used in *WITBD*] socialist theory to the workers from without. The *Friends of the People* passage seems to go even further than *WITBD*, since one might get the impression that Lenin here says that the Social Democrats are needed even to create the worker movement in the first place (although I do not think this is correct, since Lenin is here talking about how to obtain a worker movement fully capable of carrying out its historical mission). So the question arises: why has this passage from 1894 not given rise to the same sense of scandal as the famous passage from *WITBD*? If the 1902 version is heresy, then so is the 1894 version.

The reason why scholars have not pounced on the 'from without' heresy in its 1894 form is that the confidence underlying the merger formula is too evident here to be missed. Why does Lenin insist on the fact that the worker movement and socialism were separated in Western Europe for decades until German Social Democracy got underway? Because he has gloomy forebodings about the Russian workers' lack of revolutionary inclinations? No, rather because he wants to *refute* the pessimistic outlook of his opponents. He therefore argues somewhat as follows: You say that there is no revolutionary

---

[8] Lenin 1958–65, 1, pp. 332–3 (Lenin's emphases).

worker movement in Russia? Well, maybe so – but the worker movement in Western Europe was also non-revolutionary at the beginning and look what happened there! So just wait till we Social Democrats spit on our hands and get down to work, and you'll soon see a revolutionary worker movement. The 'history of all countries' / 'from without' argument always occurs in this same polemical context of refuting scepticism about the chances for Social Democracy in autocratic Russia.

Indeed, the shortest summary of Lenin's programme for the Russian Social Democrats is: look at the Germans, then go thou and do likewise – with appropriate changes for local conditions. Thus the Russians should take their watchword from Wilhelm Liebknecht, one of the founders of German Social Democracy: 'Studieren, Propagandieren, Organisieren'. In other words, bring insight and organisation to the worker class.

> The political activity of the Social Democrats consists of the following: assist in the development and organisation of the worker movement in Russia; assist in the transformation from its present condition of scattered attempts at protest, riots and strikes that lack any unifying and guiding idea into an organised struggle of the ENTIRE Russian working CLASS – a struggle that is directed against the bourgeois regime [as such], one that aspires to the expropriation of the expropriators and to the utter destruction of the social order that is based on the oppression of the labourers. The basis of this activity is the general conviction of Marxists that the Russian worker is the natural and sole representative of the entire labouring and exploited population of Russia.[9]

One central reason the factory worker is the natural leader of the whole people is that capitalism has shook him up and started him thinking – and once the worker starts thinking, the Social Democrats are assured of victory. All that is needed for the worker to actualise his leadership potential is 'a simple explanation to him *of his own position*' (Lenin's emphasis).[10] Once the Russian Marxists have worked out a solid theory of class antagonisms in Russia, then

> any awakening of the protesting thought of the proletariat will inevitably lead this thought into the channel of Social-Democratism. The more we

---

[9] Lenin 1958–65, 1, pp. 309–10.
[10] Lenin 1958–65, 1, p. 311.

move forward in working out this theory, the faster will be the growth of Social-Democratism, since even the cleverest preservers of the present order lack the power to interfere with the awakening of the thought of the proletariat.[11]

Where did Lenin get this confidence in the inspiring power of Social-Democratic doctrine? No prizes for guessing the answer: the experience of German Social Democracy. In the midst of his attack on Marx, the populist writer N.V. Mikhailovsky admitted that Marx's ideas had been 'assimilated' by the German worker class. Mikhailovsky attributed this to the workers' uncritical acceptance of an essentially unscientific prediction of a better future. He sneered at a 'science' that could easily fit into a pocket-size dictionary. Lenin's sarcastic reply: 'Oh yes, how truly awful – science and Social-Democratic pamphlets that cost a penny and fit into your pocket!!'.[12] Lenin took at face value and felt genuinely inspired by the German Party's claim to combine science and penny pamphlets.

## 'Friedrich Engels' (1895)

In late 1895, Lenin wrote a short eulogy for Engels who had died a few months earlier. In the previous chapter, we noted that, in this article, Lenin gave credit to Engels's *Condition of the Working Class* as the first exposition of the merger formula. Here, I want to show how Lenin enlisted Engels for the fight for political freedom in Russia.

One of the mainstays of the textbook interpretation is Lenin's admiration for Narodnaia volia [People's Will], the group of populist revolutionaries who assassinated the tsar in 1881. Due to his rejection of European Social Democracy, it is said, Lenin turned for inspiration to these conspiratorial terrorists. Yet the main significance of Narodnaia volia for the Russian Social Democrats was that this group was the first in the Russian socialist revolutionary tradition to understand and act on the imperative of achieving political freedom.[13] This meant that, in Lenin's mind, Narodnaia volia and Marx and Engels were all

[11] Lenin 1958–65, 1, pp. 307–8.
[12] Lenin 1958–65, 1, p. 189. For other passages that throw light on Lenin's Erfurtianism, see Lenin 1958–65, 1, pp. 183, 202, 300–12, 343–4.
[13] See Chapter Three For a detailed discussion.

sending the same message on this crucial issue. Lenin reminded his readers that Marx and Engels 'both became socialists after being *democrats*, and a democratic feeling of *hatred* toward political arbitrariness was particularly strong in them'. Their support for Narodnaia volia was therefore no surprise:

> The heroic struggle of a small band of Russian revolutionaries against the mighty tsarist government found a hugely sympathetic echo in the hearts of these tried-and-true revolutionaries [Marx and Engels]. On the other hand, to turn away from the most immediate and important task of Russian socialists – the conquest of political freedom – for the sake of imaginary economic gain was something suspicious in their eyes; they even considered it direct treason to the mighty cause of the social revolution. 'The liberation of the proletariat must be their own deed' – this is what Marx and Engels constantly taught. And in order to fight for their economic liberation, the proletariat must conquer for itself certain *political* rights.[14]

Marx and Engels also clearly recognised the immense international significance of a free Russia that did not oppress nationalities or increase military tensions in Europe. 'This is why the progress of the worker movement in the West provided another motive for Engels to desire fervently the establishment of political freedom in Russia'.[15] The international significance of the Russian anti-tsarist revolution is stressed again in WITBD.

At the time of writing, Lenin knew of no Russian Social Democrats who downplayed the task of achieving political freedom. His evocation of the democratism of Marx and Engels makes it easy to guess how he would react when such Social-Democratic 'economists' appeared a few years later.

## Prison Programme Draft (1895–6)

In December 1895, Lenin, along with other leading Petersburg Social Democrats, was arrested and spent over a year in Petersburg jails before being shipped off to Siberia. Jail conditions allowed him a fair amount of contact with the outside world and he was able to comply with the request of some younger activists to draft a programme and commentary for the fledgling Social-

---

[14] Lenin 1958–65, 2, pp. 13–14.
[15] Lenin 1958–65, 2, p. 14.

Democratic groups. The activists had begun to feel the need for a declaration that would define the basic principles of Social Democracy. Lenin wrote a four-page programme and a twenty-three-page commentary on the first half of the programme. Neither programme nor commentary was published until the 1920s.

The overall form of Lenin's programme is clearly modelled on the Erfurt Programme. First comes a description of the effects of capitalism, then a statement of basic party aims and finally a list of concrete goals, divided into the two categories of general political reforms and specific worker protection measures. The main contrast with the German programme is the special attention given in Lenin's draft to the battle for attaining elementary political freedoms, that is, to the imperative of overthrowing the tsar and the basic strategy for doing so. Lenin also added a third category of concrete measures aimed at protection of peasant interests.

If we take the formal imitation of the Erfurt Programme as a fairly open statement of allegiance, then all eight parts of our checklist are reflected in the 1895 programme and commentary. We will focus here on the description of the Party's central tasks and in particular on the relationship between the Party and the worker movement. The Erfurt Programme formulated the basic task of the Social-Democratic Party in the following way:

> Diesen Kampf der Arbeiterklasse zu einem bewussten und einheitlichen zu gestalten und ihm sein naturnotwendiges Ziel zu weisen – das ist die Aufgabe der Sozialdemokratischen Partei.
>
> To shape this fight of the worker class into a purposive and united effort, and to show to it its naturally necessary end – this is the task of the Social-Democratic Party.

The corresponding passage in Lenin's programme is clearly based on its German counterpart: 'The Russian Social-Democratic Party announces as its task: to help the struggle of the Russian working class by development of the class self-awareness of the workers, by assistance to their organisations and by pointing out the tasks and aims of the struggle.'

In his commentary on this passage, Lenin ties it firmly to the merger formula:

> This paragraph of the programme is the most important and central one because it shows what should be the activity of a party that defends the interests of the worker class and what should be the activity of all purposive

workers. It shows the way by which the aspiration of socialism – the aspiration of ending the eternal exploitation of man by man – must be merged with movement of the people that arose out of the conditions of life created by large-scale factories and workshops.[16]

As we saw in *Friends of the People*, Russian Social Democrats had placed their wager on the eventual appearance in Russia of a genuine worker movement, that is, of organised and militant resistance. When he wrote *Friends of the People*, Lenin could only exude confidence that the worker movement would indeed make its appearance in Russia. By the time the prison draft was written at the end of 1895, however, genuine contact had been made between Social Democrats and workers in Petersburg. These contacts bore fruit the following year with a series of strikes by textile workers that continued on and off for over a year and struck all observers with their impressive organisation and discipline. The Petersburg strikes were an epochal event in the history of Russian Social Democracy because they appeared to be concrete proof that the merger between socialism and the worker movement could really happen in Russia. Boris Gorev recalls how delighted he and his companions were by this confirmation. 'We were literally drunk from happiness and pride'. He remembers coming to the apartment of two Social-Democratic women and finding them dancing ecstatically around the floor.[17]

These developments allowed Lenin to talk about a worker movement already in existence:

> Everywhere in Russia is beginning a transition of the workers to an unremitting struggle for their essential needs – a struggle for concessions, for better conditions of life, of pay and of working hours. This transition is a giant step forward made by the Russian workers. The attention of the Social-Democratic Party and all purposive workers must be focused on this struggle and on giving assistance to it.[18]

Thus the task of the Party was 'to attach itself to the movement of the workers, bring light to it [*vnesti v nego svet*], and to help the workers in the struggle

---

[16] Lenin 1958–65, 2, p. 101.
[17] Gorev 1924, p. 24. The dancing Social Democrats were Liubov Radchenko and Apollinaria Iakubova (later married to K.M. Takhtarev).
[18] Lenin 1958–65, 2, p. 103.

that they themselves have started'.[19] Lenin's mission statement makes a careful distinction between help in the form of developing class self-awareness and help in the form of pointing out the final aim. In essence, this is the same distinction made in WITBD between 'tred-iunionist awareness' and 'Social-Democratic awareness'. To use the language of WITBD, 'tred-iunionist awareness' means a conviction of the need to unite in unions, to carry on struggle with the owners and so on, up to and including a political fight for favourable legislation.

In WITBD, Lenin's polemic is aimed at those who, he claims, would *stop* at this level and who would neglect the further duty of pointing out the final aim – whence the derogatory term 'tred-iunionist awareness'. Readers of WITBD who are not aware of the technical definition of 'worker movement' nor its role in the merger narrative and who, to boot, misread the term tred-iunionist, naturally read this as contemptuous and dismissive of mere protection of worker interests. In 1895–6, Lenin held the same position as he did later: the worker movement in isolation is insufficient. But, at that time, it did not occur to him that any Social Democrat would challenge this position. His aim is, rather, to set out in a non-polemical way the *importance* of helping the worker movement as such. In WITBD, due to polemical context, this importance is taken for granted and not amplified. For today's reader of WITBD, therefore, the 1895–6 discussion fills in a crucial gap when it describes the crucial but limited task of 'developing class self-awareness'.

Following Lenin's usage, 'class self-awareness' can be defined as the workers' awareness of themselves as a distinct interest group – but not necessarily the necessity for socialist transformation of society and the workers' mission to carry out this transformation. How do the workers attain this pre-socialist awareness? First and foremost, they learn it from the struggle upon which they themselves embark out of self-defence. Following the stages of the class struggle set down in the *Communist Manifesto*, Lenin describes the original phase of violent revenge against individual capitalists. This is a necessary phase, since 'hatred toward the capitalist is everywhere and always the first stimulus for the awakening of the workers' striving to defend themselves. But the Russian worker movement has already grown out of the first phase'.[20]

---

[19] Lenin 1958–65, 2, p. 102.
[20] Lenin 1958–65, 2, p. 103.

After this phase, the workers move on to strikes, and every strike, win or lose, is valuable education for the workers. They learn the methods of capitalist exploitation and the sources of their own strength, and they begin to acquire political awareness.

This whole process is extremely encouraging for the Russian Social Democrats, since 'the transition of the Russian workers to this kind of struggle points to the huge step forward made by them. This struggle places the worker movement on the direct road and serves as a reliable guarantee of its further progress'.[21] The task of the Social Democrats is therefore to speed up this development of class self-awareness by participating in the workers' own defence of their essential needs. For example, a strike leads directly to political awareness when the workers listen to factory inspectors who themselves patiently explain that the abusive actions of the bosses are entirely legal. To this useful lesson about the class nature of the state are added 'leaflets and other explanations of the socialists', so that 'during such a strike the workers receive in full measure their political education'.[22]

In this way, the Russian Social Democrats work for the great merger from the side of the worker movement. The Social Democrats also work for the merger from the other side, from the side of 'socialism', when they explain the 'real' goals of the struggle. In order to carry out their mission, the workers have to understand *why* the interests of the capitalists and the workers are antagonistic and will continue to be antagonistic until private property is abolished.

We see that Lenin in 1895–6 makes a *conceptual* distinction between the understanding that arises directly out of the struggle of the worker movement and the understanding that comes from the explanations of the socialists. The 1895–6 commentary shows how the stress on original separation in no way implies a pessimistic or dismissive attitude toward the worker movement. Worker resistance is heroic and admirable, it moves steadily onward in organisation and insight, and all Social Democrats have a duty to participate in it. Nevertheless, they *also* have a duty to explain socialism. Both duties tend toward the same result: the merger of socialism and the worker movement.[23]

---

[21] Lenin 1958–65, 2, p. 104.
[22] Lenin 1958–65, 2, p. 105.
[23] Lenin's insistence on the double duty of the Party is overlooked by those who

Lenin's commentary touches only briefly on organisational questions. One task is to set up strike organisations and worker funds. Another quite distinct task is the 'ever more necessary organisation' of protection from the police, keeping worker organisations and their relations secret, provision of illegal literature and other tasks arising out of tsarist repression.[24] There is a straight line from this brief evocation of the challenge posed by tsarist repression to WITBD's stress on *konspiratsiia* and the 'revolutionary by trade' (= 'professional revolutionary').[25]

I conclude our survey of the 1895–6 programme by citing a couple of passages from the commentary to bring out Lenin's emotional commitment to the hegemony scenario. One emotion is hatred of tsarist lawlessness and its *chinovniki* [a contemptuous term for bureaucrat]:

> Citizens [in Russia] are deprived of any right to demand an account from the *chinovniki*, verify their actions, bring legal action against them. Citizens are even deprived of the right to deliberate on state matters: they do not dare to set up assemblies or organisations without the permission of these same *chinovniki*. Thus the *chinovniki* are irresponsible in the full sense of the word: they constitute a separate caste that stands over citizens. The irresponsibility and arbitrariness of the *chinovniki*, coupled with the population's utter lack of voice gives birth to such crying abuses of the *chinovnik's* power and to such violation of the rights of ordinary people that is hardly possible in any European country.[26]

The other emotion is the inspiring nature of the crusade against the tsar:

> And if even now, when the struggle of the workers and their closing of ranks is just beginning, the government hurries to make concessions to the workers to order to halt the further growth of the movement, then without a doubt, when the workers close ranks and unite under the leadership of a single political party, they will know how to compel the government to

---

see Lenin proclaiming here that class consciousness grows 'automatically' (Cliff 1975, p. 52) or 'of its own accord' (Schapiro 1987, p. 232) out of the economic struggle, and thus the 'exact opposite' (Schapiro 1987, p. 232) of WITBD.

[24] Lenin 1958–65, 2, pp. 105–6.

[25] *Konspiratsiia* and the 'revolutionary by trade' are discussed in detail in Chapter Eight.

[26] Lenin 1958–65, 2, pp. 99–100.

surrender – they will know how to conquer political liberty for themselves and for the entire Russian people![27]

## Tasks of the Russian Social Democrats (1897)

This twenty-five-page pamphlet, written in Siberian exile in 1897 and published abroad the following year, is Lenin's most important political writing prior to *Iskra*. For us, as interpreters of *WITBD*, it is crucial in a couple of ways. First, its appearance set off the chain-reaction of back-and-forth polemics that only ended four years later with *WITBD*. Although both of the Social-Democratic émigré groups in Geneva rated the pamphlet and its author very highly, one group made a mild criticism and the other group refuted the criticism. Lenin sided passionately with the group making the mild criticism. But more of that in Chapter Five.

*Tasks of the Russian Social Democrats* also serves as a touchstone for the orthodoxy or lack thereof of *WITBD*. When *Tasks* was first published in Geneva in 1898, the pamphlet came equipped with a glowing foreword by Pavel Akselrod, one of the founding fathers of Russian Social Democracy, who described the unnamed author as

> a revolutionary who happily combines the experience of an excellent *praktik* with theoretical education and wide political views. . . . For émigrés [such as myself] who have left the homeland long ago, it is exceptionally pleasant to feel and acknowledge oneself in complete solidarity with the most thoughtful and active leaders of the revolutionary movement in Russia.

Akselrod even gave the pamphlet semi-official status by calling it a commentary on the Manifesto issued earlier in 1898 by the abortive first congress of the newly formed Russian Social-Democratic Worker Party (RSDWP).[28]

Lenin also had a high opinion of this pamphlet. He republished it three times – in 1902, 1905 and 1907 – each time with the express purpose of bringing

---

[27] Lenin 1958–65, 2, p. 108.
[28] Akselrod's preface as printed in Lenin 1926–35, 2, pp. 603–5. Vladimir Akimov, a Social Democrat extremely hostile to *WITBD*, wrote in 1904 about *Tasks* that 'the booklet still expresses views shared by us all and still formulates correctly the tactical principles which distinguish us, the Social Democrats, from socialists of other schools. But it is no longer adequate for us . . . It contains theses which, as they have evolved, have proved open to too many different interpretations' (Akimov 1969, p. 319).

out the continuity in his views. In a foreword to the 1902 edition, he wrote that *Tasks* came from a period when Russian Social Democrats were united in their views. If *WITBD* was a reaction to a period of wavering, then *Tasks* expressed the original orthodox viewpoint that the waverers had come to doubt. In 1905, he wrote that *Tasks* gave an outline of general tasks, while later works like *Two Tactics* presented the specific tasks of the moment.[29] Finally, in 1907, in the introduction to a collection of his writings from 1895 to 1905, he stated that 'the views that in other articles and brochures of the present collection are set forth as polemics with the right wing of Social Democracy are here set forth in positive form'.[30]

Akselrod's and Lenin's views on this pamphlet confirm the thesis advanced here that Lenin never swerved from basic Social-Democratic principles. They also pose something of a dilemma for the textbook interpretation. *Either* the heretical views found in *WITBD* are already set forth in *Tasks* in 1897. But, then, how do we account for Akselrod's glowing endorsement?[31] *Or* Lenin had a conversion experience at some point between 1897 and late 1901 and rejected the truly Social-Democratic outlook of *Tasks*. But, then, how do we account for Lenin thrusting his rejected views before his readers on so many occasions? The usual line is that Lenin was a self-deceiving *unconscious* heretic – but, still, would not he have found his earlier views to be embarrassing, at least unconsciously?

The tone of *Tasks* is much less stridently polemical than either *Friends of the People* or *WITBD*. Lenin explains that, since people now have a clear idea of what Social Democracy stands for, there is no need for a 'heated defence of the foundations of Social Democratism'. Lenin's aim is only to dispel the prejudice that, somehow, Social Democracy is indifferent to the political struggle against the autocracy. Lenin little knew how soon he would again be engaged in a heated defence of basic principles – but this time against fellow Social Democrats. His defence of Social-Democratic politics in 1897 is aimed at people who criticised Social Democracy for *ignoring* the revolutionary

---

[29] Lenin claimed in 1905 that 'a simple comparison' of *Tasks, What Is to Be Done?*, and his writings of 1905 would show a continuity of general views even while his stand on concrete issues such as the feasibility of an armed uprising evolved in relation to circumstances (Lenin 1958–65, 2, pp. 443–4; see also 11, pp. 138–9 [1905]).

[30] Lenin 1958–65, 16: 98.

[31] Akselrod himself was not one of those who rejected *WITBD* as theoretically heretical.

political struggle, while, in following years, it is aimed at people who criticised Social Democracy for being *obsessed* with revolutionary political struggle.[32]

In *Tasks*, Lenin responds to scepticism about the possibility of applying the Erfurtian strategy to Russia. One form of scepticism rejected SPD-style enlightenment: does not this strategy concentrate too much on the urban factory workers and ignore the great numbers of exploited workers in Russia who do not fit this category? Another form of scepticism rejected SPD-style organisation: is not this kind of mass organisation impossible in absolutist Russia? If so, a political conspiracy remains the only way to achieve the political freedom needed for a genuine mass movement.

In his reply to the objection about SPD-style enlightenment, Lenin uses two terms central to Russian Social Democracy, *propaganda* and *agitation*. We need to examine the specialised meaning of these terms, especially since *agitprop* later acquired such justly negative associations.

For us, 'propaganda' means simplified slogans aimed at exploiting the irrationality of the masses. Thus, one scholar reproaches Lenin for openly advocating propaganda as a way of overcoming the natural moderation of the workers.[33] In Social-Democratic discourse, 'propaganda' meant the exact opposite. It meant individualised, intensive study embracing a wide range of social knowledge. 'Propagandised worker' was a title of respect accorded to the graduates of the study circles. Propaganda was criticised, not because it was a cheap shortcut to unconsidered support, but rather because it was a labour-intensive method that produced only a few highly knowledgeable individuals.

---

[32] A note to those who wish to read *Tasks* in full. Lenin uses the expression 'the merger of the socialist and the democratic struggle'. This may look like the canonical merger formula, but it is not. Rather, it expresses the hegemony scenario: all socialists should make political freedom their main priority and all who desire political freedom should realise that the democratic revolution will only happen when the worker movement understands the need for revolutionary overthrow. Accordingly, 'socialism' means here something like 'the worker movement that has already merged with socialist doctrine at least to the extent of accepting Social-Democratic guidance'. Thus the two merger formulae use 'socialism' in confusingly different and even directly opposed ways. I have the feeling Lenin wanted to use the 'socialists should be democrats and democrats should be socialists' formula (which he may have taken from a famous speech by Wilhelm Liebknecht in 1869) as a framework for this article, even though it did not exactly fit the two main prejudices he wanted to combat. Fortunately, Lenin did not insist on this version of the formula or use it in other writings, so that we can ignore it even in our exposition of *Tasks* itself.

[33] Meyer 1957, pp. 47–50.

'Agitation' was closer to what we now call 'propaganda': simplified rhetoric meant to capitalise on specific abuses and outrages. The Social Democrats, of course, did not concede in any way that agitation exploited worker irrationality. It was, rather, meant to be a vivid teaching tool useful in getting across what the revolutionaries themselves fervently believed to be the case: the connection between day-to-day abuses and the existence of capitalism and the autocracy. The emphasis on propaganda and agitation does not stem from a pessimistic conviction that the workers were not fulfilling the Marxist scenario. It arose, rather, from the heart of the SPD model as well as the Marxist political strategy informing that model. Propaganda and agitation meant bringing the good news to the workers.

In Lenin's exposition, the spreading circle of awareness starts with the basic truths about the worker mission. 'Socialist' propaganda teaches the worker about 'the central task of international Social Democracy and the Russian worker class', while 'democratic' propaganda leads up to the truth that 'a successful struggle for the worker cause is impossible without the achievement of political freedom and the democratisation of Russia's political and social order'. Lenin stresses that 'while propagandising among the workers, Social Democracy *cannot* avoid political questions and considers any attempt to avoid such questions or even simply put them off as a profound mistake and as a retreat from the basic principles of world Social Democratism'.[34] Agitation then brings these truths in simplified form to a wider circle by 'fusing' [*slit'*] them with the everyday concerns of the worker movement.

Because he is responding to criticisms that the Social Democrats concentrate too exclusively on the factory proletariat, Lenin is here more explicit than earlier about the way he sees the spread of awareness reach the outer circles. Social Democrats concentrate on the factory proletariat not because they wish to ignore the wider proletarian mass – the artisans, the rural proletariat, the 'devastated peasants' – but, rather, because the focus on the factory worker is the most rational use of very scarce resources. In Russia, the 'worker-socialist' continues to have close personal contact with these more 'backward' categories and implants in them the ideas of socialism, class struggle, and the crucial importance of political freedom. Thus, Lenin envisages an almost unstoppable spread of awareness:

---

[34] Lenin 1958–65, 2, pp. 447, 450.

Agitation among the advanced strata of the proletariat is the most reliable and the unique path toward the awakening (as the movement becomes wider) of the whole Russian proletariat as well. The dissemination of socialism and of the idea of the class struggle among the urban workers inevitably pours these ideas into ever more narrow, ever more small-scale channels. For this to happen, it is necessary that these ideas first put forth deep roots in a more prepared milieu and saturate this vanguard of the Russian worker movement and the Russian revolution.[35]

Further out than the wider proletarian mass is the outermost circle of awareness, namely, the 'democratic elements', those sections of the people (the *Volk* or the *narod*) that are capable of energetic support of *democratic* transformation but who are hardly open to socialist ideas at present. Lenin wants these people to be organised – but not directly by Social Democracy. Lenin is so convinced by the basic Marxist axiom that energetic political action comes from clearly perceived class interests that he feels only non-socialist parties can really mobilise the 'democratic elements'. The Social-Democratic contact with this outer circle comes from Social Democracy's leadership in society's struggle to overthrow the autocracy. This leadership consists primarily in *telling the workers* about the abuses of the autocracy toward *all* classes of Russian society. Seeing the genuinely revolutionary workers on their side will encourage other discontented elements to actually *do* something to get rid of the hated tsar. This concept of 'political agitation' was put into practice by *Iskra*.

Confidence in the spread of awareness goes together with a concern for purity of doctrine. A fledgling Social-Democratic movement needs to be even more concerned with getting the essential message right than an older one. Lenin expounds this characteristic theme by using what was for him the highly emotional symbol of 'the banner'.

Convinced that the revolutionary theory that serves as the banner of the revolutionary movement can today only be the teaching of scientific socialism and of the class struggle, Russian Social Democrats will disseminate it with all their strength, preserve it from misleading interpretations, and rebel against any attempt to saddle the still young worker movement with vaguer doctrines.[36]

---

[35] Lenin 1958–65, 2, p. 449.
[36] Lenin 1958–65, 2, p. 450.

Lenin thus responds to scepticism about the applicability of SPD-style enlightenment by saying: yes, granted, we do not have the opportunity to openly spread our ideas among the Russian proletariat as a whole. Yet the conditions of Russian life are such that our underground activity among the factory proletariat can have a multiplier effect as it trickles down via personal contact to the wider masses.

Lenin also responded to scepticism about the applicability of SPD-style organisation. One of the icons of revolutionary populism, Petr Lavrov, expressed this scepticism in an article published abroad in 1895. Lavrov granted that the Russian Social Democrats seemed to be having success with SPD-style enlightenment.

> But for socialists the propaganda of ideas is no more than one element of [preparation for socialist tasks]. The other element is organisation. In the West, whose [Social-Democratic] activity serves as an unconditional model for Russian Social Democrats, history has created the soil for this organisation. It has to be strengthened, widened, defended, but the soil *of juridical forms and social customs* is already there. *In Russia this soil is absent.* The organisation of the Russian worker party must be created under the autocracy and all its charms.[37]

For Lavrov, theoretical questions about economic materialism or the fate of the peasant commune were secondary compared to this practical problem. If an effective mass political organisation were possible under the autocracy, then, of course, the Social-Democratic strategy would be the best. *'But [such a strategy] is extremely dubious, if not impossible'.* Lavrov concluded that the challenge for Russian socialists was to combine propaganda of socialist ideas with the organisation of a revolutionary conspiracy – the only serious kind of political struggle under autocratic conditions. And the only ones tackling this kind of political struggle were revolutionaries who remained loyal to the traditions of Narodnaia volia.[38]

In his response, Lenin granted that the organisational resources of the Russian Social Democrats were pitiful indeed compared to the Germans. Yet

---

[37] Lavrov's article as printed in Lenin 1926–35, 2, p. 607.
[38] Lavrov's article as printed in Lenin 1926–35, 2, pp. 605–9.

he paradoxically turned this fact into an argument for confidence by saying: look at the mighty effect even this weak Social Democracy is having already! Look at the experience of the Union of Struggle in Petersburg (Lenin was one of the founders of the Union of Struggle, although it achieved its greatest success after his arrest). The Petersburg proletariat accepted the Union's guidance and proceeded to carry out long-term strikes in so effective a fashion that the Russian government was forced to respond with a major piece of reform legislation.

If the Social Democrats could accomplish so much with so little, owing to the support we found in the Petersburg worker class, then what miracles could they not accomplish if they got their act together in entirely possible ways? Lenin's underlying confidence is rarely expressed more concretely than in the following:

> This concession [the law of 2 June 1897 on working hours] was a tiny one, the change a very insignificant one – but remember, the organisation of the worker class that successfully compelled this change was also not distinguished either by breadth or strength or length of existence or wealth either in experience or money. The Union of Struggle, as we know, was founded only in 1895/6 and its appeals to the workers were confined to some badly printed broadsheets. Can one possibly deny that if a similar organisation united at least the largest centres of the worker movement in Russia (the St. Petersburg region, Moscow-Vladimir, the south and the most important towns, such as Odessa, Kiev, Saratov and so on) and had a revolutionary press organ at its disposal and enjoyed as much authority among the Russian workers as the Union of Struggle did among the St. Petersburg workers – can anyone doubt that such an organisation would be a political factor of the highest order in contemporary Russia, a factor that the government would have to take into account in both internal and external policy?[39]

Lenin tells Lavrov: we know as well as you do that we cannot have an open legal party like the SPD and that the fight for political freedom cannot be separated from the fight for socialism. But *we* do not restrict our concept of political struggle to revolutionary conspiracies as do you and others who

---

[39] Lenin 1958–65, 2, pp. 460–1.

have not fully liberated themselves from the Blanquist traditions of *Narodnaia volia*. We believe rather that 'the struggle against absolutism must consist not in the creation of conspiracies but rather in the education, disciplining and organisation of the proletariat, in political agitation among the workers'.[40]

Robert Service cites the words just quoted and comments: 'The imagery is trenchantly hierarchical; it bursts through all the qualifying language of the sentences around it. Discipline was always a key theme in [Lenin's] thought'.[41] Evidently, Lenin was trying to keep hidden his deep personal desire to dominate and discipline – unsuccessfully, thanks to sharp-eyed commentators like Service. Yet the emphasis on discipline was not some personal quirk of Lenin's but a fundamental goal, not only of Social Democracy, but of any worker movement. (I would not like to go down to the local trade-union branch during a strike and announce that only trenchantly hierarchical intellectuals care about discipline.) As an example, we might cite the following comment from one of Lenin's polemical foes within Russian Social Democracy, the 'economist' underground newspaper *Rabochaia mysl*.

> The worker movement in Russia can now consider itself as part of the pan-European worker movement. . . . Now dying down to a barely flickering spark, now growing into a sea of fire, [the Russian worker movement] conquers the worker masses ever more widely and deeply, while it slowly but surely disciplines them as it teaches how to struggle with the enemy.[42]

Contrary to Service, Lenin does not in the least qualify his language when talking about discipline – he is too involved in responding to scepticism about whether an illegal underground party *can* bring about the disciplined struggle that everybody desires:

> Leading the class struggle of the proletariat, developing discipline and organisation among the workers, helping them fight for the economic needs and forcing capital to concede one position after another, educating the workers politically, systematically and continually pursuing absolutism, badgering any tsarist bashibazouk that makes the proletariat feel the heavy

---

[40] Lenin 1958–65, 2, p. 460.
[41] Service 1985–95, 1, p. 77.
[42] Lead article from *Rabochaia mysl* No. 1 (October 1897), as printed in Lenin 1926–35, 2, pp. 611–12.

hand of the police government – any organisation that does all these things will be at one and the same time a worker party adapted to our conditions and a mighty revolutionary party directed against absolutism.[43]

Thus, the aim of Lenin's pamphlet is to make Russian Social Democracy more attractive by instilling confidence in its ability to deliver even under absolutist conditions. Lenin's confidence does not mean that he is *less* activist (as many scholars seem to expect should logically be the case) but *more* activist. The peroration of his pamphlet seeks to inspire his fellow Social Democrats by showing them the vast potential for success if only they will be up and doing:

> Before Russian Social Democracy stands a field for work that is huge and barely begun. The awakening of the Russian working class, its *stikhiinyi* aspirations for knowledge, for [organisational] merger, for socialism, for struggle against its exploiters and oppressors reveals itself every day more clearly and more extensively. The giant strides that Russian capitalism has made recently guarantees that the worker movement will grow without halt ever more widely and more deep . . . [Russian Social Democrats must take pains to ensure that when the inevitable economic crisis comes,] the proletariat will be capable of standing at the head of Russian democracy in a decisive struggle against the police absolutism that ties Russian workers and the whole Russian people hand and foot.
>
> And so – to work, comrades! We mustn't waste valuable time. Russian Social Democrats face a mass of work: we must satisfy the demands of the awakening proletariat, organise the worker movement, strengthen revolutionary groups and their mutual ties, provide the workers with propagandistic and agitational literature, and unite the worker circles and Social-Democratic groups that are scattered all over Russia into a single *Social-Democratic worker party!*[44]

## Three protests (1899)

Can the people who are writing this really be Social Democrats? (Lenin, 1899)

---

[43] Lenin 1958–65, 2, p. 461.
[44] Lenin 1958–65, 2, p. 466.

When he wrote *Tasks* in late 1897, Lenin felt that the battle to explain the essence of Social Democracy was over and the Party could move to more practical matters. In the latter half of 1898, he found he had been over-optimistic. There were still people around who from Lenin's point of view just didn't get it – and these were underground Social-Democratic activists! Startled and indignant, Lenin penned three protests. The first was occasioned by a short document called the *Credo*. Lenin drafted 'A Protest by Russian Social Democrats', had it signed by sixteen other exiled Social Democrats and sent it to Geneva, where it was published. The other two protests were also written at some time before Lenin's exile ended in early 1900 but were only printed in the 1920s. One was entitled 'A Retrogressive Tendency in Russian Social Democracy' and directed against the Separate Supplement issued by the newspaper *Rabochaia mysl*. The other unpublished protest was aimed at a 'Profession de foi' issued by Kiev Social Democrats.[45]

In Chapter Four, we will take a closer look at the statements that provoked such a fierce response from Lenin. Here, we will look at Lenin's protests as a passionate reaffirmation of his core beliefs. We shall take at face value Lenin's description of his opponents' views, since this will allow us to see what Lenin was defining himself against. Lenin charged his opponents with distorting the essence of Social Democracy, so his protests are an excellent source for capturing his own conception of that essence.

At first the dispute seems to be overwrought – all this uproar over the relative significance of political vs. economic struggle! Scholars have often concluded that the motive force behind the protests was hysteria (opinions differ over whether the hysteria was genuine or cynically whipped up). But 'politics' had long been something of a code word for two key planks in the Social-Democratic platform: the necessity of an independent class-based political party and the urgency of political freedom. 'Anti-political' trends in international and Russian socialism – for example, Bakuninist anarchism – rejected these two planks. The correct appreciation of 'politics' was indeed at the heart of Marx-based Social Democracy.

---

[45] For 'A Protest by Russian Social Democrats', see Lenin 1958–65, 4, pp. 163–76. For 'A Retrogressive Tendency in Russian Social Democracy', see Lenin 1958–65, 4, pp. 240–73. For 'On the Profession de foi', see Lenin 1958–65, 4, pp. 310–21.

Lenin had another motive for being upset by the appearance of Social-Democratic writing that could be perceived as anti-political. A common charge against the Russian Marxists, especially from those in the Narodnaia volia tradition, was that the Marxists were passive fatalists who at most organised economic protest while ignoring revolutionary political struggle. Lenin's reaction in his earliest writings was to say, more or less, 'you must be getting your idea of Marxism from glib talkers in literary salons. No genuine Russian Social Democrat ever believed anything like that'. His confidence on this score was increased by the Founding Congress of the RSDWP in 1898. The Congress had been organised by South Russian activists without any contribution from Lenin or his group. The Congress proved abortive in organisational terms: the delegates were arrested *en masse*, no central institutions were set up, plans to establish a 'central organ' (official party newspaper) fell through. Yet a nation-wide party now had at least a notional existence, giving rise to various schemes for giving it a more corporeal existence. Local Social-Democratic organisations who previously had called themselves 'Unions of Struggle' renamed themselves 'committees of the RSDWP' and this renaming had a real influence on the way they thought of themselves. Best of all, from Lenin's point of view, the Congress had issued a Manifesto that affirmed Lenin's sense of the essence of Social Democracy. In particular, the 1898 Manifesto announced that political freedoms were light and air to the Russian worker class and that 'the Russian worker class must carry and will carry on its strong shoulders the cause of the conquest of political freedom'.[46]

And, now, a year later, Social-Democratic activists were making statements that repudiated the assertions of the 1898 Manifesto and that justified the scorn toward Social Democracy expressed by other Russian revolutionaries. This was especially true of the underground Petersburg newspaper *Rabochaia mysl* [*Worker Thought*]. Lenin's other two protests were aimed at fugitive underground writings that would have vanished without the attention Lenin paid to them. *Rabochaia mysl* was another matter. One of the first underground newspapers to survive for any length of time, it was a truly impressive achievement, both because of its ability to outwit the enraged police and

---

[46] *Kommunisticheskaia partiia . . . v rezoliutsiiakh* 1983, pp. 15–18.

because it published invaluable material from worker correspondents. The opponents of Social Democracy would be certainly justified in citing it as the authentic voice of Russian Social Democracy. Lenin's protest against *Rabochaia mysl*'s programmatic statements – entitled 'A Retrogressive Tendency in Russian Social Democracy' or 'Retrogression' for short – is the longest and most passionate of the three protests. In fact, 'Retrogression' contains some of the most eloquent assertions of his basic beliefs and I particularly recommend it as the most revealing of Lenin's early writings.

Taken together, the protests of 1899 provide excellent documentation of Lenin's commitment to Erfurtianism. As we go through the check list, we shall see that Lenin accused the new Social-Democratic voices of denying or at least moving away from every plank in the platform.

(i) *Erfurtian allegiance*. A central theme throughout the three protests is that the new voices in Russian Social Democracy (as expressed by the *Credo*, *Rabochaia mysl* and the 'Profession de foi') are rejecting the model of Western Social Democracy and the key lessons of European experience, even though the new Russian Party was officially committed to this model and these lessons.

> With an almost infinite lack of concern, our latest perverters of Social Democratism throw overboard all that is dear to Social Democracy, all that gives us the right to see the worker movement as a world-historical movement. They don't care at all about the fact that the age-old experience of European socialism and European democracy teaches the necessity of striving toward the formation of independent worker political parties. They don't care at all that the history of the Russian revolutionary movement has gone through a long and difficult path to bring about the merger of great social and political ideals with the class struggle of the proletariat. They don't care at all that the advanced Russian workers have already laid the foundations of the 'Russian Social-Democratic Worker Party'. Down with all that![47]

(ii) *Merger formula*. The protest writings contains Lenin's most elaborate retelling of the merger narrative, as we shall see later.

(iii) *Good news*. Lenin accused the new voices of reneging on the duty of inspiring the worker class with high ideals. They excused themselves by

---

[47] Lenin 1958–65, 4, p. 248.

grossly underestimating the willingness of the workers to receive the message. In response, Lenin elaborated his own sense of how awareness spread through the different levels of the worker class.

(iv) *Party ideal*. The new voices either ignored or expressed aggressive scepticism about the possibility of an independent class-based nation-wide political party under repressive Russian conditions. Lenin's response was: you say that the autocracy has a 'highly structured organisation' with 'competent and resourceful' officials dedicated to stamping out worker and socialist groups? True enough, but only a cowardly liberal therefore concludes that an organised underground struggle is impossible. A real Social Democrat will instead set about building our own 'highly structured organisation' that will turn workers and socialists into 'competent and resourceful' experts in fighting the political police.[48]

Lenin's remarks on this point is an important stage in the crystallisation of the idea of the revolutionary by trade or professional revolutionary. We see that the emphasis on revolutionary expertise is in response to *Rabochaia mysl*'s emphasis on the expertise of the police. This serves to demonstrate the purpose of the revolutionary by trade: not to *substitute* for a mass movement, but to make a mass movement *possible* under the autocracy.

(v) *Political freedom*.

> Why should the overthrow of the autocracy be the first task of the Russian worker class? Because under the autocracy the worker class cannot broadly develop its struggle, cannot conquer for itself strong positions either economically or politically, cannot create strong, mass organisations and cannot unfurl before all the labouring masses the banner of social revolution and teach them to fight for it.[49]

Instead of fighting for political freedom, the new voices asked the older leaders of Russian Social Democracy: why are you so obsessed about a parliament that we don't have? Why don't you concentrate on worker participation in such local representative institutions as tsarism allows? To which Lenin replies: 'If we don't put the advantages of a parliament in the foreground, then from what source will the workers learn about political rights and political freedom?'.

---

[48] Lenin 1958–65, 4, pp. 260–1, citing phrases from *Rabochaia mysl*.
[49] Lenin 1958–65, 4, pp. 252–3.

Social Democrats are all for worker participation in local institutions – but participation by worker-*socialists*, who are illegal by definition in tsarist Russia.[50]

(vi) and (vii) *Popular leadership and hegemony*. The new voices did not believe that the conquest of political freedom needed to be Russian Social Democracy's most urgent task. Lenin retorted that

> when Social Democracy makes the overthrow of absolutism its most urgent
> task, it must show itself to be the advanced fighter for democracy and just
> for that reason must provide any and all support to all democratic elements
> of the Russian population, enlisting them as allies.[51]

(viii) *Internationalism*. A constant theme throughout the protest writings is that Russian Social Democracy is part of international Social Democracy and as such is committed to its political strategy and the high ideals animating this strategy.

All these propositions were fused together and given emotional content by the merger narrative. There is no ambiguity about the moral Lenin draws from the 'the experience of all countries' in 'Retrogression': the Western-European experience should be an inspirational model for us – what happened there *is* happening *here*, right before our very eyes – we must reject the naysayers who claim the workers are not eagerly moving toward the merger. Lenin tells the story in order to pound these lessons home.

Given the importance in Lenin's writings and especially in WITBD of what can be called the 'history of all countries' argument, we shall look at Lenin's narrative from 'Retrogression' in some detail. Instead of 'merger' [*soedinenie*], Lenin uses here the even stronger word 'fusion' [*sliianie*].

> In all European countries, socialism and the worker movement at first existed
> separately one from the other. The workers carried on a struggle with the
> capitalists and set up strikes and unions; meanwhile, the socialists kept their
> distance from the worker movement and created teachings that criticised
> the contemporary capitalist bourgeois social system and demanded the
> replacement of that system with a higher, socialist system. The separation

---

[50] Lenin 1958–65, 4, p. 261.
[51] Lenin 1958–65, 4, p. 175.

of the worker movement from socialism meant weakness and lack of development in both the one and the other. Socialist teachings that did not merge with the worker struggle remained only utopias – good intentions without any influence on real life. The worker movement remained petty and fragmented; it didn't acquire political significance, it wasn't illuminated by the advanced science of its time. For this reason we see in all European countries a stronger and stronger striving to *fuse* socialism and the worker movement into a single *Social-Democratic* movement.

Given such a fusion, the class struggle of the workers became an *purposive struggle of the proletariat* for its liberation from the exploitation of the owner classes; this class struggle worked out the highest form of the socialist worker movement – *an independent worker Social-Democratic party*. The central contribution of K. Marx and F. Engels was to direct socialism toward a merger with the worker movement: they created a revolutionary theory that explained the necessity of this fusion and gave socialists the task of organising a class struggle of the proletariat.

Lenin immediately applies this master narrative to Russia:

Exactly the same process occurred here in Russia. With us as well socialism existed for a very long time – for many decades – *at a distance* from the struggle of the workers with the capitalists, the strikes of the workers and all the rest. On one hand, the socialists didn't understand Marx's theory and considered it inapplicable to Russia; on the other hand, the Russian worker movement was still in a completely embryonic form.

In the 1870s, the *worker* organisations were the first to understand the vital importance of political freedom while the socialists stood aside, owing to their 'backward, mistaken theory'. Thus, the Russian workers were perfectly justified to stand apart from socialism as long as Russian socialism stood apart from them due to its infatuation with peasant and conspiratorial socialism. But, as soon as the socialists got their act together and became Social Democrats, the worker movement was happy to move toward fusion, as shown in all its large-scale manifestations in the mid-1890s.

The *fusion* of the advanced workers with Social-Democratic organisations was completely natural and inevitable. It was the result of that important historical fact that during the 1890s two profound social movements met in Russia: one was the *stikhiinyi* people's movement in the worker class and the other was the movement of social thought toward the theories of Marx and Engels, to the teaching of Social Democracy . . .

At the present time, the *central* task of all Russian socialists and all purposive Russian workers is to make this fusion durable, to strengthen and organise the Worker Social-Democratic Party. He who doesn't want to recognise this fusion, he who strives artificially to bring some kind of division between the worker movement and Social Democracy in Russia – that person brings *harm*, not benefit, to the cause of worker socialism and the worker movement in Russia.[52]

But some people mistake the central task of the day. They 'call on the workers in essence to separate from Social Democracy and in so doing [they] throw overboard all the achievements of European and Russian experience!'. Although the fusion that is now completing itself is *'natural'* and 'inevitable', the new voices among Social Democrats who want to *'artificially* tear apart the tie between the worker movement and socialism'.[53]

It is instructive to compare the American scholar John Kautsky's summary of the argument of WITBD: 'under capitalism the labour movement spontaneously tends to come "under the wing" of the bourgeoisie unless *artificially* diverted from this *natural* tendency by the Social-Democratic Party'.[54]

Lenin uses the European experience to illustrate the two-front polemical war. One of the new voices (the *Credo*) claimed that the European worker parties are now making a radical shift away from a political focus toward an economic focus. No, says Lenin, already in the 1840s, Marx and Engels were polemicising against utopian socialists who believed that the economic struggle had no importance. From early on, the Marxist movement warned against both exaggerating the significance of economic struggle, as the English workers tended to do, or minimising its significance, as some French and German groups such as the Lassalleans tended to do. The same with politics. Marxism warned against the obsession with politics of the conspiratorial Blanquists *and* against the dismissal of the political struggle in the manner of both wild anarchists and staid professorial socialists.[55]

---

[52] From Lenin 1958–65, 4, pp. 244–7 (order of passages changed).
[53] Lenin 1958–65, 4, p. 262. Emphasis added.
[54] J. Kautsky 1994, 59–62. Emphasis added.
[55] Lenin 1958–65, 4, pp. 170–2.

In the typical Social-Democratic manner, Lenin defined Social Democracy by contrasting it with all the Others who remained outside the synthesis and exaggerated the significance of their little bit of the truth.

Lenin's whole Erfurtian strategy rests on his confidence that the Russian workers will enthusiastically respond to the socialist message. For this reason, he was especially outraged when one of the new voices asserted 'the Russian worker in the mass has not yet matured for political struggle'.[56] Lenin exploded:

> 'The Russian worker in the mass has not yet matured for political struggle'. If this is true, then it is equivalent to a death sentence on all Social Democracy, since it means that the Russian worker in the mass has not yet matured for Social Democratism. In fact, nowhere in the world has there been nor is there now a Social Democracy that is not utterly and completely tied to political struggle. Social Democracy without political struggle – this is a river without water, this is a crying contradiction, this is a return to either to the utopian socialism of our forefathers who despised 'politics', or to anarchism, or to *tred-iunionizm*.[57]

Throughout the protest writings, Lenin is therefore insistent that the worker class has always and everywhere striven for political freedom. He rejects as slander the assertion that Western workers did not support democratic struggles. They did so, he asserts, at a time when the socialists themselves still rejected the primordial importance of political freedom (with the exception, of course, of Marx and Engels).[58] In the 1870s, Russian workers strove for freedoms long before the socialists and things have not changed in the interim:

> Hasn't the Russian worker in the mass over the course of more than twenty years put his best, most developed, most honest and daring comrades into the ranks of revolutionary circles and organisations? . . . The Russian worker in the mass has not only matured for political struggle but has demonstrated his maturity many times over, he has many times carried out acts of political struggle and indeed quite often carried them out in *stikhiinyi* fashion.[59]

---

[56] From the 'Profession de foi' of the Kiev Social Democrats (Lenin 1958–65, 4, p. 311).

[57] Lenin 1958–65, 4, p. 311. *Tred-iunionizm* is an ideology advocating restriction of the worker movement to economic struggle.

[58] Lenin 1958–65, 4, pp. 169–70.

[59] Lenin 1958–65, 4, pp. 314, 313 (order of passages rearranged).

The workers make their political protests in *stikhiinyi* fashion, that is, without the insight and organisation that Social Democracy has dedicated itself to providing – and what do the new Russian Social Democrats do? Instead of devoting all their efforts to supply insight and organisation, they show themselves to be indifferent or even begin to polemicise against the whole idea of political struggle. Scandal![60]

Our survey of the protest writings of 1899 must create a strange impression for anyone raised on the textbook interpretation of *WITBD*. According to this line of thought, the new voices within Russian Social Democracy led to such 'worry about workers' on Lenin's part that he lost all confidence in the socialist inclinations of the workers, he demanded that party activists artificially divert the workers from their natural leanings, he gave up on the idea of a mass movement in autocratic Russia, he rejected the Western model in favour of the Russian revolutionary tradition and, in general, he showed himself an enemy of political freedom.

In 1899, we see Lenin's immediate reaction to the new voices. And, indeed, he is very angry and upset. He is pounding on the table, he is shouting at his adversaries: how dare you lose confidence in the political maturity of the workers? How dare you artificially forestall the natural and inevitable merger of socialism and the worker movement? How dare you become defeatist about our ability to keep the political police from crushing a real mass movement? How dare you throw overboard as of no value the inspiring record of the Western worker parties? How dare you forget the primordial importance of political freedom?

### Articles for *Rabochaia gazeta* (1899)

At the end of 1899, there was a project afoot to resuscitate *Rabochaia gazeta* [*Worker Newspaper*], the newspaper that had been designated by the abortive first party congress as the official organ of the party. As was typical of the underground newspapers in the 1890s, *Rabochaia gazeta* came out with only two issues prior to the congress in 1898 and none afterwards. Lenin was asked to contribute articles for the revived newspaper and he complied with

---

[60] Lenin 1958–65, 4, p. 315.

three short articles. The project fell through, the newspaper never appeared, and the articles were not published in Lenin's lifetime (Lenin discusses the episode in WITBD).[61]

The articles are valuable mainly because Lenin here first set out the organisational themes that became the basis of the *Iskra* group's activity in the following years. The role of a central newspaper in unifying the Party, the need to overcome 'artisan'-like localism, the imperative of inculcating a culture of *konspiratsiia*, and, finally, the need for a clear programme – these themes are the ones WITBD sets out to defend. In many ways, the original formulations of the 1899 articles are preferable to later versions that are more bogged down in polemics. Here, we will touch on only a few points to round out the picture of Lenin's Erfurtianism.

> Social Democracy cannot be reduced to simply providing services for the worker movement: it is 'the merger of socialism with the worker movement' (to use K. Kautsky's expression that reproduces the basic ideas of the *Communist Manifesto*): its task is to bring in definite socialist ideals to the *stikhiinyi* worker movement, to connect the worker movement to socialist convictions that must stand on the level of contemporary science, to connect it with systematic political struggle for democracy as a means for the realisation of socialism – in one word, fuse this *stikhiinyi* movement in one unbreakable whole with the activity of the *revolutionary party*.[62]

After reading this sentence, the reader will stifle a pardonable yawn. Lenin here repeats what he has been saying in every programmatic article since 1894 when he wrote *Friends of the People*. But wait – the reader is uninstructed. According to Leonard Schapiro, this sentence actually reveals fruits of a 'complete transformation of Lenin's outlook' that had occurred a month or two earlier. He argues that in these articles 'there appeared for the first time, in embryonic form, the basic ideas which were to become the characteristic features of what would later be called "Bolshevism" or "Leninism"'.[63] Schapiro

---

[61] Lenin 1958–65, 6, pp. 158–9 [817].
[62] Lenin 1958–65, 4, p. 189.
[63] Schapiro 1987, pp. 234–5. Schapiro ends his citation after the reference to '*stikhiinyi* worker movement', thus leaving out the point about striving for democracy. Schapiro claims that the instigation for Lenin's Paul-like conversion from genuine Social Democracy was the appearance of the new Social-Democratic voices in 1899. But,

does not explain why quoting Kautsky in 1899 signifies a radical change from quoting the same words by Kautsky in 1894.

In these articles, Lenin sets forth the core of the 'organisational plan' expounded in WITBD, namely, using a national Social-Democratic newspaper as a tool for creating a unified and nation-wide party structure. Lenin asserts that his scheme is based on 'the history of socialism and democracy in Western Europe, the history of the Russian revolutionary movement, the experience of our worker movement'. Nevertheless, both Europe today and Russia in the days of Narodnaia volia are quite different from Russia today.[64] Let us see whether Lenin's organisational dreams lead him to reject the European model in favour of models taken from the Russian revolutionary tradition.

Lenin's tone when talking about revolutionary parties such as Narodnaia volia is *concessive*. When his opponents point to the continued relevance of Narodnaia volia, Lenin responds: yes, yes, of course we acknowledge the need for underground technique. At the same time, he wants to set a fairly stringent limit to this concession:

> Russian Social Democracy is distinct from early revolutionary parties in Russia in highly essential matters, so that the necessity of learning revolutionary technique and the technique of *konspiratsiia* from the old Russian leaders [*korifei*] (we have no hesitation at all in conceding this necessity) in no way relieves us of the responsibility to take a critical attitude toward them and to work out independently our own form of organisation.[65]

The 'not particularly elaborate methods of *konspiratsiia*' of the past will help an underground newspaper get sufficient material – but *distribution* of the newspaper goes beyond the old techniques, since previous forms of the revolutionary movement in Russia simply did not set themselves the task of distributing newspapers to 'the masses of the people'.[66]

Lenin's newspaper plan also takes into account an essential difference with European models:

---

since he passes over all the protest writings in silence, he neatly avoids confronting the difficulties for the textbook interpretation pointed out in the previous section.

[64] Lenin 1958–65, 4, pp. 189–90.

[65] Lenin 1958–65, 4, p. 190.

[66] Lenin 1958–65, 4, p. 195. *Konspiratsiia*, the set of rules for surviving in the underground, is quite distinct from conspiracy as a political strategy (see Chapter Eight for full discussion).

> The necessity of concentrating *all* our forces on the organisation of a party organ that comes out regularly and is properly distributed shows the originality of our situation in comparison both to Social Democracy in other European countries and to older Russian revolutionary parties. Besides newspapers, the workers of Germany, France and elsewhere have a mass of other means of announcing publicly what they are doing as well as other means of organising the movement: parliamentary activity, electoral agitation, popular meetings, participation in local social institutions (rural and urban), open activity of craft (trade, guild) unions and so on and so on. With us, the revolutionary newspaper is *the substitute for all of that* – and I mean *all* of that – until such time as we conquer political freedom. Without a revolutionary newspaper it is impossible for us to have *any* kind of broad organisation of the whole worker movement.[67]

Lenin is saying: we differ from earlier Russian revolutionaries because, on the whole, we are *superior* – we have better theories, we set ourselves wider tasks. We differ from Western Social Democrats because we are perforce *inferior* – we can only envy the broad range of outlets available to French and German workers. Nevertheless, with our one newspaper, we will strive to accomplish the essence of what the Germans are doing: 'Studieren, Propagandieren, Organisieren'.[68] The reader will recall that Lenin quoted this same Liebknecht slogan in his first programmatic writings in 1894.

Lenin evokes both European experience and Russian experience in justifying his own proposals. But these two sources do not have equal rhetorical weight. When speaking about the Russian revolutionary model, Lenin contents himself with the general statement that there is much to learn from these people. We never hear of any concrete example of success in *konspiratsiia*, or the name of any individual particularly noted for expertise in this matter, or even any specific techniques. In contrast, when Lenin talks about the experience of the European worker movement, concrete examples spill out of him. Let us use front organisations, just like the French workers did under Napoleon III and the German workers did under the emergency laws. Let us off-load as much underground activity as we can to legal organisations, as we are advised to

---

[67] Lenin 1958–65, 4, p. 192.
[68] Ibid.

do by *Vorwärts*, the central organ of the SPD. Let us be inspired by the German experience with an underground newspaper:

> During the epoch of the exceptional laws against the socialists (from 1878 to 1890), the German political police worked no worse and perhaps even better than the Russian police, and yet the German workers, thanks to their discipline and organisation, were able to ensure that an illegal weekly newspaper was brought into the country from abroad and delivered to all subscribers, so that even government ministers could not help praising the Social-Democratic post (the 'red post'). We, of course, do not even dream of success on this scale.[69]

We have seen how Lenin invokes the example of both present-day Western Europe and the earlier Russian revolutionaries to support his plan for a nation-wide newspaper. Lenin also makes a highly characteristic assertion about present-day Russia to boost the plausibility of his ambitious schemes. 'Among the worker youth can be found a passionate and unstoppable striving towards the ideas of democracy and socialism' – so, if we can get these people to understand the importance of organisation, then the plan of a regularly appearing paper need not remain a dream. Successful distribution is entirely possible because we can direct copies to industrial districts where 'the worker is factually master of the situation with hundreds of ways to outwit the vigilance of the police'.[70] Clearly, if Lenin ever does lose his confidence in the workers and in the fundamental relevance of the Western model, he is going to find his organisational plan much harder to defend.

Looking ahead, Lenin evokes the West-European worker movements to explain to his worker readers why political freedom must be their most urgent goal.

> No economic struggle can bring firm improvements to the workers – none can even be carried out on a broad scale – if the workers do not have the right to freely set up meetings, set up unions, have their own papers, send their own representatives to popular assemblies, as do the workers of Germany and all other European countries (except Turkey and Russia).[71]

---

[69] Lenin 1958–65, 4, p. 196. Chapter Seven documents this rhetorical imbalance in *WITBD*.

[70] Lenin 1958–65, 4, pp. 195–6. Chapter Eight shows how the assumption of the underground party's roots in the worker milieu informs Lenin's organisational schemes.

[71] Lenin 1958–65, 4, p. 185.

The *Rabochaia gazeta* articles bring out clearly the logic behind Lenin's plan: we must build a party as much like the SPD as possible under absolutist conditions, so we can overthrow the tsar and obtain the political liberties we need to make the party even more like the SPD!

## 'A Draft Programme for Our Party' (1899)

We end our survey with yet another stab at coming up with an actual programme for the fledgling Social-Democratic Party. 'A Draft Programme for Our Party' was also written for *Rabochaia gazeta* and remained unpublished. It is more a discussion piece about the principles of a Social-Democratic programme than an actual programme draft.

Lenin's continued efforts to provide a programme is itself a consequence of his Erfurtian outlook. A proper Social-Democratic party has a clear statement of principles that serves as a banner for the army of fighters for socialism. The party banner raises the morale of the combatants and sends a message to outsiders.[72] According to Lenin, 'a programme should grasp the *whole* movement, while in practice, of course, now one, now another side of the movement must be moved into the foreground'.[73] In this sense, WITBD is a practical book, not a programmatic one, since it deals with specific issues that occupied the forefront at a particular time. Much misunderstanding of WITBD results from treating it as a programmatic book that attempts 'to grasp the whole movement'. Our long journey through Lenin's genuinely programmatic writings provides us with a context for avoiding these errors.

For the actual text of the programme, Lenin goes back to a draft programme issued by Plekhanov's Emancipation of Labour group in 1885. He announces that this draft is still basically sound and needs only partial corrections. In the course of our survey, we have seen Lenin assert several times that he is defending the tradition both of international Social Democracy and Russian Social Democracy. His adoption of a fourteen-year-old draft programme as a basic text is a striking expressing of his loyalty to Russian Social Democracy as defined by the Plekhanov group. How does this loyalty fit into the Erfurtian framework?

---

[72] Lenin 1958–65, 4, pp. 213–15.
[73] Lenin 1958–65, 4, p. 238.

Earlier, we looked at an article by the populist Petr Lavrov arguing that Social Democracy was mostly inapplicable to Russian political conditions. In that article, he scoffed that the Russian Social Democrats 'let the Germans write their programmes for them'.[74] This sort of remark must have rankled, since Lenin responds four years later:

> Not in the slightest are we afraid to say that we wish to imitate the Erfurt Programme. There is nothing bad about imitating something good. Precisely because one so often hears opportunist and half-hearted criticism of this programme, we consider it our duty to openly speak up for it.[75]

The Erfurt Programme is thus the essential model. The draft of the Plekhanov group is acceptable because it passes the test presented by the German Programme. As Lenin says, the theses of the Plekhanov programme 'have again and again received confirmation in the development of socialist theory as well as the development of the worker movement in all countries'.[76] When there is a clash between the Erfurt Programme and the Plekhanov programme – for example, in the demand found in the Russian Programme for 'direct popular legislation' to supersede representative parliaments – the Erfurt Programme takes precedence.[77]

Of course, the Erfurt Programme must be adjusted to meet Russian conditions. Lenin mentions two main issues requiring creative adaptation: the lack of political freedom and the peasant question. We have discussed the first issue at length throughout this chapter. Lenin's treatment of the peasant issue in this article is his first statement of his proposals of a peasant strategy for Russian Social Democracy. His elaboration and defence of his strategy is a major theme in his writings of the *Iskra* period. Since WITBD does not take up the peasant question – another reason why it is *not* a programmatic work – we will not go into the details of Lenin's strategy. All that is necessary here is to show that Lenin is searching for an answer to an Erfurtian problem.

The Erfurtian outlook calls on Social Democracy to become a tribune of the people, to act as the most resolute defender of their current non-socialist

---

[74] Lavrov's article as printed in Lenin 1926–35, 2, pp. 605–9.
[75] Lenin 1958–65, 4, p. 219.
[76] Lenin 1958–65, 4, p. 217.
[77] Lenin 1958–65, 4, pp. 223–4; Lenin cites Kautsky's *Parliamentarism* on the subject. Plekhanov also writes somewhere that Kautsky has shown that this demand is outmoded.

interests and to mobilise their support in the fight for political freedom. Many people will ask whether this strategy is even possible in the case of the peasants, since (it is said) the Marxists saw the peasants as nothing more than a sack of potatoes, had only contempt for the mental capacities of the peasants, saw them as the *main* barrier to social progress, and so forth.[78] Although these assumptions about the Marxist outlook have no basis, Lenin does proceeds with uncharacteristic defensiveness here, because he feels there are valid Social-Democratic suspicions that he must dispel. These suspicions concern peasant *interests* and peasant *revolutionary qualities*.

Lenin's view of peasant interests can be summarised as follows: modern economic development is ending the possibility of *independent* small-scale production. This is inevitable and there is nothing we can do about it, nor should we want to. But the loss of independence can take place in three different contexts. The best context for small producers like the peasants would be a socialist society under proletarian class rule. In this case, the process of losing independence will take place voluntarily and without victimisation. When the process takes place under capitalism, the human costs are much higher: expropriation, impoverishment, ruin. But even worse is a third possibility: the peasants face the onslaught of capitalism, while bound hand and foot by the autocratic order, by the restrictions imposed by the peasant commune and by artificial economic dependence on the noble landowners. To try to protect the peasants against capitalism by preserving this kind of restriction – for example, protecting the peasant commune by not permitting the peasant to refuse or to sell his allotment land – is nonsense. It will not stop capitalism, but it will stop peasants from using their resources as *they* best see fit. On the contrary, Social Democracy must push for the removal of all these restrictions and enlist peasant support for the removal of the most repulsive restriction of them all – the tsarist autocracy.

Lenin is somewhat defensive when it comes to devising the specific measure to implement this strategy, because he does not want to be seen – either in the eyes of other Social Democrats or *in foro interno* – as encouraging small-scale at the expense of large-scale production. So, he makes a distinction between ending dependence (progressive) and encouraging small-scale production (reactionary). The hostility to restrictions on individual peasants

---

[78] I discuss the 'sack of potatoes' image in Lih 2001a.

implies a large overlap with a standard liberal definition of the situation. Lenin is perfectly well aware of this overlap and even brings it out in another article written around this time.[79] The overlap with liberalism on this point is somewhat similar to the overlap about political freedom.

Besides these calculations, there would seem to be a moral dimension to Lenin's programme, as we see from this version of the 'sooner or later' argument addressed to fellow Social Democrats:

> Of course, the development of capitalism is leading and will lead in the final analysis to the removal of these holdovers [of serfdom] 'all by itself, in the natural way of things'. But, in the first place, these holdovers possess extraordinary tenacity so that one cannot rely on their swift removal. In the second place – and this is the main point – this 'natural path' means nothing other than the dying out of the peasants who are *factually* (thanks to labour services and the like) tied to the land and enserfed to the landowner. It goes without saying that under these circumstances Social Democrats cannot pass over this question in silence in their programme . . .
>
> Social Democrats cannot remain indifferent spectators of the starvation of the peasants and their destruction from death by starvation. Never could there be two opinions among Russian Social Democrats about the necessity of the broadest possible help to the starving peasants. And is there anyone who will affirm that such help is possible without revolutionary measures?[80]

The other prejudice to which that Lenin responds somewhat defensively concerns the peasant's *revolutionary qualities*. Lenin assures the reader that he is well aware of peasant 'lack of development and darkness' and that violent peasant outbursts are not the same as purposive revolutionary struggle. Certainly, the Social Democrats cannot *count* on the peasant. But times are changing and Social Democrats would be derelict if they did not cheer and encourage the growing peasant purposiveness. Here, Lenin cites a classic Marx passage about the emerging conflict within the peasantry between the

---

[79] The article 'Which Heritage Do We Renounce' was written in 1897 (1958–65, 2, pp. 505–50). For an attack on Lenin precisely for this overlap with the liberals, see Kingston-Mann 1999.

[80] Lenin 1958–65, 4, pp. 235, 233 (order of passages reversed). According to memoir evidence, Lenin was opposed to famine help in 1891. I cannot here undertake to reconcile this discrepancy. For a good discussion of the context of Lenin's views in 1891, see Ingerflom 1988.

tendency to support despotic régimes such as Napoleon III and the tendency to fight against them.[81]

The actual strategy proposed by Lenin in 1899 is hardly bold: return some of the peasant land taken at the time of the peasant emancipation in 1861 and adopt a 'maybe so, maybe no' attitude to peasant revolutionary action. But, if we look at Lenin's *reasoning* and the direction in which he is moving, we will easily see the continuity in his peasant strategy throughout his career. My point here is that this innovative strategy arose out of his search for a way to fulfill Erfurtian guidelines. To support this contention, let us leap ahead a few years and look at Kautsky's remarkable 1906 article 'The Driving Forces of the Russian Revolution and Its Prospects'.[82] Here, Karl Kautsky, the authoritative spokesman for Erfurtianism, turns to Russia and lays out the basic hegemony strategy that (as I argued earlier) was implied in his 1893 book *Parliamentarism*. Only the overthrow of the autocracy will unleash economic progress among the Russian peasants; the Russian bourgeoisie has good reason to shy away from revolutionary measures; the proletariat must lead the peasantry on the basis of genuine and durable common interests. The coming revolution will not be a standard 'bourgeois revolution', but who cares?

Particularly striking is Kautsky's account of the transformation of the Russian peasant in recent years 'from a good-natured, sleepy unreflective creature of habit into a energetic, restless and untiring fighter who strives toward something new and better'. Oppression that earlier would have crushed him now makes him stand taller.

> He no longer allows others to think for him – he is compelled to think for himself, compelled to use all his mother wit, all his energy, all his recklessness, and to cast out all his prejudices so that he can firmly assert himself in the incredible whirlwind of events into which he has been drawn.[83]

Lenin was in ecstasy. He promptly translated Kautsky's article into Russian and provided it with a preface that began

---

[81] Lenin 1958–65, 4, pp. 131–2. The citation is from Marx's *18th Brumaire*. For a discussion of the Marx passage, see Lih 2001a.

[82] Kautsky 1906. Both Lenin and Trotsky translated Kautsky's article into Russian; Trotsky's translation can be found in Trotsky 1993. An English translation of Kautsky's article can be found in Harding 1983, pp. 356–72.

[83] Kautsky 1906, p. 330.

> The advanced Russian workers have long known K. Kautsky as *their* writer,
> one who can not only explain and provide foundations for the theoretical
> teachings of revolutionary Marxism but can also apply them on the basis
> of real knowledge and serious analysis of the facts to the complicated and
> confused questions of the Russian revolution.

Lenin saw Kautsky's argument as a complete vindication. 'A bourgeois
revolution carried out by the proletariat and the peasantry despite the
unreliability of the bourgeoisie – this fundamental proposition of Bolshevik
tactics is completely confirmed by Kautsky'.[84]

In his 1899 critique of the new voices in Social Democracy, Lenin presented
himself as having *more confidence* in the workers than his opponents. In
arguments with fellow Social Democrats about the peasants, Lenin (along
with Kautsky) presents himself as having more confidence in the peasants
as well. Lenin's wager is that the peasants will become more and more
independent and purposive, they will understand their interests better and
they will realise that the rational way to achieve their interests is revolutionary
struggle under the guidance of the Social-Democratic proletariat. Lenin hedges
his bets with the peasants in a way that he does not with the workers. If the
workers do not respond, Social Democracy is dead. If the peasants do not
respond, well, it's too bad, but life and struggle go on. Nevertheless, Lenin
placed hopes on the peasantry that struck many then and strike many now
as unrealistically optimistic. We should keep this fact in mind when assessing
the debates over *WITBD*'s alleged worry about workers.

We have ended our trek through Lenin's programmatic writings from the
beginning of his career in 1894 to the end of his Siberian exile in 1899. We
leave him as he goes abroad in preparation for a new phase in his career. The
reader may feel our journey has been somewhat monotonous at times. In
fact, I hope so – because one of my main points is the unwearying regularity
with which Lenin presents his Erfurtian outlook. The continuity is nicely
symbolised by the quotations from Kautsky ('Social Democracy is the merger
of socialism and the worker movement') and Liebknecht ('Studieren,
Propagandieren, Organisieren') that we find both in 1894 and 1899.

The presentation changes in emphasis according to polemical context. Lenin
passes lightly over points when he believes that his audience agrees with

---

[84] Lenin 1958–65, 14, pp. 221, 225.

him and concentrates on points where he thinks his audience needs convincing. But the entire Erfurtian checklist can almost always be found. The narrative underpinning the outlook – the inspiring story of the European worker parties as interpreted by the *Erfurt Programme* – is usually in evidence. When Lenin feels that core Social-Democratic values are under attack, as in the protest writings of 1899, this narrative surfaces in passionate detail.

The 1890s were a time of great change for Russian society and for the worker movement in particular, and Lenin's rhetoric reflects these changes. For the most part, developments only strengthened Lenin's Erfurtian faith. Things seems to be proceeding according to the Erfurtian scenario. In the 1890s, the workers began to stage militant protests, began to accept Social-Democratic guidance, and forced the government to make concessions. The Social Democrats themselves were weak and disorganised, so this success could only mean they had correctly identified a vast and powerful social force. In 1898, the merger took a giant step foreword with the creation of at least a notional Russian Social-Democratic Worker Party. Lenin had nothing to do with this step forward, a circumstance which must have increased his confidence in the universality of the merger narrative that predicted a drive in all countries toward a independent worker party as the highest form of the class struggle.

True, Lenin was surprised and shocked by the Social-Democratic voices that emerged in 1899. This scepticism within Social-Democratic ranks was something he had not predicted. His first reaction was to re-assert his core Erfurtian values. His second or third reaction was not any different. In 1899, Lenin begins to set out some of the policy proposals that he later defended in *WITBD*. We shall look at these proposals in more detail in later chapters. Here, we note only that the proposals were presented and defended in Erfurtian terms.

Why do we read *WITBD*? For most people, no doubt, the interest of the book is not in the specific policies it advocates but in the general framework of ideas used to justify the proposals, since *WITBD* is supposed to tell us about the core values that Lenin later applied to very different situations. But, if that is the case, our work is done. Lenin does not develop any new core values between late 1899 and late 1901. The examination of *WITBD* will tell us nothing about these values that we do not know already.

Nevertheless, we shall proceed to give the background context for the concrete policies and polemics of *WITBD*. This context is necessary for understanding *WITBD* as a historical document, that is, as an event in the life of Russian Social Democracy. It is also necessary to clear away the misconceptions that have prevented readers from seeing *WITBD*'s Erfurtian heart. And so we now focus our attention on one particular episode in the story of Russian Social Democracy: *Iskra*'s drive to consummate the merger between socialism and the Russian worker movement.

# Chapter Three
## The *Iskra* Period

In Lenin's view, the great historic fact of the 1890s in Russia was the emergence of all the elements needed for genuine Russian Social Democracy. On the one side, a militant worker movement had grown up and, on the other, the socialists finally understood the need for a merger. The two were already working together and had achieved astonishing successes, considering that both partners were still in an embryonic condition. They had compelled – yes, compelled – the tsarist government to make a highly visible legislative concession (the law of 2 June 1897 on working hours), something no Russian social group acting independently had ever done before. Both of these natural partners were, for their own reasons, yearning for closer contact. The highest form of merger was an independent, class-based nation-wide political party. Many people assumed that such a party was impossible under tsarism – but, in 1898, the foundations were laid for a Russian Social-Democratic Worker Party.

Surely, thought Lenin, only those with eyes that did not see would deny that the merger scenario set forth in the canonical documents of European Social Democracy was being confirmed yet again by the course of events in Russia. The central task for Russian Social Democrats in the immediate period ahead was clear: to consummate the merger, to give the notional

Social-Democratic Party a flesh-and-bones existence and to turn all energies toward fulfilling the historic task of bringing political freedom to Russia. What this meant in concrete terms can be summarised by the popular triadic formula of organisation, programme, tactics. Organisation: create functioning national party institutions that would be granted enough legitimacy by local organisations to make genuine co-ordination possible. Programme: adopt a precise Social-Democratic programme and clear the way for this programme by criticising prevalent misunderstandings of what Social Democracy was all about. Tactics: continue to galvanise the society-wide onslaught against the autocracy by revealing the worker movement as the front-line fighter for democracy.

The instrument for all these tasks was to be the underground newspaper *Iskra*. The first issue of this remarkable publication was published abroad in December 1900 and some fifteen issues had appeared by the time *WITBD* was completed in early 1902. *WITBD* was a manifesto of *Iskra*-ism (although, as we shall see, not an expression of all aspects of *Iskra*'s outlook). *WITBD*'s positive aim was to set out the details of *Iskra*'s plan for accomplishing the three tasks just mentioned. Its polemical aim was to combat various criticisms of *Iskra* that had appeared in the autumn of 1901 in response to *Iskra*'s first seven or so issues. The more concrete an idea we have of what *Iskra* was all about, the easier it is for us to enter into the world of *WITBD*.

The layout of a typical issue of *Iskra* would not win any journalism awards today. The masthead on the first page said '*Iskra*' in large letters. On the left-hand side were the words 'Proletarians of the world, unite!' On the right-hand side was an explanation of the name of the newspaper (*iskra* means 'spark'): 'From a spark will burn a flame! . . . the response of the Decembrists to Pushkin' (ellipsis in original). Thus the masthead combined Social Democracy on the left side with the Russian revolutionary tradition on the right side (the Decembrists were aristocratic rebels who tried to overthrow the tsar in 1824).

Right underneath the masthead was the date and issue number. In *Iskra*'s case, the date was perhaps more than just informative, since part of its prestige came from the frequency and regularity of its issues. Although *Iskra* did not live up to its own goals on this score, it did outshine all other Russian underground newspapers.

Each page of *Iskra* consisted of three columns of small print. An issue contained four to eight pages and each page was 42 by 46 centimetres. A lead article of two columns takes up about six pages when reprinted in Lenin's complete works. At that rate, if the first fifteen issues of *Iskra* were printed in book form, they would take up 774 pages. (More approximately, the 51 issues that came out while Lenin was on the editorial board would take up 2,700 pages and the full run of 112 issues – *Iskra* ceased publication at the end of 1905 – would take up 6,000 pages.)

The newspaper itself contained no indication of the identities of the editorial board. Only very rarely were articles by-lined. At the end was a German post-office box address for correspondence. This coyness was mainly due to considerations of *konspiratsiia* [underground secrecy], but it also strengthened the impression that *Iskra* spoke with a single voice. At the Second Congress in 1903, when the members of the editorial board were at each other's throats, many party members were aghast because they had become so accustomed to thinking of the *Iskra* group as a model of teamwork and unity of outlook.

The prose style of *Iskra*'s columns matched the fiercely small print. While journalistic, it was dense, difficult and not meant for the faint of heart or the newly literate. Two opinions existed, then and now, about this prose style. One is that it was an insult to the workers since it was clearly not meant for them but, rather, for revolutionary intellectuals. The other view is that it was a compliment to the workers. It did not condescend to them, dumb down the issues or hide away questions that deeply concerned the intellectuals. The top strata of the workers would be fully equal to it and the middle strata would be challenged rather than discouraged.

The lead articles taking up the first and second page were either polemics against other revolutionaries or indictments of some current outrage by the tsarist government. On the remaining pages came a number of regular sections contributed mainly by *Iskra*'s correspondents – that is, by anyone who took the effort to write in with a description of this or that abuse or strike or protest. The first section was 'From Our Social Life'. Here, the reader found a running account of the battle between government and society – all of society, not just the workers. The next section was 'Chronicle of the Worker Movement and Letters from Factories and Workshops'. The spatial priority of the section 'From Our Social Life' was deliberate. The aim of *Iskra* was to broaden horizons beyond local conflicts with individual capitalists so as to include all of tsarist oppression as well as the resistance engulfing Russian society as a whole.

Two other regular sections were 'Foreign Survey' and 'From the Party'. The 'Foreign Survey' section was almost exclusively devoted to developments within European Social Democracy: party congresses, ideological disputes, electoral successes. The section 'From the Party' contained documents and communiqués from local committees, along with *Iskra's* comments.

What message would be received by the diligent Russian reader – whether 'advanced worker', Social-Democratic *praktik*, or police official – from these first fifteen issues? First of all, the priority of political freedom. The first issue announced that political freedom was 'the same vital necessity for the worker class as air for a living being'.[1] Almost a year later, the new banner of the workers was contrasted to the programme of earlier Russian revolutionaries:

> 'Land and Liberty' was written on the banner of socialist intellectuals of the 1870s. 'Political freedom in order to fight for socialism' – this is the banner under which the workers will finally take their place in the common democratic struggle with tsarism.[2]

Thus political freedom was, for the time being, in the front seat, while socialism was in the back seat. It would be hard to find articles in *Iskra* on the attractiveness of socialist society, the necessity for common ownership, the meaning of surplus-value, or even the wickedness of capitalist owners. Making propaganda for socialism was not *Iskra's* mission. *Iskra* was a revolutionary newspaper and so it preached the overthrow of tsarism in order to obtain political freedom.

One cannot help observing that, despite *Iskra's* mythical status, many of its arguments would have been seen as scandalous in Soviet times. According to the reactionaries, announces *Iskra*, a free press in a bourgeois country is a fraud because rich capitalists corrupt it and use it to dupe the workers. (Now, who would be using this same argument twenty or thirty years later?) These reactionaries forget that a free press provides its own antidote by allowing bourgeois lies to be combatted.[3]

The battle for political freedom was fast approaching its climax – *Iskra* sent this message on every column on every page. 'The autocracy is living out its

---

[1] *Iskra*, No. 1 (December 1900) ('Achievements of International Social Democracy'). For the background of the 'light and air' metaphor, see Chapter One.

[2] *Iskra*, No. 11 (20 November 1901).

[3] *Iskra*, No. 8 (10 September 1901).

last minutes and the pressure of this huge, dying and rapidly disintegrating carcass is vividly felt everywhere – in industrial centres and in sleepy villages'.[4] *All* sections of Russian society were exasperated with this clumsy monster, *all* wished to destroy this barrier to Russian progress.

The section entitled 'From Our Social Life' brought out the sheer ubiquity of dissatisfaction with the government. Protests broke out everywhere. In one issue, this section contained reports from Petersburg, Moscow, Saratov, Vilna and Kostroma.[5] Protest could be found in all strata of society – not only the workers and peasants, but the urban petty bourgeoisie, the school teachers (who were told that the fight for political freedom was the fight for genuine enlightenment of the people), the statisticians, the *zemstvo* activists, and even a voice or two from among the noble landowners. The sympathy of these strata for *Iskra*'s cause was dramatically demonstrated by the secret documents provided by whistle-blowers and printed in *Iskra*. All nationalities were up in arms. 'In each ethnic group of the Russian state a worker movement is growing and becoming stronger as it strives to become a Social-Democratic movement'. Freedom was indivisible, *Iskra* preached, and the tsar's Russification policies were forcing 'wider and wider strata of the Russian people to join under the watchword: long live free Finland! long live free Russia!'.[6]

The 'Chronicle of the Worker Movement' section painted a corresponding picture of an increasingly militant proletariat. 'From Ivanovo-Voznezensk we hear of a whole series of small factory protests that show that the growth of poverty caused by the [economic] crisis plus the agitation carried out by local Social Democrats has not been without effect'.[7] The workers are more than ready and willing – as one of the lead articles put it, 'without waiting for their [Social-Democratic ] leader/guides, the proletariat threw itself into battle'.[8]

The other sections of the newspaper contributed to the picture. According to the 'Foreign Survey', the strong and advancing Social-Democratic movement in Europe had the deepest interest in Russian developments and the deepest sympathy for its revolutionary struggle. Within the Russian Party, the current

---

[4] *Iskra*, No. 7 (August 1901).
[5] *Iskra*, No. 6 (July 1901).
[6] *Iskra*, No. 1 (December 1900).
[7] *Iskra*, No. 6 (July 1901).
[8] *Iskra*, No. 3 (April 1901).

was running strongly against the 'economist' fallacies of the past, as shown by the documents discussed in the section 'From the Party'. Even the more extended polemics in the lead articles usually sought to give this impression (the exception being the breakout of war between *Iskra* and the émigré journal *Rabochee delo*, of which more in Chapter Five).

I have not said anything up to now about who was putting together *Iskra* issue after issue because I wanted to suggest how little *Iskra*'s first readers themselves knew. It is now time to provide this information. The editorial board of *Iskra* was a coalition between the émigré elder statesmen who had founded Russian Social Democracy in the 1880s (Plekhanov, Alsekrod, and Zasulich) and younger Russian *praktiki* who had been directly involved in organising and publishing activities in Russia during the 1890s. The younger men – the first two had just finished up exile in Siberia – were Vladimir Ulianov (Lenin), Iulii Martov and Aleksandr Potresov. After various negotiations in 1900 that almost fell through (one of the very few personal documents we have from Lenin is a poignant description of 'how the Spark was almost extinguished'), a workable editorial routine was set up. The main literary contributors were Plekhanov, Martov and Lenin. It is fair to say that without the utter dedication of Lenin and his wife Nadezhda Krupskaya the ambitious project would have fallen through many times over.

The newspaper was printed first in Zurich and later in London and smuggled into Russia by a variety of means. Part of the mystique of *Iskra* came from the double-bottomed suitcases, the false passports, the disappearing ink, the heartbreaking failures and the gleeful successes that were part of distributing *Iskra*. Like the 'red post' of *Sozialdemokrat* during the anti-socialist laws in Germany, *Iskra* thumbed its nose at the tsarist government merely by existing.[9]

As I have said, about fifteen issues had come out by the time WITBD was completed. The Party's Second Congress in August 1903 was *Iskra*'s triumph and failure – triumph because an effective party congress had been one of the newspaper's principal aims and because *Iskra* was now declared the official organ of the Party, failure because the editorial board fell apart in mutual recriminations. After the Second Congress there was always one or more prominent party figures outside the editorial board and hostile to it. For the

---

[9] For an English-language memoir description of various smuggling methods, see Piatnitsky 1925.

first few issues after the Second Congress the editorial board consisted of just Lenin and Plekhanov. Starting with issue 52 in fall 1903, Lenin was out and, very soon thereafter, everybody else (Akselrod, Zasulich, Martov, Potresov) came back in, although unity remained fragile. *Iskra* continued as more or less an organ of the Menshevik faction until its 112th issue in October 1905. The term '*Iskra* period' in this commentary refers to the period of the original editorial board from December 1900 to August 1903.[10]

*Iskra* had a sister journal, *Zaria* [*Dawn*], that contained long serious articles, book reviews and the like. Besides contributions from the *Iskra* board, *Zaria* printed articles by (among others) Kautsky, David Riazanov (the future Marx scholar), Parvus and the young philosopher Liubov Akselrod. Three volumes came out (one was a double issue, No. 2–3 in December 1901), two before WITBD's completion and the final one in 1902. *Zaria* was Plekhanov's chance to tear revisionism to shreds. Lenin contributed articles to *Zaria* but his main interest was *Iskra* and its more practical concerns.

To an unappreciated extent, Karl Kautsky directly supported the *Iskra* enterprise. He contributed an autobiographical essay to *Zaria* (a valuable and overlooked one) and an article to *Iskra* entitled 'The Slavs and Revolution' which became a classic (Lenin was still quoting it with approval after the Revolution). He also intervened in a pro-*Iskra* manner in one of the disputes between *Iskra* and *Rabochee delo*. When the *Iskra* board fell apart, Kautsky had little compunction about wading in with his opinion. In short, Kautsky knew a champion of Erfurtianism when he saw one.[11]

*Iskra* was not just making it up when it described the growing revolutionary excitement in Russia. The years 1900–3 were indeed enveloped in an atmosphere of a growing revolutionary storm – a storm that broke out in 1905. The meaning of *Iskra*-ism cannot be separated from this atmosphere. To help evoke it, I will rely on two documents from 1904, both written to explain Russian developments to foreign audiences and therefore most apt for our purposes. One was based on a series of lectures given in America by the historian and liberal party leader Paul Miliukov, the other was a small book whipped together by Lenin and his lieutenants to present the Bolshevik side to the

---

[10] Chapter Nine of this commentary is devoted to the polemics that the former *Iskra* colleagues aimed at each other during 1903–4.

[11] For Kautsky's relations with the Russians, see Donald 1993 and Weill 1977.

delegates at the international Social-Democratic congress in Amsterdam in August 1904. Together they will help us grasp what *Iskra* meant to informed readers of the time.

## A view from the side: Paul Miliukov

Miliukov was a type we do not see much of these days: a liberal revolutionary. Like the Social Democrats, he wanted to overthrow the autocracy to obtain political freedom. Unlike the Social Democrats, he wanted political freedom more or less for its own sake. After getting into various kinds of trouble with the tsarist government, he went on a long trip abroad in 1903 and in the summer of that year gave a series of lectures in America (written by him in English – he was something of a linguistic prodigy). The aim of the lectures was to set out a comprehensive interpretation of Russian history *and* to bring home to Americans the seriousness of Russia's revolutionary situation. After a trip to London – where he looked up Lenin, presumably as the author of WITBD, and found him 'a stubborn debater and a slow-thinking scholar', as he put it many years later – he returned to America and revised his lectures for publication.[12] The chapter on the socialist tradition was especially reworked in the light of the great collection of Russian revolutionary pamphlets at Harvard.[13] In the last pages of his book, we see Miliukov receiving the exciting news from Russia in January 1905 that a massacre had taken place on Bloody Sunday and that the revolution had begun in earnest.

I believe that *Russia and Its Crisis* remains today the best introduction in any language to the historical background of the *Iskra* enterprise. Not that there is a great deal in the book about *Iskra* itself. The book is a unique resource because Miliukov combined a historian's detachment with a keen interest in the forces driving Russia toward revolution – one of which was *Iskra*. Miliukov's study provides us with three essential components of *Iskra*'s context: the Russian socialist tradition as understood in 1900, the European context for socialist political strategy, and the accelerating revolutionary crisis in Russia itself.[14]

---

[12] The description of Lenin is from Miliukov 1922, p. 48.

[13] For background on Miliukov and particularly on the writing of this book, see Stockdale 1996.

[14] Miliukov 1962.

Miliukov viewed *Iskra* itself with a sardonic but essentially sympathetic eye, for he was glad to see a champion of political freedom triumph over its Social-Democratic rivals. He presents *Iskra* to his American audience as on the right side. He never mentions Lenin or any of the younger Social-Democratic leaders. Nevertheless, I am fairly certain he had read WITBD and, indeed, wrote a perceptive review of it for the underground liberal journal *Osvobozhdenie*. In an Appendix to this chapter, I provide a text of this anonymous review and give my reasons for assigning it to Miliukov.

Miliukov's book sets out for us what 'absence of political freedom' meant in tsarist Russia. The overwhelming temptation when reading this sort of description is to say to oneself: you think tsarism is bad – wait till you see tsarism's successor. And this is a valid reaction. But let us abstract from the grim ironies of the twentieth century and see tsarist Russia as a liberal and a patriot would see it.

Miliukov notes the large number of institutions and persons 'whose particular duty it is to observe, to discover, and to punish political offences'.[15] Secret police informers are everywhere, not only in revolutionary and Social-Democratic organisations but also in private circles for self-education and even among school children. The 'janitors' – the concierge-type figures installed in apartment buildings – are forcibly enlisted as spies on private residences. Judicial controls barely exist; prescribed formal procedures are but 'legalised arbitrariness'.[16] Nero's Rome pales by comparison.

Every Russian citizen must carry an internal passport, which must be shown to the 'janitors' at all times. 'You are not permitted to pass the night, were it with your friends or relatives, without showing your passport to the janitor, or your host and landlord may be punished by a fine of as much as \$250'.[17] This requirement applies to everybody, while people marked as untrustworthy come under various sorts of special 'surveillance' associated with restrictions of movement. The police can at any time enter the lodgings of someone under strict surveillance – although, Miliukov remarks sardonically, 'this last arrogance cannot be particularly resented, because actually, though not legally, such is the general condition of the Russian citizen'.[18] The dimensions of the current

---

[15] Miliukov 1962, p. 144.
[16] Miliukov 1962, p. 147.
[17] Miliukov 1962, p. 148.
[18] Miliukov 1962, p. 149.

revolutionary crisis is shown by an explosion in the number of people under surveillance: in 1880, 2,873 people under internal exile, in 1901, 16,000 or so exiled from the Russian provinces alone.

There is no right of assembly, so that any crowd in the street or any private gathering is considered illegal. 'This may explain why mere crowding in the streets is considered both by the government and the revolutionists as a means of revolutionary action'.[19] If professors want to invite their own students to their lodgings to discuss paedogicial matters, they must petition for the right to do so.

Do you want to give a public lecture? You have to inform the authorities of the subject matter and sometimes even provide the text. Occasionally, a government agent shows up to check that the text has not been changed. Getting permission is all the more difficult if you want to give a lecture in the provinces or to peasants and workers. Libraries meant for the lower classes are also under strict control. 'Thus we have two official catalogues for reading: that of books prohibited for general libraries, and that of books permitted for the people's libraries'.[20]

Besides various other methods of censorship, the government can simply forbid topics of discussion. 'When a movement among workingmen began, during the present reign, this subject also was withheld from public discussion. . . . There is no burning question of the times that is accessible to the Russian press.'[21] Miliukov goes on to discuss the repressive régime in the educational system, with the result that the students are all socialistic, and since 1899, 'the revolution is, as it were, insistent within the walls of our universities and academies. Thus the task of the government superintendence has grown much more complicated'.[22]

Miliukov sums up the situation in a passage denying the possibility of meaningful reform as long as the autocracy exists – a passage that reveals the intransigence that Miliukov shared with *Iskra*:

> Can the government, while it remains what it now is, namely, a mere system of police, hypocritically supporting itself on fictitious nationalistic tradition,

---

[19] Miliukov 1962, p. 150.
[20] Miliukov 1962, p. 153.
[21] Miliukov 1962, pp. 156–7.
[22] Miliukov 1962, p. 164.

leaving to legislation a merely fictitious independence, to administrative power a likewise fictitious responsibility, to the judiciary not even a shadow of its original freedom and competency – can a government such as this lighten the system of oppression it is obliged to use against any free utterance of an enlightened public opinion? Can it, for instance, abolish the *Okhrana*, the gendarmes, the system of political spies, re-establish regular justice, respect the rights of the individual, forbear arbitrary arrest and exile, allow the population liberty to meet, to read whatever they wish, to speak publicly about politics? Can it free the press from censorship, the schools from police duties? Of course it cannot, without denying itself in essence.[23]

Having shown the intolerable lack of political freedom in Russia, Miliukov sets out the historical evolution of the main oppositional currents, the 'liberal idea' and the 'socialistic idea'. When he talks about the developments in Russian socialist thought, our lecturer puts the emphasis on a different set of issues from the ones stressed by present-day lecturers on Russian history. The way the story is usually told now focuses on the shift from a revolutionary wager on the peasants to a wager on the urban workers. Attention is also given to a ferocious debate over the future of capitalism in Russia that accompanied this shift: would capitalism destroy Russia, as the populists argued, or would it lay the foundations of Russia's eventual salvation, as the Social Democrats argued? There were also tactical debates, particularly on the use of terror.

All of these were indeed crucial developments. But Miliukov is much more interested in the gradual acceptance by socialist revolutionaries of the primordial importance of political freedom. For him, *this* development is the meaning of the triumph of Marx in the Russian socialist movement. For a liberal revolutionary such as Miliukov, the socialist emphasis on political freedom was obviously very good news indeed. But, when the Russian Social Democrats themselves looked back, they did not see things very differently.[24]

It is worth looking closely at Miliukov's account of the evolution of the Russian socialist tradition from Narodnaia volia to the rise of Russian Social Democracy. The thrust of my commentary is to link Lenin's outlook with European Social Democracy as opposed to the Russian revolutionary tradition.

---

[23] Miliukov 1962, p. 165.
[24] For Martov's view of these developments, see Martov 1900.

Nevertheless, readers will rightly feel that a commentary on WITBD that says nothing about Narodnaia volia is an odd one. Besides, Lenin was indeed very proud of the Russian tradition and inspired by its heroes. This pride in no way weakened his Erfurtian loyalties, for Narodnaia volia was, among other things, a crucial step forward in the evolution toward Social Democracy.

For Miliukov's American audience, Russian revolutionaries were exotic types called 'nihilists'. Miliukov puts the figure of the 'nihilist' firmly in context as 'a specifically Russian variety of the socialism of western Europe'. These early peculiarities of Russian socialism 'disappear as the movement grows. The more it spreads and develops, the more cosmopolitan it becomes'.[25] When Miliukov talks about European socialism, he means the SPD model. 'Russian socialism, then, differs from German socialism in that it carries to an extreme the features which have made German socialism differ from English and American'.[26]

The trajectory in Russia, then, is toward German-style socialism. This trajectory is best shown in the shift from a Proudhon/Bakunin-style rejection of political freedom as on outright obstacle to socialist revolution to a Marx-style insistence on it. For the anarchists, political freedom was for the bourgeoisie, not for the *narod* who perhaps could not even read newspapers and who instinctively just wanted to run their own affairs in 'an autocracy of popular communes, popular gatherings, popular bands'. These are the words of Petr Lavrov – the same Lavrov who, as we saw in the previous chapter, twitted the Russian Social Democrats in the 1890s for not being political enough. In the mid-1870s, Lavrov held quite different views and angrily rejected any revolution prior to the real, the socialist one. Lavrov asked Russian revolutionary youth

> whether they would like to follow the same path as those constitutionalists who also may form a conspiracy in order to limit the imperial power by an all-Russian representative assembly, requesting nothing but liberal checks and guaranties; or whether they forgot that the people were always cheated whenever an alliance between the popular party and the bourgeoisie was concluded; or whether they thought that there was anything in common between a social revolution and revolution for a liberal constitution? . . .

---

[25] Miliukov 1962, pp. 244–5.
[26] Miliukov 1962, p. 247.

> The revolution we look for must be popular and social; it must be directed
> not only against the government, and its aim must be not only to deposit
> the power in some other hands, but it must at once overthrow the economic
> foundations of the present social order.[27]

What accounted for the shift of Lavrov and most other Russian socialists
away from these views? Miliukov explained that one force was an almost
unconscious evolution among the revolutionary populists.[28] First, they found
themselves spending more and more time propagandising the workers instead
of peasants, because the workers were the ones they could get to and who
would listen to them. But, as government repression made this task more
and more difficult, the revolutionaries 'found that they had not sufficiently
appreciated the obstacles put in their way by the complete absence of legal
forms for any political propaganda in Russia'. They therefore fought back,
using terrorist means. But this use of terror was something of a heresy – not
because terror was violent, but because it represented *political* struggle, that
is, an attempt to attain political freedom instead of social transformation. In
an early version of the hegemony strategy, Andrei Zheliabov – one of the
leaders of Narodnaia volia – explained why socialist revolutionaries had
decided to act like liberal revolutionaries:

> The party does not strive to attain political reforms. This task should belong
> entirely to the men who call themselves liberals. But these men are entirely
> powerless in Russia, and, whatever the reasons are, they have proved
> incapable of giving Russia free institutions and guaranties of personal rights.
> However, such institutions are so necessary that no activity appears to be
> possible without them. Therefore the Russian socialistic party is obliged to
> assume the duty of crushing despotism.[29]

The terrorists who formed the Narodnaia volia group tried their best to square
the circle by positing a 'constitutional convention' that, of course, would have
a large socialist majority – so the populist terrorists assured each other – and

---

[27] Miliukov 1962, p. 289.
[28] Miliukov's account here is clearly deeply influenced by Plekhanov's own various
autobiographical accounts.
[29] Miliukov 1962, p. 302.

that would therefore instantly inaugurate the social revolution. Their opponents within the revolutionary-populist movement (who included the future founders of Russian Social Democracy) laughed at this self-deception and re-iterated that a constitution 'would rather delay than accelerate the advent of the social revolution, and, furthermore, it would compromise its success'.[30]

Thus, by the late 1870s, the populist revolutionaries had fallen into two camps, one with a completely unrealistic idea of what could be achieved without political freedom (wide-scale propaganda and agitation) and the other with a completely unrealistic idea of what could be achieved with political freedom (instant socialism). Marx to the rescue!

> It is well known that the doctrines of Marx represent a synthesis of the ideas of economic emancipation and political struggle; and it was just such a synthesis that the revolutionaries of the [Narodnaia volia] party needed so badly. . . . Marx's starting-point, as well as theirs, was that the economic emancipation can be achieved only by the workingmen themselves; but Marx wanted the workingmen to unite for this purpose in a large political party and to fight their battles of class interest, not by way of small riots in isolated villages, but by the large, centralised organisation of a labour party whose aim should be to come into possession of political power.[31]

The man who realised that Marx's political strategy could reunite the shattered revolutionary movement was Georgii Plekhanov. Plekhanov had been one of the populist hard-liners who opposed terrorism by pointing out that political freedom would benefit the bourgeoisie. Now he said to his erstwhile opponents: in our debate a few years ago, our side was completely right in arguing that a political revolution only means the triumph of capitalists. But we now realise, thanks to reading Marx, that this is acceptable – let the bourgeoisie triumph for a while, so long as we get political freedom. We will adopt your strategy of political struggle (although not necessarily your terrorist tactics) but we will do it, and we invite you to do it, with eyes open, without fantastic expectations of instant socialism.[32]

---

[30] Miliukov 1962, p. 301.

[31] Miliukov 1962, p. 308. Compare Miliukov here to John Rae on Marx's desire to 'introduce the large system of production into the art of conspiracy' that I quoted at the end of Chapter One.

[32] This paraphrase of Plekhanov's argument is based on my own reading of his

In one sense, Plekhanov's call to unity failed, since Social Democracy and neo-populist currents remained separate and, eventually, became two separate parties, the RSDWP and the Socialist Revolutionaries. But, in another sense, Plekhanov succeeded, because both sides now fought for political freedom not in the expectation of instant socialism but, rather, in the hope of applying the SPD model. As a prominent terrorist of the 1870s, Stepniak (Sergei Kravchinsky), wrote in 1890,

> The violent actions to which we now have recourse are purely temporary measures, which will give place to peaceful, intellectual work as soon as popular representation is substituted for the present despotism. ... The German Socialist party, which has astonished the world with its titanic growth, presents the most brilliant example of political discretion and self-control.[33]

The difference that still divided the two Russian revolutionary currents concerned the application of the SPD model *before* the overthrow of the autocracy. Despite their endorsement of political freedom as a goal, Stepniak in 1890 and Lavrov in 1895 continued to think that conspiracies – 'bombs and dynamite', in Stepniak's words – were central and essential means of obtaining political freedom in the first place. Social-Democratic success in the late 1890s changed the terms of debate. By 1900, when the Socialist-Revolutionary Party was formed, the emphasis of the neo-populists had strongly shifted to a mass movement even under the autocracy, with terror as only (at least officially) a supplementary means.

Miliukov does not use the term 'Erfurtianism', since it did not exist until a chapter ago, but that is what he is talking about. Commentary on WITBD usually devotes much time to the Russian revolutionary tradition, especially Narodnaia volia, and very little time to European Social Democracy. Miliukov's account provides one more reason for my opposite emphasis. According to Miliukov, the whole trend of Russian socialism was toward acceptance of the SPD model and the primordial importance of political freedom. Narodnaia volia in particular played a crucial part in this development, so that admiration

---

seminal 1883 publication *Socialism and Political Struggle* rather than Miliukov's account. *Sotsializm i politicheskaia bor'ba* can be found in Volume 2 of Plekhanov 1923–7.

[33] Miliukov 1962, pp. 235–6.

for Narodnaia volia is no indication of a sneaking atavistic Russian rejection of Western models.

We turn now to Miliukov's account of the current situation in Russia and *Iskra*'s role in it. The big point that emerges from Miliukov's remarks is that *Iskra* was successful because its original position was confirmed by the growing 'revolutionism' of the situation and also because *Iskra* was flexible enough to become even more revolutionary as the situation heated up.

Miliukov wanted to demonstrate to his American audience of 1903–4 that a revolutionary crisis had been brewing in Russia for at least a decade (and, of course, his diagnosis was confirmed by what was happening even as he sent his book off to press in early 1905). The Russian crisis was an explosive compound of economic downturn and widespread anger at the government. 'Material want, growing more and more acute, finally takes the shape of a general crisis – agricultural, industrial, and financial. Political disaffection, becoming permanent, forms an atmosphere of social unrest which finds expression in individual or combined violent action'.[34] After giving statistics on the economic problems of the country, Miliukov rings through the same gamut of protest that was featured in the pages of *Iskra*. Of course, the university, the factory and the villages are prominent venues for protest, since these are the 'more or less customary and habitual spheres of revolutionary agitation', but, even in these milieus, the dimensions of protest are unprecedented.[35] In the 1870s, the peasants themselves turned the revolutionaries over to the police.

> But at present the peasants do their best to conceal the propagandists from the police, and, when directly requested to hand over seditious leaflets distributed by socialists, they often answer with plain refusal. To watch them more closely, thirty-five thousand special village policeman had to be introduced by Mr. Plehve.[36]

National groups from Finland to the Caucasus are in revolt. And new and more unexpected groups are joining the roster of protest, groups such as

---

[34] Miliukov 1962, p. 313.
[35] Miliukov 1962, p. 371.
[36] Miliukov 1962, p. 262. Plehve was the Minister of the Interior. Compare *Iskra*'s comments on him in the next section.

teachers in lower schools and the army. The number of political criminals is rising rapidly (Miliukov gives statistics), and, indeed, 'to be branded as a political criminal by the police is a mark of distinction, gradually becoming a quite necessary qualification for everybody who claims to advocate liberal public opinion'.[37]

The two protest groups that are forcing the pace of transformation from dissatisfaction to revolutionary upheaval are the students and the workers. Miliukov traces the galvanising role of the militant worker movement, starting with the strikes of 1896, when 'Petersburg was roused by a startling movement of workingmen, the like of which it had never before seen'.[38] Furthermore, the conditions of Russian life ensure that no purely apolitical, *tred-iunionist* movement is possible.

> The very fact of a strike – independently of its causes, its character, or its demands – constitutes a crime. . . . The strike from a professional [= trade] contest becomes at once a political demonstration – even before the workmen themselves have had time to realise it. Thus they generally begin with a protest against the manufacturer, but invariably finish by protesting against autocracy; and very often the manufacturer himself, in his inmost heart, feels inclined to join them.[39]

In the beginning, perhaps, strikes became political before the workers realised it, but no longer. 'Political disturbances similar to those endemic in the Russian universities have now become a permanent feature of factory life. . . . They are gradually becoming better organised, more simultaneous, and more conscious of their political significance'. Miliukov appends to this remark a list of worker demonstrations from September 1901 to May 1902 – that is, the very months Lenin was churning out *WITBD*. In September, Kishenev and Petersburg; in November, Moscow and Kharkov; in December, Kharkov and Ekaterinoslav; in February, Kiev, Moscow, Ekaterinoslav, Rostov-on-the-Don, Odessa; in March, Petersburg; in April, Krasnoyarsk, Rostov-on-the-Don, Baku; in May, Sormovo and Saratov. (I wonder why January was such a slow month?) The worker demands are all the more dangerous for the government

---

[37] Miliukov 1962, p. 376 (Miliukov himself had served time).
[38] Miliukov 1962, p. 350.
[39] Miliukov 1962, p. 354.

since 'the workingmen in the larger factory' are the 'vanguard' of the Russian masses, so that 'now the people in the village are trying to imitate their example'.[40] Alongside the mass dissatisfaction, there is a large and growing corps of dedicated activists who ensure that protests will never cease in spite of the barbarous and violent repression.

All this ensured *Iskra*'s success. Miliukov treats *Iskra* as the organ of the Plekhanov group and never mentions the younger members of the board – mainly, no doubt, because even the pseudonyms of the younger members were barely known at the time. The decades-long struggle of the Plekhanov group was vindicated by the emergence of a radical worker movement in the mid-1890s.

> The fact was that the struggle of the workingmen against autocracy was of itself coming to the front; and such a struggle offered the best chance of success to a theory which had always taught that this was the only kind of struggle which led directly to the advent of socialism, in strict accordance with the teachings of scientific socialism.[41]

*Iskra*'s first success was against 'economists' and 'revisionists' within Social-Democratic ranks. Miliukov sides with *Iskra* on both counts, although, of course, he gives a different analysis of the issues. The 'economists', he says, were young Russian revolutionaries who had grown up in the Russia of the 1880s and imbibed more than they realised of its reactionary, passive apolitical pessimism about social action. Thus they were delighted when events confirmed the Marxist analysis – but drew the conclusion that they could allow events to complete the job.

> Social revolution was now safely expected to come as an unavoidable result of an organic and spontaneous material evolution; and people in possession of that 'scientific' prognosis looked down with contempt upon their predecessors, who were short-sighted enough to rely upon a weak individual effort. . . . The consequence was that, in spite of the influence of the elder Marxists, the active and individual – the political – element in the revolution was disregarded, and the chief attention was drawn to the passive and

---

[40] Miliukov 1962, pp. 367, 351.
[41] Miliukov 1962, p. 352.

spontaneous – the economic – side of the movement. Strikes of workingmen – their struggle for better wages – were to become the main, if not the only, object of the socialistic propaganda and agitation.[42]

The 'passive' outlook of the 'economists' soon dissipated:

> The old Marxists were the first to dispel the charm. . . . Not strikes on professional [= trade] lines with demands for a shorter workday and better wages, but direct political demands for the destruction of autocracy; not local work, but party work on a large scale – such was now the watchword of socialistic democratism. A new literary organ of the 'orthodox' Marxists was founded (*The Spark*), and it carried the day against the inexperienced 'economism' of the younger generation.[43]

Attempts to import revisionist-style reformism from the West also failed because they were out of tune with the Russian situation. In Germany, perhaps, revisionism made sense to large currents in the Party, but not in Russia, where the Party's role was necessarily revolutionary. Revisionism had to be rejected for the sake of sheer self-preservation. Thus, the success of the *Iskra* group 'is easily explained by the fact that their tendency coincided with the ascending line of the whole movement and was powerfully supported by the whole trend of the increasing revolutionism of the Russian socialists'.[44]

Miliukov goes on to describe the rise of the Socialist Revolutionaries. This new party treated *Iskra*-style Social Democrats as the latter had treated the 'economists', namely, as conservatives out of touch with increasing revolutionism in Russia. Miliukov himself felt that the Social Democrats were too obsessed with preparatory organisation of the labour party of the future and that in fact 'all the revolutionary blows which have essentially determined the change in the political situation during the last three or four years have been struck by Social Revolutionaries'.[45] (Miliukov is referring to terroristic assassination of government officials.) In any event, both the competition with the Socialist Revolutionaries and the trend of events forced the Social Democrats to move away 'from their preparatory work for the "organisation"

---

[42] Miliukov 1962, pp. 352–3.
[43] Miliukov 1962, pp. 353–4.
[44] Miliukov 1962, p. 355.
[45] Miliukov 1962, p. 359.

of a labour party into an active, and a revolutionary, struggle. Their strikes, at first purely economic, soon became political, and their mass demonstrations from peaceful became armed'.[46] As a result, the two parties were rivals in the polemics of the leaders but partners on the ground and in their practical activity. (Needless to say, *Iskra* would have strongly disputed this picture.)

Miliukov's participant account evokes the atmosphere in which *Iskra* made its appearance – an atmosphere of growing revolutionary excitement. Throughout the 1890s, as we have seen, Lenin was wagering his political reputation on the claim that the workers *could* be the large-scale revolutionary force that would galvanise the whole society to overthrow the tsar – and, now, this was really happening for all to see. The *Iskra* group was exhilarated, not worried, by the way the workers seemed to living up to their role in the Social-Democratic script. *Iskra* came into the world with an 'I told you so' attitude in everything it said or did.

### Bolsheviks look back: the Amsterdam Report, 1904

By August 1904, the once united *Iskra* editorial board had been shouting at each other for a solid year. The whole thing was a scandal at home and abroad, especially now that the congress of international Social Democracy at Amsterdam was drawing near. Since the Mensheviks had control of most top party positions at this time, they dominated the delegation sent to Amsterdam – in fact, only Lenin was included from the Bolshevik faction. Not exactly happy with this situation, Lenin feigned illness and asked if other Bolsheviks could replace him. The Mensheviks said no, the Bolsheviks showed up anyway, and the whole wretched dispute was brought before the International Bureau. Although leaders such as Bebel, Kautsky and Victor Adler were probably inclined to side with the Menshevik leaders, some of whom they had known personally for a long time, they also felt that it was only fair to give both factions a voice, and the Bolsheviks were allowed to sit as delegates.

The conflict had a curious literary by-product. About a week before the Congress, Lenin learned that one of the members of the delegation, the

---

[46] Ibid.

Menshevik Fyodor Dan, had written a historical report to be distributed to members of the Congress. Lenin decided to come up with a party history to represent the Bolshevik standpoint. Gathering together three of his lieutenants – Vlatislav Vorovskii, P.A. Krasikov and M. Liadov – he assigned a chapter to each one (he himself wrote the final one) and they got to work. While Krupskaya fed them and provided lots of strong coffee, the four managed to write, translate into German, and print an eighty-page report in ten days.[47]

The last two chapters are a polemic concerning organisational disputes at the Second Congress and after.[48] The first two chapters, however, are a valuable historical account of the pre-*Iskra* period and the *Iskra* period – valuable because they show what the *Iskra* experience meant to Lenin and his supporters fresh after events and also how they wanted to present it to their European comrades. I will give a detailed paraphrase of the twenty-page chapter on the *Iskra* period itself. Since we know that Liadov wrote the first chapter and Lenin the last, this chapter must have been written by Vorovskii or Krasikov. In any event, the whole text was closely edited by Lenin (so Liadov informs us) and can be taken to represent his own viewpoint. Beyond the question of authorship, the chapter is an informative survey of all the issues that came up during the *Iskra* period. Thus, it helps put the particular range of issues of concern to WITBD into context. Of WITBD itself, we learn nothing in this chapter – or, rather, we learn that it is possible for Bolsheviks to write a detailed history in 1904 without so much as mentioning WITBD.[49]

For purposes of this paraphrase, I adopt the persona of the mythical M. Lydin, the name found on the cover of the German report (with occasional comments from my own authorial persona in brackets).[50]

[47] Background information comes from M. Liadov's introduction to Lydin 1963. The Menshevik report was Dan 1904. The text I consulted is not the original Russian draft, which is lost, but a re-translation by Liadov from the 1920s. The original German title was *Material zur Erläuterung der Parteikrise in der Socialdem. Arbeiterpartei Russlands* [Materials for a Clarification of the Party Crisis in the SDRWP] (Lydin 1963, p. 22).
[48] Trotsky's pamphlet *Our Political Tasks*, which came out only a week or so later, contained a contemptuous reference to an 'utterly ungrammatical German text' that announced to Europe of all the details of the Russian party dispute. Trotsky was fairly sure no German had read it and completely sure no German had understood it (Trotsky 1904, pp. viii–ix).
[49] WITBD is mentioned in later chapters in the book that deal with post-Second Congress disputes.
[50] This paraphrase is based on Chapter Two of the Amsterdam Report entitled 'Iskrovskii period' (Lydin 1963, pp. 39–61).

In 1898 our party proclaimed a purely symbolic unity. In actual fact, each committee worked pretty much on its own. At most, neighbouring committees would sometimes exchange a report or more rarely help each other out. Equally fragmented were programmatic and tactical views – one could find everything 'from the purest Bernsteinism to the purest revolutionism'.[51] The worker movement continued to expand without interruption, the revolutionary mood of the proletariat continued to intensify, and more and more people – as many workers as intellectuals – began to find the party situation intolerable. Practical work itself demanded a clear theoretical base.

This situation defined the mission of *Iskra* whose first issue came out in December 1900. The best theoreticians of the Party joined the editorial board of this newspaper that eventually drew the Party from the dark alleyways of mutual isolation and theoretical helplessness to the broad highway of *common* party work. To understand the great changes of the last four years, we need to look at the intense ideological work of *Iskra* as well as the new and complicated tasks thrown up by the progress of the worker movement.

A united party required an end to the chaos of opinions. Thus, *Iskra* from its first issues polemicised against 'economists' of various stripes who ignored the tasks of *political* struggle. Social Democracy cannot content itself with *tred-iunionist* politics of economic reform. 'It must lead the proletariat to a free democracy, the one true path to the dictatorship of the proletariat'.[52]

In spring 1901, the workers *on their own initiative* supported the political protests of the university students. *Iskra* wrote at that time that

> we, the advocates of the revolutionary political struggle of the proletariat, can feel a sense of triumph: the Russian proletariat has demonstrated to its myopic friends the correctness of the point of view that we have defended. . . . Russian Social Democracy must base its practical activity on this clear striving of the worker masses to participate actively in the liberation struggle of Russian democratic forces as a whole.[53]

But the events also showed that the Russian Social Democrats were not yet capable of acting as leaders of the workers.

---

[51] Lydin 1963, p. 39.
[52] Lydin 1963, p. 40.
[53] The quoted words are from a Martov article in *Iskra*, No. 3, April 1901.

One problem was the proper attitude toward protests by bourgeois groups. The 'economists' merely repeated truisms about the hostility between proletariat and bourgeoisie and about the bourgeois nature of the government. *Iskra*'s more profound analysis showed that there were many reasons why the Russian bourgeoisie might rebel against the lawlessness and incompetence of the tsarist government. In any event, insofar as bourgeois protests led to further democratisation, the proletariat should support them. 'The basic thought of *Iskra* – one that it emphasised at every opportunity – was that political freedom is the necessary presupposition for the struggle for socialism'.[54]

More than that, *Iskra* called on the proletariat to take upon itself 'the function of leader [*vozhd*'] of the whole democratic revolutionary movement'.[55] Of course, this mission did not mean forgetting 'the class point of view', the antagonism between capitalists and worker, the final aim of socialism. On the contrary, only by stressing these antagonisms can we build an independent class party that will not be politically exploited by the bourgeoisie. Thus *Iskra* fought 'for purity of dogma' and exposed all who tried to hush up the gulf separating bourgeoisie and proletariat. [In 1904, the Mensheviks charged the Bolsheviks with overlooking 'the class point of view' and putting exclusive focus on the anti-tsarist revolution.]

All this showed that a political proletarian party 'had to be united enough and powerful enough so that after the overthrow of the autocracy it will be in a position to conquer a maximum of political weight in the free political institutions of a future free bourgeois Russia'.[56]

The swift upsurge of the worker movement was meanwhile calling all sorts of non-proletarian groups into active political life. The progressive strata of the bourgeoisie began to wake up after a long sleep and to dream about political democracy [the 'wake-up-to-dream' mixed metaphor is in the original]. Petr Struve and others [including Miliukov] started to publish the journal *Osvobozhdenie* [*Liberation*]. At first, *Iskra* greeted the new journal, but soon discovered that *Osvobozhdenie* was trying to hush up the contradictions between worker and bourgeoisie, in other words, to politically exploit the workers. Even worse, the journal did not issue a clarion call to *revolutionary* struggle

[54] Lydin 1963, p. 43.
[55] Lydin 1963, p. 42.
[56] Lydin 1963, p. 43.

but tried to impress the government with its propaganda of moderation. '*Iskra* began to sharply denounce attempts to fool the revolutionary proletariat and explained the whole futility of liberal attempts to bargain with the autocracy for political freedom by renouncing struggle'.[57]

Exposing the liberals was relatively easy, exposing the Socialist Revolutionaries much more difficult. The *political* programme of the new Party is a good one, since they are radical and thorough-going democrats. But their social and economic views are eclectic to the point of chaos. They do not even understand what it means to have a principled programme. They like to call themselves Marxists, but also like to think of themselves as broad-minded 'critics' of Marxism, much superior to the sectarian dogmatism of orthodox Social Democrats. Their views on class relations are superficial and naïve. They think the peasant is a socialist by his very nature. They claim that 'the labouring people' (a concept covering everyone from peddlers to craftsmen to workers to peasants) are all one united class. And they believe that 'floating above the whole class like God's spirit over the waters is the intelligentsia who – so they think – is utterly foreign to bourgeois class ideology and who is guided in all its activity exclusively by ethical principles'.[58]

The trouble is that their pseudo-socialist rhetoric has acquired an unfortunate influence on many workers and threatens to undermine the loyalty of the worker class to Social-Democratic principles. Thus, *Iskra* had to devote a great many articles to exposing the true class position of the Socialist Revolutionaries and to explaining what is really going on in the villages. *Iskra* called on Russian Social Democrats to enlist rural proletarians [*batraki*] into the proletarian army and, in this way, fulfilled its *socialist* duty. But *Iskra* never forgot that the peasantry as a whole faced purely *democratic* tasks, since the peasants faced a double yoke, oppressed as they were by capital *and* by the landowners and other survivals of serfdom. Stamping out all these survivals, rooting out the spirit of caste inequality that permeated all Russian political institutions – this is a *common national* task. A party that aspires to be the leader in the fight for Russian freedom cannot ignore it. 'Anyone who honestly and seriously dreams of a radical improvement in the peasant position must call on the peasants to fight for political freedom'.

---

[57] Lydin 1963, p. 45.
[58] Lydin 1963, p. 46.

In spring of 1902, peasant disorders in the south of Russia electrified the country. 'The Russian peasant presented to society the bill written by centuries of blood and tears'. Revolutionaries were dumbfounded by this unexpected phenomenon [as Miliukov points out, the Socialist Revolutionaries were as surprised as any]. How to interpret the disorders? Some said that they proved once more the socialist nature of the peasants. Others dismissed them entirely, saying they were blind, aimless and *stikhiinyi* protests. Only *Iskra* gave the correct interpretation and stressed the potential importance of such uprisings without exaggerating their immediate impact. True, the disorders of 1902 were *stikhiinyi* and disorganised, but this characteristic just defined the task of Social Democracy: teach the peasants how to conduct a political struggle. And, in fact, Social-Democratic committees did try to establish connections with the villages and to devote resources to explanatory pamphlets. Lenin's little book *To the Rural Poor* (1903) enjoyed great success among the peasants.

The workers had already awakened to political struggle, so that they and *Iskra* were moving toward each other. One of *Iskra*'s tasks was to widen their perspective and show the Russian workers that they were one part of a great whole, the international proletariat. Thus the overthrow of Europe's gendarme – tsarism – would not only liberate Russia but serve as a mighty impetus to the international movement. *Iskra* pointed to the mighty battles, the brilliant victories and heartbreaking defeats of the European proletariat, while at the same time explaining 'all the advantages of struggle that exist in the West-European countries that have political freedom in comparison to the struggle of the Russian workers under the autocracy'. At the same time, *Iskra* remembered to warn their readers that 'political freedom was in no way an open door leading immediately into the socialist paradise'. This helped the workers keep their perspective. *Iskra* also tried to make sure that Russian workers were kept abreast of factional disputes in the European parties, so that they could understand the terrible dangers of the introduction of bourgeois ideology into a Social-Democratic Party.

*Iskra*'s commitment to internationalism had practical consequences at home, since one heritage of the precapitalist era was mutual suspicion between Russia's many nationalities. Thus, *Iskra* had to conduct polemics not only against bourgeois nationalists but various worker groups infected by nationalist tendencies. Articles appeared against Zionism, the Polish Socialist Party, the Caucasian nationalists and the Jewish Bund.

When the workers went out on the streets, they presented Social-Democratic Russia with wider tasks and forced it to consider the whole arsenal of methods of struggle – not only old methods, such as strikes, propaganda, and agitation, but the new one discovered by the workers, namely, the demonstration. Take strikes, for example. *Iskra* may have inveighed against the earlier obsession with strikes to the exclusion of all else, but it was certainly not opposed to them. On the contrary, it urged all party members to conduct economic agitation and to guide strikes. Of course, it did not fail to emphasise that a purely economic strike – even in conjunction with political activity, if confined to economic reforms – was not yet a Social-Democratic strike.

*Iskra*'s analysis of the relative significance of economic vs. political struggle was confirmed by the plans of the ingenious police official Sergei Zubatov. 'The Russian autocracy observes with horror the rapid growth of the political struggle of the proletariat. They could not cope with it even with the help of the most energetic police prosecution'. So, the government listened to Zubatov's scheme: allow legal but strictly non-political trade unions to defend worker economic interests. The government went so far as to put pressure on entrepreneurs to make a few timid concessions. Zubatov sent his own agitators to the workers with the message that the Social Democrats were bourgeois intellectuals who were trying to dupe the workers into fighting for bourgeois political freedom – something for which the workers had no use. For a while, Zubatov managed to fool some of the backward strata of the workers. But, as *Iskra* conducted its campaign against this Russian form of police socialism, it discovered that the class self-awareness of the workers was sufficiently high to quickly see through this pseudo-democratic policy. The temporary enthusiasm of the backward strata turned to scorn and indignation.

But the rapid development of the revolutionary worker movement soon outstripped the available forces of Russian Social Democracy. There were all sorts of *stikhiinyi* anti-tsarist explosions that were wasted, simply because the Party did not have enough trained and purposive leaders. *Iskra* called attention to this problem and particularly stressed the importance of *political agitation*. 'In the period from 1901 to 1903, the issue of the political education of the Russian proletariat by means of a detailed consideration and analysis of all political and social problems became the common task of all party activists'.[59]

---

[59] Lydin 1963, p. 53.

Just how much this emphasis on political agitation corresponded to the needs of the workers can be seen in a letter to *Iskra* from a rank-and-file worker. The letter thanked the *Iskra* editors because 'it was the first to show us workers that we should interest ourselves not only in the worker movement alone, but in the life and movement of the people as a whole and of all of society'. Each *Iskra* article breathes 'the spirit of the times'.[60]

A Social-Democratic Party cannot restrict itself just to showing the proletariat where it should be going – it also has the responsibility of teaching it how to fight. In 1901, the proletariat 'almost instinctively' seized on the method of political demonstrations. All that remained for Social Democracy to do was to popularise the tactic, explain its significance and to step forth as leaders and organisers of these political protests. Pointing out the weakness of the early demonstrations, *Iskra* argued that they would achieve their true educational significance only when they became the act of the workers themselves, that is, when they attained truly mass dimensions.

The revolutionary mood of the workers grew so quickly that the mass political protests advocated by Social-Democratic committees started to occur by the end of 1902. Tens of thousands of workers participated in a grandiose political demonstration in Rostov-on-the-Don, listened to Social-Democratic speeches and fought back against the Cossacks. And this was just the beginning. In summer 1903, workers all over the south of Russia joined in massive political protests that shook up even such previously out-of-the-way corners of the country as Kostroma. The government had to call in the troops. The power of the proletariat was so evident in these demonstrations that even the bourgeois press spoke of it.

While saluting the enormous significance of the demonstrations, *Iskra* did not idealise them. After an exhaustive analysis, it announced that 'our worker mass, maturing literally not in days but in hours, is nevertheless not completely ready for purposive political action. ... There is no other remedy than the one we have recommended so often . . . : *agitation and organisation; organisation and agitation, and more agitation, and more organisation*'.[61]

As the proletariat grew more powerful, attempts by misguided revolutionaries to foist terrorist tactics on it grew more frantic. *Iskra* declared

---

[60] The quoted words are from a letter that appeared in *Iskra*, No. 14, January 1902.
[61] The quoted words are from a Plekhanov article in *Iskra*, No. 46, August 1903.

merciless war on the tactic of individual terror. Terrorism sucked away the Party's best and most energetic forces and distracted it from its basic task: educating the proletariat in the principles of Social Democratism.

A couple of examples will show how deeply *Iskra*'s ideas have entered the thinking of the guiding strata of the proletariat. In the early 1880s, the then police director Plehve organised the first anti-Jewish pogroms and many industrial workers took part. In 1903, the same Plehve tried the same trick, but the proletariat had grown up. As *Iskra* wrote, 'the Russian proletariat has already grown out of its swaddling clothes and the primitive fairy tales spread by the reactionaries no longer confuse it'. During the gigantic strikes in the summer of 1903, the workers *protected* the Jewish population. 'This conduct on the part of the workers is the fruit of the influence of Social-Democratic propaganda and gives us the measure of that influence. Messrs Anti-Semites *are too late. The [workers] in the large [industrial] centres will no longer follow them'.*[62]

Another example. Of late (1902–3), the tsarist government has not relied so heavily on administrative exile but, instead, adopted the tactic of turning arrested Social Democrats over for open trial. The speeches given in these trials by rank-and-file members of our Social-Democratic army show that not only the party leaders but the workers themselves have fully assimilated the tasks of the movement and are fully capable of putting Social-Democratic ideas into action. In Saratov comrade Denisov, an ordinary worker, said at his trial:

> Since I consider that Social Democracy and it alone is the true expression of the interests of the proletariat generally and the Russian workers specifically, I consider it my duty to follow its principles, to act according to its programme.... Preaching socialist ideas, the Social Democrats hope that these ideas, as they penetrate into the masses of the people, will make it possible to implement reforms that will bring happiness not only to the labouring classes but to all mankind.[63]

---

[62] The quoted words in this paragraph come from an article by Plekhanov in *Iskra*, No. 50, October 1903. Plehve was assassinated in July 1904, the very month the Bolshevik report was written. The assassination is not mentioned in the report.

[63] Lydin 1963, p. 58. For a memoir account of Denisov, see Kanatchikov 1986.

In Nizhni-Novgorod, the worker Petr Zalomov described in his courtroom speech the horrifying conditions of the Russian worker and went on to explain why the freedom to strike, to assemble, to speak and publish, and to elect representatives is necessary for a civilised life. 'And that is why I wrote on our banner: Down with the autocracy and long live political freedom.'

One other *Iskra* achievement must be mentioned before we end our survey. As the wave of revolutionary activity grew higher, the old party organisational forms were felt to be more and more of a burden. Isolated local committees wanted a way to share experiences, co-ordinate actions, and speak with a single voice. Party members wanted a unified national leadership consisting of respected figures with solid theoretical principles and great practical experience. *Iskra* responded to this widespread desire and took on the task of fusing the scattered Social-Democratic forces into a single centralised organisation not just in words but in actual fact.

But how could a *newspaper* accomplish all this? *Iskra* helped create unity by involving all local committees in one common task, namely, in preparing (by sending material) and distributing *Iskra* itself. Merely the technical demands of this project required setting up a network of agents that would be the skeleton of the kind of organisation we need. Of course, this whole plan depended on getting the local committees on board. But this is exactly what happened, as more and more committees declared their acceptance of *Iskra* as a guiding voice for the Party. By the end of 1902, the factual unity of the Party was almost assured. Only after this task was accomplished was it expedient to have a party congress. In December 1902 an Organising Committee was formed and so successful was the preparatory work that the great event actually took place in August 1903.

And so,

> *Iskra*'s work over three years did not go to waste. It succeeded in creating ideological unity for Russian Social Democracy, in educating the class self-awareness of the proletariat, in broadening and deepening the struggle for socialist freedom and in working out new methods of the worker class struggle, methods that were well calculated to achieve their goal and that turned out to be extremely effective.[64]

---

[64] Lydin 1963, p. 56.

Thus ends the Bolshevik account of the glory days of *Iskra*, looking back only a year later when *Iskra*'s accomplishments seemed to be submerged in pettiness. I probably do not need to remind the reader that this is a partisan account whose version of events would be challenged by all other participants.

The paraphrased chapter represents *Iskra* as speaking with a single voice. The authors of the individual articles (which, as mentioned before, were not by-lined) are not mentioned. Lenin's articles are cited at length, but so are Plekhanov's and Martov's. The only mention of a specific member of the *Iskra* editorial board is of Lenin, identified as the author of *To the Rural Poor*.[65]

It is rather striking that WITBD is not mentioned. Some of the book's concerns are identified – for example, broad political agitation – but others are not. The idea of the 'revolutionary by trade' is discussed only in a later chapter in relation to organisational disputes between the two Social-Democratic factions. There is no discussion anywhere in the book of the 'from without' formulation (the same is true of Dan's Menshevik report). I assume this is because the Mensheviks had not yet seized on the formulation as vulnerable or particularly significant.

The general impression of this whole historical period that is conveyed by 'M. Lydin' is the same as in Miliukov's account: growing revolutionary excitement, fuelled by the militancy of the workers which increases in a way that fulfils *Iskra*'s fondest hopes and justifies its political outlook. Of course, *Iskra* is here presented as well-nigh infallible. But the author is careful not to make *Iskra* a demiurge that summons up worker militancy with a 'Let there be struggle!'. The worker movement is charging ahead on its own steam and certainly does not need *Iskra* to push it into action. The Social Democrats are often presented as flummoxed by the unexpected dimensions of the movement. *Iskra*'s merit is rather that it understands what the worker movement wants and needs in order to be effective.

The workers are presented throughout as students who need the education provided by the Social Democrats. But they are not recalcitrant children who have to be rapped on the knuckles to pay attention. Rather, they are adult students who know what it is they do not know and why they need to know it. They are a volunteer army asking for training, not a conscript army being forcibly drilled.

---

[65] The Menshevik report (Dan 1904) praises *To the Rural Poor* in similar terms.

The Social Democrats are presented as teachers who know two major things: the importance of political freedom and how to conduct a political struggle. The author of the chapter wants to bring out how often *Iskra* also emphasised the final goal of socialism. This emphasis is a defensive one since, in 1904, the Bolsheviks were being accused by the Mensheviks precisely of neglecting the class point of view in favour of the multi-class onslaught on the tsar.

The Social Democrats are teachers who are delighted and impressed with the eagerness of their students and who are occasionally abashed to see that the students move ahead of them in finding new methods of struggle. The teachers are also aware that they themselves could be doing a much better job – or, if they are not aware of this, *Iskra* is there to scold them.

The workers are beset with a great many temptations and *Iskra*'s mission is to fend them off. Economists, nationalists, police socialists, Socialist Revolutionaries, liberals and anti-Semites – no wonder *Iskra* seems to be permanently polemicising. The 'backward strata' of the workers are sometimes duped for a while. But experience has shown that such errors are only temporary. The Bolshevik report reflects a general sense of pride in the class awareness of the proletariat. Only in the case of the rivalry with the Socialist Revolutionaries do we pick up a note of failure and unfinished business.

One important aspect of Erfurtianism is the two-front polemical war. Since the paraphrased chapter is a survey of all of *Iskra*'s various stands, we see how the two-front war becomes part of a general polemical style that is always situating itself between two extremes. Some overestimate peasant revolutionary potential, some underestimate it, but *Iskra* gets it just right. Some get carried away with strikes, some ignored them, and *Iskra* warns against both errors. It is a style of thought that shows up later in the idea of right deviation vs. left deviation.

Perhaps most resonant is the story of the rank-and-file workers who stand up in court and witness for the Social-Democratic faith. Indeed, we see here the germ of one of Soviet civilisation's constitutive myths. Petr Zalomov, one of the workers quoted above, had been arrested in 1902 in a suburb of Nizhni-Novgorod at a May Day celebration where he had picked up a fallen red flag. Nizhni-Novgorod was the birthplace of the novelist Maxim Gorky, who was acquainted with Zalomov and his family. In 1906, while visiting in America, he wrote a novel based on these events called *Mother*. This novel turns the spread of awareness into a potent myth as it shows how the high purposiveness of the Zalomov character is transmitted to his downtrodden and unaware mother. (In historical fact, Zalomov's mother was already an active member of the revolutionary cell.) Gorky's *Mother* was later recognised as the ur-socialist-realist novel. As Katerina Clark has shown, the spread of awareness is the foundation myth behind all socialist realism. If you want to get an idea of the emotional meaning of Russian Erfurtianism, I recommend Gorky's *Mother*.[66]

## The unknown Lenin: political agitation, 1901–3

> But the Russian worker class will level to the ground this cursed all-Russian prison and conquer for itself class representation in a bourgeois democratic state. (Lenin, August 1903)

After the fall of the Soviet Union, many hitherto unpublished Lenin documents were made available in collections with titles like *The Unknown Lenin*.[67] But, as this commentary suggests, the Lenin that emerges from a careful reading of works that have long been sitting on library shelves is in many ways more unknown and more surprising than anything found in new archival documents. In this section, I will push this process one step further. I believe I have discovered a whole new book by Lenin that has, up till now, remained ignored and unread – a book that poses a greater challenge to received ideas about Lenin than any new archival revelation by far.

Lenin wrote a total of fifty articles for *Iskra* and *Zaria* during the years 1900–3. These articles can be divided into two groups. One group can be called party polemics, devoted to programmatic and strategic questions. The other group is devoted to what Lenin called political agitation. The articles in this group describe the growing crisis in Russian society and urge all sections of society to step up their revolutionary action.

It is this second group – the political agitation series – that I consider Lenin's undiscovered book. The direct interest of the series for this commentary is that WITBD devotes much of its space to defending political agitation as an

---

[66] See the discussion of *Mother* in Clark 1981. Clark's discussion of socialist realism shows the continuing power of the scenario of the spread of awareness.

[67] Pipes 1996. See Lih 2001b for a discussion of the many serious errors in this edition.

appropriate and effective Social-Democratic strategy. The series reveals what Lenin meant by political agitation and why *Iskra*'s critics were uneasy about it. But, beyond this aspect, the series constitutes a remarkable whole that paints a vivid portrait of Russian society, shrewdly analyses the autocracy's political dilemmas and mounts a pugnacious defence of political freedom. The tone is Lenin's usual angry sarcasm but even this tone grates less when it is directed against the common enemy on the other side of the barricades. I personally rate the political agitation series as one of Lenin's most remarkable achievements.

First, some statistics to put the political agitation series into context. Out of fifty Lenin articles in *Iskra* and *Zaria*, twenty-three are devoted to party polemics.[68] Given the usual image of *Iskra* as obsessed with 'economism', it is remarkable that exactly one Lenin article is devoted to this target. Various pot-shots against economism can also be found in the four articles that are primarily devoted to setting out *Iskra*'s goals. I call these articles *Iskra* manifestos.[69] The remaining articles can be broken down as follows: against the liberals, three; on various forms of nationalism within and without the party, seven; against the Socialist Revolutionaries, five; defending Lenin's proposed agrarian plank in the party platform, three. (These totals include one long *Zaria* article against the liberals and two on agrarian issues.)

The remaining twenty-seven articles constitute the political agitation series (see Table 3.1 for a list of titles). The balance between political agitation and party polemics shifted drastically toward polemics in the second half of the *Iskra* period, as shown below.

**Lenin *Iskra* Articles**

|  | Political Agitation Articles | Others |
| --- | --- | --- |
| Period I, to summer 1902 | 20 | 7 |
| Period II, from summer 1902 | 7 | 16 |

---

[68] Articles in the sister journal *Zaria* were usually much long than *Iskra* articles. Lenin's two political agitation articles for *Zaria*, however, are actually a collection of seven *Iskra*-size smaller articles and have been counted accordingly.

[69] In this category I put 'The Urgent Tasks of our Movement' (December 1900), 'Where to Begin' (May 1901), 'Political Agitation and the Class Point of View (February 1902), 'Announcement of the Formation of an Organising Committee' (January 1903) (both here and in Table 2, I use the titles as given in the English Collected Works).

The political agitation articles have escaped notice, partly because they are scattered among more attention-grabbing party polemics. If published together in a separate volume, however, they would take up a hefty 240 pages. For purposes of comparison, *WITBD* is 170 pages, *Imperialism* (1916) is 127 pages, *State and Revolution* (1918) 120 pages. In other words, *Political Agitation* would take its place as one of Lenin's weightier works. Read together as a unit, moreover, the series possesses a striking unity, despite the wide variety of topics. Accordingly, I make no distinction in the following discussion between the majority of articles published before the appearance of *WITBD* in early 1902 and those that appeared afterwards.[70]

### Table 3.1
### Titles in Lenin's Political Agitation Series

'The War in China' (December 1900)

'Beat – But Not to Death!' (April 1901)

'Why Accelerate the Vicissitudes of the Times' (April 1901)

'Objective Statistics' (April 1901)

'The Drafting of 183 Students into the Army' (February 1901)

'Another Massacre' (June 1901)

'A Valuable Admission' (July 1901)

'The Lessons of the Crisis' (August 1901)

'The Serf-Owners at Work' (September 1901)

'Fighting the Famine Stricken' (October 1901)

'Penal Servitude Regulations and Penal Servitude Sentences' (November 1901)

'The Protest of the Finnish People' (November 1901)

'Famine' (December 1901)

'Attitude Towards the Crisis and the Famine' (December 1901)

'The Third Element' (December 1901)

'Two Speeches by Marshals of the Nobility' (December 1901)

'Demonstrations Have Begun' (December 1901)

'Concerning the State Budget' (January 1902)

---

[70] If someone were to prepare an edition of *Political Agitation*, I would suggest also including 'The Class Point of View' (an *Iskra* manifesto defending political agitation) and the first article in the two-part series 'Revolutionary Adventurism' (a polemic against the SR use of terrorism as a substitute for *Iskra*-style political agitation).

'Signs of Bankruptcy' (February 1902)

'From the Economic Life of Russia: The Savings-Banks' (February 1902)

'A Letter to the Zemstvoists' (March 1902)

'The Draft of a New Law on Strikes' (September 1902)

'Political Struggle and Political Chicanery' (October 1902)

'New Events and Old Questions' (December 1902)

'Moscow Zubatovists in St. Petersburg' (January 1903)

'The Autocracy is Wavering' (March 1903)

'An Era of Reforms' (August 1903)

The central theme of the series is the same as in Miliukov's book: Russia and its crisis, the last days of an autocracy that is compulsively alienating all sections of Russian society.

> We are living through stormy times, when the history of Russia is moving forward with seven-league boots, when each year often has more significance than decades of peaceful periods. A final reckoning of the half century since the abolition of serfdom is being made, the foundation stones are being laid for social/political structures that will determine the fate of the whole country for long and for long.[71]

Lenin's sense of urgency is based on the standard Social-Democratic reading of European history, and particularly of Germany, where the legacy of the half-hearted revolution of 1848 was an incomplete democratisation that hampered the SPD at every turn. The revolutionary crisis in Russia thus sharpened the 'sooner or later' argument we have seen earlier. That argument reconciled urgency with inevitability: yes, socialism will inevitably come sooner or later but we have a duty to avoid the tragedy of later rather than sooner. Lenin argues: yes, full democratisation will come to Russia sooner or later, but 'sooner' is right now, and 'later' could be decades away. The choices made right now will determine how much breathing room Russian Social Democracy will have in post-tsarist Russia for many a long year.

Lenin seizes on anything that comes his way – from the tsar on his throne giving frightened speeches all the way to a drunken *muzhik* beaten to death by policemen for talking back – to paint a portrait of a society about to

---

[71] Lenin 1958–65, 7, p. 377, *Iskra*, No. 23 (1 August 1902).

explode. An unjust war in China, illegal Russification in Finland, persecution of religious sectarianism, drafting students into the army as punishment for exercising rights of assembly, heavy-handed government restrictions on local authorities who are trying to deal with famine – the autocracy seems intent on alienating everybody. And the autocracy cannot help itself – it knows that it is surrounded by inflammable material so that a mere spark [*iskorka*] can start a conflagration. ('Iskorka' is a diminutive of 'iskra'.)[72] It is compelled to rely on frantic repression.

> The struggle against the enemy within is going on at full blast. Hardly at any time in the past have fortresses, lock-ups, prisons, special detention facilities at police stations and sometimes private houses and apartments temporarily converted into prisons been filled to such an extent with persons under arrest. . . . This is open and undisguised war, one that is not only observed by the mass of ordinary Russians but is more or less immediately felt by them.[73]

The intensity of the crisis is also revealed by protests circulating even among the élite. Several articles in the series give the complete text of speeches or privately circulated protest letters composed by dissatisfied members of the gentry, particularly those associated with the *zemstvo* (the *zemstvo* was a local self-government institution with limited powers). Lenin even found signs of protest in draft legislation emanating from the more progressive part of the bureaucracy. In one article, regarded by many Social Democrats as more than a little scandalous, Lenin published two mildly oppositional speeches by Marshals of the Nobility – local gentry representatives – and predicted that even these comfortable members of the élite would support Social Democracy:

> Anyone who clearly grasps the contradiction between the 'cultural development' of the country and the 'oppressive regime of bureaucratic dictatorship' will sooner or later by led by life itself to the conclusion that this contradiction cannot be removed without removing the autocracy. Having drawn this conclusion, such a person will inevitably assist – he will grumble, but he will assist – a party that knows how to set in motion a threatening force against the autocracy (a force that is threatening not just

---

[72] Lenin 1958–65, 4, p. 392, *Iskra*, No. 2 (February 1901).
[73] Lenin 1958–65, 7, p. 34, *Iskra*, No. 26 (15 October 1902).

in its own eyes but in everybody's eyes). . . . And so to the marshals of the nobility we say as we take our leave: we shall meet again, gentlemen, our allies of tomorrow![74]

The tsarist government responded to the crisis not only by repression but also by attempts at reform. A substantial fraction of the political agitation articles is devoted to detailed analysis of various proposed laws or regulations concerning famine relief, legalising strikes, elected worker representatives and compensation for job-related injuries. These extended analyses remind us of Lenin's own training as a lawyer.[75] It is, indeed, somewhat surprising to see a Marxist revolutionary take tsarist reform legislation so seriously and even compliment some of the legislation for progressive intentions. But Lenin has a number of agitational goals in mind. One is to show once more the universal exasperation with the government. For example, Lenin claims that a proposed legalisation of strikes is different from earlier such attempts because

> the new draft features much greater roots in real life – you hear in it not just the voice of a few theoretically advanced ideologists of the bourgeoisie, but the voice of an entire strata of industrial *praktiki* . . . This is intolerable! We're fed up! Keep out of it! – this is what the Russian factory owner is saying to the Russian police through the lips of the author of the ministerial memorandum.[76]

Lenin also uses these attempts at reforms to reveal the autocracy's essential dilemma. The tsarist government desperately needs to make concessions to society, to provide a carrot as well as a stick. Occasionally it tries to do this by material subsidies to both élite and non-élite (for example, a proposed worker compensation law). But it also feels compelled to offer social groups a little independence, a little breathing room. Yet, since any such independence runs counter to the very nature of autocracy, these offers are hedged around with so many restrictions and second thoughts that the end result is ludicrous and more calculated to exasperate than appease. In an article with the characteristic title 'Signs of Bankruptcy', Lenin dissects some provisional regulations on student organisations and comments:

---

[74] Lenin 1958–65, 5, p. 347, *Zaria*, No. 1 (December 1901).
[75] Burbank 1995.
[76] Lenin 1958–65, 6, p. 401, *Iskra*, No. 24 (1 September 1902).

Indeed, one does not have to be a revolutionary, one does not have to be a radical, to recognise that such a (if you will excuse me) 'reform' not only fails to give the students anything resembling freedom, but is also worthless as a means of bringing any tranquillity into university life. . . . Can it be doubted, for example, that by presiding at such meetings, the inspectors who exercise police functions will constantly annoy some, push others to protest, and intimidate and gag yet others? And is it not clear, that the Russian students will not tolerate the fact that the content of these meetings is brazenly determined by the 'discretion' of the authorities?

And yet the 'right' of assembly and organisation granted by the government in the absurd form set up by the 'provisional regulations' is the *maximum* that the autocracy can give the students while remaining an autocracy. Any further step in this direction would mean a suicidal disturbance of the equilibrium upon which the relations between the authorities and the 'loyal subjects' rest.[77]

And, Lenin taunts the government, you are absolutely correct to be so worried, since we Social Democrats fully intend to take complete advantage of your feeble attempts to allow independent protection of interests. You are thinking of allowing factory workers to elect representatives? Go ahead: our exposure of the contemptible features of the bill will awaken the most backward workers. Remember the fiasco of the Zubatov police unions, a much more ambitious attempt to entice the workers with legal, loyalist and apolitical unions.

We sent purposive workers to the Zubatov assemblies where they themselves learned and where they taught others, and the whole Zubatov saga ended in a miserable failure that benefited Social Democracy much more than the autocracy.[78]

(As we shall see, Lenin's confident attitude toward the Zubatovshchina is a highly characteristic one that also manifests itself in *WITBD*.)

The goal of all this activity is the overthrow of the autocracy or, in positive terms, the achievement of political freedom. The imperative necessity of

---

[77] Lenin 1958–65, 6, pp. 274–5, *Iskra*, No. 17 (15 February 1902). Lenin's reasoning about the autocracy's inability to reform can be compared to Miliukov's very similar argument cited earlier and written not long after Lenin's *Iskra* article.

[78] Lenin 1958–65, 7, p. 319, *Iskra*, No. 46 (15 August 1903).

political freedom is the central theme of Lenin's political agitation, so much so that often it is difficult to remember that the author is a Marxist socialist. Of the twenty-seven articles in the series, only two contribute to the reader's strictly Marxist education. One of these two articles analyses statistics on Russian savings banks in order to refute revisionist claims about the diffusion of wealth. (This article was meant to be the first of a series on economic themes, but no others were written.) In another article, Lenin gave Marxist reasons for seeing Russia's present economic crisis as inevitable and bound to recur. But, even here, the moral of the story is that

> the effect of a crisis in Russia is ever so much greater than in any other country. . . . The workers and the peasants are being drawn closer to each other, not only by unemployment and starvation, but also by the police oppression that takes away from the workers the possibility of [organisational] merger and defence and takes away from the peasant even the philanthropic aid sent to him.[79]

The prominence of political freedom provides a possible explanation of why the political agitation series has remained so obscure all these years. The academic establishment in both the Soviet Union and America had this much in common: they both wanted a Lenin who at all times acted as befits the father of the Soviet system. The passionate advocate of political freedom is hard to squeeze into this role. Indeed, one wonders why some group of Soviet dissidents did not issue a *samizdat* version of the political agitation articles with a title such as 'Lenin vs. the Kremlin'.

Let us take the Social-Democratic hostility to restrictions on the peasant's ability to dispose of his own property and even to move freely around the country. The Social Democrats believed that the peasant commune was a lynchpin in this systematic restriction of peasant rights – this function was a central reason for their desire to destroy it. In his political agitation articles, Lenin focused on more recent government restrictions on mobility:

> The law of 15 September puts the peasant in a serf-like position not only because it takes from the peasant the freedom to move around. The law

---

[79] Lenin 1958–65, 5, p. 86, *Iskra,* No. 7 (August 1901). This same passage also predicts that workers exiled from the towns will rouse the peasants from their past subservience and teach them to *demand.*

also gives the bureaucrats the right *to withhold a part of wages* to send to the family of the [peasant] workers, if 'the gubernatorial authorities of the localities in which the family resides' finds this necessary. The money earned by the peasant to be disposed of without the consent of the [peasant] workers themselves! The muzhik is stupid: he is unable to take care of his own family himself. The authorities can do this oh so much better.[80]

In reaction to bureaucratic talk of restricting peasant migration to Siberia, while at the same time granting Siberian lands to gentry, Lenin pictured the United States of America as a land where lack of restrictions on individual farmers directly benefited the worker class:

There no one *dares* to argue about permitting or not permitting population movements because each citizen has the right to move his home to wherever seems best to him. There anyone who wishes to farm has the right *by law* to occupy the free lands in the frontier regions of the country. There is built up not a class of Asiatic satraps but a class of energetic farmers who will develop all of the productive forces of the country. There the worker class, thanks to the abundance of free land, leads all others in terms of high living standards.[81]

Restriction of the peasants' ability to organise and to protest also ensures a callous attitude toward the casualties of famine:

The bosses of the capitalist state are no more concerned about the vastness of the numbers of the victims of famine and crises than a locomotive is concerned about those whom it crushes in its path. The dead bodies retard the wheels; the train stops, it may (if the engine driver is excessively energetic) jump the rails; but after a delay of lesser or greater duration it will in any event continue on its way. You hear of death from starvation and of the ruin of tens and hundreds of thousands of small owners, but at the same time, you hear stories about the progress of agriculture in our country, about the successful conquest of foreign markets by Russian noble landowners . . . you hear about the broader market for improved equipment, the dissemination of fodder grass cultivation, and so on.[82]

---

[80] Lenin 1958–65, 5, p. 291, *Iskra*, No. 10 (November 1901).
[81] Lenin 1958–65, 5, pp. 91–2, *Iskra*, No. 8 (10 September 1901).
[82] Lenin 1958–65, 5, p. 324, *Zaria* No. 2/3, (December 1901).

One can see why Soviet scholars did not want to give prominence to sentiments such as the ones just quoted or such as the following:

> In Nizhni-Novgorod a small but successful demonstration was called for November 7 to see off Maxim Gorky. This writer of European fame, whose weapons consist entirely – as one of the speakers at the demonstration justly remarked – of free speech, is being deported from his home town by the tsarist government without trial or examination. The bashibazouks accuse him of being a bad influence on us – continued this speaker in the name of all Russian people who have even the least striving for light and freedom – but we assert that he has been a good influence. The tsarist minions carry out their abuses in secret and we try to make these abuses open and public. In our country they beat the workers who are defending their right to a better life, in our country they beat the students who protest against lawlessness, in our country they crush any honest and audacious word![83]

By a nice irony, the Soviet bashibazouks shut up the inconvenient dissident Andrei Sakharov by sending him *to* Nizhni-Novgorod – renamed 'Gorky' in the meantime.

The exclusive focus of *Iskra*'s political agitation articles on political freedom excited suspicions among some Social-Democratic readers. But, for Lenin, the Russian Erfurtian, the connection between political freedom and the proletariat's historical mission was a bedrock truth, as he shows in this application of Kautsky's 'light and air' metaphor:

> Without political freedom all forms of worker representation will remain pitiful frauds, the proletariat will remain as before in prison, without the light, air and space needed to conduct the struggle for its full liberation. In this prison the government is cutting a tiny little hole instead of a window and setting up this opening in such a way as to bring more benefit to the gendarmes and spies who are guarding the prisoner than to the prisoner himself.
>
> And this is the kind of reform that the butchers of the Russian people want to pass off as the great good deed of the tsarist government! But the Russian worker class with the help of this opening will breathe into itself

---

[83] Lenin 1958–65, 5, pp. 369–70, *Iskra*, No. 13 (20 December 1901).

new strength for struggle, it will level to the ground this cursed all-Russian prison and conquer for itself class representation in a bourgeois-democratic state.[84]

Some readers might find Lenin's final words a rather anti-climactic and uninspiring message to be inscribed on the banner of an army of militant revolutionaries. But Lenin, imbued as he was to his fingertips with the Social-Democratic narrative, did not see it this way. Using the biblical story of Jacob and Esau as a metaphor, Lenin asserted that the mess of pottage represented by the tsarist government's pitiful reforms would never induce the workers to renounce their struggle for their essential birthright, namely, 'the freedom for the proletariat's struggle against *all* economic and social oppression'.[85]

So far, Lenin has looked mainly at the Russian élite, whether panicky tsarist bureaucrats or fed-up protesters from respectable society. It is time to turn to his invocation of 'the new mighty movement among the people that is gathering strength to wipe all brutality from the face of the Russian land and to realise the highest ideals of mankind'. The development of urban life, the growth of industry, the spread of literacy – all of this had brought a new awareness of human dignity even to the most downtrodden masses. The tsarist government therefore has a new and most deadly enemy – all the forces that make it their business to bring to the dark Russian masses 'the light of awareness of their rights and faith in their strength'.[86]

The main force bringing this awareness and faith to society at large is the worker movement. The worker movement is the hero of the political agitation series. From its earliest beginnings in 1885, the Russian worker movement has been ready to fight and that readiness has only been growing over the years. Repression cannot stop it:

> Penal servitude will not terrify workers whose leaders were not afraid to die in open street battles with tsarist minions. The numbers of these heroic comrades killed and tortured in prison will increase the strength of new fighters ten-fold and attract thousands of helpers like eighteen-year old Marfa Yakovleva who will openly say 'We stand by our brothers'.[87]

---

[84] Lenin 1958–65, 7, p. 321, *Iskra*, No. 46 (15 August 1903).
[85] Lenin 1958–65, 6, p. 357, *Iskra*, No. 18 (March 1902).
[86] Lenin 1958–65, 4, p. 416, *Zaria*, No. 1 (April 1901).
[87] Lenin 1958–65, 5, p. 294, *Iskra*, No. 10 (November 1901). According to Lozhkin

The support of student protests in 1901 by the workers shows their revolutionary idealism, since higher educational institutions were hardly filled with the sons and daughters of the workers themselves.[88] By actions like this, the worker movement has set all Russian society into movement. The militancy of the workers compels the government to search for reforms and galvanises élite grumblers into actually doing something. The workers take advantage of every small opening provided by the tsarist government in order to spread the word to other sections of the people.

The amazing events going on in Russia show again and again the basic correctness of the Social-Democratic wager on the worker movement. Take the current conflict between the government and the statisticians employed by the *zemstvo*. Would the statisticians have dared to openly resist the government if the worker movement had remained quiescent? Lenin points the moral:

> For us, Social Democrats, this little picture of the crusade against the 'third element' [= *zemstvo* employees] should serve as an important lesson. We should draw new faith in the immense strength of the worker movement guided by us when we see how the ferment in the advanced revolutionary class is transferred to other classes and strata of society as well, how it leads not only to the unheard-of upsurge in the revolutionary spirit of students but also to the village that is beginning to awaken, how even in social groups that as a group have remained up till now unresponsive [to events], the worker ferment leads to strengthened faith in oneself and readiness to fight.[89]

What, then, is the relationship between Social Democracy and this heroic worker movement? The textbook interpretation of WITBD tells us that Lenin wanted a strong centralised party to guide the proletariat because he had lost faith in the proletariat's innate revolutionary feelings. The political agitation articles make it crystal-clear that Lenin based his case for a strong centralised party to guide the proletariat precisely on his abiding faith in the worker movement's heroic militancy.

---

1986, pp. 112–13, Marfa Yakovleva as a small child met Lenin when he conducted study classes in her father's apartment.

[88] Lenin 1958–65, 6, p. 276, *Iskra*, No. 17 (15 February 1902).

[89] Lenin 1958–65, 5, p. 334, *Zaria*, No. 2/3 (December 1901).

In the first place, the Social-Democratic mission of bringing insight and organisation to the class struggle only made sense because of the worker movement's inexhaustible rebelliousness. After a bloody encounter in May 1901 between workers and police (the so-called 'Obukhov defence'), Lenin argues that

> we do not mean to say that fistfights with the police are the best form of struggle. On the contrary, we have always told the workers that it is in their interest to make the struggle calmer and more controlled and to try to direct all dissatisfaction to the support of the organised struggle of the revolutionary party. But the main source that nourishes revolutionary Social Democracy is precisely this spirit of revolt in the worker masses that, despite the oppression and violence that surround the worker, breaks through from time to time in desperate outbursts. These outbursts awaken to purposive life the widest strata of workers crushed by need and darkness. They disseminate in them the spirit of a noble hatred of the oppressors and the enemies of freedom.[90]

But Social Democracy must get its act together, must build up its own organisational strength, because, otherwise, it will fail the worker movement in its time of need. The following comment is polemically directed against terrorist tactics, yet is making essentially the same point Lenin makes against 'economism' in WITBD:

> Anyone who genuinely conducts his revolutionary work in connection with the class struggle of the proletariat knows, sees and feels very well what a mass of the immediate and direct demands of the proletariat (and the strata of the *narod* capable of supporting it) remains unsatisfied. He knows that in a mass of places, in whole entire districts, the worker population is literally bursting to fight, while this fervour is entirely without effect due to insufficient literature, leader/guides, due to the absence of resources and means in the revolutionary organisations. And we find ourselves – we see that we find ourselves – in the same cursed vicious circle that like an evil fate has pursued the Russian revolution for so long. On the one hand, the revolutionary

---

[90] Lenin 1958–65, 5, pp. 14–15, *Iskra*, No. 5 (June 1901). According to Reginald Zelnik, Lenin was so unconcerned with the struggles of actual workers that he ignored the 'Obukhov defence' (Zelnik 2003b).

fervour of the insufficiently enlightened and unorganised crowd is entirely without effect. On the other hand, the pistol shots of 'uncatchable individuals' who have lost faith in the possibility of going into the ranks and working hand in hand with the mass is also entirely without effect.

But the matter can still be completely put to rights, comrades! Loss of faith in a real cause is no more than a rare exception. The infatuation with terror is a passing mood. So let the Social Democrats close their ranks, and we shall meld together into one single whole the fighting organisation of the revolutionaries and the mass heroism of the Russian proletariat![91]

I have cited these passages at length because they are fundamental pieces of evidence in the clash of interpretations over WITBD. The same can be said about the article that in many ways is the climax of the series (although not the last chronologically). The six-page article 'New Events and Old Questions' appeared in December 1902 (almost nine months after the publication of WITBD) in reaction to a series of worker demonstrations that had just occurred over a period of several weeks in Rostov-on-the-Don. The polemical edge of the article is directed against the terrorist tactic. In Lenin's post-WITBD *Iskra* articles, 'economism' is almost forgotten while the terrorist tactic advocated by the Socialist Revolutionaries (and highly attractive to many Social Democrats) became the main target.[92]

A close paraphrase of 'New Events and Old Questions' follows.

It should be clear to everyone that the lull in the revolutionary movement for the last six months or so is over. Of course, any informed observer should have realised that the absence of open manifestations of worker indignation in no way implies that this indignation is not growing in scope and intensity. But many revolutionary intellectuals lack a solid connection with the worker movement and this short lull was enough to trigger voices among them of gloom and lack of faith. Other revolutionaries do not lose hope in the revolution but they are free from what they call our dogmatic Marxist faith in the worker movement. Thus the newly formed party of Socialist Revolutionaries insists on isolated political murders as an absolutely necessary tactic, undeterred by

---

[91] Lenin *PSS*, 6, pp. 386–7, *Iskra*, No. 23 (1 August 1902).
[92] For more on Lenin's and *Iskra*'s hostility to the terror tactic, see Chapters Five and Six.

our no doubt boring insistence on the primary tasks of agitation among the mass of the people and organisation of *mass* resistance.

Consider the course of events in Rostov-on-the-Don – events which show the absurdity of the Socialist Revolutionaries' return to the tactics of Narodnaia volia. It all began with what seemed like ordinary economic strikes but quickly grew into a political event – all this despite the completely inadequate participation of organised revolutionary forces. Crowds of people – up to twenty or thirty thousand strong – improvised political meetings that struck observers with their seriousness and organisation. The crowd listened with great eagerness to Social-Democratic proclamations and speeches and to explanations of some elementary truths about socialism and the political struggle, even though these explanations were offered by chance members of the labouring people with no serious preparation. The authorities seemed paralysed and, for several days, Rostov-on-the-Don saw something never before seen in Rus' – mass political meetings under an open sky. And, when the troops were finally called in, the crowd resisted fiercely, people were killed, and a new round of political demonstrations started again the next day at their funeral.

No doubt the Socialist Revolutionaries would have preferred the six murdered comrades to have given their lives in an attempt to assassinate some tsarist official or other. We, in contrast, think that the only 'revolutionary act' worthy the name is one that sets the *masses* in motion and that is tied to the growth of the worker class' political awareness and revolutionary activity – a growth evident to all. But we need to see not only the heroic resistance of the crowd but also how unprepared, unorganised and *stikhiinyi* this resistance still is – and remember our own duty of bringing organisation and training to the crowd that is out there fighting right now.

You do not need a few pistol shots aimed at easily replaceable official criminals to instigate and excite the crowd.[93] Rather, you should learn to use for effective agitational purposes the outrages that Russian life provides in all too splendid profusion. Much more inspiring and much more educational than showy assassinations are events that grow out of the masses' genuine feelings – for example, when tens of thousands of workers gather together

---

[93] 'Excite' and 'instigate' are digs at the writer L. Nadezhdin, as explained in Chapter Six.

to deliberate on their vital interests and to consider how political action can further these interests. More and more, this mass participation in the struggle will truly *raise up* as yet untapped strata of the proletariat to a more purposive life and a broader revolutionary struggle.

In fact, the Rostov events should make us start thinking about the possibility of a genuine popular uprising. Precisely the banality of the original strike action underscores the proletariat's mighty solidarity as it instantly perceived that the cause of the striking railroad workers was its *own* cause. The Rostov drama reveals the proletariat's receptivity to the preaching of political action and its readiness to defend in open battle its right to a free life, to free development. Indeed, all thinking workers already insist on these rights. So we can see that an armed uprising of the whole people against the autocracy is not just something that revolutionaries dreamed up and put in their programmes, but the inevitable, natural and practical result of the movement itself – the result of the growing indignation, growing experience and growing audacity of the workers.

Inevitable and natural next step, I say – *if only* we do not forget for a minute the task that is incumbent on us and becoming more urgent all the time, namely, the task of helping the masses who are already rising up to do so in ever more daring and compact fashion. Every street demonstration should have not just one or two, but a dozen street orators and leader/guides. We need to create a genuine fighting organisation – not the purely intelligentsia outfit created for terrorist purposes by the Socialist Revolutionaries, but an organisation that can really direct the fighting masses.

Comparable to the Rostov events as signs of the times are the courtroom speeches given by worker participants in demonstrations in Nizhni-Novgorod. These outstanding speeches are by workers who are by no means advanced in terms of development and who speak not as members of any organisation but as people of the crowd. These workers use the facts of proletarian life in Russia to explain why they deliberately and purposefully took part in demonstrations against the autocracy. These same facts are a guarantee that thousands, tens and hundreds of thousands, will inevitably come to the same conclusion – *if* we work systematically to broaden and deepen our revolutionary influence.

The four workers in Nizhni-Novgorod say: once we have felt the breath of freedom, we will brave the threat of arrest and forced labour in order to fight for it. As if in answer, thousands of workers in Rostov conquered for themselves – by dint of heroic fighting – a few days of free political assembly.[94]

Thus concludes 'New Events and Old Questions'. As the title of the article indicates, Lenin uses the exciting events in Rostov to bolster the definition of the situation he had been pushing throughout the political agitation series: the worker movement is growing ever more militant and powerful, thus confirming the fundamental Social-Democratic wager. The only drawback is the Social Democrats themselves, since they are shamefully behindhand in providing their own proper contribution, namely, effective agitation and organisation. If the Social Democrats could get their act together, the rising flood of worker militancy would soon demolish the autocracy.

We have completed our survey of the main themes of the undiscovered work to which we have given the title *Political Agitation*. To repeat: when these twenty-seven or so articles are placed together and read as a unit, we are confronted with a work more surprising than any recent archival revelation. Of course, the diligent reader of this commentary will be much less surprised than the unenlightened. Speaking for myself, I already knew, by the time I read the political agitation articles, that Lenin consistently expressed confidence in the worker movement and that political freedom was a top priority for him. Yet even I was taken aback by the exuberance of his romantic characterisation of the worker movement and by his obsessive insistence on the virtues of political freedom. I was also surprised by a hitherto unsuspected side of Lenin. Evidently when he wanted to (or should I say, had he wanted to, for he never did so again), Lenin could get beyond the party polemics and the abstract statistical generalities that fill up his writings and actually talk about real people in real situations. Of course, even here, he did so by analysing laws, speeches and newspaper articles; nevertheless the change is refreshing. The case study of the drunken *muzhik* beaten to death in a tsarist jail seems to me to be one of Lenin's best, if most atypical, productions.[95]

One person who might have been surprised by the political agitation series is Rosa Luxemburg. In her 1904 attack on Lenin, she asserted (with almost no textual documentation, let it be said) that Lenin was so intent on total

---

[94] Lenin 1958–65, 7, pp. 58–64, *Iskra*, No. 29 (1 December 1902).

[95] 'Beat, but not to Death' can be found in Lenin 1958–65, 4, pp. 401–16, *Zaria*, No. 1 (April 1901).

central control that he overlooked the creative role of the worker movement itself. Meanwhile, Luxemburg continued, the Russian worker movement had at three crucial moments had made tactical breakthroughs without benefit of Social-Democratic guidance: the strikes of 1896, the demonstrations in support of students in spring 1901, and the Rostov events of late 1902. She describes the Rostov events as

> the mass strike that broke out 'all by itself' in Rostov-on-Don, with its improvised street agitation, its popular assemblies under open skies, its public speeches – something that the most audacious enthusiast of Social Democracy would have considered a few years back as a fantasy not to be thought of.[96]

Where did Luxemburg, living in Germany, get her information about events in far-off Rostov-on-the-Don? Naturally, from *Iskra* – in fact, as is easily seen by the details of her description, directly from the article 'New Events and Old Questions'.[97] These articles were not by-lined, so Luxemburg was no doubt unaware that she was quoting Lenin to show the sort of thing that Lenin overlooked.

The series constitutes a severe problem for today's textbook interpretation. Take, for example, Robert Tucker's excellent description of *WITBD*:

> To understand Lenin's political conception in its totality, it is important to realise that he saw in his mind's eye not merely the militant organisation of professional revolutionaries of which he spoke, but the party-led popular *movement* 'of the entire people'. The 'dream' was by no means simply a party dream although it centred in the party as the vanguard of conscious revolutionaries acting as teachers and organisers of a much larger mass following in the movement. The dream was a vision of an anti-state popular Russia raised up by propaganda and agitation as a vast army of fighters against the official Russia headed by the tsar.[98]

Tucker's description is a direct challenge to the textbook interpretation and most scholars would say that he gives much too romantic a picture of Lenin's

---

[96] Luxemburg 1970, p. 432 (Harding 1983, p. 301 for English translation). Luxemburg's article is discussed in more detail in Chapter Nine.

[97] Note Lenin's phrase 'under open skies' [*pod otkrytym nebom*] and Luxemburg's 'unter freiem Himmel' (see Lenin 1958–65, 7, p. 59).

[98] Tucker 1987, p. 39.

outlook. Yet, when we compare it to the political agitation series, we find that the only problem with this description is that it is *not romantic enough*. We need to intensify it in three ways: Lenin is saying that the tsar's final hour is fast approaching *right now*; he includes many *élite* elements in the army of outrage that is closing in on the tsar; he gives the worker movement itself a major leadership role vis-à-vis the rest of society.

The political agitation series had many potential audiences in mind. One such audience was Lenin's fellow Social Democrats, and the moral he wanted them to draw is expounded at length in WITBD. It runs something like this: an effective organisation of revolutionaries can certainly overturn the autocracy now, small as such an organisation would be, because such an organisation could count on the vast and unstoppable power of a popular movement whose fervour grows ever deeper and that is ready to accept Social-Democratic guidance. Fellow Social Democrats, look at what is going on around you and realise that *we* are the bottleneck, *our* shortcomings are all that stands between the worker movement and a free Russia.

Even as they were living through it, the Russian Social Democrats saw the *Iskra* period as an episode in a larger narrative. In Chapter One, we looked at the two highest levels of this movement and explored how the top level of Marx's world-historical narrative determined the political strategy of Social Democracy as an episode within that narrative. In Chapter Two, we saw how a Russian Erfurtian viewed his own country as an episode within the Social-Democratic narrative. The present chapter took a look from a variety of angles at the *Iskra* episode that constituted one phase within the history of Russian Social Democracy. Our three witnesses – Miliukov's lectures on the Russian crisis, the Amsterdam report on Russian party history, and Lenin's political agitation series – bring out different aspects. Miliukov shows the historical roots of the growing clash between Russian society and tsarism, the Amsterdam report described the various polemics *Iskra* conducted with all and sundry, and Lenin evoked the desperate flailing of a doomed system. Yet all three agree on one key theme: the central role of a radicalised worker movement in galvanising society-wide revolutionary opposition to absolutism.

In Part II, we will train the narrative zoom lens on the fifth and final level and look at a particular set of polemics conducted by *Iskra* in 1901. By the autumn of that year, enough issues of *Iskra* had appeared to enable critics to mount serious accusations against this new contender for Social-Democratic leadership. *WITBD* thus had a double task – to set out *Iskra*'s positive recommendation, but also to respond to this criticism. We must descend into the maelstrom of this polemical infighting before we can emerge into the clear day of a real understanding of what *WITBD* is all about.

## Appendix to Chapter Three

*Miliukov's Review of* WITBD

I discovered this review by accident. I was reeling through some microfilm on my way to another document and was surprised, when I paused for a moment, to see the words 'N. Lenin' on the page. What I had found was a review of *WITBD* that appeared in 1903 in the underground liberal oppositional journal *Osvobozhdenie*.[99] Miliukov was one of the principal collaborators in this journal. This review is a revealing document no matter who wrote it, but I am certain that Miliukov is the author.

The review is signed with the initials 'R.D.', but I am informed by Melissa Stockdale, Miliukov's American biographer, that *Osvobozhdenie* used deliberately misleading initials to indicate authorship. According to Stockdale, Miliukov in later life made a list of the articles in *Osvobozhdenie* for which he was responsible. The *WITBD* review is not on this list, but other omissions have already been found by scholars.[100]

There is thus no reason why Miliukov could not have written the review. The external reasons for identifying Miliukov as the author are these. First, to whom would this review assignment have been given except to the man who was then working on a study of Russian socialism for his book *Russia and Its Crisis*? Indeed, the set of people who were both liberal spokesman *and* experts on the internal politics of Russian Social Democracy must have been very small (perhaps only Petr Struve is another candidate). Finally, the sentiments expressed by the review about the significance of *WITBD* account for the effort that Miliukov made to look up Lenin in London in 1903–4.[101]

---

[99] *Osvobozhdenie*, Kn. 1 (1903), pp. 253–5.
[100] Melissa Stockdale, personal communication.
[101] According to Thomas Riha, however, it was Lenin who asked to meet Miliukov (Riha 1969, pp. 54–5).

The internal evidence for Miliukov's authorship is even more compelling. The review expresses exactly the same attitudes toward issues – for example, toward Social-Democratic 'economism' – that we find in *Russia and its Crisis*.[102]

In my view, Miliukov's brief account of WITBD is more to the point than almost anything available in Western scholarship. I am glad to place it here at the end of Part I because it provides an excellent introduction to the rest of the commentary. Miliukov adumbrates some of my central theses in Part II of the Commentary, devoted to WITBD's polemical context. The theoretical pronouncements that scholars see as a major statement of Lenin's innovative views are dismissed by Miliukov as polemical 'side-swipes' that often ascribe views to opponents that nobody actually held. Insofar as the polemics had substance, the clash was between 'economist' scepticism versus Lenin's confidence in the revolutionary inclinations of the workers. Miliukov's review also takes a calm view of Lenin's organisational proposals and sees them (much as I do in Part III) as a straightforward and 'not very complicated' deduction from Lenin's desire to have Social Democracy lead the struggle to bring political freedom to Russia.

**N. Lenin.** *What Is to Be Done? Burning Questions of Our Movement*. J.H.W. Dietz Nachf. Verlag, Stuttgart 1902. Price 1 rouble = 2 marks = 2.50 francs

> 'Our movement' is the movement of that part of intelligentsia Russia that has set itself the goal of creating in Russia an independent worker party that would pursue a social revolution [*perevorot*] as its *final goal*, and the elimination of the tsarist régime of lawlessness in order to replace it with a legal constitutional order as its *immediate* goal. There are a great many 'burning questions' in this movement, since along with purely tactical and organisational problems, the party is going through a difficult struggle about purely theoretical questions. The party must now subject to a critical examination the entire philosophical, sociological, economic and historical foundation upon which the Social-Democratic programme has arisen. Mr. Lenin, however, does not set himself such a wide task and in the book under review limits himself for the most part to questions of tactics and organisation. Only in passing, in various digressions, does he send his theoretical opponents

---

[102] In particular, compare Miliukov 1962, pp. 353–4.

more or less weighty *Seitenhiebe* [side-swipes], which, however, do not always hit their target.

Mr. Lenin's book falls into five sections, of which the first talks about 'dogmatism' and 'freedom of criticism'. This section is very incoherent, very angry and very uninteresting. Here in general terms is what this section is all about:

A certain part of our Russian and of foreign Social Democracy, having expressed doubts concerning certain points in the programme and the theoretical ideas that lay at its foundation, has met with sharp rejection and condemnation from the majority of the party. There have even been hints about the exclusion of the heretics and the 'apostates' from the party. It is therefore natural that among these doubters should arise the thought that the party forbids any doubt in the truth of certain ideas and does not permit any 'criticism'. Our author on the first page rejects any accusation that the party has any designs on 'the constitutional law of the majority of European countries that guarantees freedom of science and scientific investigation' (p. 1). But, in his opinion, there is an 'innate hypocrisy' in the 'present-day use of the term "freedom of criticism"', since the aforesaid freedom of criticism 'is the freedom of the opportunist tendency in Social Democracy, the freedom to transform Social Democracy into a democratic party of reform, the freedom of instilling bourgeois ideas and bourgeois elements into socialism' (p. 3). And, for this reason, he is nothing loath to help the 'removal' of all 'critics' into the 'swamp', by which he means all those who are not in the camp of the 'dogmatists'. In other words, he is nothing loath to exclude all dissenters from the party. We do not agree with Mr. Lenin's attitude toward 'critics', but we do not consider it necessary to get into a polemic with him here. We will just say that this entire chapter could with great success have remained unwritten – the book would have lost nothing, in fact it might have gained.

The remaining chapters are entirely devoted to organisational and tactical questions. To clarify these questions, we need to briefly set out the development of Social-Democratic ideas and the Social-Democratic movement in Russia.

Russian Social Democracy has already existed for a couple of decades. Its beginning goes back to 1883, when the newly organised group Emancipation of Labour first stepped into the literary arena with two small publications.

Starting at this period and continuing approximately to 1894, Social-Democratic ideas were propagandised in Russia for the most part in circles of the intelligentsia youth that occasionally also included workers. These ideas still did not have, however, any wide social resonance. Its literary expression consisted almost exclusively of the émigré 'illegal' press. But then 1894 arrived, the first legally-permitted Marxist books appeared, and (in 1897) a Marxist journal was founded – and Marxist ideas spread in a wide and rapid flood over the face of the Russian land, seizing wide strata of intelligentsia youth, pushing them on the one hand to a struggle against the world-view then reigning [populism] and on the other hand to organisational and enlightenment work among the urban proletariat.

At that time, neither among the literary, theoretical nor the practical leader/guides of the movement did there exist any noticeable disagreements. Work went ahead smoothly, energetically, not weakened by internal disputes.

Already by the end of the nineties, however, there was observable, if not a schism, then in any event a certain drifting apart. Among the active Social Democrats new voices were heard that proposed to the Russian Marxist a new programme, formulated in one document [the *Credo*] with the following words: 'participation, that is, helping the economic struggle of the proletariat, and participation in liberal oppositional activity'. This programme would thus have put a wooden stake through the heart of Russian Social Democracy as a worker political party. The programme maintained that the dream of creating a political party based on the workers could not be carried out and, just for that reason, was harmful. The Russian proletariat – said the advocates of this programme – had not yet matured enough to understand specific political demands; all that it was capable of now was the struggle for its *economic* needs. The Russian worker did not yet feel any need for political freedom, he was unable to lift itself up to a struggle with the autocracy, he was attracted only by the struggle for high wages and a short working day.

But such a programme, given the whole nature of present-day Russian life, did not have and could not have any success. In a country that has a despotic régime such as our Russian one, in a country where such elementary democratic rights as the right of free speech, assembly and so on, do not exist, where each worker strike is accounted a political crime and workers are forced by bullets and whips to return to work – in such a country, no party can restrict itself to the narrow framework of an exclusively economic struggle. And Mr. Lenin justly protests against such a programme.[103] Basing himself on the fact that a definite section of the Russian proletariat has now already matured to an understanding of the necessity of the struggle with autocracy, he finds it possible and necessary to conduct a struggle not only for the immediate economic demands of the proletariat, but also for the transformation of the existing form of government. He assumes that 'the ideal of the Social Democrat should not be a secretary of a *tred-iunion* but a *people's tribune* who can respond to each and every manifestation of abuse of power and oppression, wherever it occurs, whatever stratum or class it concerns and who can generalise all these manifestations into one big picture of police violence and capitalist exploitation, who is able to use each small affair to set *before everybody* his socialist convictions and his democratic demands and to explain to each and *all* the world-historical significance of the liberation struggle of the proletariat' (p. 62).

Thus Mr. Lenin places before Russian Social Democracy the task of becoming an advanced detachment in the great struggle with the régime of lawlessness that governs us. Since he does not believe that the Russian liberal opposition can carry out in Russia what the liberals of Western Europe carried out, that is, a successful campaign for a constitution, he finds it necessary to put this problem before Russian Social Democracy, assuming that it and only it is in a position to solve this task that is becoming more pressing for all of progressive Russia. In order to do this, Russian Social Democracy must win hegemony in the guidance of the Russian revolutionary and oppositional struggle. He writes that 'we' – that is, Social Democrats – 'must take care to push people who are personally dissatisfied only with their university or with their *zemstvo* institutions to face the thought that it is our political institutions as a whole that are worthless. We must take upon ourselves the task of organising an all-sided political struggle under the guidance of our party so that as much help as possible can be given and will be given to that struggle and to that party by each and every oppositional stratum. We must take the *praktiki* of Social Democrats and make them political leaders, leaders capable of guiding all manifestation of the all-sided

---

[103] The author's wording suggests that he was aware that the anonymous 'Protest' against the *Credo* written in 1899 was authored by Lenin.

struggle, capable at the crucial moment "to dictate a positive programme of action" to the turbulent students, the dissatisfied *zemstvo* people, the indignant sectarians, the offended rural teachers and so on and so on' (p. 64–5). Such all-sided political work demands a corresponding organisation. Given our autocratic régime, this 'organisation must consist for the most part of people who treat revolutionary activity as a full-time trade [*professional'no*]' (p. 94), capable at the least sign of danger to quickly change their passport or their living quarters – in general, people experienced in the struggle with police lawlessness. How does one start creating such an organisation? Mr. Lenin recommends starting with an all-Russian newspaper. A newspaper, he says, is 'not only a collective propagandist and a collective agitator, but also a collective organiser. In this latter respect it can be compared to scaffolding erected around a building under construction: it brings out the contours of the building site, it facilitates relations between individual builders, it helps them distribute the work and look over the general results that are obtained by means of their organised labour' (p. 126).

Not contenting himself with just recommending, Mr. Lenin has started to implement his plan as well – and *Iskra*, the newspaper guided by him and his comrades, should be the 'collective organiser' of which he speaks in his book.

Mr. Lenin develops his not very complicated thoughts in the form of an angry polemic with comrades who see things differently, and, it must be said, his polemical sorties are not always successful. The author often does not understand or does not wish to understand his opponents and ascribes to them ideas that they never stated.

This book is being read with passion, and will continue to be read, by our revolutionary youth. Several of the ideas that lay at its basis – one can state with confidence – will continue for a long time to serve as practical guidance for the activity of Russian Social Democrats. Therefore we recommend to any Russian who is not completely indifferent to what our revolutionary youth is doing and thinking to become acquainted with this book.

R.D.

Part Two

# Lenin's Significant Others

# Chapter Four
## Russian Foes of Erfurtianism

At one point in WITBD, Lenin portrays himself at his writing desk, telling us that 'I am starting to leaf through Martynov's article' in order to find appropriate phrases.[1] This verbal snapshot is extremely revealing. Lenin seems always to have an opposing text lying open on his writing desk, always to be quoting offending phrases, always to be expostulating 'can you *believe* they're saying such things!'. Indeed, Lenin often allows his opponents' arguments to organise his own argument and to supply the vocabulary with which he presents his own ideas. He even states, at one point, that he prefers to wait until he can present his ideas in attack mode.[2] These polemical opponents are WITBD's 'significant others'.

The dramatic personae of WITBD's polemical drama are the writers and groups against whom Lenin directs his fire. One or more of the following six characters is present on almost every page of Lenin's book. (After the group name, I add in parentheses the main individual names associated with the group.)

[1] Lenin *PSS*, 6, p. 81 [747].
[2] 'We were looking for a suitable opportunity or a well-formulated expression of this popular accusation [that *Iskra* neglected the class point of view] in order to answer it. And we are accustomed to answer an attack not by a defence but by a counter-attack' (Lenin *PSS*, 6, p. 91 [755]).

*Credo* (Elena Kuskova, Sergei Prokopovich)

*Rabochaia mysl* (K.M. Takhtarev)

*Rabochee delo* (Boris Krichevskii and Aleksandr Martynov)

B-v, a contributor to *Rabochee delo* (Boris Savinkov)

*Joint Letter* (sent to *Iskra* in late 1901 by a group of political prisoners within Russia)

*Svoboda* (L. Nadezhdin)

I have chosen to keep the names of periodicals and political groups in Russian while translating other titles. Other scholars consider it more reader-friendly to use English translations for these names:

*Iskra* = *The Spark*

*Rabochaia mysl* = *Worker Thought*

*Rabochee delo* = *Worker Cause*

*Svoboda* = *Freedom*

WITBD cannot be understood without grasping what these significant others stand for and why Lenin opposed them. The protagonist is WITBD's polemical drama is *Rabochee delo*, the main rival of the *Iskra* group for leadership in the inchoate party of 1901. In later 1901, *Rabochee delo* published some severe criticisms of *Iskra* based on its first six or so issues. Lenin's original intention was to confine his book to setting forth his positive proposals, but, by the time he sat down to write in late 1901, he felt compelled to respond to the attack mounted by *Iskra's* rivals. When Lenin mentions his WITBD in correspondence in 1901, he usually says something like 'I'm working away on the book against *Rabochee delo*'.

Lenin's central polemical stragegy is to associate *Rabochee delo* with 'economism', even though *Rabochee delo* was on record as stoutly opposed to economism as an ideology. The classic exemplars of economism were the first two names on my list: the *Credo* and *Rabochaia mysl*. We have met them before as targets of Lenin's protest writings in 1899. By 1901, owing both to the horrified reaction of all shades of Social-Democratic opinion (including *Rabochee delo*) and to the course of events, economism was completely discredited. Thus Lenin's aim is not to show that economism is wrong, for he takes it for granted that all readers of his book agree on this. His aim is to take the formulations in which *Rabochee delo* clothed its criticism of *Iskra* and show that they smack of this dreaded ideological error. Lenin's argument can be paraphrased: '*Rabochee delo* today is nothing but a confused and half-hearted version of what the discredited, although bolder and more logical, *Credo* and *Rabochaia mysl* were yesterday'.

Although the onslaught against *Rabochee delo* is the main campaign in Lenin's polemical war, he fights skirmishes on the side with the last three names on our list: Savinkov, the *Joint Letter*, and L. Nadezhdin. None of these persons or groups were particularly significant figures within Russian Social Democracy in their own right, but Lenin used their writings issued in 1900–1 to make various points in aid either of his polemic against *Rabochee delo* or of his explanation of his positive policy proposals.

The group of six thus falls naturally into three groups. In this chapter, we examine the first group, the *Credo* and *Rabochaia mysl*, the paradigmatic instances of economism. The common thread that connects these two otherwise disparate groups is scepticism about the applicability of the SPD model of a national class political party to absolutist Russia. In the following chapter we look at WITBD's polemical protagonist, *Rabochee delo*. I show that *Rabochee delo* was not really guilty of economism but that the *Iskra*-ites had sufficient motivation to accuse their rivals of this mortal Social-Democratic sin. In a third chapter, I examine Lenin's disputes with the three remaining polemical others. The common thread in this group is, in one way or another, scepticism about the empirical spread of awareness under tsarist conditions.

Before turning to 'economism', we need to look more closely at this term that plays such a major role not only in the polemics of the time but also in later commentary on WITBD. WITBD was so successful in pinning the label 'economist' on *Rabochee delo* that this group is regarded as 'economist' even by those who correctly see that its position was strongly opposed to the classic economism of the *Credo* and *Rabochaia mysl*.[3] More often, *Rabochee delo* is presented as simply the more moderate ally of *Rabochaia mysl* with essentially the same outlook.[4] This is historically and analytically confusing. In this commentary, 'economism' is restricted to the position of the *Credo* and *Rabochaia mysl*. Only by restricting the terms in this way can we understand what is going on in WITBD, as Lenin builds his paradoxical case that *Rabochee delo*, the

---

[3] Nicolaevsky 1927, p. 17.
[4] Haimson 1999, pp. 153–6; Haimson 2004, p. 60.

explicit opponent of economism, was itself guilty of it. I judge Lenin's accusation to be unfounded, but even those who disagree will lose nothing in clarity by defining Russian economism as 'the position defended in different ways by the *Credo* and *Rabochaia mysl'*.

Another common misunderstanding is to equate the statement 'I am opposed to economism' to the statement 'I am opposed to the economic struggle as such, that is, to strikes, trade unions, factory laws'. But '-ism' means an *ideology*, which in this case is: 'a *restriction* to economic struggle defended as a matter either of principle or of long-term tactics'.

'Economic' also had a special Social-Democratic meaning which can best be appreciated by looking at what 'politics' meant in nineteenth-century debates among socialist revolutionaries. 'Politics' essentially meant 'insisting on the importance of political freedom' and, in the Russian context, 'insisting on the urgent priority of overthrowing the autocracy in order to obtain political freedom'. This is what people had in mind when they said that anarchists or populists 'rejected politics'. But, under this definition, certain kinds of political activity – working for factory legislation or even working to obtain partial political rights from the autocracy – were not 'political'. Anyone who *restricted* himself on *principle* to these kinds of activity was still an economist. For this reason, even at the time, the term was felt to be somewhat clumsy and misleading. Lenin apologises for his use of the term in WITBD and explains that it is a concession to common usage.[5]

Once we grasp these background assumptions, the term economism is precise enough as this sort of political label goes. The essential point is that economism, so defined, was anathema to Social Democracy. Recall Kautsky's words in the *Erfurt Programme*: political freedoms are 'light and air for the proletariat; he who lets them wither or withholds them – he who keeps the proletariat from the struggle to win these freedoms and to extend them – that person is one of the proletariat's worst enemies'.[6] It is no surprise, then, that the Russian economists are conscious and determined foes of Erfurtianism at home and abroad. Their critique not only confirms the existence of such a thing as Erfurtianism but helps delineate its features more precisely. In particular, the economists bring out the difficulties and paradoxes of applying

---

[5] Lenin 1958–65, 6, pp. 33, 42 [705, 712].
[6] Kautsky 1965, p. 219.

Erfurtianism to Russia – difficulties and paradoxes that Lenin spent his career trying to overcome.

## The *Credo*: Kuskova and Prokopovich

> If the *Communist Manifesto* is taken as gospel, then our point of view is heresy. (Sergei Prokopovich)

The *Credo* assumed an almost mythical status in the history of Russian Social Democracy. Every faction accused the other of trying to implement 'the programme of the *Credo*'. And what was the *Credo*? It was a five-page document scribbled down by Elena Kuskova as part of a private debate among some young Russian Social Democrats in Petersburg in 1899. It certainly was not meant for publication and no one was more surprised than Kuskova when some months later it was published in the West under the imposing title of *Credo* and accompanied by a long 'Protest of Russian Social Democrats' that had been drafted by Lenin in Siberian exile and signed by sixteen other Russian Social Democrats in exile. It later transpired that Lenin's sister Anna ilyanova had somehow got a hold of a copy of the document, given it the title of *Credo* and sent it to Lenin, who had no idea who had written it.[7]

What, then, was 'the programme of the *Credo*'? We will get to that at the end of this section, but first we should introduce the author Elena Kuskova and her husband Sergei Prokopovich. This remarkable couple had been shopping around for a political home in the 1890s and after going through various forms of latter-day populism they ended up in Social Democracy for a few years. They quickly identified themselves with what they considered the progressive wing of the movement, namely, the revisionism associated with Eduard Bernstein. Kuskova and Prokopovich later occupied an area somewhere between Social Democracy and the liberals.[8] In 1917 Prokopovich became Minister of Food Supply for the Provisional Government (in which capacity he makes an appearance in an earlier book of mine).[9] In 1921–2, the

---

[7] For the origins of the *Credo*, see Kuskova 1906; editorial notes in Lenin 1925–36, 2, pp. 637–8.
[8] Judging from David Riazanov's review of a 1908 edition of Prokopovich's book on German socialism, Prokopovich still regarded himself as a Social Democrat, much to Riazanov's amazement (Riazanov 1908).
[9] Lih 1990.

couple helped organise a Russian committee to combat the famine in the Volga region and were deported from Russia by Lenin for their pains. In emigration, Prokopovich continued to produce valuable studies of the Soviet economy.

Luckily, we have other sources for their views than a solitary scribbled document, although all of their writings from this period have a similarly odd publication history. In early 1900, as part of his ongoing war with *Rabochee delo*, Plekhanov published his *Vademecum* consisting primarily of unpublished material by Kuskova and Prokopovich. Included was an unpublished pamphlet by Prokopovich that contained a stinging attack on the Emancipation of Labour group, a letter written by Kuskova to Akselrod, and other private letters from a member of the *Rabochee delo* editorial staff (Timofei Kopelzon) who knew Prokopovich and described his views. The ethics of Plekhanov's publication of this material can surely be questioned (as well as his bad taste in mocking grammatical errors in correspondence not meant for publication), but the historian must be grateful.

In 1900, Prokopovich finally published something intentionally: a substantial study (over three hundred pages) entitled *The Worker Movement in the West: An Essay in Critical Investigation*.[10] This study of Germany and Belgium also had its publication ups and downs. Kuskova had returned to Russia in 1899 and smuggled in a manuscript of the book, but, when Prokopovich himself returned to Russia, he was promptly arrested. The publisher, L.F. Panataleev, decided he should play it safe and handed the manuscript over to the official censorship. The officials sat on it for another six months but, finally, allowed publication in January 1900. According to *Iskra* No. 10, the book had at least one Russian fan. Sergei Zubatov, the police chief who tried to introduced legal anti-revolutionary trade unions, recommended Prokopovich's book to workers under his influence as an antidote to more mainstream Social-Democratic views.[11]

As we shall see, Zubatov had cause. A couple of cautionary remarks before proceeding. First, I am making the simplifying assumption that this body of writing all expresses the same set of views, despite the weird publication

---

[10] The full title is *Rabochee dvizhenie na Zapade, Opyt kriticheskogo issledovaniia. Tom I. Germaniia. Bel'giia* (Prokopovich 1899).

[11] Lenin 1958–65, 4, p. 479; 6, p. 482; Kindersley 1962, pp. 95–6.

history and the double authorship (or triple, if we count the letter-writer who describes Prokopovich's views). As a matter of fact, I do see some apparent minor differences between Kuskova and Prokopovich, but their basic unity of outlook is remarkable. Furthermore, it is unclear to what degree readers in 1901 understood that all this material came from the same source. In particular, Kuskova's authorship of the *Credo* only became officially public knowledge when Kuskova herself announced the fact in 1906.

### Short-circuiting the spread of awareness

Taken together, these writings constitute as concerted and slashing an attack on Erfurtianism as has ever been penned. Let us go through the check-list. *Erfurt allegiance*: Prokopovich's book explicitly attacks Kautsky, the *Erfurt Programme*, and the SPD model. *Merger formula, good news, circles of awareness, and the ideal of an independent political class party*: all explicitly repudiated. *Political freedom*: Kuskova and Prokopovich did not reject political freedom as a value, but they were certainly blasé about its importance and definitely argued that overthrowing the autocracy was not an urgent priority at the moment. *Popular leadership and hegemony*: Kuskova and Prokopovich thought that it was Social Democracy that needed to 'recognise society' and abandon its outworn creed. Perhaps the two writers did not reject internationalism – I have found nothing to the contrary – but they did reject imitating alien models and in particular transferring the SPD model to Russia.

And yet Kuskova and Prokopovich still thought of themselves as Social Democrats! This is because they assumed that Social Democracy was itself rejecting the Erfurtian model of the past. They were certainly not merely tame disciples of Eduard Bernstein. They considered Bernstein as a useful but somewhat confused spokesman for a massive shift in party outlook. Indeed, Prokopovich criticises Bernstein for spending too much time on correcting socialist doctrine – as if the Party's actual practice was ever really guided by doctrine! What needs to be rejected (continues Prokopovich) is, rather, the mythical self-image of a party guided by doctrine.[12]

I myself am encouraged by the attack mounted by Kuskova and Prokopovich because it confirms not only the existence of Erfurtianism but its basic contours

---

[12] Prokopovich 1899, pp. 187–98, particularly pp. 197–8.

as described here. I also agree with Prokopovich that his critique goes to the heart of the matter more incisively than Bernstein's. Instead of dithering on about whether small-scale agriculture was increasing or decreasing, Kuskova/Prokopovich zeroed in on the Social-Democratic narrative – on the very possibility of a class having an exalted historical mission or of a party that brings insight to the wide masses. Prokopovich laughed at Lassalle's illusions on this score: 'The masses are not aware of any "grand historical ideas" that they are supposed to carry out – and indeed, are the masses even capable of striving in purposive fashion to carry out such ideas?'.[13]

Erfurtians visualised their political strategy as a series of spreading circles of awareness and their aim was to break down all barriers to this spread. Kuskova and Prokopovich tried in every possible way to subvert this scenario. First, they blocked the spread of awareness at the root by denying that the party programme itself should contain anything but immediately realisable aims. The proletariat was not going to take power in the near future and therefore 'to put socialisation of the means of labour into the programme or to talk about the *Zukunftsstaat* [future state] is utopian and childish'.[14] In fact, even the SPD's 'minimum programme' – the so-called 'practical' and non-socialist part of the programme – was utopian as well, since many of the reforms were simply not acceptable to contemporary bourgeois society.[15] The same reasoning applied to Russia. Since the actual overthrow of the autocracy was not on the immediate agenda, the demand for it should be removed from the Social-Democratic programme.

Another barrier to the spread of awareness was set up by Prokopovich's idiosyncratic concept of propaganda vs. agitation. The job of creating a new awareness of basic interests was left to propaganda, while agitation restricted itself to help in implementing interests of which the workers were already aware. But this meant that the mission by which Social Democracy defined itself – spreading awareness – should be confined to a small number of, it would seem, rather marginal individuals.

---

[13] Prokopovich 1899, p. 116.
[14] Description of Prokopovich's views by Timofei Kopelzon in Plekhanov 1923–7, 12, p. 496 (all references to writings included in Plekhanov's *Vademecum* are to this edition).
[15] Prokopovich 1899, pp. 144–5.

> Propaganda about the future, socialism and all the rest of it can *for the time being* serve as an excellent means for attracting *individuals* from the intelligentsia and from among the workers (in the majority of cases sentimental types who are not very purposive), but *never* the masses.[16]

(The dismissive 'and all the rest of it' is eloquent.)

In contrast, agitation among the mass of workers was in some way phoney if revolutionary intellectuals were involved:

> Just as economic agitation begins only when a strike movement begins *by itself* in the worker mass (without the immediate participation of intellectuals), just so can political agitation be started when the workers by themselves (without the revolutionary bacilli/intellectuals) begin the struggle with the autocracy.[17]

Well, did Kuskova and Prokopovich have *any* conception of class leadership? Yes, and here is how it worked. The Social Democrats help the masses *organise* on the basis of their perceived interests (trying to increase the workers' *insight* into their own interests on a mass scale is impossible and undesirable). The job of the Social Democrat is thus to fight *stikhiinost*, that is to say, disorganisation and indiscipline.[18]

As these mass organisations fight for worker interests, they will run into tsarist repression, an experience that will broaden the workers' sense of their interests. Not agitation by the party but 'life continually makes the worker aware of more and more new interests . . . Since it develops in strict dependence on the conditions of time and place, the awareness of the masses renders fruitless all attempts to force [*nasilovat'*] the natural course of the worker movement's development'.[19]

Kuskova and Prokopovich were not worried about *domination* of the workers by the 'revolutionary bacilli/intellectuals'. They just thought that trying to 'revolutionise minds' on a mass scale was a plentiful waste of time. The phrase

---

[16] Kuskova letter in Plekhanov 1923–7, 12, p. 492 (emphasis in the original).

[17] Prokopovich in Plekhanov 1923–7, 12, p. 512 ('by itself' = *samoproizvol'no*).

[18] For the reasons that I have chosen to keep *stikhiinost* untranslated, see Annotations Part Two, where I demonstrate the unsatisfactory nature of the usual translation of 'spontaneity'. The reader's sense of the word's connotations will increase as we see it in use in Social-Democratic discourse.

[19] Prokopovich in Plekhanov 1923–7, 12, p. 505.

'revolutionising minds' had been used by Kautsky to express the modus operandi of the party. Prokopovich sided with the revisionist leaders who mocked this phrase. For example, the German agrarian specialist, Eduard David, responded as follows:

> We didn't obtain the sympathy of the masses in the way described by Kautsky: revolutionising minds. We conquered the sympathy of the masses by practical activity that responded to the needs of the day. The revolutionising of minds will get us only a few students. We can't get the sympathy of the masses by awakening hopes for the future in them or by ideas that are not so easy to understand. The revolutionising of the masses doesn't start from the mind but from the stomach.[20]

Prokopovich records similar sentiments in the Belgian worker party that he and Kuskova saw as a model. One Bertrand asks: 'What is the reason for the success of the worker party up till now – the socialist ideal or our programme of practical reforms?' His answer is reforms, since 'the [socialist] ideal allures only the more enlightened and more intellectual part of the working class'. Most striking of all, Prokopovich summed up the general feeling of Belgian socialists in the following way: 'The masses are like children: visual demonstration is what strikes them. Like children, the masses are allured only by immediate and current results – not by high, abstract ideals'.[21]

Erfurtian Social Democrats such as Plekhanov and Lenin also assume that 'life' in the form of the political obstacles experienced by workers in their economic struggle would be an important source of increased class awareness. Who would be foolish enough to deny it? What struck them about the 'line of least resistance' interpretation was, instead, that it relegated all political leadership to a unimportant superstructure. In his *Vademecum*, Plekhanov responded that correct leadership could *accelerate* historical development, using a version of the 'sooner or later' argument:

> 'The workers know only two things: their own clearly perceived concrete interest and their position among other classes.'[22] This also needs to be

---

[20] Comment made at the 1895 SPD Congress, cited by Prokopovich 1899, p. 166.
[21] Prokopovich 1899, Part II, pp. 102, 107.
[22] Plekhanov is here quoting the Kuskova letter published in the *Vademecum* (Plekhanov 1923–7, 12, p. 488).

analysed. Do the workers *always* know their own interests and their position among other classes? We, the partisans of the materialist view of history, believe the answer is: *far from always*. We do not doubt that the *awareness* of people is determined by their *social existence*. The appearance of new aspects of reality are the cause of a new content of awareness. But this determination of awareness by existence is *an entire process* that is completed in the course of a more or less extended period. For this reason, the workers do not always know their 'real interests'. For this reason, for example, some German workers do not support the Social Democrats but the 'free-thinkers', or the party of the centre, or even the large-scale landowners.[23]

If workers did not immediately or automatically perceive their true interests, then there was a role for what Prokopovich dismissively termed the 'revolutionary bacilli/intellectuals'. This term became something of a catch-phrase (Lenin alludes to it in *WITBD*).[24] Plekhanov's comment brings out the essential disagreement:

> Mr. N.N. [Prokopovich] wants to say that the awareness of the masses always *falls behind* the development of social relations. This is more or less correct. But the only logical conclusion that follows from this is that the '*revolutionary bacilli*' (it makes no difference whether these come from the intelligentsia or the workers) *should use all means in their power to ensure that the awareness of the worker falls as little behind the development of the real relations of a given society*. The task of the bacilli is precisely this: to further the development of the self-awareness of the proletariat.[25]

At bottom, the issue was not for or against intellectuals, it was for or against inspired and inspiring leadership. Plekhanov saw the mission of Social Democrats as *accelerating* historical development by increasing class awareness, while Kuskova and Prokopovich worried about Social Democracy trying to *force* or even *violate* [*nasilovat'*] the course of development.[26] No wonder that Kuskova and Prokopovich scorned the Erfurtian ideal of inspired and inspiring leadership as futile self-deception. Any attempt at such leadership was

---

[23] Plekhanov 1923–7, 12, pp. 14–15.
[24] Lenin, *PSS*, 6, p. 73 [740].
[25] Plekhanov 1900, pp. xxxi–xxxii (original edition).
[26] Prokopovich in Plekhanov 1923–7, 12, p. 505 (one of the meanings of *nasilovat'* is 'to rape').

equivalent to assuming the workers were dough that could be moulded at will. It was knocking on the doors of closed hearts.[27]

### Erfurtianism pro et contra: Parvus and Prokopovich

Prokopovich's big book on the European worker movement provoked a long review by Parvus, a Russian-born Social Democrat who became a prominent spokesman of the left wing of the German Social-Democratic Party. The review was published in the first issue of *Zaria*, the theoretical journal published by the *Iskra* group.[28] Thus we have a major debate between two informed Russians about the meaning and relevance of the SPD model. Perhaps nowhere else can we find the essential issues stated with such clarity and conviction.

Prokopovich's history of German Social Democracy was a wholesale attack on the SPD model. His view of the party past is well summed up by Timofei Kopelzon, one of the editors of *Rabochee delo* (in a letter to Akselrod):

> For a person as gifted [as Prokopovich], the path of criticism, the path of negation, is a path that is very rewarding, but it is also a very slippery path. In his criticism of the programmes and the views set forth in the European Social-Democratic literature, he positively does not leave stone on stone. He has a completely different view of the Social-Democratic past from the one found in the German literature. The communism of Marx, the views of Lassalle, the tendencies of the 1848 revolution – all of these appear in a completely different light.[29]

In his review, Parvus described Prokopovich's views of the SPD present sarcastically but fairly accurately:

> The basic presuppositions of Social Democracy are mistaken, its final goal is mistaken, its entire theory is unscientific – there is not a 'grain' of scientific value in it. Despite all this backwardness, fuzzy thinking, immaturity, contradictions and nonsense, Social Democracy just keeps growing and

---

[27] For these metaphors, see Plekhanov 1923–7, 12, p. 509 (Prokopovich); 12, p. 493 (Kuskova).

[28] Parvus 1901 ('European Workers and their Russian Historian'). Lenin also penned an unfinished review of the book in late 1899 (Lenin 1958–65, 4, pp. 299–309).

[29] Plekhanov 1923–7, 12, p. 495. 'Criticism' means specifically revisionist criticism of Marx. The first sentence shows that Kopelzon (a member of *Rabochee delo*) is not endorsing Prokopovich's views, as implied by Plekhanov.

growing. Why does it keep growing? – Hard to say, since the conditions for a social revolution have not matured and indeed they never will mature! All of Social Democracy is just one big mistake. It should have been a bourgeois-democratic party. It developed completely in the wrong direction. Old Man History got things all screwed up.[30]

According to Prokopovich, party tactics follow the line of least resistance: they go where circumstances push them, not where party leaders want them to go. Official programmes are thus self-deceiving myths. Prokopovich divided SPD history into three periods and the men who symbolise the three periods – Lassalle, Kautsky and Bernstein – actually had very little idea of what was really going on.[31] We can paraphrase in the following way Prokopovich's account of SPD history.

The founder of German Social Democracy, Ferdinand Lassalle, was essentially a Catiline, that is, a déclassé enthusiast who assumed that reforms were useless because the revolution was coming soon. Thence came his dismissal of the rest of society as 'one reactionary mass'; thence his contempt for trade unions and economic organisations in general. Thence came the whole idea of a separate worker party. But, in the Lassalle period, the workers were too undeveloped to be capable of anything much. They certainly had no role in obtaining political freedom: that was done by others. Lassalle was forced to use propaganda to tell the workers about the *content* of their interests and thus was not in a position to use agitation to help them *defend* their interests – a stage that had already been reached by the workers in France and England but not yet in Germany. Thus Lassalle's attempt to create a class movement and to imbue it with a sense of mission was bound to end in failure. 'The most eloquent speech cannot create new needs.'[32]

Genuine political independence was also an illusion during this period: the workers had only the choice of whether to be the 'tail' (that is, passively accept the leadership) of the liberals or of the conservatives. And unfortunately, Lassalle chose the conservatives, thus *weakening* the progressive opposition.

---

[30] Parvus 1901, p. 224. Prokopovich's remark about the scientific value of Social-Democratic theory is in Prokopovich 1899, p. 156. Prokopovich was more confident that the SPD was evolving in the desired direction than the Parvus paraphrase would suggest.

[31] Prokopovich 1899, pp. 101–98.

[32] Prokopovich 1899, p. 113.

He bequeathed to the Party an erroneous belief in the 'cowardly German bourgeoisie' – even though later capitalist development would make nonsense of this negative assessment.

The spirit of the second period, 1867–90, is best summed up by the Erfurt Programme and Kautsky's commentary. Kautsky tried to tie the 'abstract' final goals to concrete interests, without much success. Prokopovich quotes some of the passages I quoted in Chapter One from Kautsky's *Parliamentarism* in which Kautsky argues that great goals help unite the movement. Prokopovich just laughs, since Kautsky obviously had no idea of the real variety of interests within the worker class.[33]

Prokopovich gives his own sarcastic version of the merger formula:

> In the programme of the Party we are evidently dealing with aims of two kinds: (a) aims that arise out of the immediate interests of the workers and that develop along with the growth of the economic strength of the working class, and (b) aims taken from without [*izvne*], from the conclusions of social science, and introduced [*privnesennnyi*] to the worker movement.[34]

What Kautsky thought of as a marriage made in heaven between socialism and the worker movement was, for Prokopovich, a shotgun wedding leading straight to divorce.

The third period – 1890 to the time of writing in 1899 – was a period when the Party realised its own growing influence and integration into society and therefore began to discard the baggage of hostility to society and of earlier dreams of revolution. Bernstein was the symbol of this change but, actually, he was as deluded as Lassalle and Kautsky because he also thought that abstract principles determine tactics. Not theoreticians like Bernstein but practical leaders like Georg Vollmar are the ones who are helping the Party make the necessary adjustments and who propagate the new tactics. Of course, the struggle against outmoded principles does take time and effort – which is why putting principles into programmes is a bad idea. This lag explains why the new outlook has not yet (1899) triumphed. But circumstances determine tactics, and the basic circumstance at present – the Party's new-found strength – ensures a rapid victory of the new outlook.

---

[33] Prokopovich 1899, pp. 141, 155–7.
[34] Prokopovich 1899, p. 147.

Prokopovich's all-out attack on the SPD model provoked Parvus's classic exposition and defence of it. For Parvus, 'the essence of Social-Democratic tactics lies in the synthesis of reformism and revolutionism'.[35] The English workers were narrowly reformist. As yet, they did not realise that a genuinely independent worker party was necessary if for no other reason than to preserve Parliament from degeneration. In contrast, the French workers were so disgusted with the bourgeois state that they remained stuck in 'pure revolutionism'. They busied themselves in organising the 'social-revolutionary army of the proletariat' but they had nothing for this army to *do*. As a result, they did nothing more than oppose 'the democratic chatter of the bourgeois parliamentarians with chatter about the social revolution'.[36]

As opposed to either of these, the German model was based on 'using parliamentarism for revolutionary aims'. Parvus was not advocating a cynical exploitation of an institution that would later be discarded, since the nature of parliament depended on the class nature of the state and not the other way around. This meant that

> the capitalist character of the state is not changed in the slightest by the parliamentary growth of Social Democracy. . . . The essential point is not a shift in the composition of parliament but a redistribution of the political forces of the country. But this redistribution will find its final expression in the changed composition of parliament. Usually this will be preceded by an epoch of political troubles [*smuta*].[37]

From Parvus's extensive description of how the SPD strategy works out in practice, I will concentrate on the SPD's role as tribune of the people and as leader in the fight to defend and extend democracy. The liberal-bourgeois opposition in Germany is disheartened by Social Democracy's successful campaign to end the political dependence of the workers. It therefore inclines more and more to joining the reaction in a common crusade against Social Democracy.

> The result is that Social Democracy more and more becomes the only opposition party. As it fights in parliament against the capitalist nature of

---

[35] Parvus 1901, p. 224.
[36] Parvus 1901, p. 213.
[37] Parvus 1901, p. 217.

government policy, against the exploitative strivings of the parliamentary majority, against the impotence and disingenuousness of the bourgeois opposition, it not only strengthens its position among the workers but draws to its side the democratic elements [of society].[38]

One way that a truly Social-Democratic party exercises this strictly democratic leadership is to interest itself in *everything* happening around it. 'The final result is that in the whole wide world of political and social life there is not one fact that does not sooner or later call for Social-Democratic intervention. Everything, starting from major political shifts and ending with petty scandals, is transformed into a means of social revolutionary agitation.'[39] As we shall see, Parvus here expresses one of Lenin's key theses in WITBD.

Needless to say, Parvus rejects Prokopovich's picture of Lassalle as a romantic self-deceiving dreamer. For Parvus, Lassalle was 'the *practical* politician par excellence'. It was he who grasped the tactical implications of the *Communist Manifesto* and applied them to Germany by making the social-revolutionary energy of the proletariat a political factor on a continuing day-to-day basis. No longer would the revolutionary party only emerge on days of revolution and then afterwards subside back to quiet theoretical propaganda.

In his very strong defence of Lassalle, Parvus particularly rebutted Prokopovich's charge that by breaking away from the liberal Progressive Party Lassalle had helped reactionary forces by undercutting bourgeois liberalism. On the contrary, Lassalle had awakened the workers to political life instead of leaving them in indifference and apathy.

> And this is a much greater bulwark of political freedom and democracy than any provided even by a liberal majority in Parliament. . . . Even apart from the social revolution, the fact that in Germany the organised proletariat stands on guard for the constitution is the deed of Social Democracy, the deed of Lassalle.[40]

Since Prokopovich had no conception of the basic Social-Democratic synthesis of reform and revolution, he misinterpreted the events of the 1890s, the so-called post-Erfurtian period. Prokopovich saw any manifestation of reform

---

[38] Parvus 1901, p. 216.
[39] Ibid.
[40] Parvus 1901, pp. 223–4.

activity as evidence of evolution *away from* an earlier pure revolutionism. He made his case by pointing to current SPD support of trade unions and the Party's attempts to gain peasant support, but he did not realise that both of these efforts had a long past in Social-Democratic activity.

A further proof of the soundness of the Social-Democratic synthesis is the characteristic fact that

> all deliberate deviations from the policy we have described have up till now suffered a complete fiasco. Deviations to the Left lead to pure revolutionism and peter out into nothingness. Deviations to the Right turn bit by bit into bourgeois radicalism and fuses with it. And, indeed, present-day Social Democracy has no *raison d'être* without the idea of social revolution. Its continued separation from the democratic bourgeoisie becomes incomprehensible.[41]

Far from being rejected by the SPD itself, the logic of the 'German model' was imposing itself everywhere. The English workers were swiftly moving toward an independent worker party, while the French-style 'pure revolutionism' was quietly evolving toward the German model. 'The policy of German Social Democracy is being deliberately taken over by the worker parties of other countries. This would be an impossibility if this policy did not correspond to the general historical tasks of the class struggle of the proletariat'.[42]

The debate between Prokopovich and Parvus about the 'German model' confirms my description of the basic content of Erfurtianism and, even more important, my thesis that there *was* such a thing as Erfurtianism. The debate also shows that the clash between economist and orthodox in Russian Social Democracy was, at heart, a clash over the relevance of the SPD model. Prokopovich's critique zeroed in on the heart of this model, namely, the story the Party told itself about its own past, combined with its sense of mission about the future.

Of particular interest is Prokopovich's sarcastic version of the merger formula that we quoted earlier. He contrasts the aims coming from the worker class to the aims brought in [*privnesti*] from without [*izvne*]. When Lenin uses

---

[41] Parvus 1901, pp. 217–18.
[42] Parvus 1901, p. 218.

almost the same words in an approving way, they are taken to be proof of his rejection of European Marxism and Social Democracy.[43] Is it not more natural to see these terms as his *affirmation* of that model against attack? Let others take Prokopovich's advice and focus on the worker's stomach – he, Lenin, would continue to bring them the socialist good news that would revolutionise their minds.

### Erfurtianism as an alien importation

It is now time to turn to the notorious 'programme of the *Credo*'.[44] Kuskova's *Credo* is an application of Prokopovich's reading of Western Social Democracy to the situation in Russia. The formula that summed up this reading was tactics always followed the line of least resistance. In fact, circumstances determine tactics 'with the precision of an astronomer', thus rendering irrelevant all conscious tactical decisions of the leaders. In the case of German Social Democracy, circumstances had imposed a 'negative' phase in which the proletariat opposed itself to society and dreamed of revolution, but circumstances had now changed and the Party was now in the process of 'recognising society'.[45]

In the case of Russia, the circumstances of tsarist repression severely limited possibilities, so that the tactics imposed by 'the line of least resistance' were meagre indeed:

> In Russia, the line of least resistance will never lead in the direction of political activity. The incredible political repression compels us to talk a lot about [politics] and focus our attention precisely on this question, but it will never compel any sort of practical activity. In the West the weak forces of the proletariat were strengthened and formed by being drawn into political activity. In Russia, in contrast, these weak forces stand before a wall of political repression. Not only are there no practical ways of fighting against this repression and therefore no practical ways of developing, but even the weakest shoots [of practical activity] are systematically smothered and cannot grow.

---

[43] For this famous passage, see Lenin 1958–65, 6, p. 30 [702].

[44] The text of the *Credo* can be found in Lenin's *Protest* of 1899 (Lenin 1958–65, 4, pp. 165–9). English translations of the complete text can be found in Harding 1983, pp. 250–3 and Lenin's *Collected Works*, Volume 4, pp. 171–4.

[45] Lenin 1958–65, 4, pp. 165–7.

If you add to this that our worker class has not received the legacy of the organisational spirit that distinguished the fighters of the West, the resulting picture is depressing and capable of plunging the most optimistic Marxist – someone who believes that every additional factory smokestack brings great well-being by the mere fact of its existence – into gloom.

The economic struggle is difficult, infinitely difficult, but it is possible – it is indeed being carried out by the masses themselves. Getting used to organisation by means of this struggle and being pushed every minute up against the political régime, the Russian worker will finally create something we can call a form of worker movement – will create the organisation or the organisations that best fit Russian conditions.

At the present time we can say with assurance that the Russian worker movement is still in an amoeba-like condition and has created no [organisational] form at all. The strike movement, which occurs at any level of organisation, cannot yet be called a crystallised form of the Russian movement. Illegal organisations do not merit any attention from a purely quantitative point of view, not to speak of their usefulness under present conditions.[46]

What, then, did Kuskova think was possible in Russia under the autocracy? Some kind of non-political worker movement that would work out organisational forms that 'best fit Russian conditions' and that would studiously avoid connections to an irrelevant revolutionary underground. What was impossible? A worker movement capable of fighting against political repression, much less revolutionary overthrow. Based on these premises, Kuskova sets out the following programme of action (she does not herself say 'programme').

Any talk about an independent worker political party is in essence nothing more than the product of the transfer of alien tasks, alien results, onto our soil. The Russian Marxist is still a pitiful spectacle. . . . The slightest attempt to concentrate attention on social manifestations of a liberal-political nature calls forth the protest of orthodox Marxists, who forget that a whole series of historical conditions prevent us from being Marxists of the West and demand from us another Marxism, appropriate and necessary for Russian conditions. . . . For the Russian Marxist there is only one conclusion:

---

[46] Lenin 1958–65, 4, pp. 167–8.

participation by helping the economic struggle of the proletariat, and
participation in liberal oppositional activity.[47]

In his *Vademecum*, Plekhanov dotted the i's and crossed the t's about the
political meanings of Kuskova's recommendations. 'In the absence of an
independent political worker party, this kind of "participation" necessarily
turns into a straightforward fusion with the radical and liberal bourgeoisie.'[48]

In *WITBD*, Lenin summarises (accurately enough, as it seems to me) the
'programme of the *Credo*':

> have the workers carry out the economic struggle (to speak more precisely:
> the *tred-iunionist* struggle, for this embraces a specific worker politics as
> well), and have the Marxist intellectual fuse with the liberals for a political
> 'struggle'.[49]

Lenin is careful to underline that 'the economic struggle' encompasses what
we might now call 'interest group politics', in contrast to régime change. A
major part of his polemic throughout *WITBD* is that his Social-Democratic
opponents had unwittingly embarked on a realisation of the 'programme of
the *Credo*'.

Lenin's comment, in which he says, in effect, that there is such a thing as
'economist politics', brings up an important issue: what does it meant to say
that the economists rejected political struggle? Kuskova herself wrote in 1906
that any talk about the economists' principled refusal of political struggle 'is
a despicable untruth that belongs to those political methods that so strongly
compromise the Social-Democratic Party'.[50] And Kuskova and Prokopovich
did indeed think that political rights were very important and that organising
the worker movement would indirectly lead to genuine worker support for
the expansion of political rights in Russia, since the workers would continuously
'be pushed up against' their lack of political rights. Kuskova even writes
elsewhere that one advantage of Russia over Western Europe is 'the white

---

[47] Kuskova in Lenin 1958–65, 4, p. 168.
[48] Kuskova in Plekhanov 1923–7, 12, p. 36.
[49] Lenin 1958–65, 6, p. 18 [691].
[50] Kuskova 1906, p. 326. Kuskova is justified in protesting against the use of writings
not meant for publication, but I am surprised that she is surprised that her views met
strong condemnation among Social Democrats and not just because they were
misrepresented.

terror that the government directs against the workers and that will swiftly purify their minds and will quickly place political interests among their *real* interests'.[51]

Nevertheless, Kuskova and Prokopovich did strongly reject political struggle in the Russian Erfurtian sense. First of all, any struggle for political rights would *not* be carried out by an independent worker political party.[52] Vladimir Akimov, an editor of *Rabochee delo* who evidently knew Kuskova, summed up her views as follows:

> The author of the *Credo* was an extreme political, who maintained that the working-class was not capable of overthrowing the autocracy and therefore urged the socialists to look elsewhere, to look to the intelligentsia, for support in its struggle against the autocracy.[53]

Further, Kuskova made clear her feeling that a constitutional system was, in itself, no big prize. Kuskova pointed out that the reactionary bourgeoisie in the constitutional West was making workers fear for their established rights. The Russian bourgeoisie would certainly learn from their Western colleagues. Thus 'it is utopian to think the overthrow of the autocracy would cause the Russian bourgeoisie to change the political position of the workers. . . . One must not expect any [particular benefit] from a constitution in Russia'.[54]

Prokopovich and Kuskova were also dead set against any agitation aimed at overthrow of the autocracy. Propaganda on this subject was acceptable, because propaganda was, by definition, impractical and aimed at marginal individuals. But, since agitation was always a call to action, and since a call for an immediate attack on the autocracy could only end in a bloodbath, it followed that Russian Social Democrats should fear political agitation worse than any provocateur.[55] Not even the party programme should mention a

[51] Kuskova in Plekhanov 1923–7, 12, p. 489.

[52] Kuskova wrote in 1906 that she and Prokopovich were 'fervently devoted to the idea of a Social-Democratic worker party', but her discussion makes clear she means *after* the achievement of political freedom (Kuskova 1906).

[53] Akimov 1969, p. 246. Akimov takes pains to disassociate Kuskova from *Rabochee delo* (I have substituted 'political' for 'politician' in Jonathan Frankel's translation).

[54] Kuskova in Plekhanov 1923–7, 12, p. 489.

[55] This statement acquires a measure of irony when we learn that Prokopovich and Kuskova were among the close advisors of Father Gapon. He conferred with them the day before the demonstration that sparked off the Bloody Sunday massacre in January 1905 (Surh 1989, p. 140).

direct political struggle within the autocracy. 'In the interests of the future political struggle we must avoid with all our strength a parody of it at the present time.'[56]

The effort to foist a programme of revolutionary overthrow on the worker movement was deemed wrong-headed not because it stymied worker self-activity (as implied by Kuskova in 1906), but because it was futile. According to Prokopovich, revolutionary-democratic intellectuals, such as Plekhanov and Akselrod, looked around after the defeat of Narodnaia volia for some real force that would help them attain their aims. They settled on the worker movement and tried for fifteen years to foist their programme of political freedom via revolutionary overthrow on the workers. They had never succeeded and they never would.

> At the same time that the Emancipation of Labour group strives with its typical energy toward a direct struggle with the government, our Russian comrades, with their 'indifferent' attitude toward politics, have for a long time carried out an indirect struggle with the autocracy. There are no loud triumphs in this struggle, no noisy battles; it is the work of the mole that undermines the very foundations of the existing political order. Which side claims our just sympathies? The side of the commanders without armies who do not know the paths that lead to the desired goal and who have over the course of a decade and a half tirelessly waved a *paper sword* – or the side of the humble activists who toil on without noisy publicity from day to day, doing the job that needs to be done?[57]

Prokopovich's accusation that the Emancipation of Labour group wanted to exploit the worker movement in order to fulfill the dreams of the democratic intelligentsia about political freedom is still influential among scholars today. We should therefore note that it is the opposite of the truth. Plekhanov and Akselrod were not advocates of political freedom who decided that the workers would be good revolution fodder, but, rather, *socialist* revolutionaries who only adopted the watchword of political freedom *after* they were convinced that it was in the interests of the workers.

It is an unfortunate oversimplification to say that the economists rejected all political struggle on principle. Nevertheless, it hardly advances matters

---

[56] Prokopovich in Plekhanov 1923–7, 12, p. 513
[57] Prokopovich in Plekhanov 1923–7, 12, pp. 514–15.

simply to correct this oversimplification by stating 'the economists *did* support political struggle' and leave it at that. The Russian Erfurtians had a vision, squarely based on the SPD model, of an independent worker political party leading the struggle for democratic transformation of Russia. Kuskova and Prokopovich were fervently opposed to this vision and built up an impressive case against it.

What Aleksandr Potresov (an *Iskra* editor who was later on the right wing of Menshevism) wrote in 1909 about economism in general applies with particular force to Kuskova and Prokopovich: economism was the product of a 'disenchantment' with the workers and with the 'primitiveness, *stikhiinost*, and meagre purposiveness' of the strike movement. 'This concrete movement of the concrete proletariat' did not square with its assigned 'historical mission of universal liberation'.[58]

As Kuskova truly said in the *Credo*, the picture that she and Prokopovich painted was 'depressing and capable of plunging the most optimistic Marxist into gloom'.[59] The Russian émigré Kopelzon who had talked with Prokopovich noted his conviction that 'to talk to the worker mass in Russia about the abolition of capitalism, about socialism, and indeed, about the abolition of the autocracy is in general absurd and an unproductive waste of forces'.[60] The couple felt that Russian Social Democrats had deceived themselves by a 'schematic application of the path of development in the West to our situation'.[61] They explicitly noted their distance from some of the arguments of the *Communist Manifesto*: 'if this work is taken as gospel, then [our] point of view is heresy'.[62]

For Lenin, the *Communist Manifesto* was indeed 'the "gospel" [*evangelie*] of international Social Democracy'.[63] The history of the Western-European worker movement, as presented by Kautsky, remained Lenin's basic source of inspiration. He stoutly maintained that talking to the Russian workers about

---

[58] Potresov 1909, 1, p. 583. Note the negative attitude toward *stikhiinost*, which, in this context, means lack of organisational structure and discipline. This negative attitude was shared by the economists and the orthodox, as documented at the end of this chapter and in Annotations Part Two.

[59] Kuskova in Lenin 1958–65, 4, p. 167.

[60] Kopelzon in Plekhanov 1923–7, 12, p. 497.

[61] Kuskova in Plekhanov 1923–7, 12, p. 491.

[62] Prokopovich in Plekhanov 1923–7, 12, pp. 493–4; see also Kuskova in Lenin 1958–65, 4, p. 166.

[63] Lenin 1958–65, 6, p. 267 (*Iskra* article from February 1902).

socialism and about the abolition of autocracy was the most productive possible use of available forces. Lenin was one Russian Social Democrat who refused to be plunged into gloom. Thus we can see why the accusation of 'implementing the programme of the *Credo*' was just about the most serious one Lenin could fling at any Social Democrat.

## Rabochaia mysl

*Rabochaia mysl* [*Worker Thought*] was a St. Petersburg underground newspaper that began publication in late 1897 and managed to put out sixteen numbers by the time of its final issue in late 1902. This five-year run is an impressive one as underground newspapers go (*Iskra* itself only lasted five years altogether, although it published many times more issues). *Rabochaia mysl* billed itself as the voice of the Petersburg workers. Starting with the fifth issue in early 1899, it was also the official organ of the St. Petersburg Social-Democratic committee (the Union of Struggle) – a status in possible conflict with the aspiration to be the voice of the workers. Indeed, along with the *Credo*, *Rabochaia mysl* soon became a symbol of extreme economism. In WITBD, Lenin does not really polemicise with *Rabochaia mysl*. Rather, he uses it as a well-known exemplar of economism and then attempts to demonstrate that *Rabochee delo* – his real target – is following in the dreaded path of *Rabochaia mysl*.

Why was *Rabochaia mysl* so unpopular in orthodox Social-Democratic circles? Our answer to this question is crucial to our interpretation of WITBD. There are two approaches to *Rabochaia mysl*, divided by the key issue of whether the newspaper spoke with one voice or with many voices. If the newspaper spoke with one voice, then the views of the editorialists should be considered the views of at least some of the St. Petersburg workers. In this case, Lenin's attack on *Rabochaia mysl* betrays his anxiety about the outlook of the workers themselves – a conclusion that fits in nicely with the textbook interpretation. If, on the contrary, many conflicting views can be found jostling side by side on the pages of the newspaper, then this conclusion need not follow.

The claim that *Rabochaia mysl* spoke with one voice goes back to a 1904 party history by a former member of *Rabochee delo* editorial board, Vladimir Akimov, who argued that Russian Social Democrats were hostile precisely because *Rabochaia mysl* *was* a worker newspaper.

For decades the Russian socialists sought to make the workers think for themselves. And gradually the mind of the worker came to life. . . . At last, on the peripheries of Russia, in Vilna and Petersburg, the workers managed in the same year to create their own newspapers, *Arbeter Shtime* and *Rabochaia mysl*. The Jewish *intelligenty* – Social Democrats – caught the voice of the workers, supported it, made it loud, strong and glorious. But it was actually the orthodox wing of the 'revolutionary' Social Democrats that ridiculed and condemned the thinking of the Petersburg worker. True, his ideas were untutored, clumsy, unsubtle! Nevertheless, it is a matter for rejoicing that there were Social Democrats, *Economists*, in Petersburg who supported and served those workers who thought for themselves! For this they should be forgiven all the errors that were forced upon them on this difficult road.[64]

Akimov saw *Iskra* as the inheritor of this arrogant attitude toward actual workers. He cites a case where *Iskra* ridiculed a letter by workers as illiterate.[65]

The same basic approach is found in the work of Allan K. Wildman, author of the only detailed study in Western scholarship of *Rabochaia mysl*. Wildman argues that *Rabochaia mysl* had a consistent message:

Despite the variety of sentiments which found refuge on the pages of *Rabochaia mysl*, a consistent line of thought threaded its way through the successive issues and underlay the spirit of the whole enterprise. This way of thinking squarely opposed, both in letter and spirit, the mainstream of Russian Social Democracy, from the theoretical precepts of its founders to the workaday philosophy of its underground practitioners in Russia.[66]

The content of *Rabochaia mysl*'s message was 'the workers' bid for self-liberation'.[67] Wildman – followed on this point by Reginald Zelnik and Gerald Surh – draws the conclusion that Lenin's hostility to the worker's drive for self-liberation is the key to Lenin's 'worry about workers'. By the end of the 1890s, Lenin (as Zelnik puts it)

---

[64] Akimov 1969, p. 273.
[65] Akimov 1969, p. 273 fn.
[66] Wildman 1967, pp. 148–9.
[67] Wildman 1967, p. 89.

had learned from afar that some of Russia's most militant, dedicated workers were now engaged in the dramatic (though in some ways ambivalent) rejection of intelligentsia tutelage, a 'worker-phile' trend that echoed trends in other parts of Europe, and one that Lenin fought with all his heart.[68]

Thus, (in Surh's words) what Lenin called 'economism' was in actuality 'the trend among workers in the 1890s to seek control of their own party organisations'. Since he himself was committed to an 'élitist conception of intelligentsia hegemony in the revolutionary party', Lenin could not but be opposed to such a trend.[69] WITBD was designed to be Lenin's heavy artillery in his campaign to systematically exclude workers from leadership positions.[70]

The alternative view – that *Rabochaia mysl* spoke with many voices – also goes back to some of the newspaper's first Social-Democratic readers. Among these early readers were Plekhanov and his associates in the Emancipation of Labour group (starting in 1898), many of the writers associated with *Rabochee delo* (also starting in 1898), Lenin (starting in 1899), and M. Liadov in his party history of 1906 (where he explicitly challenges Akimov). Remarkably enough, included in this group is K.M. Takhtarev, one of the main editors of *Rabochaia mysl*, in his 1902 history and defence of the newspaper. We also have evidence of private reactions by a number of observers.

These readers encompass a wide range of Social-Democratic opinion and also a wide range of attitudes toward *Rabochaia mysl*: some are hostile to it (Liadov), some defensive (Takhtarev), and some are trying their best to say something nice (*Rabochee delo*). The basic consensus in their reactions is therefore quite striking. As opposed to Akimov and Wildman, all these writers insist on a *separation* between the voices of the workers writing in the pages of *Rabochaia mysl* and the voices of the editorialists. They are all dissatisfied with the voices of the editorialists, asserting that the editorialists had no particular right to speak in the name of the Petersburg workers and that their views went beyond the pale of Russian Social Democracy.

After listening to all sides, going through the issues of *Rabochaia mysl*, and assimilating the valuable factual material assembled by Wildman, I believe

---

[68] Zelnik 2003a, p. 28. The term 'worker-phile' is a coinage of Wildman's and was not used by *Rabochaia mysl* to describe its own position.
[69] Surh 2000, pp. 119, 123.
[70] Wildman 1967, pp. 213–53.

the second approach is the most convincing. The Akimov / Wildman tradition has overestimated the unity of the newspaper's voice and underestimated the offensiveness to *any* Social Democrat of many of the views set forth by the editorialists. As far as Lenin is concerned, his opposition to *Rabochaia mysl* arose out of genuine programmatic differences and not out of hostility to a worker bid for self-liberation. Lenin's hostility to *Rabochaia mysl*'s editorial stand belongs to a consensus that includes staunch *Iskra* foes such as *Rabochee delo* and even – from his 1902 vantage point – the writer of many of the offending editorials, K.M. Takhtarev.

Three lines of evidence support these conclusions. The first is information about who actually controlled the newspaper. The second is the conflicting views that found expression in *Rabochaia mysl*. The third is the consensus of informed Social-Democratic readers. We shall examine these three lines of evidence in turn.

*The auspices of 'Rabochaia mysl'*

We are interested only in the first eight issues of *Rabochaia mysl*'s sixteen-issue run, since these early issues are the ones that led to controversy and scandal in Social-Democratic ranks. Who controlled the content of the newspaper during this period? For whom did it claim to speak? We have to answer these questions issue by issue because the auspices under which the newspaper came out kept changing. I will give the date of each issue and then explain the circumstances under which it was composed.

Issue No. 1 – October 1897

Issue No. 2 – December 1897

These first two issues were the creation of a group of St. Petersburg workers along with some sympathetic intellectuals. These issues did not have wide circulation and, in fact, they are no longer extant. We have access to some of their contents only to the extent that writers such as Takhtarev and Liadov reprinted material from these issues.[71]

---

[71] Takhtarev 1902, Takhtarev 1924, Liadov 1906.

Issue No. 3 – July 1898

Owing to arrests, the original St. Petersburg worker group behind *Rabochaia mysl* 'ceased to exist' after the second issue.[72] A newly constituted group was composed mostly of intellectuals. *Rabochaia mysl* would probably have ceased publication at this point, but salvation came from an unexpected quarter. An individual by the name of Karl August Kok – who might best be described as an intellectual of worker origin – arrived from Berlin and offered to publish *Rabochaia mysl* abroad. Kok was an Estonian born in the Caucasus who had travelled throughout Russia and emigrated to Berlin in the mid-1890s. As far as I can tell, he had no Petersburg roots prior to his contact with the reconstituted group in 1898.[73] From Issue No. 3 on, *Rabochaia mysl* was published abroad, a situation that sometimes led to conflict.

Issue No. 4 – October 1898

Starting with this issue, K.M. Takhtarev joined the émigré editorial group. Takhtarev had emigrated from St. Petersburg sometime previously. He was introduced to Kok by Elena Kuskova, the author of the *Credo*. Kuskova herself felt that Kok was too anti-intellectual.[74] The editorial articles in Issue No. 4 first excited hostility to *Rabochaia mysl* from other Social Democrats.

Issue No. 5 – January 1899

Issue No. 6 – April 1899

Issues Nos. 5 and 6 marked a crucial change in the status of *Rabochaia mysl*. Owing to negotiations among St. Petersburg groups, *Rabochaia mysl* now became the official journal of the local Social-Democratic committee. Since *Rabochaia mysl* was now the most authoritative voice of Social Democracy from within Russia, all Social-Democratic activists had even more reason to be interested in the content of its editorials. The immediate result of the new situation was conflict between the Petersburg group (now a combination of

---

[72] Wildman 1967, p. 127.
[73] My biographical data comes from Wildman 1967, pp. 127–8; Takhtarev leaves a different impression.
[74] Takhtarev 1924, p. 113.

the reconstituted *Rabochaia mysl* group and the Social-Democratic Union of Struggle) and Kok over editorial content. The fifth issue was held back by the local group because they did not like Kok's editorials, and the sixth issue had no lead editorial.

Issue No. 7 – July 1899

Separate Supplement – September 1899

While No. 7 was being prepared, arrests destroyed the Petersburg reconstituted group and much of the Social-Democratic committee. The foreign editorial board decided to go ahead with the publication of prepared material, plus adding some editorials without sanction from the now non-existent Petersburg group. The same can be said for the 36-page Separate Supplement published in September 1899, which was a completely theoretical, learned, non-worker production.

Issue No. 8 – February 1900

After the Separate Supplement, arguments arose about how to deal with the 'absurdity' of a paper that claimed to be the voice of St. Petersburg workers yet was published under the exclusive control of a foreign editorial board.[75] Furthermore, the St. Petersburg Social Democrat Apollinaria Iakubova (Takhtarev's future wife) arrived in Europe from Russia and objected to Kok's anti-intelligentsia outlook:

> A.A. Iakubova, although she defended the independent significance of worker organisations and the entry of workers into the central groups of our Social-Democratic organisations on the basis of equality with the intellectuals, was nevertheless very much opposed to the tendency represented by Kok.[76]

The result was a chaotic Issue No. 8. On p. 8 of this issue appeared the following comment: 'All pamphlets and Nos. 3, 4, 5, 6, 7 and the first four pages of No. 8 of *Rabochaia mysl* were published with P. Petrov [Kok] as chief

---

[75] Takhtarev 1902, p. 79.
[76] Takhtarev 1924, p. 149.

editor. Starting from page 5 of No. 8, the newspaper appears under a new editorial board.' The editors also profusely apologised for a particular article in the Separate Supplement that had managed to offend just about everybody in the Russian revolutionary movement. Certainly, Issue No. 8 did not seem a very professional affair!

At this point, midway in its career, we can take leave of *Rabochaia mysl*. A 'Worker Organisation' was soon thereafter founded in Petersburg that was eventually able to take over editorial functions. The editorial stance grew more 'political' and revolutionary, in line with the times. Takhtarev himself engineered this change of direction in early 1900.[77] In WITBD, Lenin made clear that his critique did not refer to the current *Rabochaia mysl*.

This history shows that editorial control of *Rabochaia mysl* was never firm or stable. In Petersburg, we have the original *Rabochaia mysl* group, the reconstituted group and the Social-Democratic committee. All of these groups were severely damaged by arrests. Abroad, we have Kok, who subsequently co-opted Takhtarev and then was forced to hand over editorial control to him. There were conflicts and confusion within the local groups in St. Petersburg, within the foreign editorial board, and between the local groups and the émigrés. These conflicts showed up very visibly in the newspaper itself.

After the first two issues, the editorial voice came mainly from abroad. Neither Kok nor Takhtarev had any particular claim to speak for the Petersburg workers. As noted earlier, Kok had no prior Petersburg roots, although he did travel incessantly between Berlin and Petersburg when he was editor. Takhtarev, although an intellectual born and bred, had hands-on experience in the Petersburg Social-Democratic underground. But, as we shall see, the views he expressed immediately upon emigration from Russia were quite different from those he expressed in his later *Rabochaia mysl* editorials. He changed his outlook under the impact of his work in the Belgian worker movement as well as his interest in academic sociology.

*The many voices of 'Rabochaia mysl'*

It is time to listen more closely to the different voices of *Rabochaia mysl*. The distinctive voices include:

---

[77] Nikolaevsky 1927, p. 34.

Worker Contributors

Worker Letters

Editorials in Issue No. 1

Short editorials in Issues 4 to 8

Takhtarev editorials (No. 4, No. 7, Separate Supplement)

The heart of *Rabochaia mysl* and the cause of its success among the workers was the contribution from worker correspondents describing factory conditions and economic struggle. Unfortunately, this commentary must restrict its attention to abstract programmatic questions and so I refer the reader to Wildman's study for more discussion of the worker contributions.[78] Important for our argument here is that in these contributions we find no explicit statements of worker resentment toward intellectuals or any considered rejection of the need for revolutionary overthrow of tsarism. Worker contributors also revealed their hopes for what I will call the de facto tolerance strategy that was set out in elaborate form in some of the editorials, as discussed below.

Distinct from the factory correspondents were workers who sent in letters to comment on the newspaper or to urge revolutionary action, since the letter-writers were often 'advanced' workers in the Social-Democratic sense. For example, a large group of political exiles wrote a letter that hailed 'the struggle for improved living standards [*byt*], for political freedom, for the final liberation of the worker class from all oppression. Down with despotism! Long live the first of May! Long live international Social Democracy!'.[79]

Ironically, these worker letters sometimes contained criticism of *Rabochaia mysl* for being overly intellectual and over the heads of ordinary workers – the same kind of criticism later levelled at *Iskra*. A letter from a 'Worker *Praktik*' criticised the paper because of its evident desire to be a 'scientific' organ devoted to heavy-duty thinkers such as Marx and Chernyshevsky. The many foreign words in the articles were comprehensible only to a worker aristocracy. The ordinary worker was left baffled – and all this 'in his own organ, one that calls itself *Worker Thought*'. Worker *Praktik* called for living words, evocations of heroism, including romantic heroes such as Vera Perovskaia of Narodnaia volia fame.

---

[78] Wildman 1967, pp. 118–51.

[79] *Rabochaia mysl*, No. 7 (July 1899).

> You will see that the worker is not simply a worker – someone who needs
> a crust of bread – but is also a decent human being who has the sense of
> duty of the citizen and the self-sacrificing nature of the member of the
> intelligentsia.[80]

Recall that Akimov blamed *Iskra* for sneering at the illiteracy of its worker
critics. Alas, this failing also was not unique to *Iskra*. *Rabochaia mysl* reacted
badly to the letter from Worker *Praktik*. It mocked the author for a factual
mistake (the Narodnaia volia heroine was Sophia, not Vera, Perovskaia) and
complained that he himself did not express himself very comprehensibly –
typical put-downs of workers by intellectuals.[81]

We now move on to the editorial voices that constituted the real source of
irritation with *Rabochaia mysl*. We start with the two lead editorials in Issue
No. 1. These editorials represent the voice of the original *Rabochaia mysl* group
before the foreign editorialists came on board. One of the editorials was
written by a worker (V. Poliakov) and the other by an *intelligent* (N.A. Bogoraz),
although, of course, this was not known at the time.[82] In fact, owing to the
limited circulation of these issues, these editorials only became known when
reprinted elsewhere. The intelligentsia editorial was reprinted in 1898 in an
article about *Rabochaia mysl* written by the émigré Vladimir Ivanshin. The
worker editorial became available only after it was reprinted by Takhtarev
in his 1902 book – that is, *after* Lenin's WITBD. Thus, Lenin's view of *Rabochaia
mysl* prior to 1902 was unaffected by the worker editorial. As Takhtarev said
in 1902, the two editorials leave quite different impressions.[83]

The intelligentsia editorial in Issue No. 1 established the profile of *Rabochaia
mysl* in Social-Democratic circles. Lenin uses it as a target in WITBD and, as
we shall see, he was far from the first to subject the editorial to withering
criticism. A full translation of this short editorial is given in the Appendix to
this chapter.

---

[80] *Rabochaia mysl*, No. 8 (February 1900).

[81] *Rabochaia mysl* No. 8 (February 1900).

[82] For the names of the authors, see Wildman 1967, pp. 123–5. By tone and style,
Liadov correctly identified the origins of the authors of the two editorials (Liadov
1906, 2, pp. 103–4).

[83] The text of the intelligentsia editorial can be found in Lenin 1925–36, 2, pp. 611–12;
my citations for the worker editorial are to Takhtarev 1924.

The central point of the editorial that the average worker will not be passionately involved in the movement until he is fighting for everyday economic interests. Whatever the merit of this point, the editorialist defended it in a way that was bound to put everybody on edge. What had earlier prevented the movement from engaging the workers on the basis of their economic interest? The repentant *intelligent* who devoted himself to the movement only for personal psychological reasons. The irrelevance and lack of influence of the isolated *intelligentnye* workers who were the only ones capable of true dedication for non-economic reasons. The preoccupation with the 'political ideal', that is, with the importance of political freedom. These obstacles were only removed when the workers asserted control of their own fate by 'tearing [their fate] out of the hands of the leader/guides', that is, Social-Democratic intellectuals.

When the editorialist looked ahead, he still did not forecast any useful role for non-repentant intellectuals, or for 'advanced' workers in leadership positions, or for a commitment to political freedom on the part of average workers. Perhaps he wanted all these things, but he forgot to say so. Rather, he forecast a continually expanding worker movement that moved from success to success with no evident need for sacrifices or revolutionary battle:

> Now, of course, no one will doubt that the man in the blue uniform [the gendarme] will not hold back [the worker movement's] gradual and undeviating development. . . . In this struggle every step forward is an improvement in one's life and a new means for further victories.[84]

Kautsky, we recall, argued that a sense of historical mission would preserve the worker movement during inevitable defeats and periods of depression. In contrast, the *Rabochaia mysl* editorialist is so confident that such defeats will not occur that he seems actually hostile to the idea of workers doing things for future generations.

> Let the workers conduct their struggle, knowing that they are not fighting for just some kind of future generation but for themselves and their children – let them remember that every victory, every foot of ground taken from the enemy, is one more step in the ladder leading to their personal well-being. . . .

---

[84] As given in Lenin 1926–35, 2, p. 612.

> Victory is ahead, and the fighters will win only when their watchword is
> *'workers for the workers'*.[85]

What is striking about this editorial is the confidence in steady improvement
in the worker condition and in the uninterrupted expansion of the worker
movement. Liadov's comment sums up the Erfurtian response (when Liadov
wrote this in 1906 he only guessed on the basis of its style and outlook that
the editorial was written by an intellectual):

> After liberating themselves from their previous leader/guides, the workers
> were supposed to liberate themselves [as well] from the ideology of these
> leader/guides and to abdicate from the struggle for future generations –
> and go to prison and exile, go hungry during strikes, die in times of
> [government] pacification – and all this in the name of an immediate
> improvement of their personal well-being! Only a semi-educated intellectual
> who fancied himself the interpreter of the will and desires of the workers
> could attribute to the workers this absurd and low-minded point of view.[86]

We turn now to the worker editorial from Issue No. 1. The key contrast
between this editorial and the intelligentsia editorial just discussed is precisely
the sense of historical mission. The worker editorialist's sense of empowerment
is expressed in Lassallean language. (He may have been one of the Petersburg
workers mentioned by Takhtarev who were excited by Lassalle's ideas.)[87]

> Our historic position as the worker class is such that at the same time that
> we are working to achieve our own well-being, we are also fulfilling work
> for society. We are the last class. After us there is no one. The domination
> of the worker class is universal domination or, better, universal equality of
> rights, and we should strive to achieve this: only then can we say that we
> have not lived in vain, and our children will affirm this.[88]

In contrast to the intelligentsia editorial, this writer believes that today's
workers *should* think of future generations ('our children' should be read in
a wide sense). Perhaps as a consequence, there is no trace in this editorial of

---

[85] As given in ibid.
[86] Liadov 1906, 2, p. 104
[87] Takhtarev 1924, p. 24.
[88] Takhtarev 1924, p. 119.

hostility between intellectuals and workers. True, the editorialist insists that 'the improvement of our position as workers depends on us ourselves', but this dictum is aimed at the capitalists and not at the intellectuals. The editorialist goes on to explain that isolated individual efforts will fail and that the workers must stand together. Workers in different factories should think of themselves as one class and not accept the prevailing fragmentation.

> This fragmentation is not without consequences. One result is that worker circles who have lost their leader/guide search for the restoration of new ties through comrades in other factories, while all the time they could have renewed them through someone no further away than a workshop [in the same factory]. In the same way I have come across comrades organised into a group who remained off by themselves and did not know how to attach themselves to the [local Social-Democratic committee] and receive books.[89]

This editorialist does not dismiss the 'political ideal' nor does he look forward to continuous economic improvement. He tells his readers that the law in autocratic Russia is one link in the chain that binds them, since the capitalist and the government stand together. 'We are all fettered by a single chain of arbitrary abuse that we can break apart only by pooling our strength. . . . We see before us the gloomy wall of the monarchy that prevents our access to the light.' The power of autocratic lawlessness is so great that it can only be defeated by a united worker class, strong in the awareness of its independence.

The worker editorialist is not an Erfurtian, but, on the crucial question – the sense of historical mission – he certainly can be called a proto-Erfurtian. He does not call for a revolutionary party to overthrow the autocracy, but he also makes no complaints about intellectuals who obsess about political freedom. No monumental change of circumstances would be required to convince this editorialist that the overthrow of the autocracy had to be a priority task. At the very least, then, these two voices of the original *Rabochaia mysl* group differ in their tone of voice and their imagery. No doubt, Takhtarev was right to regret that the intelligentsia editorial was the one that came to be seen as the banner statement of the newspaper.

---

[89] Ibid. Note the contrast with the intelligentsia editorial that tells the workers to tear their fate from the hands of the leader/guides and to set up strike funds that will *not* be spent on books.

Another of the many voices of *Rabochaia mysl* finds expression in a number of short editorial statements in Issues 4 to 8 that respond to criticisms of *Rabochaia mysl*'s position. These truculent statements seemed to go out of their way to be insulting while, at the same time, avoiding any real discussion of the issues. They were instrumental in alienating the rest of Social Democracy from *Rabochaia mysl*.

The author of these shorter editorials is not known. The obvious candidates are Kok, Takhtarev, or both. I wanted to believe that the author was Kok, since, in quality, they are a cut below Takhtarev's larger editorials. But there is some indication that Takhtarev might indeed be responsible (I now lean toward this position). If so, Takhtarev rather than (as Wildman asserts) Kok was responsible for setting the 'basic tone' of the newspaper after Takhtarev joined in Issue No. 4. No doubt, however, the two men agreed on basic outlook. I will discuss these short editorials in more detail in the following section on reader response to *Rabochaia mysl*.

*Rabochaia mysl*'s most elaborate programmatic statements came from the pen of K.M. Takhtarev. His two substantive lead editorials in Issues No. 4 and No. 7, plus the fifteen-page article 'Our Reality' in the Separate Supplement, constitute an ambitious effort to present and defend a course of action for Russian Social Democracy.[90] The Separate Supplement as a whole sparked off the most extensive of Lenin's 1899 protest writings, 'A Retrogressive Tendency in Russian Social Democracy' (see Chapter Two).

I find Takhtarev's basic beliefs hard to pin down. When Takhtarev emigrated from Russia in the mid-1890s, no one would have suspected that he would turn out to be the theoretician of *Rabochaia mysl*. In fact, the Plekhanov group was extremely encouraged by his first-hand account of the strike movement in Petersburg and especially by his views that these strikes represented the first major step in Russia toward the long-awaited merger. The Emancipation of Labour group published an article by him on the subject which reads like a paean to Russian Erfurtianism.[91]

---

[90] In 1927, Boris Nicolaevsky identified Takhtarev as the author of 'Our Reality' on the basis of the testimony of K.A. Kok (Nikolaevsky 1927, p. 34). This information was unknown to later scholars and the identification had to be re-established by L.I. Komissarova in 1970 on the basis of circumstantial archival evidence (Komissarova 1970). Translated excerpts from Takhtarev's 'Our Reality' can be found in Harding 1983, pp. 242–50.

[91] The article 'Po povodu s.-peterburgskoi stachki' ('On the St. Petersburg Strike') was published under the pseudonym Peterburzhets in *Rabotnik*, 1897, Nos. 3/4.

Arising in isolated circles of intellectuals and workers, Russian Social Democracy becomes a mighty force only when it fuses its intentions and ideals into one unbreakable intellectual and class movement along with the immediate needs and demands of the Russian worker. . . . The mass movement of the workers and the Social-Democratic organisations had been isolated one from the other before the big St. Petersburg strike – what was *new* in that strike was *the link between the Russian worker mass and the Social-Democratic movement.*[92]

Takhtarev was also completely loyal to Plekhanov's hegemony scenario:

The Russian worker movement, thoroughly imbued with Social-Democratic ideas, is the first and the foremost force that with its uninterrupted development will overthrow the existing political system in Russia. . . . Every Russian person will help to move forward the great cause of the whole nation: *the conquest of political freedom.*[93]

This article (published in 1897 prior to the existence of *Rabochaia mysl*) strengthened the faith of the Plekhanov group in their anti-economism.[94] Takhtarev obviously changed his mind. What happened? In emigration, Takhtarev left the Russian milieu and became much more involved in the Belgian and English worker movements. This led him to reject the SPD model and consequently, as he himself well understood, mainstream Russian Social Democracy. In the 1920s, he wrote that

the Russian Social-Democratic movement, just like the English movement of the Chartists and the German Social-Democratic movement, was to a significant extent the merger of a mass worker movement with a movement of an intelligentsia that was inclined to revolution and that strove to become the head of the worker movement and to guide it – to a significant extent in order to accomplish its own political strivings.[95]

In later conversations with Lenin in London, Takhtarev realised that the root of their disagreements was that Lenin regarded 'the German Social-Democratic

---

[92] Takhtarev 1897, pp. iii–iv (order of passages changed). On intellectuals, see also p. xii.
[93] Takhtarev 1897, pp. vii, xvi (the entire first sentence is emphasised in the original).
[94] The Takhtarev article was cited with approval by Akselrod in an influential pamphlet (Akselrod 1898) and even several years later in an article in *Iskra*, No. 2 (February 1901).
[95] Takhtarev 1924, p. 121.

party as a model worker-class party'.[96] (I hope that the reader notices that this first-hand account confirms the basic thesis of this commentary.)

Following a hint of M. Liadov in his party history of 1906, we may see a final influence on Takhtarev emanating from the optimistic hopes of the Petersburg workers themselves about the possibility of large-scale worker organisations in autocratic Russia. Takhtarev was aware of these hopes through written submissions to *Rabochaia mysl*, not direct contact with the workers. In the late 1890s, an economic upswing and the novelty of the worker movement created a situation in which illegal strikes were tolerated and successful. To many workers, it seemed as if this situation would continue indefinitely and permit the worker movement to expand and grow strong within the framework of tsarist absolutism. Temporary strike committees would turn into permanent militant unions, strike funds would become the basis for large-scale organisations built from below. A worker cited by Takhtarev put the case thus: 'Are not strikes . . . forbidden – and yet nevertheless occur more and more often?'. And are not strikes really the same things as a militant union, only the latter is permanent? And therefore do we need to worry overmuch about official prohibition of trade unions?[97]

Other worker correspondents in *Rabochaia mysl* expressed the same outlook. One worker writes that 'the bigger and wider are worker strikes, the weaker and more cowardly become our enemies'. Another worker exhorts his fellows:

> Nothing can be dangerous for us if we hold on to our fellows and stand together like one man, because in that case our word alone is equivalent to action. Then there won't be enough prisons or gallows [to stop us] and besides, there won't be anybody to carry out the orders. Even our enemies will cross over to our side, since the majority of them are the kind of people who side with the strongest.

---

[96] Takhtarev 1924, pp. 179–81 (the whole discussion is pertinent). Kuskova and Prokopovich also rejected the SPD model in favour of Belgian and English models. As Vera Zasulich observed in 1902, 'In the beginning of the movement the generally acknowledged model for Russian Social Democrats was German Social Democracy. In contrast, during the time of economism, the model that was set forth was that of the English trade unions and the Belgian party with its co-operatives'. Zasulich 1983, p. 366 (from an article written for a German audience). Takhtarev's interest in academic sociology may also have led to his great emphasis on the power of custom.

[97] Takhtarev 1899, p. 15 (Separate Supplement), citing worker -r-v from *Rabochaia mysl*, No. 7 (July 1899).

A third sums up: 'As soon as we fuse together [*splotimsia*] into one army, there will be no more sorrow and need'. In other words: if the workers stand together – and what is to prevent them from doing just that? – their enemies will fold.[98]

These expectations form the basis of what I call the *de facto* tolerance strategy. The worker movement could continue to expand and organise without revolutionary overthrow of tsarism – indeed, without any *de jure* removal of legal prohibition of worker strikes and unions. In its hopes for a revolutionary outcome solely by means of a militant worker movement, the *de facto* tolerance strategy might be compared to European syndicalism, except that the syndicalists expected and perhaps even looked forward to a bloody struggle, while these Russian workers wanted to avoid bloodshed and seemed woefully unprepared to confront determined opposition and repression.

In his editorials, Takhtarev provided a theoretical rationale for this optimistic outlook by claiming that custom [*obychai*] was the basis of law so that that *de jure* legalisation was unnecessary. In one of his editorials, Takhtarev stated and then responded to the obvious objection that autocratic repression would stifle the growth of the worker movement.

> *Russian law still does not acknowledge any right of the workers* to establish unions for the improvement of their position. Russian law so far only acknowledges the right of the workers to establish peaceful mutual aid societies.
>
> But – life itself with the greatest possible insistence compels the workers to establish militant 'strike' unions for raising wages, shortening working hours, and so on. And until our law acknowledges the right to the official existence of this kind of union, these unions – as was the case everywhere abroad – will exist secretly. Worker unions are at first everywhere persecuted, then they are tolerated, then they become customary, then openly and officially acknowledged by the law and finally they are protected by the law.[99]

Takhtarev elaborated the de facto tolerance strategy into a more explicitly anti-political message than one finds in the worker contributors. Expanded political rights are no doubt a good thing.[100] But there is no need to get

---

[98] Liadov 1906, 2, pp. 123–5, all citations from *Rabochaia mysl*, No. 3 (July 1898).

[99] *Rabochaia mysl*, No. 4 (October 1898) and No. 7 (July 1899).

[100] Wildman incorrectly says that Takhtarev denied the utility of political rights (Wildman 1967, p. 138).

obsessed about it. To fixate on a non-existent parliament instead of using existing representative bodies is 'revolutionary nihilism'. Fighting the political police is a side issue of concern only to the 'revolutionary intelligentsia'. (Both these comments particularly enraged Lenin, as shown by his 1899 protest as well as by *WITBD*.[101])

But political freedom is not something one fights for, it just *happens* as the worker movement gets stronger and more recognised:

> No! – we've had enough of the lie that the worker movement develops because political freedom is already available . . . No! Real freedom develops because the worker movement starts moving and cannot be held back in its striving ahead. The truth is that every strike, every worker fund, every worker union only becomes legal when it has already become a matter of custom – when it makes not the slightest bit of difference whether it is allowed or forbidden. The actual law is only a registration of contemporary everyday mutual (estate, class) relations. The force of the law is the force of custom. If you can make something customary, then you have made it legal.[102]

It follows from the *de facto* tolerance scenario that there is no particular need for a revolutionary political party. Takhtarev does not so much polemicise against the idea of a party as ignore its existence. His attention is exclusively focused on the worker movement, and since it is obvious that the worker movement *cannot* overturn the autocracy on its own and also that it does not *need* to overthrow it in order to expand and accomplish its basic purposes – then why talk about revolutionary overthrow? The worker movement definitely has political tasks, but these tasks – worker protection legislation and specific political rights – can be accomplished under the autocracy. The worker movement can also team up with various élite groups fighting for their interests, since the autocracy is hostile to *any* independent social activity.

Takhtarev summed up in a passage that became notorious:

---

[101] Takhtarev 1899, pp. 13 and 15 (Separate Supplement); Lenin 1958–65, 6, p. 68, 109 [736, 772]. 'Existing representative bodies' were weak organs of local self-government.

[102] *Rabochaia mysl*, No. 4 (October 1898), lead article (ellipsis in original). This passage is discussed by Liadov 1906, 2, p. 125. Takhtarev in 1902 protested that this editorial was incorrectly interpreted as anti-political.

What is the struggle that it is desirable that the workers conduct? Isn't it the struggle that is the only possible one to conduct under the given circumstances? And isn't the possible one in the present circumstances that very struggle that they are conducting in actuality at the given moment?

And it is to this struggle – the particular and the political struggle for the improvement of their position – that we call the workers. By *particular struggle* we understand the struggle the workers conduct with their bosses, with their particular interests in view, for the improvement of their particular position. . . . We call *political struggle* the struggle that the workers carry out for the improvement of their common position, having in view the improvement of the position of all workers.[103]

I believe that Takhtarev meant this conclusion to be an empirical one: the present worker movement is *in fact* the best one under present Russian circumstances. But this passage certainly reads as almost a philosophical statement: whatever is, is right. As such, it is scornfully rejected in WITBD.[104] Takhtarev's definition of 'political struggle' illustrates what Lenin in WITBD called 'tred-iunionist politics' as opposed to the 'Social-Democratic politics' that was aimed at revolutionary overthrow of tsarism on the basis of the interests of society as a whole.

*Reader reaction*

We now turn to the history of the Social-Democratic reaction to *Rabochaia mysl*. For our purposes, this reaction is just as important as what *Rabochaia mysl* was actually saying, perhaps more so. The timing of the reaction also helps establish just what it was about *Rabochaia mysl* that everybody found so offensive.

The reaction to the first two issues of the newspaper was highly positive. Vera Zasulich of the Emancipation of Labour group was the first to record her response, although she had seen only Issue No. 2 (the editorials in Issue No. 1 might have cooled her enthusiasm). She wrote in April 1898 (by mistake,

---

[103] Takhtarev 1899, p. 14 (Separate Supplement). One might ask what is the point of the socialists calling the workers to a struggle that is the only one possible and that they are now conducting?

[104] Lenin 1958–65, 6, pp. 47–8 [717].

Zasulich thought that part of Issue No. 2 was a separate newspaper entitled *Bor'ba* or *Struggle*):

> We wish yet again the widest possible development for this purely worker literature of which *Rabochaia mysl* and *Borb'a* are model examples. . . . If accounts of strikes were written by participants who can write as well as the correspondent of *Borb'a*, then in their descriptions every strike would have its own particular character, precisely because the authors would give us not only the facts but their own impressions of the facts. Newspaper correspondence of this kind would acquaint us not only with the general course of the struggle but also with the mental and moral profile of the fighters.[105]

Vladimir Ivanshin, later an editor of *Rabochee delo*, was also enthusiastic. He heartily praised the appearance of 'the *first* Russian worker paper' as a sign that the Russian worker movement was alive and thriving. He also reprinted one of the two editorials in Issue No. 1. In the long run, this turned out to be a disservice to *Rabochaia mysl*, since otherwise the offensive editorial would never have attracted notoriety, given the extreme rarity of copies of the first issue. Lenin used Ivanshin's text for his critique in WITBD.[106]

Despite his welcoming tone, Ivanshin struck a note that became more and more forceful in reactions to *Rabochaia mysl*:

> Our task is to acquaint the reader with *Rabochaia mysl* only in general terms and therefore we cannot go into a detailed analysis of the article just printed [the intelligentsia editorial from *Rabochaia mysl* No. 1]. We will simply note that this article reveals the clear traces of a purely local character and – what is particularly important – does not completely or exactly express the general tendency and character of this organ of the Petersburg workers.[107]

The first real attack on *Rabochaia mysl* came in response to Issue No. 4, that is, the first issue in which the Kok-Takhtarev team made their voice heard.

---

[105] As cited in Liadov 1906, 2, p. 110; originally in *Listok Rabotnika*, No. 7 (April 1898).
[106] Ivanshin's review of *Rabochaia mysl* appeared in *Listok Rabotnika*, No. 9/10 (November 1898), pp. 47–53.
[107] *Listok Rabotnika*, No. 9/10 (November 1898), p. 50. Ivanshin evidently helped *Rabochaia mysl* in various ways such as serving as its Zurich address and so forth (Nikolaevsky 1927, p. 34).

Issue No. 4 contained a long editorial by Takhtarev that seemed to cast aspersions on the priority of political freedom and a short editorial that went out of its way to be offensive to the intelligentsia as a group. In response, D. Koltsov, a member of the Plekhanov group, criticised the anti-intelligentsia tone of the editorials while praising the correspondence coming from the workers themselves.[108]

*Rabochaia mysl* responded in Issue No. 7 to Koltsov in a short editorial note. The tone of these short statements did as much damage to *Rabochaia mysl*'s reputation as did the programmatic heresies of the larger editorials. This particular note managed to be both abrasive and evasive. It announced that two abusive articles had recently appeared in the journal *Rabotnik*, one of them directed against *Rabochaia mysl* which, however, did not respond to abuse [*rugan'*]:

> We do not consider it necessary to analyse the quasi-serious 'positive' part of D. Koltsov's article about us, since his 'revolutionary theory' – the organisation by *intelligenty* of small circles of advanced workers for ... overthrow of the autocracy – seems to us to be a theory that has outlived its time, a theory that everybody has left behind, in which there is very little sense indeed of reality or any understanding of it.[109]

This note in *Rabochaia mysl* led in return to a harsh attack on *Rabochaia mysl* by *Rabochee delo* editor Pavel Teplov under the penname of Sibiriak [The Siberian]. Teplov's attack was a response not only to Issue No. 7 but the Separate Supplement of September 1898. The title of the article – 'Polemical Beauties of the *Rabochaia mysl* Editorialists' – sets out the basic thesis, namely, that the voice of the editorials was *not* the voice of the local *Rabochaia mysl* group nor of Russian Social Democracy (recall that, since Issue No. 5, *Rabochaia mysl* billed itself as the official organ of the local Social-Democratic committee):

> Bitter necessity compels us to a clarification of [our attitude toward] the editorial board of *Rabochaia mysl*. We definitely mean '*editorial board*', because

---

[108] Koltsov 1899. I was unable to locate the text of the Koltsov article and rely on the various reactions to it. My description is mainly based on the short citation in Liadov 1906, 2, pp. 110–11.

[109] *Rabochaia mysl*, No. 7 (ellipses in original). The other *Rabotnik* article mentioned here was critical of the Jewish Bund.

the question does not concern the 'newspaper of the Petersburg workers' itself nor the articles and reports that are written by comrades working in Russia and that provide excellent reading matter for the *wide mass* of Petersburg workers [that is, as opposed to more advanced workers]. The question concerns exclusively the articles and polemical remarks of the *editorial board*.[110]

Teplov pointed to the tactlessness of *Rabochaia mysl*'s polemics. A newspaper intended for a mass worker audience tells its readers there is an abusive journal called *Rabotnik* and then refuses to inform them what the issues are (beyond a caricature of Koltsov's position). And *Rabochaia mysl* complains of uncomradely polemics!

Teplov also reacted strongly to the anti-intelligentsia stand of the newspaper, a stand that in the Separate Supplement was blown up into a full-scale rejection of the Russian revolutionary heritage. For example, one article in the Separate Supplement dismissed the 'to the people' crusade of the 1870s as 'fantastic hocus-pocus'. As noted earlier, *Rabochaia mysl* later retracted this particular article.[111]

For our purposes, the most important item is Teplov's critique of the intelligentsia editorial in Issue No. 1. This editorial is the main *Rabochaia mysl* document cited in WITBD, where Lenin's whole aim is to cast *Rabochee delo* as a follower of the spirit of *Rabochaia mysl*. Yet here is *Rabochee delo* attacking this very editorial in 1899:

> In the programmatic article of *Rabochaia mysl* No. 1, the editorial board comes forward with grave and unjust accusations against the revolutionary intelligentsia, labelling the *intelligentnye* leader/guides as the chief reason for the failures of the Russian worker movement. 'As long as the movement was only a means for soothing the bad conscience of the repentant (for what?) *intelligent*, it was alien to the actual worker.' This same 'repentant *intelligent*' is also accused of not knowing 'what to fight for, with whom and for what motive' as well as for an 'unceasing striving not to forget the

---

[110] Teplov 1899.

[111] The Teplov article says that the offensive article was published as a separate brochure, which indicates that *Rabochaia mysl* took this article more seriously than *Rabochaia mysl*'s apologetic retraction in Issue No. 8 would lead us to believe (Teplov 1899, p. 63).

political ideal' – a striving very harmful, in the opinion of the editorial board of *Rabochaia mysl*, to the success of the worker movement. Evidently, the editorial board got an earful of very bitter truths about its views from Russian comrades and was compelled to explain itself.[112]

Finally, Teplov criticised the anti-political tone of the lead editorial in Issue No. 7 (by Takhtarev). Takhtarev had criticised May Day proclamations issued by Russian Social-Democratic committees because they made broad political demands that did not fit the workers' real demands. Takhtarev claimed that the real demands of the workers were much more narrow and apolitical. In response, Teplov also quoted another May Day proclamation that was issued in 1898 by the local *Rabochaia mysl* group itself:

> Fraternally, tirelessly, showing no fear of the gendarmes, showing no fear of the government, we will acquire . . . the right of strikes, the right to join in unions, to set up worker funds and meetings . . . freedom of speech and press, political freedom.[113]

Thus the émigré *Rabochaia mysl* editorialists seemed to be polemicising not only with the local Social-Democratic committee but with the local St. Petersburg *Rabochaia mysl* group!

*Rabochaia mysl* replied to this criticism in another short editorial note with the familiar truculently evasive tone:

> In reference to Sibiriak's article in No. 4/5 *Rabochee delo*: he has not given himself the trouble to examine the least bit attentively the outlook of *Rabochaia mysl* nor to understand it thoroughly, and for that reason we consider it completely superfluous to respond to the article of Mr. [that is, not Comrade] Sibiriak and to demonstrate that *Rabochaia mysl* 'acknowledges politics'. . . . We do not consider it possible to initiate our comrades, the workers, into all these petty details of mutual recrimination. *Rabochaia mysl* has been and remains the practical organ of the Petersburg workers.[114]

---

[112] Teplov 1899, pp. 67–8. The last sentence refers to the explanatory short editorial published in *Rabochaia mysl*, No. 4 – an explanation that infuriated critics even more.

[113] Teplov 1899, p. 64. Teplov also pointed out that the May Day proclamation specifically criticised by Takhtarev was issued by the Petersburg Social-Democratic committee in 1898, although by 1899 *Rabochaia mysl* was supposed to be the official organ of the committee.

[114] *Rabochaia mysl*, No. 8, p. 7 (February 1900).

I have examined Teplov's criticism in detail because it establishes a number of important points. A negative view of the *Rabochaia mysl* editorials was a Social-Democratic consensus by 1899 (despite the fact that *Rabochee delo* and the Plekhanov group were at loggerheads, Teplov supported Koltsov's criticism).[115] Contrary to the impression given both by Lenin and modern scholars, *Rabochee delo* was not an advocate in 'moderate' form of *Rabochaia mysl*'s economism but, rather, a determined enemy from the beginning. Teplov also makes a good factual case that the émigré editorial board did *not* represent the views even of the Petersburg *Rabochaia mysl* group, which seems to have been more 'political' and revolutionary than its reputation.[116]

We return to our survey of reader response to *Rabochaia mysl*. Takhtarev's Separate Supplement came out in September 1899. We happen to have a private reaction to it by M.I. Tugan-Baranovsky, a noted 'legally-permitted Marxist' (someone who was able to publish censor-approved Marxist articles in the Russian press) and 'critic,' that is, revisionist. Tugan-Baranovsky's actual stay in Social Democracy was brief but his reputation as an economic historian lives on today. Evidently Takhtarev had shown him a draft of the programmatic article in the Separate Supplement. 'This article made my hair stand on end. A high-school student could have done as well. I pointed out and corrected some of the most glaring errors, but the article is still really awful.'[117]

The Separate Supplement also roused Lenin, out in Siberian exile, to respond. Besides the programmatic article by Takhtarev just mentioned, the Separate Supplement contained an article by Eduard Bernstein, a sympathetic analysis of Bernsteinism, and articles on Chernyshevsky that used Lenin's hero to discredit the entire Russian revolutionary tradition. In his critique, Lenin made a distinction between the useful side and the harmful side of *Rabochaia mysl*:

> As long as *Rabochaia mysl*, evidently adapting itself to the lower strata of
> the proletariat, assiduously avoided the issue of the final aim of socialism
> and the political struggle but made no [explicit] declaration of a special

---

[115] *Rabochee delo* did not enjoy coming to the defence of the Plekhanov group and in fact the chief editor Boris Krichevskii wanted to cut the relevant passage. Fellow editor Timofei Kopelzon wrote to Krichevskii that 'we are *obliged* to defend them, if they are attacked by wretches like these' (Nikolaevsky 1927, p. 35).

[116] This conclusion is confirmed by Takhtarev 1902, p. 88.

[117] Letter of August 1899 to Plekhanov, cited by Komissarova 1970, p. 169. For Tugan-Baranovsky's brief stay in Social Democracy, see Kindersley 1962.

tendency of its own, many Social Democrats only shook their head, hoping that with the development and broadening of their work, the members of the *Rabochaia mysl* group would on their own easily free themselves from their narrowness.

But when people who have previously carried out the useful work of a preparatory class start to make a noise all over Europe, latching on to fashionable theories of opportunism, and declare that they want to put all of Russian Social Democracy in the preparatory class for many years (if not forever) – when, in other words, people who have been labouring usefully over a barrel of honey begin 'in full view of the public' to pour ladles of tar into it – then we must resolutely rise up against this retrograde tendency.[118]

Lenin's very important article is discussed in other places in this commentary. Here, I will only point out that Lenin is not at all exercised by *Rabochaia mysl*'s anti-intellectualism (his critique does not mention the anti-intelligentsia editorial in Issue No. 1 that is his main text in WITBD). Rather, he focused exclusively on the empirical question of whether the Russian worker movement will or will not respond to revolutionary appeals. Lenin's only comment on the worker / intelligentsia issue is the following ('R.M.' is the pseudonym used by Takhtarev for the Separate Supplement):

R.M. says: 'The attitude of the advanced strata of the workers to such a government (the autocracy) . . . is as easy to understand as the attitude of the workers to factory owners'. This means – healthy common sense concludes – that the advanced strata of the workers are no less purposive than the socialists from among the *intelligenty*, and that therefore the striving of *Rabochaia mysl* to separate the two is absurd and harmful. This means that the Russian worker class has already created and has independently pushed forward elements for the formation of an independent political worker party.[119]

---

[118] Lenin 1958–65, 4, pp. 272–3. 'A barrel of honey spoiled by a spoonful of tar' is a Russian proverb. Note that Lenin incorrectly gives responsibility for the Separate Supplement to the original St. Petersburg *Rabochaia mysl* group.

[119] Lenin 1958–65, 4, p. 262. Wildman seems unaware of this article, Lenin's most extensive discussion of *Rabochaia mysl*. This is a major lacuna in an interpretation that stresses so heavily Lenin's horrified reaction to the spirit of this newspaper. Lenin's article also does not support Zelnik's assertion that Lenin learned from afar that militant dedicated workers were rejecting intelligentsia tutelage. As this passage shows,

*Rabochaia mysl* became an issue in the war between the Plekhanov group and *Rabochee delo* that broke out into the open in early 1900. Plekhanov accused *Rabochee delo* of refusing to combat economism even when carried to the point of absurdity, as in the case of *Rabochaia mysl*. Boris Krichevskii, the chief editor of *Rabochee delo*, was able to point to the Teplov critique of *Rabochaia mysl* discussed earlier. But, continued Krichevskii, there were no grounds to equate even the editorial views of *Rabochaia mysl* with economists of the *Credo* type – the newspaper's editors were 'confused and tactless' but no worse. In any event, those views had nothing to do with Social-Democratic workers in St. Petersburg:

> The 'tendency' of the *editorial board* of *Rabochaia mysl* contradicts *sharply* the overall character of the activity and views not only of the St. Petersburg Committee of the Russian Social-Democratic Party in general but the Petersburg worker movement in particular. The explanation of this seemingly incredible fact is given by the outrageous conditions of illegal publishing created by the tsarist bashibazouks. If you remove the confused and tactless articles of the *editorial board*, the 'newspaper of the Petersburg workers' is not a model of the 'economist tendency' 'pushed to absurdity', but rather the first attempt at creating in Russia an organ for the *broad masses* of the worker class, accessible to their understanding, dedicated to their urgent needs and to topical issues, to specific clashes, especially those arising from *economic struggle*.[120]

Krichevskii wanted to defend *Rabochaia mysl*. The only way he could do so was to say, 'Ignore the editorials'.[121]

By 1901, *Rabochaia mysl* had changed editorial direction and critiques were no longer directed at its current stance. Nevertheless, the old *Rabochaia mysl* continued to be bandied about in polemics. In the very first issue of *Iskra* (December 1900), Martov devoted an article to Zubatov and his police unions.

---

the Separate Supplement confirmed Lenin in his belief that the advanced workers would be the backbone of Russian Social Democracy.

[120] Krichevskii 1900, p. 47.

[121] Some critical remarks about *Rabochaia mysl* can be found in *Rabochee delo* articles by Boris Savinkov and the same Vladimir Ivanshin who so notoriously praised the first issue. The relevant passages are cited in Chapter Six (Savinkov) and Eight (Ivanshin).

The police official Zubatov promised workers that the tsarist government would support their just demands and some workers took the bait. Martov added a sarcastic aside about these deluded workers: 'probably the poor guys had been reading too much *Rabochaia mysl'*. Martov went so far as to ironically dedicate his article – an attack on police unions – to *Rabochaia mysl*.[122]

Martov's sally was directed against the *de facto* tolerance strategy discussed earlier. Programmatically, Martov may have had a point, but, polemically, he could not have been more tactlessly offensive. Martov's implied accusation that *Rabochaia mysl* and Zubatov were working together became a symbol of *Iskra*'s take-no-prisoners polemical belligerence. A worker in Petersburg wrote an indignant letter into *Rabochee delo* defending his comrades who had risked their safety and freedom to distribute *Rabochaia mysl* – they definitely had *not* done all this to help Zubatov. The worker also included an eloquent description of how *Rabochaia mysl'*s hard-driving exposés of factory abuses had gradually opened the minds of many of the less developed workers to more kindly thoughts about the socialists.[123]

*Rabochee delo* was glad to print this letter that was so critical of *Iskra* and also glad to document 'the revolutionising significance of economic struggle and its printed propaganda'. Even so, the editorial introduction to the letter (undoubtedly written by Martynov) felt compelled to argue with the author of the letter and to utter one of the sharpest critiques of *Rabochaia mysl* to date. The result is rather ironic. When this issue of *Rabochee delo* came out, Lenin was already busy writing WITBD, which sought to prove that *Rabochee delo* was the *Rabochaia mysl* of today.

Martynov insisted that there was no excuse for the deliberate downplaying of political struggle in the early issues of *Rabochaia mysl* nor for its narrowing of political tasks in all issues until recently. *Rabochaia mysl* claimed not to be programmatic, but the notorious call not to obsess about political freedom was nothing if not programmatic. *Rabochaia mysl'*s claim that it represented the view of 'advanced Russian workers' had no foundation:

> The editorial articles of the former *Rabochaia mysl* were in no way dictated
> by the condition of the Petersburg movement at that time nor by the character

---

[122] *Iskra*, No. 1 (December 1900).
[123] *Rabochee delo*, No. 11/12, pp. 48–50.

of the newspaper itself. The editorial board acted in a way directly opposed to the basic task of a Social-Democratic newspaper when it attempted to inject into the worker mass false views about political struggle. The only value of these views was their *inaccessibility* and therefore lack of harm for the mass. But if the theoretical confusion of the editorial articles was unheeded by the mass reader, it undoubtedly had a harmful influence on more developed readers and in particular on the activity of Social-Democratic organisations.[124]

*Rabochaia mysl* plays a small but vital role in *WITBD* itself. Lenin did not use his extensive 1899 critique of the Separate Supplement, although he does mention that the Supplement sums up the whole spirit of *Rabochaia mysl* and quotes it once or twice. Instead, he went back to the intelligentsia editorial from *Rabochaia mysl*, No. 1. Why did he dig up an article that he himself described as 'little known and practically forgotten today'?[125] Lenin wanted to present *Rabochaia mysl* as the bottom of the slippery slope down which *Rabochee delo* – his real foe – had begun to slide. *Rabochaia mysl* was the 'the most direct and open advocate of economism', while *Rabochee delo* was a confused and evasive one.[126] Lenin's aim is simply to ensure that the can of *Rabochaia mysl* was firmly tied to the *Rabochee delo* tail. This rhetorical strategy depends on the audience taking it for granted that the old *Rabochaia mysl* was indeed a bad thing.

Later in 1902 appeared K.M. Takhtarev's history of the Petersburg worker movement, written partly in reaction to *WITBD*. Much of the book was devoted to *Rabochaia mysl*. If there was one person responsible for *Rabochaia mysl*'s bad reputation, it was Takhtarev, whose lead editorials – especially in issues 4, 7 and in the Separate Supplement – set out the views so universally condemned in Social-Democratic circles. By 1902, the revolutionary atmosphere was quite different from 1898–9, and Takhtarev and his wife Iakubova now supported *Iskra* and wrote a public letter to that effect.[127] What is remarkable

---

[124] *Rabochee delo*, No. 11/12, pp. 47–8.

[125] Lenin 1958–65, 6, p. 43 [125, 713].

[126] Lenin 1958–65, 6, p. 19 [126, 691].

[127] *Iskra* No. 33, 1 February 1903. The letter is signed 'Former members of the central group of the Petersburg Union of Struggle and collaborators in the earlier *Rabochaia mysl*'. On its authorship, see Gorev 1924, pp. 57–8. The letter was a result of Gorev's conversations with Takhtarev and Iakubova in London.

about his 1902 book is that Takhtarev *apologised* for his editorials and asked that *Rabochaia mysl* itself not be held responsible for them.

Takhtarev's apology has not been noticed heretofore because he issued the apology without stating directly that he had written the offending articles. Armed with the knowledge that Takhtarev did write these editorials, we can better appreciate what he is trying to say. Takhtarev first describes the situation in 1898 when *Rabochaia mysl* began to be printed abroad. There was a down side to this situation:

> It must be admitted that the most negative aspect [of an émigré editorial board] was that owing to the transfer abroad of the printing, the [St. Petersburg] group publishing *Rabochaia mysl* was deprived of the unconditional guarantee of their exclusive editorial rights that this group enjoyed when it held directly in its hands the entire business of publishing *Rabochaia mysl*. And it seems to me that this negative aspect of the transfer abroad of the printing of *Rabochaia mysl* made itself known partly in Issue No. 4.[128]

Later, he tells us about the situation in 1899, after arrests had wiped out the *Rabochaia mysl* group in St. Petersburg. The foreign editors decided to go ahead with prepared material for Issue No. 7 – *and* to add on an editorial.

> A lead article was hastily written . . . by members of the group that found themselves abroad at that time – and one must recognise that it was written in rather one-sided fashion. This article really could be called a sort of preaching of *tred-iunionizm*, but responsibility for it should fall neither on the Petersburg *Rabochaia mysl* group nor on the Petersburg Union of Struggle. The same thing can be said with even greater justice about the Separate Supplement.[129]

These remarks are the only negative comments Takhtarev makes about *Rabochaia mysl*. He then asks that *Rabochaia mysl* be judged only according to early issues. The import is clear: the spirit of *Rabochaia mysl* should not be judged by my editorials in No. 4 and No. 7 nor by my article in the Separate Supplement, since they were one-sided and in any event not the responsibility of the local group.

---

[128] Takhtarev 1902, p. 76. Takhtarev's own editorials began to appear in Issue No. 4.
[129] Takhtarev 1902, p. 79.

Takhtarev's comments, veiled as they are, are creditably gallant. His gallantry is somewhat dimmed by his refusal to come clean about his authorship in the expanded version of his book in 1924 (the second comment is missing and Takhtarev does not even mention the Separate Supplement). One reason for his coyness may have been that his wife and Lenin's wife were very close friends and that Takhtarev continued to be a personal friend of Lenin after Takhtarev left political activity to become a sociologist.

In 1904, Akimov came out with the rather superficial defence of *Rabochaia mysl* quoted earlier. He simply assumed all opposition to it came from a condescending attitude toward the workers. Even Akimov felt that the St. Petersburg economists had made 'errors', although forgivable ones.[130] In 1906, M. Liadov published his party history from a pro-*Iskra*, pro-Lenin perspective (although in later years Liadov lost his faith in Lenin). He challenged both Takhtarev and Akimov about *Rabochaia mysl*. Liadov added two new thoughts about the division that previous writers had made between worker voice and editorial voice. He described the anti-intellectualism of the editorialists as an expression of intelligentsia self-abasement that had nothing to do with the attitudes of real workers. He also argued that in one respect the *Rabochaia mysl* editorialists *did* reflect the outlook of the many workers who made an overly sanguine extension of their 1896–9 successes into the future. But, instead of countering this naïve view, the editorialists erected it into a matter of principle (see my earlier discussion of the *de facto* tolerance strategy).[131]

This survey of Social-Democratic reaction to *Rabochaia mysl* (which is at the same time a survey of the earliest and most fundamental historiography on the topic) shows that *Rabochaia mysl* was welcomed insofar as it was the expression of militant worker protest. The newspaper caused scandal because of the elaborate programmatic claims made by intelligentsia and émigré editorialists, principally Takhtarev. The hostility to *Rabochaia mysl*'s programmatic stance was strikingly unanimous across the Social-Democratic spectrum – from Kuskova and Tugan-Baranovsky on the extreme right through *Rabochee delo* and on to *Iskra* and Liadov. Even the main author of the programmatic articles, Takhtarev, condemned them in 1902 as one-sided and *tred-iunionist*.

---

[130] Akimov 1969, p. 273.
[131] Liadov 1906.

All these critics argued that the *Rabochaia mysl* editorials did *not* reflect the views of the workers in general or even the St. Petersburg *Rabochaia mysl* group. This assertion is most convincing coming from those who were best disposed and best informed about *Rabochaia mysl* – namely *Rabochee delo* and Takhtarev himself. I conclude that the burden of proof is on anyone who argues that the *Rabochaia mysl* editorials were the voice of the workers or that opposition to *Rabochaia mysl*'s programmatic stance meant opposition to the workers.[132]

*Workers vs. intellectuals?*

We have completed our survey of *Rabochaia mysl*. There remains one further question to explore. Perhaps *Rabochaia mysl* was just one symptom of a long-standing clash between revolutionary intellectuals and workers who resented their tutelage. In 1924, Takhtarev claimed that this kind of concrete issue was the inspiration of *Rabochaia mysl*.

> *Rabochaia mysl* arose against the position that was created in Russian Social-Democratic organisations in which intellectuals, thanks to the conditions of the development of the Russian Social-Democratic movement, took over for themselves the role of exclusive leader/guides and pushed out the workers from the guidance of their own movement.[133]

The clash is symbolised by a meeting that took place in Petersburg in early 1897 and that later became famous. Present at the meeting were some activists on their way to Siberian exile – Lenin, Martov and others – as well as some of the local activists still at large. This meeting would have been totally forgotten if Lenin had not described it briefly in WITBD as an early manifestation of the later division between economist and orthodox. According to Lenin, the dispute that arose at the meeting was whether priority should be given to worker strike funds or to an organisation of revolutionaries. Takhtarev's book that came out later in 1902 disputed Lenin's account of the issues, claiming that Lenin and other 'veterans' opposed the entry of workers into

---

[132] The case might be put this way: the person who subverted 'the workers' bid for self-liberation' in this case was Takhtarev, who used his entrée into the editorial board as an opportunity to substitute his voice for that of St. Petersburg workers.

[133] Takhtarev 1924, p. 120.

the Social-Democratic committee. After that, various participants weighed in with memoir accounts.[134]

Wildman and others have seen the clash at this meeting as an early sign of the central split within Russian Social Democracy. The workers wanted to take over their own revolution while Lenin and Co. insisted on preserving an intelligentsia monopoly of leadership. It was this practical challenge rather than any ideological revisionism that worried and indeed frightened Lenin. It is outside the purview of this commentary to write the history of Russian Social Democracy that would be needed to fully explore this issue, but I will briefly outline my reasons for rejecting the Wildman interpretation.

First, did anybody ever oppose the entry of workers as such into leadership positions, simply because they were workers? I find this impossible to believe.[135] After going through various descriptions of the 1897 meeting, I conclude there is no reason to accept Takhtarev's partisan account of his opponents' case. Even Takhtarev's account does not quite accuse his opponents of seeking to exclude workers on principle as implied by Wildman and others. Much more plausible is Liadov's description (based on first-hand experience) of the general mood among the Social-Democratic intelligentsia. 'The ideal for all *praktiki* was to carry out matters in such a way that purposive workers would stand at the head of [Social-Democratic] work'. There were, indeed, arguments about whether this or that individual worker was sufficiently purposive to be recruited into the leadership. But the more experienced *praktiki*, while not automatically idealising each and every worker like many neophytes, regarded purposive workers as their equals and saw their participation as leader/guides not only as desirable but necessary.[136] Of course, the actual interaction was fraught with much more ambiguity than Liadov's account suggests, yet I see no reason to reject his description of strongly held beliefs.

Second, granted that there was dissatisfaction among some Petersburg workers about their lack of membership on the Social-Democratic committee,

---

[134] For a survey of accounts, see Lenin 1926–35, 4, pp. 607–12. Takhtarev himself was not present at the meeting and relied on his wife's first-hand account.

[135] After writing these words, I came across a statement made in early 1903 made by one of the participants in these events, B.I. Goldman, who responds to the charge that the veterans wanted to exclude workers as such: 'I must categorically state that *in this absurd form we never said anything like this* nor did we think it' (*Perepiska* 1969–70, 3, pp. 90–3).

[136] Liadov 1906, 2, pp. 19–20. The quoted sentence is emphasised in the original.

can we accept Takhtarev's claim that this issue inspired *Rabochaia mysl*, either at the beginning or later? Takhtarev relies on written evidence (he was in Western Europe when *Rabochaia mysl* originated in late 1897). He points to the intelligentsia editorial in Issue No. 1 discussed earlier. He also provides the text of other unpublished worker submissions, but these admittedly fascinating documents do not really say what Takhtarev claims they do.[137] Most of the anti-intelligentsia pot-shots published in *Rabochaia mysl* were added by the foreign editors and do not seem related to the local organisational issue. Also relevant is the defence of *Rabochaia mysl* discussed in the previous section that was published in *Rabochee delo* by a St. Petersburg worker. This valuable letter describes the reaction of both advanced workers and average workers to *Rabochaia mysl*. There is not a trace of the worker / intellectual tension that Takhtarev claims was central.[138]

A worker group did arise in St. Petersburg based on this organisational clash: the Worker Self-Liberation Group. The manifesto of this group did complain about workers being denied entry into top Social-Democratic institutions. The group's resentment on the behalf of advanced workers seems distant from *Rabochaia mysl*'s emphasis on the average worker and the economic struggle.[139]

Third, was the kind of clash described by Takhtarev the real meaning of the later division between economists and the orthodox 'politicals'? An affirmative answer to this question is the heart of the Wildman interpretation. On this issue, I agree with Takhtarev himself. When he challenged Lenin in 1902 about the 1897 meeting, his whole point was to *deny* that it reflected later divisions. In setting forth his account of the clash, he further assumed that his readers in 1902 would barely be able to conceive the issues at stake in 1897:

---

[137] Takhtarev 1902 and Takhtarev 1924.

[138] *Rabochee delo* No. 11/12 (February 1902), pp. 48–52. Wildman himself notes that the worker editorial in Issue No. 1 – the *one* editorial in the first eight issues of *Rabochaia mysl* that we know was written by a worker – was 'far more imbued with the spirit and overall goals of the Social-Democratic movement' than the intelligentsia editorial in the same issue. Yet in his summary of the spirit of *Rabochaia mysl*, Wildman says it was sharply opposed to the Social-Democratic mainstream (Wildman 1967, pp. 126, 148–9).

[139] The group's manifesto was published in the émigré journal *Nakanune* [*On the Eve*], No. 7 (July 1899), pp. 78–80, and condemned by the journal's neo-populist editors. Lenin briefly discusses the manifesto in Chapter II of *WITBD*.

> At the present time there will be hardly anybody among the active Petersburg comrades who will dispute or, even more, object on any grounds to the significance of the present mixed make-up of the Union of Struggle [the local Social-Democratic committee] into which both workers and intellectuals enter on equal grounds. There hardly could be anybody these days who would have any objection to the idea that an educated and practical worker can fulfil the role of an organiser of the workers more competently and at a higher level of *konspiratsiia* than an intellectual who does not know the worker milieu so well nor is known so well by this milieu. But these self-evident truths were not so self-evident in 1896.[140]

There were, of course, various kinds of tension between Social Democrats of different class origins. Nevertheless, I see little evidence of a fundamental clash between the people Wildman calls 'worker-philes' vs. the others that he implies were worker-phobes. I see no actual Social-Democratic currents that can be usefully described as either pro-intelligentsia or anti-worker. There *were* anti-intelligentsia currents and, in response, an anti-anti-intelligentsia backlash, that is, people opposed to any exclusionary policy aimed at intellectuals. But this was a relatively minor clash, since almost the entire range of Social Democracy was anti-anti-intelligentsia, as shown by the reaction to *Rabochaia mysl*.[141]

After WITBD was published, serious conflict arose over the status of 'worker committees' in several city organisations in Russia, ending with the disbandment of special worker committees in favour of unified committees. This episode has yet to be fully described.[142] My belief is that *Iskra*'s campaign against these organisations was not motivated by any sort of distrust of workers or by any anti-worker outlook but, if anything, by an over-confidence that workers could be fully represented on the unified committees without any need of affirmative action. Such, in any event, is the brunt of a Menshevik criticism of Lenin on this issue.[143]

Next, did *Rabochaia mysl* set forth a philosophy of leadership that was fundamentally different from orthodox Russian Social Democracy? Such is

---

[140] Takhtarev 1902, p. 66.
[141] See Chapter Nine for Menshevik affirmation of the anti-anti-intelligentsia position.
[142] For a pioneering effort, see Surh 1999 and Surh 2000.
[143] Cherevanin 1904, pp. 39–40. See also Kuskova 1906.

the opinion of Wildman, who sums up the spirit of Takhtarev's editorials, which he believes to be the spirit of *Rabochaia mysl* as a whole, in the following way: 'worker initiative alone was to determine the direction of the movement, obviating the need for "Social-Democratic leadership" [or, in other words,] an opting for "spontaneity" in place of "consciousness"'.[144]

Wildman's statement is plainly an attempt to extend the framework of the textbook interpretation of WITBD to Russian Social Democracy as a whole. Thus, he equates 'spontaneity' with 'worker initiative' and 'consciousness' with 'Social-Democratic leadership'. He then claims *Rabochaia mysl* is for spontaneity and therefore against Social-Democratic leadership. But this affirmation is doubly wrong. 'Spontaneity' is a translation of *stikhiinost*, a Russian word that connotes chaotic and disorganised struggle, and the whole argument of the economists was that the most crying need of the Russian worker movement was organisation, by which they meant 'conscious' or purposive organisation. And, on the other hand, while *Rabochaia mysl* was certainly for worker initiative (was anybody against it?), it was just as certainly not against Social-Democratic leadership. It separated from the Social-Democratic mainstream primarily on the empirical possibilities of that leadership.

It is worthwhile documenting *Rabochaia mysl*'s desire to replace *stikhiinost* with 'consciousness' as quickly as possible. According to the intelligentsia editorial in Issue No. 1, previous strikes were *stikhiinyi* explosions. This era was moving into the past and current organisational striving among the workers represented 'the transition to a fully purposive [= conscious] era of the movement'.[145]

In Takhtarev's editorials, he pictured a ladder that started with non-purposive protests and strikes and then moved on to higher and higher stages in which the workers acquired a greater 'feeling of social responsibility and a more correct understanding of their interests'.[146] Takhtarev did not deny the role of Social-Democratic leadership but maintained that it had to set its sights low for the time being, given the present lack of awareness among the workers of their actual interests:

---

[144] Wildman 1967, 139.
[145] As given in Lenin 1926–35, 2, p. 612.
[146] Takhtarev 1899, p. 4 (Separate Supplement). 'Non-purposive' = *malosoznatel'nye*; 'feeling of social responsibility' = *obshchevstvennost'*.

> Unity and organisation without awareness [= 'consciousness'] is impossible
> but the job is already half-done [when we see] the first glimmer of awareness. .
> . . Of course, not all workers completely understand their own cause; the
> time is still remote when the workers of an entire factory will come together
> purposively [*soznatel'no*], as one person.[147]

At present, 'the degree of awareness of their social interests and of what is
to their advantage that exists even among, say, urban and capital-city workers
leaves much to be desired'.[148]

Both orthodox and economists thought that a *stikhiinyi* level of organisation
was entirely undesirable and should be replaced by purposive organisation
as soon as possible. The crucial dispute was: how soon *was* this possible?
And, on *this* empirical dispute, we find the usual division. The economists
insisted on the low existing level of the workers' purposiveness, while the
orthodox insisted on both a higher present level of awareness and the potential
for a more rapid movement forward.

I also cannot accept Wildman's view of Takhtarev as someone who believed
that 'worker initiative alone was to determine the direction of the movement'.
Takhtarev was an intellectual who had a strong sense of the workers' real
interests and used the leadership mechanisms available to him – in this case,
an editorial board onto which he was co-opted – to ensure that the workers
accepted his vision of their interests. Takhtarev's political programme was
based on his view of worker interests, his empirical contact with the workers,
his reading of their aspirations, his view of the dynamics of the autocracy,
and finally on a choice between the various strategies pursued in Western
Europe. Exactly the same is true of Lenin. Both men wanted to raise the
consciousness of the workers and not just to reflect their current mood. Both
expected the workers to eventually accept their respective visions of worker
interests. Both accused the other of neglecting the actual aspirations of the
workers. Since both men were émigrés, their empirical contact with Russian
workers was mainly through written material or second-hand accounts. So I
find it difficult to see why one should be called a worker-phile advocate of
'worker initiative' and the other an enemy of it.

---

[147] *Rabochaia mysl*, No. 4 (October 1898).
[148] Takhtarev 1899, p. 14 (Separate Supplement).

I should add a personal opinion here. I gather that Wildman and others in his tradition very much favour the self-effacing worker-phile intellectual, who either has no concrete view of worker interests or who feels honour-bound to suppress or muffle his own opinion. From this point of view, my description of Takhtarev will be taken as a critical exposé. But from my point of view, an intellectual (or anybody else) who is involved in worker affairs *should* have firm opinions about the workers' real interests and should strive to persuade the workers to accept his views. The important clashes in Russian Social Democracy were never between intellectuals on the one hand and workers allied with self-effacing worker-philes on the other. Rather, *some* workers and *some* intellectuals had a different concrete concept of worker interests than *some* other workers and *some* other intellectuals. And this is how it should be.

Finally, did Russian Social Democrats have other good reasons to get upset at *Rabochaia mysl* apart from their alleged desire to quash the worker bid for self-liberation? Yes. If *Rabochaia mysl* had just expressed the voice of the militant workers, no one would have strongly objected. If *Rabochaia mysl* had merely restricted itself to the economic struggle, there would have been complaints and calls for a more advanced and more political newspaper (we shall later cite such complaints by *Rabochee delo* writers). If *Rabochaia mysl*'s one venture into programmatic assertions had been the editorials in the first issue, its transgressions would soon have been forgotten.

What made *Rabochaia mysl* a hissing and a by-word in Russian Social Democracy was its status as the official organ of a Social-Democratic committee combined with Takhtarev's ambitious and aggressive programmatic articles in No. 4, No. 7 and the Separate Supplement. This combination could not be ignored. Takhtarev's editorials, along with the shorter editorial statements that he might have also written, attacked other Social-Democratic groups while claiming immunity from counter-attacks because *Rabochaia mysl* was the *soi-disant* voice of the Petersburg worker. This claim was widely and (as I think) accurately felt to be very shaky. The Takhtarev editorials carried the anti-intellectualism expressed *en passant* in the first issue to the extreme of rejecting the entire previous Russian revolutionary tradition. The Separate Supplement even provided a platform for Eduard Bernstein, thus (among other things) giving credence to Bernstein's claim that Russian groups supported him. Takhtarev later claimed that his editorials were not 'anti-political', but practically every reference to political freedom and to revolution in these writings was sarcastic and dismissive. The de facto tolerance strategy may have reflected workers' opinions, but most Social Democrats thought it was based on illusion and profoundly harmful. And all this was trumpeted to friend and foe alike as *the* authoritative voice of Social Democracy in Russia!

When we looked at the editorials in Issue No. 1, we noted that the worker editorial affirmed the idea of a worker mission while the intelligentsia editorial implicitly dismissed it. Takhtarev's editorials explicitly dismissed the idea of mission – and, given his anti-Erfurtian rejection of the SPD model, this is no surprise. Ironically – given that WITBD itself is supposed to be a homage to Chernyshevsky – Takhtarev did so by means of a Chernyshevsky quotation that he used to provide a climax to his Separate Supplement.[149] This quotation appropriately ends this chapter because it expresses the basic clash between the economists – Kuskova, Prokopovich and the editorialists of *Rabochaia mysl* – and the Erfurtians. This issue was not intelligentsia hegemony vs. worker autonomy, but a romantic sense of a proletarian mission vs. a sceptical refusal to enter into a world-historical narrative.

> Do you think to measure the distant future with your habits, conceptions, and means of production? Do you think that your great-great-grandchildren will be the same as you? – Don't worry, they will be smarter than you. Just think about how to arrange your own (social) life, and leave any worries about the fate of your great-great-grandchildren to your great-great-grandchildren.[150]

---

[149] The main reason for seeing WITBD as an homage to Chernyshevsky is that Lenin's title *What Is to Be Done?* is the same as Chernyshevsky's famous novel. For the sources of Lenin's title, see the Annotations Part One.

[150] Takhtarev 1899, p. 16 (Separate Supplement). Takhtarev gave this passage in quotation marks without identifying the source in any way (Takhtarev himself added the parenthetical 'social'). He had previously used the same passage in the lead article in *Rabochaia mysl*, No. 4 (October 1898), this time giving the source as Chernyshevsky, *Ocherki Politicheskoi Ekonomii* (1861), p. 395. It is doubtful whether Chernyshevsky himself would have approved the use that Takhtarev made of his protest against utopianism.

## Appendix to Chapter Four

Intelligentsia Editorial from *Rabochaia mysl*, No. 1 (October 1897)

The worker movement in Russia can now consider itself as part of the pan-European worker movement. Now, of course, no one will doubt that the man in the blue uniform [the gendarme] will not hold back its gradual and undeviating development. Now dying down to a barely flickering spark, now growing into a sea of fire, it conquers the worker masses ever more widely and deeply, while it slowly but surely disciplines them as it teaches how to struggle with the enemy. The worker movement is indebted for this kind of vitality to the fact that the worker himself has finally taken over his own fate, since he has torn it out of the hands of the leader/guides.

This is completely understandable. As long as the movement was only a means for soothing the bad conscience of the repentant *intelligent*, it was alien to the actual worker. The mass [of workers] were cold and indifferent to the cause. Workers with convictions – fighters for their own cause – were exceptions and in any case could not give any noticeable qualitative colouring to the cause. Means came from the emaciated purse of the student. What to fight for, with whom, for what motive? To these questions there was no answer at all for the worker who was not an *intelligent* but a rank-and-file worker from the mass, that is, precisely the one who means everything for the movement. And there could not have been an answer, because the economic foundation of the movement was obscured by the unceasing striving not to forget the political ideal. The question was put in such a way that the answer was not automatic – and there is no possibility of explaining things to each worker, since the usual *study courses* take in a comparatively small number of people. In a word, one can say that the average worker stood outside the movement.

The strikes of 1896 can be called the first and to date the only manifestation of independent worker thought, embodied in structured form – if you do not count the strikes that occurred earlier, arising more or less in *stikhiinyi* fashion as explosions and not as a struggle according to a thought-out plan. Once the question 'what are we fighting for?' is clear, once the enemy is before one's eyes, the Russian worker knows how to fight, he has already proved this. The struggle for one's economic interests is the most stubborn struggle and the strongest, due to the number of people to whom it is understandable and due to the heroism with which the ordinary person defends his right to existence. This is a law of nature.

Politics always obediently follows after economics, and, in the final analysis, political fetters burst apart along the way. The struggle for [one's] economic position, the struggle with capital on the field of everyday essential needs and strikes as the means of this struggle – this is the watchword of the worker movement. Everyone understands this struggle, it tempers energy and consolidates the workers. In this struggle every step forward is an improvement in one's life and a new means for further victories. Once the whole mass of workers is drawn in, the means for the struggle are guaranteed by that fact alone.

The movement ceases to be a beggarly one that gets by through handouts from outside. Means should be provided by the fighters themselves, and each penny earned by labour that is contributed to the cause is worth a thousand contributed from outside. The drive of the workers to set up [strike] funds heralds a transition to a fully purposive era of the movement. These funds should in the future provide means not for study courses, not for books, but for bread on the table when the struggle is at its most heated – during a strike. Workers should group themselves around these funds, each of which is more valuable for the movement than a hundred other organisations. Of course, the work of self-education should also proceed on its way, educating an *intelligentnyi* handful.

Let the workers conduct their struggle, knowing that they are not fighting for just some kind of future generation but for themselves and their children – let them remember that every victory, every foot of ground taken from the enemy, is one more step in the ladder leading to their personal well-being. Let those who have strength call the weak to struggle and place them in the ranks themselves, not relying on anybody's help. Victory is ahead, and the fighters will win only when their watchword is *'workers for the workers'*.

## Chapter Five
# A Feud Within Russian Erfurtianism

> With its negative attitude toward other Social-Democratic organisations that have a different view than itself on the course and tasks of the Russian worker movement, *Iskra* at times forgets the truth in the heat of polemics. Obsessed about isolated expressions that are indeed clumsy, it attributes to its opponents views that they do not hold, it emphasises points of disagreement that are often quite inessential and they stubbornly remain quiet about all the many points of agreement. We have in mind *Iskra's* attitude toward *Rabochee delo*.

Thus did a group of critics describe *Iskra's* polemics in the *Joint Letter* they sent to *Iskra* in fall 1901.[1] The description is accurate enough and indeed applies to Russian Social-Democratic polemics in general. But the clash between *Iskra* and *Rabochee delo* was a special case that often took on a rather absurd cast. Sometimes, the major issue in dispute was whether or not there were major issues in dispute.

Kuskova, Prokopovich and the *Rabochaia mysl* editorialists were, in their different ways, principled opponents of Russian Erfurtianism. In contrast,

---

[1] For the text of the *Joint Letter*, discussed in detail in Chapter Six, see Lenin 1958–65, 5, pp. 361–3.

*Rabochee delo* was a principled *advocate* of Erfurtianism. As will become clear as we proceed, we could go through the checklist and document the journal's support for each point. If we read *Iskra*'s polemics with care, we will see that it did not really deny this fact (although the *Iskra*-ites were not loath to obscure it). The charge was rather that *Rabochee delo* did not understand what was needed to apply Erfurtianism in the current Russian context. This lack of understanding manifested itself in tactical advice to Russian *praktiki* that was not so much bad as unclear, shifting and empty.

In outlining this feud, therefore, we cannot just outline the programmatic stands of the two sides. Politics and personality play a much greater role than in earlier debates. The chronological back-and-forth of mutual accusation, of growing irritation and anger, is just as important as the substantive issues for understanding the nature of Lenin's attack on *Rabochee delo*. WITBD is the final shot in a pamphlet war that had been going on for some years.

The feud started some years before *Iskra* came into existence. At first, the feud was between 'veterans' and 'youngsters' among the Russian émigrés in Switzerland in the late 1890s – that is, between the Emancipation of Labour group who had been preaching Social Democratism for over a decade and the young Social-Democratic activists who had emigrated only recently. These two groups were at first united in the Union of Russian Social Democrats Abroad. It certainly seems regrettable that they could not have worked effectively with each other. Nevertheless, by November 1898, relations were strained enough that the Emancipation of Labour group refused any further participation in the Union's editorial board. From this point on, the younger group controlled the Union's publications – in other words, its official voice. The Union had been publishing a periodical called *Rabotnik* but the new editorial board decided to start up a new journal called *Rabochee delo*. The first issue came out in April 1899 and, over the next two and a half years, the ten issues of *Rabochee delo* that were published were the closest thing to an official Social-Democratic voice. The last issue, No. 11/12, came out in early 1902, just as Lenin was completing WITBD. Thus *Rabochee delo* never got a chance to respond to WITBD – a pity, from the historian's point of view.

In the early days of the feud, the youngsters could with some plausibility present the dispute as one between out-of-touch émigré theorists vs. the real Social-Democratic movement in Russia, as represented abroad by recent émigrés such as themselves. Such is the picture painted by Prokopovich in the pamphlet written when he was close to the Union.[2] This bright picture was muddied when the *Iskra* organisation was formed in 1900. Now, the Emancipation of Labour had formed an alliance with its own group of youngsters who were armed with practical experience in Russia (Lenin, Martov, Potresov). *Rabochee delo*'s claim to represent the Social-Democratic committees working in Russia also came under attack when *Iskra* began a systematic campaign to win over the committees. *Iskra*'s campaign really got going only after WITBD's publication in 1902 – that is, at a time when *Rabochee delo* had ceased publication.

Before getting into the disputes and conflicts, we should stress a fact that probably determined the outcome of the feud as much as any other cause: as revolutionaries go, the *Iskra* team were heavyweights and the *Rabochee delo* team were lightweights. The *Iskra* team consisted of Plekhanov, Akselrod, Zasulich, Lenin, Martov and Potresov. The *Rabochee delo* team consisted at different times of Boris Krichevskii, Vladimir Ivanshin, Pavel Teplov, Aleksandr Martynov, Vladimir Akimov. The first set of names are all major figures in Social-Democratic history even apart from their association with *Iskra*. The second set of names have no more than footnote status.[3]

Besides the contrast in individual calibre, the two opponents differ in the quality of their teamwork. During the period 1900–3, the *Iskra* editors projected an image of unity and consistency. They agreed with each other on basic principles and on the needs of the day. They stood for something. The *Rabochee delo* editors lacked this energising sense of mutual mission. No one, at the time or since, was able to identify a consistent *Rabochee delo* outlook that united the various editors. Toward the end, the contradictions within the editorial board got completely out of hand.

This is not to say that *Rabochee delo* did not have many useful things to say, or that in particular the journal did not make many insightful digs at *Iskra*. But the points that *Rabochee delo* made always seem to be criticism, warnings, caveats, rather than a positive message. For all of *Iskra*'s aggressive polemical

---

[2] This pamphlet was published without Prokopovich's consent by Plekhanov in the *Vademecum* (Plekhanov 1900).

[3] Martynov was the only one to remain visible in later Russian Social Democracy. Akimov was totally forgotten until his pamphlets of 1904 were translated and edited by Jonathan Frankel (Akimov 1969).

stance, it also had a positive and indeed inspirational message. For all of *Rabochee delo*'s common sense and inclusive tone, they always seem to be reacting to something else – usually Plekhanov or *Iskra*.

Finally, *Rabochee delo* simply made too many mistakes. The journal at first praised the French socialist minister Millerand when he joined the government cabinet but, later, admitted that he had proved a big disappointment. In 1901, it called for aggressive May Day demonstrations and later had to admit that this call had been premature. And so on. In each case, *Rabochee delo* could say with plausibility, 'Well, how were we to know?'. Nevertheless, this record cannot have helped its prestige.

In *WITBD*, *Rabochee delo* is incarnated by Boris Krichevskii and Aleksandr Martynov, the authors of the articles in *Rabochee delo*, No. 10 (September 1901) that are Lenin's principal polemical targets. Krichevskii was the chief editor of *Rabochee delo* throughout its existence. I feel somewhat apologetic toward the shade of Krichevskii, since he will appear in these pages in an unflattering light that does not do justice to his journalistic talents or his activity in providing the Russian Social-Democratic movement with illegal literature. The descriptions we have of Krichevskii come from the period when his Social-Democratic career was sinking fast. At one time, Krichevskii was a friend and indeed a mentor of Rosa Luxemburg. But, by 1899, she could take her companion Leo Jogiches to task by saying 'your behaviour befits a sourpuss like Krichevskii but not a strong and noble person [like yourself]'.[4] Luxemburg's biographer Peter Nettl describes her attitude toward him:

> Certainly by 1903 the political friendship between them was at an end. . . . Consistent lack of success and the resulting personal humiliation were not marketable commodities in Rosa Luxemburg's polity; looking back in 1910 she recalled: 'Poor Krichevskii in Paris [after 1900] – a wreck perpetually complaining about his debts, his children, his ailments. . . . He failed to keep up with me mentally and when I saw him again it was like being visited by a provincial cousin whom one had known ten years ago as a brisk young man and found now nothing but a worried provincial hick and *pater familias*.'[5]

---

[4] Nettl 1966, 1, p. 253.
[5] Nettl 1966, 1, p. 85, quoting from an archival letter.

Especially in 1901, Krichevskii appeared to be flailing and permanently off-balance. After 1901, he plays almost no role in Russian Social Democracy.

Aleksandr Martynov joined the *Rabochee delo* editorial board rather late and made a valiant attempt to infuse the organisation with energy even as he helped bring it down. After the RSDWP Second Congress in 1903, he became a Menshevik, in which faction he played a visible if not terribly important role. During the Russian Civil War, he first retreated from politics and then decided to become a Bolshevik. This decision, he tells us, was not because he had been wrong to call Lenin a Jacobin dictator in 1904 but because he now realised that such a dictator was necessary.[6]

The memoirist N. Valentinov recalls meeting Martynov in Geneva in 1904 at a time when Valentinov was still a Lenin loyalist and thus had major political differences with Martynov:

> In his youth, as a member of *Narodnaia volia*, he had spent many years in exile in the most remote corner of Northern Siberia. . . . He was a remarkable story-teller. No one could have imagined that this fat, unattractive-looking man with a lisp, who suffered from a dreadful form of eczema on his hands and head (which many people found repulsive) had a tremendous gift of poetical description. If Martynov had written a book about his Siberian impressions and his observations of nature there instead of writing on political subjects, I am sure it would have been a brilliant and original work. To avoid arguments, we made a firm bargain not to bring up our factional differences; when conversation flagged, Martynov would teach us old French revolutionary songs, and we sang *'Peuple en avant, c'est dans la barricade que l'avenir cache la Liberté'*.[7]

## Soft on opportunism?

A common thread to all the conflicts between the *Iskra*-ites and *Rabochee delo* is the *Iskra* group's suspicion that *Rabochee delo* was soft on opportunism and *Rabochee delo*'s exasperation and resentment of those suspicions. 'Opportunism'

---

[6] Martynov 1989 (a short memoir account written in the 1920s). In this account, Martynov claims to have been the first Menshevik and a case can be made for this claim.

[7] Valentinov 1968, pp. 132–3.

was the catch-all term in international Social Democracy for deviations from orthodoxy in the direction of reformism. The main versions of opportunism that upset the *Iskra*-ites were Bernstein revisionists abroad and economism at home.

The suspicion about *Rabochee delo*'s softness did not arise because *Rabochee delo* itself openly advocated or endorsed such views. On the contrary, *Rabochee delo* printed and endorsed the Lenin-drafted 'Protest by Russian Social Democrats' against the *Credo*, and, as we saw, severely criticised *Rabochaia mysl*'s editorial line. Nevertheless, even while criticising these views, it refused to get excited about them. According to *Rabochee delo*, such views were only the isolated opinions of a few activists without any widespread influence in the movement. If the local *praktiki* focused on economic agitation, this was entirely appropriate at the early stages of the movement and actually prepared the way for higher, more political, stages.

The 'spring events' of 1901 transformed the terms of debate. After workers in Moscow, St. Petersburg, Kharkov and other cities went out on the streets to support student protests, it became a commonplace among Russian Social Democrats that the workers were entering a phase of rapid politicisation and that the Social-Democratic committees would have to scramble to catch up and provide effective leadership. But the spring events did not settle the factional dispute. Each side claimed that the new militancy of the workers proved that it had been right all along.

*Rabochee delo* argued roughly as follows: 'The spring events showed that *Iskra* was wrong to have such a negative attitude toward the Social-Democratic movement of recent years and to worry so much about economism. The economic struggle of recent years actually prepared the political outburst of last spring.'

*Iskra* argued something like the following: 'The spring events showed just how right we were to criticise the local committees for insufficient attention to politics. The committees did not realise the political potential of the worker movement (and *Rabochee delo* did not make it their business to tell them), with the result that the worker movement has now left the committees behind. Not only is the workers' current protest much less effective than it could have been, but the very real danger exists that non-Social-Democratic revolutionaries, who are more prepared than we are to assume leadership, will take control away from us.'

Thus, underlying the many specific causes of mutual irritation were two more substantive issues. The first was, were economist views ever widespread among the *praktiki*? We need to formulate the *Iskra* claim here more precisely. The *Iskra*-ites focused on the sentiments found in the *Credo* not because they felt that a substantial number of *praktiki* were ready explicitly to endorse the *Credo*, pen in hand. In spring 1901, Martov asserted that the *Credo* was not just the confusion of a few individuals as claimed by *Rabochee delo* – rather, it 'expresses most sharply the logical conclusions [to be drawn] from the views that have become popular among very many comrades'.[8] This is a vague assertion, harder to pin down but also harder to refute. We might formulate the *Iskra* claim as follows: a great many *praktiki* not only concentrate on economic struggle and bypass the political struggle, but they believe – without thinking about it too much – that this is the proper way for a Social Democrat to behave. When the workers themselves move to political activity, the *praktiki* are caught flat-footed. Even when the *praktiki* verbally admit the urgency of the political anti-tsarist struggle, they have very little idea of what exactly this entails.

The second underlying issue was, which did more harm to the movement, *Rabochee delo*'s easy-going, tolerant attitude or *Iskra*'s more hard-line, intolerant attitude? Was *Rabochee delo* too complacent or was *Iskra* too dogmatic?

It is not the job of this commentary to settle these disputes. Nevertheless, to help explain why *Rabochee delo* lost the battle, I am going to bring forward a number of witnesses who line up, often reluctantly, on *Iskra*'s side. These witnesses are Russian revolutionaries from the liberal or populist traditions. These traditions had always been somewhat suspicious that Russian Social Democracy would turn out to be a basically non-revolutionary movement devoted to the particular interests of the workers. Observers from these traditions therefore had a tendency to side with *Iskra*, even when they were dismayed by its aggressive and divisive polemics.

These witnesses will document the general image of *Rabochee delo* and *Iskra* in Russian revolutionary circles. 'Revolutionary Social Democrats' such as Lenin were very sensitive to Social Democracy's image in these circles, especially given Social Democracy's ambitious hegemony scenario. One reason

---

[8] *Iskra*, No. 4 (May 1901).

for their anger against *Rabochee delo* was that they felt it provided ammunition for the contemptuous dismissal of Russian Social Democracy as a movement that was, deep down inside, not revolutionary. The support these non-Social-Democratic witnesses give to *Iskra* also creates difficulties for a widespread opinion among modern supporters of the textbook interpretation that *Iskra's* campaign against economism was no more than a cynical or hysterical witch-hunt with no basis in fact.[9]

Our first witness is the liberal revolutionary Paul Miliukov, whom we have met before. Miliukov had his own ideas about the sources of economist attitudes, but he had no doubt about their existence:

> The strikes of 1896 and 1897 definitely persuaded the young generation of revolutionists that the evolution of socialism would take place all by itself. . . . Strikes of workingmen – their struggle for better wages – were to become the main, if not the only, object of the socialistic propaganda and agitation. The young reformers took particular pains to emphasise the peaceful character of the new movement, as the best proof of its spontaneity and omen of its final success . . .
>
> This stage of the movement did not last long, and the old Marxists [the Emancipation of Labour group] were the first to dispel the charm. . . . A new literary organ of the 'orthodox' Marxists was founded (*The Spark*), and it carried the day against the inexperienced 'economism' of the younger generation.[10]

Looking at the matter from a neo-populist, proto-Socialist-Revolutionary angle was E. Lazarev, editor of the revolutionary émigré newspaper *Nakanune* [*On the Eve*], published in London. Lazarev's testimony is revealing because it was expressed *before* the dispute in Social-Democratic ranks became public knowledge with the publication in 1900 of Plekhanov's *Vademecum* (discussed below). Lazarev writes in late 1899 that

> the contradictions of the doctrine of class struggle are revealed especially sharply in Russia at the present time. On the basis of the same doctrine [but] in contradistinction to many Western-European Marxists, many Russian

---

[9] For example, Keep 1963.

[10] *The Spark* = *Iskra*. Miliukov's testimony, written in 1903–4, shows the clear influence of *WITBD*, but his account must still be seen as an independent validation of the existence of economism. Miliukov 1962, pp. 353–4.

Marxists recognise in Russia only the trade-union struggle, the struggle of worker strikes, while they have a negative attitude to the political, revolutionary struggle against tsarist abuses . . .

There are Marxists in Russia . . . who on the basis of the 'class struggle' try to smother the indignation of a citizen and a human being [that should be felt by] the purposive worker. [These Russian Marxists] have announced that the struggle with political despotism for freer political forms, for representative institutions, for civil freedom, has nothing to do with the proletariat, that it is all a family squabble of the bourgeoisie.[11]

Despite his opposition to this kind of Russian Marxist, Lazarev also strongly objected to the arrogance and intolerance of Plekhanov's fratricidal declaration of war against *Rabochee delo*. Lazarev put the blame for the split in Social Democracy squarely on Plekhanov's dictatorial tendencies.

After the exchange of pamphlets came cutting speeches in different Swiss towns *pro* and *contra* the *Vademecum*. There arose and bubbled over a mutual hatred among many people who yesterday saw themselves as comrades – a hatred that was heated and active to an extent that probably neither of the warring sides ever felt toward the Russian autocracy itself, toward the age-old foes and exploiters of the proletariat.

Nevertheless, Lazarev granted that there was something absurd about the position of Kuskova and Prokopovich that 'a socialist must not talk to the worker mass about socialism'.[12]

Writing in *Nakanune* a year later was the young up-and-coming leader of the Socialist Revolutionaries, Viktor Chernov. Chernov specifically refuted *Rabochee delo*'s argument that Social Democracy as a whole had been unable to foresee the revolutionary energy displayed by the workers during the spring events.

According to *Rabochee delo*, the workers of the large centres 'displayed [during the spring events] a *political sense and political flair* that no doubt not a single Social Democrat and *not a single revolutionary in general* expected from them'

---

[11] From *Nakanune*, No. 11, probably December 1899, as cited by the same author in No. 15, April 1900. Note the contrast Lazarev sees between the Russian economists and Western-European Marxists.

[12] *Nakanune*, No. 17–18 (June 1900), p. 208 (third of three articles). Lenin alludes to these articles in WITBD; see Lenin 1958–65, 6, p. 140 [800].

(our emphasis). This last assertion, unfortunately for *Rabochee delo*, is completely untrue. For example, the *Rabochee znamia* and *Sotsialist* groups in *January* of the present year [1901, before the worker demonstrations] motivated their opposition to the Petersburg Committee of the 'Russian Social-Democratic Party' precisely by the latter's 'lack of faith in the growth of the *political* self-awareness of the worker class'.

These groups found it necessary to unite 'as a counterweight' to this tendency while at the same time 'sharply emphasising the necessity above all of the struggle for political freedom. We base ourselves on the conviction that the worker class in Russia has matured to the point where it understands not only its *economic but its political* interests and that it has increased in strength to the point that it can begin the struggle for both *in the near future.*' Even earlier, in a *December* proclamation of the *previous* year they announced in a similar fashion that 'the worker class is ready in the near future to *openly* commence the struggle for their political rights'. In its day *Rabochee delo* passed over these proclamations *in silence* while *Nakanune* greeted them with fervour.[13]

Chernov agreed with *Rabochee delo* (and, of course, with *Iskra* as well) that party organisations of all revolutionary tendencies were not up to the task of directing the movement. In making this point, *Rabochee delo* had mentioned that the Social-Democratic committees were the strongest of the local revolutionary organisations. Chernov felt it necessary to go even further than *Rabochee delo* on this point: at the present time, the Social Democrats were the *only* truly functioning local revolutionary organisations – all others were only *in statu nascendi.*[14] Coming as it does from a leader of the Socialist Revolutionaries, this is an important admission.

---

[13] *Nakanune*, No. 33 (September 1901), p. 400 (Chernov writing under the pseudonym of Boris Olenin). *Rabochee znamia* [*Worker Banner*] was the newspaper of a short-lived Social-Democratic group in St. Petersburg (see Savinkov's discussion of the Petersburg situation presented in Chapter Six). Chernov cites the words of *Rabochee delo*, from 'Historical Turning Point' (*Rabochee delo*, 1901). Note the mortifying emphasis on the fact that an official Social-Democratic party organisation was accused of non-revolutionary attitudes. Chernov's comments are also a challenge to modern scholars who tend to agree with *Rabochee delo* that the spring events caught all of Russian Social Democracy off-guard.

[14] *Nakanune*, No. 33, September 1901, pp. 399–401. Zasulich brought this comment to the attention of German readers in Zasulich 1983 [1902].

Our final witness, L. Nadezhdin, was a recent convert to Social Democracy, although he still leaned toward the Socialist-Revolutionary position on issues such as terrorism. As we shall see when we look at Nadezhdin in more detail in Chapter Six, he was in no sense an *Iskra* partisan. An even more recent émigré than most of the *Rabochee delo* editors, Nadezhdin believed that Russia was undergoing a 'rebirth of revolutionism' (the title of his political pamphlet published in 1901). Although Nadezhdin had observed a shift toward a more political outlook in Social-Democratic circles starting a year or two before the events of spring 1901, he nevertheless insisted that economism was still around. Scotching it was, therefore, a priority task of Russian Social Democracy. His tirade on this subject is useful because it lists all the mitigating circumstances that can be made in defence of economism:

> We should give all that is due to the people representing the economist tendency in revolutionary thought. We should recognise the useful contribution that they made in the first stages of the development of the worker movement and understand the extent to which this worldview is really the fault of Russian history when it threw revolutionary thought over to the completely opposite pole [away from the maximalism of *Narodnaia volia*]. We should also understand the extent to which this kind of work was caused by the embryonic nature of the worker movement in Russia several years ago. Finally, we should understand a weakness common to all humans who are compelled to specialise in one particular kind of work and end up considering it as the end-all and be-all.
>
> We should take all of this into account. Nevertheless, we cannot have a tolerant attitude toward narrow economism and its current incarnation, namely, Bernsteinism. It is a thousand times easier to bear the blows of governmental oppression than the propaganda of Bernsteinism, diligently nourished in the place where revolutionary struggle should be! The whip brandished by the government does not destroy anything for long – on the contrary, it calls forth resistance. The Bernsteinist propaganda of economic struggle pushes revolutionaries toward a swampy mire, and this mire sucks people down.[15]

---

[15] *Rebirth of Revolutionism*, Nadezhdin 1903 [1901], pp. 22–3. Compare Lenin's use of the swamp metaphor in WITBD; see Lenin 1958–65, 6, pp. 9–10 [684].

In Nadezhdin's view, the shift in mood toward a more political outlook did not remove the need for a determined pro-political, anti-economism campaign. The new mood, the growing popularity of slogans like 'struggle for political freedom' – these by themselves did not ensure a concrete sense of *how* to conduct political struggle. According to Nadezhdin, both the new political mood *and* the continuing lack of concreteness found their spokesman in *Rabochee delo*. 'In one and the same issue you can find a whole kaleidoscope of attitudes towards politics', ranging from an all-out war on tsarism to hopes for small concessions. Thanks to *Rabochee delo*'s tendency to get carried away with this or that tack, no definite message emerged from its pages.[16] This was intolerable when the task of the day was to oppose 'economist pettifoggery' ever more firmly and instill a clear sense of the significance and necessity of political struggle.[17]

These witnesses do not prove that *Rabochee delo* was necessarily wrong to minimise the impact of economism within Russian Social Democracy. All the writers I have quoted had a bias in favour of anti-tsarist revolution that might have led them to exaggerate the economist threat in the same way *Iskra* did. Nevertheless, these witnesses tell us why, as the situation become more and more revolutionary, *Rabochee delo* was more and more at a disadvantage.

## Early clashes

We have looked at some of the background differences in outlook and attitudes that explain why the two groups of Russian Erfurtians were bound to get on one another's nerves. Like a married couple on the brink of divorce, *Rabochee delo* and the Emancipation of Labour were capable in 1898–9 of taking the smallest incident and turning it into a raging argument.

*Rabochee delo*'s first year of publication was 1899. The journal could not have made its Erfurtian sympathies more plain. The first issue of *Rabochee delo* had a highly enthusiastic review of Lenin's *Tasks of the Russian Social Democrats*. The as-yet-anonymous author of *Tasks* was called an outstanding representative of the Social-Democratic movement in Russia and *Rabochee delo*

---

[16] Nadezhdin 1901a, pp. 102–6.
[17] Nadezhdin 1903 [1901], pp. 34–5.

announced its full solidarity with the views of the pamphlet.[18] *Rabochee delo* also joined the crusade against the *Credo*. It published Lenin's 'Protest by Russian Social Democrats', both in the journal and as a separate pamphlet, and later praised it as 'brilliantly demonstrating the entire theoretical baselessness and practical groundlessness of the *Credo*, its contradiction with the conditions of the Russian life and with the actual character of the Social-Democratic movement in Russia'.[19] Finally, *Rabochee delo* published a harsh criticism of *Rabochaia mysl*'s editorialists.[20]

Thus, in 1899, Russian Social Democracy was represented abroad by two émigré groups – the Emancipation of Labour group and *Rabochee delo* – who differed hardly at all in their programmatic views or in their rejection of both the *Credo* and the *Rabochaia mysl* editorials. Yet, within a year, a passing remark by Akselrod had led to a full-scale explosion in Social-Democratic ranks. When Lenin's *Tasks of the Russian Social Democrats* was published in early 1899, it came with an introduction by Akselrod in which he praised the work very highly. Akselrod felt, however, that the author overestimated the consensus within Social-Democratic ranks, since Akselrod felt that many young Social Democrats coming out of Russia lately had rather one-sided views on economic struggle. Akselrod had Kuskova and Prokopovich particularly in mind, but was also plainly worried about their influence among the young émigrés who now controlled the Union of Russian Social Democrats Abroad. The first issue of *Rabochee delo* soon came out with their own glowing review of Lenin's *Tasks*. The review took exception to Akselrod's remark about 'younger émigré comrades', remarking that *Rabochee delo* did not know what younger comrades Akselrod meant, since all the younger comrades they knew did not have any such views. Indeed, these younger comrades (themselves) were encouraged by the complete coincidence between their views and the views of the best of the Russian *praktiki*, as exemplified by the author of *Tasks*.[21] (The review's

---

[18] *Rabochee delo*, No. 1 (April 1899), pp. 139–42. On the status of Lenin's *Tasks* as a statement of Erfurtian orthodoxy, see Chapter Two.

[19] Krichevskii 1900, p. 35. Lenin's 'A Protest' appeared in *Rabochee delo*, No. 4/5 (September/December 1899).

[20] Teplov 1899 in *Rabochee delo*, No. 4/5 (September/December 1899). *Rabochee delo*'s view of *Rabochaia mysl* is documented in Chapter Four.

[21] *Rabochee delo*, No. 1 (April 1899), pp. 139–42. Krichevskii was the author of this anonymous review. Archival letters quoted by Boris Nicolaevsky show that the *Rabochee delo* editors admitted in private that it was no 'myth' that some members of their organisation inclined toward economism (Nicolaevsky 1927, pp. 20–1).

high praise cut no ice with Lenin – in *WITBD*, he rather humourlessly accused *Rabochee delo* of lying when it said it did not know which comrades Akselrod had in mind.[22])

Akselrod in response prepared a twenty-two-page open letter to *Rabochee delo* that tried to show that he indeed had cause to worry about the younger comrades. To make his point, he cited an unpublished manuscript by Prokopovich (later published in the *Vademecum*).[23]

Boris Krichevskii started work on a response to Akselrod's open letter. Meanwhile, the protest against the *Credo* drafted by Lenin arrived in Geneva. *Rabochee delo* published the protest, condemned the *Credo*, and praised the protest itself as a fine piece of work. Nevertheless, it could not help adding that the *Credo* was the mistaken opinion of a few isolated individuals and did not have wide significance.[24]

This remark, plus various other mutual irritations, led Plekhanov to deliver a bombshell. In early 1900, he published *Vademecum for the Editorial Board of 'Rabochee delo'*, in which he inserted not only Prokopovich's unpublished pamphlet but various letters never meant for publication. The idea was that this publication would serve as a guide ('vademecum', 'go with me' in Latin, refers to travel guides) to the younger comrades so that they could grasp the fact that they were – or in any event had been – infested with economism. Plekhanov's analysis of the issues in his introduction is useful, but, in general, the pamphlet is a striking example of the sarcastic yet strangely insecure arrogance that made Plekhanov such a disaster as a Social-Democratic leader. The low point was reached when Plekhanov made fun of grammatical errors contained in friendly private letters written with absolutely no thought of publication.[25]

---

[22] Lenin 1958–65, 6, p. 44 [714]. The polemical ping-pong between the two sides was so complicated that even Lenin gets a little mixed up on this point. He says that *Rabochee delo* feigned unbelief about a comment Akselrod made in his pamphlet of 1898 'On the Question of the Present-Day Tasks and Tactics of the Russian Social Democrats'. As shown here, *Rabochee delo* was actually responding to another article by Akselrod, namely, his introduction to Lenin's *Tasks*. *Rabochee delo* did have occasion elsewhere to make critical remarks about Akselrod's 1898 pamphlet. (A summary of this important pamphlet can be found in the Annotations Part One.)

[23] Akselrod 1899; Prokopovich 1900.

[24] *Rabochee delo*, No. 4/5 (September/December 1899). These comments were penned by Pavel Teplov (Nicolaevsky 1927, p. 35).

[25] Plekhanov 1900.

The stunned *Rabochee delo* team drafted an 'answer to Plekhanov' and tacked it on to their previous 'answer to Akselrod', thus creating an eighty-page pamphlet. Angrily referring to 'Mr. Plekhanov' instead of 'comrade Plekhanov' throughout the pamphlet (it is hard to convey just how insulting this usage is), Krichevskii (the drafter of the *Rabochee delo* response) pointed out that Prokopovich's outlook had been rejected by the younger members of the Union as soon as they understood what it was. Not entirely without cause, Krichevskii attributed the aggressiveness of the old guard to their loss of organisational power within the Union. Anyone who knows of Lenin's later campaign against *Rabochee delo* will find it odd to read Krichevskii's pamphlet and to see the author of *Tasks* – that is, the still anonymous Lenin – treated by *Rabochee delo* as an almost unimpeachable authority and as a weapon in the fight against Plekhanov and friends.[26] Thus, in the space of a year, a parenthetical remark about a pamphlet with which both parties expressed agreement had led to an all-out war and mutual excommunication.

Later in 1900, Krichevskii wrote an article explaining the *Rabochee delo* position in a way that I believe was meant to be conciliatory and to focus attention on fundamental agreement rather than tactical disagreements. The article clearly reveals Krichevskii's Erfurtian outlook – indeed, through selective quotation I could make Krichevskii out to be a forerunner of *Iskra*-ism. Consider the final sentences of the article:

> Only the political education of the proletariat will guarantee the success of the struggle for freedom and only freedom will guarantee the success in the further struggle of the proletariat for its final liberation, for socialism.
>
> Working ceaselessly in this direction, the Social-Democratic Party of Russia, as in the West, fuses in actual fact with the fighting proletariat and forges in the crucible of class struggle the mighty hammer that will smash to dust the chains of the autocracy.[27]

Krichevskii's conception of the 'fusion' process was the standard Erfurtian vision of the spread of awareness. Social-Democratic organisations should act as 'the leader/guides and the teachers, as the purposive vanguard (advanced detachment)' of the worker masses.[28] The job of these advanced detachments

---

[26] Krichevskii 1900.
[27] Krichevskii in *Rabochee delo*, No. 7 (August 1900), p. 22.
[28] Krichevskii in *Rabochee delo*, No. 7 (August 1900), pp. 8–10.

was to bring insight and organisation to the worker movement. Anyone who did not accept the basic task of 'accelerating the transition from a *stikhiinyi* mass movement to a purposive class movement' was no Social Democrat.[29] The leadership role of Social Democracy did not stop at the boundaries of the worker movement. Eventually, the Social Democrats should conduct their agitation on the basis of political issues that had no direct link to economic struggle or immediate reward – issues that concerned the proletariat only in its capacity as 'the advanced detachment of the entire oppressed people in its struggle with the autocracy'.

Krichevskii advanced his soon-to-be notorious 'stages theory' *within* this Erfurtian framework. Workers advanced to political class awareness through a series of predictable stages. The first and lowest stage was 'purely economic agitation'. Next was political agitation still strongly tied to immediate economic interests. Then came agitation still linked to economic interests but intended to show how the wider political planks in the Social-Democratic platform (for example, political freedom) were necessary for economic struggle. Finally, came political agitation not tied to economic interests but, rather, to the proletariat's role as leader of the people. At this stage, political agitation should 'embrace without exception all questions of social-political life', since everything affects the class interests of the proletariat. (Recall that this definition of political agitation was written before the appearance of *Iskra*.)

Krichevskii quickly emphasised that he did not advocate waiting until all or even a majority of workers understood the need for political agitation. The pace should not be set by the unaware elements among the workers. The transition to full political agitation was possible wherever 'the mass had already pushed forth an advanced detachment of fighters'. Nevertheless, a certain gradualness or step-by-step-ness [*postepennost'*] was called for, not as an opportunistic muffling of final aims but as a 'paedagogical' device that allowed adaptation to the low level of the average Russian worker.[30]

These are the basic contours of the notorious 'stages theory'. This theory cannot usefully be called economism or even 'moderate economism'. On all fundamental questions, Krichevskii and Lenin stood on one side, while the *Credo* and the *Rabochaia mysl* editorialists stood on the other. Krichevskii did

---

[29] Krichevskii in *Rabochee delo*, No. 7 (August 1900), p. 2.
[30] Krichevskii in *Rabochee delo*, No. 7 (August 1900), p. 18.

not argue that the Social Democrats should wait until the workers themselves worked out this or that interest. He wanted a vigorous, activist Social Democracy to bring socialist ideas to the worker movement. What he did advocate was a 'paedagogical' approach to bringing these ideas. And, in some sense, no one could deny that such an approach was necessary. Agitation that did not take the existing outlook of the workers into account was bound to fail.

Krichevskii wanted to use his stages theory in order to chill the fervent crusaders against economism. Do not worry, he argued, what you see as a dangerous 'economist tendency' is just people who are still at the lower stages. In the actual movement itself, there were not two tendencies – economist and political – but rather two *stages* of one mighty struggle for worker liberation. Remember Marx's words, 'each step of actual movement is worth a dozen programmes'.[31] But Krichevskii pushed his point too far and ended up with a Pollyannish assurance that everybody would sooner or later get all the way to full political agitation without anybody prodding or criticising the local *praktiki*.

When the stages theory turned into prescriptive tactical advice that mandated passing through each stage in an invariable order (of course, as quickly as possible), it ran into further difficulties eagerly pointed out by adversaries. The insistence on 'paedagogy' – tailoring your message to suit the audience – could easily be carried to the point of confusion and even dishonesty. A political party should (both a moral 'should' and a prudential 'should') project the same message to all and sundry. It should, to use a favourite image of Lenin and others, fight under a clear and consistent banner. The 'stages' theory implied that workers in different localities, or even workers in the same locality but at different 'stages', should receive substantially different messages.[32]

Krichevskii argued that even now (1900) Social Democrats in a new locality had to start with 'purely economic agitation'.[33] Meanwhile the rise in the political temperature in Russia and the growing need for a single society-wide message from Social Democracy made this advice sound rigid and

---

[31] An earlier version of this point can be found in the answer to Plekhanov (Krichevskii 1900, pp. 46–8).

[32] For an *Iskra*-ite critique of the stages theory, see Liadov 1906, 2, pp. 174–88.

[33] Krichevskii in *Rabochee delo*, No. 7 (August 1900), pp. 13–15.

out-of-date. Workers might now be first attracted not by the economic struggle but by the growing political excitement. This objection was cogent enough that *Rabochee delo* officially retreated from Krichevskii's argument the following year.[34]

One final squabble between *Rabochee delo* and Emancipation of Labour / *Iskra* is highly instructive because it reveals the growing interdependence of the international Social-Democratic world. The imbroglio started in 1899 when a Russian (Krichevskii) wrote a set of dispatches on French affairs for the central German party newspaper *Vorwärts*. 1899 was a dramatic year in French politics and especially for socialists, because the French socialist Alexandre Millerand had accepted a ministerial post in a 'bourgeois cabinet', a cabinet that also included General Galliffet, known as 'the butcher of the Paris Commune'. Krichevskii's dispatches started a dispute that pulled in a stellar cast: Martov, Plekhanov, Kautsky, Liebknecht, Bebel, Parvus, Luxemburg, Clara Zetkin and the French socialist leaders Jules Guesde and A.M. Brache. Only Lenin seems not to have been directly involved.[35]

The dispute concerned the objectivity of Krichevskii's description of French socialism. Did he favour reformist types such as Millerand and Jean Jaurès while systematically slandering the left wing of French socialism represented by Guesde and Paul Lafargue, thus misleading German readers? Or was he properly objective? The dispute really got going in late 1901, when Martov, writing in *Zaria*, stoutly maintained the first alternative, accusing Krichevskii of 'constantly throwing filth at the representatives of French revolutionary socialism'.[36] Martov was the master of putting infuriating personal twists into his polemics, in this case with the following words: Krichevskii attacks 'the Guesdists who have grown and developed in close accord with German Social Democracy and who have always been accused by the Krichevskiis of French possibilism [= reformism] of having sold themselves to the Germans'.

*Vorwärts* responded by defending Krichevskii's objectivity. At this point, Kautsky got involved by sending a letter to *Vorwärts* that may have been

---

[34] Krichevskii signed a resolution condemning the stages theory in June 1901 (as discussed in the next section).

[35] For accounts of the scandal, see *Rabochee delo*, No. 11/12, pp. 73–80; *Zaria*, No. 4 (August 1902), pp. 105–17; Weill 1977, pp. 141–57. *Zaria* reprints the basic German interventions; Weill delineates the backstage manoeuvering with the help of archival letters.

[36] *Zaria*, No. 2–3 (December 1901), p. 405.

meant as conciliatory but came across as an intervention in favour of Martov and *Iskra* / *Zaria*. Please note, said Kautsky, that Martov did not say that *Krichevskii himself* had accused the Guesdists of selling themselves to the Germans. (Kautsky's intervention strikes me as missing the point, since Martov's remark was clearly meant to be a provocative political and personal insult to Krichevskii.)

*Vorwärts* barked at Kautsky and Kautsky responded with another, still conciliatory letter, also refuted by *Vorwärts*. Then the French socialists got involved with an article in *Le Socialiste* by the Guesdist A.M. Brache, attacking Krichevskii and claiming that Kautsky had sided with Martov. Martov prepared his own lengthy proof of his charges but *Vorwärts* refused to print it unless Martov removed all his documentation, on the grounds that German readers were not interested in such details. Martov and his lieutenant Fyodor Dan looked up Rosa Luxemburg, who passed them on to Bebel. Luxemburg was opposed to Krichevskii on this particular issue but she also made clear that she disdained the polemical methods of Plekhanov and Co.

Meanwhile, one German party member showed himself very interested in the details of the dispute. In his Munich publication *Aus der Weltpolitik*, Parvus wrote a long analysis entitled 'Millerand and *Vorwärts*: A Characterisation of the Psychology of Opportunism'. Here, he made Martov's case for him by going through the Krichevskii articles in search of compromising phrases. Parvus's aim was to point to a growing split in the *German* Party between an opportunist *Vorwärts* and a more radical provincial press. Parvus also claimed that, before his recent death, Wilhelm Liebknecht had been dissatisfied with the Krichevskii reportage.[37]

*Vorwärts* finally printed an abridged version of Martov's letter in February 1902 and allowed Krichevskii a very detailed refutation. Krichevskii thus had the last word in the German press. The last issue of *Zaria* in August 1902 allowed Martov the final Russian word.

Behind the scenes, we see the Russians desperately trying to get influential comrades involved in their dispute. Krichevskii writes to Kautsky about 'a method and tone of "polemic" hitherto unknown in the Russian revolutionary literature, a polemic directed by the other party against my organisation and

---

[37] The article by Parvus was republished in *Zaria*, No. 4 (August 1902), pp. 105–17.

my person'.[38] Plekhanov writes to Guesde asking for an open letter accusing Krichevskii of bias. 'This is in the interest of the French Worker Party as well as our party. We should seize the occasion to *écraser l'infame*. So, my friend, help us out, strike and strike hard.' (Guesde wrote no letter but, as noted previously, the French socialists did intervene.)

Besides documenting the enormous personal and political bitterness between the two factions, this episode can be interpreted in a number of ways. For Russians – as emphasised by Lenin in the first chapter of WITBD – the contretemps revealed the growing internationalisation of the basic revolutionary/opportunist split. Guesde vs. Millerand in France, Parvus vs. *Vorwärts* in Germany, Martov vs. Krichevskii in Russia – were not the fault lines basically the same in all cases, and did not the participants recognise this and side naturally with the foreign comrades closest to them? In a way, Krichevskii agreed with this, when he compared the dictatorial and intolerant *Iskra* faction to the equally intolerant Guesde party: both of these factions constituted the real stumbling blocks to the socialist unity that was so vitally necessary.[39]

Another view was taken by *Vorwärts* when it dismissed the whole affair as a squabble by the incomprehensibly factional Russians, especially those who were eager to discredit themselves on the international stage by accusing the central SPD party organ of systematic bias. Insofar as *Vorwärts* could distinguish between the Russian groups, it particularly disliked the scandal-mongering *Iskra*-ites.

## A divisive attempt at unity

We have now arrived at the events of 1901 that form the immediate background to WITBD. The appearance of *Iskra* in late 1900 obviously changed the nature of the debate between the two factions. Even more crucial were 'the spring events' of February/March 1901, in which workers came out on the streets in support of student protests. These events were widely interpreted as

---

[38] Weill 1977, p. 149.
[39] Krichevskii 1901 in *Rabochee delo*, No. 10 (September 1901) (that is, before Martov's original attack). Krichevskii's comment seems to show that he was, indeed, opposed to the Guesdists.

marking a new phase for both the Russian worker movement and the anti-tsarist liberation movement.

From the beginning, *Iskra* had defined itself partly in opposition to *Rabochee delo*. In the statement issued in 1900 to announce the new publication, the editors claimed that *Rabochee delo* was utterly incorrect to dismiss the *Credo* and *Rabochaia mysl* as isolated and unrepresentative of any actual trend in the Russian worker movement.[40] In the first issue of the new newspaper, a short notice announced *Iskra*'s intention to side with the Emancipation of Labour group against *Rabochee delo*. *Iskra* did not deny 'the contribution made by *Rabochee delo* which has put in a great deal of work in publishing literature and organising its distribution'. Nonetheless, *Rabochee delo* defended a profoundly mistaken tactic of passing over in silence the extremism of some economist statements and abstaining from open struggle with them. *Iskra* sided with Plekhanov in his fight against 'unsteadiness of thought'.[41] Both these items were drafted by Lenin. Plekhanov was irritated by the single compliment paid to *Rabochee delo* and tried to get it removed.

The most extensive attack on *Rabochee delo* came in the first issue of the sister journal *Zaria* (April 1901) in the form of a long article by David Riazanov on the *Rabochee delo* programme issued in 1899. This was a project worthy of Riazanov's world-class nit-picking talents: the *Rabochee delo* programme is no more than a couple of pages, Riazanov's article is eighteen densely packed pages. The aim was to show that *Rabochee delo* was 'eclectic'. The flavour of the analysis can be illustrated by Riazanov's crusade against 'not only . . . but also'.

The *Rabochee delo* programme stated:

> The activity [of Russian Social Democracy] can be effective only under the condition, first, that it is guided *not only* by the general principles of scientific socialism *but also* by the concrete relations between social classes in Russia and the essential needs of the Russian worker movement at a given degree of its development and, second, that it takes into account the variety of local conditions and the level of development of the different strata of the worker class.[42]

---

[40] This statement was drafted by Lenin; see Lenin 1958–65, 4, p. 356.
[41] Lenin, 1958–65, 4, pp. 384–5.
[42] *Zaria*, No. 1 (April 1901), p. 119. Emphasis added.

At first glance, you or I might think this is mildly boring boilerplate. On second glance, we might see that the second condition is a defence of the stages theory. But Riazanov zeroed in on the first condition in order to show that the wording 'not only . . . but also' was far from innocent.

First, did not the whole point of scientific socialism consist in its claim to be guided precisely by 'the concrete relations between classes'? If *Rabochee delo* meant specifically Russian conditions, why state it in the form of a contrast? Riazanov suggested a motive. Populists had long accused Social Democrats (especially the Emancipation of Labour group) of uncritically transferring abstract Marxist principles to Russian soil and, nowadays, Social-Democratic *praktiki* also complained of the 'doctrinairism' of the Emancipation of Labour programme. *Rabochee delo* wished to avoid such reproaches, saying in effect '*we* (unlike some others we could name) want to take into account Russian conditions'. But this would only make sense if there was a Social-Democratic group that did *not* want to take into account Russian conditions. Was *Rabochee delo* suggesting there existed such a group?[43]

This kind of attack was just a 'same old, same old' continuation of earlier polemics. *Rabochee delo* was still not itself accused of economism, but only of not grasping the need to fight against it. This polemical context was sharply changed by the evidence of worker militancy displayed in the 'spring events' of 1901. Both factions were highly enthusiastic about these events. *Iskra* claimed that they vindicated its own stand. As Martov wrote in May 1901:

> The active participation of the workers in the political demonstrations of the stormy month gives these demonstrations a completely special significance and inaugurates a new epoch in Russian history. . . .
>
> We, the advocates of the revolutionary political struggle of the proletariat, can celebrate: the Russian proletariat has proved to its near-sighted friends the correctness of the point of view that we have defended. Ignoring its [Social-Democratic] leader/guides, the proletariat threw itself into battle when it saw that the radical section of society was ready to take on the government in a serious way.[44]

---

[43] *Zaria*, No. 1 (April 1901), pp. 119–20 (see p. 122 of this article for a comment on the stages theory). *Rabochee delo* may have had the last laugh because Riazanov later devoted a whole book to tearing apart *Iskra*'s own draft for a party programme.

[44] *Iskra*, No. 3 (April 1901), lead article 'Stormy Month'. The article says that Social Democrats in Kiev and Kharkov did play some role in guiding proletarian protest.

*Iskra*'s positive reaction paled before *Rabochee delo*'s excitement. Krichevskii and his team thought that these events would go down in history in the way that Bloody Sunday in January 1905 did in actual fact, namely, as the signal for the beginning of open revolution. They issued a special leaflet in April entitled 'Historical Turning-Point' in which they announced the events had transformed the country with 'the unstoppable strength of a natural force [*stikhiia*]'. The Social-Democratic committees had been caught flat-footed and were forced to catch up with the workers who were 'qualitatively transformed' and thirsting for action. No doubt the proletarian masses were not yet fully purposive, but revolutionary *feeling* was the most important indication of their political maturity. Therefore, the Social Democrats should *radically change* (these words emphasised in the original text) their tactics, following Liebknecht's advice: 'if circumstances change in twenty-four hours, then we must change our tactics in twenty-four hours'. In particular, the Social Democrats must rethink the question of terror, since 'the *white terror* of the tsarist government will again, with the unstoppable force of a law of nature, create the soil for a *red terror* of the revolutionaries'. We must be prepared to meet force with force, answer blood with blood.

In concrete terms, the *Rabochee delo* leaflet called upon local committees to organise further street demonstrations, to summon *all* revolution-minded sections of society into active support, and make the coming May Day demonstrations into a signal for revolution. The leaflet ended with these ringing words:

At the present time, only one thing is reasonable: audacity!

Let us remember that the revolution casts away those who do not recognise from afar its fateful stride. Go to meet it, comrades, and you will speed its steps!

This is a new and – for the first time – a mass storming of the fortress of despotism. Assemble in serried ranks for the storming!

*Our* Bastille is not yet destroyed, but the storming of it has already begun. Hurry to place yourselves in the front ranks of the columns of this storming![45]

---

[45] *Rabochee delo*, 1901. The expression 'blood for blood' can be found in an earlier issue of *Listok 'Rabochee delo'*.

I could easily take out selected passages from this leaflet and pass them off as the excited rhetoric of Lenin and others in 1905. Unfortunately, it was still 1901. *Rabochee delo* called the revolution and nobody came. *Iskra's* cold response was: *you* may change your tactics at a moment's notice, but *we* have always said that strengthening Social-Democratic organisations and their political orientation was our first task. You ask too much of a movement that is still barely organised. Not hysterical cries for terror but 'extreme caution' is required. And are not the economist currents *you* refused to attack responsible for our lack of organisation? A historical turning-point indeed – a shift of 180 degrees by people without any firm principles.[46]

Viktor Chernov noted with some bemusement that the spring events had knocked the moderate, eclectic, half-and-half elements of Social Democracy – elements that had found themselves a home in *Rabochee delo* – for a loop. The good grey 'centre' had bounded all the way to the extreme Left of Social Democracy, leaving *Iskra* and *Zaria* behind. Perhaps *Iskra* described this surprising evolution in excessively uncomradely terms – hysterical nerves, lack of firm principles, and the like – but *Iskra's* attack did not misrepresent the facts.[47]

The result of *Rabochee delo's* unexpected lurch to the left was thus that the journal ended up looking rather foolish. Its vulnerability may account for the next unexpected lurch, when it decided to join in a common organisation with *Iskra*. I do not know *Rabochee delo's* motivation for this decision. Perhaps there was pressure from its constituency in Russia to end the émigré dispute now that the spring events had removed earlier sources of friction. What is important for us, spectators of the feud, is the resolution on principles signed by both parties at a preliminary conference in June 1901 in Geneva. This resolution – an important programmatic statement in its own right – represents a full victory for *Iskra* on the disputed issues.[48]

The Geneva resolution could be described as a programmatic contract signed by both *Rabochee delo* and *Iskra*, although *Rabochee delo* later tried to

---

[46] *Iskra*, No. 4 (May 1901), articles by Martov and Lenin (the words 'extreme caution' come from Martov).

[47] *Nakanune*, No. 33 (September 1901), p. 400.

[48] The text of this resolution can be found in Martynov 1901b and *Kommunisticheskaia partiia . . . v rezoliutsiiakh* 1983, pp. 37–8.

back out. This is how Lenin treats it in his account of *Iskra*'s 1901 conflict with *Rabochee delo* that he wrote up as an appendix to WITBD. This account shows Lenin's lawyerly training – it is a cool, calm, and persuasive brief, in contrast to much of the ideological polemics directed against *Rabochee delo* in the main body of WITBD itself. (I have placed my translation of Lenin's account as an appendix to the present chapter.)

The Geneva resolution was clearly drafted with the intention of leaving *Rabochee delo* no loopholes. The first paragraph committed *Rabochee delo* to join the war against opportunism:

> Recognising the basic principles of scientific socialism and acting in solidarity with international revolutionary Social Democracy, we reject any attempt to introduce opportunism into the class movement of the proletariat, as expressed in so-called economism, Bernsteinism and Millerandism.[49]

Several other formulations were aimed against the stages theory. The signatories rejected the idea that 'Social Democracy can set forth general political tasks in its agitational activity only after the proletariat has gone through preliminary stages of an exclusively economic struggle and of a struggle for partial political demands'. Rather, the urgency of the task of overthrowing the autocracy should 'not for a minute' be dropped from view in all organisational and agitational activity.

On organisational questions, the resolution reads:

> Recognising that, in its relation to the elementary forms of the manifestation of the class movement of the proletariat, Social Democracy must always be a force for moving forward, we for this very reason consider as important for the movement to criticise currents that elevate elementarity and elevate the narrowness that elementarity imparts to these lower forms into a principle of socialist activity.[50]

'Lower forms' of organisation are non-party (or better, pre-party) worker organisations such as strike funds and mutual assistance societies, while party

---

[49] Martynov 1901b, p. 4.

[50] Martynov 1901b, p. 5. I apologise for 'elementarity [*elementar'nost'*]', but luckily the word occurs only here. This clause in the resolution is the embryonic form of the catch-phrase 'kow-towing to *stikhiinost'*' that plays such a role in WITBD.

organisations are the desired higher forms. *Iskra* also proposed a clause condemning the terror tactic but *Rabochee delo* abstained until a proposed unity congress scheduled for the autumn considered the issue.

Lenin seems to have regarded the Geneva conference in June with a mixture of wariness and optimism, judging from a letter of May in which he asks Akselrod to give speedy consent to the conference. Lenin recounts a conversation with Riazanov who had played an important mediating role in setting up the conference:

> In relation to a rapprochement with the Union [*Rabochee delo*'s parent organisation], Riazanov at first announced that he put absolutely no hopes on the conference. . . . But when he found out that we did not make the destruction of the Union a *conditio sine qua non,* that side by side with a scientific journal (*Zaria*) and a political newspaper (*Iskra*) we are ready to concede a popular collection or journal for workers (*Rabochee delo*) – then he definitely changed direction and announced that he had already talked about this a long time ago to Krichevskii and that he considered this a natural finale to the dispute and that he himself was ready to work for the implementation of a such a project. Let him work! Perhaps a unification *or federation* will actually take place on this basis – this would indeed be a giant step forward.

Nevertheless, Lenin cautioned against letting one's guard down:

> Our desire to speed up [the scheduling of] the conference is really to be explained by the fact that it would be more advantageous to us to get it over quickly so as to begin our own organisation sooner and, in case of a break, have time to prepare for a decisive war against the Union. And [such a] war would probably be shifted to Russia as well this summer.[51]

---

[51] Lenin 1958–65, 46, pp. 109–12 (letter of 25 May 1901). A peep into the workshop of our Lenin scholars: in his account of this episode, Jonathan Frankel describes Lenin as acting in deliberate bad faith and with the full intention of making the conference fail. As proof, he cites this very letter. He leaves out the first quoted paragraph entirely. In his quotation of the second paragraph, Frankel replaced the words 'in case of a break' by an ellipsis. Frankel probably did not consciously distort Lenin's letter. Since Lenin was obviously a cynical manipulator, his words expressing hope and approval must be a fake. And if they are a fake, why burden the reader with the useless knowledge of their existence? (Frankel 1969, p. 51.)

Fortunately, we have direct memoir evidence of what was transpiring on the *Rabochee delo* side after the Geneva conference. Martynov had emigrated to Berlin in late 1900. He faced a difficult choice deciding between *Iskra* and *Rabochee delo*. On the one hand, he opposed economism and thought that *Rabochee delo* was too soft on this issue. On the other hand, he sided with *Rabochee delo* on organisational questions and resented *Iskra*'s splitting tactics. He wrote an article for *Rabochee delo* in which he opposed the stages theory. When this article was accepted, he consented (his expression) to join the editorial board of *Rabochee delo*. The rest of the story can be told in his own words:

> My attempts to restore health to the Union [*Rabochee delo*'s parent organisation] and to galvanise its corpse suffered a complete failure. It led only to a severe worsening of relations between me and the *Iskra*-ites. When I learned while lying in my hospital bed that an agreement had been concluded in Geneva at a conference of the *Iskra*-ites and the *Rabochee delo* people, I mutinied and demanded a review of the agreement. At my insistence *Rabochee delo* entered into polemics with *Iskra*. In our journal were placed two anti-*Iskra* articles by me and Krichevskii – these two articles, by the way, were completely at odds with each other, something possible only with such a 'democratic' editorial board as that of *Rabochee delo*.
>
> At the second, Zurich, conference between the *Rabochee delo* people and the *Iskra*-ites, the *Rabochee delo* people, at my insistence, did not put the notorious 'stages theory' into their platform but contented themselves with other corrections to the Geneva agreement. The *Iskra*-ites rejected all the corrections and declared war on us – a war that ended with our defeat. A particularly devastating blow against us came from Lenin's book *What Is to Be Done?*.[52]

As we learn from this account, the third lurch of the year for *Rabochee delo* was the decision to pull out of the proposed union with *Iskra*. But how was this to be accomplished? If *Rabochee delo* simply announced that it had reconsidered, it would confirm every prejudice against it: eclectic, acting without principles, prone to making turns of 180 degrees. Better to fix the

---

[52] Martynov 1989, p. 528. The *Iskra* delegation actually accepted one or two of the proposed corrections.

onus of the split on *Iskra*. This could be accomplished by making demands that were certain to be unacceptable to *Iskra*. But even this had to be done with care. *Rabochee delo* had all along insisted there was no *principled* division between itself and *Iskra*. Furthermore, *Rabochee delo* had recently signed on to the Geneva resolution. So differences had to be found that were serious enough to justify making changes to the terms of the Geneva resolution – changes calculated to provoke *Iskra* to walk out of the unity congress.

Such, I surmise, was the calculation of *Rabochee delo*. (NB: I would not feel justified in making this kind of speculation if we did not have Martynov's direct avowal that *Rabochee delo* fully intended to torpedo the proposed union.) If so, it helps explain certain aspects of *Rabochee delo*'s next move. First, Martynov and Krichevskii wrote long articles lambasting *Iskra* on every page in angry terms and then piously ending with a statement that there was no reason why the two organisations could not work together.[53]

Second, *Rabochee delo* knew perfectly well that its suggested changes to the Geneva resolution would act as a red flag. For example, it asked that the words 'so-called economism' and 'Millerandism' be removed from the first paragraph cited earlier. Justification? The terms were excessively vague. Of course, *Rabochee delo* was against economism properly defined, but other parts of the resolution made this point without using the actual term – so there was no need to condemn 'economism' in so many words. *Rabochee delo* also proposed to remove the words 'not for a minute' from the injunction to make anti-tsarist revolution a priority. These words sounded too much like giving orders.[54] Such was *Rabochee delo*'s explicit justification for the proposed changes. But, given the polemical context – *Iskra*'s long-held suspicion that *Rabochee delo* was likely to waffle on these very points – *Rabochee delo* knew perfectly well that these changes were unacceptable.

If I have read the *Rabochee delo* strategy correctly, then, in the short run, it succeeded admirably. The *Iskra*-ite delegation to the unity congress in October in Zurich refused the changes and then walked out of the congress. The Zurich congress briefly brought together all the principal actors in the mini-drama we have been exploring, so we are lucky to have a detailed account by the

---

[53] Martynov 1901a and Krichevskii 1901 (these two articles are discussed in detail below).

[54] Martynov 1901b.

young *Iskra*-ite Liubov Akselrod, which I reproduce here.[55] She begins her story with a preliminary caucus meeting of the *Iskra*-ites just prior to the congress itself. Only after arriving in Zurich did the *Iskra*-ites become aware of the anti-*Iskra* articles in *Rabochee delo* that had just come off the press, so the caucus had to hurriedly decide on a response.

> The conversation [among us] took place without chairman and without secretary, in comradely style, without formalities.
>
> The subject was the programme of the congress and of the position that we revolutionary Social Democrats should take at the upcoming congress. Lenin stood for a final break with the 'economists'. It was his strong conviction that the 'economists' had started down the path of revisionism, so that working together with them seemed to him completely impossible. He supported his position by pointing to the lead articles in *Rabochee delo* [No. 10]. *Rabochee delo*-style opportunism had now received a theoretical illumination and there was a pressing necessity to conduct a determined battle with it.
>
> Lenin's position was shared by P.B. Akselrod and V.I. Zasulich. Georgii Valentinovich [Plekhanov] defended the opposite point of view. He stood for union with the 'economists', pointing to the necessity of such a union in the struggle against the threatening danger coming from reviving populism [that is, the beginnings of the Socialist Revolutionary Party]. This consideration prompted him to advise concessions, of course, not principled ones. Martov and I supported Plekhanov. These differences of opinion, however, did not cause any irritation among the disputing parties. The whole conversation went off extremely peacefully and, as far as I remember, no final decision was made at the caucus.

At first, the caucus assumed that Plekhanov would be the *Iskra* speaker, but Plekhanov insisted on Lenin.

> The congress opened on the morning of the next day (4 October). The floor was given to Lenin. Lenin's report was elaborate and well thought out; his positions followed logically one after the other; the material and facts were

---

[55] As far as I know, Liubov Akselrod is no relation to Pavel Akselrod. Her account is in Lenin 1926–35, 4, pp. 592–4. Her remarks are not dated but they presumably were written in the 1920s.

selected to hit the opponents at vulnerable spots. He spoke with a great deal of spirit, freely but controlled, with conviction and in a business-like fashion, sometimes repeating and emphasising significant words. He clearly influenced the audience and carried it with him completely. Our opponents got angrier and angrier as he talked, as could be seen by the expressions on the faces of their leaders. Our side, in contrast, listened with great satisfaction and enthusiasm. The 'veterans' were especially enthusiastic: Akselrod, Zasulich, Plekhanov.

Lenin was answered by one of the editors of *Rabochee delo*, the theorist of their point of view, the well-known émigré B. Krichevskii. Generally speaking Krichevskii was not a bad orator at all, he spoke clearly, energetically and insistently, with an appropriate fund of facts at his disposal. But Lenin's great and obvious success threw him off his stride and ripped apart his prepared remarks. Krichevskii alternated between speaking with apathy and speaking with excessive and unnatural pathos, and in the final analysis he pushed his revisionist position to its extreme limit. His speech was a total failure. The success of one side and the failure of the other irritated the 'Union' people even more. Even at this first session the atmosphere was strained to the limit: the inevitable schism had clearly matured.

Later sessions did not improve matters, rather, they intensified the antagonism of the two points of view. Of the speakers that followed Lenin only Martov's highly excited speech stood out. G.V. Plekhanov and P.B. Akselrod limited themselves to a few minor remarks and abstained from giving speeches, since they reckoned that it made sense to leave the struggle with the 'economists' to comrades who had more recently emigrated from Russia, since the economists ceaselessly accused the Emancipation of Labour group of dogmatism and explained this dogmatism by its isolation from Russian reality.[56]

On the morning of the second day on the congress, after the *Iskra*-ites received the proposed corrections to the Geneva resolution, they called a short break, huddled together, came back to read a short statement, and walked out.

Judging from Krupskaya's much briefer account, both Martov and Plekhanov got into the spirit of things at this congress. She tells us that 'Martov got completely carried away . . . he even tore off his necktie – it was the first time

---

[56] Lenin 1926–35, 4, pp. 592–4.

I had seen him like this'. She also reports that 'Plekhanov was in an excellent mood, since the foe that he had been compelled to fight for so long was now on the ropes. Plekhanov was happy and talkative'.[57]

In the long run, as Martynov noted in his memoir, the *Rabochee delo* strategy backfired in a big way. Martynov's account puts neither himself nor Krichevskii in a good light. Krichevskii comes across as someone who had lost any sense of direction or firm leadership. As for Martynov himself, he does not seem to realise that his strategy, far from galvanising *Rabochee delo*, gave it the *coup de grâce*. As we shall see in the following sections, his claim to be a foe of economism in contrast to Krichevskii is paradoxical in more than one way.

We have now reached the point where we can look directly at the notorious articles in *Rabochee delo*, No. 10 by Krichevskii and Martynov that play such a central role in the polemical economy of WITBD. Each article mounted a broadside against *Iskra* and each buttressed its attack with reasoning of a 'theoretical' nature. The two articles present a somewhat similar critique of *Iskra*. Nevertheless, the theoretical superstructures erected by Martynov and Krichevskii were 'completely at odds with each other', as Martynov truly remarked in his memoir account.[58] We shall discuss the articles in turn.

## Boris Krichevskii's article in No. 10

*Tolkuiut o stikhiinosti*. They consider, they talk about, *stikhiinost*. Thus Lenin introduces one of the most famous passages in WITBD. But 'they' were *not* talking about *stikhiinost*. Neither the word nor the concept was on the polemical agenda in 1901. Not 'they', but 'he' – Boris Krichevskii in *Rabochee delo*, No. 10.[59]

---

[57] Krupskaya 1969, 1, p. 249. Basing themselves on the account given by Martov, some scholars have assumed a serious disagreement between Plekhanov, Martov and Lenin about how to deal with *Rabochee delo*. Martov wrote his account in 1919 without access to documents and, consequently, makes chronological mistakes in his description of these events. He also has an anachronistic description of *Rabochee delo*, No. 10 as a criticism of Lenin's organisational ideas. Nevertheless, nothing in Martov's account contradicts Liubov Akselrod's assertion that the dispute was a momentary and purely tactical difference. Note that the first two printed sallies against the articles in *Rabochee delo*, No. 10 came in *Iskra* articles by Martov and Plekhanov immediately after the abortive unity congress. Martov's account is in *Istoriia Rossiiskoi Sotsial-Demokratii*, reprinted in Martov 2000, pp. 53–5.

[58] Martynov 1989, p. 528.

[59] Krichevskii 1901; Lenin *PSS*, 6, p. 40 [710].

Judging from WITBD, we naturally assume that *stikhiinost* – especially when translated 'spontaneity' – has something to do with the worker movement by itself and without Social-Democratic help, or with *tred-iunionism*, or with economic struggle. After all, Krichevskii is an economist, albeit a 'moderate' one, is he not? But Krichevskii's polemical use of the word has *nothing to do* with any of these things. Krichevskii's focus is entirely on proper party leadership of purely 'political' explosions such as the worker demonstrations in spring 1901 in support of the students. Underneath all the abstractions about *stikhiinost* lies the concrete argument that *Rabochee delo*'s reaction to the spring events was more revolutionary than *Iskra*'s coldness and caution.

Krichevskii's attack on *Iskra* from the left is not inconsistent with his 'stages' theory. After all, the theory defined the final and highest stage as political protest that was not tied to any economic or immediate self-interest. Krichevskii now felt that this final stage had commenced in Russia. Of course, in his defence of the leaflet 'Historical Turning-Point' and its call for immediate action, Krichevskii was playing with a weak hand. Not only had no further demonstrations followed, but Krichevskii himself emphasised that the local committees had been caught off guard and were hardly prepared for immediate action. He nevertheless stoutly maintained that 'we *carried out our revolutionary duty* when we took the attitude toward the [spring] events as if they must be the *immediate prologue to revolution*'.[60]

Let us recall the polemics of spring 1901. In April, *Rabochee delo* published 'Historical Turning-Point' in which it heralded the worker demonstrations as a prelude to immediate revolution. Lenin and Martov poured cold water on this enthusiasm in *Iskra* articles in May. By signing the Geneva resolution in June, Krichevskii seemed to admit defeat in this battle.

When seeking to reopen the battle in September, Krichevskii's eye fell on Lenin's May article. Here Lenin not only criticised *Rabochee delo* but set forth *Iskra*'s own 'plan' for the Social-Democratic movement. In the following remark by Lenin, Krichevskii thought he saw a vulnerable point, a clue to the weakness of *Iskra*'s outlook. Lenin's use of *stikhiinyi* in this passage illustrates yet another vernacular connotation of this word: a *stikhiinyi* explosion is an unplanned, chaotic, sudden, surprising and unstoppably powerful event:

---

[60] Krichevskii 1901, p. 17 (Krichevskii's emphasis).

We have spoken all the while only of systematic and plan-like [*planomernyi*] preparation, but in no way do we wish to imply by this that the autocracy can fall exclusively from a correctly executed siege or from an organised storming. Such an attitude would be absurd doctrinairism. On the contrary, it is fully possible and historically much more likely that the autocracy will fall under the pressure of one of those *stikhiinyi* explosions or unexpected political complications that constantly threaten it from all sides.

But no political party, unless it falls into adventurism, can base its activity solely on the expectation of such explosions and complications. We must travel along our own path, carrying out our systematic work without deviation, and the less we base our calculations on unexpected occurrences, the greater the possibility that no 'historical turning-point' will catch us flat-footed.[61]

Krichevskii did not disagree with the substance of Lenin's remark. In fact, his point was this: if *Iskra* finds it necessary to say something so obvious, does not this show that *Iskra* usually neglects the *stikhiinyi* aspect of things? Is not its 'pale, semi-pessimistic' reaction to the spring events proof positive of this failing?

Lenin had praised the firmness of *Iskra*'s 'plan' and contrasted it favourably with *Rabochee delo*'s 'Historical Turning-Point'. For Krichevskii, Lenin's contrast revealed the rigidity that *Iskra* had inherited from the Emancipation of Labour. *Iskra* was in love with dogma, cut off from Russian life and without any 'flair for real life' in its reaction to unexpected events. Instead, it tried to impose its lifeless abstractions on the living movement. Krichevskii dressed up this old accusation – disastrously, as it turned out – in some fancy talk about underlying 'tactical philosophies', using Lenin's words 'tactical plan' as a springboard. *Iskra* believed in 'tactics-as-plan' while *Rabochee delo* believed in 'tactics-as-process' (something that looked suspiciously like the officially repudiated stages theory).[62]

The accusation of rigid and arrogant doctrinairism runs through all of Krichevskii's specific charges:

*Iskra* insists that in the solution of tactical issues, 'the opinion of theorists' must dominate over 'the practical experience of struggle'.

---

[61] Lenin 1958–65, 5, p. 13.
[62] Krichevskii 1901 (*taktika–plan* vs. *taktika–protsess*).

*Iskra* refuses to acknowledge that *all* currents within international Social Democracy – 'including the most extreme Bernsteinians' – genuinely represent proletarian class interests. Instead, it emulates the Guesde faction in France that rejected freedom of criticism within the party. (The contretemps over Krichevskii's correspondence from France had not yet broken out.)

*Iskra* refuses to admit the valuable preparatory work done by local committees during the years 1898–1901.

*Iskra* refuses to 'answer force with force', a necessary tactic in revolutionary times. It claimed that the question of terror had been decided long ago.

> Here [in regard to the question of terror] the doctrinaire attitude toward tactics, the disdain for concrete circumstances of the struggle, goes to extreme lengths – to the downright unbelievable arrogance of imposing on party organisations a 'decision' on tactical questions, made by a group of émigré writers over fifteen years ago, when the Party still had no hint of existence![63]

Finally, *Iskra* does not see that the unification and creation of central institutions for a *mass* party with ties to the workers – as opposed to a conspiratorial party – could only be carried out *from below* (that is, at the initiative of the local committees).

But – unexpectedly concludes Krichevskii – we are only talking here of differing 'shades' of opinion and so there is no reason we cannot work together.

I will quote some extended excerpts from Krichevskii's article in order to document his use of the term *stikhiinost*. Given the crucial importance of Lenin's counter-formulations, paraphrase would be inappropriate. The passages will also illustrate Krichevskii's style of argument.

The following passage is intended to lay the groundwork for Krichevskii's attack on *Iskra*'s 'tactical philosophy' and to show that 'tactics-as-plan' 'contradicts the basic spirit of Marxism'. This passage is also useful because it shows how *stikhiinost* could be used in a retelling of the merger narrative. The passage also illustrates Krichevskii's Erfurtian credentials since it is clearly based closely on Kautsky's *Erfurt Programme*:

> From the time when socialism fused with the worker movement – that is, from the time of the emergence of Social Democracy as the political class organisation of the proletariat – programmatic principles on the one hand and tactics on the other separated themselves out step by step into two

---

[63] Krichevskii 1901, pp. 24–5.

distinct categories in the awareness of socialists. In the earliest period of the [mutually] isolated existence of utopian socialism in its various guises [vs.] the *stikhiinyi* worker movement, this differentiation did not exist.

For utopian socialism, the achievement of the final aim was not a *process of struggle* that took place according to certain social laws in specific social conditions, but rather a *sudden act* that occurred either as the result of the good will of the ruling classes or else (in the case of the '*stikhiinyi*' socialism of worker utopians and old-style Blanquists) the result of a successful uprising or plot. Where there is no process of struggle and no militant class, there can be no tactics in the wide, present-day meaning of the term, in the sense of adapting one's entire activity to concrete circumstances in the interests of achieving the final aim – in the sense of working out new forms of struggle that correspond to the growth of the militant class and its final struggle. *Principles devour tactics.*

On the other hand, a *stikhiinyi* worker movement or even a trade-union [*sindikal'noe*] movement that is purposive but isolated from socialism (the English worker unions) – one that has no purposive final aim, no programme in the precise sense of the word – such a movement acts haphazardly, from day to day, guided only by the tangible conditions of achieving the most urgent small-scale aim. It continually and non-purposively sacrifices the solid and general successes of the future for the ephemeral and partial success of the current day. In this case, therefore, *tactics devour principles.*

I cited these extreme cases in a somewhat 'sharpened' aspect in order to bring out my thought. Today it is impossible to find either the one or the other extreme in the ranks of international Social Democracy. (Perhaps the anarchists – who deny the minimum programme, the struggle for reforms within the framework of the existing system and thus the political struggle as well – can be thought of as the inheritors or more precisely the *remnants* of *stikhiinyi* worker socialism.)[64]

If we focus entirely on word usage, this passage seems to be somewhat contradictory. At the end of the first paragraph, 'stikhiinost' is first used to describe any *worker movement* prior to the great synthesis. It is then applied in the second paragraph with a different shade of meaning to one type of pre-synthesis *socialism*. We next learn (in the third paragraph) that even a *stikhiinyi*

---

[64] Krichevskii 1901, pp. 4–5 (the parenthesis on anarchism is a footnote in the original).

pre-synthesis worker movement can be 'purposive', a word that is usually the antonym of *stikhiinyi*. We then learn that the 'purposive' English trade-union movement has no 'purposive' final aim and continually acts in a 'non-purposive' manner. Finally, Krichevskii follows Kautsky in describing anarchism as the inheritor of *stikhiinyi* worker socialism, an inheritor that as such continues to reject the Social-Democratic synthesis.

It would be inaccurate to blame Krichevskii for these inconsistencies, since they arise from the varied connotations in the common usage of *stikhiinyi* and 'purposive'. Furthermore there is little ambiguity in Krichevskii's actual meaning. In fact – except for the final claim about the absence of extremes within international Social Democracy – this passage is uncontroversial.

After Krichevskii lays his groundwork, he proceeds to explain the difference in the respective 'tactical philosophies' of *Rabochee delo* and *Iskra*. A translation of an extensive excerpt is provided in an appendix to this chapter. In my opinion, Krichevskii's argument is very confused and haphazard – obviously the result of a last-minute theoretical improvisation. Just for that reason, I feel that my analysis here needs to be supplemented with the actual text (all quotations are from the passage translated in the appendix).

The real inspiration for Krichevskii's argument is his continuing anger about the spring events:

> What is so characteristic of *Iskra*'s doctrinairism is the fact that it could not forgive us our actively revolutionary attitude toward these events. . . . At the moment of *stikhiinyi* explosions, any revolutionary party is obliged with all its strength to try to ensure that the explosion leads to revolution and to victory.

*Iskra* not only has forgotten this responsibility but 'finds it possible to spill cascades of inky anger' on those who try their best to live up to it.

Krichevskii then makes the same point but in a more abstract, general way. He takes the phrase from Lenin's *Iskra* article about a '*stikhiinyi* explosion' and argues: *Iskra* has to *assure* people that it does not underestimate the role of *stikhiinyi* explosions because it feels, with justice, that all its talk of tactical 'plans' reveals that it *does* underestimate this role. As a matter of fact, any political revolution is inconceivable *without* a *stikhiinyi* explosion. 'The appearance of a new social order here below . . . will continue to be the result *primarily* of *stikhiinyi* explosions.'

Thus, the concrete dispute over the spring events is now represented by the formula: 'plan-like [*planomernyi*] preparation vs. *stikhiinyi* explosion'. Krichevskii now kicks the level of abstractness up another notch:

> But the immense significance that Marxism justifiably gives to purposive revolutionary work draws *Iskra* away in practice – *thanks to its doctrinaire view on tactics* – toward an *underestimation of the significance of the objective or stikhiinyi element of development.*

'*Stikhiinyi* explosion' has now become 'the objective element of development'. But what does this phrase mean? To put it another way: if *Iskra* underestimates the objective element, what does it overestimate? It seems to me that Krichevskii gives two completely opposed answers to this question.

The first answer is that *Iskra* overestimates the *subjective* element, that is, *Iskra* is similar to the conspirators from before the great synthesis. But this conclusion is highly implausible. *Iskra* is conspiratorial, first, because it proposes a tactical 'plan'. The *content* of the plan is immaterial, since merely to propose a plan is conspiratorial. *Iskra* is conspiratorial, second, because it disparages *stikhiinyi* explosions. But why must a conspirator disparage *stikhiinyi* explosions? Lenin is in fact very often called a conspirator who successfully took advantage of *stikhiinyi* explosions.

Krichevskii's other answer to the question 'what does *Iskra* overestimate?' is more surprising. Recall that 'objective element of development' is for Krichevskii a highly abstract way of saying '*stikhiinyi* explosions'. The opposite of a *stikhiinyi* explosion is a large, purposive, aware, well-organised proletariat – and *this* is what *Iskra* is overestimating.

> Social Democracy is and can only be the *purposive* movement of the proletariat fighting for its emancipation. No class has had even a remotely similar degree of clarity in its understanding of the conditions of its emancipation, of the final aim of its struggle and of the paths leading to it, as does the proletariat fighting under the banner of Social Democracy. All this is true. But scientific socialism would stop being itself, if it threw out of its calculations or in any way decreased the significance of the *stikhiinyi* element – not only in an evolutionary period (that goes without saying) but also in a time of revolution.

Even in the West, 'where the proletariat can throw on the scales of history an unparalleled force of awareness and organisation', *stikhiinyi* explosions dominate. In Russia, the organised and aware proletariat will play an even smaller role.

Thus Krichevskii. I actually think Krichevskii's last point is a good one. *Iskra*, and Lenin in particular, probably did get carried away with the image of a purposive and organised class acting as a single protagonist in a grand historical drama. But this accusation is highly inconsistent with Krichevskii's other accusation of being a conspirator. Still, by now, we should not be surprised that Krichevskii accuses *Iskra* and Lenin of being *over-optimistic* about the possibility of proletarian awareness and organisation.

I conclude that, theoretically and logically, Krichevskii's argument is an incoherent mess. On a purely rhetorical level, there is much more consistency. Krichevskii asserts:

(a) *Iskra*'s criticism of 'Historical Turning-Point' shows its doctrinaire rigidity;
(b) *Iskra*'s talk of a tactical 'plan' shows its doctrinaire rigidity;
(c) *Iskra*'s comment on *stikhiinyi* explosions shows its doctrinaire rigidity.

These points come together in the formula that 'in practice', *Iskra*'s 'doctrinaire view on tactics' leads it toward an 'underestimation of the significance of the objective or *stikhiinyi* element of development'. Once having arrived at this purely rhetorical formula, Krichevskii is completely unable to make logical sense of it.

Krichevskii's article in *Rabochee delo*, No. 10 is perhaps the least distinguished piece of writing that we will see in this commentary. It is also one of the most important, since it establishes a number of vital points.

Readers of WITBD tend to assume that Lenin was obsessed with the issue of *stikhiinost*. Lenin's 'insistence' on *stikhiinost*, we are told, is what needs to be explained.[65] But Lenin *had no choice* in the matter. *Rabochee delo* issued a very public challenge: *Iskra* is responsible for the organisational split, since we could have worked together. In response, Lenin *had* to show that *Rabochee delo* had violated its obligations under the ideological contract it had signed in the form of the Geneva resolution. Since Krichevskii insisted on using the language of *stikhiinost*, Lenin had to respond in kind and show that Krichevskii's comments not only violated the contract but showed *Rabochee delo*'s sneaking affinity for opportunism. The glove had been flung down by Krichevskii and Lenin had to pick it up.

---

[65] Zelnik 2003a, p. 28.

No doubt the responsible and statesmanlike thing to do would have been to straighten out the conceptual confusion and state Krichevskii's underlying point in more reasonable language. Obviously, however, Krichevskii's polemical foes had a much greater interest in taking his vulnerable formulations and beating him over the head with them. Given Krichevskii's motives in making the argument in the first place, I do not think we can blame the *Iskra*-ites too harshly. In any event, we should not expect any great enlightenment from the result.

Finally, the Krichevskii passage shows the inner link between the abstract formula 'the *stikhiinyi* element of development' and the concrete episode of worker militancy in spring 1901. This helps us understand Lenin's polemical response. He understood the charge '*Iskra* underestimates the *stikhiinyi* element of development' to mean the following: '*Iskra*'s plan spends not enough time on the problem of worker militancy and too much time on the problem of improving leadership'. As we shall see in the following chapters, Lenin's reply is: worker militancy is *not* the problem because it is increasing in leaps and bounds all on its own. The problem, the weak link, is effective party leadership of all this militancy. *Iskra* very properly focuses attention precisely on this problem – on Social-Democratic deficiencies, not worker deficiencies.

## Martynov's tactical plan

Like Krichevskii, Martynov's article in *Rabochee delo*, No. 10 attacked *Iskra* from the left: *Iskra* was too stodgy and dogmatic to provide leadership in revolutionary times. Like Krichevskii, Martynov improvised a theoretical superstructure for his critique. But Martynov went off in a completely different rhetorical direction from Krichevskii. Whereas Krichevskii found the root of the trouble in *Iskra*'s belief that tactics should be governed by a systematic plan, Martynov berated *Iskra* precisely for its failure to provide any such plan. According to Martynov, *Iskra* only tells its readers what *not* to do, but never tells them 'what we need to do [*chto nuzhno delat'*]'. It fails to provide direction on 'how we must act [*kak nuzhno deistvovat'*]'. The verbal echoes between these demands and the title of Lenin's work are not coincidental.[66]

---

[66] Martynov 1901a, pp. 46–7. See Annotations Part One for a discussion of the origin of the title of WITBD.

Martynov's theoretical superstructure is a redefinition of 'propaganda' and 'agitation'. Propaganda now covers any 'revolutionary illumination' of society as a whole or in part, while agitation is a 'call to the mass to carry out definite concrete actions'. Lenin devotes an entire section in WITBD to tearing this new definition apart.[67] Here, we are interested in the role it plays in Martynov's article. According to Martynov, what *Iskra* calls 'political agitation' – using instances of oppression to indict the autocracy – is really only propaganda, since it issues no call to specific action. Plekhanov and his spiritual heirs have always pretty much confined themselves to propaganda, to abstract preaching of revolutionary ideas. This one-sidedness was acceptable back in the early 1890s, when the proletariat was still 'politically inactive and unorganised'. It was tolerable during the following decade when Russian Social Democrats were confined to guiding the economic struggle and when they were 'weakly connected one to another and overwhelmed by [purely] local activity'.[68] But (Martynov continues) it is no longer acceptable today, in a revolutionary period when the proletariat is systematically destroying the underpinnings of the autocracy. Now we need 'a broad theoretical foundation of party tactics . . . guiding principles of the mass struggle of the proletariat'.[69] In other words, we need tactics-as-plan!

Martynov uses his propaganda/agitation redefinition to set up a whole series of rhetorical contrasts:

Propaganda vs. Agitation
Polemics vs. 'Current struggle'
Passive vs. Active
Elite oppositional activity vs. Worker revolution
*Iskra* vs. *Rabochee delo*

Thus *Rabochee delo*, unlike *Iskra*, puts 'the revolutionising of life higher than the revolutionising of dogma'. When *Iskra* talks about 'extreme caution', *Rabochee delo* advises the use of force to meet force. *Rabochee delo* has 'close organic ties' to the workers in their revolutionary struggle, while *Iskra* confines

---

[67] Martynov 1901a, p. 39; 'The story of how Martynov made Plekhanov deep' in Lenin 1958–65, 6, pp. 65–8 [733–6].

[68] As we shall see in Chapter Eight, this is a good formula for what Lenin meant by 'artisanal limitations'.

[69] Martynov 1901a, pp. 38, 42.

itself to indictments of the obstacles that the autocracy places on the workers' path. '*Iskra* has a tendency to disparage the significance of the forward march of the grey ongoing struggle in comparison with the propaganda of brilliant and self-sufficient ideas'.[70]

Martynov expressed himself very badly with this last remark and acquired an inaccurate reputation as an 'economist'. Taken by itself, it looks very much like an endorsement of the old economist/revisionist contempt for final aims and an embrace of economic struggle as the main content of Social Democracy. This is the way Lenin took it and this is the way it has been taken by commentaries ever since. But what Martynov means by 'grey current struggle' is actually, as his whole article shows, the dramatic current *political* struggle to bring down the tsar ('grey' only to ivory-tower doctrinaires). Martynov does not indict *Iskra* for ignoring the day-to-day economic struggle of the workers with the employers but, rather, for leaving the workers in the lurch when they went out in the streets to protest against the government.

Thus Martynov – who, as his memoir states, prided himself on his anti-economism – has gone down in history as a model economist. Another reason for Martynov's reputation is perhaps more substantial. Not content with criticising *Iskra*'s lack of a tactical plan, Martynov actually spends the first third of his article – ostensibly devoted to a critique of the first five issues of *Iskra* – to setting out his own tactical strategy. Before looking at this strategy, we should note that its formal status is quite vague. Although Martynov spends many pages on it, he refers to it merely as an example to illustrate his redefinition. Evidently his proposals did not represent a consensus of the *Rabochee delo* editorial board – especially given Krichevskii's critique of tactics-as-plan in the very same issue of *Rabochee delo*. This ambiguous status seems typical of *Rabochee delo*.

The essence of Martynov's tactical advice was to use the energy of economic struggle to 'raise the activeness of the worker mass' as a way to achieve political and revolutionary ends. Thus the day-to-day economic struggle should be made as political as possible while anti-government actions should be given an economic basis. Concretely, this meant presenting the government with concrete demands that promised tangible results – in the serene expectation

---

[70] Martynov 1901a, pp. 60–1.

320 • Chapter Five

that the government would refuse the demands or botch their implementation. The economists of yore had a *de facto* tolerance strategy. In contrast, Martynov's proposed tactic can be described as a *de facto* intolerance strategy.

Furthermore (continues Martynov), while *Iskra* only *talked* about autocratic oppression, this kind of real *action* would 'make the workers push up against' their lack of political rights. Thus Martynov advocated (in a phrase Lenin particularly detested) an 'economic struggle of the workers with [both] the employers and the government' *in order to hasten* the overthrow of the autocracy. In other words, this was *not* a reformist strategy.

In this connection, and only in this connection, I think we can trace some continuity between the anti-*Iskra* critique and later Menshevism, at least in its 1904–6 phase (when Martynov himself was an active Menshevik spokesman). The tactics proposed during this time by Pavel Akselrod, leader of the Menshevik faction, were based on a similar logic. But, we must realise – and this comment applies to both Martynov and Akselrod – that this strategy is *not* aimed at the independence or initiative of the workers, it does *not* favour following the workers' 'spontaneous' sense of their own interests, nor is it primarily aimed at satisfying economic interests or improving worker living standards. On the contrary, the strategy is controlling and manipulative. The party makes demands it knows will fail, in order to involve the workers and drive home the appropriate lesson. It organises specific worker campaigns because disciplined action by the workers, one that gives 'active expression' to embryonic revolutionary feelings, is an effective teaching tool.[71]

In his memoir account, Martynov implies that Krichevskii's article was economist while his was not.[72] Yet Krichevskii concentrated completely on political '*stikhiinyi* explosions' and said hardly a word about economic struggle.[73] Martynov, on the other hand, insisted at some length on the necessity of making economic struggle the centre of tactics. True, economic struggle was to be used for political and revolutionary ends.

---

[71] Martynov 1901a, p. 45. On Menshevik advocacy of similar campaigns in 1904, see Chapter Nine.

[72] Martynov 1989.

[73] Krichevskii 1901, p. 33. This one sentence seems to be the only mention of the topic: 'We have not spoken here about the difference in our estimation of the economic struggle as a means of drawing in the masses to political struggle. *Iskra* and *Zaria* evidently underestimate this means both in the past and the present, or in any event accords it less significance than we do'.

Martynov's central polemical point – *Iskra* confines itself to 'propaganda' and refuses to give concrete tactical advice – is more than a little artificial, as his own article shows. *Iskra* gave plenty of advice, but Martynov just did not like it very much. In his criticism of specific concrete points – *Iskra*'s stand on terrorism, Lenin's 'plan' for using *Iskra* as an organising tool – Martynov rang the same notes as Krichevskii. Only people without true revolutionary fervour would refuse to rethink terror in the current revolutionary circumstances. *Iskra* wanted to become an autocratic legislator over the Party and had only contempt for the local committees. There is evidently some dissonance between Martynov's denunciation of *Iskra* arrogance on specific points and his earlier claim that it evaded its responsibility to give concrete advice.

## Opening rounds of the pamphlet war

The unsuccessful unity congress in early October started off a round of polemics and finger-pointing. The *Iskra* side published two articles, one by Plekhanov mocking Krichevskii's 'philosophy of tactics' and the other by Martov containing a vicious swipe made in passing at Krichevskii. *Rabochee delo* published their side of the story in a pamphlet entitled *Two Congresses*.[74]

Both sides went overboard in this period, even compared to earlier polemics. Here is *Rabochee delo* (in this instance, Martynov) describing *Iskra*:

> Even if *Iskra* managed to fulfil its mission to the end, even if it succeeded in 'purifying' the Russian Social-Democratic movement from everything 'low', material and economic, it would in so doing throw the movement back ten years, it would return us to the period of propaganda in small study circles – it would 'throw the baby out with the bath water'. But luckily, its mission is utterly unfulfillable. And no matter how annoyed it may be by the fact, yet even *Iskra* is compelled whether it likes it or not to take account of the powerful demands of life and at least insert the news that they receive about the worker movement.[75]

---

[74] Plekhanov in *Iskra*, No. 10 (November 1901); Martov in *Iskra*, No. 9 (October 1901). *Two Congresses* (the title refers to the abortive unity congress and the regular congress of the Union of Russian Social Democrats Abroad) seems to have been written by Martynov; see Martynov 1901b.

[75] Martynov 1901b, p. 27.

Thus Martynov seriously asserts that *Iskra* printed worker correspondence only under constraint.[76] In turn, the *Iskra*-ites accused *Rabochee delo* of abdicating any effort at Social-Democratic leadership. Both these descriptions aroused justifiable indignation on the other side. Despite the fact that they are too distorted even to qualify as caricatures, historians have by and large accepted them as accurate descriptions of both warring parties.

Both Plekhanov and Martov issued attacks on Krichevskii, but neither took much notice of his idiosyncratic use of the phrase 'the *stikhiinyi* element'.[77] Lenin, in contrast, reacted to it immediately in his remarks at the congress itself, and later made it the basis of his own anti-*Rabochee delo Iskra* article in December.[78] We trace the rhetorical evolution of *stikhiinost* during this crucial period in Annotations Part Two. Suffice it to say here that at least six different meanings were floating about, with no effort from anyone to sort them out.

In its pamphlet *Two Congresses*, *Rabochee delo* claimed that *Iskra* wanted to push all disputed issues into obscurity and to 'work in the shadows' like a tribunal of the Inquisition. In contrast, *Rabochee delo* openly called to all comrades for support.[79] Thus *Rabochee delo* practically dared *Iskra* to justify its sectarianism, splitting tactics, and so on. *Iskra* had to show that the disagreements uncovered at the unity congress were serious enough to prevent organisational unity – in other words, to make the disagreements as principled and theoretical as possible (following the precedent of *Rabochee delo*, No. 10). Lenin undertook to combine this task with the book that he had already promised would set forth his positive plan – that is to say, in WITBD.[80]

We shall be returning to the polemics of late 1901 at various points in the commentary, since WITBD's most famous formulations cannot be understood outside this context. We can conclude this chapter by summing up the clash between *Iskra* and *Rabochee delo*.

The real point of the theoretical superstructure created by the articles in *Rabochee delo*, No. 10 was a practical indictment of *Iskra* as a political rival.

---

[76] Lenin responds to this accusation in WITBD, see Lenin 1958–65, 6, p. 55 [725].

[77] Martov and Plekhanov published their attacks in *Iskra*, No. 10 (November 1901).

[78] For Lenin's remarks at the unity congress, see Lenin 1958–65, 5, pp. 269–76. Lenin's anti-*Rabochee delo* article in *Iskra*, No. 12 (6 December 1901) is discussed in Chapter Six in connection with the *Joint Letter* (Lenin 1958–65, 5, pp. 360–7).

[79] Martynov 1901b, p. 31.

[80] Lenin's promise is contained in 'Where to Begin?' in *Iskra*, No. 4 (May 1901).

('*Iskra*' here includes *Zaria*, the Emancipation of Labour group and other supporters.) The case against *Iskra*, using the evidence provided by its first four or five issues, can be summed up in four charges:

(i) *Iskra*'s dogmatic obsession with theoretical chastity leads to harmful campaigns against non-existent heresies. This obsession reveals itself in *Iskra*'s hostility to freedom of criticism within the Party, its condescending view of the recent past of Russian Social Democracy, and its overestimation of the danger of 'bourgeois democracy', that is, political leadership of the workers by non-Social-Democratic revolutionaries.

(ii) *Iskra* is tactically rigid and frigid. This failing is graphically revealed by its pedantic under-reaction to the 'spring events', when *Iskra* poured cold water on *Rabochee delo*'s own calls for action. Instead, *Iskra* talked about 'extreme caution' and polemicised against terror. *Iskra* is fixated on its abstract tactical 'plan' and unable to see what is really going on in Russia.

(iii) *Iskra* pays too much attention to non-proletarian classes, as shown by its obsession with 'indictments' of the oppression suffered by other classes, including élite classes. This failing goes hand in hand with its relative lack of interest in the source of the workers' *revolutionary* energy, namely, economic struggle.

(iv) *Iskra* is undemocratic. It tries to force its ideas and its organisation on the local Social-Democratic committees or even to by-pass the committees altogether.

*Iskra* obviously had to answer these charges. The structure of WITBD is, in part, determined by the need to provide a point-by-point refutation.

Chapter I of WITBD answers the charge of dogmatism. It says: 'What you call dogmatism is what we call a proper recognition of the need for a firm programme of principle. The slogan "freedom of criticism" is a cover for passivity and eclectic meandering.'

Chapter II responds to the charge of tactical rigidity by tearing apart Krichevskii's slogans about not underestimating *stikhiinost* and about the importance of 'tactics-as-process'. Lenin argues that both of these formulae betray the Social-Democratic duty of providing guidance and leadership.

Chapter III defends the *Iskra* strategy of political agitation and 'all-sided indictments'.

Chapters IV and V, in the course of setting out Lenin's thoughts on party organisation and the role of a party newspaper, defend the *Iskra* plan against the charge of being undemocratic.

Thus, WITBD was a weapon in *Iskra*'s rivalry with *Rabochee delo* for leadership within Russian Social Democracy. It is worth noting two issues that were *not* brought up by *Rabochee delo*: first, Lenin's campaign for improving organisation and for overcoming the 'artisanal limitations' faced by local committees and second, 'intellectuals' vs. 'workers'. That is to say, in 1901, there was a general Social-Democratic consensus on the need to improve local organisations (although, in September 1901, Lenin's specific plan was not known in its details). There was also a consensus that certain economists had indulged in inappropriate intelligentsia-baiting. This provisional consensus needs to be kept in mind when interpreting WITBD's polemical strategy.

Underneath all the specific contentious issues, perhaps the crucial contrast between the two factions – the one that spelled the difference between victory and defeat – was that *Iskra had* a plan for the *praktiki*, whatever one's opinion of this plan, and *Rabochee delo* did not. The *Iskra* plan shall occupy our attention in Part Three of the commentary. Here I want to say a few words about *Rabochee delo*'s lack of one.

*Rabochee delo* did not deny the need for Social-Democratic leadership nor the necessity to move to a political stage as fast as possible. On the contrary. But it did assume that it was unnecessary and even insulting to provide aggressive leadership of the *praktiki*. The *praktiki* understood perfectly well what was needed, and if they did not completely understand, there was no need to get all upset, because the worker movement was progressing anyway. *Rabochee delo* was thus hostile to any attempt on *Iskra*'s part to win the committees over to its side. Any such attempt was arrogant, dictatorial, and contemptuous of the committees. *Rabochee delo* argued that national party institutions should rather be built up by the committees from below, in democratic fashion. *Rabochee delo*'s 'from below' strategy was of a piece with its attitude elsewhere, whether we call it a 'go with the flow' abdication of leadership or whether we call it trust in the local committees.

*Rabochee delo* did show some leadership on tactics, but these efforts were confused and halting. *Rabochee delo* criticised *Iskra* for throwing cold water on its excitement over the spring events, but one is hard put to say what exactly *Rabochee delo* wanted the committees to do in fall of 1901. *Rabochee delo* objected to *Iskra*'s doctrinaire view on terror, but its own resolution on the topic was vague and evasive,[81] and also implied rather implausibly that *Iskra* rejected economic struggle. Martynov's emphasis on economic struggle was certainly not an endorsement of letting the workers follow a putative natural bent for petty aims. Rather, he wanted vigorous Social-Democratic leadership of the economic struggle in order to ensure its effective use for revolutionary political struggle. But Martynov's only concrete tactical proposals were put forth in a tentative 'for instance' mode.

At the same time that Martynov made these tentative tactical suggestions, he also expressed rather forcefully a 'why worry?' attitude about possible political rivals that might supplant Social-Democratic leadership of the workers. He assured his readers that Russia's repressive political situation in and of itself made all of *Iskra*'s worries baseless. More than once, he asserted that the worker movement was pushed 'with the force of fate [*fatal'no*]' toward a revolutionary political stance.[82] In fact, he claimed, there was no chance that non-Social-Democratic forces could ever lead the workers. 'Bourgeois democracy' – that is, all non-Social-Democratic anti-tsarist revolutionaries – was 'a phantom'.[83] This line of argument could not have helped *Rabochee delo*'s credibility at a time when two major revolutionary rivals to the Social Democrats – the Socialist Revolutionaries and the liberal Constitutional Democrats (Kadets) – were springing into existence.

Certainly, one can easily sympathise with *Rabochee delo*'s complaint about *Iskra*'s arrogance, its aggressive and sometimes nasty polemics, its self-righteousness, its magnification of all disagreements. But you can't beat something with nothing. That is why it was imprudent for Martynov to argue that *Iskra* refused to give an answer to the question, *chto delat'* – what should the *praktiki* actually *do*? Such a challenge might prompt the *Iskra* forces to issue a book devoted precisely to answering that question.

---

[81] Martynov 1901b, p. 18; for Lenin's comment in WITBD, see Lenin 1958–65, 6, p. 51 [720].

[82] Martynov 1901b, p. 32; Martynov 1902, pp. 6, 8.

[83] Martynov 1901b, p. 32.

## Appendices to Chapter Five

1. *Excerpt from Boris Krichevskii*

(*Rabochee delo*, No. 10 (September 1901), pp. 17–20)

What is so characteristic of *Iskra*'s doctrinairism is the fact that it could not forgive us our actively revolutionary attitude toward these events. These events may not have been the result of a 'systematic plan carried out with determination' [a quotation from Lenin's 'Where to Begin'], but nevertheless – indeed, *all the more* – they promised a successful revolutionary outcome.

It is evident that the general disagreement between us and *Iskra* concerning the question of the foundations of tactics is also reflected in our differing evaluation of the *relative* significance of the *stikhiinyi* element and the purposive, 'plan-like' element for the final success of the revolutionary struggle. For the conspirators of bygone days, the [projected] overturn was exclusively the result of their own plans, efforts, cleverness and flexibility. They did not take into account the objective laws of social development and the process of the development of the class struggle. The teaching of Marx and Engels forever put an end to the conspiratorial outlook and methods of revolutionary struggle. The purposive work of revolutionising minds and social relations that took pride of place with Social Democracy had nothing in common with the well-thought-out planning of the conspirator. The Social Democrat who was also a revolutionary had the following task: only to *accelerate* objective development with his purposive work, *not* to replace it or substitute his subjective plans for it.

In theory, *Iskra* knows all this. But the immense significance that Marxism justifiably gives to purposive revolutionary work draws *Iskra* away in practice – *thanks to its doctrinaire view on tactics* – toward an *underestimation of the significance of the objective or stikhiinyi element of development*. We earlier showed that *tactics-as-plan* contradicts the basic spirit of Marxism. It is not surprising that *Iskra* – inclined as it is toward tactics-as-plan – is by this very fact also *compelled*, against its will, to approach the conspiratorial outlook on the 'preparation' of revolution – in other words, to give the objective or *stikhiinyi* process a secondary place even in the *final act* of revolutionary development.

It is characteristic [of *Iskra*] that the author [Lenin] of the lead article of No. 4 – the one that sets out a 'systematic plan' in detail (we'll talk about the plan itself later on) – is compelled at the end of his article to make the following proviso: although he talks 'all the time about systematic and plan-like preparation', he 'in no way wants to imply that the autocracy can fall exclusively from a correctly executed siege or from an organised storming. On the contrary, it is fully possible and historically much more likely that the autocracy will fall under the pressure of one of those *stikhiinyi* explosions', etc. This is probably the first time that a *Social-Democratic* writer, a *Marxist*, had to *make a proviso* that a political change as radical as the fall of the autocracy in Russia will not be *'exclusively'* the result of subjective 'plan-like preparation', that is, that the objective laws of social development also have a not unimportant significance for the preparation and triumph of the revolution. Probably for the first time a *Marxist* felt the need – and with good reason – to warn against the 'misunderstanding' that readers will take him for an advocate of . . . idealism and subjectivism. Besides, even in his proviso the author of the lead article only admits the 'full possibility' and the 'much greater likelihood' that the fall of the autocracy will result from an *'stikhiinyi* explosion' – as if a political revolution is conceivable *without* an *'stikhiinyi* explosion'! . . . [ellipses in original]

One might think that for the author, the revolutionary flame can flare up only from *Iskra* [*The Spark*] (with a capital letter), in the editorial laboratory of the 'all-Russian newspaper' that has worked out and is now dictating a 'systematic' plan 'carried out undeviatingly'. One cannot help recalling the prototype of lifeless doctrinairism – Goethe's Wagner with his laboratory homunculus.

Without a doubt, the purposiveness of the militants plays a greater and greater role in history. The most important laws of social development were discovered by Marx and Engels. Scientific socialism is justly termed 'the algebra of revolution'. Social Democracy is and can only be the *purposive* movement of the proletariat fighting for its emancipation. No class has had even a remotely similar degree of clarity in its understanding of the conditions of its emancipation, of the final aim of its struggle and of the paths leading to it, as does the proletariat fighting under the banner of Social Democracy. All this is true. But scientific socialism would stop being itself, if it threw out of its calculations or in any way decreased the significance of the *stikhiinyi* element – not only in an evolutionary period (that goes without saying) but also in a time of revolution.

Despite the progress of natural science, people still reproduce themselves in the same old ancestral way. In similar fashion, the appearance of a new social order here below – despite all the progress of social science and the increase in purposive fighters (or militants) – will continue to be the result *primarily* of *stikhiinyi* explosions. This applies *even* to the social revolution in the West, where the proletariat can throw on the scales of history an unparalleled force of awareness and organisation. The *stikhiinyi* element will thus predominate to an even greater degree in the upcoming Russian political revolution.

Of course, we completely agree with *Iskra* that 'no political party, unless it falls into adventurism, can base its activity solely on the expectation of such [*stikhiinyi*] explosions'. But: *at the moment of stikhiinyi explosions, any revolutionary party is obliged with all its strength to try to ensure that the explosion leads to revolution and to victory*. It is this responsibility that *Iskra* has forgotten, due to the reasons mentioned and to its doctrinaire approach – indeed, *Iskra* finds it possible to spill cascades of inky anger on those who do remember this responsibility and try their best to live up to it.

## 2. *Lenin's Appendix to WITBD on the Disputes of 1901*

(Lenin 1958–65, pp. 184–90)

### *The Attempt to Unite 'Iskra' with 'Rabochee delo'*

It remains for us to describe the tactic *Iskra* adopted towards *Rabochee delo* in organisational matters. This tactic was already fully expressed in *Iskra*, No. 1, in an article entitled 'The Split in the Union of Russian Social Democrats Abroad'. From the outset we adopted the point of view that the *actual* Union of Russian Social Democrats Abroad recognised the first congress of our party as the Party's representative abroad, had *split* into two organisations; – that the question of the Party's representative remained an open one and that the settlement reached at the International Congress at Paris by the election of two members [Krichevskii and Plekhanov] to represent Russia on the International Socialist Bureau, one from each of the two sections of the divided Union, was only a temporary and conditional settlement. We declared that on essentials *Rabochee delo was wrong*; we emphatically took the side of the

Emancipation of Labour group in matters of principle, but at the same time we refused to enter into the details of the split and noted the services rendered by the 'Union' in the sphere of purely practical work. [Lenin puts 'Union' in quotation marks because he regards it as only half of the original Union.]

Consequently, ours was, to a certain extent, a waiting policy. We made a concession to the opinion prevailing among the majority of the Russian Social Democrats that even the most determined opponents of 'economism' could work with the 'Union' because, it was said, the 'Union' had frequently declared its agreement in principle with the Emancipation of Labour group and did not claim an independent profile on fundamental questions of theory and tactics. The correctness of the position we took up was indirectly demonstrated by the fact that almost simultaneously with the publication of the first number of *Iskra* [December 1900], three members separated from the 'Union' and formed the so-called Group of Initiators and offered their services as mediators in negotiations for reconciliation (1) to the foreign section of the *Iskra* organisation, (2) to the revolutionary organisation 'Social Democrat', (3) to the 'Union'. The first two [*Iskra*-ite] organisations immediately responded with agreement, while the third *refused*. It is true that when a speaker [probably Lenin himself] related these facts at the Unity Congress last year, a member of the administration of the 'Union' declared that their rejection of the offer was due *entirely* to the fact that the 'Union' was dissatisfied with the composition of the group of initiators. While I consider it my duty to cite this explanation I cannot, however, refrain from observing that the explanation is an unsatisfactory one; knowing that the two [*Iskra*-ite] organisations had agreed to enter into negotiations, the 'Union' could have approached them through other intermediaries, or directly.

In the spring of 1901 both *Zaria* (No. 1, April) and *Iskra* (No. 4, May) entered into open polemics with *Rabochee delo*. *Iskra* particularly attacked *Rabochee delo*'s 'Historical Turning-Point' that appeared in its *April* supplement – consequently, already after the spring events. *Rabochee delo* revealed its lack of stability by getting carried away with terror [as a tactic] and by its calls for 'blood'. Notwithstanding these polemics, the 'Union' agreed to the resumption of negotiations for reconciliation through the mediation of a new group of 'conciliators'. A preliminary conference of representatives of the three organisations named above took place in June at which a draft agreement was drawn up on the basis of a detailed 'agreement on principles' (published later by the 'Union' in the pamphlet *Two Congresses* and by the [*Iskra*-ite] League in a pamphlet entitled *Documents of the Unity Congress*).

The contents of this agreement on principles (or as it is more frequently named, the resolutions of the June conference) show with utter clarity that we put forward as an absolute condition for a merger *the most emphatic repudiation of all manifestations of opportunism generally and of Russian opportunism in particular*. Section 1 reads: 'We reject any attempt to introduce opportunism into the class struggle of the proletariat as expressed in so-called "economism", Bernsteinism, Millerandism, and so on.' 'The sphere of Social-Democratic activities include . . . ideological struggle against all opponents of revolutionary Marxism' (4, C); 'In every sphere of organisational and agitational activity Social Democracy must not for a moment forget the immediate task of the Russian proletariat – the overthrow of the autocracy' (5, A); '. . . agitation, not only on the basis of the every-day struggle between wage-labour and capital' (5, B); '. . . not accepting . . . stages either of exclusively economic struggles or of a struggle for partial political demands' (5, C); '. . . we consider as important for the movement the criticism of the currents which elevate the elementarity [*elementar'nost'*] . . . and the narrowness of the lower forms of the movement into a principle' (5, C-D).

Even a complete outsider who has read these resolutions at all attentively will realise from the very way in which they are formulated that they are directed against those who are opportunists and 'economists', against those who, even for a moment, forget about the task of overthrowing the autocracy, who accept the theory of stages, who have elevated narrowness into a principle, etc. And anyone who has any acquaintance at all with the polemics conducted by the Emancipation of Labour group, by *Zaria* and by *Iskra* against *Rabochee delo* will not doubt for a second that these resolutions repudiate point by point the very errors into which *Rabochee delo* had wandered. Consequently, when one of the members of the 'Union' declared at the unity congress that the articles in No. 10 of *Rabochee delo* were prompted, not by a new 'historical turning-point' on the part of the 'Union,' but by the fact that the June resolutions were too 'abstract',[84] this assertion was quite justly ridiculed by one of the speakers. The resolutions are not abstract in the least, the speaker said, they

---

[84] This expression is repeated in *Two Congresses*, p. 25.

are incredibly concrete: a single glance at them is sufficient to see that 'someone was trapped' here.

This last remark served as the occasion for a characteristic episode at the congress. From one side, B. Krichevskii seized upon the word 'trapped' in the belief that this was a slip of the tongue which betrayed our evil intentions (to set up an entrapment) and exclaimed with pathos 'who exactly, who here was trapped?' 'Who indeed?' ironically rejoined Plekhanov. B. Krichevskii responded 'Allow me to aid comrade Plekhanov's lack of perspicacity and explain to him that it was *the editorial board of Rabochee delo* that was trapped here (laughter from the audience). But we will not let ourselves be trapped!' (A remark from the left: so much the worse for you!)

From the other side, a member of the *Borba* group (the conciliators), while opposing the 'Union's' amendment to the resolution and wishing to defend our speaker, declared that no doubt the word 'trapped' escaped without forethought in the heat of polemics. For my part, I think the speaker responsible for uttering the word under discussion [probably Lenin himself] was not helped much by this 'defence'. I think the expression 'someone was trapped' could be called a 'true word spoken in jest'. We had always accused *Rabochee delo* of lack of stability, of unsteadiness, and naturally we *had* to try to *trap* it in order to put a stop to this unsteadiness. There is no evil intent in all this, for the issue was instability in principles. And we succeeded in 'trapping' the 'Union' in such a comradely manner[85] that B. Krichevskii himself and one other member of the administration of the 'Union' signed the June resolutions.

The articles in *Rabochee delo*, No. 10 (our comrades saw this issue for the first time when they arrived at the congress, a few days before the sessions began) clearly showed that the 'Union' had taken a new turning-point in the

---

[85] Indeed: in the introduction to the June resolution we said that Russian Social Democracy as a whole always took its stand on the basis of the principles of the Emancipation of Labour group and that the merit of the 'Union' lay particularly in its publishing and organising activity. In other words, we expressed our complete readiness to forget the past and to recognise the usefulness (for the cause) of the work of our comrades in the 'Union' *on the condition* of a complete end to the unsteadiness that we were tracking with our 'trapping operation'. Any impartial person reading the June resolutions will interpret them only in this way. If the 'Union', having *caused* a split by its new turn towards 'economism' (in its articles in No. 10 and in the proposed amendments), now solemnly accuses us of an *untruth* (*Two Congresses*, p. 30) because of our words of recognition of its services, then, of course, such an accusation can only raise a smile.

period between the summer and the autumn and that the 'economists' had again got the upper hand. The editorial board, one that turned with every 'wind', started in again to defend 'the most dyed-in-the-wool Bernsteinists' and 'freedom of criticism', to defend '*stikhiinost*' and (through the mouth of Martynov) to preach a 'theory of narrowing' the sphere of our political influence (with the aim, so it was said, of complexifying this influence). Once again Parvus's apt observation was proved correct: it is difficult to trap an opportunist with a [programmatic] formula. An opportunist will put his name to *any* formula and as readily abandon it, because opportunism is precisely a lack of definite and firm principles. Today, the opportunist repudiates *all* attempts to introduce opportunism, repudiates *all* narrowness, solemnly promises 'never for a moment to forget the task of overthrowing the autocracy', to carry on 'agitation not only on the basis of the every-day struggle between wage labour and capital', and so on and so on. But tomorrow they will change their forms of expression and revert to their old ways by way of a defence of *stikhiinost*, of the forward march of the grey ongoing struggle, of putting forth demands that promise tangible results, and so on. Continuing to affirm that 'the Union did not and does not now see [in the articles in No. 10] any heretical departure from the general principles of the draft of the [June] conference' (*Two Congresses*, p. 26), the 'Union' reveals a complete lack of ability, or a lack of desire, to understand the essential points of disagreement.

After the appearance of *Rabochee delo* No. 10, only one thing remained for us to try and that was to open a general discussion in order to ascertain whether the 'Union' as a whole agreed with these articles and with its editorial board. The 'Union' is particularly displeased with us because of this and accuses us of sowing discord in the 'Union', of not minding our own business, and so on. These accusations are obviously unfounded because with an elected board which 'executes a turning-point' with every breeze, everything depends precisely upon the direction of the wind, and we determined the direction of the wind at private meetings at which no one was present except members of the organisations who had gathered together for the purpose of uniting. The amendments to the June resolutions submitted in the name of the 'Union' removed the last shadow of any hope for an agreement. The amendments are documentary evidence of the new turning-point towards 'economism' and of the fact that the majority of the members of the 'Union' are in agreement with *Rabochee delo*, No. 10. Amendments were offered to delete the words 'so-called economism' from the reference in the resolution to manifestations of opportunism (allegedly because 'the sense was vague' – but if that were so, all that was required was a more precise definition of the nature of this widespread error), and to delete the word 'Millerandism' (although B. Krichevskii defended Millerandism in *Rabochee delo*, Nos. 2/3, pp. 83–4 and still more openly in *Vorwärts*).[86] The June resolutions definitely indicated that the task of Social Democracy was 'to guide *every* manifestation of the proletarian struggle against *all* forms of political, *economic* and social oppression', and by this they called for the introduction of system and unity to all these manifestations of the struggle. Nevertheless, [at the unity congress] the 'Union' added an absolutely superfluous sentence to the effect that 'the economic struggle is a powerful stimulus to the mass movement' (taken by itself, this assertion cannot be disputed, but in view of the existence of narrow 'economism' it cannot but give occasion for false interpretations). More than that, a *narrowing* of [the meaning of] 'politics' was introduced into the June resolutions by the deletion of the words 'not for a moment' (should the aim of the overthrowing the autocracy be forgotten) as well as by the addition of the words 'the economic struggle is the *most widely* applicable means of drawing the masses into active political struggle'. It is quite understandable that after such amendments had been introduced, all the speakers on our side should one after another refuse to take the floor, on the grounds that further negotiations were useless with people who were again turning towards 'economism' and who were striving to secure for themselves a freedom of unsteadiness [under the guise of 'freedom of criticism'].

'Precisely what the Union regarded as the *sine qua non* of the durability of our future agreement – the preservation of the independent profile and the autonomy of *Rabochee delo* – was from *Iskra*'s point of view the stumbling block preventing an agreement' (*Two Congresses*, p. 25). This is very inexact. We never had any designs against *Rabochee delo*'s autonomy.[87] We did indeed *absolutely refuse to recognise* the independence of its profile, if by this is meant

---

[86] A controversy over this subject arose in *Vorwärts* involving its editorial board, Kautsky, and *Zaria*. We shall not fail to acquaint Russian readers with this polemic.

[87] That is, if the editorial consultations that were proposed in connection with the establishment of a joint supreme council of the combined organisations are not to be regarded as a restriction of autonomy. But in June *Rabochee delo* agreed to this.

an 'independent profile' on principled questions of theory and practice. The June resolutions did indeed absolutely repudiate *this* independence of profile because, in practice, such an 'independent profile' means, as we have already said, all sorts of unsteadiness – an unsteadiness that supports the intolerable confusion in party affairs that now prevails. With the articles in No. 10 and its 'amendments', *Rabochee delo* clearly revealed its desire to preserve precisely this kind of independence of profile, and such a desire naturally and inevitably led to a rupture and a declaration of war. But all of us were ready to recognise *Rabochee delo*'s 'independent profile' in the sense of its concentration on specific literary functions. The appropriate distribution of functions was obvious: (1) a scholarly journal [*Zaria*], (2) a political newspaper [*Iskra*], and (3) popular article collections and popular pamphlets [*Rabochee delo*] . Only by agreeing to such a distribution of functions would *Rabochee delo* prove that it *sincerely* desired to abandon once and for all its erring ways against which the June resolutions were directed. Only such a distribution of functions would have removed all possibility of friction and would have guaranteed a durable agreement that at the same time would serve as a basis for a new upsurge and new successes of our movement.

Not a single Russian Social Democrat can have any doubts now about the fact that the final rupture between the revolutionary and opportunist tendencies was brought about, not by any sort of 'organisational' clash, but by the desire of the opportunists to perpetuate an independent profile for opportunism and to continue to sow confusion in people's minds with the arguments advanced by the Krichevskiis and the Martynovs.

## Chapter Six

# The Purposive Worker and the Spread of Awareness

We now turn to the remaining three of Lenin's interlocutors in WITBD: the *Joint Letter* of September 1901 criticising *Iskra* from an economist point of view, Boris Savinkov's article in *Rabochee delo* on the Petersburg worker movement in 1900, and the copious writings of the energetic but solitary Social-Democratic journalist L. Nadezhdin. Unlike the first three interlocutors – Kuskova / Prokopovich, *Rabochaia mysl*, *Rabochee delo* – the members of this second set are not of any particular importance in the history of Russian Social Democracy. The authors of the *Joint Letter* remain anonymous, Boris Savinkov was only passing through Social Democracy on his way to becoming a prominent terrorist for the Socialist Revolutionaries, and L. Nadezhdin remained marginal until his early death in 1905.

On the other hand, all three play a substantial role in WITBD. The *Joint Letter* had as great an influence as any other document in setting up the framework of Lenin's polemic against 'kow-towing to *stikhiinost*'. Savinkov is called in as a valuable witness at some crucial points in the argument. The second half of WITBD almost turns into a debate with Nadezhdin. Furthermore, although these particular writers may be marginal, the issues they bring up were later to become very important indeed. These include terror as a revolutionary tactic, 'the class point of view' (how the worker movement should relate to other classes), and 'writerism' [*literaturshchina*, focusing too much on polemical disputes and journalistic exposés instead of action]. Economism was on its death bed by the time Lenin wrote WITBD, which is why Lenin found it a convenient stick with which to belabour *Rabochee delo*. But these other issues remained very much alive and in years to come they served as a basis for energetic attacks on the *Iskra* of 1900–3 and on Lenin.

It is with relief that we turn away from the squabble between *Iskra* and *Rabochee delo*. In that clash, such substantive issues as existed took a decided back seat to organisational rivalry, hastily improvised 'theoretical' generalisations, and almost deliberately confusing verbal formulae. In contrast, the issues in this chapter are much more straightforwardly expressed by both sides, albeit with the inevitable quotient of mutual misunderstandings and polemical distortions. The disputes are also much more empirically based. Each writer has a specific view of the dynamics of the Russian worker movement circa 1900–1 and derives organisational and tactical conclusions from these empirical claims.

The central *problématique* that unites all these writers is *the spread of awareness* within the Russian worker class. What groups within the Russian workers have what views? What forces determine these views? How fast and how reliably is the spread of awareness occurring? Each writer has a greater or lesser degree of confidence in the ability of the ongoing spread of awareness to create a revolutionary, anti-tsarist outlook on the part of the workers. The degree of confidence in this process was the key factor determining a person's views on party tactics. We can schematically set out our three writers (counting the authors of the *Joint Letter* as one) on a grid from right to left on this crucial issue.

The *Joint Letter* is sceptical about the spread of awareness and in consequence defends unambitious party tactics, calls on *Iskra* to eschew polemics and advises against overestimation of the impact of leadership of any sort.

Savinkov is much more confident that a revolutionary outlook is spreading among the workers. He therefore calls for a more effective party to take advantage of this shift in outlook. His own scepticism is not about the workers but rather about the forces available for party work.

Nadezhdin maintains that Russia is on the eve of revolution and that the bulk of the worker class is ready to go into battle right now. He is therefore sceptical about any strategy based on a slow spread of awareness via the usual methods of intense propaganda or even via the long, prosy newspaper articles that *Iskra* calls 'political agitation'. Nadezhdin calls for *real* political agitation, that is, calls to action that will get the eager masses moving. The masses are already on the move – and if the Social Democrats do not lead them into action immediately, they may well find themselves trampled by them.

In each case, Lenin situates himself as more confident than his opponent in the spread of awareness. As opposed to the scepticism of the *Joint Letter*, Lenin asserts that workers *are* ready to become revolutionary and that proper leadership can make a difference. He welcomes Savinkov's confident reading of the workers' mood, but opposes his organisational scepticism and asserts that party organisation *can* be vastly improved with the human resources now available. In response to the scepticism of Nadezhdin, Lenin asserts that the spread of awareness must remain the key goal of the Party not only in times of quiet but also in times of revolutionary excitement.

The key figure in the spread of awareness is the *purposive worker*. Both as a sociological type and as a character in the Social-Democratic narrative, the purposive worker was central to the empirical disputes between Lenin and his interlocutors. Before turning directly to the disputes, therefore, we will take a look at the purposive worker.

## The purposive worker

Russian Social Democrats talked about the *soznatel'nyi rabochii* as a worker with the right kind of *soznanie*. According to the usual translation, the figure under discussion is the *conscious worker* with the right kind of *consciousness*. According to the translation adopted in this commentary, he or she is the *purposive worker* with the right kind of *awareness*.

I chose my translation after creating a concordance of all uses in WITBD of *soznatel'nost'*, *soznanie* and related words.[1] I found 'purposiveness' in association with words such as 'energy', 'initiative', 'systematic [*planomernyi*]', 'guidance [*rukovodstvo*]' and 'organisational talent'. In contrast, 'awareness' was associated with 'knowledge' and 'point of view'. For example, Lenin uses it to translate

---

[1] My thanks to Anna Krylova who first urged me to investigate the distinction between the two Russian words.

the German words *Einsicht* and *Erkenntniss* as well as *Bewusstsein*. There are different kinds of *soznanie*, that is, different theories of the world: Social-Democratic, *tred-iunionist*, and so on. *Soznanie* is often used in WITBD in the much less political sense of simple awareness of the world and one's own actions.[2]

These associations show the relationship between 'awareness' and 'purposiveness' as terms in Social-Democratic discourse. The simplest way to put the relationship is that 'awareness' is knowledge that guides action while 'purposiveness' is action guided by knowledge.[3] 'Awareness' is not just neutral knowledge, but the kind of knowledge that impels and compels action – the knowledge, for example, of one's historical mission. 'Purposiveness' is a quality of action. When action is controlled by knowledge – by a firm and clear sense of purpose and by a solid grasp of ends and means – it is purposive.

Workers can be purposive long before they have socialist awareness. Impelled by their situation to resist their exploiters, the workers first realise that purposive action is even possible, they then realise that only *collective* action has a chance of success, and more and more they shape their means to effectively serve their ends. As Lenin put it in 1899,

> Strikes are carried out successfully only where the workers are already
> sufficiently purposive, where they are able to select the time for strikes, are
> able to put forth demands, have ties with the socialists so that they can get
> hold of leaflets and brochures.[4]

In contrast, awareness is a matter of doctrine, of the teaching of scientific socialism. Of course, the idea of a mission contained in these teachings is not just intellectual – it is also profoundly emotional and has manifold implications for action. Nevertheless, Social-Democratic awareness is basically a matter of mental outlook. Thus, roughly speaking, purposiveness is a quality of the

---

[2] For example, Lenin says that the shoddy performance of the *praktiki* is forgivable as long as they have an awareness of the need to do better – the real disaster is when they lose that awareness (Lenin 1958–65, 6, p. 33 [704]).

[3] In Russian, both these terms have a common root in the verb 'to know [*znat'*]'. This root meaning of 'to know' is further reinforced in WITBD by the frequent use (especially in Chapter III) of *znanie*, knowledge. The phrase *politicheskoe znanie*, political knowledge, sometimes seems equivalent to *politicheskoe soznanie*, political awareness.

[4] Lenin 1958–65, 4, p. 297 (an 1899 article on strikes). Lenin gives a very similar account of the development of worker resistance at the beginning of Chapter II of WITBD.

worker movement and awareness is a quality of socialism. The merger narrative is, therefore, also the story of awareness and purposiveness coming together. To use Kautsky's metaphor from the *Erfurt Programme*, the purposive workers are the main recruiting ground for Social Democracy, and there is a tendency for Social Democracy and 'purposive workers' to become synonymous.[5]

The purposive worker – also known as the 'advanced worker', '*intelligentnyi* worker', 'worker revolutionary', and so on – is thus an absolutely central figure in the Social-Democratic narrative.[6] It is also the label for an identifiable social group in Russia in this period that used 'purposive worker' as a name for themselves that embodied their self-image and their aspirations. A look at this social group will serve as an introduction to the empirical disputes about the spread of awareness in Russia.

The purposive workers saw themselves as the natural leaders of the worker movement, but, at the same time, they were intensely aware of the threat of marginality and despair. The best evocation in English of the social environment and the outlook of the Russian purposive worker is the autobiography of Semën Kanatchikov, a worker of peasant origins who later became a Bolshevik 'revolutionary by trade' and wrote his memoirs in the 1920s. I cannot recommend this book highly enough, not only as background to WITBD but as a vivid and revealing historical document.[7] A few passages from this memoir will give us an idea of why Kanatchikov and his like chose the label 'purposive worker'.

> Sufficiently fortified by now by my awareness that I was 'adult, 'independent', and, what is more, 'purposive', I bravely entered into combat with 'human injustice'. I stood up for the abused and the oppressed, enlightened and persuaded the 'non-purposive', and argued passionately with my opponents, defending my ideals. . . .

---

[5] See the discussion of Kautsky's circles of awareness in Chapter One (in the terminology of the relevant passage in the *Erfurt Programme*, the fighting proletariat tends to become aware of the proper goal of struggle) (Kautsky 1965, pp. 216–17).

[6] The term 'purposive worker' is a basic one for Lenin but *not* in WITBD. Here he most often uses 'advanced workers'. No doubt the complicated polemics about *stikhiinost* vs. purposiveness motivated this atypical usage.

[7] Kanatchikov 1986. The value of this publication is much enhanced by the notes and introduction of the editor and translator, Reginald Zelnik, although I cannot agree with Zelnik's overall argument that Kanatchikov is covertly stressing the limitations of *Iskra* and Lenin in this period. Zelnik has written extensively on the purposive

Until this time, as was customary in a workers' milieu like ours, we had looked upon the woman worker as a creature of a lower order. She had no interest in any higher matters, was incapable of struggling for ideals, and was always a mere hindrance, an encumbrance in the life of a purposive worker. How great, then, was my surprise and admiration when, for the first time, I made the acquaintance of two purposive women workers, women who argued logically and debated just like the rest of us. Henceforth we met with them frequently and joined them on big holiday excursions in the country. Our life proceed happily, joyfully, sensibly; we enjoyed the present and looked with hope to the future.[8]

Kanatchikov brings out the happy, excited and youthful side of the life of the purposive workers, banded together in intense and self-involved groups. The purposive worker also had an exalted sense of mission. Much of Kanatchikov's memoir is devoted to his reading, allowing us to see the immense influence on him of fiction, poetry and all sorts of romantic and exhilarating narratives of revolutionary heroism. Kanatchikov recalls his emotions on reading Gorky's prose poem 'Song of the Falcon'.

True, there was nothing said in it about workers as such, but the ideas, the words, were so familiar, so truthful, appropriate and authentic! As I read it, I felt as if I was being transported from the face of the earth, rising high above the vulgarity and injustice of human existence. I wished to rush at once into battle with our mortal enemy, the autocracy, to arouse the sleeping mass of workers and summon them to combat! I wished they all would recognise at once the greatness of the force and power that lay within them![9]

But this sense of exhilaration and community was fragile. Russian life had many ways of forcing the purposive worker out of any supportive environment and confining him to the isolation of, say, army life or village life. Even surrounded by the industrial urban worker class, the purposive worker was likely to feel a sense of isolation and frustration, coupled with a despairing contempt for the less purposive. Kanatchikov recalls the vast, milling crowds of workers and the incessantly ringing bells on religious holidays:

---

worker; see in particular Zelnik 1976. I have used Zelnik's excellent translation, except that after consultation with the original text I have changed 'conscious' to 'purposive'.

[8] Kanatchikov 1986, pp. 70, 93 (Kanatchikov 1929, pp. 60, 78).
[9] Kanatchikov 1986, p. 129 (Kanatchikov 1929, pp. 109–10).

The question naturally arose in the mind of any purposive worker who viewed this crowd of peacefully parading workers: 'And what couldn't this mass accomplish if only it were purposive? If by some miracle one could awaken this powerful force and turn it against the tsarist autocracy, the police, the capitalists?! Why we'd level the old slave system to the ground!' Such were the thoughts and dreams of the few solitary revolutionary youths, who, as they observed this harsh and unattractive reality, continued to founder among the inert and sometimes even hostile masses.[10]

Naturally, Kanatchikov and his fellows felt rather superior to *Rabochaia mysl.*

> Sometimes individual issues of the journal *Rabochaia mysl* would come our way, and we would read them with great interest. But despite this interest, we considered the journal not very suitable to our own needs. True, we were unable to define its shortcomings analytically, since we were still too ill-equipped intellectually, but to us it simply seemed insufficiently militant. On the other hand, we considered it great material for conducting propaganda among less purposive workers: it contained much information about the workers' basic needs, it printed correspondence from factories, and it criticised management. . . . The mass of workers, as I would later have many occasions to learn, eagerly swallowed this shop-floor bait, but still their political development failed to advance.[11]

This passage reveals that along with the condescension toward the average worker, the purposive worker had the humility of the eager learner. He did not define himself as someone possessed of the truth but as one determined to seek it out.

The sense of isolation could turn into despair.

> It usually happened that no sooner did a worker become purposive than he ceased being satisfied with his social environment; he would begin to feel burdened by it and would then try to socialise only with persons like himself and to spend his free time in more rational and cultured ways. At that moment his personal tragedy would begin. . . . The active, purposive

---

[10] Kanatchikov 1986, p. 98 (Kanatchikov 1929, p. 82).
[11] Kanatchikov 1986, p. 98 (Kanatchikov 1929, pp. 82–3). I have substituted 'militant [*boevoi*]' for Zelnik's 'belligerent'.

worker saw himself as a doomed man, with prison, exile, want, famine, privations, and often even death looming before him.[12]

One of the aims of the Social-Democratic underground was to provide a home for the purposive worker and to provide him with a narrative in which he was the hero. Later in his book, Kanatchikov inserts a long account from a 1903 *Iskra* article describing the strategy of the underground propaganda circles – that is, the intense initiation process that turns a purposive worker into a Social-Democratic militant. The proposed course aimed to be a therapeutic journey from despair to confidence. In the beginning, the worker is angry but prone to debilitating doubts.

> Remember the words of the worker [who wrote in a letter to *Iskra*]: 'Teach us how to go into battle!'[13] The worker who despite the danger comes to our circles is above all a fighter whose soul is boiling over, and our task is to unfold the forces and capacities of this fighter, put into his hands the sharply honed sword of revolutionary socialism, teach him to use it. . . . Pay attention to the psychology of a worker who enters the circle. Even earlier he felt all the hopelessness of his position. Sometimes despair and gloom will have crept into his soul about the grey, dim life of the slave of capital. He cannot reconcile himself with his fate and perhaps for a long time has vainly sought an escape.

The course of study starts with the glorious deeds of the older Russian revolutionaries that the worker regards as semi-legendary figures. The worker is shown their moment of triumph – the assassination of Tsar Alexander II – which is also the moment of crushing defeat. At this point in the story [*rasskaz*], the listener's heart dies within him: 'The listeners have lived through a lot [in the circle], and if silence now reigns among them, it is not the silence of the sleepy. This moment is like the dead stop of a fly-wheel'. Life returns to the mighty machine as the listeners learn how Social Democracy will avoid replaying the defeat of Narodnaia volia: 'You [the propagandist] point to the necessity for a revolutionary/socialist party to rely on the masses, on the broad mass movement.'[14]

---

[12] Kanatchikov 1986, p. 102 (Kanatchikov 1929, pp. 85–6).
[13] For more on this letter, see the discussion of Nadezhdin later in this chapter.
[14] *Iskra*, No. 34 (15 February 1903), excerpts in Kanatchikov 1986, pp. 289–91. I have

## The purposive worker in Lenin's scenario

> When all purposive workers become socialists – that is, when they strive
> toward a liberation [of the whole class] – when they merge [organisationally]
> among themselves throughout the whole country in order to spread socialism
> among the workers, in order to teach the workers all the means of battle
> against their enemies – when they constitute a socialist worker party, fighting
> for the liberation of the whole people from the oppression of the government
> and the liberation of all labourers from the oppression of capital – only then
> will the worker class completely join itself to the mighty movement of the
> workers of all countries that unites all workers and lifts up the red banner
> with the words: 'Proletarians of all countries, unite!'[15]

As this passage shows, Lenin took the *Erfurt Programme*'s scenario of the
growing identity between purposive workers and Social Democracy and
applied it to Russia, making it the basis of his entire political strategy.[16] Lenin's
views on the role of the purposive worker in Russia, as formulated on the
eve of the *Iskra* period, can be paraphrased as follows.

The history of all countries shows that the worker movement always creates
purposive workers in great numbers. They learn purposive ways while leading
strikes and they naturally go on to become socialists and even theorists of
the movement. This same process is going on in Russia, and we Social
Democrats must encourage it with all our forces. The purposive workers are
an utterly essential link in the spread of awareness. They are the first to hear
and to heed the Social-Democratic good news. In turn, they are able to pass
it on to the mass of workers who turn to them instinctively as their leaders

---

translated directly from the *Iskra* article. I call attention to one translation error in the
English edition of Kanatchikov's memoirs. According to the translation, the circles
taught 'hatred toward our cursed mother country!' (Kanatchikov 1986, p. 290). The
Social Democrats did not preach hatred of Russia. The words should read 'hatred
toward the curse of our mother country' – that is, tsarism.

[15] Lenin 1958–65, 4, p. 298. All the quotations in this section come from 1899 unless
otherwise noted.

[16] Reginald Zelnik brings out the centrality of the purposive worker in Lenin's
scenario in Zelnik 2003b. He struggles valiantly but without avail to bring this fact
into line with the 'worry about workers' paradigm. By using the term 'worker *intelligent*',
Zelnik strives to make Lenin's confidence in the purposive worker look like pessimism
about ordinary workers. Zelnik himself is rather sceptical about the purposive worker's
ability to play the role assigned to him and evidently projects this scepticism on to
Lenin.

in the fight against oppression. Without the protective influence of the Social-Democratic purposive worker, the more backward workers can be led astray by the competing messages of the bourgeois and government élite. Russian Social Democracy must, therefore, take the purposive worker as its principal target audience in all its propaganda and agitation. Under no circumstances should Social Democracy ignore the purposive worker in the hope of appealing to the lower standards of the average worker. The growing crisis in Russia – the increasing clashes with employers and with police – is summoning genuine heroes and heroines from out of the Russian worker class. This steadily expanding army of purposive workers ensures the success of Russian Social Democracy's project of bring political freedom to Russia – *if* we do not lose our bearings and bypass the purposive worker.

Following the lead of the *Erfurt Programme*, Lenin also affirms that 'the history of the worker movement of all countries shows that the ones who accept the ideas of socialism before anyone else and easier than anyone else are the strata of better situated workers'.[17] This hypothesis about the social location of the purposive worker is important but not crucial. Lenin could change his opinion about where to look for purposive workers (and perhaps did so in later years) and still remain Lenin. The same is not true about the scenario of the spread of awareness and the central role assigned to the purposive worker in that scenario.

Lenin's scenario was the basis of his own political programme, but it was also the basis of a recruitment drive among the Kanatchikovs of Russia.[18] The exalted and urgent tone of voice in which Lenin presented his scenario is not the least of the qualities that seem designed to appeal to this group. Recall Kanatchikov's romantic reading habits as we listen to Lenin make his pitch.[19]

The purposive workers, says Lenin, are 'genuine heroes' who show a 'passionate drive toward knowledge and toward socialism'. Despite the oppressiveness of their environment, they have enough strength of will to continue to study and to make out of themselves 'purposive Social Democrats,

---

[17] Lenin 1958–65, 4, pp. 268–9.
[18] I am here extending an argument first made by Henry Reichman in his groundbreaking article, Reichman 1996.
[19] Chapter Seven is devoted to an exploration of what Potresov called the poetry of *WITBD*.

a "worker intelligentsia"'.[20] Lenin informs these heroes that Social Democracy is *their* party – a party that is aimed at them and will eventually be taken over by them.

> In Russia this 'worker intelligentsia' already exists, and we must make every effort to ensure that their ranks are continually broadened, that their high intellectual needs are fully met, that out of their ranks come the leader/guides of the Russian Social-Democratic Worker Party. . . . [When these needs are met, the worker intelligentsia] will take into its own hands the cause of the Russian workers, and *therefore*, the cause of the Russian revolution.[21]

While affirming the purposive worker's highest view of themselves, Lenin's scenario also addresses their fears of marginality and isolation. He assures these aspiring leaders that they will have eager followers.

> The central point is this: it's not true that the masses will not understand the idea of political struggle. The most backward [*samyi seryi*] worker will understand this idea, on the following condition: if an agitator or propagandist knows how to approach him in a way that will communicate this idea – knows how to translate it into understandable language while relying on facts well-known to him from everyday life. . . . The same thing happens in the area of politics: of course, only the *intelligentnyi* worker assimilates the general idea of political struggle and the mass will follow him, because they have an excellent feeling for their lack of political rights . . . and the most immediate everyday interests lead them into conflict with all sorts of manifestations of political oppression.[22]

The West-European experience, a major source of Lenin's own political confidence, also addresses the anxieties of Kanatchikov and his fellows. If it happened there, it will happen here, despite the depressing day-to-day realities that crowd in on the Russian purposive worker. And when it happens here, Russians will be able to take pride in their contribution to a world-wide movement. 'Any vital worker movement will put forth worker leaders, its Proudhons, and Vaillants, its Weitlings and Bebels. And our Russian worker

---

[20] Lenin 1958–65, 4, p. 269.
[21] Ibid.
[22] Lenin 1958–65, 4, p. 316.

movement promises that in this connection it will not fall behind the European movement.'[23]

When Lenin asserts that the present Russian crisis is producing new worker leaders, he not only allays anxiety about isolation but also gives the purposive worker an outstanding role in the current dramatic events. In commenting on a clash between workers and government in 1901, Lenin assures his readers that

> The government was victorious. But each victory of this kind will steadily bring the hour of its final defeat closer. Each battle with the people will increase the number of indignant workers ready for war, will push forward more experienced, better armed, more audacious leaders [*vozhaki*].[24]

Of course, Lenin's whole scenario might be completely unrealistic. The actual Kanatchikovs might be unable or unwilling to play the role assigned to them. Social Democracy might be unable or unwilling to fulfil its part of the bargain. Certainly, there were voices of scepticism and caution among Russian Social Democrats, and we turn now to the clash between these voices and Lenin. Lenin had staked his political career on the existence of a category of advanced, purposive workers who

> know how to obtain the full confidence of the worker masses, workers who dedicate themselves utterly to the cause of enlightening and organising the proletariat, workers who accept socialism in completely purposive fashion and who even have worked out socialist theories.[25]

What did other first-hand observers of the Russian scene have to say about this?

## The *Joint Letter*

In September 1901, a group of Social Democrats in internal exile wrote a joint statement which they entitled 'Letter to Russian Social-Democratic Newspapers' (henceforth *Joint Letter*). They signed themselves Tovarishchi (Comrades) and announced that they were writing at the behest of their comrades in exile in

---

[23] Lenin 1958–65, 4, pp. 268–9.
[24] Lenin 1958–65, 5, p. 18 (an *Iskra* article on the so–called 'Obukhov defence', a major clash in June 1901 between workers and government).
[25] Lenin 1958–65, 4, pp. 268–9.

order to set forth the reasons for their disagreements with *Iskra* (*Iskra* had only come out with six or so issues by this time.) The resulting three-page statement is a concise and well-written critique that compares favourably with the over-the-top rhetoric of *Rabochee delo*, No. 10. In contrast to *Rabochee delo*, the standpoint of the authors tends toward classic economism.[26]

When one of *Iskra*'s agents in the field sent Lenin the letter, he decided to publish it in full along with his response. 'Conversation with Defenders of Economism' appeared in *Iskra*, No. 12, 6 December 1901. In the introduction to WITBD, Lenin announced that this article explained his new definition of 'economism in a broad sense' and that the article could be seen as an outline of WITBD.[27] Indeed, Lenin's critique of the *Joint Letter* was a crucial step toward erecting the polemical framework of WITBD. In one sense, it was a step toward *obfuscation*. Lenin did his best to conflate the standpoint of the *Joint Letter* with the quite different standpoint of *Rabochee delo*. In so doing, he added another element to the verbal confusion sparked by Krichevskii's use of *stikhiinost*. If *stikhiinost*, translated as spontaneity, is the most famous word from WITBD, a close rival is *sovlech*, usually translated 'divert'. This word comes from the *Joint Letter* and can only be understood in its polemical context.

In another sense, Lenin's article was a step toward *clarification* of the real issues in dispute. For the most part, the *Joint Letter* stated issues clearly and Lenin responded in kind, in contrast to the sorry polemics kicked up by *Rabochee delo*, No. 10. Our job is to use the clarification in order to dissipate the smokescreen of obfuscation.

The argument of the *Joint Letter* can be paraphrased as follows: *Iskra*'s basic fault is its overestimation of the impact of Social-Democratic leadership. Material conditions determine outcomes, not the efforts of ideologues, no matter how inspired. This basic fault reveals itself in a number of ways. *Iskra* is too hard on the *praktiki* of the last few years. Leading an economic struggle was the best that could be done, given the material elements of the time. Because *Iskra* puts undue stress on theoretical rectitude, it conducts polemics in an uncomradely way and creates unnecessary conflict. 'All the differences [among Russian émigrés] have practically no influence whatever on the factual

---

[26] Lenin 1958–65, 5, pp. 360–2. The Soviet editors of Lenin's works provide no information on the identity or the location of the authors.
[27] Lenin 1958–65, 6, p. 4 [678].

course of the Russian Social-Democratic movement', except, perhaps, to introduce undesirable schisms.

Finally, *Iskra*'s theoretical ruminations have led it to define the overthrow of the autocracy as Social Democracy's immediate task, when, clearly, the Russian worker class has not yet accumulated sufficient strength for such a task. *Iskra* must feel that it has given the worker class too difficult a task, because it seeks help from élite oppositional forces such as the *zemstvo*. The hopes placed by *Iskra* on these forces lead it not only to overestimate their oppositional fervour, but – much worse – to abandon the class point of view. Instead of telling the workers why they should be hostile to élite groups, *Iskra* obscures class antagonism and urges the workers to make deals and compromises.

Lenin's response can be paraphrased as follows: to set up a contrast between 'material elements' and 'ideologues' is a parody of Marxism, since the 'ideologues' – that is, the various political forces of society working actively to drum up support – are themselves a part of the 'material elements'. More important than this theoretical error is the motivation behind it: a desire to shift the blame for the shortcomings of Social Democracy from the *praktiki* to the workers. In actuality, the upsurge of the Russian worker movement has been growing in leaps and bounds and has galvanised all society. The *praktiki* are the ones who have fallen behind. Of course, the shortcomings of the *praktiki* are forgivable, given the will to do better. What is unforgivable is the *theoretical* justification of such backwardness *in principle* – a justification that can be called 'economism in a broad sense'. *Iskra* fights such justifications with all its might, and its polemical sharpness in this cause is entirely appropriate.

The *Joint Letter* (continues Lenin) says that 'the class point of view' requires us to put less emphasis on the common anger against the government that is so widespread in Russia today. But since Social Democracy should be a front-line fighter for democracy, *Iskra* is *proud* of its work in raising political dissatisfaction and only wishes it could do much more. Russia is undergoing an upsurge of the democratic movement of the *narod* as a whole. If Social Democracy refuses to play a leadership role, bourgeois democracy will. And this might very well happen – the spring events have energised *non*-Social-Democratic revolutionary forces, whereas, if we had done our job adequately, the worker militancy revealed by these events would have increased *our* prestige and authority.

These paraphrases outline the main clash between the *Joint Letter* and Lenin. The central dispute is empirical rather than theoretical. Lenin sees a revolutionary upsurge going on in Russia, both among the workers and the broad 'democratic' strata of the people. The *Joint Letter* is highly sceptical about both. The theoretical debate about 'material elements' is simply a reflection of this empirical dispute. The *Joint Letter* is sceptical about the impact of 'ideologues' *because* of its scepticism about the workers' 'accumulation of strength' at present. Lenin thinks leadership choices can make a difference *because* he is optimistic about the popular upsurge.

This underlying empirical clash will become clearer as we go through the polemical back-and-forth on specific points and allow the disputants to make their case in their own words. The *Joint Letter* opens with its main accusation against *Iskra*:

> *Iskra*'s fundamental fault – one that runs like a red thread through all its columns and determines all its remaining faults both big and little – is that it pays so much attention to the ideologues of the movement on the assumption that they have an influence on this or that direction of the movement. At the same time, *Iskra* takes little account of that material environment and those material elements of the movement whose interaction creates a specific type of worker movement and determines its path. All the efforts of ideologues – even though inspired by the best possible theories and programmes – cannot cause the movement to stray from this path.[28]

Lenin is opposed to this dismissal of 'ideologues' precisely because of his enthusiastic confidence about the revolutionary attitudes of the Russian worker movement:

> This profound theoretical error [not seeing that the efforts of 'ideologues' are themselves part of the 'material elements'] must necessarily lead – at the moment we are living through now – to the greatest possible tactical mistake, one that has caused and is causing untold harm to Russian Social Democracy. The point is this: the *stikhiinyi* upsurge of both the worker mass and (thanks to its influence) other social strata has been taking place in

---

[28] Lenin 1958–65, 5, p. 360. This passage seems to show the clear influence of Prokopovich and Kuskova and their 'line of least resistance' theory (tactics are determined entirely by circumstances and not at all by programmes). If so, we must revise the common assumption that these two writers had no impact on the movement in Russia and that economism had disappeared without a trace by 1901.

recent years with striking swiftness. The 'material elements' of the movement have grown tremendously even in comparison with 1898, but *the purposive leader/guides* (Social Democrats) *have fallen behind this growth.*

This is the fundamental reason for the crisis in Russian Social Democracy that we are living through now. The mass (*stikhiinyi*) movement does not have enough 'ideologues' who are sufficiently prepared in theory that they are safe from any unsteadiness, not enough leader/guides who have the kind of broad political outlook, the kind of revolutionary energy, the kind of organisational talent needed to create a fighting political party on the basis of the new movement.[29]

The empirical clash between Lenin and the *Joint Letter* about the revolutionary potential of the worker movement manifests itself in differing views of the movement's past, present and future. As regards the past, the *Joint Letter* argues that *Iskra* is wrong to blame the *praktiki* of the late 1890s, given 'the absence of conditions at that time for any other work except the struggle for petty demands'. In response, Lenin states in WITBD that 'this affirmation of the "absence of conditions" is *diametrically opposed to the truth*'. In actuality, all conditions were present – except on the part of the woefully unprepared Social Democrats.[30]

The same line of division appears in the assessment of the current situation. As we saw in Chapter Five, both *Iskra* and *Rabochee delo* were, in their ways, enthusiastic about the spring events of 1901. The *Joint Letter* throws cold water on this enthusiasm, remarking that *Iskra* has 'significantly overestimated' worker participation in the spring events of 1901. When *Iskra* dreams of an immediate transition to a struggle against the autocracy, it ignores 'the entire difficulty of this task for the workers under present circumstances'. In actual fact, responds Lenin, this task appears *less* difficult to the workers than it does to intellectuals who treat the workers like children. 'The workers are ready to fight even for demands that do not promise . . . any "tangible results".'[31]

Looking to the future, the *Joint Letter* states that *Iskra* would be better advised to wait for a 'further accumulation of strength by the workers'.[32] *Iskra*'s political agitation strategy is a sign of desperation:

---

[29] Lenin 1958–65, 5, pp. 363–4.
[30] Lenin 1958–65, 6, p. 33 [704].
[31] Lenin 1958–65, 6, p. 91 [756]. The catch-phrase 'tangible results' is taken from Martynov.
[32] Lenin 1958–65, 5, p. 361.

After deciding through a purely theoretical exercise that the [present] task is the immediate transition to the struggle against absolutism, and feeling, no doubt, the full difficulty of this task for the workers under present circumstances but also lacking the patience to wait for a further accumulation of strength by the workers for this battle, *Iskra* is beginning to search for allies in the ranks of the liberals and the intelligentsia and in its search often slips from the class point of view.[33]

The 'class point of view' means sticking to 'the basic task of Social-Democratic literature – a task that consists in a critique of the bourgeois system and a clarification of class interests, and not in obscuring the antagonism between them'. In reply, Lenin mounted a defence of *Iskra*'s campaign of anti-tsarist political indictments as an effective 'political education' of the workers.

In reaction to the *Joint Letter*, Lenin comes up with a four-part definition of 'economism in a broad sense'. Not coincidentally, each aspect of this definition has a chapter of WITBD devoted to it. 'Economism in the broad sense' has the following features:

- A refusal to polemicise against revisionist 'critical' views in the Party (refuted in Chapter I of WITBD).
- A *principled* defence of a leadership that falls behind the *stikhiinost* of the masses (refuted in Chapter II).
- A striving to narrow political agitation, coupled with a refusal to understand that Social Democracy must lead the whole people against the tsar (refuted in Chapter III).
- A failure to realise that the mass character of the movement requires *more* urgency in creating a solid, centralised organisation of revolutionaries (refuted in Chapter IV).

So far, Lenin's polemic with the *Joint Letter* has *clarified* the issues. As we see at every point in the debate, the underlying clash is between the *Joint Letter*'s scepticism and Lenin's enthusiasm about the revolutionary inclinations of the Russian workers in 1901. Unfortunately, the same polemic has obfuscated the issues – in fact, it has left the impression that Lenin is himself sceptical and pessimistic about the 'material elements' in general and the worker movement in particular. How did this happen?

---

[33] Lenin 1958–65, 5, p. 361.

The first reason is Lenin's determination to use the extreme views of the *Joint Letter* as a stick to beat *Rabochee delo*. Thus, he insists that 'the fundamental mistake of the authors of the letter is exactly the same as the one made by *Rabochee delo* (see especially No. 10)'. He proves this by the simple expedient of translating the arguments of the *Joint Letter* into the language of '*stikhiinost* vs. purposiveness' introduced by Krichevskii. Both sides, says Lenin, 'get completely confused by the question of the mutual relations between the "material" (*stikhiinyi*, as *Rabochee delo* puts it) elements of the movement and the ideological (purposive, acting "according to a plan")'.[34]

This purely polemical attempt to equate the Joint Letter's 'material elements' and Krichevskii's '*stikhiinost*' obscures the fact that Krichevskii and the *Joint Letter* had completely different empirical readings of the Russian worker movement at the present time. Take the 'spring events' of 1901. From *Iskra*'s point of view, the *Joint Letter* underestimated the revolutionary significance of the worker actions at that time while Krichevskii overestimated it.

While obscuring his opponent's position, Lenin also obscures his own. He makes it sound as if he were somehow suspicious and fearful of *stikhiinost* and 'the material elements' while his opponents confidently accepted them. But as soon as we get past abstract and cloudy phrases like 'the material elements', Lenin's confidence in the ongoing revolutionary upsurge among the workers is crystal clear.

The other reason why the polemics with the *Joint Letter* obfuscated the actual issues is a quaint vocabulary item used by the *Joint Letter*. The last sentence in the letter's opening paragraph (quoted earlier) goes like this (I have broken the sentence in two for clarity):

> At the same time, *Iskra* takes little account of that material environment and those material elements of the movement whose interaction creates a specific type of worker movement and determines its path. All the efforts of ideologues – even though inspired by the best possible theories and programmes – cannot cause the movement to stray from this path.

In my translation, 'to cause to stray' translates the Russian word *sovlech*. The translation of this word in the standard translation of WITBD is 'divert'. In this case, the sentence in the *Joint Letter* looks like this: 'All the efforts of

---

[34] Lenin 1958–65, 5, p. 363.

ideologues – even though inspired by the best possible theories and programmes – cannot divert the movement from this path'.

My justification for translating the Russian word *sovlech* as 'to cause to stray' is given in Part Two of the Annotations. For the moment, we will use the familiar translation 'divert'. In his immediate response to the *Joint Letter* in the *Iskra* article of December 1901, Lenin did not particularly react to 'divert'. In WITBD, however, in what, in retrospect, must be adjudged a very bad move, Lenin decided to make his point more vividly and say, in effect: you claim that we cannot divert the worker movement from the path determined by material elements? Well, I say that the task of Social Democracy is precisely to divert the worker movement from this path.[35]

Lenin seems to be saying: the path determined by material elements is a bad one. The worker movement is headed in the wrong direction. Marxist determinism and optimism must be rejected. The only way to avoid disaster is to – somehow – divert the worker movement from its natural path. The *Joint Letter* is naïve to place its confidence on the direction of this path.

But, as we have become abundantly aware, the *Joint Letter* was *pessimistic*, not confident, about the 'material elements' at the present time. Its message was: right now, the Russian workers are not at a high level of revolutionary energy, and all of your Social-Democratic piety and wit is unable to cancel out this sad reality. In response, Lenin insists that inspiring Social-Democratic leadership can make a big difference and especially at the present time, precisely because a revolutionary upsurge is taking place among the workers.

The case of the *Joint Letter* is the case of WITBD, only on a smaller scale. When we look at Lenin's case against the *Joint Letter* only in terms of a vocabulary used originally by his opponents and adopted strictly for polemical reasons *and* we ignore the polemical context completely, we receive one impression. When we look at the actual empirical disputes about Russia in 1901 and about concrete political strategy, we get a very different impression. The aim of this commentary is to enable people to look at the disputes in the second way. Once this happens, I am fairly confident which of these two impressions will be felt to be the most accurate.

---

[35] Lenin 1958–65, 6, p. 40 [711]; compare the similar formulation on 6, p. 50 [719]. The word *sovlech* is not used in the business part of WITBD, that is, the last three chapters that set forth Lenin's plan.

## Boris Savinkov: a valuable witness

The issue of *Rabochee delo* published in April 1900 contained an article entitled 'The Petersburg Movement and the Practical Tasks of Social Democracy'. The article was signed 'B-v', a pseudonym for Boris Savinkov. It attempted to clarify, on the basis of first-hand observations, 'the degree of political maturity [= revolutionary leanings] of the Petersburg workers and the most developed part of the Russian proletariat'.[36]

This article served as an extremely valuable witness for Lenin at several crucial points in his *WITBD* argument. Not only was Savinkov an on-the-spot participant in Petersburg Social Democracy but his conclusions were endorsed by Lenin's arch-rivals, the editors of *Rabochee delo*, as 'a valuable communication from a close observer'. Lenin could even label Savinkov himself as an economist – quite without foundation, as we shall see. Thus he could say, in effect, 'even a truthful economist endorsed by *Rabochee delo* admits', and so forth.

And what did Savinkov say that was so useful to Lenin? First, he supported Lenin's optimistic view of the present state of the spread of political awareness among the Russian workers and he also drew what for Lenin was the indicated tactical implications. *Because* he was optimistic, Savinkov called for a better organised, more centralised party organisation that would insist on higher standards of *konspiratsiia* [rules for survival in the underground]. Like Lenin, Savinkov pointed to the division between economist and politicalist currents within Social Democracy as an unfortunate weakness that needed to be overcome. No wonder Lenin asserted that Savinkov's article was remarkable for its truth and vividness.[37]

Lenin took issue with Savinkov only when Savinkov himself began to sound sceptical. Although Savinkov called for organisational reforms in the direction desired by Lenin, he seemed to imply that the needed reforms were unattainable, since sympathetic intelligentsia forces were meagre and the circumstances of factory life made worker participation in the Social-Democratic organisations very difficult. Lenin responded emphatically that the Social Democrats could make much more efficient use of the sympathisers in élite society and, even more crucially, could and must enlist workers into the party organisation.

---

[36] Savinkov 1900, p. 28
[37] Lenin 1958–65, 6, p. 73 [741].

As we go over the testimony of this valuable witness, we should bear in mind Lenin's strong endorsement of Savinkov's definition of the situation. The distinctive quality of the present revolutionary movement, according to Savinkov, is

> the ever-growing and natural [sic] emergence of purposive worker revolutionaries out of the proletariat on the one hand, and, on the other, a fusion of circle activity [= intensive propaganda aimed at individuals] with mass agitation and the success of the latter. This fusion is to a certain extent caused by the appearance of a new, politically developed stratum of workers, standing between the worker revolutionaries and the mass.[38]

In other words, there is an active link between the few highly committed graduates of 'propaganda circles' and the ongoing changes of outlook among workers as a whole. Savinkov's claim that a new intermediate strata of workers has arisen is a remarkable duplication of Lenin's own argument in his unpublished protest writings of 1899. Also note Savinkov's use, here and below, of the word 'natural', since so many writers are convinced that Lenin was pessimistic about the *natural* course of events.

Savinkov describes each of the resulting three divisions – purposive worker revolutionaries, middle layer, mass – in turn. The purposive worker revolutionaries – all determined enemies of the autocracy – are, unfortunately, few in number but they are active and capable organisers and agitators, better, indeed, than are the intelligentsia revolutionaries. Savinkov is at pains to warn against overestimating the influence of intelligentsia agitators in the creation of this top stratum. True, intelligentsia revolutionaries most often have contact with this type of worker. Nevertheless the swift growth in the number of these advanced workers has other, deeper causes: the ever higher 'cultural' level of the proletariat and the huge progress of the Russian revolutionary movement. Thus it is 'inevitable and natural' that 'life pushes all the more energetic, all the capable and daring workers, onto the road of revolution'.[39]

The middle strata – the 'advanced strata of the proletariat' as a whole – are much more numerous and less 'developed' than the worker revolutionaries.

---

[38] Savinkov 1900, pp. 28–9
[39] Savinkov 1900, pp. 28–31.

They are extremely interested in politics, more so even than in their own direct economic interests. *Rabochaia mysl* – 'an organ of the economist tendency, edited according to the pattern of German trade newspapers' – bores them. They are the main audience for illegal agitational literature (the worker revolutionaries in contrast can handle both the censor-caused obscurities as well as the academic ones inherent in legally published literature). 'Books are preserved with extreme care, they are read at night with all-absorbing interest.'[40]

Intelligentsia revolutionaries who conduct face-to-face agitation have a greater influence on this stratum. Yet even these workers hardly need the guidance of underground agitators. 'The *intelligent* in the circle is an older comrade from whom one expects explanations, but not the direction of thought in this or that direction.'[41]

The third, mass, stratum has a much clearer idea of its economic interests than of its political ones. Nevertheless, there is no doubt about the 'revolutionary mood' of these workers. Intelligentsia agitators rarely make contact with them, but

> *any illegal book* will be read – of course, if the book is properly disseminated. The extent to which these revolutionary publications are properly understood is another question – no doubt to a significant extent they are interpreted improperly, but the important fact here is the continually growing interest in illegal literature.[42]

These workers strive to make sense as best they can of the aspects of tsarist oppression that directly affects them: the police lawlessness and agents of the secret police within the factories.

In conclusion, Savinkov makes the following bold prediction – one that was vindicated within a year in remarkable fashion by the 'spring events' of 1901:

> The overall mass of the workers of Petersburg still do not have a clear awareness of their political interests, but the course of development of the Russian revolutionary movement, as expressed in the ever-growing number

---

[40] Savinkov 1900, p. 31. Compare to the description by Robert Hunter quoted at the end of Chapter One.

[41] Savinkov 1900, p. 31.

[42] Savinkov 1900, p. 32.

of politically mature workers, leads to this conclusion: *in the near future the Petersburg worker movement will take on the character of a mass struggle of the proletariat for its political and economic liberation.*[43]

Savinkov then passes on to the struggle between economic and political tendencies within Petersburg Social Democracy. On the economist side was *Rabochaia mysl* and the Petersburg Union of Struggle (the local Social-Democratic committee), on the political side was *Rabochee delo* and the local group *Rabochee znamia* [*Worker Banner*].[44]

How to explain these clashes? Savinkov's explanation is remarkably similar to Lenin's 1899 writings.

> To the extent that the active organisation gives itself the aim of reflecting the demands, views, and mood of the less developed part of the factory proletariat, while leaving without attention the political maturity of its advanced strata – to that extent its practical activity unwittingly must for the most part take on the character of agitation on the basis of immediate economic interests, while the centre of gravity of this activity must come to rest on the publication of proclamations that exploit each individual fact and each local abuse in a factory.[45]

Thus the economist tendency merely reflected the most immediate demands of the least developed section of the proletariat. The economists were insufficiently aware of the fact that 'dissatisfaction with the contemporary political system penetrates deeper and deeper into the masses', even though these dissatisfactions did not yet find clear and coherent expression. Therefore 'agitation based on exclusively economic interests has outlived its time' and the continued presence of the economist tendency was harmful to the Party.

> The practical disagreements of the active organisations is explained by the fact that the political dissatisfaction of the mass of workers is still not clearly expressed – and, contrariwise, these same disagreements [among the activists] slow down the development and the possibility of a manifestation of this

---

[43] Savinkov 1900, pp. 33–4 (emphasis in the original).

[44] Savinkov 1900, pp. 34–5. The *Rabochee delo* editors inserted a footnote here disputing the 'economist' label given to the Petersburg Union of Struggle. They did *not* dispute the implication that they and *Rabochaia mysl* represented opposed tendencies. Bear in mind that *Iskra* had not yet appeared.

[45] Savinkov 1900, p. 35.

dissatisfaction, destroy the proper course of political development of the workers.[46]

The rest of Savinkov's article deals with the need for organisational reform in order better to carry out the mission of raising the political awareness of the mass of workers. His views are much in Lenin's spirit. Like Lenin, his call for a 'single, strong and disciplined organisation' arises out of his own optimistic empirical assessment of the spread of political awareness. Also like Lenin, Savinkov blamed both intelligentsia and workers for their lack of *konspiratsiia* skills and that he opposed the fulfilment of more than one revolutionary 'function' by a single person as detrimental to underground secrecy. Since, however, Lenin has placed a very long excerpt from this part of Savinkov's article at the beginning of his chapter in WITBD on artisanal limitations,[47] we do not need to say anything further here.

The reader may recall, with some puzzlement, Lenin's description of Savinkov as an economist! The only support Lenin gives for this characterisation is that Savinkov even regards *Rabochee delo* as a 'political' journal.[48] Lenin's description, when read in WITBD, gives the impression that Savinkov was such an *extreme* economist that he rejected even *Rabochee delo* as too political. In reality, Savinkov supported *Rabochee delo* because it expressed a political and revolutionary tendency as opposed to *Rabochaia mysl*. In my view, Savinkov's statement is just another indication of just how baseless is Lenin's own attempt to label *Rabochee delo* as an economist journal.

Not only was Savinkov not an economist, he rapidly revealed himself as an ultra-political. By the time WITBD was being written, Savinkov had already been arrested for his participation in *Rabochee znamia*, the Social-Democratic group of political tendency mentioned in Savinkov's article (as noted above). After being sentenced to internal exile, Savinkov rapidly shifted his allegiance to the newly-born Socialist-Revolutionary Party and, within the Party, to the top-secret Fighting Organisation devoted to terrorist actions. There he became known for his virtuoso skills in *konspiratsiia* (which is *not* the same as conspiracy, as explained in Chapter Eight) although he himself completely taken in by the police spy Azef who headed the Fighting Organisation. Savinkov was a

---

[46] Savinkov 1900, p. 36.
[47] Lenin 1958–65, 6, pp. 102–3 [760–7].
[48] Lenin 1958–65, 6, p. 73 [741].

central participant in the murder of such prominent officials as the Minister of the Interior Plehve in 1904. He later wrote several novels exploring the terrorist mindset (republished in Russia in the 1990s).[49] His own end was improbably novelistic: he fought against the Bolsheviks during the Revolution and Civil War, was lured back into Russia in the 1920s, was tried, sentenced to death but had his sentence commuted, and finally ended his days with an alleged prison suicide in 1925.[50]

His memoirs do not cover his Social-Democratic days. Is there anything in his *Rabochee delo* article that explains his evolution into a terrorist? Savinkov might have decided that Social Democracy was never going to be sufficiently political and revolutionary, at least not in comparison to the Socialist Revolutionaries. His scepticism about the availability of organisational resources and the chances of democratising *konspiratsiia* might have killed his faith in a successful mass movement under tsarist repression.

Lenin is thus inexcusably misleading when he labels Savinkov an economist. His motive was to make Savinkov an even more valuable witness to empirical developments that gave the lie to economism. Nevertheless Lenin underscored the essential similarity of Savinkov's outlook and his own. He cites Savinkov's words 'the growth of the worker movement has outpaced the growth and development of revolutionary organisations'. This observation, said Lenin, confirms *my* formula about the leader/guides falling behind in comparison to the *stikhiinyi* upsurge of the worker movement. Therefore, continues Lenin, Savinkov and I stand together against *Rabochee delo* and the *Joint Letter*. These two groups accuse *Iskra* of underestimating the *stikhiinyi* element. The artisanal limitations that Savinkov describes – these grave defects in party organisation – show the *practical* harm of such statements, namely, they are *inappropriate at the present time*. The *stikhiinyi* element is doing just fine, thank you, but the Social Democrats need to pay attention to getting their *own* act in order.[51]

Savinkov's article is thus especially useful for us because it sets out Lenin's basic point more clearly than Lenin is able to do himself, entangled as he is in the language of *stikhiinost* imposed by his campaign against *Rabochee delo*. Thus Savinkov is a valuable witness not only for Lenin but for this commentary.

[49] Savinkov 1990.
[50] Spence 1991 (this biography is unreliable on Savinkov's Petersburg period).
[51] Lenin 1958–65, 6, pp. 105–6 [769].

## L. Nadezhdin

When republishing *WITBD* in 1907, Lenin freely admitted that much of it was taken up with disputes between émigré 'circles', that is small, tight-knit groups, each hoping to set the tone for a still amorphous party. This was inevitable, he argued, given the circumstances in which a Social-Democratic party could emerge in an autocratic country. Besides, the issues at stake in those days were much more fundamental than any later disputes between Bolsheviks and Mensheviks – the argument was not what the Party should do in particular cases but defining the basic tasks of *any* Social-Democratic politics.

On one point, however, Lenin was rather defensive. He reminded his readers of 1907 that, back in 1901–2, 'there was no possible criterion of the strength and *seriousness* of this or that circle. Much was overblown that is now forgotten but which in its day wanted to struggle in order to prove its right to existence'.[52] It sounds like Lenin had been teased for aiming his heavy guns at nonentities. This criticism would not apply to the polemics with *Rabochee delo*, a group that in 1901 was more solidly established than *Iskra*. It did apply to the polemics aimed at L. Nadezhdin, a person who, by 1907, was already an almost forgotten footnote in Social-Democratic party history yet one who plays a curiously large role in *WITBD*.

Nadezhdin's real name was E.O. Zelenskii. As we shall see, his pseudonym – Man of Hope – was well chosen. Starting off as a populist, he joined the Social-Democratic organisation in Saratov in 1898. He was arrested a year later and ended up in Switzerland in 1900. The 'youngsters' of *Rabochee delo* had long criticised the Emancipation of Labour for losing touch with Russian realities, but now there appeared an even younger youngster – Nadezhdin was only twenty-three in 1900 – who thought that *Rabochee delo* itself had lost touch. To establish, as Lenin puts it, his viewpoint's right to existence, Nadezhdin founded the circle *Svoboda* [*Freedom*]. B.I. Gorev, who arrived in Switzerland at the end of 1902, remembers meeting Nadezhdin in the same sanatorium in the mountains around Lausanne in which his sister, ill with tuberculosis, lived.

> There I became acquainted with one of the interesting figures of that time, the talented revolutionary writer Nadezhdin. . . . He occupied an idiosyncratic position between Social Democracy and the Socialist Revolutionaries, merging

---

[52] Lenin 1958–65, 16, pp. 105–6.

Marxism and the class point of view with terrorism. He wrote a series of works that were bright and interesting but confused as to content. He even created a small group of followers, one of whom – Sladkopevtsev (later, I believe, a Socialist Revolutionary) – had shortly before my own departure from Siberia escaped on the way to internal exile together with Skrypnik, now a rather well known communist, then a young student.[53]

As far as I can tell, Nadezhdin wrote everything in the group's publications himself. The names of two small books that came out in 1901 tell us the essence of his particular viewpoint: *Eve of Revolution* and *Rebirth of Revolutionism*.[54] Based on his first-hand observations of Russian workers – observations made *prior* to the spring events of 1901 that proved decisive for Russian Social-Democratic opinion as a whole – Nadezhdin felt that large strata of the Russian workers were ready to explode in revolutionary anger. For better or for worse, revolution was just around the corner, and Social Democracy had to deal with it. Following on this empirical assessment, Nadezhdin was very hostile to economism (in the previous chapter, I cited him as a witness in the dispute over economism's existence). He was also sarcastically dismissive of *Rabochee delo* as a representative of the half-and-half mood of the preceding period.

Nadezhdin might therefore seem a natural ally of *Iskra*, and, indeed, he had good things to say about *Iskra*. But, in the end, Nadezhdin thought *Iskra* had no real sense of the urgency of the situation. The *Iskra*-ites were still talking calmly about organisation and the spread of awareness – good things in themselves, no doubt, but long-term projects without relevance to the actual Russian situation. *Iskra*'s idea of 'political agitation' was to write learned articles, at a time when it should have turned to the mass of workers with direct calls for action. What most starkly revealed *Iskra*'s distance from 'life', its 'writerism', its inappropriate 'educational priority', was its dismissive attitude toward terrorism, a necessary element of any genuinely revolutionary situation.

One has to admire Nadezhdin's cockiness – a young unknown arrives in Geneva and promptly publishes two long (circa one hundred pages each) pamphlets energetically criticising the entire Social-Democratic establishment

---

[53] Gorev 1924, 52.
[54] *Kanun Revoliutsii* (Nadezhdin 1901a) and *Vozrozhdenie revoliutsionizma v Rossii* (I consulted the second edition, Nadezhdin 1903).

across the board. Besides these two pamphlets, Nadezhdin undertook to provide a Social-Democratic journal aimed specifically at the middle strata of workers. This journal was entitled *Svoboda* [*Freedom*] and, it seems, appeared only in two issues, one in late 1901 and one in 1902.[55] The two pamphlets from 1901 and the first issue of *Svoboda* are the ones to which Lenin responded in WITBD.

In late 1902, Nadezhdin intervened (in yet another 'newspaper-journal', *Otkliki* [*Responses*]) on the side of *Rabochaia mysl* against *Iskra*'s supporters in Petersburg. I have been unable to locate the relevant article, but it must have been something, judging from the ecstatic response from *Rabochaia mysl* and the angry response from *Iskra*.[56] The *Svoboda* group folded in 1903.[57] We last hear from Nadezhdin in early 1905 joyfully greeting the outbreak of revolution in Russia.[58] Nadezhdin died in 1905 at the age of 28, presumably of tuberculosis.

Nadezhdin is the main interlocutor for Lenin in two important sections of WITBD ('What do economism and terrorism have in common?' in Chapter III and 'Organisation of workers and organisation of revolutionaries' in Chapter IV) plus all of the substantive part of Chapter Five. If we put together all the WITBD references to Nadezhdin's writings in WITBD, we come up with a curiously disjointed picture: sometimes, Nadezhdin is an economist and, sometimes, an ultra-political, sometimes he has lost faith in the workers and sometimes he thinks they are ready to burn down the Winter Palace. One reason for this is that Lenin himself has not quite made up his mind whether he is dealing with a single group or just a single writer. 'L. Nadezhdin' becomes a name for him only in Chapter Five, due to the pamphlet *Eve of Revolution* 'just received by us'. The other two publications – *Rebirth of Revolutionism* and the journal *Svoboda* – were published only under the name of the *Svoboda* group. Thus, at one point, he remarks: has L. Nadezhdin, just like the author of the article on organisation in *Svoboda*, forgotten, etc.?[59] But Nadezhdin *was* the author of the *Svoboda* article.

---

[55] Nadezhdin 1901b.
[56] *Rabochaia mysl*, No. 16 (November/December 1902); *Iskra*, No. 30 (15 December 1902).
[57] In July 1903, Krupskaya noted to a correspondent that '*Svoboda* and *Rabochee delo* have closed up shop for a time' (*Perepiska* 1969–70, 3, p. 432).
[58] Nadezhdin 1905.
[59] Lenin 1958–65, 6, pp. 167, 120 [824, 782].

Lenin also made two or three plain mistakes in defining Nadezhdin's position. In a second edition of *Rebirth* published in 1903, Nadezhdin admitted – a rare and admirable occurrence! – that his own lack of clarity had been responsible for some major misapprehensions. For purposes of this chapter, I shall deal with Nadezhdin's actual position, as I understand it from his writings, and point out Lenin's clear errors as they arise.

As a factor within the Social-Democratic movement, the *Svoboda* group (if 'group' is the appropriate word) had no discernible influence. As a writer, Nadezhdin is vivid and insightful, able to convey more of the actual texture of Russian life than other émigré writers. His critical shafts, aimed with impartiality at *Rabochee delo* and *Iskra*, often strike home. His two main tactical proposals – Social-Democratic embrace of terrorism and direct calls to action aimed at the middle strata of workers – were found unconvincing.

Nevertheless, despite Nadezhdin's own limited historical importance, the issues he brought up are just as important and, in some ways, more so than the ones involved in *WITBD*'s main polemic directed at economism and *Rabochee delo*. *WITBD* was the stake in the heart of these two foes, while the issue of terror became a central one shortly after *WITBD*'s publication with the assassination of the tsarist Minister of Internal Affairs D.S. Sipiagin in April 1902 and with the rise of the Socialist-Revolutionary Party. Nadezhdin's attack on *Iskra*'s 'writerism [*literaturshchina*]' also found strong echoes later. In 1904, Trotsky called him a forerunner of the Menshevik way of looking at things, although (Trotsky added) Nadezhdin seemed deliberately to go out of his way to minimise his influence within Social Democracy.[60] Potresov, the *Iskra* editor who later turned decisively against *Iskra*-ism, noted in 1905 that all of *Iskra*'s critics shared its basic presumptions so that an empirical *praktik* such as Nadezhdin was almost the only one to see the real problem. Unfortunately, Potresov continued, Nadezhdin's insights had no effect because he could not present a *system* of ideas that could stand up to the imposing system of *Iskra* ideas set forth in *WITBD*.[61]

All this goes to show that Nadezhdin is worth the attention we are spending on him and that we do not have to be as apologetic as Lenin was in 1907. Three issues require closer examination, two of which have been already

---

[60] Trotsky 1904, p. 47.
[61] *Iskra*, No. 111 (24 September 1905).

mentioned: Nadezhdin's take on the spread of awareness and his defence of terror. Another issue brought up by Nadezhdin's presence in WITBD is Lenin's relation to Petr Tkachev, a Russian revolutionary writer of the 1870s. Tkachev himself is mentioned once in passing in WITBD – a good indication of his overall significance for Lenin. Yet a long tradition of writers have insisted on Lenin's debt to Tkachev and this theme has received new prominence recently in the writings of Robert Service, a writer accepted by many as a genuine Lenin expert. A final section of this chapter is therefore devoted to Tkachev.

## A new form of scepticism

Like Savinkov, Nadezhdin's policy recommendations are based squarely on his empirical reading of current worker attitudes. The present situation differed greatly from the situation in the early 1890s, when the workers could still be divided into two parts: a insignificant percentage of worker *intelligenty* and a vast majority of various shades of grey (a colour that to Russians denotes a dull facelessness). But, by the end of the 1890s, a three-part division was necessary in which the new and surprising element was the middle stratum [the *seredniaki*].[62]

The top stratum was still the worker intelligentsia. Generalising from his own observations, Nadezhdin estimated that three-quarters of this group were revolutionary socialists in the full sense of the word. His description of the remaining quarter contains a revealing use of the word 'purposive': 'These are developed people, relating to everything in purposive fashion, interested in global life, not allowing anybody to walk all over them, but who take no active, constant participation in the struggle'. For Nadezhdin, this non-revolutionary attitude on the part of purposive workers was a puzzle that called for explanation. As for the revolutionary majority of the worker intelligentsia, Nadezhdin thought they were remarkable examples of the beauty of the human soul – a full harmony between thought and deed, motives and actions, ideals and practicality.[63]

---

[62] Nadezhdin elsewhere cites with approval Savinkov's somewhat similar three-part division. (*Svoboda*, No. 1, 1901).

[63] Nadezhdin 1903, pp. 4–5.

The new element on the Russian scene was the middle stratum, which Nadezhdin here labels 'semi-*intelligenty*', 'intuitive *intelligenty*'. They rise above their environment by *feeling* rather than understanding. They have an interest in everything, and while their explanation of events is fantastic, their evaluations are correct. They say 'I'm a socialist', 'I'm a Social Democrat' with almost religious pride.

> 'I have long been *initiated* in this matter', a worker semi-*intelligent* told me,
> and in the tone of his voice, in the shining of his eyes, in the whole way he
> held himself, in all of his movements, a pure child-like soul revealed itself
> and, at the same time, the firm conviction and the inexorable energy of the
> fighter.[64]

The middle workers are fighters who understand the 'power of organisation'. When they read leaflets, pamphlets or newspapers, they always pay close attention to which political group is publishing them. They have a profound need for action. These middle workers are the ones who participate in demonstrations. The spring events of 1901, when the workers supported student protestors, strikingly revealed the insistence of these workers – 'partly instinctive, partly worked out by awareness' – on actively supporting anyone involved in a real struggle with government abuse.[65]

The third stratum, the worker mass, is more numerous than the middle stratum. These workers are very interested in economic questions, although they are 'uncultured' and have only vague ideas about politics. Nevertheless, as compared to the past, their sense of their economic position is a broad one that takes in the entire country and even the world. They no longer allow themselves to be exploited like lambs taken to the slaughter – they are always ready to fight the bosses.

To sum up – and this is obviously a conclusion that *Iskra* liked very much: 'A rich soil has been formed among the mass of workers for a transition from a struggle for petty improvements in individual life to a struggle under the

---

[64] Nadezhdin 1903, p. 5.

[65] In a footnote to the second edition of 1903, Nadezhdin mentions the objection of some of his readers that he placed the Russian worker above the European worker. Nadezhdin's answer: thou hast said! Because of the overall revolutionary environment in Russia, the Russian worker at this juncture *is* in some respects higher than the European.

banner of broad political demands for the democratic status of the state'. This soil was created by the joint action of Russian life in the form of government repression, of 'the books and the voice of propagandists and agitators', and of a general widening of horizons due to capitalist development. The workers demanded democracy both because they saw it was necessary for genuine economic struggle and because they were proud human beings who demanded the right to speak their words of anger.[66]

Since the *Iskra*-ites shared much of Nadezhdin's optimistic assessment, there was also much overlap in their policies. Nadezhdin was himself clearly a strong supporter of political revolution (although I recall no Erfurtian praise of political freedom as the necessary condition for raising worker awareness.) He scorned both economism and half-and-halfers like *Rabochee delo* – indeed, because of his first-hand observation, he is more vivid and eloquent than *Iskra* in his denunciation of the baneful influence of economist small-mindedness among the *praktiki*. He saw the existing revolutionary mood of the worker movement as the key factor in the overall situation in Russia and urged the worker to take a great interest in other potentially revolutionary forces.

Similarly, Nadezhdin was as caustic as *Iskra* about the wretched state of party organisation. The local committees had only become revolutionary after the workers pressured them from below. The lack of central co-ordinating party institutions was intolerable. The intelligentsia revolutionaries did not throw themselves into their work with the passion and full-time commitment that was necessary.

And yet Nadezhdin and *Iskra* ended up at dagger points. The reason was that in the final analysis Nadezhdin was as sceptical and dismissive of the spread of awareness as the *Joint Letter*. He was not hostile or opposed to it as such – no doubt it was a worthy long-term task. But the times were changing with such rapidity that the spread of awareness was at best irrelevant and at the worst – if it deflected attention from revolutionary tasks – harmful.

The middle workers were already eager to bring down the tsar, so no awareness-raising was needed on that score. The task of Social Democracy was, rather, to put itself immediately at the head of this drive for action. The revolutionary explosion was coming, like it or not, and the only question was

---

[66] Nadezhdin 1903, pp. 3–9.

whether it would be a mindless pogrom or a purposive revolutionary battle. If the Social Democrats myopically focused on setting up a long-term organisational framework, they would find themselves swept away and trampled by the *stikhiinyi* explosion.

> When the longing for desperate battles boils over in the masses [as is currently the case], we [Social Democrats] cannot take the risk of *not* assuming responsibility [for leadership of the revolt], no matter what the consequences. Yes, we know that the numerical preponderance is not on our side – but since the clash is now inevitable, we must increase our energy ten times over, we must conquer with the spirit of Garibaldi that which we are not in a position to conquer with simple physical strength.[67]

In view of the urgency of the situation, the intermediary role of the top stratum of 'worker *intelligenty*' – despite Nadezhdin's high praise of the beauty of their souls – could be ignored. They were too few and with too little influence on the masses. The existing committees had ties mainly to this top stratum – a central cause of their ineffectiveness. The intelligentsia revolutionaries should put themselves in direct contact with the middle workers.

This demand led to Nadezhdin's urgent insistence on providing suitable political literature for the middle workers. This insistence in itself might seem like a wager on the spread of awareness. But, for Nadezhdin, the aim of this literature was to be *a call for direct action*. To illustrate his point, Nadezhdin made great use of a letter of support written by a worker to *Iskra*. *Iskra* was very proud of this letter (Lenin refers to it in WITBD) and yet, Nadezhdin asks, should *Iskra* really be encouraged by what the worker actually said? As an epigraph to his book *Eve of Revolution*, Nadezhdin quoted from this letter: 'And what we need now is not strike funds, not circles, not even books, now just teach us this: how to go into battle, how to fight in the battle'. Precisely (argued Nadezhdin), *not* books *but* a summons to battle.[68]

Intensive propaganda that relied on exposition of general principles might work in the West, but in Russia it could only give insignificant results since it was aimed not at the masses but only at isolated 'circles'. Mass 'political

---

[67] Nadezhdin 1901a, pp. 52–3.
[68] The letter originally appeared in *Iskra*, No. 7 (August 1901); for Lenin's allusion in WITBD, see Lenin, 1958–65, 6, p. 89 [754].

self-awareness' came not from this sort of propaganda based on basic principles, but from action-packed agitation in times of revolutionary struggle.[69]

This positive evaluation of action/agitation in comparison to word/propaganda is central to Nadezhdin's outlook. All Russian writers in this period like to talk of 'life' – how life proves this or that position correct or incorrect. With Nadezhdin, this becomes almost a tic, with 'life' appearing every other paragraph. We sometimes hear of 'living life [*zhivaia zhizn'*]'. And this outlook leads to his final damning dismissal of *Iskra* as incorrigibly infected with 'writerism [*literaturshchina*]' – the overestimation of theoretical polemics and printed 'political indictments'. While *Iskra* spent its time refuting bad arguments, real life was impelling the workers to take action to correct bad conditions.

Thus, Nadezhdin impatiently wanted to bypass the spread of awareness. Putting together his various arguments, I came up with the following scenario for what Nadezhdin thought would be the best outcome.

Acts of terror will start the whole process. Terror was not needed to galvanise the workers – they were already champing at the bit – but, rather, to galvanise the intelligentsia revolutionaries who would never be stirred up by the worker movement itself, no matter how revolutionary. The intellectuals will throw themselves with full-time passion into direct connection with the middle workers. A literature aimed at these workers will arise – a literature not based on refuting false theories but rather based on facts that reflected real life and on calls to action. This intense interaction between intelligentsia revolutionaries and the workers will, in turn, lead to strong and energetic local organisations. Once these local organisations get going, the problem of central co-ordination will easily solve itself: the locals will tell the central institutions how to act, and people who can effectively transport and distribute illegal literature will be found. (Nadezhdin is really no more precise than that.) The revolution will break out and be supported by massive peasant disorders and 'agrarian terror'.

From the *Iskra* point of view, Nadezhdin was too dismissive of the spread of awareness and too insouciant in his expectation that 'life' and revolutionary excitement would solve all organisational problems. Social Democrats should not place all their bets on the immediate outbreak of a revolutionary storm but, rather, must keep their eyes fixed on a goal that would serve in times of peace

---

[69] Nadezhdin 1903, p. 14.

*and* in times of revolution, namely, a SPD-like organisation committed to spreading awareness and to turning that awareness into disciplined organisation.[70]

According to Lenin, Nadezhdin formulated in an insightful way the underlying problem of creating effective national organisations: the national organisations had to be supported by local committees who shared a similar outlook, but the committees obtained a similar outlook only via common nation-wide institutions. But from *Iskra*'s point of view, Nadezhdin's own solution to this dilemma was magical – he called on everyone simply to inoculate themselves with the revolutionary fervour of the middle workers. Much more solid was *Iskra*'s plan, according to which a proto-national institution (such as *Iskra* itself) created sufficient unity, both ideologically and practically, prior to the creation of central institutions. (Although *Iskra*'s plan was carried out, Nadezhdin could well argue that it created only a magical 'paper' unity that promptly fell apart.)

*Iskra*'s reaction to the disparagement of theoretical polemics as 'writerism' can easily be guessed. The basic political and emotional clash between *Iskra* and Nadezhdin comes out most strongly on the related question of 'literature for the middle workers'. Officially, Nadezhdin was not against literature for advanced workers, nor was *Iskra* against popularising literature. Yet their respective sense of priorities were poles apart, as revealed in their reaction to each other's attempt at political literature.

Nadezhdin affirmed that middle workers simply did not read *Iskra* and *Zaria* and that, therefore, the message was not getting through. In consequence, *Iskra*'s 'wide political agitation' could not accomplish much:

> N. Lenin writes a very eloquent treatise about a periodical for the 'leader/guides', and dozens of Lenins set themselves to create such a periodical (an enterprise to which we of course wish every success), but as far as a periodical for the worker mass goes, at a time when the mass movement is growing as it is, we hear not a word, not a sound – as if this wasn't the most essential need of the moment![71]

---

[70] Lenin, 1958–65, 6, pp. 176–7 [833]. In 1905, Plekhanov expressed amazement that people regarded Nadezhdin's popular style as 'talented'. In Plekhanov's view, it was an insult to the workers (Plekhanov 1923–7, 13, pp. 252–61).

[71] Nadezhdin 1903, p. 32 (a footnote added in the second edition responding to Vera Zasulich's criticism).

In a review of Nadezhdin's *Rebirth of Revolutionism*, Zasulich explained why directing literature at the higher strata of workers was not an abdication of Social-Democratic duty but, rather, a wager on the spread of awareness.

> Not everybody in the worker milieu reads books, pamphlets, newspapers, but the concepts [contained therein], assimilated by their comrades who do read them, penetrate gradually into the heads of the non-readers as well. Sometimes a feisty and talented worker who catches a few ideas on the fly is able to explain them to others even better than the well-read worker can – although, of course, this worker also has a greater chance than the well-read worker to get confused and to combine nonsense with insight. But this is true of *intelligenty* as well.[72]

Workers who did not read would turn for explanation to other better-read workers, who would certainly not limit themselves to literature marked 'for workers'. Zasulich predicted that Nadezhdin's *Rebirth* would be far more widely read by workers than his *Svoboda*, even though *Rebirth* was a programmatic statement aimed at worker *intelligenty* while *Svoboda* was intended to serve as 'literature for middle workers'. Why? – because *Rebirth* was incomparably better written than *Svoboda*, where the author was so intent on being popular in his style that he ended up being condescending and vulgar.[73]

*Svoboda* became, for Lenin, an emblem of vulgarised 'literature for workers'.[74] A confidential letter in 1903 expressed his profound irritation. One of the *Iskra* agents in Russia had passed along a long letter to *Iskra* written in a Nadezhdin spirit that was guaranteed to enrage Lenin. Here is Lenin, working himself to the bone getting out *Iskra*, operating with pitifully few resources, and painfully aware of the many inadequacies and lacunae in the *Iskra* operation. And here is the critic in Russia who says: you should have much better information about events in Russia, you should combine *Iskra* with more popular newspapers aimed at the lower strata of the workers. Lenin's extensive response was a highly revealing one in which he let off steam about his frustrations and the misunderstandings he encountered. We will limit ourselves

---

[72] Zasulich 1983a, p. 359.
[73] Zasulich 1983a, p. 362.
[74] In an unpublished note from late 1901, Lenin expressed his almost visceral distaste for *Svoboda*'s artificially popular style laced with folk sayings and folk vocabulary (Lenin 1958–65, 5, pp. 359–60).

to a light paraphrase of his feelings about various attempts to provide popular Social-Democratic literature.

My critics seem to think that it is no bad thing that we have never seen such a 'popular' newspaper, since a newspaper as opposed to leaflets has to talk about a whole range of subjects. It is evidently no bad thing that *all* attempts at this kind of literature, starting with *Rabochaia mysl* and continuing with *Rabochee delo* and others, inevitably turn out to be mongrels – not newspapers, not popular. It is no bad thing that these attempts to create 'worker' newspapers perpetuate the absurd division into a worker movement and an *intelligentnyi* movement (a division created in the first place by the myopia of certain *intelligenty*). It is no bad thing that *all* such attempts only increase artisanal limitations in our movement and are responsible for so many 'original', 'profound' and deeply provincial theories. None of that is a bad thing when we have such *charming* publications as *Svoboda*! It's no bad thing that it is all shit – as long as it is shit *for the masses*![75]

## Terror

> Long live terror as the vanguard of a wide political movement in the masses!
> (L. Nadezhdin, 1901)

Terror nowadays seems to mean killing a lot of innocent bystanders. Terror in the Russian sense meant selective assassination of individual guilty parties. When Russians talked about 'individual' terror, they meant 'terror carried out by individuals or small groups', not 'terror directed against individuals', since terror, as they understood it, was always directed against individuals. Similarly, the 'mass terror' that *Iskra* contrasted to individual terror was not 'terror directed against large groups' but 'terror directed against individuals by large groups'. Mass terror was appropriate only to open revolution. As described by *Iskra*, mass terror looks a lot like lynch law: one hypothetical example was hanging Zubatov from a lamppost.

There were a lot of reasons why individual terror might be useful to the revolutionary cause, all of them discussed at length by the revolutionaries. Terror could protect the revolutionary movement as a whole, either by removing

---

[75] Lenin 1958–65, 46, p. 273 (letter of February 1903 addressed to F.V. Lengnik).

specific enemies or deterring the government by fear of reprisals. It could protect a specific revolutionary group by, say, executing police spies. It could disorganise the government, either by 'decapitating' it or spreading panic and confusion. This kind of terror was only appropriate as part of an attempted overthrow of the government based on some combination of conspiracy and uprising. Terror could also have agitational significance, showing that the government was not all-powerful, thus imbuing slavish subjects with a spirit of resistance. Finally, terror could be an outlet for what the terrorists viewed as honest indignation or generous revenge.

One of the first heroines of Russian terrorism was Vera Zasulich herself, who shot an abusive official in 1878, got acquitted by a Russian jury, and escaped abroad. There she became a Social Democrat as part of Plekhanov's group and, as such, an opponent of individual terror. The sympathy shown her crime by non-revolutionary educated society – the basic cause of her acquittal – remained an important part of the Russian terrorist equation.[76] The great success of Russian terrorism was the assassination of the Tsar in March 1881 – a terrorist success but a complete revolutionary failure. The last major terrorist attempt in this period was an attack on the new Tsar by a group headed by Aleksandr Ulianov, Lenin's older brother, in 1887. This attempt was a terrorist *and* a revolutionary failure.

All Russian revolutionaries around the turn of the century, very much including the *Iskra*-ites, honoured and respected, indeed hero-worshipped, the earlier terrorist revolutionaries. As a political tactic, however, terror fell into disrepute for a simple reason: it had not worked. But, at the turn of the century, the new revolutionary atmosphere led to a reconsideration of terror. No doubt terror could not single-handedly bring about a revolution, but perhaps it could accelerate the arrival of a revolution that was inherent in the prevailing atmosphere of mass protest. The question acquired topicality in February 1901 when the student P.V. Karpovich assassinated the Minister of Education N.P. Bogolepov. *Iskra* had a restrained and frosty reaction to this deed, while *Rabochee delo* felt that revolutionaries with red blood in their veins should applaud it.

*Rabochee delo*, true to itself, nevertheless remained wishy-washy on the subject of terror. Nadezhdin was more forthright. He has not received the

---

[76] See Sally Boniece's study of a later terrorist heroine, Maria Spiridonova (Boniece 2003).

attention he deserves as one of the first Russian revolutionary writers who, inspired by 'the rebirth of revolutionism' at the turn of the century, offered a reasoned case for terror under the new conditions of genuine mass protest.[77]

Nadezhdin started off by rejecting any creational or founding [*sozidaiushchii*] role for terror. Terrorism could not be a substitute for mass protest or for revolution. He also rejected one of the main rationales for the terror in the earlier revolutionary era of the 1870s, namely, the hope of introducing panic and disorganisation in the government. (Nadezhdin calls this the *ustrashaiushchii* role of terror, a coinage which I have translated 'paralysing with fear'.) Yes, there had been some signs of panic and disorganisation back then, but that was because the government was as new to the game as the terrorists. It was utopian to expect similar results today.

Nevertheless, terror could still play an important, if transitory, role today – a role that arose out of Nadezhdin's empirical definition of the situation. All the separate elements of revolution were already present: workers ready to fight, revolutionaries committed to overthrowing the tsar. What was still required was somehow to bring these elements together in dynamic, passionate interaction. The merger of socialism and the worker movement by means of the spread of awareness was too slow and too crippled by Russian conditions. What was needed was a shotgun marriage between revolutionaries and the workers. The heroic assassination of government officials would overcome the inertia of Russian life and galvanise all participants who would then seek each other out to begin intense revolutionary work.

Nadezhdin coined a new term to describe this role: *excitative* [*ekstsitativnyi*] or, as he glossed it with a more Russian sounding word, 'instigating [*vozbudaiushchii*]'. Once the logic of the new rationale was grasped, the very term 'terrorism' is seen to put a misleading emphasis on fear. According to Nadezhdin, *excitarism* would be a better name for the tactic he advocated. He retained the more familiar term only for convenience.

The excitative influence of acts of terror was aimed, in the first place, at the revolutionary intellectuals. Even though the worker movement was continually growing in energy and revolutionary commitment, it was still

---

[77] The first extensive Socialist-Revolutionary manifesto on terror was published in June 1902. Drafted by Viktor Chernov, it contained a sarcastic reference to the debate between Lenin and Nadezhdin (manifesto reprinted in Budnitskii 1996, reference on p. 196).

not carrying out the role assigned to it by *Iskra* of inspiring the revolutionaries to throw themselves heart and soul into revolutionary work.

> At present [the intellectual] does not give himself to the revolutionary cause completely, three quarters of his life slips away in working at some statistical office or running around to teach lessons, and only a pitiful fraction of the day is devoted to revolutionary work. This last is not the only and not the exclusive motor of his existence, but something that is subordinated to a significant extent to personal and family concerns. When asked about his trade [*professiia*], the present-day revolutionary cannot, putting his hand on his heart, say, as Zheliabov did: my job is revolutionary activity.[78]

Terror would not only galvanise these lackadaisical revolutionaries but give them something to talk about with the workers:

> Why are these pistol shots ringing out? Why does the government answer them with fearful punishments that sow death everywhere? From these first two why's come a whole round of other why's about the conditions of Russian political life.[79]

The role of terror was, therefore, the transitory one of breaking the ice and getting the passionate conversation going.

> The opponents of terrorism, if they even feel any need to criticise terror and present it from a negative point of view, will themselves advance by way of *argumentum heroicum* the necessity of intensified political agitation in the masses. Modest political *propaganda* – which does not know the day or the hour when its ideals will be realised in life – will be replaced by untiring *agitation*, calling for the burial of the existing political system and the creation of another.
>
> But that is precisely the goal that terror is striving to advance. Once intensive, energetic agitation begins among the masses, then the excitative (instigating) role of terror is done.[80]

---

[78] Nadezhdin 1903, p. 79. Zheliabov was one of the leaders of Narodnaia volia. As we shall see in Chapter Eight, this passage is the direct source of Lenin's coinage 'revolutionary by trade'.

[79] Nadezhdin 1903, p. 81.

[80] Ibid. (emphasis added). Nadezhdin goes on to say that 'life' will then decide whether terror has other uses.

To sum up,

> Terror cannot help but to intensify the movement if only because it initiates
> political struggle. It is the clear symptom of the beginning of the end. The
> reason for its existence is to throw a spark into that inflammable material
> that has already been collected. The availability of such material is known
> to any observer of Russian life, and if that is the case, then terror is an
> essential, necessary step forward in revolutionary struggle.[81]

In Nadezhdin's view, the workers themselves were quite ready to explode,
although perhaps not in a focused way. It was the focusing force, the
revolutionary intellectuals, that needed to be galvanised. But no amount of
rhetoric could have the effect created by dramatic acts of terror.

> The word – no matter the passion and the power that it breathes – is not
> in a position to break down the sluggishness of Russian life. Many such
> words have swept across Russia and all they do is enrich our political lexicon
> – they do not electrify the head that remains bowed down.[82]

But Nadezhdin's comments reveal the deeper clash between Nadezhdin and
*Iskra*: his close-to-contemptuous dismissal of 'the word'. Nadezhdin wanted
terror to be replaced by agitation, but, for him, 'agitation' meant 'call to action',
in opposition to the 'word' of propaganda – including the wordy articles that
*Iskra* called 'political agitation'. Nadezhdin felt that terror 'could not help'
having a strong effect because it was a 'clear symptom of the beginning of
the end'. The slow spread of awareness was irrelevant during a 'revolutionary
storm'.

The *Iskra*-ites rejected Nadezhdin's dismissal of the allegedly irrelevant
spread of awareness, just as they had mocked *Rabochee delo*'s 'Historical
Turning Point' for its over-excited call for immediate revolutionary attack. In
her review of *Rebirth of Revolutionism*, Zasulich responds directly to Nadezhdin's

---

[81] Nadezhdin 1903, p. 80.
[82] Nadezhdin 1903, p. 79. To some extent, Lenin and Zasulich misunderstood
Nadezhdin's case (as he himself admitted in his second edition, his exposition was
not entirely clear). Lenin summarised Nadezhdin's message in these words: 'we need
to instigate the sluggish course of the worker movement by means of excitative terror'
(Lenin 1958–65, 6, p. 105 [769]). Nadezhdin did not say or mean that the worker
movement was sluggish, but 'Russian life' in general and the intellectuals in particular
were sluggish.

assertion: 'Thus, in a movement that is developing and accelerating but is still closer to the beginning than to the end, the author would like to artificially call forth symptoms of the end'.[83]

The polemic against terrorism inspired by Nadezhdin takes up only a few pages in WITBD and yet its presence helps give the book balance. One of the fundamental characteristics of Erfurtianism is the two-front polemical war against isolation of the worker movement on the one hand and against the isolation of socialist intelligentsia on the other. Much of WITBD is occupied with clean-up skirmishes on the first of these two fronts, namely, 'economist' isolation of the worker movement. In this sense, the book closes a period in party history, since the real fighting on the other front was just about to commence. By including a polemic against terrorism, WITBD looks toward the future.

The title of the section devoted to terrorism is 'What do economism and terrorism have in common?'.[84] This title re-affirms more explicitly than anywhere else in WITBD the Erfurtian logic of the two-front war. What Lenin sees in common between the two is (in the polemical phrase invented for WITBD) 'kow-towing to *stikhiinost*' – either the *stikhiinost* (meaning, in this context, isolation) of the worker movement or the *stikhiinost* of revolutionary *intelligenty* who 'do not have the ability or who do not find it possible to link revolutionary work into one whole with the worker movement'.[85] The great sin, from either side, is to lose faith in the goal of linkage, since the worker movement cannot 'with its own forces' make an effective revolution, and *intelligenty* 'with their own forces' cannot do it either.[86] According to Lenin, these terrorist *intelligenty* have unjustifiably lost faith – they do not see the eagerness of the workers for revolutionary ideas and revolutionary activity, the 'greed' of the workers for political literature, their genuine indignation at the 'disgusting outrages of Russian life'. In fact, these *intelligenty* that Lenin attacks so fiercely bear a curious resemblance to the portrait of Lenin that we find in the textbook interpretation.

---

[83] Zasulich 1983a, p. 361. Zasulich's comment is cited by Lenin in WITBD; see Lenin 1958–65, 6, p. 127 [797].

[84] Lenin 1958–65, 6, pp. 74–8 [741–4].

[85] Lenin 1958–65, 6, p. 75 [742].

[86] Lenin 1958–65, 6, pp. 30, 75 [702, 742].

The polemic against terror is a brief excursion placed smack in the middle of the book. It tends to get lost in the shuffle. I highly recommend to those determined to grasp the spirit of *WITBD* that they read it early on and give it due attention.

## Tkachevs great and small

There has been a persistent effort in Western scholarship to tie Lenin as closely as possible to the Russian revolutionary tradition and, by so doing, to distance him as far as possible from European socialism. The aim, one speculates, is to 'Orientalise' Lenin and to make him the voice of a so-called Eastern Marxism: Marx, for all his sins, was a solid European, while Lenin the non-European Russian misunderstood Marx so completely *because* he was a Russian.[87]

The odd thing is that Lenin's foes among the Russian Social Democrats were more prone then he was to invoke the earlier Russian revolutionaries as concrete models for the present day. *Rabochaia mysl* devoted much of the notorious Separate Supplement to extravagant praise of Chernyshevsky, while Lenin testily responded that Chernyshevsky had his weak sides as well as strong sides.[88] *WITBD* is chock-full of invocations of the SPD model and barely mentions Narodnaia volia (as documented in Chapter Seven). In contrast, during the debate at the 1903 Second Congress over the definition of a party member, Akselrod – who opposed Lenin's definition and soon became the ideological mentor of the Mensheviks – praised the organisational structure of Narodnaia volia and said the same principle should be strictly carried out in Social-Democratic organisations.[89] The perplexing conclusion that many scholars draw from this record is that Lenin based his organisational ideas on Narodnaia volia, while the Mensheviks based themselves on the 'European' SPD.

The same pattern holds for Petr Tkachev, a Russian revolutionary writer of the 1860s and 1870s. Tkachev called for political conspiracy, minority revolution, the use of terror, and an organised, disciplined (but not mass)

---

[87] One of the first to argue in this way is Nicolas Berdyaev (Berdyaev 1960, first published in 1937).

[88] Lenin 1958–65, 4, p. 259 (*Retrogression*, Lenin's 1899 protest writing against *Rabochaia mysl*). The author of the Chernyshevsky article in the Separate Supplement was Takhtarev (Nicolaevsky 1927, p. 34).

[89] *Vtoroi s"ezd . . .* 1959, p. 262.

party. As a result, many writers believe that in one way or another Tkachev was in fact 'the first Bolshevik'.[90] Yet the Social-Democratic writer most obviously influenced by Tkachev was Nadezhdin, who adopted his specific vocabulary and many of his specific arguments. Lenin picked up on this and openly mocked Nadezhdin as a 'little Tkachev'. In all of Lenin's writings, this polemic sally is the only substantive comment on Tkachev. The conclusion drawn by some writers is that Lenin has here revealed his admiration of Tkachev.

Let us turn to Tkachev himself to get an idea of his outlook and the catch-phrases that became associated with him. Here, I must first correct a bizarre error put about by Robert Service, who tells us that Tkachev was 'one of Europe's most distinguished Marxologists in the 1870s' and, in fact, claimed to understand Marx better than Engels.[91] I do not know where Service picked up this idea, but certainly not from the responsible scholars who have previously written about the putative Tkachev-Lenin link.[92]

Tkachev was, indeed, one of the very first to quote Marx in Russian legally published literature (in 1865) and was influenced by Marx's economic materialism, although he certainly never claimed to be a disciple.[93] Scholars both in Russia and the West argue about how far Tkachev actually assimilated Marxist principles. At present, there seems to be general agreement (which I share) that Tkachev was somewhat influenced by Marxist economic materialism but not at all by Marxist political strategy. In 1874, he wrote an open letter to Engels in which he made no distinction between Marx and Engels but attacked both men impartially for their ideas as well as their

---

[90] This is the title of Weeks 1968; see also Hardy 1977 (these studies contain references to journal literature).

[91] Service 1985–95, p. 38; Service 2000, p. 98; editorial notes to Lenin 1988. Service writes that Tkachev 'argued that Engels, after Marx's death, had been insufficiently "Marxist" inasmuch as his *Anti-Dühring* had offered an excessively deterministic analysis of world history' (Service 2000, p. 98). By the time Marx died in 1883, Tkachev had already suffered a complete mental breakdown and had been confined to an insane asylum, where he remained until his death in 1886. *Anti-Dühring* was published during Marx's lifetime.

[92] For example, Service cites Andrzej Walicki as an authority, but Walicki's accurate account of Tkachev has nothing in common with the claims made by Service (see Walicki 1979, pp. 244–52).

[93] Leonard Schapiro claims that Tkachev called himself as a 'Marxist' and speculates at length why he did this. Schapiro's error comes from his misunderstanding of a remark by Boris Koz'min. Compare Schapiro 1986, pp. 139–40 with Koz'min 1961, p. 374.

activities in the International Working Men's Association. This open letter defended not Marx but Bakunin – oddly enough, since Tkachev was generally a caustic and effective critic of anarchism. In emigration, Tkachev collaborated with the French Blanquists, participated in their newspaper *Ni dieu ni maître*, and the French Blanquist Eduard Vaillant gave an eulogy at his funeral.[94]

Tkachev's view of the Russian situation in his day is summed up by the title of the journal he published in emigration: *Nabat* [*The Tocsin*]. The name was chosen because Tkachev had an eve-of-revolution standpoint: just as a peasant village rings the tocsin bell to summon the villagers in time of emergency, just so Tkachev used his writings to summon all and sundry to drop everything in view of the impending revolutionary storm. Precisely on this point is revealed the deepest difference between Tkachev and Lenin the Russian Erfurtian. Tkachev insisted over and over again that revolutionaries would never be able to propagandise to the masses under tsarist repression and any such attempt was a lily-livered excuse to avoid the genuine revolutionary action that was needed. Thus, WITBD is a book-long refutation of one of Tkachev's central points. Tkachev also would have contemptuously rejected the idea of a revolution aiming for political freedom rather than for socialism. For Tkachev, putting the bourgeoisie in power would only delay the socialist revolution, perhaps forever.[95]

Terror was not an intrinsic or distinctive part of Tkachev's outlook. He insisted, rather, on the necessity of a political conspiracy for the conquest [*zakhvat*] of power by an enlightened minority for the purposes of socialist transformation (*not* political freedom). Toward the end of his career, he wrote articles advocating the use of terror in aid of such a conspiracy. This shift to terror came about partly under the influence of Polish émigrés who gradually took over *Nabat* and partly due to the adoption of terror tactics by Narodnaia volia in Russia. The function Tkachev gave to terror was (in Nadezhdin's terminology) 'paralysing'. In 1879, in one of Tkachev's last articles for *Nabat*, he summed up his current programme : 'Organisation as a means, terrorisation, disorganisation and annihilation of the existing governmental power as the immediate and most essential goal'.[96]

---

[94] Weeks 1968, p. 62.
[95] This is my own summary of Tkachev's standpoint, based on the writings collected in Tkachev 1932–7 and Tkachev 1975.
[96] Tkachev 1932–7, 3, pp. 441–7 (1879 article in *Nabat*).

Although Nadezhdin was aiming at a political rather than a socialist revolution, his 'eve-of-revolution' standpoint reveals a clear affinity with Tkachev. His use of Tkachev's catch-phrases such as 'tocsin' is illustrated by the following passage from his *Rebirth of Revolutionism*:

> What is needed is for the political tendencies in the worker masses to cut extremely deep furrows so that we hear on all highways and byways about the disturbances in the worker masses who are aiming at political goals – only in this case will all that is alive but still sleepy rouse itself and beat the tocsin. But the political worker movement is just starting, and therefore, in the *ordinary course of things*, it is not in a position to create such an atmosphere of life and creation. A strong shove is needed for this movement, and terror will give this.[97]

In the second edition of 1903, Nadezhdin cut this passage because he felt his wording gave rise to the false impression that he thought terror was needed to 'excite' the worker movement. Thus, as a result of *Iskra*-ite polemics against Nadezhdin, the sum total of Tkachev-style catch-phrases in Social-Democratic circulation went *down*.

Lenin immediately seized on this affinity between Tkachev and Nadezhdin and used it to discredit Nadezhdin:

> Yes – the most sincere indignation about [party] narrowness, the most passionate desire to lift up the people who are kow-towing before this narrowness is not enough, if the indignant person proceeds without a rudder and without sail, in the same '*stikhiinyi*' fashion as the revolutionaries of the 1870s, if he latches on to 'excitative terror', to 'agrarian terror', to a 'tocsin' and so on.[98]

The principal 'revolutionary of the 1870s' that Lenin has in mind is Tkachev.

The following comment by Lenin is even more sarcastic about Nadezhdin's use of Tkachev-style catch-phrases:

> They say that history does not repeat itself. But Nadezhdin is trying with all his might to do so. He zealously copies Tkachev by denouncing 'revolutionary cultural uplift', shouting about 'the tocsin bell of the parish

---

[97] Nadezhdin 1903, Appendix p. 81 (response to Zasulich where he quotes from his own first edition).

[98] Lenin 1958–65, 6, p. 166 [824].

church', about the special 'eve-of-revolution point of view', and so forth. He forgets, evidently, the well-known saying that, if the original of a historical event is a tragedy, then a copy of it is merely a farce. The attempt to seize power that Tkachev's preaching helped to prepare and that was carried out by means of a 'paralysing' terror that really did paralyse, had grandeur – but the 'excitative' terror of the little Tkachev is simply ridiculous and especially ridiculous when it is supplemented by the idea of an organisation of middle workers.[99]

The 'attempt to seize powers by means of paralysing terror' to which Lenin refers was the assassination of the Tsar in 1881 by Narodnaia volia. In calling Narodnaia volia's attempt 'magnificent', Lenin reflected a *consensus omnium* of Russian (indeed international) Social Democracy. All stood in awe of the heroic struggle of a small band of dedicated revolutionaries engaged in a duel with the mighty autocratic government – and so on, the phrases called forth by the theme being rather stereotyped.

Narodnaia volia's use of terror did, in fact, momentarily paralyse the government. It also conclusively proved (at least for Social Democrats) that this kind of terror did not justify the hopes placed on it. Even Nadezhdin conceded that the 'paralysing' function of terror was outdated. Lenin pounces on this concession in order to reject unambiguously any application of Tkachev's ideas to the situation Russian revolutionaries faced in 1901: 'To admit that today one cannot "paralyse" – and therefore, disorganise – means, in essence, to completely condemn terror as a system of struggle, as a sphere of activity sanctified by a programme.'[100]

Lenin's comment on Tkachev does pay him one compliment: Lenin asserts that Tkachev's preaching helped prepare the way for Narodnaia volia. This factual assertion was controversial then and remains controversial today. The shift in Russian revolutionary thinking at the end of the 1870s away from earlier strategies (Bakunin-style attempts to instigate peasant riots and Lavrov-style attempts to propagandise to the peasants) toward political conspiracy was one that had long been advocated by Tkachev, who was highly supportive of Narodnaia volia. But these facts do not necessarily mean that Tkachev and

---

[99] Lenin 1958–65, 6, p. 173 [830]. The particular phrases quoted by Lenin can be found in *Eve of Revolution* (Nadezhdin 1901a, pp. 60–7).
[100] Lenin 1958–65, 6, p. 77 [743].

his émigré writings had any actual influence on debates inside Russia. Vera Figner, one of the leaders of the conspiracy, denied that Tkachev had any influence at all. Other scholars have found connections between Tkachev and specific individuals in the Russian underground. The question continues to be a disputed one (a thorough examination of the topic has recently been made by the Russian historian E.L. Rudnitskaia).[101]

Lenin was aware that his views on Tkachev's influence were personal opinion rather than generally accepted fact. N. Valentinov was a young Russian Social Democrat who was close to Lenin for a few months in Geneva in 1904. Perhaps historians have taken too literally his claim that he could remember decades-old conversations accurately word-for-word. Nevertheless, the essence of the following conversation does seem confirmed by the Tkachev passage in *WITBD*. Valentinov had just said he agrees with every word with Plekhanov's *Our Differences* (1885). In *Our Differences*, one of the seminal works of Russian Marxism, Plekhanov uses Tkachev as a central example of the dead-end reached by populist political strategy. Lenin responds to Valentinov's remark as follows:

> Well, now, you are going a bit too far in the other direction there. . . . That book had an enormous influence on men of my generation. Yet, no matter how great our respect for the book, it's not necessary to agree with every word of it. That's too much! There's something glaringly wrong in the introduction. Plekhanov's attitude to Tkachev is wrong. In his day, Tkachev was a great revolutionary, a real Jacobin, who had a great influence on the most active section of *Narodnaia volia*. But Plekhanov has never had a sufficiently objective attitude to that movement. I know, from talking to him about it, that he had personal clashes with some members of it and this has coloured his attitude to the whole *Narodnaia volia* movement.[102]

Tkachev is thus not personally a negative image for Lenin. He is, for Lenin, a dedicated and, in many ways, insightful revolutionary of the 1870s and deserved to be honoured as such. In particular, Lenin feels he had not been given due credit as a forerunner of Narodnaia volia, and he takes the

---

[101] Rudnitskaia 1992.
[102] Valentinov 1968, p. 203. Valentinov nowhere suggests that Lenin prefers Tkachev to Plekhanov on any substantive issue.

opportunity in *WITBD* to give him that credit. And what is the opportunity? The opportunity is a scornful rejection of Tkachev's *outlook* as even conceivably appropriate to Russia in 1901. For Lenin, Nadezhdin's use of Tkachev-style language and concepts refutes itself. What was a justifiable, indeed inevitable and therefore tragic error in the 1870s is merely ridiculous now.[103]

Advocates of a Tkachev-Lenin link also point to other memoir evidence of admiring remarks made by Lenin about Tkachev in 1904. I cannot go into detail here about what this memoir evidence actually shows. Suffice it to say that Lenin's remarks were about Tkachev as a historical figure. The idea that Lenin used Tkachev as a reliable guide to on-going political decisions in 1904–5 or any other time is totally absurd.[104]

Lenin's attitude toward Tkachev was the standard Erfurtian one toward pre-Marxist predecessors. Each of them had, in Kautsky's phrase, *ein Stückchen des Richtigen*, a little bit of the truth. Since they wrote prior to the great synthesis, they pushed their little bit of truth to one-sided extremes. Tkachev's bit of truth was the anti-anarchist emphasis on political power and on the need for a strong party organisation, themes that he bravely pushed in an atmosphere dominated by anarchist prejudices. These themes found their place in the Social-Democratic synthesis, although their meaning was profoundly altered when placed in the context of a class-based mass movement. Lenin did not pick up the emphasis on party organisation from Tkachev. He learned it from Marx, Kautsky and the SPD, and then, looking back, saw that Tkachev was to be commended for his early advocacy of it. (I can only assume he saw this, since he never felt moved to compliment Tkachev in print.) On any point where Tkachev was at odds with the Erfurtian synthesis, Lenin did not even think of taking Tkachev seriously.

In Part II we have had to go into great detail about the infighting and polemics among Russian Social Democrats. Many of the issues at dispute

---

[103] I have gone into detail about Lenin's attitude toward Tkachev and his tactics partly because of the attempt by Robert Service to use Lenin's mention of Tkachev to prove that mass revolutionary murder 'pervaded the thoughts of the future Russian Marxist Vladimir Ulyanov' (Service 1985–95, 1, pp. 29, 99). Service's astounding misrepresentation of the *WITBD* passage serves as a pillar of his interpretation of Lenin's whole career (see also Service 1985–95, 1, p. 200, Service 1988, p. 39; Service 2000, p. 139).

[104] For such claims, see Service 1985–95, 1, p. 135; Service 2000, pp. 170–1.

represented genuine and crucial political choices, many others were only the verbal froth of mutually willed misunderstanding. In rejecting the economism of the *Credo* and the editorials in *Rabochaia mysl*, Lenin stood within what was, by 1901–2, a Social-Democratic consensus. In attacking *Rabochee delo*, Lenin was engaged in a fight for influence within the Party, during which both sides indulged in a higher percentage than usual of unscrupulous and obfuscating polemics. Lenin's aim in these polemics was to affirm Social-Democratic commonplaces and to take advantage of his opponents' gaffes to make them look marginal. In evaluating the assessments of the current Russian situation given by the *Joint Letter*, Savinkov and Nadezhdin, Lenin made clear his own highly optimistic assessment of the empirical potential of the spread of awareness. In all three cases, Lenin portrayed himself as fighting the good fight against scepticism and defeatism.

Since Lenin was not writing to make his outlook on life clear to those reading WITBD decades later, but, rather, to ensure the triumph of his faction and to see his proposals accepted in the Russia of 1902, the journey through these polemics has been absolutely necessary. But, now, we are in a position to go to WITBD, push the polemics aside, and see clearly the view of the world Lenin wanted his readers to adopt.

Part Three

## The World of *What Is to Be Done?*

# Chapter Seven
## Lenin's Erfurtian Drama

One of the very first readers of *WITBD* was Lenin's editorial colleague Aleksandr Potresov. After looking at the book in proofs, Potresov wrote Lenin that while he was a little uneasy about some of Lenin's generalisations concerning the *stikhiinyi* worker movement, he very much liked the book. Indeed, he felt that many passages were genuine poetry.[1]

In 1905, looking back at *WITBD* at a period when he opposed Lenin, it was precisely the poetry that repelled Potresov. Now he felt that *WITBD* was the perfect expression of the unrealistic self-glorifying dreams of the revolutionary *praktiki*. Potresov was repelled by the exalted rhetoric that invoked the 'proletariat awakening in *stikhiinyi* fashion', whose allegedly enthusiastic support allows the underground *praktik* to accomplish miracles. *WITBD*'s grandiosely utopian optimism, its 'romantic' dreams 'foreign to any scepticism' – this is the heart of Potresov's case against *WITBD*.[2]

Poetry – whether good or bad, romantic or otherwise – is not a word often used for describing Lenin's book.[3] *WITBD* is a book of angry polemics and

---

[1] Potresov's letter to Lenin was written in March 1902; it can be found in Lenin 1926–35, 4, p. 599.

[2] Potresov in *Iskra*, No. 107 (29 July 1905), reprinted in Potresov 2002, pp. 67–120.

[3] But see Marie 2004, p. 72: 'Lénine évoque avec lyrisme les perspectives radieuses' of a underground newspaper regularly produced on a weekly basis.

nuts-and-bolts practical proposals, and it takes historical empathy and contextual knowledge to see the poetry lurking between the angry rejoinders. And, yet, digging out this poetry is necessary if we want to grasp the impact the book made on its intended audience. This is true whether we agree with the Potresov of 1902 that the poetry was impressive or with the Potresov of 1905 that the poetry was meretricious.

A would-be leader always situates his recommendation for action in the framework of a broader *definition of the situation*. This definition locates both problems that need to be overcome and opportunities for an effective solution to these problems. Once the leader gets people to accept his definition of the situation, his work is two-thirds done.[4] The political poetry of WITBD is located in this larger definition of the situation within which the polemics and the proposals are embedded.

Given Lenin's Erfurtian loyalties, we would expect this definition to include such things as the fundamental relevance of the SPD model, the workers' eagerness to hear and understand the Social-Democratic message, the willingness of other social forces to accept the Social-Democratic worker movement as a leader in the fight for democratic rights and political freedom. And we do find all of these things. What is less predictable is the excitement and intensity with which Lenin portrays Russia's ongoing revolutionary crisis and the exalted vistas he presents to the Social-Democratic *praktiki*.

Lenin's definition of the situation is, in fact, a heroic Erfurtian drama. WITBD invited the young Social-Democratic revolutionaries to think of themselves as inspiring leaders, indeed as heroes. It told these aspiring heroes that they could accomplish great things because they had available to them the tidal force of a great popular movement. The *praktiki* inspire the workers and the workers inspire the rest of society. Despite police-state repression, the proletariat was on the move, the mass of the people were ready to follow the workers, and even educated society was riddled with anti-tsarist indignation. Yet this vast army could not accomplish its great deed of bringing political freedom to Russia unless the Social-Democratic revolutionaries got their act together and applied the SPD model in a creative way so as to provide an effective organisation for all this bubbling protest.

---

[4] On a leader's definition of the situation, see Tucker 1981.

The political poetry of WITBD is thus the spark set off by the contact of the highly charged SPD model with Lenin's highly charged definition of the revolutionary situation in Russia. Together, these two create an intense political drama that portrays a volcanic spread of awareness sweeping over Russia. The heroes of this drama are the Social-Democratic activists and workers who are inspired by the socialist message and inspire others in turn.

In order to perceive this drama, we need to look past the polemics and proposals to the Erfurtian assumptions that sustain them. The present chapter is devoted to this task. We will start by pushing aside a veil that has effectively hidden Lenin's political poetry from view: his famous pronouncements on 'consciousness from without' and 'combating spontaneity'. We will then examine the motivation of the actors in Lenin's political drama. Lenin inhabits a rational political universe where people always act for good reasons – but this rationality is a highly dramatic one.

We will then follow Lenin's picture of the spread of awareness from its source in Germany to its final incarnation in the Russian revolutionary crisis. German Social Democracy was Lenin's own inspiration and WITBD is permeated with invocations of the success of the SPD in inspiring the workers. We then look briefly at the Social-Democratic activist, the *praktik* whom Lenin wishes to raise up to be a *vozhd* or inspiring leader. Lenin assigns an exalted role not only to the Social-Democratic leader/guide but also to the worker follower. Perhaps nowhere else is Lenin's confidence in the spread of awareness so clearly revealed as in his portrait of the worker rank-and-file that strives to receive and pass on the message.

The spread of awareness rolls on and becomes an enormous *stikhiinyi* upsurge enveloping all of Russian society. This vision of the *stikhiinyi* upsurge is what unites the definition of the situation found in WITBD to Lenin's outlook expressed during later revolutionary crises, as we will see by a brief look beyond WITBD to 1905 and 1912. Only this wider view will enable us to understand the full meaning of Lenin's famous Archimedean cry: 'give us an organisation of revolutionaries – and we will turn Russia around!'.[5]

---

[5] Lenin 1958–65, 6, p. 127 [789]. The usual translation is 'and we will overturn Russia!'.

## Raising the curtain

A curtain stands before most readers and the Erfurtian drama displayed on the pages of *WITBD*. This curtain consists of the two most famous passages in the book, the ones that are endlessly recycled in secondary accounts as the essence of Lenin's outlook (I cite these in the standard English translation because some of the scandal caused by these passages is a direct result of translation decisions). In one passage Lenin says that

> Social-Democratic consciousness could only have been brought to the workers from without. The history of all countries shows that the working class exclusively by its own effort is able to develop only trade-union consciousness.[6]

In the other, Lenin announces that

> the task of Social Democracy is *to combat spontaneity, to divert* the working-class movement from this spontaneous, trade-unionist striving to come under the wing of the bourgeoisie, and to bring it under the wing of revolutionary Social Democracy.[7]

The implications of these statements *seem* clear. Do not they show that Lenin stood Western Marxism and Social Democracy on its head? Marx and his Social-Democratic followers believed that the proletariat was a naturally revolutionary class that could be, must be, entrusted with the task of introducing socialism. Lenin did not believe that the workers were capable of even understanding this task, since all they wanted was material improvements. Instead of leading the workers, any self-respecting group of revolutionaries must *combat* their spontaneous strivings and *divert* them from their actual inclinations. From this position, it logically follows that a narrow, élite and conspiratorial band of revolutionaries recruited from the intellectuals must substitute themselves for the revolutionary class. A remarkable argument for a self-professed Marxist! Probably the only way we can account for such an aberration is to point to the similarly élitist and conspiratorial tradition of Russian populism.

There have been two approaches to these passages since *WITBD* was published. One is to see these couple of paragraphs as the key to understanding

---

[6] Lenin 1958–65, 6, pp. 30–1 [702]; Lenin 1988, p. 98.
[7] Lenin 1958–65, 6, p. 40 [711]; Lenin 1988, p. 107.

Lenin. All other Lenin material should be seen through the prism of what these passages seem at first sight to be saying. The other approach is to dismiss these passages as polemical formulations that are unlikely to shed much light on Lenin's outlook. In 1904, the Bolshevik Mikhail Olminskii put the case in the following terms:

> The immediate historical circumstances determined the general content of the literary productions of *Iskra* and *Zaria*. (The pamphlet *What Is to Be Done?* obviously falls in this category. One therefore mustn't look on this pamphlet as a complete catechism for Social Democrats nor as a full expression of the opinions of its author.) For example, it would have been pointless to talk about the enlistment [*vovlechenie*] of the masses into the political movement at a time when it was precisely the masses who were enlisting their intelligentsia leaders into politics. It was unnecessary to defend the role of *stikhiinost*, because it was fully acknowledged anyway. It *was* imperative to concentrate on the issue of organisers and purposive tactical leaders at a time when the lack of both of these things was the sore spot of the movement.[8]

The textbook interpretation is built on the first of these two approaches. As a curtain-raiser to Lenin's Erfurtian drama, I will briefly sketch out an aggressive version of the second approach. A more exhaustive analysis can be found in Annotations Part Two.

Why did Lenin pen these two passages? Lenin's original intention in writing *WITBD* was to set forth in a relatively non-polemical way a package of practical proposals concerning political agitation, organisational professionalism, and the use of a party newspaper as an aid to party unification. These were the themes announced in his *Iskra* article of spring 1901. He changed his mind and made the book intensely polemical because of the squabble with *Rabochee delo* that broke out in autumn 1901. *Rabochee delo*'s full-scale attack on *Iskra*'s claim to leadership in Russian Social Democracy caused Lenin to tack on at the last minute two new polemical chapters at the beginning of the book.

---

[8] Olminskii 1904b, p. 7 (the parenthetical comment on *WITBD* is a footnote in the original). In an article in 1924, Olminskii recalled that Lenin's clumsy [*neudachnaia*] phrase led to confusion even among Bolsheviks, but Lenin scornfully refused to clear it up. And, Olminskii adds, this was understandable, since none of his accusers had a conscious theory that took more account of the elemental force of the proletarian movement than did Lenin's (*Proletarskaia revoliutsiia*, 1924, No. 3, pp. 28–30).

The second of these two tacked-on chapters is devoted to Boris Krichevskii's article in *Rabochee delo*, No. 10 (September 1901), entitled 'Principles, Tactics and Struggle'. As we saw in Chapter Five, this article mounted a pseudo-theoretical critique of *Iskra*'s 'underestimation of the *stikhiinyi* element'. In response, Lenin wrote Chapter II entitled 'The *Stikhiinost* of the Masses and the Purposiveness of Social Democracy'. The two scandalous passages are both in this chapter.

*Stikhiinyi* is a rich Russian word with a variety of meanings arising from a root metaphor of an unstoppable natural force. Any minimally coherent theoretical dispute would require some sorting out of the various definitions and conflicting connotations. No one involved in the *Iskra/Rabochee delo* dispute made the slightest effort to do this. On the contrary, the angry polemics only made the word more unfocused and confusing. In Annotations Part Two, I list six distinct meanings of *stikhiinyi* that emerge from this debate, plus a couple more from WITBD. Clarity was further dimmed by the shift of attention from the relatively concrete and vivid adjective *stikhiinyi* to the nebulous abstract noun *stikhiinost*.

The polemical waters were further muddied by the *Joint Letter* that arrived in *Iskra* offices soon after the fall-out with *Rabochee delo* (see Chapter Six). This letter asserted a thesis very close to the Prokopovich/Kuskova 'line of least resistance', namely, that material elements determine the path from which no leaders can cause the movement to stray. For the most part, Lenin's critique of the *Joint Letter* is substantive and based on genuinely disputed issues. But Lenin also decided to use the out-and-out economism of the *Joint Letter* as a stick with which to beat Krichevskii. Thus, he tried his hardest to mix together Krichevskii's vocabulary [*stikhiinost*] and the *Joint Letter*'s vocabulary ('stray from the path') as a way of demonstrating to his own satisfaction that the two were really saying the same thing – which they were not.

One more item from autumn 1901 was thrown into this polemical stew. As Lenin was working on WITBD, the latest issue of Kautsky's *Neue Zeit* arrived with an article by Kautsky on some proposed changes in the party programme of the Austrian Social-Democratic Party. One passage in particular seemed to Lenin to support the accusation he was making against *Rabochee delo* and the *Joint Letter*, namely, that they ignored the fundamental mission of Social Democracy to bring the socialist message to the workers. (This accusation had some justification in the case of the *Joint Letter* and very little in the case of *Rabochee delo*.) The Kautsky passage reiterated the canonical merger narrative by saying that the socialist message comes to the worker movement 'from without' (just as the message about worker militancy comes to the socialist movement from without). Lenin was so taken with this phrase as ammunition against his polemical targets that (as I argue in the Annotations) he inserted the passage and the terminology into an already existing draft.

Thus, Lenin insists on making his point with a heterogeneous vocabulary taken from three distinct polemical formulations of other writers: Krichevskii [*stikhiinost*], *Joint Letter* ('stray from the path'), Kautsky ('from without'). The resulting confusion is further compounded for English readers by the standard translation of the first two items: 'spontaneity' and 'divert'. 'Spontaneity' is a rich and powerful English word with only a tangential overlap with the Russian word 'stikhiinost'. I cannot recall a single discussion of *WITBD* that makes an effort to define the English word 'spontaneity' or that allows for the possibility that the English word might not be a good guide to Lenin's meaning. The same holds true for 'divert'. On the contrary, for many writers these two English words taken in isolation sum up Lenin's outlook.[9]

The polemical argument Lenin is making with the help of this off-the-cuff vocabulary can be paraphrased as follows: right now the *stikhiinyi* upsurge of the Russian workers is galvanising all of Russian society and preparing the way for the imminent overthrow of tsarism. If this uprising were given adequate Social-Democratic leadership, it could carry out the revolution in a way most advantageous to Social Democracy, that is, achieving a maximum extension of political freedom. The potentiality for this kind of leadership exists, and so we must fight against any obstacle to realising this potential. One such obstacle is the confused attitude of *Iskra*'s main rivals in the Russian movement, *Rabochee delo*. The accusation Boris Krichevskii has flung at *Iskra* – *Iskra* allegedly underestimates the *stikhiinyi* element – is a perfect example of this unfocused attitude. If we take it to its logical conclusion, is it not tantamount to denying the need for any active Social-Democratic leadership at all? Is Krichevskii not really saying the same thing as the *Joint Letter* when it asserts that active Social-Democratic leadership has no impact at all? What is

---

[9] For example, Bertram Wolfe writes that, for Lenin, 'stikhijnost', spontaneity, the natural liberty of men and classes to be themselves, was the enemy and opposite of consciousness' (Wolfe 1984, p. 30).

Krichevskii's position but the parody of Marxism concocted by its Russian foes who accused it of passive fatalism?

From this paraphrase we learn the most important thing to keep in mind about the scandalous passages, namely, that Lenin's aim is not to assert a bold new proposition, but to make his opponents look marginal by claiming that they reject a universally accepted commonplace. His polemical strategy is a standard one: take your opponent's arguments to their 'logical conclusion', that is, draw ridiculous conclusions from them. This is the same game that was played against Lenin with some success a couple of years later.

It is easy to show just how common is the commonplace affirmed by Lenin, because, as it happens, *Rabochee delo* also accused *Iskra* of exactly the same crime: remaining passive in the face of *stikhiinyi* forces, that is, refusing the primary Social-Democratic duty of providing enlightened leadership.

In late 1901, before WITBD appeared, Martynov accused *Iskra* of giving too *much* scope to *stikhiinost*:

> *Either* Social Democracy takes upon itself the immediate guidance of the economic struggle of the proletariat and by so doing turns it into a revolutionary class struggle. . . . *Or* this perspective: Social Democracy distances itself from the guidance of the economic struggle of the workers and by so doing, on the one hand, clips its own wings, and on the other hand, gives scope to the *stikhiinost* of the worker movement, thereby making the movement less dangerous to the autocracy.[10]

Martynov explained in detail why Social Democracy had to combat the *stikhiinyi* character of the worker movement.

> It could be objected that the economic struggle of the workers arose outside of the influence of Social Democracy and earlier than that influence [NB: Lenin argues precisely this in WITBD]. True; but this struggle has a *stikhiinyi* character. Often workers, aware of only their transitory and special interests, act in opposition to the interests of the whole worker class. There have been and there continue to be cases where the workers themselves demand longer shifts and non-compliance with factory laws. There have been and there continue to be times when their boiling rage unleashes itself against

---

[10] Martynov 1902, pp. 18–20.

Jews . . . against foreigners, and so on. By taking into its hands the guidance of this struggle, Social Democracy significantly widens it and, most of all, brings into it light and awareness.[11]

Martynov's article appeared in time for Lenin to respond to it in WITBD, although only in a tacked-on footnote. Lenin's whole rhetorical campaign against *Rabochee delo* was based on the charge of 'kow-towing to *stikhiinost'*. How could Lenin quote Martynov without undercutting his entire polemical framework? Simple: he ends his quotation right before the accusing words 'gives scope to the *stikhiinost* of the worker movement' and replaces them with an ellipsis.[12]

At the Second Congress, Martynov was the most vociferous critic of WITBD. Yet Martynov took for granted Social Democracy's responsibility to bring light and awareness to the *stikhiinyi* worker movement and he even accused *Iskra* of giving scope to *stikhiinost*. This highly revealing exchange shows that Lenin was trying to affirm something that was utterly non-controversial.

Unfortunately, he did not do it very well, for all the reasons I have just set out: hasty polemical improvisation, use of borrowed vocabulary, and an insistence on equating *Rabochee delo* with people holding quite different views. The sorry result is exemplified by the phrase 'the history of all countries shows', and so forth. We have encountered this phrase a number of times in our survey of Lenin's writings. It always introduces a refutation of Russian sceptics and pessimists. Lenin says to these sceptics: granted, the Russian worker movement does not at present equal the mighty German worker movement, but so what? So what if Russian Social Democracy is pitifully weak compared to the mighty German Party? The history of all countries shows that the worker movement *always* starts off small, weak, and disorganised. Our disappointing present is their past, and so we can be confident that their inspiring present is our future.

It would be strange if Lenin used the same words in WITBD in order to make a totally different argument. And, in fact, a close reading of this 'from

[11] Ibid. These statements also show that Haimson is mistaken to attribute to *Rabochee delo* and Martynov in particular the view that 'workers *by their own devices* would be able to set their own political objectives, rather than having them dictated to them by outside political actors' (Haimson 2004, p. 60 [emphasis in the original]).

[12] Lenin 1958–65, 6, p. 76 [743].

without' passage in *WITBD* shows that he was, indeed, making his usual point.[13] Nevertheless, Lenin managed to convey the impression that he was refuting overconfidence and optimism rather than scepticism and pessimism. And it cannot be denied that the scandalous passages, taken in isolation without knowledge of the polemical context (and especially in the standard English translation), do seem to convey a pessimistic attitude about the socialist awareness of the workers. How, then, to proceed?

To defenders of the textbook interpretation, I suggest the following. Either Lenin's alleged 'worry about workers' is expressed elsewhere in his writings or it is not. If it is, then why not document your case without using the scandalous passages, since doubt has been thrown on the usefulness of these? Your case will be all the more convincing. If, on the contrary, Lenin's 'worry about workers' only finds expression here, then you might want to give us an explanation as to why Lenin revealed his real outlook only in a confused, last-minute, polemical improvisation.[14]

In any event, if you choose to adopt the intensive method of mining these couple of paragraphs for the heart of Lenin's outlook, then you need to do it right. You need to go into detail about the actual meaning of 'spontaneity' and 'divert', about the sources of this vocabulary and Lenin's polemical intentions in adopting it, and finally about what precisely these passages do say and what they do not say. I myself have gone into all these details and the results are set out at perhaps excruciating length in Annotations Part Two. My conclusions are unfavourable to the textbook interpretation, so you will need to refute the contentions contained therein.

To those interested in what *WITBD* can tell us about Lenin's outlook, I suggest that, for reasons given, the scandalous passages are just about the last place to look for something genuinely revealing about Lenin's outlook. So why not bracket these passages, at least for the time being? Why not examine *WITBD* as a whole to see what Lenin thinks about the Russian worker movement, the Russian socialists, and the chances of a merger of the two forces? Why not examine what Lenin actually says about the intellectuals, the revolutionary

---

[13] See Annotations Part Two.

[14] In the Introduction, I gave some examples of the difficulties encountered by advocates of the textbook interpretation when they try to take into account a wider range of textual evidence.

by trade, and the need for *konspiratsiia*? We may find out why so many Russian *praktiki* found the book inspiring and exhilarating. After we are finished, we can, if we feel curious, delve into the detail necessary for understanding the scandalous passages.

And so, let us proceed to raise the curtain and become spectators of Lenin's Erfurtian drama.

## Dramatic rationality

We now turn to the psychology and the motivations of the actors in Lenin's political drama. When we look at the way Lenin defines the current Russian situation, an unexpected fact emerges: Lenin inhabits a thoroughly rational political universe. Everybody in it acts for good reasons, on the basis, that is, of the information available to them. Everybody, especially the workers, is strongly motivated to search out information and arguments in order to better understand their true interest. Not everybody has a correct view of their true interest at present, but the teaching brought by the Social Democrats and still more by events will remedy this situation, and that very soon.

When I say that political actors are portrayed by Lenin as acting for rational reasons, I do not mean the individualistic utility calculations of 'rational-choice' theory. Lenin assumes a steady supply of heroic and self-sacrificing actions. But he also assumes that these heroic actions stem from a correct view of the interests of one's group or the group in whose name one is acting. Indeed, the more people realise their true interests, the more heroically they will act. I also do not mean that Lenin is necessarily correct about what constitute good reasons – only that what he himself regards as rational reasons are what he assumes motivated social actors.[15]

Lenin's views on this matter are worth exploring for a couple of reasons. Lenin's strong faith in the *stikhiinyi* upsurge may give the impression that he saw the workers themselves as akin to a natural force, that is, acting on instinct, without reflection. On this view, the job of the Party is not to transform the outlook of the workers but simply to utilise their pent-up force, much as an engineer uses the *stikhiinyi* force of rivers to create electricity. Lenin is also

---

[15] On the difference between 'rational-choice' model and a wider 'good reasons' model, see Boudon 2001.

sometimes associated with theories of 'false consciousness' and irrationalism, that is, theories that posit a studied rejection of one's true interest even when one is aware of the case for it.[16] As we shall see, nothing could be more foreign to Lenin's outlook than any theory of false consciousness.

At one point, Lenin observes that bourgeois ideology is older, better worked out and more widely disseminated than the rival ideology of the socialists.[17] No doubt some such observation is a constitutive part of any theory of 'false consciousness'. But that is not how Lenin uses it here. The workers are not acting irrationally when they rely on bourgeois explanations of social life, if these are the only explanations available to them. The indicated course for the socialists is, therefore, to put all their energy in making sure the workers are provided with a better explanation. Such is the power of a genuinely sound explanation that the German socialists won over the bulk of the workers despite the inferiority of their means of dissemination. The Russian Social Democrats are at an even greater disadvantage in this respect and yet Lenin's whole scenario depends on socialist success in convincing the workers.

When reading WITBD, we automatically tend to picture the vast state-sponsored propaganda campaigns of the Soviet Union and other Communist states. These states could also simply eliminate anyone with a competing message. Not only did Lenin face a diametrically opposite situation in 1902, but his central political goal at the time was political freedom, that is, open competition between clashing ideologies. Thus his pitch is barely comprehensible without a very strong assumption of the motivating power of good reasons.

Accordingly, it never occurs to Lenin to advocate anything but the use of good arguments. We saw in Chapter Two how one scholar accused Lenin of consciously resorting to 'propaganda', that is, distortion, simplifications and lies.[18] This assertion rested on a simple misunderstanding of the meaning of 'propaganda' in the Social-Democratic discourse of the period, but the mistake is a revealing one. If Lenin really believed that the workers were innately reformist and thus (by his lights) irrational, how could he help advocating some way of using this irrationality in order to cajole them into a revolutionary

---

[16] Meyer 1957.
[17] Lenin 1958–65, 6, p. 41 [712].
[18] Meyer 1957, pp. 47–50.

attitude? Yet Lenin struck readers at the time as someone who considerably *over*estimated the power of rational argument. Strict economists such as Prokopovich and the authors of the *Joint Letter* scoffed at the idea that 'theories' and programmes could really influence events. Nadezhdin was nonplussed by *Iskra*'s 'writerism', that is, an exaggerated sense of the importance of refuting bad arguments. Krichevskii's 'stages' theory gave considerably more active power to good reasons, and yet it too advocated keeping one's basic convictions under wraps for the duration. Many Social Democrats also felt that the workers should not be bothered with intelligentsia and émigré disputes, and they saw Lenin's attempts to get rank-and-file support for his sides in these disputes as demagogic. One historian has observed that, in the period after the 1917 revolution, Lenin's *Pravda*, in contrast to the *Pravda* of the Stalin era, was rationalistic to the point of being dry.[19] A similar observation can be made about Lenin's approach throughout his career.

One reason that many people overlook Lenin's assumption of rationality is that they automatically assume that a rational actor should not require anything coming 'from without' in order to make a correct decision. Lenin combines a deep sense of the rationality of political actors with an equally deep sense of the urgency of providing effective leadership that will prevent the workers from making avoidable mistakes. Consequently, Lenin's assumption about the essential rationality of social actors does not make WITBD any less dramatic. Providing people with good reasons is a grave challenge that may or may not be met. To grasp the dramatic rationality of WITBD is therefore key to understanding Lenin's outlook.

To say that people act for good reasons is not to say they cannot make mistakes and very serious ones, since people act on the basis of the information available to them and acquiring this information (particularly in an absolutist environment) can be very costly indeed. It follows that the key task of the Party – the key battle – is to get information and arguments to the workers and indeed to all the subjects of the autocracy. Getting the word out under the autocracy is a highly dangerous, highly exciting, cat-and-mouse game against some very determined opponents. Thus Lenin asks, why has the Russian worker not reacted in a revolutionary way to all the various outrages in Russian life. Because he simply does not care about any outrages that do

---

[19] Brooks 2000.

not have a direct connection to his economic interests? Not at all – the reason is simply that he does not yet even know of the existence of these outrages. And whose fault is that? Put the blame on the Social Democrats who have fallen behind the mass movement and whose unprofessional carelessness helps the government suppress information.[20]

The job of the Social Democrats is not only to get information to the workers. They must also, as it were, create some good reasons by providing effective leadership. One essential type of argument is the visible existence of inspired and inspiring leaders. Many 'less developed' workers start on the path to a Social-Democratic outlook when they realise that dedicated Social-Democratic activists as their natural guides and leaders. The Social Democrats make good arguments in their propaganda and agitation, but, thinks Lenin, probably their most compelling argument is their own tireless and effective leadership.

That is, if it *is* effective. If the Social Democrats fail to provide effective leadership, the workers will quite rationally seek elsewhere. Why does Lenin fear that the Social Democrats may lose the leadership of the workers to other parties? Because the Social Democrats are preaching a revolutionary message that falls on the deaf ears of the reformist workers? Precisely the opposite. The workers are searching for revolutionary leadership and the Social Democrats are failing to provide it.[21]

In the world of WITBD, 'bourgeois democracy' is a revolutionary, anti-tsarist force that includes both the liberals and the Socialist Revolutionaries (both political camps *in statu nascendi* when WITBD was being written). If the non-Social-Democratic revolutionaries are providing the most energetic and flexible leadership available, then the workers will support them and not the Social Democrats. This outcome would of course be highly unfortunate, since the revolutionary energy of the workers would be exploited and the chance for a genuinely radical conquest of political freedom would be lost. But again, whose fault would that be? The Social Democrats, of course. As usual, the German Social Democrats show the way – *they* provide vigorous political leadership for democratic reform and are rewarded with prestige and support.[22]

For workers to follow the most effective revolutionary leadership on offer is definitely rational. Yet Lenin also expresses fears that some workers will

---

[20] Lenin 1958–65, 6, pp. 70–1 [738].
[21] Lenin 1958–65, 6, p. 182 [839].
[22] Lenin 1958–65, 6, pp. 95, 97–8 [759, 761–2].

be led astray by bad reasons and act mistakenly. In WITBD, for example, he asserts that the success of his Social-Democratic opponents, such as it was, had stemmed from their appeal to the 'less-developed' worker. His opponents were demagogues who tried to activate the base instincts in these workers by sowing suspicion of anyone who brought them knowledge and revolutionary experience. But 'it is not possible for less-developed workers to recognise these enemies who present themselves, sometimes quite sincerely, as their friends'.[23]

This description of the less-developed worker occurs in the context of justifying intra-party polemics. Lenin does not suggest that these workers might be confused about whether, say, the employers are their friend or not. Nor does he suggest any special difficulty about demonstrating that the government is not a friend: the Social Democrats (all of them) and the gendarmes are working in tandem to get that point across. The person whom the less-developed worker might not recognise correctly is the Social Democrat whose opinions Lenin finds mistaken. In pointing out the danger of the less-developed worker being led astray, Lenin wants to justify breaking the taboo against harsh polemics between Social-Democratic comrades ('Oh yes! Don't rush to raise a howl about the "un-comrade-like methods" of my polemic!').[24] We *must* polemicise against the likes of *Rabochee delo* and Nadezhdin, says Lenin, so that the less-developed worker, unable to recognise his true Social-Democratic friends without such polemics, will see the light.

As usual, the template is the German experience. The German Party also had demagogues who tried to evoke base instincts by flattering the 'horny-handed fists' of the rank-and file worker as against party leaders. German socialism grew strong by exposing such attempts, presumably by good arguments.[25]

Mistaken fellow socialists do not consciously intend to lead the workers astray. In contrast, from Lenin's point of view, government attempts to set up police unions are deliberate attempts to deceive. Police officials such as

---

[23] Lenin 1958–65, 6, pp. 72, 121–3 [739, 785–7]. In this connection, Lenin warns against the *razvrashchenie* of the less-developed workers. This word is usually translated 'corruption', but I believe 'leading astray' is more accurate. For two discussions of Lenin that bring his fear of worker 'corruption' to the fore, see Mayer 1993b and Zelnik 2003b.

[24] Lenin 1958–65, 6, p. 123 [785].

[25] Ibid.

Zubatov do have this intention (at least, as Lenin sees it) when they set up semi-legal police unions. During the *Iskra* period, Sergei Zubatov, the head of the Moscow security police, tried to convince workers that they could have effective economic unions if they only renounced the project of overthrowing the tsar.

Lenin's attitude toward the *Zubatovshchina* is extremely revealing about his key assumptions. A crucial passage in WITBD displays his feelings on the subject.[26] The point of this passage is this: we Social Democrats should *welcome* tsarist attempts to trick the workers by legalising or at least tolerating loyalist and apolitical unions. Of course, we should expose such attempts as the fraud they are. Nevertheless, the gains to us are substantial. First, why not let the police unions take over the function of 'drawing the attention of ever broader worker strata, including the most backward, to social and political issues' – one less job for us revolutionaries to do. If the legalisers try to lead the workers astray with revisionist doctrines, we will expose them. While they try to use provocateurs to catch socialists, we will use the opportunity to recruit socialists. In sum, even the smallest room for manoeuvre for the workers, even the faintest whiff of political freedom, is real progress. The Social Democrats should say to Zubatov, 'please go right ahead – you're doing us a favour'.

As the American historian of the *Zubatovshchina* correctly observes, the events of 1905 were frequently cited by Lenin as confirmation of his 'optimistic view' of Zubatov's efforts to seduce the workers.[27] The worker demonstration on Bloody Sunday (9 January 1905) had been organised under the auspices of a Zubatov-type union led by Father Gapon in January 1905 (Zubatov himself had lost his job by this time). Lenin saw the revolutionary outcome of Bloody Sunday as a vindication of WITBD. Had he not predicted that 'even the most backward workers would be drawn into the [revolutionary] movement by the Zubatovists'?[28] Had he not assured his readers that 'once they are

---

[26] Lenin 1958–65, 6, pp. 114–16 [778–9]. This passage is somewhat opaque because of the way it mixes references to Gogol and to New Testament parables together with polemics with *Rabochee delo* and the specific case of Zubatov. The reading presented here is confirmed by Lenin's 1905 references to this passage (see the following footnote).
[27] Schneiderman 1976, p. 206. Schneiderman lists the following 1905 passages: Lenin 1958–65, 9, pp. 174–5, 210–11, 218, 220–1, 262, 300. On the Zubatov movement, see also Kavtorin 1992 and Pospielovsky 1971.
[28] Lenin 1958–65, 9, pp. 220–1.

brought into movement and become interested in the issues of their own fate, the workers will go further'?[29]

A healthy respect for the ideological apparatus of bourgeois society was an essential part of the Erfurtian outlook. As Liebknecht said in 1875, 'Our most dangerous enemy is not the standing army of soldiers, but the standing army of the enemy press'.[30] Yet, as compared to other revolutionary currents, the Social Democrats were relatively confident in the power of good reasons. Lenin too shared the basic Erfurtian assumption that 'the socialist awareness of the worker masses' was 'the sole foundation that can guarantee us victory'.[31] Indeed, so intense was Lenin's focus on awareness that he was regularly accused of 'writerism' – of being obsessed (as Nadezhdin put it) with fighting bad arguments rather than bad actions.

While Lenin assumes that social actors are motivated by good reasons, this assumption does *not* commit him to assuming that workers cannot have mistaken opinions or that the Social Democrats do not have to work very hard to ensure that the workers receive correct opinions. In fact, it commits Lenin to making every possible effort to ensure that the workers receive good reasons. What is characteristic of Lenin is his confidence that, if they try hard enough, the Social Democrats *can* get the good news to the workers, despite tsarist repression. They *can* build the effective organisation that will give the workers a good reason to accept Social-Democratic leadership. They *can* use vigorous polemics to thwart the efforts of mistaken socialists to lead astray the awareness of the more backward workers. And, finally, the Social Democrats can rest assured that the efforts of the government to seduce workers will certainly backfire.

## 'Look at the Germans'

'Look at the Germans.'[32] 'Take the Germans.'[33] 'Remember the example of Germany.'[34] 'Take German Social Democracy.'[35] Whenever Lenin wants to

---

[29] Lenin 1958–65, 9, pp. 174–7.
[30] Steenson 1981, p. 129.
[31] Lenin 1958–65, 6, pp. 8–9 [683].
[32] Lenin 1958–65, 6, p. 132 [793].
[33] Lenin 1958–65, 6, p. 121 [783].
[34] Lenin 1958–65, 6, p. 40 [711].
[35] Lenin 1958–65, 6, p. 97 [761].

illustrate a point or clinch an argument, he resorts to the SPD model. This model was authoritative for all of international Social Democracy, but probably nowhere else in the socialist literature is the SPD so exhaustively and so admiringly made the basis for argument as in Lenin's WITBD. To match it, we must look ahead to the use made of the Soviet or Chinese models by twentieth-century Communists in their internal polemics. It is therefore ironic that the one thing on which both Soviet and Western scholars agree is that WITBD contains Lenin's plea for 'a party of a new type'.

The SPD was not only the ultimate model but the original starting point of the heroic spread of awareness that Lenin wanted to see in Russia. The inspired and inspiring activists whom Lenin regarded as the heart of the process received their inspiration in the first place from observing the mighty German Party. The most important step toward putting WITBD in proper historical context is thus to see the full scope of Lenin's use of the SPD model in his polemics, in his practical proposals, and in his exalted definition of the current situation in Russia.

The meaning of the German model is brought out in WITBD by means of a continual contrast with the 'English' model.[36] The clash between these two models structures the overall rhetoric of WITBD. When Lenin contrasts, say, Social-Democratic politics to *tred-iunionist* politics, he is also contrasting, even on a linguistic level, the German model to the English model, since 'Social Democracy' in the relevant sense is a German coinage, while '*tred-iunionist*' flaunts its English-ness. Germany is the country where the worker class built up its own independent, class, political and socialist party as the centre of a wide-ranging movement seeking to embrace all manifestations of worker life. England is the country where the workers contented themselves with building up strong and effective trade unions that defended the interests of particular trades but where these same workers accepted a position of political dependence and refused to undertake the great historical mission of introducing socialism. To choose Germany over England was what it meant to *be* a Social Democrat, and so Lenin makes the most of the Germany/England contrast in his effort to reveal the heretical leanings of his opponents.

---

[36] I apologise for the inaccurate use of 'English' rather than 'British' but I am constrained to follow the usage of my texts.

In this section, we will list and paraphrase all the explicit references to the SPD model in *WITBD*. The only reference in *WITBD* to the SPD that contains even a hint of criticism is the very first one. We will save this one until the end but otherwise proceed in the order of the text. This procedure will bring out the sheer volume and weight of these references. They are detailed, they are passionate, and they are closely tied to the course of the argument. The SPD references create problems for the textbook interpretation on two central points. If Lenin rejected Western-style parties for a conspiratorial party in the populist tradition, then what are all these SPD references doing here and why do they outweigh the references to the populist revolutionaries by any measure? Furthermore, for Lenin and his readers, the SPD is the future of the RSDWP in the coming days of Russian political freedom. If Lenin was pessimistic and anxious about workers in general, we should expect these feelings to show up in his invocation of the accomplishments of the German workers.

*SPD model in Chapter I (on 'freedom of criticism')*

(i) *Engels on the German Party.* In order to show the importance of a party's theoretical clarity, Lenin gives a long citation from Engels about the German workers. From Engels we learn that the German workers have a remarkable aptitude for theory (as opposed to the English workers among others). They have been able to benefit from the earlier experience of workers in other countries; they exploit the advantages of their own situation 'with rare ability'. The German workers were the first to build a co-ordinated movement that combined political, economic and theoretical aspects. If the German workers continue as they have done, they will meet the challenges ahead of them.

Lenin adds that a few years after Engels wrote this passage, the German workers did indeed acquit themselves splendidly when they defeated Bismarck's anti-socialist laws. Lenin expresses the hope that the Russian workers will occupy a similar place of honour in the international movement when they overthrow the tsar.[37]

---

[37] Lenin 1958–65, 6, pp. 25–8 [697–9].

*Chapter II (attacking 'Rabochee delo' as 'economist in a broad sense')*

(ii) *Failure of tred-iunionizm in Germany*. *Rabochaia mysl* expresses ideas similar to the German bourgeois reformist Max Hirsch who tried to transplant English *tred-iunionizm* to German soil, that is, to convince the German workers to restrict themselves to trade-union battles and not to worry about future generations.[38]

(iii) *Lassalle as paradigmatic leader*. Lassalle is a good example of how an inspiring leader can make a difference. In no way did he simply accept the given situation as the best that could be accomplished. He directly tackled the bourgeois reformers who were trying to entice the workers down a conservative path. The result of his impassioned struggle? The workers of Berlin moved from being supporters of the liberals to becoming a stronghold of Social Democracy. Even today, many workers are not yet Social Democrats, so the struggle must go on.[39]

(Note that Lassalle's 'struggle' consisted entirely of eloquence and shrewd agitational techniques. Lenin's insistence that the Party can never relax in its effort to spread the word was close to the German Party's own self-image, as we see in a passage from Bebel's memoirs where he looks back to Lassalle's *Open Letter* and comments that 'if we remember that even today, after more than fifty years of intensive efforts to enlighten the worker classes as to their true interest, there are still millions of workers who follow the various bourgeois parties, it is not to be wondered at that the majority of the workers in the sixties regarded the new movement with sceptical eyes'.)[40]

(iv) *'Rabochaia mysl' and English workers*. *Rabochaia mysl* can hardly be called Social-Democratic, since the kind of worker politics it advocates is common to *all* workers, including the English workers. (The fact that something is done by the English workers does not mean it is a bad thing in itself. On the contrary. But it *does* mean that it is not in and of itself Social-Democratic.)[41]

(v) *Legitimacy of having tactical plans*. Why does Boris Krichevskii reject the idea of tactical *plans*? Germany furnishes several examples of leaders defending competing plans. The outcome of these disputes was crucial to the history of the SPD.[42]

---

[38] Lenin 1958–65, 6, p. 36 [707].
[39] Lenin 1958–65, 6, pp. 40–1 [711].
[40] Bebel 1912, p. 54.
[41] Lenin 1958–65, 6, pp. 42–3 [713].
[42] Lenin 1958–65, 6, pp. 48–9 [717–18].

*Chapter III (on political agitation)*

(vi) *Economic agitation.* Lenin introduces his discussion of political agitation by talking about the previous success of economic agitation and emphasises that economic agitation will always be required. To bring home the point, he states that socialists 'in the most advanced European countries' use the indictment of abuses in some forgotten sweatshop or cottage industry in order to awaken class awareness and to inspire resistance to employers.[43]

(vii) *Example of a party campaign.* In order to show the absurdity of Martynov's attempt to equate propaganda with lack of action and agitation with calls to action, Lenin uses the example of the current struggle of the German Social Democrats against grain duties. The party theorists write treatises on the economic issues involved, propagandists popularise their conclusions in journals, and agitators do the same in public speeches. Workers make the rounds of the factories and homes to get signatures for the petition campaign. (What is striking about this description is the picture of the Party working together as a united whole on political issues of society-wide import.)[44]

(viii) *Role of 'political indictments'.* Political indictments of the sort found in *Iskra* are one of the most important functions of international Social Democracy. 'For example, the German Party particularly strengthens its position and widens its influence due directly to the unremitting energy of its campaign of political indictments.'[45]

(ix) *'Economistic' politics.* The economic struggle can become political – that is, aim at worker protection legislation and the like – without the slightest intervention of purposive Social Democracy, as the English example shows.[46]

(x) *Liebknecht as ideal leader.* The immediate occasion for this crucial passage is to show that Martynov's suggested strategy is perfectly compatible with English *tred-iunionizm.* Like Hamlet showing his mother the portraits of her past and present husbands – 'look here upon this picture, and on this' – Lenin presents us Wilhelm Liebknecht, the Social-Democratic tribune of the people, vs. Robert Knight, the resourceful leader of the United Society of Boilermakers and Ironshipbuilders.

---

[43] Lenin 1958–65, 6, p. 55 [725].
[44] Lenin 1958–65, 6, p. 67 [735].
[45] Lenin 1958–65, 6, p. 69 [737].
[46] Lenin 1958–65, 6, p. 73 [740].

Lenin's source of information about Knight is *Industrial Democracy* by Sidney and Beatrice Webb, a book whose translation into Russian he had overseen. The Webbs tell us that the Boilermakers, established in 1832, remained 'one of the most powerful and best conducted of English trade societies'. Knight had been general secretary of the union since the late 1870s. He was 'a man of remarkable ability and strength of character, who has remained the permanent premier of this little kingdom'. The Webbs use him as an example of the way in which the rules of 'primitive democracy' do not prevent oligarchic rule, although in Knight's case they note that his 'upright and able government' worked well without the safeguards of democracy. He seems to have done very well for the 40,000 or so members of his union by an impressively disciplined and organised application of collective bargaining.[47]

Knight is thus a strong example of an effective trade-union leader. Nevertheless, from a Social-Democratic point of view, his activities benefited only a small group of workers and not the class as a whole. It was no part of his job description to work for democratic reform of society, much less socialism. Liebknecht, in contrast, is the very type of an inspired and inspiring leader. He illuminates the real nature of the society as a whole, he provides leadership for the German democratic movement as a whole – for example, during the Franco-Prussian War – and he directs his journalistic activity toward wide-ranging political indictments.[48]

(xi) *Social-Democratic hegemony in the democratic struggle in Germany*. The backwardness of the Russian Social Democrats will allow non-Social-Democratic revolutionaries to take over leadership of the liberation struggle. The German example should inspire us. Why is it that not a single major political event occurs in Germany without *strengthening* the authority of the SPD? Not because the Social-Democratic activists in that country sat around waiting for the economic struggle to revolutionise workers! These activists are always in the lead, awakening political dissatisfaction in all classes, rousing the torpid, dragging the backward, helping the proletariat develop its awareness and activeness. Thus they inspire the respect even of enemies, and 'it often happens

---

[47] Webb, Sidney and Beatrice Webb 1965, pp. 28–30, 204. Knight retired in 1899. A recent history of British trade unions notes that Knight was a pioneer in the imposition of national agreements on employers (Reid 2004, p. 172).

[48] Lenin 1958–65, 6, pp. 80–1 [746–7].

that an important document not only from bourgeois but even from bureaucratic and court circles ends up by some miracle in the editorial offices of *Vorwärts* [the central party newspaper]'.[49]

*Chapter IV (on organisational improvement)*

(xii) *Party's relationship to trade unions.* Although the SPD is not mentioned in this passage by name it is clearly the main model for Lenin's description of the relationship between trade unions and party 'in countries with political freedom'. Even though the two types of organisation should always be kept separate, they must also be as closely linked as possible.[50]

(xiii) *Continuity of leadership.* Lenin thinks Nadezhdin is imposing a false dilemma: *either* roots in the masses *or* reliance on leaders. Take the Germans. No one can deny that, in Germany, the party organisation is based on the masses, that everything in the German Party comes from the masses and that the German worker movement has learned to walk on its own two feet. (Lenin is here repeating Nadezhdin's own list of good things.) And yet these masses also have faith in their leaders and put a high value on continuity of leadership. The Germans have enough political maturity to know that without talented and experienced leaders [*vozhdi*] who have learned to work together as a team, *no* class can fight effective battles in today's world. Various demagogues within the German Party tried to convince the workers otherwise, but they were exposed and discredited, thus strengthening the Party. (In other words, *Iskra* is justified in its campaign to expose and discredit fellow socialists.[51])

(xiv) *Stable leadership.* Lenin asserts a five-part proposition about the importance of stable leadership. This passage is often quoted as Lenin's plea for a party of a new type. But, when we look closer, we note that Lenin meant the first three parts of the definition to be a description of revolutionary organisations under any circumstances while restricting the last two clauses to the situation in autocratic countries. Since the SPD is the paradigm of a revolutionary organisation in a non-autocratic country, the first three parts

---

[49] Lenin 1958–65, 6, pp. 97–8 [761–2].
[50] Lenin 1958–65, 6, pp. 112–13 [775–6].
[51] Lenin 1958–65, 6, pp. 121–2 [783–4]. Lenin uses Nadezhdin's word *tolpa*, crowd, to refer to German workers in this passage.

must be understood as a description of the SPD. Indeed, these first three parts merely recapitulate the argument just made about demagogues.

Lenin asserts that (1) any revolutionary movement requires a stable organisation of leader/guides; (2) the broader the masses who are drawn in to support this organisation, the greater the need for stable continuity in order to combat demagogues within the Party (Lenin has just shown that the German Party does this successfully); (3) the organisation will be composed of people who do their jobs in a professional manner.[52]

(xv) *Workers as revolutionaries by trade.* Lenin maintains that it is criminally wasteful not to use the talents of revolutionary workers to best advantage. Although the Germans have far greater personnel resources than do the Russians, they eagerly snap up workers who show talent for, say, agitation, and give them the opportunity to become thoroughly skilled at their new revolutionary trade. Thus, they obtain the Bebels and Auers needed to fight the good fight. While this process occurs more or less automatically in free countries, we Russians will have to set about it as a deliberate policy of encouraging talent.[53]

(xvi) *Party democracy.* In order to show that full democratisation within the Party is impossible under autocratic conditions, Lenin cites the example of a truly democratic party, the SPD. One basic elements of its internal democracy is *glasnost*, full openness of all proceedings. Only *glasnost* turns the elective principle into the democratic weapon of control by the masses that it is. (Lenin is of course assuming that, come the anti-tsarist revolution and the achievement of political freedom, the RSDWP will operate on similar principles.[54])

(xvii) *Division of labour.* By way of exception, the English and German experience both confirm the same point, namely, that specialisation and division of labour are necessary for efficient organisation. Lenin cites the Webbs (authority on the English worker organisations) and Kautsky (authority on German Social Democracy) to show the naïveté of 'primitive democracy' (the Webbs' term). Kautsky scorns those who demand that the people's

---

[52] Lenin 1958–65, 6, pp. 124–5 [786–7]. The last two parts of Lenin's five-part proposition concern the underground party in an absolutist state and so are discussed in Chapter Eight.
[53] Lenin 1958–65, 6, pp. 132–3 [793–4] (for a full discussion of revolutionaries by trade, see Chapter Eight).
[54] Lenin 1958–65, 6, pp. 138–9 [798–9].

newspaper be edited directly by the people, who deny the need for professional journalists and parliamentarians and the like.[55]

(xviii) *Local underground press*. In this passage, Lenin is arguing that an extensive local press is beyond the present powers of Russian Social Democracy so that exclusive attention should be given for the time being to a single central newspaper. The SPD is not mentioned, but its flourishing network of newspapers is the implicit point of comparison. Lenin states that the reader will search local Russian underground newspapers in vain for lively and interesting articles with indictments covering a wide range of abuses: diplomacy, military, church, city, financial, and so on. He notes that, if a Social-Democratic party possesses a local press that is more flourishing than its central press, then this is a sign that the party is either in a state of luxury or of poverty. Lenin assumes that his readers will understand that the extensive local press of the SPD is a sign of luxury while the relative preponderance of the local press in Russia is a sign of poverty.[56]

(xix) *Condemning revisionism*. In only one case (in Chapter I) did Lenin have to respond to an invocation of the German model against *Iskra*. In order to show the dangers of *Iskra* intolerance, Krichevskii made a contrast between Germany and France. The SPD allows freedom of criticism within the Party – for example, it did not expel Bernstein – and it is strong and flourishing. French Marxists are obsessed with pure doctrine in the same way as are Plekhanov and *Iskra*. The result? Socialism in France lacks organisational unity and consumes its energy in internecine squabbles.

Lenin responds to this contention first by suggesting a multitude of other reasons why the Germany socialists were united and the French socialists were not. He then points out that, while the SPD did not actually expel Bernstein (he does not hide the fact that he wished Bernstein *had* been kicked out), it did officially condemn revisionism at two party congresses, warning Bernstein by name at one of them. (Although Lenin does not bring this out, it was the intellectuals in the German Party who wanted freedom of criticism and the worker rank-and-file who supported doctrinal purity.)[57]

---

[55] Lenin 1958–65, 6, pp. 142–3 [801–2].

[56] Lenin 1958–65, 6, pp. 149–50 [809–10]. There are no SPD references in Chapter V, which is focused more than the others on a specifically Russian problem, namely, creating central institutions on the basis of pre-existing local committees (see Chapter Eight).

[57] On this topic, see Pierson 1993. For Plekhanov's strong argument in favour of

Finally, Lenin argues that in this one respect *Iskra* has to act differently from the German Party. The SPD has a long, solidly established revolutionary tradition and can afford to be somewhat easy-going about a few intellectual gadflies. In Russia, revisionist 'legally-permitted Marxism' is the only easily available theoretical literature, while economist theories and economist moods are still dominant among *praktiki*.[58] Thus, the German Party stands for the preservation of the existing situation while *Iskra* must attack the status quo. (Of course, Lenin is not saying that the Germans are conservative while the Russian are revolutionary, but the reverse: the Germans are *already* revolutionary, while the Russians have to fight to *become* revolutionary.[59])

Lenin generalises his point by arguing that a young Social-Democratic movement *must* be more intolerant than an established party.[60] In the early days of a party, theoretical confusion is bound to exist, if only because the established 'bourgeois' outlook still reigns mostly unchallenged. Choices made at this point will establish the foundations of party life, with consequences down the years. (This passing comment in WITBD can be seen as the seed of a major development in Lenin's aims for the Party, one that bore full fruit in the Third International's effort to create simon-pure revolutionary parties. In WITBD, however, Lenin's remark is not a critique of the SPD model but a sigh of envy: the German are established, powerful and determined, while we are embryonic, weak and confused.)

In the midst of his polemics with Krichevskii in the first chapter of WITBD, Lenin mocks *Rabochee delo* for slavishly imitating the Germans. This stands in contrast with Lenin's own response a few years earlier to a similar charge, when he responded: what's wrong with imitating something excellent? It turns out that *Rabochee delo* only imitates the *weak* sides of SPD – presumably,

---

kicking Bernstein out of the Party, see his article 'Red Congress in a Red Country', in Plekhanov 1923–7, 12, pp. 451–60 (originally published in *Iskra*, No. 49 [1 September 1903]).

[58] 'Legally-permitted Marxism' (usually translated 'legal Marxism') refers to a number of writers, including Struve and Tugan-Baranovsky, who wrote Marxist articles in the mid-1890s that were abstract enough to be passed by the censor. As a group, these writers tended toward revisionist 'criticism' of orthodox Marxism as a way-station to leaving Social Democracy completely. On the history of this group, see Kindersley 1962.

[59] Lenin 1958–65, 6, pp. 11–12, 21–2 [685–6, 693–4].

[60] Lenin 1958–65, 6, pp. 23–4 [696]; p. 42 [712].

its over-tolerant side.[61] This polemical thrust at *Rabochee delo* as slavish imitators, especially coming in the first chapter, gives a quite misleading impression of the role of the SPD model in Lenin's own outlook and rhetoric.

In the 1960s, Oxford University Press published an English translation of WITBD that systematically removed most of the passages in which Lenin evoked the SPD.[62] What this English translation did explicitly has been done implicitly by the bulk of scholarly commentary on Lenin's book. Partly through not enough interest in the SPD model and partly through too much interest in Lenin's links with the Russian revolutionary tradition, the rhetorical as well as ideological centrality of the SPD model has been effaced. Scholars have thus condemned themselves and their readers to missing the heart of Lenin's vision.

The picture of the SPD painted in WITBD is what we should expect from this intensely Erfurtian Russian. The SPD is a democratic and worker-controlled party that nevertheless is genuinely revolutionary. It is led by talented, experienced leaders who have gained the justified confidence of the rank and file through devoted service. It understands the importance of theory. It is an energetic tribune of the people, tirelessly exposing abuses and acting as the leader of all democratic forces in Germany. What do I mean, says Lenin, when I advocate all-sided political agitation, political indictments, overcoming artisanal limitations, 'revolutionaries by trade', and the worker's role as the advanced fighter for democracy? If you want to know, just look at the Germans!

## Inspired and inspiring activists

The German model was the original inspiration for the Social-Democratic activists who were at the heart of the spread of awareness in Russia. We will now see how Lenin portrays the way these inspired activists went on to inspire others.

Whether these would-be leader/guides come from the workers or the intelligentsia, the most striking feature of their role in Lenin's Erfurtian drama

---

[61] Lenin 1958–65, 6, p. 97 [761].
[62] The editor, S.V. Utechin, tells us that he omitted 'examples given by Lenin from the practice of German Social-Democracy in order to illustrate points he was making, examples which would now be more likely to obscure than to elucidate his reasoning' (Lenin 1963, p. v).

is that they enjoy the boundless confidence of the masses. This is Lenin's promise to *all* the *praktiki* who are willing to work at becoming true political leaders [*vozhdi*]: they will be able to inspire their followers. The image of the inspiring leader is central to the four purple-prose passages of WITBD that come close to the emotional heart of the book. These four passages contain Lenin's political poetry in its most concentrated form.

The first is the one in which Lenin contrasts the *tred-iunionist* secretary to the tribune of the people. The people's tribune – Lenin's ideal leader – responds to *all* instances of oppression, no matter which class they are directed against. He can take the smallest instances of abuse and use them to paint a single awe-inspiring picture of police violence and capitalist exploitation. He uses every chance to present to the world his socialist convictions and democratic demands, for he wants *all* to know about the world-historical significance of the liberation struggle of the proletariat.[63]

The next passage arises out of the earlier polemical clash between the Emancipation of Labour group and *Rabochee delo*. Here, Lenin asserts that the revolutionary heroes of the 1870s were inspiring leaders – their impassioned preaching found an echo in the masses that were awakening in *stikhiinyi* fashion and they, in turn, were supported by the energy of the revolutionary class. So Plekhanov was a thousand times right, even back in 1885, to identify the workers as the revolutionary class, to assert the *inevitability* (my emphasis) of their *stikhiinyi* awakening, and to give great and grand political tasks to 'worker circles'.

Many years later (Lenin continues), in 1900, when the mass movement had begun in earnest, *Rabochee delo* still refused to enjoin the overthrow of the autocracy as a principal theme of Social-Democratic agitation. Thus, it underestimated the revolutionary potential of the masses. It also underestimated the Social-Democratic *praktiki*. 'You brag about your practicality and you don't see (a fact known to any Russian *praktik*) what miracles for the revolutionary cause can be brought about not only by a circle but by a lone individual.' If the *praktiki* diligently worked at it, they too could be as inspiring as the heroes of the 1870s and – given the existence of a genuine mass movement – could accomplish much greater things.

---

[63] Lenin 1958–65, 6, pp. 80–1 [746]. We have looked at this passage earlier in this chapter because it uses Wilhelm Liebknecht, one of the founding fathers of the SPD, as its paradigm of a people's tribune.

It is precisely at the present time that the Russian revolutionary – guided by a genuinely revolutionary theory and relying on the class that is genuinely revolutionary and that is undergoing a *stikhiinyi* awakening – can at last – at last! – draw himself up to his full stature and reveal all his heroic [*bogatyrskii*] strength.[64]

The *bogatyri* were the giant marvellous heroes of the Russian folk epics. Lenin could have chosen no better word to evoke his romantic conception of the Social Democrat as people's hero.

Lenin evoked the heroes of the Russian revolutionary tradition much less often than he did the contemporaneous SPD, but, when he did, he pointed primarily to their ability to inspire (of their organisation he says little beyond that they had one, thus demonstrating that an effective nation-wide organisation is not an impossibility).[65] In the third of our purple-prose passages, Lenin again alludes to earlier revolutionaries as a way of shaming today's pitiful artisans. Someone who wavers in theoretical matters, who is apathetic and without energy, who is more like a secretary of a trade union than a people's tribune, and who is not even skilled enough to keep from getting arrested – such a person lowers the prestige of the revolutionary hero that was once so great in Rus' (this poetic name for Russia evokes the same heroic world as the *bogatyr*).[66]

In our final passage, Lenin actually labels his vision a 'dream'. The dream starts small although not unambitiously: a newspaper published regularly on a weekly basis and distributed throughout Russia. But the newspaper becomes part of a Cyclopean forge blowing every spark of popular indignation into a massive fire of protest. The work in this forge toughens up a corps of experienced warriors. Lenin then brings together his two personal sources of inspiration: Russian revolutionary heroes in the person of Alexei Zheliabov, the leader of Narodnaia volia, and the SPD in the person of August Bebel. Lenin called on his reader to envision Social-Democratic Zheliabovs and Russian Bebels as part of a grand army of revolutionaries and workers who march at the head of the entire people to settle accounts with the shame and curse of Russia. '*That* is what we must dream about!'[67]

---

[64] Lenin 1958–65, 6, p. 107 [770–1].
[65] Lenin 1958–65, 6, pp. 25, 28 [697, 699].
[66] Lenin 1958–65, 6, pp. 126–7 [788].
[67] Lenin 1958–65, 6, p. 171 [828].

## Workers as followers

> The mass of workers are already roused and they are ready to follow socialist leaders. (Lenin, 1900)

If the Social-Democratic activists are cast in the role of inspiring leaders, then the workers at large are cast in the role of inspired followers. Much attention has been paid to Lenin's concept of leadership, but very little to his conception of followership. Yet, given his overall insistence on dramatic rationality, we should not be surprised to discover that this concept is a complex and exalted one.

Lenin's *WITBD* portrait of the Social-Democratic workers is not addressed to the workers themselves; that is, he is not exhorting them to live up to his exalted picture. Rather, it is addressed to the *praktiki*: look, this is how the workers really are at this point in time, so you had better deal with it in your strategies and goals. If the 'worry about workers' approach were correct, we would expect Lenin to say to his polemical opponents: you are overestimating the workers, you cannot count on them, trim down your plans. But, in actuality, his consistent argument is: you are underestimating the workers, they demand more than you are giving them, you need to learn to think big and be more ambitious. In fact, the workers play many roles in Lenin's drama. They appear as dedicated *fighters*, as *organisers* of their own economic struggle, as an eager and appreciative *audience*, and as diligent *students*. They are also expected to actively *push forward* leaders from their own midst. We shall examine these roles in turn.

The workers are assigned the central role in the coming revolutionary drama because, first of all, they are *fighters*. Like the proverbial British tar, their fists are ever ready for a knock-down blow. The workers can be counted on to take to the streets and provide the muscle power without which the anti-autocratic revolution will dwindle away into mere grumbling.[68] Some writers claim that this is *all* Lenin expects of the worker majority – all fists and no brains.[69] And it is true that Lenin, like Social Democrats in general, views the

---

[68] Lenin 1958–65, 6, p. 109 [773].

[69] 'Destructive mass action on the streets, if *What is to be Done?* is to be taken as having represented [Lenin's] current viewpoint, seemed to be the limit of working-class potentiality' (Service 1988, p. 40).

workers as the rank and file of the revolutionary army. In May 1901, he proudly announced that the workers were making it evident to everybody that a mass anti-tsarist force was now in existence. 'There *is* such a force and it is the revolutionary proletariat. It has already proven its readiness not only to hear and support the call to political struggle, but to audaciously throw itself into battle.'[70] But, as a good Erfurtian, he also expects that the proletarian class army will be effective fighters because they understand the reasons for the conflict better than other class armies, because they have greater organisational capacity than other classes, and because they are energetic participants in the ongoing spread of awareness. Their effectiveness as fighters thus depends on their ability to fulfil the other roles assigned to them.

Workers, then, are also *organisers* who can be counted on to mount their own economic struggle. At one point, Lenin defines '*tred-iunionist* politics' as the common aspiration of all workers to obtain state measures to improve their position, protect themselves against disaster, limit exploitation and so forth, but without hitting at the roots of the capitalist system. This kind of activity, he says, is common to all workers, including members of organisations hostile to socialism, such as English *tred-iunionist*s, German Catholic workers, and members of Russian police-sponsored unions.[71] This sort of remark, coupled with the opprobrious epithet 'tred-iunionist', has caused many readers to assume (incorrectly) that Lenin looks down on the workers as irredeemably addicted to trivial reformism. At the very least, he seems to be setting limits to what workers can do without Social-Democratic inspiration. But let us look at Lenin's remarks from the other direction, not as setting limits, but as praise for what the workers can do without any help from anybody.

This polemical point is driven home by Lenin's fictional Social-Democratic worker who reproaches the intellectuals for wasting their time doing what the workers are fully capable of doing themselves. Look, he says, even out in the Russian boondocks, the workers are doing what comes naturally, that is, resisting the employers with strikes. They are perfectly capable of figuring out for themselves whose side the gendarmes are on. But what no one has yet told them is what socialism is or even that there is such a thing – and that is where you Social-Democratic intellectuals come in. Do not treat us

---

[70] Lenin 1958–65, 5, p. 10.
[71] Lenin 1958–65, 6, p. 42 [713].

workers like children who cannot handle our daily economic affairs – rather, satisfy our desire to learn about *all* aspects of Russian life.[72]

Lenin's desire to make this point leads him to minimise the role of intellectuals in conducting the economic struggle. In the Petersburg strikes of the mid-1890s, for example, Social-Democratic intellectuals played a significant role in putting together an organisational framework, preparing demands, and so forth. But in *WITBD* Lenin wants to picture the mid-1890s as a time when the workers, on one side, and Social-Democratic intellectuals, on the other, were moving toward each other in order to merge. He therefore passes over in complete silence the role of the Social-Democratic intellectuals in the Petersburg strikes and ascribes all advances in purposiveness solely to the workers.[73]

As we saw earlier, the English trade unions, usually a rather negative image in *WITBD*, are cited at one point as authorities on the subject of purposive organisation. Lenin points to the experience of the English trade unions who (according to the Webbs) learned through bitter experience the imperative of a specialised division of labour. Lenin then cites Kautsky's *Parliamentarism* to the same effect and observes that the learned Marxist arrives at the same conclusion as the English workers who united 'in *stikhiinyi* fashion'.[74] Thus, the Russian *praktiki* can learn something from non-Social-Democratic English workers. The workers – all of them, not just the Social-Democratic ones – can handle the economic struggle.

In a metaphor that, as far as I can tell, is unique to Lenin, the workers also fulfill the crucial role of providing a great *audience*. The workers are not just motivated by good reasons – they are greedily eager for knowledge. They are avid to hear the Social-Democratic message and they applaud vigorously when they hear it, thus stimulating propagandists and agitators to greater heights. The workers are an ideal audience for political indictments because they feel they need political knowledge and because they are capable of turning political knowledge into active struggle. For this reason, the underground press was already a power in Russia even a generation ago.

---

[72] Lenin 1958–65, 6, pp. 72–3, see also 6, pp. 109, 112–13 [773, 775–6].
[73] Lenin 1958–65, 6, p. 30 [740–1].
[74] Lenin 1958–65, 6, pp. 142–3 [802–3].

And, today, in comparison, the strata of the people ready to read the non-censored press and take rules for living from it are several times broader and deeper than before.[75]

The potential enthusiasm of the worker audience for political indictments is revealed by the way it reacted earlier to economic indictments. As soon as leaflets exposing factory abuses started to appear, a positive passion for such indictments exploded among the workers. When the workers saw the Social Democrats telling the truth about their life, they flooded the *praktiki* with descriptions and reports. *Rabochaia mysl* was part of this popular urge to tell the real story. This declaration of war against existing society had both moral and practical significance, and similar economic exposés continue to play an awakening role even in the most advanced European countries.[76]

One of the accusations Lenin needed to counter was that political indictments of the type Lenin was churning out for *Iskra* – denouncing abuses perpetrated by the autocracy against *all* classes of society – were inappropriate for a class-based worker newspaper. He therefore wants to show that the workers are ready and, indeed, eager to move on from economic to political indictments. Accordingly, Lenin cites Savinkov and Nadezhdin to document his claim that not only the advanced workers but also the mass of workers are very interested in political life.[77] The economists are wrong to treat the workers as if they were children who are unable to respond to any issue except those promising immediate tangible results.[78]

The terrorists reveal the same underestimation of the workers' readiness to respond to outrages when they advocate 'excitative terror', since anyone who is not stirred to his depths by the outrages of the Russian autocracy is unstirrable. In fact, the workers are already highly indignant about all that is going on, as shown by their 'greediness' for illegal political literature.[79]

In a striking image, Lenin claims that all that needs to be done is simply to *throw* journalistic indictments to the worker mass. Just do this, and even

---

[75] Lenin 1958–65, 6, p. 89 [753–4]. The original use of the audience metaphor in *Iskra*, No. 4 (May 1901) is revealing (Lenin 1958–65, 5, pp. 5–13).

[76] Lenin 1958–65, 6, pp. 54–6 [724–6].

[77] Lenin 1958–65, 6, pp. 73–4 [740–1].

[78] Lenin 1958–65, 6, p. 91 [755–6].

[79] Lenin 1958–65, 6, p. 77 [744]. The theme of the workers' greed for illegal literature recurs throughout Lenin's writings in this period.

a completely unenlightened [*seryi*] worker 'will understand or will *feel*' that the same evil force that is crushing him is also crushing other Russians. In other words, although the less-developed worker may not be able to articulate his case or be able to back it up with wide-ranging information, he will certainly draw the right conclusions about the connection between his own life and the outrages perpetrated by the autocracy. And, once the less-developed worker feels this, he will experience an overpowering desire to respond in some way and will himself find ways to do so – and, here, Lenin indulges in a fantasy list of possible popular protests, for example, against censorship.[80]

*Iskra*'s political indictments were needed not simply to stir up indignation but to bring understanding – Social-Democratic awareness – to the worker mass. Thus, the workers are also expected to act as *students*. Lenin's description of what this entails is almost unbelievably ambitious. The worker masses – not just the worker élite, mind you – must be able to apply a materialist analysis to *all* aspects of the life of *all* classes of society. The worker has to grasp the social and political profile of everybody from the tramp to the landowner, know their strong and weak sides, see through their deceptive slogans, expose the ways in which legislation serves particular economic interests.[81]

For the more diligent worker-student, Lenin urges the *praktiki* to provide lectures and talks on the history of the revolutionary movement, the internal and external policies of the government, on the current economic position in Europe and Russia, and the present situation of Russian social classes.[82]

One final reason why the temptation to dumb down 'writing for workers' should be resisted is the hope of preparing the way for outstanding worker theoreticians. Broad horizons are required for original contributions of this kind, and these are hardly encouraged by artificially limited 'writing for workers'. Workers wish to read and in fact are now reading everything written for educated society, and only some poor quality intellectuals think otherwise.[83]

This assertion brings us to Lenin's portrayal of the workers as actively pushing forward those among them with leadership abilities in order to build

---

[80] Lenin 1958–65, 6, p. 71 [738].
[81] Lenin 1958–65, 6, pp. 69–70 [737–8]. This passage sounds like a prospectus for the imaginary book *Political Agitation* discussed in Chapter Three.
[82] Lenin 1958–65, 6, p. 80 [746].
[83] Lenin 1958–65, 6, p. 39 fn. [710].

up a national party organisation. The word he uses to express this process – *vydvigat'*, to push forward – had a future in Soviet culture. Later, during the 1930s, the *vydvizhentsy* were workers who experienced rapid promotion to leadership roles.[84] But Lenin consistently uses the word to show the workers creating and sending forth their own leaders. In 1899, he writes:

> Not a single class in history has achieved a position of dominance if it did not push forward its own political leaders [*vozhdi*] and its own advanced representatives who were capable of organising the movement and guiding it. The Russian worker class has already shown that it is capable of pushing forward such people: the overflowing struggle of the last five or six years has shown what a mass of revolutionary forces are hidden in the worker class.[85]

In 1901, he argues that common work will push forward leaders:

> If we unite our forces in producing a newspaper common to all, then this work will prepare and push forward not only the most able propagandists, but the most expert organisers, the most talented political leaders of the party, capable at the right time to give the watchword for the decisive battle and to guide it.[86]

In *WITBD*, he again uses the 'push forward' image as one more way to make his ambitious plans sound plausible. 'We *will* be able to do these things precisely because the mass that is awakening in *stikhiinyi* fashion will push forward from its own milieu a greater and greater number of "revolutionaries by trade".'[87] The deeper and wider is this vast awakening, the more the worker masses will push forward talented agitators, propagandists, and *praktiki* in the best sense of the word. No political police in the world will be able to cope with a party based on such a corps of worker revolutionaries, since these revolutionaries will be entirely devoted to the cause and they will also enjoy the unlimited confidence of the worker masses.[88]

---

[84] See Mokienko and Nikitina 1998 for a sense of the Soviet connotations of *vydvigat'*.
[85] Lenin, 1958–65, 4, p. 375.
[86] Lenin 1958–65, 5, pp. 12–13.
[87] Lenin 1958–65, 6, p. 111 [774].
[88] Lenin 1958–65, 6, p. 133 [794]. Lenin adds here a parenthetical slam at Russian intellectuals who are sloppy and in fact not very practical.

In the 1930s, the term *vydvigat'* was redolent of the pathos of promotion. This pathos can be found in WITBD as well. Lenin promises the worker who becomes a full-time revolutionary that he will get a chance to apply his talents and improve himself in his chosen party speciality. He will expand his horizons and his knowledge, he will rub elbows with the leaders of other localities and of other parties, and, in general, see the world.[89] If one is looking for a direct link between WITBD and the Soviet Union, this appeal to the excitement of rising up in the world might be a good place to start.

All these aspects of worker followership – militancy, organisational ability, appreciative audience that is eager for knowledge, and participation in underground revolutionary organisations – are mobilised by Lenin in order to make his practical proposals sound plausible. For example, the project of a nation-wide underground newspaper is feasible only because the worker youth show 'a passionate and unstoppable striving towards the ideas of democracy and socialism'. The difficulties encountered in distributing the newspaper will be eased by worker support and worker cleverness.

> The French workers under Napoleon III and the German workers under the exceptional laws against socialists were able to contrive all sorts of pretexts for their political and socialist meetings. The Russian workers will be able to match this feat.[90]

In WITBD, Lenin expands on this theme by showing how a secret underground organisation can have strong roots in the worker milieu (a basic assumption of his organisational plan, as shown in Chapter Eight). There he presents a vision of a thriving, bustling underground Russia. The Social-Democratic organisation will flood the worker districts with illegal literature, the workers will greedily snap it up, with the result that reading and contributing to illegal literature will occur on such a scale that it will practically cease to be an underground activity. The same applies to 'worker trade unions, worker circles for self-education and the reading of illegal literature, socialist as well as democratic circles in *all* other strata of the population and so on and so on'.[91]

---

[89] Lenin 1958–65, 6, pp. 132–3 [794].
[90] Lenin 1958–65, 4, pp. 195–7 (1899).
[91] Lenin 1958–65, 6, pp. 125–6 [788].

In relation to Social-Democratic leaders, the workers are cast as passionate followers. But the spread of awareness rolls on, and in relation to Russian society as a whole the worker movement acts as a leader. For Lenin, the growing revolutionary crisis in Russia is unthinkable without the *stikhiinyi* upsurge of the workers, as we shall see in the next section.

## The *stikhiinyi* upsurge

> The *stikhiinyi* upsurge of both the worker mass and (thanks to its influence) other social strata has occurred in recent years with striking swiftness. . . . The leader/guides have fallen *behind* this *stikhiinyi* upsurge of the masses and they have turned out to be unprepared to carry out their responsibilities as leader/guides. (Lenin, 1901)

The *stikhiinyi* upsurge of the workers is galvanising all of Russian society and creating the possibility of the imminent overthrow of tsarism and the conquest of political freedom. All that is lacking is for the natural leader/guides of the workers – the Social Democrats – to provide an effective organisational and ideological framework for the revolutionary onslaught. This is Lenin's basic definition of the situation. In order to understand what the *stikhiinyi* upsurge means to him, we have to put it in the context of WITBD's Erfurtian drama and the volcanic spread of awareness Lenin thought was taking place in Russia.

The standard English translation 'spontaneous upsurge' is much too weak (and no doubt this is one reason the centrality of this concept has been completely overlooked). *Pod"em*, the word translated as 'upsurge', connotes a swelling of energy and enthusiasm, while *stikhiinyi* endows this upsurge with the unstoppable strength of a natural force. As we have seen, *stikhiinyi* was often used in a primarily negative sense in Social-Democratic rhetoric. '*Stikhiinyi* protest' was disorganised, violent, explosive and needed to be turned into 'purposive protest' as fast as possible. But the root metaphor of 'ungovernable natural force' could have positive connotations if it designated a force of nature moving with unstoppable force *in the right direction*. Within the framework of the merger narrative, the right direction meant, first, towards militant protest against the exploiters and the government, and, second, towards a merger with the revolutionary socialists who are themselves moving towards the workers.

As far as I have been able to trace, the earliest occurrence of the phrase *'stikhiinyi* upsurge' is in late 1900.[92] The concept itself emerges somewhat earlier and, in fact, cannot be separated from Lenin's package of practical proposals first put forth in 1899. Lenin's concept has three facets: the workers' rapid politicisation, worker leadership of the Russian people's struggle against the tsar, and the bottleneck of inadequate Social-Democratic organisation.

These three facets are strikingly present in a piece written in late 1900, that is, before the first issue of *Iskra* was published. It is a preface to a pamphlet compiled by the local Kharkov Social-Democratic committee based on worker descriptions of May First events in Kharkov earlier in the year. The May First demonstrations had turned into a general strike, thus marking the opening of a new phase in the Russian worker movement. Lenin uses these descriptions as a basis for his definition of the situation. First, rapid worker politicisation:

> In the history of the Russian worker movement, an epoch of excitement and outbursts has commenced, occasioned by a very wide variety of causes. . . . There exists a fairy tale that says that the Russian workers have not yet grown up enough for political struggle, that their main cause is a pure economic struggle that will imperceptibly and bit by bit be supplemented by partial political agitation for individual political reforms and not by a struggle against the entire political system of Russia. This fairy tale is decisively refuted by the May First events in Kharkov.[93]

This rapid politicisation shows the spread of awareness within the worker class. But central to Lenin's definition of the *stikhiinyi* upsurge is the spread of awareness *beyond* the boundaries of the worker class to all strata of the *narod* and even élite society. The following vivid scenario of worker leadership is, I think, one of the most revealing Lenin citations in this commentary:

> They say that a certain individual who was passing through Kharkov during the May events asked a cabbie what it was that the workers wanted, and he answered, 'Well, they're demanding eight hours of work and their own

---

[92] 'We must study . . . the forms and conditions of the awakening of the worker class, of its struggle that is now commencing, in order to link, in one indivisible whole, the Russian revolutionary movement and the *stikhiinyi* upsurge of the masses of the *narod*' (preliminary draft of the announcement of *Iskra*'s publication, Lenin 1958–65, 4, p. 328).

[93] Lenin 1958–65, 4, pp. 364–6.

newspaper'. That cabbie already understood that the workers will not be satisfied by petty concessions, that they want to feel that they are free human beings, that they want to freely and openly talk of their needs and fight for them.

But the cabbie's answer still does not reveal any awareness that the workers are fighting for the freedom of the whole people, for its right to participate in the workings of the state. When the demand that the Tsar call together representatives of the people is repeated with full purposiveness and invincible firmness by the worker masses in all the industrial towns and factory areas of Russia – when the workers arrive at the point where the entire urban population and all the village people near the towns understand what the socialists want and what the workers are fighting for, then we have not long to wait for the great day of the liberation of the people from police autocracy![94]

In the parable of the cabbie, Lenin gives most attention to the workers' impact on various sections of the *narod*. But he also believes that when 'the worker class lifts up the banner of struggle', *all* of the decent elements of Russian society will rally round. Lenin's whole political programme depends on this assertion of the power of the *stikhiinyi* upsurge. As he argued in 1899,

The Russian worker class is able to conduct its economic and political struggle all by itself, even if it receives no help from any other class. But in the political struggle the workers do *not* stand alone. The complete absence of rights for the people and the savage abuses of the bashibazouk bureaucrats infuriate all educated people who are the least bit decent and who cannot reconcile themselves with the harrying of free speech and free thought. They infuriate the persecuted Poles, the Finns, the Jews, the Russian sectarians – they infuriate the petty merchants, the industrialists, the peasants who cannot find any defence from anyone against the oppression of the bureaucrats and the police.

All these groups in the population, taken singly, are incapable of sustained political struggle, but when the worker class lifts up the banner of struggle like this, then from all sides come hands offering help. Russian Social Democracy will stand at the head of all fighters for the rights of the people, of all fighters for democracy – and when it does, it will be invincible![95]

---

[94] Lenin 1958–65, 4, pp. 369–70.
[95] Lenin 1958–65, 4, p. 186.

Thus there exists a vast potential for immediate revolutionary change. But Lenin uses the May First events to underscore his constant motif: the 'political capabilities of the Russian workers' will be wasted if we Social Democrats do not get our act together:

> While proving again and yet again the political capabilities of the Russian workers, the May First events in Kharkov at the same time show what is still lacking for the full development of those capacities.... If we do not wish to remain in the rear of the battle, we must direct all our efforts toward the creation of a nation-wide organisation that is capable of guiding all the separate outbursts and in this way ensure that the approaching storm ... will not be a *stikhiinyi* storm but a purposive movement of the proletariat standing at the head of the whole people against the autocratic government.[96]

In WITBD, the 'spring events' of February–March 1901 – when workers took to the streets to support student protests – are used as a metonymy for the *stikhiinyi* upsurge as a whole. But, as we have seen, these events did not surprise Lenin or provoke any change of outlook on his part (as is sometimes asserted). On the contrary, Lenin used the spring events to confirm his pre-existing definition of the ongoing *stikhiinyi* upsurge and the inadequate Social-Democratic response. In *Iskra*, No. 4 (May 1901), where he first sets forth his plan in public form, he asks his readers to

> recall the recent events: before our eyes the broad masses of the workers of the cities and the ordinary people of the cities are straining at the bit to begin the struggle – and among the revolutionaries there is no staff of leader/guides and organisers.[97]

In WITBD, the spring events are cited to point the same moral that Lenin derived from the May Day events in Kharkov. Moral Number One: the workers will undertake radical action even when no 'tangible' results' are forthcoming. Moral Number Two: 'the *stikhiinyi* striving of the workers to come to the defence of students who were beaten by the police and the Cossacks overtook the purposive activity of the Social-Democratic organisation'.[98]

---

[96] Lenin 1958–65, 4, pp. 364–6.
[97] Lenin 1958–65, 5, p. 7. The word *rvat'sia*, 'straining at the bit', 'bursting to do something', often shows up in Lenin's writings of this period. See Lenin 1958–65, 4, pp. 327, 375 and (in WITBD) 6, p. 31 [702]).
[98] Lenin 1958–65, 6, p. 93 [757–8]. This reading of the spring events as confirming

The third moral Lenin derives from the *stikhiinyi* upsurge in WITBD is the potential created by the worker movement's ability to inspire all of Russian society. A truly revolutionary Social Democracy can count on sympathisers in all classes of society. The economists are still sceptical about the possibility of such support, but they overlook the 'gigantic change' undergone during the years from 1894 to 1901. Under the influence of the worker movement, a wider and wider range of social strata are becoming dissatisfied and ready to help Social Democracy in its fight against absolutism in any way they can. Of course, the many millions of peasants and small artisans will always greedily hear the preaching of a competent Social Democrat. But (Lenin asks) is there really even a single class in society where contact cannot be made with individuals or groups who are disgusted with autocratic abuses?[99]

The Social Democrats, therefore, have a positive duty to overcome their limitations and transform this potential energy into actual energy. An effective party organisation will 'go to all classes' and mobilise all this support, ranging from inside information sent in by whistle-blowers to small but needful services such as providing a roving revolutionary with a roof over his head for a night or two. Lenin instances a factory inspector who was frustrated because he could not hand over his valuable information to a 'revolutionary centre' that could put it to good use. Lenin insists that similar support could come from civil servants and bureaucrats of all shades: the postal service, the customs service, gentry organisations, indeed, even police and court circles.[100]

These people should be used for information and small services without dragging them into the underground. But there are many impetuous people whose 'revolutionary instincts' must find satisfaction. If they perceive that Social Democracy is not adequately militant, they will turn to self-defeating and disruptive terrorist acts.[101] Once again, the growing revolutionary excitement makes a strong party organisation possible and therefore necessary.

There are hints in WITBD that the *stikhiinyi* upsurge will have ripple effects even beyond Russian society. The upcoming Russian revolution will galvanise

---

the existence of the *stikhiinyi* upsurge is not a self-evident one. Other Social-Democratic observers looked at the same events and concluded that revolutionary initiative still belonged to radical elements of élite society such as the students.

[99] Lenin 1958–65, 6, pp. 87–8, 128–9 [752–3, 790–1].
[100] Lenin 1958–65, 6, pp. 129–30 [791].
[101] Lenin 1958–65, 6, p. 137 [798].

all of international Social Democracy and perhaps lead to momentous events in Western Europe.[102]

We have traced the progress of Lenin's Erfurtian drama, starting from the original inspiration provided by German Social Democracy and going on to the Social-Democratic activists in Russia, then to the workers and finally on to the Russian people and élite society. From Lenin's point of view, the course of events was stunning. Within a decade, the efforts of isolated *praktiki* to read and apply the *Erfurt Programme* had snowballed into an avalanche that promised to sweep away the autocracy. Lenin holds out an intoxicating perspective indeed to the underground *praktik*. As he claims in WITBD, the energy and initiative of the *praktik* will be given an enormous boost by the perspective of having at his disposal the combined strength of millions and millions of workers arising in *stikhiinyi* fashion in the proletarian class struggle.[103]

## The Archimedes of Social Democracy

One of the most famous lines from WITBD is the Archimedean boast 'give us an organisation of revolutionaries – and we will turn Russia around!'.[104] This phrase may look like a complete sentence and a summation of Lenin's message. If taken this way, it is a *proposition* about the ability of a revolutionary organisation – presumably all by itself – to turn Russia around. But, as presented in WITBD, it is not a compete sentence but a clause in an larger sentence. When we read the full sentence, we realise that it is a line of dialogue given to a character in a historical narrative, namely, to Lenin himself along with his comrades in St. Petersburg in the mid-1890s, just before their arrest on the eve of the great strikes of 1895–6. Following a tirade against the deficiencies of the 'artisanal' *praktik*, Lenin admits that he too has felt inadequate and unprepared. He then goes on to relate the circumstances:

> I worked in a circle that took upon itself very broad and all-embracing tasks – and all we members of this circle had to suffer agonies to the point of illness from our awareness that we were showing ourselves to be [nothing

---

[102] Lenin 1958–65, 6, pp. 27–8 [698–9].
[103] Lenin 1958–65, 6, p. 48 [717].
[104] Lenin 1958–65, 6, p. 127 [789]. The usual translation is 'and we will overturn Russia!'.

but] artisans at a historical moment such that it could have been said, modifying a well-known saying: give us an organisation of revolutionaries – and we will turn Russia around![105]

How does the meaning of Lenin's Archimedean boast change when we see it embedded in its narrative context? We see, first of all, that it is not a boast at all but, rather, a confession of failure – of 'the burning feeling of shame that I felt then'. Given the circumstances of a specific historical moment, there *could* have been an anti-tsarist revolution in Russia, since the people were already on the move – but Lenin and his friends were not up to the task. And, now, in 1901–2, when the *stikhiinyi* upsurge is electrifying all Russia, the lack of organisation is even more unforgivable.

What is the moral of this story, when seen in the context of WITBD's overall argument? Archimedes's lever is a device able to give almost infinite power under the right circumstances to a single person: 'Give me a place to stand and I can move the earth!'. In Lenin's application, a properly organised party was the place to stand, but the lever itself was the cascading spread of awareness that will amplify the message of the Social Democrats and turn it into a revolutionary onslaught against the autocracy. The success of the revolution now depends on the revolutionaries, because, once they do their part, they can be sure the proletariat and *narod* will do theirs. Organisation must be the Russian Social Democrats' top priority because everything else – the enthusiasm of the masses, the universal hatred of the autocracy – is at hand.

The Archimedean lever thus sums up Lenin's Erfurtian drama. The power of the *stikhiinyi* upsurge and the speed of the spread of awareness means that Social Democracy itself is now the bottleneck. Russian Social Democracy has therefore a great responsibility and a great opportunity. This moral continues to be Lenin's message in the years to come. It is worth taking a look ahead to see this continuity.

The *stikhiinyi* upsurge – and in particular the revolutionary actions of the workers in 1905 and the strike movement that broke out in Russia after the massacre of striking workers in the Lena gold fields in 1912 – remained the centre of Lenin's message. The two upsurges of 1905 and 1912 are great historical landmarks for Lenin. His reaction to both can accordingly be predicted

---

[105] Ibid.

from *WITBD* and his political agitation articles for *Iskra*. He instantly and instinctively reacted by putting events into the framework of the Erfurtian drama. In each case, he emphasises that the actions of the workers began in *stikhiinyi* fashion, that is, without the instigation of Social-Democratic leaders. This proves that the revolutionising of the workers is as unstoppable as a force of nature, despite the nay-saying of intellectuals whose weak faith was shaken by intervening months and years of worker quiescence. In each case – 1905 and 1912 – the workers' action sparks off effective widespread protest against the tsar, thus proving the essential correctness of the Social-Democratic wager on the proletariat's ability to be the leader of the whole Russian liberation movement. The growing dimensions of these great *stikhiinyi* upsurges show that Social-Democratic propaganda, agitation and guidance in the past has paid off – they have planted seeds of awareness that did their subterranean work unnoticed by many. Nevertheless, the *stikhiinyi* nature of the upsurge is a standing reproach to the Social Democrats and an urgent reminder of how much they have yet to do.[106]

Lenin's reaction to events following the massacre of workers in the Lena gold fields in 1912 reveal Lenin's loyalty to his Erfurtian drama a decade after the publication of *WITBD*.[107] In an article entitled 'Revolutionary Upsurge', Lenin claimed that a living tradition of revolutionary mass strikes existed among the workers and gave rise to the present strikes. These mass strikes accomplished what no other force could accomplish: a huge country with a population of 150 millions, scattered and isolated over a huge expanse, oppressed and without rights, protected from dangerous influences by an army of police officials and spies – this *entire* country had been set into motion. Even the most backward workers and peasants came into direct or indirect

---

[106] Many writers both in the academic and activist wings of the textbook interpretation see Lenin's 1905 writings as evidence that Lenin was now 'intoxicated' with the 'spontaneous' revolutionary actions of the Russian proletariat (Haimson 2004, p. 64). Indeed he was, but he was hardly sober before. In the very writings used to document Lenin's new outlook, Lenin himself affirms continuity. See Lenin 1958–65, 9, pp. 174–5, 210–11, 218, 220–1, 262, 300 (reactions to Bloody Sunday); 12: 84 (the article on party reorganisation used by Haimson and others, who do not notice that Lenin here assumes the existence of political freedom in Russia and most predictably advocates new modes of party organisation).

[107] For contrasting views on the impact of the massacre in the Lena gold fields, see Haimson 2005 and the forthcoming study by Michael Melancon. Melancon shows the tremendous anti-tsarist impact of these events on all Russian society.

contact with the strikers. Immediately there also appeared on the scene hundreds of thousands of revolutionary agitators whose immense influence derived from the fact that they were also fighting for the most urgent needs of the workers. The autocracy itself was sowing deep hatred toward itself and ensuring at least an elementary understanding of its real nature. And, now, the advanced workers in the capital shouted out the message – long live the democratic republic! – and this message went out by a thousand channels (a favourite image of Lenin's) into the depths of the Russian people.[108]

The moral for the Social Democrats? We need organisation and more organisation, in order to support and widen the movement of the masses.[109] The masses have begun to move and they are all the more insistently asking the Social Democrats for guidance and leadership: where are we going? How do we get there? What should be our immediate aims? Even if the upsurge does not now turn into revolution, the seeds sown by bold revolutionary watchwords will go deep and bear fruit later. The target of Lenin's polemics, as usual, is intelligentsia scepticism.[110]

A year later, in 1913, after May First strikes and demonstrations in Petersburg, Lenin is ecstatic about the quarter of a million workers that he claims took part in the strikes. And even more inspiring are the street demonstrations.

> Singing revolutionary songs, with loud calls for revolution in all suburbs of the capital and from one end of the city to another, with red banners waving, the worker crowds fought over the course of several hours against the police and the Okhrana [security police] that had been mobilised with extraordinary energy by the government.[111]

Lenin takes the occasion to demonstrate the power of the Archimedean lever that arises out of the spread of awareness. He quotes a sarcastic Menshevik comment: 'If the Party equals the underground, then how many members does it have? Two or three hundred?'. Lenin indignantly responds that, in fact, there were already thousands of workers in the Party by 1903 and that tens of thousands of workers do underground work even today. But suppose the critics were right. What then?

---

[108] Lenin 1958–65, 21, pp. 342–3.
[109] Lenin 1958–65, 21, pp. 339–46.
[110] Lenin 1958–65, 22, p. 173.
[111] Lenin 1958–65, 23, p. 297 (1913).

'A miracle!' First, a decision made by five or six members of the executive group of the Central Committee. Next, a leaflet prepared and distributed by the two or three hundred workers in the party underground. The leaflets do not talk about this or that reform but about the anti-tsarist revolution and how political freedom is the only way out of the situation. Next the entire population of Petersburg – we are up to two million now – see and hear these calls for revolution. And then the message goes forth to all of Russia, with millions and tens of millions hearing the message. The message is conveyed through a thousand connections between workers and the rest of the population (not to mention by means of the bourgeois newspapers forced to carry news of the strike). The peasants – and the peasant army – hear of the workers' fight for a republic and for confiscation of gentry land.

Thus, owing to the initiative of the two or three hundred individuals at whom the Mensheviks scoffed, 'slowly but surely, the revolutionary strike shakes up, awakens, enlightens and organises the mass of the people *for revolution*'.[112] The strike brings the good news, and the power of the good news does the rest.

Let other historians assess the accuracy of Lenin's facts and analyses. My aim here is to show the continuity of Lenin's vision. The '*stikhiinyi* upsurge' of 1901 that forms the backdrop for WITBD is small potatoes compared to what came in 1902, 1903, 1905–7, 1912–14 (not to mention later events). Yet Lenin the Russian Erfurtian works all of them into the same ongoing story – the story in which Social-Democratic Zheliabovs from the revolutionaries and Russian Bebels from the workers take their place at the head of an outraged army of the whole people in order to settle accounts with the shame and curse of Russia.

---

[112] Lenin 1958–65, 23, pp. 303–4.

## Chapter Eight

# The Organisational Question:
# Lenin and the Underground

> The Russian socialists must work out a form of
> organisation appropriate to our conditions, for
> the purpose of spreading Social Democratism
> and for the cohesion of the workers into a political
> force. (Lenin, 1894)

In 1902, Lenin published WITBD, a book in which he
insisted that the time had come to give priority to
the organisational question. In 1904, there was a great
debate about organisational questions among Russian
Social Democrats, during which Lenin was described
as an advocate of a 'bureaucratic centralism' that
would pave the way for a personal dictatorship within
the Party. In 1917 the Bolsheviks took power in Russia
and the ultimate result was a very bureaucratic, very
centralised and very dictatorial system.

These facts make it highly tempting to see WITBD
as the founding document of a party of a new
type – the Bolshevik Party – which eventually got into
power and put its views into effect. In other words,
Soviet history made easy. But fuller knowledge of
the context of WITBD again makes Soviet history a
somewhat harder subject. The context in this case is
the institutions and norms of the Russian socialist
underground that emerged in the 1890s and lasted
until 1917 when the political environment that helped
create these institutions suddenly disappeared. To

understand the role of *WITBD* in the history of these institutions, we need to take a wider view than merely the disputes between *Iskra* and the economists or between the Bolsheviks and the Mensheviks during 1900–4. Not only do we have to keep in view the whole period but also the whole range of political parties and in particular the Socialist-Revolutionary Party that was coming into existence at exactly the time that *WITBD* was being written.

In *WITBD*, Lenin gave a particularly clear expression to a number of the basic norms that animated the underground. The actual institutions of the underground did not much resemble the ideal organisation sketched out by Lenin. Nevertheless, the *norms* embodied in Lenin's ideal did play a crucial role in the actual functioning of the system. Lenin did not invent these norms but, rather, gave forceful expression to what 'oft was thought' by the *praktiki* on the ground. The norms were common to both factions of the Social Democrats. When the Mensheviks in 1904 attacked Lenin's specific organisational proposals – proposals that Lenin put forth *after* the publication of *WITBD* – they did so while invoking the common norms set forth in *WITBD*. When the Socialist-Revolutionary Party arose, it also took over these same norms.

The central insight behind this interpretation of *WITBD*'s role comes from Lenin supporters who were writing during the period 1904–6, including M. Liadov, N. Baturin, M. Olminskii, A. Bogdanov, V. Vorovskii and I. Dzugashvili (Stalin).[1] We should not think of these people as Lenin clones who simply repeated his views and his thoughts. They followed Lenin because they thought that his writings (as Stalin put it in 1920) 'generalised in masterly fashion the organisational experience of the best *praktiki*'.[2] They use different arguments from Lenin and often make a better case for his position (in any event, a more readable one) than can be found in his own writings. They mark their disagreement with him on a variety of points and two of them – Liadov and Bogdanov – rejected Lenin personally a few years later without renouncing their own reasons for supporting him in 1900–6.[3] Rather than

---

[1] Liadov 1906; Liadov 1911; Baturin 1906; Olminskii 1904a; Olminskii 1904b; Olminskii and Bogdanov 1904; Stalin 1946–52; Vorovskii 1955. The Bolshevik polemics of 1904 are collected together in Shutskever 1925.

[2] Stalin 1946–52, 4, pp. 308–9.

[3] Liadov 1911; Bogdanov 1995.

being plunged into oblivion (as is now the case), these views should be taken seriously, coming as they do from informed *praktiki* with experience on the ground. At the very least, their arguments tell us how WITBD was understood by its first enthusiastic audience.

The core of the Russian underground before 1917 was the local revolutionary committees, found mainly in the large industrial cities, with strong roots in the worker milieu. As Liadov argued, these committees were democratic in spirit, even if not in composition or formal rules.[4] Although non-workers always remained a majority at committee level, there was a strong norm in favour of recruiting workers into higher positions. Furthermore, and most crucially, the committees' only chance to survive and thrive came from the support of the worker milieu and the demands for 'guidance' arising out of that milieu.

These local committees felt themselves to be the local representatives of a nation-wide party. Central party institutions existed but could hardly enforce their will – indeed, factional disputes made it hard to come up with a coherent will or, once having got that far, making that will known to local committees. Such unity as there was came about principally through the message preached by central party newspapers and by roving 'illegals', that is, full-time activists not tied to any one locality but providing informational links among local units and between them and the centre.

The bread-and-butter activity of the underground revolved around illegal literature: getting it from outside, creating it locally, distributing it, discussing it. Out of this central task arose several well-defined specialities, such as propaganda, agitation, transport of literature and so forth. In times of greater excitement, the underground aimed at 'guiding [*rukovodit'*]' strikes, street demonstrations, or any combination of the two, up to and including an uprising aimed at overthrow of the autocracy.

The main threat to the viability of the underground was unrelenting tsarist repression, not only in the direct form of arrests but also in the intensely demoralising form of infiltration by informers, a problem which only grew larger as the years went on. It is a miracle that the underground survived at all. It managed to do so because of its roots in the worker milieu and because

---

[4] Liadov 1906, 2, pp. 49–50.

of the creation of a nation-wide framework. It also developed a series of rules for preserving secrecy – so-called *konspiratsiia* – that did not come close to eliminating, but at least minimised, the damage done by repression and infiltration.

Given the very nature of an illegal underground, the Russian revolutionary movement had to rely on widespread shared norms. I hesitate to label these 'the culture of the underground', since 'culture' all too often signifies an unreasoning, unreflecting inheritance, thus giving rise to empty explanations of the type 'Group A did or believed X or Y because it had a culture of X or Y'. The norms of the underground were widely shared because people had good reasons to believe they were essential to the working of a valued institution.[5] Among these norms could be found a commitment to preserving roots in the worker milieu, to recruiting workers into party structures, to maintaining high standards of *konspiratsiia*, to according high status to full-time illegals, to creating an efficient division of labour, to overcoming local horizons and seeing oneself as part of a larger whole, and, finally, to using party newspapers to give concrete content to this sense of unity. All these norms found eloquent expression in *WITBD*.

This description of a relatively long-lasting institution abstracts from its history: its period of gestation, its days of defeat and of triumph, the conflicts within it, its manner of leaving the world and finally its impact on the society around it. This history has yet to be written.[6] Here, I will describe the early development of the Russian Social-Democratic underground as described in the historical accounts of the Lenin loyalists of 1904–6 (most extensively by Liadov in his party history of 1906). All these writers saw this history as an instance of the overarching narrative of the merger of socialism and the worker movement.

Starting in the early 1890s, a Russian Social-Democratic movement began to emerge in various places throughout Russia. The activities of these early *praktiki* were not co-ordinated in any way and, indeed, were usually not even aware of each other's existence. Two local Social-Democratic groups could start up in the same city in complete mutual ignorance. Nevertheless, because

---

[5] Boudon 2001.
[6] Important chapters in this history can be found in Lane 1969, Elwood 1974, Melancon 1985, Rice 1988, Melancon 1990, Morozov 1998, Melancon 2000.

of their common sources of inspiration, these scattered local groups shared certain common features. One was 'the principles of world-wide Social Democracy'. Liadov states that the main inspiration for the *praktiki* did not come from Plekhanov or the draft programme of the Emancipation of Labour group but rather directly from Kautsky's *Erfurt Programme*, that is, from practical Social Democracy rather than theoretical Marxism.[7] The SPD model – a revolutionary party tied to a mass worker movement and demonstrating in practice the value of political freedom to a socialist movement – showed the way.

In similar fashion, the home-grown source of inspiration was not the theoretical 'legally-permitted Marxism' that became a fad among the Russian intelligentsia in the mid-1890s but the actual local militant worker movement. If there was a local *stikhiinyi* movement of worker resistance to employees, a local Social-Democratic group survived and thrived – if not, not. The contribution of *praktiki* was to give purposive form to this already existing movement. According to Liadov, the workers were the ones who transformed the *intelligenty* who came in contact with them into Social Democrats and revolutionaries.[8] Perhaps Lenin himself is an example of this process, if we can take seriously the remarks made by his widow Krupskaya at Lenin's funeral:

> His work among the workers of Piter [St. Petersburg], conversations with these workers, attentive listening to their speeches gave Vladimir Ilich an understanding of the grand idea of Marx: the idea that the worker class is the advanced detachment of all the labourers and that all the labouring masses, all the oppressed, will follow it: this is its strength and the pledge of its victory.[9]

Thus, in contrast to Narodnaia volia, the Social-Democratic Party grew up out of the periphery and was not implanted from the centre.[10] Liadov describes three possible paths forward from Russian Social Democracy's original state of scattered organisations that had durable local roots but no connection to anything larger. One was represented by the Plekhanov group who were

---

[7] Liadov 1906, 2, p. 49; Liadov 1911, p. 7.
[8] Liadov 1906, 2, pp. 3–15, 50.
[9] *Pravda*, 27 January 1924, reprinted in *Vospominaniia o V.I. Lenine* 1969, 1, pp. 574–5.
[10] Liadov 1906, 2, p. 49.

conditioned by the experience of Narodnaia volia, as well as the many long years spent abroad with no sign of a home-grown Social-Democratic movement. They put forth a plan of 'a militant, strictly centralised organisation, with strict rules of *konspiratsiia* – an organisation of revolutionary Social Democrats, a staff that would prepare itself for recruiting an army', once political freedom was obtained. They did not understand the nature of the already existing Social-Democratic movement and they overestimated the possible contribution from the 'freedom-loving' intelligentsia as a whole. This plan was a non-starter.[11]

A second organisational current was so eager to recruit and organise an army that they forget the aims of the battle. 'The old banner of revolutionary Social Democracy frightened off the average [*massovoi*] worker – this banner must be furled and, finally, thrown aside'.[12] This was the economist current.

The third current slowly and gradually took shape among the veteran *praktiki* (of whom Liadov himself was one). The plan here was 'to expand as much as possible the framework of a secret organisation, and, while preserving intact the *konspiratsiia* character of the [party] staff, connect it with a whole series of threads to the mass'.[13] Lenin's 1897 pamphlet *Tasks of the Russian Social Democrats* was an expression of the views of this whole generation of Social-Democratic *praktiki*.

Combining the necessary secrecy of an illegal underground with the preservation of 'threads' to the workers was, of course, no easy task. Two things made it possible. One was that (as Mikhail Olminsky put it in 1904) 'a Social-Democratic milieu, one that is revolutionary in mood and outlook even if in not completely purposive fashion, already exists'.[14] Olminsky illustrates with the example of the job of distributing leaflets. The police are perforce reconciled to the existence of a thriving Social-Democratic milieu and do not persecute opinion but only action, such as the distribution of leaflets. Yet a local Social-Democratic organisation is able to quickly and efficiently do this job without detection. If several people simply grabbed a

---

[11] These automatic assumptions about organisation may account for Akselrod's stand in the 1903 debate over the definition of a party member. For more discussion, see Chapter Nine.
[12] Liadov 1906, 2, p. 63.
[13] Liadov 1906, 2, p. 64.
[14] Shutskever 1925, pp. 146–7.

pack of leaflets and started handing them out right and left, they would very
soon be arrested or even be followed by the police to the underground printing
press. So a special distribution organisation exists under local committee
guidance. One person breaks up the original shipment and hands them to
several agents. Each of these distributes only to, say, five apartments, but
each of these, in turn, distributes to five more apartments, and so on through
several levels. So, at least when running properly, we see a specialised technical
apparatus that preserves the rules of secrecy while still working within a
thriving Social-Democratic milieu.[15]

The other factor making possible a secret organisation with links to the
mass was a drive for organisation from below. According to Liadov, already
by the 1890s

> the worker masses had pushed forward from their milieu significant cadres
> of rank-and-file, [under-officers] and officers, who insistently desired to be
> *genuinely organised* so that their revolutionary energy, their already awakened
> thirst for activity, could be used as it should.[16]

These two factors – the existence of a specifically Social-Democratic milieu
and the drive for organisation from below – meant that the workers set the
tone, no matter what the formal rules were or what the composition of the
city committee itself. Olminsky adds the point that the intelligentsia participants
in the movement were usually still quite young and, at least for the time
being, isolated from their own intelligentsia milieu.[17]

The great challenge facing these local committees that they could not solve
entirely with their own resources was isolation. Even getting all the Social-
Democratic groups in one locality into constant contact with each other was
a problem, much less maintaining contact with Social-Democratic committees
in other towns. Isolation was a threat not only in space but in time, since the
local committees faced a massive challenge in maintaining any sort of continuity
given the constant arrests and the police break-ups of organisations. Add to
this the chance personal disputes and the sheer inexperience of the young
*praktiki*, and the odds favouring continuity were slim. Liadov describes the

---

[15] Ibid.
[16] Liadov 1906, 2, p. 44.
[17] Shutskever 1925, pp. 146–7.

situation in Petersburg after arrests led to the arrival of fresh blood. There was a Moscow *praktik* who scorned the intelligentsia, a Tula *praktik* who felt the intelligentsia should set up a 'socialist university', and a Kazan *praktik* whose experience had not given him any clear idea of what the 'purposive worker' (the key figure in the Social-Democratic movement) was all about.[18] Under these circumstances, the actual direction of policy was erratic and unpredictable. Thus the hopes placed on greater centralisation had strong roots in the experience of the local *praktiki*. The young Stalin, writing in 1905, evoked the hopes that the party *praktiki* placed on the Second Congress in 1903: 'At last! – we exclaimed in joy – we have lived to see unification into a single party, and we will receive the possibility of acting according to a united plan!'.[19]

For Liadov, the slow and empirical work of adapting the basic principles of international Social Democracy to Russian conditions was not carried out 'by individuals or by circles of theorists, but by the collective creativity of all Social-Democratic organisations'. This assertion also applied to the tactical innovations in the movement's history, from strikes in the mid-nineties to the general strike in autumn 1905.

> I affirm without fear and I undertake to prove with facts in hand that not a single tactical method of struggle that was actually applied in practice was ever dictated by one or other of the 'leaders' [*lidery*]. In every case at the beginning was a nameless collective groping. The 'leaders' caught up these methods brought forth by life in a fashion more or less appropriate, more or less timely, and raised them up into a general watchword.[20]

From this point of view, what accounted for *Iskra*'s success in 1901–3? Was it (using the rhetoric of Soviet historians) Lenin's insights of genius that inspired a generation of revolutionaries – or (making the same kind of Lenin-centred explanation from a different point of view) Lenin's plan for a party of a new type that would disenfranchise the inherently reformist workers? No, the cause was rather that *Iskra*, and Lenin in particular, showed that they understood the problems and aspirations of the *praktiki*. Given the prior

---

[18] Liadov 1906, 2, pp. 15–26 (on the purposive worker, see Chapter Six).
[19] Stalin 1946–52, 1, p. 90.
[20] Liadov 1911, p. 8 (written by Liadov after his break with Lenin).

existence of many scattered local Social-Democratic groups, national party unity could not be created by fiat from above, and given the need for secrecy and *konspiratsiia*, it could not for practical reasons be built from below, that is, by having the committees connect with each other, build up regional organisations, and so forth. It could only be achieved, so to speak, from the middle – by winning over the local committees to a common platform via an émigré newspaper. Thus, *Rabochee delo* got it completely wrong when it accused *Iskra* of by-passing the existing committees and trying to create the party out of nothing, like God's spirit moving over the waters.

*Iskra*'s and WITBD's organisational plan also showed a close acquaintance with the concrete problems of the *praktiki*. Lenin always made his pitch for his organisational plan by showing how it could help the *praktiki* do their job better. As the Bolshevik writers saw the situation when looking back, it was not *Iskra* but the workers who won over the committees. Initial resistance and incomprehension on the part of the committees crumbled as *Iskra*'s wager on the *stikhiinyi* upsurge – the explosive politicisation of the workers – proved justified. The workers put demands on the committees of a kind that could only be satisfied by reorganisation in an *Iskra* direction. 'The complete success of *Iskra* was secured by the very course of events in Russia.'[21]

Needless to say, this entire picture is disputed by Western scholars. Or, rather, not disputed, but completely ignored. For these Western scholars, any sign of worker creativity or self-assertion is a protest and rebuke to the plans for intelligentsia domination made by Russian Social Democracy in general, by *Iskra* in particular, and by Bolshevism without doubt. For my part, I support the main thrust of the early Bolshevik analysis, once we broaden it beyond factional partisanship and include other Social-Democratic organisations (most importantly the Jewish Bund and the Poles) and non-Social-Democratic organisations (the Socialist-Revolutionary Party). The non-ethnic-Russian Social Democrats were often in advance of the ethnic Russians, and the Socialist Revolutionaries successfully took over much of this Russian underground model once it was in place.

The core of the case made by Liadov, Baturin, Olminsky, Bogdanov and others is the collective creativity of local *praktiki* in adapting Erfurt principles to Russian conditions, creating a set of institutions based on a partnership of

---

[21] Baturin 1906, p. 78.

revolutionary intellectuals and purposive workers. These institutions claimed to give purposive form to the innate revolutionary drive of the workers. One certainly does not need to subscribe to the Russian underground's self-narrative to argue that there was sufficient popular revolutionary feeling and sufficient purposive organisation during the years 1895–1917 to permit the socialist underground not only to play a major role in Russian politics but, perhaps, to constitute the essential motor that forced the pace of events.

The general plausibility of this conclusion can be established by some statistics gathered by late-Soviet and post-Soviet Russian historians. These statistics are based on an impressively comprehensive set of data concerning the worker movement, revolutionary organisations, and the participants of the Social-Democratic movement in particular. They show a fairly steady growth in the worker movement, in the revolutionary underground, and in worker participation in the overall anti-tsarist 'liberation movement'. It is difficult to believe that these trends are not interconnected.

The total of strikes and non-strike forms of protest in each year are as follows:[22]

|      | Total actions | Number of Worker Participants |
|------|---------------|-------------------------------|
| 1895 | 350 | 80,000 |
| 1896 | 364 | 64,000 |
| 1897 | 732 | 152,000 |
| 1898 | 815 | 165,000 |
| 1899 | 880 | 163,000 |
| 1900 | 655 | 100,000 |
| 1901 | 911 | 176,000 |
| 1902 | 694 | 147,000 |
| 1903 | 2,244 | 363,000 |
|      | (29% of total) | (24% of total) |

During these years, there was thus a total of 7,600 strike and non-strike actions, involving something like 1.5 million participants (about 30% of the total of worker actions occurred in 1903). Note that 1901 – the year in which WITBD was conceived and written – was a year of relative upsurge.

During the same years, the organisational structure of the socialist underground was proliferating. The following figures represent Social Democracy (including the Jewish Bund), Socialist Revolutionaries and illegal trade unions:[23]

---

[22] Pushkareva 2003, p. 5.
[23] Pushkareva 2003, p. 8.

|      | Committees, circles, groups | Provinces |
|------|-----------------------------|-----------|
| 1895 | 50                          | 25        |
| 1898 | 135                         | 37        |
| 1901 | 163                         | 52        |
| 1903 | 405                         | 68        |
|      | (plus 300 lower groups)     |           |

In 1898, there were organisations in 54 populated centres. By 1903, this figure had grown to 312. In 1903, 85% of these organisations were Social-Democratic (again including the Bund). 'Iskra-oriented committees' were something like 35% of all underground organisations.

Combined with this growth in the number of local organisations were energetic attempts to create central co-ordinating party institutions. In 1903, besides the Second Congress of the Social Democrats, there took place a conference of the Latvian Social-Democratic Party, a congress of Rosa Luxemburg's Polish party and a conference of the Polish Socialist Party, a congress of Bund organisations, a Belorussian socialist assembly, the Revolutionary Ukrainian Party and the Jewish organisation Poalei-Zion.[24]

Our next set of numbers is based on an extraordinarily complete set of biographical data on the Social-Democratic movement compiled by V. Nevsky and others in the 1920s and early 1930s but never completely published or properly analysed. In the 1980s, the Soviet historian Vladilen Lozhkin used the data to come up with a figure of approximately 3,500 members of Social-Democratic organisations in all the years prior to the Second Congress. Based on a sample of over one-third of the total, Lozhkin came up with these percentages for worker membership in the Party.[25]

| Years                          | Percentage of Worker Membership |
|--------------------------------|---------------------------------|
| 1883–93                        | 42%                             |
| 1892–3                         | 47%                             |
| 1895–6                         | 51.6%                           |
| 1902–3                         | 56.1%                           |
| Joined in 1904                 | 62%                             |
| Revolutionary period (1905–7)  | 71%                             |

Two-thirds of the worker Social Democrats at the turn of the century were under the age of twenty-four (a fact that should be kept in mind when assessing their participation in higher party bodies). Only a very small percentage – seven per cent – were women, and most of these came in the 1902–3 period.

---

[24] Pushkareva 2003, p. 8.
[25] Lozhkin 1983, p. 69. The figures for the revolutionary period come from M. Volin.

Of course, the percentage of workers drops as we go up the hierarchy. Given the general impression in the Western literature of a party entirely run by the intelligentsia, I was rather struck to read that 45% of local committee members during the period 1883–1903 were workers, with a preponderance of worker committee members in the last two years (76% of all worker committee members).[26] The following figures are also revealing. Lozhkin's sample (35% of all participants) includes 167 authors of books, articles and leaflets. These include 108 intelligentsia authors and 59 worker authors. A similar proportion obtains for propagandists.[27]

At the same time, the number of worker participants in the overall liberation movement was going up. According to the Soviet historian Iurii Kirianov, workers constituted 15% of all those arrested for political crimes in the years 1884–90. By 1901–3, the percentage had gone up to 46%. Kirianov also notes the steady rise in the number of street demonstrations by workers, a clear sign of politicisation.

| Year | Number of Street Demonstrations |
|------|-------------------------------|
| 1901 | 51 |
| 1902 | 61 |
| 1903 | 142 |
| 1904 | 178 |

Kirianov notes that, although the strike movement greatly abated in 1904, the number of demonstrations continued to go up. Kirianov's statistics also show the great preponderance of the non-ethnic Russian border provinces in the demonstration movement, including Poland, Belarus (home of the Jewish proletariat), Baltic provinces and Ukraine.[28]

This whole complex of institutions can also be considered a gigantic machine for getting out the word. In this connection, one of the most eloquent statistics is the astounding rise in the number of leaflets issued by the underground. In 1901, 459 leaflet titles were issued.[29] By 1903 this figure had risen to 1,400 titles – on the order of thirty times the amount issued in 1895. During the

---

[26] Lozhkin 1983, p. 79. According to Allan Wildman, workers were 'systematically excluded' from local Social-Democratic committees during these last two years (Wildman 1967, p. 251). I do not know how to reconcile this statement with Lozhkin's findings.

[27] Lozhkin 1983, p. 78.

[28] Kirianov 1987, pp. 134–5, 188.

[29] *Rabochee dvizhenie* 2000, p. 601 (this figure is based on leaflets that still leave traces in the archives).

whole period (1895–1903), something like three and a half thousand titles were issued.[30]

This enormous increase in the number of illegal leaflets could hardly have occurred if the organisations issuing them had not felt that their message was being greeted by a receptive audience – not necessarily a convinced one but certainly an interested one. We also have to assume that the organisations had effective roots in the worker milieu that made possible proper distribution of the leaflets. Some idea of the potential impact of these leaflets can be gleaned from remarks of V. Ivanshin writing in 1900 about the Social Democrats in Ekaterinoslav:

> The proclamation issued about the beating of workers by army troops in Mariupol was disseminated in 3,000 copies. 'In March, No. 1 of the newspaper *Iuzhnyi rabochii* came out in 1,000 copies – too little. Soon afterwards was issued a pamphlet 'Dream before May 1' in 3,000 copies; this had a big success – 3,000 was too small. 12,000 copies of 'May Day Leaflet' were prepared for May 1. . . . The demand for literature from the workers is enormous.[31]

And what was the message sent by the leaflets – ultimately a common message despite the great variety of specific subjects? First, the socialists are on the workers' side and are ready to help them fight their battles – this was the message coming through all the leaflets describing specific factory abuses.[32] Second, the worker movement cannot achieve any of its goals without the overthrow of the autocracy and the achievement of political freedom. This message came through more insistently as the years went on. Thirdly, workers everywhere have a special mission to fight injustice. This three-part message was summed up in the watchwords that became more and more a standard feature of the leaflets: 'Proletarians of all countries, unite! Down with the autocracy! Long live political freedom! Long live the worker movement!'[33]

The leaflets were not the only medium for this message. The street demonstrations conveyed the same basic message with dramatic intensity:

---

[30] Pushkareva 2003, p. 9.
[31] Ivanshin 1900, p. 5 (quoting *Listok Rabochego dela*, No. 1, p. 12).
[32] Surh 1999.
[33] A sense of the leaflets can be found in the various volumes of *Rabochee dvizhenie v Rossii 1895–fevral' 1917 g.: Khronika*. This series has by now reached the year 1903.

red banners carrying the essential watchwords, revolutionary songs, visible violation of tsarist decorum, violent scuffles and heroic dedication. Face-to-face agitation, ranging from one-on-one conversations to mass rallies during general strikes, also continually conveyed the message.

It is hard to assess the impact of the underground's message because it cannot be measured by, say, the number of workers demonstrating at any one time at the urging and with the guidance of underground committees. Still, the 'channels' of which Lenin spoke must have been extraordinarily blocked up for the essential content of the message not to have percolated to very wide strata of the workers and other non-élite classes. The message may have been rejected or shrugged off at any one time but its existence would be noted. The insightful remarks of Michael Melancon point to the ultimate impact of the socialist underground. Melancon asks why, in February 1917 after the overthrow of the Tsar, were the Russian masses able to clearly distinguish between socialists on the one hand and liberals and conservatives on the other, and why did they unambiguously chose socialists to represent them as soon as they could speak freely? Melancon's answer is based on his study of the anti-war agitation during the First World War, but I believe his conclusions have wider import:

> The workers, soldiers, peasants, and large portions of the intelligentsia elected socialists to represent them because the SRs [Socialist Revolutionaries] and SDs [Social Democrats] had been involved not only in underground organisations but in other groups such as unions, health funds, co-operatives, factory circles, student organisations, and zemstvos and had taken part in strikes, demonstrations, and campaigns. . . . The socialists and their programmes were familiar to the mass segments of society. Dramatic proof of this arose when, on the very first day of the revolution in each locality, workers and soldiers (followed a little later by peasants) elected individual SRs, Mensheviks, and Bolsheviks, in many cases from among their midst, to represent them in soviets and other political bodies. Thus their socialist preferences were not only clear but instantaneous. Only long-time socialist activism on a mass basis would account for this development.[34]

---

[34] Melancon 1990, p. 280.

## Terms of art

How do the organisational arguments of WITBD fit into the evolution of the institutions of the underground? The best approach to this question is to elucidate Lenin's use of technical terms used by members of the underground. Two of these terms – 'artisanal limitations' [*kustarnichestvo*] and 'revolutionary by trade' [*professional'nyi revoliutsioner*] – are original coinages by Lenin. Others, such as *konspiratsiia* and *proval*, were current previously. On the assumption that widely accepted coinages and technical terms fill a felt need by those involved in a concrete activity, and in view of the translation problems posed by these terms, a detailed look is called for.

Most short summaries of WITBD tell us that Lenin advocated a 'conspiratorial organisation' or a 'conspiratorial élite'. And indeed Lenin uses the term *konspiratsiia* and allied forms often enough in WITBD (forty times, to be precise).[35] Yet his usage of the term is effectively concealed from readers of English translations. The first translator, Joe Fineberg, occasionally translated, say, 'principles of *konspiratsiia*' as 'principles of conspiracy', but later translators correctly felt that this was seriously misleading. They therefore substituted 'secrecy' or some such term.

In its way, 'secrecy' is not a bad translation. Nevertheless, hiding Lenin's use of the term *konspiratsiia* is not a satisfactory solution. The reader of English translations is barred from having a grounded opinion on the accuracy of the textbook description of his views. The profound contrast between *konspiratsiia* and conspiracy is totally obscured. The very existence of a central theme in the outlook of all Russian underground activists remains unknown. In his memoirs, Trotsky recalls that as a young man the very word *konspiratsiia* was endowed with romantic prestige ('We knew that links with the workers demanded a great deal of *konspiratsiia*. We pronounced this word seriously, with a respect that was almost mystical').[36] He did not mean that he could hardly wait to plot and scheme.

A concise definition of *konspiratsiia* is 'the fine art of not getting arrested'. It encompassed all the rules of secrecy necessary to carry on illegal activities without the knowledge of the police – rules that were supposed to become

---

[35] This figure includes derivatives such as *konspirativnost'*.
[36] Trotskii 1991, p. 113.

second nature to underground activists. Lack of skill in *konspiratsiia* would lead to a disastrous *proval*, that is, arrests that gutted a local organisation. The technical meaning of *proval* and *konspiratsiia* are thus closely linked.

This technical meaning of *proval* – one which is not reflected in modern dictionaries – was part of the slang of underground activists faced with the grim probability of arrest.[37] The root meaning of the parent verb is to fall down or to collapse. This meaning is extended metaphorically to mean 'to disappear' and 'to fail disastrously', and in particular 'to fail an exam'. In his memoirs, Martov recounted how embarrassed he felt as a young man when he gave away too much information in a conversation with some more experienced activists. He felt as though he had failed [*provalilsia*] his exam in *konspiratsiia*.[38] And indeed, a *proval* was not only a waste of scarce resources and at least a major disruption for a local organisation – a *proval* also carried a charge of humiliating failure, of letting one's comrades down. Translators have always faced difficulties with *proval*.[39] The best solution is to keep it in Russian, thus preserving the aura of an expressive technical term.

The aim of *konspiratsiia* – to avoid a *proval* by the police – meant inculcating secrecy and to this extent *konspiratsiia* overlaps with 'conspiracy' [*zagovor*], as Lenin points out in WITBD.[40] Yet, as political strategies, the two are fundamentally opposed. Russian Social Democracy defined itself against the earlier *Narodnaia volia* strategy of a conspiracy aimed at government overthrow, as we saw earlier in Lenin's 1897 polemic against Lavrov.[41] Instead of focusing on a conspiracy, a one-time event carried out by a few individuals (even if the conspirators found it expedient to take advantages of simultaneous popular disorders), Social Democracy focused on the long-term project of raising the awareness and purposiveness of the worker class. *Konspiratsiia* was needed in order to protect the integrity of this project under autocratic repression.

---

[37] When Lenin used the term in 1900, he still felt the necessity to put it in quotes (Lenin 1958–65, 4, p. 323).

[38] Martov 1975, p. 174.

[39] For example, in the Penguin edition edited by Robert Service (Lenin 1988), *proval* is translated as break–up, discovery and arrest, arrests, raids, police raids, police raids and arrests, round-up, police break-up.

[40] Lenin 1958–65, 6, p. 136 [797]. I originally intended to translate the Russian word *zagovor* as 'plotting', but I switched to 'conspiracy' in order to bring out the essential contrast between *konspiratsiia* and conspiracy.

[41] This polemic is contained in *Tasks of the Russian Social Democrats*, discussed in Chapter Two.

Thus, while conspirators seek to restrict information to as small a circle as possible, the aim of *konspiratsiia* is to get the word out to as wide a circle as possible. Both populist conspiracies and Social-Democratic *konspiratsiia* set out to achieve the political freedom that would make conspiracies and *konspiratsiia* unnecessary, but *konspiratsiia* did so by creating a space for open politics even under police-state conditions. Thus a more recent example of *konspiratsiia* is the *samizdat* of the dissident movement during the post-Stalin era.

A vivid example of the significance of *konspiratsiia* is found in Lenin's riposte to Prokopovich's remark that *konspiratsiia* was necessary for a conspiracy but not for a mass movement. Prokopovich argued that 'the mass certainly cannot proceed along secret paths. Is a secret strike possible?'. In reply, Lenin asserts that a strike indeed cannot be a secret for its immediate participants, but it surely can remain a secret for the Russian worker class and society as a whole. The job of *konspiratsiia* is to *overcome* the secrecy imposed by the police.[42]

Given this meaning of *konspiratsiia* – one that existed long before WITBD – what are Lenin's specific arguments in WITBD? Lenin directly confronted the following issue: is a mass organisation possible given the necessity of strict *konspiratsiia*? Using Liadov's terms, the question can be phrased: how can we combine *konspiratsiia* with threads to the worker milieu?[43] Lenin advocates centralising the *konspiratsiia* functions of the movement and restricting participation in them to as few people as possible. But Lenin's proposal to limit participation in *konspiratsiia* is presented alongside his proposals to *expand* participation in other kinds of party organisations. He argues that this semi-mass participation is made possible only by relieving such organisations of *konspiratsiia* tasks. He also hopes that the combination of strict and loose *konspiratsiia* will allow the Russian underground at least to emulate the SPD model of a party-led movement. Whatever the cogency of Lenin's proposal to centralise and restrict *konspiratsiia* functions, his aim is clear: to make a mass movement possible under the autocracy.[44]

---

[42] Lenin 1958–65, 6, pp. 110–11 [773–4].

[43] Lenin 1958–65, 6, p. 125 [787].

[44] Later in 1902, Lenin wrote his *Letter to a Petersburg Comrade* which gave more concrete recommendations for local organisation (Lenin 1958–65, 7, pp. 1–32). The *Letter* is often said to reveal Lenin's hyper-centralised and conspiratorial outlook, but the picture that emerges in it follows the picture described here: an underground organisation with manifold threads that connect it to a supportive worker milieu. A full examination of the *Letter*, unfortunately, cannot be undertaken here.

Lenin also argues that formal democratic institutions such as elections within local organisations are dangerous because they violate *konspiratsiia*. Elections and other kinds of formal rules allow the police to infiltrate and to locate the leaders.[45] On the other hand, a culture of *konspiratsiia* – a widespread recognition of its importance and of the need to train oneself to follow its rules – could strengthen the democratic nature of the movement. One of the reasons for intelligentsia predominance in leadership positions was a widespread perception of worker carelessness at *konspiratsiia*. The more the workers understood the need for *konspiratsiia*, the easier to recruit them into the leadership. Lenin also felt that only a more solid grounding in *konspiratsiia* skills would make an elected national party congress and central committee possible.[46]

Lenin also used *konspiratsiia* considerations as an additional argument against wasting time and resources on local underground newspapers. The elaborate apparatus of *konspiratsiia* needed for such an newspaper would hardly be able to recoup its losses given the narrow scope of the enterprise.[47] Carter Elwood writes in his study of the Social-Democratic underground that

> the establishment of an underground printing press and the publication of an illegal paper was the most difficult act in the Social-Democratic repertoire. It required money to buy the typographical equipment, men with experience to run the presses and education to write the articles, and good conspiratorial technique plus a bit of luck to keep one jump ahead of the police.[48]

It was rare for any of these papers to publish as many as ten issues. Semën Kanatchikov, later a Bolshevik, recalled with pride the ten issues of *Rabochaia gazeta* [*Worker News*], a newspaper he and his worker comrades (without intelligentsia participation) published in Saratov in 1901–2.

> From a [*konspiratsiia*] standpoint, the printing and publication of *The Workers' Newspaper* were so well organised that, when many of us were later arrested, and the gendarmes charged some of us with direct or indirect participation

---

[45] Lenin 1958–65, 6, p. 119 [781].
[46] Lenin 1958–65, 6, pp. 159, 179 [818, 835]. See Chapter Nine for the importance of the principle of congress sovereignty for the Bolsheviks.
[47] Lenin 1958–65, 6, p. 168 [826].
[48] Elwood 1974, pp. 142–3.

in putting out the newspaper, they were incapable of proving anything. And today, when we find ourselves in possession of the archives of the gendarme office, we can see how little was revealed there about the identities of the paper's organisers and collaborators.[49]

Martov's memoir account of the evolution of the norms of *konspiratsiia* in the early 1890s gives us what we cannot get from *WITBD*, namely, a concrete sense of what some of these norms were. Newly arrived in Vilno, Martov was talking to some of his new Social-Democratic comrades and telling them about underground circles in Petersburg. At one point, he mentioned that his own circle kept apart from populist circles because of their inadequate *konspiratsiia*. At this remark, his new friends smiled at each other and proceeded to lecture Martov on his own lack of *konspiratsiia*. True, he had not mentioned names, but he nevertheless had provided useful clues to the whereabouts of these circles in the course of conversation with people he hardly knew – a violation of elementary rules. Martov felt he had failed a test and was extremely irritated with himself.[50]

The stress on *konspiratsiia* grew up not only in Vilno but in several other of the Social-Democratic organisations that sprouted up in other towns, since it was a simple matter of survival. Martov recalled that 'long experience of work in one place developed these elementary rules of *konspiratsiia* to the point of virtuosity, and I later had occasion to realise how these elementary rules had become part of my flesh and blood'.[51] Never name each other or others in the organisation, even when talking face to face; never appear on the streets with a package, no matter how innocent looking; never give signs of recognition when passing others on the street; never go straight to a meeting place; lower your voice when talking in an apartment (these were the days before room bugs); never ask unnecessary questions. The elementary rules worked out in this period achieved results, although at the expense of a great deal of psychological and even physical energy.

When the Social Democrats moved from an exclusive focus on propaganda (small circles concentrating on education of a small number of workers) to broad-based agitation, this original system seemed too unwieldy. Before the

---

[49] Kanatchikov 1986, p. 215.
[50] Martov 1975, p. 174.
[51] Martov 1975, pp. 173–7.

St. Petersburg textile strikes, for example, a Social-Democratic activist would walk from one neighbourhood of Petersburg to another rather than taking a street car on which a police tail could less easily be detected. When the strikes started and the tempo of Social-Democratic work increased, this particular bit of *konspiratsiia* was regarded as a luxury. But, as often happens when a system of strict morality is rejected, there followed a period of 'de-*konspiratsiia*' and excessive carelessness.

> Only in the succeeding stage of development, in the *Iskra* period, was there a resurrection of *konspiratsiia*, enriched by new experience and relying on an infinitely more developed technique that allowed organisations to operate with illegal activists, with genuinely *konspirativnyi* apartments and using division of labour. But this *konspiratsiia* was already more complex and flexible, shorn of those features of naïveté and dogmatism that characterised the first half of the 1890s.[52]

In absolute terms, the underground's *konspiratsiia* was never very effective. Especially in the years following the 1905 Revolution, arrests and especially infiltration led to repeated *provaly*. Lenin himself was responsible for a spectacular breach of *konspiratsiia*: the unknowing election of the police informer Roman Malinovskii to the Bolshevik Central Committee in 1912.[53] When reading memoirs from this period, one wonders how the underground managed to stay in existence. The conclusion must be, not that *konspiratsiia* was useless, but, rather, that a strong emphasis on the norm of *konspiratsiia* was absolutely necessary for the survival of the underground.

The textbook description of WITBD as arguing for a 'conspiratorial organisation' is, thus, highly misleading. If it means that Lenin advocated the organisation of conspiracies or that he wanted party organisation that had no ties to the workers, the textbook interpretation is simply wrong. If this description really refers to *konspiratsiia* – that is, the fine art of not getting arrested – then Lenin did not advocate *konspiratsiia* so much as he simply took it for granted as a valued organisational norm. All other Social Democrats, including those used as polemical targets in WITBD, also took this norm for

---

[52] Ibid.
[53] On the Malinovskii case, see Elwood 1977 and Rozental 1994 (Rozental has much to say on the relations between workers and Social Democrats).

granted. The textbook description of *WITBD* thus does not clear up but, rather, compounds the confusion between *konspiratsiia* and conspiracy.

*Konspiratsiia* was a long-standing term in the argot of the underground but *kustarnichestvo* was a Lenin coinage. Translators have had difficulty with the term, rendering it variously as 'primitive methods', 'primitiveness', 'amateurism' and Utechin's rather charming 'rustic craftsmanship'. I have decided to translate *kustarnichestvo* as 'artisanal limitations'. This rendition aims at bringing out the system of images Lenin meant to evoke with this term.

The *kustar* was an artisan or a handicraftsman who worked in a very small establishment and for a very restricted market. The *kustar* himself may have been very skilled but his work (at least from a Marxist standpoint) was inefficient, time-consuming, costly and liable to disruption, due mainly to the small scale of his activities. According to the *Communist Manifesto* and Kautsky's *Erfurt Programme*, *kustar*-type production is the starting point of a process that leads to the growth first of a national and then an international market. A larger scale of production allows technical advance and an organisational division of labour that consigned *kustar* production, without regret, into eventual oblivion (Social Democrats were not William Morris types). Paralleling the nationalisation and then internationalisation of the economy is the formation of nation-wide classes. As these nation-wide classes grow aware of their common interests, they create modern political parties analogous to modern industry because of their reliance on the functional specialisation made possible by the national scale of their activities. Modern political parties thus stand in contrast to the earlier face-to-face politics of personal dependence in the same way that modern industry stands in contrast to the *kustar*.[54]

Lenin was invoking this scenario when he labelled the existing state of party relations as *kustarnichestvo*. The key themes in the *kustar* metaphor were fragmentation, isolation and narrow horizons of local party organisations. The resulting inefficiencies were not caused by the lack of skill on the part of the local *praktiki* but rather by the constraints of their position. The *kustar* was a necessary stage of institutional evolution but it was a stage that must also necessarily be transcended. The time had come to modernise. The move beyond the *kustar* stage had always been a goal but now it was urgent, due to the *stikhiinyi* upsurge and the growth of a *nation-wide* revolutionary situation.

---

[54] Marx and Engels 1959; Kautsky 1965.

The scenario informing Lenin's argument also lay behind the remark of British scholar John Rae writing in 1883: 'Marx sought, in short, to introduce the large system of production into the art of conspiracy'.[55]

I came up with the term 'artisanal limitations' after listening to a Montreal radio news show on which an official of a Quebec savings-and-loan association was being interviewed. The official – a francophone speaking English – said that the savings and loan banks had now 'passed the artisanal stage'. No English speaker would have put it this way and yet it showed me that something resembling the Social-Democratic scenario about artisans/*kustari* was alive and well. Taking my cue from the francophone official, I translate *kustar* as 'artisan', the representative of a certain stage in economic and organisational evolution. *Kustarnichestvo* becomes 'artisanal limitations' in order to bring out Lenin's essential point: the present party organisational framework has become too cramped and restrictive – only a national framework is up to the demands of the moment.

In his pre-*WITBD* writings, Lenin's use of *kustarnichestvo* was meant to evoke a stage in institutional evolution rather than any negative attitude toward the party 'artisans' – the local *praktiki* – or any condescending attitude toward the problems caused by this objective situation.[56] In 1901, Lenin's use of the term becomes more hostile and charged. *Kustarnichestvo* becomes an 'ism', that is, not only an objective situation but a resistance to change justified by theoretical arguments. The disputes with *Rabochee delo* and Nadezhdin undoubtedly contributed to this change. Perhaps the essential reason, however, was Lenin's growing conviction that the narrow horizons of the local *praktiki* were the cause of economism, rather than economist ideology being the cause of narrow horizons.

An explosion in a letter of July 1901 to an *Iskra* agent in Russia illustrates this feeling. Lenin was highly exasperated that even *Iskra* supporters just did not understand about the necessity of *one* national newspaper being the only

---

[55] Rae 1884, pp. 127–9. The full passage is given in Chapter One.

[56] This usage of the term is reflected later in a passing remark by Nikolai Bukharin, when in 1914 he wrote that the Moscow 'liquidators' (a Social-Democratic faction) 'were then [1910] still to a considerable extent going through a *kustar* period, and many liquidators carried out exclusively *kustar* work in legal institutions, not giving any thought to the creation of an all-Russian organisation of whatever type' (*Voprosy istorii*, No. 9, 1993, p. 118).

efficient use of very scarce resources. He lectured his correspondent, who had proposed setting up of a regional underground newspaper:

> Instead of a struggle with the narrowness that compels the Petersburger to forget about Moscow, the Moscovite to forget about Petersburg, the Kievan to forget about everything except Kiev – instead of accustoming people to carry out an all-Russian cause (we'll need years to accustom people to this, if we want a political party worthy of the name) – instead of all that, to encourage limited artisanal work and local narrowness. . . .
>
> Artisanal limitations are a much fouler enemy than 'economism', because it is my deep conviction that the most profound roots of economism *in life* come precisely from artisanal limitations.[57]

Thus, in WITBD, the 'wretched *kustar*' becomes someone who besmirches the prestige of the Russian revolutionary with his narrow horizons and his refusal to hone his *konspiratsiia* skills.[58] But, despite outbursts of this sort, the key element in the *kustar* image remains the fragmentation and isolation that is inevitable prior to the existence of effective national institutions.

In 1901–2, when no central party institutions existed, Lenin could scold the *praktiki* and urge them to put more of their energy into overcoming *kustarnichestvo* by co-operating with *Iskra*. Later on, the tables were turned and the *praktiki* put the blame for their own devastating sense of isolation on the inefficiency of the central institutions. One member of the Kiev Social-Democratic organisation later recalled the alarming situation in 1911:

> [there were] no satisfactory ties with the Central Committee of the party. Party literature was received infrequently from abroad, individual leaflets and odd newspapers of various factions reached us by chance and usually from unexpected sources. We were generally poorly informed about intra-party matters . . . and to a remarkable extent carried out work on our own initiative.[59]

The mention of newspapers in this description points to their key role in overcoming isolation and providing a sense of unity. Lenin's arguments in

---

[57] Lenin 1958–65, 46, pp. 139–41 (letter of July 1901 to S.O. Tsederbaum [Martov's brother]).

[58] Lenin 1958–65, 6, p. 127 [788].

[59] Elwood 1974, p. 86, citing a Soviet article of 1928.

*WITBD* are specifically focused on the use of a newspaper in providing unity
prior to the existence of central institutions and thus making possible the
creation of such institutions. Nevertheless, much of his discussion describes
the unifying role of party newspapers in the underground at all times. No
party newspaper came close to matching Lenin's ideal party organ – and
yet, once again, we can say that the existence of a strong norm about the role
of newspapers was vital to the underground. The norm is expressed in a
resolution of a Bolshevik-dominated party meeting (Prague conference) in 1912:

> It is necessary to keep in mind that fact that systematic written Social-
> Democratic agitation and especially the dissemination of a regularly and
> frequently issued illegal party newspaper can have great significance in the
> establishment of organisational ties between illegal cells as well as between
> Social-Democratic cells in legal worker associations.[60]

This resolution uses the term 'cell' for the lowest unit of party organisation.
This term was not yet current when Lenin was writing *WITBD* and instead he
uses *kruzhok* or 'circle' (more literally, 'little circle'). The term 'circle' was first
used in Social-Democratic jargon in the early 1890s to mean the study circles
aimed at propaganda, that is, intensive instruction of a small number of
workers. Thus, the term *kruzhkovshchina* often means 'the period when the
main activity of the Social-Democratic movement was propaganda circles',
with the implication of excessive focus on this type of activity. In this sense,
*kruzhkovshchina* stands in contrast with the following period of mass agitation.

Over the next decade, the local Social-Democratic circles took on new tasks –
including agitation itself – and gradually became the lower level organisations
of the proto-party.[61] The circles represented the local parts of the party
organisation at a time when the whole as such had no institutional expression.
After functioning central institutions were created by the Second Congress
in 1903, the term 'cell' was adopted, precisely to emphasise that these lower-
level organisations were parts of an existing whole.

In 1904, after central party institutions had been created, the term 'circle'
was used to evoke the earlier period when local circles had acted independently

---

[60] *Kommunisticheskaia partiia . . . v rezoliutsiiakh* 1983, p. 394.
[61] Scholars sometimes seem unaware of this shift in usage and translate *kruzhok*
inappropriately as 'study circle'.

and without organisational discipline – because, of course, there existed no central organisation that could discipline them. Both Bolsheviks and Mensheviks accused each other of still acting in the spirit of *kruzhkovshchina*, the time when circles reigned.[62] These later negative usages should not be projected back into *WITBD*. In his 1902 book, Lenin discusses the problems besetting the circles with critical sympathy and presents himself as a circle *praktik* himself.[63] Despite all the inadequacies he describes, the only unforgivable sin for Lenin is to refuse to try to better oneself or – even worse – to encourage complacency in others by pseudo-theoretical arguments.[64]

Some idea of the circle system can be gleaned from a set of rules for the Petersburg organisation in autumn 1900. Lenin sharply criticises these rules in *WITBD*.[65] He nevertheless takes for granted that their general picture of local Social Democracy is correct and aims his strictures toward the excessive formality and complication of the rules as violating *konspiratsiia*.[66] The rules state 'Political conditions require organising the workers via separate groups (circle system)'. In each factory, there is a central group composed of 'the most purposive and energetic workers'. This group seems to be self-selected, at least in the beginning. One of their duties is to organise further circles. (Although Lenin ridicules for its extensive formality a rule stating that circles should be no more than ten people, ten appears to have been the normal size of a circle or cell.) Members of a circle strictly supervise the entry of new members (only on the recommendation of two current members and only when not blackballed by any existing member). The member of the central group who organised the circle is assumed to be its representative to higher bodies until such time as someone else is elected by the circle.

Thus, the circles were organised, as it were, from the middle (factory central group) down. It is hard to get a clear idea of the actual operation of the

---

[62] For a detailed discussion of these charges, see Chapter Nine.

[63] Lenin 1958–65, 6, p. 127 [788–9].

[64] Lenin 1958–65, 6, p. 33 [704]. Lenin's most extensive descriptions of circle activity can be found on Lenin 1958–65, 6, pp. 80 and 100–2 [704, 746, 764–6].

[65] Lenin 1958–65, 6, pp. 117–19 [779–81].

[66] Lenin does not give the full text of the rules, which can be found in Takhtarev's book on the Petersburg movement: Takhtarev 1924, pp. 154–5; see also Surh 1999, pp. 118–19. Lenin also uses his discussion of the rules to set out his ideas about the relation of economic struggle to the Social-Democratic struggle as a whole. This theme is not germane to our present discussion.

elective principle within this system (that is, within a small elite of 'purposive workers' chosen in the first place by co-optation). Sometimes, Carter Elwood's study of the underground in Ukraine gives the impression of an organisation controlled from below by the cells (the erstwhile circles under a new name).[67] Thus, the key position of a secretary-organiser for a party committee above the factory level is supposed to have been chosen *by* circle representatives from among their own number. But, elsewhere, we are told that 'other officers, especially the secretary-organiser and the treasurer, were if possible professional revolutionaries employed full-time by the party. But such professionals were always in short supply [and] professionals stayed in a town on average only about three to six months'.[68]

The lack of clarity in Elwood's account is probably accurate. The link between the circles and the higher bodies had to be mutually acceptable to both for the system to work – to the circle/cells because the members of these groups could leave at any time and to the upper bodies both for reasons of *konspiratsiia* and because of the team feeling (what was then called comradeship) that was a necessary precondition for underground work. Neither election nor delegation could be applied in strict logic, and they were not. The system rested on informal adjustments.

When Lenin scoffs at the possibility of elections within the underground, he seems to have in mind, not elections of a representative by a small circle of less than ten people, but broad, contested open elections involving a whole factory or more. Furthermore, he assumes that anyone familiar with the underground will realise the absurdity of the 'utopian' dream of relying on such elections under the autocracy.[69] He seeks to give the impression that opponents such as *Rabochee delo* favour this type of election, his aim being to make them look foolish. In reality, neither *Rabochee delo* nor the St. Petersburg rules advocate elections of this type.[70] Everyone knew that such elections

---

[67] See, for example, the organisation chart on Elwood, 1974, p. 91. For useful information on the social composition of the underground, see Lane 1969.

[68] Elwood 1974, pp. 92–3, 102.

[69] Lenin 1958–65, 6, pp. 120, 143 [782, 802–3]. For Lenin's views on 'democratism', see the section 'Democracy in the underground' later in this chapter.

[70] *Rabochee delo*'s advocacy of a 'broad democratic principle' was meant as an attack on *Iskra*'s undemocratic attitude toward local committees. Institutional rules within local organisations were not part of the dispute between *Iskra* and *Rabochee delo*. I know of no *Rabochee delo* discussion of this latter issue. Martynov 1901b, p. 18; Lenin 1958–65, 6, p. 138 [798].

were impossible. The practical dilemma underlying the problem of elections and 'democratism' was yet another aspect of the central dilemma confronting the underground as a whole: how to preserve a democratic spirit without formal democratic rules, how to combine roots in the worker milieu with *konspiratsiia*.

## Revolutionaries by trade

Lenin's most famous coinage in WITBD is *revoliutsioner po professii* or *professional'nyi revoliutsioner*. This is always translated, naturally enough, as 'professional revolutionary', but this rendition creates difficulties. In Russian, at least when Lenin wrote, *professiia* meant 'trade', that is, a specialised branch of economic activity. Thus, any factory worker was associated with a *professiia*, so that the word was not restricted to the 'liberal professions' of the middle class. In particular, 'trade unions' were *professional'nye soiuzy*.

This use of the word *professiia* is not an arcane linguistic fact but a blatant textual reality in WITBD, since Lenin has a fair amount to say about trade unions, organising by trade, and so forth. Other types of *professiia* are not mentioned. Thus, the metaphor of the *revoliutsioner po professii* has strong links within Lenin's text to the *professii* of the workers in general. To preserve these echoes, I translate both *revoliutsioner po professii* and *professional'nyi revoliutsioner* as 'revolutionary by trade'.

What are some of the aspects of a worker's trade (or 'skill', another possible translation of *professiia*) that might be activated in Lenin's metaphor of underground activity as a trade? A trade implies a set of skills that need to be learned in order to do a good job. Someone who is outstanding at their trade probably has special aptitude for it but even more crucial to their success is the seriousness with which they seek to acquire the necessary skills. Long experience is also needed for true excellence. A trade is a full-time occupation, as opposed to an amateur diversion. Being good at one's trade is a source of pride and of esteem both from self and others.

A factory worker's trade or skill stands in contrast to a rural artisan's craft skills. A worker's trade allows (or forces) them to be part of a large impersonal organisation. Workers can apply their trade anywhere that a similar organisation exists. A worker's trade can lead to feelings of solidarity not only with those in the same trade but also with all workers who share a sense of pride in what they do. On the other hand, learning a trade and becoming skilled in it is a way to move up in the world.

At one point or another Lenin activates all these aspects of the 'trade' metaphor. Especially striking is the appeal to workers to take up the trade of underground activist. Several times Lenin urges the worker to 'make himself over' [*vyrabotyvat'sia*] into a skilled revolutionary by trade. Doing so requires high seriousness and (here, the connotations of the English word are appropriate) a professional attitude. As noted earlier, Lenin surrounds the image of the full-time revolutionary by trade with an aura of social mobility. Within the brotherhood of this trade, there will be no division either among the workers themselves or between the workers and the intelligentsia.

We should note aspects of the metaphor that are not activated by Lenin. Members of a trade try to band together to protect their interests against their employers. As Lenin himself points out, following Kautsky, one of the limitations of the economic struggle taken by itself is that it tends to divide the workers by trade rather than give them a sense of general class solidarity. Lenin sometimes uses '*professional'nyi* struggle' to mean 'pursuing one's special interests'. In this sense, all groups in society engage in a *professional'nyi* struggle.[71] But Lenin never implies that the revolutionaries by trade will act in this self-regarding manner. Perhaps he should have.

The metaphor of a trade does not carry some of the implications an English-speaker might import into the word 'professional revolutionary'. A 'professional revolutionary' might be thought of as akin to a professional soldier, a mercenary who goes from trouble spot to trouble spot, selling his skills. Or a 'professional revolutionary' might be like a doctor or a lawyer – a prestigious middle-class expert who tells the ignorant worker what to do. There is, in fact, no implication in the metaphor itself that the revolutionary by trade is a non-worker intellectual (of course, Lenin realises that, at the time of writing, a majority of full-time revolutionaries in Russia were non-workers). On the contrary – the intellectual is satirised for lack of seriousness in learning a trade. Thus the ultimate aim of the metaphor is to portray the revolutionary as *part* of the worker's world, as a fellow skilled labourer in the great factory of revolution.

'Revolutionary by trade' was an evocative metaphor and it caught on fast. Yet, upon examination, there are some peculiarities in the way Lenin presents

---

[71] Lenin 1958–65, 6, p. 57 [726], 6, p. 85 [750].

it in *WITBD*. Unlike Lenin's other coinage, 'artisanal limitations', Lenin had never used 'revolutionary by trade' previously.[72] Yet he never says 'I have a new term here which I'd like to introduce and here's what it means'. Reading *WITBD*, you might get the impression that it was already a term in common circulation. Furthermore, it is found exclusively in Chapter IV (plus one mention in the final chapter). During the first three chapters, Lenin discusses all sorts of crucial topics, including the ideal leader (people's tribune vs. trade-union secretary) – but nary a mention of the revolutionary by trade.

It is also quite hard, in fact impossible, to pin down who exactly the revolutionaries by trade are and the exact role Lenin sees them playing in the Party. Mostly, it appears that the specific skill of the revolutionary by trade is *konspiratsiia*, the fine art of not getting arrested or (as *Rabochaia mysl* put it) the fight with the political police. (The term *konspiratsiia* also does not appear prior to Chapter IV.) On other occasions, however, the *professiia* metaphor is associated with division of labour, with expertise in various underground specialities such as propaganda, agitator, distribution of literature, agent for false passports, and the like. There is more than a little clash between the images of romantic *konspiratsiia* and these prosaic cogs in the revolutionary organisation. Finally, the idea of long experience and skill in one's trade is associated with the top leaders of a party such as Bebel and Liebknecht in Germany.

Similar difficulties arise when we try to identify the place in the party organisation occupied by the revolutionaries by trade. Is it all party members? Probably not.[73] Is it all those who are occupied with *konspiratsiia* functions? Sometimes this seems to be the case, but other times this definition seems too narrow (since a propagandist or agitator by trade need not be heavily involved with *konspiratsiia*) or too broad (since revolutionary by trade sometimes connotes a full-time specialist, on salary from Social-Democratic organisations, moving from place to place). Although the full-time specialist was later seen as the archetypal revolutionary by trade, the textual links in *WITBD* itself

---

[72] The closest I have found is the statement in the published announcement for *Iskra* (1900) that *Iskra* would represent all the various *professii* (Lenin puts the term in quote marks) of the revolutionary movement (Lenin 1958–65, 4, p. 358).

[73] The 'probably' is here because I restrict myself to the *WITBD* text. If I took into account Lenin's statements at the time of the debate over party membership in 1903–4, I would say 'definitely not' (see Chapter Nine for further discussion).

between the term and this particular definition are few, vague and rather off-hand.[74] In any event, this group was truly a small number of people.

I believe we must accept 'revolutionary by trade' as an evocative metaphor but *not* as a fully thought-out or even partially thought-out conception. In fact, the term seems to have been a last-minute improvisation prompted by the following passage in Nadezhdin's *Rebirth of Revolutionism*:

> At present [the intellectual] does not give himself to the revolutionary cause completely, three quarters of his life slips away in working at some statistical office or running around to teach lessons, and only a pitiful fraction of the day is devoted to revolutionary work. This last is not the only and not the exclusive motor of his existence, but something that is subordinated to a significant extent to personal and family concerns. When asked about his *professiia*, the present-day revolutionary cannot, putting his hand on his heart, say, as Zheliabov did: my job is revolutionary activity.[75]

Lenin does not cite this passage, but we know he read it, most likely just prior to writing Chapter IV.[76] The origin of the phrase shows that the first meaning of the metaphor is 'full-time commitment', as exemplified by Aleksei Zheliabov, one of the leaders of Narodnaia volia. It also shows that his use of the term comes from a chance remark encountered at the last minute rather than any long-held definition. This origin helps account for the way the metaphor is used in the text. After he started using the term, he realised how evocative it was and started applying it rather opportunistically whenever some aspect of the metaphor served his turn. For example, in the second use of the term (about ten pages into Chapter IV), Lenin uses it to make a contrast between the qualities shared by *all* workers that are sufficient for economic

---

[74] Lenin 1958–65, 6, pp. 133, 171 [794, 828].

[75] Nadezhdin 1903, p. 79. This passage is discussed in another context in Chapter Six.

[76] In the section in Chapter III entitled 'What is common between "economism" and terrorism', Lenin analyses Nadezhdin's arguments in favour of terrorism and cites passages right before and after this passage (Lenin cites pp. 64 and 68 of the first edition of *Rebirth of Revolutionism*). Even more conclusively, in a footnote in Chapter IV, he says about Nadezhdin's *Svoboda* group that 'their heart is in the right place but not their brain. Their inclinations are excellent, their intentions are of the best, and the result is sheer confusion'. An example of their good intentions is the attempt 'to call to life again the revolutionary by trade'. He gives *Rebirth of Revolutionism* as his source but without page number (Lenin 1958–65, 6, p. 125 [786–7]).

struggle vs. the *special* aptitudes needed for revolutionary underground work.[77] But he did not take the time for any sort of focused discussion of what exactly he had in mind – partly because he did not have anything exact in mind. I have the feeling that, since he had just read it in Nadezhdin, he did not fully realise the novelty of the term. In any event, neither in the introduction to the book as a whole nor in the epilogue did it occur to him to use the term in summarising his message.

'Revolutionary by trade' was thus a rhetorical enforcement of Lenin's various organisational arguments and not a new conception in itself. We should take care not to read too much into it and, in that spirit, I will go over a number of things the term does *not* represent, at least in WITBD. First of all, the term is not the centrepiece of a 'party of a new type'. The content of the term as it emerges in WITBD is (unsurprisingly) based on the SPD model of a party organisation made up of full-time specialists. The connection to the SPD model is stated fairly overtly in a famous five-part description of the organisation of the revolutionaries by trade.[78] The first three parts of this description are said to apply to revolutionary organisations in general and only the last two are restricted to autocratic countries. These first three parts state (a) *any* revolutionary movement requires a permanent organisation of leader/guides [*rukovoditeli*]; (b) the broader the mass participation in the movement, the greater is the need for a secure organisation to avoid going off-course; (c) this organisation will for the most part be made up of people who treat this activity as their trade [*professiia*]. This portrait of a revolutionary organisation in a free, non-autocratic country could only be the SPD and, in fact, each of these points can be illustrated by Lenin's invocations of the German example.[79]

Lenin does not waste time defending the necessity for an organisation of full-time revolutionary activists. He rather treats it as a commonplace that his opponents will find impossible to refute. He quickly turns his attention exclusively to the parts of the description relevant to the underground in an autocratic country. The last two parts in the five-part definition summarise

---

[77] Lenin 1958–65, 6, pp. 109–10 [773]. The first use is in the paragraph introducing Chapter IV.
[78] Lenin 1958–65, 6, pp. 124–5 [786].
[79] See in particular Lenin 1958–65, 6, pp. 121–2, 142–3 [783–4, 802–3].

an argument we have examined earlier: if you restrict participation in *konspiratsiia*, you will be able to broaden participation in other aspects of the movement.

What else does the term 'revolutionary by trade' *not* mean? The term is not used to imply any new conception of the tasks of the underground. The broad tasks remain the same: propaganda and agitation that spread enlightenment and organisation, guidance in the class struggle. The more technical functions – distributing literature, running an underground printing machine, forging passports – were also long familiar ones. Lenin is not telling the *praktiki* to reconceive their jobs. Lenin's message to the *praktiki* is: you can increase the efficiency of what you are now doing, if you take *konspiratsiia* skills more seriously and if you become part of a nation-wide organisation that can provide support services (for example, providing illegal literature or faking passports).

Lenin is not proposing any monopoly of decision-making by the revolutionaries by trade. In general, WITBD has little to say about party governance. Take the following vignette concerning economic struggle:

> Again, there is here no particular reason to formalise things. Any agitator with even a spark of understanding of what he is doing can find out in complete detail from a simple conversation what kind of demands the workers want to bring forward. Having found out, he will be able to transfer it to the narrow – *not* broad – organisation of revolutionaries so that they can make an appropriate leaflet available.[80]

Taken by itself, this vignette implies that the crucial decision in this situation – what demands to fight for – flows upwards from the workers to the agitators, while the specific job of the revolutionaries by trade is just to prepare the leaflet. Presumably, somebody tells the agitator to write down worker demands; presumably, the basic source of local authority is the city committee; and, presumably, this committee is formed by a combination of self-appointment, co-optation and elected representatives of lower circles. We have to presume all this because Lenin himself has his attention fixed on other problems.

Certainly, there is not the slightest hint that the trade of revolutionary is restricted to the intellectuals – on the contrary, the recruitment of workers to

---

[80] Lenin 1958–65, 6, pp. 118–19 [781].

this trade is treated as a goal of the highest priority.[81] The opposite impression comes from running together Lenin's comments about intellectuals and his comments about 'revolutionaries by trade'. But the scandalous passages about the intellectuals are in Chapter II of WITBD, whereas the 'revolutionary by trade' is confined to Chapter IV. There is no textual justification for taking the alleged arguments about 'intellectuals' and applying them to the 'revolutionary by trade'.

Of course, Lenin recognises that at the time of writing, most full-time revolutionaries are not originally from the worker class. But neither then nor later is there any logical or factual reason for us to equate 'revolutionaries by trade' with intellectuals. According to the study of worker membership quoted earlier in this chapter, 48% of pre-Second Congress 'revolutionaries by trade' were of worker origin. The same study indicates that the total number of revolutionaries by trade during this period is quite small – no more than two hundred.[82]

During the years 1907–14, intelligentsia support for Social Democracy dropped away and the full-time roving revolutionary was even more likely to be a worker (or, if you prefer, an ex-worker). Indicatively, Lenin was sanguine about this shift in social composition while others, such as Trotsky, were more worried.[83] The lesson for us is that these shifts in social composition could take place without altering the concept of 'revolutionary by trade' one iota.

Textbooks commonly suggest that Lenin's definition of a party member at the Second Congress was meant to restrict the membership to revolutionaries by trade. This is incorrect. First, Lenin explicitly said at the Congress that his definition was meant to include not only the members of the *konspiratsiia* parts of the organisation but all the looser organisations discussed in WITBD.[84] Second, as we see from Lozhkin's numbers, the revolutionaries by trade were only a small fraction of those who were party members according to Lenin's definition.

The revolutionary by trade cannot be equated with Lenin's ideal revolutionary leader. As we saw in the last chapter, the core of Lenin's ideal

---

[81] For more discussion of this topic, see Chapter Nine.
[82] Lozhkin 1986, p. 138. Lozhkin defines a 'revolutionary by trade' as anyone to whom sources give this label and who carried out party work as an 'illegal'.
[83] Elwood 1974, p. 69 (see Elwood 1974, pp. 60–73 on 'the loss of the intelligentsia' during this period).
[84] Lenin 1958–65, 7, p. 287 (further discussion in Chapter Nine).

is the image of the inspired and inspiring leader. To this core, Lenin now adds the idea that the revolutionary leader should take seriously the skills of his own trade. In explaining why he thinks a party organisation staffed by workers will be invincible, Lenin lists the freshness of the worker's socialist convictions (the inspired leader), the unbounded confidence given him by the worker mass (the inspiring leader), and, finally, the *professial'nyi* skill [*vyuchka*], without which the proletariat cannot fight its highly trained enemies.[85] A similar evocation of the ideal revolutionary lists *konspiratsiia* skills along with theoretical understanding, initiative, and resemblance to a people's tribune.[86]

Lenin's other words for leaders all seem more highly charged than 'revolutionary by trade'. *Korifei* summons up the inspiring heroes of the 1870s, *vozhd'* indicates a widely-known spokesman for a class or outlook, '*narodnyi* tribune' is meant to be highly dramatic, and even the standard word 'leader/guide' [*rukovoditel'*] evokes images of strikes, demonstrations and, in general, being in the thick of things. In contrast, the passionately anonymous custodian of an underground press or the secretive forger of passports are no doubt serving the cause but in a rather undramatic way. No wonder that the revolutionary by trade is associated in WITBD with such low wattage terms as 'specialisation', 'function', division of labour', and 'detail worker'.[87]

In autumn 1905 – just as the revolution was approaching its climax – the Menshevik-controlled *Iskra* thought it proper to devote its pages to two long articles with hostile analyses of a book published by Lenin three and a half years earlier. Despite their different approaches, both Parvus and Potresov agreed that WITBD expressed (in Potresov's words) a cult of the revolution by trade.[88] This theme of a cult has been taken up by academic specialists. But the Russian revolutionary underground did not need Lenin to give it a romantic self-image or inspire it with the idea of heroic self-sacrifice for the revolution. Take Rakhmetov, the striking figure depicted in Chernyshevsky's *What Is to Be Done?*. Rakhmetov gave up all personal life for the revolution, slept on a bed of nails to test his own toughness, and so on. Rakhmetov was a role

---

[85] Lenin 1958–65, 6, p. 133 [794].
[86] Lenin 1958–65, 6, p. 127 [788].
[87] For a memoir available in English of a Bolshevik 'revolutionary by trade', see Piatnitskii 1925.
[88] *Iskra*, No. 111 (24 September 1905).

model for Social-Democratic activists long before *WITBD*, as revealed by none other than Lenin's foe Boris Krichevskii, the editor of *Rabochee delo*, in 1899. Krichevskii praised Chernyshevsky's novel because it 'brought forth in it the mighty figure of Rakhmetov, the type, just emerging then, of the revolutionary, or more precisely, the prototype of future heroic martyrs for freedom and the welfare of the working people'.[89]

The underground as a whole took Lenin's rather prosaic image of the revolutionary by trade and moulded it in a Rakhmetov spirit that was alien to the way Lenin had used it in *WITBD*. Take this revealing if telegraphic comment by Viktor Chernov, the *vozhd'* of the Socialist Revolutionaries:

> Revolutionary by trade. A roving apostle of socialism, a knight who punishes evil-doers. In his way, a magnificent type of person. His university: prison. His degree exam: police interrogation. His life-style: *konspiratsiia*. His sport: a contest with the police in cleverness and elusiveness. The episodes of his life: escape from prison. His vocational training: techniques of passport, dynamite, and coding. His life: propaganda and agitation.
>
> The London Social-Democratic Congress [in 1907]: 338 persons with 597 years of police supervision, prisons, exiles, forced labour. Average age: 28. 710 arrests, 201 escapes. The London conference of the Socialist Revolutionaries [in 1908]: 61 people with 228 police searches, 146 prison stretches, 121 years of internal exile, 104 years of prison, 88 years of forced labour.[90]

In Chernov's account, the revolutionary by trade gains authority because he is tough enough to be arrested and to escape. In *WITBD*, the revolutionary by trade gains authority because he is too smart to get arrested. Lenin wants the revolutionary by trade to be careful and self-controlled, while, for Chernov, he is tough and energetic. Lenin's image is the creation of the man who later collected a fine from his leather-coated commissars when they were late for Politburo meetings.[91]

---

[89] *Rabochee delo*, No. 4/5 (September/December 1899), p. 11 (article marking the tenth anniversary of Chernyshevky's death). For more on Social-Democratic admiration of Chernyshevsky, see the discussion in Annotations Part One of *WITBD*'s title.

[90] Morozov 1998, p. 40. Unfortunately, Morozov does not give the date of this unpublished note by Chernov. For full statistics on the membership of the 1908 London conference of the Socialist Revolutionaries, see Morozov 1998, pp. 614–15.

[91] Rigby 1979.

Chernov's comment shows us that, like some of Lenin's other terms of art, 'revolutionary by trade' quickly became the property of the entire underground (although, obviously, not always in the same spirit as the original usage). Another indication of this broad usage comes from Vladimir Akimov, a *Rabochee delo* editor who stood on the far Right of Russian Social Democracy. While Akimov violently attacked WITBD for its formulations about bringing awareness from without, he was also angry at Lenin personally – for asserting that he, Akimov, did not see the necessity for an organisation of revolutionaries. Did not Lenin know that Akimov had been a revolutionary by trade for over a decade![92] So soon and so universally did 'revolutionary by trade' become a term of honour. (In fairness to Akimov, he did have a particularly good claim to the title of 'revolutionary by trade'. Despite all the talk about inculcating the skills of *konspiratsiia*, one of the few textbooks in this matter was Akimov's popular pamphlet *How to Conduct Yourself Under Questioning*.[93])

Lenin, I think, did himself have a cult of the inspired and inspiring Social-Democratic leader. The specific aim of the image of the revolutionary by trade was to inject some sobriety into *this* cult. It is not enough to be brave and energetic, it is also vital to be skilled enough to be able to continue work for more than a few months. Not everybody can have dashing, dramatic roles in the great revolutionary drama – the detail man, the anonymous cog in the machine, should also be appreciated for his service to the cause.

This combination of enthusiasm and modesty is very much in the Erfurtian spirit. Kautsky calls on anybody who wants to carry out the tasks set out by Marx and Engels to do their *Kleinarbeit*, their prosaic job, as diligently as possible, while filling their thoughts with a broad-ranging sense of socialism that united all aspects of the proletarian movement into one *ungeheure Ganze*, a giant whole.[94] In the 1920s, Stalin coined an even more striking formula: combine Russian revolutionary sweep [*razmakh*] with American attention to

---

[92] Akimov 1969, p. 322. Describing his own organisational plan, Akimov emphasised the need to base the organisation on the purposive workers in the factories. 'Connected with these organisations there should be organisations of professional revolutionaries to lend them their experience, knowledge, and skill [in *konspiratsiia*], and the advantage of their education' (Akimov 1969, p. 362).

[93] Akimov 1900 (Akimov's pamphlet was 47 pages long and saw a second edition in 1902).

[94] Kautsky 1908, p. 37.

business [*delovitost'*].[95] All of these formulae have the same aim of combining the organisation man with the revolutionary.

Lenin's thoughts on the organisational question can be expressed – perhaps can only be expressed – in the argot of the underground. Brush up your *konspiratsiia* skills and become a revolutionary by trade so that your *kruzhok* is not destroyed by a *proval*. Working together on a nation-wide newspaper and its political agitation will help the *praktiki* escape from the 'artisanal limitations' inherent in isolated and fragmented committees and make their guidance of the worker movement more effective. Such are Lenin's proposals. They arise out of the common aspirations and the practical problems of the underground. Even those who opposed Lenin's specific proposals used this vocabulary – and what is more important, the implied norms – to explain why.

## Democracy in the underground

> Lenin was originally a democrat in the true Marxist sense. He believed in democracy inside the party; and he also believed that the party could never carry out a successful revolution until Russia had become an industrial country with a large urban proletariat, politically organised and converted to socialism. He wanted to create a highly disciplined, revolutionary party restricted to militants, but not because he thought that such a party could establish socialism without the help of a large and democratically organised proletariat. The party must be kept pure so that it could pass on the pure doctrine to the masses; but until the masses were indoctrinated there could be no socialist revolution. This was his genuine belief until the very eve of the October revolution; but when the opportunity offered he did not hesitate to seize it.[96]

John Plamenatz – a British scholar who was in no sense a Marxist or a Lenin partisan – wrote these words in 1947. As a description of Lenin's views in the *Iskra* period, I endorse Plamenatz's words one hundred per cent. My aim in

---

[95] Stalin 1946–52, 6, p. 186.
[96] Plamenatz 1947, p. 83. Plamenatz also noted that, in WITBD, 'Lenin did not mean either to deny the political capacity of the workers or to flatter the Marxist intellectuals: he meant only to show that they were necessary to each other' (Plamenatz 1954, pp. 223, 225).

this section is to sort out the issues so that we are not bogged down in vague assertions about who was and who was not 'for democracy'. Democratic organisation is an issue for Lenin at three levels: society as a whole, relations between party and class, relations within the party. We shall take these up in turn.

As Lenin said again and again, the most urgent priority in his political programme was achieving political freedom in Russia. Anyone – within or without Social Democracy – who did not share this priority was Lenin's political enemy. In his writings from this period, the advantages of political freedom are much more vividly brought out than the advantages of socialism. When he talks about 'revolution', he means 'the revolution to overthrow absolutism and establish political freedom'. Our commentary has stressed this point throughout and no further discussion is needed here.

We next consider the relations between party and class. A Social-Democratic party did not see the worker class as just another interest group nor did it see itself as an interest group association serving the views of the worker class at any one time. Consequently, Social Democracy did not hold itself democratically accountable to the worker class as a whole – on the contrary, it rejected such accountability as contrary to its own mission of bringing socialist awareness to the workers. Lenin accused various Social-Democratic opponents of erasing the distinction between party and class but his charges are not plausible if taken literally. Any and all Social Democrats believed in the mission of bringing the good news of socialism.[97]

On the other hand, Social Democracy could only survive and thrive to the extent that it gained support from the worker class through democratic means under conditions of political freedom. It simply did not enter the conceptual universe of any Social Democrat – including Lenin – to consider any other way of doing it. Lenin passionately desired political freedom *because* he wanted to duplicate the SPD success in convincing the workers of the historical mission by means of good reasons vividly presented. This simple and central fact in itself reduces the plausibility of the standard interpretation of the *stikhiinyi* passages almost to zero.

Turning now to democracy within the Party – that is, within the community of those committed to the Social-Democratic mission – we remind ourselves

---

[97] Chapter Nine makes clear that the Mensheviks did not confuse party with class.

that mass parties were a relatively new phenomenon. Many observers who took a close look at these new parties decided that they were not and perhaps could not be democratic. One such observer was a Russian writer who completed his magnum opus on party organisation in March 1902. This writer's name was Moishe Ostrogorski, whose massive classic investigation of the British and US mass parties was published in English and French. Ostrogorski demonstrated at length the anti-democratic nature of such modern innovations as machine politics.[98] Another classic on party organisation focused directly on Social Democracy and particularly the SPD. Robert Michels's book of 1912 used the SPD as an *a fortiori* argument to support his proposed 'iron law of oligarchy'. The SPD was a party with the strongest possible commitment to internal democracy and yet was essentially run by a permanent oligarchy. This outcome arose not because of any evil plot but through the immanent laws of organisation that were stronger than any ideological commitment to democratic procedure.[99]

'The party organisation "substitutes" itself for the party, the Central Committee substitutes for the party organisation, and finally, a "dictator" substitutes himself for the Central Committee.'[100] This famous quotation can be read in two different ways, depending on what meaning we give to 'substitute'. We can understand this word the normal way, or we can understand it in the way Trotsky actually used the word in his anti-Lenin pamphlet of 1904. Trotsky's actual meaning is elucidated in the next chapter. The sentence only seems prophetic when we use the normal meaning rather than Trotsky's. But understood this way, Trotsky's dictum is little more than a dramatic paraphrase of the iron law of oligarchy. Michels even has a chapter on the 'cult of personality' that surrounded the top leaders of the Western socialist parties.

Trotsky's statement seems prophetic because it predicts later developments in the Bolshevik Party. But as the overlap with Michels shows, to see Trotsky's words as a prophecy about Lenin in particular is highly misleading. We should also be wary about easy connections between Lenin's 'undemocratic' proposals for centralism, discipline and professionalism on the one hand and the political

---

[98] Ostrogorski 1902.
[99] Michels 1962.
[100] Trotskii 1904, p. 54.

culture of Russian autocracy on the other. Lenin's organisational values were completely in the mainstream of Western Social Democracy. As Michels demonstrates, they did indeed have undemocratic consequences, but they did so under conditions of political freedom and with the participation of activists whose democratic convictions cannot be doubted. One might, in fact, argue that the Russian underground was forced to be *more* democratic than the SPD in some respects, because the constant arrests prevented the formation of a permanent élite and because support for the Party remained not only voluntary but highly dangerous.

Russian Social Democrats were forced to live in the underground and, as they themselves were well aware, this situation did place grave limitations on party democracy. Problems existed on two levels: the relation between the local leadership and the central party institutions, and the relation between the local leadership and the bulk of local activists. Very few Social Democrats of either faction were prepared to argue for local 'democratism' – that is, control of underground committees by local party members using elective procedures. This comes out in Martov's comments at the Second Congress in support of his membership definition. Martov wanted to expand the number of party members, but he certainly had no intention of allowing these party members to run or even to control in any way the workings of the secret parts of the organisation. He wanted people who provided various services for the Party to feel like genuine members of the Party but 'the question of rights and responsibilities is decided by the declaration: "Okay, here's your work [*Vot vam rabota*]"'.[101] There *were* people at the Second Congress who genuinely wanted to expand elective democracy at this local level – Vladimir Akimov and his sister Lydia Makhnovets – but these people accurately saw that Martov was working from very different assumptions.

At the higher level – the relation between local committees and the centre – there was a greater effort to observe democratic norms. As the Menshevik writer Panin put it in 1904:

> The local committees, headed by their [nation-wide] central institutions, as
> a system of organisations complete unto itself, carries out within its boundaries

---

[101] *Vtoroi s"ezd* 1959, pp. 262–3. These words were cited by the Bolshevik Olminsky to show the undemocratic implications of Martov's loose membership definition (Shutskever 1925, p. 225). For more on the definition of party membership and Menshevik rejection of 'democratism', see Chapter Nine.

in the most thorough-going fashion the 'principle of democratism'. The congresses, the highest instance of the Party, to which committees send their delegates – the election at these congresses of central institutions responsible to them – this is thorough-going democratism. In the same way, the most effective organisation of party activity presupposes full organisational centralism to the greatest extent possible.[102]

WITBD's argument stands within this Russian Social-Democratic consensus about democratic norms within the Party. On the local level, Lenin labels any attempt to use electoral procedures to control the workings of the local organisations as 'playing at democracy'. Lenin's rationale for this phrase is as follows: you ask for democratic procedures under underground conditions? That shows you do not have a clue about what *real* democracy is all about. In a real democracy, such as the German SPD, there is full *glasnost* and the activities of party officials are completely transparent. Transparency is impossible in the underground, where no one is supposed even to know any leader's real name. To try to have democratic elective procedures without transparency is to be *un*democratic. In rejecting these formal elective procedures under underground conditions, we are not criticising democracy but, rather, a parody that 'plays at democracy'.[103] The most striking thing about Lenin's argument is not its widely-shared feelings about 'democratism' in the underground, but its naïveté about the power of elections, transparency and *glasnost* in Western Social-Democratic parties.

If we take Lenin's argument in WITBD seriously, then we would predict that if political freedom came to Russia, he would dramatically alter his views on local party organisation. For a brief moment in late 1905, Lenin was convinced that 'the proletariat had conquered political freedom for Russia' and he instantly called for a very broad electoralism in the Party. His sigh of relief in escaping the stifling underground is heartfelt.[104]

---

[102] Supplement to *Iskra*, No. 57 (15 January 1904), under the pseudonym *Praktik*. The term 'democratic centralism' was first used by Menshevik writers.

[103] Lenin 1958–65, 6, pp. 134–43 [795–803]. As noted earlier in the chapter, it is unclear whether anybody held the views Lenin here attacks.

[104] Lenin 1958–65, 12, pp. 83–93 ('On the Re-organisation of the Party'). Those who cite this article as evidence of a turnabout in Lenin's views (for example, Haimson 2005) seem to think that Lenin preferred underground organisation on principle.

Lenin was a supporter, even under underground conditions, of the second level of democracy within the Party: the relation between local committees and central institutions. Democracy at this level meant that the sovereign authority in the Party was a congress comprised of representatives of local organisations. *Iskra*'s whole strategy of winning local committees over to *Iskra* was based on this assumption. In 1904, the charge of violating the principle of congress sovereignty was the main accusation of the Bolsheviks against the Mensheviks (see Chapter Nine).

Another topic bearing on democracy is 'freedom of criticism' within the Party. Chapter I of WITBD is devoted to this topic and makes clear Lenin's hostility to the slogan 'freedom of criticism'. Does this show Lenin's lack of understanding of the basics of political freedom? We can skip over the details of the polemic with *Rabochee delo* for the time being (see Annotations Part One). To understand the general argument, we must be aware that 'criticism' was a code word in both German and Russian Social Democracy for 'revisionism', that is, criticism of basic Marxist tenets. The question brought up by the presence of revisionists within the Party is: to what extent can a voluntary organisation dedicated to propagating a particular world-view tolerate influential voices in its ranks that cast doubt on important aspects of this world-view? How does one decide when legitimate debate within the world-view crosses the line to challenging the fundamentals of the world-view itself?

This is, of course, a difficult problem for any principled political organisation (and not only political ones). In the particular case before us, *Rabochee delo* opined that even Eduard Bernstein had not crossed the line and Lenin (speaking for *Iskra*) was scandalised by such an assertion. Lenin thus comes heavily down of the side of ideological purity. His argument may strike us as illiberal, especially given later heresy-hunting in the Communist movement. Nevertheless, the argument as presented in WITBD is *not* illiberal. This is because Lenin is assuming that Social Democracy is a voluntary organisation without coercive power and that alternatives for political action exist. In a liberal society (one with political freedom), voluntary organisations are not only allowed to enforce ideological conformity – they are *encouraged* to do so. The vigour of a liberal society depends on the effective presentation of coherent and competing world-views.[105]

---

[105] For a discussion of this chapter and the challenges it raises for Marxist theory,

Lenin is not a liberal and does not use the argument I made in the previous sentence. He *is* a Marxist Social Democrat, and this means he assumes the desirability of political freedom and voluntary choice. Even under the underground conditions created by the repressive autocracy, the existence of free choice among political alternatives is simply a bedrock reality. Thus, in one of Lenin's *Iskra* articles, he actually welcomes 'criticism':

> And you know something? – I'm prepared to agree with the widespread opinion that we should welcome 'criticism', since it brings movement into an allegedly stagnant theory. . . . Yes, I am ready to shout 'Long live criticism! – *on the condition* that we socialists bring an analysis of all the bourgeois sophisms of fashionable 'criticism' *as widely as possible* into our propaganda *and agitation among the masses*.[106]

'Criticism' outside the Party is fine, it may keep the Social Democrats on their toes – 'criticism' of basic values inside the Party is intolerable, it is the first step toward the dreaded *Credo* programme of turning Social Democracy into a tool of bourgeois radicals. Throughout this period – and, I believe, all the way to 1917 – Lenin actually urges non-Marxist groups to organise and to represent social strata that (according to Marxism) do not have a direct interest in socialism but will fight for political freedom.

Lenin was not alone in advocating intolerance toward revisionism in the Party. Plekhanov in particular was even more obsessed with kicking Bernstein out of the German Party and repudiating 'criticism' than Lenin. In an *Iskra* article of 1903, Plekhanov argues that there is a great difference between freedom of speech within the Party and freedom of speech in the society at large.[107] As far as I know, Lenin's argument against 'freedom of criticism' was not brought up by any Social-Democratic critique of WITBD.

Political freedom barely existed in the Soviet Union for most of its history. At some future date, I hope to explore why this happened and what role

---

see Alan Shandro's forthcoming *Lenin and the Logic of Hegemony* (I am grateful to Alan Shandro for letting me read this chapter in advance).

[106] Lenin 1958–65, 6, p. 289, from *Iskra*, No. 17 (15 February 1902) (that is, before Lenin could have received any reaction to his argument against 'freedom of criticism' in WITBD).

[107] Plekhanov, 'Red Congress in a Red Country' in *Iskra*, No. 49 (1 September 1903), reprinted in Plekhanov 1923–7, 12, pp. 451–60.

Lenin played in the eventual outcome. Just for that reason, I say nothing on this topic here. All that needs to be said is that WITBD's arguments about democracy do not make Stalinist tyranny easier to explain – they make it harder to explain.

## Reader survey

Would the first readers of WITBD be surprised or perhaps even shocked by its organisational arguments? Or did Lenin express ideas that were in the air and searching for an effective spokesman? We can approach an answer to this question by looking at some organisational opinions produced before, during and shortly after the appearance after WITBD. We cannot say how widespread these opinions were among Social-Democratic *praktiki*, but we can certainly say they existed.

In November 1900 – before the first issue of *Iskra* had seen the light – there appeared an article in *Rabochee delo* called 'Organisational Tasks of the Russian Worker Movement'. The author was V. Ivanshin, pilloried in WITBD because of his compliment (a restrained one, as we noted earlier) to *Rabochaia mysl*. Judging from WITBD's description of *Rabochee delo* and of Ivanshin in particular as 'economist', we should expect arguments that stand in strong contrast to those of WITBD.

I give a detailed paraphrase of this article because its author and its date allow us to establish a number of important points. In itself, the article is a good account of the organisational evolution of Russian Social Democracy up to 1900. The extensive overlap with Lenin's organisational programme strengthens my case that the *Rabochee delo* group cannot seriously be labelled 'moderate economist'. The article also shows that the thrust of many of Lenin's proposals in WITBD were already in the air. This fact, in turn, helps to explain *Iskra*'s success.

Looking back, Ivanshin divides the development of the Social-Democratic movement in Russia into three periods, each marked by a distinctive means of reaching the workers. The first, corresponding to the period of small propaganda circles, relied mainly on face-to-face verbal messages. The second period began in 1895–6, when Social Democracy began to take on the attributes of a mass movement. 'Social Democracy stood at the head of the *stikhiinyi* movement and began to bring into it awareness, that is, to facilitate the development of class awareness among the workers.'[108] The principal means of influence in this second period was illegal printed literature, particularly in the form of leaflets inspired by local economic disputes. The leaflets were a substitute for the various channels of influence open to Social Democracy in free countries: worker meetings, public speeches, worker newspapers and other printed literature.

The transition to the third period is going on now. Of course, the two earlier means of influence – the spoken word and the local leaflet – will always remain valid, but, for Ivanshin, the urgent need at present was for Social-Democratic newspapers, particularly ones with a broad, national, political orientation. After the transition to the third period had been successfully negotiated with the appearance of local political newspapers, the Russian movement could then set its sights on the further goal of open political demonstrations. Here, as elsewhere, the Polish and Jewish party organisations were showing the way.

Ivanshin illustrated the type of political newspaper now required is illustrated by a contrast between *Rabochaia mysl* in Petersburg and *Iuzhnii rabochii* [*Southern Worker*] in Ekaterinoslav. Life had already outgrown *Rabochaia mysl*, since a significant stratum of workers had arisen in Petersburg that demanded more from a worker newspaper.

> They search in their newspapers for guiding articles and not just raw material, they demand as much enlightenment as possible on all the highly important aspects of social and political life both in Russia and abroad – aspects to which the worker class cannot and must not remain indifferent.[109]

*Rabochaia mysl* needs to be transformed from a paper serving the 'elementary needs' of the workers to an 'all-sided and consistent' (key words for Lenin and *Iskra*) newspaper that would facilitate 'the upsurge in the politicisation of the movement'. (These remarks render somewhat ironic *WITBD*'s portrayal of 'V.I.' as an enthusiastic defender of *Rabochaia mysl*.)

If *Rabochaia mysl* were to be revamped, *Iuzhnii rabochii* could serve as a model.

---

[108] Ivanshin 1900, p. 3. (The reader may note the similarity to Lenin's seemingly much more scandalous formula about bringing awareness 'from without'.)

[109] Ivanshin 1900, p. 9.

> From the very first issue, *Iuzhnii rabochii* went beyond the limits of *local* life
> and considered the *common* position of the worker class throughout all
> Russia It pointed to the *common* reasons for the oppression of the workers,
> to the political system and the necessity of struggle against it . . . and sharply
> underlined the fact that the local Ekaterinoslav organisation was only one
> part, a *Committee* of the Russian Social-Democratic Worker Party that is
> uniting all the isolated forces 'into one structured whole, into one general
> common worker army all using the same methods of struggle directed
> towards one common goal'.[110]

Ivanshin wanted all major local committees to produce such a newspaper,
but he admitted that this was beyond the power of many committees. In any
event, the top priority for local committees should be a newspaper that
appeared regularly and much more often than the usual two or three times
a year. (This comment sheds light on *Iskra*'s ambitiousness in producing 11
issues in 1901 and hoping to do better.) And not only local newspapers: a
nation-wide authoritative Social-Democratic organ was another urgent necessity.
A central organ would help prevent the continual *provaly* that played such
havoc with local organisations, because it would allow the sharing of
experiences between local activists. Most importantly, an authoritative central
organ promoting a programme common to the whole movement could speak
to the workers with a single message, thus increasing Social-Democratic
influence. In turn, the unified message would help the workers speak to the
government and society with one voice.

Not only a central newspaper but functioning central party institutions
were imperative. 'Life itself is pushing toward unification: our movement has
grown out of the narrow framework of isolated local work – it is, so to speak,
suffocating within these limits.'[111] The challenges of arranging common
proclamations and similar tasks had already forced local committees to make
mutual contact, although still haphazard ones. The local activists had been
able to handle the tasks of the first two periods (spoken word and local
leaflets) with their own resources, but no longer. Without outside help, they

---

[110] Ivanshin 1900, p. 11. The words quoted by Ivanshin come from *Iuzhnii rabochii*.
It comes as no surprise that this newspaper and *Iskra* were mostly allies during the
*Iskra* period.
[111] Ivanshin 1900, p. 19.

could not create their own literature or even effectively receive literature published abroad. A functioning central committee would make possible the overall 'distribution of forces and means' (this is as close as Ivanshin gets to the idea of the full-time roving revolutionary by trade). For all these reasons, 'the demand began to arise to create a single Social-Democratic party out of the previously scattered local organisations.'[112]

Social Democrats should not put off party unity until each local worker movement had made the transition from economic to political agitation (this comment is a slam at extreme versions of the stages theory). A truly unified party would in fact accelerate this transition. Local organisations must never forget for a moment that

> only the *common* efforts of the worker class can conquer better political conditions for itself in Russia, that all local work prepares only individual regiments in the grand army of workers – an army that is the only force capable of entering into a decisive battle with the tsarist government.[113]

Thus Vladimir Ivanshin, in late 1900, prior to the appearance of *Iskra*. He does not use precisely the same vocabulary as Lenin, his arguments are somewhat different and he sometimes arrives at different practical suggestions (Lenin argued strongly against local newspapers for the time being). Yet the overlap with Lenin's definition of the situation is extensive. Ivanshin calls for effective party unification, a unified programme and tactics, central party organisation and common action aimed against the tsarist government on the part of all local organisations. The move toward political agitation, the unifying role of newspapers, the belief in 'the upsurge in the politicisation of the movement', the assumption of worker support, the exasperation with local organisational isolation, the emphasis on the destructiveness of *provaly*, the hopes for an efficiently centralised distribution of resources – all these are expressed, prior to *Iskra*'s appearance, in *Rabochee delo*, the journal set up in *WITBD* as a punching bag. It is no wonder that Ivanshin himself jumped ship in early 1903 and wrote a public letter explaining his shift of loyalty to *Iskra*.[114]

---

[112] Ivanshin 1900, p. 15.
[113] Ivanshin 1900, p. 19.
[114] *Iskra*, No. 33 (1 February 1903) (letter dated 8 February 1903). *Iskra* printed Ivanshin's letter but not the accompanying critique of *Rabochee delo*, saying that it did not want to re-open wounds. As a historian, I must regret that *Iskra*'s political tact prevented the publication of an insider account of *Rabochee delo*.

We next look at the views of some *Iskra* supporters written prior to the appearance of *WITBD*. In autumn 1901, the Georgian newspaper *Brdzola* [*Struggle*] was launched with programmatic articles that show the newspaper to be in the *Iskra* camp, although *Iskra* is not explicitly named. The text of these unsigned articles are found in Stalin's *Collected Works*, so possibly he was their sole or main author, or possibly he merely participated in their drafting. Our interest in them, however, has nothing to do with Stalin's biography but only in their status as documents revealing the sentiments of one group of *praktiki* in 1901. These articles could also serve as evidence for the canonical status of the merger narrative even for Social Democrats as far removed geographically and culturally from Erfurt as Tblisi.[115]

The articles call for the organisation of a party that will be united not only in name but in fact. 'Our task is to work for the creation of a strong party that will be armed with firm principles and indestructible *konspiratsiia*.'[116] The articles say no more than this about organisational principles or structures. What merits remark is the fact that, although these articles predate *WITBD*, the need for *konspiratsiia* is firmly placed in the context of what Lenin would call the *stikhiinyi* upsurge. The articles contain a long litany of all the groups that 'groan' under the autocratic system. The underfed and overtaxed peasants groan, so do the urban lower classes as well as the petty and even middle bourgeoisie. The 'free professions' groan under the suppression of free thought, and a long list of nationalities and sectarians also groan under tsarist oppression. All these groups hate the tsar, but they are either incapable of acting in revolutionary fashion or will act only after the workers have shown the way.

The *Brdzola* articles are particularly taken with the potentiality of street demonstrations, even claiming that they diffuse awareness more efficiently than illegal literature. A demonstration shows to the curious and intrigued urban crowd a host of brave fighters for the cause, and the government is so worried by this infectious curiosity that it punishes onlookers as severely as demonstrators. But in vain.

> We will still be beaten on the street more than once, and more than once
> the government will emerge victorious from these street battles. But it will
> be a 'Pyrrhic victory'. A few more such victories and the defeat of absolutism

---

[115] Stalin 1946–52, 1, pp. 1–3 (autumn 1901).
[116] Stalin 1946–52, 1, p. 28.

will be inevitable. Today's victories prepare it for its own defeat. And we, firmly convinced that this day will come, that this day is not far off, go to meet the blows of whips in order to sow the seed of political agitation and socialism.[117]

In two or three years, predicted *Brdzola*, the government will be confronted with the spectre of a people's revolution.

In the passage just cited, the author stresses the importance of *confidence* in victory (here I catch a glimpse of the future Stalin). A newspaper is needed in order to get information through to the worker despite all the obstacles put up by the autocracy – otherwise the worker will remain without the big picture and 'often an insignificant defeat at some factory close by is enough to chill the revolutionary mood of the worker, to cause him to lose faith in the future. The leader/guide once more has to pull him into [revolutionary] work'. The recipe is to provide the workers with grand horizons and ambitious goals – unlike the economists, who treat the worker as a baby who will be frightened by bold ideas. On the contrary, 'great energy is born only out of great goals' – and so a mere strike movement is doomed to peter out if its horizons are not expanded.[118]

Several months later, on the eve of WITBD's publication, *Iskra* proudly published some letters from workers who supported the plan presented by the still anonymous Lenin in *Iskra*, No. 4. The editorial introduction to these letters was written either by someone who had written WITBD or someone who had read it in proofs – probably the latter (I am guessing Krupskaya, Lenin's wife and secretary for the *Iskra* organisation). This introduction contains what is undoubtedly the first use in print of 'revolutionary by trade'. The passage contains a nuance not found in WITBD itself.

> Our author [of one of the worker letters to *Iskra*] understands that precisely at this point, when the error of the previous one-sided enthusiasm with the *'massovik'* – that is, the *stikhiinyi* movement – has become evident, it is high time to stop continually putting off working toward an 'organisation of revolutionaries' and not just of workers [that is, for economic struggle]. He understands that what is now necessary is an organisation of revolutionaries

---

[117] Stalin 1946–52, 1, pp. 27–8.
[118] Stalin 1946–52, 1, pp. 5, 18–20.

*by trade*, without which we will continue to remain in the intolerable situation where the revolution stops for the summer while the 'gentlemen relax at their dacha'.[119]

For purposes of our survey, the letter signed Rabotnitsa [Woman Worker] is also revealing. Her pseudonym is the only direct clue to the writer's social origins, but the linguistic style of the letter makes the identification plausible. Rabotnitsa was arrested in 1898; she spent her time in prison (which she refers to as 'the Russian university for workers') with the painful sense that she had not done enough to deserve the distinction. It was the unending *provaly*, one after the other, that led her to write to *Iskra*. The worst thing about the *provaly* was the disruption to organisational continuity:

> Worse than anything else is the fact that others cannot immediately replace [arrested activists] and the comrades who replace them cannot immediately get down to the work already started – in a word, with rare exceptions, they cannot be continuers of their predecessors, they cannot use either their mistakes or their successes. As yet, there exists nothing that would serve as a connecting link between the comrades removed from the ranks and those who come to replace them. And the biggest evil that I see in our work is this: we are not yet fully organised, we all work, so to speak, completely on our own. We have absolutely no tradition.[120]

It was, therefore, imperative to start work up again as soon as possible after a *proval*. One reason was to convince the gendarmes themselves that no amount of repression could halt the movement even temporarily. An even more compelling reason was to avoid the depressing effect on less purposive workers, who might panic and lose their faith in those who had been arrested. Avoiding this loss of faith would redouble the energy of those who came to replace the ones removed from the ranks.[121]

Both Rabotnitsa and the Georgian activists around *Brdzola* confronted the greatest existential problem of the underground: maintaining confidence and faith, on the part of the workers and just as importantly on the part of the

---

[119] *Iskra*, No. 14 (1 January 1902). Compare the letter from I.I. Radchenko quoted in Chapter Nine.
[120] *Iskra*, No. 14 (1 January 1902).
[121] *Iskra*, No. 14 (1 January 1902).

*praktiki* themselves. As Rabotnitsa makes clear, a crucial source for a *praktik*'s own energy was his or her strong sense of the fervour of at least some parts of the worker milieu.

Having stated the problem, Rabotnitsa goes on to call for the solution: 'a central organisation that will guide the whole movement in Russia'. She places some very high hopes on this central organisation. It will diminish, perhaps even eliminate, the *provaly*; it will allow the Party to react properly to any unexpected event; it will send reinforcements immediately whenever and wherever the workers are on the move; it will maintain ties through its agents with all the local organisations; it will be able to distribute forces in such a way that all who desire to work can contribute. For, after all – continues Rabotnitsa – our principal weakness compared to the police is that they are organisationally unified and work according to single well-thought-out plan, whereas 'in our case the most dedicated and outstanding activists cannot work successfully precisely because they are fragmented' and cannot link up fruitfully with other party organisations.[122]

Neither Rabotnitsa nor the young Dzugashvili/Stalin have a clear idea of what their central organisation would look like or propose any concrete steps to attain it. Nevertheless, they both want it very much, due to their very clear perception of the concrete organisational and psychological problems faced by the local *praktiki*. We might call the unrealistic hopes they placed on a central organisation 'the utopianism of the *praktik*'. We can imagine their reaction to a book by a learned émigré Social Democrat who had a genuine sense of their problems, who proposed a definite programme for achieving the desired organisation and who exuded confidence about Russia's revolutionary drama as well as about the benefits flowing from a nation-wide party organisation. Such an author could scold and polemicise and it would still come across as a pep talk.

We will conclude our brief reader survey with statements by members of the émigré community from 1902–3, that is, after the publication of *WITBD*. In later years, one of these readers, Vera Zasulich, became a Menshevik on the Right of the movement while the other, Nadezhda Krupskaya, became an exemplary Bolshevik. Their statements on the organisational questions

---

[122] *Iskra*, No. 14 (1 January 1902).

can be taken to represent the *Iskra* consensus before there existed any suspicion of the later party split.

Zasulich was invited in 1902 to write an article for Kautsky's journal *Neue Zeit* on Russian terrorism, then attracting much excited and favourable attention from socialists in Western Europe. She took the opportunity to lay out basic *Iskra* principles, thus making her article the first exposition of *Iskra*-ism for a foreign audience. Her brief discussion of organisational issues sums up what the other *Iskra*-ites saw as the essence of WITBD's organisational arguments and why they lent their authority to it.[123]

Writing toward the end of 1902, Zasulich informs the German reader that 'economism' has now a purely archival interest and that unity of outlook had been restored in the Russian Party. Not so with organisational unity. The Russian Party had grown up in various localities, doing the purely practical work of propaganda and agitation in worker circles. (In a footnote, Zasulich tries to impress the German reader by giving a long list of Russian towns with Social-Democratic committees.) In the early stages of Social-Democratic work, lack of co-ordination was not felt so strongly, and the end result was a series of internally cohesive but completely independent committees. 'Nothing acted as a divisive element among these committees, but there was equally nothing that united them into one whole, except the common goal itself.' The only nation-wide organisation during the previous two years was *Iskra* itself.

The work done by the committees was, of course, absolutely necessary, but under present circumstances – the acceleration of the worker movement and the pressing political tasks whose urgency was now undisputed – hardly satisfactory. Nation-wide unity was needed not only in outlook but in action. If the Party was to make effective use of all the people now available to it, it had to create a central organisation that would be linked to the existing local committees and that, in turn, would make them a single active whole.

> The pressing necessity of the creation of a 'Central Committee', a central organisation that would stand over and above the local organisations, is felt by everybody, although not everybody has a clear idea of its character. We think, however, that to some extent this central organisation will be formed

---

[123] Zasulich 1983b (a Russian translation of the published *Neue Zeit* article). For the German interest in Russian terrorism and, more generally, the interaction between the SPD and the Russian Social Democrats, see Weill 1977.

and already gradually is being formed according to the only model possible under a regime of unlimited despotism. This is an organisation of carefully selected 'illegal' revolutionaries – an organisation consisting of people for whom revolution is, so to speak, their only trade, who devote themselves exclusively to revolutionary activity and who are ready at any moment to change their name or change their mode of life in order to escape from persecution and constantly serve the cause.

Only under these conditions is intensive revolutionary activity that is measured in years thinkable in Russia. Only such people will be able to hold out for several years, as opposed to the present time when a single revolutionary can barely be active for a few months. Only under these conditions will they acquire the knack for *konspiratsiia*, the skill in revolutionary matters, that is unattainable in other conditions even given outstanding revolutionary abilities.

At the end of the 1870s [at the time of Narodnaia volia], secret organisations were thought of as some kind of general staff without an army, a cohort only of leaders [*vozhdi*] without anyone to be guided. Now, when the awakening of the worker class is obvious, when its militant spirit is finding expression whenever possible, it has become clear that such an army exists. On the other hand, the number of cases where revolutionaries successfully escape from prison and exile is increasing, and this circumstance serves as a guarantee that we will soon have at our disposal the cadre of revolutionaries operating illegally that is needed under Russian conditions for the mobilisation of this army.[124]

Zasulich goes on to argue that recently revived terrorism showed the need for 'strict discipline' within the Party. Indeed, the Social Democrats themselves were partly to blame for the waste represented by individual terrorists, since the Social-Democratic organisation was not yet able to turn the energies of these individuals into effective revolutionary action.

Thus Zasulich, giving a particularly valuable gloss on the concept of 'revolutionary by trade'. Some months later, Krupskaya – who had served as secretary for the *Iskra* organisation and was no doubt better informed than anybody else about the ups and downs of *Iskra*'s agents in Russia – wrote a

---

[124] Zasulich 1983b, pp. 369–70.

report on *Iskra*'s activities for the Second Congress. From the resulting extremely valuable historical document we take one or two points that shed light on *Iskra*'s view of the underground.

Krupskaya was painfully aware of two popular charges against *Iskra* on organisational questions, first that *Iskra* was embarked on a power grab aimed against the local committees (thus *Rabochee delo*) and second that the committee reorganisations that took place in 1902–3 were anti-worker. Thus, she emphasises in her report that in the beginning the opposition to *Iskra* came from intelligentsia committees, who often actively kept *Iskra* from the workers. She details various efforts by the *Iskra* agents to get the newspaper in the hands of the workers, while citing reports that the workers responded more favourably than the intellectuals to *Iskra*'s message. She announces proudly that the first local organisation to choose *Iskra* as its 'guiding organ' – in October 1901 – was the purely worker organisation in Orekhovo-Bogorodsk in north Russia.

According to Krupskaya, the workers should receive the credit for the conversion of the intelligentsia committees – not in the direct sense that they angrily stormed the committee offices demanding *Iskra*, but in the indirect sense that their revolutionary mood changed the committee's attitude from abstract approval to an urgent priority.

> In the majority of cases [the committees] looked on the *Iskra* enterprise as something that had nothing to do with them. The attitude of the committees to *Iskra* was put very insightfully by one of our correspondents: 'In general the committee is well-disposed to *Iskra*, but people still say "that newspaper" and not "our newspaper".' For the majority of committees, *Iskra* remained 'that' newspaper for a long time. 'Their own' work was the local work that monopolised the attention of the activists of that period. It was this work – not all-Russian work – that kept them awake at nights. . . .
>
> Of course, few people denied the necessity of common party work, a common party organ, unification and so on. But it all seemed something far off and remote.
>
> Meanwhile everybody was more or less clearly aware of the need to broaden the framework of local work. 'They sit there as in a deep pit and know nothing about what is going on in other localities', wrote one correspondent about the Kiev committee. I do not know how fair this is to the Kiev committee, but generally speaking, during that period there was

more than enough of such sitting around in a pit. The revolutionary mood in the worker masses compelled the committees to start thinking about how to climb out of the pit. The enormous demand for illegal literature, the feverish interest on the workers' part about the movement in other towns, all showed the committees as clear as day that they could not go on living as they had before.[125]

In Krupskaya's account, much of the pressure for a better organisation of *Iskra* itself came from *Iskra's* own *praktiki* in the field. Their efforts to distribute *Iskra* brought them face-to-face with the reigning 'chaos', 'anarchy', and 'artisanal limitations'. In their view, practical success in distributing *Iskra* was infinitely more important in raising its prestige than (in the words of one *Iskra* agent) 'all these theoretical ruminations and endless disputes about economism'. Thus they themselves demanded better division of labour and organisational discipline. Lenin and the central *Iskra* organisation are represented by Krupskaya as responding to this initiative. Unfortunately, in February 1902 (perhaps ironically, on the eve of *WITBD's* publication), the *Iskra* network itself suffered a devastating *proval* which destroyed most of the previous organisational work. Nevertheless, devoted *Iskra*-ites in Russia took the initiative and built up an even more effective organisation.

*WITBD's* specific role in the *Iskra* fight is described in the following terms:

> *What Is to Be Done?* had a strong influence on Russian activists and a whole series of people became, on their own admission, partisans of *Iskra* thanks to the influence of this book. Many of them who had been upset by various legends about *Iskra's* 'seizure of power', of *Iskra's* desire to annihilate all committees, to become the Central Committee itself and so on, now became defenders of its organisational plan.[126]

Thus we see that, prior to the Second Congress and the outbreak of factional struggle among the *Iskra*-ites, *WITBD's* organisational principles were presented as an *Iskra* consensus and as a way of achieving widely shared goals. The quickening of the revolutionary tempo in 1901–2 was Krupskaya's explanation for the acceptance by local committees of *Iskra's* proposals.

---

[125] *Vtoroi s"ezd* . . . 1959, pp. 569–70 (ellipsis in original).
[126] *Vtoroi s"ezd* . . . 1959, pp. 579–80.

I have outlined an emerging consensus on the basic norms of the Russian underground. These include centralism, discipline, opposition to artisanal limitations, opposition to conspiratorial organisations without links to the worker milieu, the need for revolutionaries by trade, at least *some* division of labour, *konspiratsiia*, inapplicability of formal electoral principles in the underground. These norms were the sensible and empirically worked-out implications of the original project of applying the SPD model to the extent that Russian autocratic conditions permitted. Ultimately, they derived from a common commitment to the merger of socialism and the worker movement. In *WITBD*, Lenin describes the ideal organisation that would result if all these norms were fully realised. The actual underground never remotely approached this ideal state. Nevertheless, the norms that Lenin picked up from the Russian Social-Democratic *praktiki* and trumpeted back to them and to all other socialist activists were vital to the survival and to the accomplishments – not lightly to be dismissed – of the Russian underground of 1890–1917.

# Chapter Nine

## After the Second Congress

The *Iskra* editors came into the Second Congress as a united team, they left it bitterly and permanently divided. For over a year, the two sides exchanged barbed polemics, sometimes claiming that deep issues of principle were at the bottom of the dispute, sometimes reducing the scandalous split to the personal failings of their opponents. Only toward the end of 1904 did the impending revolution impose new and more substantial controversies on the factional contenders. Although various issues came and went in the years that followed, the top leaders usually split along the lines of the original 1903–4 schism.

According to the textbook interpretation, WITBD was at the centre of the split. Lenin tried to put into effect the vision of the Party put forth in his book by means of a restrictive definition of party membership, by a hyper-centralised organisational scheme, and by a dictatorial purge of all who disagreed. Their eyes finally opened, Lenin's former colleagues on the *Iskra* editorial board saw the dangerous consequences of Lenin's innovations. In response, they reaffirmed the democratic nature of the party and made worker 'self-activity [*samodeiatelnost*]' the centre of their platform. Or, as the activist tradition would have it, they reverted to the standard Social-Democratic confusion of party and class and in this way rejected a vanguard role for the party.

Two outstanding revolutionaries, Rosa Luxemburg and Lev Trotsky, immediately saw the evil consequences of WITBD (continues the standard story, complimenting Luxemburg and Trotsky in view of their anti-Lenin stance). Their words are prophetic. In Luxemburg's stirring words, 'the mistakes made by a truly revolutionary worker movement are historically immeasurably more fruitful and more valuable than the infallibility of the best possible Central Committee'.[1] Trotsky's prophecy is intensely ironic, given his own later fate: 'The party organisation "substitutes" itself for the party, the Central Committee substitutes for the party organisation, and finally, a "dictator" substitutes himself for the Central Committee.'[2]

I had not originally intended to carry my story beyond the Second Congress. Yet I began to realise that the story I have just told – a powerful and attractive narrative, with its ironies, prophecies and reversals – is an essential prop of the 'worry about workers' interpretation. If WITBD was not a charter document of a party of a new type or an innovative vanguard party, then why the dramatic rejection of it by all shades of Social-Democratic opinion, from Akimov on the Right to Luxemburg on the Left? If WITBD was not the first step toward Stalin, then how do we account for the insightful prophecies of Luxemburg and Trotsky?

How is it possible, I also asked myself, that anyone who had actually read WITBD could write the following: 'How could Martov and Trotsky who wholeheartedly supported Lenin's *What is to be Done?*, which proposed that absolute authority should be given to the Central Committee of the party, reject Lenin's definition of party membership?'.[3] WITBD has absolutely nothing to say about the (as yet non-existent) central institutions of the Party. It offers no opinions about their make-up or their powers vis-à-vis local committees. Lenin has a plan for attaining a national unified party structure and he addresses himself to people who share the same goal. The question of degrees of centralism in the make-up of the yet-to-be-created Party simply does not arise in WITBD.

---

[1] Luxemburg 1970, p. 444.
[2] Trotskii 1904, p. 54.
[3] Cliff 1975, p. 110. See also Haimson 2004, p. 62: 'Lenin's highly centralized scheme for the party's underground organisations outlined in *What Is to Be Done?*'. The debate over party membership is discussed below.

Lenin never even mentions the party Central Committee in *WITBD*. Or rather, he does, once, in a revealing passage. He asks, what would be the best way to prepare for the national uprising that we see looming in the near future? Should the Central Committee appoint agents to mastermind the uprising? Well, we do not even have a Central Committee yet, but even if we did, that procedure is obviously not the answer. We need to build up local organisations who are so politically sophisticated and so aware of national developments – thanks to their participation in a national underground party newspaper such as, say, *Iskra* – that they will not have to wait for orders when choosing the right moment for an uprising.[4]

So where does the idea come from that *WITBD* is all about the 'absolute authority' of the Central Committee? Not from Lenin's writings, but from Luxemburg's. Every page of her attack on Lenin pounds away on the accusation that Lenin wants an all-powerful Central Committee to do the thinking for the Party as a whole. She never gives the least documentation for this description of Lenin's views. She does not even mention *WITBD*. Her description of his views was denied directly by Lenin himself. Once we think about it, her account is highly implausible. Yet such is the power of her rhetoric and such is her stature as a revolutionary martyr that her version of Lenin takes precedence over the most glaring textual evidence to the contrary.

The polemical attacks on Lenin in 1904 and their status as a critique of *WITBD* can only be assessed in the context of the actual issues in dispute. But there exists no adequate account of what those issues actually were. Indeed, both the main Bolshevik charge against the Mensheviks and the main Menshevik charge against the Bolsheviks have been almost forgotten – because they are so counter-intuitive in terms of the standard story. The main Bolshevik charge was based on the democratic principle of the sovereignty of an elected party congress. The main Menshevik charge was based on the vanguardist principle of vigorous, centrally-directed mobilisation campaigns both inside and outside the Party.

The first aim of the present chapter, then, is to explain what the real issues of 1904 were. The Bolshevik case will be documented using an unmined source, namely, the Bolshevik pamphlets of 1904. The Menshevik case will

---

[4] Lenin 1958–65, 6, pp. 178–9 [835–6].

be documented mainly by Trotsky's *Our Political Tasks*. I then turn to Menshevik attempts to find a smoking gun in support of their portrait of Lenin as a hyper-centralist and demagogic dictator-in-waiting. This partisan portrait, whatever its merits, was not based on WITBD, but mainly on various ad hoc comments made by Lenin and his supporters. A closer examination of Luxemburg's article comes in this section.

The always contentious issue of intellectuals and workers within the Party was prominent in 1904 and so a section of the present chapter is devoted to this topic. Here, again, the results are counter-intuitive, with Lenin indulging in anti-intellectual rhetoric and insisting on worker representation on the committees, while the Mensheviks defend the role of the intellectuals as teachers of the workers.

In much of this chapter, I shall be documenting WITBD's relative absence from the disputes of 1904. The inflated role that the standard story of the party split gives to WITBD is one of the barriers to an accurate account of Lenin's book. But the polemics of 1904 do provide some valuable data about the impact of WITBD. As I argued in Chapter Eight, Lenin successfully made explicit the norms that had evolved over the years in the Social-Democratic underground. The authority of these norms is nowhere more evident than in the polemics directed with such passion against Lenin personally, as shown in the final section of this chapter.

Like any highly partisan debate, the Menshevik-Bolshevik split of 1904 poses challenges for the non-partisan historian. Yet there is a certain quality to the partisanship of this particular debate that makes it somewhat different from the earlier polemics we have examined. This quality was noticed early on by the Bolshevik Mikhail Olminskii. I will give Olminskii's own example, since it illuminates a difficulty I must still confront today.

Olminskii was struck when he came across the following summary by Martov of the issues at dispute:

> A proletarian party or an organisation of intellectual leader/guides of the non-purposive proletarian masses – thus stands the question. . . . A diverse Social-Democratic tactic, developing the elements of *this kind* of party, or a simplistic tactic of 'enlisting the masses' into the common revolutionary struggle with the autocracy, on the immovable basis of the political passivity of the advanced stratum of the proletariat? The political self-activity of the proletarians or an eternal tutelage of a non-proletarian organisation over

them? Thus stands the question to which each member of the Party should give himself a definite and clear response.[5]

Olminskii praised Martov for clearing up the dispute. Of course, the labels 'Menshevik' and 'Bolshevik' were now obsolete, since the Mensheviks were obviously the 'heroes' and the Bolsheviks just as obviously the 'villains'. Adopting this more precise vocabulary, we can state the disputed issues as follows:

What do the 'heroes' want? A proletarian party. What do the 'villains' want? An organisation of intelligentsia leader/guides of the non-purposive proletarian masses.

The 'heroes' want a variegated Social-Democratic tactic that would develop elements of a proletarian party. The 'villains' want a simplistic tactic of enlisting the masses into the struggle against the autocracy on the immovable condition of the passivity of the advanced stratum of the proletariat.

The 'heroes' want the political self-activity of the proletariat. The 'villains' want eternal tutelage of a non-proletarian organisation over the proletarians.

The 'heroes' want parents to be respected, free and equal marriages and proper bringing-up of children. The 'villains' want people to scorn their parents, violate maidens and smash babies' heads against rocks.

Olminskii congratulated Martov for setting out the issues in a way that was bound to restore party unity. Obviously, everybody in the Party wanted a proletarian party, no one wanted eternal tutelage over the workers, and so on. And there was no reason to eliminate the final point – added by Olminsky and not by Martov – because it had exactly the same intellectual value as the first three. Besides, it added artistic verisimilitude to an otherwise bald and unconvincing narrative. After all, if you cast Lenin as a melodrama villain, do not spoil the effect by suggesting he is not utterly evil![6]

Olminskii's mockery brings out the tinge of hero/villain melodrama that is still dominant in accounts of the party split. One sometimes gets the impression that the real split within the Party was between the faction of Decent and Attractive Individuals vs. the faction of Amoral and Fanatical

---

[5] Martov in *Iskra*, No. 69 (10 July 1904), as cited by Olminskii in the pamphlet *Our Misunderstandings* (Shutskever 1925, p. 154) The meaning of the term 'self-activity [*samodeiatelnost*]' will be discussed later.

[6] Shutskever 1925, pp. 155–6.

Thugs. Compare Martov's formulation to the way that Abraham Ascher sums up the controversial issues.

> Axelrod's and Lenin's concept of the party could not have been more at variance with each other: Lenin favoured a small, restrictive membership, Axelrod the largest one possible; Lenin advocated a hierarchical structure with control exercised at the top, Axelrod decision making by the rank and file; Lenin stressed the importance of discipline in the organisation, Axelrod the development of the political initiative of the masses. Both distrusted spontaneity, and both looked to the intelligentsia to blunt it, but in Lenin's view it was the party professionals who were to be prepared for the revolution, whereas in Axelrod's it was the masses. In short, their conceptions were bound to come into conflict because one was an elitist and the other a democratic approach to politics.[7]

My account of the party split is intended to be non-partisan and based strictly on the sources. Given the previous climate, however, my account will surely be perceived as pro-Lenin, since I will be forced to bring out that the Bolshevik had a more defensible case than the usual 'villains' outlook attributed to them. I believe mine is the first scholarly account systematically to use sources other than Lenin to document the Bolshevik case. This adds to my perception of the strength of this case, since the other Bolshevik pamphleteers often made points more clearly and effectively than Lenin does himself. Particularly important are pamphlets by two Russia-based *praktiki*, Olminskii and Aleksandr Bogdanov. The readability of these pamphlets compares favourably with the émigré literature, all of which (including Lenin) is so wrapped up in clashing personalities that real issues get obscured. Olminskii and Bogdanov, while highly partisan, are detached enough to be genuinely witty rather than just angrily sarcastic.

I nevertheless believe that my non-partisan approach will also benefit the Mensheviks. Basing themselves on some polemical sallies by Lenin, writers in the activist tradition regularly portray the Mensheviks as hopelessly confused

---

[7] Ascher 1972, p. 199. Every one of Ascher's contrasts is incorrect. Compare Wildman on the reaction to WITBD: 'Indeed, many disciples so fully assimilated the spirit of *Chto delat'* that they outdid their master in zeal for the cause, contempt for opponents, and fondness for manipulations' (Wildman 1967, pp. 234–5).

on the issue of class vs. party. As I shall show, the Mensheviks had a very strong sense that the Party was not the class nor the representative of the class but rather a vanguard whose job was to fill up the class with socialist awareness. Furthermore, even present-day partisans of the various Menshevik spokesmen – Akselrod, Martov, Trotsky – have overlooked or thoroughly misunderstood the core of the Menshevik case.

## After the Second Congress: the real issues

The oddity of the debate in 1903–4 was that each side overlooked or minimised the issue most important to the other side. The newly-minted Bolsheviks accused the Menshevik leaders of 'organisational opportunism', of 'anarchist individualism', of 'intelligentsia indiscipline'. The Mensheviks laughed off these charges ('What kind of opportunist is Martov? What kind of opportunist is Akselrod or Starover? When Kautsky heard that people are calling them opportunists, he laughed out loud') and accused their opponents of letting relatively trivial issues blind them to the truly serious danger – the danger of 'tactical opportunism' that arose out of the old *Iskra*'s emphasis on the merely political revolution for political freedom.[8] The Bolsheviks did not join battle on tactical issues until the end of 1904, when the Menshevik leaders proposed a specific campaign (the so-called '*zemstvo* plan') that embodied their thinking. The debate that then erupted over the Menshevik plan was a sign that a new chapter in the history of Russian Social Democracy had commenced.

The somewhat frustrating debate of 1903–4 was not over the profound issues many people have wanted to read into it. On the other hand, it was not just a trivial squabble either. We can best call it a characteristic split over empirical questions. The ins and outs of the conflict among the émigré leaders were complicated and full of zigzags. At first, the Mensheviks posed as the defender of the newly-elected Central Committee, then they led a crusade against it. Lenin first had his base in the new *Iskra* editorial board, then in the new Central Committee, and finally turned against both. Without going

---

[8] The parenthetical statement was made by Plekhanov at a meeting on 2 September 1904 ('Starover', Old Believer, was the pseudonym of Potresov) (Plekhanov 1923–7, vol. 13, p. 376). In later years, Plekhanov himself bitterly attacked all three.

into all these institutional details, we need to have an outline of events in order to make sense of the polemics.

When the Second Congress met in Brussels and later in London, a majority of delegates were representatives from committees that had declared their loyalty to *Iskra*. The main opposition was led by the delegation from *Rabochee delo* and from the Jewish Bund, and both of these groups abandoned the Congress midway. The *Iskra* majority stayed together on programmatic matters and (for the most part) on tactical matters. A serious split occurred over the clause in the party rules that defined the status of party member. We shall look at this famous clash later, but please note that the labels 'majority [*bol'shinstvo*]' and 'minority [*men'shinstvo*]' did not arise from this clash, since the Mensheviks led by Martov won on this issue.

Much the more important split came over the choice of editors for *Iskra*. The Congress had designated *Iskra* the official party newspaper, but this new status raised a delicate but fundamental question: did the Party, in the form of the Congress, have the right to name the editors of what had previously been solely the affair of the *Iskra* group itself? Lenin and Plekhanov thought so and, furthermore, proposed only a three-man editorial board: themselves plus Martov. Martov and the other three editors (Akselrod, Potresov and Zasulich) did not really deny the formal right of the Congress to name the editors, but they considered it politically disastrous not to appoint the old editorial board as a whole. Martov refused to serve on the newly elected three-man board and joined the other three (along with Trotsky and a few others) in declaring a boycott on their own participation in party institutions. It was 'the general strike of the generals'.[9]

Thus, for the first three months, *Iskra* was run by the two-man board of Lenin and Plekhanov. During most of this period, Plekhanov was an uncompromising Bolshevik. Then, he developed into a compromising Bolshevik – he decided that, for the sake of peace, the old editors needed to be co-opted onto the editorial board, even though they might through misunderstanding or inertia have shown opportunist tendencies. But any such co-optation required a unanimous decision, and Lenin felt enough had already been conceded to the boycotters (offering them space in *Iskra* to state their objections or even

---

[9] From the Menshevik point of view, it was Bolshevik intolerance and persecution of dissenters that led to their non-participation (see Dan 1964).

providing them their own newspaper). He therefore refused to co-opt the old editors. Plekhanov threatened to resign and Lenin, under pressure, was forced himself to resign. The new one-man editorial board then 'unanimously' decided to co-opt all the old editors. Thus, by the end of November, there had occurred something like a palace coup at *Iskra*. An editor selected by the Congress was out, the editors rejected by the Congress were in.

How would the new editorial board comport itself? Would it declare itself a representative of the congress majority and strive for party peace, as Plekhanov rather piously hoped? Or would it justify Lenin's gloomy prediction that peace would be further away than ever? The answer came with the very first issue of the new board, which featured a rewritten version of an anti-majority polemical broadside originally entitled 'Again in the Minority'. This article, now entitled 'Our Congress', argued that the decisions of the Congress had been mistaken in various sorts of ways. For the Bolsheviks, this article by Martov in *Iskra* No. 53 was the turning point of the dispute. The article signified that the Party's official 'central organ' had declared its freedom from and, indeed, its hostility to the will of the party congress.

What, then, was the positive programme of the new editors? The answer to this question came a few issues later in a signed article by Akselrod entitled 'The Unification of Russian Social Democracy and Its Tasks'. According to Akselrod, the most pressing task facing the Party was to work out a political tactic that was truly Social-Democratic and emphasised the class *distinctiveness* of the workers. The previous *Iskra* period had neglected this task because the merely anti-tsarist revolution had monopolised everyone's attention. The workers and the bourgeoisie both needed political freedom, but only the workers needed socialism – and the Party had to get the workers to appreciate this fact. For the Mensheviks, this article by Akselrod in *Iskra* Nos. 55 and 57 was the turning point in the dispute. It provided wise and instructive guidance from a founder of the Party about the urgent tasks now facing the Russian Social Democrats.

The lines were drawn, both sides had a healthy sense of grievance – let the polemics begin! Lenin no longer had a journalistic outlet for his views and expressed his frustration in two separate pamphlets. The first was an official publication of his influential article from 1902 entitled *Letter to a Comrade on Organisational Questions*. Lenin now accompanied the *Letter* was a postword bitterly attacking Akselrod's *Iskra* article.

Lenin's second pamphlet was *One Step Forward, Two Steps Back*. This book was a blow-by-blow account of the Second Congress (made possible by the publication of the congress records in early 1903). Its aim was to show that there was a solid *Iskra* majority led by Plekhanov and himself. The *Iskra* minority led by Martov and Akselrod owed what success it had to support from non-*Iskra* delegates – dubious allies that revealed the incipient opportunism of the *Iskra* minority. In fact, had *Rabochee delo* and the Bund not walked out midway, the *Iskra* minority would have been the congress majority. Thus, Lenin made the claim that the Bolsheviks deserved their name 'majority' not just because they represented a slim majority of the party Congress but also – what was politically more important – a solid majority of *Iskra*-ites.

Lenin's two broadsides absolutely infuriated his former colleagues. Their impact was overwhelmingly more important than WITBD in defining the context and the tone of the Menshevik case. The Menshevik writers were personally angry at Lenin, not only for portraying them as opportunists, but, more fundamentally, for undermining the legitimacy of the party leadership at a time when the Party needed to be even more united in the face of new challenges. Lenin seemed to them to be devoting all his energy to wrecking the party he had helped to build up.

So, in response, they organised a vast literary anti-Lenin campaign. One front consisted of their own long and obsessive *Iskra* articles attacking Lenin's *Letter* and especially *One Step*. A second front called in heavy artillery from the West: prestigious party authorities such as Kautsky and Rosa Luxemburg, who were persuaded to weigh in with *Iskra* articles attacking Lenin. A third front was Trotsky's extensive pamphlet *Our Political Tasks*, published in summer 1904 with the official imprimatur of the *Iskra* editorial board.

The Bolsheviks fought back with committee resolutions and a few pamphlets (including the report to the Amsterdam International Congress examined in Chapter Three), but their literary response was quantitatively unimpressive, given their lack of a press outlet and their relative poverty of literary talent (Lenin himself was exhausted after *One Step* and contributed little). The more telling Bolshevik response was a campaign to convene an extraordinary party congress as a way of settling the dispute. The central party institutions (including the Central Committee which had turned against Lenin) claimed that a party congress would be a divisive diversion of scarce resources and even forbade any intra-party agitation in its favour.

Finally, in November 1904, the Mensheviks carried out their promise to come up with a new, truly Social-Democratic, political tactic. They proposed a campaign to stiffen the anti-government opposition of élite groups such as the *zemstvos* (local bodies with mild self-governing powers). The Menshevik plan may have saved Lenin from terminal obsession with his own intra-party grievances. In any event, his blistering attack on the Menshevik plan opened up a new chapter in Menshevik-Bolshevik relations in which the sides argued about the actual balance of class forces in Russia and the crucial political choices facing revolutionary Social Democracy. Unfortunately, we must take our leave of the Menshevik-Bolshevik debate just as it enters this more instructive and substantive phase.

## The Bolshevik case: *partiinost* vs. *kruzhkovshchina*

Looking back a few years later, the Bolshevik M. Liadov defined the heart of Bolshevism in 1904 as the defence of *partiinost*, a word that in this era can be defined as 'acting as befits a modern political party'.[10] A historian of French socialism calls Jules Guesde's Marxist party 'the first modern political party' in France because it had the following characteristics: 'a large national base, an annual national congress, an executive committee, a programme, and an insistence on discipline'.[11] This also defines what the Bolsheviks meant by *partiinost*.

*Kruzhkovshchina* was the opposite of *partiinost*. The *kruzhok* ('little circle') was the basic unit of party organisation prior to the existence of a national organisational framework.[12] The *kruzhok* did not recognise a higher authority because there was no higher authority to recognise. It was essentially self-appointed and voluntary and it acted (had to act) only as it saw fit. Under the circumstances, this behaviour was necessary and, indeed, praiseworthy. *Iskra* itself was such a *kruzhok* that took upon itself the task of giving the Party a common programme. It possessed no authority except its own persuasiveness and bowed to no authority except its own sense of mission.

*Iskra*'s mission was to transcend its own status as a *kruzhok* contending against other *kruzhki*. The Second Congress ended – or should have ended –

---

[10] Liadov 1911 (my definition of *partiinost*, a word with a considerably different meaning in the Soviet era).
[11] Derfler 1998, p. 3.
[12] For further discussion, see Chapter Eight.

the era of the *kruzhok*. Now *Iskra* had acquired legitimate authority, namely, the status of the official central organ of the Party. By the same token, it now accepted authority – namely, the authority of the Party as an organised, institutional whole, as expressed by the decisions of the Second Congress and the institutional rules there adopted. The editors were now party spokesmen, chosen by the Party to carry out the programme and tactics adopted by the party Congress.

But old habits die hard, especially for individualistic intellectuals. The old *Iskra* editors felt that had a personal right to the editorial chairs of the party newspaper. They felt they had a right to advocate whatever policies they felt best, even if those run directly against the policies of the Congress. They were eager for the authority conferred by the Party, but had no time for the discipline that went with it.

This accusation was the heart of the Bolshevik case. When they talked about the 'anarchistic individualism' of the intellectuals, they were not referring to local intellectuals refusing to follow the orders of the local committees or of local committees refusing to follow the orders of an all-powerful Central Committee. Their paradigmatic example of intelligentsia indiscipline was the boycott followed by the take-over of the central organ by Martov, Akselrod, Potresov and Zasulich. Lenin stated the essence of the Bolshevik case when he responded to Luxemburg's charge of hyper-centralism by wondering rhetorically 'if the comrade finds it normal – can she allow – has she observed in *any* party – that central organs that call themselves *party* organs are dominated by the minority of the party congress?'.[13]

Olminskii framed the issue using Western political systems as a source of metaphor. The party congress was a sovereign parliament. The party rules were a constitution that should never be violated. Legality – abiding by agreed-upon formal rules – was henceforth a vital norm. The party leaders – including the editors of the central organ – should think of themselves as representatives of the Party.

The Menshevik editors, in contrast, were Bonapartists who, like Louis Napoleon, carried out a *coup d'état*, using methods of dubious legality. They were aristocrats who thought of themselves as irreplaceable and rejected

---

[13] Lenin 1958–65, 9, pp. 42–3.

criticism as *lèse-majesté*. Since the old *Iskra* board had split five against one, the five were able to accuse the one of dictatorial ambitions – all the while acting as a compact oligarchy and taking one high-handed action after another. The Menshevik editors were so imbued with the political culture of absolutism that they automatically reverted to the leadership style of the Russian conspirators of the 1870s. They had so little idea of how a loyal opposition operates that they panicked when not chosen as *Iskra* editors and could think of no better reaction than the typical *kruzhok* methods of boycott and threats of resignation.

Olminskii concluded with a plea for congress sovereignty as the best chance for democracy in the underground party:

> A millionaire can easily waste roubles but a poor beggar must hoard every kopeck. The autocracy has deprived us of a great deal, of practically everything, that is essential to citizens of a free country. All the more is our responsibility to defend those aspects of democratism of the Party that are left to us or that have been achieved by us. It still remains possible for us to have congresses that express the will of the Party and we must give special value to this. We must employ all our sensitivity and all our attention to ensure that the central institutions do not destroy the will of the Party.[14]

The Bolshevik slogan of '*partiinost* vs. *kruzhkovshchina*' implied that the Second Congress was a great turning point in party history. This implication had the surprising effect of making WITBD rather irrelevant to present concerns, since it was written in the days when the *kruzhok* reigned supreme. Olminskii made this point by looking at Lenin's 1901 article 'Where to Begin', which contained a précis of the forthcoming WITBD. Olminskii directed attention to the title of this article: Where to *Begin*. 'In it the author speaks only of how to begin the creation of an all-Russia organisation, and not about how that party should be organised.'[15]

What was the Menshevik response to the accusation of usurpation brought against them by the Bolsheviks? One response was to paint Lenin as a monster who needed to be removed from the leadership. We shall examine this part

---

[14] Olminskii 1904b (reprinted in Shutskever 1925, here p. 236); see also Olminskii 1904a (reprinted in Shutskever 1925, see p. 210).

[15] Olminsky 1904b, p. 8. A similar point is made by Lenin in *One Step Forward* (1958–65, 8, pp. 354–5).

of the Menshevik case later. Less energetically and less explicitly, the Mensheviks also put forth a reasoned case against applying the principle of congress sovereignty in an underground party. Like Lenin's, this case was self-serving but, also like Lenin, it reflected a coherent and defensible view of how a vanguard party operated in a specific context. The Menshevik argument has to be pieced together from scattered remarks.[16] After connecting the dots, I came up with the following.

A Social-Democratic party is held together by two principles. One is, indeed, the ideal of a democratic national organisation as embodied in congress sovereignty. The other is the continuity and prestige of the top leaders – the Bebels, the Guesdes, the Akselrods. The best situation is when these two principles work together – as they could and should have worked together in Russia. But who is to blame for the fact that the Second Congress made the decision that split apart the existing leadership core and discarded some of the most prestigious *vozhdi*? Lenin and no one but Lenin. (Plekhanov's role in these events was consciously air-brushed out.[17])

Thus Lenin created a highly unfortunate situation in which a choice had to be made between the two basic unifying principles. Under underground conditions, the only *real* guarantee of party unity was the cohesiveness of the top leaders. The anomalous situation created by the Second Congress was thus best repaired by having as much of the old editorial board as possible back at the old stand.

The principle of congress sovereignty was deficient for all the reasons set forth by Lenin in his polemic against 'playing with democratism' in *WITBD*.[18] Open elections, the *glasnost* necessary to enable people to make an informed choice, wide discussion of principles and tactics – all of this was out of the question. The committees who chose representatives were themselves without democratic credentials, due to *konspiratsiia*, heavy turnover, local factionalism.

---

[16] The most explicit statements on this subject can be found in Martov 1904b and in Kautsky's intervention published in *Iskra*, No. 66 (15 May 1904).

[17] Evidently the originally circulated version of Trotsky's *Report of the Siberian Delegation*, written immediately after the Second Congress, harped on the theme of Plekhanov as a tool in Lenin's hands. All such references were removed when the *Report* was published a few months later (Shutskever 1925, p. 25).

[18] This point was made by Martov 1904b, pp. 1–9 and responded to by Olminsky 1904b.

A committee would declare itself for *Iskra* and then next week there would be a coup and the committee would reject *Iskra*.[19] Given these problems, it was ludicrous to take a slim majority at the Second Congress (even Lenin admitted the outcome would have been entirely different had certain delegates not walked out) and use it to eliminate senior leaders.

Besides, there was the unpleasant fact that the *praktiki* themselves could hardly be trusted with final say. Unlike the Western parties, there was no solidly established proletarian vanguard – only revolutionary intellectuals and backward workers. Furthermore, the *Iskra* period immediately preceding the Second Congress had created a one-sided emphasis on the merely political revolution and, connected to this, unrealistic views on organisation. These problems needed to be corrected by the 'progressive' minority who pointed out the correct path to follow.

Thus Lenin's invocation of the Western SPD model was simply too 'optimistic' for Russia.[20] As Akselrod stated sarcastically, the ideal of the majority – a 'strictly centralised organisation' headed by 'authoritative political *vozhdi* and central leadership institutions' and acting on the basis of a genuinely Social-Democratic programme – was much too ambitious for the primitive Russian Party: 'it suits the political embryo [that is our party] no better than a uniform, a parade hat and an imposing staff suits a baby'.[21]

Since the principle of congress sovereignty was radically insufficient, the principle of united leadership was all the more necessary for carrying out the tasks of the Party. The party campaigns that the Mensheviks called for required a prestigious and united leadership. The Menshevik vision of how the Party worked is revealed by Martov's description of what could have been, had Lenin not fissured the leadership core. The Party would have left the Congress as a united and energised organisation. The new Central Committee would have set itself the task of raising the qualitative level of local work both by its direct influence and by sending out agitators and propagandists. From them, the committees would have learned new methods of influencing the masses. When the war with Japan broke out, the Central

[19] Trotskii 1904, pp. 64–6.
[20] Luxemburg 1970 (see later discussion of centralism as a common value).
[21] *Iskra*, No. 68 (25 June 1904), reprinted in *Iskra za dva goda* 1906 (here p. 151).

Committee would have undertaken the mobilisation of the Russian proletariat by sending a small group of agitators to all centres of the movement. And so on.[22]

Emblematic of the Menshevik outlook is the name they chose for themselves: 'the minority'. I emphasise 'chose for themselves', because there exists a widespread opinion that Lenin cleverly foisted the label on the naïve Mensheviks. This opinion arose not on the basis of any facts but because, in the eyes of later observers, 'majority' is politically more prestigious than 'minority'. But the Mensheviks in 1903–4 thought differently. They retained from the pre-Congress period a feeling that 'minority' signified a progressive vanguard leading the way. This view of the matter was widespread and even comes out in a complaint by Akimov that the *Rabochee delo* group was unjustly accused of going along with the majority, with being conservative and in the tail of the movement, instead of acting as a minority that advanced new and broader tasks.[23]

In 1901, Martov wrote an article entitled 'Always in the Minority' as a response to the accusation made by *Rabochee delo* that *Iskra* was arrogantly laying down the law to the rest of the Party. Martov explained why legally-permitted Marxism, economism and so forth had briefly attained majority status and why *Iskra*, even if alone, had a duty to combat them. He ended by announcing that

> the socialist intelligentsia will find support in its scientific worldview that will allow it to purposefully break all the chains laid down by the ideology of bourgeois society. And then it will not be afraid if the 'whole world' regards them as 'sectarians'. And then it will understand the whole moral duty, in certain circumstances, of remaining *always in the minority*.[24]

Immediately after the Second Congress, Martov wrote a pamphlet entitled 'Once More in the Minority'. As soon as 'the minority' took over the *Iskra* editorial board, a rewritten and retitled version of this pamphlet was printed in *Iskra* as a manifesto of the new editors. Thus, the Mensheviks were proud

---

[22] Martov in *Iskra*, No. 69 (10 July 1904). For more on Mensheviks' campaignism, see next section.

[23] *Vtoroi s"ezd*, p. 687.

[24] *Zaria*, No. 2–3 (December 1901), p. 203.

to be the progressive minority and they had a coherent view of the Party to back up their pride.

Yet they were in a false position and could never escape from it. Lenin was right about one thing: the status of 'progressive minority' and the status of 'editors of the official central organ of the Party' were barely compatible. The false position of the Menshevik leaders created a polemical literature in which the rational case I have presented was drowned out by other elements.

The false position of the Mensheviks is the ultimate cause of another striking feature of their polemics: the constant and obsessive personal vilification of Lenin throughout the year. Lenin's views are not just attacked, his actions are not just criticised – his motives are impugned, his abilities mocked, his character blackened. Lenin is a power-hungry demagogue out to destroy the Party for his own dark and discreditable motives. The drumbeat of personal accusation starts the day after the Congress with Trotsky's *Report of the Siberian Delegation*, in which Lenin is called an egomaniacal Robespierre ready to execute fellow party members.[25] It continues throughout the year without let-up, with each of Lenin's former colleagues weighing in with their contribution.

There is no real counterpart to this in the Bolshevik polemics, angry and partisan as they are. This discrepancy requires explanation. For some (the majority of the academic tradition), the explanation is simple. Lenin *was* a power-hungry scoundrel and the Mensheviks were only being responsible when they pointed it out. For others (the majority of the activist tradition), there is also no particular mystery. Naturally, such a dedicated revolutionary would become the main target for enraged opportunists.

A more political explanation points to the underlying Menshevik feeling that a united, prestigious and authoritative leadership core should run the Party. In 1903–4, it seemed that the only reason this was not happening was because of Lenin. It also seemed that if the rest of the leadership core remained united against him, there was no force that could keep Lenin from being annihilated.

The first feeling was expressed by Akselrod in a letter to Kautsky:

> Given this condition of our party [an 'intellectual regression' on the part of the majority], it is easy to carry out a policy of Bonapartist demagoguery

---

[25] Shutskever 1925, pp. 484, 493–4.

and put up obstacles to the concentration of all our forces for searching out new ways and means for lifting the Party up to a new level of development in a principled proletarian sense. . . . Lenin and Co., with their disorganising methods and their systematic casting of suspicion on our critical and positive explanations, are pushing the Party not only to a schism but to complete disintegration.[26]

The second feeling was expressed by Plekhanov, as Zinoviev recalled many years later:

Let me recall my first conversation with Plekhanov . . . when he frightened us by saying: Who are you going along with? You should consider who is on our side: Martov, Zasulich, Akselrod and the rest; but over on your side is only Lenin. And you know, things will eventually turn out that in a few months all the sparrows will be laughing at your Lenin! And you go along with him![27]

Thus the Mensheviks thought that Lenin could be easily disposed of and were unpleasantly surprised to discover differently. Lenin had a power base outside the leadership core and the Mensheviks glumly ascertained that Lenin was the 'idol' of the *praktiki*.[28] If Lenin managed to survive the onslaught against him, this had to be because he was a demagogue. But a demagogue requires an easily deluded audience. The Mensheviks were therefore compelled to widen their critique to include the majority of *praktiki*.

The bitterness and contempt toward the party *praktiki* is another striking feature of Menshevik polemics in 1904. While officially the abuse is directed at Lenin's supporters, it is not counterbalanced by any praise or encouraging words for Menshevik *praktiki*. One discerns a feeling of exasperation on the part of the educated and cosmopolitan émigrés toward the young, semi-educated and provincial *praktiki* in Russia. The most thorough-going expression of this attitude is a series of articles published in 1905 by Potresov. These

---

[26] This letter, with its virulent denunciation of 'Lenin and Co.' and the party majority, was published in *Iskra*, No. 68 (25 June 1904) and reprinted in *Iskra za dva goda* 1906 (here p. 154). What Akselrod means by 'new level of development' is discussed in the following section.

[27] Zinoviev 1973, pp. 112–13.

[28] Akselrod so described Lenin in his letter to Kautsky, published in *Iskra*, No. 68 (25 June 1904) and reprinted in *Iskra za dva goda* 1906 (here p. 149).

articles portray the history of the Russian revolutionary underground as a series of misadventures by the utterly provincial and comically self-absorbed *praktiki*. Lenin acquired influence among the *praktiki* because he shared and faithfully reflected these delusions.[29]

There is nothing similar to this in Bolshevik polemics, which are directed solely against the *Iskra* editors and allies such as Trotsky. Olminskii and Bogdanov quickly picked up on this feature of Menshevik writings. Olminskii even took his pseudonym from a remark in this vein by Martov, who attributed Lenin's success to his pandering to the 'cheap seats [*galerka*]'. Thus Olminskii signed his pamphlets Cheap Seats, while Bogdanov adopted the pseudonym Rank-and-Filer [*Riadovoi*]. They portrayed the party split as a clash of the party aristocracy and of prestigious émigré writers on the one side and the party plebians and the rank and file on the other.[30]

The sheer oddity of the position in which the Menshevik leaders now found themselves needs to be appreciated. *Iskra* was the central organ of a militant political party. Yet from its pages in 1904 (and from the pages of Trotsky's *Our Political Tasks*) can be drawn an absolutely devastating portrait of the RSDWP, its policies and its personnel – a portrait written in anger and hostility. Olminskii collected a number of typical passages and indignantly asked why people raised to leadership positions by precisely these despised *praktiki* should insult the Party in this way.

> It is also characteristic that these sneers at the Party, this attempt to discredit the Party, are published in the central organ which we are compelled to distribute as a propaganda weapon in order to uphold the prestige of the Party, and risking our freedom while doing so.'[31]

The original false position of the Mensheviks – their politically illegitimate control of the central organ – fatally undermined their case, and *Iskra* was eventually perceived to be – because it was – a factional newspaper rather than a party organ. In fact, Lenin won this debate. The principle of congress sovereignty was later accepted by both sides, as shown most graphically by

---

[29] Potresov 2002, pp. 67–120.
[30] Olminskii and Bogdanov 1904 (a better known pseudonym of Bogdanov is 'Maximov').
[31] Shutskever 1925, p. 229; see also Shutskever 1925, pp. 149–50.

the Menshevik adoption in 1905 of Lenin's definition of party membership (as discussed below).

Lenin won this debate because, as the Mensheviks discovered, he had the stronger case. With all its difficulties, the principle of congress sovereignty proved indispensable, if for no other reason than the impossibility of winning a factional fight without winning a majority at a party congress. Furthermore, the unity and prestige of the original leadership core – the counter-principle of the Mensheviks – proved to be a will-of-the-wisp. In 1903–4, the troublemaker Lenin might plausibly be perceived as the only threat to unity. But, even by the end of 1904, the rest of the 'tight leadership nucleus' was fissuring. Eventually, from out of the top group of Menshevik spokesmen in 1904, there emerged at least four distinct tendencies: Plekhanov, Martov and Akselrod, Potresov and Zasulich, Trotsky.

Finally, the calculation that the prestige of the top leadership could provide unity in action proved misinformed. The émigrés learned that eventually it was they who were dependent on the *praktiki* and the participation of the Russian underground. So argued M. Liadov in 1911, claiming that both factions were forced, unexpectedly for themselves, to stop being obsessed with leadership positions in Geneva and to align themselves with the tactics advanced by their supporters in Russia.[32]

The Mensheviks lost and the penalty for their defeat was that they were stuck with the name 'the minority'. This is not to say that they were incorrect when they pointed out the many difficulties of applying congress sovereignty in underground conditions (and, in fact, also in Western Europe). The frail and finally non-existent unity of the RSDWP shows that these difficulties were very real indeed.

## The Menshevik case: campaignism vs. substitutionism

In the usual telling of the party split, Lenin is the focus of attention. It is he who makes innovations and imposes his organisational vision, while the others react to him and define themselves only as they begin to plumb the

---

[32] Liadov 1911. 'Look at the proceedings of the Bolshevik Third Congress [spring 1905] and you will immediately see the extent to which the lower ranks [*nizy*] had overtaken their leader at that time.'

depths of his political and personal depravity – or, from the point of view of the activist tradition, only as they are forced by his revolutionary challenge to reveal their own opportunist assumptions.

At the time, both Lenin and the Mensheviks preferred to see the split the other way around: as Lenin reacting to the aggressive innovations of the Mensheviks. Lenin portrayed Bolshevism as the inheritor of *Iskra*-ism, protecting it against the attack of the Mensheviks. In turn, the Mensheviks accepted the label 'the minority' because they associated 'minority' with progressive leadership. They had a new message and a new set of tasks to set before the Party, in an effort to move the Party on to the necessary next stage of its development. This message and these tasks were not in reaction to Lenin. The progressive minority would have undertaken this mission, even had there been no split and no Lenin.[33] Lenin only entered the picture as the incarnation of hide-bound party conservatism and as an unscrupulous demagogue who prevented the progressive minority from carrying out its mission.

From this point of view, Akselrod rather than Lenin is the protagonist of the drama of 1904. At the beginning of the year, Akselrod set out the Party's new tasks in two articles in *Iskra*, Nos. 55 and 57. These articles were constantly described in Menshevik literature as groundbreaking, insightful, inspiring. In mid-year, Trotsky penned *Our Political Tasks* as a popularisation of Akselrod's message. At the end of the year, Akselrod's message finally achieved concrete form in the plan for the so-called 'zemstvo campaign'. A rationale for the plan penned by Akselrod was sent around by the *Iskra* editors to the local committees.[34] Thus, at each step, Akselrod and the Mensheviks took the initiative.

My name for the positive content of Akselrod's message is 'campaignism'. This word did not exist in 1904, but the need for a certain sort of party-directed political campaign was at the heart of Akselrod's concerns. According to Akselrod, Russian Social Democracy had yet to become a genuine *class* party. A class party was one that received mass support – but not just any support. Only support based on an understanding of specifically proletarian

---

[33] Akselrod already had begun to write of these concerns in an article drafted in summer 1902, although it was only published in 1905 (Akselrod 1905).

[34] Akselrod's original exposition and the rebuttal by the *Iskra* editors of Lenin's criticism of the *zemstvo* campaign plan can be found in *Men'sheviki* 1996, pp. 69–89.

interests made a party a class party. Joining the revolutionary onslaught against the tsar in order to obtain political freedom was, of course, in the interest of the Russian proletariat, but nevertheless not a distinctive proletarian interest. Rather, it was one shared with most of the rest of Russian society, including the exploiters. Support for Social Democracy as a *revolutionary* party was, therefore, insufficient for its mission as a *class* party. What was needed were campaigns that would set the proletariat in motion in such a way as to bring out the *clash* between proletarian interests and elite interests.

Trotsky's *Our Political Tasks* was consciously and explicitly meant to be the Menshevik WITBD and modelled itself on WITBD in a variety of ways. Just as Lenin coined an effective term for the besetting sin of the time ('artisanal limitations'), Trotsky coined a term for what he regarded as the basic fault inherited from the past, substitutionism [*zamestitel'stvo*]. Just as Lenin polemicised against *Rabochee delo*, Trotsky polemicised against Lenin. Trotsky's polemic with Lenin was meant both to destroy a leadership rival and to expose various more widespread theoretical misconceptions. But, as with WITBD, these polemics were meant to clear the way for the question: what is to be done?

Trotsky no doubt hoped that *Our Political Tasks* would take its place in party history alongside *On Agitation* and WITBD as a literary production marking and in part causing a major transformation in party outlook. No such luck – the book had little resonance even among Mensheviks, it did not win over the *praktiki* to the Menshevik position, 'substitutionism' did not catch on.

I have created the term 'campaignism' because the heart of the new Menshevik tactic is the insistence on a particular type of party-organised campaign. What Akselrod meant by *samodeiatelnost* and what Trotsky meant by 'substitutionism' can best be appreciated when we have seen a concrete example. At the centre of Trotsky's pamphlet is an outline of just such a campaign in a section that is appropriately titled 'What, then, is to be done? [*Chto zhe delat'?*]'. The occasion for Trotsky's hypothetical campaign is a Congress for Activists in Technical Education that actually took place in St. Petersburg and gave rise to a clash between the government and the liberal opposition. After criticising the actions of the actual Petersburg Social-Democratic committee, Trotsky sets out the following scenario of what should have been done.

The committee issues a proclamation. It then summons its propagandists and makes sure they understand how this proclamation is related to the party programme and to the resolutions passed by the Second Congress. The same message is passed on via channels of oral propaganda. The committee issues yet more proclamations. As the campaign unfolds, the workers – or, at least, the upper levels of the worker class – begin to take an interest.

The committee now prepares a resolution to be addressed to the technical congress. A member of the committee briefs the propagandists on the resolution and they take it to all the factory cells. When enough support has been expressed, 'agitators by trade [*professionalnye agitatory*]' start rounding up both signatures on petitions and endorsements by show of hands. The results are relayed back to the committee which then presents the resolution to the congress. Each worker feels that the demands expressed by the resolution are *his* demands.

One of two: either the congress of technical education activists will accede to the demands or it will not. The first outcome is not unlikely, since the 'radical-democratic intelligentsia' wants to preserve its prestige in the eyes of the workers. This outcome means that the workers will get a taste of being the actual 'vanguard of the general democratic revolution'. If the congress refuses, the workers will receive a salutary lesson in the half-heartedness of the bourgeois opposition. They will be weaned away from bourgeois influence and won over to Social Democracy. Thus we have a win-win situation. However the congress reacts, the workers will receive a salutary class 'political education'.[35]

As a the result of the campaign, the decision of 'an official group of Petersburg Marxist *intelligenty*' will be transformed into a genuine 'formulation of the political will of the progressive Petersburg proletariat'. The same logic should be applied at the national level – say, in opposition to the war. All the local committees will push the same message and point to the same weaknesses of the liberal opposition. At the appropriate time, resolutions are prepared, accompanied where appropriate with mass demonstrations. If the Party could carry out one – just one – such militant campaign, it would 'immediately grow by a whole head!'.[36]

According to Trotsky and Akselrod, this kind of campaign would represent a decisive step forward in Social-Democratic tactics. They base their claim on

---

[35] Martynov had already defended this 'win-win' logic in his article in *Rabochee delo*, No. 10, a forerunner of Menshevik campaignism.

[36] Trotskii 1904, pp. 39–42.

a double contrast with the typical activities undertaken by the Party during the recent *Iskra* period. In the past, the Party has tried to bring the *socialist* message to the workers, it has tried to inculcate a sense of class distinctiveness, of the clash between proletariat and bourgeoisie. But it did so only by means of the written or spoken *word*. It did not do so through *actions*, through *deeds*. But organised action is a much more effective way of raising awareness than reading a Social-Democratic newspaper. Words vs. deeds is thus the first contrast.

The central meaning of 'substitutionism' is this substitution of words for action.[37] After describing the hypothetical campaign aimed at the technical education congress, Trotsky looks at what the Party had actually done instead of undertaking such a campaign. Nothing but an editorial in *Iskra*, No. 55! What is this but 'substitutionism and substitutionism!'?[38] Thus, substitutionism strongly recalls Nadezhdin's 'writerism', and Trotsky explicitly underscores Nadezhdin's role as a forerunner of Menshevism on this point.[39]

'Words vs. action' is not the only contrast with the past. The Party did not completely confine itself to the word – political actions such as demonstrations, mass strikes and the like were undertaken with some success in the immediately preceding period. But these were *revolutionary* actions, not *Social-Democratic* actions. They aimed at overthrowing the tsar in concert with other classes, not at preparing the workers to introduce socialism in opposition to other classes. 'Revolutionary vs. Social-Democratic' is the second contrast with the past. The title of Trotsky's pamphlet should thus be read with the emphasis on the first word: *Our* Political Tasks, the tasks of Social Democracy in particular.

For this reason, Trotsky grants that substitutionism of words for action is not such a problem for 'us as [merely] revolutionaries', since the Party has successfully organised anti-tsarist campaigns. But the 'class will' of the proletariat demands more specific expression.

---

[37] The meaning of substitutionism arises out of Trotsky's whole argument, but specific passages of interest include Trotskii 1904, pp. 16 (first use), 35–9, 41, 47, 50–1, 54–5, 59, 67–8.

[38] Trotskii 1904, p. 41. The same contrast is made by Martov after describing a hypothetical campaign in very similar terms: 'The political action [*deiatelnost*] of Social Democracy is now expressed not by isolated committee proclamations or articles in the central organ, it becomes the political action of a *class*' (*Iskra*, No. 69, 10 July 1904).

[39] Trotskii 1904, p. 47.

> The guiding Social-Democratic groups do not understand that enlisting the proletariat for a 'demonstration' of its class will in *opposition* to the liberal and radical democracy is just as necessary for us as enlisting the proletariat for a demonstration of its revolutionary democratism against the autocracy.[40]

The use of the word 'revolutionary' in this contrast can be confusing, yet I have adopted it because the word was used in this way by Akselrod and Trotsky to make their case. In this period, 'revolutionary' *tout court* in Russian Social-Democratic discourse referred only to the upcoming anti-tsarist revolution. The Mensheviks were not only intellectually but emotionally engaged in the anti-tsarist struggle and they fully shared in the growing revolutionary excitement. And yet – they did not want to get so carried away that they forgot their own Social-Democratic identity. After all, the Social Democrats were not the only ones who were revolutionary – so were the Socialist Revolutionaries, so were even the liberals in their way.

In order not to be swallowed up in the anti-tsarist crusade, Social Democracy had to emphasise what made it distinct: the final goal of the dictatorship of the proletariat. Even in the hurly-burly of the present revolution, the Social Democrats had to remember their essential mission of preparing the workers for this ultimate class dictatorship. And this meant bringing out the *conflict* between the workers and élite classes *now*, even or especially while fighting together with these classes against tsarist absolutism. The essence of opportunism was to sacrifice the final goal for momentary successes. What was it, then, but tactical opportunism, if all party activity was dedicated exclusively to tsarist overthrow?[41]

The same double contrast is what Akselrod and Trotsky meant (at least in 1904) by the word *samodeiatelnost*. This word is usually translated something like 'initiative' or 'self-reliance' and, indeed, this is how most speakers understood it even it in 1904. When Akselrod and Trotsky called for worker *samodeiatelnost* in the context of their tactical proposals, however, they meant something more specific and quite different. *Samodeiatelnost* was part of a wider process of class self-definition [*samoopredelenie*]. This wider process is the familiar one of the spread of awareness, of the workers coming to

---

[40] Trotskii 1904, pp. 54, 51 (emphasis added).
[41] For an argument to this effect, see Martov in *Iskra*, No. 69 (10 July 1904).

understand and accept the great world-historical mission. *Samodeiatelnost* refers to the specific part played in this process by *action* [*deiatelnost*]. Thus *samodeiatelnost* is Trotsky and Akselrod's writings of 1904 is better translated 'distinctive action', or, unpacking the term, 'action that pits the workers against other classes and thus gives them a better sense of the distinctiveness of their own class interests'.

We can, therefore, state the double contrast as follows. In the past, Russian Social Democracy have organised *actions* – but they have not been *self*-actions, that is, actions that taught the workers what was distinctive about their class position. In the past, the Social Democrats have taught the workers about their distinctive class position, but they did so through propaganda and agitation, not through self-*action*.

The aim of *samodeiatelnost*, in this context, is therefore not the 'encouragement of the development of a capacity of independent activity and self-organisation on the part of Russia's workers'.[42] We can see this by returning to Trotsky's proposed campaign and observing *samodeiatelnost* at work.

We note, first of all, the Lassallean logic of the campaign. A campaign consists of focused mobilisation around a single slogan carried out by a dedicated and centrally directed corps of agitators. Trotsky is perfectly aware of his debt to Lassalle and, in fact, cites him at length, including some of the same passages cited earlier in this commentary.[43]

Thus an effective campaign requires a party that is unified and directed from the top. In a formula Trotsky repeats more than once, a national campaign will be 'guided by a centre that thinks politically and that is politically inspiring'. The authority of this centre ensures that 'one and the same theme is brought up in all circles and groups, in closed discussion groups and open assemblies, in [all] proclamations'.[44] Campaignism is thus linked to the Menshevik view of the party we examined in the previous section.

The ultimate goal of the campaign is to turn the Party's official decisions into the purposive will of the workers. There is no hint in Trotsky's version of *samodeiatelnost* that the initiative for the campaign or the text of the resolutions will be a result of initiative from below. Nor does it appear that the widespread

---

[42] Haimson 2004, p. 61.
[43] Trotskii 1904, pp. 87–8, cf. pp. 42, 85–6.
[44] Trotskii 1904, pp. 42 and 48 [*politicheski mysliashchim i politicheski bodrstvuiushchim*].

discussion of the proposed resolution will result even in any modification of the text (for one thing, the necessary unity of the campaign would be destroyed). No, the initiative comes from a centre that thinks politically and that is politically inspiring, and stays there.

Campaignism also governs Trotsky's vision of intra-party relations. Just as the workers need to be educated in Social Democratism, so do a large proportion, perhaps a majority, of the *praktiki*. The progressive minority that controls the centre thus has the additional responsibility of educating the *praktiki*. Once more, Trotsky provides us with a concrete example of what he has in mind, namely, the ongoing Menshevik campaign to unify the Party around new tasks. This campaign started even before the Second Congress at the top, with Akselrod conducting word-of-mouth propaganda for his vision of the Party's 'new tactical tasks'. Akselrod knew he had to prepare 'the necessary psychological foundation in the awareness of the comrades guiding the movement'. These comrades evidently did not include anyone who could not go abroad and meet Akselrod in person. Then, the real needs of the movement having been identified, 'the most valuable and influential elements of the Party' will be united around the task of meeting these needs (that is, conducting appropriate campaigns). As to the raw recruits who make up the opposing wing of the Party – well, most of them will leave the Party anyway, and the sooner the better.[45]

We saw earlier how Trotsky condemned the 'substitution' of an *Iskra* editorial for a full-blooded petition campaign. In similar fashion, substitutionism within the Party is revealed by a refusal to mount educational campaigns. When Trotsky says, in the oft-quoted passage, that 'the party organisation "substitutes" itself for the Party', he is not complaining that the party organisation is unresponsive to the will of the Party as a whole. On the contrary, he is angry at the demagogue Lenin for expressing the will of the less advanced outer circles of the Party. Trotsky's complaint is that the party organisation does not see it as its task to *shape the will* of the Party as a whole, to create 'politically thinking *Parteigenossen*' out of the present narrow party specialists.[46]

---

[45] Trotskii 1904, pp. 49, 72, 95–6.
[46] Trotskii 1904, p. 64. See below for Menshevik dislike of Lenin's stress on division of labour.

The substitutionism of the Bolsheviks within the Party is not revealed by the actual content of their organisational schemes. Trotsky has very little to say on this score, either as criticism or as positive suggestion. At one point, he even grants that 'there is not a shade of bureaucratism' in an organisational blueprint proposed by some local Bolsheviks.[47] What *is* evidence of substitutionism is the very Bolshevik obsession with organisation. This obsession with organisational trivialities can only be explained as a semi-conscious evasion of the *real* task of the Party, namely, preparing educational mobilisation campaigns of an Akselrodian sort. Bolshevik organisational schemes may or may not have a shadow of bureaucratism, but they definitely do not have a shadow of reality. They remain paper utopias with no relation to the dismal realities. A majority of the *praktiki* were so obsessed about organisational trivialities that their thinking (in Trotsky's striking phrase) was caught like a mouse in a mousetrap.[48]

Substitutionism, both within and without the Party, is the refusal to organise *actions* that involve both the workers and the *praktiki* aimed at getting them to act and think in truly Social-Democratic fashion. Trotsky does not want the Party to 'think for the proletariat' and he insists that party decisions become real decisions only when they express the purposive will of the factory circles. But as he truly remarks, 'the point here is not "democratic" fictions'.[49] Indeed: the point for Trotsky is not for the Party to be guided by the thinking of the workers or the *praktiki*, but, rather, to undertake the essential but neglected task of getting them to think like the guiding elements of the Party. Thus the principled choice set out by Trotsky is between substitutionism on one side vs. 'political education' and 'political mobilisation' on the other.[50]

Trotsky does not seriously argue that the party majority does not *want* to have the workers and *praktiki* think and act in Social-Democratic fashion. He suggests that the majority deludes itself that this is already the case, thus evading the difficult task of educating and mobilising. The majority does not realise that there is a huge gap between *objective* class interests and the

---

[47] Trotskii 1904, p. 83.
[48] Trotskii 1904, p. 86. The charge of organisational fetishism was first advanced by Akselrod in *Iskra*, Nos. 55 and 57.
[49] Trotskii 1904, p. 68.
[50] Trotskii 1904, p. 50.

subjective understanding of them by empirical workers. It does not realise that there is a long and thorny path between objective interest and subjective assimilation – a path that can only be traversed under the guidance of Social-Democratic intellectuals.[51]

When we read this passage, we realise how distinct Trotsky's actual understanding of substitutionism is from the one we automatically assign to him. We understand substitutionism as a protest against pessimistic worry about workers, against intellectuals who wish to think for the workers. And, here, we see that Trotsky uses 'substitutionism' to condemn the reluctance of Social-Democratic intellectuals to educate and mobilise workers who are unaware of their own interests.

The term 'substitutionism' is unique to Trotsky. I do not recall any other writer, Bolshevik or Menshevik, even so much as using it. In all other respects, *Our Political Tasks* is a useful compendium of Menshevik arguments in 1903–4. The meaning of substitutionism can be grasped only in the context of Trotsky's concrete tactical proposals. Those proposals, as Trotsky himself insists, are taken straight from Akselrod's campaignism. They are the heart of Menshevism in 1904.

## The case against Lenin

The Mensheviks wanted to show that Lenin had put himself out of the Social-Democratic mainstream, not only because of his irresponsible actions, but because he actually preached hyper-centralism, personal dictatorship within the Party, a narrow party confined to conspirators, Jacobinism as a Social-Democratic ideal and the like. In the influential picture of Bolshevism in 1904 contained in Martov's history of Russian Social Democracy (written in 1918), the words 'dictator' and 'dictatorial' occur quite frequently – although, as we know, Lenin never had the chance to be an actual party dictator in this period.[52] We have examined some real differences between the Mensheviks and the Bolsheviks. But on the issues of centralism, personal dictatorship within the Party and so on, one is hard put to find principled differences between the two sides even with a microscope.

---

[51] Trotskii 1904, p. 52, see also p. 74.
[52] Martov 2000, pp. 70–82.

The Mensheviks did not claim that Lenin openly and explicitly advocated in *WITBD* or elsewhere the views attributed to him – rather, these views were inadvertently revealed by various off-the-cuff comments made by Lenin and his supporters in 1903–4. The Mensheviks cannot be blamed too severely for taking isolated phrases out of context, drawing absurd conclusions and then beating Lenin over the head with them. This was the way the game was played and Lenin was by no means averse to playing it himself. But a problem arises when scholars uncritically take these partisan sallies as accurate descriptions of Lenin's actual outlook, and then, to compound the confusion, assume that Lenin preached these views in *WITBD*.

In this section I will look briefly at the most influential of these allegedly revealing episodes: the debate over party membership, the report of the Bolshevik committees in the Urals, the factory metaphor, the Jacobin metaphor, and Luxemburg's accusation of hyper-centralism.

## The rules debate

The real source of the party split at the Second Congress was the non-election of three members of the old *Iskra* board. Much more famous than this conflict is the clash over the definition of a party member in Paragraph One of the party rules. Admittedly, the actual difference between the formulations proposed by Lenin and Martov respectively seems rather thin. Lenin proposed that a member was someone who acknowledged the party programme and supported the Party in one of the party organisations. Martov defined a member as anyone who acknowledged the programme and gave the Party regular assistance under the guidance of one of its organisations.

Nevertheless (we are told), these seemingly insignificant differences in wording are symbolic of vast differences in political outlook. Lenin's definition points to a narrow party, fearful of contamination, confining itself to a closed band of intelligentsia conspirators, turning away from Western Social Democracy toward Narodnaia volia and other Russian populist revolutionaries. Martov's formulation points in the opposite direction: open, democratic, moving toward the Western idea of a party that genuinely represented the workers, and so forth. Two paths opened up during the rules debate – the vanguard party and the democratic party – and the fateful first steps were taken.

This is a pretty story, but without historical foundation. A few facts need to be kept in mind as we evaluate it. First, the clash over the rules was not a cause of the party split. The Bolsheviks were a minority on this question. They lost and Martov's formulation became the official definition of a party member. The Bolsheviks did not think it was a good formulation, but the principle of congress sovereignty meant they had to live with it, and they had no problem doing so. It was a minor issue. The rules debate came up once or twice in the ensuing polemics, but it was far overshadowed by other concerns.

Second, from the point of view of people at the time, it was Martov's formulation that represented the spirit of Narodnaia volia, while Lenin's formulation that represented the spirit of Western Social-Democratic parties. In his defence of Martov's formulation at the Second Congress, Akselrod explicitly brought up Narodnaia volia as a positive model that exemplified Martov's logic. Later on, Kautsky also sided with Martov – because of the special circumstances of the Russian underground. In the case of a party operating under political freedom, Lenin's formulation would be preferable.[53]

Third, and most striking: the Mensheviks themselves decided that Lenin's formulation was superior. A Menshevik party conference in late 1905 passed a resolution defining a member according to Lenin's logic, as someone who was a member of a party organisation. At the Unity Congress in 1906, the Mensheviks had a majority. Nevertheless, a new set of rules containing Lenin's definition was passed unanimously and without debate. The only comment made on the shift was that time had erased all differences on this subject.[54]

Finally, Lenin's definition – now accepted by the whole Party – did not have the dire practical consequences predicted by its opponents at the Second Congress. Membership was *not* restricted to committee members or to 'revolutionaries by trade', both of which categories remained small fractions of the total membership.[55] The membership definition was not a restrictive or exclusionary bottleneck that kept membership low. There were lots of other very good reasons why membership was low in repressive tsarist Russia. In

---

[53] *Iskra*, No. 66 (15 May 1904). A contemporary observer notes the norms of the SPD: 'the keynote of the Party is solidarity, which is a synonym for discipline. . . . The membership of the Party includes all those who pay party dues and will oblige themselves to party fealty, to do any drudgery demanded of them' (Orth 1913, pp. 176–7).

[54] *Chetvertyi s"ezd* 1959, p. 461.

[55] For figures, see Chapter Eight.

practice, the Social Democrats were desperate for members and anyone who wanted could join.[56]

So what was all the fuss about? What was so objectionable about Lenin's formulation? I believe the whole row originated from a simple misunderstanding. Owing to the lack of a definite article in Russian, Lenin's formulation could be read as demanding that a party member be a member of 'the party organisation' or 'a party organisation'. Those who, in the congress debates, opposed Lenin's formulation assumed the first reading and used 'organisation' in the singular in their speeches. Those who supported Lenin's formulation (including Lenin himself) assumed that a party member could belong to one of many organisations and so talked of 'organisations' in the plural.

Behind these automatic grammatical assumptions were different experiences of the nature of the underground. Akselrod and Zasulich, who had last been in Russia in the days of Narodnaia volia, tended to think of the underground as a closed, secret organisation that was strictly walled off from the surrounding society. The *praktiki* with experience in the new Social-Democratic underground that had arisen since the mid-1890s thought in terms of the many 'threads' that connected the secret structure with the worker milieu (as discussed in Chapter Eight). For people with this concept of the underground, 'member of a party organisation' did not primarily mean members of the *konspirativnyi* parts of the structure, but, rather, members of the factory cells.

Akselrod wanted the secret *konspirativnyi* 'organisation' to be as protected and closed off as possible. Just for that reason, many members of the Party had to be *excluded* from 'the organisation'. Thus for him and others of his generation such as Zasulich, when Lenin's definition demanded that a party member belonged to 'the organisation', it restricted the Party to a 'narrow band of conspirators'.[57] No wonder they thought it denied the core of Social Democracy, namely, the expanding circle of awareness.

Why did the Mensheviks so quickly change tack and adopt Lenin's definition? The record is thin on their rationale, but I should imagine there were three major reasons. First, the misunderstanding was cleared up and

---

[56] Elwood 1974.

[57] One of the few discussions of the dispute over membership is Vera Zasulich's article in *Iskra*, No. 70 (25 July 1904) in which she argues that Lenin restricts the Party to a narrow band of conspirators, a 'small little corner' of the Party.

people realised that Lenin did not mean to restrict party membership to revolutionaries by trade and to *komitetchiki*. Second, Martov's formulation was deficient for practical reasons. Already at the Second Congress, Takhtarev (the former editor of *Rabochaia mysl*) had insisted on the difficulty involved in supervision [*kontrol*] of an individual who was not a member of an actual party organisation.[58] Finally, the Mensheviks realised that if the words 'party minority' and 'party majority' were to make any sense, there had to be a fairly strict and unambiguous boundary between 'member' and 'non-member'. In other words, the democratic principle of congress sovereignty was incompatible with a vague membership definition.[59]

Years later, in the strikingly different context of the Third International, when the Bolsheviks were a ruling party and when Lenin was highly suspicious of prominent European socialists who wanted to join the new Communist Parties, the criterion of membership proposed at the Second Congress seemed much too broad. Let anyone into the new parties who says he accepts the programme and is willing to work in a party organisation? What about all those who claimed to be orthodox Social Democrats, who even wrote eloquent books on the subject – and who then showed their true colours when the War broke out?

In 1903, Lenin proposed a membership definition that, by the end of 1905, was supported by a consensus of Mensheviks and Bolsheviks. After 1914, he proposed stringent membership tests – aimed not at the rank and file but at well-known members of the old parties – that were intended to split the Second International and did so. These two phases of Lenin's view of the party should not be confounded.

### Urals Committees

In late 1903, representatives of three party committees in the Urals (Ufa, Middle Urals, Perm) sent in a protest to *Iskra* about one of Plekhanov's articles. This protest contained several unfortunate phrases that were seized on by Menshevik polemicists. One passage in particular was used by Trotsky in the

---

[58] *Vtoroi s"ezd* 1959, pp. 266–7.
[59] On the connection between the membership definition and party democracy, see Olminskii 1904b, the rules debate at the Bolshevik Third Congress, and the Menshevik resolutions of 1905 (*Men'sheviki* 1996, pp. 147–8).

very last section of *Our Political Tasks* as the crushing proof of the dictatorial ambitions of Lenin and his supporters. The Urals Bolsheviks are arguing that the Party's organisation must help prepare the Party for its supreme task of leading the proletariat in power, that is, the dictatorship of the proletariat:

> The preparation of the proletariat for dictatorship is such an important organisational task that all others must be subordinated to it. This preparation consists, among other things, in the creation of an attitude in favour of a strong and authoritative [*vlastnaia*] proletarian organisation, in an explanation of all its significance. The objection might be made that dictators have appeared and will appear by themselves. But that is not always the case, and a proletarian party should not act in a *stikhiinyi* or opportunistic fashion. Here we should combine the highest degree of purposiveness with unconditional obedience – one calls forth the other (the awareness of necessity is freedom of the will).[60]

According to Trotsky and Martov, this passage calls for the Party itself to be run by individual dictators. Is this a plausible reading? I think not. The use of the word 'dictator' is unusual – a more practised party writer would have avoided it – but it clearly means 'the proletarians who are implementing the dictatorship of the proletariat'. One of the tasks of the Party is to prepare the workers to fulfill this role, and one mode of preparation is a disciplined political organisation. The underlying thought is the purest Erfurtian orthodoxy (despite the tactlessness of the phrase 'unconditional obedience').

Valentinov recalls in his memoirs how delighted Martynov was when the Urals report arrived in Geneva.[61] The great attention given by the Mensheviks to this unsophisticated provincial report speaks very eloquently, it seems to me, of their inability to document Lenin's views with Lenin's own words.

*Factory analogy*

Lenin's major contribution to the 1904 polemics was his long *One Step Forward, Two Steps Back*. In his summary section at the end, Lenin made two remarks that were immediately used by his opponents. One of these was the claim

---

[60] *Iskra*, No. 63 (1 March 1904).
[61] Valentinov 1968. The Urals committee report still makes an appearance in the party history of Menshevik Fyodor Dan (Dan 1964 [1945], pp. 253–4).

that workers understood discipline better than intellectuals because the workers had undergone the factory experience whereas intellectuals had not.

> The factory, which seems only a bogey to some, represents that highest form of capitalist co-operation which has united and disciplined the proletariat, taught it organisation, and placed it at the head of all the other strata of the labouring and exploited population. And it is Marxism, the ideology of the proletariat schooled by capitalism, that has taught and is teaching unstable intellectuals the distinction between the exploitative side of the factory (discipline based on fear of starvation) and its organising side (discipline founded on collective work unified by conditions of production that are highly developed technically).[62]

Both Rosa Luxemburg and Trotsky pounced on this remark and lectured Lenin about the evils of mind-numbing factory discipline.[63] In response, the Bolshevik Aleksandr Bogdanov penned a rejoinder in which, he said, he rose to the defence of his revolutionary colleague Karl Marx. After noting that the passage showed that Lenin was well aware of the bad side of factory discipline, Bogdanov asserted that if the factory really had the thoroughly evil consequences described by Trotsky and Luxemburg, then the whole Marxist project was a washout. Bogdanov was later the most prominent theorist of 'proletarian culture' as a higher type than individualist bourgeois culture.[64]

I agree with Bogdanov. Anti-Lenin fervour incited Trotsky and Luxemburg to make arguments that from a Social-Democratic point of view were extremely peculiar. One of the deepest strands in Social-Democratic discourse was the claim that the industrial workers were capable of emancipating society in a way that other oppressed classes – the peasantry and the petty bourgeoisie – were not. Worker protest against exploitation was more effective than peasant protest because the workers had gone through the school of large-scale organisation.

The factory metaphor was behind Lenin's coinage 'artisanal limitations'. As I showed in Chapter Eight, the imagery behind this neologism was taken straight

---

[62] Lenin 1958–65, 8, p. 379.
[63] Somewhat oddly, Trotsky rejects the 'barracks discipline' of the factory, but calls, instead, for 'one fighting army' of labour as a positive model of discipline (Trotskii 1904, pp. 74–5).
[64] Olminskii and Bogdanov 1904.

from the *Communist Manifesto* and the *Erfurt Programme*. Lenin's metaphor was accepted by Russian Social Democrats as a whole and even used in polemics against Lenin. For example, Parvus criticised Lenin's organisational plan because it merely unified a series of local 'artisans' and did not really achieve the co-ordinated division of labour of a 'large-scale capitalist enterprise'.[65]

### Jacobin analogy

The other vulnerable remark from *One Step* was Lenin's assertion that the Bolsheviks were the Jacobins of Russian Social Democracy. Everybody rushed to inform Lenin that the Jacobins were bourgeois revolutionaries whose organisation was no model for Social Democracy. Trotsky added that the remark was further confirmation of Lenin's resemblance to Robespierre, a resemblance that accounted for Lenin's 'malicious and morally repulsive suspiciousness'.[66] Martynov devoted a whole pamphlet to the remark and displayed the results of impressive historical research on the Jacobins in the French revolution.[67] Lenin's comment is still cited by scholars today as a clue to his outlook.

A glance at the context shows us that Lenin had not given a single thought to a comparison with the historical Jacobins. He is thinking entirely of divisions within Social Democracy and particularly of the issues separating Bolsheviks and Mensheviks. As usual with Lenin's vulnerable remarks, he is making a pugnacious response to his opponent's polemics. In his *Iskra* articles setting out the Menshevik case against tactical opportunism, Akselrod made an allusion to Jacobins as an example of bourgeois revolutionaries. Lenin seized on this.

> Comrade Akselrod is probably well aware that the division of present-day Social Democracy into revolutionary and opportunist has long since given rise – and not just in Russia – to 'historical analogies with the era of the great French revolution'. Comrade Akselrod is probably well aware that the *Girondists of present-day Social Democracy* everywhere and always resort to the terms 'Jacobinism', 'Blanquism', and so on to describe their opponents.[68]

---

[65] *Iskra*, No. 111 (24 September 1905). As shown in the final section of this chapter, the Mensheviks (including Trotsky) all accepted the term 'artisanal limitations'.

[66] Trotskii 1904, p. 98. In 1907, upset at the use by liberal journalists of the 'Jacobinism' label for Social Democracy, Trotsky indirectly retracted these remarks as exaggeration for polemical effect (Trotskii 1907).

[67] Martynov 1905.

[68] Lenin 1958–65, 8, pp. 368–9.

He then goes on to show that the anti-*Iskra*-ites used similar accusations against the *Iskra*-ites at the Second Congress. In particular, the people labelled as Jacobins supported party rules that favoured proletarian participation, while Akselrod joined with anti-*Iskra*-ites in his concern to make room for professor and high-school students.

Lenin sums up:

> Absolutely nothing but opportunism is expressed by these 'fearsome words': Jacobinism and so forth. A Jacobin, inextricably linked with the *organisation* of the proletariat that *has become aware* of its class interests – this is a *revolutionary Social Democrat*. A Girondin, who sighs after professors and high-school students, who fears the dictatorship of the proletariat, who gets dewy-eyed about the absolute value of democratic demands – this is an *opportunist*.[69]

The final sentence – never quoted – reveals quite clearly how we should read this passage. Obviously, he is not claiming that the historical Girondins had anything to say about high-school students. His real argument is as follows.

International Social Democracy is split into 'revolutionary Social Democrats' and 'opportunists'. These two groups are sometimes called 'Jacobins' and 'Girondins' – for instance, by Plekhanov in 1901.[70] At the Second Congress, the people who were called Jacobins by their opponents were revolutionary Social Democrats who wanted a truly proletarian organisation, as shown by their stand on the definition of a member. The people who opposed the revolutionary Social Democrats in the rules debate – that is, Akselrod himself – showed by their solicitude for professors that they were 'opportunists' and as such can also be called Girondins.

## Centralism and the Central Committee

'Centralism' is not a prominent theme in Lenin's polemics, either in WITBD or in 1903–4. In WITBD, he sets forth a plan to establish the central national political organisation desired by all. In 1903–4, he protests that the actions of a handful of top leaders have been destructive of the principle of congress

---

[69] Lenin 1958–65, 8, p. 370. Lenin has just given examples of how 'opportunists' at the Second Congress did all the things here ascribed to Girondins.

[70] Lenin alluded to Plekhanov's comparison in WITBD (1958–65, 6, p. 10 [685]). In the 1907 edition, he added a footnote underlining the fact that Plekhanov had used the comparison before he did himself.

sovereignty and thus of any effective national centre. In neither case does he focus on advocating one particular organisational scheme that is more or less 'centralised' in comparison to others. His thoughts on the specific powers of the party Central Committee take up a vanishingly small space in his output.

These exists a strong impression to the contrary and the reason is not far to seek. Rosa Luxemburg's 1904 attack on Lenin, still in print, still highly regarded, portrays Lenin as someone totally obsessed with an all-powerful Central Committee.[71] Luxemburg's prestige as an icon of the Left has given her anti-Lenin broadside an uncriticised authority both among academic and activists. Given the damage done to historical understanding by her article, I feel it my duty as a historian to point out that it is not a perceptive or prophetic critique but an unscrupulous hatchet job.[72]

Luxemburg's articles provides no evidence that she had even read WITBD. It purports to be a review of Lenin's *One Step Forward*. Lenin's book is a blow-by-blow, hour-by-hour account of the Second Congress. Every vote, every debate is analysed in terms of the emerging split. Two themes predominate. One is that the *Iskra*-ite minority tended more and more to end up voting with the anti-*Iskra*-ites. The other theme is the inexcusability of the actions of the *Iskra* minority, first in boycotting, then in taking over, the central organ. Luxemburg passes over all of this in total silence.

I believe that Luxemburg was handed *One Step* by the Mensheviks who were organising the literary campaign against Lenin and who pointed out to her the notorious passages about factory discipline and Jacobins. Luxemburg had better things to do than actually read Lenin's long, obsessive polemic but, instead, relied on the anti-*Iskra* critique earlier deployed by her friend and mentor Boris Krichevskii. Indeed, her article can be called 'Krichevskii's revenge'. Due to this article's prestige, Krichevskii's main charge – that *Iskra* was so obsessed with a rigid tactics/plan that it would miss the revolution – became inextricably attached to Lenin and to WITBD.[73]

---

[71] Luxemburg 1970 [1904]. The English translation in Luxemburg 1961 and Luxemburg 1970a is inadequate and politically tendentious. For a more accurate translation by Richard Taylor, see Harding 1983.
[72] Even most of those who side with Lenin against Luxemburg do not dispute the basic accuracy of her account of his views. Two writers who have properly rejected this article are Hal Draper and Paul Le Blanc.
[73] Lenin saw the resemblance (Lenin 1958–65, 10, p. 16). Luxemburg's article was

Throughout her article, Luxemburg keeps pounding away at one theme: Lenin wants a dictatorial Central Committee to reduce everyone else in the party to automata.

> Ultracentralist tendency . . . the Central Committee is the only active nucleus in the party and all the remaining organisations are merely its tools for implementation . . . absolute blind submission of the individual organs of the party to their central authority . . . mechanical submission of the party's militants to their central authority . . . a central authority that alone thinks, acts and decides for everyone . . . the lack of will and thought in a mass of flesh with many arms and legs moving mechanically to the baton . . . zombie-like obedience [*Kadavergehorsam*] . . . absolute power and authority of a negative kind . . . sterile spirit of the night watchman . . . strict despotic centralism . . . the strait-jacket of a bureaucratic centralism that reduces the militant workers to a docile instrument of a committee . . . an all-knowing and ubiquitous Central Committee.[74]

I find it surprising that this rhetorical overkill did not arouse anyone's suspicions. Do people really believe that Lenin desired and indeed openly advocated unthinking, zombie-like obedience? We may, if we wish, excuse Luxemburg's melodramatic characterisation as exuberant polemics. A more direct proof of her article's lack of connection with reality is the exclusive focus on the power of the Central Committee.

If there is one issue that did *not* separate Mensheviks and Bolsheviks, it was the official definition of the functions of the Central Committee. In the rules accepted unanimously at the Second Congress, the Central Committee is given the power to organise committees, guide their activity and unite the entire activity of the Party. These basic powers, along with more specific ones such as administering party finances, remain unchanged in all later prewar versions of the party rules, including the Fourth Unity Congress (1906) at

---

published simultaneously in *Neue Zeit* and *Iskra*. Lenin wrote a reply and sent it to Karl Kautsky, editor of *Neue Zeit*, who refused to print it on grounds of lack of reader interest. Lenin's reply (unpublished at the time) can be highly recommended as the best short exposé of what was on his mind in 1904 (see the discussion in Le Blanc 1990, pp. 79–87).
[74] Luxemburg 1970. English is powerless to reproduce the rich rotundity of her rhetoric, for example, 'eines allwissenden und allgegenwärtigen Zentralkomitees' (p. 443).

which the Mensheviks had a majority. At no time in 1904 did the Mensheviks demand a change in this definition.

The rules adopted at the Second Congress also specified that all party organisations were autonomous in regard to activities exclusively within their functions. The Bolsheviks supported these rules and did not demand that local committees leave all their thinking to the Central Committee.

What did change in the rules over time were the relations between the various central institutions. The positions taken on this issue are rather unexpected. Lenin had a scheme (one of his few concrete organisational proposals) which he persuaded the Second Congress to adopt. According to this scheme, the Party had three central institutions: a Central Committee, a Central Editorial Board, and a Party Council. Both the Central Editorial Board and Central Committee were elected directly by a party congress. The Central Editorial Board was given the task of 'ideological guidance', while the Central Committee was restricted to directing practical activity.

Thus the Central Editorial Board and the Central Committee were completely independent institutions with independent missions. In order to adjudicate the (inevitable?) conflicts, Lenin's scheme included a Party Council. The Central Editorial Board and the Central Committee would each name two members of this Council, with a fifth member elected directly by the Congress. Since this fifth member would cast the deciding vote, he would have the closest thing to dictatorial power within the Party. The Second Congress elected Plekhanov as fifth Council member.[75]

The Mensheviks first defined their organisational position in opposition to this scheme – because it subordinated the Central Committee to the Central Editorial Board! They accused Lenin of using the Central Editorial Board to impose a 'theocracy' (Akselrod's term) over the Party. They therefore took up the cudgels *for* the Central Committee.[76] Of course, when they themselves took over the Central Editorial Board, they made no attempt to limit its power.

---

[75] A few years later, after he had broken with Lenin, Bogdanov described Plekhanov as the one real party dictator in this period (Bogdanov 1995).

[76] In Trotsky's anti-Lenin *Report of the Siberian Delegation*, written immediately after the Second Congress, he writes: 'We did all we could, comrades. . . . We defended the independence and autonomy of the militant leader [*vozhd*] of the Party, *the Central Committee*, because we are centralists' (Shutskever 1925, p. 489). See also Dan, cited in Martov 1904b, p. 96 and Trotskii 1904, p. 31.

On the contrary, they opened up a campaign against the Central Committee because it appeared to be a bastion for Lenin and his supporters.

Meanwhile, many Bolsheviks were also having second thoughts. Bogdanov pointed out in 1904 that Lenin's scheme almost guaranteed destructive conflict because it set up two independent central institutions.[77] Consequently, the purely Bolshevik Third Congress in early 1905 changed the rules and subordinated the Central Editorial Board to the Central Committee. Lenin himself remained unconvinced by Bogdanov's reasoning and protested against the change.

The following picture results: in the name of more efficient centralism, the Bolsheviks defy Lenin and move in the direction of Menshevik complaints about the 'theocratic' Central Editorial Board.[78] All this shuffling and reshuffling of central party institutions are perhaps of minor significance in themselves. But they do reveal Rosa Luxemburg's picture of Lenin's devotion to an all-devouring Central Committee as the baseless nonsense it is.

### Intelligenty and workers

> I have long advocated in my published works that workers should be recruited on to the committees in the greatest possible number. (Lenin, 1905)

The Bolsheviks are usually cast in the role of the defenders of intelligentsia hegemony in the Party. In WITBD (according to this scenario), Lenin demanded a party consisting of intelligentsia 'professional revolutionaries', since workers could not be trusted. In 1904, the Mensheviks rose up against this intelligentsia hegemony in the name of proletarian samodeiatelnost. Some writers (particularly those in the activist tradition) add an ironic coda to this story. In 1905, Lenin was so carried away with the unexpected revolutionary actions of the workers that he reversed track and demanded that workers be recruited into party

---

[77] Bogdanov in Olminskii and Bogdanov 1904, pp. 64–8 ('A centralist organisation with two separate centres!').

[78] The Menshevik-dominated Fourth Congress (1906) returned to direct election of the Central Editorial Board. Administrative convenience was the stated rationale for this decision. Unlike Lenin's earlier 'dual centrism', the Central Editorial Board was given no independent mission and the Central Committee was given the job of uniting all, not just 'practical', activity. The Bolshevik faction nevertheless protested against 'the old dual centrism. . . . We all remember its unfortunate and gloomy features' (Chetvertyi s"ezd 1959, pp. 461–3). Recall that the originator and main defender of this dual centrism was Lenin himself.

committees. This shocked the Bolsheviks, who had grown up on the WITBD philosophy of excluding workers. At the Bolshevik Third Congress in 1905, the Bolshevik faction defeated their own leader's resolution on the subject.

At earlier points in this commentary we have touched on the various profound difficulties of this story. In Chapter Four we looked at the Social-Democratic consensus on the subject – a consensus that was neither 'worker-phile' nor 'worker-phobe', neither anti-intellectual nor anti-worker. In Chapter Seven, we looked at the role assigned to workers in WITBD. In Chapter Eight, we saw that party members were not restricted to 'revolutionaries by trade' and that 'revolutionaries by trade' were not restricted to intellectuals. We also looked at figures on the actual composition of the Party by social origin. In this chapter, we will wrap things up by taking the story through the party debates of 1904 and the Bolshevik Third Congress in 1905.

In 1904, neither Mensheviks nor Bolsheviks stepped outside the earlier consensus on this issue. No one wanted to exclude workers as such from the Party or from local and central leadership. On the contrary, everyone saw purposive workers (or '*intelligentye* workers') as the key to the party's future. Everyone wanted to increase the number of purposive workers and to encourage them in every way. A viable underground organisation was unthinkable without the participation of purposive workers at all levels.

Everyone realised that *intelligenty* had played the major role in bringing the Social-Democratic message to Russia and laying the foundations of party organisation. Everyone thought that this was an inevitable anomaly in the course of being corrected. All would have agreed with Lenin's statement that 'the role of the "intelligentsia" comes to this: to make it unnecessary to have special leader/guides from the intelligentsia'.[79]

On the other hand, all opposed the slogan of a 'purely worker movement [*chisto rabochee dvizhenie*]'. Social Democracy wanted to convert the workers, not reflect their views, democratically or otherwise. In order to join the Party and even more to be placed in a position of leadership, a worker had to be 'purposive', that is, someone who understood what Social Democracy was all about and who was fully committed to it. The 'purely worker movement'

---

[79] This statement occurs in Lenin's first major writing *Friends of the People* (Lenin 1958–65, 1, p. 309). Note: not 'eliminate intellectuals from leadership positions', but 'eliminate the special reliance on them necessary in the early stages of the movement'.

slogan had anti-intellectual implications that were roundly rejected, especially since the anti-intellectual card was also played by police socialists such as Zubatov, who told workers they were being politically exploited by revolutionary intellectuals.

Within the Party, workers and intellectuals were comrades, for whom distinction of social origin should be effaced. Connected to this ideal was the complete rejection of any institutional separation between intellectuals and workers within the Party. There should be no two-tier newspaper system, with one aimed at intellectuals and the other at workers. There should be no separate worker organisations within the Party, but, rather, a single party committee on which both workers and intellectuals served.

When this last demand was put into practice during the *Iskra* period (1901–3), it meant disbanding the existing worker organisations in the expectation of increasing worker representation directly on party committees. The bitterness caused by the break-up of separate worker organisations was not assuaged by the poor record of the committees in recruiting workers – although the percentage of workers on party committees did go up during this period.[80]

Finally, all agreed that democratic control by party members of local committees was an excellent ideal but impossible to put into practice under present Russian conditions. The resulting difficulties in the relations between the committees and the 'subcommittee world' or 'party periphery' – the factory circles and other ground-level party organisations – were sometimes interpreted as antagonism between intellectuals and workers. Nevertheless, the consensus was that these difficulties, however painful, did not represent real or fundamental antagonisms.

These views constituted the strong consensus of Russian Social Democracy. No doubt, personal interaction gave rise to tensions and resentments that did not always reflect the official democratic ideal. No doubt, party policies did not always succeed in advancing the goal of worker participation. Yet the ideal of Social Democracy as a genuine worker party was held by all.

Within this consensus, there could be different emphases, different priorities. During the pre-Congress *Iskra* period and after, there was one prominent Social Democrat who insisted with particular vehemence on the need to recruit workers into the leadership. This Social Democrat was Lenin. During the 1904

---

[80] See Chapter Eight for figures.

debate, one faction was particularly insistent on the leadership role of the intellectuals both in the past and present. This faction was the Mensheviks.

Lenin's pre-Congress views on this issue were expressed in WITBD and the *Letter to a Comrade on Organisational Questions* written later in 1902. WITBD takes up a number of topics: political agitation, organisational questions, the role of a party newspaper. One topic the book does *not* take up is the role of the intelligentsia. All the book contains is a number of isolated remarks, almost all parenthetical to the topic at hand. Even if we gather all the comments together, views that Lenin expressed with some vehemence before and after WITBD will not be found.

The lack of systematic attention is reflected in the profusion of undefined terms. Lenin makes no effort to tell us what exactly the following locutions – all found in WITBD – mean or how they relate to each: Marxist intelligentsia, revolutionary intelligentsia, socialist intelligentsia, revolutionary-socialist intelligentsia, non-worker intelligentsia, *intelligentnyi* worker, liberal intelligentsia, *zemstvo* intelligentsia, 'intelligentsia in general'. Terms that are *not* used include 'Social-Democratic intelligentsia' and 'Social-Democratic *intelligenty*'. The overall portrait of the party *intelligenty* that emerges from these various offhand remarks is not a particularly flattering one. Running through the book is a contrast between the revolutionary workers and the party *intelligenty*, who have failed to fulfil their own responsibilities.[81]

Lenin argues that one of the Social Democracy's urgent priorities must be to encourage and push forward as many worker leaders as possible. This is partly because intelligentsia forces are thin on the ground, partly because Russian *intelligenty* are often sloppy and impractical, but mainly because Social Democracy as a merger of socialism and the worker movement will succeed only when it is embodied in a corps of inspired and inspiring worker activists. In his most eloquent passage on this theme, he says that the *stikhiinyi* upsurge of the worker mass will lead to more and more workers being pushed forward as genuine *praktiki*. When the Party has a corps of workers who have learned the skills of the revolutionary trade, it will be unbeatable, because these activists will be completely dedicated to the revolution and also enjoy

---

[81] Robert Himmer argues that Stalin may have been surprised to discover that Lenin himself was an *intelligent*, such was the animus against *intelligenty* in WITBD (Himmer 2001).

the utmost trust of the wide worker masses. And, Lenin adds, it is the direct fault of present party members that they do not urge the workers to acquire revolutionary skills in the same way as *intelligenty*.[82]

In WITBD, Lenin is talking about underground revolutionary activists in general. The *Letter to a Comrade* is focused more on institutional details, including the membership of the local party committees. On this subject, he gives the following advice:

> The [local party] committee should include, to the extent possible, all the chief leaders [*vozhaki*] of the worker movement from among the workers themselves.... It is especially necessary to try to ensure that as many workers as possible become completely purposive revolutionaries by trade and end up on the committee.[83]

At the end of 1904, Lenin quoted these words and issued a challenge: show me any statement in the Russian Social-Democratic literature that calls for worker recruitment on the committees as clearly and urgently as I did in 1902. Nobody responded to this challenge, which still stands for advocates of the textbook interpretation.[84]

In 1903–4, Lenin's rhetoric took on a more stridently anti-intellectual tone. As we have seen, the central Bolshevik accusation was that the *Iskra* editors refused to submit to the authority of the party congress and regarded *Iskra* as their personal property. Lenin accompanied this accusation with much rhetoric about 'intelligentsia indiscipline' and 'intelligentsia anarchism' as opposed to a proletarian sense of discipline and collectivism. This new emphasis in his polemics was not inconsistent with his remarks in WITBD and elsewhere.

Lenin's contrast between worker aptitude and intelligentsia lack of aptitude for organisation was something of a Social-Democratic commonplace and Lenin was able to cite Kautsky on the issue.[85] This did not prevent some Social Democrats from concluding that Lenin's aggressive use of this theme

---

[82] Lenin 1958–65, 6, pp. 132–4 [793–5].
[83] Lenin 1958–65, 7, p. 9 (order of sentences reversed).
[84] In *Iskra*, No. 86 (3 February 1905), a correspondent with the pseudonym 'A Worker As Well' said he would respond to the challenge but did not even try to produce any statements.
[85] Lenin 1958–65, 8, pp. 309–11. The basic thesis about proletarian aptitude for disciplined organisation can be found in *Parliamentarism* (Kautsky 1893).

strayed close to impermissible intelligentsia-baiting. One such Social Democrat was Rosa Luxemburg. What, she asked in her 1904 critique of Lenin, is Lenin's greatest fear? Answer: the fear that the worker movement will be turned into 'a tool of the bourgeois intelligentsia's lust for power'. She speaks of a 'Lenin-type fear of the catastrophic influence of the intelligentsia on the proletarian movement'. She warns Lenin that he is outside the Social-Democratic consensus on this point: 'an intense emphasis on the innate propensity of proletarians for Social-Democratic organisation and a suspicion of the "intelligentsia" elements in the Social-Democratic movement is in and of itself no expression of "revolutionary Marxism"'. As examples of Lenin-style worker worship, she points to French syndicalists, English trade-unionists and even 'the pure "economism" of the former Petersburg paper *Rabochaia mysl* with its transfer of *tred-iunionist* narrowness into autocratic Russia'. Thus – amazingly – Luxemburg insists on the similarity of Lenin's outlook to *Rabochaia mysl*.[86]

Combatting what they considered to be Lenin's anti-intellectual demagoguery was not the only Menshevik motive for stressing the positive role of the intellectuals. The central Menshevik proposal of 1904 was the tactic of organising campaigns with true Social-Democratic content (as discussed in a previous section). This proposal was grounded in a historical narrative about Russian Social Democracy. Owing to a variety of factors (went this narrative), Russian Social Democracy was built up completely by intellectuals. This intelligentsia party had scored some success in awakening the workers to economic struggle and (merely) revolutionary struggle. This Party had also been preparing itself for its culminating task: bringing Social-Democratic content to the workers, creating the 'purposive proletarian vanguard' as yet missing in Russia. But at the present time, Russian Social Democracy was still an 'intelligentsia party', a worker party only in name and aspiration.

Many people, at the time and at the present day, seized on the Menshevik description of Social Democracy as a 'intelligentsia party' as a de-legitimising critique. But the Menshevik leaders did not mean it that way. They saw the intelligentsia path to a worker party as historically inevitable in Russia and,

---

[86] Rosa Luxemburg in *Iskra* No. 69 (10 July 1904). ('*Tred-iunionist* narrowness' in German is 'trade-unionistischen Borniertheit' [Luxemburg 1970, p. 436]). Looking back in 1927, Miliukov also saw Lenin as anti-intellectual, affirming that at the Second Congress Lenin stood for 'the removal of wavering "*intelligenty*" and for the promotion [*vydvizhenie*] of workers ready to submit to discipline' (Miliukov 1927, p. 125).

therefore, as perfectly justifiable. They did not see the Social-Democratic intellectuals as motivated by lust for power or imbued with an alien class interest, but, rather, as dedicated activists laying the necessary groundwork for true Social Democracy. Of course, the time had come to turn potential Social-Democratic energy to actual energy by enlisting the workers in appropriate campaigns. And, now, in 1904, it seemed as if one faction of the Party was intent on throwing a spanner into the works by hindering the proposed Menshevik tactics. Nevertheless, the intelligentsia had played and were still playing an absolutely essential role in turning workers into Social Democrats. Trotsky made the point in a sarcastic riposte to Lenin:

> Without fear of revealing my 'bourgeois intellectual psychology', I affirm . . . that between the objective conditions [of proletarian life] and the purposive discipline of political action, there is a long road of struggle, errors, education [in] the school of political life. The Russian proletariat enters into this school only under the leadership – good or bad – of the Social-Democratic intelligentsia. I affirm that the Russian proletariat, in whom we [sic] have barely begun to develop political *samodeiatelnost*, is not yet able . . . to give lessons in discipline to its 'intelligentsia'.[87]

When they looked back at the history of Russian Social Democracy, the Menshevik and Bolshevik polemicists of 1904 saw things differently. The Mensheviks tended to give an initiatory role to the intellectuals. Thus Akselrod described Social Democracy as 'a revolutionary movement of the intelligentsia' that 'called the worker movement to life'.[88] Similar remarks can be found in other Menshevik writings.

Bolshevik accounts relied on a more interactive version of the merger narrative in which the worker movement had a more independent existence and often influenced and inspired the socialists. Olminskii and Bogdanov presented a much different picture of the history of the Party:

> [According to the Menshevik version of events], it is the intelligentsia which thinks up tactics, the intelligentsia which criticises and changes them, the intelligentsia which draws the worker into the movement – in a word, it is

---

[87] Trotskii 1904, p. 74. Trotsky criticised the old *Iskra* for its double standard: hard on intellectuals, easy on workers (p. 23).

[88] *Iskra*, 68, 25 June 1904 (in the letter to Kautsky reprinted in *Iskra za dva goda* 1906, here p. 153).

the navel of the universe. [In reality,] when the underground worker movement [in the latter half of the 1890s] revealed itself to the world, it shone with a bright flame that illuminated the path for the intelligentsia and awoke its desires for liberation from autocratic oppression: the sunflower/intelligentsia strained toward the worker sun.[89]

In the pamphlet by Panin published by the minority, you will find a concrete picture of how the proletarian vanguard [actively] *adjusted* the intelligentsia and its tactics to the needs of the worker movement.[90]

The Bolsheviks also disputed the term 'intelligentsia party' as an appropriate label for Russian Social Democracy in 1904. Bogdanov granted that the intelligentsia played a relatively larger role in Russia than in other countries, and also that the party committees – the key link in the local hierarchy – were mostly staffed by intellectuals. Nevertheless, he insists that only someone unacquainted with the realities of the Russian underground would deny its essentially proletarian character.

Our party is a proletarian party even in regards to its quantitative make-up. Its foundation is not a couple of dozen committees each containing just a few people, but the numerous worker groups and organisations standing behind those committees. According to available data, each of 27 organisations represented at the Second Congress has behind it hundreds, and some of them thousands, of organised workers. In actuality, for every Social Democrat/*intelligent* there are *dozens* of organised workers – and these are in no way passive, non-purposive political neophytes who allow themselves to be led down any road. From among their number are recruited many members of the committees, many more of them stand at the head of city sections [*raion*] and factory organisations, they work as professional agitators, and so forth.

Do you think that all of this is not a 'vanguard' but a non-purposive mass? Do you think that they slavishly follow after the '*intelligenty*'?[91]

---

[89] Olminskii in Olminskii and Bogdanov 1904, pp. 14–15.

[90] Bogdanov in Olminskii and Bogdanov 1904, p. 57. Panin was a second-tier Menshevik writer. Note the way the Bolshevik writer seizes on the discrepancy between Panin and the leaders of the Menshevik faction.

[91] Bogdanov in Olminskii and Bogdanov 1904, p. 56. As we shall see, Akselrod and Trotsky both had occasion to retract the 'intelligentsia party' label and essentially endorse Bogdanov's picture.

The label 'intelligentsia party' came out of Akselrod's long-standing views (*not* out of a horrified reaction to Lenin) and was also used to respond to Lenin's anti-intelligentsia rhetoric (the Bolsheviks flail the *intelligenty* but they themselves prolong the existence of the intelligentsia party). I have the impression the Menshevik leaders were somewhat taken aback when the label was used to de-legitimise Social Democracy as a whole. It was bad enough that liberal and conservatives made use of the Menshevik 'admission'. Even more upsetting were Social-Democratic voices who declared themselves fervent Mensheviks but used Menshevik rhetoric to justify an anti-intelligentsia crusade within the Party. Such a voice was an anonymous pamphlet signed Rabochii [A Worker], published under *Iskra* auspices in later 1904.[92]

This pamphlet is the most full-bodied literary expression of the anti-intelligentsia feelings among many workers. Rabochii was not content with saying 'we need more workers on party committees'. He wanted an energetic purge of most *intelligenty* and their replacement by 'true proletarians'. The intellectuals were led by their 'class instinct' to despise the workers and to exclude them systematically from party life. All ills of party life were due to this alien class influence. Did frequent arrests of *praktiki* lead to lower quality replacements? It was the fault of the intellectuals. Did stringent *konspiratsiia* intended to prevent arrests lead to difficulties in the relationships between committees and lower-level organisations? It was the fault of the intellectuals. And writers such as Bogdanov, who painted a different picture of committee life, were demagogic liars.

Menshevik intellectuals (continued Rabochii) were no better than Bolshevik ones. True, the top Mensheviks had issued a clarion call for the workers to take over. But they had addressed this call only to intellectuals. And Rabochii could assert through personal experience that Menshevik committees were no better than Bolshevik ones in allowing workers access to leadership positions.

Rabochii's pamphlet was sent in to the *Iskra* editorial board with a request that it be published, and *Iskra* duly did so. But Akselrod realised that Rabochii's politics of suspicion and purge would make party life impossible and he was deeply embarrassed by Rabochii's claim to be a faithful Menshevik. He

---

[92] Rabochii 1904. According to Zinoviev 1975, p. 111, Rabochii was a St. Petersburg worker named Glebov-Putilovsky (although Zinoviev gives a very inaccurate picture of Akselrod's preface).

therefore accompanied Rabochii's pamphlet with an unrequested foreword almost one-half the size of Rabochii's own text in which he pointed out the dangers of Rabochii's 'one-sided' and 'formal/organisational' approach to the problem. 'Proletarian *samodeiatelnost'* was not a question that could be solved by a crude comparison of the number of intellectuals vs. workers on the party committees.[93]

Akselrod's foreword is a remarkable re-assertion of the Social-Democratic consensus that Rabochii had violated. At times, he sounds more like WITBD than WITBD does. If Rabochii's practical suggestion were adopted, Akselrod warned, the result would be the resurrection of the late unlamented slogan, a 'purely worker movement' – a slogan that led to 'the corruption of the workers and the disorganisation of the Party'. The English trade unions were 'purely' proletarian too, but that did not help them escape the 'political and moral tutelage' of bourgeois intellectuals.

Does not Rabochii remember how bad so-called 'democratism' was? Democratism – electoral control of local committees from below – is impossible under Russian conditions. Not only that, democratism 'served as a cover for ambitious intriguers and even provided clever provocateurs with a access to the organisation'. (This is a harsher critique of 'democratism' than can be found in WITBD.)

There should be no distinction between workers and intellectuals in today's Party. There is only one meaningful distinction: party member vs. non-member. A non-member worker has no rights, a non-worker member has full rights, in deciding on the questions of party life. If workers have not hitherto played the leadership role that one could hope, this is due to historical circumstances, not the individual qualities of workers or intellectuals, and certainly not to the class origin of the intellectuals, their evil will, or their alleged aspiration to exclude workers.

Akselrod does blame the Bolsheviks for the frustration felt by Rabochii and his peers – but not because he sees the Bolsheviks as defenders of 'intelligentsia hegemony'.[94] Rather, their factionalism has crippled local party life, so that

---

[93] Rabochii 1904, pp. 3–16 (the text in the pamphlet differs from the one published in *Iskra* No. 80 [15 December 1904] or reprinted in *Iskra za dva goda* 1906, pp. 155–66).

[94] Indeed, there is at least a hint that the unscrupulous Lenin would latch on to Rabochii's anti-intelligentsia crusade in order to make further trouble (*Iskra za dva goda* 1906, p. 160).

eager workers like Rabochii do not receive directives for action even as they observe the advancing revolutionary storm. The implication is that if Rabochii had been given something useful to do, he would stop worrying so much about whether or not he was on the committee.

Akselrod again reaffirms the historical role of the intellectual as the exclusive 'uniting and organising element in the process of the formation of our party'.[95] Back in the days when the Party was starting up, even the purposive workers were extremely backward compared to the intellectuals.[96] On the other hand, Akselrod seems to retract his label of 'intelligentsia party' for present-day Russian Social Democracy. In fact, he sounds much closer to the Bolshevik Bogdanov than he does to the Menshevik Rabochii. After reaffirming that the Party was a 'purely intelligentsia' one in the beginning, he goes on to say:

> At the present time, purposively revolutionary workers make up the main detachments of the Social-Democratic Party, a party that has pushed into the background the purely intelligentsia revolutionary factions, that expresses the interests and aspirations of the proletariat, and that strives for an unbreakable fusion with its actively revolutionary elements.[97]

Lenin wrote a review of Rabochii's pamphlet and Akselrod's foreword. Of course, much of what Rabochii said about the overt hostility of the *praktiki* toward the workers was misinformed (Lenin announced). Misled by his Menshevik mentors, Rabochii would be surprised to read in Lenin's *Letter to a Comrade* the only clear call in Russian Social-Democratic literature for worker recruitment onto the committees. But his demand for results and his exposé of the gap between Menshevik words and deeds showed proletarian good sense. As for Akselrod, his foreword showed that even the Mensheviks were aghast at the results of their demagoguery.[98]

---

[95] *Iskra za dva goda* 1906, p. 165.

[96] *Iskra za dva goda* 1906, pp. 162–5.

[97] Rabochii 1904, pp. 15–16. This passage is not in the other published versions of Akselrod's preface. In 1907, Trotsky also retreated from the 'intelligentsia party' label: 'That Russian Social Democracy is a proletarian party not only because of its programme but because of its social composition is as difficult to prove as any other obvious fact' (Trotskii 1907, p. 89).

[98] Lenin 1958–65, 9, pp. 161–5. At the Third Congress, Lenin cited Rabochii as authority for the claim that 'in the era of "economism", workers were the bearers of revolutionary ideas, not the intellectuals' (1958–65, 10, p. 162).

Lenin's review of Rabochii (published at the end of 1904) forms the immediate background to Lenin's intervention on this issue at the Bolshevik Third Congress a few months later. While praising himself for the advice he had given on worker recruitment, Lenin was constrained to admit in his review that the advice had not been taken. The record on worker recruitment, especially since the Second Congress, was poor. No guarantee on this issue was possible, given the lack of feasibility of 'democratism'. But perhaps something stronger than just the unofficial, private advice that he had already given – say, an official congress resolution?

The story of the consequent debate at the Bolshevik Third Congress (April 1905) has been told many times, especially by those in the activist tradition, and provides substantial support to the textbook interpretation. According to this story, WITBD had done such a good job in urging the praktiki to mistrust workers that, when Lenin himself changed his mind, he could not convince his own followers! The most elaborate modern retelling is by Tony Cliff, who gives substantial excerpts from the debate and concludes that

> most of the delegates to the Congress were committee-men who were opposed
> to any move which would tend to weaken their authority over the rank and
> file. Buttressing themselves with quotations from *What is to be Done?*, they
> called for 'extreme caution' in admitting workers into the committees and
> condemned 'playing at democracy'. . . . The unfortunate Lenin had to persuade
> his supporters to oppose the line proposed in *What is to be Done?*.'[99]

All this is totally false. No one at the Congress was opposed to the idea of having as many workers as possible on the committees. In fact, one motive for opposition to the proposed resolution was that it stated a self-evident goal without saying how to achieve it. WITBD was not even mentioned in the debate, and everyone was well aware of Lenin's long-standing position in favour of workers.[100] The Congress majority had various objections to the text of the resolution drafted mainly by Bogdanov and supported by Lenin.[101]

---

[99] Cliff 1975, p. 175.

[100] 'In his *Letter to a Petersburg Comrade*, Comrade Lenin has also spoken about the necessity of introducing workers to the committees in the great possible number' (M.G. Tskhakaia, *Tretii s"ezd* 1959, p. 258); 'Comrade Lenin has shown the solution completely correctly, affirming the ideas that he spoke about in his well-known *Letter to a Petersburg Comrade*' (D.S. Postolovskii, *Tretii s"ezd* 1959, p. 263).

[101] Among the objections: the resolution paid too much attention to 'Menshevik

Thus, while the Bogdanov/Lenin resolution was defeated, another resolution passed by the Congress emphasised the extreme importance of having as many workers as possible on the local committees. All in all, the debate as it actually transpired at the Third Congress does fatal damage to the textbook interpretation.

The case of the congress majority opposed to the Bogdanov/Lenin resolution might be paraphrased as follows: we all agree that there should be as many workers as possible on the committees and we all agree that the number of such workers at present is very unsatisfactory. The cause of this situation, however, is not the attitude of the present committee members or anything that can be fixed by passing a resolution. There are a host of objective problems that need to be addressed. To pass a resolution making worker recruitment *obligatory* would be ridiculous. To pass a resolution that repeats platitudes about worker recruitment without pointing out concrete means of improvement would also be useless. To pass a resolution that points out all the objective problems would also be counter-productive, since we would go on record as saying 'nothing much can be done immediately'. Better not to have a resolution at all. Or, preferably, we should state our commitment to worker recruitment in a resolution that points out a practical solution, such as the resolution on 'propaganda' (in the technical sense of intensive preparation of a few outstanding individuals).[102]

The congress debate was thus about empirical ways and means rather than a clash in values. As a supporter of the resolution said,

> we have always stood and stand now for the preparation of advanced worker Social Democrats and for the participation of all purposive leaders of the worker movement in our committees and other organisations, and this has been shown empirically in the organisation of committees and in recruitment to them.[103]

---

demagoguery', it mixed up a variety of issues that should be handled separately, it did not give directives on how to achieve the stated goals, and, in general, it was too 'watery' (Aleksei Rykov).

[102] In the English translation of her memoirs, Krupskaya is made to imply that the *komitetchiki* wanted a resolution that directly excluded workers (Krupskaya 1960, p. 126). This is a mistranslation of the original passage, which refers to the reasoning I have just summarised (Krupskaia 1969, p. 290).

[103] *Tretii s"ezd* 1959, p. 257, comment of Tskhakaia, who nonetheless believed there was a serious problem to be addressed.

What the Bogdanov/Lenin resolution essentially demanded was affirmative action to increase worker representation, and the opposing sides adopted attitudes familiar from other debates over affirmative action. One side resented the pious wishes of people with little hands-on experience being forced down the throats of the people out in the trenches. They resented the insulting implication that they were prejudiced, they insisted on unpleasant realities such as a paucity of acceptable worker candidates at the present time, and they worried about lowering standards. In contrast, the other side was also impatient with pious wishes about increasing worker recruitment without a firm commitment to improve the situation *now*, by means of quotas if necessary. They strongly suspected that the reference to objective conditions was indeed the excuse of people prejudiced for some reason against workers on the committees. They argued that inappropriate standards had artificially lowered the number of workers on the committees.

The clash about standards was revealing. The supporters of the resolution insisted that different standards should be applied to worker candidates, with popularity and influence among the mass of workers as the basic criterion.[104] Opponents warned of the dangers of making popularity more important than a purposive commitment to Social Democracy and of having too low expectations for workers.

> The very distinction made between workers and *intelligenty* is in my view an incorrect one. When a new person arrives in town, no one asks whether he is a worker or an *intelligent*. They ask: where did he work, how long, and what function did he carry out. This information is what guides them in taking him into the organisation. If he is a worker, all the better, all the more ties will he have [with workers] and all the better will the work go.[105]

The back-and-forth in the debate about the presence or absence of objective conditions is very instructive about life in the underground. Here, I will only list the various concerns. Have we gone too far away from 'propaganda' aimed at creating worker leaders and toward 'agitation' aimed at awakening the mass of workers? Are we so rigid about *konspiratsiia* that the necessary contact and consultation between the committee and 'the periphery' (lower-

---

[104] *Tretii s"ezd* 1959, p. 263 (D.S. Postolovskii), p. 335 (P.A. Krasikov).
[105] *Tretii s"ezd* 1959, p. 266 (V.N. Losev).

level party organisations) is eroded? Can we overcome the difficulties created by the necessary absence of electoral 'democratism'? Have we allowed the party split to make us too timid about recruiting newcomers? Are we rising to the challenge presented by the rapid expansion of worker activity in the present (spring 1905) revolutionary atmosphere?

The overall impression of the debate is a group of people who are all committed to the same goal – increasing worker representation on the committees – and who are arguing about the empirical causes of and remedies for the present unsatisfactory situation. And, as usual in an empirical debate of this kind, Lenin is energetically on the side with the more optimistic assumptions. At one point, he observes 'Here's a strange thing. There are all of three *littérateurs* at the Congress and the rest are committee members, yet the *littérateurs* are for getting workers on the committees while the committee members are for some reason getting all upset.' Reading this comment, the thought might occur that perhaps the committee members had a more realistic understanding of conditions on the ground that émigré *littérateurs* such as Lenin.[106] In any event, Lenin's emotional commitment cannot be gainsaid. Constantly interrupting, shouting 'Bravo!' or 'Shame!' as the case required, he made his feelings perfectly known. As he truly said, 'I cannot sit here calmly when people say that there are no workers capable of committee work.'[107]

Our long survey of Lenin's various intra-party disputes ends with the Third Congress in spring 1905. Perhaps the best picture of the hopes and expectations reflected in WITBD about worker participation in Russian Social Democracy comes from an earlier document. This is a letter written to him in summer 1902, right after the publication of WITBD, by I.I. Radchenko, a life-long Bolshevik. He wrote to Lenin from Petersburg and was full of unrealistic optimism about *Iskra*'s chances for easy success in Petersburg. This circumstance only strengthens the interest of this not-for-publication document as an indication of what Lenin and the people close to him counted on from the workers.

Radchenko had some trouble locating workers to interview, but he finally tracked down 'some purposive metal workers'. He informed Lenin that 'you

---

[106] *Tretii s"ezd* 1959, p. 333 (Lenin's comment is misleading, since he was supported by a number of *praktiki* and the final vote was quite close). On later difficulties with worker recruitment to leadership positions, see Rozental 1994.

[107] *Tretii s"ezd* 1959, p. 333.

cannot imagine how disgusted the workers here are with the intelligentsia'. Radchenko puts the blame for this situation entirely on the intelligentsia. Radchenko reports that the workers took kindly to him personally partly because they were surprised, given the summer season, that he was not at his *dacha*. In his long conversation with these workers, he heard many complaints about sloppy and ineffective organisation of, for example, demonstrations.

> In this conversation I heard citations from *What Is to Be Done?* – if not word for word, then in its spirit. I sat there and was happy for Lenin: this shows, I thought, what he was able to do. It was clear to me that the people talking with me had read him and there was no need for me to summarise his argument. I had only to touch on some points of principle and set out in concrete detail the plan for all-Russian work that Lenin recommended. So I mentioned to them: 'Well, you've read *What Is to Be Done?*, haven't you?'
>
> 'What's that? We haven't read any such book'.
>
> 'Maybe one of your comrades?'
>
> 'No', they answered in one voice, 'we haven't run across it'. (*Those jerks on the [present Social-Democratic] committee, they gobbled up 75 copies but didn't give any to the workers.*)
>
> I was struck: before me sat the Lenin type – people longing for the revolutionary trade. I was happy for Lenin, who sits a million miles away, barricaded by bayonets, cannon, borders, border guards and other attributes of the autocracy – and he sees how people work here on the shop floor, what they need and what they will become. Believe it, my friends, soon we will see our Bebels. Genuine lathe turners / revolutionaries. Before me sat people longing to get down to business – not like the local intelligentsia, who treat [revolutionary work] like a dessert after dinner, no, these people want to get down to business in the way you take up a chisel, a hammer, a saw, take it with your two hands and don't let it go until you've finished what you've started, doing everything for the cause with the profound faith 'I *will* do this'. I say it one more time: this was the happiest moment of my life.[108]

---

[108] *Perepiska* 1969–70, 2, pp. 28–9 (letter of 6 June 1902).

## Party norms and the party split

As we have seen, *WITBD* played a rather marginal role in the polemics of 1904. The issues that were closest to the heart of the two factions – the violation of congress sovereignty for the Bolsheviks and the demand for truly Social-Democratic campaigns for the Mensheviks – had no place in *WITBD* and would have arisen had Lenin not written the book. The Menshevik attack on Lenin did not focus on *WITBD*.[109] Of the two most famous 'prophecies', one (Luxemburg) did not even mention *WITBD*, and the other (Trotsky) only in passing. Insofar as the Mensheviks document their picture of Lenin's views, they relied on various of his off-hand remarks from 1903–4. On the issue of worker-intelligentsia relations, the consensus is much more fundamental than any clash, but insofar as there is a factional clash on this issue, the Bolshevik downplayed the positive role of the intellectuals and the Mensheviks emphasised it.

And yet, the party discussion of 1904 can hardly be understood without *WITBD*. *WITBD* provides an invaluable guide, not to what separated the two factions, but what united them, namely, the norms of the Russian socialist underground and the vocabulary used to describe them (I say 'socialist underground' in order to include the Socialist Revolutionaries). The evidence on this point is all the more compelling because the Mensheviks had every motivation to disown these norms or at least shed the Lenin-associated vocabulary of 'revolutionary by trade' and 'artisanal limitations'.

Let us start our documentation with *WITBD*'s most notorious terminological innovation: 'revolutionary by trade'. The concept, if not the term itself, was endorsed by Akselrod in the *Iskra* articles of December 1904/January 1905 that quickly acquired the status of a Menshevik manifesto. There he states that 'a rather large corps has been formed of Social Democrat revolutionaries who have cut their ties with their legal positions and their regular jobs – a corps that under contemporary Russian conditions is so necessary for forming a political party'.[110]

---

[109] See the discussion in the section 'Lenin rediscovered' in the Introduction.

[110] *Iskra*, Nos. 55 and 57 (December 1903 and January 1904). Trotskii 1904 remarks on the necessity of revolutionaries by trade (pp. 32–3), but then uses the term to refer to the present-day *praktiki*, especially those of the majority, whom he despises.

An even stronger endorsement of both the concept and the vocabulary was penned by Plekhanov in an article for the German party paper *Vorwärts*. Perhaps Plekhanov felt less constraint in using Lenin's vocabulary because he was not writing for Russian readers. Plekhanov explains that only a mass movement can topple tsarism and that a mass movement requires revolutionaries by trade.

> Our contemporary political system places an extremely high number of obstacles in the way of the influence of the purposive socialists on the mass of the people. Overcoming these obstacles requires the expenditure of a great deal of material means and moral effort. Life has created in our country a whole stratum of so-called *revolutionaries by trade*, that is, people who dedicate all their time and all their forces to revolutionary activity. These revolutionaries by trade serve as the central and hardly replaceable source of ferment in the masses. And if these people were to devote themselves to terror instead of agitation and propaganda in the worker mass, then the dissemination of revolutionary ideas in these masses would not of course stop, but it would undoubtedly become much *weaker and slower*.[111]

The Menshevik writer Panin took for granted the role of the revolutionary by trade in local organisation. In an article mainly devoted to a critique of Lenin's organisational schemes, he writes that 'at the head of the worker movement of a town stands the committee of the Party, consisting as far as possible of revolutionaries by trade who give all their time and all their strength to the revolutionary cause'.[112] Thus Lenin was perfectly justified when he wrote in 1907 with some pride that the idea of the revolutionary by trade had been implemented by both Social-Democratic factions. If there was anything unique to Bolshevism, it was not the concept of the revolutionary by trade.[113]

---

[111] Plekhanov 1923–7, 13, pp. 143–4. Plekhanov reproduces WITBD's argument even more closely when he says that terrorists either do not understand the significance of the mass movement or have lost faith in it. This article is dated 11 August 1904, that is, exactly at the time when he was penning his anti-WITBD broadside for home consumption.

[112] Supplement to *Iskra*, No. 57 (15 January 1904), under the pseudonym Praktik. Panin emphasises that the local revolutionaries by trade should be personally acquainted with as many workers as possible and that as many worker-revolutionaries as possible should be on the committee.

[113] Lenin 1958–65, 16, pp. 101–3 (1907 introduction to a collection of Lenin's earlier writings).

The obverse of the *revoliutsioner po professii* is *kustarnichestvo*, artisanal limitations. Lenin's coinage was taken up because it responded to a felt need, so much so that Mensheviks used it even to make their anti-Lenin points. Martov responded to the Bolshevik taunt that none of the *Iskra* editors had criticised Lenin's organisational plan until they fell out with him by saying, yes, we failed to give his detailed organisational proposals a proper critical analysis – but this was due to 'the "artisanal limitations" that reigned at that time and against which *Iskra* had fought'.[114]

Any new organisational proposal in 1904 had to show that it was not reinforcing artisanal limitations. Typical is Cherevanin's defence of his concept of committee autonomy.

> But perhaps [this proposal will lead to] disorganisation, or, at the very least, to decentralisation and the artisanal limitations that flow from thence? Won't the 'autonomy' defended by the minority demolish first of all any kind of party discipline? Not in the least.[115]

Centralism was another common value for the two factions. Martov affirmed that WITBD's overall advocacy of centralism represented a collective *Iskra* position. Nevertheless, there was no reason to see '*all* the detailed proposals of WITBD and especially of *Letter to a Comrade* [as] necessary consequences of "the old organisational views"'.[116] The Mensheviks attacked Lenin not for his centralism but for his bureaucratic centralism, barracks centralism, hyper-centralism, even ego-centrism (Trotsky's gibe). We will pass by the question of what content if any these phrases have and inquire into the good kind of centralism defended by the Mensheviks.

Akselrod continued to endorse the campaign of the old *Iskra* for a nationally centralised party based on rejecting 'economism, ideological wavering and organisational anarchy as elements incompatible with the historical tasks of our movement'.[117] Trotsky went out of his way to show his centralist pedigree

---

[114] Martov 1904a, pp. 3–4. The same anti-Lenin use of 'artisanal limitations' can also be found in Trotsky's writings; see Shutskever 1925, p. 489 (*Report of the Siberian Delegation*).

[115] Cherevanin 1904, p. 29.

[116] *Iskra*, No. 58 (25 January 1904). One wonders exactly what 'detailed proposals' in WITBD Martov had in mind, if any.

[117] *Iskra*, Nos. 55 and 57, December 1903/January 1904.

by citing an unpublished work of his from 1901 – that is, as he himself took pains to point out, *before* the appearance of WITBD.

> My report was written under the influence of fragmentary information about the spring massacre of 1901 [presumably the 'Obukhov defense']. The starting point of the report was as follows: 'We appear (to use for a hundredth time this comparison) to be in the position of those inexperienced sorcerers who call to life an enormous force by stereotyped methods but who are revealed as bankrupts when it becomes necessary to control them'. The conclusion must be: an all-party organisation with a Central Committee to head it. A congress called ad hoc will not resolve the issue. The centre must be *created* before it is *proclaimed*. Such was the train of thought of this unpublished report.[118]

Rosa Luxemburg attacked Lenin for his 'merciless centralism', but her own centralism was fairly stern. In her anti-Lenin article, she advocates revising the rules of the German Party in the direction of tighter organisational discipline in order to ward off the opportunist danger. But what is possible in Germany is not possible in Russia. Luxemburg endorses a central thesis of the present commentary when she chides Lenin for thinking that 'all the preliminary conditions for the creation of a large and highly centralised worker party already exist in Russia' and for 'optimistically' assuming that the indiscipline of the intelligentsia is the source of all problems. Luxemburg tells Lenin that he needs to cast away 'ready-made clichés' from Western Europe and, instead, base his organisational prescriptions on conditions in Russia.[119]

The flip side of centralism was party discipline and the Mensheviks realised they could not afford to be perceived as anti-discipline. As the Menshevik writer Cherevanin announced:

> Party discipline is necessary in general and needed at the present moment in particular, in view of the struggle against such a disciplined enemy as the autocracy. . . . Each member of the Party must be imbued with the conviction that in certain cases he can and must act against his convictions on this or that particular case.[120]

---

[118] Shutskever 1925, pp. 492, 489. Note Trotsky's assertion that 'we' called an enormous force to life.

[119] The word 'optimistically' is dropped from the translation used by Bertram Wolfe and others (Luxemburg 1961).

[120] Cherevanin 1904, pp. 29–30.

Martov argued for greater autonomy for local committees, but he was careful to specify that any dependence on the local purposive workers would be 'factual' and 'political', that is, *not* based 'of course, on "playing at democratism", playing at elections'. And (somehow) this local autonomy 'must not weaken the dependence of committee policies on the will of the *entire* Party as a whole'.[121] Thus Martov must be added to the comments cited in the previous section about the unacceptability of 'democratism' under conditions of absolutist repression.

Tied to the rejection of democratism was the endorsement of the norm of *konspiratsiia*. *Konspiratsiia* was a central value long before WITBD and Lenin's only contribution was to insist on a more professional commitment to learning the appropriate skills. If Lenin did put forth a specific organisational proposal on this subject, it was the idea of a small, centralised organisation of revolutionaries by trade with high *konspiratsiia* standards linked informally to mass organisations with a lesser degree of *konspiratsiia*. In this light, Kautsky's intervention into the debate on the Menshevik side takes on a certain interest. Kautsky endorsed the Menshevik stand on the definition of a party member – but only because of the repressive underground conditions faced by the Party in absolutist Russia. In the case of open societies such as England, Switzerland and France, announced Kautsky, Lenin's formulation would be the better one.

In justifying his opinion, Kautsky unwittingly and ironically paints a picture of the underground much like the one in WITBD. Kautsky remembered the period of the Bismarck anti-socialist laws when the German Party became something of a *Geheimbund* or secret society. 'We tried to include in our organisations only people actually needed – someone to work on publication, shipment and distribution of literature, someone whose job was acquiring and spending financial resources, or setting up demonstrations, etc.' Such organisations could not go beyond certain minimal boundaries if they wanted to remain workable and secure from *provaly*. Attached to these narrow party organisations were wider peripheral organisations such as trade unions and singing societies.[122]

---

[121] Martov 1904a, p. 13.
[122] *Iskra*, No. 66 (15 May 1904). *Provaly* is the Russian word used in the *Iskra* version of Kautsky's letter.

The dispute over whether members of these wider organisations should or should not be called 'party members' is a superficial one compared to the overlap between Kautsky and Lenin on actual underground institutions. Kautsky obviously was not familiar with WITBD, but had he been, he probably would have been *more* sympathetic to Lenin. No wonder that Bolshevik polemicists such as Bogdanov claimed that Kautsky really supported Bolshevik organisational principles.[123]

To all of this favourable use of Lenin-associated vocabulary we must add Plekhanov's defence both of the phrase and of the tactic 'go to all classes' – a defence mounted against Lenin himself. When Lenin attacked the Menshevik *zemstvo* campaign plan in late 1904, Plekhanov supported the plan by saying it was an implementation of Lenin's WITBD slogan. This argument undoubtedly irritated Plekhanov's fellow *Iskra* editors even more than it did Lenin.[124]

There was *one* party norm for which Lenin made a strong case in WITBD that was openly rejected by the Mensheviks. This norm was division of labour and specialisation of functions. Without denying that some such arrangement was expedient, the Mensheviks were concerned lest people confined to a narrow speciality turn into soulless cogs in the machine. Cherevanin warned against assigning just one function to one individual. This was too restrictive – each individual should have two or three functions.[125] Trotsky also chided the Bolsheviks for leaving the local *praktiki* without wide political horizons.[126] This dislike of over-specialisation was a common theme in other Menshevik polemics.

The ubiquity of WITBD's technical vocabulary is only a partial tribute to WITBD. Menshevik leaders adapted these norms because they made sense, which is unsurprising since they had evolved in practice before Lenin wrote them down.

Instead of providing support for the textbook interpretation, the factional polemics of 1904 undermine it. WITBD itself had a relatively low profile, especially in comparison with *Letter to a Comrade* and *One Step Forward, Two*

---

[123] Shutskever 1925, pp. 160–1.

[124] Plekhanov 1905 (reprinted in Plekhanov 1923–7, 13, pp. 169–87). Compare to Potresov 2002, pp. 67–120, articles written at the same time but attacking WITBD for its 'go to all classes' programme.

[125] Cherevanin 1904, p. 51, see p. 16.

[126] See Trotskii 1904, pp. 59–64 on division of labour. Trotsky seems to think that

*Steps Back*, both published in 1904. Even more revealing is the ragbag of offhand comments by Lenin and careless expressions by unsophisticated *praktiki* that the Mensheviks of 1904 felt compelled to use in documenting their anti-Lenin case. But at least the Mensheviks made an effort to provide documentation, which is more than can be said for Rosa Luxemburg's fantasies.

On close inspection, the famous prophecies of 1904 look somewhat tarnished. Luxemburg's prophecy seems to be that Lenin's hyper-centralism will cause the Party to be so conservatively suspicious of popular unrest that it will miss the revolution – a prediction hardly borne out by the events of 1917. Trotsky's prediction at first sight looks better: the party organisation will substitute itself for the Party, and so on. There are only two problems. The first is that the dynamics of substitution are hard at work in the most democratic of organisations, as shown by Robert Michels's study of 'the iron law of oligarchy' in the SPD. The existence of a similar process within Bolshevism proves nothing about the consequences of Lenin's particular vision.

The other problem is that Trotsky himself meant something quite different by his accusation. For him, 'substitutionism' is defined by the contrast with what I call Menshevik campaignism, since the heart of the positive Menshevik programme in 1904 was the call for a certain type of centrally-directed mobilisation campaign. *Our Political Tasks* can be considered a prophetic critique only if we believe that future Leninist parties did not undertake massive propaganda and mobilisation campaigns aimed at instigating the workers against the bourgeoisie. Thus, Trotsky's prophecy is either true but misleading, or false but based on Trotsky's actual argument.

Another Menshevik prophecy of 1904 specifically about Lenin has, unfortunately, been forgotten. In his programmatic articles in December 1903/January 1904, Akselrod predicted that Lenin would turn out to be another Struve in a somewhat different guise, that is, an orthodox Marxist who ended up doing more for the liberal cause of political freedom than for socialism. 'To complete its malicious irony, history will perhaps place at the head of this bourgeois revolutionary organisation, not just a Social Democrat, but the very one who by origin is the most "orthodox".'[127] This prediction

---

Lenin defends division of labour as a specifically Social-Democratic principle, although WITBD clearly argues the opposite.

[127] Akselrod in *Iskra*, No. 57 (15 January 1904). Akselrod explicitly drew the parallel with Struve. Trotsky also predicts that people like Lenin would be reformists under conditions of political freedom (Trotskii 1904, pp. 77–8).

grew out of the Menshevik critique of Bolshevism in 1904 and tells us a lot about it. After the 1917 revolution, Martov still defended Akselrod's words as a brilliant prophecy.[128]

On the other hand, the polemics of 1904 do provide support for the interpretation advanced in this commentary. I have depicted Lenin as a fervent Erfurtian who made optimistic (from the point of view of critics, over-optimistic) assumptions about the applicability of the SPD model to the underground conditions of tsarist Russia. Exactly this case is made against Lenin by Akselrod, Luxemburg, Kautsky, Potresov and even the Bolshevik *praktiki* who resented Lenin's over-sanguine demands for immediate worker recruitment. One way or another, they all accused Lenin of an over-optimistic unrealism about Russian conditions.

I argue that WITBD presents an Erfurtian drama which portrays a *stikhiinyi* upsurge that accelerates the spread of awareness and pushes forward both worker followers and worker leaders, while intelligentsia revolutionaries lag behind. This picture is confirmed by polemics in 1904 over the label 'intelligentsia party' and over worker recruitment. The Bolsheviks insisted that Russian Social Democracy had been and was now a genuine worker party in which the workers, along with the local *praktiki* in close contact with them, called the tune.

In WITBD, Lenin did not so much set forth an organisational plan as insist on the general norms needed for effective operation in the underground. Lenin did not invent these norms. Instead, he gave a name and a rationale to what had emerged from the experience of the *praktiki*. This accounts for the continued deployment of WITBD vocabulary in the polemics of people who were violently opposed to Lenin personally. It also helps to account for the Menshevik retreat on issues such as congress sovereignty, membership definition, and 'intelligentsia party'.

Lenin emerges from this commentary as a man whose urgent priority at this stage in his career was to bring political freedom to Russia. This picture is supported by the Menshevik complaint that the Bolsheviks were too obsessed with the anti-tsarist democratic revolution and paid too little attention to socialism and the class struggle with exploiters. As the Menshevik Fyodor

---

[128] Martov 2000, p. 81.

Dan wrote in his party history many years later, 'Bolshevism took shape as the bearer of predominantly *general-democratic* and *political* tendencies of the movement, and Menshevism as the bearer predominantly of its class and *socialist* tendencies'.[129]

These words, first published in 1945, found no place in the emerging postwar scholarly consensus about Lenin, WITBD, and Russian Social Democracy. In fact, the issues closest to the heart of the two factions in 1904 have been forgotten. The aim of this chapter has been to show why the Bolsheviks were so upset with the organisational opportunism of the Mensheviks and why the Mensheviks were so upset with the tactical opportunism of the Bolsheviks.

---

[129] Dan 1964, p. 259.

# Conclusion

At the Bolshevik Third Congress of 1905, one delegate – M.G. Tskhakaia – gave his personal reaction to WITBD. These cool but appreciative remarks of a life-long Bolshevik allow us to put Lenin's book in proper perspective. Tskhakaia was disturbed at the way some delegates spoke of 'Leninism' and the 'Leninist spirit' of the party rules. He explained his own attitude somewhat as follows:

Two or three years ago I read WITBD and I had a very favourable impression. I did not feel any need to pore over it (I do not think I have read anything by Lenin more than once), because I did not see anything particularly earthshaking or difficult in it. I was simply glad to see that a decade of practical experience had not passed in vain for Russian Social Democracy and that it had found someone who could sum up the implications of its *praktika* for organisational, tactical and party questions. Of course, Lenin makes mistakes and sometimes comes up with incorrect or clumsy formulations. No doubt he himself would now do a better job of formulating and supporting the same basic ideas set forth in WITBD. Still, I admire him more than any of the other writers of the younger generation. But let's not go overboard and start talking about 'Leninism', a term invented by our irritated comrades in the other faction. After all, outstanding leaders such as Kautsky and Bebel (not to mention Engels) do not have '-ism' attached to their names. When asked, I certainly do not call myself a 'Leninist' but a Marxist, a socialist, a revolutionary Social Democrat.[1]

Tskhakaia's remarks help us use WITBD to rediscover Lenin. WITBD is a fascinating historical document, but not because it is an pathbreaking new innovation or a charter document of a new type of party. It sums up the aspirations and the practical experience of people who tried to apply a particular set of assumptions to a particular situation. Making the effort to put WITBD into context will allow us to recover a sense of those assumptions and that situation.

The consensus 'worry about workers' interpretation has created, instead, a barrier between WITBD and its context. To make 'worry about workers' the keynote of WITBD and of Lenin's outlook is not just one-sided or distorted – it is to get Lenin completely wrong. This dire result occurred because scholars allowed themselves to be hypnotised by a non-issue, Lenin's attitude toward 'spontaneity'. 'Spontaneity' is a misleading translation of *stikhiinost* at the best of times. But the reason that Lenin used *stikhiinost* so much in WITBD is not because of any *crise de foi* or deep malaise, but simply because Boris Krichevskii used the word at length in an attack on *Iskra* in September 1901. The resulting polemical free-for-all leached all coherent meaning out of the word. Outside of Lenin's clash with Krichevskii in Chapter II of WITBD, the word *stikhiinost* occurs only fitfully in Lenin's writings.

Owing to the fatal fascination with 'spontaneity vs. consciousness', the creators of the textbook interpretation looked in the wrong places. They looked at Tkachev, Chernyshevsky and Bakunin instead of Kautsky and Bebel, Lafargue and Guesde. They did not uncover the shared assumptions and the empirical clashes that inform Lenin's polemics with fellow Social Democrats. They did not look at the extensive range of Lenin's writings produced in the *Iskra* period. When advocates of the textbook interpretation do make a good faith effort to incorporate a wider range of evidence, their picture of Lenin dissolves in a flurry of flip-flops and stick-bending.

---

[1] *Tretii s"ezd* 1959, pp. 340–1. This is the only mention of WITBD at the Third Congress. Contrary to Cliff 1975, it does not occur in the debate over worker recruitment (Tskhakaia himself supported Lenin's resolution). In 1920, Stalin spoke in similar terms of WITBD as a book that 'completely corresponded to Russian reality and generalised in masterly fashion the organisational experience of the best *praktiki*' (Stalin 1946–52, 4, pp. 308–9).

As we set about the task of rediscovering Lenin's actual outlook, the terms 'party of a new type' and 'vanguard party' are actually helpful – but only if they are applied to the SPD as well as the Bolsheviks. The SPD was a vanguard party, first because it defined its own mission as 'filling up' the proletariat with the awareness and skills needed to fulfil its own world-historical mission, and second because the SPD developed an innovative panoply of methods for spreading enlightenment and 'combination'. The term 'vanguard party' was not used during this period (I do not believe the term can be found in Lenin's writings), but 'vanguard' was, and this is what people meant by it. Any other definition is historically misleading and confusing.

Ultimately, the vanguard outlook derives from the key Marxist assumption that 'the emancipation of the working classes must be the work of the working classes themselves'. Sometimes this dictum is viewed as the opposite of the vanguard outlook, but, in actuality, it makes vanguardism almost inevitable. If the proletariat is the only agent capable of introducing socialism, then it must go through some process that will prepare it to carry out that great deed. Even though Martynov was a violent critic of WITBD, he brought out as well as anyone the vanguardist implications of Marx's dictum when he explained its meaning in a 1902 article aimed at a worker audience:

The autocratic government and the élite classes – our foes – all have experience, knowledge and organisation. The proletariat must attain these things, but they cannot be accomplished in a day. Each separate worker would be unable to arrive at all of this by his own thought alone – but, fortunately, this is not necessary. Since all workers everywhere have the same class interest, Russian workers can benefit from the century-long worker liberation struggle in Europe. 'During this time the socialist intelligentsia, devoted to the proletariat and in part itself emerging from its ranks, flesh of its flesh, using the knowledge of the present century and the experience of proletarian struggle, succeeded in working out a socialist science.' The Western proletariat has also worked out appropriate political methods – in particular, the Social-Democratic party that represents the interests of the class as a whole. 'Only this party is capable of creating and of guiding the liberation struggle of the worker class, only this party is capable of guiding the proletariat at the present moment of revolution.'[2]

---

[2] *Krasnaia znamia* (a short-lived newspaper edited by Martynov between the end of *Rabochee delo* and the Second Congress), No. 1 (November 1902), lead article.

Lenin's commitment to the SPD model and to the Kautsky merger narrative was not just intellectual. The essential source of data from which he derived his vision was the history of the European worker class from 1848 to the end of the century – particularly, of course, the history of German Social Democracy. No doubt Lenin had thoroughly studied *Das Kapital* and understood the doctrine of surplus-value, no doubt he had read Chernyshevsky and Tkachev and wanted to live up to the glorious tradition of earlier Russian revolutionaries. But the fund of knowledge that is the palpitating, living source of his key arguments and his rhetoric – the examples that bubble to the surface in those manifold asides that occur when he really wants to drive home his point – these come from the Erfurtian epic, the grand story of the merger of socialism and the worker movement that he thought had taken place in Europe.[3]

Lenin's political programme thus became: let us build a party as much like the SPD as possible under underground conditions so that we can overthrow the tsar and become even more like the SPD. Achieving political freedom was the centre of this programme. Lenin wanted political freedom because he thought it would bring immeasurable benefit to Russia, to the workers, and to Social Democracy. He gave advice on how to build an effective party in the underground, but the reason he wanted an effective party was to be able to leave behind forever the stifling atmosphere of the underground.

The vanguard outlook was coupled with an empirical wager on the spread of awareness. No one was so naïve as to think this would happen automatically, painlessly, without setback and crises. The influx of newcomers to the worker class would constantly slow the process down, and probably it would be far from complete at the time of the socialist revolution. All this was known to Kautsky and other spokesmen of European Social Democracy. Lenin knew it too, and yet the distinctive feature of his own outlook was an insistence on the speed and power of the spread of awareness.

The wager on the spread of awareness in Russia, despite all the obstacles placed in its way by tsarism, predicts Lenin's position in all the disputes surveyed in this commentary, starting with his cocky polemic against the

---

[3] 'It goes without saying: there must be, linked inextricably with questions of general theory, knowledge of the worker movement in the West, its history and its current condition.' Lenin 1958–65, 4, p. 326 (the 1900 draft of the announcement of *Iskra*'s publication).

venerable populist Petr Lavrov in the mid-1890s and ending with his indignation at the scepticism of Bolshevik *praktiki* in 1905. Starting in 1900, Lenin identified a new, powerful phase in the spread of awareness in Russia, a phase to which he gave the name 'the *stikhiinyi* upsurge'. The workers were beginning to take militant political action and by so doing they galvanised all of Russia. A revolutionary crisis was approaching and the days of tsarism were numbered.

The *stikhiinyi* upsurge forms the backdrop to the Erfurtian drama of WITBD, with its workers greedy for illegal literature and for political action, and its *praktiki* achieving miracles of inspiration. 'Give me an organisation of revolutionaries and I will turn Russia around!' – because an effective organisation was the only thing lacking.

Lenin's organisational proposals grew out of this context of excitement and opportunity. The revolutionary by trade, *konspiratsiia*, transcendence of artisanal limitations – their reason for being was not to substitute for a mass movement but, rather, to make a mass movement possible in the underground. But Lenin did not think up these norms, he observed them. Therein lies the real source of his influence within Russian Social Democracy – his perception of the needs and outlook of the *praktiki* and his ability to suggest wider horizons to them. To use Boris Nicolaevsky's expression, he was not just an empirical *praktik* but a *praktik* on an all-Russia scale.[4] Even Social Democrats who could not stand Lenin, even non-Social Democrats, had to respect this quality at least to the extent of adopting the vocabulary and norms he popularised.

I have tried to convey in this commentary the tone of voice of European and Russian Social Democrats at a time of revolutionary excitement. It is fitting to end with one more outburst, this time from a 1907 article written by Lenin's literary lieutenant Vatslav Vorovskii.[5]

> Russian Social Democracy finds itself in exceptionally propitious circumstances. Not a single other worker party was formed and began its struggle with such a high level of purposiveness in the proletariat. If other worker parties had to forge the class awareness of the proletariat by means of long, stubborn and often unsuccessful blows on cold metal, – our Social

---

[4] Nicolaevsky 1927.
[5] Vorovskii 1955, p. 392.

Democracy works on fiery hot iron that easily takes the desired shape. We do not yet have the historical tradition of the [European] worker movement that often becomes a huge brake on its development. Our entire tradition is this: the passionate faith in the good news [*evangelie*] of socialism and an inextinguishable longing for knowledge and struggle.

Annotations Part One
## Section Analysis

The aim of this part of the commentary is to briefly situate each section of WITBD in the overall argument of the book and to discuss passages that might present difficulties. I will not repeat information given in the overall commentary but rather provide appropriate cross-references. Brief biographical information on historical figures mentioned in passing in WITBD can be found in the English-language edition of Lenin's *Collected Works* and Robert Service's English-language edition of WITBD.[1] My aim is to provide information that clarifies the course of Lenin's argument. The chapter numbers of WITBD are given in Roman numerals while the chapter numbers of the commentary are spelled out. The location in my translation of each section discussed is shown by the page numbers in marginal brackets.

### Front Matter (Title, Epigraph, Table of Contents, Foreword) [673–9]

*Title*

'What Is to Be Done?' is a translation of *Chto delat?*. A more literal and perhaps a more vivid English translation is 'What to Do?'. *Chto delat?* is also the

---

[1] Lenin 1988, pp. 249–61.

title of a famous novel by Nikolai Chernyshevsky, the major figure among the radical writers of the 1860s and, in many ways, the father of the Russian revolutionary-socialist tradition. His novel set forth rules for radical living that had an immense influence on Russian radicals and revolutionaries in the second half of the nineteenth century. In particular, his ascetic revolutionary hero Rakhmetov became an iconic figure. Lenin greatly admired Chernyshevsky and his choice of title is rightly seen as a homage to Chernyshevsky.[2] But Lenin had other strong reasons to choose this title and, consequently, his choice does not indicate anything specifically Chernyshevskian about Lenin's argument.

We first observe that the title has little textual connection with the bulk of the book. Lenin's foreword does not explain the choice of title and, in fact, makes no allusion to it at all. Hardly anywhere in the book is the phrase used. Only in the last sentence of WITBD does Lenin really seem to remember the name of his book: '. . . by way of putting together everything said above, we can answer the question, what is to be done, with the short reply: liquidate the third period'.

The phrase *chto delat?* was commonly used by Russian radicals to demand concrete answers to practical questions: tell us, you who wish to be leaders, what we should actually *do* in the kind of situation that we are likely to encounter. *Iskra*, in particular, wanted to show that it could answer this question because it realised that people were wary of its emphasis on rooting out doctrinal errors and were inclined to dismiss it as 'merely theoretical'. Lenin's *Iskra* article of May 1901, entitled 'Where to Begin', announced that its aim was to answer this question.[3] In another article in the same issue, Martov made fun of *Rabochee delo* for saying that the 'spring events' of 1901 had given rise to 'a completely new question':

> For those Social Democrats who have never lost confidence in the historical
> task of the Russian proletariat, the 'completely new question' that the recent
> events have put forward is: 'what is to be done in order to organise the

---

[2] Valentinov 1968; Drozd 2001.

[3] The first sentence of the article is: 'The question "what is to be done?" has in recent years placed itself before Russian Social Democrats with particular force.' Lenin then explains that the basic *theoretical* choices have been made and that the issue is now how to take *practical* steps to advance along the chosen path. Thus Lenin uses the phrase *chto delat* to indicate that he is *not* addressing fundamental questions (Lenin, 1958–65, 5, p. 5).

proletariat into a political force such that each new crisis will find it in a condition of militant readiness [instead of catching it unawares]?' . . . The reader will find our own answer to the question 'what is to be done' in a special article in this very issue [that is, Lenin's 'Where to Begin'].[4]

In the autumn of 1901, *Rabochee delo* and Martynov in particular began criticising *Iskra* for failing to give the *praktiki* the answer to this fundamental question (phrased in various ways, for example, 'what needs to be done?'). After Lenin was well into the writing of WITBD, Martynov came out with another article that, I believe, directly inspired Lenin's choice of title. Martynov first demonstrated to his own satisfaction (using methods as intellectually fast and loose as Lenin's own polemic against *Rabochee delo*) that Plekhanov accorded only secondary significance to practical questions. While Plekhanov and *Iskra* represented the abstract theorising of the émigrés, *Rabochee delo* was the voice of the Russian *praktiki*:

> Social-Democratic activists in Russia, naturally, are interested first of all in the question: what is to be done and how is it to be done in the interests of the development of political struggle? But the Emancipation of Labour group, who are placed far from the immediate arena of struggle and who could be said to occupy only an observational position, do no more than warn the activists away from mistakes and only show them what should not be done, what should not be forgotten, and so forth. This unnatural relation between the Emancipation of Labour group and the Social Democrats in Russia has created the ground for mutual misunderstanding.[5]

Martynov also praised Chernyshevsky for giving a genuine answer to the question *chto delat?*, unlike Plekhanov and his friends.

We know that Lenin read this article too late to respond to it in the text of WITBD, although it is mentioned in footnotes. I surmise that Lenin made a final choice of title after reading Martynov's article. The title of his book was meant to say something like this: you claim that the Plekhanov group does not answer the question: *chto delat?*. Well, that may be somewhat true of Plekhanov personally but not of the *Iskra* group as a whole and particularly not of N. Lenin (a pseudonym only used once or twice previously). You

---

[4] *Iskra* No. 4 (April 1901) (both Lenin's and Martov's articles were unsigned).
[5] Martynov 1902, p. 13.

further claim that *Rabochee delo* stands more in the Chernyshevsky tradition than does *Iskra*? I will choose a title that will directly respond to your challenge that the *Iskra* group evades this fundamental question. It will also re-affirm *Iskra*'s legitimacy as the true heir of Chernyshevsky. I will call my book *What Is to Be Done?: Burning Questions of our Movement*.

This reconstruction accounts for the last-minute quality of the way the title is treated and for the otherwise remarkable coincidence that Martynov's challenge to *Iskra* in late 1901 used precisely the title of Lenin's half-written book. In any event, Lenin's little homage to Chernyshevsky is not a challenge to Russian Social-Democratic orthodoxy, nor a call to return to the ideals and prescriptions of the 1860s. Chernyshevsky was a hero for all Russian revolutionaries of this period. In fact, Chernyshevsky was more explicitly praised by Lenin's opponents during this period than by Lenin. Takhtarev, the editor of *Rabochaia mysl*, was a great admirer. He not only wrote a long article on Chernyshevsky for the Separate Supplement, but used Chernyshevsky in his editorials to underscore his point about not worrying about later generations. In response, Lenin protested that Chernyshevsky had his weak sides as well as strong sides.[6]

The editors of *Rabochee delo* were greatly inspired by Chernyshevsky's portrayal of Rakhmetov. In 1899, Krichevskii praised 'the mighty figure of Rakhmetov' as the prototype of future Russian revolutionaries.[7] Martynov later recalled that in his youth, 'I slowly crushed cigarettes on my hand in imitation of Rakhmetov, while a school friend of mine went even farther: he used a penknife to score his hand'.[8]

As with Lenin's other arguments in WITBD, the Chernyshevsky reference was a way of presenting *Iskra* as the voice of Russian Social Democracy's legitimate mainstream.

*Epigraph*

Lenin ended his *Iskra* article on the *Joint Letter* (6 December 1901) with a quotation from a 1852 letter from Lassalle to Marx.[9] The epigraph for WITBD

---

[6] For Takhtarev's authorship of the Chernyshevsky article, see Nicolaevsky 1927. For the evocation of Chernyshevsky in Takhtarev's editorials, see Chapter Four. For Lenin's protest, see Lenin 1958–65, 4, p. 259.

[7] *Rabochee delo*, No. 4/5 (September/December 1899), p. 11.

[8] Martynov 1989, p. 525 (a memoir written in the 1920s).

[9] According to the Soviet editors, Lenin got this quotation from a collection published

is taken from this quotation. The quotation as a whole reads like a defence of vigorous intellectual life, while the epigraph taken by itself seems to lay somewhat sinister emphasis on the party 'purifying' or even 'purging [*ochishchaet*]' itself. Lassalle's words as quoted in the *Iskra* article are as follows (the phrase used for the epigraph is in brackets):

> Probably few difficulties will be created by the police for the publication of your tract against the 'great men', Kinkel, Ruge and so on. . . . The government, I should think, would even be happy at the appearance of such tracts, for they will think 'the revolutionaries are squabbling among themselves'. The fact that [struggle within the party gives the party strength and vitality, the fact that the greatest sign of weakness of the party is vagueness and the blunting of sharply drawn boundaries, the fact that the party is strengthened when it purifies itself] – all of this is something that bureaucratic logic does not suspect and does not fear.[10]

*Table of Contents and Foreword*

In May 1901, Lenin informed the public that he was writing a small book that would put forth his proposed plan in a relatively non-polemical manner. There was many a slip betwixt *Iskra* No. 4 and WITBD nine months later, the main one being the dispute with *Rabochee delo*. As the Foreword states, the result was a hybrid: half-polemic with *Rabochee delo*, half exposition of plan. The chapter titles reveal the nature of this hybrid:

Chapter I: Dogmatism and 'Freedom of Criticism'

Chapter II: The *Stikhiinost* of the Masses and the Purposiveness of Social Democracy

Chapter III: *Tred-iunionist* and Social-Democratic Politics

Chapter IV: The Artisanal Limitations of the Economists and the Organisation of Revolutionaries

Chapter V: The 'Plan' for an All-Russian Political Newspaper

---

in Stuttgart in 1902. But Lenin's *Iskra* article is dated 6 December 1901. I assume that, although the book carried a 1902 publication date, it was available in late 1901. Lenin must have got this book literally hot off the press. This is another example of WITBD's extraordinary reliance on material published immediately before and during the time of writing.

[10] Lenin 1958–65, 5, p. 367. Note that 'party' in this period meant people of the same political outlook rather than an organised institution.

Only the last chapter is not given a polemical 'Good vs. Bad' title (and, even in the case of Chapter V, Lenin ironically refers to his opponents' use of ironic quotation marks around 'plan'). As the Foreword makes clear, the book can be divided into two parts. The first two chapters are concerned solely with issues brought up by the dust-up between *Iskra* and *Rabochee delo* (these are also the two shortest chapters). The next three chapters are devoted to the three prongs of the plan: political agitation, organisation, and the party newspaper's role as a catalyst.

Another two-part division of WITBD uses principal polemical target as a criterion. In this case, the division is between the first three chapters and the last two. The first three chapters are devoted to *Rabochee delo* (Chapter I to *Rabochee delo* in general, Chapter II to Krichevskii's article in issue No. 10 and Chapter III to Martynov's article in issue No. 10). In the last two chapters, Nadezhdin takes over as principal interlocutor, with an immediate gain in readability. Indeed, Lenin ends his Foreword with a quasi-apology for the obsessive polemics with *Rabochee delo*.

## Chapter I: Dogmatism and 'freedom of criticism'

*Section (a) What does 'freedom of criticism' mean?* [681–4]

'Criticism' was a code word in both Russian and German Social Democracy for revisionist criticism of Marxism. 'Freedom of criticism' was a slogan put forward specifically by revisionists within the Party. It thus brought up the issue of the proper limits of tolerance for ideological heterodoxy in a Social-Democratic party. Lenin makes clear he is talking only about intra-party affairs, not society at large. For Russian Social Democrats, the concrete question was not whether they should expel the 'critics', since the Party was not yet institutionalised enough to do this. The question was whether *Iskra* was justified in its aggressive polemical stance against fellow Social Democrats.

For Lenin, the essence of the conflict between orthodoxy vs. criticism can be formulated as: the reality of struggle vs. the hope of conciliation. This conflict was an international one. Eduard Bernstein and Alexandre Millerand were both *causes célèbres* in international Social Democracy. Bernstein was the originator of ideological 'revisionism' within the SPD and international Social Democracy at large, while Millerand was the first prominent socialist politician to join a 'bourgeois' cabinet. Boris Krichevskii of *Rabochee delo* supported Millerand's entry into the French cabinet until Millerand joined in official greetings to mark the Russian Tsar's state visit to France. Georg von Vollmar was a symbol of the more practical, less theoretical 'revisionist'.

The image of a 'swamp' was a common one, applied to people or groups without sharply defined positions and who felt uncomfortable with conflict. The fable of the empty barrel is taken from the works of the great Russian poet Ivan Krylov. Two barrels fall from a cart into the streets. The empty one makes a huge clatter while the full one is much less noisy. Just so, the revisionists want a noisy 'freedom of criticism' but have little of real substance to contribute.

*Section (b) New defenders of 'freedom of criticism'*                    [684–8]

According to Krichevskii, *Iskra* was intolerant and did not allow 'freedom of criticism'. In response, Lenin argues: by 'criticism' you must mean revisionism. Thus you want to allow revisionism a right to exist in the Russian Party – but you do not say anything concrete about who exactly these revisionists are.

*Rabochee delo*'s argument was actually: there are *no* serious revisionist or economist currents at present in Russian Social Democracy. *Iskra*'s crusade against this non-existent enemy shows its intolerance, and if we join in a single organisation with *Iskra*, we are afraid that we will be gagged. Krichevskii's defence of dyed-in-the-wool Bernsteinists quoted here by Lenin gives him a more legitimate grievance (and I wager others at *Rabochee delo* were uncomfortable with Krichevskii's remark).

The Mountain (Jacobins) and the Gironde were the radical and the moderate wings of the French revolutionaries after 1789. These names became symbols of any other radical/moderate split, and many authors talked about the Mountain and the Gironde in international Social Democracy. Plekhanov did so in the article in *Iskra*, No. 2 (February 1901), to which Krichevskii is here responding. Use of the 'Mountain vs. Gironde' terminology did *not* imply any *concrete* similarity between the Jacobins and 'revolutionary Social Democrats' or between the Gironde and Social-Democratic 'opportunists'. This is why Krichevskii's riposte to Plekhanov misses the point. This is also why the reaction to similar comparisons later made by Lenin – a reaction first by his factional rivals and later by modern scholars – equally misses the point. Lenin was not seriously comparing the *content* of 'revolutionary Social

Democracy' to French Jacobinism, but only its *relation* to the moderate wing of Social Democracy.[11] Since Lenin had been raked over the coals in 1904 for his use of the Jacobin/Gironde terminology, he was glad to add a comment to the 1907 edition of WITBD pointing out that Plekhanov had been the first to use it.

Lenin claims that 'the *stratum* of educated people' rather than the workers are responsible for revisionism in Germany. He uses a Russian variant of the German word *Akademiker*, which does *not* mean an 'academic' but anyone with an university education. The *Akademikers* in the German Party had been associated with various theoretical disputes in the 1890s.[12]

A. Mühlberger and E. Dühring provoked lengthy attacks from Engels. The 'socialists of the chair' are discussed in more detail below.

D.I. Ilovaiski was an author of monarchist textbooks. Starover (= 'Old Believer') was the pseudonym of Lenin's fellow *Iskra* editor Aleksandr Potresov. Nozdrev is a character in Gogol's *Dead Souls* with many unpleasant qualities. I assume the one meant here is his tendency to tell tall tales about the past. As in this comment, Lenin often calls *Rabochee delo* 'historical'. All these references are sneers at the *Rabochee delo* article 'Historical Turning-Point' (see Chapter Five).

*Section (c) Criticism in Russia*                                    [689–94]

In the famous 'from without' paragraph in Chapter II, Lenin describes the infatuation with Marxism among the Russian intelligentsia in the mid-1890s. The impression given in that account is that intellectuals in general are revolutionary. Section (c) of Chapter I (plus scattered remarks throughout WITBD) gives Lenin's actual view of this episode. Lenin describes the original flourishing of legally-permitted Marxism as a temporary alliance between future liberals and future revolutionary Social Democrats, both of whom wanted to topple populist ideology (the 'outmoded social-political worldview' mentioned by Lenin) from its dominant position among the radicals. The archetypal legally-permitted Marxist was Petr Struve. Lenin mentions here

---

[11] For more discussion of Lenin's 1904 comparison with Jacobinism, see Chapter Nine.

[12] Pierson 1993.

that more than one writer got 'became full of himself'. This is an allusion to the title of a story by Maxim Gorky.[13]

After the censor got wise and prohibited books and articles with real revolutionary content (Lenin continues), the legally-permitted Marxists used their privileged access to publication to propagate *tred-iunionizm*. This word is a *faux ami* that *cannot* be translated as 'trade unionism' (trade unions were not legal in Russia at the time). As explained in the commentary, it was the name current in international Social Democracy for an ideology that explicitly rejected both socialism and an independent class-based party and that urged the workers to limit themselves to economic improvement.

According to *Iskra*, the duty of *underground* activists – *Rabochaia mysl* and *Rabochee delo* both fall into this category – was to combat the open 'criticism' of legally-permitted Marxism as well as the *tred-iunionizm* that (according to *Iskra*) characterised the outlook of many underground *praktiki*. Given the urgency of such combat, talking about 'freedom of criticism' was not only dubious in principle but highly inappropriate in the specific Russian situation in practice. The tendency to reject theoretical debate as irrelevant only made matters worse.

In notes added to the 1907 edition, Lenin documented his own role in these events. He calls attention to his 1895 article 'Economic Content of Populism' that criticised Struve (that is, Lenin was among the 'one or two people' who had suspicions about Struve early on). Lenin also mentions that he 'participated in putting together' (actually, drafted) the 'Protest by Russian Social Democrats' against Kuskova's *Credo* (by 1907, Kuskova had publicly announced her authorship).

In a footnote found near the end of this section, Lenin says that '999/1,000' of the Russian population is corrupted by political servility and by a lack of understanding of party honour. According to Zelnik, this comment shows Lenin's contempt for the masses and stands in stark contradiction to the heroic role he assigns the workers. Note, however, that Lenin's target is not the Russian masses but a learned Russian academic. Note also that Lenin's comment praises the way a German Social-Democratic intellectual feels bound

---

[13] On legally-permitted Marxism, see Kindersley 1962. For an amusing memoir view of the superstar quality of some of the legally-permitted Marxists, see Gorev 1924.

by the decisions of the worker-dominated SPD. The comment is thus aimed at educated Russians who cannot comprehend the voluntary discipline of a party operating under political freedom. Thus the contradiction with the heroic mission of the Russian proletariat (whom Lenin sees as inspired by the SPD model) seems merely verbal.[14]

Herostratus jumped into a volcano just to ensure that his name would be remembered. Lenin's contrast between German and Russian Social Democracy is discussed in the 'Look at the Germans' section in Chapter Seven.

*Section (d) Engels on the significance of theoretical struggle*                    [695–99]

Lenin continues his attack on *Rabochee delo*'s indifference to theory (as shown by its dislike of *Iskra*'s aggressive polemics). Krichevskii cites Marx's epigram: 'Every step of a genuine movement is more important than a dozen programmes.' Lenin makes a joke that he repeats later in the book: 'To repeat these words in an era of theoretical disarray is the same as crying "Many happy returns of the day!" to a funeral procession'. This joke is much closer to the heart of Lenin's real concerns than his attempts in Chapter II to show the theoretical falsity of *Rabochee delo*'s various formulations. Throughout his career, Lenin makes this kind of argument: what you say is an undoubted general truth but to insist on it now, under the present concrete circumstances, shows that your priorities are all wrong.

Lenin says (and no Social Democrat, including the *Rabochee delo* group, would disagree): 'the role of an advanced fighter can only be fulfilled by a party guided by an advanced theory'. His following comment is a bit cryptic but I assume it means: the great revolutionaries of the past were *eager* to use the most advanced theory of their day, and in our time Russian writers such as Plekhanov are significant players on the international scene, for example, in the fight against Bernstein.[15] (It is highly unlikely that 'literature' here

---

[14] Zelnik 2003b, p. 219. Compare Kuskova's comment in the *Credo* about the 'the absence in every Russian citizen of political feeling and flair' (Lenin 1958–65, 4, p. 168). In Kuskova's case, this observation is tied in strongly with her entire political programme.

[15] An English observer writes in 1903: Socialism's 'growth in Russia has, of course, been wholly underground, and it is driven to be violent and non-constructive. Its party organisations are much divided, and have still to fight for political freedom before Socialism. Its chief doctrinal influence is that exerted by Russian exiles in Western Europe. These have included a surprising number of able men; but their

means great novels and poetry, which was not one of Lenin's concerns and in any event irrelevant to the point being made. 'Literature' in WITBD always means party literature: leaflets, pamphlets, newspapers, and journals such as *Zaria*.)

Lenin then gives a long citation by Engels on the importance of theory. This is one of two long *positive* quotations in WITBD, the other being the Kautsky quotation in Chapter II. The Kautsky passage has attracted much attention and seems scandalous to many. And yet the scenario outlined in the Engels passage is essentially the same: scientific socialism is worked out by intellectuals and then is brought to the German workers who accept it eagerly thanks to their innate theoretical sense. 'Without this sense of theory among the workers [says Engels], this scientific socialism would never have entered into their flesh and blood to the degree that we see today . . . The ever more clear awareness acquired in this way must be disseminated among the worker masses with ever greater zeal . . .' This is a classic statement of the good news scenario.

The Russian proletariat's immediate and urgent task is, of course, not to take power and introduce socialism but to overthrow the tsar and introduce political freedom. But such is the importance of political freedom, that this non-socialist task makes the Russian proletariat the temporary vanguard of international Social Democracy. Lenin was not alone in this view. Indeed, an important aspect of the enthusiasm generated by the impending political storm in Russia was precisely the growing revolutionary prestige of the Russian proletariat among European socialists. Plekhanov and Krichevskii sent a joint letter to the Paris Congress of the International in April 1901 in which they said that the recent worker demonstrations in support of the students 'exceeded the most optimistic hopes of the Russian socialists' and showed that 'Russia has entered into a revolutionary period with enormous significance not only for the socialist and revolutionary movement in Russia but for international socialism'.[16]

As so often, Lenin could find confirmation for his dreams in Kautsky's writings. Inspired by the events of 1901, Kautsky wrote in an article published in *Iskra* in early 1902:

---

ideas, conceived with reference to a despotic and agrarian environment, are not always of service to industrial democracies' (Ensor 1910, pp. xxiii–xxiv).
[16] Kirianov 1987, p. 206.

At the present time it is possible to believe that not only have the Slavs entered into the ranks of revolutionary peoples, but also that the centre of gravity of revolutionary thought and revolutionary practice is more and more shifting to the Slavs. . . . The new century is starting off with events that lead one to think that we are seeing a further movement of the [international] revolutionary centre, namely its movement to Russia.[17]

## Chapter II: The *Stikhiinost* of the Masses and the Purposiveness of Social Democracy

Chapter II contains the most famous and influential passages in WITBD and, at the same time, is the most neglected and unknown chapter in the book. An overall account of the chapter and detailed readings of the famous scandalous passages can be found in Annotations Part Two.

Chapter II of WITBD presents one of the strangest cases in the annals of interpretation. The whole chapter is focused on the situation in Russia. Lenin is completely unambiguous about his definition of this situation. In the opening paragraph, he says

> the strength of the present-day movement is the awakening of the masses (and principally the industrial proletariat), while its weakness is the inadequate purposiveness and initiative of the revolutionaries and leader/guides.

At the end of the chapter he says:

> The upsurge of the masses proceeded and became wider continually and with gathering momentum – it proceeded without stopping in places where it already started as well as conquering new localities and new strata of the population (ferment among the students, the intelligentsia in general and even the peasantry gained energy due to the influence of the worker movement).

His main historical argument is the assertion that Russian workers would have responded enthusiastically much earlier to the Social-Democratic message, had anybody made it available. If this message had been made available in printed form,

---

[17] Kirianov 1987, pp. 207–8. For more on Kautsky's views on Russia, see Donald 1993.

> nobody who is in the slightest degree acquainted with the state of the
> movement at that time [the mid 1890s] will doubt that it would have met
> with full sympathy both from the workers of the capital and from the
> revolutionary intelligentsia and that such a newspaper would have received
> the widest dissemination.

Any assertion that the workers would not have responded in this enthusiastic
way is 'diametrically opposed to the truth' and a shabby excuse for one's
own failings.

The only theoretical pretension of the chapter consists of attempts to show
that various formulae put forth by his opponents contradicted the most
obvious, the most widely accepted, axioms of Social Democracy. And yet
this chapter has gone down in history as Lenin's bold theoretical challenge
to Marxist optimism, as his anxious and pessimistic response to the inertness
of the masses, as an argument that the intelligentsia leadership is reliably
revolutionary while the masses are reliably reformist.

Some of the responsibility for this paradoxical result goes to Lenin: his
hasty carelessness, his 'polemical panache', and, in particular, his brief
parenthetical remarks on a tangential issue he had not thought through
carefully (the social origins of the creators of scientific socialism). Yet one
cannot help regret that historians – professional putters-into-context – have
remained blissfully unaware of the resulting challenge to their interpretation
and, in fact, have energetically assured the educated public that pessimism
about the workers is unambiguously the theme of this chapter, of WITBD as
a whole, of Lenin as a whole, of Bolshevism as a whole, and even of Soviet
and world Communism as a whole.

The chapter has three sections. The first section sets up the over-all story
about the inadequate Social-Democratic response to the *stikhiinyi* upsurge.
The second section introduces *Rabochaia mysl* as the open and unashamed
economists. The third section introduces *Rabochee delo* as the wishy-washy,
mealy-mouthed and shamefaced economists. Much later, Lenin summed up
the resulting picture more straightforwardly than anywhere in WITBD. In 1909,
he was exasperated with his erstwhile supporter Aleksandr Bogdanov and
compared the dispute with him to the long-ago dispute with *Rabochee delo*:

> It is an *exact* repetition of the story of the attitude of the *rabochedeltsy* (in the
> years 1897–1901) to the *Rabochaia mysl* people. 'We are not economists', cried
> the *rabochedeltsy*, beating their breasts, 'we do not share the views of *Rabochaia*

*mysl*, we openly dispute them . . . it is only those wicked *Iskra*-ites who have laid false charges against us, slandered us, "blew up" economism into a big deal, and so on and so forth'. Meanwhile among the *Rabochaia mysl* people – open and honest economists – there were not a few who had sincerely gone astray, who were not afraid of defending their convictions, whom it was impossible not to respect. But the émigré clique of *Rabochee delo* particularly specialised in intrigues, in covering up their tracks, playing hide-and-seek and deceiving the public.[18]

## Section (a) The beginnings of the stikhiinyi upsurge [701–5]

Lenin mentions a newspaper named *Rabochee delo* that his group, the Petersburg Union for the Liberation of the Worker Class, planned to publish in 1895. This paper has no connection with Lenin's émigré foes of 1901. Lenin says he got the information about this 1895 newspaper and about other matters from Anatoly Vaneev. This is mystification for the sake of *konspiratsiia*, since Lenin had first-hand knowledge of these events. Vaneev's death from tuberculosis caused by imprisonment evokes the heroic and difficult life of the underground *praktik*.

Lenin pays a compliment to the pamphlet *On Agitation*. This pamphlet was written in 1894 by A. Kremer with additions by Martov. It signalled a change in focus within Russian Social Democracy from 'propaganda' (intense study with a few individuals) to 'agitation' (enlisting support from the workers at large, mostly on the basis of economic struggle). Some within Social Democracy saw it as an early manifestation of economism.[19]

## Section (b) Kow-towing to stikhiinost: 'Rabochaia mysl' [705–13]

For the anonymous origins of the phrase 'kow-towing to *stikhiinost*', see the word history of *stikhiinost* in Annotations Part Two. Lenin tries to make this phrase the connecting thread for all his various polemical battles, although his pursuance of this theme becomes rather half-hearted later in the book.

---

[18] Lenin 1958–65, 19, pp. 85–6. Two of the people associated with *Rabochaia mysl* – K.M. Takhtarev and A.A. Iakubova – were in 1909 personal friends of Lenin and Krupskaya.

[19] *Ob agitatsii* 1896 (the year of its publication abroad with comments by Akselrod). An English translation can be found in Harding 1983, pp. 192–205.

I chose 'kow-towing' to translate *preklonenie* in order to bring out the proper note of servile obeisance.

Lenin analyses the early editorial line of *Rabochaia mysl* not because these views were still widespread in 1901–2, but, rather, the reverse: he feels they are so discredited that they will be an effective albatross to hang around the neck of *Rabochee delo*. For a translation of the editorial in *Rabochaia mysl* No. 1, see the Appendix to Chapter Four.

In *WITBD*, the document I have labelled the *Joint Letter* is usually called 'the economist letter in *Iskra* No. 12'. Lenin's fullest discussion of the *Joint Letter* is in the section 'The worker class as advanced fighter for democracy' in Chapter III.

For the meeting discussed in the first paragraph, see Chapter Four of the commentary. The 'V.I.' mentioned in the second paragraph and elsewhere is Vladimir Ivanshin, one of the editors of *Rabochee delo*. For his views on *Rabochaia mysl*, see Chapter Four and for his (not very economist) views on organisation, see Chapter Eight.

Lenin calls his opponents 'V.V.'s of Social Democracy'. V.V. was the pen name of V.P. Vorontsov, a writer in the populist tradition who tried to prove the impossibility of a viable capitalism in Russia. Probably Lenin has mainly in mind here a small book that Vorontsov wrote in the early 1890s called *Our Tendencies* that contained one of the earliest attacks on Russian Social Democracy from the populist camp. Vorontsov argued that Russian Social Democracy actually contradicted Marx's own historical materialism. He called the Russian Social Democrats 'neo- or pseudo-Marxists', 'Marxists turned inside out', who completely misunderstood the true nature of scientific socialism. A genuine materialist analysis would show them the absurdity of actually working to bring capitalism to Russia. Furthermore, a materialist analysis would show the absurdity of assigning to the proletariat – a class whose material position condemned it to passive execution of other people's orders – the role of a creative historical mission.[20] Martov recounts how he tried his hand at refuting Vorontsov's book in one of his first polemical efforts but got too bogged down in objecting to every phrase and finally gave it up.[21]

---

[20] Vorontsov 1893, pp. 137–9.
[21] Martov 1975, p. 179.

N.K. Mikhailovsky and N.I. Kareev are other writers who pictured Marxism as a creed of passive fatalism – a portrait naturally regarded by Social Democrats as a parody of the real thing.

Lenin's translation of the Kautsky passage has received criticism. John Kautsky objects that by translating *urwüchsig* as 'spontaneous', Lenin is illegitimately piggy-backing his own viewpoint onto Kautsky. John Kautsky is probably correct that *urwüchsig* is not a good translation of 'spontaneous' – but this does not mean it is an inadequate translation of *stikhiinyi* ('elemental' is one English translation of *urwüchsig* found in dictionaries). As it happens, Krichevskii used *stikhiinyi* when he paraphrased Kautsky's point in the *Erfurt Programme* about *urwüchsig* proletarian socialism.[22] Robert Mayer similarly argues that Lenin's innovation is due to a simple mistranslation of Kautsky.[23]

I have my own, milder objection to Lenin's translation. In the penultimate sentence, Lenin translates the word *Satz* as 'thesis': 'The new draft takes this thesis [*polozhenie*] from the old programme and then attaches to it the thesis mentioned above.' This is certainly possible, but I believe the correct translation is 'sentence'. Kautsky is pointing to a *drafting* problem: in the proposed new Austrian programme, the words 'the proletariat comes to an awareness' are cheek by jowl in the same paragraph with the seemingly contradictory words about Social Democracy filling up the proletariat with awareness.

In his picture of Lassalle's activities in Germany, Lenin evokes Hermann Schulze-Delitzsch. Schulze-Delitzsch was the archetypal German exemplar of what in Russia was called 'the *Credo* programme': economic self-improvement by the workers (in his case by co-operatives) and political leadership by a liberal reform party (in his case by the German Progressive Party). One of Lassalle's most extensive popularisations of Marxist ideas was a polemic entitled *Herr Bastiat-Schulze von Delitzsch* (1864).[24]

*Section (c) The Self-Liberation Group and 'Rabochee delo'* [713–22]

The very title of Section (c) is an insult to *Rabochee delo*, since it puts the émigré journal on the same footing as a fleeting group of workers in St. Petersburg (discussed in Chapter Four). Polemical as this section is, it is a step up from

---

[22] Krichevskii 1901.
[23] J. Kautsky 1994; Mayer 1994.
[24] Steenson 1981, pp. 7, 11.

the demagoguery of the previous section. Here, Lenin is making his real case, namely, that *Rabochee delo* is wishy-washy, eclectic, unsteady in principle, and with a narrow idea of leadership. There is more substance in these accusations than in the charge that *Rabochee delo* was crypto-economist.

Prior to *WITBD*, L. Nadezhdin had made very similar accusations against *Rabochee delo*: the journal represented an inadequate, half-and-half, and uninspiring response to the heightening of the political temperature in Russia and the on-going 'rebirth of revolutionism'.[25] But, while Lenin presents *Rabochee delo* as semi-economist, Nadezhdin presents them as semi-political. As a historian, I prefer Nadezhdin's version.

Lenin discusses Krichevskii's 'stages' theory in a long footnote. For the 'stages' theory, see Chapter Five. Lenin's shock that the article was written in August 1900 presumably arises from his feeling that the *'stikhiinyi* upsurge' in worker politicisation had already commenced. Ludwig Woltmann was a proto-racist German sociologist.

Lenin likes to cite the writer Narcissus Tuporylov. Tuporylov is the invention of Martov, who wrote a satirical *Hymn of the Modern Socialist* as the expression of the economism of the *praktik*. Martov gave Tuporylov, the purported author, a name evoking complacent lack of imagination. The phrase 'timid zigzag' mentioned in one footnote comes from this poem: the economist *praktik* wants to advance toward revolution, but softly, carefully, in small steps, without bold gestures.[26]

Lenin quotes R.M., the author of the Separate Supplement to *Rabochaia mysl*. We know, although Lenin possibly did not, that R.M. was in fact K.M. Takhtarev, one of the 'sincere' economists mentioned earlier. R.M's article in the Separate Supplement is discussed in Chapter Four.

Lenin likes to repeat sarcastically certain phrases found in his opponents' writings. The main catch-phrases found in this chapter are:

'The worker himself has finally taken over his own fate, since he has torn it out of the hands of his leader/guides' (from *Rabochaia mysl*, No. 1).

*Iskra* tends toward 'the underestimation of the significance of the objective or stikhiinyi element of development' (from Krichevskii's article in *Rabochee delo*, No. 10).

---

[25] Nadezhdin 1903 [1901], pp. 34–5 (*Rebirth of Revolutionism*).
[26] Martov's poem was published in *Zaria*, No. 1 (April 1901), pp. 152–3.

*Iskra* prefers 'tactics-as-plan' and this contradicts the spirit of Marxism. 'Tactics-as-process' is preferable (from Krichevskii's article in *Rabochee delo*, No. 10).

Any worker movement develops 'along the line of least resistance' (from Kuskova's *Credo*).

'The desirable struggle is one that is possible and the possible struggle is the one that is going on at a given minute' (Lenin's paraphrase of R.M. in *Rabochaia mysl*'s Separate Supplement).

## Chapter III: *Tred-iunionist* and Social-Democratic Politics

Chapter III begins the business part of WITBD in which Lenin sets out *Iskra*'s organisational programme. In this chapter, Lenin defends 'political agitation' as it was carried out by *Iskra*, that is, in the form of written 'indictments' of the tsarist system as a whole. Since Martynov's article in *Rabochee delo*, No. 10 was specifically devoted to a critique of *Iskra*'s brand of political agitation, he is the main polemical target. The chapter has six sections, three more substantive ones alternating with shorter polemical forays.

*Section (a) Political agitation and its narrowing by the economists* [724–33]

Lenin first describes *economic* agitation and then urges Social Democrats to move on to the higher level of political agitation. The description of economic agitation in the first paragraph – even though it is devoted to what Lenin regards as only the first and 'lower' stage of Social-Democratic agitation – is a crucial one, since it gives us a paradigmatic instance of the effect of the Social-Democratic good news. The key sentence is:

> As soon as the workers saw that a circle of Social Democrats wished and was able to provide them with the new kind of leaflet that said the whole truth about their poverty-stricken life, their boundlessly heavy labour and their lack of all rights – they began, so to speak, to bombard the circles with material from factories and workshops.

Thus the Social Democrats begin the process, provide a framework for it, and the workers respond with passion. Economic indictments had been a great success, so why not political indictments? (The line about the 'instigating' effect of leaflets is a dig at Nadezhdin who seemed to give the instigating function solely to terror.)

'Political agitation' is *like* economic agitation in that it is based on 'indictments', that is, vivid depictions of concrete although typical abuses. Political agitation is *unlike* economic agitation first because it deals with the state as opposed to factory life, but also (Lenin is very concerned to make this point) because it deals with abuses and outrages directed at *all* classes, not just workers. This is the feature of *Iskra*'s political agitation that upset many Social Democrats who felt that the movement might lose support from the workers if it concerned itself overmuch with the problems of other groups. They also feared that the wrong message would be sent to the workers if the Social Democrats stressed too much what the various classes had in common (antipathy to tsarism) rather than what separated them (exploitation).

Lenin argues strongly that the workers *will respond* to political agitation as passionately or more so than they did to economic agitation. They will respond first because political oppression affects them in their daily lives and second because they have the capacity to be indignant at abuses that do not concern them directly.

Lenin then turns his attention to Martynov's formulation. Lenin never quite comes to grips with Martynov's specific tactical suggestion, although no doubt it is a vulnerable one (Liadov provides a good critique in his 1906 party history). Martynov did not want to *narrow* political agitation down to economic reforms but, rather, use a campaign for reforms as a way of demonstrating to the workers the impossibility of serious reform under tsarism and therefore the need for revolution. For understanding Lenin's outlook, however, the accuracy of Lenin's critique is not central. We should instead note that Lenin is here trying to occupy the common ground of Social Democracy and exclude Martynov. He thus insists on the commonplace that Social Democracy should not restrict itself to reforms.

In the penultimate paragraph, Lenin gets down to cases and lists political agitation articles from *Iskra* and *Zaria*. All these examples come from Lenin's pen (see Chapter Three for a discussion of Lenin's political agitation series). In a footnote to this section, Lenin underscores that *Iskra* did *not* neglect economic agitation.

Lenin ironically says that the 'politicals', such as the *Iskra* group, must have invented economism 'as a way of giving people mortal insults'. Many modern scholars think that this is the unironical truth (for a discussion, see Chapter Five).

The final paragraph in the section is an amusing example of how Lenin wrote *WITBD*. He clearly only at this point really noticed the phrase 'economic struggle of the workers with the owners and the government'. As the reader will soon discover, it becomes Lenin's favourite catch-phrase and, in line with his usual rhetorical technique, he repeats it incessantly.

*Section (b) The story of how Martynov made Plekhanov deep*    [733–36]

This brief section mocks Martynov's attempt to come up with a new and improved definition of propaganda vs. agitation. This issue is not entirely terminological and somewhat similar disputes on this matter arose with Prokopovich and Nadezhdin. It can also be seen as a forerunner to the Menshevik critique of Lenin in 1904. All these writers tend to see 'agitation' as a direct call to immediate concrete action. Prokopovich therefore condemned revolutionary agitation as untimely, while Nadezhdin condemned merely abstract revolutionary propaganda as untimely. The Plekhanov definition used by Lenin makes both propaganda and agitation a matter of changing the worker's mental outlook, of providing good reasons. Change the *awareness* of the workers, says Lenin, and concrete revolutionary action can be left to circumstance (see the next section, Chapter III, and the final section of Chapter V). For the critics, this mind-oriented definition of agitation leaves unanswered the question, what is to be *done*?

Lenin's concrete example taken from German experience has the odd effect of making it difficult to categorise Lenin himself. Is he a propagandist or an agitator? I suppose that he saw himself as providing agitational material in a *printed* newspaper for others to use in direct *oral* agitation. In the next section, he refers to himself as a *publitsist*, which I have translated 'journalist'.

Mikhail Lomonosov was a genuine self-taught genius who had a distinguished career in the reign of Catherine the Great. The sarcastic use of his name here does not imply any disrespect toward Lomonosov himself.

Lenin comments on 'how [Martynov] *begins* to understand, for example, that we cannot ignore the oppositional mentality of this or that stratum of the bourgeoisie (*Rabochee delo*, No. 9, pp. 61, 62, 72 and compare the *Answer to Akselrod* by the editorial board of *Rabochee delo*, pp. 22, 23–4)'. This remark is unimportant in itself, but does give a revealing glimpse into the nature of the polemical clash between the two émigré groups. If we look up the page references provided by Lenin, we will see that, indeed, in 1900, *Rabochee delo*'s

*Answer* scoffed at the idea of a significant bourgeois opposition to the autocracy, while, in 1901, Martynov gave a limited role to this opposition.

Two comments suggest themselves. First, note the care (not to say obsessiveness) with which Lenin has dug up and carefully documented a contradiction between two pronouncements of *Rabochee delo*. He seems to have gone through all the writings of this group like a lawyer gathering material for his brief. Second, note that Lenin makes Martynov responsible for the *Answer* of 1900. But Martynov was not then a member of *Rabochee delo* and never did hold the views expressed there. The real case against *Rabochee delo* that emerges from a comparison of these writings is not (as Lenin would have it) a timid evolution toward correct views, but, rather, the incoherence of an editorial board that by 1901 contained people with clashing views (as Martynov himself stated in his memoir).[27]

At the end of the section, Lenin quotes R.M. (= K.M. Takhtarev) of *Rabochaia mysl* to show that R.M. makes the same point as Martynov. This passage is a vivid example of Lenin's rhetorical tactic of using *Rabochaia mysl* as a universally acknowledged Bad Example in order to discredit *Rabochee delo*.

*Section (c) Political indictments and 'education for revolutionary activeness'* [736–41]

This extraordinary section shows Lenin's exalted view of the transformative power of a Social-Democratic understanding. The key passage is:

> if we do this [organise timely indictments] the very simplest worker will understand, *or will feel*, that the dark force that mocks and oppresses the student and the sectarian, the *muzhik* and the writer, is the same that oppresses and weighs on him at each step of his life. And when he does feel this, he will himself desire, with an overwhelming desire, to respond – and he will know how to do it.

In this section, Lenin also gives a speech to a fictional Social-Democratic worker – that is, the purposive, advanced worker discussed in Chapter Six – whose central demand is: give us knowledge! (The picture of the workers in this section is further discussed in Chapter Seven.)

---

[27] Martynov 1989.

In the first paragraph, Lenin demands 'all-sided' political agitation. This term is in explicit contrast to the term of abuse flung by both sides, the charge of being 'one-sided'.

Lenin mentions the *Iskra* articles in issue No. 2 that called for protests against the students being drafted into the army. This is yet another example of Lenin defending his own *Iskra* material. As it happened, there *were* worker protests, namely, the 'spring events' often mentioned in *WITBD*.

The phrase 'adding a kopeck to a rouble' was originally used by Petersburg economists (at least according to Plekhanov's horrified report in *Vademecum*).[28] The *Iskra* group did not argue 'the worker cares only about adding a kopeck to a rouble, we must change his outlook'. Rather, it argued 'it is a scandalous slander to affirm that the worker only cares about adding a kopeck to a rouble'.

At the end of the section are two important footnotes. The first sets forth the standard Social-Democratic conception of the economic struggle as a stepping stone to political struggle. This footnote contains the phrase 'revolutionary bacilli, the intelligentsia'. Lenin puts the phrase in quotes, but – no doubt assuming his readers were all closely following the *Iskra-Rabochee delo* dispute with bated breath – does not give its origin. The phrase was used by Sergei Prokopovich in one of his anti-Emancipation of Labour writings. Plekhanov responded by affirming the role of the revolutionary bacilli but denying that the role was restricted to intellectuals.[29] Lenin does the same thing here *en passant* by using ironical quotes and then substituting what Prokopovich *should* have said: 'purposive Social Democrats'. Lenin does *not* agree with Prokopovich about the equation of Russian Social Democracy with intellectuals.

The second footnote backs up Lenin's portrayal of the Social-Democratic worker by citing two first-hand reports, the first by the alleged economist Savinkov and the other by the Social-Democratic advocate of terror L. Nadezhdin (see Chapter Six for further discussion).

---

[28] 'The Petersburg comrades told us that they were willing to preach political struggle to the *intelligentsia* but to the *workers* they were only going to talk about adding "a kopeck to a rouble".' Plekhanov 1900, p. xlviii.

[29] Plekhanov 1900, p. xxxii.

*Section (d) What do economism and terrorism have in common?*　　　[741–44]

In the first three sections of Chapter III, when Lenin was making his own passionate case for political agitation, the word *stikhiinost* retreated into the background. The word comes back to centre stage in this section as Lenin uses the formula 'kow-towing to *stikhiinost*' to explain what Martynov and Nadezhdin (writing in *Svoboda*) have in common. 'Kow-towing to *stikhiinost*' now means 'accepting the continued isolation of *either* socialism *or* the worker movement'.

As soon as Lenin begins his substantive critique of Nadezhdin's ideas, *stikhiinost* again drops out of his vocabulary. Lenin's critique is discussed in the commentary in the sections on terror and on Tkachev in Chapter Six.

Lenin charges that the *Svoboda* group (= Nadezhdin) 'openly admits' that it wanted to 'replace [*zamenit'*]' terror for agitation in the opening phases of the struggle. This comment led to the only instance I know of a writer attacked in WITBD responding to a specific accusation. In his second edition of *Rebirth of Revolutionism* in 1903, Nadezhdin responded: 'Amazing logic! What kind of "replacement" is this, when we "openly admit" that the excitative role of terror ends at the threshold of energetic agitation among the masses'.[30]

Nadezhdin misunderstands Lenin's remark, which can be paraphrased as follows: the very fact that Nadezhdin sees terror handing the baton over to agitation after completing its excitative role shows that he replaces agitation with terror in the opening stages of the process. On the other hand, Lenin incorrectly accuses Nadezhdin of underestimating the 'revolutionary activeness' of the masses, since the excitative role of terror in Nadezhdin's eyes is mainly to galvanise the revolutionaries, not the masses.

A number of times in WITBD, Lenin mentions Akselrod's pamphlet *On the Question of the Present-day Tasks and Tactics of the Russian Social Democrats* (written in 1897 and published in 1898). In Lenin's view, this pamphlet was one of the first statements of what became the *Iskra* platform. Although Akselrod and Plekhanov became Social Democrats before Erfurtianism *sensu strictu* took shape in the early 1890s, Akselrod's 1898 pamphlet showed the solid basis for the alliance between the Emancipation of Labour group and

---

[30] Nadezhdin 1903, Appendix, p. 82 (I added the quote marks around 'replacement').

the newly emigrated *praktiki* such as Lenin and Martov.[31] A summary of what Lenin terms Akselrod's 'famous two perspectives' is called for.

Akselrod first asserts that although the Russian worker movement is in good shape and will not succumb to tsarist repression, it is still in the first stage of development. Whether or not the worker movement will accept 'the banner of Social Democracy' remains an open question. There are thus two possible perspectives or paths of development. One possibility is that the worker movement would remain apolitical and reject Social-Democratic leadership. Of course, the advanced workers as individuals will still fight for the cause of political freedom, but they will do so in the way workers did in Western Europe in the old days: not as an independent political force but as a weapon in the hands of the radical bourgeois intelligentsia.

*Or* the worker movement could develop along the path shown by German and Austrian Social Democracy. This path will require much more political independence and awareness on the part of the workers and (Akselrod remarks optimistically) there are factors in Russian life that can potentially contribute to this awareness. 'But of course, without the energetic influence of Social Democracy, these factors might operate in an sluggish and sleepy manner, so far as the political development of our proletariat is concerned.'[32]

As Lenin says in this section, the fight between orthodox and economist was adumbrated in Akselrod's 1898 pamphlet. Thus, whatever 'worry about workers' is inherent in Lenin's position (the worker movement *might* not become an independent revolutionary force, even though advanced workers can always be counted on to fight for political freedom) was already expressed by Akselrod in 1898.

Toward the end of the section, there is a long footnote that attacks an article by Martynov entitled 'Social Democracy and the Worker Class'. As pointed out in Chapter Seven (in the section 'Raising the curtain'), Lenin distorts this citation by leaving out Martynov's accusation that *Iskra* did not sufficiently understand the importance of a struggle with *stikhiinost* (*Iskra* gives too much

---

[31] Harding 1977 argues that Akselrod's pamphlet was a turning-point for Lenin. In my view, this assertion is exaggerated and based on an inaccurate reading of Akselrod's argument.

[32] Akselrod 1898, pp. 18–29. Ironically, Akselrod backs up his argument by citing the 'excellent article' by Peterburzhets on the strikes in St. Petersburg. As discussed in Chapter Four, this article was written by K.M. Takhtarev who went on to become chief editor of *Rabochaia mysl*.

'scope to the *stikhiinost* of the worker movement'). Martynov's words would have ill fit Lenin's campaign against *Rabochee delo* for kow-towing to *stikhiinost*.

Lenin employs the metaphor of a flood that unites all the droplets of protest in Russia. The same idea is repeated later using different metaphors – for example, blowing all the sparks of protest into a vast conflagration. The idea behind these metaphors is this: Russia is seething with protest and indignation against the tsar. But each protesting individual or group feels isolated and helpless. This will change drastically when word gets out, first, about just how widespread protest is, second, about the existence of a mass force that is strong enough and motivated enough to transform revolutionary overthrow into a matter of practical politics. Under these circumstances, an underground, worker newspaper dedicated to political agitation is in a position to start off a stunning multiplier effect.

*Section (e) The worker class as advanced fighter for democracy*          [744–59]

In this section – one of the longest in the book – Lenin elaborates on the strategy I have just outlined:

> But 'we', if we wish to be advanced democrats, must take care to *push* people who are personally dissatisfied only with their university or with their *zemstvo* institutions to face the thought that it is our political institutions as a whole that are worthless. *We* must take upon ourselves the task of organising an all-sided political struggle under the guidance of *our* party such that as much help as possible can be given and will be given to that struggle and to that party by each and every oppositional stratum.

(Note the sarcastic use of Martynov's word 'push [*natalkivat'*]': do not wait for circumstances to push workers and others to revolutionary opposition, but do some pushing yourselves!)

In this passage, Lenin says that Social Democracy should 'organise' and provide 'guidance [*rukovodstvo*]' for non-worker groups. How strongly should we take these words? We should remember that, when WITBD was written, other oppositional social strata had almost no revolutionary or even oppositional organisation. This situation quickly changed with the rise of the liberal Constitutional Democrats (Kadets) and the Socialist Revolutionaries. Perhaps Lenin was misled by Social Democracy's temporary monopoly of organised opposition and thought that Social Democracy could actually be the sole organised voice of all Russian oppositional groups and direct their protest in the same way as it aspired to guide and direct worker protest. This conclusion about Lenin's expectations was later drawn by Aleksandr Potresov, which was one reason Potresov gave up on the whole idea of hegemony as megalomaniacal nonsense.[33]

My reading of this section leads me to believe that Lenin meant 'organise' and 'guidance' in the much looser sense of changing people's perception of what was desirable and possible, primarily by *Iskra*'s role as tribune of the people and also by face-to-face contact where circumstances allowed. As the quoted passage states, the main aim of 'organising' non-worker strata was to obtain help from these strata, and the main help envisioned was providing materials for further journalistic indictments and exposures. Paradigmatic here is the factory inspector mentioned in Chapter V who wanted to be assured that his information was being properly used by a proper organisation. The main charge to be levelled against this conception of hegemony was not one of megalomania but rather the charge of being so abstract, intellectual and 'writerly' that not even the workers were really being organised to actually *do* things. This is the charge mounted by Martynov, Nadezhdin and later by Menshevik writers such as Trotsky in 1904.

The polemics in this section are more concrete than usual because Lenin is responding to direct criticism of *Iskra*'s political agitation campaign – criticism coming from both Martynov and the *Joint Letter*. The key charge, in Martynov's words, is this:

> *Iskra* is an organ of revolutionary opposition that indicts our system and mainly our political system, insofar as it conflicts with the interests of the most diverse strata of the population. We, on the other hand, work and will continue to work for the cause of the workers in a close and organic link with the proletarian struggle.[34]

The implication is that a group that displays so much concern about the problems of non-worker groups is no longer really genuinely Social-Democratic. (When Lenin was later criticised as Jacobin and as copying Narodnaia volia,

---

[33] Potresov 2002, pp. 67–120.

[34] Martynov 1901a. This kind of comment gives credence to Martynov's later assertion that he was the first Menshevik (Martynov 1989 [1925–6]) (see Chapter Nine for further discussion).

this charge is often what is meant.) Lenin responds by evoking the Erfurtian image of the Social Democrat as the people's tribune, in contrast to a secretary of a *tred-iunion*. The eloquent double portrait of Wilhelm Liebknecht vs. Robert Knight brings this out. Lenin says that his indictments are *vsenarodnyi*, addressed to the whole people. The ringing and emotional word *narod* should be given its full weight.

Lenin also responds to this criticism by claiming that all groups in Russia are ready and waiting to hearken to the Social-Democratic voice. In the previous section, he emphasised how eagerly the workers will respond to the good news and, in this section, he expands this picture to all of anti-tsarist Russia.

If you want to understand why a young Social-Democratic *praktik* might feel inspired, empowered and indeed ennobled by WITBD, this is the section to read. Through all the polemics emerges the glamorous picture of a tribune of the *narod*, protesting against all the wrongs perpetrated by tsarism and using inspirational words to raise up (in Robert Tucker's words) 'a vast army of fighters against the official Russia headed by the tsar'.[35]

In the opening paragraph of this section, Lenin talks about 'the general democratic tasks' of Social Democracy. These essential 'democratic tasks' consist of the achievement of the political freedom that is light and air both for the proletariat fighting for its interests and for Social Democracy fighting to bring socialist enlightenment and organisation to the proletariat. This task is particularly urgent in absolutist Russia. Since Lenin is an Erfurtian Social-Democratic sparring with people that he knows (although he sometimes affects not to know) are also Erfurtian Social Democrats, he does not spend much time in WITBD stressing the crucial role of political freedom. His views on this matter must be sought elsewhere. The debate in WITBD is not *whether* political freedom is an urgent goal but, rather, what needs to be done to achieve it. (At one point in this section, Lenin quotes 'the impatient reader' as saying 'Everybody agrees with this!'. Even the more patient reader should keep this thought in mind when assessing Lenin's polemics.)

In the 1870s, there was a movement among the young revolutionaries to 'go to the people', that is, go to the peasant villages to try to stir them up.

---

[35] Tucker 1987, p. 39.

Lenin plays with this hallowed phrase when he contrasts the strategy 'go to the workers' to the strategy he advocates: 'go to all classes of the population'.

Later Lenin supports his 'go to all classes' strategy by quoting the statement 'the communist supports any revolutionary movement'. This statement from the *Communist Manifesto* was particularly crucial for Russian Social Democracy.

Toward the end of the section, Lenin quotes his *Iskra* article from May 1901 (where he first set forth the basic elements of his concrete proposals) about the tremendous effect that an underground, Social-Democratic, all-Russian worker newspaper could have. The most detailed examination of these proposals is in Chapter V.

M.N. Katkov and V.P. Meshcherskii were iconic examples of reactionary journalists with financial ties to the government.

While discussing the *Iskra* article, Lenin cites the worker letter that complimented *Iskra* on telling the worker 'how to live and how to die'. For Nadezhdin's anti-*Iskra* reading of this letter, see Chapter Six.

In a single sentence later in the section, Lenin sets forth his complicated ideal for Russian Social Democracy:

> The party that will carry out this all-sided political agitation is one that merges an attack on the government in the name of the whole people with the revolutionary education of the proletariat and the preservation of its political independence, along with guidance of the economic struggle of the worker class and the utilisation of its *stikhiinyi* clashes with its exploiters – clashes that lift up and draw in to our camp ever new strata of the proletariat!

Note the expectation that *stikhiinyi* clashes with exploiters will 'draw in to our camp ever new strata of the proletariat'. The verb here is *privlech'*, a member of the same word family as *sovlech'*, that is, the word usually translated as 'divert' and which I translate as 'cause to stray'. The *-vlech'* family (equivalent to the *tractare* family in Latin) is widely employed in WITBD. Unfortunately, my translation was not able to preserve these verbal echoes. But note the following revealing contrast. When Lenin sarcastically used his *opponent's* word *sovlech'*, he gets into trouble by seeming to suggest that the regular economic struggle pushed workers *away* from Social Democracy. In this passage, when he sets forth his views in his own words, he uses another *-vlech'* word to set forth the expectation that the regular economic struggle will bring workers *to* Social Democracy.

The final part of the section is an extended polemic with the *Joint Letter* (see Chapter Six for further discussion). In his response to the *Joint Letter*, Lenin writes 'we really have already lost the "patience" "to wait" for the blessed time promised us by all manner of "conciliators" when our "economists" stop blaming the workers for *their* backwardness'.[36] By 'conciliators', he means people who keep saying 'why can't we all just get along?' – for example, David Riazanov, who wanted to bring *Rabochee delo* and *Iskra* together. Lenin's dislike of 'conciliators' often exceeded his dislike of his direct foes. His life-long campaign against such people had a great impact on his political career, often leading to isolation but sometimes, as in 1917, leading to victory.

Appropriately for an argument whose inner content is defence of the political agitation series, the section ends with a listing of *Iskra* articles. The first article mentioned – 'The Autocracy and the *Zemstvo*' – is by Petr Struve, the archetypal 'legally-permitted Marxist'. This article is a late-blooming fruit of the 'alliance' between the legally-permitted Marxists and the 'revolutionary Social Democrats' that Lenin discusses earlier in WITBD. Most of the other articles are by Lenin.

*Section (f) Once more 'slanderers', once more 'mystifiers'*                    [759–62]

The chapter ends with a short polemical blast against *Rabochee delo* on the subject of 'bourgeois democracy'. To understand the debate, we need to grasp that 'bourgeois democracy' in the 1902 Russian context means *all non-Social-Democratic anti-tsarist revolutionaries*. According to the textbook interpretation, Lenin is worried that the reformist workers will follow the reformist bourgeois democrats instead of the revolutionary Social Democrats. In actuality, he is worried that the revolutionary workers will follow, *faute de mieux*, the revolutionary bourgeois democrats instead of the shamefully reformist Social Democrats.

The interpretational challenge of this section is a miniature version of the one presented by Chapter II and the 'combat spontaneity' passage. Lenin faces the same kind of polemical problem, namely, defending the heated accusation made by *Iskra* in 1901 that *Rabochee delo* was helping to turn the worker movement into a tool of bourgeois democracy. Lenin uses the same method as earlier: seize on *Rabochee delo*'s criticism of *Iskra* for

---

[36] Lenin 1958–65, 6, p. 92 [756].

underestimating *stikhiinost*, and maintain that *any* 'kow-towing to *stikhiinost*' is a betrayal of Social Democracy's leadership mission. The same polemical strategy leads to the same seemingly scandalous assertion: 'a *stikhiinyi* worker movement in and of itself creates (and inevitably creates) only *tred-iunionizm*'. Upon examination, what this assertion actually says is 'a worker movement without Social Democracy is a worker movement without Social Democracy'.

As in Chapter II, there is a startling contrast between the usual reading of this general assertion (the workers are letting us down) and Lenin's *concrete* argument about the Russian workers in 1901–2 (we are letting the workers down). Lenin asserts that 'the activeness of the worker masses turned out to be higher than our own activeness'. The workers are so determinedly revolutionary that they bypass Social Democracy in search of 'more flexible, more energetic' revolutionary leaders.

The section and the chapter appropriately ends with one of Lenin's more eloquent evocations of the SPD model that lies at the foundation of not only the 'go to all classes' strategy but also of Lenin's image of Social Democracy as a people's tribune. (In the 1907 edition, Lenin cut the final paragraph mocking *Rabochee delo*, so that the final word in the chapter is '*Vorwärts*', the SPD newspaper.)

One wonders if Lenin was well-advised to make the charge that *Rabochee delo* 'demonstrates with its hasty abuse that it lacks the ability to grasp the train of thought of its opponents'.

Lenin makes a joke about a publication entitled 'How may I serve you?'. This is a reference to Mikhail Saltykov-Shchedrin, the great Russian satirist of the second half of the nineteenth century. Saltykov-Shchedrin describes a wishy-washy 'liberal' editor who likes to think of himself as progressive and as battling the censor, but who is really quite ready to hide his views in order to keep out of trouble. Lenin loved Saltykov-Shchedrin and particularly his heavy satire against spineless liberals. Only a very small range of Saltykov-Shchedrin's writings is available in English translation. If we want to get a good sense of the *Russian* side of Lenin's outlook and upbringing, Saltykov-Shchedrin is the place to start.

Lenin refers to 'liberals who carry the Brentano view of class struggle and a *tred-iunionist* view of politics to the workers'. Lujo Brentano was a German economist (that is, someone who studied economics!) and a member of the group called the *Katheder-Sozialisten* (socialists of the chair, meaning professorial socialists). This group is actually better categorised as welfare-state liberals. John Rae described Brentano's outlook as follows:

> Brentano, who is one of the most moderate, as well as one of the ablest of [the socialists of the chair], takes nearly as grave a view of the state of modern industrial society as the socialists themselves do; and he says that if the evils from which it suffers could not be removed otherwise, it would be impossible to avoid much longer a socialistic experiment. But then he maintains that they can be removed otherwise, and one of the chief motives of himself and his allies in their practical work is to put an end to socialistic agitation by curing the ills which have excited it.[37]

Brentano was much inspired by the English trade unions and wanted to give such unions guild-like powers to regulate working conditions. He recognised that trade unions split the worker class into unionised and non-unionised sections, but felt that society was at least moving in the right direction if (in Rae's words) 'at least a large section of the working class has been brought more securely within the pale of advancing culture'.[38]

Catch-phrases from his opponents that Lenin likes to repeat in this chapter (except for the last, all from Martynov's article in *Rabochee delo* No. 10) include:

Social Democracy should have a 'close and organic link with the proletarian struggle'.

'Now the task stands before the Social Democrats of imparting a political character to the economic struggle itself.'

Social Democracy should put forth demands that 'promise tangible results'.

The 'economic struggle of the workers with the owners and the government' will 'push the workers up against the issue of their political lack of rights'.

'*Iskra* has a tendency to disparage the significance of the forward march of the grey ongoing struggle in comparison with the propaganda of brilliant and self-sufficient ideas.'

'The economic struggle is the most widely applicable means of drawing the masses into active political struggle' (from *Two Congresses*, also authored by Martynov).

---

[37] Rae 1891, p. 204.
[38] For Brentano and the 'Socialists of the Chair', see Rae 1891, pp. 195–217.

## Chapter IV: The Artisanal Limitations of the Economists and the Organisation of Revolutionaries

In Chapter IV, Lenin sets forth the norms he thinks should govern Social-Democratic political organisation in an autocratic country such as Russia. In Chapter Eight of the commentary, I argue (basing myself on M. Liadov and other *praktiki* writing in 1904–6) that Lenin's organisational proposals should not be seen as innovative or as advocating a 'party of a new type', nor should they be seen as a throwback to Narodnaia volia or other earlier Russian revolutionaries. Rather, they are a summing-up and an explicit exposition of the results of almost a decade of experimentation by Russian *praktiki* in adopting the SPD model to the political conditions imposed by repressive tsarist absolutism.

Lenin's organisational proposals are often reduced by modern scholars to his demand for narrowing the membership of the 'organisation of revolutionaries' to 'revolutionaries by trade'. He does, indeed, argue for something like this (although it bears repeating that Lenin's conception of party membership was much wider than 'revolutionaries by trade'). A better question to ask of this chapter, however, is the following: what is Lenin's view of the Russian Social-Democratic movement as a whole? The answer provided by Chapter IV is a rather expansive and participatory model, stressing links with the worker milieu, contributions from anybody willing to help, and wide recruitment efforts even into the secret parts of the organisation. Thus a typical argument reads

> The centralisation of the *konspirativnyi* functions of the *organisation* does not at all mean centralisation of all the functions of the *movement*. The active participation of the broadest mass in [distributing] illegal literature will not decrease but will *intensify* ten times over if the 'dozen' revolutionaries by trade centralise the *konspirativnyi* functions of this business.

The first two sections approach the question negatively: how *not* to do it. The next two sections sketch out Lenin's vision of the underground movement as it could be. The final sections respond to possible objections about 'democratism' and neglect of local work.

*Section (a) What are artisanal limitations?*                    [764–7]

Lenin defines the term 'artisanal limitations' or *kustarnichestvo* and then illustrates it firstly by a generalised version of his own experiences and then by using the first-hand observations of Boris Savinkov. Noteworthy in Lenin's portrait of a typical 'circle' is the expectation of sympathy and support from both workers and élite society. The vitality of the movement is stronger even than the incompetence of the *praktiki*. For the meaning of 'circle', artisanal limitations, *konspiratsiia* and *proval* (a police raid that succeeds in destroying a local underground organisation at least temporarily), see the discussion of underground terms of art in Chapter Eight. For Savinkov, see Chapter Six.

*Section (b) Artisanal limitations and economism*                    [768–74]

This section links up Lenin's long-held idea of the need to overcome artisanal limitations with his current polemic against *Rabochee delo*. In a manner completely typical of Lenin, the section combines tedious, clause-by-clause rebuttal of *Rabochee delo* (mercifully dropped from the 1907 edition) with one of his most eloquent evocations of the heroic *revolutionary* leader standing at the head of an enthusiastic mass movement.

Lenin recycles Plekhanov's joke about Social Democrats who 'gaze with beatitude on the posterior of the Russian proletariat'. This comes from the same imagery as the term 'tailism [*khvostizm*]'. The Russian proletariat is facing in the right direction and moving in the right direction. It is, rather, the Social Democrats who have been left behind by the proletariat and can only see its past.

For Narcissus Tuporylov, Martov's fictional economist *praktik*, see my earlier remarks on Section (c) of Chapter II.

*Section (c) Organisation of workers and organisation of revolutionaries*   [774–89]

This section, one of the longest in WITBD, sets out Lenin's basic proposal about the proper relation under the autocracy between the broad Social-Democratic organisations and the narrow ones.

In the first paragraph, Lenin recalls a conversation with a 'fairly thorough-going economist'. Some have speculated that this interlocutor was Martynov himself, who indeed did have a somewhat similar conversation with Lenin around this time, as described in Martynov's memoirs.[39] Nevertheless, unless Lenin has completely misrepresented his interlocutor's views, the conversation described here cannot have been with Martynov.

Lenin says that the economists 'continually stray from Social Democratism over to *tred-iunionizm* not only in political tasks but in organisational ones'. This statement is a good example of why we should not translate *tred-iunionizm* as 'trade unionism'. Lenin refers here to a non-Social-Democratic ideology that systematically restricts the worker movement to defending its sectional interests.

To those who find my rendering 'revolutionaries by trade' somewhat clumsy, I call attention to Joe Fineberg's translation of these lines from the second paragraph:

> A workers' organisation must in the first place be a trade organisation. . . .
> On the other hand, the organisations of revolutionaries must consist first
> and foremost of people whose profession is that of a revolutionary. . . . In
> view of this common feature of the members of such an organisation, all
> distinctions as between workers and intellectuals, and certainly distinctions
> of trade and profession, must be obliterated.

In the Russian original, both the workers and the revolutionaries have a *professiia*. In the English translation, the workers have a trade and the revolutionaries have a profession. Fineberg then talks about the need to erase 'distinctions of trade and profession'. Fineberg thus implies that only workers have trades, while professions are restricted to intellectuals. In contrast, the Russian text talks about ending 'the distinction between separate *professii*' of both the workers and the intelligentsia. All other English translations follow Fineberg in this regard. In this way the English translations import a whiff of middle-class élitism that is absent from the Russian original.[40]

Lenin's remark that 'all distinctions between workers and *intelligenty* must be completely eliminated' is usually understood as creating a place for *workers* in the revolutionary organisation. On this standard reading, Lenin is saying

---

[39] Editorial comments in Lenin 1926–35, 4, pp. 618–19.
[40] The Hanna and Service translations read 'the workers' organisation must in the first place be a trade-union organisation'. This further distorts Lenin's point (see Lenin 1988, p. 174).

in effect: 'we intelligentsia revolutionaries must make room for workers and make them feel at home'. Lenin's remark perhaps reads more naturally in context as making room for the *intelligenty*. Lenin insists that they have a legitimate role to play in a revolutionary organisation, so that their social origin should not be held against them.

Lenin mocks those who want a 'new model' of 'close and organic links with the proletarian struggle' (Martynov's phrase). Thus, ironically, the closest Lenin gets to the phrase 'party of a new type' is for purposes of mockery.

Lenin's discussion of the likely failure of the Zubatov unions – one that he felt was confirmed by events and to which he often referred in the future – is a highly instructive one for those wishing to grasp Lenin's outlook. N.V. Vasilev was a gendarme official like Zubatov himself, while I.Kh. Ozerov and A.E. Worms were liberal professors who read lectures at meetings of the Zubatov workers. The rhetorical trick of pluralising names – depersonalising and typicalising – is a common one for Lenin.

'By pulling up the tares, we are at the same time clearing the soil for the possible germination of wheat seeds.' Perhaps Lenin's metaphor can be paraphrased as: the brutal polemics in which we *Iskra*-ites like to indulge will help to remove the weeds that hinder the (natural?) growth of worker awareness.

The final sentence of this paragraph actually reads 'while the Afanasii Ivanovichs together with the Pulkheria Ivanovnas occupy themselves with their flowerpot crops . . .'. These are the names of an elderly married couple from the Gogol short story 'Old-World Landowners'. Pulkheria Ivanovna is much involved with her flowerpots yet hardly knows what is happening on her estate, much less in the world outside. I have taken the liberty of basing my translation on the rhetorical meaning of the allusion.

In his discussion of the St. Petersburg rules, Lenin concludes that they turn the Social-Democratic organisation into an 'implementation group' for the worker organisation. Allow me to record at least a doubt about this conclusion, since the rules give us only a foggy glimpse of actual relations within the Petersburg underground. More unbiased research is needed here.

The end of the section takes on Nadezhdin's article in *Svoboda*. Lenin makes a mistake: the quoted passage is not Nadezhdin speaking in his own voice, but his rendition of the words of an Ivanovo-Voznesensk worker. The mistake is a pardonable one, owing to the way the *Svoboda* text is punctuated (the identity of the speaker only becomes clear a few pages later). I doubt that Lenin would have been as sarcastic and aggressive as he is if he had realised that a worker was speaking.

The German demagogues that Lenin cites as examples, Johann Most and Wilhelm Hasselmann, were left-wing German Social Democrats who were eventually (1880) excluded from the Party, after which they adopted anarchist positions. Johann Most advocated 'propaganda of the deed' and terror tactics and, thus, Lenin's mention of him is part of his polemic against terrorism as a tactic. Ironically, in 1904, Rosa Luxemburg warned Lenin against following the example of these same flatterers of the worker's muscular fist.[41]

In the final sentence of the section, Lenin expresses his anger at Social Democrats who 'bring shame to the high calling of a revolutionary [*pozoriat' revoliutsionera san*]'. This is an allusion to a poem written in the 1820s by the poet and member of the Decembrist conspiracy K.F. Ryleev: 'Will I, at the fateful hour, bring shame to the high calling of citizen?'. The poem was a well-known one in the Russian revolutionary tradition.

## Section (d) The sweep of organisational work [789–95]

In this section, Lenin argues for obtaining more *part-time* work from educated society and more *full-time* work from the proletariat. The plausibility of both demands rests on an assumption of widespread eagerness to support the revolutionary cause. The passage at the end of the section on worker revolutionaries is one of Lenin's most eloquent evocations of the scenario of the inspired and inspiring leader.

In this section at least, the slogan 'send Social-Democratic organisers to all classes of the population' means 'make use of all the small services that only more established and above-ground people can provide'.

While responding to Savinkov's argument, Lenin happens to be reminded of Nadezhdin's thesis about 'middle workers' and veers off into an irritated polemic on this point. As often, in the midst of arid polemics we find a statement of a crucial aspect of Lenin's outlook:

> You must understand that these very issues of 'politics' and of 'organisation'
> are serious enough that we should only talk about them completely seriously:

---

[41] Luxemburg 1970 [1904].

we can and we must *prepare* the workers (and students and secondary-school pupils) sufficiently so that we will *be able to start a discussion* about these issues.

In the footnote at the end of this paragraph, the first quoted sentence is Nadezhdin speaking in his own voice. The second one is not. The person who sneers at intellectuals is not Nadezhdin himself (Nadezhdin explicitly opposed anti-intellectualism) but, rather (as noted earlier), a worker with whom Nadezhdin has conversed.

Saltykov-Shchedrin's joke about 'but' is one that Lenin liked and used often. Saltykov-Shchedrin relates that he was travelling in France and was listening to a conversation by French radicals about the need for an amnesty for survivors of the Paris Commune. They ended by saying 'But . . .', followed by an eloquent silence, indicating that, instead of actually doing something to obtain the amnesty, the Frenchmen just felt there was nothing to be done. Saltykov-Shchedrin translated this 'but' with a Russian proverb meaning 'there are some things that are just impossible'.[42] Lenin uses the proverb to scoff at any 'but' clause that thoroughly undercuts what the speaker had just said (for example, 'I'd like to help you, but . . .').

*Section (e) A 'conspiratorial' organisation and 'democratism'* [795–803]

This section responds to a miscellany of current criticisms of *Iskra*'s organisational proposals and the whole idea of a centralised national organisation. (i) *Iskra* is reverting to Narodnaia volia-ism. (ii) *Iskra* advocates a 'conspiratorial' organisation. (iii) A centralised organisation might engage in destructive revolutionary adventures. (iv) *Iskra* is undemocratic and should be countered with 'the broad democratic principle'. (v) Specialisation, expertise and division of labour harm democratic organisations. This section may give the impression that the goal of a nationally centralised organisation was more controversial than it was in reality. As shown in Chapter Eight, this goal was widely shared and might even be called a Social-Democratic consensus.

(i) Narodnaia volia, the revolutionary organisation of the 1870s that assassinated the Tsar in 1881, is discussed in Chapter Three of the commentary.

---

[42] Saltykov-Schedrin's anecdote is in *Za rubezhom* [*Travels Abroad*], published in 1881 (Saltykov-Schedrin 1972, pp. 122–3).

Lenin's comment that *Iskra* should be flattered by the accusation of Narodnaia volia-ism is not an endorsement of Narodnaia volia. Lenin is saying: any orthodox revolutionary Social Democrat will be accused by the 'economists' of being an advocate of Narodnaia volia-ism. Even *Rabochaia gazeta*, the short-lived newspaper that was designated the party's official organ by the First Congress in 1898, faced this accusation. *Iskra* would certainly feel slighted if it were left out.

Instead of an endorsement, the actual implication of Lenin's comment is: what *unites* us with Narodnaia volia is something *common* to all serious revolutionary organisations, including Zemlia i volia (the predecessor organisation of Narodnaia volia) and others (primarily, of course, the SPD). What *separates* us from Narodnaia volia is the very core of our being, namely, the aspiration to merge socialism and the worker movement. Such an aspiration was not even within the ken of Narodnaia volia.

This passage thus creates difficulties for the common assumption that Lenin's organisational proposals were inspired by Narodnaia volia. In his translation, S.V. Utechin faces up to the difficulty with the following intriguing footnote:

> The organisation of *Zemlia i Volya* was rather loose and decentralised. This was one of the reasons for dissatisfaction on the part of those members who later formed *Narodnaia volia*. It was in fact the latter's organisation that served Lenin as a model. Lenin may have been genuinely mistaken here – possibly taking the known views of the *Zemlia i Volya* group in St. Petersburg as representing the actual state of affairs in the organisation.[43]

Utechin is so sure where Lenin got his ideas that, if Lenin says something different, then he must be mistaken. Lenin evidently did not know much about the Russian revolutionary tradition that nonetheless was his central inspiration. As shown in the Introduction, this kind of convoluted reasoning is typical of the more knowledgeable defenders of the textbook interpretation.

(ii) Lenin here responds to the charge that *Iskra* advocates an 'conspiratorial organisation' by making clear the distinction between *konspiratsiia* and conspiracy (even though he makes a play on words to show how they overlap). He refers to his own article of 1897, 'Tasks of the Russian Social Democrats', discussed in Chapter Two of the commentary.

---

[43] Lenin 1963, p. 155.

Lenin alludes to the following statement by Krichevskii in *Rabochee delo*, No. 10:

> The teaching of Marx and Engels forever put an end to the conspiratorial outlook and methods of revolutionary struggle. The purposive work of revolutionising minds and social relations that took pride of place with Social Democracy had nothing in common with the well-thought-out planning of the conspirator. [The full passage can be found in the Appendix to Chapter Five.]

(iii) Lenin here answers the worry that a centralised organisation will push local organisations into battles beyond their strength. Note the contrast with the better-known accusation of Rosa Luxemburg that Lenin's organisational scheme would lead to *lack* of action even when revolutionary action was possible. The V.Z. cited here is Vera Zasulich, from her article on Nadezhdin mentioned in Chapter Six.

(iv) Lenin interprets *Rabochee delo*'s call for a 'broad democratic principle' as a call for elections and referenda in local underground organisations. *Rabochee delo* was actually talking about *Iskra*'s relation to *Rabochee delo* itself and to local committees as a whole. The issue of elections within local organisations became more of an issue *after* the publication of WITBD and the protest stemmed not from émigré circles, as asserted by Lenin here, but rather from local *praktiki*.

Lenin points to the open sessions of the party congresses in Germany as a sign of the SPD's democratism. In 1904, the principle of congress sovereignty was the key plank in the Bolshevik platform (see Chapter Nine).

Lenin's evocation of the 'selection of the fittest' that is imposed by 'full glasnost, elections and universal monitoring' could have been used by informed observers such as M. Ostrogorski and Robert Michels as an example of utter naïveté about the reality of intra-party democracy in the West.[44] Lenin's comparison of the 'open political arena' to a stage open before spectators perhaps reveals this naïveté, since what spectators see on stage is an elaborate illusion and much necessary machinery is carefully hidden from view.

During the *perestroika* era in the late 1980s, I kept up with the use of Lenin in polemics of the time. I do not recall that anybody remembered Lenin's stirring defence of glasnost in WITBD.

---

[44] Ostrogorski 1902 and Michels 1962 [1911].

Lenin asks: 'Is it thinkable here in Russia that everybody "who accepts the party programme and supports the party insofar as he can" will monitor each step of a revolutionary/*konspirator*?'. As pointed out in Chapter Nine, this was *not* the issue at dispute between Mensheviks and Bolsheviks when they clashed over the definition of a party member at the Second Congress, since Martov and Akselrod made clear that they did not envision any such monitoring by party members at large of the activities of the secret part of the organisation.

The revolutionaries mentioned in the quotation from E. Serebriakov – I.N. Myshkin and the rest – are figures from the 1870s. The original Areopagus in ancient Athens was a body of elders with vast indefinite powers to control social mores.

(v) Here, Lenin stands up for division of labour and specialisation against the 'primitive democracy' that is hostile to representative institutions and the use of expert civil servants. As witnesses, Lenin calls on Kautsky as well as Sidney and Beatrice Webb. Lenin seems to have completely forgotten about the existence of this passage by 1917, since otherwise, one imagines, he would not have written as he did in *State and Revolution*:

> One of the 'founders' of modern opportunism, the former Social Democrat Eduard Bernstein, has more than once exercised his talents in repeating the vulgar bourgeois jeers at 'primitive' democracy. Like all opportunists, including the present-day Kautskyists, he fails completely to understand that, first of all the transition from capitalism to socialism is *impossible* without a 'return', in some measure, to 'primitive' democracy. . . .
>
> Bernstein's renegade book *The Presuppositions of Socialism* wars against 'primitive' democracy, against what he calls 'doctrinaire democratism' – imperative mandates, officials who receive no pay, the central representative without power and so forth. To prove that 'primitive' democratism is not viable, Bernstein refers to the experience of the English *tred-iuniony*, as interpreted by the Webbs.[45]

Beatrice and Sidney Webb already had an international reputation by the 1890s (we might call them 'world-wide Webbs'). Lenin translated into Russian their 929-page book *Industrial Democracy*, an exhaustive examination of the world of English *tred-iunionizm*. Lenin's Russian edition of 1900 is an impressive

---

[45] Lenin 1958–65, 33, pp. 43, 115–16.

achievement that must have given him a solid grounding on the subject. One thing that Lenin learned from the Webbs is a recurring theme in WITBD: *tred-iunionizm* does have a political side, called by the Webbs 'the method of legal enactment'. The implication for Lenin is that 'economism' is a somewhat misleading label. The real division between is *tred-iunionist* politics and Social-Democratic politics. The contrast Lenin makes is somewhat analogous to special-interest politics vs. the politics of social reform.

Kautsky's book on parliamentarism was directed against Moritz Ritting-hausen's advocacy of 'direct popular legislation' that would by-pass a representative parliament.[46]

The rule about local elections cited in the final paragraph comes from the same set of St. Petersburg rules discussed earlier in Section (c).

*Section (f) Local and all-Russian work* [803–12]

Many *praktiki* at the period wanted to focus on creating local or regional underground newspapers. In this section, Lenin explains why he thinks that a nation-wide press organ should be the most urgent priority. This section shows Lenin at his best. His Erfurtian vision and the concrete example of the awe-inspiring party press of the SPD are applied to concrete Russian problems in support of a proposal to which Lenin has obviously given careful and detailed thought. Even the polemics with Nadezhdin are more business-like than usual.

Lenin's sources for the number of local newspapers is the report by the Russian Social Democrats for the Paris Congress of the Second International held in 1901. The report was written by Boris Krichevskii. Miliukov makes use of this report in his useful description of the underground circa 1900.[47]

The 'famous remark' about non-existent parliaments comes from Takhtarev's Separate Supplement to *Rabochaia mysl* in 1898. It is also quoted by Lenin in Section (b) of Chapter II.

The sarcastic remark thrown back at Nadezhdin – 'it always greatly upsets me', and so on – had been quoted in an footnote in the previous section. As noted earlier, Nadezhdin was relaying the words of his worker interlocutor, not speaking in his own voice.

---

[46] Kautsky 1893.
[47] Miliukov 1962, pp. 360–2.

In the final part of the section, Lenin talks about trade pamphlets [*brochiury*]. The Russian vocabulary for types of publications is different from ours, and *brochiury* can be fairly hefty – for example, WITBD itself was sometimes called a *brochiura* or a *knizhka* [little book]. Similarly, leaflets, or *listki*, can be fairly meaty by our standards.

In a footnote to this part of the chapter, Lenin recalls his experience quizzing a worker about factory conditions. The full details of this episode have only recently been established. In 1894 in Petersburg, Lenin organised a survey of factory conditions and composed a rather lengthy questionnaire. Only in 1985 was a copy of this questionnaire found and published. The 'one factory' mentioned by Lenin was the Port (New Admiralty). Vladilen Lozhkin (who uncovered the questionnaire) makes a persuasive case that an anonymous pamphlet from late 1894 describing conditions at this factory was written by Lenin on the basis of the material gathered by his survey. The WITBD footnote indicates that Lenin became somewhat disillusioned about this method of acquiring factory information.[48]

## Chapter V: The 'Plan' for an All-Russian Political Newspaper

In his *Iskra* article of May 1901, Lenin's plan for a party newspaper was the centre of attention. By the time WITBD was completed, it somehow got tucked away into this final chapter, which has not received the attention it deserves. The newspaper plan was Lenin's baby – his own original idea, one that he had laboured long and hard to bring to fruition. His ambitious dream that a nation-wide underground newspaper could galvanise Russian Social Democracy into effective and unified action is here supported with a great deal of ingenuity. Even the polemics of this chapter are more solidly based in substantive disputes than is usual. Appropriately enough, Lenin in this chapter defends the right to dream.

*Section (a) Who was offended by the article 'Where to Begin?'*                    [814–18]

Lenin dropped this entire section from the 1907 edition of WITBD as too involved in bygone organisational disputes. Nevertheless, the section does bring out

---

[48] *Leninskii sbornik*, vol. 40, 1985, pp. 19–26; Lozhkin 1986. The questionnaire attributed to Lenin in Harding 1983 is much less extensive than this new discovery.

some important aspects of Lenin's plan. We can perhaps see this section as Lenin's defence against mainstream Western scholarship. The basic charge made by Martynov and Krichevskii – *Iskra* had a dictatorial attitude toward the local committees – is one that is supported by modern scholars.[49]

Lenin first argues that *Rabochee delo* seems to think that merely proposing a plan – a plan that *Iskra* had no means of imposing on anyone – was arrogant.

> Can our party develop and move forward if merely an attempt to lift up
> local activists to broader views, tasks, plans and so forth is rejected not only
> from the point of view of whether the views are true or not, but from the
> point of view being 'offended' because someone 'wants' to 'lift us up'?

This issue is still a live one, as can be seen by Zelnik's similar accusation.[50]

Lenin then argues that other attempts to create central party institutions have failed. Individual members of the *Iskra* group made good-faith efforts to co-operate with these attempts, but the practical difficulties of creating a set of institutions from the ground up proved to be insurmountable, due to police-state conditions.

*Iskra* is indeed a self-appointed saviour of the Party – but what is wrong with that, since it makes no claim to official status and will only succeed if it can persuade existing committees? Somebody has to take the initiative. The 'network of agents' envisioned by *Iskra* was not an oppressive 'Agenten-partei' (Dietrich Geyer's term) intended to replace the committees, but rather a nucleus of locally-based leader/guides that would be 'created by the committees'.[51] (This issue is further discussed in the remarks on Section (c) below.)

I believe we should take Lenin's remarks here at face value in regard to his intentions. As Liadov argues, the distinctive dilemma facing Russian Social Democracy was that separate underground organisations that had grown up locally with roots in the local worker milieu had to somehow come together to create central institutions. Lenin's plan is an ingenious strategy for getting from A to B: from a series of independent local committees to a set of central institutions with enough legitimacy to provide genuine co-ordination (Lenin

---

[49] This scholarly case against the '*Iskra* juggernaut' (Allan Wildman's words) is based primarily on events occurring after *Rabochee delo* made its accusation (see Wildman 1967).

[50] Zelnik 2003b.

[51] Geyer 1962.

has this situation in mind when he talks about constructing the Party 'from all directions').

Whether Lenin's original intentions were carried out in practice during the actual *Iskra* campaign of 1902–3 is another matter. Getting a whole series of independent organisations to join the *Iskra* bandwagon inevitably proved a messy matter. In my view, there is no fully adequate scholarship on the subject of the *Iskra* campaign. Soviet scholars tend to assume that the plan was carried out according to intention (with only some obstreperous 'economists' causing trouble), while Western scholars tend to assume the plan was evil and dictatorial in its very conception.

In his recital of four damning facts, Lenin responds not only to *Rabochee delo* but also to the Jewish Labour Bund, the Social-Democratic organisation of the Jewish proletariat.[52] The relations between *Iskra* and the Bund, their disputes over the national question, were important issues of this period and had a widespread impact on intra-party rivalries. Since these issues play no role in WITBD, I have scanted them in this commentary.

Lenin announces this his four facts are not in chronological order. This is mystification for purposes of *konspiratsiia*. Lenin is the 'member of the *Iskra* group' mentioned in facts one and three. These episodes (1897 for first fact and 1899 for third fact) gave rise to the *Rabochaia gazeta* articles discussed in Chapter Two. The *Iskra*-ite mentioned in the second fact was Martov. The 'various circumstances' that prevented Martov from knowing about the status of the Emancipation of Labour was his exile to remote parts of Siberia.

The fourth fact refers to a failed attempt by *Rabochee delo*'s parent organisation, the Union of Russian Social Democrats Abroad, to convene a second party congress in Smolensk in May 1900. The actual Second Congress took place in August 1903 under *Iskra* auspices.

*Section (b) Can a newspaper be a collective organiser?*  [819–30]

More precisely, the question is: can a common, all-Russian, but, as yet, unofficial newspaper serve at the present time to help organise functioning nation-wide party institutions as well as a 'common assault' of Russian society against the autocracy? Both Lenin and Nadezhdin want to organise and lead the

---

[52] For a detailed analysis of the episode from which Lenin takes his four facts, see Nicolaevsky 1927.

actual assault on the autocracy, both of them feel there is vast revolutionary potential in the *narod*, and both feel that local organisations are the weak links at present. Nadezhdin's proposed scenario is: the local *praktiki* organise the people, the *narod*, for an assault on the autocracy. This activity 'cultivates [*vospitat'*]' strong local organisations which are then in a position to unify the Party. But, argues Nadezhdin, an all-Russian newspaper is not much use for the crucial first step of organising the *narod*, because of its inevitable distance from concrete local issues and its 'writerism'. In contrast, Lenin's proposed scenario is: use the all-Russian newspaper to cultivate the local organisations and then let these newly prepared leader/guides go out and organise the *narod*.

In the passage quoted at the beginning of the section, Nadezhdin talks about recruiting (or gathering, mustering) and organising the *narod*, the people. By the end of the section, Lenin is talking about recruiting and organising 'an army of experienced fighters', that is, the local *praktiki* themselves. Although the shift from one recruiting target to the other is the core of the disagreement between the two men, Lenin never makes it quite explicit. Nadezhdin stated the issue more clearly in his 1903 remark:

> N. Lenin writes a very eloquent treatise about a periodical for the 'leader/ guides', and dozens of Lenins set themselves to create such a periodical (an enterprise to which we of course wish every success), but as far as a periodical for the worker mass goes, at a time when the mass movement is growing as it is, we hear not a word, not a sound – as if this wasn't the most essential need of the moment![53]

Lenin does emphasise very strongly that recruiting and organising the *praktiki* is *not* the final goal. It is 'where to begin', a preliminary stage. The metaphor of brick-layer and scaffolding make the same point. Lenin rebuts the charge of 'writerism' by pointing to the final goal of revolutionary action. (Later on, the charge of writerism resurfaced with the argument that Lenin overestimated the role of a newspaper and its political agitation even as a way of cultivating militant organisations of the *praktiki*.[54])

This section presents two challenging translation problems, neither of which I managed to solve. The first comes from Nadezhdin's term *intelligentnye*

---

[53] Nadezhdin 1903, p. 32.
[54] Trotsky 1904 and Potresov in *Iskra*, No. 107 (29 July 1905).

*rabochii*. The connotations of this term are so difficult to catch that, very unusually, each of the four earlier translations has a different rendering. Fineberg has 'intelligent workers', Hanna has 'enlightened workers', Service has 'intellectually enlightened workers' and Utechin has 'educated workers'. To these we might add Zelnik's 'worker *intelligenty*'.[55] In my view, all of these are misleading and so I have given up and just used '*intelligentnye* workers'. The term is a label for the same group of people who were also called 'advanced workers' or 'purposive workers' (see Chapter Six for further discussion).

The other translation problem goes to the core of Lenin's argument in this section. We inquire of Lenin, *how* does the newspaper help organise the *praktiki*? The key word in his answer is *obshchii*, a word that occurs with striking frequency throughout the section. Unfortunately, neither I nor any other translator has been able to reproduce this effect by finding a single-size-fits-all equivalent for all uses of this one word. For example, in a single sentence, all translations (including this one) translate *obshchii* as '*common* cause', '*general* outline', and '*all*-Russian activity'. (I was tempted to add '*overall* mechanism' to this, but decided this was overdoing it.) I have also translated '*obshchii* press organ' as 'nation-wide [= all-Russian] press organ', since context makes clear that this is what is meant.

All these various facets of *obshchii* – common, general, all-Russian, nation-wide – point to a strategy of improving co-ordination by sharing information. This is done first of all by the political agitation articles that give the *praktiki* the big picture and (one hopes) teach them to be effective political leaders. Effective leader-guides 'are cultivated *exclusively* by systematic, on-going assessments of *all* sides of our political life, of *all attempts* at protest and of struggle by a variety of classes and for a variety of reasons'.

Next, the common/all-Russian newspaper will help local activists get out of 'the pit' that condemns them to ignorance of what is going on in the rest of the movement. 'The sweep of organisational work would immediately become many times broader, and the success of one locality would be a constant encouragement to further perfection, to a desire to utilise the experience of a comrade at the other end of the country without having to discover it oneself.'

---

[55] Zelnik 2003b, pp. 218–19.

Finally, actually working together on a common task would lead to practical co-ordination between different local organisations and eventually to the efficient transfer of forces, a corps of full-time roving revolutionaries by trade, and so on.

The first of Lenin's two metaphors (both taken from his *Iskra* article of May 1901) evokes bricklayers who need a thread to co-ordinate their individual activity. I unlock the allegory as follows: the bricklayers are the *praktiki* and the bricks are 'any protest and any flare-up'. The aim of the newspaper is to co-ordinate the local response to these protests so that they will eventually lead to tsarism's overthrow, instead of being easily 'blown away' by the big bad wolf of the autocracy.

While setting out this comparison, Lenin says that 'if we wanted to give commands, gentlemen, we would have written not *Iskra*, No. 1 but *Rabochaia gazeta*, No. 3'. *Rabochaia gazeta*, No. 3, if it had ever come out, would have had the prestige of being designated the Party's official organ (see the previous section).

Lenin's second metaphor for demonstrating how a newspaper can be an collective organiser is scaffolding. He remarks that scaffolding of this kind was not needed back in the 1870s, presumably because the problem at that time was for an existing central organisation to *establish* new local organisations rather than to create central institutions by co-ordinating existing local ones. But now, Lenin says, scaffolding is absolutely necessary. This explicit rejection of the 1870s as a model for 1902 is confirmed in the following paragraph. We again observe that Lenin seems to be blissfully unaware that the populists of the 1870s were actually his chief inspiration!

At the end of the section is one of the book's most eloquent passages. It describes Lenin's dream of an army that would raise up the whole people. (Note the links in the chain: a small group of exceptional Social-Democratic Zheliabovs and Russian Bebels, next a wider army of mobilized *praktiki*, and finally the whole people.) Lenin then cites Dmitri Pisarev on the topic of useful as opposed to harmful dreaming. Pisarev was a radical literary critic of the 1860s for whom Lenin had a great admiration. His wife Krupskaya tells us that Lenin kept four photographs of five individuals: Marx, Engels, Herzen, Chernyshevsky and Pisarev.[56]

---

[56] Pozevsky 2003, pp. 196–7.

Lenin's quotation comes from Pisarev's discussion of Lev Tolstoy's trilogy *Childhood, Boyhood, Youth*. Lenin's citation somewhat misrepresents Pisarev's argument. Pisarev identifies two kinds of dreams: those that run ahead of the natural course of events and those that go where the natural course of events could never go. The implication created by *WITBD*'s citation is that the first kind of dream is useful and the second harmful. But actually Pisarev argues strongly that the second kind is *also* useful – in fact, this kind of bold dream is more admirable and more important than dreams which simply run ahead of the natural course of events. This kind of dreamer indeed sounds somewhat like Lenin himself:

> The dreamer himself sees in his dream a great and sacred truth; and he works, works conscientiously and with full strength, for his dream to stop being just a dream. His whole life is arranged according to one guiding idea and it is filled with the most strenuous activity. He is happy, despite deprivations and unpleasantness, despite the jeers of unbelievers and despite the difficulties of struggling with deeply rooted ways of thought.[57]

In Pisarev's view, the harmful kind of dreaming is neither of these two kinds of dreams but rather the kind of idle day-dream that does not lead to any work or any action whatsoever.

*Section (c) What type of organisation do we need?*                              [830–6]

Nadezhdin advocated a Tkachev-style 'eve of revolution' viewpoint, something like: 'act today as if the revolution will break out tomorrow'. In other words, any long-term perspective or exaggerated interest in theoretical questions is likely to be an evasion of today's urgent tasks and to lead to 'overlooking the revolution'. Lenin proposes a more exalted criterion: a political tactic or organisational plan should be one that is 'definitely calculated on the expectation of *work over a very long period* and also guarantees *through the very process of the work itself* the readiness of our party to remain at its post and fulfil its duty during any kind of unexpectedness, during any acceleration of the course of events'.

He then argues that his newspaper plan fulfils this criterion, that is, it is appropriate for quiet periods when trying to recover from *provaly* caused by

---

[57] Pisarev 1956, p. 148.

arrests, for stormy periods when the *narod* rises up to overthrow the tsar, and for the task of turning the first kind of period into the second kind of period. Lenin again stresses the theme of co-ordinating action by sharing information.

At the beginning of this section, Lenin contemptuously dismisses Nadezhdin as a 'little Tkachev'. For the significance of this description, see Chapter Six on 'Tkachevs great and small'. The 'attempt to seize power that Tkachev's preaching helped to prepare' was the assassination of the Tsar in 1881 by Narodnaia volia. It seems that the central reason Lenin does not want terror introduced 'into the programme' is that this status implies a permanent organisational commitment to carrying out terrorist activity.

Lenin later argues that political agitation is an activity that will 'bring closer and merge into one the crowd with its *stikhiinyi* destructive force and the organisation of revolutionaries with its purposive destructive force'. This is easily recognisable as a version of the merger formula. Note that this way of stating the question – including the phrase about 'the *stikhiinyi* destructive force' of the crowd – comes straight from Nadezhdin. Lenin, as often, is making his point while using his opponent's vocabulary. It is, therefore, unwise to cite this comment (as sometimes happens) as a concise summary of Lenin's outlook. The concrete point of Lenin's argument here is the contrast between organised terrorism and political agitation. Political agitation responds (as Lenin thinks) to the concerns of the workers at large and therefore enables Social Democracy to be actual leaders of the masses whenever the masses take revolutionary action.

In a footnote toward the end of the section, Nadezhdin scoffs at 'revolutionary culturalists [*kultur'niki*]' who do not have an eve-of-revolution standpoint. Nadezhdin comment was not aimed directly at *Iskra* but, rather, at people who wanted to raise up the revolutionary awareness of the peasant masses – a tactic Nadezhdin felt was impossible in the short period before the day of reckoning. Nadezhdin called for more immediately destructive actions, such as arson and 'terrorisation' of landowners. This sort of action would 'beat the tocsin bell'.[58]

Lenin briefly considers two possible labels for activists who participate in his newspaper plan: 'collaborators' and 'agents'. The term 'collaborators [*sotrudniki*]' had a specifically journalistic flavour appropriate to Lenin's project

---

[58] Nadezhdin 1901, pp. 60–7.

for making a newspaper a central revolutionary project. Soon after WITBD was written, 'agent' came to mean the 'Iskra agents' who were appointed by the Iskra editorial board and who set up their own specific organisation in Russia. It seems clear from context, however, that this 'Iskra organisation' is not what is meant here, or, rather, is only part of what is meant. In fact, Lenin makes a specific contrast between his plan and agents appointed by a central authority. What he hopes to see is a network of agents that 'forms by itself' and that consists of all those chosen by the local committees to participate in the Iskra project. Local activists do this by contributing correspondence and accounts of local conditions, making arrangements to receive and distribute the newspaper, reading it carefully and using it as a guide for local agitation. Lenin's dream is that people involved in this activity will be able to link up local protest to the growing nation-wide assault on the autocracy.

Perhaps as a result of the connotation that 'agent' developed after WITBD was written, Lenin removed the sentence 'But we need a military [voennaia] organisation of agents' in the republication of 1907.[59]

## Conclusion                                                   [837–40]

In a brief epilogue, Lenin sums up the basic message of the book. How does he do this? Not by general formulae about consciousness and spontaneity, not by the slightest hint that intelligentsia revolutionaries have to prod innately reformist workers. Instead, Lenin sums up by telling the story of Russian Social Democracy: its brief moment of potential glory when 'Social Democracy made its appearance in the world as a social movement, as an upsurge of the masses of the people, as a political party', followed by its fall from grace into a period of confusion and unsteadiness. The polemical vocabulary of purposiveness and stikhiinost is used to summarise this story: 'the purposiveness of the leader/guides abdicated in reaction to the broadness and strength of the stikhiinyi upsurge'. Lenin's actual point is stated more directly in the following words:

> Only the leader/guides wandered about separately or went backwards: the movement itself continued to grow and to make enormous steps forward.

---

[59] Marie 2004, p. 74.

The proletarian struggle seized new strata of the workers and was disseminated throughout Russia, while at the same time also indirectly influencing the enlivening of the democratic spirit among the students and other strata of the population.

With the horror of a true Erfurtian, Lenin outlines the anti-merger that he feels is characteristic of the 'third period': 'the merger of a submersion in petty practical work with the utmost lack of concern in theoretical matters'. The ringing call to reverse *this* merger in favour of the true Erfurtian merger ends the book.

## Scandalous Passages

The vast majority of comment on *WITBD* – perhaps on Lenin's outlook in general – confines itself to two notorious paragraphs. In this commentary, I have bracketed these two paragraphs and proceeded pretty much as if they did not exist. I have also presented an interpretation of Lenin's outlook that is deeply opposed to the standard picture on every count. The question naturally arises, how do I account for these two notorious passages that seem to give such support to the textbook interpretation? This part of the Annotations provides the answers.

These passages were found scandalous at the time – as Vladimir Akimov put it at the Second Congress, 'no Social Democrat has, to my knowledge, ever attained such paradoxes!' – and they continue to scandalise today.[1] Both are found in Chapter II of *WITBD*, the chapter devoted to a polemic against Boris Krichevskii, the editor of *Rabochee delo*. I call the first one the 'from without' passage. I give it here in the standard English translation that is the basis from almost all previous comment:

---

[1] Akimov 1969, pp. 118–21.

We have said that *there could not have been* Social-Democratic consciousness among the workers. It could only have been brought to them from without. The history of all countries shows that the working class exclusively by its own effort is able to develop only trade-union consciousness, i.e., the conviction that it is necessary to combine in unions, fight the employers, and strive to compel the government to pass necessary labour legislation, etc. The teachings of socialism, however, grew out of the philosophic, historical and economic theories elaborated by educated representatives of the propertied classes, by the intelligentsia. By their social status, the founders of modern scientific socialism, Marx and Engels, belonged themselves to the bourgeois intelligentsia.[2]

My label for the second passage is 'combat spontaneity'. Here is the 'combat spontaneity' passage in the standard English translation:

There is much talk of spontaneity. But the *spontaneous* development of the working-class movement leads to its subordination to bourgeois ideology, *to its development along the lines of the Credo programme*; for the spontaneous working-class movement is trade-unionism, is *Nur-Gewerkschaftlerei*, and trade-unionism means the ideological enslavement of the workers by the bourgeoisie. Hence, our task, the task of Social Democracy, is *to combat spontaneity*, *to divert* the working-class movement from this spontaneous, trade-unionist striving to come under the wing of the bourgeoisie, and to bring it under the wing of revolutionary Social Democracy.[3]

The remarkable thing about these two passages is the contrast between the vast theoretical and even world-shaking significance people attribute to them and their origin in an improvised polemical squabble that took place in autumn 1901. Take the striking polemical vocabulary: spontaneity, divert, and from without. All of them are taken straight from polemical productions that came out between September and November 1901. 'Spontaneity' comes from an attack on *Iskra* published in late September in *Rabochee delo*, 'divert' comes from an attack on *Iskra* that arrived in *Iskra* editorial offices probably in October, and 'from without' comes from Kautsky's polemical article on the Austrian party programme that came out in October. Chapter II was almost surely

---

[2] Lenin 1958–65, 6, pp. 30–1 [702]; Lenin 1988, p. 98.
[3] Lenin 1962, pp. 384–5; see Lenin 1958–65, 6, p. 40 [710–11].

written before the end of the year.[4] Whatever Lenin was trying to say with this vocabulary, he did not leave himself much time for careful reflection.

One thing is sure. Lenin's immediate aim was not to announce new theoretical views or to make a breakthrough in Marxist thought, but, rather, to rebut certain concrete criticisms of *Iskra*. His polemical method was a standard one: seize on isolated formulations, take them to their 'logical conclusion', show how these 'logical conclusions' lead to a denial of Social-Democratic ABCs. Precisely the same method had been used by Krichevskii and Martynov in their critique of *Iskra*. Of course, it is not inconceivable that such a down-and-dirty polemic would produce a major theoretical innovation. But before making such a claim, we need to be thoroughly conversant with the polemical context.

While I emphasise polemical context, I am *not* making the argument often heard in the activist tradition that polemical overkill led Lenin to 'bend the stick' and overstate a valid point. My argument is, rather, that when we grasp Lenin's polemical aims, we discover that he is affirming something rather banal and non-controversial for Social Democrats. He is affirming the mission of Social Democracy to bring the socialist message to the workers as vigorously as possible. He is affirming that *tred-iunionizm* – an ideology that explicitly denies the need for Social Democracy – is a bad thing and needs to be combatted. He affirms these precisely because he assumes, correctly, that his intended readers and even his opponents regard them as axioms. The scandalous overtones of his words arise solely from his insistence – for strictly polemical motivations – on using a confusing and ambiguous vocabulary to express his accusations.[5]

We will proceed as follows. First, we will look at each of the striking vocabulary items: spontaneity / *stikhiinost*, divert / *sovlech*, and 'from without'. We will trace their varied meanings and the way they become involved in the partisan bickering of Russian Social Democracy. We will then turn to the two passages as they occur in *WITBD*. After giving an overall account of the argument of Chapter II as a whole, we will provide a line-by-line reading of both the 'from without' passage and the 'combat spontaneity' passage.

---

[4] At the beginning of Chapter V, Lenin mentions that 'it is now mid-January 1902' (Lenin 1958–65, 6, p. 156 [814]).

[5] The assertion in Haimson 1999 that Lenin introduced *stikhiinost* to Social-Democratic discourse is tied to his misperception that the articles in *Rabochee delo*, No. 10 were written in reaction to *WITBD*, instead of the other way around.

## Stikhiinost: adventures of a word

For many writers, the key interpretative question not only for WITBD but Lenin's outlook as a whole is: what was Lenin's attitude toward spontaneity or *stikhiinost*? Zelnik remarks on Lenin's

> insistence on adhering to the language of 'consciousness and spontaneity', a decision that obviously lies at the roots of the importance conferred on that language by Leopold Haimson and other scholars a half century later.[6]

I would go further and say that scholars are, in fact, hypnotised by this language and therefore give their attention almost exclusively to texts bearing on this issue. This is highly unfortunate, since Lenin only used this language for ad hoc reasons and mostly in Chapter II of WITBD, not before or after. The insistence that Lenin's views on *stikhiinost* are the keys to his whole outlook virtually guarantees an extremely impoverished textual base. The problem is compounded because, as we shall see later, there is no such thing as *stikhiinost*.

Why *did* Lenin insist on adhering to the language of consciousness and spontaneity? Is this because, as some have suggested, 'spontaneity vs. consciousness' is a deep theme in Russian culture?[7] Or, perhaps, Lenin himself felt for either intellectual or psychological reasons that this was the appropriate word to communicate something important to him? Not at all – he did it because, like Kipling's kangaroo, he *had* to. Boris Krichevskii had used *stikhiinost* in order to argue that *Iskra*'s tactical plan contradicted the basic spirit of Marxism and that *Iskra*'s doctrinaire rigidity was responsible for the failure of the Russian émigrés to achieve organisational unity.[8] Lenin could not ignore this attack and in return, he tried to show that Krichevskii's phrase 'underestimation of the *stikhiinyi* element' meant that *Rabochee delo* had no understanding of the very foundations of the Social-Democratic mission.

*Word history*

The Russian word *stikhiinyi* is a rich one with a variety of meanings that all emanate from the central metaphor of a natural force but end up with different,

---

[6] Zelnik 2003a, p. 28.
[7] Haimson 2004.
[8] Krichevskii 1901, as discussed in Chapter Five.

even opposed connotations. It is unlikely that anybody will have a consistent attitude toward *stikhiinost,* just as it is unlikely they will have a consistent attitude toward, say, 'power'. Given the extraordinary importance the word has assumed in our understanding of Lenin and Bolshevism, we must start our investigation at the very beginning. *Stikhiinyi* is of Greek, not Slavic, origin. The original root word in ancient Greek is *steikho,* to walk or to go in line, and from thence *stoikhos,* a row or line, and *stoikheion,* one thing in a row. The basic metaphor of a row led to the word being used for anything that could be lined up in rows, such as letters of the alphabet. From 'letters', we proceed to the idea of constitutive elements making up a whole and, also, to the idea of the elementary subjects in a discipline (its ABCs). The philosophers seized hold of the word – Plato may have been the first – and *stoikhea* became the basic elements of the universe: earth, air, fire and water.

This image of the basic elements of the universe became associated somewhere along the line with vast 'elemental' powers. Perhaps a key step in this process was St. Paul's phrase 'the *stoikheia* of the cosmos'. What exactly he meant by the term is unclear. The New English Bible gives as alternate readings 'the elemental spirits of the universe', 'the elements of the natural world', and 'elementary ideas belonging to this world'. What is clear is that they are powerful enough to require Christ to liberate us from them but that after our liberation by Christ they appear 'mean and beggarly'.[9]

I do not know at what date *stikhiia* entered the Russian language. In any event, the Russian word means an element of the universe, a force of nature that is powerful and uncontrollable. From *stikhiia* comes the adjective *stikhiinyi,* and then, at double remove, *stikhiinost,* an abstract noun denoting '*stikhiinyi*-ness'.

The history of *stikhiinost* is a vivid case-study of the ways an original metaphor can expand and mutate. The same original Greek metaphor of a row was also at the beginning of another series of permutations, but, this time, arriving at a very different destination. A *stoikhos* or row could be applied to the ranks and files of a military formation and, from thence, to the written lines marshalled by the poets. This is why the word *stikhi* in modern Russian means 'poetry'. It is pleasant to think of the same original word ending up

---

[9] New English Bible translation of Galatians 4: 9; see also Galatians 4: 3, Colossians 2: 8, 20. The Vulgate translates *stoikheia* as *elementa.*

at the end of one line of development meaning a vast, uncivilised, unorganised pre-social force [*stikhiia*] and, at the end of another line, meaning a delicate, civilised, highly organised ornament of society [*stikhi*].

The natural translation for *stikhiinyi* is 'elemental'. In fact, this has been its translation since ancient times, when *elementa* was used by Latin writers to translate *stoikheia* (the Latin word may indeed have been coined for that purpose). The existing English translations of WITBD occasionally use 'elemental' for *stikhiinyi*, thus obscuring the variegated ways in which Lenin uses the single word *stikhiinyi*.

Why then did earlier English translations not consistently use 'elemental' for *stikhiinyi*? They could not, for two technical and essentially accidental reasons which I quickly discovered when I attempted to use 'elemental' in my own translation. First, English happens to lack a familiar word for the abstract noun form of 'elemental'. One can find in dictionaries words such as 'elementalness' and 'elementality', but they grate on the ear (my computer spell-checker rejects them). Second, the phrase 'the *stikhiinyi* element', used originally by Krichevskii, plays a large role in WITBD polemics. After a few pages bravely writing 'the elemental element', I gave up and just used *stikhiinyi*.

*Spontaneity*

The previous English translations sometimes do translate *stikhiinyi* as 'elemental', thus adding to the confusion. But *stikhiinyi* is usually translated 'spontaneous' and *stikhiinost*, the abstract noun, is always translated 'spontaneity'. A word history of spontaneity is needed to show why it is a profoundly misleading translation for *stikhiinost*. This may seem like a digression, but spontaneity is far from a simple word – rather, it points to a profoundly important theme in our own culture. All sorts of irrelevant associations are imported into Lenin studies by the use of the word 'spontaneity'. The only way to gain a critical handle on this problem is to be consciously aware of the full range of connotations of the English word.

Spontaneity also has roots in classical civilisation, but this time on the Roman side. *Sponte* is a rather oddball Latin word because it exists only in the ablative and mainly in the phrase *sponte sua*, according to one's own will. Its etymological origins are obscure, but the Romans themselves linked it to *spondeo*, to promise solemnly, from whence our 'spouse', 'sponsor' and the like. The conceptual link was that for a promise or contract to be binding and reliable, it had to be uncoerced, *sponte sua*. So we see that a word which for the Romans suggested the most grave and binding obligation ends up for us as the lightest of whims, the merest of impulses.

The phrase *sponte sua* was early associated with the idea that a free and unconstrained expression of will and personality is not only more valid but more admirable. It is associated in Virgil and Ovid with the Golden Age: 'Aurea prima sata est aetas, quae vindice nullo, Sponte sua, sine lege fidem rectumque colebat' (in the Golden Age, humans kept faith and righteousness of their own will, without need of public laws or private revenge).[10] The same feeling in a private sphere turns up in Terence's *The Brothers*, where an easy-going father says that a parent's aim should be to have his son act do the right thing *sua sponte*, of his own accord, rather than *alieno metu*, through fear of another.[11]

Only in post-classical Latin does the concept behind *sponte sua* become embodied in other forms such as the adjective *spontaneus*. In the Vulgate, we find a highly significant New-Testament use in the first epistle from Peter, who tells the elders of the church: 'Pascite qui in vobis est gregem Dei, providentes non coacte, sed spontanee secundum Deum: neque turpis lucri gratia, sed voluntarie' ('Feed the flock of God which is among you, taking care of it, not by constraint, but willingly, according to God: not for filthy lucre's sake, but voluntarily').[12] Thus, already in the New Testament, we see a contrast between the ancestor of 'spontaneous' associated with pastoral care [*spontanee*] and the ancestor of *stikhiinyi* associated with vast powers of the cosmos [*stoikheia*].

In modern English, two broad sets of connotations can be discerned for 'spontaneous'. One, the high road, is a free civilisation. Writing in Lenin's era, Woodrow Wilson writes 'The highest and best form of efficiency is the spontaneous co-operation of a free people'.[13] The other and more popular

---

[10] Ovid, *Metamorphoses*, 1, ll. 89–90; see also Virgil, *Aeneid*, 7, ll. 203–4.

[11] Terence, *Adelphoe*, ll. 74–5.

[12] I Peter 5:2 (English version from the Douay Rheims translation of the Vulgate). The King James Version translates *non coacte, sed spontanee* as 'not by constraint, but willingly'; the New English Bible gives it as 'not under compulsion, but of your own free will'. The original Greek word translated by *spontanee* is *hekousios*. The words *secundum Deum* are not in all manuscripts, and they bring up one of the paradoxes of spontaneity: spontaneously, but according to God.

[13] As cited in *American Heritage Dictionary*, third edition, s.v. 'spontaneous'.

meaning is connected to fun: to be spontaneous is to be impulsive in a cheerful way, to be charmingly unexpected – a key value of the consumer culture. In a discussion of the film classic *Bringing Up Baby*, Morris Dickstein writes that

> this is not the Freud who saw a tragic conflict between civilisation and impulse, but the popular Freudianism of the 1920s and 1930s, pitting spontaneity and instinct against Victorian shackles of repression.[14]

'Spontaneity' seems like a plausible translation of *stikhiinost* because both words revolve around *lack of control* – but *stikhiinost* connotes the self's lack of control over the world, while spontaneity connotes the world's lack of control over the self. Thus, our attitude to *stikhiinost* is usually hostile, or at least wary, while our attitude toward spontaneity is usually positive. Furthermore, 'spontaneity' carries an enormous cultural and even political baggage of its own and summons up deep and emotional feelings about, say, American vs. Soviet civilisation, capitalism vs. communism. This allows Bertram Wolfe to cast Lenin as the enemy of all that is true and good, merely on the basis of his alleged hostility to spontaneity: 'Thus [for Lenin] *stikhijnost'*, spontaneity, the natural liberty of men and classes to be themselves, was the enemy and opposite of consciousness'.[15]

*Lenin translates 'spontaneity'*

As it happens, we have Lenin's own opinion, so to speak, about the appropriateness of 'spontaneous' as a translation of *stikhiinyi*. In the late 1890s, Lenin translated *Industrial Democracy* by Sidney and Beatrice Webb from English into Russian. The word 'spontaneous' is used several times by the Webbs, but Lenin never translated it as *stikhiinyi*. Looking at his renderings, we see that there was no one Russian word that Lenin thought was adequate for 'spontaneous', forcing him to resort to paraphrase – always, be it noted, with positive connotations.

The Webbs write that, when workmen meet to discuss their grievances and carry on their own affairs on a national scale, 'they are forming, within

---

An informative usage note is appended to the definition. (A full word history of 'spontaneous' would examine concepts such as 'spontaneous generation' and 'spontaneous combustion'.)

[14] Morris Dickstein in Carr 2002.

[15] Wolfe 1984, p. 30.

the state, a spontaneous democracy of their own'. For this sentence, Lenin translates 'spontaneous' as 'self-determining [*samoopredeliaiushchuiusia*]'. The Webbs then contrast the Russian autocrat's attitude toward the 'spontaneous activity' of the peasant commune and the liberal's approval of the 'voluntary spontaneity of [the union's] structure'. Lenin translates the first 'spontaneous' as 'independent [*samostoiatel'nii*]' and the entire second phrase as 'freedom of organisation'.[16] Later, when the Webbs refer to the 'spontaneous democracies of Anglo-Saxon workmen', Lenin translates 'free democracies'.[17]

In talking about modern division of labour, the Webbs assert that 'the crowding together of dense populations, and especially the co-operative enterprises which then arise, extend in every direction this *spontaneous delegation to professional experts* of what the isolated individual once deemed "his own business"' (emphasis added). Lenin translates the emphasised words as 'striving voluntarily [*dobrovol'no*] to transfer into the hands of specialists'.[18]

Whatever Lenin meant by *stikhiinyi*, it was *not* what the Webbs meant by 'spontaneous'.

## Stikhiinost *in Social-Democratic discourse*

The basic metaphor of an uncontrollable natural force was a rich one and various aspects of it could be activated at various times to varying effect. For example, if the revolution itself or the growth of awareness among the workers was moving forward like an unstoppable natural force, that was a good and encouraging thing. If, on the other hand, a strike action was called *stikhiinyi* and thus implicitly compared to a hurricane, that was mostly a bad thing: violent, unpredictable, disorganised, short-lived, destructive, exhausting. Clearly, even though this kind of *stikhiinost* was better than passive acquiescence and was a harbinger of better things, it had to be overcome and replaced with purposive and organised militancy.

---

[16] Compare Webbs 1965, p. 808 and Webbs 1900, p. 659 (Lenin's edition). For another instance of 'self-determining' as a translation of 'spontaneous', compare Webbs 1965, p. 842 and Webbs 1900, p. 686. (Lenin may have worked primarily from a German translation of *Industrial Democracy*.)

[17] Webbs 1965, p. 845; Webbs 1900, p. 688.

[18] Webbs 1965, p. 846; Webbs 1900, p. 689. Undoubtedly arguments of this nature (also found in Kautsky) influenced Lenin's concept of the revolutionary by trade. It is still noteworthy that Lenin does not use *professional'nyi* to translate 'professional expert' but *spetsialist*. Mayer 1993a argues that the Webbs are the chief source of Lenin's concept of the 'revolutionary by trade'.

Prior to 1901, most uses of *stikhiinost* I have encountered were in this second and more negative sense. Economist writers such as Kuskova and Takhtarev – writers whose central aim is to *organise* the workers for economic struggle – tend to see *stikhiinost* as the main obstacle to be overcome. The actions of the Russian worker class are still so *stikhiinyi* that merely getting the workers to organise effectively for economic struggle will leave the Social Democrats with little time for more ambitious tasks. This usage remained standard among Social Democrats. An article in 1912 by S.O. Tsederbaum (Martov's brother) was entitled 'From *Stikhiinost* to Organisation' – a journey desired by all Social Democrats.[19]

In Chapter Seven, we noted another more positive use of *stikhiinyi* in which the aspect of the underlying metaphor that is activated is the image of moving forward with unstoppable force. This is the connotation deployed in the phrase '*stikhiinyi* upsurge'. Lenin often used *stikhiinyi* in this sense prior to the polemics of 1901. For example, he wrote in 1900:

> Recent years have been characterised by a strikingly swift dissemination of the ideas of Social Democratism among our intelligentsia, and coming to meet this current of ideas within society is a completely independent and *stikhiinyi* movement of the industrial proletariat that is beginning to unite and fight against its exploiters and to show an ardent drive for socialism. . . . [Social Democracy must respond] to the requirements of the worker masses that are straining at the bit in *stikhiinyi* fashion toward socialism and political struggle.[20]

*The polemics of 1901*

Thus, prior to 1901, *stikhiinyi* was an expressive word that was used occasionally but did not become the subject of attention or dispute. Accordingly, one rarely finds the noun form, only the adjectival form. People had no trouble understanding what those who used it were intending to convey. This all changed in 1901. In May of that year, an offhand but conventional use of the word by Lenin snowballed into its seemingly obsessive use in WITBD. We

---

[19] Editorial reference in Lenin, 1958–65, 21, p. 602; for Lenin's discussion of this article, see 21, pp. 321–4, 353–4. For further discussion of this meaning of *stikhiinyi*, see Chapter Four.

[20] Lenin 1958–65, 5, pp. 322, 327 (the draft of the announcement of *Iskra*'s publication).

have covered the polemics of 1901 in Chapter Five and, here, we need only summarise developments insofar as they affect the meaning of the words *stikhiinyi* and *stikhiinost*. Three streams flowed into its polemical use by late 1901.

The first stream goes through the Boris Krichevskii article in *Rabochee delo*, No. 10. Lenin mentioned in his earlier May article in *Iskra* that an actual revolution would probably be sparked by a *stikhiinyi* explosion (powerful, unexpected, with profound subterranean forces revealing themselves). This phrase was seized on by Krichevskii to argue rather perversely that *Iskra* *under*estimated the *stikhiinyi* element (why else would *Iskra* find it necessary to affirm such an obvious truth?). In his article of September 1901, Krichevskii paved the way to WITBD by using *stikhiinost* in a variety of confusing ways, all with the purpose of polemicising against *Iskra* (the relevant passages can be found in Chapter Five). When Lenin read this, he saw it immediately as a 'principled defence of *stikhiinost*' and as proof that *Rabochee delo* was irredeemably opportunist.

Stream Number Two is the one that gave the world the phrase 'kow-towing to *stikhiinost*' that is so ubiquitous in WITBD. This stream begins with the following comment in the lead article in *Iskra*, No. 1 (December 1900):

> 'Organise!' – this is what *Rabochaia mysl* repeats to the workers at every turn and what all advocates of the 'economist' tendency repeat. And we, of course, united ourselves wholeheartedly to this call, but we add the following without fail: organise not only in mutual-aid societies, strike funds and worker circles, organise also in a political party, organise for the decisive struggle against the autocratic government and against the whole capitalist society.[21]

This comment makes a distinction between the more elementary forms of worker organisation and what an Erfurtian would regard as the highest form, namely, a political party. In the Geneva resolution of June 1901 – the unfortunate treaty that *Rabochee delo* and *Iskra* signed when they still thought they might be able to work together – the *Iskra* side put in a clause on this theme. The *Iskra*-ites wanted to ensure that *Rabochee delo* would also criticise this aspect of economism or at least not hinder *Iskra*'s own crusade:

---

[21] Lenin 1958–65, 4, p. 375.

Recognising that, in its relation to the elementary [*elementarnye*] forms of the manifestation of the class movement of the proletariat, Social Democracy must always be a force for moving forward, we for this very reason consider as important for the movement the criticism of currents that elevate elementarity [*elementarnost'*] into a principle of socialist activity and similarly elevate the narrowness imparted by elementarity to these lower forms.[22]

At the autumn congress, the *Rabochee delo* group did not object to the substance of this point, but proposed changing 'elementary and *lower* forms' to 'elementary and *narrow* forms'. *Rabochee delo* claimed that its proposed wording was less insulting to economic struggle. I do not find in the summary records of the Congress any indication that *Iskra* specifically objected to this wording change. Nevertheless, *Rabochee delo* accused *Iskra* of looking down on the economic struggle as 'low'.

At the Congress, when the *Iskra*-ites decided to quit the proceedings, they huddled together and hastily drafted a statement in which they accused *Rabochee delo* of breaking the terms of the Geneva resolution and returning to past errors. In the statement, said that the Geneva resolution asserted the full solidarity of the two organisations on the necessity of 'a sharply critical attitude toward kow-towing to the elementary *stikhiinyi* forms of the worker movement'.

Comparing the Geneva resolution with the wording of this later statement, we see that 'lower' is indeed dropped, that 'elevate into a principle' becomes 'kow-towing' and 'stikhiinyi' is thrown in as a synonym for 'elementary' – obviously because of Krichevskii's use of this word. Thus, the notorious phrase 'kow-towing to *stikhiinost*' originates in a collective brain-storm by the *Iskra*-ites. The identity of its actual author is lost to history.

The last step in the history of this phrase is when Lenin takes it up, removes any reference to organisational forms, and makes it the slogan for explaining *all* of *Rabochee delo*'s disagreements with *Iskra* ('In the following chapters we shall see how this kow-towing before *stikhiinost* manifested itself in the area of political tasks and in the organisational work of Social Democracy').[23] This decision may have given WITBD a rhetorical unity, but it also guaranteed that

[22] Martynov 1901b, p. 5.
[23] Lenin 1958–65, 6, p. 53 [722] (end of Chapter II).

*stikhiinost* would be further bent out of shape, or, rather, made even more shapeless.

Stream Number Three arises from the *Joint Letter* from the critics of *Iskra* – not that the authors of the *Letter* themselves use the word *stikhiinost* (the letter was written prior to the appearance of *Rabochee delo*, No. 10). The key sentence is the following:

> *Iskra* takes little account of that material environment and those material elements of the movement whose interaction creates a specific type of worker movement and determines its path. All the efforts of ideologues – even though inspired by the best possible theories and programmes – cannot cause the movement to stray from this path.[24]

This assertion, taken literally, comes very close to affirming a fatalistic inability to influence events. Lenin found it in his interest to tie the *Joint Letter*'s formulation as closely as possible to *Rabochee delo*, which he does in the following remark:

> The fundamental mistake of the authors of the letter is exactly the same as the one made by *Rabochee delo* (see especially No. 10). They get completely confused by the question of the mutual relations between the 'material' (*stikhiinyi*, as *Rabochee delo* puts it) elements of the movement and the ideological (purposive, acting 'according to a plan'). . . . The theoretical views of the authors of the letter (like those of *Rabochee delo*) do not represent Marxism but rather the parody of it with which our 'critics' and Bernsteinians are so enamoured, since they don't understand how to tie together *stikhiinyi* evolution with purposive revolutionary activity.[25]

By this means, Lenin associates the word *stikhiinost* with an overt denial of Social Democracy's leadership mission or even its capacity to influence events at all.

At this stage – autumn 1901 – we can discern at least six quite distinct meanings of *stikhiinyi*:

(i) Disorganised, lacking purposiveness, as in a *stikhiinyi* strike movement without any sort of long-term organisational structure.

---

[24] Lenin 1958–65, 5, p. 360 (further discussion in Chapter Six).
[25] Lenin 1958–65, 5, p. 363.

(ii) A *stikhiinyi* explosion, for example, the worker defence of students in spring 1901. A *stikhiinyi* explosion is massive and unpredictable action of the kind that could spark off a genuine revolution (according to Krichevskii, a revolution can *only* be sparked off by such an explosion).

(iii) A worker movement prior to the merger with Social Democracy – a worker movement that lacks not so much purposiveness [*soznatel'nost'*] as socialist awareness [*soznanie*]. Krichevskii uses the word in this way.

(iv) A vast, unstoppable force, as in '*stikhiinyi* upsurge' (this term is used in Lenin's response to the *Joint Letter*).

(v) The 'elementary' organisational forms of the movement, such as mutual-aid societies.

(vi) Objective circumstances (Krichevskii accuses *Iskra* of an 'underestimation of the significance of the objective or *stikhiinyi* element of development').[26]

To these, we must add at least two more from *WITBD* itself. First, Lenin applies the term as an insult to his opponents and also to unprepared *praktiki*:

> In the first chapter we demonstrated how *Rabochee delo* lowered our theoretical tasks and pointed to their '*stikhiinyi*' repetition of the fashionable catchword 'freedom of criticism'.[27]

> We still have done very little, almost nothing, to *toss* into the worker masses fresh and all-sided indictments. Many of us are not even aware that this is our *responsibility* and so follow in *stikhiinyi* fashion the 'grey ongoing struggle' within the narrow framework of factory life.[28]

> 'Economists' and terrorists kow-tow before different poles of *stikhiinyi* currents: the 'economists' before the *stikhiinost* of the 'exclusively worker movement' and the terrorists before the *stikhiinost* of the passionate indignation of *intelligenty* who do not have the ability or who do not find it possible to tie revolutionary work into one whole with the worker movement.[29]

Another meaning found throughout *WITBD* is 'the *stikhiinyi* awakening of the masses'. Plekhanov was right to predict the *stikhiinyi* awakening of the masses.[30]

---

[26] Krichevskii 1901.
[27] Lenin 1958–65, 6, p. 53 [722].
[28] Lenin 1958–65, 6, p. 71 [738].
[29] Lenin 1958–65, 6, p. 75 [742].
[30] Lenin 1958–65, 6, p. 106 [770].

The preaching of inspiring leaders will meet with an impassioned response from the masses awakening in *stikhiinyi* fashion.[31] The masses awakening in *stikhiinyi* fashion will push forward revolutionaries by trade from out of their own ranks.[32] The whole crisis of Russian Social Democracy is that the masses who are awakening in *stikhiinyi* fashion are not provided with prepared and experienced guides.[33] And so forth.

In the business part of the book – Chapters Three to Five – the predominating meanings are (a) *stikhiinyi* upsurge, (b) *stikhiinyi* awakening, (c) the *stikhiinyi* failures of Social-Democratic activists.

Lenin saw no difficulty in using violently contrasting usages cheek by jowl in the same paragraph, as, for example, in the following highly revealing remark:

> True, in the stagnant waters of 'an economic struggle against the bosses and the government', a certain film has unfortunately formed – people appear among us who get down on their knees and pray to *stikhiinost*, gazing with beatitude (as Plekhanov puts it) on the 'behind' of the Russian proletariat. But we will be able to free ourselves from this stagnant film. And it is precisely at the present time that the Russian revolutionary – guided by a genuinely revolutionary theory and relying on the class that is genuinely revolutionary and is undergoing a *stikhiinyi* awakening – can at last – at last! – draw himself up to his full stature and reveal all his heroic strength.[34]

*Iskra*'s opponents worship *stikhiinost* and that is very bad, because it signifies abdication of leadership. Iskra itself is thrilled by the 'the class that is genuinely revolutionary and is undergoing a *stikhiinyi* awakening', and that is very good because the *stikhiinyi* awakening ensures that Social-Democratic leadership will be effective. If we simply look at the word *stikhiinost*, this remark seems self-contradictory nonsense. If we look at the actual rhetorical force of the remark, its argument is clear and straightforward. Each of the two contrasting uses of *stikhiinost* allows Lenin to insist on the necessity and effectiveness of Social-Democratic leadership of the worker movement.

---

[31] Ibid.
[32] Lenin 1958–65, 6, p. 111 [774].
[33] Lenin 1958–65, 6, p. 122 [784].
[34] Lenin 1958–65, 6, p. 107 [770–1].

This survey of the uses of the word *stikhiinost* has descended down to very small details of the polemical free-for-all in autumn 1901. Taken together, however, these details explain why Lenin used *stikhiinost* in Chapter II of WITBD as if his entire philosophy of life depended on it, while barely using the word both before and after.[35] They also explain why it is so pointless and potentially misleading to ask the question 'what is Lenin's attitude toward *stikhiinost?*' *There is no such thing as stikhiinost* – or, perhaps, there are too many things. There is an adjective, *stikhiinyi*, used in a variety of contexts with a variety of usually comprehensible meanings. Lenin's attitude in each of these contexts is just what we would expect, given his views copiously expressed in the good old pre-*stikhiinost* days.

I hope this trek through so many tangled connotations of a single word will give the reader a feel for how *stikhiinyi* was used, so that the crippling crutch of 'spontaneous' can be thrown away. In regard to our interpretation of Lenin, the moral of this section can be summed up in a warning: ambiguous word being used – extreme caution is advised.

## Divert/sovlech

The case of 'spontaneity' is very similar to the case of 'divert', the other highly influential word in these passages. The Russian word *sovlech* is embedded in a multifaceted metaphor of leaving the correct path. Lenin found it in one of his polemical texts (the *Joint Letter*) and used it obsessively when attacking that target but nowhere else. An accidental choice of 'divert' by the first translators further misled readers of WITBD in English translation.

According to the standard translation of the 'combat spontaneity' passage, Lenin asserts that 'the task of Social Democracy . . . is to *divert* the worker movement'. John Kautsky (Karl's grandson) therefore ascribes to Lenin the belief that

> under capitalism the labor movement spontaneously tends to come 'under the wing' of the bourgeoisie unless artificially diverted from this natural tendency by the Social-Democratic Party.

---

[35] A German observer in the 1920s well described Lenin's polemical technique: 'In Lenin's written style, the inverted commas with which his articles swarm are highly characteristic. He loved to use his opponent's words, set them in a contemptible

Of course, Lenin himself does not describe Social-Democratic activity as being an *artificial* attempt to work against the *natural* order of things. On the contrary, as we have seen, he believes that keeping Social Democracy and the workers separate is artificial and unnatural.[36] But the word 'divert' does seem logically to imply these adjectives. 'Divert' is so important to John Kautsky's presentation of Lenin's views that he uses the word six times in the three pages following the sentence I have just quoted.[37] And he is no exception in this regard.

'Divert' translates the Russian word *sovlech*. Is 'divert' an adequate translation? This is somewhat hard to answer, because the word is a rather obscure one – for instance, it does not appear in the *Oxford Russian-English Dictionary*.[38] Etymologically, 'divert' seems inappropriate, since the respective Latin and Slavic roots of the two words have different meanings. The *-vlech'* root means to draw something in a certain direction and, thus, is closer to Latin *tractare* than *vertere*. A translation such as 'attract away' is thus closer to etymological logic.

After much poking around in dictionaries and after encountering other uses of the word from the period, however, I finally understood that the crucial context for understanding *sovlech* was its use in the idiomatic phrase *sovlech s pravil'nogo puti*, 'to draw away from the right path' – that is, to seduce from the path of virtue. My own translation is therefore 'to cause to stray'.

Thus, the word *sovlech* in the relevant meaning is always used in connection with leaving a path. Although the word 'true' is usually dropped in the instances I have seen, the standard implication of the idiom is that someone is unfortunately leaving the correct path. An example of this straightforward use of the idiom can be found in WITBD:

> Our party is just now beginning to form, is just now working out its profile and is still far from settling accounts with other tendencies of revolutionary thought that threaten to cause the movement to stray [*sovlech*] from the correct path.[39]

---

light, rob them of their force, as it were, strip off their shell' (Fueloep-Miller 1965 [1926], p. 34).

[36] See Chapter Two.

[37] J. Kautsky 1994, pp. 59–62. 'Divert' is not the only aspect of the standard English translation that has misled J. Kautsky and other commentators (see the discussion of the 'combat spontaneity' passage below).

[38] Wheeler 1984 (2nd edition).

[39] Lenin 1958–65, 6, p. 24 [696].

But could Lenin really be asking Social Democracy to draw the worker movement away from the right path? To answer this question, we must return to the polemical context of autumn 1901. Lenin encountered the word in a very striking sentence in the *Joint Letter*. As part of their critique of *Iskra*, the authors of the *Joint Letter* asserted that the *Iskra* group badly overestimated the possible impact of activists or 'ideologues'. Thus they wrote:

> *Iskra* takes little account of that material environment and those material elements of the movement whose interaction creates a specific type of worker movement and determines its path. All the efforts of ideologues – even though inspired by the best possible theories and programmes – cannot *sovlech* the movement [cause it to stray] from this path.[40]

The use here of the word *sovlech* is somewhat ironical, since the letter-writers are not suggesting that the path determined by material circumstances is the path of virtue or that the path toward which *Iskra* wished to draw the worker movement was the path of vice. Their point is the *ineffectiveness* of the activists. They are saying, in effect, 'it might be nice if all your propaganda and agitation would cause the workers to stray away from the objectively-determined path – but sorry, it's not going to happen'. Lenin's retort is similarly ironical: 'You say we Social-Democratic activists can have no impact on the worker movement? Well, I say we can, must and will cause it to stray from the path laid down by other forces.' In other words, the Social Democrats *can* make a difference. It is *not* a matter of perfect indifference how they conceive their jobs. The fatalism expressed by the *Joint Letter* is a parody of Marxism.

As shown in the discussion of the *Joint Letter* in Chapter Six, the writers of the letter were the ones who felt that Social-Democratic efforts to provide revolutionary leadership were artificial (at least in Russia in 1901), given the existing low revolutionary potential of the worker movement. In response, Lenin insisted that improved Social-Democratic leadership was the natural response to the ongoing *stikhiinyi* upsurge: 'the material elements of the movement have grown tremendously even in comparison with 1898, but the purposive leader/guides (Social Democrats) have fallen behind this growth'.[41] The insistence on the existence of a *stikhiinyi* upsurge was so basic to Lenin's outlook that it never occurred to him that his sarcastic use of his opponents'

---

[40] Lenin 1958–65, 5, p. 360 (a single sentence in the original).
[41] Lenin 1958–65, 5, p. 364.

term *sovlech* could leave a totally opposite impression, namely, scepticism about the 'material elements'.

But the *Joint Letter* was not Lenin's principal text in the first two chapters of WITBD. This honour belongs to Krichevskii. Lenin brings up the *Joint Letter* and the *sovlech* sentence so often in these chapters because he wants to leave the reader with the impression that Krichevskii and the *Joint Letter* are saying the same thing. Thus 'causing the movement to stray from the path' (*Joint Letter*'s vocabulary) is equated with 'combat *stikhiinost*' (Krichevskii's vocabulary). Lenin uses *sovlech* in this sense *only* when scoffing at the *Joint Letter* and *only* in the two chapters directed against Krichevskii.

As usual, clarity returns when Lenin switches away from an artificial vocabulary chosen for sarcastic polemical reasons and provides a concrete example of what he has in mind. Right after the 'combat spontaneity' passage, Lenin invokes Ferdinand Lassalle, the paradigm of the Erfurtian inspiring leader, as an illustration of 'combating spontaneity' and 'causing the movement to stray from the path laid down by the interaction of material elements'. Lassalle did not sit around with his arms folded because he knew in advance he could not make an impact. He went out there and fought the good fight with eloquence and energy. His only weapon was the power of his message; his only hope was that the workers could respond with passionate enthusiasm. And he and his successors met with stunning success.[42]

## In search of *Erfüllungstheorie*

At the Second Congress in 1903, one of the members of the *Rabochee delo* group, Vladimir Akimov, accused Lenin of advocating *Erfüllungstheorie*. Lenin was frankly baffled by the accusation. In Lenin's notes, we read: 'not only our dispute, but also in Europe, *Erfüllungstheorie*???'.[43] Akimov took the word *erfüllen* from the original German text of Lenin's long Kautsky quotation in WITBD. Kautsky, in turn, took the word from the party programme of the Austrian Social-Democratic Party – but Akimov was unaware of this. In fact, he believed the word expressed a dangerous heresy dreamed up by Kautsky and taken over by Lenin.

---

[42] Lenin 1958–65, 6, pp. 40–1 [711–12].
[43] Lenin 1958–65, 7, p. 410.

Akimov was completely mistaken about the status of the word *erfüllen*. He, nevertheless, has done us a service in focusing attention on it because this word constitutes a visible and meaningful link between the official programmatic statements of Western Social Democracy and WITBD. Tracing the peregrinations of the term *erfüllen* from text to text will also help us put WITBD's crucial Kautsky citation – the source of the term 'from without' – into proper context.[44]

The word *erfüllen* is first found in the programme of the Social-Democratic Party of Austria that was adopted at the Hainfeld Congress in December 1888/January 1889. The term comes in the crucial definition of the Party's mission: 'to organise the proletariat politically, to fill [*erfüllen*] it with the awareness of its position and its task, and to make and keep it spiritually and physically fit for struggle'. The author of the programme was the main leader of the Austrian Party, Victor Adler. Kautsky – on the eve of his move from Austrian to German Social Democracy – went over the draft but stated later that his contribution consisted of expressing approval.[45]

Kautsky had a very high opinion of the Hainfeld Programme. His approval is echoed by the noted American scholar of European Social Democracy, Gary Steenson, who calls the Hainfeld Programme not only 'the first marxian political programme for a mass workers' party' but even 'perhaps, the best statement of late nineteenth-century political marxism'.[46] *Erfüllen* certainly seems an appropriate symbol of the spirit of the Programme. One delegate, Rudolf Pokorny, introduced the Programme to the delegates by saying that the task of the Party was 'to bring enlightenment to the minds of the proletariat, to fill it with consciousness of its class condition, to make it trust in the task assigned to it by history'.[47]

In 1892, a few revisions were made to the Programme, but *erfüllen* was retained. Adler took the opportunity to re-affirm the ongoing mission of Social Democracy: 'we absolutely may not give in to the illusion that our work has already been done, that the proletariat actually has already been revolutionised'. He later expanded this point:

---

[44] Kautsky 1901b. I would like to thank Alan Shandro for discussion of this article and for providing me with his translation.
[45] Kautsky 1901b.
[46] Steenson 1991, pp. 185–96.
[47] Steenson 1991, p. 190.

Social democracy should be and is above all the mouthpiece, the spokesmen [sic] of the proletarian movement. Certainly! But the movement of the proletariat, as it develops immediately and unconsciously out of economic conditions, is something much broader, larger, and more powerful than social democracy. Social democracy will first come to power . . . when it completely becomes an expression of this proletarian movement.[48]

Steenson comments: 'No clearer statement of the marxian concept of worker self-liberation was ever given by a leader of a mass, workers' movement; no clearer rejection of the party as the vanguard could be imagined'.[49] I am not sure what Steenson means by 'vanguard'. In actuality, no *better* statement of the thinking behind the vanguard metaphor can be imagined. The job of Social Democracy is to bring the inspiring message of the workers' mission to the hitherto imperfectly aware worker movement.

The next episode in our story is the more substantial revision of the Austrian Programme carried out by the Vienna Congress of November 1901. The Kautsky article from which Lenin took the 'from without' passage was devoted to a critique of the changes suggested by Adler himself, the author of the original Hainfeld version. The proposed changes did *not* include the *erfüllen* passage – the statement of the Party's essential mission. This was retained without modification. The Kautsky comment used by Lenin was provoked by a proposed change elsewhere in the Programme.

Adler wanted to refute a typical dig at Marxism – one that has never died away – that points to a contradiction between historical determinism and the will of the proletariat. Adler therefore felt it necessary to emphasise that Social Democracy was 'a purposive and willed deed [*eine bewusste und gewollte Tat*]' on the part of the proletariat.[50] He thus proposed the following new passage: 'The more the development of capitalism swells [the ranks of] the proletariat, the more is the proletariat compelled and enabled to take up the struggle against it. The proletariat comes to the awareness [*Bewusstsein*]' of the reality that private production is harmful, that new forms of society have to be created, that socialism must be the goal of the workers' struggle. Adler's

---

[48] Steenson 1991, pp. 194–6. Note that if the first sentence of this passage were cited in isolation, it would give the impression that Adler was denying the leadership role of Social Democracy.

[49] Steenson 1991, p. 196.

[50] Adler, September 1901, cited by Kautsky 1901b, p. 78.

formulation was not intended to make worker awareness look more automatic and 'spontaneous'. His ultimate aim was, in fact, to stress the role of Social Democracy in preparing the proletariat to carry out its purposive deed.

In his critical remarks on the new Programme, Kautsky agreed with Adler's aim, but pointed out a possible misunderstanding that might arise from the new passage. Adler's new passage implied the following scenario: capitalism develops, the class struggle develops in tandem, and proletarian awareness develops at the same time and at the same rate. Now (says Kautsky) the class struggle is indeed an inevitable accompaniment of capitalism. In the long run, so is proletarian awareness. But can we say that socialist awareness grows at a steady pace in tandem with the development of capitalism?

Kautsky was worried that the language of Adler's new passage might be taken to imply that the growth of proletarian awareness was a 'necessary and direct result [*notwendige und direkte Ergebnisse*]' of the class struggle. The new passage thus opened the door to another standard objection to Marxism: why does England, the country of the most advanced capitalism, have a worker class whose awareness is so distant from Social Democracy? More generally, the new wording, thus interpreted, raises the question: if capitalism will do the job by itself, what is the point of Social Democracy? What happens to the mission of Social Democracy so eloquently expressed in the earlier Hainfeld Programme?

> Accordingly [says Kautsky], the old Hainfeld Programme quite rightly stated that it belongs to the task of Social Democracy to fill [*erfüllen*] the proletariat with the awareness of its position and its task. This would not be necessary if this awareness arose of itself out of the class struggle. The new draft has taken this sentence [*Satz*] from the old Programme and attached it to the sentence mentioned above. But in so doing the train of ideas is completely disrupted. In the new draft, [in one passage] we see in the proletariat an awareness of its historical task that arises out of the class struggle itself and then [in another passage] the same awareness once more, [but this time] brought in by Social Democracy. The matter is in no way clarified and misunderstandings are virtually invited.[51]

---

[51] Kautsky 1901b, p. 80. My citation includes the last four sentences cited by Lenin in WITBD plus two further sentences that Lenin omitted. I have translated directly from Kautsky's German, while, in my WITBD translation, I base myself on Lenin's Russian. In particular, Lenin translates *Satz* as thesis or position [*polozhenie*]. (Akimov also read *Satz* as 'thesis'.)

Kautsky argues that, while a militant worker movement may be said to spring up more or less automatically with capitalism, the time of its conversion to socialism depends on various other independent factors. The original discovery of the necessity to merge happens at a certain time and place, and the subsequent process of spreading the good news is influenced not only by the rise of capitalism but all sorts of political, social and even cultural peculiarities. This is Kautsky's essential argument, which seems rather commonsensical to me.[52]

In response, Adler asserted that he did not see any contradiction between the old *erfüllen* passage and the new language.[53] Thus Adler and Kautsky disagreed only about possible misunderstanding. The two men did *not* disagree about the use of the word *erfüllen* to describe the Social-Democratic mission.

In his attack on WITBD at the Second Congress, Akimov described *Erfüllungstheorie* as an 'ultra-Kautsky standpoint' and as a rejection of the views of Adler and the Austrian Party.[54] Not only Lenin and Kautsky but Victor Adler and Austrian Party as a whole felt that *erfüllen* was an entirely adequate term to express Social Democracy's mission of bringing the good news about socialism to the working class – in other words, its role as vanguard.

The case of *Erfüllungstheorie* is not merely a misapprehension by one of Lenin's less intelligent critics. For one thing, Akimov is taken very seriously indeed by modern scholars. He and he alone has had his writings of the period made available in a scholarly translation and commentary.[55] One can certainly say that his attack on WITBD as heretical *Erfüllungstheorie* is enshrined in today's textbook interpretation. It is no credit to the textbook interpretation that one of its forefathers was a man who literally did not know what he was talking about.

## Kautsky provides help to Lenin from without

We now have a clear idea of the origin of the Kautsky passage from which Lenin lifted the notorious phrase 'from without'. It is time to take a closer

---

[52] Kautsky often found occasion to make this same point; see, for example, Kautsky 1908.

[53] Akimov 1969, p. 118.

[54] *Vtoroi s"ezd* 1959, p. 257.

[55] Akimov 1969 (translated with an introduction by Jonathan Frankel).

look at the passage itself and the impact it had on Lenin's text.[56] Kautsky asserts that the grand discovery of the need for a merger, based as it is on profound scientific insight, could only come from someone who had mastered the most advanced economic and historical science of the day. This argument may or may not be cogent, may or may not be genuinely Marxist. In any case, it does not by itself tell us much about the process by which the message is brought to the workers from without.

Kautsky himself goes on to describe this process in the following words:

> The vehicle of science is not the proletariat, but the *bourgeois intelligentsia*: modern socialism arises among individual members of this stratum and then is communicated by them to proletarians who stand out due to their intellectual [*geistig*] development, and these then bring it into the class struggle of the proletariat where conditions allow.[57]

These words show that Kautsky's scenario is not 'bourgeois intellectuals bring the message to the *worker class* from without' but rather 'proletarian Social Democrats bring the message to the *worker movement* from without'. Did Lenin agree with Kautsky about the central role of 'proletarians who stand out due to their mental development' in bringing the message to the worker class as a whole? Of course he did. Chapters Six and Seven of this commentary document in detail that this was one of his core beliefs. It is no wonder, then, that Lenin endorsed this passage as 'profoundly true and important'.

We next turn our inquiry to the question: how did the Kautsky passage get itself into Lenin's text? The following reconstruction, although speculative, will establish some guidelines. Kautsky's article was written in the latter half of October 1901 and immediately published in *Neue Zeit* (I date the writing of the article from internal evidence). Lenin, who was in Munich at the time, sent the relevant issue to Plekhanov and asked for it to be returned. In a letter dated 2 November 1901, he told Plekhanov – working at this time on a draft programme for the Russian Party – that he might find Kautsky's article of use.[58]

These dates help us get a sense of the possible impact of Kautsky's article on Lenin's argument in WITBD. Lenin had begun work on WITBD immediately

---

[56] See Lenin 1958–65, 6, pp. 38–9 [709–10] for his citation of Kautsky.

[57] Kautsky 1901b, pp. 79–80. Note the phrase 'where conditions allow', an important point for Kautsky's general argument outlined above.

[58] Lenin 1958–65, 46, p. 150.

after the abortive Unity Congress of 4–5 October 1901. By the time Kautsky's article came out, h*r* must have been well into it. It therefore seems implausible that Kautsky's argument, even if it intended to make an original theoretical contribution, could have determined the basic thrust of Lenin's polemic.

In fact, the Kautsky passage was probably inserted into an existing draft. I do not know, reader, if you have ever had the experience of arguing something or writing something and then coming across a passage in one's reading on a tangential topic, and saying to oneself, 'yes, yes, that makes my point exactly, that would floor my opponents'? I have had this experience more than once and I think Lenin had it when he read the Kautsky article. Kautsky's phrase 'brought in from without' – especially coming from such an authority – struck him as providing additional support to his general argument in Chapter II that *Rabochee delo* ignored its duty to bring socialist awareness to the workers. He therefore sought for a place in his draft where he could invoke Kautsky's authority.

One place was just prior to the scandalous 'combat spontaneity' passage. Lenin has just observed that the ideology ascribed to the workers by *Rabochaia mysl* was nothing but the same old 'trade-unions-are-all-the-workers-need' ideology used by Western-European bourgeois opponents of Social Democracy. Lenin reminds his readers that there are only *two* ideologies, bourgeois and socialist. To abdicate one's duty to bring socialist awareness is *ipso facto* to strengthen bourgeois ideology. In the middle of this argument, Lenin announces that 'to supplement what we have just said, we will also cite the following profoundly true and important words of K. Kautsky, speaking about the draft of the new programme of the Austrian Social-Democratic Party'. He then gives a very long excerpt from Kautsky's article. He makes no comment whatsoever on the excerpt nor does he defend or explicate it in any way. The passage just sits there by itself. He immediately resumes his argument about *Rabochaia mysl*, so that the entire Kautsky passage could be cut and there would be no perceptible seam, either logically or stylistically, in the resulting text. For all these reasons, I assume that the Kautsky passage was thrown in *ex post facto*. It was literally brought into WITBD from without.

Lenin saw the Kautsky passage as useful because it provided one more reason why Social Democracy was needed to bring the message to the workers. A complicated and elaborate doctrine like Marxism, based on the advanced economic science of the day, could only have been worked out by a highly learned individual who could devote full time to the task and who was, for this reason alone, not a worker. It was, therefore, the responsibility of Social Democracy to bring the basic insights of scientific socialism *to* the worker.

Thus Kautsky and Lenin are talking about the *origins* of socialist *doctrine* and particularly of scientific socialism. Since scientific socialism necessarily originates from without, Social Democracy is *needed* to bring the message. But this argument tells us nothing about whether or not the message will be *heeded*. Or, rather, the argument shows that Kautsky and Lenin strongly believed that the message *would* be heeded by the workers – or why else take the trouble to bring it to them?

This basic point will be reinforced when we look at Lenin's 'from without' passage. But the Kautsky passage will also help us clear up some vocabulary issues that have hindered comprehension in the past.

First, the expression 'modern socialism' was a fairly common synonym among Social Democrats for 'scientific socialism' or Marxism. Thus, Kautsky writes, 'modern socialism emerges in the heads of individual members' of the bourgeois intelligentsia. He does not mean that the *ideal of a socialist society* originates only in those heads. As a historian of socialism, Kautsky is perfectly well aware that this is not the case. He means that Marx and Engels – the 'individual members' here referred to – developed scientific socialism, a very elaborate *version* of socialist doctrine.

Next, the term 'awareness [*Bewusstsein, soznanie*]' *can* mean simply 'doctrine', 'der Sozialismus als Lehre'. Kautsky writes: 'Modern socialist awareness can emerge only on the basis of profound scientific knowledge'. This does not mean that only those with deep scientific knowledge can be committed socialists. It means that the doctrine of scientific or 'modern' socialism could only have been discovered by someone who had assimilated Smith, Ricardo and their ilk and was capable of advancing beyond them.

'Awareness' is used to mean 'doctrine' in the key 'from without' sentence of the passage. Kautsky has just described the process by which the doctrine of 'modern socialism' is disseminated in the worker milieu by purposive workers. He sums up:

> Socialist awareness is thus something brought in to the class struggle of the
> proletariat from without [*von aussen Hineingetragenes*], and not something
> that arises from it in elemental fashion [*urwüchsig*].[59]

---

[59] Kautsky 1901b, pp. 79–80. The translation of *urwüchsig* is disputed; see Annotations Part One on Lenin's citation of this passage.

Unfortunately, 'awareness [*soznanie, Bewusstsein*]' is also used to describe the end result of the process: the transformed *outlook* of the workers. So, for example, Kautsky also says in this passage (quoting the Austrian Programme) that the task of Social Democracy is to fill the proletariat with an awareness of its task. Thus 'awareness' is used to mean both the doctrinal starting-point of the spread of awareness and its subjective end-point. Despite the confusing shifts in meaning, Kautsky's actual scenario is straightforward: a scientific *doctrine* about the true interests of the proletariat is discovered by a few geniuses, this doctrine becomes the basis of the message brought to the workers by Social Democracy (consisting mainly of workers), and eventually this message transforms the *outlook* of broader and broader circles of the worker class.[60]

One final vocabulary item is used only by Lenin but was clearly inspired by the Kautsky passage. The word in question is *vyrabotat*, 'to work out', in the specific meaning of working out, devising, elaborating, socialist *doctrine*. I am going to present the evidence on the use of this word in detail because it supports my argument about the insertion of Kautsky's passage into a pre-existing text and also (more importantly) will help us understand Lenin's 'from without' passage.

*Vyrabotat* is used once in Lenin's translation of Kautsky and three more times in the sentences immediately preceding and following Kautsky's passage, each time in connection with the working out of *ideology*. In Lenin's translation of the Kautsky passage, we find the following words:

> On the basis of the [proposed new] draft, one would think that the commission that *worked out* the Austrian Programme shared this allegedly orthodox-Marxist view . . .[61]

On comparison with Kautsky's German text, we find that Lenin added the words 'that worked out the Austrian Programme' as a gloss to make clear

---

[60] At each stage of the translation process from German to Russian to English, distinctions becomes smudgier and the argument harder to follow. Kautsky used both *Erkenntnis* [subjective recognition] and *Bewusstsein* [meaning both doctrine and outlook]. Lenin translated both German words with a single Russian word, *soznanie* or awareness. The existing English translations of Lenin compound the confusion by using 'consciousness' not only for *soznanie* but *soznatel'nost'* or purposiveness, even though this latter term is used in implicit *contrast* to 'awareness' in the paragraph preceding the 'from without' paragraph.

[61] Lenin 1958–65, 6, p. 38 [709] (emphasis here and in the following citations added).

the nature of 'the commission' in question. Immediately preceding the Kautsky passage in Lenin's text, we find the sentence:

[My opponents] imagine that a purely worker movement can *work out* all by itself and is now working out an independent ideology, if only the workers 'tear their fate out of the hands of their leader/guides'.[62]

Immediately after the Kautsky passage is the following:

Once we realise that there can be no question of an ideology *worked out* by the worker masses in the very course of their movement, then the question stands only in this way: bourgeois or socialist ideology.[63]

A footnote is attached to this last sentence, which begins: 'This does not mean, of course, that workers do not participate in this *working-out*' of socialist ideology.[64] Lenin's use of this word is opaque even to the careful reader of English translations because *vyrabotat* is rendered differently every time it appears. In the passages cited above, it is translated as 'to develop', 'to elaborate', 'to formulate' and 'to create'. Furthermore, although *vyrabotat* is a rather common word in WITBD, only here and in the 'from without' passage is it used to mean 'to work out an ideology'.

This verbal evidence strengthens our conclusion that, due entirely to the Kautsky passage, Lenin got interested in the theme of who did or did not 'work out' ideological doctrines. It also strengthens the conclusion that Lenin's interest in this topic is strictly localised and not part of the ongoing argument of WITBD.

## The immediate context of the scandalous passages: Chapter II of WITBD

The aim of Chapter II is to discredit *Rabochee delo* with the help of the formulations found in Boris Krichevskii's article in the issue dated September 1901. This intention is announced at the beginning of the chapter, and, after

---

[62] Ibid. ('tear their fate', etc. is a catch-phrase from *Rabochaia mysl*).

[63] Lenin 1958–65, 6, p. 39 [710].

[64] Ibid. The concentration at this point in the text of *vyrabotat'* in the meaning of 'working out an ideology' implies that, when Lenin inserted the Kautsky passage, he added one or two sentences before and after, using *vyrabotat'* as suggested to him by Kautsky's argument.

a certain amount of groundwork has been laid, it is carried out explicitly in the last third. We can best appreciate the overall course of the argument if we paraphrase it without resort to any of the special polemical vocabulary used by Lenin – in particular, *stikhiinost*.

*Iskra*'s definition of the current Russian situation (says Lenin) is that the revolutionary inclinations and actions of the workers have at present far outstripped the capacity of the Social Democrats to provide effective guidance. Since this is the weak link at present, we at *Iskra* have concentrated our attention on improving precisely this aspect. One might have thought that any informed person would agree with our priorities, even if they disagree with any particular suggestion. But no – in the latest issue of *Rabochee delo*, Boris Krichevskii charges that *Iskra* pays too *much* attention to improving Social-Democratic leadership. This accusation, carefully considered, shows that *Rabochee delo* is advocating yet another variety of economism and is advancing yet another denial of the need for any Social-Democratic leadership.

To explain why, we need to go back in history a bit. Already by 1895–6, the worker movement was moving ahead in leaps and bounds, showing its capacity for organisation and militancy. At the same time there also existed a corps of potential *praktiki*, ready to bring the socialist good news to the workers and to provide necessary organisational skills for their struggle. There can be no doubt that the workers would have responded enthusiastically to this message and that the resulting merger of socialism and the worker movement would have accomplished great things. But, even then, the weak link was the Social Democrats themselves. Due to their clumsiness and inexperience, they were removed from the scene. (Lenin only mentions in a later chapter that he himself was one of those clumsy Social Democrats.)

This particular failure was in itself no disaster, since there were always plenty of new revolutionaries ready to take their place. The real disaster was that the new generation of *praktiki* was seduced by an ideology that denied the need for energetic Social-Democratic leadership. Naturally, these *praktiki* did not make the improvement of Social Democracy's organisational capacity an urgent priority. These mistaken ideas were expressed in pure form by the newspaper *Rabochaia mysl*, which saw the absence of Social-Democratic leader/guides as a victory for the workers.

Perhaps the reader thinks this is all ancient history (since even *Rabochaia mysl* itself has renounced these ideas by now). Not at all, *Rabochee delo* – a group that in the past has always defended economists against *Iskra* polemics – is now basing its case against *Iskra* on what is essentially the *Rabochaia mysl* position in attenuated form. When the *rabochedeltsy* accuse us of overestimating the need to improve leadership, does this not show that they have no conception of *why* Social-Democratic leadership is so important – in fact, that they think the worker movement can get along fine *without* Social-Democratic leadership? Not only do the formulations of Boris Krichevskii's anti-*Iskra* article show that he and his friends do indeed think along these lines, but their objections to specific *Iskra* proposals all stem from the same underlying tendency to isolate the worker movement and socialism from each other and therefore to underestimate if not dismiss the urgency of providing competent Social-Democratic guidance to the workers now openly fighting against the tsar. Unlike *Iskra*, *Rabochee delo* is outside the Social-Democratic mainstream. It is the *Rabochaia mysl* of today.

Thus Lenin in Chapter II. On the question of whether the workers *heed* the Social-Democratic message, there is a genuine, substantive dispute between *Iskra* and *Rabochee delo*, although it only concerns the past. *Rabochee delo* argued that the *praktiki* of the 1890s could not have done much better than they did, given the conditions of the time. Lenin stoutly denies this, saying that, on the contrary, the workers would have responded enthusiastically to better leadership from the *praktiki*. Note that both sides agree on what 'doing better' meant – in the main, getting the workers to understand the priority of a revolutionary overthrow of tsarism.

As usual, Lenin is *more* optimistic and confident than is *Rabochee delo* about the receptivity of the workers in the recent past to the Social-Democratic message. Indeed, Lenin is more optimistic on this point than almost all Western specialists on the period, who side with *Rabochee delo* (although usually for different reasons) and believe that Russian workers would have rejected the *Iskra* message had it been presented to them in the 1890s. And yet instead of accusing Lenin of unrealistic optimism, most of these specialists accuse him of a dour pessimism.

The other question that seems to be at dispute is: is Social Democracy *needed*? I say, 'seems to be at dispute,' because, on this issue, Lenin is attacking a straw man. As I demonstrated in Chapter Five, the editors of *Rabochee delo* were mainstream Russian Erfurtians who fervently believed in the leadership mission of Social Democracy and the necessity of enlisting the energies of the worker movement for the revolutionary overthrow of autocracy. In 1901, they also insisted that the 'spring events' had outstripped Social-Democratic leadership capacities and that improving this weak link was the highest priority. In fact, the particular formulation used by Lenin as his main target – '*Iskra* underestimates the *stikhiinyi* element' – was intended to make exactly this point. According to Krichevskii, *Iskra* was so rigid that it was unable to adjust when faced with a *stikhiinyi* explosion of revolutionary action by the workers, thus failing to provide proper leadership in revolutionary times.

Let me introduce a spectre who haunts these pages, the Parody Marxist who defines himself with a speech such as the following: 'Marx taught that the social revolution is the result of inevitable forces and that proletarian class awareness is determined by the material environment. Therefore, as a logical and optimistic Marxist, I realise I need do nothing except sit back with hands folded and observe with satisfaction the advent of revolution. Crusader-like activism would be in logical contradiction to my beliefs and betray anxiety on my part.'

Many commentators on Lenin evidently believe that the Parody Marxist is the real thing. We need not assess this belief but merely point out that Lenin thought that this figure *was* a parody of Marxism and fully expected his readers to agree.[65] The Parody Marxist helps us see what is going on in these polemics. Lenin's insistence on the urgency of purposive leadership is not meant to be daring, controversial or innovative in any way. It is meant rather to make his opponents look marginal and extreme. The point is important enough for me to put it in italics. *The aim of these passages is not to reveal Lenin's own views on these matters but to expose Krichevskii and Martynov of Rabochee delo as Parody Marxists.* As he says in the 'combat spontaneity' passage, if my opponents thought through the consequences of what they are saying, then, like the Parody Marxist, they would sit in a house by the side of the road and leave it to non-Social-Democrats to make real efforts to lead the workers.[66] Unfortunately for Lenin, he had a very weak case, since in point of fact the

---

[65] The Parody Marxist arose out of the earlier polemics between populists and Social Democrats, since populists liked to tease the Marxists that their philosophy condemned them to passive fatalism or, at most, starting up a factory or village tavern in order to hurry capitalism along. In WITBD, Lenin mentions N.K. Mikhailovsky (a populist) and N.I. Kareev (a liberal) as writers who fought against Plekhanov on this issue. See Lenin 1958–65, 6, p. 50 [719].

[66] Lenin 1958–65, 6, p. 40 [711].

*rabochedeltsy* were not Parody Marxists but card-carrying Erfurtians. Lenin was thus reduced to the standard polemical technique of seizing on vulnerable phrases and spinning out absurd conclusions.

Chapter II thus has two over-arching polemical positions:

(i) *Rabochee delo* thinks that the workers of the 1890s would not have *heeded* the full Social-Democratic message, but I, Lenin, argue that they would have.

(ii) *Rabochee delo* thinks or implies that vigorous and effective Social-Democratic leadership is not *needed*, but I argue (along with all right-minded Social Democrats) that it is.

In the first case, Lenin was disputing views actually held by his opponents. On the second one, he is pummelling a straw man. The 'from without' passage is primarily in aid of the first position. The 'combat spontaneity' passage is primarily in aid of the second position.

## The 'from without' passage

We are now in a position to examine Lenin's 'from without' passage. Here is the text of the relevant paragraph in my translation. For convenience, the sentences are numbered.

(1) We said that *there could not have been* a Social-Democratic awareness among the workers.

(2) It could have been brought in only from outside.

(3) The history of all countries bears witness that exclusively with its own forces the worker class is in a condition to work out only a *tred-iunionist* awareness, that is, a conviction of the need to unite in unions, to carry on a struggle with the owners, to strive for the promulgation by the government of this or that law that is necessary for the workers and so on.

(4) The doctrine of socialism grew out of those philosophical, historical, and economic theories that were worked out by the educated representatives of the propertied classes, the intelligentsia.

(5) The founders of modern scientific socialism, Marx and Engels, belonged themselves, according to their social origin, to the bourgeois intelligentsia.

(6) In exactly the same way, in Russia as well the theoretical doctrine of Social Democracy arose completely independently from the *stikhiinyi* growth of the worker movement, arose as a natural and inevitable development of thought among the revolutionary-socialist intelligentsia.

(7) At this same time – that is, the middle of the 1890s – this doctrine of scientific socialism had not only fully taken shape in the form of the programme of the 'Emancipation of Labour' group, but had also won to its side the majority of the revolutionary youth in Russia.

Let us first put the 'from without' paragraph into its immediate context, namely, the paragraph preceding and following it. Lenin is telling the story of how two great forces were moving toward each other in Russia during the 1890s. One force – the revolutionary intelligentsia inspired by Social Democracy – had been discussed in Chapter I of WITBD, so, now, Lenin is going to tell us about the *other* force, that is, the great strike movement of the mid-1890s. He describes the strike movement, compliments the workers on their growing purposiveness, and asserts that the workers at this period were not yet convinced Social Democrats. The moral of the story is that the two forces *needed* each other and were moving towards each other with unstoppable force:

> In *this* sense, the strikes of the 1890s, despite the enormous progress in comparison with the 'riots', remained a purely *stikhiinyi* movement. Thus there was on hand both the *stikhiinyi* awakening of the worker masses – the awakening to purposive life and purposive struggle – and the availability of a revolutionary youth armed with Social-Democratic theory, who were straining at the bit to get to the workers.[67]

Now, I must confess that I deliberately misquoted this passage. I should have put an ellipsis between the two sentences. This ellipsis stands for the 'from without' passage. In other words, the 'from without' passage is a *digression*, a parenthetical remark that breaks the flow of the narrative.

What inspired Lenin to make this digression? The answer is clear: the Kautsky passage. The connection is established by the verbal echoes – not only 'from without', but 'modern socialism' and 'working out' socialist doctrine.

---

[67] Lenin 1958–65, 6, pp. 30–1 [702].

All of these occur only here and in the immediate vicinity of the Kautsky passage.[68]

But this connection brings out a rather strange fact: an *allusion* is made to the Kautsky passage before the reader knows of its existence. Would Lenin have proceeded in this way if making the Kautsky argument was in any way important to his overall argument? What I think happened was this: Lenin read Kautsky's *Neue Zeit* article as he was working on WITBD and decided to find some place where he could use Kautsky's 'from without' argument. The first place he found was later in Chapter II: he seized on the opportunity to give the whole long Kautsky passage in order 'to supplement what we have just said'. Having done so – and having started to use the verb 'to work out' in the surrounding text – he realised that Kautsky's argument was also tangentially relevant to his description of the Russian workers prior to the great merger. So he inserted another digression, again finding a verbal hook as a point of entry. He starts his digression by saying more or less: a few sentences ago I mentioned that we could hardly expect the Russian workers in the mid-1890s to be committed Social Democrats. Let me expand on this, using an argument that I came across the other day.

Thus, the two crucial uses of 'from without' (the 'from without' paragraph and the Kautsky citation) were most likely inserted into a pre-existing text. Obviously, we cannot set great store on these speculative textual arguments. But we should set great store by what is revealed by the very possibility of making them, namely, what seems to the textbook interpretation as the very heart of WITBD could be erased from the book without trace by snipping a couple of paragraphs.

I urge some reader with access to university students to try the following experiment in practical interpretation. Take the paragraphs preceding and following the 'from without' paragraph and type them up as a united text, eliminating the paragraph with the digression concerning 'from without'.

---

[68] One exception is this use of 'from without' in Chapter III: 'Class political awareness can be brought to the worker *only from without*, that is to say from outside the economic struggle, from outside the sphere of the relations of workers to owners'. The phrase 'from without' has no connotation here of workers vs. intellectuals, but only of limited economic struggle vs. more general political struggle. Lenin 1958–65, 6, p. 79 [745]. In the only other use of 'from without', Lenin states that local *praktiki* should not wait for a push from without before pitching in to help with a central newspaper. Lenin 1958–65, 6, p. 146 [805].

Announce to your students that there were some Russian Social Democrats who opposed Lenin's anxiety, pessimism, and worry about workers. Here, for example, is a text by a lesser-known activist of the same period, V. Ulyanov. Observe how optimistic *he* is. Note his assurance that, if a Social-Democratic newspaper could have been published in the mid-1890s, 'such a newspaper would have met with full sympathy both from the workers of the capital and from the revolutionary intelligentsia and the newspaper would have received the widest dissemination'. Ah, what a difference to Russian history if V. Ulyanov had won out in the leadership race instead of Lenin! – and then inform them that historians have used this same section of the book to construct the pessimistic portrait of Lenin.

Having established the relation of the 'from without' passage to the surrounding text, let us go through the passage itself sentence by sentence.

> **Sentence 1**: We said that *there could not have been* a Social-Democratic awareness among the workers.

How has Sentence 1 been usually read? Luckily, we have some evidence on this score. In his book *The Bolsheviks*, Adam Ulam quotes the 'from without' passage in order to convey the heart of Lenin's outlook. His quotation is inside quote marks and Ulam provides a footnote reference to WITBD. Thus readers are given to understand that they are getting Lenin's actual words. I believe that Ulam's quotation is indeed an accurate rendition – *not* of Lenin's actual words, but of how these words are automatically read by many people. Ulam translates Sentence 1 as follows: 'Socialist consciousness cannot exist among the workers.'[69]

There are three mistakes in Ulam's translation of Sentence 1. First, Ulam says 'socialist' instead of 'Social-Democratic'. But 'socialist' awareness can also refer to pre-Marxist, pre-synthesis socialist doctrine, and, in fact, Lenin uses it in this sense in Sentence 4.

Second, Ulam leaves out the words 'we said'. But these are crucial, because they refer us back to the earlier paragraph. In this paragraph, Lenin was talking about the strikes of the mid-1890s. He there stated that these strikes

---

[69] Ulam 1965, p. 178. Although Ulam provides a footnote reference to the Soviet English-language edition of Lenin's *Complete Works*, he does not follow the Fineberg/Hanna translation. I assume he translated directly from the Russian text.

showed steady growth of *purposiveness* among the Russian workers but that the workers at that period did not have Social-Democratic *awareness* nor could anyone have expected them to.[70]

So Lenin is not saying 'the workers cannot have Social-Democratic awareness', he is saying 'the Russian workers who carried out the heroic strikes of the mid-1890s did not yet have socialist awareness nor could we have expected them to'. This leads to the third and perhaps most crucial translation error: the tense is wrong. According to Ulam, Lenin says that Social-Democratic awareness *cannot* exist among the workers. In reality, Lenin says that Social-Democratic awareness could not have existed among a specific set of workers *at some time in the past*.

Ulam's rendition turns Lenin's historical statement into a general proposition about workers as such, everywhere, at all times. Some such misreading must be behind some extraordinary assertions by scholars. In 1956, Alfred Meyer wrote that Lenin's 'generally prevailing opinion was that the proletariat *was* not and *could* not be conscious'. More recently, James D. White makes the same point by contrasting Lenin to Kautsky. Kautsky believed (in White's words) that

> once the socialist consciousness had been communicated to the workers, the workers would then be in possession of the consciousness. Not so with Lenin; in his view the socialist consciousness *always* remained outside the working class because it could *never* see beyond its narrow material class interests.[71]

Lenin did not believe that the workers could ever have Social-Democratic awareness! Amazing.

Even when we correctly see Sentence 1 as a statement about the past, we still might be tempted to see the Sentence 1 as the second half of the following exchange:

*Lenin's opponent*: The workers in 1895 did have Social-Democratic awareness (that is, they understood the necessity of revolutionary overthrow of the tsar)

---

[70] The words 'there could not have been' are italicised in Sentence 1 as a way of indicating the relevant clause in the previous paragraph. Lenin does not use quotation marks because the wording is slightly changed. (I thus account for the italics differently from Zelnik 2003b, who sees it as indicative of Lenin's insistence on intelligentsia mentoring.)

[71] Meyer 1957, p. 29; White 2001, p. 59. Emphasis added in both citations.

or, in any event, they could have had Social-Democratic awareness without any help from anybody.

*Lenin*: No, you are over-optimistic: they could not have had Social-Democratic awareness, at least not without help.

But no one maintained the position we have ascribed to Lenin's opponent and, for that reason, Lenin had no interest in refuting it. The real dispute went like this:

*Rabochee delo and Joint Letter*: *Iskra* is wrong to criticise the activists of the 1890s because there was no Social-Democratic awareness at the time and therefore no basis for any other activity except economic demands.

*Lenin*: Of course there was no Social-Democratic awareness at the time, but then, there could not have been, could there? The history of all countries shows that the worker class begins without such awareness and acquires it through the activity of Social Democracy. Russia is no exception, and so the fact that the workers did not have Social-Democratic awareness is no excuse for the *praktiki* of the time, for they should have been busy bringing the message. If they had done so, the workers would have received it enthusiastically.

> **Sentence 2**: It [Social-Democratic awareness] could have been brought in only from outside.

Sentence 2 is short. Short and enigmatic. From the outside of what? Who brings it, and how? What kind of process is going on here?

The 'from without' formula only makes sense within the framework of the merger narrative, which informs us that socialism and the worker movement are *both* originally exterior to each other and have to be brought to each other. 'Modern socialism' – that is, Marx's scientific socialism – corrects the one-sidedness and the isolation of *both* sides. It brings the message of socialism to the worker movement 'from without' but it also brings the message of class struggle and the need for a militant worker movement to the original socialists 'from without'. Socialism as a doctrine can and does originate in either bourgeois or proletarian heads, but (according to the Kautsky narrative) in both cases it is originally separate and indeed hostile to the worker movement.

Neither in the Kautsky passage cited in WITBD nor in this particular Lenin passage do these writers set out this mutual and symmetrical 'from-withoutness'. Their aim in these passages is not to expound the merger narrative but to apply one aspect of it to the issue at hand. After *WITBD* was published, Lenin did, in fact, aim his polemics mainly in the *other* direction – toward intelligentsia terrorists who needed to hear the good news brought to them from without about the revolutionary worker movement. An early example of this argument can be found in *WITBD* itself.[72]

The 'from without' passage thus says nothing about the concrete *process* of bringing the message from without, even though, as we know, Lenin actually had a lot to say about the nuts and bolts of the spread of awareness.

> **Sentence 3**: The history of all countries bears witness that exclusively with its own forces the worker class is in a condition to work out only a *tred-iunionist* awareness, that is, a conviction of the need to unite in unions, to carry on a struggle with the owners, to strive for the promulgation by the government of this or that law that is necessary for the workers and so on.

This sentence begins with the phrase 'the history of all countries . . .'. This phrase should be a tip-off to what kind of argument Lenin is making. From the beginning of his career, Lenin has used almost these exact words to introduce an argument intended to knock down Russian sceptics: You say that the Russian worker movement is embryonic, unorganised, apolitical, *stikhiinyi*, and so on and so forth? Well, maybe so, although you neglect the enormous strides made recently. But look at the workers in the West – I recall *they* started small, and look at where they are now. The history of all countries shows that you *have* to start small, so don't let the sceptics get you down!

Lenin made this argument in 1894, in 1899 and in *WITBD* (each time emphasising the enormous strides made recently). Unfortunately, Lenin's presentation of one of his favourite arguments is botched in the *WITBD* version, primarily because of the influence of the Kautsky passage. Lenin wanted to use Kautsky's point about the origin of ideology as a supplementary argument explaining why the worker movement was originally isolated from socialism. As a result of shoe-horning this argument into his polemic, Lenin made a number of 'mistakes' – that is, he said or implied things that he clearly did not believe. This will become more clear later, when we look at Sentences 4 and 6.

---

[72] See the section 'What do economism and terrorism have in common' in Chapter III of *WITBD*.

The next phrase in Sentence 3 is 'exclusively with its own forces [*svoimi sobstvennymi silami*]'. I take this phrase to be a description of a worker movement isolated from Social Democracy. On this reading, Lenin's point is almost tautological, since *tred-iunionizm* is *defined* as the ideology of a worker movement without Social Democracy. Lenin himself is only tangentially interested in the question 'what are the workers able to do exclusively with their own forces?'. His political programme is built on another question: 'what can the workers achieve *with* Social Democracy?'.

Nevertheless, let us examine Lenin's answer to the first of these two questions. According to the standard English translation, Lenin says that the worker class, exclusively with its own forces, 'is able to develop only trade-union consciousness'. These words suggest to many readers that Lenin thinks that workers are perfectly content with trade-union activity and want nothing more, that trade unions are reformist by nature, that Lenin disapproves of trade-union activity as petty or even finds it dangerous, and, finally, that workers can never develop anything but a reformist, non-socialist outlook.

In reality, Lenin is not talking about subjective outlook at all, but the *origins of ideological doctrine*. Readers can be excused for not seeing this, because the English words 'develop', 'trade-union' and 'consciousness' are all misleading. First, 'develop' is a translation of *vyrabotat'*, and, as we have established, this word means 'work out or elaborate an ideological doctrine'. 'Consciousness' translates *soznanie*, awareness, and, as we have established, this means 'doctrine' in this passage. Finally, 'trade-union' translates *tred-iunionist*, and, as we have established, this refers to an *ideology*, not to actual trade-union activity.[73]

This reading of Sentence 3 is confirmed by Sentence 4, which establishes a contrast between the workers who work out *tred-iunionist* awareness and the intellectuals who work out the doctrine of socialism.[74] So, first of all, we transform 'the working class is able to develop only trade-union consciousness' into 'the worker class is able to work out only *tred-iunionist* awareness'. We then further translate the sentence into less technical language: the worker class with its own forces could not have discovered the doctrine of scientific socialism.

---

[73] A more extensive discussion of *tred-iunionizm* can be found later on in the discussion of the 'combat spontaneity' passage.

[74] The word for 'to work out' in Sentence 4 is *razrabatyvat*, a near synonym of *vyrabotat*.

Once we see that Lenin is talking about *the origins of doctrine*, the sense of scandal in the paragraph starts to go down. It is one thing to say that only a learned intellectual could have created (elaborated, formulated, developed, worked out) scientific socialism, it is another thing to say that only intellectuals can be aware socialists. The first proposition might very well be true, the second proposition is clearly false, and we know that Lenin believed it to be false.

> **Sentence 4**: The doctrine of socialism grew out of those philosophical, historical, and economic theories that were worked out by the educated representatives of the propertied classes, the intelligentsia.

Sentence 4 talks about the doctrine [*uchenie*] of socialism. Those who are familiar with the merger narrative will realise that Lenin is referring here to pre-synthesis socialism as opposed to 'modern socialism' or Marxism. According to the narrative, the socialists at this early stage were hostile to the militancy of the worker movement and to its efforts to unite in unions, fight the owners, pressure government, and so on. These original socialists had to learn a thing or two from a couple of other intellectuals who were ten times more learned than they were. And what they had to learn from Marx and Engels was precisely the necessity for the workers to unite in unions, fight the owners, and so on. The socialists had to learn that only a militant worker movement – once it became converted to socialism – could realise their dreams.

Nevertheless, from an Erfurtian standpoint, Sentence 4 is a mistake and a serious one too. The merger narrative says that socialist doctrines grew up separately from the *worker movement*, so that even individual workers who became socialists were also hostile to the worker movement. Lenin here says or strongly implies (especially in conjunction with Sentence 3) that socialist doctrines grew up separately from the *worker class*, that is, that *only* non-workers could come up with socialist doctrines. But this is clearly false, from the point of view both of the merger narrative and of elementary historical knowledge. Lenin himself notes a few pages later that workers such as Proudhon and Weitling participated in the working out of socialist ideology. True, he then says they did so 'not in their capacity as workers but in their capacity as theoreticians'.[75] Whatever the validity of this distinction, it does

---

[75] Lenin 1958–65, 6, p. 39 [710].

not make Sentence 4 any more correct in locating the origin of socialist doctrine exclusively in the propertied classes.

> **Sentence 5**: The founders of modern scientific socialism, Marx and Engels, belonged themselves, according to their social origin, to the bourgeois intelligentsia.

The reference in Sentence 5 to 'modern scientific socialism' is another of the many verbal echoes in this paragraph from the Kautsky quotation. Note that the socialists of Sentence 4 are representatives of the propertied classes, while Marx and Engels are bourgeois intellectuals only because of their social origin.

> **Sentence 6**: In exactly the same way, in Russia as well the theoretical doctrine of Social Democracy arose completely independently from the *stikhiinyi* growth of the worker movement, arose as a natural and inevitable development of thought among the revolutionary-socialist intelligentsia.

Sentence 6 starts to segue back from the Kautsky-inspired excursus about the origins of scientific socialism to the historical narrative about Russia in the 1890s. The strain of the stitching together shows in two unfortunate phrases. First, 'in exactly the same way'. Is Lenin comparing developments in Russia in the 1890s to the developments described in Sentence 4? But Russian intellectuals did not work out socialist doctrines in the 1890s. Socialism had triumphed among the radical intelligentsia long before then. What Lenin is describing in Sentence 6 is the new-found popularity in Russia of 'scientific socialism'.

Surely Lenin is not suggesting that the conversion of Russian intellectuals to Marxism is in any way comparable to the discovery of scientific socialism mentioned in Sentence 5? Marx and Engels were bourgeois intellectuals, yes, but they were the greatest of their kind. The Russian revolutionary intellectuals made no original discoveries whatsoever – they were young and inexperienced people who were inspired by their reading of Marx and his populariser Kautsky and perhaps even more by the shining example of the German Party. They were committed to bringing to the Russian worker 'from without' the inspiring news about the accomplishments of the *German* workers.[76] They were, at best, intermediaries.

---

[76] Liadov 1906, 2, pp. 251–66.

In various places throughout *WITBD*, Lenin goes into more detail about this episode of Marxism's temporary triumph among the Russian intelligentsia in the mid-1890s. Lenin's rather sardonic view of this whole episode emerges from these accounts and contrasts strongly with his enthusiasm about the worker movement in the same period. Certainly, Lenin does not intend here to put down the workers and exalt the intelligentsia.

Lenin also says in Sentence 6 that the triumph of Marxism took place 'completely independently from the *stikhiinyi* growth of the worker movement'. The words 'completely independently' were seized upon by Plekhanov in his anti-Lenin article of 1904, where – in the manner to which we have become so wearily accustomed – he repeats them obsessively as an indication of Lenin's failure to understand Marxism. The words 'completely independently' suggest that Marx would have come up with scientific socialism even the absence of a proletarian movement. Why, this is idealism, not historical materialism! And I, Plekhanov, am here to tell you that my conversion to Marxism would not have taken place in the absence of a industrial worker class.[77]

The Bolshevik response to this argument was simply to laugh it off. Yes, it is absurd to think of Marx coming up with scientific socialism in the absence of a worker movement – and it is also absurd to think that Lenin did not realise this.[78] In 1907, Lenin also dismissed Plekhanov's critique as nit-picking on the basis of individual phrases in *WITBD* that were not completely successful or exactly formulated.[79] And, indeed, 'completely independently' has not made it into the pantheon of scandalous phrases regularly trotted out to show Lenin's heresy.[80]

A more discreet and more pertinent criticism of Lenin's remark comes from the Bolshevik picture of Social-Democratic history. According to these writers, *some* intellectuals such as Struve and Tugan-Baranovsky were converted to Marxism 'completely independently' of the actual worker movement – but not those intellectuals who became real Social-Democratic *praktiki* (including

---

[77] *Iskra*, No. 70 and 71 (25 July and 1 August 1904), reprinted in Plekhanov 1923–7, 13, pp. 116–40.

[78] Stalin 1946–52, 1, pp. 89–130; Olminskii and Bogdanov 1904.

[79] Lenin 1958–65, 16, p. 106.

[80] Exceptions are Baron 1963 (Plekhanov's biographer) and Le Blanc 1990 (following Baron).

Lenin). Contact with the workers was a direct inspiration for them and central to their full conversion to Social Democracy.[81]

Although no one seems to have noticed it, Lenin's picture of two completely independent forces moving toward each other is also an insult to the intellectuals. His narrative implies that Social-Democratic *intelligenty* had nothing to do with the strikes of 1896–7, whereas they actually played a major role. I believe that Lenin distorts the picture here because of his rhetorical need to impose the merger narrative, with its emphasis on original separation, on the messier reality of Russian Social Democracy in the 1890s.

> Sentence 7: At this same time – that is, the middle of the 1890s – this doctrine of scientific socialism had not only fully taken shape in the form of the programme of the 'Emancipation of Labour' group, but had also won to its side the majority of the revolutionary youth in Russia.

The reader will be relieved to know I have nothing to say about Sentence 7, the final sentence in the 'from without' paragraph. To make up for this lapse, I do have something to say about Sentence 8, that is, the first sentence in the next paragraph. This sentence is the pay-off, the punch-line, of the whole exercise:

> Sentence 8: In this way, there was on hand both the *stikhiinyi* awakening of the worker masses – the awakening to purposive life and purposive struggle – and the availability of a revolutionary youth armed with Social-Democratic theory, who were straining at the bit to get to the workers.

After our exhausting trek through the Lenin's digression about the origins of doctrine, we now return to the story Lenin wants to tell about the *stikhiinyi* upsurge: the workers are moving with unstoppable force toward purposive revolutionary struggle and the Social Democrats are doing their usually inadequate best to help them.

Let us now review what we have learned about the 'from without' passage. The passage was a last-minute addition inspired by some remarks of Kautsky published after Lenin had already started serious work on WITBD. Most probably, the 'from without' passage and the Kautsky quotation itself were inserted into an already existing draft.

---

[81] See Chapter Eight for more discussion.

The impact of the Kautsky passage on Lenin's text can be seen in Lenin's vocabulary – not only 'from without' itself, but 'to work out' in the sense of elaborating a doctrine, 'awareness' meaning an elaborated doctrine, and 'modern socialism' meaning Marxism. As in the case of a meteorite hitting earth, the disturbance is most pronounced at the point of impact, in other words, mainly in the sentences preceding and following the quotation of the Kautsky passage and in the 'from without' passage itself. The vocabulary items just mentioned are much harder to find anywhere else in *WITBD*. This observation strengthens the impression that the 'from without' argument was indeed brought into Lenin's text from without, with little connection to the warp and woof of Lenin's overall argument.

The 'from without' passage seeks to provide more reasons why Social Democracy is *needed*. One of these reasons is that 'scientific socialism' – meaning essentially the great insight into the necessity of a merger – could only have been developed by learned intellectuals. Kautsky used this argument in his article and Lenin adopted it from thence, but it was widely accepted within Social Democracy. Lenin goes on to say or imply things that Kautsky did *not* say, in particular, that only non-workers originated all *other* forms of socialism. In my view, this implication should be seen as an infelicity due to a careless scissors and paste operation, like the phrase 'completely independently' in Sentence 6. But, for purposes of argument, let us assume that Lenin's considered view was that *only* non-workers came up with pre-Marxist socialist doctrines.

Even so, is there *anything* in this passage that says or implies that the workers will not *heed* the message brought to them by Social Democracy? Is there any suggestion that the workers can not or will not receive the Social-Democratic message with open arms, open hearts and open minds? No.

First of all, Lenin did *not* say what many people evidently read him as saying: 'Socialist consciousness cannot exist among the workers' (Ulam's translation of Sentence 1). Next, we observe that 'intellectuals' are *not* equated with Social Democracy. Kautsky described the advanced workers as assimilating and passing on scientific socialism to workers in the outer circles of awareness. Lenin evidently had no problem with this description, since he endorsed Kautsky's words as 'profoundly true and important'. Nothing in the 'from without' passage casts the slightest doubt on what we know from elsewhere to be Lenin's fervent belief in the advanced worker's crucial role in the spread of awareness.

There is no suggestion in Lenin's 'from without' passage, the Kautsky passage, or any of the other Social-Democratic pronouncements about the origins of scientific socialism that intellectuals should run the Party. Because Marx and Engels were bourgeois intellectuals, how does it follow that bourgeois intellectuals have the right to rule the Party forever?

Finally, we do not find in the 'from without' passage any hint of what is indeed present in the 'combat spontaneity' scandalous passage, namely, the strong impression that the isolated worker movement is actually moving in the wrong direction, *away* from socialism. On the contrary, when we read the 'from without' passage together with the paragraph preceding and following, we see that Lenin is painting a vivid picture of 'the *stikhiinyi* awakening of the worker masses – the awakening to purposive life and purposive struggle'.

This reading of the 'from without' passage is not just an over-subtle interpretation of a scholar writing a hundred years after the event. As evidence to the contrary, I will cite a passage which shows how the young Lenin loyalist Dzugashvili (Stalin) read this passage. Stalin immediately latched on to the importance of the word 'to work out' and emphasised it strongly in his defence of WITBD. Stalin announces that the task of Social Democracy is 'to bring socialist awareness (that Marx and Engels *worked out*) into the *stikhiinyi* worker movement and to unite the advanced forces of the worker class into one centralised party'.[82]

Stalin then quotes a Menshevik critic who says that Lenin believed that workers, exclusively with their own forces, could never *assimilate* socialist ideals. Stalin quotes WITBD to the effect that the workers *do* assimilate socialist theory very easily. Stalin triumphantly concludes: 'As you see, according to the "majority" [the Bolsheviks], the workers easily assimilate those "high ideals" that are called socialism'.[83]

Where, then, did An, the Menshevik writer, get this wrong-headed idea? By his reading of the 'from without' passage:

> [The Menshevik An] is thinking of the place in the book *What Is to Be Done?*
> where Lenin speaks of the *working out* of socialism, where he affirms that

---

[82] Stalin 1946–52, 1, p. 106 (emphasis in the original). The parenthetical comment about Marx and Engels is a footnote in the original.

[83] Stalin 1946–52, 1, p. 107. Stalin's WITBD citation comes from Lenin 1958–65, 6, p. 41 [712]. The citation is not quite the knock-down blow that Stalin claims, since, while Lenin does say that the workers can easily assimilate socialist theory, he does not say that they can do it exclusively with their own forces.

the worker class with its own forces *cannot work out* scientific socialism. But you will say: how is this? The *working out* of socialism is one thing and its *assimilation* is another. . . . Reader, you are correct.[84]

The reader of the standard English translation of WITBD learns that, according to Lenin, the worker class 'is able to develop only trade-union consciousness'. After minute philological investigation, I was able to demonstrate in my comments on Sentence 3 that what Lenin really argued was that the workers were not in a position to make the epochal discovery of scientific socialism.[85] I am happy to discover that the young Stalin, a reader steeped in the atmosphere of Russian Social Democracy, automatically read the passage as I do, and even happier to report that Lenin particularly praised Stalin's article for its treatment of the vexed question of 'bringing in awareness from without'.[86]

The *working out* of socialism is one thing and its *assimilation* is another. Lenin thought that Social Democracy was needed to bring the message *and* he thought the message would be heeded.

## The 'combat spontaneity' passage

We are now in a position to analyse the 'combat spontaneity' passage. In my opinion, this is by far the most unsettling of the two scandalous passages, which I give here in the official Soviet English translation of 1961:

There is much talk of spontaneity. But the *spontaneous* development of the working-class movement leads to its subordination to bourgeois ideology, *to its development along the lines of the Credo programme*; for the spontaneous working-class movement is trade-unionism, is *Nur-Gewerkschaftlerei*, and trade-unionism means the ideological enslavement of the workers by the

---

[84] Ibid. Although Plekhanov later polemicised against WITBD, he made what in essence is the same point in his defence of the book at the Second Congress: 'Comrade Martynov cites the words of Engels: "Modern socialism is the theoretical expression of the modern worker movement". . . . But Engels's words express a *general* position. The issue [we are now discussing] is, who was the first to formulate this theoretical expression' (*Vtoroi s"ezd*, p. 125).

[85] Note that, in the view of Kautsky and Lenin, not only workers but almost all intellectuals were incapable of making this discovery.

[86] Lenin 1958–65, 11, pp. 386–7 (October 1905). Lenin's short statement should be taken as authoritative comment on the 'from without' passage. (Mayer 1996 was the first to note the significance of Lenin's endorsement of Stalin.)

bourgeoisie. Hence, our task, the task of Social Democracy, is *to combat spontaneity, to divert* the working-class movement from this spontaneous, trade-unionist striving to come under the wing of the bourgeoisie, and to bring it under the wing of revolutionary Social Democracy.[87]

Why is this passage so unsettling? Because it is one thing to say that the worker movement needs Social Democracy in order to understand its proper final goal, but quite another thing to suggest that the worker movement is actively and 'spontaneously' moving *away* from socialism toward bourgeois ideology. Vladimir Akimov immediately picked up on this implication in his 1904 pamphlet:

> In Lenin's view . . . the 'intelligentsia' develops in one direction. The 'theory of socialism' 'grows out' of 'philosophical, historical, and economic theories'. But the proletariat moves in a different direction, it moves toward 'its subordination to bourgeois ideology'; the spontaneous worker movement is trade-unionism. Hence, the intelligentsia must launch a struggle against spontaneous development and '*divert* [Lenin's italics] the worker movement from this spontaneous striving'.[88]

Note that, in his indictment of Lenin, Akimov cites phrases from the earlier 'from without' passage ('intelligentsia', 'theory of socialism' and so on) and ties them together with phrases from the 'combat spontaneity' passage we are now considering. But this procedure brings out a paradox. There is no hint in the earlier passage that the worker movement is actively moving in the wrong direction – nay, more, anyone who takes the trouble to read the paragraphs immediately proceeding and following the 'from without' paragraph will see that Lenin vividly presents the workers as moving *toward* Social Democracy, as awakening to purposive life and purposive struggle. Thus, the two scandalous passages do not propound a single teaching but, rather, directly contradict each other.[89]

---

[87] Lenin 1962, pp. 384–5; see Lenin 1958–65, 6, p. 40 [710–11].

[88] Akimov 1969, p. 118. I use Frankel's translation, except that I have substituted 'worker movement' for 'labour movement'. I assume that the bracketed editorial comment is by Akimov.

[89] Note also that the 'combat spontaneity' passage has nothing to say about the intelligentsia.

Another source of scandal is present only to the reader who does not speak either Russian or Socialdemocratese. The 'combat spontaneity' passage seems to equate trade-union activity with the worst sort of ideological enslavement to the bourgeoisie. Lenin, it would seem, wants the workers to scorn such petty things as strikes and material improvement and to concentrate solely on socialist revolution. But Lenin is not talking about trade unionism in this passage, he is talking about *tred-iunionizm*. *Tred-iunionizm* is an explicitly anti-socialist *ideology* that urges the workers to restrict their class activity to the economic struggle (with related legal enactments). To drive home the point here, Lenin borrows a term from German Social Democracy: *Nur-Gewerkschaftlerei*. This term might be rendered as 'shamefully propounding the theory that the workers need nothing but trade unions'. The emphasis in this term falls on the *Nur*, 'nothing but'. The first English translation by Joe Fineberg made a feeble effort to bring this out by translating 'pure and simple trade unionism' but this was unfortunately removed by later English translations.

No Social Democrat would have disagreed with Lenin that *tred-iunionizm* is a bad thing. Akimov is not shocked that Lenin insulted *tred-iunionizm*, he is shocked that Lenin associates it with the spontaneous worker movement. Rosa Luxemburg was merely stating a commonplace when she railed against 'trade-unionistischen Borniertheit [*tred-iunionist* narrowness]'.[90] This Social-Democratic commonplace did not imply that Social Democracy was against trade unionism, that is, against trade-union activity. On the contrary, Marxist Social Democracy encouraged trade-union activity, in contrast to, say, Lassalleanism or Proudhonism. Of course, this trade-union activity was supposed to be part of a larger whole, namely, the party-led Social-Democratic movement. But even isolated trade-union activity was not bad in itself. It was better, much better, than no resistance at all to the exploiters. To repeat, the enemy was an *ideology* that preached that workers should *limit* themselves to trade-union activity and to legal enactment of economic reforms.[91]

---

[90] Luxemburg 1970, p. 436.

[91] Leonard Schapiro translates the German term (inaccurately transcribed as 'nur Gewerkschaftlerei') as 'mere trade union stuff' (Schapiro 1987, p. 244). He argues that Kautsky's use of this term is evidence of his contempt for trade-union activity and that Lenin picked up the term in order to validate his similar attitude. Schapiro's translation and argument illustrates how a scholar with an impressive feel for the Russian context can misunderstand elementary Socialdemocratese.

The problem is compounded by a serious mistranslation in the standard English translations (not Utechin). According to the three synoptic translations, Lenin says that Social Democracy's task is 'to divert the working-class movement from this spontaneous, trade-unionist striving to come under the wing of the bourgeoisie'. But, in fact, Lenin does not say either that the worker movement has a striving toward the bourgeoisie or that the spontaneous striving of the worker movement is trade-unionist in nature. He says:

> Therefore our task – the task of Social Democracy – consists of a *struggle with stikhiinost*, consists in *causing* the worker movement *to stray* away from this *stikhiinyi* striving of *tred-iunionizm* toward accepting the leadership of the bourgeoisie and in causing the worker movement to go toward accepting the leadership of revolutionary Social Democracy.[92]

*Tred-iunionism*, a bourgeois ideology that rejects the need for a Social-Democratic party, has a *stikhiinyi* striving to seduce the worker movement. Social Democracy must combat it.

All this underscores the fact that what is truly scandalous about this passage is the sense of movement in the wrong direction: 'the *spontaneous* development of the working-class movement leads to its subordination to bourgeois ideology'. The words 'development' and 'leads to' (or, more accurately, 'moves toward') bring this out. For the reader of the English translation, there is the further suggestion that the worker class actually *strives* to come under the wing of the bourgeoisie. This passage may be only two or three sentences that are directly and indirectly contradicted by everything else Lenin wrote, but, still, we have to admit, they are a very striking couple of sentences. Is there anything we can do to lessen the sense of scandal?

Yes, I think so. First of all, for reasons already explained, several key words in the English translation – 'spontaneous', 'divert' and 'trade unionism' – are highly misleading. More importantly, if we examine the polemical context of this passage, we will discover that the passage occurs in a passage with a more than usually high content of polemical flimflammery. People have been so preoccupied with a sense of scandal that they have not noticed the astonishing weakness of the actual argument being made. The point Lenin

---

[92] Lenin 1958–65, 6, p. 40 [711]. The Russian text does literally say 'under the wing [*pod krylyshko*]', but I have translated according to what I take to be the meaning of the idiom in this case.

is trying to make in the 'combat spontaneity' passage is invisible if we read it in isolation (which is the only way almost everyone does read it). We must put it back at least into its immediate context, namely, the section of Chapter II entitled 'Kow-towing to *stikhiinost. Rabochaia mysl*'.

Let us ask of Lenin what he is trying to prove. His answer is clear: he wants to prove in this section that *Rabochee delo* is making a principled defence of *stikhiinost* and thus sees no need for Social-Democratic leadership in general, much less the need for improved leadership upon which *Iskra* insisted. Lenin first made this accusation at the Unity Congress in autumn 1901, fresh after reading *Rabochee delo*, No. 10.

> Not only is there no noticeable principled break with opportunism in the articles of *Rabochee delo* No. 10, but there are even some things that are worse: fulsome praise for the predominance of the *stikhiinyi* movement. I'm not picking at words. All of us – the comrades from *Iskra* and *Sotsial-demokrat* and myself – want to focus only on the basic tendencies of the articles, but these words, as the Germans say, *ins Gesicht schlagen* [hit you right between the eyes].[93]

In December 1901, Lenin made the same kind of accusation in print. *Rabochee delo*

> has raised kow-towing and slavishness before *stikhiinost* into a theory, it [has begun] to preach that Social Democrats should not go ahead of but drag along in the *tail* of the movement [and it makes] a principled defence of *stikhiinost* – that is, a principled defence of refusing to lead.[94]

Finally, earlier in Chapter II, he announces in a footnote that he will later prove the ideological enslavement of *Rabochee delo* to the ideas of *Rabochaia mysl*.[95]

As I have shown in Chapter Five, Lenin could not make good these accusations by means of a serious examination of Krichevskii's article, since Krichevskii made no such principled attack on the need for Social-Democratic leadership. In any event, Lenin makes little effort to give us an accurate sense of Krichevskii's argument (even his engagement with Martynov is more

---

[93] Lenin 1958–65, 5, p. 274. *Sotsial-demokrat* was an émigré organisation associated with the Plekhanov group, who were among its delegates at the Unity Congress.
[94] Lenin 1958–65, 5, p. 364.
[95] Lenin 1958–65, 6, p. 37 [708].

substantive). I suspect that, when he sat down to document his charges, he found he was unable to find the textual smoking gun he thought he remembered reading. Therefore, when he gets down to it, he does not actually argue that *Rabochee delo* made a principled defence of *stikhiinost*, but something quite different. 'What *Rabochee delo* simply cannot understand', say Lenin, is the following:

> *Any* kow-towing before the *stikhiinost* of the worker movement, any disparagement of the role of the 'purposive element', the role of Social Democracy, *means* just by itself, – *completely independent of whether the disparager wishes this or not* – *the strengthening of the influence of bourgeois ideology on the workers.*

Lenin is essentially arguing that the mere fact that *Rabochee delo* criticised *Iskra* for overestimating the purposive element means that *Rabochee delo* does not understand the need for Social-Democratic leadership:

> All those who talk about the 'overvaluation of ideology' [letter of the 'economists' in No. 12 *Iskra*], of the overestimation of the role of the purposive element [*Rabochee delo*, No. 10] and so forth, imagine that a purely worker movement can work out all by itself and is now working out an independent ideology, if only the workers 'tear their fate out of the hands of their leader/guides'.[96]

Really? Merely by accusing somebody – anybody – of overestimating the purposive element, I am committed to arguing that the workers should get rid of their Social-Democratic leader/guides and work out a new ideology that is neither socialist nor bourgeois?

But the real rhetorical force of this tirade comes from the references in brackets (these are footnotes in the actual text). Lenin wants to equate Krichevskii's phrase 'overestimating the purposive element', with phrases that say something quite different. He takes a phrase from the truly economist *Joint Letter* and a phrase from the truly economist *Rabochaia mysl* (the final quoted words in the passage) and throws them together with *Rabochee delo*'s criticism of *Iskra*, and hopes to show thereby that *Rabochee delo*'s formula must lead to economist conclusions.

---

[96] Lenin 1958–65, 6, p. 38 [708–9].

The other arguments Lenin makes to back up his claim are no more cogent. Lenin continues to attack genuine economists as if this procedure strengthens his case against *Rabochee delo*. The following monster sentence uses the *Joint Letter* and Prokopovich to expound at length what *Rabochee delo* 'simply does not understand':

> The words used by the authors of the 'economist' letter in *Iskra* No. 12 – i.e., that the efforts even of the most inspired ideologues cannot cause the worker movement to stray from the path determined by the interaction of material elements and the material environment – is therefore *utterly equivalent* to the *renunciation of socialism*, and if the authors were capable of thinking through what they are saying fearlessly and logically to the end – as anyone who steps forward in the arena of literary and social activity should do – then nothing would be left for them to do but 'rest their useless arms on an empty breast' and – and leave the field of activity to Messrs. Struve and Prokopovich, who drag the worker movement 'along the line of least resistance', that is, along the line of bourgeois *tred-iunionizm*, or to the Zubatovs of the world who drag it along the line of a priest/gendarme 'ideology'.[97]

The strong implication is that, if *Rabochee delo* was only courageous enough to follow their line of thought to the end, they would arrive at the passive fatalism of the Parody Marxist. The argument is also a tacit admission that *Rabochee delo* did *not* preach passive fatalism.

Lenin tries to strengthen his argument by inserting the Kautsky passage that he had just read in the latest issue of *Neue Zeit* (as discussed earlier). Kautsky was often used as a rhetorical club in various disputes within Russian Social Democracy. In 1904, he was used by the Mensheviks against the Bolsheviks. In 1907, the tables were turned and Lenin used a Kautsky article to discomfit Plekhanov.[98] In this case as well, the Kautsky passage was meant to be heavy artillery, although it actually deals with an issue tangential to the subject at hand (the reasons why capitalist development does not

---

[97] Lenin 1958–65, 6, p. 40 [711] ('line of least resistance' is a catch-phrase associated with Kuskova and Prokopovich).

[98] For more on these episodes, see Chapter Nine (1904) and Chapter Two (1907) in the preceding commentary. For Kautsky's role in Russian disputes more generally, see Donald 1993 and Weill 1977.

automatically lead to a corresponding growth in socialist awareness). But there is no doubt that Krichevskii himself was an advocate of *Erfüllungstheorie*, namely, the idea that Social Democracy had a mission to fill the proletariat with awareness of its mission.

Next, Lenin gives a concrete example of the 'combatting *stikhiinost*' for which people like Krichevskii allegedly see no need: Lassalle's career in Germany. Lassalle was, of course, *the* archetypal example of the inspired and inspiring leader. Lenin wants us to walk away with the impression that Krichevskii would be confounded by the example of Lassalle, but this is highly implausible.

The 'combat spontaneity' passage is found in the midst of these arguments and is a fit companion for them. Here is the passage, this time in my translation:

> People talk about *stikhiinost*. But the *stikhiinyi* development of the worker movement goes precisely to its subordination to bourgeois ideology, goes precisely *according to the Credo programme*, because the *stikhiinyi* worker movement *is tred-iunionizm, is Nur-Gewerkschaftlerei* – and *tred-iunionizm* is precisely the ideological enslavement of the workers by the bourgeoisie. Therefore our task – the task of Social Democracy – consists of a *struggle with stikhiinost*, consists in *causing* the worker movement *to stray* away from this *stikhiinyi* striving of *tred-iunionism* toward accepting the leadership of the bourgeoisie and in causing the worker movement to go toward accepting the leadership of revolutionary Social Democracy.[99]

This passage makes more or less the following argument: You, Krichevskii, talk about *stikhiinost*. One meaning of *stikhiinyi* is 'without Social-Democratic influence'. (This is indeed *one* of the ways in which Krichevskii used the word in *Rabochee delo*, No. 10, although, of course, he did not in any away approve of *this* kind of *stikhiinost*.) A worker movement that is without Social-Democratic influence is, by definition, one that sees no need for an independent class political party devoted to socialism. Again, by definition, such a movement – for instance, the one in England – is a *tred-iunionist* one. The development of a worker movement in which no one makes a case for Social Democracy will not be in the direction of Social Democracy. You must not realise this. You must think that Social Democracy has no responsibility to try to convert a

---

[99] Lenin 1958–65, 6, p. 40 [710–14].

non-Social-Democratic worker movement into a Social-Democratic one. You thereby are indirectly helping the bourgeois ideology of *tred-iunionizm* influence the workers.

So intent was Lenin on his hatchet-job that he did not realise that '*stikhiinyi* development' could be understood with another meaning of *stikhiinyi*, one that he himself often used: a development moving in a certain direction with elemental, unstoppable force. Lenin himself used *stikhiinyi* in *this* sense when he evoked the *stikhiinyi* upsurge of the workers, their *stikhiinyi* awakening, their *stikhiinyi* drive toward revolutionary action that was leaving Social Democrats behind. Precisely because he saw so clearly the *stikhiinyi* drive of the workers in one direction, he did not realise that his words in this passage could imply a *stikhiinyi* drive in another direction.

To conclude: to evaluate the 'combat spontaneity' passage, we must put it in its polemical context. Three points in particular need to be grasped. First, Lenin is trying to invoke, for strictly polemical reasons, the spectre of a world without Social Democracy, the better to show the dire outcome of what Lenin claims is the logical consequence of his opponent's views. This rhetorical strategy is clearly stated by V. Vorovskii in an article from 1905:

> Already at the congress of the party Plekhanov, at that time *defending* Lenin and his book *What Is to Be Done?*, said with complete truth: 'Lenin was not writing a treatise on the philosophy of history but a polemical article against the economists, who said: we should wait until the worker class itself arrives at a certain point without the help of the "revolutionary bacilli".'
>
> These words set out with complete truth the sense and the significance of Lenin's book. . . . Indeed, *What Is to Be Done?* was a polemical pamphlet, entirely dedicated to a critique of the tailist wing of the Social Democracy of that time, to pointing out and refuting the special mistakes of that wing.[100]

All we need to add to Vorovskii and Plekhanov's description is that *WITBD* is not really aimed at economism but, rather, in using economism as a stick to beat *Rabochee delo*.

Second, Lenin is bound and determined – again, for strictly polemical reasons – to use the words *stikhiinyi* and *stikhiinost* at every turn, whatever

---

[100] Text given in Lenin 1926–35, 4, p. 546. According to the Soviet editors, all the words starting with 'entirely' were added by Lenin, thus strengthening my interpretation of his 'bend the stick' remark (see Introduction).

the cost to clarity. For example, Lenin remarks that the triumph of *stikhiinost* over purposiveness itself occurred in *stikhiinyi* fashion. What he means is that the temporary predominance of economism in Russian Social Democracy occurred not through open debate but through the accidental circumstance of the arrest in Petersburg of older leaders such as himself.[101] 'This may seem like a play on words', says Lenin about his formulation, and indeed, that is exactly what it is. Lenin is determined to use *stikhiinyi* in every possible way.

Another example occurs in the section we have been examining. Lenin writes: 'Therefore the workers assimilate [socialist theory] very easily, *if* only this theory does not abdicate before *stikhiinost*, *if* only it subordinates *stikhiinost* to itself'.[102] I honestly do not know what Lenin is trying to say here. My guess is that he is trying to say 'Social Democracy must take an active role in bringing theory to the workers'. But this is only a guess.[103]

Third, Lenin is not engaged here in setting out a new thesis important to him nor in defending his practical proposals. Nor is he really talking about genuine disagreements. He is trying to prove the unproveable, namely, *Rabochee delo*'s ideological enslavement to the ideas of *Rabochaia mysl* – even though, as documented in Chapter Four, *Rabochee delo* had a more extensive record of hostile remarks about *Rabochaia mysl* than did *Iskra*. Through determined shuffling of verbal formulae, he seeks to give the impression that *Rabochee delo* preaches what are, from a Social-Democratic point of view, absurdities. The result has the same intellectual value as Martynov lecturing *Iskra* that Social Democracy has a duty to bring light and awareness to the worker movement.[104]

Lenin tried to show that *Rabochee delo* had scandalous opinions. Such was his polemical overkill that he ended up giving the impression that he himself held scandalous opinions. One is tempted to say 'serves him right' – if only the cause of historical understanding did not also have to be served right.

---

[101] Lenin 1958–65, 6, p. 37 [707–8]. Trotskii 1904 cites this argument as revealing Lenin's arrogance.

[102] Lenin 1958–65, 6, p. 41 [712].

[103] For another analysis of the confusions of this passage, with different conclusions, see Zelnik 2003b.

[104] On this episode, see Chapter Seven.

# Translation

# Note on the Translation

*What Is to Be Done?* was first published in early 1902. This edition included an appendix in which Lenin presented *Iskra*'s side in the organisational dispute with *Rabochee delo* in 1901. A translation of this material can be found as an appendix to Chapter Five of the commentary.

Lenin republished WITBD in 1907 as part of a collection of his writings. For the 1907 edition, he dropped some of the more dated polemics and he added some brief explanatory notes. I have translated the full 1902 edition (following the text given in the fifth edition of Lenin's *Complete Works*). The information provided by Lenin's explanatory notes of 1907 can be found in the commentary.

Lenin began writing WITBD in early October 1901 and the Foreword is dated February 1902. As he says in the Foreword, although he promised the book in his *Iskra* article of May 1901, he delayed writing until he knew the outcome of the unity negotiations with *Rabochee delo*. He sat down to write immediately after the failed Unity Congress.

The memoirs of his wife Nadezhda Krupskaya state that he began work on WITBD in April 1901 and sat down to complete the work after the Unity Congress in October.[1] Since she was living with Lenin in Munich at the time, her testimony must be taken

---

[1] Krupskaya 1969, pp. 248–9.

seriously. But it is easy to see from the text of *WITBD* that no substantial portion of the published version was drafted prior to *Rabochee delo*, No. 10 and the abortive Unity Congress in early October. The entire framework of Lenin's presentation is built around the polemic with *Rabochee delo*. Furthermore, the published text of *WITBD* contains many other references to works published in late 1901. This textual evidence is confirmed by letters by both Lenin and Krupskaya in late 1901.[2]

After looking carefully at Krupskaya's account, I think it highly probable that she was thinking of Lenin's original *Iskra* article 'Where to Begin?', which was published soon after her arrival in Munich in April 1901. The drafting of this article might in some sense be called working on *WITBD*, since the basic outline of the book's argument was first made public by this article.

In his Foreword, Lenin apologises for his hasty writing. One result of this haste was that, instead of revising his draft, Lenin simply added footnotes when he wanted to clarify or expand a point. As a result, the footnotes – particularly in the first two chapters – are important parts of the text and often more revealing than the text on the page.

The style back then was in favour of long paragraphs, sometimes several pages in length. I have broken these up, both for purposes of sheer readability and for bringing out the course of the argument. On the other hand, the convoluted sentences seem more an integral part of Lenin's style and I have tried to avoid breaking these into smaller units.

Following the Russian text, Lenin's frequent interjections to quoted material are placed in parentheses. Square brackets indicate my own additions aimed at increasing clarity.

In my opinion, the ratio of polemical chaff to substantive wheat is much higher in the first two chapters than in the last three chapters. Readers have been drawn to Chapter II because it appears to be the most general ('The history of all countries bears witness . . .'), not realising that it is actually the most parochial (for reasons detailed in the commentary). Readers might instead consider beginning with Chapter III, continuing to the end and then going back to the first two chapters. This procedure will give the reader a sense of Lenin's political outlook that will help in interpreting the scandalous passages in Chapter II.

---

[2] The evidence from the letters can be found in Tikhonova and Stepanov 1971 and *Perepiska V. I. Lenina i redaktsii gazety 'Iskra'* 1969–70.

*What Is to Be Done?*

**Burning Questions of Our Movement**

by

**N. Lenin**

*'... struggle within the party gives the party strength and vitality, the greatest sign of weakness of the party is vagueness and the blunting of sharply drawn boundaries, the party is strengthened when it purifies itself...'*

(from a letter of Lassalle to Marx, 24 June 1852)

# Foreword

According to the original plan of the author, the present pamphlet would have been dedicated to a detailed development of the ideas set forth in the article 'Where to Begin?' (*Iskra* No. 4, May 1901). And, first of all, we have to apologise to the reader for the tardy fulfillment of the promise given there (and repeated in response to many private inquiries and letters). One of the reasons for the delay was the attempt to unify all the émigré Social-Democratic organisations undertaken in July of the previous (1901) year. It was natural to wait for the results of this attempt, since if it had succeeded, then perhaps it would have been necessary to set out the organisational views of *Iskra* from a somewhat different point of view. In any event, a success would have promised a very quick end to the existence of two tendencies in Russian Social Democracy. As the reader knows, the attempt ended in failure; as we will try to show later, it could not have ended otherwise, given the new turn in No. 10 of *Rabochee delo* toward 'economism'. It turned out to be absolutely necessary to commence a decisive struggle with this tendency that is diffuse and indeterminate but is all the more tenacious and capable of reviving in various forms. Accordingly, the original plan of the pamphlet changed and broadened very significantly.

The main theme of the pamphlet was supposed to be the three questions set forth in the article 'Where to Begin?', namely: the character and main content of our political agitation, our organisational tasks, and the plan for building a militant all-Russian organisation simultaneously and from different starting points. These questions have long interested the author, who already tried to raise them in *Rabochaia gazeta* during one of the unsuccessful attempts at its resuscitation (see Chapter V). But the original idea of limiting the pamphlet to an analysis of only these three questions and to set out my views as far as possible in a positive form, without or almost without resorting to polemics, has proved completely unrealisable for two reasons. On the one hand, 'economism' has shown itself to be much more vital than we had supposed (we use the word 'economism' in the broad sense explained in *Iskra*, No. 12, December 1901, in the article 'A Conversation with Defenders of Economism' – an article which is, so to speak, an outline of the book now presented to the reader). It became very clear that the different views on these three questions were explained by a radical opposition of the two tendencies in Russian Social Democracy to a much greater degree than by disagreements over details. On the other hand, the inability of the 'economists' to understand the views set forth in *Iskra* demonstrated clearly that we are often talking literally in different languages and that, for this reason, we *cannot* arrive at any sort of agreement if we do not begin *ab ovo*. This makes it necessary to undertake a *systematic 'explanation'* in as popular a form as possible, illustrated with a great many concrete examples, of *all* the underlying points of our differences. And I decided to try such an 'explanation', completely aware that it would severely extend the dimensions of the book and slow down its publication, but seeing no *other* way to fulfil the promise I made in the article 'Where to Begin?'. I must therefore add to my apology about the tardiness of the pamphlet an apology about the many inadequacies in its literary presentation. I was forced to work *at the highest possible speed* along with interruptions from all other sorts of work.

The analysis of the three questions mentioned above remains as before the main theme of the pamphlet, but I had to begin with two more general questions. First, why has such an 'innocent' and 'natural' slogan as 'freedom of criticism' become such a red flag for us? Second, why cannot we come to an understanding with each other about even the basic question of the role of Social Democracy in relation to the *stikhiinyi* mass movement? Furthermore, an exposition of our views about the character and content of political agitation turned into an explanation of the differences between *tred-iunionist* and Social-Democratic politics; an exposition of our views on the organisational tasks turned into an explanation of the differences between the artisanal limitations that satisfy the 'economists' and what we believe to be the necessary organisation of revolutionaries. I also insist all the more on the 'plan' for an all-Russian political newspaper because the objections made against it are so baseless and respond so little in essence to the question posed in the article 'Where to Begin?' about starting simultaneously and from all points. Finally, in a concluding part of the pamphlet, I hope to show that we did all that lay within our power to ward off a decisive break with the 'economists' – a break that was nevertheless inevitable. *Rabochee delo* acquired, if you wish, the 'historic' significance of revealing so fully and so vividly, not 'economism' in a straightforward and logical form, but the confusion and the unsteadiness that constituted the defining trait of a *whole period* in the history of Russian Social Democracy – and, therefore, what may seem at first glance as an excessively detailed polemic with *Rabochee delo* also acquires some significance, since we cannot go forward if we do not liquidate this period once and for all.

February 1902                                                                 N. Lenin

# Chapter 1

# Dogmatism and 'Freedom of Criticism'

### a) What does 'freedom of criticism' mean?

'Freedom of criticism' – this is undoubtedly the most fashionable slogan of the present time, used most often in the disputes among socialists and democrats of all countries. At first glance, it is difficult to imagine anything stranger than these solemn appeals of one of the disputing parties to freedom of criticism. Are there voices really raised in the ranks of the advanced parties against the constitutional law of the majority of European countries that guarantees freedom of science and scientific investigation? 'Something's not right here!' – any person looking at this dispute from the side must be saying to himself when he hears this fashionable slogan repeated at every turn, but before he has penetrated into the essence of the disagreements between the disputing parties. 'This slogan, evidently, is one of those catchwords that are sanctified by use like nicknames and have become a normal vocabulary item.'

Indeed, it is not a secret to anyone that in contemporary international[1] Social Democracy two

---

[1] Incidentally. In the history of recent socialism, there is a close to unique and in its way comforting phenomenon: the disputes between various tendencies within socialism have been transformed from national ones to international ones. In earlier times the disputes between Lassalleans and Eisenachers, between Guesdists and Possibilists, between Fabians and Social Democrats, between those loyal to Narodnaia volia and [Russian] Social Democrats have all remained purely national disputes that reflected purely national peculiarities and took place, as it were, on different levels.

tendencies have formed. Here the struggle between them breaks out in a fierce flame while there it subsides and smoulders under the ashes of edifying 'resolutions of truce'. The content of the 'new' tendency – the one that regards 'old' dogmatic Marxism 'critically' – is defined with ample precision by what Bernstein *says* and what Millerand *does*.

Social Democracy must transform itself from a party of social revolution into a democratic party of social reform. Bernstein shored up this political demand with a whole battery of 'new' arguments and considerations that were placed together in a rather impressive system. The possibility of giving socialism a scientific base and proving its necessity and inevitability on the basis of the materialist view of history was denied. The fact of growing poverty, proletarianisation and intensification of capitalist contradictions was denied. The very concept of a *'final aim'* was shown to be baseless and the idea of the dictatorship of the proletariat was unconditionally rejected. The opposition in principle between liberalism and socialism was denied. The *theory of class struggle* – allegedly inapplicable in a strictly democratic society that is administered according to the will of the majority – was denied. And so forth.

In this way, the demand for a decisive turn from revolutionary Social Democracy to bourgeois social-reformism is accompanied by a no less decisive turn toward bourgeois criticism of all the fundamental ideas of Marxism. And, since this bourgeois criticism has been conducted for a long time against Marxism from the political tribune as well as the university chair – in a mass of pamphlets and a whole series of scholarly treatises – since the whole new generation of the youth of the educated classes has been systematically brought up on this criticism over the course of decades – then it is unsurprising that the 'new critical' tendency in Social Democracy emerged in no time at all as something completely finished, like Minerva from the head of Jupiter. As far as content is concerned, this tendency did not need to develop and take shape: it was transferred directly from bourgeois literature into socialist literature.

---

In the present time (as is now perfectly clear) the English Fabians, the French Ministerialists, the German Bernsteinians, the Russian Critics are all one family – they all praise one another, teach one another and conduct a war together against 'dogmatic' Marxism. Perhaps, in this first international skirmish with socialist opportunism, international revolutionary Social Democracy will acquire strength sufficient to put a final end to the political reaction that has long reigned in Europe?

Furthermore: If Bernstein's theoretical criticism and his political desires still remained unclear to anybody, then the French went to the trouble of providing an object lesson in the 'new method'. France again justified its ancient reputation as 'the country in whose history the struggle of classes are brought to their full conclusion' (Engels, from the foreword to Marx's work *The Eighteenth Brumaire*). The French socialists did not theorise, but acted; the political conditions of France, more developed in a democratic sense, permitted them to move right away to 'practical Bernsteinism' with all its consequences. Millerand gave an excellent example of this practical Bernsteinism – not for nothing did Millerand throw himself with such zeal to defend and exalt both Bernstein and Vollmar! Indeed: if Social Democracy is in its essence nothing but a party of reform that should have the audacity to admit this openly, – then a socialist not only has the right to enter into a bourgeois government but is even obligated to strive for this at all times. If democracy in its essence means the abolition of class dominance, – then why shouldn't a socialist minister charm the entire bourgeois world with speeches about class collaboration? Why shouldn't he stay in the ministry even after the murder of workers by the gendarmes showed for the hundredth and thousandth time the true character of the democratic collaboration of classes? Why shouldn't he personally participate in official greetings for the tsar, for whom the French socialists have no other name than the hero of the gallows, knout and exile (*knouteur, pendeur et déportateur*)? And the reward for this endlessly humiliating self-abasement of socialism before the whole world, for this leading astray of the socialist awareness of the worker masses – the sole foundation that can guarantee us victory – the reward for all this are some pompous *proposals* for some pitiful reforms, so pitiful that more has been won from bourgeois governments!

Anyone who doesn't deliberately shut his eyes cannot help seeing that the new 'critical' tendency in socialism is nothing other than a new variety of *opportunism*. And if one judges people not by the brilliant uniform that they themselves put on, not by the noisy nickname that they themselves have adopted, but by how they act and what they really propagandise, – then it becomes clear that 'freedom of criticism' is the freedom of the opportunist tendency in Social Democracy, the freedom to transform Social Democracy into a democratic party of reform, the freedom of instilling bourgeois ideas and bourgeois elements into socialism.

Freedom is a glorious word, but the most predatory wars are conducted under the banner of freedom of industry – under the banner of the freedom of labour the labouring classes are looted. The same innate hypocrisy is found in the present-day use of the term 'freedom of criticism'. People who are genuinely convinced that they are moving science forward do not demand freedom for the new views alongside of the old, but the replacement of the latter by the former. And the present-day shouting of 'long live freedom of criticism!' is too reminiscent of the fable of the empty barrel.

We proceed in a closely knit group along a precipitous and difficult path, holding each other with a firm grip. We are surrounded by enemies on all sides and almost always we must proceed under fire. We have joined together by a freely taken decision, precisely in order to fight with enemies and not to get stuck in the neighbouring swamp, whose inhabitants have from the very beginning condemned us because we separated out into a special group and chose the path of struggle rather than the path of conciliation. And, now, several of us take up the cry: let's go into the swamp! – And, when people begin to scold them, they object: aren't you people backward! And aren't you ashamed to deny us our freedom to urge you on to a better path! – Oh yes, gentlemen, you are free not only to urge but to proceed wherever you want, even into the swamp; we even consider that your real place is precisely there, and we are ready to give all the assistance we can for *your* removal thither. But let go of *our* hands, don't cling to us and don't disgrace the glorious word of freedom, because we also are 'free' to proceed where we wish, free to fight not only against the swamp but against those who turn us toward the swamp!

## b) New defenders of 'freedom of criticism'

And now, just the other day, this very slogan ('freedom of criticism') is solemnly advanced by *Rabochee delo* (No. 10), the organ of the émigré 'Union of Russian Social Democrats'. It is advanced not as a theoretical postulate but as a political demand, as an answer to the question: 'is it possible to unify the active Social-Democratic organisations operating abroad?' [*Rabochee delo*'s answer is:] 'Freedom of criticism is necessary for a long-lasting unification' (p. 36).

From this announcement comes two completely definite conclusions: 1. *Rabochee delo* has decided to defend the opportunist tendency in international Social Democracy; 2. *Rabochee delo* demands freedom of opportunism in Russian Social Democracy. Let us examine these two conclusions.

*Rabochee delo* is not pleased 'in particular' by 'the tendency of *Iskra* and *Zaria* to prophesy a break between the Mountain and the Gironde of international Social Democracy'.

> In general (writes the editor of *Rabochee delo* B. Krichevskii) this talk of *Mountain* and *Gironde* in the ranks of Social Democracy seems to us to be a superficial historical analogy, a strange one to see used by Marxists: the Mountain and the Gironde did not represent differing temperaments or intellectual tendencies, as it might appear to an ideologue/historian, but different classes or strata – small artisans together with the proletariat on one side and middle bourgeoisie on the other. Within the contemporary socialist movement there is no clash between class interests. The entire movement, in *all* (B. Krichevskii's emphasis) its varieties, including the most died-in-the-wool Bernsteinists, stands on the ground of the class interests of the proletariat, its class struggle for political and economic liberation. (pp. 32–3.)

A courageous assertion! Hasn't B. Krichevskii heard of the fact pointed out long ago that it was precisely the widespread participation in the socialist movement in recent years of the *stratum* of educated people that assured such a rapid dissemination of Bernsteinism? And, most importantly – on what does our author base his opinion that even 'the most died-in-the-wool Bernsteinists' stand on the ground of the class struggle for the political and economic liberation of the proletariat? There is no way of telling. The resolute defence of the most died-in-the-wool Bernsteinists is shored up by absolutely no arguments or reasoning. The author evidently thinks that since he is repeating what even the most died-in-the-wool Bernsteinists say about themselves – why, then his assertion doesn't need proofs. But can we imagine anything more 'superficial' than this judgement of an entire tendency on the basis on what this tendency says about itself? Can we imagine anything more superficial than the following 'story with a moral' about the different and even diametrically opposed types or roads of party development (*Rabochee delo*, pp. 34–5)? The German Social Democrats, don't you see, recognise full freedom of criticism, – the French do not, and precisely their example shows all the 'harm of intolerance'.

Precisely the example used by B. Krichevskii – we will answer – shows that some people who call themselves Marxists use history literally 'in the Ilovaiskii style'. In order to explain the unity of the German socialist party and the fragmentation of the French socialist party, we evidently don't need to delve into the particularities of the history of the two countries, or compare militarist semi-absolutist conditions with republican parliamentarism, or analyse the consequences of the Commune and the exceptional law against the socialists, or compare economic life and economic development, or recall that the 'unexampled growth of German Social Democracy' was accompanied by an energy of struggle against errors not only theoretical (Mühlberger, Dühring,[2] socialists of the [professorial] chair) but also tactical (Lassalle) – an energy itself unexampled in the history of socialism – and so on and so forth. Nothing like this is necessary! The French fight among themselves because they are intolerant, the Germans are united because they are such nice people.

And note that a fact that completely refutes the defence of the Bernsteinists is pushed aside by means of this inimitable profundity. Whether the Bernsteinists *do* actually stand on the ground of the class struggle of the proletariat is a question that can be decided finally and irrevocably only by historical experience. Therefore, it is precisely France that has much more significance in this connection, since it is the only country in which the Bernsteinists have tried to *stand* independently on their own feet, accompanied by the warm approval of their German colleagues (and partly also by Russian opportunists: cf. *Rabochee delo*, No. 2–3, pp. 83–4). The reference to the 'intolerance' of the French – besides its 'historical' (in the Nozdrev sense) significance – turns out to be simply an attempt to cover up a most unpleasant fact with angry words.

And we certainly don't intend to make a present of the Germans to B. Krichevskii and the other multitudinous defenders of 'freedom of criticism'. If 'the most died-in-the-wool Bernsteinists' are still tolerated in the ranks of

---

[2] When Engels attacked Dühring with such fervour, there were more than a few representatives of German Social Democracy who inclined to Dühring's views, so that accusations of sharpness, intolerance, uncomradely polemics and the like were showered on Engels even publicly at a party congress. At the 1877 Congress, Most and his comrades submitted a resolution to remove Engels's articles from *Vorwärts* as 'presenting no interest for the great majority of readers', and Wahlteich announced that the publication of this articles had brought great harm to the Party, that Dühring had shown great services to Social Democracy: 'We should utilise everybody in the interests of the Party and if professors are disputing among themselves, *Vorwärts* is not the place to conduct such disputes' (*Vorwärts*, 6 June 1877, No. 65). As you can see, this is an example of the 'freedom of criticism' – an example that our legally-permitted critics and our illegal [underground] opportunists, who love to point to the example of the Germans, would do well to reflect upon!

the German Party, then only to the extent that they *subordinate themselves* both to the Hanover resolution, resolutely rejecting Bernstein's 'corrections', and the Lübeck resolution that contains (despite its diplomatic nature) a direct warning to Bernstein. From the point of view of the interests of the German Party, we can dispute whether diplomacy of this sort is appropriate here, whether in this case a bad peace really is better than a good quarrel – we can differ, in a word, in our evaluation of the expediency of this or that *method* of rejecting Bernsteinism, but we cannot deny the fact that the German Party *did* reject Bernsteinism twice over. Therefore, to think that the German example confirms the thesis that 'the most died-in-the-wool Bernsteinists stand on the ground of the proletariat's class struggle for political and economic liberation' – to think this is to completely misunderstood what is going on right before our eyes.[3]

And that's not all. As we have already noted, *Rabochee delo* presents itself to *Russian* Social Democracy with its demand for 'freedom of criticism' and with its defence of Bernsteinism. It is evident that they have convinced themselves that among us someone is unjustly insulting our 'critics' and Bernsteinists. Which ones, precisely? By whom? Where? When? And why unjustly? – *Rabochee delo* is silent on these questions and does not say a single word about a single Russian critic or Bernsteinist! We are left to draw one of two possible conclusions. *Either* the unjustly insulted party is none other than *Rabochee delo* itself (this is confirmed by the fact that both articles of Issue No. 10 talk only about insults delivered by *Zaria* and *Iskra* to *Rabochee delo*). Then how do you explain the oddity that *Rabochee delo* – so stubbornly denying

---

[3] We should note the fact that, when discussing Bernsteinism in the German Party, *Rabochee delo* always confines itself to a bare recital of the facts with a complete 'abstention' from its own evaluation. See, for example, No. 2–3, p. 66, on the Stuttgart Congress: all differences are reduced to 'tactics' and all that is asserted is that the vast majority remained faithful to the previous revolutionary tactic. Or No. 4–5, p. 25 ff.: a simple paraphrase of the speeches at Hanover along with Bebel's resolution, while an exposition and criticism of Bernstein is again (as in No. 2–3) deferred to a 'special article'. Curiously enough, on p. 33 in No. 4–5 we read: '. . . the views set forth by Bebel were supported by the vast majority of the Congress', and a little later: '. . . David defended the views of Bernstein . . . who tried first of all to show, that . . . after all is said and done (sic!) Bernstein and his friends stand on the ground of the class struggle . . .'. This was written in December 1899, and in September 1901 *Rabochee delo* must have changed their minds about Bebel's correctness and now repeat the views of David as their own!

any solidarity with Bernsteinism – cannot defend itself without blurting out some remark about 'the most died-in-the-wool Bernsteinists' and about freedom of criticism? *Or* some third parties have been unjustly insulted. Then what could be the motive for silence about them?

We see, in this way, that *Rabochee delo* continues the game of hide-and-seek that it has indulged in (as we will show later) from its very origins. But, for now, direct your attention to this *first* application in practice of the laudable 'freedom of criticism'. In actual fact, it leads not only to the absence of any criticism but even to the absence of any independent judgement whatsoever. The same *Rabochee delo* that remains silent about the secret sickness (to use Starover's very apt expression) of Russian Bernsteinism, proposes as a cure for this sickness *nothing more than to copy* the latest German prescription against the German variety of the disease! Instead of freedom of criticism, a slavish . . . worse, a simian imitation! The social and political content of present-day international opportunism is the same everywhere but it appears in different varieties according to national peculiarities. In one country, a group of opportunists has stood for a long time under its own banner [the Fabians in England]; in another, the opportunists spurn theory and carry out in practical terms the policy of those Radicals who call themselves socialists [Millerand in France]; in a third, we see a few members of the revolutionary party cross over to the camp of opportunism and try to attain their aims not by an open struggle for principles or for a new tactic but by a gradual, unnoticed and (if I may put it this way) unpunishable leading astray of their party [Bernstein in Germany]; in a fourth, we see the same kind of renegades use these same methods in the shadows cast by political slavery with a completely original combination of 'legal' and 'illegal' activity ['legally-permitted Marxists' and underground economists in Russia] and so on. To undertake to talk about freedom of criticism and of Bernsteinism as a condition for the unity of *Russian* Social Democrats, and, at the same time, not to take the trouble to analyse how exactly *Russian* Bernsteinism manifests itself and what fruit it has produced – why, this is to undertake to talk in order not to say anything.

Let us ourselves try to say something, if only in a few words, about what *Rabochee delo* doesn't want to say (or, perhaps, doesn't dare to understand).

## c) Criticism in Russia

The fundamental peculiarity of Russia in the present context is that the *very beginning* of the *stikhiinyi* worker movement on one side and the turn of advanced public opinion toward Marxism on the other was marked by the merger of obviously heterogeneous elements under a common flag in order to conduct a struggle with the common opponent (an outmoded social-political worldview). We are speaking of the honeymoon period of 'legally-permitted Marxism'. This was, in general, a very unique phenomenon: nobody in the 1880s or the beginning of the 1890s could even have believed in the very possibility of it. In an autocratic country, where the press is fully enslaved, in an era of extreme political reaction that persecutes even the tiniest appearance of dissatisfaction and protest, – the theory of revolutionary Marxism, set out in an Aesopian language that was completely understandable to all 'interested' parties, suddenly finds itself a road into the *censored* press. The government was used to regarding the theory of (revolutionary) Narodnaia volia-ism as the only dangerous one, not noticing, as usual, its internal evolution [toward moderation] and delighting in *any* criticism directed against it. Before the government got its bearings and before the weighty army of censors and gendarmes recognised the new enemy and rushed to smash it, there passed a not inconsiderable (by our Russian standards) amount of time. And, during this time, Marxist books appeared one after the after, Marxist journals and newspapers were started, literally everybody became Marxists, Marxists were flattered and courted, publishers were delighted by the exceptionally brisk sale of Marxist books. It is completely understandable that, among the novice Marxists who were surrounded by this incense, there appeared more than one 'writer who became full of himself' . . .

At present, we can speak of this period calmly as something in the past. It is no secret for anybody that the brief flowering of Marxism on the surface of our literature was called forth by an alliance between people with extreme views and people with very moderate views. In essence, the latter were bourgeois democrats and this conclusion (confirmed to the point of obviousness by the later development of 'criticism') suggested itself to one or two people even while the 'alliance' was intact.

But, if that is the case, then doesn't the great responsibility for the following 'time of confusion' fall precisely on the revolutionary Social Democrats who entered into this alliance with future 'critics'? This kind of question, together with an affirmative answer, is heard now and again from people who look at the matter in a very simplistic fashion. But these people are completely wrong. The only ones who fear temporary alliances even with unreliable people are those with no confidence in themselves, and not a single political party could exist without such alliances. But the merger with the legally-permitted Marxists was, in its way, the first genuine political alliance of Russian Social Democracy. Thanks to this alliance, a strikingly quick victory was achieved over populism as well as a huge dissemination of the ideas of Marxism (even though in a vulgarised form). Besides, the alliance was concluded not entirely without any 'conditions'. The proof: *Materials on the Question of the Economic Development of Russia*, the Marxist collection burned in 1895 by the censor. If the agreement to publish along with the legally-permitted Marxists can be compared to a political alliance, then this book can be compared to a political treaty.

The break was caused, of course, not because the 'allies' turned out to be bourgeois democrats. On the contrary, the representatives of this tendency are the natural and desirable allies of Social Democracy, insofar as its democratic tasks are concerned – tasks that are brought to the forefront by the present-day position of Russia. But a necessary condition of such an alliance is the full possibility for socialists to reveal to the worker class the hostile opposition between its interests and the interests of the bourgeoisie. But Bernsteinism and the 'critical' tendency to which a clear majority of the legally-permitted Marxists belong removed this possibility: they led socialist awareness astray, they vulgarised Marxism, preached a theory of the blunting of social contradictions, labelled the idea of social revolution and the dictatorship of the proletariat as absurd, reduced the worker movement and the class struggle to a narrow *tred-iunionizm* and a 'realistic' struggle for petty, gradual reforms. This is entirely equivalent to bourgeois democracy's negation of socialism's right to independence and, therefore, its right to exist; it signifies, in practice, a striving to transform the worker movement that is now commencing into a tail of the liberals.

Naturally, a break was inevitable under these conditions. But the 'unique' particularity of Russia shows itself in this: the break meant a simple elimination of the Social Democrats from 'legally-permitted' literature of the kind most accessible to everybody and widely disseminated. In this literature were now entrenched the 'used-to-be Marxists' who arose 'under the sign of criticism' and received close to a monopoly of 'denunciation' of Marxism. The slogans 'against orthodoxy' and 'long live freedom of criticism' (now repeated by *Rabochee delo*) immediately became fashionable catchwords. That censors and the gendarmes had no problems at all with this fashion is evident from such facts as the appearance of *three* Russian editions of the book of the notorious (notorious à la Herostratus) Bernstein or the recommendation by Zubatov of the books of Bernstein, Prokopovich and so on (*Iskra*, No. 10). On Social Democracy now lay the difficult task – a heavy one in and of itself and made unbelievably more difficult by purely external obstacles – of a struggle with the new current [of 'criticism']. And this current did not confine itself to the literary arena. The turn toward 'criticism' was met by a corresponding infatuation with 'economism' on the part of the *praktiki* of Social Democracy.

The interesting issue of how the link and interdependence between legally-permitted criticism and illegal 'economism' originated and grew up could be the subject of a special article. For us, it is sufficient to note the undoubted existence of this link. The notorious *Credo* acquired such well deserved renown just for the reason that it openly formulated this link and blurted out the basic political tendency of 'economism': have the workers carry out the economic struggle (to speak more precisely: the *tred-iunionist* struggle, for this struggle embraces a specific worker politics as well), and have the Marxist intellectuals fuse with the liberals for a political 'struggle'. *Tred-iunionist* work 'among the people' would be the fulfilment of the first half of this task and legal criticism the second half. This declaration was such a excellent weapon against 'economism' that if the *Credo* didn't exist, it would be worth inventing it.

The *Credo* wasn't invented, but it was published without the knowledge and, perhaps, even against the will of its authors. At least, the writer of these lines, a participant in bringing the new 'programme' to the light of God's world, had to hear complaints and reproaches that a brief summary of views thrown together by participants in a conversation was disseminated in copies, received the label *Credo* and was even printed along with a protest! We touch on this episode because it reveals a very curious trait of our 'economism': its fear of publicity [*glasnost*]. This is indeed a trait of 'economism' in general and not only the authors of the *Credo*: it appears in *Rabochaia mysl*, the most direct and open advocate of 'economism', and in *Rabochee delo* (indignant about the publication of 'economist' documents in *Vademecum*), and in the

Kiev committee that two years ago refused permission for the publication of its 'Profession de foi' along with a written refutation of it,[4] and in many, many individual representatives of 'economism'.

This fear of criticism manifested by the partisans of freedom of criticism cannot be explained only by cunning (although, undoubtedly, sometimes cunning is not absent: it would be unwise to expose the new and as yet weak growths of the new tendency to the attacks of opponents!). No, the majority of 'economists' are completely sincere when they regard (and, by the very essence of 'economism', must regard) with disapproval any kind of theoretical disputes, factional disagreements, broad political questions, projects to organise the revolutionaries and so forth. 'Leave all that to the émigrés!' – this is what one of the more thorough-going 'economists' once said to me, and he expressed in this way a widely disseminated (but still purely *tred-iunionist*) view of things: our business is the worker movement along with the worker organisations that are here in our locality – and as for the rest, it's all something made up by doctrinaires, an 'overvaluation of ideology', as the authors of the letter in No. 12 *Iskra* put it in unison with No. 10, *Rabochee delo*.

Let us now ask ourselves: in view of these peculiarities of Russian 'criticism' and Russian Bernsteinism, what should have been the task of those who wish to be opponents of opportunism in deed and not just in word? Firstly, it was imperative to take over the job of renewing theoretical work that had only just begun in the era of legally-permitted Marxism and that now fell again to the lot of illegal activists – the successful growth of the movement is impossible without such work. Secondly, it was necessary to come out actively in the struggle with the legally-permitted 'criticism' that so strongly leads people's outlook astray. Thirdly, it was imperative to come out actively against confusion and unsteadiness in the practical movement, exposing and refuting any attempts to consciously or unconsciously lower the level of our programs and our tactics.

It is a well-known truth that *Rabochee delo* did not do the first nor the second nor the third, and, later on, we will have explain this well-known truth in detail and from a number of angles. All I want to do now is to show the glaring contradiction between the demand for 'freedom of criticism' and

---

[4] As far as we know, the composition of the Kiev committee has changed since that time.

the specific features of our own home-grown criticism and our Russian 'economism'. And, in this connection, look at the text of the resolution with which the 'Union of Russian Social Democrats Abroad' [the parent organisation of *Rabochee delo*] endorsed the point of view of *Rabochee delo*:

> In the interests of the further ideological development of Social Democracy we see freedom of criticism in party literature to be unconditionally necessary, insofar as this criticism does not stand opposed to the class and revolutionary character of this theory. (*Two Congresses*, p. 10.)

The resolution is supported as follows: the resolution 'in its first half coincides with the resolution of the Lübeck party congress [of the SPD] about Bernstein . . . (in their charming naïveté, the Union people do not even notice what a *testimonium paupertatis* (proof of poverty) they provide for themselves by means of this copy-catting!) . . . but . . . in the second half we limit freedom of criticism more stringently than the Lübeck party congress'.

So, the resolution of the Union is directed against Russian Bernsteinists? Otherwise, it would be completely absurd to refer to Lübeck! But it is not true that the Union resolution 'stringently limits freedom of criticism'. The Germans, in their Hanover resolution, rejected point after point of *precisely those* revisions proposed by Bernstein, and the Lübeck resolution gave a warning to *Bernstein in person*, naming him in the resolution. Meanwhile, our 'free' imitators do not mention *in any way* a *single* manifestation of specifically Russian 'criticism' and Russian 'economism'; given this silence, the bare reference to the class and revolutionary character of theory leaves a very wide space open for misinterpretation, especially when the Union refuses to categorise 'so-called economism' as opportunism (*Two Congresses*, p. 8, remark on point 1).

But this is only in passing. The main point is that the position of the opportunists vis-à-vis the revolutionary Social Democrats is entirely different in Russia and in Germany. In Germany, revolutionary Social Democrats stand, as we know, for the preservation of what exists: the old programme and tactics that everybody knows and that have been worked out to the last detail by long decades of experience. The 'critics' are the ones who want to introduce changes, and, besides, since these critics are an insignificant minority and their revisionist strivings are very timid, the majority understandably can limit itself to a dry rejection of these 'innovations'. But, for us Russians, it is the critics and the 'economists' who stand for the preservation of what exists: the 'critics' want people to consider them still to be Marxists and to guarantee them their 'freedom of criticism', which they enjoy in every sense of the word (because they basically do not recognise[5] any *party* tie, especially since we have no generally recognised party organ that could 'limit' their freedom of criticism even with good advice); the 'economists' want the revolutionaries to admit 'the full rights of the movement now existing' (*Rabochee delo*, No. 10, p. 25), that is, the 'legitimacy' of the existence of that which exists; they demand that the 'ideologues' should not try to cause the movement 'to stray' from the path which 'is determined by the interaction of material elements and the material environment' (Letter in No. 12, *Iskra*); they demand that we acknowledge as desirable the struggle 'that is the only possible one for the workers to conduct under the present circumstances', and that we acknowledge, as the only one possible, the struggle 'that they are actually conducting at the present moment' ('Separate Supplement' to *Rabochaia mysl*, p. 14). We revolutionary Social Democrats, on the other hand, are unhappy with this kow-towing to *stikhiinost*, that is, that which exists 'at the present moment'; we are the ones demanding changes in the dominant tactic of recent years; we openly state that 'before uniting and for the sake of uniting, it is necessary resolutely and firmly to draw lines of demarcation' (taken from the announcement of *Iskra*'s publication). In a word, the Germans stand for the given situation and reject changes; we demand changes in the given situation and strive against kow-towing to this situation and any reconciliation with it.

It is this 'little' difference that our 'free' copycats of German resolutions have not noticed!

---

[5] Just by itself, this absence of an open party tie and party traditions constitutes a cardinal difference between Russia and Germany that should warn off any reasonable socialist from blind imitation. And here is a good example of what 'freedom of criticism' leads to in Russia. A Russian 'critic', Mr. Bulgakov, made the following rebuke to a Austrian critic, Hertz: 'For all the independence of his conclusions, Hertz on this point (on co-operatives), evidently still remains somewhat bound by the opinion of his party and, while he differs in details, cannot bring himself to break with the common principle' (*Capitalism and Agriculture*, vol. 2, p. 287). Here, we see the subject of a politically enslaved state in which 999/1,000 of the population is led astray to the very marrow by political servility and by a complete lack of understanding of party honour and party ties, and he grandly rebukes the citizen of a constitutional state because he is excessively 'tied by the opinion of his party'! All that remains is for our illegal organisations to start composing resolutions about freedom of criticism . . .

## d) Engels on the significance of theoretical struggle

'Dogmatism, doctrinairism', 'ossification of the party – the inevitable punishment for the forcible bottling-up of thought' – these are the enemies against which the gallant knights of *Rabochee delo* make battle for the sake of 'freedom of criticism'. – We are very glad that this issue has been raised and would only propose adding another question:

Who are the judges?

Lying in front of us are two announcements of literary ventures. One is the 'Programme of *Rabochee delo*, the periodic organ of the Union of Russian Social Democrats' (offprint from No. 1 of *Rabochee delo*). The other is 'Announcement of the renewal of the publications of the Emancipation of Labour group'. Both are dated from 1899, when the 'crisis of Marxism' had long been placed on the order of the day. And what do we find? In the first of these productions, you will search in vain for any reference to this phenomenon or any definite exposition of the stand that the new publication intended to take on this issue. There is not a word in this programme about theoretical work and its present tasks, nor is there in the supplements to it that were adopted by the third congress of the Union in 1901 (*Two Congresses*, pp. 15–18). During all this time, the editors of *Rabochee delo* neglected theoretical issues, although these issues were of absorbing interest to all Social Democrats all over the world.

In contrast, the other announcement [from the Emancipation of Labour group] first of all points to the weakening of interest in theory in recent years, insistently demands 'vigilant attention to the theoretical side of the revolutionary movement of the proletariat' and calls for 'a merciless critique of Bernsteinist and other anti-revolutionary tendencies' in our movement. The issues of *Zaria* that have since come out show how this programme of action was fulfilled.

Thus we see that pompous phrases about the ossification of thought and so on conceals lack of concern and lack of ability in the development of theoretical work. The example of Russian Social Democrats illustrates with particular clarity a pan-European phenomenon (already long noted by German Marxists) that the vaunted freedom of criticism does not mean the substitution of one theory for another but freedom from any consistent and thoroughly considered theory – it means eclecticism and lack of principle. Anyone who is at all familiar with the actual state of our movement cannot help seeing that the wide dissemination of Marxism was accompanied by a definite lowering of theoretical standards. Thanks to its practical significance and practical successes, the movement attracted quite a few people who had very little and even no theoretical preparation. One can therefore judge the lack of judgement shown by *Rabochee delo* when it promotes with a triumphal flourish Marx's epigram: 'Every step of a genuine movement is more important than a dozen programmes.' To repeat these words in an era of theoretical disarray is the same as crying 'Many happy returns of the day!' to a funeral procession. And, besides, these words are taken from Marx's letter about the Gotha Programme, in which he *sharply denounces* its eclecticism in the formulation of principles: if it is necessary to merge – wrote Marx to the leaders of the Party – then strike an agreement for the sake of achieving the practical aims of the movement, but don't make deals at the expense of principles, don't make theoretical 'concessions'. This is how Marx thought, and yet we find people who try in his name to weaken the significance of theory!

Without a revolutionary theory there can be no revolutionary movement. It is impossible to emphasise this thought too much at a time when along with the fashionable preaching of opportunism people are carried away with the narrowest possible forms of practical activity. And, for Russian Social Democracy in particular, the significance of theory is intensified by three circumstances that people often forget. First, our Party is just now beginning to form, is just now working out its profile and is still far from settling accounts with other tendencies of revolutionary thought that threaten to cause the movement to stray from the correct path. On the contrary, we see that it is precisely the recent period that has seen a new vitality in non-Social-Democratic revolutionary tendencies (as Akselrod forecast to the 'economists' long ago). Under these circumstances, a mistake that seems at first to be 'unimportant' can have the most unfortunate consequences, so that only myopic people can regard factional disputes and a strict separation of nuances to be premature or superfluous. The whole future of Russian Social Democracy for many years to come can depend on the relative strength of this or that 'nuance'.

Second, the Social-Democratic movement is international in its very essence. This does not only mean that we must struggle with national chauvinism. It also means that a movement starting up in a young country can be successful only if it assimilates the experience of other countries. And this kind of assimilation requires more than a simple familiarity with this experience or a simple copying of the latest resolutions. It requires the ability to have a critical attitude toward this experience and to verify it independently. Anyone who takes the trouble to reflect on how enormously the present-day worker movement has grown and developed will realise what a reservoir of theoretical forces and of political (as well as revolutionary) experience is necessary for the fulfilment of this task.

Third, the national tasks of Russian Social Democracy are unlike those confronted by any other socialist party in the world. Later, we will have occasion to talk about the political and organisational obligations that are assigned to us by the task of liberating the whole people from the yoke of autocracy. Now, we wish only to underline that *the role of an advanced fighter can only be fulfilled by a party guided by an advanced theory*. And to have some concrete idea of what this means, let the reader recall such forerunners of Russian Social Democracy as Herzen, Belinsky, Chernyshevsky and the brilliant galaxy of revolutionaries of the seventies; let him remember the world significance that Russian literature has now acquired; let him . . . but let that suffice!

We will now quote some remarks of Engels from 1874 on the issue of the significance of theory in the Social-Democratic movement. Engels recognises *not just two* forms of the great struggle of Social Democracy (political and economic) – as is customary with us – *but three, putting theoretical struggle alongside the other two*. His words of advice to the German worker movement – one that was already strong politically and practically – are so educational from the point of view of present-day issues and disputes that the reader will forgive us, we hope, for the long citation from the preface to the pamphlet 'The German Peasant War', copies of which have long since become extremely rare:

> The German workers have two essential advantages compared to the workers in the rest of Europe. The first is that they belong to the most theoretical people of Europe and that they preserve the sense of theory that has almost completely been squandered by the so-called 'educated' classes in Germany. Without the German philosophy that preceded it, in particular the philosophy of Hegel, German scientific socialism – the only scientific socialism that has ever existed – would not have been created. Without this sense of theory among the workers, this scientific socialism would never have entered into their flesh and blood to the degree that we see today. And how unimaginably great is this advantage is demonstrated, on the one hand,

by the indifference to any theory that constitutes one of the principal reasons why the English worker movement moves forward so slowly, despite its magnificent organisation of separate crafts – and on the other hand, it is demonstrated by the confusion and unsteadiness that Proudhonism sowed among the French and the Belgians in its original form and among the Spanish and the Italians in the caricature form given to it by Bakunin.

The second advantage is that the Germans took part in the [international] worker movement later than almost anybody else. German theoretical socialism will never forget that it stands on the shoulders of Saint-Simon, Fourier, and Owen – three thinkers who despite all the fantastic utopianism of their teaching were among the greatest thinkers of all time and who anticipated with genius an infinite number of those truths whose correctness we have demonstrated scientifically only now. In just the same way, the German practical worker movement should never forget that it developed on the shoulders of the English and French movements, that it enjoyed the possibility of simply taking over for its own use the experience acquired with so much difficulty and of avoiding those errors today that for the most part were impossible to avoid earlier. Where would we be now without the image of the English *tred-iuniony* and the French political struggle of the workers, without the colossal push forward given in particular by the Paris Commune?

It is only fair to the German workers to note that they have used the advantages of their position with rare ability. For the first time since the existence of the worker movement, the struggle is conducted systematically in all three of its aspects that are co-ordinated and linked among themselves: theoretical, political and practical-economic (resistance to the capitalists). In this, so to speak, concentric attack lies the strength and the invincibility of the German movement.

As a consequence of this advantageous position on the one hand and of the insular particularities of the English movement and the violent repression of the French one on the other, the German workers at the present moment are placed at the head of the proletarian struggle. How long events will allow them to occupy this responsible post cannot be predicted. But as long as they do occupy it, one may hope that they will carry out the responsibilities given to them in a fitting way. This requires a doubled intensification of forces in all areas of struggle and agitation. In particular it is the responsibility of the leaders [*vozhdi*] to enlighten themselves more and more in theoretical issues, to liberate themselves more and more from the influence of traditional phrases that belong to the old worldview and to always keep in mind that from the time it became scientific, socialism demands to be treated as a science, that is, that it must be studied. The ever more clear awareness acquired in this way must be disseminated among the worker masses with ever greater zeal – the solidarity of the organisation of the party and the organisation of the trade unions must be ever more powerfully strengthened. . . .

. . . If the German workers will go forward in this way, then they will – not so much march at the head of the movement, since it is not at all in the interests of the movement that the workers of any one nation march at its head – but they will occupy a place of honour in the ranks of the fighters; and they will stand ready and armed if unexpectedly heavy tests or great events demand from them even greater courage, even greater resoluteness and energy.

Engels's words proved to be prophetic. Within a few years, the German workers did face an unexpectedly heavy test in the form of the exceptional law against socialism. And the German workers indeed stood ready and armed and were able to emerge victoriously from this test.

The Russian proletariat faces tests that are incomparably heavier, faces a struggle against a monster in comparison with which the exceptional law in a constitutional country is a mere pygmy. History has put before us an immediate task that is *the most revolutionary* of all the *immediate* tasks of any other country. Carrying out this task – the destruction of the most powerful support not only of European but also (we can now say) Asiatic reaction – will make the Russian proletariat the vanguard of the international revolutionary proletariat. And we have the right to assume that we will attain this honourable calling that our predecessors, the revolutionaries of the seventies, already merited, if we know how to inspire our own movement, one that is a thousand times broader and deeper [than the movement of the 1870s], with the same dedicated resoluteness and energy.

# Chapter II

## The *Stikhiinost* of the Masses and the Purposiveness of Social Democracy

We said that our movement, much broader and deeper than the movement of the seventies, must be inspired with the same dedicated resoluteness and energy as then. Indeed, up to recently, it would seem, no one doubted that the strength of the present-day movement is the awakening of the masses (and principally the industrial proletariat), while its weakness is the inadequate purposiveness and initiative of the revolutionaries and leader/guides.

Just recently, however, a truly astounding discovery has been made that threatens to overthrow all the hitherto dominant views on this issue. This discovery was made by *Rabochee delo* in its polemic with *Iskra* and *Zaria*: not limiting itself only to specific objections, it tried to bring 'the general disagreement' to deeper roots – to 'a different evaluation of the *relative* significance of the *stikhiinyi* element and the purposive-"systematic" element'. The bill of indictment of *Rabochee delo* states: '*underestimation of the significance of the objective or stikhiinyi element of development*'.[1] In response, we say: if the polemic conducted by *Iskra* and *Zaria* led to no other results than prompting *Rabochee delo* to think up this 'general disagreement', then this result alone would give us

---

[1] *Rabochee delo*, No. 10, September 1901, pp. 17 and 18. *Rabochee delo*'s emphasis.

great satisfaction, so highly significant is this thesis, so bright a light does it shine on the essence of the present-day theoretical and political disagreements among Russian Social Democrats.

This is why the issue of the relationship between purposiveness and *stikhiinost* presents enormous general interest. It behooves us to dwell on this issue in great detail.

## a) The beginnings of the *stikhiinyi* upsurge

We have already noted the *wholesale* enthusiasm for Marxist theory among Russian educated youth in the middle of the 1890s. Just around this time, worker strikes took on the same wholesale character, after the famous Petersburg industrial war of 1896. Their dissemination throughout all Russia was a clear witness to the depth of the people's movement that was newly rising up, and if we are going to talk about the '*stikhiinyi* element', then, of course, it is precisely this strike movement that one must call '*stikhiinyi*' before anything else. But there are different kinds of *stikhiinost*. Strikes took place in Russia even in the 1870s and 1860s (and even in the first half of the nineteenth century), accompanied with '*stikhiinyi*' destruction of machines and so on. In comparison with these 'riots', the strikes of the 1890s can even be called 'purposive' – so significant is the step forward that the worker movement had made by this time. This shows us that the '*stikhiinyi* element' is, in essence, nothing other than the *embryonic form* of purposiveness.

Even primitive riots already express a certain awakening of purposiveness: the workers lost their age-old faith in the unshakability of the order that oppressed them, they began . . . I won't say to *understand*, but to *feel* the necessity of collective resistance, and they broke once and for all with slavish humility before the bosses. But this was still much more an expression of despair and revenge than of *struggle*. The strikes of the 1890s reveal much more of the rudiments of purposiveness: specific demands were set forth, the most convenient moment was calculated ahead of time, known occurrences and examples in other places were considered, and so forth. If the earlier riots had been the uprisings simply of oppressed people, then these systematic strikes already expressed the embryo of a class struggle – but, indeed, no more than the embryo. Taken in isolation, these strikes were simply a *tred-iunionist* struggle, but not yet a Social-Democratic one: they bore witness to the awakening of the antagonism between workers and owners, but there did not exist among these workers – nor could it have existed at that time – an awareness of the irreconcilable opposition of their interests to the entire political and social order, in other words, a Social-Democratic awareness. In *this* sense, the strikes of the 1890s, despite the enormous progress in comparison with the 'riots', remained a purely *stikhiinyi* movement.

We stated that *there could not have been* a Social-Democratic awareness [at that time] among the workers. It could have been brought in only from outside. The history of all countries bears witness that exclusively with its own forces the worker class is in a condition to work out only a *tred-iunionist* awareness, that is, a conviction of the need to unite in unions, to carry on a struggle with the owners, to strive for the promulgation by the government of this or that law that is necessary for the workers and so on.[2] The doctrine of socialism grew out of those philosophic, historical, and economic theories that were worked out by the educated representatives of the propertied classes, the intelligentsia. The founders of modern scientific socialism, Marx and Engels, belonged themselves, according to their social origin, to the bourgeois intelligentsia. In exactly the same way, in Russia as well, the theoretical doctrine of Social Democracy arose completely independently from the *stikhiinyi* growth of the worker movement, arose as a natural and inevitable development of thought among the revolutionary-socialist intelligentsia. At this same time – that is, the middle of the 1890s – this doctrine of scientific socialism had not only fully taken shape in the form of the programme of the 'Emancipation of Labour' group, but had also won to its side the majority of the revolutionary youth in Russia.

Thus there was on hand both the *stikhiinyi* awakening of the worker masses – the awakening to purposive life and purposive struggle – and the availability of a revolutionary youth armed with Social-Democratic theory, who were straining at the bit to get to the workers. In this connection, it is especially important to establish the often forgotten (and comparatively little known) fact that the *first* Social Democrats of that period – who *zealously carried on economic agitation* (and, in so doing, took full account of the genuinely useful

---

[2] *Tred-iunionism* certainly does not exclude any kind of 'politics', as is sometimes thought. *Tred-iuniony* always carry on some (non-Social-Democratic) political agitation and struggle. We will discuss the distinction between *tred-iunionist* and Social-Democratic politics in the next chapter.

instructions of *On Agitation*, then still in manuscript) – not only did not consider such agitation their sole task, but on the contrary *from the very beginning* put forward both Russian Social Democracy's broadest historical tasks in general and the task of the overthrow of the autocracy in particular.

For example, already at the end of 1895, the first issue of a newspaper entitled *Rabochee delo* had been put together by the group of Petersburg Social Democrats who founded the 'Union of Struggle for the Liberation of the Worker Class'. This issue was completely ready to go to press when it was seized by the police on the night of 8 December in a raid on the quarters of one of the members of the group, Anatolii Alekseev Vaneev,[3] and so this original *Rabochee delo* was not destined to see the light. The leading article of this newspaper (which, perhaps, some thirty years from now some Russian historical society will extract from the archives of the police department) outlined the historical tasks of the worker class in Russia, putting the conquest of political freedom at the head of these tasks. Along with this was an article about police persecution of the Literacy Committees entitled 'What Are Our Ministers Thinking Of?'; there was also a series of reports not only from Petersburg but also from other localities of Russia (for example, about the slaughter of the workers in Yaroslavl province). In this way, this (if I am not mistaken) 'first try' of the Russian Social Democrats was a newspaper without a narrow local character, much less an 'economistic' one – a newspaper that strove to merge the strike struggle with the revolutionary movement against the autocracy and to attract all those oppressed by the policies of reactionary obscurantism to the support of Social Democracy.

And nobody who is in the slightest degree acquainted with the state of the movement at that time will doubt that such a newspaper would have met with full sympathy both from the workers of the capital and from the revolutionary intelligentsia and that the newspaper would have received the widest dissemination. The failure of the enterprise proves only that the Social Democrats back then did not have the forces to satisfy the demands of the moment, due to their lack of revolutionary experience and practical preparation. [Other Social-Democratic pronouncements of that period] – the *St. Petersburg*

---

[3] A.A. Vaneev died in 1899 in East Siberia from the tuberculosis picked up while in solitary confinement in pre-trial detention. We therefore judge it permissible to publish the information given in the text. We guarantee its reliability since it came from persons who were intimately acquainted with A.A. Vaneev.

*Rabochii Listok*, the *Manifesto* issued by the newly-formed Russian Social-Democratic Party in spring 1898, and especially *Rabochaia Gazeta* – had [a similar content, prospects and fate].

It goes without saying that it would never occur to us to blame the activists of that period for this lack of preparation. But in order to draw some practical lessons from this first try and to gain some benefit from the experience of the movement, it is necessary to be frank about the reasons and significance of this or that failing. Therefore it is extremely important to establish the point that a section (perhaps even the majority) of Social Democrats active during 1895–8 considered – with complete justice – that it was possible even then, at the very beginning of the '*stikhiinyi*' movement, to come forward with a very broad programme and a militant tactic.[4]

The lack of preparation of the majority of revolutionaries is completely natural and should not worry us overmuch. Given that there was a correct definition of tasks and also the energy to try again and again to fulfill those tasks, these temporary failures were only half-misfortunes. Revolutionary experience and organisational skills are things that come with time – *if* there is the desire to develop the necessary qualities in oneself. In a revolutionary cause, an awareness of our failings is more than halfway to fixing them!

But a half-misfortune became a real misfortune, when this awareness began to fade (and it was very much alive among the activists of the groups mentioned above) and when there appeared people – and even Social-Democratic periodicals – who came up with theoretical arguments that turned such failings into virtues, who even tried to justify *theoretically* their own *slavishness and kow-towing toward stikhiinost*. It is time to sum up the results of this tendency,

---

[4] '*Iskra* has a negative attitude toward the activity of Social Democracy at the end of the 1890s and ignores the absence during that time of the conditions for any other work than the struggle for petty demands' – so announce the 'economists' in their 'Letter to Russian Social-Democratic Organs' (*Iskra*, No. 12). The facts given in the text above demonstrate that this affirmation of the 'absence of conditions' is *diametrically opposed to the truth*. Not only at the end, but even in the middle of the 1890s, conditions were completely ready for work *other* than the struggle for petty demands – except for adequate preparation of the leader/guides. And now, instead of openly admitting this lack of preparation on our part – by us, the ideologues, the leader/guides – the 'economists' want to shift the blame to the 'absence of conditions', to the influence of the material environment that determines the path from which no ideologues can cause the movement to stray. What is this if not slavishness toward *stikhiinost*? What is it if not the infatuation of the 'ideologues' with their own inadequacies?

whose content is very inexactly characterised by the overly narrow label of 'economism'.

## b) Kow-towing to *stikhiinost: Rabochaia mysl*

Before moving on to the literary manifestation of this kow-towing, let us take note of the following characteristic fact (given to us by the source mentioned earlier), one that throws some light on how the split between the two future tendencies of Russian Social Democracy emerged and grew up in the milieu of comrades active in Petersburg. At the beginning of 1897, just before they were sent into internal exile, A.A. Vaneev and several of his comrades happened to participate in a private meeting that brought together the 'old' and the 'young' members of the Union of Struggle for the Liberation of the Worker Class. The conversation mainly focused on organisation and in particular on the same 'Rules for a Worker Fund' that were published in their final form [in late 1898] in No. 9–10 of *Listok Rabotnika* (p. 46). Between the 'veterans' (the 'Decembrists', as Petersburg Social Democrats then called them as a joke) and several of the 'youngsters' (who later collaborated with *Rabochaia mysl*) immediately arose a sharp disagreement, and a heated polemic broke out. The 'youngsters' defended the main principles of the Rules as they were printed. The 'veterans' said that what we needed most of all was not that, but a strengthening of the Union of Struggle into an organisation of revolutionaries to which would be subordinated various worker funds, circles for propaganda among students and so forth. It goes without saying that the disputants were far from seeing this disagreement as the beginning of a parting of the ways – on the contrary, they assumed it was unique and accidental. But this fact demonstrates that the emergence and dissemination of 'economism' took place in Russia not without a struggle from the 'old' Social Democrats (the current 'economists' often forget this). And if this struggle, for the most part, has not left any 'documentary' traces, the *sole* reason is this: the composition of active circles changed unbelievably often, no continuity could be established and, therefore, disagreements were not fixed in written documents.

The emergence of *Rabochaia mysl* brought 'economism' into the light, but also not right away. One must concretely grasp the conditions of work and the short duration of the existence of Russian [underground] circles (and only those who lived through them could grasp these concretely) in order to understand what a role chance played in the success or failure of the new tendency in various towns and why for a long time neither the supporters nor the opponents of the 'new' tendency could not – were literally unable – to determine whether this was a real tendency of its own or whether it was simply the expression of the lack of preparation of particular individuals. For example, the first hectographed issue of *Rabochaia mysl* remained utterly unknown to the vast majority of Social Democrats, and if we now can refer to the editorial contained in this first issue, this is only because it was reprinted in the article by V.I. (*Listok Rabotnika* No. 9–10, p. 47 ff.), who did not neglect, of course, to zealously (over-zealously) praise the new publication that distinguished itself so sharply from the newspapers and the projects for newspapers mentioned earlier.[5] And it is worth dwelling on this editorial, so clearly does it bring out the *whole spirit* of *Rabochaia mysl* and 'economism' in general.

After noting that the man in the blue uniform [the gendarme] cannot halt the development of the worker movement, the editorial continues: '. . . the worker movement is indebted for this kind of vitality to the fact that the worker himself has finally taken over his own fate, since he has torn it out of the hands of their leader/guides', and this basic thesis is then developed in detail. In actuality, the leader/guides (that is, the Social Democrats, the organisers of the Union of Struggle) were so to speak torn out of the hands of the workers by the police[6] – and yet the matter is presented as if the workers struggled with these leader/guides and freed themselves from their yoke! Instead of urging people forward – toward the strengthening of the revolutionary organisation and the broadening of political activity – the writers urge people *back* to nothing but a *tred-iunionist* struggle. They pompously announce that 'the economic foundation of the movement is obscured by the

---

[5] By the way, this praise of *Rabochaia mysl* in November 1898, when 'economism,' especially abroad, was completely formed, comes from the same V.I. who soon thereafter became one of the editors of *Rabochee delo*. And *Rabochee delo* denied even the existence of two tendencies in Russian Social Democracy and continues to deny it still today!

[6] The correctness of this comparison can be seen from the following characteristic fact. When, after the arrest of the 'Decembrists,' the news was disseminated among the workers in the region of the Schlüsselburg highway that the *proval* was aided by the dentist and provocateur N.N. Mikhailov (who was close to one of the groups attached to the 'Decembrists'), these workers were so outraged that they decided to kill him.

unceasing striving not to forget the political ideal', that the watchword of the worker movement is 'the struggle for [one's] economic position' (!) or, even better, 'workers for the worker'; it is announced that strike funds 'are more valuable for the movement than a hundred other organisations' (compare this statement from October 1897 with the dispute of the 'Decembrists' with the 'youngsters' at the beginning of the year) and so forth. Various catchwords – our focus should not be on the 'cream' of the workers but on the 'middle' worker, the mass worker, or 'politics always obediently follows after economics'[7] and so forth and so on – became fashionable and acquired an overwhelming influence on the mass of young people who were attracted into the movement and who were familiar in most cases only with fragments of Marxism as set forth in legally-permitted publications.

Purposiveness was completely overwhelmed by *stikhiinost* – the *stikhiinost* of those 'Social Democrats' who parroted the 'ideas' of Mr. V.V., the *stikhiinost* of those workers who succumbed to the argument that adding a kopeck to the rouble is nearer and more to be valued than any socialism or any politics, that they should conduct a struggle 'knowing that they are not fighting just for some kind of future generation but for themselves and their children' (editorial of *Rabochaia mysl*, No. 1). Phrases like this have always been the favourite tool of those Western-European bourgeois who hate socialism and therefore work (like the German *Sozialpolitiker* Hirsch) to transplant English *tred-iunionizm* to their own home soil, telling the workers that it is the exclusively-trade-union struggle[8] that is precisely the struggle for themselves and their children – without worrying about future generations with their future socialism – and now the 'V.V.'s of Russian Social Democracy' set about repeating these bourgeois phrases. It is important at this point to focus on three circumstances that will be very useful to us as we continue to analyse *present-day* disagreements.[9]

---

[7] This comes from the same editorial in the first issue of *Rabochaia mysl*. This statement allows one to judge the theoretical preparation of these 'V.V.'s of Russian Social Democracy' who repeat the crude debasement of 'economic materialism' at the same time as the Marxists were conducting literary war against the real V.V., long ago given the moniker 'reactionary par excellence' for the *same* understanding of politics and economics.

[8] The Germans even have a special word, *Nur-Gewerkschaftler*, signifying the supporters of 'exclusively-trade-union' struggle.

[9] The emphasis on 'present-day' is aimed at those who shrug their shoulders in

First, the replacement of purposiveness by *stikhiinost* mentioned above itself occurred in a *stikhiinyi fashion*. This seems like a play on words, but it is – alas! – the bitter truth. It happened not by way of open struggle between two completely opposed outlooks and the victory of one over the other, but by way of the gendarmes who [to use the words of *Rabochaia mysl*] 'tore away' a greater and greater number of revolutionary-'veterans' and by way of a greater and greater appearance on the scene of 'young' 'V.V.'s of Russian Social Democracy'. Anyone who – I won't say participates in the *present-day* Russian movement but only sniffed its air, knows very well that this is exactly how the matter stands. And if, none the less, we insist that the reader completely grasps this well-known fact, if for ocular proof, so to speak, we provide data about the original [and never published] *Rabochee delo* and about the dispute between 'veterans' and 'youngsters' at the beginning of 1897 – this is because some people who boast of their 'democratism' speculate on the lack of knowledge of this fact on the part of the broad public (or on the part of some especially young people). We will return to this matter later.

Second, already in this first literary manifestation of 'economism', we are able to observe something to the highest degree original and extremely characteristic for the understanding of all disagreements in the ranks of present-day Social Democrats. The supporters of a 'purely worker movement', worshippers of the closest and most 'organic' (the expression of *Rabochee delo*) link with the proletarian struggle, opponents of any non-worker intelligentsia (even if it is a socialist intelligentsia) are compelled for the defence of their position to resort to the conclusions of *bourgeois* 'exclusively *tred-iunionists*'. This shows us that *Rabochaia mysl*, from the very beginning, undertook – itself unaware of the fact – to implement the programme of the *Credo*. This shows – (what *Rabochee delo* simply cannot understand) – that *any* kow-towing before the *stikhiinost* of the worker movement, any disparagement of the role of the 'purposive element', of the role of Social Democracy, *signals* just by itself, – *completely independent of whether the disparager wishes this or not – the strengthening of the influence of bourgeois ideology on the workers*. All those who talk about the 'over-valuation of ideology', of the exaggeration of the role of the purposive

---

pharisaical fashion and say: it is easy nowadays to tear *Rabochaia mysl* apart, but really the whole issue is dead and buried! *Mutato nomine de te fabula* – this is our answer to these present-day Pharisees whose complete enslavement to the ideas of *Rabochaia mysl* is *proven* below.

element and so forth, imagine that a purely worker movement can work out all by itself and is now working out an ideology standing by itself [apart from socialist ideology], if only the workers 'tear their fate out of the hands of their leader/guides'. But this is a profound error. To supplement what we have just said, we will also cite the following profoundly true and important words of K. Kautsky, speaking about the draft of the new programme of the Austrian Social-Democratic Party:[10]

> Many of our revisionist critics assume that Marx affirmed that economic development and class struggle create not only the conditions for socialist production, but also immediately generate the *awareness* (Kautsky's emphasis) of its necessity. And then these critics object that the country with the highest capitalist development, England, is the one most foreign to this awareness. On the basis of the [proposed new] draft, one would think that the commission that worked out the Austrian programme shared this allegedly orthodox Marxist view that has been refuted in the indicated way. This draft reads: 'The more capitalist development increases the proletariat, the more the proletariat is compelled to conduct the struggle against capitalism and receives the possibility of doing so. The proletariat comes to the awareness' of the possibility and necessity of socialism. In this context socialist awareness is presented as the necessary immediate result of the proletarian class struggle.
>
> But this is completely untrue. Naturally, socialism as a doctrine is as deeply rooted in modern economic relations as is the class struggle of the proletariat, just as both of them flow from the struggle against the poverty and desperation of the masses generated by capitalism. Nevertheless, socialism and the class struggle emerge side by side and not one from the other – they arise with different preconditions. Modern socialist awareness can emerge only on the basis of profound scientific knowledge. In fact, modern economic science is as much a condition of socialist production as modern, say, technology. The proletariat, even if it wanted to, cannot create either the one or the other: both emerge from the modern social process.
>
> The carrier of science is not the proletariat, but the *bourgeois intelligentsia* (Kautsky's emphasis): modern socialism emerges in the heads of individual

---

[10] *Neue Zeit*, 1901–2, XX, I, No. 3, p. 79. The commission draft of which K. Kautsky speaks was adopted by the Vienna Congress (at the end of the past year) in a somewhat modified form.

members of this stratum and then is communicated by them to proletarians who stand out due to their mental development, who in turn bring it into the class struggle of the proletariat where conditions allow. In this way, socialist awareness is something brought in to the class struggle of the proletariat from without (*von aussen Hineingetragenes*), and not something that emerges from the class struggle in *stikhiinyi* fashion (*urwüchsig*).

Correspondingly, the old Hainfeld Programme said with complete justice that the task of Social Democracy is bringing to the proletariat (literally: filling the proletariat up with) the *awareness* of its position and the awareness of its task. But there would be no need for this if such awareness flowed out of the class struggle all by itself. The new draft takes this thesis from the old Programme and then attaches to it the thesis mentioned above. But the train of thought is completely disrupted thereby . . .

Once we realise that there can be no question of an ideology standing by itself and worked out by the worker masses in the very course of their movement,[11] then the question stands *only in this way*: bourgeois or socialist ideology. There is no middle way (for humanity has not worked out any kind of 'third' ideology, and in general, in a society torn apart by class contradictions there can never be a non-class or supra-class ideology). Therefore *any* disparagement of socialist ideology, *any* distancing from it signals in and of itself a strengthening of bourgeois ideology.

People talk about *stikhiinost*. But the *stikhiinyi* development of the worker movement goes precisely to its subordination to bourgeois ideology, goes precisely *according to the Credo programme*, because the *stikhiinyi* worker movement *is tred-iunionizm, is Nur-Gewerkschaftlerei* – and *tred-iunionizm* is

---

[11] This does not mean, of course, that workers do not participate in this working-out. But they participate not *qua* workers, but *qua* theoreticians of socialism – as Proudhons and Weitlings. In other words, they participate only insofar as they succeed to a greater or lesser extent in attaining a command of the knowledge of their century and in advancing that knowledge. In order for workers to *succeed in doing this more often*, it is necessary to occupy ourselves as much as possible in raising the level of purposiveness of workers in general – it is necessary for workers not to confine themselves within the narrow framework of *'writing for workers'* but to study to achieve a greater and greater command of *what is written for all*. Instead of saying 'confine themselves,' we should really say 'are confined' – because the workers themselves read and want to read all that is written for the intelligentsia, and only some (bad) intellectuals think that it is sufficient 'for the workers' to talk about factory conditions and chew over what has long been known.

precisely the ideological enslavement of the workers by the bourgeoisie. Therefore our task – the task of Social Democracy – consists of a *struggle with stikhiinost*, consists in *causing* the worker movement *to stray* away from this *stikhiinyi* striving of *tred-iunionism* toward accepting the leadership of the bourgeoisie and in causing the worker movement to go toward accepting the leadership of revolutionary Social Democracy. The words used by the authors of the 'economist' letter in *Iskra*, No. 12 – i.e., that the efforts even of the most inspired ideologues cannot cause the worker movement to stray from the path determined by the interaction of material elements and the material environment – is therefore *utterly equivalent* to the *renunciation of socialism*, and if the authors were capable of thinking through what they are saying fearlessly and logically to the end – as anyone who steps forward in the arena of journalistic and social activity should do – then nothing would be left for them to do but 'rest their useless arms on an empty breast' and – and leave the field of activity to Messrs. Struve and Prokopovich, who drag the worker movement 'along the line of least resistance', that is, along the line of bourgeois *tred-iunionizm*, or to the Zubatovs of the world who drag it along the line of a priest/gendarme 'ideology'.

Remember the example of Germany. What historical service did Lassalle perform for the German worker movement? It was this: he *caused* the movement *to stray* from the path of the Progressive Party's *tred-iunionizm* and co-operativism – the path along which it was moving in *stikhiinyi* fashion (*with the benign participation of Schulze-Delitzsch and his like*). To carry out this task, Lassalle needed something a lot different from talk about underestimating the *stikhiinyi* element, about tactics-as-process, about interaction of elements and environment and so on. This task required a *desperate struggle with stikhiinost*, and only as a result of this struggle carried out over many long years were results obtained like this one: the worker population of Berlin changed from a bulwark of the Progressive Party to one of the finest fortresses of Social Democracy. And this struggle is in no way finished today (as it might seem to people who get their history of the German movement from Prokopovich and its philosophy from Struve). And even now the German worker class, if I may so express it, is fragmented among a number of ideologies: a portion of the workers are merged with the Catholic and monarchical unions, another portion in the Hirsch-Duncker unions founded by bourgeois supporters of English *tred-iunionizm*, and a third portion in the Social-Democratic unions.

This last portion is immeasurably larger than all the rest, but Social-Democratic ideology was able to achieve this primacy and will be able to preserve this primacy only by way of unremitting struggle with all other ideologies.

But why – the reader will ask – does the *stikhiinyi* movement, the movement [that goes] along the line of least resistance, go precisely to the domination of bourgeois ideology? For the simple reason that bourgeois ideology originated much longer ago than the socialist ideology, that it has been worked out in a more all-encompassing manner, and that it disposes of *immeasurably* greater means of dissemination.[12] And the younger the socialist movement is in any particular country, the more energetic must be the struggle against all attempts to strengthen the non-socialist ideology, the more resolutely must the workers be warned against those bad counsellors that cry out against 'the overestimation of the purposive element' and so forth. The authors of the 'economist' letter grumble in unison with *Rabochee delo* about the intolerance characteristic of the youthful period of the movement. Our answer is: yes, our movement really does find itself in a youthful condition – and, in order to grow to man's estate, it needs to be infected with intolerance toward people who hold back its growth by their kow-towing toward *stikhiinost*. There is nothing more harmful and nothing more laughable than to pose as veterans who have long ago lived through all the decisive episodes of the struggle!

Third, the first number of *Rabochaia mysl* shows us that the label 'economism' (which of course we will not refuse to use since this nickname has established itself one way or another) does not quite give us the essence of the new tendency. *Rabochaia mysl* does not completely deny the political struggle: the rules for a worker fund that are printed in *Rabochaia mysl*, No. 1 speak of a struggle with the government. *Rabochaia mysl* simply assumes that 'politics always obediently follows after economics' (while *Rabochee delo* varies this thesis by stating in its programme that 'in Russia more than any other country,

---

[12] It is often said: the worker class is drawn toward socialism *in stikhiinyi fashion*. This is completely true, in the sense that socialist theory defines the reasons for the distress of the worker class more profoundly and more truly than any other. Therefore the workers assimilate it very easily, *if* only this theory does not abdicate before *stikhiinost*, *if* only it subordinates *stikhiinost* to itself. Usually this goes without saying, but *Rabochee delo*, as it happens, forgets and distorts what goes without saying. The worker class is drawn in *stikhiinyi* fashion to socialism, but nevertheless bourgeois ideology, more broadly disseminated (and constantly resurrected in the most various forms), all the more thrusts itself on the worker in *stikhiinyi* fashion.

the economic struggle is *inextricably tied* to the political struggle'). These positions of *Rabochaia mysl* and *Rabochee delo* are completely untrue, *if we understand by 'politics' Social-Democratic politics*. Very often, the economic struggle of the workers is tied (although not inextricably) to a bourgeois politics, to a clerical politics and so on, as we have seen. The positions of *Rabochee delo* are true, if we understand by 'politics' a *tred-iunionist* politics – the general striving of all workers to obtain from the government that or that measure aimed against the misfortunes inherent in their position but not as yet aimed at eliminating that position, that is, not at annihilating the subordination of labour to capital. This striving is indeed common to the English *tred-iunionisty* who are hostile toward socialism, to the Catholic workers, to the 'Zubatov' workers and so forth. There is politics and politics. Thus, we see that *Rabochaia mysl* is an example not so much of an outright rejection of political struggle as of kow-towing to its *stikhiinost*, to its lack of purposiveness. Fully recognising a political struggle – or rather, not [necessarily] struggle, but [just] the political desires and demands of the workers – that grows in *stikhiinyi* fashion out of the worker movement itself, *Rabochaia mysl* completely refuses *to work out independently* a specifically *Social-Democratic politics* that answers to the general tasks of socialism as well as to present-day Russian conditions. Later we will show how *Rabochee delo* makes the same kind of mistake.

## c) The Self-Liberation Group and *Rabochee delo*

We have analysed with such detail the editorial of the first issue of *Rabochaia mysl* – little known and at the present time almost forgotten – because it expresses earlier than all others and more vividly than all others the general stream that later came into God's world in an infinite number of trickles. V.I. was completely right when he said, in praise of the first number of *Rabochaia mysl* and its editorial, that it was written 'sharply, with panache' (*Listok Rabotnika*, No. 9–10, p. 49). Anyone who has a firm opinion and believes he has something new to say writes 'with panache' and writes so as to express his views vividly. Only people who are accustomed to sit between two chairs lack all 'panache' – only such people are capable of praising one day the panache of *Rabochaia mysl* and attacking its opponents the next day for their 'polemical panache'.

Without dwelling on the Separate Supplement to *Rabochaia mysl* (for various reasons, we will have to refer later to this production which expresses more consistently than anywhere else the ideas of the 'economists'), we will take a short look here at the 'Appeal of the Worker Self-Liberation Group' (March 1899, reprinted in the London journal *Nakanune*, No. 7, July 1899). The authors of this appeal say very truly that 'worker Russia is *only just awakening*, only starting to look around and *instinctively to latching on to the first available* means of struggle'. But they draw from this the same incorrect conclusion as did *Rabochaia mysl*, forgetting that instinctiveness *is* the lack of purposiveness (*stikhiinost*) to whose aid socialists are supposed to come. They forget that the 'first available' means of struggle will in modern society always be the *tred-iunionist* means of struggle and that the 'first available' ideology will be the bourgeois (*tred-iunionist*) ideology. Also exactly like *Rabochaia mysl*, the authors do not reject politics but say only (only!), following Mr. V.V., that politics is a superstructure and that therefore 'political agitation should be a superstructure in relation to agitation in favour of the economic struggle, should grow out of that struggle and follow after it'.

As far as *Rabochee delo* is concerned, it began its activity with a straight-out 'defence' of the 'economists'. After saying a *direct untruth* in its very first issue (No. 1, pp. 141–2) – as if it 'did not know about what young comrades Akselrod was speaking' when he warned against the 'economists' in his well-known pamphlet[13] – *Rabochee delo* had to admit during the polemics that flared up with Plekhanov and Akselrod that 'under the guise of perplexity [it] wanted to *defend* all the young émigré Social Democrats from this unjust accusation' (Akselrod's accusation that the 'economists' were too narrow). As a matter of fact, the accusation was completely fair, and *Rabochee delo* knew very well that among those targeted was V.I. [Vladimir Ivanshin], a member of its editorial board. I note in passing that, in this polemic, Akselrod was completely correct and *Rabochee delo* completely incorrect in the interpretation of my pamphlet *Tasks of the Russian Social Democrats*. This pamphlet was written in 1897, that is, before the appearance of *Rabochaia mysl*, when I considered and had a right to consider the *original* tendency of the St. Petersburg Union of Struggle (as described above) as the dominant one [in Russian Social

---

[13] *The Contemporary Tasks and Tactics of Russian Social Democrats*. Geneva, 1898. Two letters to *Rabochaia gazeta*, written in 1897.

Democracy]. And up to the middle of 1898 at the very least, this tendency really was the dominant one. *Rabochee delo* had not the slightest right, therefore, to use a pamphlet that set forth views that were *pushed aside* by 'economist views' in St. Petersburg in 1897–8 as a support for their denial of the existence and danger of 'economism'.[14]

But *Rabochee delo* not only 'defended' the 'economists' but also constantly strayed off itself toward the basic confusions of the 'economists'. The source of this straying lies in the ambiguous interpretation of the following thesis from the *Rabochee delo* programme: 'we consider the most important phenomenon of Russian life, the one that for the most part *will determine the tasks* (our emphasis) and the character of the literary activity of the Union, to be the *mass worker movement*' (*Rabochee delo*'s emphasis). There can be no disputing that the mass movement is indeed the most important phenomenon. But the question is: what do we mean when we say that this mass movement 'determines tasks'? There are two possibilities: *either* in the sense of kow-towing before the *stikhiinost* of this movement, that is, reducing the role of Social Democracy down to a simple servicing of the worker movement as such (the possibility adopted by *Rabochaia mysl*, the Self-Liberation Group and other 'economists'); *or* in the sense that the mass movement puts before us *new* theoretical, political, organisational tasks, much more complicated than those found satisfactory in the period before the emergence of the mass movement. *Rabochee delo* tended and tends precisely toward the first understanding, because it never said anything that was at all definite about any kind of new tasks, but continually reasoned just as if the 'mass movement' *relieves* us of the necessity of being clearly aware and of solving the tasks brought forward by this movement. We need only point out that *Rabochee delo* considered it impossible to set before the mass worker movement the

---

[14] In defending its first untruth ('we don't know of which young comrades P.B. Akselrod was speaking') *Rabochee delo* added another, when it wrote in its *Answer*: 'After the review of *Tasks* was written, tendencies emerged or became more or less clearly defined in the direction of an economist one-sidedness that is a step backwards in comparison to the condition of our movement that was pictured in *Tasks*' (p. 9). Thus speaks the *Answer* that came out *in 1900*. But the first issue of *Rabochee delo* (containing the review) came out *in April 1899*. Does this mean that 'economism' only emerged in 1899? No, for in 1899 was distributed the first protest of *Russian* Social Democrats against 'economism' (protest against the *Credo*). But 'economism' emerged in 1897, as *Rabochee delo* knows perfectly well, because V.I. already *in November 1898* (*Listok Rabotnika*, No. 9–10) lauded *Rabochaia mysl*.

overthrow of the autocracy as its *first* task. It lowered this task (in the name of the mass movement) to the level of the task of fighting for immediate political demands (*Answer*, p. 25).

Without stopping at the article by the editor of *Rabochee delo* B. Krichevskii in No. 7 – 'Economic and Political Struggle in the Russian Movement', an article that repeats the same old mistakes[15] – let us move on directly to *Rabochee delo*, No. 10. Of course, we are not going to nit-pick with B. Krichevskii and Martynov about their various objections to *Zaria* and *Iskra*. All that interests us are the positions of principle that *Rabochee delo* takes up in No. 10. We are not going to analyse, for example, the following oddity: *Rabochee delo* sees a 'diametrical opposition' between what is said in *Iskra*, No. 1 and *Iskra*, No. 4.

*Iskra*, No. 1: 'Social Democracy does not tie its own hands [in advance], does not narrow its activity to any plan thought up ahead of time or to any one method of political struggle – it recognises all means of struggle, as long as they correspond to the available forces of the Party' and so forth.

The position set forth in *Iskra*, No. 4: 'If there is not a strong organisation that is tested in political struggle under all circumstances and during every period of time, then we cannot even talk about a systemic plan of activity that is illuminated by bedrock principles and steadfastly carried out – the kind of plan that alone deserves the name of tactics.'

---

[15] The 'theory of stages' or the theory of the 'timid zigzag' in the political struggle, for example, is expressed in this article in the following way: 'Political demands, which are by their very character common to all of Russia, must, however, during the first phases' (this was written in August 1900!) 'correspond to the experience drawn from the economic struggle by a given stratum (sic!) of the workers. Only (!) on the ground of this experience can one and should one move on to political agitation', etc. (p. 11). On p. 4, the author, protesting against what he regards as completely unfounded accusations of economist heresy, cries out with pathos: 'What kind of Social Democrat does not know that according to the teaching of Marx and Engels the economic interests of separate classes play a decisive role in history and, *therefore*, in particular, the struggle of the proletariat for its economic interests must have a paramount significance for its class development and liberation struggle?' (our emphasis). This 'therefore' is completely out of place. From the fact that economic interests play a decisive role, *no conclusion at all* can be drawn about the paramount significance of economic (= trade) struggle, for the most essential and 'decisive' interests of classes can be satisfied *only* by radical *political* changes in general, and in particular, the basic economic interest of the proletariat can be satisfied only by means of a political revolution that replaces the dictatorship of the bourgeoisie with the dictatorship of the proletariat. B. Krichevskii repeats the reasoning of the 'V.V.'s of Russian Social Democracy' (– politics follows economics and so on) and the reasoning of the Bernsteinists of German Social Democracy (for example, Woltmann tries to show by exactly this reasoning that the workers must first acquire 'economic strength' before they can even think about political revolution).

To confuse the recognition *in principle* of all means of struggle, all plans and methods, so long as they are expedient, with the insistence – if you want to say something useful about tactics – on the need *at the given political moment* to be guided by a plan steadfastly carried out, is tantamount to confusing the recognition of various systems of cure by medical science, on the one hand, with its insistence on one definite system in order to cure a given illness, on the other. But that's just it: *Rabochee delo*, although it itself suffers from the disease that we have named kow-towing before *stikhiinost*, does not want to recognise any 'system of cure' against *that* illness.

It therefore makes the remarkable discovery that 'tactics-as-plan contradicts the basic spirit of Marxism' (No. 10, p. 18), that tactics are '*a process of growth of party tasks that grow together with the Party*' (p. 11, *Rabochee delo*). This last pronouncement has a good chance of becoming a famous one that will provide an undying monument of the 'tendency' of *Rabochee delo*. In response to the question 'whither?', a guiding organ gives the answer: movement is a process of changing the distance between the beginning point and subsequent points of movement. This incomparable profundity is, however, not only a curiosity (in which case it would not be worth specially dwelling on) but the programme of *an entire tendency*, namely, the same programme that R.M. (in the Separate Supplement to *Rabochaia mysl*) expressed with the words: the desirable struggle is one that is possible and the possible struggle is the one that is going on at a given minute. This tendency is, in fact, unbounded opportunism that passively adapts itself to *stikhiinost*.

'Tactics-as-plan contradicts the basic spirit of Marxism'! But this is nothing but a slander on Marxism, a distortion that turns it into the very same caricature that the populists set up in their war with us. It is nothing but a lowering of the initiative and energy of purposive activists, since, on the contrary, Marxism gives a gigantic incitement to the initiative and energy of the Social Democrat, turning over to his disposal (if I may express myself this way) the mighty forces of the millions and millions of the worker class rising up 'in *stikhiinyi* fashion' for struggle!

The entire history of international Social Democracy swarms with the plans that were advanced first by this and then by that political leader – plans that confirmed the foresight and the truth of the political and organisational views of one leader while exposing the myopia and political mistakes of another. When Germany went through an extremely important historical turning-point – the formation of the empire, the opening of the Reichstag, the granting of universal suffrage – Liebknecht had one plan for Social-Democratic politics and its work in general while Schweitzer had another. When the exceptional laws came down on the heads of the German socialists, one plan was advanced by Most and Hasselman who were prepared simply to appeal to violence and terror. Another plan was advanced by Höchberg, Schramm and (partly) Bernstein, who started preaching to the Social Democrats that they themselves had provoked the [anti-socialist] law by their unreasonable sharpness and revolutionary fervour and that they should now earn forgiveness by exemplary behaviour. A third plan came from those who prepared and carried out the publication of an illegal press organ.

Looking back, many years later, when the struggle over the issue of the choice of path has ended and history has given a final judgement about the suitability of the path actually chosen, it is, of course, not too difficult to show one's profundity with pronouncements about the growth of party tasks that grow together with the Party. But in a time of real confusion,[16] when the Russian 'critics' and the 'economists' lower Social Democracy to *tred-iunionizm*, and terrorists zealously preach the adoption of a 'tactics-as-plan' that simply repeats old mistakes – to limit oneself to this kind of profundity is equivalent to issuing oneself a 'certificate of poverty'. At a time when many Russian Social Democrats suffer precisely from a lack of sufficient initiative and energy, from a lack of sufficient 'sweep in political propaganda, agitation and organisation',[17] from a lack of sufficient 'plans' for a broader conception of revolutionary work – at such a time, to say 'tactics-as-plan contradicts the basic spirit of Marxism' means not only to vulgarise Marxism theoretically but to *drag the Party backward* in practice.

*Rabochee delo* instructs us:

> A revolutionary Social Democrat has the task only to accelerate objective development with his purposive work and not to eliminate it or substitute his subjective plan for it. *Iskra* knows this well enough in theory. But the enormous significance that Marxism justly gives to purposive revolutionary

---

[16] *Ein Jahr der Verwirrung* (year of real confusion) – this is the title Mehring gives to the section in his 'History of German Social Democracy' in which he describes the vacillations and irresoluteness that the socialists at first displayed when they were confronted with selecting a 'tactic-as-plan' that corresponded to the new conditions.

[17] From the lead article in *Iskra*, No. 1.

work carries it in practice, thanks to its doctrinaire view of tactics, toward
*the underestimation of the significance of the objective or stikhiinyi element of*
*development.* (p. 18.)

Another outstanding theoretical mishmash worthy of Mr. V.V. and his ilk. We
might ask our philosopher: how does the 'underestimation' of objective
development on the part of a creator of subjective plans manifest itself?
Evidently, when he does not notice how objective development creates or
strengthens, destroys or weakens, such and such a class, stratum, group,
such and such a nation or group of nations and so forth, as conditioned by
such and such an international grouping of political forces, the position of
revolutionary parties and so on. But the fault of such a creator of plans will
then consist not in the underestimation of the *stikhiinyi* element but, on the
contrary, in the underestimation of the *purposive* element, for he does not have
enough 'purposiveness' for the correct understanding of objective development.
Therefore even to start talking about the 'evaluation of the *relative* (emphasis
by *Rabochee delo*) significance' of *stikhiinost* and purposiveness exposes a
complete lack of 'purposiveness'.

If particular '*stikhiinyi* elements of development' are in general accessible
to human awareness, then an incorrect evaluation of them is equivalent to
an 'underestimation of the purposive element'. And, if they are not accessible
to awareness, then we do not know them and cannot speak of them. So what
is B. Krichevskii talking about? If he finds *Iskra*'s 'subjective plans' to be
mistaken (and indeed he does call them mistaken), then he should show
exactly what objective facts the plans overlook and accuse *Iskra* therefore of
an 'underestimation of the purposive element', to use his vocabulary. But if,
dissatisfied as he is by subjective plans, he has no other argument than to
refer to 'the underestimation of the *stikhiinyi* element' (!!), then he thereby
demonstrates that (1) he theoretically understands Marxism in the manner
of the Kareevs and the Mikhailovskys who were fully ridiculed by Beltov
[Plekhanov] and (2) in practical terms, he is completely satisfied with those
'*stikhiinyi* elements of development' that led our legally-permitted Marxists
into Bernsteinism and our [underground] Social Democrats into 'economism',
and that he is 'full of wrath' against people who have resolved to do whatever
they can to *cause* Russian Social Democracy *to stray* from the path of '*stikhiinyi*'
development.

And, now, we come to some things that are really quite amusing.

Just as people continue to be fruitful and multiply in the good old-fashioned way despite the advances of natural science – just so the appearance in this world of a new social order, despite any advances of social science and increases in the number of purposive militants, will in the future still result from *stikhiinyi* explosions *for the most part*. (p. 19.)

Just as good old-fashioned wisdom told us that it doesn't take much brains to produce offspring – just so the wisdom of 'the latest socialists' (*à la* Narcissus Tuporylov) tells us that everybody has enough brains to participate in the *stikhiinyi* appearance in this world of a new social order. We also think everybody has enough brains for this. For participation of this sort, all you have to do is *give in* – to 'economism' when 'economism' reigns, to terrorism when terrorism emerges. Thus, last spring, when it was very important to issue a warning against being carried away by terrorism, *Rabochee delo* stood dumbfounded before an issue that was 'new' for it. And, now, half a year later, when this issue is no longer so current, it can at one and the same time announce to us that 'we think that it is not the task of Social Democracy, nor should it be, to counteract the upsurge in terrorist moods' (*Rabochee delo*, No. 10, p. 23), and announce as a resolution of its congress [in fall 1901]: 'The congress states that systematic aggressive terror is inopportune' (*Two Congresses*, p. 18). How remarkably clear and consistent! We don't counteract it – but we do declare it inopportune, and do our declaring in such a way that the 'resolution' does not tell us anything about unsystematic and defensive terror. You have to admit that such a resolution is very safe and completely guaranteed from error – just as a person who talks in order to avoid saying anything is free from error!

And only one thing is needed to put together such a resolution: the ability to keep oneself in the *tail* of the movement. When *Iskra* mocked *Rabochee delo* for calling the terror issue a new one, *Rabochee delo* angrily accused *Iskra* of 'the really unbelievable pretension of imposing on the party organisation the solution of tactical issues given by a group of émigré writers 15 years ago' (p. 24). Oh yes, what pretension and what an overestimation of the purposive element: to try to resolve issues theoretically so that afterwards the organisation, the Party and the mass can be persuaded of the correctness of this solution.[18]

---

[18] We also should not forget that when it 'theoretically' resolved the issue of terror, the Emancipation of Labour group *generalised* the experience of the preceding revolutionary movement.

How much better simply to give us the same old stuff and not 'impose' anything on anybody but simply submit to every 'turning point', now towards 'economism' and now towards terrorism. *Rabochee delo* even generalises this grand precept of worldly wisdom, accusing *Iskra* and *Zaria* of 'opposing its programme to the movement like a spirit brooding over the formless chaos' (p. 29). But isn't this the role of Social Democracy – to be a 'spirit' that does not merely brood above the *stikhiinyi* movement but *lifts up* this movement *to 'its programme'*? Its role is certainly not to drag along in the *tail* of the movement: this is useless for the movement in the best case and extremely harmful in the worst case. But *Rabochee delo* not only adopts this 'tactics-as-process' but elevates it into a principle, so that a better name than opportunism for its tendency would be *tailism*. And you have to admit that people who have definitely decided always to follow after the movement as its tail are absolutely and for all time guaranteed against 'underestimation of the *stikhiinyi* element of development'.

\* \* \*

Thus we are convinced that the basic mistake of the 'new tendency' in Russian Social Democracy consists in kow-towing toward *stikhiinost*, in the inability to understand that the *stikhiinost* of the mass demands from us, the Social Democrats, a mass of purposiveness. The greater is the *stikhiinyi* upsurge of the masses and the wider becomes the movement, so much the more does the demand increase for a mass of purposiveness in the theoretical, the political and the organisational work of Social Democracy.

The *stikhiinyi* upsurge of the masses in Russia has taken place (and continues to take place) with such speed that Social-Democratic youth found itself unprepared to carry out these gigantic tasks. This lack of preparation is our common misfortune, the misfortune of *all* Russian Social Democrats. The upsurge of the masses proceeded and became wider continually and with gathering momentum – it proceeded without stopping in places where it had already started as well as conquering new localities and new strata of the population (ferment among the students, the intelligentsia in general and even the peasantry gained energy due to the influence of the worker movement). But the revolutionaries *fell behind* this upsurge both in their 'theories' and in their activity – they did not succeed in creating an uninterrupted and continuous organisation with gathering momentum that was capable of *guiding* the entire movement.

In the first chapter, we demonstrated how *Rabochee delo* lowered our theoretical tasks and we pointed out their '*stikhiinyi*' repetition of the fashionable catchword 'freedom of criticism'. The repeaters did not have sufficient 'purposiveness' to understand the diametrical contrast between the relationship between 'critics'/opportunists vs. revolutionaries, on the one hand in Germany and on the other in Russia.

In the following chapters, we shall see how this kow-towing before *stikhiinost* manifested itself in the area of political tasks and in the organisational work of Social Democracy.

# Chapter III

## *Tred-iunionist* Politics and Social-Democratic Politics

We start once more by praising *Rabochee delo*. 'Indictment literature and the proletarian struggle' – this is the title Martynov gives to his article in *Rabochee delo*, No. 10 about the disagreements with *Iskra*. 'We cannot limit ourselves just to indictments of the system that blocks the path of its (the worker party's) development. We must also react to the urgent and current interests of the proletariat' (p. 63) – thus does he formulate the essence of these disagreements. '... *Iskra* ... is in actuality an organ of revolutionary opposition that indicts our system and mainly our political system. ... We, on the other hand, work and will continue to work for the cause of the workers in a close organic link with the proletarian struggle' (p. 63). We must be grateful to Martynov for this formulation. It takes on great general interest because it encompasses, in essence, not just our disagreements with *Rabochee delo* but, in general, all the disagreements between us and the 'economists' on the issue of political struggle. We have shown already that the 'economists' do not unconditionally reject 'politics', but merely stray continually from a Social-Democratic understanding of politics to a *tred-iunionist* one. Martynov strays in the same way, and so we are ready to take him and no one else as a *model* of economist confusions on this issue. As we shall demonstrate, the choice of Martynov is one which neither the authors of the Separate Supplement to *Rabochaia mysl*, nor the authors of the Worker Self-Liberation group proclamation, nor the authors of the economist letter in *Iskra*, No. 12 have a right to dispute.

## a) Political agitation and its narrowing by the economists

Everybody knows that the wide dissemination and consolidation of the economic[1] struggle went hand in hand with the creation of a 'literature' of economic (factory and trade) indictments. The main content of the 'leaflets' was the indictment of factory rules, and among the workers there quickly flared up a genuine passion for indictments. As soon as the workers saw that a circle of Social Democrats wished and was able to provide them with a new kind of leaflet that said the whole truth about their poverty-stricken life, their boundlessly heavy labour and their lack of all rights – they began, so to speak, to bombard the circles with material from factories and workshops. This 'literature of indictment' created a tremendous sensation not only at the factory excoriated by a given leaflet but at all factories where anything was heard about the facts being exposed. And, since the needs and distress of the workers in different enterprises and different trades have much in common, this 'truth about the worker life' exhilarated *everybody*. Among the most backward workers there developed a real passion for 'getting into print' – a noble passion for this embryonic form of the war against the entire present-day social system that is built on looting and oppression. And the vast majority of 'leaflets' were indeed a declaration of war, because the exposure had a highly instigating effect and called forth from the workers a common demand to remove the most crying abuses and a readiness to support these demands with strikes. The factory owners themselves were in the final analysis forced to recognise the significance of these leaflets as a declaration of war, so much so that sometimes they had no desire to await the opening of hostilities [before making concessions]. The indictments, as indeed is always the case, became

---

[1] To avoid misunderstandings, please note that, in the following discussion, we always understand 'economic struggle' (following the accepted usage) to mean the 'practical-economic struggle' that Engels (in the citation given above) called 'resistance to the capitalists' and which in free countries is called the trade, syndicalist or *trediunionist* struggle.

powerful by the very fact of their appearance, acquired the significance of a mighty moral pressure. It happened more than once that the mere appearance of a leaflet was enough to get all or some of the demands satisfied. In a word, the economic (factory) indictments were and remain today an important tool of economic struggle. And they will retain this significance as long as capitalism exists and necessarily calls forth the self-defence of the workers. In the most advanced European countries, it is possible to observe how the indictment of abuses of some out-of-the-way business or some completely overlooked area of cottage industry serves as the starting point of the awakening of class awareness, of the beginning of the trade [*professial'nyi*] struggle and the dissemination of socialism.[2]

The overwhelming majority of Russian Social Democrats in the period just passed were almost completely taken up with this work of organising factory indictments. It is enough to recall *Rabochaia mysl* to realise the extent of this absorption and how it was forgotten in all of this that *taken by itself*, organising economic indictments is in essence not yet Social-Democratic but only *tred-iunionist* activity. The indictments encompassed, in essence, only the relation of workers *of a given trade* to their bosses and all they accomplished was that the sellers of labour-power learned how to sell their 'commodity' more advantageously and to fight the buyer on a ground of a purely commercial deal. These indictments could have become (given some utilisation of them by an organisation of revolutionaries) a beginning and a component part of Social-Democratic activity, but they could also (and, in the context of kow-towing toward *stikhiinost*, must) lead to a 'exclusively-trade-union' struggle and to a non-Social-Democratic worker movement.

---

[2] In the present chapter, we speak only of *political* struggle, of a broader or narrower conception of it. Therefore, only in passing will I mention as a curiosity the accusation of *Rabochee delo* against *Iskra* for 'excessive abstention' in relation to the economic struggle (*Two Congresses*, p. 27, and rehashed by Martynov in his pamphlet *Social Democracy and the Worker Class*). If the accusers would measure, let's say, in pounds or printed pages (since they love doing this sort of thing) the section on economic struggle in *Iskra* for one year and compare it to the corresponding section in *Rabochee delo* and *Rabochaia mysl* taken together, then they would clearly see that they are backward in this area as well. Evidently, the awareness of this simple truth forces them to resort to statements that clearly show their embarrassment. They write that '*Iskra* is compelled (!) whether they like it or not (!) to take account of the powerful demands of life and at least (!!) to insert the news that they receive about the worker movement' (*Two Congresses*, p. 27). Now there's an argument that really destroys us!

Social Democracy guides the struggle of the worker class not only for advantageous conditions in the sale of labour-power but also for the abolition of the social system that forces the have-nots to sell themselves to the rich. Social Democracy understands the worker class not only in its relation to a given group of entrepreneurs but in its relation to all classes of modern society, to the state as organised political power. It is therefore understandable that Social Democrats must not confine themselves to an economic struggle and also that they must not allow the organisation of economic indictments to be their predominant activity. We must also actively take up the political education of the worker class, the development of its political awareness. 'All are agreed' on this *now*, after the first onslaught against 'economism' by *Zaria* and *Iskra* (although some agree only in words, as we shall see soon).

Let us now consider, what should political education be? Can we limit ourselves to propagandising the idea of the enmity of the worker class towards the autocracy? Of course not. It is not enough to *explain* the political oppression of the workers (just as it is not enough to *explain* to them the opposition between their interests and that of the owners). It is necessary to agitate in relation to each concrete manifestation of this oppression (just as we have come to agitate in relation to concrete manifestations of economic oppression). And since *this* oppression falls on the most various classes of society, since it appears in the most various areas of life and activity – occupational [*professial'nyi*], general citizenship, personal life, religion, science, and so on and so forth – surely it is obvious that *we will not carry out our task* of developing political awareness of the workers, if we do not *take upon ourselves* the organisation of *an all-sided political indictment* of the autocracy? And, if we want to carry on agitation on the basis of concrete manifestations of oppression, we must create indictments of these manifestations (just as it is necessary to indict factory abuses in order to conduct economic agitation)?

This is all very clear, one would think? But it is precisely here that it turns out that people 'all' agree on the necessity of developing political awareness in an *all-sided* fashion only in words. Just here, it turns out that, for example, *Rabochee delo* not only did not itself take upon itself the task of organising (or laying the foundations for organising) all-sided political indictments – it also tried to *drag back Iskra*, the newspaper that did take on this task. Listen to this: 'The political struggle of the worker class is merely' (no, *not* 'merely'!) 'the most developed, broad and active form of economic struggle' (the programme of *Rabochee delo* in *Rabochee delo*, No. 1, p. 3). 'Now the task stands before the Social Democrats of imparting a political character to the economic struggle itself' (Martynov in No. 10, p. 42). 'The economic struggle is the most widely applicable means of drawing the masses into active political struggle' (resolution of the congress of the Union and its proposed corrections [to the draft agreement with *Iskra*]: *Two Congresses*, pp. 11 and 17). All these theses permeate *Rabochee delo* (as the reader will see) starting with its very emergence and going right up to the most recent 'instructions of the editorial board', and they all express, clearly, a single outlook on political agitation and struggle. Let us look closer at this outlook from the point of view of the opinion dominant among all the 'economists', namely, that political agitation must *follow after* economic agitation.

Is it true that economic struggle is in general[3] 'the most widely applicable means' of drawing the masses into the political struggle'? Completely untrue. A no less 'widely applicable' means of 'drawing in' is *each and every* manifestation of police oppression and autocratic outrage – and definitely not just manifestations tied to the economic struggle. The *zemstvo* captains and their corporal punishment of the peasants, the bribe-taking of bureaucrats and the way the police treat the urban man-in-the-street, the fight against starving people and the mockery of the people's striving toward light and knowledge, the extortion of taxes and the persecution of sectarians, the harsh drill of soldiers and the treatment of students and liberal intelligentsia as if they were in the military – speaking generally, why should we consider that all of these and a thousand other similar manifestations of oppression that are not tied to the 'economic' struggle are a *less* 'widely applicable means'

---

[3] We say 'in general', because *Rabochee delo* is talking precisely about general principles and general tasks of the Party as a whole. No doubt, there are occasions in practice where political [struggle] *should* follow after economic [struggle], – but to talk this way in a resolution that is aimed at all of Russia is something only 'economists' would do. There are also some occasions when 'at the very beginning' conducting political agitation 'only on economic grounds' is the only possibility – and nevertheless *Rabochee delo* has managed to work its way to the conclusion that 'there is no need [even at the very beginning to conduct political agitation only on economic grounds'] (*Two Congresses*, p. 11) [that is, on the issue of agitation *Rabochee delo* grasped the difference between individual cases and programmatic generalisation]. In the following chapter we will show that the tactics of the 'politicals' and revolutionaries not only do not ignore the *tred-iunionist* tasks of Social Democracy but on the contrary they and they alone provide a *guarantee* that these tasks are completely carried out.

and an occasion for political agitation and drawing in the masses to political struggle? In fact, the opposite is the case: in the general sum of the day-to-day occurrences in which the worker suffers (either in his own person or in the person of those close to him) from lack of rights, abuse of power and violence, there is no doubt that only a small minority consists of police oppression that is specific to the economic struggle. So why *narrow* in advance the sweep of political agitation, why call only *one* of the means 'the most widely applicable', when a Social Democrat should recognise others that are, speaking generally, no less 'widely applicable'?

In the days of long ago (last year! . . .), *Rabochee delo* wrote: 'Urgent political demands become accessible to the masses after one or at the most a few strikes', 'as soon as the government puts the police and the gendarmes into action' (No. 7, *August* 1900). This opportunist theory of stages has today already been rejected by the Union when they made a concession to us and wrote 'there is no need, even at the very beginning, to conduct political agitation only on economic grounds' (*Two Congresses*, p. 11). Simply this repudiation by the Union of part of its past mistakes will be more useful than any number of lengthy arguments in showing a future historian of Russian Social Democracy to what depths the 'economists' brought socialism! But what naïveté on the part of the Union to imagine that, by rejecting one form of narrowing politics, it could induce us to agree to another form of narrowing! Wouldn't it have been more logical to say instead that the economic struggle should be conducted on the widest possible basis, that it should always be used for political agitation, but that [nevertheless] 'there is no need' to consider economic struggle the *most* widely applicable means for drawing in the masses into active political struggle?

The Union imparts significance to the fact that it substituted the expression 'the most widely applicable means' for the expression 'best means' used in the corresponding resolution by the Fourth Congress of the Jewish Worker Union (Bund). It would be difficult, true, to say which of these resolutions is better: in our opinion, *both are worse*. Both the Union and the Bund are led astray here (in part, perhaps, even without their awareness, under the influence of tradition) toward an economist, *tred-iunionist* conception of politics. In essence, the matter is not changed a whit whether this occurs by means of the formula 'best' or by means of the formula 'most widely applicable'. If the Union had said that 'political agitation on economic grounds' is the most widely applied (not 'applicable') method, then it would have been correct in relation to a certain period in the development of our Social-Democratic movement. It would have been correct precisely in relation to the *'economists'*, in relation to many *praktiki* (if not to a majority of them) from 1898 to 1901, since these *praktiki-*'economists' did really *apply* political agitation (insofar as they applied it at all!) *almost exclusively on economic grounds. This kind* of political agitation is recognised and even recommended, as we saw, by *Rabochaia mysl* and the Self-Liberation Group! *Rabochee delo* should have *resolutely condemned* the fact that the useful work of economic agitation was accompanied by a harmful narrowing of political struggle. Instead, it announced that the most widely app*lied* means (*by 'economists'*) is the most widely app*licable*! It is not surprising that when we call such people 'economists', they are forced to resort to loudly swearing at us and calling us 'mystifiers' and 'disorganisers' and 'papal nuncios' and 'slanderers'[4] – or that they must needs sob before all and sundry that they have received a mortal insult and to state, practically with oaths: 'Not one single Social-Democratic organisation is now guilty of "economism"'.[5] Oh, these slanderers, these evil politicals! They must have invented this whole 'economism', out of sheer hatred of mankind, as a way of giving people mortal insults!

When Martynov formulates the task of Social Democracy as 'imparting a political character to the economic struggle itself', what concrete, real sense does this formulation have? The economic struggle is the collective struggle of the workers with the owners for advantageous conditions of the *sale of labour-power*, for the improvement of the conditions of labour and life for the workers. This struggle is by necessity a trade [*professial'nyi*] struggle, since the conditions of labour vary extremely in different trades and consequently the struggle for the *improvement* of these conditions must be conducted along trade lines (trade unions in the West, leaflets and temporary [illegal] associations for trade struggle in Russia and so forth). To impart 'a political character to the economic struggle itself' means, therefore, to attain the implementation of these trade demands, these improvements of the conditions of labour in a particular trade by means of 'legislative and administrative measures' (as Martynov puts it on the following page of his article, p. 43). This is exactly

---

[4] All expressions taken right out of *Two Congresses*, pp. 31, 32, 28 and 30.
[5] *Two Congresses*, p. 32.

what all worker trade unions are doing and have always done. Look at the writing of those weighty scholars (and 'weighty' opportunists), the Webbs, and you will see that the English worker unions have long, long ago become aware and have implemented the task of 'imparting a political character to the economic struggle itself'. They long ago have been fighting for the freedom of strikes, for the removal of each and every legal obstacle to the co-operative and trade[-union] movement, for the promulgation of laws in defence of women and children, for the improvement of conditions of labour by means of sanitary and factory legislation and so on.

Thus behind the eloquent phrase 'imparting a political character to the economic struggle *itself*', which sounds so profound and revolutionary, is hidden in essence the traditional striving to *lower* Social-Democratic politics to *tred-iunionist* politics! Under the guise of correcting the one-sidedness of *Iskra* – which, don't you know, places 'revolutionising of dogma higher than the revolutionising of life'[6] – we are given as something new *the struggle for economic reforms*. In fact, absolutely nothing but the struggle for economic reforms is contained in the phrase 'impart a political character to the economic struggle itself'. And Martynov himself would be able to arrive at this straightforward conclusion if he would just think a bit about the meaning of his own words. 'Our party' (he says while training his heaviest artillery on *Iskra*) 'can and must present the government concrete demands for legislative and administrative measures against economic exploitation, against unemployment, against hunger and so on' (pp. 42–3 in *Rabochee delo*, No. 10). Concrete demands for measures – isn't this the demand for social reforms? And we once more ask impartial readers: are we slandering the *Rabochee delo* people when we call them secret Bernsteinians, since they advance as a point of their *disagreement* with *Iskra* the thesis of the necessity of the struggle for economic reforms?

Revolutionary Social Democracy has always included and still includes in its activity the struggle for reforms. But it uses 'economic' agitation to present to the government not only the demand for this or that measure but also (and first of all) the demand to cease being an autocratic government. More

---

[6] *Rabochee delo*, No. 10, p. 60. This is the Martynov variant of the application to the present-day chaotic state of our movement the thesis: 'each step of genuine movement is more important than a dozen programmes' (as discussed earlier). In essence, this is only a translation into Russian of the notorious Bernstein motto: 'the movement is everything and the final aim is nothing'.

than that, it regards as its responsibility to present this demand to the government *not only* on the grounds of the economic struggle, but also on the grounds of all the manifestations in general of social/political life. In a word, it subordinates the struggle for reform to the revolutionary struggle for freedom and for socialism as one part to a larger whole. Martynov resurrects the theory of stages in another form when he prescribes as obligatory a (so to speak) economic path of development for political struggle. But when he comes forth, in a moment of revolutionary upsurge, with a special so-called 'task' of a struggle for reforms, he drags the Party back and plays into the hand both of 'economist' and of liberal opportunism.

There's more. Coyly hiding the struggle for reforms under the elegant thesis 'imparting a political character to the economic struggle itself', Martynov puts forth *economic reforms* (and even factory reforms) as something special *in and of themselves.* We don't know why he has done this. Perhaps, through carelessness? But if he has in view not just 'factory' reforms, then, in that case, his entire thesis that we have just examined loses all sense. Perhaps [he talks this way because] he considers it possible and plausible that the government will make 'concessions' only in the economic area?[7] If that is the case, then it is a strange misconception: concessions are possible and happen in other areas as well – in the field of legislation concerning corporal punishment, or internal passports, or redemption payments, or sectarian groups, or censorship, and so and so forth. 'Economic' concessions (or pseudo-concessions) are the cheapest and most advantageous for the government, obviously, since it hopes by this means to inspire the confidence of the worker masses [toward the government]. But just for this reason we, as Social Democrats, *should not* in any way whatsoever give grounds for the opinion (or misunderstanding) that economic reforms are the ones that we most value or the ones that we consider the most important and so forth. 'Such demands', says Martynov about the concrete demands for legislative and administrative measures advanced by him above, 'are not just an empty noise, since they promise tangible results and thus can be actively supported by the worker mass'.... We are not 'economists', oh no! All we do is grovel before

---

[7] Page 43: 'Of course, if we recommend to the workers to make certain economic demands to the government, we do this because in the *economic* area the autocratic government is ready if need be to make certain concessions.'

the 'tangibility' of concrete results just as slavishly as Messrs. Bernsteins, Prokopovichs, Struves, R.M. and *tutti quanti*. All we do is let it be understood (along with Narcissus Tuporylov) that everything that does not 'promise tangible results' is 'an empty noise'! All we do is express ourselves in such a way that it seems as if the worker mass is not capable (and has not already demonstrated its capability, in spite of all those who endow them with their own small-mindedness) of actively supporting *each and every* protest against autocracy – even when *it promises absolutely no tangible results at all!*

Let's take even the examples, adduced by Martynov himself, of 'measures' against unemployment and hunger. At the same time as *Rabochee delo* is busying itself, judging by its own promise, with working out and elaborating 'concrete' (in the form of legislative drafts?) 'demands of legislative and administrative measures' that 'promise tangible results' – at the very same time, *Iskra* ('invariably placing the revolutionising of dogma higher than the revolutionising of life') tried to explain the unbreakable connection between unemployment and the capitalist system as a whole, warned that 'famine is coming', indicted the police 'struggle against the starving' and the outrageous 'provisional rules for forced labour', while *Zaria* published for agitational purposes a separate offprint of material dedicated to the famine. Good heavens! – These incorrigibly narrow orthodox types are so 'one-sided', these dogmatic types are so deaf to the imperatives of 'life itself'! Not a single one of these articles – horrors! – has *even one* (can you imagine it? – not even the slightest) 'concrete demand' that 'promises tangible results'! These poor unfortunate dogmatic types! Turn them over to Krichevskii and Martynov so that they can hear and be persuaded that tactics are a process of growth, growing with, etc., and that one must impart a political character to the economic struggle *itself.*

'The economic struggle of the workers with the owners and the government (*'economic* struggle with the government'!!), besides its immediate revolutionary significance, is also significant because it continually pushes the workers up against the issue of their political lack of rights' (Martynov, p. 44). We copied out this citation not in order to repeat for the hundredth and thousandth time what has already been said but in order to congratulate Martynov for this novel and outstanding formulation: 'economic struggle of the workers with the owners and the government'. What a beauty! With what inimitable talent and masterly elimination of all specific differences and distinctions in nuance between 'economists' do we find expressed here in a concise and clear thesis *the entire essence* of 'economism'. [Russian 'economism' started with] an appeal to the workers to 'a political struggle that they conduct for the common interest, having in mind the improvement of the position of all workers';[8] it continued with the theory of stages and ended up with the resolution of the [Union] congress about 'the most widely applicable' and so on. 'Economic struggle of the workers with the government' is precisely *tred-iunionist* politics, and there is a great gulf between it and Social-Democratic politics.

## b) The story of how Martynov made Plekhanov deep

'Have you noticed how many Social-Democratic Lomonosovs one sees around lately!' remarked one comrade the other day. He had in mind that striking inclination of many of those inclined to 'economism' to arrive strictly with their own brainpower to great new truths (such as that economic struggle pushes the workers to face the issue of their lack of rights) and, at the same time, to ignore with the grand contempt of a self-educated genius everything that earlier revolutionary thought and revolutionary movement has given us. Lomonosov-Martynov is just such a self-educated genius. Take a look at his article 'Current Issues' and you will see how he with his own brainpower *comes close* to what was said long ago by Akselrod (about whom our Lomonosov of course preserves a total silence) – how he *begins* to understand, for example, that we cannot ignore the oppositional mentality of this or that stratum of the bourgeoisie (see *Rabochee delo* No. 9, pp. 61, 62, 72 in comparison to the [earlier] *Answer* to Akselrod by the editorial board of *Rabochee delo*, pp. 22, 23–4) and so forth. But – alas! – only 'comes close' and only 'begins', no more than that, because Martynov still shows he does not grasp Akselrod's meaning when he talks of 'economic struggle of the workers with the owners and the government'. In the course of three years (1898–1901), *Rabochee delo* has tried hard to understand Akselrod and – and still can't quite understand! Perhaps this is because Social Democracy, 'like mankind', always presents itself with tasks that can be carried out?

---

[8] *Rabochaia mysl*, Separate Supplement, p. 14.

But Lomonosovs stand out not only because they don't know a lot (not so bad in itself!) but also because they themselves are unaware of their ignorance. This *is* bad, so bad that they are immediately moved to take to make Plekhanov more 'deep'. Lomonosov-Martynov tells us:

> Since the time that Plekhanov wrote this book (*On the Tasks of the Socialists in the Struggle with Famine in Russia* [1892]), a lot of water has flowed under the bridge. The Social Democrats who for a decade have guided the economic struggle of the worker class . . . have not yet succeeded in giving a broad theoretical foundation to party tactics. Now this issue has come to a head, and if we wish to provide such a theoretical foundation, we undoubtedly would significantly deepen the principles of tactics that Plekhanov worked out earlier. . . . We would now make the distinction between propaganda and agitation in a different way than Plekhanov did. . . . (Martynov has just cited Plekhanov's formula: 'the propagandist gives many ideas to one person or a few persons, while the agitator gives only one or a few ideas, but he gives it to a whole mass of people'.) . . . By 'propaganda' we understand the revolutionary illumination of the whole existing system or its partial manifestations, irrespective of whether it is done in a form accessible to individuals or to the broad mass. By 'agitation' in the strict sense of the word (sic!), we understand the call to the mass to undertake certain concrete actions that enables the immediate revolutionary intervention of the proletariat in social life.

We congratulate Russian – and international – Social Democracy on acquiring this new Martynov-style terminology, one that is much stricter and deeper. Up to this time, we had thought (along with Plekhanov and, indeed, with all the leaders of the international worker movement) that, if the propagandist takes up the issue, for example, of unemployment, he should explain the capitalist nature of crises, demonstrate the reason for their inevitability in present-day society, describe the necessity of their transformation in socialist society and so forth. In a word, he should give 'many ideas' – so many that all these ideas in all their interconnections can only be assimilated right away by a few (comparatively few) individuals. When the agitator talks about the same issue, he will select for his example something notorious that is very well known to all his listeners – let's say, an unemployed family who perished from hunger, or the intensification of poverty, and so on – and then directs all his energy to use this fact known to each and all in order to give to the 'mass' *one idea*: the idea of the insanity of the contradiction between the growth of riches and the growth of poverty. He will try to *awaken* in the mass dissatisfaction and indignation about this crying injustice while leaving its full explanation to the propagandist. The propagandist thus acts for the most part by the *printed* word while the agitator acts by the *living* word. A good propagandist has different qualities than a good agitator. For example, we call Kautsky and Lafargue propagandists while Bebel and Guesde are agitators. To carve out a third area or third function of practical activity and define this function as 'the call to the mass to undertake certain concrete actions' is a complete hodgepodge, since any such 'call' as a separate act is *either* a natural and inevitable supplement to a theoretical treatise, to a propagandistic pamphlet, to an agitational speech, *or* it is part of direct implementation [of a particular mass action].

Take, for example, the current struggle of the German Social Democrats against grain duties. Theoreticians write investigations of customs policies and 'call', let us say, for a struggle for trade treaties and for free trade. A propagandist does the same thing in a journal and the agitator in public speeches. The 'concrete actions' of the mass in this case consists of signing petitions to the Reichstag against raising grain duties. The call to carry out these actions comes indirectly from the theoreticians, propagandists and agitators, and directly from those workers who bring around the signature lists to factories and to all sorts of living quarters. According to the 'Martynov terminology', it seems that that Kautsky and Bebel are both propagandists, while the people who bring around signature lists are agitators – have I got that straight?

This German example brings to mind the German word *Verballhornung*, which, literally translated, is 'Ballhorning'. Johann Ballhorn was a Leipzig publisher in the sixteenth century who published an alphabet book in which there was the usual picture of a rooster – only, instead of the usual representation of a rooster with spurs, he printed one without spurs but with a pair of eggs lying near. And on the cover of the book he added: 'A *corrected* edition by Johann Ballhorn'. Since that time the Germans use *Verballhornung* to describe an 'improvement' that is really a worsening. And we can't help recall Ballhorn when we see how the Martynovs 'deepened' Plekhanov . . .

Why did our Lomonosov 'invent' this confusion? He wanted to illustrate the charge that *Iskra* 'pays attention only to one side of the matter, just as Plekhanov did fifteen years ago' (p. 39). 'In *Iskra*, at least at the present time,

the tasks of propaganda push the tasks of agitation into the background'
(p. 52). If we translate this last thesis from Martynov language to normal
human language (since humanity is not yet able to absorb the newly created
terminology), then we come up with the following: in *Iskra*, the tasks of
political propaganda and political agitation push to the background the
task of 'presenting the government concrete demands for legislative and
administrative measures' that 'promise tangible results' (or, demands for
social reforms, if it is permitted to use the old terminology of backward
humanity that hasn't yet got as far as Martynov). We invite the reader to
compare the Martynov thesis with the following eloquent passage:

> What strikes us in these programmes (the programmes of the revolutionary
> Social Democrats) is their eternal insistence on the advantages of the activity
> of the workers in parliament (which we don't have) while at the same time
> ignoring (due to their revolutionary nihilism) the importance of the par-
> ticipation of the workers in the legislative assemblies for factory owners on
> factory matters that do exist here [in Russia] . . . or, say, the participation of
> workers in urban self-government . . .

The author of this eloquent passage expresses somewhat more straight-
forwardly, clearly and more openly the same thought that Lomonosov-
Martynov arrived at with his own brainpower. This author is – R.M. in the
Separate Supplement to *Rabochaia mysl* (p. 15).

### c) Political indictments and 'education for revolutionary activeness'

When he advances against *Iskra* his 'theory' of 'raising the activeness of the
worker mass', Martynov actually reveals an striving to *lower* this activeness,
since he announces that the preferred, most particularly important, and 'most
widely applicable' means of awakening and support for this activeness is the
same old economic struggle before which all 'economists' grovel. This error
can be called characteristic, because it certainly is not original to Martynov
alone. In fact, 'raising the activeness of the worker mass' can be attained *only*
under the condition that we *do not limit ourselves* to 'political agitation on
economic grounds'. And one of the basic conditions of the necessary widening
of political agitation is the organisation of *all-sided* political indictments. The

masses *cannot* be educated in political awareness and revolutionary activeness other than on the basis of these indictments. Therefore this kind of activity is one of the most important functions of international Social Democracy as a whole, since political freedom in no way eliminates but only somewhat shifts the scope of these indictments.

For example, the German Party particularly strengthens its position and widens its influence precisely because of the unremitting energy of its campaign of political indictments. The awareness of the worker class is not genuine political awareness if the workers are not taught to respond to *each* and *every* occurrence of abuse of power and oppression, violence and malfeasance, *no matter which class* is affected; – and, in so doing, respond precisely with a Social-Democratic point of view and no other. The awareness of the worker masses cannot be a genuine class awareness if the workers do not learn, on the basis of concrete and (this is essential) topical political facts and events, to observe *each* of the other social classes in *all* the manifestations of their intellectual, moral and political life – if they do not learn to apply in practice a materialist analysis and a materialist evaluation of *all* sides of the activity and life of *all* classes, strata and groups of the population. He who focuses the attention, powers of observation and awareness of the worker class exclusively or even primarily on itself is no Social Democrat: the self-knowledge of the worker class is inextricably tied to full clarity in its conceptions of the mutual relations of *all* classes of present-day society – conceptions that are not only theoretical . . . more precisely, not so much theoretical as they are worked out via experience of political life. That is why the preaching of our 'economists' (the economic struggle is the most widely applicable means of drawing the masses into the political movement) is so deeply harmful and so deeply reactionary in its practical significance.

In order to become a Social Democrat, a worker must have a clear conception of the economic nature and the social/political profile of the landowner and the priest, the bureaucrat and the peasant, the student and the homeless tramp – know their strong sides and their weak ones, be able to analyse the catchwords and the sophisms of all possible kinds by which each class and each stratum *conceals* its selfish desires and its actual essence – a worker must be able to analyse how various institutions and laws reflect this or that interest and how they do so. And this 'clear conception' cannot be taken from any book: it can be given only by living pictures and up-to-the-minute indictments of what is happening at any given time around us – the things about which everybody has something to say or at least about which people whisper among themselves. A 'clear conception' comes when people realise what is expressed in such and such an event, in such and such statistics, in such and such a judicial decision, and so on and so on and so on. These all-sided political indictments are a necessary and *fundamental* condition of the education of the masses in revolutionary activeness.

Why does the Russian worker still show in so limited a fashion his revolutionary activeness in connection with the police's bestial treatment of the people, the persecution of sectarians, the corporal punishment of peasants, the outrages of the censor, the torment of the soldiers, the persecution of the most harmless cultural undertakings and so forth? Is it because the 'economic struggle' does not 'push him to face' the need for such activeness or that revolutionary activeness promises him so little in the way of 'tangible results', so little in the way of 'positive' results? No – such a view is, let us repeat it, nothing other than an attempt to shift the blame and to shift one's own philistinism (and Bernsteinism) over to the worker mass. We must blame ourselves, our falling behind the movement of the masses, since we have yet not been able to organise indictments of these despicable things in a sufficiently broad, clear and timely fashion. If we do this (and we must do it and we can do it), – the very simplest worker will understand, *or will feel*, that the dark force that mocks and oppresses the student and the sectarian, the *muzhik* and the writer, is the same that oppresses and weighs on him at each step of his life. And, when he does feel this, he will himself desire, with an overwhelming desire, to respond – and he will know how to do it, today setting up a chorus of catcalls for the censor, tomorrow demonstrating before the home of a governor who repressed a peasant riot, the day after tomorrow giving a lesson to the priests who are nothing but policemen in cassocks doing the work of the Holy Inquisition, and so forth. We still have done very little, almost nothing, to *throw* into the worker masses fresh and all-sided indictments. Many among the Social Democrats are not even aware that this is our *responsibility* and so they follow in *stikhiinyi* fashion the 'grey ongoing struggle' within the narrow framework of factory life. Under these circumstances, to announce that '*Iskra* has a tendency to disparage the significance of the forward march of the grey ongoing struggle in comparison with the propaganda of brilliant and self-sufficient ideas' (Martynov, p. 61) is to drag the Party backward, to defend and glorify our lack of preparation and our falling behind.

As far as the call to the masses to action is concerned, it will come of itself, once we have on hand energetic political agitation, clear and living indictments. To catch somebody red-handed and brand him immediately so that everybody knows about it – this just by itself will act as the best possible 'call'. Often, it will act in such a way that afterwards one cannot say definitely who exactly 'called' a crowd into action or who exactly came forth with this or that plan for a demonstration, and so on. To call [to action] in this way – not in the general but in the concrete sense of the word – can only be done on the field of action, and only he who himself goes there at a particular time can do the calling. But our business – the business of the Social-Democratic journalists – is to deepen, broaden and intensify political indictments and political agitation.

By the way, on the subject of 'calls'. *The only publication* that *prior* to the spring events *called* on the workers to intervene energetically in an issue that definitely *promised no tangible results* at all for the worker – for example, drafting the student [protesters] into the army – *was Iskra*. Immediately after the publication of the decree of January 11 about 'the drafting of 183 students into the army', *Iskra* published an article about it (No. 2, February) and – *before* any kind of demonstration began – directly *called* on the 'worker to help the student', called on 'the people' to openly respond to the government's contemptuous challenge. We ask everybody: how can we explain the extraordinary circumstance that Martynov, the one who talks so much about 'calls' and even makes 'calls' a special form of activity, does not refer to *this* call by so much as a word? And isn't it philistinism for Martynov to label *Iskra* 'one-sided' because it does not issue enough 'calls' for a struggle based on demands that 'promise tangible results'?

Our 'economists' – and *Rabochee delo* is included – met with success because they pandered to less developed workers. But the worker/Social Democrat, the worker/revolutionary – and the number of such workers grows every day – will reject with indignation all this reasoning about the struggle for demands that 'promise tangible results', and so on and so on, because he understands that all this is just a new variant of the old song about adding a kopeck to a rouble. Such a worker will say to his counsellors from *Rabochaia mysl* and *Rabochee delo*:

You worry too much to no purpose and intervene with excessive zeal in matters that we can handle ourselves, while not bothering to carry out your real responsibilities. It is far from insightful for you to say that the task of the Social Democrats consists of imparting a political character to the economic struggle itself. That is only the beginning – the main task of the Social Democrats lies elsewhere, for everywhere in the world, including Russia, *the police themselves often themselves undertake to give* a political character to the economic struggle and the workers themselves learn to understand for whom the government stands.[9]

That 'economic struggle of the workers with the owners and the government' of which you are so proud, exactly as if you had discovered America, is being carried out in the most remote corners of Russia by the workers themselves – they've heard about strikes, even if they haven't read about or even heard of socialism. And the 'activeness' of us workers that all of you want to support by coming up with concrete demands that promise tangible results – we already have this activeness, and we ourselves, in the small, day-to-day, trade [*professial'nyi*] struggle, put forth these concrete demands, often without any help from the *intelligenty*. But *this* kind of activeness is not enough for us; we are not children whom you can feed with the thin soup of 'economist' politics by itself; we want to know everything that everyone else knows, we want to become acquainted in detail with *all* sides of political life and *actively* participate in each and every political event. For this it is necessary that the *intelligenty* spend less time repeating what we ourselves already know,[10] and more time

---

[9] The demand to 'impart a political character to the economic struggle itself' reveals in the most vivid fashion *kow-towing before stikhiinost* in the area of political activity. The economic struggle acquires a political character *in stikhiinyi fashion*, that is, without the intervention of the 'revolutionary bacilli, the intelligentsia', without the intervention of purposive Social Democrats. For example, the economic struggle of workers in England acquired a political character without any participation by the socialists. But the task of the Social Democrats is not exhausted by political agitation on economic grounds, their task is to *turn* this *tred-iunionist* politics into a Social-Democratic political struggle, – to *use* those gleams of political awareness that the economic struggle plants in the workers in order to *raise* the workers up to *Social-Democratic* political awareness. But instead of raising and pushing forward this political awareness that is awakening in *stikhiinyi* fashion, the Martynovs *fall on their face before stikhiinost* and repeat (repeat over and over to the point of nausea) that the economic struggle is what 'pushes the worker to face' the issue of their political lack of rights. It's too bad, gentlemen, that this *stikhiinyi* awakening of *tred-iunionist* political awareness doesn't '*push*' you to face the issue of your Social-Democratic tasks!

[10] To show that we haven't made up this speech of the workers to the 'economists'

giving us what we don't know, what we ourselves will never be able to learn from our own factory and 'economic' experience, namely: political knowledge. It is you, the *intelligenty*, that can bring us this knowledge, and you are *obliged* to deliver it to us a hundred and a thousand times more than you are doing up to now, and what is more, deliver it not only in the form of disquisitions, pamphlets and articles (which are often, if you will forgive my frankness, a little boring!), but, without fail, also in the form of living *indictments* of what exactly our government and our dominant classes are doing in all areas of life. Just carry out more zealously this responsibility of yours, and *talk less about 'raising the activeness of the worker mass'*. There is a lot more activeness among us than you think, and we are able to support, with open street battle, even such demands as promise no 'tangible results' at all! And it's not you who will 'raise' our activeness, because *it so happens that it is you who aren't showing enough* activeness. Less kow-towing before *stikhiinost*, gentlemen, and more thought to raising *your* activeness!

### d) What do economism and terrorism have in common?

Earlier, in a footnote, we compared an 'economist' and a non-Social-Democratic-terrorist on a point where they accidentally agreed together. But, speaking

---

out of thin air, we will refer to two witnesses who undoubtedly have an immediate knowledge of the worker movement and who are no wise inclined to be partial to us 'dogmatic types', since one of the witnesses is an 'economist' (who even considers *Rabochee delo* to be a political publication!) and the other is a terrorist. The first witness [Savinkov] is the author of an article entitled 'The Petersburg Worker Movement and the Practical Tasks of Social Democracy' that is remarkable for its truthfulness and sense of life. He divides the workers into three categories: (1) purposive revolutionaries, (2) an intermediate stratum and (3) the remaining mass [of workers]. We find that the intermediate stratum 'is often more interested in the issues of political life than their own direct economic interests, while the connection of these interests to general social conditions has long been grasped' . . . *Rabochaia mysl* is 'sharply criticised': 'it's always the same thing that we've known for a long time and have read for a long time', 'in the politics sections there is again nothing new' (pp. 30–1). But even the third stratum 'is a worker mass that is more alert, younger, not so much led astray by the tavern and the church. Although this stratum never has even the possibility of acquiring any book with political content, it interprets in distorted fashion the phenomena of political life and uses fragmentary information about the student riots as food for thought' and so forth. And the terrorist [Nadezhdin] writes: '. . . Two or three times they will read about the details of factory life in cities other than their own and then they will stop reading. . . . It's boring. . . . Not to talk about the state in a worker paper . . . means to look on the worker as on a small child . . . The worker is not a child' (*Svoboda*, published by the revolutionary-socialist group [of the same name], pp. 69 and 70).

generally, there is not just an accidental but a necessary internal link between 'economism' and terrorism. This is a topic to which we will have to return later but on which we must now touch precisely because it concerns the issue of education for revolutionary activeness. The 'economists' and present-day terrorists have one common root: the very same *kow-towing before stikhiinost* that we discussed in the previous chapter in general terms and that we are now examining in its influence in the area of political activity and political struggle. At first glance, our affirmation might appear to be a paradox, so great is the evident distance between people who emphasise the 'grey on-going struggle' and people who call for the most self-sacrificing struggle of individuals. But it is not a paradox. 'Economists' and terrorists kow-tow before different poles of the *stikhiinyi* current: the 'economists' before the *stikhiinost* of the 'exclusively worker movement' and the terrorists before the *stikhiinost* of the passionate indignation of *intelligenty* who do not have the ability or who do not find it possible to link revolutionary work into a single whole with the worker movement. It is difficult for anyone who has lost faith in this possibility or who never had it to find any other outlet for his feelings of indignation and for his revolutionary energy than terror.

This kow-towing before *stikhiinost* in both of these two tendencies is in this way nothing other than *the beginning of the implementation* of the famous programme of the *Credo*: the workers will conduct their own 'economic struggle with the owners and the government' (I hope the author of the *Credo* will forgive my use of Martynov's terminology! – we think we have the right to do this because the *Credo* also speaks of how the workers are 'pushed to face up to the political régime' in the economic struggle), while the *intelligenty* conduct the political struggle with their own forces, naturally, with the help of terror! This is a completely logical and inevitable *conclusion* on which we do not have to insist, *even though those* who are beginning to implement the programme *are not themselves aware* of its inevitability. Political activity has its own logic that does not depend on the awareness of those who with the very best intentions call either for terror or for imparting a political character to the economic struggle itself. The road to hell is paved with good intentions and, in the present case, good intentions will not save anyone from being drawn in *stikhiinyi* fashion down the 'line of least resistance', down the line of the *purely bourgeois* programme of the *Credo*. It is therefore hardly accidental that many Russian liberals – both open liberals and those who wear a Marxist mask – sympathise wholeheartedly with terror and try to give support to the upsurge in terrorist moods at the present moment.

And, now, when the 'revolutionary-socialist group *Svoboda*' has emerged and assigned itself the task precisely of providing an all-sided assistance to the worker movement, but which also includes terror *in its programme*, thus emancipating themselves, so to speak, from Social Democracy – this fact affirms yet one more time the remarkable foresight of P.B. Akselrod, who *literally foretold* these results of Social-Democratic unsteadiness *already at the end of 1897* (in *The Contemporary Tasks and Tactics of Russian Social Democrats*) and set out his famous 'two perspectives'. These two perspectives already contain, as a seed contains a plant, all of the disputes and differences between Russian Social Democrats that followed after.[11] From this point of view it becomes understandable that *Rabochee delo*, unable to stand up against the *stikhiinost* of 'economism', was also unable to stand up against the *stikhiinost* of terrorism.

It is very interesting here to note the particular argumentation that *Svoboda* advances in defence of terror. It 'completely rejects' the paralysing role of terror (*Rebirth of Revolutionism*, p. 64) and in its place advances its 'excitative (instigating) significance'. This is characteristic, in the first place, because it is one of the stages in the disintegration and collapse of a traditional (pre-Social-Democratic) set of ideas that led to a reliance on terror. To admit that, today, one cannot 'paralyse with fear' – and, therefore, disorganise – the government is essentially to condemn terror completely as a system of struggle, as a sphere of activity sanctified by a programme. It is even more characteristic in another respect – as a model of the lack of understanding of our present

---

[11] Martynov sees 'another, more real (?) dilemma' ('Social Democracy and the Worker Class', p. 19): '*Either* Social Democracy takes upon itself the immediate guidance of the economic struggle of the proletariat and by so doing (!) turns it into a revolutionary class struggle' . . . 'By so doing', that is, evidently, by the immediate guidance of the economic struggle. Let Martynov show us where we can see *even one* case where a *tred-iunionist* struggle was turned into a revolutionary class movement simply by guidance of the trade [*professial'nyi*] struggle. Doesn't he realise that to do any 'turning into' of this kind, we must actively take on the 'immediate guidance' of *all-sided* political agitation? . . . '*Or* this perspective: Social Democracy distances itself from the guidance of the economic struggle of the workers and by so doing . . . clips its wings' . . . According to the opinion of *Rabochee delo* cited earlier, it is *Iskra* that 'distances itself'. But we have seen that *Iskra* is doing *much more than Rabochee delo* for the guidance of the economic struggle, although it does not limit itself to this kind of guidance and *does not* for the sake of this guidance *narrow* its political tasks.

basic tasks in the matter of 'education for the revolutionary activeness of the masses'. *Svoboda* propagandises terror as a means of 'instigating' the worker movement, of giving it a 'powerful shock'. It would be difficult to find an argument that more obviously refutes itself! Let's think: are there really so few outrages in Russian life that we have to invent some special means of 'instigation'? And, from another angle, if someone is not instigated or not instigable even by Russian abuses of power, then isn't it obvious that he will also look on the duel between the government and a handful of terrorists with sublime indifference? The point is this: the worker masses *are* very much instigated by the despicable features of Russian life, but we do not yet know how to collect (if I may so express myself) and concentrate all those droplets and streams of popular indignation that percolate out of Russian life in vastly greater quantities than we think or can conceive but which indeed must be merged into *one* gigantic flood.

This task can be accomplished. This is proved irrefutably by the enormous growth of the worker movement and the greediness of the workers for political literature mentioned earlier. Calls to apply terror, exactly like calls to impart a political character to the economic struggle itself, are just different ways of *shirking* the most urgent responsibility of Russian revolutionaries: to organise the conduct of all-sided political agitation. *Svoboda* wants to *replace* agitation with terror and it openly admits that 'once intensive, energetic agitation begins among the masses, then the excitative (instigating) role of terror is done' (p. 68 of *Rebirth of Revolutionism*). As it happens, this demonstrates that both terrorists and 'economists' *underrate* the revolutionary activeness of the masses, in spite of the clear testimony of the spring events, even though the former busy themselves in search of artificial 'instigations' while the latter talk about 'concrete demands'. Both the one and the other pay insufficient attention to the development of *their own activeness* in the matter of political agitation and the organisation of political indictments. But one cannot *replace* this task with any other, either now or at any other time.

### e) The worker class as advanced fighter for democracy

We saw that carrying out the broadest possible political agitation and, therefore, the organisation of all-sided political indictments are unconditionally necessary tasks – the *most urgent of all* the tasks – of our activity, if it is to be genuinely

Social-Democratic activity. But we came to this conclusion based *only* on the pressing requirement of the worker class for political knowledge and political education. In itself, this way of putting the question is too narrow and ignores the general democratic tasks of any Social Democracy in general and of present-day Russian Social Democracy in particular. In order to explain this thesis as concretely as possible, let us try to approach the problem from the angle that is 'nearest' to the 'economist', that is, the practical side. 'All are agreed' that we must develop the political awareness of the worker class. Let us now ask ourselves *how* to do this and what is required for doing it. The economic struggle 'pushes the workers to face' only issues about the relation of the government to the worker class and therefore – *no matter how much we labour* over the task of 'imparting a political character to the economic struggle itself' – we will *never be able* to develop the political awareness of the workers (up to the level of Social-Democratic political awareness) within the framework of this task, because *the framework itself is too narrow*. Martynov's formula is valuable for us, not only because it illustrates his capacity to confuse issues, but also because it vividly expresses the basic mistake of all 'economists' – the conviction that it is possible to develop class political awareness *from within*, so to speak, the economic struggle, that is, proceeding only (or even just for the most part) from that struggle, basing oneself only (or primarily) on that struggle. This view is radically mistaken – precisely because the economists, angry as they are about our polemics against them, do not want to think hard about the source of our differences, with the result that we literally do not understand one another and we speak in different languages.

Class political awareness can be brought to the worker *only from without*, that is to say from outside the economic struggle, from outside the sphere of the relations of workers to owners. The only area from which this knowledge can be taken is the area of the relations of *all* classes and [social] strata to the state and to the government – the area of the interrelations between *all* classes. Therefore, one cannot answer the question 'what is to be done to bring political knowledge to the workers?' with the response that the majority of *praktiki* are contented with, namely: 'go to the workers'. In order to bring the *workers* political knowledge, the Social Democrats must *go to all classes of the population, must send the detachments of its army in all directions.*

We have deliberately chosen such a harsh formulation and deliberately expressed ourselves in sharp and simplified fashion – not because of any desire to speak in paradoxes but in order to 'push the "economists" to face' the tasks that they unforgivably disdain and the distinction that they do not want to understand between *tred-iunionist* politics and Social-Democratic politics. And, therefore, we ask the reader not to get upset but to follow us attentively to the end.

Let us examine the type of Social-Democratic circle found most commonly in recent times and look closely at its work. It has 'links with the workers' and is content with that; it publishes leaflets in which factory abuses are flayed along with police violence and the government's actions that are so biased toward the capitalists; during conferences with workers, the conversation does not ordinarily go beyond or barely goes beyond the limits of these same themes; very rarely are there reports and conversations on the history of the revolutionary movement, on issues of domestic and external policies of our government, on issues of the economic evolution of Russia and Europe and the position in modern society of this or that class and so on; nobody even thinks of obtaining and broadening links to the other classes in society. In essence, the ideal activist as pictured by members of these circles – in the majority of cases – is something much closer to a secretary of a *tred-iunion* than to a socialist political leader [*vozhd'*]. The secretary of any, let's say, English *tred-iunion* always helps the workers conduct their economic struggle, organises factory indictments, explains the injustice of laws and of measures that hinder the freedom of strikes or the freedom to establish pickets (to warn all and sundry that there is a strike at a given factory), explains the partiality of the arbitration court judges who belong to the bourgeois classes of the people, and so on and so on. In a word, any secretary of a *tred-iunion* conducts and helps others conduct the 'economic struggle with the owners and the government'. We cannot insist too strongly that this is *not yet* Social Democratism and that the ideal of the Social Democrat should not be a secretary of a *tred-iunion* but a *people's tribune* who can respond to each and every manifestation of abuse of power and oppression, wherever it occurs, whatever stratum or class it concerns, who can generalise all these manifestations into one big picture of police violence and capitalist exploitation, who is able to use each small affair to set *before everybody* his socialist convictions and his democratic demands and to explain to each and *all* the world-historical significance of the liberation struggle of the proletariat.

Compare, for example, such activists as Robert Knight (the well-known secretary and leader of the Boiler-Makers' Society, one of the most powerful English *tred-iuniony*) and Wilhelm Liebknecht – and try to apply to them the set of contrasts by which Martynov sets forth his disagreements with *Iskra*. You will observe – I am starting to leaf through Martynov's article – that Knight is more engaged in 'calling the masses to certain concrete actions' (p. 39) while Liebknecht is more engaged in 'the revolutionary illumination of the whole system or its partial manifestations' (pp. 38–9). Knight 'formulates the urgent demands of the proletariat and shows means for their implementation' (p. 41), while Liebknecht, although he does this as well, does not refuse also to 'simultaneously guide the energetic activity of various oppositional strata' and 'dictate a positive programme of action for them' (p. 41).[12] Knight is the one who tries to 'impart a political character to the economic struggle itself' (p. 42) and knows very well how to 'present the government with concrete demands promising tangible results' (p. 43), while Liebknecht is much more engaged in 'one-sided' 'indictments' (p. 40). Knight gives more significance to the 'forward march of the grey ongoing struggle' (p. 61), while Liebknecht gives more significance to 'the propaganda of brilliant and self-sufficient ideas' (p. 61). Liebknecht created out of the newspaper he guided precisely 'an organ of revolutionary opposition, denouncing our institutions and particularly our political ones, insofar as they clash with the interests of the most various strata of the population' (p. 63), while Knight 'worked for the worker cause in a close and organic link with the proletarian struggle' (p. 63) – if we understand 'close organic bond' in the sense of the kow-towing before *stikhiinost* that we observed earlier in the case of Krichevskii and Martynov – and 'narrowed the sphere of his activity', no doubt assured like Martynov that he was 'by this very fact complexifying his influence' (p. 63). In a word, you will see that Martynov is de facto lowering Social Democracy to *tred-iunionizm*, although, of course, he does not do this because he wishes anything but good for Social Democracy but simply because he was just a trifle hasty in deepening Plekhanov instead of giving himself the trouble of understanding Plekhanov.

---

[12] For example, at the time of the Franco-Prussian War, Liebknecht dictated the actions of *the entire democracy* – and Marx and Engels did this to an even greater extent in 1848.

But let us return to our exposition. We said that a Social Democrat, if he insists (more than just in words) on the necessity of an all-sided development of political awareness of the proletariat, must 'go to all classes of the population'. I will be asked: how to do this? Do we have forces to do this? Is there any ground for such work among all the other classes? Will not this mean a retreat, or lead to a retreat, from the class point of view? Let us dwell on these questions.

We should 'go to all classes of the population' as theoreticians, as propagandists, as agitators and as organisers. No one doubts that the theoretical work of Social Democrats is directed toward the study of all the particularities of the social and political position of individual classes. But extremely little is being done in this connection – disproportionately little in comparison with the work aimed at the study of the particularities of factory life. In our committees and circles, you will meet people who are genuinely learned in the special subject of something like railroad manufacture – but you will find almost no examples of members of these organisations (when they are compelled, as often, to leave practical work for this or that reason) devoting themselves especially to some topical issue of our social and political life that could provide the occasion for Social-Democratic work in other strata of the population. When we talk about the lack of preparedness of the present-day leader/guides of the worker movement, we must certainly also remember lack of preparation of this kind, since it is also tied closely to the 'economist' understanding of 'close and organic links with the proletarian struggle'.

But the main thing, of course, is *propaganda and agitation* in all strata of the people. This task is alleviated for the Western-European Social Democrat by popular assemblies and meetings that *anybody* who wants can attend; it is also alleviated by a parliament in which the Social Democrat speaks before deputies of *all* classes. We have neither parliament nor freedom of assembly – nevertheless, we have been able to set up meetings for workers who wish to hear a *Social Democrat*. We should also be able to set up meetings with representatives of each and every class of the population that only want to hear a *democrat* – since he is no Social Democrat who forgets in practice that 'the communists support any revolutionary movement' and that we are obliged therefore to lay out our views *in front of the whole people* and to underline *general democratic tasks*, not hiding for a moment our socialist convictions. He is no Social Democrat who forgets in practice about his responsibility to be *in advance of all* in presenting, sharpening and resolving *any* general democratic issue.

'Everybody completely agrees with this!' interrupts the impatient reader. Indeed, the new instructions for the editorial board of *Rabochee delo* that were adopted at the last congress of the Union states outright: 'All manifestations and events of social and political life must serve as occasions for political propaganda and agitation, whether they touch the proletariat either directly as a distinct class or as the *vanguard for all revolutionary forces in the struggle for freedom*' (*Two Congresses*, p. 17, my emphasis). Yes, these are very true, very good words, and we would be completely satisfied with them, if *Rabochee delo really understood* them, *if it did not at the same time say things that are in sharp contrast with them*. It is not enough just to call oneself a 'vanguard', an advance detachment – one has to act so that *all* other detachments see and are compelled to admit that we are indeed moving out ahead. And we ask the reader: are the representatives of the other 'detachments' really such fools simply to accept our word about being a 'vanguard'?

Just imagine the following concrete situation. A Social Democrat goes to the 'detachment' of educated radicals or liberal constitutionalists and says: we are the vanguard and 'before us stands the task of imparting, to the greatest extent possible, a political character to the economic struggle itself'. A moderately intelligent radical or constitutionalist (and there are lots of intelligent people among the Russian radicals and constitutionalists) will only smile when hearing such a speech and say (to themselves, of course, because most of these people are accomplished diplomats), 'Well, this is a rather simple-minded "vanguard"! It doesn't even understand that it is our task – the task of the advanced representatives of the bourgeois democracy – to impart a political character to the workers' economic struggle *itself*. We, like the bourgeoisie everywhere in Western Europe, want to draw the workers into politics, *but precisely into tred-iunionist and not into Social-Democratic politics*. A *tred-iunionist* politics of the worker class is precisely a *bourgeois politics* of the worker class. And the formulation by this "vanguard" of its task is precisely a formulation of *tred-iunionist* politics! So let them call themselves Social Democrats as much as they want. I'm not a child who gets all upset about labels! I just hope they don't fall under the influence of those harmful orthodox dogmatic types – let them preserve "freedom of criticism" for those who, unaware, are dragging Social Democracy into a *tred-iunionist* channel.'

And the faint smile of our constitutionalist will turn into Homeric laughter when he learns that what these Social Democrats who talk about Social Democracy as a vanguard fear most on earth – at the present time of almost complete domination of *stikhiinost* in our movement – is 'underestimation of the *stikhiinyi* element', 'underestimating the significance of the forward march of the grey ongoing struggle in comparison with the propaganda of brilliant and self-sufficient ideas' and so on and so on. An 'advanced' detachment which fears that purposiveness might overtake *stikhiinost* and which fears to put forward a daring 'plan' that would compel general recognition even from those who disagree! Haven't these people confused the word 'vanguard' with the word 'rearguard'?

Ponder, in this connection, the following reasoning of Martynov. He says on p. 40 that the indictment tactic of *Iskra* is one-sided and that 'no matter how much we sow mistrust and hatred toward the government, we will not achieve our aim, so long as we do not succeed in developing sufficient active social energy for its overthrow'. This, let us note in passing, is the already familiar worry about raising the activeness of the mass while at the same time striving to lower one's own activeness. But the main point is elsewhere. Martynov is speaking here, it follows, about *revolutionary* energy ('for its overthrow'). And at what conclusion does he arrive? Since, in normal times, the various social strata inevitably march separately, then

> in view of this fact it is clear that we Social Democrats cannot at the same time guide the activities of different oppositional strata, we cannot dictate a positive programme of action for them, we cannot show them in what way to fight for their own interests from day to day. . . . The liberal strata themselves will surely take care of the active struggle for their current interests, a struggle that will push them to a direct collision with our political régime. (p. 41.)

Thus, after starting to talk about revolutionary energy, about the active struggle for the overthrow of the autocracy, Martynov immediately strays off and talks about toward the energy of occupational concerns [*professional'naia energiia*], about the active struggle for current interests!

It goes without saying that we cannot guide the struggle of the students, the liberals and so forth for their 'current interests', but that's not the point, my most highly respected 'economist'! The point is, rather, the possible and the necessary participation of various social strata in the overthrow of the autocracy, and *this* 'energetic activity of various oppositional strata' we not only *can* but definitely must guide if we want to be a 'vanguard'. Our students, our liberals and so forth are not the only ones who will take care that they are 'pushed into direct collision with our political régime' – the police and the bureaucrats of the autocratic government will be the ones who first of all and most of all take care of this. But 'we', if we wish to be advanced democrats, must take care to *push* people who are personally dissatisfied only with their university or with their *zemstvo* institutions to face up to the worthlessness of our political institutions as a whole. *We* must take upon ourselves the task of organising an all-sided political struggle under the guidance of *our* party so that as much help as possible can be given and will be given to that struggle and to that party by each and every oppositional stratum. *We* must take the *praktiki* of Social Democrats and make them political leaders [*vozhdi*], leaders capable of guiding all manifestations of the all-sided struggle, capable at the crucial moment 'to dictate a positive programme of action' to the turbulent students, the dissatisfied *zemstvo* people, the indignant sectarians, the offended rural teachers and so on and so on.

Therefore Martynov's affirmation is *completely untrue* when he says that 'in relation to these strata we can come out *only in the negative* role of denouncers of institutions. . . . *All* we can do is dissipate the hopes placed on various governmental commissions' (our emphasis). When he says this, Martynov shows that he *understands absolutely nothing* about the issue of the actual role of the revolutionary 'vanguard'. And, if the reader keeps this in mind, then he will understand the *true meaning* of Martynov's concluding words:

> *Iskra* is an organ of revolutionary opposition that indicts our system and mainly our political system, insofar as it conflicts with the interests of the most diverse strata of the population. We, on the other hand, work and will continue to work for the cause of the workers in a close and organic link with the proletarian struggle. By narrowing our sphere of activity, we by this very fact complexify our influence. (p. 63.)

The true meaning of this conclusion is this: *Iskra* wants to *raise tred-iunionist* politics of the worker class (the politics to which our *praktiki* so often limit themselves, either through confusion, lack of preparation, or conviction) up to Social-Democratic politics. But *Rabochee delo* wants to *lower* Social-Democratic politics down to *tred-iunionist* politics. And after saying all this, they still assure all and sundry that these two positions are 'completely compatible in common work' (p. 63). O, sancta simplicitas!

Let us proceed. Do we have sufficient forces to be able to direct our propaganda and agitation to *all* classes of the population? Yes, of course. Our 'economists', often inclined to deny this, forget about the giant step forward that our movement has made from approximately 1894 to 1901. True 'tailists', they still live to some extent according to conceptions of a period at the beginning of our movement that has long since been past. At that time, we indeed had strikingly insufficient forces. The determination to go totally into work among workers and to harshly condemn any deviation from it made sense and was natural at that time. Our task at that time consisted in entrenching ourselves in the worker class. Now, a gigantic mass of forces has been drawn into the movement and the best representatives of the younger generation of the educated classes are coming to us. Everywhere throughout the provinces can be found people who are forced to live there and who are already taking part or who wish to take part in the movement – people gravitating toward Social Democracy (whereas, in 1894, you could count Russian Social Democrats on your fingers). One of the basic political and organisational inadequacies of our movement is that we *have not been able* to use all these forces, to give them all appropriate work (we will speak of this in more detail in the next chapter). The vast majority of these forces are completely deprived of the possibility of 'going to the workers', so that there is no danger of drawing forces away from our basic task. But, to provide the workers with genuinely all-sided and living political knowledge, we need 'our people', Social Democrats, to be everywhere, in all social strata, in all sorts of positions that give them the possibility to know the internal workings of our state mechanism. And these people are necessary, not only for propaganda and agitation, but even more for organisation.

Is there ground for activity in all classes of the population? He who doesn't see this is someone whose purposiveness is falling behind the *stikhiinyi* upsurge of the masses. The worker movement has called forth and will continue to call forth dissatisfaction among some, hopes for support for their opposition among others, awareness of the intolerability of the autocracy and the inevitability of its collapse in yet others. We would be 'politicals' and Social Democrats only in words (as is so very often the case) if we were not aware of our task to use all and sundry manifestations of dissatisfaction, to collect together and to cultivate every germ of even still embryonic protest. We haven't even mentioned yet the whole many-millioned mass of labouring peasantry, the artisans, the small craftsmen and so forth, who would always listen eagerly to the preaching of any decently capable Social Democrat. But really, is it possible to point to even one class of the population which does not contain people, groups and circles that are dissatisfied with their lack of rights and with abuse of power and are therefore open to the preaching of a Social Democrat as someone who expresses the most burning general democratic needs? And if anyone wishes to picture the political agitation of the Social Democrat in *all* classes and strata of the population in concrete fashion, we point to *political indictments* in the wide sense of this word as the main (but of course not the sole) means for this agitation.

As I wrote in the article 'Where to Begin', *Iskra*, No. 4, May 1901 (an article we will have to talk about in more detail later):

> We must awaken a passion for *political* indictments in all strata of the population that are in any way purposive. We do not need to worry about the fact that the voices of political indictment are so weak, timid and rare at the present time. It is certainly not a universal reconciliation to police-state abuse of power that causes this situation. The reason is this: people who are ready and able to make indictments have no tribune from which they could speak – no audience that passionately listens to and approves the orators – and they do not see anywhere in the *narod* a force to whom it would be worth their effort to complain about the 'all-powerful' Russian government. . . . We are now in a position to create a tribune for an indictment of the tsarist government addressed to the whole people [*vsenarodnyi*] – and we are obliged to create it. A Social-Democratic newspaper must be this kind of tribune.

Exactly such an ideal audience for political indictments is the worker class, which needs all-sided and living political knowledge first of all and most of all and which is the most able to turn this knowledge into active struggle, even though the struggle promises no 'tangible results' whatever. And a tribune for indictments *addressed to the whole people* [*vsenarodnyi*] can only be an all-Russian newspaper. 'In modern Europe, a movement that deserves the name of "political" is unthinkable without a political press organ' – and, in this connection, Russia undoubtedly belongs to modern Europe. The press has long ago become a force in this country – otherwise, the government would not spend tens of thousands of roubles on bribing and subsidising all of our Katkovs and Meshcherskiis. And it is no new thing in autocratic Russia that the underground press breaks through the barriers of censorship and *compels* the legally-permitted and conservative organs to talk openly about it. This happened in the 1870s and even in the 1850s. And how much broader and deeper now are those strata among the people that are ready to read the underground press and learn from it 'how to live and how to die', using the expression of the worker who sent in a letter to *Iskra* (No. 7). Political indictments are a declaration of war against the *government* in exactly the same way that economic indictments declare war against the factory owners. And this declaration of war acquires more and more moral significance as the indictment campaign becomes broader and more forceful, and the more numerous and resolute is the social *class that declares war in order to get a real war underway*. Political indictments are therefore already in and of themselves one of the most powerful means of *disintegrating* the enemy system – a means of drawing away from the enemy his accidental or temporary friends, a means of sowing enmity and distrust among those who are permanent participants in the autocratic power.

In our day, only a party that *organises* indictments genuinely addressed to the whole people [*vsenarodnyi*] can be an advance guard of revolutionary forces. And this term 'addressed to the whole people' has a very large content. The great majority of people from the non-worker classes who are engaged in indictments [of tsarism] – and to be a vanguard, it is precisely necessary to draw in other classes – are sober politicians and pragmatic, business-like people. They know perfectly well that it is dangerous to 'complain' about even the lowest bureaucrat, not to mention the 'all-powerful' Russian government. And they will turn *to us* with complaints only when they see that their complaint is genuinely capable of having a real effect and that we constitute a *political force*. In order to impress third parties this way, we must work long and hard on *raising* our purposiveness, initiative and energy – it is not enough to hang a sign saying 'vanguard' on the theory and practice of a rear-guard.

But if we are obliged to take upon ourselves the organisation of indictments of the government genuinely addressed to the whole people, then how does the class character of our movement express itself? – This is the question that will be posed and is posed to us by the overzealous worshipper of 'close and organic links with the proletarian struggle'. The class character is expressed in this: it is we, the Social Democrats, who organise these indictments addressed to the whole people. Furthermore, the illumination of all the issues raised by agitation will be carried out in an unremitting Social-Democratic spirit without the slightest indulgence toward deliberate and unintentional distortions of Marxism. The party that will carry out this all-sided political agitation is one that merges an attack on the government in the name of the whole people with the revolutionary education of the proletariat and the preservation of its political independence, along with guidance of the economic struggle of the worker class and the utilisation of its *stikhiinyi* clashes with its exploiters – clashes that lift up and draw in to our camp ever new strata of the proletariat!

But one of the most characteristic traits of 'economism' is precisely this lack of understanding of the link – more than that, the complete overlap – between the most essential need of the proletariat (all-sided political education by means of political agitation and political indictments) and the needs of the general democratic movement. This lack of understanding is expressed not only in Martynov-style phrases but also in various remarks about the class point of view that have the same basic meaning as these phrases. For example, see how the authors of the 'economist' letter to *Iskra*, No. 12 express themselves [with Lenin's interjections in parentheses]:[13]

> This same basic defect of *Iskra* . . . (the overvaluation of ideology) . . . is the reason for its inconsistency in issues concerning the relation of Social Democracy to various social classes and tendencies. Having decided through a purely theoretical exercise . . . (and *not* by means of 'the growth of party tasks growing together with the party' [as advocated by Krichevskii]) . . . that the task is the immediate transition to the struggle against absolutism and feeling, no doubt, the full difficulty of this task for the workers, given the

---

[13] Owing to lack of space, we could not give a fully detailed answer in *Iskra* itself to this letter so highly characteristic of the 'economists'. We were very happy to receive it, since allegations about *Iskra*'s inability to hold to the class point of view had come to our ears for a long time and from a great variety of sources, and we were looking for a suitable opportunity or a well-formulated expression of this popular accusation in order to answer it. And we are accustomed to answer an attack not by a defence but by a counter-attack.

> present state of things . . . (and not only feeling, but knowing very well, that this task seems more difficult to 'economist' *intelligenty* who feel they are taking care of little kids [as they see the workers] than it does to the workers, since [in reality] the workers are ready to fight even for demands that do not promise, as the never-to-be-forgotten Martynov puts it, any 'tangible results') . . . but lacking the patience to wait for an accumulation on the part of the workers of sufficient strength for this struggle, *Iskra* is beginning to search for allies in the ranks of liberals and the intelligentsia . . .

Yes indeed, we really have already lost the 'patience' 'to wait' for the blessed time (promised us for so long by all manner of 'conciliators') when our 'economists' stop blaming the workers for *their* backwardness, stop justifying their own insufficient energy by the alleged lack of forces among the workers. We ask our 'economists': what exactly will the 'accumulation on the part of the workers of sufficient strength for this struggle' consist of? Isn't it obvious that it consists of the political education of the workers, in the unmasking for them of *all* sides of our contemptible autocracy? And isn't it clear that *precisely for this work* we need 'allies in the ranks of the liberals and the intelligentsia', ready to share with us indictments of the political campaign [directed by the government] against the *zemstvo* people, the teachers, the statisticians, the students and so forth? How hard can it be to grasp this fairly simple mechanism? Did not P.B. Akselrod repeat over and over again since 1897 that 'the task of obtaining supporters and direct and indirect allies among the non-proletarian classes is decided first of all and primarily by the character of the propagandistic activity conducted among the proletariat itself'? But the Martynovs and the other 'economists' nevertheless continue to think that the workers must *first* accumulate forces (for *tred-iunionist* politics) by means of 'the economic struggle with the owners and the government', and only *then* make a 'transition' – evidently, from *tred-iunionist* 'education for activeness' to Social-Democratic activeness!

The economists continue:

> In its search [for allies] *Iskra* often strays from the class point of view by muffling class contradictions and putting the entire focus on the commonality of dissatisfaction with the government, even though the reasons and degree of this dissatisfaction among the 'allies' is extremely various. Take, for example, the relations of *Iskra* to the *zemstvo* . . .

*Iskra* allegedly 'promises noblemen unsatisfied with government handouts the help of the worker class, without a word being said about the class hostility between these strata of the population'.

If the reader will turn to the articles 'The Autocracy and the *Zemstvo*' (*Iskra*, Nos. 2 and 4) – these are *probably* the ones the authors of the letter are talking about – he will see that these articles[14] are dedicated to the *government's* reaction to 'the mild agitation of the élite/bureaucratic *zemstvo*', to 'the independent activity even of the propertied classes'. The article says that the worker cannot be indifferent to the struggle of the government against the *zemstvo* and it invites the *zemstvo* people to throw away mild speeches and to speak out with sharp uncompromising words at a time when the government is faced with revolutionary Social Democracy in its full stature. It is hard to say what the authors of the letter disagree with here. Do they think that the worker 'will not understand' the words 'propertied classes' and 'élite/bureaucratic *zemstvo*'? – or that this *pushing* of the *zemstvo* officials to move from gentle to sharp words is an 'overvaluation of ideology'? Do they imagine that the workers can 'accumulate sufficient forces' for the struggle with absolutism if they never know about the relation of absolutism to the *zemstvo as well*? The answers to these questions must remain unknown.

Only one thing is clear: the authors have a very confused idea of the political tasks of Social Democracy. This comes out even more clearly in this statement: '*Iskra* has the same attitude' (that is, one that 'obscures class antagonisms') 'to the student movement as well'. In *Iskra*, No. 2, there was an appeal to the workers to show by means of a public demonstration that the real source of violence and unbridled lawlessness was not the students but the Russian government. Instead of this appeal, we evidently should have published reasonings in the spirit of *Rabochaia mysl*! And such ideas are expressed by Social Democrats in the autumn of 1901 – after the February and March events, on the eve of a new student upsurge that will show in this sphere as well that the *stikhiinost* of protest against the autocracy *is overtaking* the purposive guidance of the movement on the part of Social Democracy. The *stikhiinyi* striving of the workers to come to the defence of students beaten by the police

---

[14] Note that *in between* the appearance of these articles (in *Iskra*, No. 3) was published an article specifically about the class antagonisms in our village.

and the Cossacks is overtaking the purposive activity of the Social-Democratic organisation!

'Meanwhile, in other articles' (continue the authors of the letter) '*Iskra* sharply condemns any compromises and comes out, for example, in defence of the intolerant conduct of the Guesdists'. We advise people who habitually pronounce on the topic of the disagreements among [Russian] Social Democrats with a good deal of self-assurance but without much thought and who say that these disagreements are on inessential matters and that no schism is justified – we advise these people to think good and hard about this statement. Is successful work in a single organisation possible if one group [*Iskra*] says that we have done strikingly little in the matter of explaining the hostility of the autocracy toward the most diverse classes as well as in the matter of acquainting the workers with the opposition to the autocracy by the most diverse strata – while the other group views all this as a 'compromise', a compromise, it would seem, with the theory of 'economic struggle with the owners and the government'?

On the occasion of the fortieth anniversary of the liberation of the peasants, we talked about the necessity of bringing the class struggle into the village (*Iskra*, No. 3). We talked about the irreconcilability between local self-government and the autocracy when commenting on Witte's secret memorandum (*Iskra*, No. 4). On the occasion of a new law [that made Siberian land available to landowners], we attacked the serf-owning mentality of the landowners and the government that serves them (*Iskra*, No. 8). We greeted the illegal *zemstvo* congress, encouraging the *zemstvo* people to move from grovelling petitions to actual struggle. We encouraged those students who are beginning to understand the necessity of political struggle and are moving towards it (*Iskra*, No. 3), and at the same time we castigated the 'primitive lack of understanding' revealed by the advocates of the 'exclusively student' movement who tell the students not to participate in street demonstrations (*Iskra*, No. 3, on the occasion of an appeal issued by the Executive Committee of the Moscow Student Association on 25 February). We exposed the 'senseless dreams' and the 'lying hypocrisy' of the liberal tricksters of the newspaper *Rossiia* (*Iskra*, No. 5) and, at the same time, noted the fury of the government torture-chamber that 'committed outrages on peaceable writers, on elderly professors and scholars and on well-known liberal *zemstvo* people' (*Iskra*, No. 5, 'Police Raid on Literature'). We exposed the real significance of the programme of 'state concern for improving the welfare of the workers' and greeted the 'valuable admission' that 'it is better to anticipate demands from below by carrying out transformations from above than to wait for the former' (*Iskra*, No. 6). We encouraged the whistle-blowing statisticians and condemned the strike-breaking statisticians (*Iskra*, No. 9).

Anyone who views the tactic [of indictments such as these] as obscuring the class awareness of the proletariat and as a *compromise with liberalism* reveals that he has absolutely no comprehension of the true significance of the *Credo* programme and that he is *de facto carrying out exactly this programme*, no matter how much he denies it! By reason of *this very view* [of Iskra's indictment tactic] he drags Social Democracy back to 'economic struggle with the owners and the government' and *abdicates before liberalism*, since he refuses the task of actively intervening in *every* 'liberal' issue while defining *his own*, Social-Democratic, attitude to that issue.

### f) Once more 'slanderers', once more 'mystifiers'

These complimentary words belong, the reader will remember, to *Rabochee delo*, which responded in this way to our accusation concerning its 'indirect preparation of the ground for turning the worker movement into a tool of the bourgeois democracy'. In all simplicity, *Rabochee delo* decided that this accusation is no more than a polemical sally: these evil dogmatic types have made up their mind (so *Rabochee delo* thinks) to say all sorts of unpleasant things about us – well, what could be more unpleasant than being a tool of the bourgeois democracy? And, so, they print in bold typeface their 'denial': 'slander without disguise' (*Two Congresses*, p. 31), 'mystification' (p. 31), 'masquerade' (p. 33). Like Jupiter (although it actually doesn't resemble Jupiter very much), *Rabochee delo* is angry precisely because it is in the wrong, and demonstrates with its hasty abuse that it lacks the ability to grasp the train of thought of its opponents. But, really, it does not take a great deal of thought to understand why *any* kow-towing before the *stikhiinost* of the mass movement, *any* lowering of Social-Democratic politics to *tred-iunionist* politics is precisely preparing the ground for turning the worker movement into a tool of the bourgeois democracy. A *stikhiinyi* worker movement in and of itself creates (and inevitably creates) only *tred-iunionizm*, and a *tred-iunionist* politics by the worker class means precisely a bourgeois politics by the worker class.

The participation of the worker class in the political struggle and even in the political revolution in no way ensures that its politics are Social-Democratic politics. Will *Rabochee delo* deny this? Will it finally set out for all to see its views on the burning issues of international and Russian Social Democracy, directly and without equivocation? – No, no, it will never get around to do anything like this, since it holds fast to the method of 'talking in negations': I'm not me, this isn't my horse, I'm not a coachman. We're not 'economists', *Rabochaia mysl* is not 'economism', there is no 'economism' in Russia at all. This is a remarkably clever and 'politic' method, having only this small inconvenience that the publications adopting it will acquire the nickname 'How may I serve you?'.

It seems to *Rabochee delo* that the bourgeois democracy in Russia is in general a 'phantom' [without existence] (*Two Congresses*, p. 32).[15] Happy folk! Like an ostrich, they hide their head under their wing and imagine that this makes everything around them disappear. A whole series of liberal journalists who give us triumphal bulletins each month about the disintegration and even the disappearance of Marxism; a series of liberal newspapers (*SPb. Vedomosti*, *Russkie Vedomosti* and many others) that encourage liberals who carry the Brentano view of class struggle and a *tred-iunionist* view of politics to the workers; a galaxy of critics of Marxism whose real tendencies were revealed so well by the *Credo* and whose literary products are the only ones which circulate freely in Russia without hindrance; the revival of revolutionary *non*-Social-Democratic tendencies, especially after the February and March events – all this, evidently, is a phantom! All of this has no relation whatsoever to the bourgeois democracy!

It would behoove not just the authors of the 'economist' letter in *Iskra*, No. 12 but *Rabochee delo* to 'think a bit about why the spring events called forth such a revival of revolutionary non-Social-Democratic tendencies instead of

---

[15] In the same publication, we find a reference to 'the concrete Russian conditions that push the worker movement onto the revolutionary path with fatal necessity'. People do not wish to understand that the revolutionary path of the worker movement can also be a non-Social-Democratic path! After all, in the days of absolutism in Western Europe, the entire bourgeoisie there 'pushed', purposively pushed, the workers on to the revolutionary path. But we Social Democrats cannot be contented with this. And if we in any way lower Social-Democratic politics down to *stikhiinyi, tred-iunionist* politics, then precisely in so doing we play into the hands of the bourgeois democracy.

calling forth a strengthening of the authority and prestige of Social Democracy'. The reason is this: we were not up to our own task, the activeness of the worker masses turned out to be higher than our own activeness, we did not have on hand enough prepared revolutionary leader/guides and organisers with an excellent understanding of the mood in all oppositional strata and who were able to stand at the head of the movement, to turn a *stikhiinyi* demonstration into a political one, to broaden its political character and so on. Under these circumstances, our falling behind will inevitably be used by more flexible, more energetic non-Social-Democratic revolutionaries; the workers, no matter how energetically and with what self-sacrifice they fight with police and troops, no matter in how revolutionary a fashion they act, will prove to be merely a force supporting these [non-Social-Democratic] revolutionaries – a rearguard of the bourgeois democracy rather than a Social-Democratic vanguard.

Take German Social Democracy – the ones from whom our 'economists' want to borrow only the weak aspects. Why is it that *not one* political event in Germany goes by without serving to increase the authority and prestige of Social Democracy more and more? Why is it that Social Democracy always shows itself ahead of everybody else in giving a revolutionary evaluation of such an event, in defending any protest made against abuse of power? Social Democracy [in Germany] does not lull itself to sleep with disquisitions about how the economic struggle pushes the workers to face the issue of their lack of rights or about how concrete conditions push the worker movement with the force of fate on to the revolutionary path. It intervenes in all areas and in all issues of social and political life: the issue of Wilhelm's refusal to confirm mayors who belong to the bourgeois Progressive Party (the Germans have not yet been enlightened by our 'economists' that this kind of intervention is in essence a compromise with liberalism!), the issue of the promulgation of a law against 'immoral' literary works, the issue of government influence on the selection of professors and so forth and so on. Everywhere they show themselves to be ahead of everybody, instigating political dissatisfaction in all classes, pushing the sleeping, prodding the backward, providing all-sided material for the development of the political awareness and the political activeness of the proletariat. And as a result, respect for Social Democracy as the advanced political fighter [for democracy] penetrates even purposive enemies of socialism – it often happens that an important document not only from bourgeois but even from bureaucratic and court circles ends up by some miracle in the editorial offices of *Vorwärts* [the main SPD newspaper].

Here is the solution to the seeming 'contradiction' that surpasses the comprehension of *Rabochee delo* so much that it can only throw up its hands and shout 'masquerade!' Just imagine: we here, at *Rabochee delo*, regard the *mass* movement as *the cornerstone* (and say so with italicised emphasis!), we warn all and sundry against underestimating the significance of the *stikhi-inyi* element, we wish to impart a political character to the economic struggle itself, *itself*, its very self, we wish to remain in a close and organic link with the proletarian struggle! And then we are told that we are preparing the ground for turning the worker movement into a tool of bourgeois democracy. And who says this? People who make 'compromises' with liberalism, who intervene in various 'liberal' issues (what a misunderstanding of the 'organic link with the proletarian struggle'!), who devote a great deal of attention to the students and even (horrors!) to the *zemstvo* people! People who, in general, want to devote a greater percentage (in comparison to 'economists') of their forces to activity among non-proletarian classes of the population! Can this be anything but a 'masquerade'?

Poor *Rabochee delo*! Will it ever manage to think its way through to the solution of this complicated affair?

# Chapter IV

## The Artisanal Limitations of the Economists and the Organisation of Revolutionaries

The affirmations by *Rabochee delo* that we analysed above – the economic struggle is the broadest applicable means of political agitation, our present task is to impart a political character to the economic struggle itself, and so on – betray a narrow understanding not only of our political but of our *organisational* tasks. The 'economic struggle with the owners and the government' absolutely does not need – and for that reason such a struggle will never give rise to – an all-Russian centralised organisation, merging each and every manifestation of political opposition, protest and indignation into one general assault, an organisation consisting of revolutionaries by trade and guided by the genuine political leaders of the whole people. And this is understandable. The character of the organisation of any institution is naturally and inevitably defined by the content of the activity of that institution. By means of the affirmations analysed above, therefore, *Rabochee delo* sanctifies and legitimates not only a narrowness of political activity but a narrowness of organisational work. And, in this case, as always, it remains a publication whose purposiveness abdicates before *stikhiinost*. And, meanwhile, the kow-towing to forms of organisation that arose in *stikhiinyi* fashion, the absence of any awareness of how narrow and primitive is our organisational work, of how we are still 'artisans' in this important area – the absence of this awareness, I say, constitutes a real sickness of our movement. It goes without saying that this is a sickness not of decline but of growth. But, precisely at this moment – when, so to speak, a wave of *stikhiinyi* indignation [against tsarism] is breaking around us, the leader/guides and organisers of the movement – the most irreconcilable struggle is more than ever necessary against any defence of falling behind, against any legitimisation of narrowness in this matter. It is particularly necessary to awaken in anyone who participates in practical work, or who intends to undertake such work, a dissatisfaction with the *artisanal limitations* dominant among us as well as an unshakeable resolution to escape from them.

## a) What are artisanal limitations?

We will try to answer this question with a short sketch of the activity of a typical Social-Democratic circle in the years 1894–1901. We have already referred to the very widespread enthusiasm for Marxism among the students of this period. This enthusiasm was, of course, not only – in fact, not so much – for Marxism as a theory but, rather, as an answer to the question 'what is to be done?' and as an appeal to march out against the enemy. And the new warriors went into battle with surprisingly primitive equipment and preparation. In very many cases, there was indeed next to no equipment and absolutely no preparation. The warriors went to war like *muzhiks* from the plough who grab a cudgel as they go. A circle of students – without any link to older activists of the movement, without any link to circles in other localities or even in other parts of the same town (or in other educational establishments), without any organisation of the separate parts of revolutionary work, without any systematic plan of activity for any significant period – establishes links with the workers and gets down to work. The circle gradually unfolds broader and broader propaganda and agitation, draws to itself by the very fact of its appearance the sympathy of fairly broad strata of the workers and the sympathy of a certain part of educated society which provides money and puts many new groups of young people at the disposal of the 'Committee'. The charisma of the committee (or 'union of struggle') grows, the scope of its activity grows, and it broadens this activity in completely *stikhiinyi* fashion: the very same people who a year or several months ago made their appearance in student circles and pondered the question 'in what direction should we go?' – who created and supported contacts with the workers, prepared and released leaflets, created links with other groups of revolutionaries, managed to find some [illegal] literature, undertook to publish a local newspaper, were starting to talk of setting up a demonstration – these people decided finally to move on to open acts of war (although such an act of war might be, according to circumstances, the first agitational leaflet or the first issue of a newspaper or the first demonstration).

And, usually, the very beginning of these actions led immediately to a complete *proval* [destruction of the organisation by arrests]. 'Immediately' and 'complete' precisely because these actions of war were not the result of a plan for stubborn and prolonged struggle – a plan that was systematic, thought-out beforehand and prepared over time – but, rather, the result of a *stikhiinyi* growth of circle-type work conducted in traditional fashion. Another reason was that the police, naturally, almost always knew all the principal activists in the local movement, who had 'made a name for themselves' already at school. The police had only been waiting for the most convenient moment for a raid and deliberately allowed the circle to expand and develop in order to have a tangible *corpus delicti*, while always deliberately letting a few people known to it stay behind 'as breeders' (to use the technical expression – one adopted, as far as I know, both by our side and the gendarmes). Is it possible to compare a war fought in this way to anything other than a gang of peasants armed with cudgels going into battle against modern troops? And we can only marvel at the vitality of a movement that continued to broaden, grow and achieve victories, despite the entire lack of preparation on the part of the fighters.

True, from a historical point of view, the primitiveness of the equipment was not only inevitable at the beginning but *even legitimate* as one of the conditions for a broad enlistment of soldiers. But as soon as serious actions of war began (and, in essence, they had already begun with the summer strikes of 1896), the inadequacies of our battle organisation started to make themselves felt with greater and greater intensity. The government, although taken aback at first and making all sorts of mistakes (for example, making appeals to society with descriptions of the evil deeds of the socialists or sending workers from the capitals to provincial industrial centres), quickly adjusted to the new conditions of struggle and managed to install where needed its own detachments of provocateurs, spies and gendarmes, all provided with the most up-to-date equipment. Raids became so frequent, seized such a mass of people and swept away the local circles so thoroughly that the worker mass literally lost all its leader/guides, the movement acquired an unbelievably sporadic character and absolutely no continuity or co-ordination of work could be established. The striking fragmentation [of the work] of local activists, the casual way circles acquired members, their lack of preparation and narrow outlook concerning theoretical, organisational and political issues – all this was an inevitable result of the conditions just described. Things got to such a pass that, in several places, the workers are imbued with a lack of trust toward *intelligenty* in general and try to keep away from them: the *intelligenty*, they say, are too careless and cause *provaly*!

Anyone who is the slightest bit acquainted with the movement knows that artisanal limitations have come to be felt as a disease by all thinking Social Democrats. And, lest the reader who is unacquainted with the movement think that we are artificially 'constructing' a special stage or a special sickness of the movement, we will refer to the testimony of a witness we have already cited once before. The reader will forgive us for the lengthy excerpt. B-v [Boris Savinkov] writes in *Rabochee delo* No. 6:

> If the gradual transition to broader practical activity – a transition that finds itself in direct dependence on the overall transition period that the Russian worker movement is now going through – is a characteristic feature [of the times] . . . there is also another, no less interesting feature that concerns the general mechanism of the Russian worker revolution. We speak here of the *general shortage of revolutionary forces fit for action*[1] that is making itself felt not only in Petersburg but all over Russia. Given the overall coming to life of the worker movement, the overall development of the worker mass, the ever more frequent occurrences of strikes, the ever more open mass struggle of the workers, the intensifying government persecution, arrests, deportations and exiles – given all these, this *shortage of revolutionary forces of high quality is becoming more and more noticeable* and, undoubtedly, is *not without influence on the overall character of the movement.*

---

[1] Our emphasis, here as elsewhere.

Many strikes take place without a strong and direct impact from revolutionary organisations. . . . A shortage of agitational leaflets and illegal literature makes itself felt . . . the worker circles are left without agitators. . . . Along with all this is a constant need of funds. In a word, *the growth of the worker movement has outpaced the growth and development of revolutionary organisations*. The available corps of active revolutionaries is much too small to be able to concentrate in its hands [the necessary] influence on the worker mass [in its present state] of unrest or to impart to all this unrest even a shadow of order and organisation. . . . Individual circles, individual revolutionaries, are not gathered together, are not merged, do not constitute a single, strong and disciplined organisation with systematically developed parts . . .

After noting that the immediate appearance of new circles to take the place of the shattered ones 'demonstrates only the vitality of the movement . . . but does not demonstrate the existence of a sufficient quantity of fully fit revolutionary activists', the author concludes:

The lack of practical preparation of the Petersburg revolutionaries makes itself known in the results of their work. The recent trials – especially those of the group 'Self-Liberation' and 'Labour's Struggle with Capital' – clearly show that a young agitator who has no detailed knowledge of the conditions of labour and therefore of the conditions of agitation at a given factory, who does not know the principles of *konspiratsiia* and who has absorbed (if indeed he has absorbed)[2] only the general outlook of Social Democracy, can continue his work only four, five or six months. Then comes an arrest, often leading to the complete break-up of the whole organisation or at least parts of it. Let us ask ourselves: is successful and fruitful activity possible for groups whose entire life-span is measured in months? Obviously, the inadequacies of existing organisations should not be blamed exclusively on the transitional period. . . . Obviously, the quantitative and, most important, qualitative [level of the] personnel of the organisations now operating plays a not unimportant role here, and the first task of our Social Democrats . . . must be *the genuine merger of [the existing separate] organisations, combined with a strict selection of members*.

---

[2] [Lenin's parenthetical comment.]

## b) Artisanal limitations and economism

We now must dwell on a question that probably has already occurred to the reader. Can we establish a link between artisanal limitations – a sign of the growing pains common to the *whole* movement – and 'economism' as only *one* of the tendencies in Russian Social Democracy? We think yes. Lack of practical preparation, clumsiness in organisational work is truly common *to all of us*, including those who have stood for revolutionary Marxism unswervingly from the very beginning. And, of course, no one can castigate the *praktiki* for this lack of preparation in and of itself. But the concept of 'artisanal limitations' includes something else besides lack of preparation: the narrow scope of all one's revolutionary work in general, the failure to understand that this narrow work cannot form the basis of a well-constructed organisation of revolutionaries, and lastly – this is the main point – attempts to justify this narrowness and to exalt it into a special 'theory', in other words, kow-towing to *stikhiinost* in this area as well.

As soon as attempts of this kind reveal themselves, we can be sure that artisanal limitations are linked to 'economism' and that we will not free ourselves from narrowness in our organisational activity without first freeing ourselves from 'economism' in general (that is, from a narrow understanding both of the theory of Marxism and of the role of Social Democracy and its political tasks). And such attempts have revealed themselves in two different ways. Some people have started to say: the worker mass has not yet itself advanced the kind of broad and militant political tasks which revolutionaries try to 'impose' upon them, the workers should therefore continue to fight for *immediate* political demands, to conduct an 'economic struggle with the owners and the government'[3] (and, naturally, corresponding to this struggle that is 'accessible' to the mass movement is an organisation that is 'accessible' even to the most unprepared young people). Other people, far removed from any form of 'gradualness', have started to say: we can and we must 'carry out a political revolution', but this does not mean there is any need to create a strong organisation of revolutionaries that will educate the proletariat in firm and stubborn struggle – all that is necessary for carrying out a revolution is to grab hold of the 'accessible' cudgel already known to us. To speak without

---

[3] *Rabochaia mysl* and *Rabochee delo*, especially *Rabochee delo*'s *Answer to Plekhanov*.

allegory: these people say that we should prepare a general strike[4] or that we need to instigate the 'sluggish' course of the worker movement by means of 'excitative terror'.[5] Both these tendencies – the opportunists as well as the 'revolutionists' – abdicate before the domination of artisanal limitations, they do not believe in the possibility of freeing themselves from it, they do not understand our first and most pressing practical task: to create an *organisation of revolutionaries* that is able to assure the energy, stability and continuity of the political struggle.

[In the previous section] we cited the words of B-v: 'the growth of the worker movement has outpaced the growth and development of revolutionary organisations'. This 'valuable communication from an on-the-spot observer' (as the editors of *Rabochee delo* describe this article) has a double value for us. It shows that we were right when we identified the basic reason for the crisis in Russian Social Democracy as *the leader/guides* ('ideologues', revolutionaries, Social Democrats) who *fall behind* the *stikhiinyi upsurge of the masses*. It shows that all the ruminations of the authors of the 'economist' letter (in *Iskra*, No. 12), of B. Krichevskii and Martynov, about the danger of underestimating the significance of the *stikhiinyi* element or of the grey ongoing struggle, about tactics-as-process and so forth – all these ruminations are exactly a glorification and defence of artisanal limitations. These people who cannot pronounce the word 'theorist' without a condescending smirk – who label their own genuflection before simple lack of preparation and lack of development as 'a feel for real life' – are, in fact, exposing their failure to understand our most pressing *practical* tasks. They shout to people who are falling behind: Keep in step! Don't get ahead! To people who are suffering from a lack of energy and initiative in organisational work, from a shortage of 'plans' for a broad and audacious approach to the issues, they shout about [the need for] 'tactics/process'. [At a time when] our fundamental sin consists in *lowering* our political *and organisational* tasks to the most immediate 'tangible' and 'concrete' interests of the on-going economic struggle, all we hear is the same old song: we must impart a political character to the economic struggle itself! To say it once again: this kind of 'feel for real life' is literally the same

---

[4] The pamphlet *Who Will Carry Out the Political Revolution?*, to be found in a collection published in Russia entitled *Proletarian Struggle*. This pamphlet was also published by the Kiev Committee.

[5] *The Rebirth of Revolutionism in Russia* and *Svoboda*.

kind as the hero of the popular epic who cries 'Many happy returns of the day!' to a funeral procession

Recall the unequalled condescension – truly in the style of Narcissus Tuporylov – with which these sages lectured Plekhanov: 'political tasks in the actual and *practical* sense of the term – that is, in the sense of a rational and successful *practical* struggle for political demands – are not in general (sic!) accessible to worker *circles*' (*Answer of the Editorial Board of Rabochee delo*, p. 24). There are circles and circles, gentlemen! Of course, a circle of 'artisans' will not find political tasks accessible, as long as these artisans are not aware of their artisanal limitations and do not free themselves from them. If, added to all this, these artisans have fallen in love with their own artisanal limitations, if they put 'practical' in italics without fail and imagine that this practicality demands a lowering of their tasks to the level of the understanding of the most backward strata of the masses, – then, of course, these artisans are hopeless and they will find *political tasks inaccessible in general.*

But a circle of inspiring leaders such as Alekseev and Myshkin, Khalturin and Zheliabov [revolutionaries of the 1870s] are capable of political tasks in the most genuine and practical sense of the word – precisely because their impassioned preaching meets with an answering call from the masses awakening in *stikhiinyi* fashion, and the leaders' seething energy is taken up and supported by the energy of the revolutionary class. Plekhanov was a thousand times right when he not only identified [the workers as] the revolutionary class, not only proved the inevitability and unavoidability of its *stikhiinyi* awakening, but also presented to the 'worker circles' a great and noble political task. But you refer to the mass movement that arose afterwards in order to *lower* this task – in order to *narrow* the energy and sweep of the activity of the 'worker circles'. What is this, except a artisan's infatuation with his own artisanal limitations? You brag about your practicality and you don't see (a fact known to any Russian *praktik*) what miracles for the revolutionary cause can be brought about not only by a circle but by a lone individual. Or do you think that our movement can't produce real leaders like those of the seventies? Why? Because we're unprepared? But we are preparing ourselves, we will go on preparing ourselves – and we will not stop until we are prepared!

True, in the stagnant waters of 'an economic struggle against the owners and the government', a certain film has unfortunately formed – people appear among us who get down on their knees and pray to *stikhiinost,* gazing with beatitude (as Plekhanov put it) on the 'posterior' of the Russian proletariat. But we will be able to free ourselves from this stagnant film. And it is precisely at the present time that the Russian revolutionary, guided by a genuinely revolutionary theory and relying on the class that is genuinely revolutionary and that is undergoing a *stikhiinyi* awakening, can at last – at last! – draw himself up to his full stature and reveal all his heroic [*bogatyrskii*] strength.

And, for this to happen, all that is needed is for the mass of *praktiki* and the even greater mass of people who have been dreaming of practical work since school days to greet the slightest attempt to lower our political tasks or the scope of our organisational work with ridicule and contempt. And we will ensure that this happens – don't worry, gentlemen!

In the article 'Where to Begin' I wrote the following against *Rabochee delo*:

> It is possible within twenty-four hours to change an agitational tactic on some special issue or a tactic on some detail of party organisation – but to change within twenty-four hours, or even within twenty-four months, one's views on whether we need, always and unconditionally, a militant organisation and political agitation among the mass is something that only people without any solid foundations can do.

*Rabochee delo* answers:

> This accusation – the only one with even a claim to factual validity – is utterly baseless. The readers of *Rabochee delo* know well that from the very beginning we not only called for political agitation (and we didn't have to wait for *Iskra* to make its appearance) . . .

(And at the same time the editors made this call, they said that it was 'impossible to present' not only to worker circles but 'to the mass worker movement the overthrow of the absolutism as the primary political task'. All that was possible was the struggle for immediate political demands, and 'immediate political demands become accessible for the mass after one or at the most several strikes'.)

> . . . but our publications provided the comrades working in Russia the *sole* Social-Democratic political-agitational material coming from abroad . . .

(And in this sole material, you applied [allegedly] broad political agitation solely on the grounds of the economic struggle – and you also managed to arrive at the conclusion that this narrowing of agitation is 'the most widely applicable' means. And you don't realise, gentlemen, that, given *this* type of *sole* material, your argument demonstrates precisely the necessity of the appearance of *Iskra* and the necessity of *Iskra*'s struggle with *Rabochee delo*?)

> ... Furthermore, our publishing activity in actual fact prepared the tactical
> unity of the Party ...

(A unity based on the view that tactics are a process of the growth of party tasks growing along with the Party? Such a valuable unity!)

> ... and by so doing prepared the possibility of a 'militant organisation' –
> an organisation for whose creation the Union has done everything within
> the reach of a émigré organisation. (*Rabochee delo*, No. 10, p. 15.)

You try to wriggle out in vain! You've done everything within your own reach – I wouldn't think of denying it. I affirmed and affirm now that the *limits* of your 'reach' are narrowed for you by the myopia of your understanding of things. It is absurd even to talk about a 'militant organisation' [if all you are interested in is] a struggle for 'immediate political demands' or 'economic struggle with the owners and the government'.

But, if the reader wants to see real pearls of 'economist' infatuation with artisanal limitations, then, of course, he must turn from *Rabochee delo*'s eclecticism and lack of stability to the thorough-going and resolute *Rabochaia mysl*. R.M. [K.M. Takhtarev] writes in the Separate Supplement, p. 13:

> And now a few words in particular about the so-called revolutionary
> intelligentsia. True, it has shown more than once in practice its complete
> readiness to 'enter into a decisive clash with tsarism'. The only trouble
> is this: because it is mercilessly persecuted by the political police, our
> revolutionary intelligentsia takes a struggle with this political police to be
> a political struggle with the autocracy. Therefore even up to the present time
> it still finds this question unresolved: 'where to get forces for a struggle with
> the autocracy?'

How truly inimitable is this magnificent contempt for the struggle with the police shown by a worshipper (in the bad sense of the word) of the *stikhiinyi* movement! He is ready to justify our clumsiness in matters of *konspiratsiia* because we have a *stikhiinyi* mass movement and, therefore, when you get down to it, the struggle with the police is unimportant!! Very, very few people will subscribe to this monstrous conclusion, since everybody is so greatly concerned by the burning question of the inadequacies of our revolutionary organisations. But if Martynov, for example, does not [explicitly] subscribe to this thesis, it is only because he is unable or lacks the courage to think through his own positions to the end. Indeed, take a 'task' such as having the mass [of workers] put forward concrete demands that promise tangible results – does such a task demand any special worries about the creation of a strong, centralised and militant organisation of revolutionaries? Isn't this 'task' already being carried out by the mass itself that, *qua* mass, does not 'struggle against the political police' at all? More than that: would this task ever be carried out if (besides a very few leader/guides) it were not taken in hand for the most part by such workers as are entirely *without the skills required* for 'struggling against the political police'? These workers, average people of the mass, are capable of showing gigantic energy and self-sacrifice in a strike, in a street battle with the police and the troops – they are capable of *deciding* the outcome of our entire movement, and only they can do this. But it is precisely a struggle with the *political* police that demands special qualities, that demands revolutionaries *by trade*. And we must take care not only that the mass 'puts forward' concrete demands, but also that the mass of workers 'puts forward' in ever greater numbers the needed revolutionaries by trade.

We have arrived in this way to the issue of the relation between the organisation of revolutionaries by trade and the exclusively worker movement. This issue is little discussed in the literature but we 'politicals' have been much occupied with it in conversations and disputes with those comrades who tend toward 'economism' in more or less pronounced fashion. It is worth considering in detail. But, first, let us finish up with one more citation that illustrates our thesis about the link between artisanal limitations and 'economism'.

N.N. [pseudonym given to Prokopovich] writes in his 'Answer' [to Akselrod]: 'The Emancipation of Labour group demands a straightforward struggle with the government, without pondering whether there is a material force for this struggle, without showing *where are the means for this struggle*.' And, underlining the last words, the author makes the following comment on the word 'means':

> This circumstance cannot be explained by considerations of *konspiratsiia*, since our programme does not speak about a conspiracy but about a *mass*

*movement*. But certainly the mass cannot proceed using secret means. Is a secret strike possible? Are secret demonstrations and petitions possible? (*Vademecum*, p. 59.)

The author himself pointed in the direction of the [required] 'material force' – those who arrange strikes and demonstrations – as well as to the 'means' for the struggle. But, nevertheless, he ends up in disarray and confusion, because he 'kow-tows' before the mass movement, that is, he regards it as something that *relieves* us of any need for our revolutionary activeness and not as something that should encourage and *push forward* our revolutionary activeness. Yes, a secret strike is impossible – for its participants and those immediately connected with it. But, for the mass of Russian workers, this strike can remain (and for the most part will remain) a 'secret', since the government takes care to cut off any contact with the strikers, takes care to make any dissemination of information about the strike impossible. And right here is where we need a special 'struggle with the political police', a struggle that will never be actively carried out by a mass as broad as that which takes part in the strikes themselves. This struggle should be organised 'according to all the rules of art' by people who engage in revolutionary activity [with the seriousness] of a trade. The organisation of this struggle does not become *less necessary* because the mass is drawn into the movement in *stikhiinyi* fashion. On the contrary, this circumstance makes such an organisation *more necessary*, since we socialists will not fulfil our direct responsibilities toward the mass, if we are not able to thwart the attempts by the police to make every strike and every demonstration a secret (and if we ourselves did not sometimes prepare strikes and demonstrations in secret). And we *will* be able to do these things, precisely because the mass that is awakening in *stikhiinyi* fashion will *push forward from its own milieu* a greater and greater number of 'revolutionaries by trade' (if we don't convince ourselves that it is a great idea on all occasions to invite the workers to mark time).

### c) Organisation of workers and organisation of revolutionaries

If a Social Democrat's concept of political struggle is coterminous with the concept of 'economic struggle with the owners and the government', then it is natural to expect that his concept of 'organisation of revolutionaries' will be more or less coterminous with the concept: 'organisation of workers'. And this is what actually happens, so that, when we talk together about organisation, we appear literally to be talking in different languages. For example, I recall a conversation with one fairly thorough-going 'economist' with whom I was not previously acquainted. We were talking about the pamphlet *Who Will Carry Out the Political Revolution?* and we quickly came to an agreement that its basic shortcoming was that it ignored the question of organisation. We thus imagined that we were in complete solidarity – but . . . the conversation continued on its course and it turned out that we were talking about different things. My fellow conversationalist accused the author of ignoring strike funds, mutual aid societies and so forth, while I had in mind the organisation of revolutionaries that was necessary for 'carrying out' the political revolution. And, as soon as this disagreement made itself known – well, I can't remember that I once agreed with this 'economist' about any principled issue at all!

What was the source of our disagreements? Precisely in this: the 'economists' continually stray from Social Democratism over to *tred-iunionizm* not only in political tasks but in organisational ones. The political struggle of Social Democracy is much broader and more complex than the economic struggle of the workers with the owners and the government. In exactly the same way (and as a consequence), the organisation of the revolutionary Social-Democratic party must inevitably be of a *different type* than the organisation of workers. The organisation of workers must be, in the first place, an organisation according to trade; secondly, it must be as broad as possible; thirdly, it must be as little *konspirativnyi* as possible (I am, of course, speaking here and later only of autocratic Russia). In contrast, an organisation of revolutionaries must consist primarily and mainly of people whose trade consists of revolutionary activity (which is why I speak of an organisation of *revolutionaries*, having in mind Social-Democratic revolutionaries). Given this common quality of the members of such an organisation, *all distinctions between workers and intelligenty must be completely eliminated*, not to speak of the distinction between the separate trades of one or the other. This organisation must necessarily be not very broad and as *konspirativnyi* as possible. Let us examine this triple distinction.

In countries with political freedom, the distinction between a trade organisation and a political one is completely clear, just as the distinction between *tred-iunionizm* and Social Democracy is clear. Of course, relations between political organisations and trade organisations will necessarily vary depending on historical, legal and other conditions (in our opinion, these relations should be as close as possible and as little complicated as possible). But, in free countries, there is never any question about a complete overlap between the organisation of trade unions and the organisation of a Social-Democratic party. At first glance, the oppression of the autocracy in Russia wipes out any distinction between a Social-Democratic organisation and a worker union, since *any and all* worker unions and *any and all* circles are forbidden, since the main manifestation and tool of the economic struggle of the workers – the strike – is, in general, a criminal (and sometimes a political!) offense. Thus, our conditions, on one hand, very much 'push' workers who are carrying out an economic struggle to face political issues, and on the other hand 'push' Social Democrats to mix up *tred-iunionizm* and Social Democratism (and our Krichevskiis, Martynovs and Co. who talk so zealously of the first kind of 'pushing' do not notice the 'pushing' of the second kind).

Indeed, picture to yourself people who are immersed ninety-nine per cent in the 'economic struggle with the owners and the government'. Some among them will never during the *entire* period of their activity (from four to six months) be pushed to confront the issue of the necessity of a more complex organisation of revolutionaries; others will be 'pushed up' against the comparatively widely disseminated Bernsteinian literature, from which they will receive the conviction of the utter importance of the 'forward march of the grey ongoing struggle'. Finally, a third group will perhaps get carried away by the seductive idea of showing to the world a new model of 'close and organic links with the proletarian struggle', links between the trade [-union] movement and the Social-Democratic one. The later a country steps into the arena of capitalism and consequently of the worker movement – such people may reason – the more will socialists be able to support and participate in the trade movement and the less room there is for non-Social-Democratic unions. Up to this point, this reasoning is completely correct, but, unfortunately, such people go further and dream of a full fusion of Social Democratism and *tred-iunionizm*. We will now see how harmfully such dreams influence our organisational plans, using the example of the 'Rules of the St. Petersburg Union of Struggle'.

An organisation of workers for economic struggle must be a trade organisation. Any worker/Social Democrat must assist as much as possible and actively work in such organisations. This is indeed the case. But it is not at all in our interests to demand that only Social Democrats can be members of such 'special-interest' [*tsekhovye*] unions: this would narrow the dimensions of our influence on the mass. Let any worker who understands the necessity of uniting for a struggle with the owners and the government participate in such a special-interest union. The very aim of special-interest unions would be unattainable if they did not unite everybody to whom at least this elementary degree of understanding is accessible, if these special-interest unions were not very *broad* organisations. And the broader these organisations, the broader will be our influence on them – an influence coming not only from the '*stikhiinyi*' development of the economic struggle but also from the direct, purposive impact that a socialist member of the union exercises upon his comrades. But, given the wide composition of the organisation, strict *konspiratsiia* is impossible (since this demands much greater preparation than is necessary for participation in the economic struggle). How can we reconcile the contradiction between the necessity of a broad composition and the necessity of strict *konspiratsiia*? How can one achieve special-interest organisations that are as little *konspirativnyi* as possible? Generally speaking, there can be only two paths: either legalisation of special-interest unions (which, in several countries, preceded the legalisation of socialist and political unions), or keeping the [special-interest] organisation secret, but so 'free' and amorphous – *lose*, as the Germans say – that *konspiratsiia* for the mass of members is reduced to almost nothing.

The legalisation of non-socialist and non-political worker unions in Russia has already begun and there is no doubt that each step of our swiftly growing Social-Democratic worker movement will multiply and encourage attempts of this kind of legalisation – attempts that come, for the most part, from supporters of the existing order, but partly from the workers themselves and from the liberal intelligentsia. The banner of legalisation has already been unfurled by the Vasilevs and the Zubatovs, assistance has already been promised and given by Messrs. Ozerovs and Wormses, and among the workers there are already adherents of the new current. And, from now on, we must reckon with this current. How should we reckon with it? – On this question there can hardly be two opinions among Social Democrats. We are obliged unremittingly to expose any and all participation in this current by the Zubatovs and the Vasilevs, the gendarmes and the priests and to explain to the workers the true intentions of these people. We are also obliged to expose any and all conciliatory, 'harmonious' overtones that make themselves heard in the speeches of the liberal activists at open meetings of the workers – it

778 • Chapter IV

makes no difference whether these overtones result from sincere conviction about the desirability of the peaceful collaboration of classes, from the desire to curry favour with the authorities or, finally, simply from clumsiness. We are obliged, finally, to warn the workers away from the trap for them set by the police when they keep a look out at open assemblies and permitted societies for any 'hotheads' and when they try via legal organisations to introduce provocateurs into illegal ones.

But doing all of these things does not at all mean that we should forget that, *in the final analysis*, the legalisation of the worker movement will be of advantage to us and not at all to the Zubatovs. On the contrary, we can separate the wheat from the tares [inherent in partial legalisation], and, as it happens, by means of our campaign of indictments. We have just discussed the tares. The wheat is, first, drawing the attention of ever broader worker strata, including the most backward, to social and political issues. Second, the liberation of us, the revolutionaries, from functions that are in essence legal ones (the dissemination of legal books, mutual aid, etc.) – functions whose development will inevitably provide us with greater and greater material for agitation. In this connection, we can and should say to the Zubatovs and Ozerovs: try your best, gentlemen, try your best! Insofar as you set traps for the workers (either in the sense of out-and-out provocation or in the sense of 'honestly' leading the workers astray with 'Struveism'), we are already taking care to expose you. Insofar as you make a genuine step forward – even in the form of a 'timid zigzag', but still a step forward – we will say: please don't stop! A genuine broadening of scope for the workers – even a miniature one – can only mean a genuine step forward. And any such broadening will be of advantage to us and will accelerate the appearance of legal organisations in which the provocateurs will not catch the socialists but the socialists will catch adherents. In a word, our business now is to fight with the tares. It is not our business to plant wheat in flowerpots. By pulling up the tares, we are at the same time clearing the soil for the possible germination of wheat seeds. And, while the people lacking any vision occupy themselves with their flowerpot crops, we must prepare reapers who will know how to cut down the tares of today as well as reap the wheat of tomorrow.[6]

---

[6] The struggle of *Iskra* against the tares brought forth this angry sally from *Rabochee*

Thus it is not in *our* power to use legislation to *solve* the challenge of creating a trade organisation that is as little *konspirativnyi* as possible and as broad as possible (although we would be very happy if the Zubatovs and the Ozerovs opened up to us even a partial possibility of such a solution – and, for that to happen, we should definitely do battle with them, as energetically as possible!). There remains the method of secret trade organisations, and *we must* show any and all assistance to the workers who are already embarking (as we know on good authority) on this path. Trade organisations are capable not only of bringing a huge advantage to the business of developing and strengthening the economic struggle but also of becoming an important adjunct to political agitation and to the revolutionary organisation. In order to attain this result, in order to direct the nascent trade movement in a channel desirable for Social Democracy, it is necessary first of all clearly to grasp the absurdity of the plan of organisation with which the Petersburg 'economists' have been obsessed for almost five years. This plan is set out both in the 'Rules of a Worker Fund' of July 1897 (*Listok Rabotnika*, No. 9–10, p. 46, taken from *Rabochaia mysl*, No. 1) and in the 'Rules of the Worker Organisation of the Union of Struggle' from October 1900 (a special leaflet printed in St. Petersburg and mentioned in *Iskra*, No. 1).

The main defect of both these sets of rules is the detailed formalisation of the broad worker organisation, combined the mixture of this type of organisation with an organisation of revolutionaries. Let us take the second set of rules as it is worked out more thoroughly. The body of the rules consists of *fifty-two* sections: twenty-three sections set out the construction, the procedures and the departmental responsibilities of the 'worker circles' that are set up in each factory ('not greater than 10 people') and that elect the 'central (factory) groups'. Section 2 announces: 'The central group keeps track of everything happening at its factory or plant and keeps a chronicle of events.' 'The central group gives a monthly report to all dues-payers about the condition

---

*delo*: 'For *Iskra* the banner of the times is not so much these large-scale events (in the spring), but rather the pitiful attempts of the Zubatov agents to "legalise" the worker movement. They do not see that these facts speak directly against them, for they testify that the worker movement has taken on very threatening dimensions in the eyes of the government' (*Two Congresses*, p. 27). Thus the blame for everything rests on the 'dogmatism' of the orthodox who are 'deaf to the imperatives of life', since they stubbornly do not see the acre of wheat and struggle with the square inch of tares! This must be a 'distorted sense of perspective in relation to the Russian worker movement', isn't that right? (ibid., p. 27).

of the fund' (No. 17) and so on. Ten sections are dedicated to the 'district organisation' and nineteen to the extremely complex intermingling of the 'Committee of the Worker Organisation' and the 'Committee of the St. Petersburg Union of Struggle' (elected delegates from each district and from 'implementation groups', that is, 'groups of propagandists, groups for relations with the provinces, for relations with émigrés, for managing stores [of illegal literature], publishing and various funds').

Social Democracy = 'implementation groups' in relation to the economic struggle of the workers! It would be hard to demonstrate more vividly how the ideas of the 'economist' stray from Social Democratism to *tred-iunionizm* and how foreign to such a person is any conception that the Social Democrat should first of all think about an organisation of revolutionaries that is capable of guiding the *entire* liberation struggle of the proletariat. To talk about the 'political liberation of the worker class', about the struggle with 'tsarist abuse of power' [phrases from the preamble of the rules] – and then to write organisational rules like these reveals a complete lack of understanding of the genuine political tasks of Social Democracy. Not one of the fifty or so sections reveals even a glimmer of understanding that we need a broad political agitation among the masses that illuminates all sides of Russian absolutism and provides a whole portrait of the different social classes in Russia. And not only political but even *tred-iunionist* aims cannot be realised with such rules, since these aims demand organisation *according to trade* and this is not even mentioned.

But probably the most characteristic feature is the striking unwieldiness of the whole 'system' as it tries to link each separate factory with the 'committee' by means of permanent threads consisting of identical and ridiculously detailed rules that involve a three-stage system of elections. Crushed by the narrow horizon of 'economism', the thinking [of the authors of the rules] becomes addicted to details of the sort that reek of red tape and office routine. In practice, of course, three quarters of these sections are never applied, although an [allegedly] *'konspirativnyi'* organisation with a central group at each factory helps the gendarmes in their efforts to carry out incredibly broad *provaly*. The Polish comrades lived through a similar phase of their movement when everybody was carried away by a broad establishment of worker funds, but they very quickly turned away from this idea, having convinced themselves that all that was gained was a luxurious crop for the gendarmes. If we want broad worker organisations and do not want broad *provaly*, if we do not want to give satisfaction to the gendarmes, then we must strive to see that these organisations remain completely without formal rules.

But in this case, [it might be objected], how can these organisations carry out their functions? Well, let's look at these functions: '. . . keep track of everything that happens at the factory and keep a chronicle of events' (Section 2 of the rules). Does this really have to be formalised? Can't this be done even better by correspondence to illegal newspapers without any formation of special groups for this particular purpose? '. . . Guide the struggle of the workers for the improvement of conditions at their factory' (Section 3 of the rules). Again, there is here no particular reason to formalise things. Any agitator with even a spark of understanding of what he is doing can find out in complete detail from a simple conversation what kind of demands the workers want to bring forward. Having found this out, he will be able to transfer it to the narrow – *not* broad – organisation of revolutionaries who will make an appropriate leaflet available. '. . . Organise a fund . . . with contributions of two kopecks per rouble' (Section 9), and along with this give everybody a report about the fund (Section 17), expel non-paying members (Section 10) and so on. The police will think they have died and gone to heaven. Nothing is easier than to penetrate into this whole [allegedly] *konspirativnyi* 'central factory fund' and confiscate the money and arrest all the best people. Isn't it simpler to issue one-kopeck or two-kopeck receipts with the stamp of a particular (very narrow and very *konspirativnyi*) organisation – or make collections without any receipts and publish reports under established code words in an illegal newspaper? The same aim will be attained and the gendarmes will find it a hundred times more difficult to pick up the threads.

I could continue this illustrative analysis of the rules but I think that I have made my point. A small, closely compact nucleus of the most reliable, experienced and toughened workers who have reliable representatives in the main districts and who are tied to the organisation of revolutionaries according to all the rules of the strictest possible *konspiratsiia* will be able to carry out fully – along with the broadest participation of the mass and without any formalisation – *all* the functions incumbent on a trade organisation and, besides, do so in a way that is most desirable for Social Democracy. Only in this way can we attain the *strengthening* and development, in despite of all gendarmes, of a *Social-Democratic* trade movement.

It will be objected: an organisation that is so *loose* that it is not even formalised at all, that does not even have any members at all who are known and listed, cannot even be called an organisation. – Perhaps. I don't insist on labels. But everything that is needed will be done by this 'organisation without members' to assure that from the very beginning there will be a solid link of our future *tred-iuniony* with socialism. And he who desires a *broad* organisation of workers with elections, reports, everything done by voting and so on, under absolutism – that person is an incorrigible utopian.

The moral of all this is simple: if we begin by firmly establishing a strong organisation of revolutionaries, then we will be able to assure the stability of the movement as a whole, to realise Social-Democratic aims along with specifically *tred-iunionist* ones. If, on the other hand, we begin with a broad worker organisation that is allegedly 'accessible' to the mass (and, in practice, accessible mostly to the gendarmes, making revolutionaries more accessible to the police), then we will achieve neither Social-Democratic aims nor *tred-iunionist* ones, we will not escape from artisanal limitations and, given our fragmentation and our eternal tendency to be destroyed by the police, we will only make the mass more accessible to *tred-iuniony* of the Zubatov or Ozerov type.

What exactly should be the functions of this organisation of revolutionaries? We will discuss this in more detail somewhat later. But, for the present, let us analyse yet another extremely typical piece of reasoning of our terrorist [Nadezhdin] who, again, turns out to be (a pitiable fate!) in closest proximity to the 'economist'. In the journal for workers *Svoboda* (No. 1) is an article entitled 'Organisation', in which the author wants to defend his friends, the worker-'economists' from Ivanovo-Vosnesensk. He writes:

> It is a bad thing when the crowd is without voice, without awareness, when the movement does not proceed from below. But look: the students in a university town disperse for the holidays or go home on summer vacation – and the worker movement grinds to a halt. Can such a worker movement, pushed from the side, really be a genuine force? Not at all! . . . It still has not learned to walk on its own two feet: it is moved around with leading strings. And it's the same all over: the students disperse – a halt occurs; the most capable ones, the cream of the crop, are snatched up [by the police] – and the milk sours; they arrest the 'Committee' – and until a new one is established, there is again a standstill; no one knows what the new committee

will be like – perhaps it will bear no resemblance to the former one, so that while the former committee said one thing, the new committee says the opposite. The link between yesterday and today is lost, the experience of the past does not teach anything for the future. And all this is because there are no roots in the depths, in the crowd – it's not the hundred fools who are at work but just a dozen clever ones. A dozen can always be wiped out in one snap, but once the organisation embraces the crowd and everything comes from the crowd – nobody, no matter how diligent, will be in a position to wreck the cause. (p. 63.)

The facts are described correctly. The portrait of our artisanal limitations is not bad. But the conclusions drawn are worthy of *Rabochaia mysl*, both because of their lack of logic and because of their political lack of judgement. It is complete absence of logic when the author confuses the philosophical and social-historical issue of the 'roots' of the movement in 'the depths' with the tactical-organisational issue of the best means for a struggle with the gendarmes. It is complete political lack of judgement because, instead of appealing from bad leader/guides to good leader/guides, the author appeals from all leader/guides to 'the crowd'. This is another attempt to drag us backward in the organisational sphere, just as [Nadezhdin's other] idea about excitative terror drags us backward in the political sphere. Truly, I face an *embarras de richesses* – I don't know where to start the analysis of the confusion presented to us by *Svoboda*.

I shall try to start, for clarity, with an example. Take the Germans. I hope that you will not deny that, in their case, the organisation embraces the crowd, everything proceeds from the crowd, and the worker movement has learned to walk on its own two feet. And, meanwhile, how this crowd of millions knows how to value its 'dozen' of tried and true political leaders, how firmly they latch on to them! More than once, the deputies from hostile parties in parliament tease the socialists: 'Fine democrats you are! only in words are you a movement of the worker class, but in reality the same old clique of leaders are always before us. Always the same Bebel, always the same Liebknecht, year after year, decade after decade. Why, your supposedly elective worker delegates are even more irremovable than the bureaucrats appointed by the Emperor!' But the Germans merely smile contemptuously at these demagogic attempts to oppose 'the crowd' to 'the leaders', to inflame in the former unworthy and envious instincts, to steal from the movement its solidity and stability by destroying the trust of the mass in the 'dozen clever ones'. Political thought has developed enough among the Germans and they have had enough experience for them to understand that, without the 'dozen' of talented (and talent is not something available by the 'hundreds') and experienced leaders who have been long schooled and prepared for their trade [as political leaders] – leaders who have learned to work together smoothly as a team – without all this, a steadfast struggle is impossible on the part of any class at all in modern society. Various demagogues have arisen from among the Germans who have flattered the 'hundred fools', flattered the 'muscular fist' of the mass, instigating it (in the manner of Most or Hasselmann) to reckless 'revolutionary' actions while instilling lack of trust toward the firm and steadfast leaders. And only thanks to an unremitting and uncompromising struggle with any and all demagogic elements within socialism has German socialism grown so much and acquired such strength. And our sages here in Russia – in a period when the entire crisis of Russian Social Democracy can be explained by the fact that there are not enough prepared, developed and experienced leader/guides for the masses who are awakening in *stikhiinyi* fashion – tell us with all the profundity of a simpleton: 'Oh, it's bad when the movement does not come from below!'.

'A committee of students is of no use and cannot be relied upon.' Absolutely correct. But the conclusion we need to draw is that we need a committee of *revolutionaries* by trade – it doesn't make any difference whether it is a student or a worker who makes out of himself a revolutionary by trade. But you draw the conclusion that one shouldn't push the worker movement from the side! Due to your political naïveté, you don't notice that you're playing into the hands of our 'economists' and artisanal limitations. May one ask what exactly is meant by the 'pushing' of our workers by our students? One thing and one thing only: the student brings to the worker those fragments of political knowledge in his possession, those crumbs of socialist ideas that have fallen his way (since the main mental nourishment of our present-day student – legally-permitted Marxism – is incapable of providing anything beyond rudiments, beyond crumbs). There is not too much of *this* kind of 'pushing from the side' but rather too little – scandalously and shockingly little in our movement, since we so zealously stew in our own juices, so slavishly kow-tow before the elementary 'economic struggle of the workers with the owners and the government'. We who are revolutionaries by trade should and will occupy ourselves with *this* kind of 'pushing' a hundred times more than we are. But precisely because you pick such a grotesque expression as 'pushing from the side' – one that will inevitably create in the worker (in any event, a worker that is just as undeveloped as you are) a lack of trust toward *all* who bring him political knowledge and revolutionary experience from the side and will call forth an instinctive desire to reject *all* such people – just for this reason, you show yourself a *demagogue*, and demagogues are the worst enemies of the worker class.

Oh yes! Don't rush to raise a howl about the 'un-comrade-like methods' of my polemic! I am far from suspecting the purity of your intentions, I already have said that someone can become a demagogue out of pure political naïveté. But I have shown that you have lowered yourself to demagoguery. And I will never tire of repeating that demagogues are the worst enemies of the worker class. 'Worst' precisely because they inflame the bad instincts of the crowd and because it is not possible for less-developed workers to recognise these enemies who present themselves, sometimes quite sincerely, as their friends. 'Worst' because, in a period of confusion and unsteadiness, in a period when the profile of our movement is just coming together, there is nothing easier than to use demagoguery to entice the crowd which recognises its mistake only through the most bitter experience. This is why the slogan of the moment for the present-day Russian Social Democrat should be a resolute struggle against both *Svoboda* when it descends to demagoguery and against *Rabochee delo* when *it* descends to demagoguery (we will talk more in detail on this subject below).[7]

'It is easier to wipe out the dozen clever ones than the hundred fools.' This magnificent truth (for which you will always be applauded by the hundred fools) seems self-evident only because, in the course of your reasoning, you have skipped from one issue to another. You started talking and continue to talk about wiping out the 'committee', wiping out the 'organisation', and now you skip over to the issue of wiping out the 'roots' of the movement 'in

---

[7] Here we notice only that everything said by us about 'pushing from the side' and all the further reasoning by *Svoboda* about organisation applies *completely* to *all* 'economists'. The *Rabochee delo* people are included in that number, since some of them actively preach and defend these views on the issue of organisation and others of them stray in that direction.

the depths'. Of course, our movement [as a whole] cannot be wiped out only because it already has hundreds and hundreds of thousands of roots in the depths, but here we are talking about a completely different subject. In relation to 'roots in the depths', it is impossible to wipe us out even now, despite all our artisanal limitations, and nevertheless we lament and cannot help lamenting when *'organisations'* are wiped out, so that any continuity of the movement is destroyed.

But once you take up the issue of wiping out *organisations* and do not stray from this issue, then I say to you that catching the dozen clever ones is much more difficult than catching the hundred fools. And I will defend this position, no matter how much you set the crowd on me for my 'antidemocratism' and so forth. By 'clever ones' in matters of organisation, we can only mean *revolutionaries by trade*, as I have already pointed out more than once, no matter whether it be students or workers that learn this trade. And thus I affirm: 1) not a single revolutionary movement can be solid without a stable organisation of leader/guides that preserves continuity; 2) the broader is the mass that is drawn into the struggle in *stikhiinyi* fashion – a mass that constitutes the basis of the movement and participates in it – the more pressing is the necessity for this kind of organisation and the more solid this organisation must be (for the easier it will be for any demagogue to entice the undeveloped strata of the mass); 3) this kind of organisation must consist for the most part of people who treat revolutionary activity as a full-time trade; 4) in an autocratic country, the more we *narrow* the membership of such an organisation so that the only ones who participate in it are those who have learned revolutionary activity as a trade and have undergone an apprenticeship in the art of struggle with the political police, the more difficult will it be to 'wipe out' such an organisation, and 5) the *broader* will be the roster of individuals both from the worker class and from other classes who will have the possibility of participating in the movement and actively working for it.

I propose to our 'economists', terrorists and 'economist-terrorists'[8] to refute

---

[8] This term – 'economist-terrorist' – is perhaps more correct in relation to the *Svoboda* group than the first two, since terrorism is defended in *Rebirth of Revolutionism* while 'economism' is defended in the article [about organisation in *Svoboda*]. About the *Svoboda* group it can be said that their heart is in the right place but not their brain. Their inclinations are excellent, their intentions are of the best, and the result is sheer confusion. The confusion is due mainly to the fact that while the group defends continuity of organisation, *Svoboda* is not interested in continuity of revolutionary

these theses. I will now look at the last two in more detail. The issue of the relative ease of wiping out a 'dozen clever ones' vs. 'a hundred fools' reduces itself to the issue analysed earlier: is a mass *organisation* possible given the necessity of strict *konspiratsiia*? If there to be any hope of a struggle with the government that is stable and that preserves continuity, we need a level of *konspiratsiia* that is unobtainable from a broad organisation. And the concentration of *konspirativnyi* functions in the hands of a few revolutionaries by trade (as few as possible) does not at all mean that these revolutionaries will 'think for everybody', that the crowd will not actively participate in the *movement*. On the contrary, the crowd will push forward a greater and greater number of these revolutionaries by trade, because then the crowd will know that it is not enough to establish a 'committee' by gathering together a few students and a few workers who conduct the economic struggle, since training oneself as a revolutionary by trade takes years, so that the crowd will 'think' not only about artisanal limitations but precisely about such training.

The centralisation of the *konspirativnyi* functions of the *organisation* does not at all mean centralisation of all the functions of the *movement*. The active participation of the broadest mass in [distributing] illegal literature will not decrease but will *intensify* ten times over if the 'dozen' revolutionaries by trade centralise the *konspirativnyi* functions of this business. In this way, and only in this way, will we achieve a situation where the reading of illegal literature, making contributions to it, and, to some extent, even dissemination of it will *almost stop being a konspirativnyi affair*, because the police will quickly understand the absurdity and impossibility of raising a judicial and administrative fuss in reaction to every copy of a publication that is distributed in the thousands. And the same thing applies not only to the press but also to all the functions of the movement, up to and including the demonstration. The most active and the broadest participation of the mass in a demonstration not only will not suffer but on the contrary will gain greatly if a 'dozen' experienced revolutionaries, schooled in their trade no less than our police, centralise all the *konspirativnyi* aspects of the matter,

---

thought and Social-Democratic theory. To try to call to life again the revolutionary by trade (*Rebirth of Revolutionism*) and to propose for this purpose, first, excitative terror and, second, an 'organisation of middle workers' (*Svoboda*, No. 1, p. 66 ff.), combined with less 'pushing from the side' – all of this is equivalent to heating one's house by chopping the house itself up for firewood.

namely, preparation of leaflets, working out an approximate plan, appointment of a detachment of leader/guides for each district of the city, for each factory neighbourhood, for each educational establishment and so on. (I know that people will object to the 'undemocratism' of my views, but I will respond to this far from intelligent objection below.)

The centralisation of the more *konspirativnyi* functions of the organisation of revolutionaries does not weaken but enriches the broadness and the content of the activity of a whole mass of other organisations that base themselves on a broad public and are therefore as informal as possible and as little *konspirativnyi* as possible. These include worker trade unions, worker circles for self-education and the reading of illegal literature, socialist as well as democratic circles in *all* other strata of the population and so on and so on. These circles, unions and organisations are necessary in all places and in the *broadest possible* number, with the most variegated functions – but it would be absurd and harmful to *mingle* them with the organisation of *revolutionaries*, erase the border between these types of organisation, extinguish in the mass the awareness (already unbelievably dim) that in order to 'serve' the mass movement, we require people who have dedicated themselves full-time to Social-Democratic activity and that such people must *train* themselves with patience and stubbornness to be revolutionaries by trade.

Yes, this awareness is unbelievably dim. Our basic sin in organisational matters is that *due to our artisanal limitations, we have injured the prestige of the revolutionary in Rus'*. A person who is flabby and shaky on theoretical issues, who has a narrow horizon, who uses the *stikhiinost* of the mass in justification of his own sluggishness, who resembles more the secretary of a *tred-iunion* than a people's tribune, who is unable to advance a broad and daring plan that would inspire respect even from opponents, who is inexperienced and clumsy even in the art of his own trade – the struggle with the political police – excuse me! This person is not a revolutionary but some kind of wretched artisan.

I hope no *praktik* will be angry at me for these sharp words since, insofar as we are talking about lack of preparation, I apply them first of all to myself. I worked in a circle that took upon itself very broad and all-embracing tasks – and all members of our circle had to suffer agonies to the point of illness from our awareness that we were showing ourselves to be [nothing but] artisans at a historical moment about which it could have been said, modifying a well-known saying: give us an organisation of revolutionaries – and we will turn Russia around! And as often as I remember to this day the burning feeling of shame that I felt then, the more anger builds in me against those pseudo-Social Democrats who 'bring shame to the high calling of revolutionary' and who do not understand that our task is not to defend the lowering of the revolutionary to the artisan but to *raise* the artisan up to the revolutionary.

### d) The sweep of organisational work

Earlier we heard from B-v about 'the shortage of revolutionary forces fit for action that makes itself felt not only in Petersburg but all over Russia'. And hardly anyone will dispute this fact. But the question is: how do we explain it? B-v writes:

> We are not going to delve into an examination of the historical reasons for this phenomenon; we will only say that a society that is demoralised by a prolonged political reaction and fragmented by the economic changes that have taken and are taking place produces from its ranks *an extremely small number of people who are fit for revolutionary work*. The worker class produces revolutionaries-workers who partially replenish the ranks of illegal organisations – but the number of such revolutionaries does not correspond to the demands of the time. All the more so because the worker, occupied 11 hours at a factory, is in a position to fulfil for the most part the function of an agitator, but the weight [of other functions] – propaganda, organisation, acquiring and reproducing illegal literature, issuing proclamations and so forth – falls, whether we like it or not, on the extremely few *intelligentnyi* forces [available]. (*Rabochee delo*, No. 6, pp. 38–9).

There is much that we disagree with in this opinion of B-v and we especially disagree with the words that we emphasised. They show particularly vividly that, although B-v is greatly upset by our artisanal limitations (just like any *praktik* who gives the matter some thought), he has no feel for a way out of this intolerable position, because he is weighed down by 'economism'. [B-v claims that only an extremely small number of people are fit for revolutionary work.] No – society produces out of its ranks extremely *many* people who are fit for 'the cause', but we do not yet know how to utilise them. In this connection, the critical and transitional state of our movement can be formulated as follows: *there are no people and – there are a mass of people*. A mass of people, because *both* the worker class *and* ever more diverse strata of society produce from their ranks each year ever greater numbers of people who are dissatisfied, who want to protest, who are ready to provide whatever assistance they can to the struggle against absolutism, and because an ever broader mass feels the intolerability of absolutism ever more sharply, even if not all are yet consciously aware of it. And, at the same time, there are no people, because there are no leader/guides, no political leaders, no organisational talents capable of arranging broad and at the same time unified and coherent work that would allow the application of all available forces, even the most insignificant ones.

'The growth and development of our revolutionary organisations' is falling behind not only the growth of the worker movement (as B-v has noted) but also behind the growth of the general democratic movement in all strata of the people. (At the present time, B-v would probably agree to this supplement to his argument.) The sweep of [our present] revolutionary work is too narrow in comparison with the broad *stikhiinyi* basis of the movement, too weighed down by the poverty-stricken theory of 'economic struggle with the owners and the government'. And meanwhile, at the present time not only political agitators but organisers/Social Democrats should 'go to all classes of the population'.[9] And hardly a single *praktik* will have any doubt that the Social Democrats could distribute a thousand detail functions of its organisational work to individual representatives of the most diverse classes. The lack of specialisation is one of the great defects of the technical side of our work, one about which B-v complains so bitterly and so justly. The smaller the individual 'operations' of the overall work, the more we can find people who are in a position to carry out these operations (and who, in a majority of cases, are not in any position to become revolutionaries by trade), the more difficult it will be for the police to 'wipe out' all these 'detail workers',

---

[9] For example, an undoubted quickening of the democratic spirit can be observed in recent times in the military milieu, in partial consequence of the ever more frequent occurrences of street battles against such 'enemies' as workers and students. And, as soon as available forces permit, we must without fail give most serious attention to propaganda and agitation among the soldiers and officers, to the creation of 'military organisations' that will be part of our party.

and the more difficult will it be for the police to arrest someone for some small offence and work it up into a 'case' that will justify the money the government spends on them to provide 'security'. And as for the number of people ready to provide assistance, we pointed in the previous chapter to the gigantic change that has occurred in this connection just in the space of five years or so.

But, on the other hand, in order to unite all these small details into one whole – in order to ensure that the movement itself is not fragmented into details in the same way as the functions – in order to inspire those who carry out these small functions with that faith in the necessity and significance of one's work without which no one will ever do the work[10] – in order for all these things to happen, what is necessary is precisely a strong organisation of tried and true revolutionaries. Given the existence of such an organisation, faith in the strength of the Party will grow stronger and be more widely disseminated as this organisation becomes more *konspirativnyi*. In war, as we know, it is important to inspire not only one's own army but also the enemy and all *neutral* elements with faith in one's strength; a friendly neutrality will sometimes decide the outcome. Given such an organisation – one standing on a solid theoretical basis and having a Social-Democratic press organ at its disposal – there is no reason to fear that the movement will be led astray from the path by the numerous 'outsider' elements attracted to it (on the contrary, right now, given the reigning artisanal limitations, we observe just

---

[10] I remember how one comrade told me how a factory inspector – someone who was ready to help and had helped the Social Democrats – bitterly complained that he could not even find out whether his 'information' had reached a genuine revolutionary centre, or whether his help was needed or whether there was a possibility of utilising his small and minor services. Of course, any *praktik* knows of more than one such case of our artisanal limitations taking allies away from us. And these services – 'minor' taken separately but invaluable taken together – could and would be provided to us by civil servants and bureaucrats, not only among factory inspectors, but among the post office, the railroads, customs officials, the gentry, the priests and *any* other sphere, up to and including the police and the tsarist court! If we already had a real party, a genuinely militant organisation of revolutionaries, we would not ask too much of these 'accomplices' nor necessarily drag them into the heart of the illegal underground. On the contrary, we would take special care of them and even prepare people for these kinds of [minor] functions, keeping in mind that many students are of more use to the party acting as our 'accomplices' among the bureaucrats than as 'short-term' revolutionaries. But it bears repeating: only a solid organisation that is experiencing no shortage of active forces has the right to apply this tactic.

how many Social Democrats hew to the *Credo* line while imagining that they are the only Social Democrats). In a word, specialisation necessarily presupposes centralisation and in its turn unconditionally demands it.

But the very B-v, who sets out so well the necessity for specialisation, does not sufficiently value it, in our opinion, in the second half of his argument quoted here. There are not enough revolutionaries from the workers, says he. This is completely correct, and we again emphasise that this 'valuable communication from a close observer' completely confirms our own view on the reasons for the present-day crisis in Social Democracy. Not only are the revolutionaries falling behind the *stikhiinyi* upsurge of the masses, but even the worker/revolutionaries are falling behind the *stikhiinyi* upsurge of the worker masses. And this *fact* confirms in the most evident way, even from a 'practical' point of view, not only the absurdity but the *politically reactionary quality* of the type of 'pedagogy' to which we are so often treated when considering the issue of our responsibilities in relation to the workers. This fact testifies that our very first and most pressing responsibility is to assist in the making of worker/revolutionaries who stand on the same level – *in relation to party activity* – as *intelligent*/revolutionaries (we emphasise the words 'in relation to party activity' because, in other respects, having the workers achieve the same level, although necessary, is far from being so easy or so pressing). Therefore, the *main* attention should be focused on *raising* workers up to revolutionaries and not in any way on *lowering* ourselves down to the 'worker mass', as the 'economists' want, or, in any event, down to the 'middle workers', as desired by the *Svoboda* group (who thus place themselves one grade up in the pedagogical scale of the 'economists').

I am far from denying the necessity of providing popularising literature for the workers and especially so for the most backward workers (although of course not made vulgar). But what makes me indignant is this constant dragging of pedagogy into political issues, into organisational issues. You defenders of the 'middle worker' are, in essence, insulting the workers with your constant desire to *condescend* to them before starting to talk about worker politics or worker organisation. Why don't you straighten up when you talk about serious things – leave the pedagogy to pedagogues but not to those concerned with politics or with organisation! Isn't it true that there are also advanced people, 'middle people' and 'the mass' among the intelligentsia as well? Isn't it true that the necessity for popular literature for the intelligentsia is generally recognised and isn't this literature being written? But just imagine that, in an article about the organisation of students or secondary-school pupils, the author repeated over and over again as some amazing new discovery that what we need most of all is an organisation of 'middle students'. Such an author would be mocked, and rightly so. He would be told: well, give us *some* organisational ideas, if you have any, and then we ourselves will figure out which of us is 'middle', which of us is higher and which lower. And if you do not have any organisational ideas *of your own*, then all this fuss about 'the mass' and 'the middle' will turn out to be simply boring. You must understand that these very issues of 'politics' and of 'organisation' are serious enough that we should only talk about them completely seriously: we can and we must *prepare* the workers (and students and secondary-school pupils) sufficiently so that we will *be able to start a discussion* about these issues. Since you have undertaken to talk about them, give straightforward answers, do not retreat back to talking about 'the middle' or 'the mass', don't try to avoid the issue with folksy sayings and phrases.[11]

In order to be completely prepared for his job, the worker-revolutionary also needs to become a revolutionary by trade. This is why B-v is wrong when he says that since a worker is occupied 11 hours at a factory, the main weight of all the other revolutionary functions besides agitation 'falls *whether we like it or not* on extremely insignificant *intelligentnyi* forces'. This happens not at all '*whether we like it or not*' but because we have fallen behind, because we are not aware of our responsibility to help any worker who has outstanding abilities turn himself into an agitator, or organiser, or propagandist, or distributor of literature, and so on, *who knows his trade*. In this regard, we are quite shamefully squandering our forces and we do not know how to preserve that which needs to be especially carefully planted and grown.

Look at the Germans: they have a hundred times more forces than we do, but they well understand that really capable agitators and the rest are produced

---

[11] *Svoboda*, No. 1, article 'Organisation', p. 66: 'the heavy tread of the worker battalions will provide strength to all the demands that are made in the name of Russian Labour' ('Labour' just had to have a capital L!). And the same author exclaims: 'Some of my best friends are *intelligenty*, but . . .' (the same 'but' that Shchedrin translated as 'ears never grow higher than the forehead'!) 'but it always greatly upsets me when a person comes up and says a great deal of very beautiful and wonderful things and then demands that they be adopted because of their (his?) beauty and other virtues' (p. 62). Yes, that 'greatly upsets me' as well . . .

from among the ranks of 'middle people' in far from huge quantities. For this reason, they try immediately to place any capable worker in conditions where his capabilities will be able to receive full development and full application: they make him an agitator by trade, they encourage him to broaden the scope of his activity, spreading it from one factory to an entire craft, from one locality to the whole country. He acquires experience and dexterity in his trade [of revolutionary activity], he broadens his horizon and his knowledge, he observes close up the outstanding political leaders of other localities and other parties, he attempts to lift himself to this level and to merge in himself a knowledge of the worker milieu plus a freshness of socialist conviction with the kind of full apprenticeship in his trade without which the proletariat *cannot* conduct a stubborn struggle with the excellently trained ranks of its enemies. Thus and only thus can Bebels and Auers be pushed forward from the worker mass.

But what, in a politically free country, takes place to a significant extent automatically must, in Russia, be carried out systematically by our organisations. Any agitator among the workers who is the slightest bit talented and who 'shows promise' *must not* work in a factory for eleven hours. We must take care to see that the Party gives him means to live, that he is able to transfer to an illegal position when the time comes, that he varies the place of his activity, since, otherwise, he will not develop vast experience, will not broaden his horizons, will not be able to hold out for at least a few years in his struggle with the gendarmes. The broader and more profound becomes the *stikhiinyi* upsurge of the worker masses, the more they will push forth not only talented agitators but talented organisers and propagandists and '*praktiki*' in the good sense of the word (of which there are so few among our intelligentsia, who, for the most part, betray something of Russian-style carelessness and clumsiness). When we have detachments of worker-revolutionaries who are specially prepared and have gone through extensive schooling (and who are, of course, revolutionaries [trained] 'in all arms of the service') – then no political police in the world will be able to cope with these detachments, because these detachments of people, boundlessly devoted to the revolution, will also be able to rely on the boundless confidence of the broadest worker mass. And it is our direct *guilt* that we 'push' workers so little onto the road – a road they share in common with the '*intelligenty*' – of an apprenticeship in the trade of revolutionary activity, and that we too often pull them back with our silly speeches about what is 'accessible' to the worker mass, the 'middle worker' and so on.

In this as in other aspects, the narrow sweep of our organisational work has an undoubted and indissoluble link (although the vast majority of 'economists' and novice *praktiki* are not aware of it) with the narrowing of our theory and our political tasks. Kow-towing before *stikhiinost* creates a sort of fear of going even one step away from what is 'accessible' to the mass – a fear of rising up too high and too far away from mere attendance on the nearest and most immediate demands of the mass. Don't be so scared, gentlemen! Recall that as far as organisation goes, we stand so low that the bare thought that we *could* rise *too* high is absurd!

### e) A 'conspiratorial' organisation and 'democratism'

And yet, there are among us many people who are so alive to 'the voice of life' that they fear just this more than anything else, and at the same time they accuse those who hold to the views expounded here of 'Narodnaia volia-ism', of a lack of understanding of 'democratism' and the like. We need to pause and look at these accusations, taken up, naturally, by *Rabochee delo* as well.

The author of these lines knows quite well that the Petersburg 'economists' had already accused *Rabochaia gazeta* of Narodnaia volia-ism (and this is understandable when we compare this newspaper to one like *Rabochaia mysl*). We are, therefore, not in the least surprised when, soon after the emergence of *Iskra*, one comrade told us that the Social Democrats of the town of X called *Iskra* an organ of 'Narodnaia volia-ism'. For us, this accusation can only be considered a compliment, since what decent Social Democrat has not been accused by the 'economists' of Narodnaia volia-ism?

These accusations are occasioned by a twofold misunderstanding. First, the history of the revolutionary movement is so little known among us that we describe as Narodnaia volia-ism any thought of a militant centralised organisation that has declared resolute war on tsarism. But the excellent organisation of the revolutionaries of the 1870s that should serve as a model for us all was not at all created by Narodnaia volia but by Zemlia i volia [Land and Freedom], which later split into Chernyi peredel [Black Repartition] and Narodnaia volia. Therefore, to see any militant revolutionary organisation as something connected specifically to Narodnaia volia is absurd both historically and logically, since *any* revolutionary tendency, if it really means business about serious struggle, cannot do without such an organisation. The mistake of the Narodnaia volia people was not that they tried to draw in to their organisation *all* the discontented and to direct this organisation toward a resolute struggle with the autocracy. On the contrary, these efforts constitute their great historical merit. Their mistake was this: they relied on a theory that in essence was not a revolutionary theory at all, and so were unable or not in a position to link their movement inextricably to the class struggle within developing capitalist society. And only the crudest misunderstanding of Marxism (or an 'understanding' of it in the spirit of 'Struve-ism') could come up with the opinion that the emergence of a mass, *stikhiinyi* worker movement *relieves* us of the obligation to create an organisation just as good as the one created by Zemlia i volia, to create indeed an incomparably better organisation of revolutionaries. On the contrary, the mass movement *imposes* upon us this obligation, because the *stikhiinyi* struggle of the proletariat does not become its genuine 'class struggle' until this struggle is guided by a strong organisation of revolutionaries.

In the second place, many people – including B. Krichevskii, judging by *Rabochee delo*, No. 10, p. 18 – have an incorrect understanding of the polemic against the 'conspiratorial' view of political struggle that Social Democrats have always conducted. We have come out against and, of course, will always come out against the *narrowing* of political struggle to the level of a conspiracy,[12] but this, of course, in no way means denying the necessity of a strong revolutionary organisation. For example, in the pamphlet mentioned in the footnote, alongside the polemic against reducing political struggle to a conspiracy, we portray as a Social-Democratic ideal an organisation firm enough to resort either to an 'uprising' or to any 'other method of attack' 'for delivering a decisive blow against absolutism'.[13] In an autocratic country, a

---

[12] See *Tasks of the Russian Social Democrats* [by Lenin], p. 21, the polemic aimed at P.L. Lavrov.

[13] *Tasks of the Russian Social Democrats*, p. 23. By the way, here is yet another illustration that *Rabochee delo* either does not understand what it is saying or changes its views as frequently as does the wind. *Rabochee delo*, No. 1 stated, with emphasis, that '*the essence of the pamphlet* [that is, Lenin's *Tasks*] *as here set out coincides completely with the editorial programme of Rabochee delo*' (p. 142). Oh really? Does the view that the overthrow of the autocracy cannot be presented to the mass movement as a priority task coincide with *Tasks*? Or the theory of 'economic struggle with the owners and the government'?

firm revolutionary organisation of this kind could be called a 'conspiratorial [*zagovorshchitskaia*]' organisation by its *form*, since the Russian word *zagovor* [conspiracy] is equivalent to the French word *conspiration*, while competence in *konspiratsiia* is necessary in the highest degree for such an organisation. The imperative of *konspiratsiia* is such a necessary condition of this kind of organisation that all other conditions (number of members, their selection, functions and so on) must be co-ordinated with it. It would therefore be extremely naïve of us to fear the accusation that we as Social Democrats wish to create a conspiratorial organisation. This accusation should be as flattering for any foe of 'economism' as the accusation of Narodnaia volia-ism.

The objection will be made: such a powerful and strictly secret organisation that concentrates in its hands all the threads of *konspirativnyi* activity – an organisation that by necessity is centralised – could very easily throw itself into a premature attack or thoughtlessly sharpen the movement before either the growth of political dissatisfaction or the ferment and indignation in the worker mass, etc., makes this either possible or necessary. Our answer is that, of course, one cannot deny abstractly speaking that a militant organisation *may* march thoughtlessly into battle that *may* end with a defeat that was not at all made necessary by other conditions. But, with this kind of issue, we cannot limit ourselves to abstract considerations, since any battle contains within itself the abstract possibility of defeat and there is no other way of *decreasing* this possibility than by organised preparation for battle. If we put the question on the concrete grounds of present-day Russian conditions, then we must arrive at this definite conclusion: a firm revolutionary organisation is absolutely necessary exactly because it gives stability to the movement and *guards* it against the possibility of thoughtless attacks. Precisely now, given the absence of such a organisation and the rapid *stikhiinyi* growth of the revolutionary movement, we *already observe* two contradictory extremes (which 'meet', as expected): on the one hand, a completely bankrupt 'economism' and the preaching of moderation, on the other hand an equally bankrupt 'excitative terror' that strives 'to artificially call forth symptoms of nearness to the final goal from a movement that is developing and strengthening but that is still closer to the beginning than to the final goal' (V.Z. in *Zaria*, No. 2–3, p. 353).

---

Or the theory of stages? We leave it to the reader to judge whether one can speak of stability in principles in a press organ that understands 'coinciding' in so original a fashion.

The example of *Rabochee delo* shows that *there still exist* Social Democrats who are unable to resist either extreme. Such a phenomenon is hardly surprising for this reason among others: the 'economic struggle with the owners and the government' will *never* satisfy a [real] revolutionary with the result that the two opposite extremes emerge now here, now there. Only a centralised militant organisation that consistently carries out Social-Democratic politics and thus satisfies, so to speak, all revolutionary instincts and aspirations, is in a position to guard the movement from making thoughtless attacks and to prepare an attack that promises success.

It is further objected that the view here set forth about organisation contradicts the 'democratic principle'. While the previous accusation had a specifically Russian origin, this one has a *specifically émigré* character. And only an émigré organisation (the Union of Russian Social Democrats) could give its editorial board, among other instructions, the following:

> *Organisational principles.* In the interests of the successful development and unification of Social Democracy, it is necessary to emphasise, develop and fight for the broad democratic principle in its party organisation. This is especially necessary in view of the antidemocratic tendency that has revealed itself in the ranks of our party. (*Two Congresses*, p. 18.)

Exactly how *Rabochee delo* fights with the 'antidemocratic tendencies' of *Iskra* will be seen in the following chapter. But for now, let us look closer at this 'principle' put forward by the 'economists'. Everyone will agree, I suppose, that a 'broad democratic principle' implies the two following necessary conditions: first, complete *glasnost* and, second, all functions subject to elections. Without *glasnost*, it is ridiculous even to talk about democratism – and, furthermore, a *glasnost* that is not just limited to members of the organisation. We call the organisation of the German Party a democratic one because everything in it is done openly, right up to the sessions of the party congress – but no one would call an organisation democratic that is closed off from non-members by a veil of secrecy. Well then, what sense is there in insisting on the '*broad* democratic principle' when the basic condition of this principle *cannot be fulfilled* by a secret organisation? The 'broad principle' turns out to be no more than a resonant but empty phrase. More: this phrase testifies to a complete lack of understanding of the essential tasks of the moment as far as organisation is concerned. Everybody knows how immense is the lack of *konspiratsiia* now prevailing among the mass of revolutionaries. We have seen how B-v bitterly complains about this when he quite correctly demands a 'strict selection of members' (*Rabochee delo*, No. 6, p. 42). And now appear people who brag about their 'sense of life' and yet, in this situation, *emphasise*, not the necessity of the strictest *konspiratsiia* and the strictest (and therefore, narrow) selection of members, but – the '*broad* democratic principle'! Doesn't this miss the point completely?

The matter stands no better with the second condition of democratism, namely, elections. In countries with political freedom, this condition is assumed as a given. 'Anyone who accepts the party programme and supports the Party insofar as he is able is considered to be a member of the Party' says the first section of the organisational rules of the German Social-Democratic Party. And, since the whole political arena is as open to everybody as the stage is to spectators in a theatre, this acceptance or refusal to accept, this support or its opposite is known to each and to all from newspapers as well as from popular assemblies. Everybody knows that such and such a political activist started at this position, underwent this or that evolution, showed himself at a difficult time in this or that manner, distinguished himself by these or those qualities – and, therefore, naturally, *all* members of the Party can elect or not elect him to a particular party post based on their knowledge of him. Universal (in the literal meaning of the word) monitoring of each step made by a party man during his political career creates an automatically acting mechanism that provides what in biology is called 'survival of the fittest'. The 'natural selection' provided by full *glasnost*, elections and universal monitoring guarantees that, in the final analysis, each activist ends up in his proper place, finds the job best suited to his talents and capacities, suffers all the consequences of his own mistakes himself and demonstrates before all eyes his capacity to become aware of his mistakes and to avoid them.

Just try putting this picture into the framework of our autocracy! Is it thinkable here in Russia that everybody 'who accepts the party programme and supports the Party insofar as he is able' will monitor each step of a revolutionary/*konspirator*? That all such people will elect from the ranks of the revolutionaries this person or the other, when a revolutionary is *obliged* in the interests of his work to hide from nine-tenths of this 'all' even who he is? Reflect just a little bit about the actual significance of the ponderous words used by *Rabochee delo* and you will see that 'broad democratism' of party organisation – given the darkness imposed by autocratic rule, given the domination of selection by the gendarmes [instead of the 'natural selection' of elective democracy] – is no more than an *empty and harmful toy*. It is an empty toy, because, in practice, no revolutionary organisation [under an autocracy] has ever put *broad* democratism into practice and could not put it into practice even if it wished. It is a harmful toy, because the attempt to put the 'broad democratic principle' into practice only makes easier the broad *provaly* carried out by the police and renders eternal the prevailing artisanal limitations, draws the thinking of the *praktiki* away from the serious and substantive task of making themselves into revolutionaries by trade while drawing it toward the creation of detailed 'paper' rules about systematic elections. Only abroad, where people who do not have the possibility of finding genuine and living work for themselves often get together, can this 'playing at democratism' develop here and there and especially in various grouplets.

In order to show the reader how improper is *Rabochee delo*'s favourite device of putting forward such a proper-sounding 'principle' as democratism in revolutionary work, we again call a witness. This witness – E. Serebriakov, the editor of the London journal *Nakanune* – displays a great weakness for *Rabochee delo* and a great hatred for Plekhanov and the 'Plekhanovists'. In articles about the schism in the émigré 'Union of Russian Social Democrats', *Nakanune* resolutely took the side of *Rabochee delo* and aimed a whole mass of wretched abuse at Plekhanov. As a witness, then, E. Serebriakov is all the more valuable on the issue now before us. In No. 7 *Nakanune* (July 1899), in the article 'On the Appeal of the Group of Self-Liberation of the Workers', he points to the 'impropriety' involved in raising the question 'of self-infatuation, of primacy, of a so-called Areopagus, in a serious revolutionary movement' and writes among other things:

> Myshkin, Rogachev, Zheliabov, Mikhailov, Perovskaia, Figner and others never considered themselves leaders, nobody elected them or appointed them – yet in reality that is what they were. This was because both in the period of propaganda and in the period of struggle with the government, they took upon themselves the greatest burden of work, went to the most dangerous places, and their activity was the most productive. Their primacy was not the result of their own desires but the result of faith on the part of their comrades in their intelligence, their energy and their devotion. To fear

some sort of Areopagus, some sort of dictatorial and self-appointed leadership
(and if you do not fear it, why write about it?) is just too naïve. Who would
obey it?

We ask the reader: in what way does worries about an 'Areopagus' differ
from worries about 'anti-democratic tendencies'? And isn't it evident that the
'proper' organisational principle advocated by *Rabochee delo* is exactly as naïve
and improper as the worries about an Areopagus? Naïve, because people
will simply not obey either the 'Areopagus' or the people with 'anti-democratic
tendencies', if there exists no 'faith on the part of their comrades in their
intelligence, their energy and their devotion'. It is improper because it is a
demagogic trick that relies on the vainglory on the part of some, lack of
knowledge about the real state of our movement on the part of others, lack
of preparation and lack of knowledge of the history of the revolutionary
movement on the part of still others.

The single serious organisational principle for the activists of our movement
should be: the strictest possible *konspiratsiia*, the strict possible selection of
members, preparation on the part of the revolutionaries by trade. Once these
qualities are present, then something bigger than 'democratism' is present,
namely: complete comradely confidence among the revolutionaries. And this
bigger thing is absolutely necessary for *us*, since, in Russia [under absolutism],
there can be no question of substituting democratic universal monitoring in
its place. And it would be a big mistake to think that the impossibility of
genuine 'democratic' monitoring means that the members of the revolutionary
organisation will not be monitored at all: they have no time for thinking about
toy forms of democratism (democratism within a tight nucleus of comrades
who have complete mutual confidence), but they feel their *responsibility* very
vividly, knowing by experience that a genuine organisation of revolutionaries
will stop at nothing to rid themselves of an unworthy member. Besides, there
exists with us a developed public opinion of the Russian (and international)
revolutionary milieu, one with a long history, that punishes with merciless
severity any falling off from the responsibilities of comradeship (and, indeed,
'democratism' – real and not toy democratism – fits into this idea of
comradeship as a part into a whole). Take all this into consideration – and
you will understand what a musty smell of émigrés acting like generals arises
out of all this talk and all these resolutions about 'antidemocratic tendencies'!

It should also be pointed out that another source of such talk – namely, naïveté – is nourished by a confusion in ideas about what democracy is. In the book by the Webbs on English *tred-iuniony*, there is an interesting chapter entitled 'Primitive Democracy'. The authors discuss how the English workers in the first period of the existence of their unions considered it a necessary sign of democracy to have everybody do everything in the administration of the unions: not only were all issues decided by taking a vote of all members but all official positions were occupied by all members in turn. It required a long historical experience for the workers to understand the absurdity of this conception of democracy and the necessity, on the one hand, of representative institutions and, on the other hand, of officials who know their trade. It required several cases of the financial ruin of union funds for the workers to understand that the issue of the proportional relationship between paid dues and benefits given out cannot be decided simply by a democratic vote but also required input from a specialist in insurance matters. Also look at Kautsky's book about parliamentarism vs. direct legislation, and you will see that the conclusions of the Marxist theorist coincide with the lessons obtained from the practical experience of many years accumulated by workers who came together in '*stikhiinyi*' fashion. Kautsky resolutely protests against Rittinghausen's primitive understanding of democracy and ridicules people who are ready to demand in the name of democracy that 'the newspapers of the people should be edited by the people'. He demonstrates why Social-Democratic guidance of the class struggle of the proletariat requires journalists, parliamentarians and so forth *who know their trade*; he attacks the 'socialism of anarchists and of *littérateurs*' who in their 'striving for effect' glorify direct popular legislation, completely failing to understand that, in modern society, this idea can only have a very conditional application.

Anyone who has worked in a practical way in our movement knows how widely this 'primitive' view of democracy is disseminated among the mass of student youth and workers. It is not surprising that this view finds its way both into [institutional] rules and into the literature. 'Economists' of a Bernsteinian persuasion put in their rules: 'Section 10. All matters that touch on the interests of the entire organisation of the Union [of Struggle] are decided by a majority vote of all its members.' 'Economists' of a terrorist persuasion back them up: 'it is necessary that decisions of the committee make the rounds of all circles and only then become actual decisions' (*Svoboda*, No. 1, p. 67). Notice that this demand for a broad application of referendums is advanced *on top of* demands to construct the *whole* organisation on the elective principle! Far be it from us to condemn *praktiki* who have too little possibility to become acquainted with the theory and practice of genuinely democratic organisations. But when *Rabochee delo*, a publication that makes claim to a guiding role, confines itself under such conditions to resolutions about the broad democratic principle, then what else can we call this but 'striving for effect'?

## f) Local and all-Russian work

If the objections made to the plan of organisation set out here because of its anti-democratic and conspiratorial character are completely unfounded, there remains another issue that is very often put forward and deserves a detailed examination. This is the issue of the relationship between local and all-Russian work. A worry is expressed: won't the creation of a centralised organisation lead to a shift in the centre of gravity from local to all-Russian work? And won't this harm the movement by weakening the solidity of our links with the worker mass and in general weakening the stability of local agitation? Our answer to this objection is that our movement in recent years suffers exactly from the fact that local activists are much too swallowed up by local work; that, therefore, it is absolutely necessary to shift somewhat the centre of gravity toward all-Russian work; that such a shift will not weaken but rather strengthen both the steadiness of our links [with the workers] and the stability of our local agitation. Let us take the question of central and local press organs, and ask the reader not to forget that newspaper work is only used here as an *example* to illustrate the much broader and many-sided work of revolution in general.

In the first period of the mass movement (1896–8), local activists made an attempt to set up a all-Russian press organ, *Rabochaia gazeta*; in the following period (1898–1900), the movement made an enormous step forward but the attention of the leader/guides was completely swallowed up by [efforts to set up] local press organs. If we sum up all these local organs taken together, it comes out to approximately one issue of a newspaper per month.[14] Isn't

---

[14] See 'Report to the Paris Congress', p. 14: 'From this time (1897) up to spring 1900, thirty issues of various newspapers came out in various localities. . . . On average this is more than one issue a month.'

this a glaring illustration of our artisanal limitations? Doesn't this make it completely evident that our revolutionary organisation is falling behind the *stikhiinyi* upsurge of the movement? If *just this many* issues were published, not by fragmented local groups, but by a united organisation, we not only would economise a whole mass of our forces but we would guarantee an immeasurably greater stability and continuity in our work. This simple consideration is too often lost from view both by those *praktiki* who work *actively* almost exclusively on local organs (unfortunately, this is how things stand in the great majority of cases) and by those journalists [such as Nadezhdin] who display in this connection a surprising Don-Quixotism.

The *praktik* usually contents himself with the idea that it is 'difficult' for local activists to work at setting up an all-Russian paper[15] and that it is better to have local papers than no paper at all. This last consideration is, of course, completely justified and we will not yield to any *praktik* in our recognition of the enormous significance and the enormous usefulness of local papers *in general*. But that is not the point at issue but rather: is it possible to escape from the fragmentation and artisanal limitations that are so glaringly expressed by [a mere] thirty issues of local papers in all Russia in a period extending two and a half years? Don't limit yourselves to the indisputable but much too general thesis about the utility of local papers in general – have the courage as well to openly recognise the negative aspects revealed by the experience of these two and a half years. This experience demonstrates that local papers, under prevailing conditions, turn out in the majority of cases to be unstable in matters of principle, deprived of political significance, extremely expensive in terms of outlay of revolutionary forces, and utterly unsatisfactory from a technical standpoint (I have in mind, of course, not the technicalities of printing but the frequency and regularity of publication). And all these inadequacies are not chance ones but the inevitable result of the fragmentation that, on the one hand, explains the predominance of local papers during this period and, on the other, *is itself maintained* by this predominance. An isolated local organisation simply *does not have the forces* to guarantee stability of principles in its newspaper nor to attain the proper level for a political organ – *it does*

---

[15] This difficulty is only a seeming one. In fact, there is *no* local circle that does not have the possibility of actively taking up one or another function of an all-Russian project. 'Don't say "I can't": say "I won't".'

*not have the forces* to collect and use enough material that can illuminate our entire political life.

And the argument used to defend the necessity of numerous local newspapers in free countries – the cheapness of using local workers for printing and the greater fullness and speed of information of concern to the local population – this *argument* becomes, as experience has shown, one that speaks *against* local newspapers in the Russian case. They turn out to be extremely expensive from the point of view of the outlay of revolutionary forces. They also come out *especially* rarely for the simple reason that an *illegal* newspaper, no matter how small, entails a huge infrastructure of *konspiratsiia* that requires [an organisation on the scale of] large factory industry, and this infrastructure cannot be prepared by [an organisation on the scale of] an artisanal workshop. The primitiveness of the infrastructure of *konspiratsiia* means – any *praktik* knows a mass of examples of this kind – that nearly always the police will use the publication and dissemination of one or two issues to prepare a *mass proval* that sweeps everything away so completely that it becomes necessary to start again from the beginning. An excellent infrastructure of *konspiratsiia* requires on the part of the revolutionaries an excellent preparation in their trade, and also a division of labour carried out in the most thorough-going fashion, and both these requirements are beyond the forces of an isolated local organisation, no matter how strong it is at any given moment. Not only the general interests of our movement (a socialist and political education of the workers that is in consistent accord with our basic principles) but even local interests taken by themselves *are better served by non-local press organs*: this seems a paradox only at first glance but in reality it is irrefutably demonstrated by our experience over a period of two and a half years. Everybody will agree that if all the local forces that managed to publish thirty issues worked together on a single newspaper, then it would be easy to provide sixty if not a hundred issues and that these would be able to reflect all the movement's particularities of a purely local nature. Without a doubt, achieving this level of organisation is not easy, but what is essential is for us to be aware of its necessity, for each local circle to think about and to *actively work* towards this goal, not waiting for a push from without, not flattering ourselves about a local organ's accessibility and proximity – qualities which on the basis of the data of our revolutionary experience have turned out to be illusory.

And a poor service to practical work is rendered by those journalists [such as Nadezhdin] who imagine themselves to be very close to the *praktiki* but who do not see this illusory quality and deliver themselves of this amazingly cheap and amazingly empty reasoning: we need local newspapers, we need regional newspapers, we need all-Russian newspapers. Of course, speaking in general terms, all of these things are indeed necessary – but it is also necessary to think about the conditions of time and place, since we are engaged in settling a concrete organisational issue. Really, isn't it Don-Quixotism when *Svoboda* (No. 1, p. 68), giving special attention to 'the *question of newspapers*', writes: 'It seems to us that any locality where any appreciable number of workers are collected should have its own worker newspaper – not one imported from somewhere or other, but precisely its own.' If this journalist himself does not want to think about the meaning of his words, then, reader, you think for him. How many tens, not to say hundreds, of 'localities where a significant number of workers are collected' are there in Russia, and what kind of perpetuation of our artisanal limitations would result if each local organisation really did undertake to publish its own newspaper! How much would this fragmentation ease the task of our gendarmes in wiping out – and without any 'appreciable' amount of trouble – the local activists at the very beginning of their activity, without letting them develop into real revolutionaries!

In an all-Russian newspaper, continues the author, the descriptions of the petty frauds of factory owners and the 'details of factory life in other than one's own town' would be boring, whereas 'an Orel resident will never tire of reading about Orel affairs. Each time that he learns that this [exploiter] was "torn to pieces" or that one "given a hiding", his spirit soars' (p. 69). Yes, yes, the spirit of the Orel resident soars, but the thinking of our journalist also soars, and much too high. Is this defence of obsession with details appropriate at the present time? – This is the question he should ask himself. We yield to no one in our recognition of the necessity and importance of factory indictments, but we should also remember [as Savinkov attests] that we have already arrived at the point where the people in Petersburg are bored reading articles about Petersburg in the Petersburg newspaper *Rabochaia mysl*. For factory indictments on the local level, we have always used *and will always continue to use* leaflets – but we should raise up the *newspaper* as a type [of agitational instrument] and not lower it to the level of the factory leaflet. For a 'newspaper', we need indictments not so much of 'details' as of large-scale and typical shortcomings of factory life – indictments based on especially vivid examples that can therefore interest *all* workers and all leader/guides of the movement, that can genuinely enrich their knowledge, broaden their horizon, begin the process of awakening a new region or a new stratum of workers engaged in a particular trade.

> Furthermore, in a local paper all the escapades of the factory bosses or of other authorities can be exposed then and there. But by the time a paper aimed at the whole country prints this news, the local people have long forgotten about the entire incident. [They'll say:] 'Now when was that? – help me remember'. (Ibid.)

That's it exactly: help me remember! Thirty issues published over two and a half years covering six towns (as we learn from the same source [of the report to the Paris Congress]). That gives an average for each town of *one issue per half-year*! And, even if our thoughtless journalist assumed a *tripling* of the productivity of local work (which undoubtedly would not be justified in relation to the average town, since any significant broadening of productivity is impossible within the framework of artisanal limitations), – we would still only get a figure of one issue every two months – that is, something that doesn't much resemble escapades being 'exposed then and there'. Yet it would be enough to unite ten local organisations and have them assign their delegates for an active contribution to setting up a nation-wide newspaper – and then we could 'expose' *for all Russia* not details but genuinely outstanding and typical outrages once every two weeks. No one acquainted with the situation in our organisations will doubt this. If we are really serious about exposing the enemy on the spot and not just indulging in fine-sounding words, then using an illegal newspaper to do this is out of the question: only the anonymous leaflet can do it, since the outside limit for catching the enemy this way does not usually go beyond one or two days (take, for example, an ordinary strike of short duration, a clash with the police at a factory, a demonstration and so on).

'The worker lives not only in a factory but in a town', continues our author who rises from the specific to the general with a strict logic that would do honour to Boris Krichevskii himself. And he points to issues concerning the town councils, the town hospitals, the town schools, and he demands in general that a worker newspaper not pass over town matters in silence. – An excellent demand in and of itself, but providing an especially glaring illustration of the empty abstractions to which people too often limit themselves when they discuss local newspapers. In the first place, if newspapers actually did appear in 'any locality where any appreciable number of workers are collected' and had the kind of detailed section on town affairs desired by *Svoboda*, then, under our Russian conditions, it would inevitably deteriorate into obsession with details and lead to a weakening of the awareness of the importance of an all-Russian revolutionary assault on the tsarist autocracy. It would strengthen the shoots – shoots that are still very much alive and far from rooted up but instead only hidden or temporarily suppressed – of the tendency already made notorious by the famous remark about revolutionaries who talk too much about parliaments that don't exist and too little about town councils that do exist. We say all this would happen 'inevitably', using this word to emphasise that *Svoboda* obviously does not want any of this to happen but rather the reverse. But good intentions by themselves are not enough.

In order to illuminate town affairs in proper proportion to our overall work, this proper proportion must be worked out fully *from the beginning* and based firmly not only on abstract reasoning but on a mass of examples so that it takes on the solidity of *tradition*. We are still a long way from this and it is something that we need to do *first*, before it is permissible to think about and discuss a broad local press.

In the second place, in order to write really well and in an interesting manner about town affairs, it is necessary to know these affairs well and not just through books. And Social Democrats with the necessary knowledge hardly exist *anywhere in Russia*. In order to write for a newspaper (as opposed to a popularising pamphlet) about town matters as well as affairs of state, it is necessary to have fresh and many-sided material that has been collected and worked up by someone competent to do so. And in order to collect and work up this material, it is not enough to rely on the 'primitive democracy' of a primitive circle in which everybody does everything and has fun playing at referendums. What is needed is a staff of specialist writers, specialist correspondents, an army of Social-Democratic reporters who establish connections here, there and everywhere, who know how to penetrate into all and sundry 'state secrets' (about which the Russian bureaucrat is so pompous and about which he so easily blabs), who can worm themselves 'behind the scenes' whenever necessary – an army of people who 'by virtue of their position' are all-knowing and all-seeing. And we, the party of struggle against *any* oppression, whether economic, political, social or national, can and must find, collect, train, mobilise and launch into a campaign this kind of army of all-knowing people – but actually accomplishing this still lays ahead!

In the vast majority of localities, not only have we not made a step in this direction but almost always the very *awareness* of its necessity is lacking. Look around in our Social-Democratic press for lively and interesting articles and indictments of the affairs and intrigues of our diplomats, military, church, towns, finances and so on and so forth: you will find *almost nothing* or very little.[16] This is why 'it always greatly upsets me when a person comes up and talks at great length about beautiful and wonderful things' about the necessity – 'in any locality where a significant number of workers are collected' – of newspapers indicting outrages in the factory, the town and the state!

Predominance of the local over the central press is a sign either of poverty or of luxury. It signifies poverty when the movement has not worked up enough forces for large-scale production and is still stuck in artisanal limitations, almost drowning in 'the details of factory life'. It signifies luxury when the movement *has already fully mastered* the task of providing all-sided indictments and all-sided agitation, so that it is necessary to have numerous local press organs besides the central one. Let each one decide for himself which of these two is indicated by the predominance of the local press among us at the present time. To avoid confusion, I shall limit myself to a precise formulation of my conclusion. Up to now, a majority of our local organisations have thought almost exclusively about local press organs and worked actively almost always for them. This is unfortunate: the opposite should be the case. The majority of local organisations should be thinking for the most part about

---

[16] This is why the example even of exceptionally good local organs completely confirms our point of view. For example, *Iuzhnii rabochii* [*Southern Worker*] is an excellent newspaper completely innocent of instability in principles. But the contribution it wishes to make to the movement is not attained because it comes out rarely and suffers from broad *provaly*. What the Party needs most pressingly at the moment – a principled statement of the fundamental issues of the movement along with all-sided political agitation – is beyond the strength of a local organ. But the sort of thing that *Iuzhnii rabochii* was so good at – such as the articles on the congress of mine owners, on unemployment and so on – does not constitute strictly local material and *is needed for all of Russia*, not just the south. Articles on this all-Russian scale were not found *anywhere* in our Social-Democratic press.

an all-Russian organ and working for the most part for it. Until this happens, we will not be able to establish *any newspaper* that is at all capable of actually serving the movement with an *all-sided* press agitation. And when it does happen, then the correct relation between a necessary central press organ and necessary local ones will come about of itself.

\* \* \*

At first glance, it might seem that the conclusion about the necessity of shifting the centre of gravity from local to all-Russian work does not apply to the area of the specifically economic struggle: the immediate enemies of the workers in this case are the individual entrepreneurs or a group of them who are not bound together by any organisation that even remotely suggests the organisation of the Russian government – our immediate enemy in the political struggle – which has an organisation that is purely military, strictly centralised and guided down to its smallest details by a single will.

But this is not so. The economic struggle – we have stated this many times – is a trade struggle and therefore it demands unification according to the trade of the workers and not only according to the place of work. And this unification by trade is becoming all the more insistently necessary, the more quickly proceeds the unification of our entrepreneurs into all sorts of syndicates and societies. Our fragmentation and our artisanal limitations get directly in the way of this unification, since unification requires a single all-Russian organisation of revolutionaries that is capable of taking upon itself the guidance of all-Russian trade unions of the workers. We have already talked about the desirable type of organisation for this purpose and we will now add a few words in connection with the issue of our press.

Hardly any one doubts that, in every Social-Democratic newspaper, there must be a *section* about the trade (economic) struggle. But the growth of the trade movement compels us to think about a trade [occupational] press. It seems to us, however, that, with rare exceptions, trade papers in Russia are out of the question: this would be a luxury at a time when we are having trouble getting enough bread on the table. The form that is necessary at the present time and appropriate to the conditions of illegal work must be *trade pamphlets* in our case. In these pamphlets, we should collect and arrange systematically both *legally-available*[17] and illegal material on the issue of the

---

[17] Legally-published material is especially important in this connection and we are

labour conditions in a given business, on the differences in this connection among the various localities in Russia, on the main demands of the workers in a given trade [*professiia*], on the shortcomings of relevant laws, on the outstanding instances of worker economic struggle in this craft, and on the beginnings of its trade[-union] organisation, its present-day condition and needs and so forth. First of all, such pamphlets would relieve our Social-Democratic press from the mass of details concerning a particular trade having a special interest only for the workers of a given craft. In the second place, they would register the results of our experience in the trade struggle while preserving and generalising the collected material, which now is literally lost among a mass of leaflets and fragments of material sent in to newspapers. In the third place, they could serve as a sort of guidance for agitators, since the conditions of labour change relatively slowly and the basic demands of the workers of a given craft are extraordinarily stable (compare the demands of the weavers of the Moscow region in 1885 to those of the Petersburg weavers in 1896) and a collection of these demands and needs could serve for years as an excellent aid for economic agitation in backward localities or among the backward strata of the people. Examples of successful strikes in one region, data about a higher standard of living or better conditions of labour would encourage the workers of other localities to ever-renewed

---

especially backward in our ability to collect it systematically and utilise it. It is no exaggeration to say that a trade pamphlet can be written up in some fashion using only legally available material while this is impossible using only illegal material. When we collect illegal material from the workers, we waste for no good reason a great deal of a revolutionary's forces (although an activist working aboveground could easily do the job instead of him) and still never get first-rate material, since the workers for the most part know only one department of a large factory and almost always know the economic results but not the general conditions and norms of their work. It is, therefore, impossible to get from them the kind of knowledge that is available to the factory office staff, to inspectors, doctors and so on – knowledge that is scattered for the most part in minor newspaper articles and in special publications by industries, hospitals, *zemstvos* and so on.

I remember as if it were yesterday my 'first attempt', one which I would never repeat. I spent many weeks grilling 'with verve' one worker about every aspect of the set-up at the enormous factory where he worked. True, I somehow managed to put together after much work a description (of only one factory!), but the worker told me with a smile, wiping the sweat away after the end of our labours, 'working overtime is not as tough for me as answering your questions!'.

The more energetically we carry out the revolutionary struggle, the more will the government be compelled to legalise part of 'trade[-union]' work, thus taking part of our burden away from us.

struggle. In the fourth place, if Social Democracy takes upon itself the initiative of bringing the trade struggle to a country-wide level and thereby strengthens the link of the Russian trade movement with socialism, it will at the same time take care that our *tred-iunionist* work occupies a place in the overall sum of our Social-Democratic work that is neither too big nor too small. It is very difficult, even sometimes almost impossible, for a local organisation to observe a proper proportion here, especially if it is cut off from organisations in other cities. (The example of *Rabochaia mysl* shows the extravagant exaggeration of *tred-iunionizm* that is possible under these circumstances.) But an all-Russian organisation of revolutionaries, standing on an unswervingly Marxist point of view, guiding the political struggle as a whole and having a staff of agitators by trade at their disposal, will never have much difficulty in determining the correct proportion.

# Chapter V
# The 'Plan' for an All-Russian Political Newspaper

'The biggest blunder of *Iskra* in this regard' – writes B. Krichevskii (*Rabochee delo*, No. 10, p. 30) as he accuses us of a tendency to 'turn theory into lifeless doctrine by isolating it from practice' – 'is its "plan" for an all-Russian organisation' (that is, the article 'Where to Begin?'). And Martynov backs him up when he tells us that

> the tendency of *Iskra* to disparage the significance of the forward march of the grey on-going struggle in comparison with propagandising brilliant and polished ideas . . . is crowned by its plan for the organisation of the Party which it sets forth in No. 4 in the article 'Where to Begin?' (*Rabochee delo*, No. 10, p. 61).

Finally, in the pamphlet *Eve of Revolution* that we have just received (a publication of the 'revolutionary-socialist group' *Svoboda* that we know from before), L. Nadezhdin has joined himself to the number of people who are indignant about the 'plan' (the quote marks must be to express an ironical attitude). He tells us that 'to speak now of an organisation stretching out from threads from an all-Russian newspaper is to propagate armchair theorising and armchair work' (p. 126), that it results from 'writerism [*literaturshchina*]' and so on.

It should not surprise anyone that our terrorist is united on this question with the defenders of the 'forward march of the grey on-going struggle'; we examined the roots of this convergence in the chapters on politics and on organisation. But we must note here that L. Nadezhdin and he alone has tried conscientiously to enter into the train of thought of an article that does not please him and has tried to respond to the essential points made by the article – whereas *Rabochee delo* said absolutely nothing about the essential point and tried only to confuse the issue with a whole series of demagogic remarks. As unpleasant as it will be, we must first waste some of our time cleaning up this Augean stable.

### a) Who was offended by the article 'Where to Begin?'

We start with a bouquet of the expressions and exclamations showered on us by *Rabochee delo*. 'A newspaper cannot create a party organisation, but just the reverse' . . . 'A newspaper standing *above* the Party, *outside the Party's ability to monitor it* and independent of the Party, thanks to the existence of its own network of agents' . . . 'By what miracle has *Iskra* forgotten about the actually existing Social-Democratic organisations of the Party to which it belongs?' . . . 'The [self-proclaimed] possessors of firm principles and of a plan to go along with them are the supreme regulators of the real struggle of the Party and dictate to it the fulfilment of its plan' . . . 'The plan drives the living and vital organisations into the kingdom of shadows and wants to call into life a fantastical network of agents' . . . 'If the *Iskra* plan was carried out, it would lead to the complete destruction of any traces of the Russian Social-Democratic Worker Party that is now coming into existence. . . .' 'A propagandistic organ will become an autocratic lawgiver, impossible to monitor, of the entire practical revolutionary struggle' . . . 'How should our party react to its *complete* subordination to an autonomous editorial board' and so on and so forth.

As the reader will see from the content and tone of these citations, *Rabochee delo* is *offended*. But it is not offended for its own sake, rather for the sake of the organisations and committees of our party that *Iskra* allegedly wants to send to the kingdom of shadows and even destroy all traces of them. Sounds awful, doesn't it? But there is one odd thing. The article 'Where to Begin?' appeared in May 1901, the *Rabochee delo* articles appeared in September 1901, and it is now mid-January 1902. During these two 5-month periods (leading up to September and from September till now), *not a single* committee and *not a single* organisation of the Party has come forward with a formal protest against this monster that wants to drive committees and organisations into the kingdom of shadows! And, yet, during this period, both in *Iskra* and in a mass of other publications, both local and non-local, appeared tens and hundreds of communications from all corners of Russia. How did it come about that the people we wanted to drive to the kingdom of shadows were not offended and did not even notice, while offense was taken by a third party?

It came about because the committees and other organisations are engaged in genuine work and not in a play 'democratism'. The committees read the article 'Where to Begin?' and saw that it was an attempt to 'work out a specific plan of organisation *that would enable people to engage in its construction from all directions'*. Since they knew very well and could see for themselves that *not a single one* of these 'all sides' would even think about 'engaging in construction' before they were convinced of the necessity and reliability of the architectural plan, they very naturally did not become 'offended' at the audacity of people who said in *Iskra*: 'In view of the importance of this issue we have decided for our part to present to the attention of our comrades a sketch of a plan that will be developed in more detail in a book being prepared for the press'. Given a conscientious approach to the issue, was it really possible not to understand that if the comrades *accept* the plan presented to their attention, then they will carry it out not because of 'subordination' but from a conviction of its necessity for our common cause, and if they *do not accept* it, then the 'sketch' (such a pretentious word, don't you think?) will simply remain no more than a sketch? Isn't it demagoguery when you battle against a sketch of a plan not only by denouncing it and advising comrades to reject it, but also by *inciting* people who are inexperienced in revolutionary matters against the author of the sketch *for this reason alone*, that he *dared* to 'hand down laws', act as a 'supreme regulator' – in other words, that he dared to *propose* a sketch of a plan? Can our party develop and move forward if merely an attempt to *lift up* local activists to broader views, tasks, plans and so forth is rejected not only because the proposed views are untrue but also because of people being 'offended' that someone 'wants' to '*lift us up*'? After all, L. Nadezhdin also roundly denounced our plan, but he did not descend to the kind of demagoguery that cannot be explained simply by naïveté or by the primitive nature of one's own political views. He resolutely rejected at the very beginning any accusation [against *Iskra*] for wanting to place an 'inspectorate' over the Party. And for that reason, one can and must respond to the essential points of his critique, while one can answer *Rabochee delo* only with contempt.

But contempt toward a writer who lowers himself to cries of 'autocracy' and 'subordination' does not relieve us of the obligation to clear up the confusion presented to the reader by such people. And, here, we can show to everyone very clearly the true nature of these catch-phrases about 'broad democratism'. We are accused of forgetting about the committees, of desiring or attempting to drive them into the kingdom of shadows and so forth. How can we answer these accusations, since we *are unable* to tell the reader *almost nothing factually* about our actual relations to the committees – unable for reasons of *konspiratsiia*? People who throw out crude accusations that irritate the crowd have the advantage of us, thanks to their recklessness, thanks to their careless attitude toward the obligations of a revolutionary who painstakingly hides from the eyes of the world those links and relations that he now maintains, that he is establishing or is trying to establish. It is easily understood why we refuse once and for all to engage in competition with such people on the subject of 'democratism'. As far as the reader who is not initiated into party matters is concerned, the only way we can fulfil our duty to him is not to talk about what exists now or what is now *im Werden*, but rather about *a small part* of what once was and what one is now permitted to talk about as something in the past.

The Bund hints about our 'pretensions to sovereignty'[1] and the émigré Union accuses us of an attempt to uproot all traces of the Party. Please excuse me, gentlemen. You will receive full satisfaction after I tell the public *four facts* from the past.

First fact.[2] The members of one of those 'Unions of Struggle' that took immediate part in the formation of our party and in sending a delegate to the founding party congress, made an agreement with one member of the *Iskra* group about setting up a special worker library that would serve the needs of the whole movement. This worker library did not become reality, and the pamphlets written for it – *Tasks of the Russian Social Democrats* and *The New Factory Law* – ended up abroad through an indirect path and through third parties and were printed there.

---

[1] *Iskra*, No. 8, answer of the Central Committee of the General Jewish Bund in Russia and Poland to our article on the national question.

[2] We purposely do not present these facts in chronological order.

Second fact. The members of the central committee of the Bund asked one of the members of the *Iskra* group to organise, as the Bund put it then, a 'literary laboratory'. In connection with this request, they pointed out that if this venture were not successful, our movement could experience a serious reverse. The result of these talks was the pamphlet *The Worker Cause in Russia*.[3]

Third fact. The central committee of the Bund, via a small provincial town, contacted a member of *Iskra* with the proposal to take on the editorship of the resuscitated *Rabochaia gazeta* and of course the proposal was accepted. Then the proposal was altered: simply a position on the editorial board was offered, owing to a new editorial combination. And this proposal was, of course, also accepted. Three articles were sent in (these have been preserved): 'Our Programme', containing a direct protest against various forms of Bernsteinism and the reversal of direction observed both in legally-permitted writers and *Rabochaia mysl*; 'Our Immediate Task' ('the organisation of an party organ issued regularly and closely linked with all local groups', plus remarks on the inadequacies of 'artisanal limitations'); 'The Essential Issue' (an analysis of the objection that we must *first* develop the activity of local groups before taking on the creation of a nation-wide press organ; insistence on the primary importance of a 'revolutionary organisation', that is, the necessity of 'bringing organisation, discipline and the technique of *konspiratsiia* to the highest degree of perfection'). The proposal to renew *Rabochaia gazeta* was not realised and the articles were never printed.

Fourth fact. A member of a committee for organising a second regular congress of our party communicated to a member of the *Iskra* group a programme for the congress and proposed the *Iskra* group as a candidate for the editorial function of the renewed *Rabochaia gazeta*. This, so to speak, preliminary step was then sanctioned both by the committee to which this person belonged and the central committee of the Bund. The *Iskra* group received notice about the time and place of the congress but (since the group was unsure for several reasons whether or not it would be able to send a delegate) composed a written report to the congress. The basic idea of this

---

[3] By the way, the author of this pamphlet [Martov] has asked me to state that this pamphlet, like his previous ones, was sent to the Union with the request that its editor be the Emancipation of Labour group (owing to various circumstances, the author could not know at that time – February, 1899 – about the changes in the editorial board). This pamphlet will soon be republished by the League [an émigré organisation of the *Iskra* group].

report was that the election of a central committee would not by itself solve the problem of unification in a period of such complete confusion as we are now going through – indeed, it risked compromising the magnificent idea of creating a party, in the event of another quick and devastating *proval*, which was all the more probable given the lack of feeling for *konspiratsiia* that reigns at present. It was therefore necessary to start with an invitation to all the committees and all the other organisations to support a renewed nation-wide press organ that would *genuinely* link all the committees with an *actual* link and that would *genuinely* prepare a group of leader/guides for the whole movement – and the committees and the Party could easily turn the group created by the committees in this way into a central committee, once such a group has grown and become strong. This congress, however, never took place owing to a series of *provaly* and the *Iskra* report was destroyed for reasons of *konspiratsiia* with the result that only a few comrades, including the delegates of one of the committees, read it.

Let the reader now judge for themselves about the nature of such methods as the hint about pretensions to sovereignty coming from the Bund or *Rabochee delo's* thesis that we wish to drive the committees into the kingdom of shades and to 'replace' the organisation of the Party with a organisation for the dissemination of the ideas of a single newspaper. It was precisely to the committees – *at their repeated invitation* – to whom we reported about the necessity of adopting a definite plan of common work. It was precisely for the party organisation that we worked out this plan in the articles intended for *Rabochaia gazeta* and in the report to the scheduled party congress – again, at the invitation of those who had such an influential position in the Party that they took upon themselves the initiative of what was (in actuality) its restoration. And only after these attempts of the party organisation *together with us* to renew an *authorised* central organ of the Party failed *twice* did we consider it our responsibility to come out with an *unauthorised* organ so that when a *third* attempt was made the comrades would have before them the known results of experience and not just vague proposals. At the present time, some of these results of experience are before the eyes of all, so that all the comrades can judge whether or not we correctly understood our obligations – and what should be thought of people who try to mislead those unacquainted with the recent past, people motivated by irritation that, in one case, we showed their lack of consistency in the 'national' question and, in the other case, their impermissible lack of steadiness in matters of principle.

## b) Can a newspaper be a collective organiser?

The central point of the article 'Where to Begin?' consists in asking precisely *this* question and giving it an affirmative answer. The only attempt known to us to analyse this question and to demonstrate the necessity of a negative answer is by L. Nadezhdin, whose conclusions we reproduce in full:

> We are greatly pleased that *Iskra*, No. 4 raised the issue of the necessity of an all-Russian newspaper, but we cannot at all agree that the issue should be discussed under the heading 'Where to Begin?'. It is one of the tasks that are undoubtedly extremely important, but neither an all-Russian newspaper, nor a whole series of popular leaflets, nor a mountain of proclamations can be the fundamental beginning of a militant organisation for a revolutionary moment [such as we now face]. What is necessary is to set to work building up strong political organisations in the localities. We have none of these at present, since in Russia [revolutionary] work took place mainly among the *intelligentnye* workers, while the masses almost exclusively conducted an economic struggle. *If strong revolutionary organisations are not cultivated in the localities, what significance does an all-Russian newspaper have, no matter how well it has been set up?* A burning bush – itself aflame, never burning down, but also not setting anyone else on fire! Around it – and in fact for it – the *narod* will be recruited and become organised – so thinks *Iskra*. *But the narod is much likelier to be recruited and organised around a more concrete task!* Such a task can and should be a broad establishment of local newspapers, the immediate preparation of worker forces for demonstrations, constant work by local organisations among the unemployed (persistently disseminating pamphlets and leaflets among them, calling on them to come to meetings, to resist the government and so forth). We must start up live political work in the localities, and when [all-Russian] unification on these real grounds becomes a necessity, [the resulting unification] will not just be an artificial one existing only on paper. It is not with newspapers that one attains this kind of unification of local work for an all-Russian cause! (*Eve of Revolution*, p. 54.)

We emphasised the sentences in this eloquent tirade that show most glaringly the author's incorrect appraisal of our plan and the incorrectness of his general point of view that is here opposed to *Iskra*. If strong political organisations are not cultivated in the localities, the best possible all-Russian newspaper will mean nothing. This is absolutely correct. But here's the point: there is *no other way to* <u>*cultivate*</u> strong political organisations than by means of an all-Russian newspaper. The author overlooked the most essential statement of *Iskra* that it made *before moving on* to an exposition of its plan: it is necessary

> to call for the creation of a revolutionary organisation that is capable of uniting all forces and guiding the movement *not merely in name* but in actual fact, that is, one that is *always prepared for the support of any kind of protest and any explosion*, using these for the increase and strengthening of militant forces fit for the final battle.

But now – continued *Iskra* – after the events of February and March 1901, everybody agrees with this, in principle at least, so that we now need a *practical resolution of the issue* rather than just a principled one. A definite plan must be immediately put forth so that right now, *from different directions*, everybody can set to work on the construction.

But we are again being pushed backward – to a truth that is true, undisputed, magnificent, but completely inadequate, conveying absolutely nothing to the broad mass of those working [in revolutionary organisations]: 'cultivate strong political organisations'! But that is not the point, esteemed author – the point is *how exactly* must we set about cultivating and later succeed in cultivating!

It is not true that 'in Russia [revolutionary] work has taken place mainly among the *intelligentnye* workers, while the masses almost exclusively conducted an economic struggle'. This thesis in such a form goes astray toward the contrast that *Svoboda* habitually sets up between *intelligentnye* workers and the 'mass' – a contrast that is radically mistaken. On the one hand, in Russia in recent years, it was the *intelligentnye* workers who 'almost exclusively conducted the economic struggle'. On the other hand, the masses will never learn to conduct the political struggle unless we help the leader/guides of this struggle *cultivate themselves*, both those leader/guides from among the *intelligentnye* workers and from among the *intelligenty*. And leader/guides like this are cultivated *exclusively* by systematic, on-going assessments of *all* sides of our political life, of *all the attempts* at protest and struggle made by a variety of classes and for a variety of reasons.

Therefore to talk about the 'cultivation of political organisations' and at the same time *set up a contrast* between a political newspaper that 'exists only on paper' and 'live political work in the localities' is simply ridiculous! It is *Iskra* who subsumes its 'plan' for a newspaper to a wider 'plan' for creating a 'militant readiness' to support the movement among the unemployed *and* the peasant riots *and* the dissatisfaction of the *zemstvo* people *and* the 'indignation of the population against the arrogant tsarist bashibazouks' and on and on. And anyone acquainted with the movement knows all too well that the vast majority of local organisations *do not even think* of this, that many of the prospects mentioned here of 'live political work' have *not once* been carried out even by a single organisation. For example, the attempt to focus attention on the growth of dissatisfaction and protest among the *zemstvo* intelligentsia calls forth a feeling of exasperated incomprehension from Nadezhdin ('Good Lord, is this newspaper for *zemstvo* people?', *Eve of Revolution*, p. 129), from the 'economists' (the letter published in *Iskra*, No. 12), and from many *praktiki*. Under these conditions, 'to begin' can *only* be done by first getting people to *think* about all this, to get them to sum up and generalise each and every flicker of ferment and active struggle. At the present time of a lowering of Social-Democratic tasks, 'live political work' can *begin only* with live political agitation, and this is impossible without an all-Russian newspaper that comes out often and is competently disseminated.

People who look at *Iskra*'s 'plan' as a manifestation of writerism do not understand the very essence of the plan. These people think that what the plan puts forward as the most appropriate means at the present moment is put forward instead as a final goal. They do not give themselves the trouble to think about two comparisons which were used for a graphic illustration of the proposed plan. The establishment of an all-Russian political newspaper (as the *Iskra* article put it) should be the *basic thread*. As we hold on to it, we will be able unswervingly to develop, deepen and broaden this organisation (that is, a revolutionary organisation that is always ready to support any protest and any flare-up). Now, please, tell me: when the bricklayers put down bricks in different places of an immense and unprecedented structure, – is it merely a 'paper' exercise to provide a thread that will help them find the correct place for each brick, that shows the final goal of the common work, making it possible to put to proper use not only every brick but every fragment of a brick, so that they join together with the ones proceeding and following to form a completed and all-embracing line? And are we not right now experiencing a moment in our party life when we have bricks and bricklayers but precisely the lack of a thread that all can see, that all can take up? Let them shout that by providing this thread we show our desire to give commands:

if we wanted to give commands, gentlemen, we would not have written *Iskra*, No. 1 but *Rabochaia gazeta*, No. 3, as several comrades asked us to do and which would have been *completely within our rights to do* after the events described above. But we did not do this: we wanted to leave our hands free for an uncompromising struggle with all pseudo-Social Democrats; we wanted our thread, if it was drawn out correctly, to become respected because of its correctness and not because it was drawn out by an official organ.

'The question of uniting local activity [by means of] central organs runs in a vicious circle', L. Nadezhdin instructs us.

> Unification presupposes the homogeneity of the elements, but this homo-
> geneity itself can be created only by a unifying force, while this unifying
> force can only be the product of strong local organisations that at present
> are in no way distinguished by homogeneity.

This is a truth just as worthy of respect and just as indisputable as affirming that we need to cultivate strong political organisations. And it is just as barren. *Any* [political] question 'runs in a vicious circle', because all of political life is an infinite chain of an infinite number of links. The whole art of politics consists in first finding and then holding as tightly as possible precisely to that link that can least easily be knocked out of our hands, that is most important at a given moment, that can best guarantee that he who controls the link controls the whole chain.[4] If we had a detachment of experienced bricklayers who had learned to work together so well that they could lay bricks exactly where needed without any thread (and this is not at all impossible, speaking abstractly) – then we would, no doubt, latch on to another link. But the trouble is that we still do not have any bricklayers who are experienced and who have learned to work well together, with the result that the bricks most of the time are not placed according to a common thread but completely at random and in such a fragmented fashion that the enemy will blow them away as if they were particles of sand and not bricks.

---

[4] Comrades Krichevskii and Martynov! I call your attention to this shocking manifestation of 'autocracy', 'unmonitored authority', 'supreme regulation' and so forth. Just imagine: he wants to 'control' the whole chain! Write a complaint on the double. Here is a theme ready-made for two editorials in *Rabochee delo*, No. 12.

The second comparison:

> A newspaper is not only a collective propagandist and a collective agitator, but also a collective organiser. In this latter respect *it can be compared to scaffolding* erected around a building under construction: it brings out the contours of the building site, it facilitates relations between individual builders, it helps them distribute the work and look over the general results that are obtained by means of their organised labour.[5]

This looks a lot like a writer's or an armchair theorist's exaggeration of his role, doesn't it? The scaffolding is not needed after one starts to live in the building, the scaffolding is built out of inferior material, the scaffolding is put up for a short time and is tossed into the furnace once the building is completed even in crude fashion. In relation to the construction of revolutionary organisations, experience shows that they can sometimes be successfully constructed without scaffolding – look at the 1870s. But for us, at the present time, one cannot conceive of any possibility of constructing the building we need without scaffolding.

Nadezhdin does not agree with this and says: 'Around it – and in fact for it – the *narod* will be recruited and become organised – so thinks *Iskra. But the narod is much likelier* to be recruited and organised *around a more concrete task!'*. Yes, yes: 'much likelier around a more concrete task' . . . The Russian proverb says: don't spit in the well, you may have to drink out of it. But there are people who are nothing loath to drink out of a well which has already been spat in. In the name of this same greater concreteness, what repulsive things had not been said by our magnificent legally-permitted 'critics of Marxism' and illegal adherents of *Rabochaia mysl*! Our whole movement is crushed by our narrowness, lack of initiative and timidity – all justified by the traditional argument about 'much likelier around a more concrete task'! And Nadezhdin – who considers himself to have a great flair for 'life', who condemns with special severity all 'armchair' types, who accuses *Iskra* (believing himself witty) of seeing 'economists' everywhere, who imagines that he stands high above the division between the orthodox and the critics – does not notice

---

[5] Martynov cites the first sentence of this citation (No. 10, p. 62), but leaves out precisely the second sentence, as if underlining either his unwillingness to discuss the essence of the issue or his inability to understand that essence.

that his arguments play into the hands of the narrowness that makes him so indignant, that he is drinking from a well that has been well and truly spat in! Yes – the most sincere indignation about narrowness, the most passionate desire to lift up people who kow-tow before narrowness is not enough, if the indignant person is swept along without a rudder and without sail, in the same '*stikhiinyi*' fashion as the revolutionaries of the 1870s, if he latches on to 'excitative terror', to 'agrarian terror', to a 'tocsin bell' and so on.

Let's look at this 'more concrete' activity around which, as he thinks, people are 'much likelier' to be recruited and organised: (1) local newspapers; (2) preparation for demonstrations; (3) work among the unemployed. From first glance, it is evident that all these activities were seized upon completely at random, haphazardly, just to say something, because, no matter how long we contemplate them, it is ludicrous to see anything special that makes them appropriate for 'gathering and organising'. Indeed, this very same Nadezhdin says a couple of pages later on:

> it is high time to recognise the simple fact that the work carried out in the localities is extremely pitiful, the committees do not do one-tenth of what they can do . . . the centres for unifying local work that we have now are fictions, a revolutionary equivalent of the bureaucrat's formalism, a mutual granting of generalships, and so it will remain until strong local organisations grow up.

Along with some exaggeration, these words contain a strong dose of bitter truth – but doesn't Nadezhdin see the connection between the pitiful work in the localities and the activists' narrow horizon, the narrowness of the sweep of their activity, a narrowness that is inevitable given the lack of preparation of the activists who remain enclosed within the framework of [merely] local organisation?

[First, local newspapers.] Has Nadezhdin forgotten, in the manner of the author of the article on organisation in *Svoboda*, that the transition to a broad local press that started in 1898 was accompanied by a particular intensification of 'economism' and 'artisanal limitations'? And even if any kind of satisfactory establishment of a 'broad local press' was possible (and we showed above that it is impossible, except under very special circumstances), still, local press organs would not be able to 'recruit and organise' *all* forces of the revolutionaries for a *nation-wide* assault on the autocracy, for guidance of a *united* struggle. Do not forget that we are now speaking *only* of the 'recruiting', of the organising significance of a newspaper, and we ask Nadezhdin, the defender of fragmentation, the same ironical question that he himself poses: 'did we receive a legacy from somewhere of a force of two hundred thousand organisers?'.

Next, 'preparation for demonstrations' cannot be *set in opposition* to *Iskra*'s plan, if only because this plan, as it happens, includes the broadest possible demonstrations *as one of its goals*. The question therefore is only one of *means*. Nadezhdin again confuses things, since he does not consider that 'preparing' a demonstration (up to now, demonstrations take place in the vast majority of cases in a completely *stikhiinyi* fashion) can only be done by troops that are already 'recruited and organised', and what we *are unable* to do is precisely recruit and organise.

'Work among the unemployed.' Again the same confusion, since this also is one of the war-time actions of the mobilised troops and not a plan for how to mobilise the troops. The extent to which Nadezhdin again underestimates the harm done by our fragmentation, our lack of 'a force two-hundred-thousand strong', is evident from the following. Many people, including Nadezhdin, reproach *Iskra* for the poverty of its information about unemployment as well as the chance nature of its reports about the most ordinary occurrences of village life. The reproach is accurate, but *Iskra* is here at fault not through its own fault. We have tried to 'draw the thread' also through the village, but we have practically no bricklayers at all there and we *are compelled* to encourage *anybody* who communicates to us even the most banal fact, – in the hope that this will increase the number of collaborators in this area and *teach all of us* to select, finally, genuinely striking facts. But the available materials usable for education are still so scanty that unless we make available what we do have on a Russia-wide scale, people will simply have nothing to learn from. Undoubtedly, a person who possesses even approximately the same talent for agitation and the same knowledge of the life of the peasant down-and-outer that Nadezhdin himself possesses could provide inestimable services to the movement by his agitation among the unemployed – but such a person is hiding his light under a bushel if he does not take the trouble to inform *all* the Russian comrades about each step of his work so that it will serve as an instructive example for those who in their mass have not yet been able to take up the new activity.

Absolutely everybody talks now about the importance of unification, of the necessity to 'recruit and organise', but, in most cases, there is no definite idea at all of where to begin and how to carry out this business of unification. Everybody agrees, no doubt, that if we 'unite' separate circles – let us say, [all the] district circles of one town – then *common institutions* are necessary for this, in other words, not simply the common name of 'union', but actual *common* work, exchange of materials, experience and forces, distribution of functions not only by district but according to speciality across the whole town. Everybody will agree that a solid and *konspirativnyi* infrastructure will not repay its investment (if I can use a commercial expression) [if it is constructed with only] the 'means' (both material and human, naturally) available in one town district, for the talents of the specialist cannot develop on this narrow scale. The same thing can be said, however, about [the need] to unify different towns, because the scale of one locality *will prove* and has already proved in the history of our Social-Democratic movement to be intolerably narrow: we demonstrated this in detail above, using the examples both of political agitation and of organisational work.

We must, we absolutely must, before anything else, broaden this scale [of organisation], create *actual* links between towns on the basis of *regular common* work, since fragmentation is smothering people who 'sit as if in a pit' (as the author of a letter to *Iskra* put it), not knowing what's going on in the wide world, nor from whom they can find out, nor how to acquire experience, nor how to satisfy the desire for broad activity. And I continue to insist that this *actual* link can *begin* to be created only by a nation-wide newspaper, as the single regular all-Russia enterprise that can sum up the results of the most various kinds of activity and by so doing *pushes* people to travel without flagging along *all* the numerous roads that lead to the revolution, just as all roads lead to Rome.

If we want unification more than in words only, then it is necessary that every local circle *allot right away* a fourth, shall we say, of their forces for *active* work for the *common* cause, and a newspaper will immediately show this circle[6] the general outline, dimensions and character of the common cause –

---

[6] *Clarification*: *if* the circle sympathises with the tendency of this newspaper and considers it useful for the cause to become a collaborator, understanding by this term not just journalistic but any revolutionary collaboration in general. *A note for Rabochee delo*: among revolutionaries who value getting things done rather than playing at democratism, who do not separate 'sympathy' from the most active and lively participation, this clarification would not be required.

show precisely which gaps in the entire all-Russian activity are making themselves felt the most, where agitation is absent, where links are weak, what cogs in the huge general mechanism can a particular circle fix or change for better ones. A circle that is not working yet but only looking for work would not then have to start off like an artisan in one separate small workshop who does not know anything about the development of the 'industry' prior to him, nor the general condition of the given production methods of this industry, but, rather, starts off as a participant in a broad enterprise that *reflects* the whole nation-wide revolutionary assault on the autocracy. And as the working of each cog becomes perfected, and as the number of detail workers for the common cause grows, the denser our network becomes and the less confusion in the ranks is caused by the inevitable *provaly*.

An *actual* link would begin to be created merely by the function of distributing the newspaper (if it really deserves to be called a newspaper, that is, if it comes out regularly not once a month, like the thick journals, but four or so times a month). At the present time, any interaction between towns on matters vital to the revolutionary cause is a tremendous rarity – in any event, it is an exception. But [if such a newspaper existed], this interaction would become the rule and would, of course, guarantee not only the dissemination of the newspaper but also (what is much more important) an exchange of experience, materials, forces and means. The sweep of organisational work would immediately become many times broader, and the success of one locality would be a constant encouragement to further perfection, to a desire to utilise the experience of a comrade at the other end of the country without having to discover it oneself.

Local work would become much richer and more many-sided than at present: political and economic indictments, gathered from all over Russia, would give mental food to workers of all trades and *all stages of development*, would give material and occasion for conversation and reading on the most varied issues – issues that furthermore are raised by hints in the legal press and by conversations in educated society, and by 'shamefaced' government communications. Each flare-up, each demonstration would be evaluated and judged from all angles in every corner of Russia, calling forth a desire not to fall behind the others, to do better than the others – (we socialists are not at all averse to *every* kind of rivalry, to every kind of 'competition'!) – to prepare purposefully what occurred the first time just somehow and in *stikhiinyi* fashion, to use the favourable conditions of a given locality or a given moment for changes in the plan of attack, and so on.

At the same time, this enlivening of local work would not entail the desperate 'do or die' stretching of *all* forces and the risking of all members that is so often the case at present with every demonstration and every issue of a local newspaper. On the one hand, it would be much more difficult for the police to get to the 'roots', since they would not know in which locality to look for them. On the other hand, regular common work would teach people how to relate the forces needed for a *given* attack with the given availability of forces of such and such a unit of the common army (at present, almost nobody ever thinks about this kind of calculation, since attacks occur nine-tenths of the time in *stikhiinyi* fashion) and would facilitate the 'transport' to another locality not only of literature but of revolutionary forces.

In the mass of cases, these forces are now bled white by narrow local work, whereas then it would be possible to transfer an agitator or organiser with any sort of talent from one end of the country to another and there would be constant occasions for doing so. Beginning with a small journey on party business at the expense of the Party, people would get used to being fully supported by the Party, would become revolutionaries by trade, would make of themselves genuine political leaders.

And if we genuinely succeed in getting all or a significant majority of local committees, local groups and circles actively to take up the common work, we would in short order be able to have a weekly newspaper, regularly distributed in tens of thousands of copies throughout Russia. This newspaper would be a small part of a huge bellows that blows up each flame of class struggle and popular indignation into a common fire. Around this task – in and of itself a very small and even innocent one but one that is a regular and in the full meaning of the word *common* task – an army of experienced fighters would systematically be recruited and trained. Among the ladders and scaffolding of this common organisational construction would soon rise up Social-Democratic Zheliabovs from among our revolutionaries, Russian Bebels from our workers, who would be pushed forward and then take their place at the head of a mobilised army and would raise up the whole people to settle accounts with the shame and curse of Russia.

That is what we must dream about!

\* \* \*

'We must dream!' I write these words and I take fright. It seems to me that I am sitting in a 'unification congress' and across me sit the editors and collaborators of *Rabochee delo*. And, now, comrade Martynov arises and turns threateningly toward me: 'And may we permitted to ask, does an autonomous editorial board still have the right to dream without a preliminary polling of the committees of the Party?'. And after him arises comrade Krichevskii who (deepening comrade Martynov's philosophy as Martynov himself had long ago deepened comrade Plekhanov) even more threateningly continues: 'I go further. I ask, does in general any Marxist have the right to dream – one who does not forget that according to Marx mankind has always set itself achievable tasks and that tactics is a process of growth of the tasks that grow along with the Party?'.

Just thinking about these threatening questions gives me the shivers, and all I can think of is where to hide. I will try to hide behind Pisarev.

On the issue of the conflict between dream and actuality, Pisarev wrote that

> There is conflict and conflict. My dream might run ahead of the natural course of events or it might attach itself to something completely off to the side – there, where the natural course of events would never go. In the first case a dream does not lead to any harm; it might even support and strength the energy of a hard-working person. . . . In such dreams there is nothing that distorts or paralyses the will to work. Indeed, just the opposite. If a person is completely without the ability to dream in this way, if he is unable from time to time to run ahead and to view in imagination a complete and finished picture of the creation that has just started to form under his hands – then I simply cannot imagine what stimulus would compel such a person to undertake and bring to completion an extensive and exhausting work in art, science or practical life. . . . The conflict between dream and actuality will not lead to any harm, if only the individual dreamer seriously believes in his dream, attentively examines life, compares his observations of life to his castles in the air and in general conscientiously works for the realisation of his fantasy. As long as there is some kind of contact between the dream and the real world, everything will turn out fine.

This is the kind of dreaming, unfortunately, of which there is all too little in our movement. And the people who are most to blame are those who make such a big affair out of their sobriety, their 'closeness' to the 'concrete': the representatives of legally-permitted criticism along with those of illegal 'tailism'.

## c) What type of organisation do we need?

From the foregoing, the reader will have seen that our 'tactics-as-plan' consists in a rejection of an immediate *call* for a storming and in the demand to set up a 'correct siege of the enemy fortress' – in other words, the demand to direct all our efforts toward recruiting, organising and *mobilising* permanent troops. When we mocked *Rabochee delo* because of its leap from 'economism' over to shouting for a storming (heard ringing out in *April* 1901, in *Listok Rabochego dela*, No. 6), it, of course, showered accusations on us of 'doctrinairism', of a lack of understanding of our revolutionary duty, of making appeals to caution and so forth. We obviously are not in the least bit surprised to hear these accusations in the mouth of people without any foundational beliefs who think they can settle all arguments with a deep-thinking 'tactics-as-process'. Nor are we surprised that Nadezhdin repeated this accusation, since he is someone who, in general, has the most sovereign contempt for solid programmatic and tactical foundations.

They say that history does not repeat itself. But Nadezhdin is trying with all his might to do so. He zealously copies Tkachev by denouncing 'revolutionary cultural uplift', shouting about 'the tocsin bell of the parish church', about the special 'eve-of-revolution point of view', and so forth. He forgets, evidently, the well-known saying that if the original of a historical event is a tragedy, then a copy of it is merely a farce. The attempt to seize power that Tkachev's preaching helped to prepare and that was carried out by means of a 'paralysing' terror that really did paralyse, had grandeur – but the 'excitative' terror of the little Tkachev is simply ridiculous and especially ridiculous when it is supplemented by [his] idea of an organisation of middle workers.

Nadezhdin writes:

> if *Iskra* ever managed to quit the realm of writerism, then it would see that these things (such as the letter from a worker published in *Iskra*, No. 7 and so on) are symptoms that indicate that the 'storming' will begin soon, very soon, and that to speak now (sic!) of an organisation stretching out by threads

from an all-Russian newspaper is to propagate armchair theorising and armchair work.

Observe the unimaginable confusion here: on the one hand, excitative terror and an 'organisation of middle workers' together with the opinion that recruiting is 'much likelier' to be done around 'something more concrete', something like a local newspaper, – and on the other hand, the opinion that to talk 'now' about an all-Russian organisation is to propagate armchair theorising, that is, to speak more simply and directly, 'now' is already too late! But according to you, most esteemed L. Nadezhdin, it's *not* too late for a 'broad setting up of local newspapers', isn't that right?

Compare this to the tactics and point of view of *Iskra*: excitative terror is nonsense and to talk about an organisation specifically based on middle workers and on a *broad* establishment of local newspapers is to open the door wide open for 'economism'. We *must* talk about a single all-Russian organisation of revolutionaries; such talk will not be 'too late' right up to the time when a real, and not just a paper, storming begins.

Nadezhdin continues:

> Yes, things are far from brilliant with us in the matter of organisation. Yes, *Iskra* is absolutely right that the main mass of our fighting forces are volunteers and [unprepared] rebels. . . . It is a good thing that you soberly present the situation of our forces, but why at the same time do you forget that *the crowd is not at all ours* and therefore *it will not ask us* when to open military operations – it will simply start 'rioting'. . . . When the crowd steps forth with its *stikhiinyi* destructive force, it *might* overwhelm and crush those 'regular troops' for whom we were always intending to bring in a highly systematic organisation but never *managed in time* to do so. (Our emphasis.)

Amazing logic! It is *precisely because* the 'crowd is not ours' that it is senseless and unseemly to shout about 'storming' this very day, because storming is an attack by regular troops and not a *stikhiinyi* explosion by the crowd. It is precisely because the crowd *might* overwhelm and crush our regular troops that we must *manage in time* to keep pace with the *stikhiinyi* upsurge by means of our work in 'bringing in a highly systematic organisation' to the regular troops, since the more we 'manage in time' to bring in this level of organisation, the more likely that the regular troops will not be overwhelmed by the crowd but will take their place in front, at the head of the crowd.

Nadezhdin gets confused because he imagines that these systematically organised troops are involved in something that cuts them off from the crowd, when, in actual fact, they are involved exclusively in all-sided and all-embracing political agitation, that is, precisely work that *brings closer and merges into one* the crowd with its *stikhiinyi* destructive force and the organisation of revolutionaries with its purposive destructive force. Indeed, you gentlemen are shifting the blame that really belongs to you because it is precisely the *Svoboda* group that introduces terror *into its programme* and by so doing calls for a organisation of terrorists – and such an organisation really does draw our troops away from getting closer to the crowd which is, unfortunately, not yet ours, and which, unfortunately, does not ask us or rarely asks us when and how to unleash military action.

Nadezhdin continues to frighten *Iskra*: [Obsessed with polemics] 'we will overlook the revolution itself, just as we overlooked the recent events that fell on us like a bolt from the blue'. This sentence, taken in connection with sentences quoted earlier, clearly shows us the absurdity of the 'special eve-of-revolution point of view' concocted by *Svoboda*.[7] This special 'point of view', if we speak plainly, reduces itself to this: it is already too late 'now' to reason and to prepare oneself. But if that is the case, my highly esteemed foe of 'writerism', what is the point of writing 132 printed pages 'on theoretical questions[8] and on tactics' [as you have just done]? Don't you think it would be more proper – from the 'eve-of-revolution point of view' – to publish 132 thousand leaflets with the concise slogan: 'beat them up!'?

The person who least risks overlooking the revolution is precisely the one who regards political agitation aimed at the whole people [*vsenarodnyi*] as

---

[7] *Eve of Revolution*, p. 62.

[8] Incidentally, in his 'survey of questions of theory', L. Nadezhdin made almost no contribution to questions of theory, unless you count the following very intriguing passage, based on the 'eve-of-revolution point of view': 'The Bernsteiniad as a whole has lost its acuteness for us at the present moment, just like the question of whether Mr. Adamovich has proved that Mr. Struve has already deserved dismissal or on the contrary Mr. Struve will refute Mr. Adamovich and will not agree to go into retirement – all that makes decidedly no difference, since the hour of revolution has struck' (p. 110). It would be hard to express more vividly L. Nadezhdin's infinite unconcern about theory. We proclaim that the 'eve of revolution' is here – and *therefore* it 'makes decidedly no difference' whether or not the orthodox manage to rout the critics! And our sage does not notice that it is precisely during a time of revolution that we will need the results of the theoretical struggle with the 'critics' in order to carry out a decisive struggle against their *practical* positions!

the cornerstone of his entire programme *and tactics and organisational work*, as does *Iskra*. The people who were engaged all over Russia in weaving the threads of organisation that stretch out from the all-Russian newspaper not only did not overlook the spring events – on the contrary, these people allowed us to predict them. These people did not overlook the demonstrations that are described in *Iskra*, Nos. 13 and 14: just the opposite, they participated in them and were vividly aware of their responsibility to come to the aid of the *stikhiinyi* upsurge of the crowd, and, at the same time, through the medium of the newspaper, they helped all their Russian comrades to learn about these demonstrations and utilise this experience. Neither will they overlook the revolution, if they are still alive – a revolution that demands of us first of all and most of all greater experience in agitation, the knowledge of how to support (in Social-Democratic fashion) every protest, of how to direct the *stikhiinyi* movement, preserving it from the mistakes of its friends and the traps of its enemies!

We arrive in this way at the final consideration that compels us to give special insistence to the plan of organisation around an all-Russian newspaper, [that is,] by means of joint work for a common newspaper. Only this kind of organisation will guarantee the *flexibility* needed by a Social-Democratic fighting organisation – that is, the ability to adapt immediately to the most varied and swiftly changing conditions of struggle, the ability 'on the one hand to refuse a battle in an open field against an enemy with crushing material superiority when he focuses all his forces on a single point and on the other hand to use the clumsiness of the enemy and attack him when and where he least expects an attack'.[9]

It would be a huge mistake to create a party organisation in the expectation either simply of an explosion and street battles or simply of a 'forward march

---

[9] *Iskra*, No. 4: 'Where to Begin?'. Nadezhdin writes: 'The length of the work ahead doesn't bother in the least the revolutionary culturists who do not stand on the eve-of-revolution point of view' (p. 62). We note in this connection: if we do not work out a political tactic, an organisational plan, that is definitely calculated on the expectation of *work over a very long period* and also guarantees *through the very process of the work itself* the readiness of our party to remain at its post and fulfill its duty during any kind of unexpectedness, during any acceleration of the course of events – then we are only pitiful political adventurers. Only a Nadezhdin, calling himself a Social Democrat only since yesterday, could forget that the goal of Social Democracy is the radical transformation of the conditions of life for all of humanity and, therefore, a Social Democrat is not permitted to be 'bothered' by the issue of the length of the work ahead.

of the grey ongoing struggle'. We must *always* carry on our day-to-day work and always be ready for everything, because it is very often almost impossible to foresee a shift between periods of explosion and periods of quiet. In those cases where this shift can be foreseen, we would not be able to use this knowledge for the restructuring of the organisation, since this kind of shift in an autocratic country happens with striking swiftness – indeed, it is sometimes connected to a single night raid by the tsarist janissaries. And the revolution itself must not be conceived as a single act (as the Nadezhdins seem to imagine) but as several rapid shifts between more or less profound explosions and more or less profound periods of quiet. Therefore, the basic content of the activity of our party organisation, the focus of this activity, should be the type of work that is possible and necessary both in a period of the most powerful explosion as well as in the period of the most complete quiet, namely: the work of political agitation that is unified across all of Russia, that illuminates all sides of life and that is directed at the broadest possible masses. And this work is *unthinkable* in Russia without an all-Russian newspaper that is issued very frequently. The organisation that forms in and of itself around this newspaper, the organisation of its *collaborators* (in the broad sense of the term, meaning everybody working [on any aspect of its operations]), will be ready precisely *for everything*, starting with saving the honour, prestige and continuity of the Party in a moment of acute revolutionary 'depression' and ending with preparing, setting the time, and carrying out the armed insurrection of the whole people.

Indeed, consider a very ordinary occurrence with us: a complete *proval* in one or several localities. In the absence of *one* common and regular task carried out by *all* local organisations, such *provaly* are often accompanied by an interruption of work for many months. But given the existence of such a task common to all, then, even in the case of the most complete *proval*, a few weeks of work by two or three energetic people would be sufficient to link the common centre to new circles of young people which, as is well known, arise extremely quickly even now. And when the common task damaged by the *proval* is visible to all, these new circles can emerge and link themselves to the centre even more quickly.

Now, consider the contrasting case of an uprising of the people [*narodnoe vosstanie*]. At the present time, probably everybody will agree that we should think about this and prepare for it. But *how* should we prepare? Not by having a central committee appoint agents to all the localities for the purpose of preparing an uprising! Even if we had a central committee, it would achieve exactly nothing by such appointments, given present-day Russian conditions. In contrast, a network of agents[10] that had formed by itself around the work of setting up and disseminating a nation-wide newspaper would not have to 'sit and wait' for a watchword from the centre about an uprising, since it would be involved in the kind of regular task that would guarantee the greatest probability of success in the event of an uprising. Exactly this kind of task would strengthen links both with the broadest masses of the workers and with all the strata that are dissatisfied with the autocracy, and these links are of the greatest importance for an uprising. Exactly a task of this kind would serve to create the ability to estimate the general political situation correctly and consequently the ability to select the appropriate moment for an uprising. Exactly this kind of task would teach *all* local organisations to react simultaneously to the very same political issues, incidents and events that trouble all Russia, to provide an answer to these 'events' as energetically as possible, as uniformly and expediently as possible, – and is not an uprising in essence, the most energetic, most uniform and most expedient 'answer' of the whole *narod* to the government? Precisely this kind of task, finally, would teach all revolutionary organisations in all corners of Russia to maintain the most constant and at the same time the most *konspirativnyi* contacts with each other, thus creating the *actual* unity of the Party, for without such contacts it will be impossible to collectively consider a plan for an uprising and to take the necessary preparatory measures on the eve of its outbreak – measures that must be taken in the strictest secrecy.

---

[10] Alas, alas! Again the horrifying word 'agent' – the word that strikes so harshly the democratic ear of Martynov – escapes my lips! But I wonder why this word did not offend the outstanding leaders of the 1870s but does offend the artisans of the 1890s? I like this word, because it clearly and sharply points to the *common task* to which all agents subordinate their thoughts and actions. If it is necessary to substitute another word, then I would just end up by picking the term '[journalistic] collaborator', except that it connotes a certain writerism and a certain vagueness. But we need a military organisation of agents. But if need be, those multitudinous Martynovs (especially among émigrés) who love to busy themselves with 'mutual appointment of one another to the rank of generals' could say – instead of 'agent for [providing false] passports' – 'the under-over-secretary of the special department for the provision of passports for revolutionaries' and so on.

In a word, the 'plan for an all-Russian political newspaper', far from being a product of the armchair work of people infected by doctrinairism and writerism (as it may seem to people who have done a poor job of considering the question) is, on the contrary, a most practical plan for starting preparation for an uprising immediately and from all directions, while, at the same time, not forgetting for a moment our essential day-to-day work.

# Conclusion

The history of Russian Social Democracy falls clearly into three periods.

The first period embraces about ten years, approximately 1884 to 1894. This was the period of the emergence and consolidation of the theory and programme of Social Democracy. The advocates of the new tendency in Russia were far and few between. Social Democracy existed without a worker movement and underwent, as a political party, a process of embryonic development.

The second period embraces three or four years, from 1894 to 1898. Social Democracy makes its appearance in the world as a social movement, as an upsurge of the masses of the people, as a political party. This is the period of childhood and adolescence. With the speed of an epidemic, a wholesale enthusiasm for the struggle against [the ideology of] populism, a wholesale enthusiasm for going to the workers and for worker strikes, was disseminated among the intelligentsia. The movement made huge progress. The majority of leader/guides were extremely young people who were far from reaching even the age of thirty-five years that had seemed to Mr. N. Mikhailovsky to be some kind of natural boundary. Thanks to their youth, they turned out to be unprepared for practical work and disappeared from the scene with striking swiftness. But the scope of their work for the most part was very broad. Many of them started to think in a revolutionary way as supporters of Narodnaia volia-ism. Practically all of them in their early youth bowed with great respect before the heroes of terror. The rejection of the charisma of this heroic tradition was at the cost of a [personal] struggle, coupled with a break with those people who were determined at all costs to remain loyal to Narodnaia volia – people that the young Social Democrats greatly respected. The struggle compelled them to study, to read illegal writings of all tendencies, to engage intensively with the issues brought up by legally-permitted populism. The Social Democrats who were educated in this struggle went to the worker movement, 'not for a minute' forgetting either the theory of Marxism that lit the world up with its bright light or the task of overthrowing the autocracy. The formation of a [national] party in spring 1898 was the most outstanding but at the same time the *final* deed of Social Democrats in this era.

The third period is prepared, as we have seen, in 1897 and finally takes over from the second period in 1898 (1898–?). This is the period of disarray, disintegration, unsteadiness. It happens that, during adolescence, a person's voice breaks. And, in the case of Russian Social Democracy during this period, the voice broke and started to sound false – on the one [legally-permitted] side, in the writings of Struve and Prokopovich, Bulgakov and Berdyaev, and on the other [underground] side, with V.I. [who praised *Rabochaia mysl*] and R.M. [K.M. Takhtarev], with Krichevskii and Martynov. But only the leader/guides wandered about by themselves or went backwards: the movement itself continued to grow and to make enormous steps forward. The proletarian struggle seized new strata of the workers and was disseminated throughout Russia, while at the same time also indirectly influencing the enlivening of the democratic spirit among the students and other strata of the population. But the purposiveness of the guides abdicated in reaction to the broadness and strength of the *stikhiinyi* upsurge; among the Social Democrats another type already predominated – the type of activist educated almost exclusively on 'legally-permitted' Marxist literature, a situation that became all the more intolerable as the *stikhiinost* of the masses demanded more purposiveness from the activists. The leader/guides turned out not only to be backward in a theoretical sense ('freedom of criticism') and in a practical sense ('artisanal limitations'), but they tried to defend their backwardness with all sorts of bombastic arguments. Social Democracy was lowered to the level of *tred-iunionizm* both by the Brentanos of legally-permitted Marxism and the tailists of illegal literature. The *Credo* programme began to be carried out, especially when the 'artisanal limitations' of the Social Democrats called forth an enlivening of revolutionary but non-Social-Democratic tendencies.

And so, if the reader scolds me because I went into excessive detail about the likes of *Rabochee delo*, I answer: *Rabochee delo* has acquired 'historical' significance because it most vividly reflects the 'spirit' of this third period.[11] Not the straightforward R.M. but precisely the weathercock Krichevskiis and Martynovs are the genuine expression of this disarray and unsteadiness, of the readiness to make concessions to 'criticism' and to 'economism' and to terrorism. The characteristic of this period is not a haughty contempt toward practical work on the part of some advocate of 'the absolute', but, rather, the merger of a submersion in petty practical work with the utmost lack of concern in theoretical matters. The heroes of this period did not busy themselves with an outright rejection of the 'great words' but, rather, vulgarised them: scientific socialism was changed from an integral revolutionary theory to a mishmash that 'freely' absorbed the contents of any new German textbook; the slogan of 'class struggle' not only did not push people forward to ever broader, ever more energetic activity but served as a tranquilliser, since 'the economic struggle is inextricably tied to the political struggle'; the idea of a party did not serve as a call for the creation of a militant organisation of revolutionaries, but justified various 'revolutionary equivalents of a bureaucrat's formalism' and a childish playing around with 'democratic' forms.

We do not know when the third period will end and when the fourth period will begin (although the shift is already presaged by many signs). We move here from talking about history to talking about the present and partly about the future. But we strongly believe that the fourth period will lead to a consolidation of militant Marxism, that Russian Social Democracy will emerge from the crisis stronger and in the full strength of manhood, that the rear-guard of opportunists will be replaced by a genuinely advanced detachment of the most revolutionary class.

---

[11] I could also answer by using the German proverb: *Den Sack schlägt man, den Esel meint man*, or, in Russian, by beating the cat, you tell the bride to behave. Not just *Rabochee delo* but a *broad mass* of *praktiki* and *theoreticians* were carried away with enthusiasm for fashionable 'criticism', got all mixed up about the question of *stikhiinost*, strayed from a Social-Democratic to a *tred-iunionist* understanding of our political and organisational tasks.

In the spirit of calling for this replacement and by way of pulling together everything said above, we can answer the question, what is to be done, with the short reply:

Liquidate the third period.

# Bibliography

Akimov, Vladimir 1900, *Kak derzhat' sebia na doprosakh*, Geneva: Rabochee delo.

Akimov, Vladimir 1969 [1904], *Vladimir Akimov on the Dilemmas of Russian Marxism 1895–1903*, Cambridge: Cambridge University Press.

Akselrod, Pavel 1898, *K voprosu o sovremennykh zadachakh i taktike russkikh sotsial-demokratov*, Geneva: Izdanie Soiuza Russkikh Sotsialdemokratov.

Akselrod, Pavel 1899, *Pis'mo v redaktsiiu 'Rabochego dela'*, Geneva: Izdanie Soiuza Russkikh Sotsialdemokratov.

Akselrod, Pavel 1905 [1902], 'Zarozhdenie u nas burzhuaznoi demokratii, kak samo-stoiatel'noi revoliutsionnoi sily', in *Bor'ba sotsialisticheskikh i burzhuazuykh tendentsii v russkom revoliutsionnom dvizhenii*, Geneva: Izdanie Rossiiskoi Sotsial'demokraticheskoi Rabochei Partii.

Akselrod, Pavel 1975 [1923], *Perezhitoe i peredumannoe*, Cambridge, MA.: Oriental Research Partners.

Ascher, Abraham 1972, *Pavel Axelrod and the Development of Menshevism*, Cambridge, MA.: Harvard University Press.

Ascher, Abraham 1988, *The Revolution of 1905: Russia in Disarray*, Stanford: Stanford University Press.

Barclay, David E. and Eric D. Weitz (eds.) 1998, *Between Reform and Revolution: German Socialism and Communism from 1840 to 1990*, Oxford: Berghahn Books.

Baron, Samuel H. 1963, *Plekhanov: The Father of Russian Marxism*, Stanford: Stanford University Press.

Baturin, N. 1906, *Ocherk istorii Sotsial-demokratii v Rossii*, Moscow: s.n.

Beaumont, Matthew 2005, *Utopia Ltd.: Ideologies of Social Dreaming in England, 1870–1900*, Historical Materialism Book Series, Leiden: Brill Academic Press.

Bebel, August 1912, *My Life*, London: T. Fisher Unwin.

Bellamy, Edward 1968 [1888], *Looking Backward*, New York: Magnum Books.

Berdyaev, Nicolas 1960 [1937], *The Origin of Russian Communism*, Ann Arbor: University of Michigan Press.

Bernstein, Eduard 1970 [1893], *Ferdinand Lassalle as a Social Reformer*, translated by Eleanor Marx Aveling, St. Clair Shores, Michigan: Scholarly Press.

Bertram Wolfe 1961, 'Introduction', in Rosa Luxemburg, *'The Russian Revolution' and 'Leninism or Marxism'*, Ann Arbor: University of Michigan Press.

Bevir, Mark 1999, *The Logic of the History of Ideas*, Cambridge: Cambridge University Press.

Bogdanov, A.A. 1995 [1914], *Desiatiletie otlucheniia ot marksizma*, in *Neizvestnyi Bogdanov* Volume 3, edited by G.A. Bordiugov, Moscow: ITs 'AIRO–XX'.

Bonch-Bruevich, V.D. 1961, *Izbrannye sochineniia*, tom 2, Moscow: Akademiia Nauk SSSR.

Boniece, Sally A. 2003, 'The Spiridonova Case, 1906: Terror, Myth, and Martyrdom', *Kritika: Explorations in Russian and Eurasian History*, 4, 3: 571–607.

Boudon, Raymond 2001, *The Origin of Values: Sociology and Philosophy of Beliefs*, New Brunswick: Transaction Publishers.

Brandes, George 1911, *Ferdinand Lassalle*, London: William Heinemann.

Brooks, Jeffrey 2000, *Thank You, Comrade Stalin: Soviet Public Culture from Revolution to Cold War*, Princeton: Princeton University Press.

Budnitskii, O.V. 1996, *Istoriia terrorizma v Rossii v dokumentakh, biografiiakh, issledovaniiakh*, 2nd ed., Rostov-na-Donu: Feniks.

Bukharin, Nikolai 1989 [1920], 'Lenin kak revoliutsionnyi teoretik', in Bukharin, *Problemy teorii i praktiki sotsializma*, Moscow: Politizdat.

Bukharin, Nikolai 1990 [1924], 'Lenin kak marksist', in Bukharin, *Izbrannye proizvedeniia*, Moscow: Polizdat.

Bukharin, Nikolai 1993, *Revoliutsiia i kul'tura*, Moscow: Fond imeni N.I. Bukharina.

Bukharin, Nikolai and Evgenii Preobrazhensky 1919, *Azbuka kommunizma*, Moscow: Gosizdat.

Burbank, Jane 1995, 'Lenin and the Law in Revolutionary Russia', *Slavic Review* 54: 23–44.

Carr, Jay (ed.) 2002, *The A List: The National Society of Film Critics' 100 Essential Films*, Da Capo Press (no place of publication).

Carver, Terrell 1983, *Marx and Engels: Their Intellectual Relationship*, Bloomington: Indiana University Press.

Chamberlin W.H. 1930, *Soviet Russia*, Boston: Little, Brown.

Cherevanin 1904, *Organizatsionnyi vopros*, Geneva: Izdanie Rossiiskoi Sotsial'demokraticheskoi Rabochei Partii.

*Chetvertyi s"ezd RSDRP, aprel'–mai 1906 goda: Protokoly* 1959, Moscow: Gospolizdat.

Clark, Katerina 1981, *The Soviet Novel: History as Ritual*, Chicago: University of Chicago Press.

Cliff, Tony 1975, *Lenin, Volume 1: Building the Party*, London: Pluto Press.

Cohen, Stephen F. 1977, 'Bolshevism and Stalinism', in *Stalinism: Essays in Historical Interpretation*, edited by Robert C. Tucker, New York: W.W. Norton.

*Collins German-English English-German Dictionary* 1981, London: Collins.

Dal', Vladimir 1978–80 [1880–2], *Tolkovyi slovar' zhivago velikoruskhago iazyka*, Moscow: Russkii iazyk.

Dan, F. 1904, *Iz istorii rabochego dvizheniia i sotsialdemokratii v Rossii, 1900–1904 g.g.*, St. Petersburg: Tip. Ia. Balianskago.

Dan, Theodore 1964 [1945], *The Origins of Bolshevism*, London: Secker and Warburg.

Daniels, Robert V. 1957, 'Lenin and the Russian Revolutionary Tradition', *Harvard Slavic Studies*, 4: 339–53.

Derfler, Leslie 1998, *Paul Lafargue and the Flowering of French Socialism*, Cambridge, MA.: Harvard University Press.

Dominick, Raymond H. 1982, *Wilhelm Liebknecht and the Founding of the German Social Democratic Party*, Chapel Hill: University of North Carolina Press.

Donald, Moira 1993, *Marxism and Revolution: Karl Kautsky and the Russian Marxists, 1900–1924*, New Haven: Yale University Press.

Draper, Hal 1977–90, *Karl Marx's Theory of Revolution*, 4 volumes, New York: Monthly Review Press.

Drozd, Andrew M. 2001, *Chernyshevskii's 'What Is to Be Done?': A Reevaluation*, Evanston: Northwestern University Press.

Eley, Geoff 2002, *Forging Democracy: The History of the Left in Europe, 1850–2000*, Oxford: Oxford University Press.

Elwood, Carter 1974, *Russian Social Democracy in the Underground*, Assen: Van Gorcum and Company.

Elwood, Carter 1977, *Roman Malinovsky, A Life Without a Cause*, Newtonville: Oriental Research Partners.

Engels, Friedrich 1959 [1845], *Die Lage der arbeitenden Klasse in England*, in *Marx Engels Werke*, Band 2, Berlin: Dietz Verlag.

Engels, Friedrich 1962a [1865], *Die preussische Militärfrage und die deutsche Arbeiterpartei*, in *Marx Engels Werke*, Band 16, Berlin: Dietz Verlag.

Engels, Friedrich 1962b [1880], *Die Entwicklung des Sozialismus von der Utopie zur Wissenschaft*, in *Marx Engels Werke*, Band 19, Berlin: Dietz Verlag.

Engels, Friedrich 1962c [1877], 'Karl Marx', in *Marx Engels Werke*, Band 19, Berlin: Dietz Verlag.

Engels, Friedrich 1989 [1878], 'The Workingmen of Europe in 1877', in *Marx and Engels Collected Works*, Volume 24, New York: International Publishers.

Engels, Friedrich 1993 [1845], *The Condition of the Working Class in England*, edited by David McLellan, Oxford: Oxford University Press.

Ensor, R.C.K. 1910 [1903], *Modern Socialism*, London: Harper and Brothers.

Frankel, Jonathan 1969, 'Introduction', in Akimov 1969.

Fueloep-Miller, René 1965 [1926], *The Mind and Face of Bolshevism*, New York: Harper and Row.

Gay, Peter 1962 [1952], *The Dilemma of Democratic Socialism: Eduard Bernstein's Challenge to Marx*, New York: Collier Books.

Geary, Dick 1987, *Karl Kautsky*, Manchester: Manchester University Press.

Geifman, Anna 1993, *Thou Shalt Kill: Revolutionary Terrorism in Russia, 1894–1917*, Princeton: Princeton University Press.

Getzler, Israel 1967, *Martov: A Political Biography of a Russian Social Democrat*, Cambridge: Cambridge University Press.

Geyer, Dietrich 1962, *Lenin in der Russischen Sozialdemokratie: Die Arbeiterbewegung im Zarenreich als Organisationsproblem der revolutionären Intelligenz 1890–1903*, Cologne: Böhlau Verlag.

Gilcher-Holtey, Ingrid 1986, *Das Mandat des Intellektuellen: Karl Kautsky und die Sozialdemokratie*, Berlin: Siedler Vertrag.

Gorev, B.I. 1924, *Iz partiinogo proshlogo: Vospominaniia, 1895–1905*, Leningrad: Gosizdat.

Gusev, K.V. et al. 1987, *Daite nam organizatsiiu revoliutsionerov . . .*, Moscow: Polizdat.

Haimson, Leopold H. 1955, *The Russian Marxists and the Origins of Bolshevism*, Cambridge, MA.: Harvard University Press.

Haimson, Leopold 1999, 'Russian Workers' Political and Social Identities: The Role of Social Representations in the Interaction between Members of the Labor Movement and the Social Democratic Intelligentsia', in *Workers and Intelligentsia in Late Imperial Russia: Realities, Representations, Reflections*, edited by Reginald Zelnik, Berkeley: University of California Press.

Haimson, Leopold 2004, 'Lenin's Revolutionary Career Revisited', *Kritika: Explorations in Russian and Eurasian History*, 5, 1: 55–80.

Haimson, Leopold 2005, *Russia's Revolutionary Experience, 1905–1917: Two Essays*, New York: Columbia University Press.

Haimson, Leopold H. (ed.) 1987, *The Making of Three Russian Revolutionaries: Voices from the Menshevik Past*, Cambridge: Cambridge University Press.

Halfin, Igal 2000, *From Darkness to Light: Class, Consciousness, and Salvation in Revolutionary Russia*, Pittsburgh: University of Pittsburg Press.

Hall, Alex 1977, *Scandal, Sensation and Social Democracy: The SPD Press and Wilhelmine Germany 1890–1914*, Cambridge: Cambridge University Press.

Harding, Neil 1977, *Lenin's Political Thought: Theory and Practice in the Democratic Revolution*, London: Macmillan.

Harding, Neil (ed.) 1983, *Marxism in Russia: Key Documents 1879–1906*, Cambridge: Cambridge University Press.

Hardy, Deborah 1977, *Petr Tkachev, the Critic as Jacobin*, Seattle: University of Washington Press.

Hildermeier, Manfred 2000 [1978], *The Russian Socialist Revolutionary Party Before the First World War*, New York: St. Martin's Press.

Himmer, Robert 2001, 'First Impressions Matter: Stalin's Initial Encounter with Lenin, Tammerfors 1905', *Revolutionary Russia*, 14, 2: 73–84.

Hobsbawm, Eric 1962, *The Age of Revolution 1789–1848*, New York: Mentor Books.

Hünlich, Reinhold 1981, *Karl Kautsky und der Marxismus der II. Internationale*, Marburg: Verlag Arbeiterbewegung und Gesellschaftswissenschaft.

Hunter, Robert 1908, *Socialists at Work*, New York: The Macmillan Company.

Ingerflom, Claudio Sergio 1988, *Le citoyen impossible: les racines russes du leninisme*, Paris: Payot.

*Iskra za dva goda, Sbornik statei iz Iskry* 1906, St. Petersburg: Saltykov.

Ivanshin, Vladimir P. 1900, 'Organizatsionnye zadachi russkogo rabochego dvizheniia', *Rabochee delo*, No. 8 (November 1900): 1–22.

Johnstone, Monty 1967, 'Marx and Engels and the Concept of the Party', in *The Socialist Register 1967*, London: Merlin Press.

Kanatchikov, Semën 1929, *Iz istorii moego bytiia*, Moscow: Zemlia i Fabrika.

Kanatchikov, Semën 1986 [1929–34], *A Radical Worker in Tsarist Russia: The Autobiography of Semën Ivanovich Kanatchikov*, edited by Reginald Zelnik, Stanford: Stanford University Press.

Kautsky, John 1994, *Karl Kautsky: Marxism, Revolution, and Democracy*, New Brunswick: Transaction Publishers.

Kautsky, Karl 1893, *Der Parlamentarismus, die Volksgesetzgebung und die Sozialdemokratie*, Stuttgart: J.H.W. Dietz.

Kautsky, Karl 1895, 'Die Intelligenz und die Sozialdemokratie', *Neue Zeit*, 13, 2: 10–16, 43–9, 74–80.

Kautsky, Karl 1899 [1895], *Friedrich Engels: His Life, His Work, His Writings*, Chicago: Charles H. Kerr.

Kautsky, Karl 1900, *Le Parliamentarisme et socialisme*, Paris: Librairie G. Jacques.

Kautsky, Karl 1901a, 'Akademiker und Proletarier', *Neue Zeit*, 19, 2: 89–91.

Kautsky, Karl 1901b, 'Die Revision des Programms der Sozialdemokratie in Oesterreich', *Neue Zeit*, 20, 1: 68–82.

Kautsky, Karl 1902, *Die soziale Revolution*, Berlin: Vorwärts.

Kautsky, Karl 1906, 'Triebkräfte und Aussichten der ressischen Revolution', *Neue Zeit*, 25, 1: 284–90, 324–33.

Kautsky, Karl 1908, *Die historische Leistung von Karl Marx*, Berlin: Vorwärts.

Kautsky, Karl 1909, *Der Weg zur Macht: Politische Betrachtungen über das Hineinwachsen in die Revolution*, Berlin: Vorwärts.

Kautsky, Karl 1925 [1908], *Foundations of Christianity: A Study in Christian Origins*, New York: International Publishers.

Kautsky, Karl 1959 [1892], *Erfurtskaia programma*, Moscow: Gospolizdat.

Kautsky, Karl 1965 [1892], *Das Erfurter Programm*, Berlin: Dietz Verlag.

Kautsky, Karl 1988 [1927], *The Materialist Conception of History*, abridged translation, edited by John Kautsky, New Haven: Yale University Press.

Kautsky, Karl 1996 [1909], *The Road to Power: Political Reflections on Growing into the Revolution*, Atlantic Highlands: Humanities Press.

Kavtorin, V. 1992, *Pervyi shag k katastrofe*, Leningrad: Lenizdat.

Kay, John 2003, *The Truth About Markets: Their Genius, Their Limits, Their Follies*, London: Allen Lane.

Keep, J.L.H. 1963, *The Rise of Social Democracy in Russia*, Oxford: Oxford University Press.

Kindersley, R. 1962, *The First Russian Revisionists: A Study of 'Legal Marxism' in Russia*, Oxford: Oxford University Press.

Kingston-Mann, Esther 1999, *In Search of the True West: Culture, Economics, and Problems of Russian Development*, Princeton: Princeton University Press.

Kir'ianov, Iu.I. 1987, *Perekhod k massovoi politicheskoi bor'be: Rabochii klass nakanune pervoi rossiiskoi revoliutsii*, Moscow: Nauka.

Kirkup, Thomas 1906 [1892], *A History of Socialism*, 3rd ed., London: Adam and Charles Black.

Knei-Paz, Baruch 1978, *The Social and Political Thought of Leon Trotsky*, Oxford: Clarendon Press.

Kol'tsov, D. 1899, 'Rabochii i intelligentsia', *Rabotnik*, No. 5–6.

Kolakowski, Leszek 1978, *Main Currents of Marxism*, 3 vols., Oxford: Oxford University Press.

Komissarova, L.I. 1970, 'Raskrytyi psevdonim', *Istoriia SSSR*, 2: 169–70.

*Kommunisticheskaia partiia Sovetskogo Soiuza v rezoliutsiiakh i resheniiakh s"ezdov, konferentsii i plenumov TsK* 1983, tom 1, Moscow: Gospolizdat.

Koz'min, B.P. 1961, *Iz istorii revoliutsionnoi mysli v Rossii*, Moscow: Akademiia Nauk.

Koz'min, B.P. 1969 [1922], *P.N. Tkachev i revoliutsionnoe dvizhenie 1860-kh godov*, The Hague: Mouton.

*Kratkii kurs: Istoriia Vsesoiuznoi Kommunisticheskoi Partii (bol'shevikov)* 1938, Moscow: Gospolizdat.

Krichevskii, Boris 1900, *Otvet redaktsii 'Rabochego dela' na pis'mo P. Akselroda i Vademecum G. Plekhanova*, Geneva: Izdanie Soiuza Russkikh Sotsial'demokratov.

Krichevskii, Boris 1901, 'Printsipy, taktika i bor'ba', *Rabochee delo*, No. 10 (September 1901): 1–36.

Krupskaia, Nadezhda 1969, *Vospominaniia o Lenine* in *Vospominaniia o Vladimire Il'iche Lenine*, tom 1, Moscow: Politizdat.

Krupskaya, N.K 1960, *Reminiscences of Lenin*, New York: International Publishers.

Krylova, Anna 2003, 'Beyond the Spontaneity-Consciousness Paradigm: "Class Instinct" as a Promising Category of Historical Analysis', *Slavic Review*, 62, 1: 1–23.

Kuskova, Elena 1906, 'Review of F. Dan, *Iz istorii rabochego dvizheniia i sotsial-demokratii v Rossii 1900–1904*', *Byloe*, No. 10 (October 1906).

Lakoff, George 1987, *Women, Fire, and Dangerous Things: What Categories Reveal about the Mind*, Chicago: University of Chicago Press.

Lane, David 1969, *The Roots of Russian Communism: A Social and Historical Study of Russian Social-Democracy 1898–1907*, Assen: Van Gorcum.

Lassalle, Ferdinand 1898 [1863], *Lassalle's Open Letter to the National Labor Association of Germany*, translated by John Ehmann and Fred. Bader, New York: International Publishing Co.

Lassalle, Ferdinand 1899 [1862], *The Workingmans' Programme (Arbeiter-Programm)*, translated by Edward Peters, New York: International Publishing Co.

Lassalle, Ferdinand 1900 [1863], *Science and the Workingmen*, translated by Thorstein Veblen, New York: International Library Publishing Co.

Lassalle, Ferdinand 1919a [1862], *Das Arbeiterprogramm*, in *Gesammelte Reden und Schriften*, Volume 2, Berlin: Paul Cassirer.

Lassalle, Ferdinand 1919b [1863], *Die Wissenschaft und die Arbeiter*, in *Gesammelte Reden und Schriften*, Volume 2, Berlin: Paul Cassirer.

Lassalle, Ferdinand 1919c [1863], *Offenes Antwort-Schreiben*, in *Gesammelte Reden und Schriften*, Volume 2, Berlin: Paul Cassirer.

Le Blanc, Paul 1990, *Lenin and the Revolutionary Party*, Atlantic Highlands: Humanities Press.

Lenin, Vladimir 1926–35, *Sochineniia*, 2nd ed., Moscow: Gosizdat (3rd edition is a reprint).

Lenin, Vladimir 1929 [1902], *What Is to Be Done?*, translated by Joe Fineberg, in *Collected Works of V.I. Lenin*, Volume 4 (2 books), New York: International Publishers.

Lenin, Vladimir 1958–65, *Polnoe sobranie sochinenii*, 5th ed., Moscow: Gospolizdat.

Lenin, Vladimir 1962 [1902], *What Is to Be Done?*, translated by Joe Fineberg and George Hanna, in *V.I. Lenin Collected Works*, Volume 5, Foreign Languages Publishing House: Moscow.

Lenin, Vladimir 1963 [1902], *What Is to Be Done?*, translated by S.V. and Patricia Utechin, edited by S.V. Utechin, Oxford: Oxford University Press.

Lenin, Vladimir 1966 [1902], *Que faire?*, edited by Jean-Jacques Marie, Paris: Editions du Seuil.

Lenin, Vladimir 1988 [1902], *What Is to Be Done?*, translated by Joe Fineberg and George Hanna with revisions by Robert Service, London: Penguin Books.

Levin, Sh. M. et al. 1969, *V.I. Lenin i russkaia obshchestvenno-politicheskaia mysl' XIX–nachala XX v.*, Leningrad: Nauka.

Liadov, M. 1906, *Istoriia Rossiiskoi Sotsialdemokraticheskoi rabochei partii*, 2 vols., St. Petersburg: Izdanie Zerno.

Liadov, M. 1911, *Po povodu partiinogo krizisa: chastnoe zaiavlenie*, Paris: Izdanie gruppy 'Vpered'.

Lidtke, Vernon L. 1966, *The Outlawed Party: Social Democracy in Germany, 1878–1890*, Princeton: Princeton University Press.

Lidtke, Vernon L. 1985, *The Alternative Culture: Socialist Labor in Imperial Germany*, Oxford: Oxford University Press.

Liebknecht, Wilhelm n.d., *On the Political Position of Social Democracy Particularly with Respect to the Reichstag*, Moscow: Foreign Languages Publishing House.

Liebman, Marcel 1975 [1973], *Leninism under Lenin*, London: Jonathan Cape.

Lih, Lars T. 1990, *Bread and Authority in Russia, 1914–1921* Berkeley: University of California Press.

Lih, Lars T. 1999, '*Vlast* from the Past', *Left History*, 6, 2: 29–52.

Lih, Lars T. 2000, 'Bukharin's "Illusion": War Communism and the Meaning of NEP', *Russian History/Histoire Russe*, 27, 4: 417–60.

Lih, Lars T. 2001a, 'Experts and Peasants', *Kritika: Explorations in Russian and Eurasian History*, 2, 4: 803–22.

Lih, Lars T. 2001b, 'Review of Richard Pipes, *The Unknown Lenin* (1996) and *V.I. Lenin: Neizvestnye dokumenty, 1981–1922* (1999)', *Canadian-American Slavic Studies*, 35, 2–3: 301–6.

Lih, Lars T. 2002, 'Melodrama and the Myth of the Soviet Union', in *Imitations of Life: Two Centuries of Melodrama in Russia*, edited by Joan Neuberger and Louise McReynolds, Durham, NC.: Duke University Press.

Lih, Lars T. 2003, 'How a Founding Document was Found, or One Hundred Years of Lenin's *What Is to Be Done?*', *Kritika: Explorations in Russian and Eurasian History*, 4, 1: 5–49.

Lozhkin, Vladilen V. 1983, 'Sostav rabochikh sotsial-demokratov i ikh rol' v sozdanii leninskoi partii', *Voprosy istorii*, 7: 64–80.

Lozhkin, Vladilen V. 1986, *Kogorta slavnykh*, Moscow: Politizdat.

Luxemburg, Rosa 1961, '*The Russian Revolution*' and '*Leninism or Marxism*', edited by Bertram Wolfe, Ann Arbor: University of Michigan Press.

Luxemburg, Rosa 1970 [1904], 'Organisationsfragen der russischen Sozialdemokratie', in Luxemburg, *Gesammelte Werke*, Band 1, Teil 2, Berlin: Dietz Verlag.

Luxemburg, Rosa 1970a, *Rosa Luxemburg Speaks*, ed. Mary-Alice Waters, New York: Pathfinder.

Lydin, M. 1963 [1904], *Material k vyiasneniiu partiinogo krizisa rossiiskoi sotsial-demokraticheskoi rabochei partii*, in *Iz istorii sozdaniia partii novogo tipa: Doklad bol'shevikov mezhdunarodnomu sotsialisticheskomu kongressu v 1904 g.*, Moscow: Gospolizdat.

Mandel, David 1982, 'The Workers and the Intelligentsia in 1917', *Critique*, 14: 67–87.

Mandel, Ernest 1971, *The Leninist Theory of Organisation: Its Relevance for Today*, London: Prinkipo Press.

Marcuse, Herbert 1958, *Soviet Marxism: A Critical Analysis*, New York : Columbia University Press.

Marie, Jean-Jacques 2004, *Lénine: Biographie*, Paris: Éditions Balland.

Martov L. 1904a, 'Predislovie', in Cherevanin, *Organizatsionnyi vopros*, Geneva: Izdanie Rossiiskoi Sotsial'demokraticheskoi Rabochei Partii.

Martov L. 1904b, *Bor'ba s 'osadnym polozheniem' v Rossiskoi Sotsial'demokratiicheskoi Rabochei Partii*, Geneva: Izdanie Rossiiskoi Sotsial'demokraticheskoi Rabochei Partii.

Martov, L. 1900, *Krasnoe znamia v Rossii: ocherk istorii russkogo rabochego dvizheniia*, Geneva: Izdanie Revoliutsionnoi Organizatsii Sotsial-Demokrata.

Martov, L. 1975 [1922], *Zapiski Sotsial-demokrata*, Cambridge, MA.: Oriental Research Partners.

Martov, L. 2000 [1923], *Istoriia rossiiskoi sotsial-demokratii*, in Iu. Martov, *Izbrannoe*, Moscow: s.n.

Martynov 1905, *Dve Diktatury*, Geneva: Izdanie Rossiiskoi Sotsial'demokraticheskoi partii.

Martynov, Aleksandr 1901a, 'Oblichitel'nai literatura i proletarskaia bor'ba', *Rabochee delo* No. 10 (September 1901): 37–64.

Martynov, Aleksandr 1901b, *Dva s"ezda*, Geneva: Izdanie Soiuza Russkikh Sotsial' demokratov.

Martynov, Aleksandr 1902, 'Sotsialdemokratiia i rabochii klass: Dva techeniia v russkoi sotsial'demokratii', *Rabochee delo*, Prilozhenie k No. 11/12.

Martynov, Aleksandr 1989 [1925–6], 'Avtobiografiia', in *Deiateli SSSR and revoliutsionnogo dvizheniiu Rossii: entsiklopedicheskii slovar' Granat*, Moscow: Sovetskaia entsiklopediia.

Marx, Karl 1984 [1860], *Herr Vogt*, in *Marx Engels Gesamtausgabe*, Abt. 1, Bd. 18., Berlin: Dietz Verlag.

Marx, Karl 1984a [1864], 'Inaugural Address', in *Marx and Engels Collected Works*, Volume 20, New York: International Publishers.

Marx, Karl 1984b [1864], 'Statutes for International Working Men's Association', in *Marx and Engels Collected Works*, Volume 20, New York: International Publishers.

Marx, Karl 1996, *Later Political Writings*, edited by Terrell Carver, Cambridge: Cambridge University Press.

Marx, Karl and Friedrich Engels 1959 [1848], *Manifest der Kommunistischen Partei*, in *Marx Engels Werke*, Band 4, Berlin: Dietz Verlag.

Marx, Karl and Friedrich Engels 1960 [1850], 'Ansprache der Zentralbehörde an den Bund vom März 1850', in *Marx Engels Werke*, Band 7, Berlin: Dietz Verlag.

Marx, Karl and Friedrich Engels 1978, *The Marx-Engels Reader*, edited by Robert Tucker, 2nd ed., New York: W.W. Norton and Company.

Marx, Karl and Friedrich Engels 2002, *The Communist Manifesto*, edited by Gareth Stedman Jones, London: Penguin Books.

Mayer, Robert 1993a, 'Lenin and the Concept of the Professional Revolutionary', *History of Political Thought*, 14, 2: 249–63.

Mayer, Robert 1993b, 'Marx, Lenin and the Corruption of the Working Class', *Political Studies*, 41: 636–49.

Mayer, Robert 1994, 'Lenin, Kautsky and Working-Class Consciousness', *History of European Ideas*, 18, 5: 673–81.

Mayer, Robert 1996, 'The Status of a Classic Text: Lenin's *What Is to Be Done?* after 1902', *History of European Ideas*, 22, 4: 307–20.

Mayer, Robert 1997, 'Plekhanov, Lenin and Working-Class Consciousness', *Studies in East European Thought*, 49: 159–85.

Mehring, Franz 1898, *Geschichte der Deutschen Sozialdemokratie*, 2 vols., Stuttgart: J.H.W. Dietz.

Melancon, Michael 1985, 'The Socialist Revolutionaries from 1902 to 1907: Peasant *and* Workers' Party', *Russian History/Histoire Russe*, 12, 1: 2–47.

Melancon, Michael 1990, *The Socialist Revolutionaries and the Russian Anti-War Movement, 1914–1917*, Columbus: Ohio State University Press.

Melancon, Michael 2000, *Rethinking Russia's February Revolution: Anonymous Spontaneity or Socialist Agency?*, Pittsburgh: Carl Beck Papers in Russian and East European Studies.

*Men'sheviki: dokumenty i materialy 1903–1917 gg.* 1996, Moscow: ROSSPEN.

Meyer, Alfred 1957, *Leninism*, Cambridge, MA.: Harvard University Press.

Michels, Robert 1962 [1911], *Political Parties: A Sociological Study of the Oligarchical Tendencies of Modern Democracy*, New York: The Free Press.

Miliukov, Paul 1922, *Russia To-Day and To-Morrow*, New York: The Macmillan Company.

Miliukov, Paul 1927, *Rossiia na perelome*, Paris: n.p.

Miliukov, Paul 1962 [1905], *Russia and its Crisis*, London: Collier-Macmillan Ltd.

Mokienko, V.M. and T.G. Nikitina 1998, *Tolkovyi Slovar' iazyka Sondepii*, St. Petersburg: Folio Press.

Molyneux, John 1978, *Marxism and the Party*, London: Pluto Press.

Moore, Barrington 1956, *Soviet Politics: The Dilemma of Power; The Role of Ideas in Social Change*, Cambridge, MA.: Harvard University Press.

Morozov, K.N. 1998, *Partiia sotsialistov-revoliutsionerov v 1907–1917 gg.*, Moscow: ROSSPEN.

Morrissey, Susan K. 1998, *Heralds of Revolution: Russian Students and the Mythologies of Radicalism*, Oxford: Oxford University Press.

N[icolaevsky], B[oris] 1927, 'Iz epokhi "Iskry" i "Zari"', *Katorga i Ssylka*, 35: 7–35 and 36: 83–100.

Nadezhdin, L. 1901a, *Kanun Revoliutsii: neperiodicheskoe obozrenie voprosov teorii i taktiki*, n.p.: Izdanie Revoliutsionno-sotsialisticheskoi gruppy 'Svoboda'.

Nadezhdin, L. 1901b, 'Organizatsiia', *Svoboda*, No. 1: 61–80.

Nadezhdin, L. 1903 [1901], *Vozrozhdenie revoliutsionizma v Rossii*, 2nd ed., n.p.: Tip. Svobody.

Nadezhdin, L. 1905, *Na rodnoi storone: otkliki s chuzhbiny*, n.p.: Tip. Partii.

Nettl, Peter 1966, *Rosa Luxemburg*, 2 vols., Oxford: Oxford University Press.

Nevskii, V. 1925, *Ocherki po istorii rossisskoi kommunisticheskoi partii*, 2nd ed., tom 1, Leningrad: Priboi.

*Ob agitatsii* 1896, Geneva: Izdanie Soiuza Russkikh Sotsialdemokratov.

Olminskii, M. [Galerka] 1904a, *Doloi Bonapartizm!*, Geneva: Rossiskaia Sotsial'demo-kraticheskaia Rabochaia Partiia.

Olminskii, M. [Galerka] 1904b, *Na novyi put'*, Geneva: Rossiskaia Sotsial'demokrati-cheskaia Rabochaia Partiia.

Olminskii, M. and A. Bogdanov [Galerka i Riadovoi] 1904, *Nashi nedorazumeniia*, Geneva: Izdanie avtorov.

Orth, Samuel P. 1913, *Socialism and Democracy in Europe*, New York: Henry Holt and Company.

Ostrogorski, Moisei 1902, *Democracy and the Organisation of Political Parties*, 2 vols., New York: The Macmillan Company.

Parvus [P. Molotov] 1901, 'Evropeiskie rabochie i ikh russkii istorik', *Zaria*, No. 1 (April 1901).

*Perepiska V.I. Lenina i redaktsii gazety 'Iskra' s sotsial-demokraticheskimi organizatsiiami v Rossii, 1900–1903 gg.* 1969–70, 3 vols., Moscow: Gospolizdat.

Piatnitsky, O. n.d. [1925], *Memoirs of a Bolshevik*, New York: International Publishers.

Pierson, Stanley 1993, *Marxist Intellectuals and the Working-Class Mentality in Germany, 1887–1912*, Cambridge, MA.: Harvard University Press.

Pipes, Richard 1968, 'The Origins of Bolshevism', in *Revolutionary Russia*, edited by Richard Pipes, Cambridge, MA.: Harvard University Press.

Pipes, Richard 1996, *The Unknown Lenin: From the Secret Archive*, New Haven: Yale University Press.

Pisarev, Dmitri 1956, *Sochineniia*, Volume 3, Moscow: 1956.

Plamenatz, John 1947, *What Is Communism?*, London: National News-Letter.

Plamenatz, John 1954, *German Marxism and Russian Communism*, London: Longmans.

Plekhanov, Georgii 1900, *Vademecum dlia redaktsii 'Rabochego Dela'*, Geneva: Tip. Gruppy starykh narodovol'tsev.

Plekhanov, Georgii 1905, *O nashei taktike po otnosheniiu k bor'be liberal'noi burzhuazii s tsarizmom*, Geneva: Izdanie Rossiiskoi Sotsial'demokraticheskoi Rabochei Partii.

Plekhanov, Georgii V. 1923–7, *Sochineniia*, 24 vols., edited by D. Riazanov, Moscow: Gosizdat.

Pospielovsky, Dimitry 1971, *Russian Police Trade Unionism: Experiment or Provocation?*, London: Weidenfield and Nicolson.

Possony, Stefan 1964, *Lenin: The Compulsive Revolutionary*, Chicago: Henry Regnery Company.

Potresov, Aleksandr 1909, 'Evoliutsiia obshchestvenno–politcheskoi mysli v predrevoliutsionnuiu epokhu', in *Obshchestvennoe dvizhenie v Rossii*, Volume 1, St. Petersburg: s.n.

Potresov, Aleksandr Nikolaevich 2002, *Izbrannoe*, Moscow: Mosgorarkhiv.

Pozefsky, Peter C. 2003, *The Nihilist Imagination: Dmitrii Pisarev and the Cultural Origins of Russian Radicalism (1860–1868)*, New York: Peter Lang.

Priimak, N.I. 1972, 'Kniga V. I. Lenina "Chto delat'?" i redaktsiia Iskry', in *Kniga V.I. Lenina "Chto delat'?" i mestnye partiinye organizatsii Rossii*, Perm: Permskoe knizhnoe izdatel'stvo.

Prokopovich, S.N. 1899, *Rabochee dvizhenie na Zapade: Opyt kriticheskogo issledovaniia. Tom I. Germaniia. Bel'giia*, St. Petersburg: Izdanie L.F. Panteleeva.

Pushkareva, I.M. 2003, 'Rabochee dvizhenie v god II s"ezda RSDRP', *Otechestvennaia istoriia*, No. 4: 3–14.

*Rabochee delo* 1901, 'Istoricheskii povorot', *Listok 'Rabochego Dela'*, No. 6 (April 1901): 1–6.

*Rabochee dvizhenie v Rossii 1895–fevral' 1917 g.: Khronika* 2000, Vyp. VII for the year 1901, St. Petersburg: BLITZ.

Rabochii 1904, *Rabochie i intelligenty v nashikh organizatsiiakh*, Geneva: Izdanie Rossiiskoi Sotsial'demokraticheskoi Rabochei Partii.

Rae, John 1884, *Contemporary Socialism*, New York: Charles Scribner's Sons.

Rae, John 1891, *Contemporary Socialism*, 2nd ed., New York: Charles Scribner's Sons.

Reichman, Henry 1996, 'On Kanatchikov's Bolshevism: Workers and *Intelligenty* in Lenin's *What Is to Be Done?*', *Russian History/Histoire Russe*, 23, 1–4: 27–45.

Reid, Alastair J. 2004, *United We Stand: A History of Britain's Trade Unions*, London: Allen Lane.

Riazanov, David 1901, 'Zamechaniia na programmu "Rabochego dela"', *Zaria*, No. 1 (April 1901): 118–36.

Riazanov, David 1902, *Sotsial-demokraticheskoi Kalendar' na 1902 god*, Geneva: Izdanie gruppy 'Bor'ba'.

Riazanov, David 1908, 'Review of Sergei Prokopovich, *Rabochee dvizhenie v Germanii*', *Neue Zeit*, 27, 1: 553–4.

Rice, Christopher 1988, *Russian Workers and the Socialist-Revolutionary Party through the Revolution of 1905–07*, London: Macmillan Press.

Rigby, T.H. 1979, *Lenin's Government*, Cambridge: Cambridge University Press.

Riha, Thomas 1969, *A Russian European: Paul Miliukov in Russian Politics*, Notre Dame: University of Notre Dame Press.

Rozental, I.S. 1994, *Provokator: Karera Romana Malinovskogo*, Moscow: ROSSPEN.

Rudnitskaia, E.L. 1992, *Russkii blankizm: Petr Tkachev*, Moscow: Nauka.

Russell, Bertrand 1965 [1896], *German Social Democracy*, London: George Allen and Unwin Ltd.

Saltykov-Schedrin, M.E. 1972 [1881], *Za rubezhom* in Saltykov-Schedrin, *Sobranie Sochinenii*, tom 14, Moscow: Izdanie Khudozhestvennaia literatura.

Salvadori, Massimo 1979 [1976], *Karl Kautsky and the Socialist Revolution 1880–1938*, London: NLB.

Savinkov, Boris [B–v] 1900, 'Peterburgskoe dvizhenie i prakticheskie zadachi sotsial'demokratii', *Rabochee delo*, No. 6 (April 1900): 28–42.

Savinkov, Boris 1990, *Izbrannoe*, Moscow: Novosti.

Schapiro, Leonard 1987 [1969], 'Lenin's Intellectual Formation and the Russian Revolutionary Background', in L. Schapiro, *Russian Studies*, New York: Viking.

Schneiderman, Jeremiah 1976, *Sergei Zubatov and Revolutionary Marxism: The Struggle for the Working Class in Tsarist Russia*, Ithaca: Cornell University Press.

Schulz, H.-J. 1993, *German Socialist Literature 1860–1914: Predicaments of Criticism*, Columbia, South Carolina: Camden House.

Service, Robert 1985–95, *Lenin, A Political Life*, 3 vols., Bloomington: Indiana University Press.

Service, Robert 1988, 'Introduction', in Lenin 1988.

Service, Robert 2000, *Lenin, A Biography*, Cambridge, MA.: Harvard University Press.

Shakhmatov, B.M. 1981, *P.N. Tkachev: Etiudy k tvorcheskomu portretu*, Moscow: Mysl'.

Shandro, Alan forthcoming, *Lenin and the Logic of Hegemony: Political Practice and Theory in the Class Struggle*.

Shutskever, A.S. (ed.) 1925, *Kak rozhdalas' partiia bol'shevikov: literaturnaia polemika 1903–04 gg.*, Leningrad: Priboi.

*Slovar' Russkogo iazyka* 1981–4, Moscow: Akademiia Nauk.

Sombart, Werner 1968 [1909], *Socialism and the Social Movement*, New York: Augustus M. Kelley.

Spence, Richard 1991, *Boris Savinkov: Renegade on the Left*, East European Monographs, Boulder: Columbia University Press.

Stalin, I.V. 1946–52, *Sochineniia*, 13 vols., Moscow: Politizdat.

Stedman Jones, Gareth 2002, 'Introduction', in Marx and Engels, *The Communist Manifesto*, London: Penguin Books.

Steenson, Gary 1978, *Karl Kautsky, 1854–1938: Marxism in the Classical Years*, Pittsburgh: University of Pittsburgh Press.

Steenson, Gary P. 1981, *'Not One Man! Not One Penny!': German Social Democracy, 1863–1914*, Pittsburgh: University of Pittsburgh Press.

Steenson, Gary P. 1991, *After Marx, Before Lenin: Marxism and Socialist Working-Class Parties in Europe, 1884–1914*, Pittsburgh: University of Pittsburgh Press.

Stockdale, Melissa Kirschke 1996, *Paul Miliukov and the Quest for a Liberal Russia, 1880–1918*, Ithaca: Cornell University Press.

Stuart, Robert 1992, *Marxism at Work: Ideology, Class and French Socialism during the Third Republic*, Cambridge: Cambridge University Press.

Surh, Gerald D. 1989, *1905 in St. Petersburg: Labor, Society, and Revolution*, Stanford: Stanford University Press.

Surh, Gerald D. 1999, 'The Petersburg Workers' Organisation and the Politics of "Economism", 1900–1903', in *Workers and Intelligentsia in Late Imperial Russia: Realities, Representations, Reflections*, edited by Reginald Zelnik, Berkeley: University of California Press.

Surh, Gerald D. 2000, 'Recent Work on Russian Labor History in the U.S.', in *Problemy vsemirnoi istorii*, St. Petersburg: Rossiiskaia Akademiia Nauk.

Takhtarev, K.M. [Peterburzhets] 1897, 'Po povodu s.-peterburgskoi stachki', *Rabotnik*, 3/4: iii–xvi.

Takhtarev, K.M. [Peterburzhets] 1902, *Ocherk peterburgskogo rabochego dvizheniia 90–kh godov: po lichnym vospominaniiam*, London: Izdanie sotsialdemokraticheskoi organizatsii 'Zhizni'.

Takhtarev, K.M. 1899, 'Nasha deistvitel'nost'', *Otdel'noe prilozhenie k 'Rabochei Mysli'* (Separate Supplement), (September 1899).

Takhtarev, K.M. 1924, *Rabochee dvizhenie v Peterburge (1893–1901 gg.)*, Leningrad: Priboi.

Tarnovskii, K.N. 1983, *Revoliutsionnaia mysl', revoliutsionnoe delo*, Moscow: Mysl'.

Teplov, Pavel 1899, 'Polemicheskie krasoty redaktsii "Rabochei Mysli"', *Rabochee delo*, 4/5 (September/December 1899): 63–71 of 2nd Otdel.

Tikhonova, Z.N. and V.N. Stepanov 1971, 'O sozdanii i rasprostranenii knigi V. I. Lenina *Chto delat'?*', *Voprosy istorii*, 4: 122–30.

Tkachev, Petr 1932–7, *Izbrannye sochineniia na sotsial'no-politicheskie temy*, 6 vols., Moscow: Gosudarstvennoe Sotsial'no-ekonomicheskoe Izdatel'stvo.

Tkachev, Petr 1975, *Sochineniia*, 2 vols., Moscow: Mysl'.

Treadgold, Donald W. 1955, *Lenin and His Rivals: The Struggle for Russia's Future, 1898–1906*, New York: Frederick A. Praeger, Inc.

*Tretii s"ezd RSDRP, aprel'–mai 1905 goda: Protokoly* 1959, Moscow: Gospolizdat.

Trotskii, Lev 1991 [1930], *Moia zhizn'*, Moscow: Panorama.

Trotskii, Lev 1993, *Permanentnaia revoliutsiia*, Cambridge, MA.: Iskra Research.

Trotskii, N. 1904, *Nashi politicheskie zadachi (takticheskie i organizatsionnye voprosy)*, Geneva: Izdanie Sotsialdemokraticheskoi Rabochei Partii.

Trotskii, N. 1907, *Verno li, chto my – intelligentskaia partiia?*, in N. Trotskii, *V zashchitu partii*, St. Petersburg: Delo.

Tucker, Robert 1981, *Politics as Leadership*, Columbia: University of Missouri Press.

Tucker, Robert 1987 [1985], 'Lenin's Bolshevism as a Culture in the Making', in *Political Culture and Leadership in Soviet Russia: From Lenin to Gorbachev*, New York: W.W. Norton.

Tudor, H. and J.M. Tudor 1988, *Marxism and Social Democracy: The Revisionist Debate 1896–1898*, Cambridge: Cambridge University Press.

Ulam, Adam 1960, *The Unfinished Revolution: An Essay on the Sources of Influence of Marxism and Communism*, New York: Random House.

Ulam, Adam 1962 [1958], *Patterns of Government: The Major Political Systems of Europe*, edited by Adam Ulam and Samuel Beer, 2nd ed., New York: Random House.

Ulam, Adam 1965, *The Bolsheviks: The Intellectual and Political History of the Triumph of Communism in Russia*, New York: The Macmillan Company.

Valentinov, Nikolay 1968, *Encounters with Lenin*, Oxford: Oxford University Press.

Van Ree, E. 2000, 'Stalin As a Marxist Philosopher', *Studies in East European Thought*, 52: 259–308.

Venturi, Franco 1960 [1952], *Roots of Revolution: A History of the Populist and Socialist Movements in Nineteenth Century Russia*, New York: Grosset and Dunlap.

Villiers, Brougham 1908, *The Socialist Movement in England*, London: T. Fisher Unwin.

Vorontsov, V. [V.V.] 1893, *Nashi Napravleniia*, St. Petersburg: Tip. M. Stasiulevicha.

Vorovskii, Vatslav 1955 [1907], 'Sotsial-demokratiia i rabochaia massa', in V.V. Vorovskii, *Izbrannye proizvedeniia o pervoi russkoi revoliutsii*, Moscow: Gospolizdat.

*Vospominaniia o Vladimire Il'iche Lenine* 1969, tom 1, Moscow: Politizdat.

*Vtoroi s"ezd RSDRP, iiul'–avgust 1903 goda: Protokoly* 1959, Moscow: Gospolizdat.

Walicki, Andrzej 1979, *A History of Russian Thought From the Enlightenment to Marxism*, Stanford: Stanford University Press.

Webb, Sidney and Beatrice Webb 1900 [1897], *Teoriia i praktika angliiskogo tred-iunionizma (Industral Democracy)*, translated by Vladimir Ilin [Lenin], St. Petersburg: Izdanie O. N. Popovoi.

Webb, Sidney and Beatrice Webb 1965 [1897], *Industrial Democracy*, New York: Augustus M. Kelley.

Weeks, Albert L. 1968, *The First Bolshevik: A Political Biography of Peter Tkachev*, New York: New York University Press.

Weill, Claudie 1977, *Marxistes russes et Social-démocratie allemande, 1898–1904*, Paris: Maspero.

Wesson, Robert 1978, *Lenin's Legacy*, Stanford: Hoover Institution.

Wheeler, Marcus 1984, *The Oxford Russian-English Dictionary*, 2nd edition, Oxford: Oxford University Press.

White, James D. 2001, *Lenin: The Practice and Theory of Revolution*, Basingstoke: Palgrave.

Wildman, Allan K. 1967, *The Making of a Workers' Revolution: Russian Social Democracy, 1891–1903*, Chicago: University of Chicago Press.

Wolfe, Bertram 1964 [1948], *Three Who Made a Revolution: A Biographical History*, 2nd edition, New York: Dell Publishing.

Wolfe, Bertram 1984, *Lenin and the Twentieth Century*, Stanford: Hoover Institution Press.

Zasulich, Vera 1983a [1901], 'Review of Nadezhdin's *Vozrozhdenie revoliutsionizma v Rossii*', in V.I. Zasulich, *Izbrannye proizvedeniia*, Moscow: Mysl' (originally appeared in *Zaria*, No. 2/3, December 1901).

Zasulich, Vera 1983b [1902], 'Terroristicheskoe dvizhenie v Rossii', in V.I. Zasulich, *Izbrannye proizvedeniia*, Moscow: Mysl' (originally appeared in *Neue Zeit*).

Zelnik, Reginald E. 1976, 'Russian Bebels: An Introduction to the Memoirs of the Russian Workers Semen Kanatchikov and Matvei Fisher', *Russian Review*, 35, 2: 249–89; 3: 417–47.

Zelnik, Reginald E. 2003a, 'A Paradigm Lost? Response to Anna Krylova', *Slavic Review*, 62, 1: 24–33.

Zelnik, Reginald E. 2003b, 'Worry about Workers: Concerns of the Russian Intelligentsia from the 1870s to *What Is to Be Done?*', in *Extending the Borders of Russian History*, edited by Marsha Siefert, Budapest: Central European University Press.

Zinoviev, Grigorii 1924 [1923], *Istoriia Rossiiskoi Kommunisticheskoi Partii (bol' shevikov)*, 4th ed., Leningrad: Gosizdat.

Zinoviev, Grigorii 1973 [1923], *History of the Bolshevik Party: From the Beginnings to February 1917: A Popular Outline*, London: New Park Publications.

# Index

The commentary and Annotations Parts One and Two contain page and section references to the translation of *WITBD* when relevant topics are discussed. The Index therefore covers only the commentary and the Annotations.